BY PHILIP S. FONER

History of the Labor Movement in the United States (4 vols.)

The Life and Writings of Frederick Douglass (4 vols.)

A History of Cuba and Its Relations with the United States (2 vols.)

The Complete Writings of Thomas Paine (2 vols.)

Business and Slavery: The New York Merchants and the Irrepressible Conflict

W. E. B. Du Bois Speaks (2 vols.)

The Fur and Leather Workers Union

Jack London: American Rebel

Mark Twain: Social Critic

The Jews in American History: 1654–1865

The Case of Joe Hill

The Letters of Joe Hill

The Bolshevik Revolution: Its Impact on American Radicals, Liberals, and Labor

American Labor and the War in Indochina

The Autobiographies of the Haymarket Martyrs

Helen Keller: Her Socialist Years

The Black Panthers Speak

The Basic Writings of Thomas Jefferson

The Selected Writings of George Washington

The Selected Writings of Abraham Lincoln

The Selected Writings of Franklin D. Roosevelt

THE
VOICE
OF
BLACK AMERICA

Major Speeches by Negroes
in the United States, 1797–1971

EDITED, AND WITH COMMENTARY, BY

Philip S. Foner

SIMON AND SCHUSTER · NEW YORK

Contents

SECTION II: *The Civil War and Reconstruction,*
1861–1876

SECTION III: *The Post-Reconstruction Period, 1877–1915*

SECTION IV: *World War I to World War II,
1917–1942*

SECTION V: *Post-World War II, 1945–1963*

SECTION VI: *Civil Rights to Black Power,*
September 1963–1971

Introduction

SEVERAL ANTHOLOGIES of speeches of black Americans have preceded this one, such as Alice Ruth Moore Dunbar's pioneering *Masterpieces of Negro Eloquence* (1913), Carter G. Woodson's *Negro Orators and Their Orations* (1925), and Roy L. Hill's *Rhetoric of Racial Revolt* (1964). There are, moreover, collections of the speeches of individual black orators such as my own four-volume *Life and Writings of Frederick Douglass* (1950–1955). Again, most of the documentary histories of the Negro American, especially the comprehensive collection edited by Herbert Aptheker, *A Documentary History of the Negro People in the United States* (1951), pay attention to speeches.

Several analyses of Negro oratory also have appeared, such as the unpublished studies by Winfred Bennett, "A Survey of American Negro Oratory, 1619 to 1925," M. A. thesis, George Washington University, 1935, and William W. Pipes, "An Interpretative Study of Old-Time Negro Preaching," Ph. D. dissertation, University of Michigan, 1942. In 1969 Marcus W. Boulware published *The Oratory of Negro Leaders: 1900–1968*. None of these studies made available speeches of Negro spokesmen not already published.

Despite the literature in the field, scores of important speeches by black Americans have never been reprinted and published in book form. Many of these appear in the present collection for the first time.

This collection of speeches of black Americans is presented in two parts and six sections. The first part opens with the earliest published speech of a black American—Prince Hall's Masonic sermon of June 24, 1797.* It closes with the last speech of Booker T. Washington on October 25, 1915, delivered less than a month before his death. The year 1915 also marked the beginning of the "Great Migration," during which hundreds of thousands of black Americans left the South to seek a better life in the North. With the more rapid growth thereafter of the

---

* There is an earlier address by a black American than the one by Prince Hall: *An Address to the Negroes of the State of New York* by the New York slave Jupiter Hammon, published in 1787 and dedicated to the members of the African Society of New York City. But it was a written piece and never delivered as a speech.

Northern black population and the more rapid rise of the black ghettos, old problems became aggravated and new ones were created. New leaders whose speeches reflected the changing conditions arose among black Americans. This development is presented in the second part of this collection covering the period 1917 to 1971.

A number of the speeches, because of their historic significance or special literary quality, are presented in their entirety, but generally the speeches have been extracted. To have reproduced all the speeches in full would have reduced the number that could be included and caused much repetitive material to remain. Every effort has been made to avoid any distortion of the original meaning in the process of excerpting.

In each case the speech is preceded by biographical and introductory notes to place the selection in its historical framework, and explanatory footnotes have been furnished wherever it was deemed necessary, to provide information on personalities and events referred to by the speaker. Except where otherwise indicated, all footnotes are the editor's. The source of each speech is provided.

In many instances the speeches included in this collection were delivered without any special covering titles. I have taken the liberty of furnishing a title where none appeared. In a few cases, I have substituted a title reflecting the theme of the speech instead of a general title originally used. In order not to interrupt the reading, I have eliminated indications of "applause," "hear, hear," "laughter," and other audience reactions. The word *Negro* has been capitalized throughout in accordance with correct usage.

Although oratory is only one form that black Americans have used throughout our history to assert their worth and to validate their claim to human rights, it is a singularly important one. Perhaps even more than writers, black orators helped to demolish the myth of the natural inferiority of black people. Many of the books authored by blacks were dismissed as ghostwritten (as quite a few before the Civil War actually were), but it was difficult to listen to speakers like Frederick Douglass, William Wells Brown, Henry Highland Garnet, Samuel Ringgold Ward, Robert Purvis, John S. Rock, and scores of other black orators, and not be convinced of the ridiculousness of the charge that Negroes were not really human beings. In 1844, six years after Douglass had escaped from slavery, a member of the audience listening to him speak in Philadelphia asked of those who questioned the Negro's human worth to explain how one who was "only six years out of bondage, and who had never gone to school a day in his life, could speak with such eloquence, with such precision of language and power of thought, and still be considered not 'a *man*.'" When Douglass lectured in Portland, Maine, in 1864, the chairman introduced him as follows: "Let no man approach Mr. Douglass in a patronizing spirit, but as an equal in every respect. He comes to us not as a black man, not as a white man, but, thank God, as a *man*."

Nor was Douglass the only one to make such a contribution. In 1864, Miss Oneida Du Bois, born a slave in Alabama, spoke in Bethlehem, Pennsylvania. Although none of her speeches has been preserved, the comment of the local paper (*The Moravian*) is an indication of the effect of the black orator: "Certainly her own lady-like proofs of high mental culture afforded by her lecture are the very best, and indeed to every candid mind an almost irresistible evidence that the poor, despised and downtrodden people to whom she belongs *are* susceptible of great elevation."

Miss Du Bois' speeches are not the only ones to have vanished either because they were not transcribed when delivered or, since they were given by black speakers, were not even deemed worthy of notice in the contemporary press. A good example of both of these tendencies is the speech delivered by J. Sella Martin, a former slave who had escaped to the North in 1855 and had become the pastor of the Joy Street Baptist Church in Boston, and one of the best-known black ministers in the North. On November 12, 1859, the *Weekly Anglo-African* reported that "this young and eloquent divine gave the third lecture of the Anglo-African course on the evening of the 2d inst., in Shiloh Church, to a very large and enraptured audience. His subject was 'Nat Turner.' A synopsis of the lecture would give but a faint idea of its merits. Mr. Martin must be heard to be appreciated."* But neither the Boston *Courier* nor the Boston *Journal* thought the speech worthy of notice in their reports of events that occurred in Boston on November 2, 1859.†

* In the Washington, D. C., *Colored American* of April 7, 1900, John E. Bruce ("Bruce Grit") wrote: "The Rev. J. Sella Martin was one of the most eloquent and able platform orators of the ante bellum period." Yet not one of the Reverend Martin's speeches has been preserved.

† Seventy-two years later, a writer describing a speech by Richard B. Moore, a radical black orator, in Los Angeles in behalf of the defense campaign for the Scottsboro youths observed: "Remarkable as was this address, not a line of it appeared in the Los Angeles newspapers, which carefully refrained from any published mention of the arrival or departure of the speaker." (George H. Shoaf in *The Open Forum*, reprinted in *Industrial Solidarity*, July 28, 1931.)

This collection centers on the use of oratory in the struggle that, from the early national period to the present, blacks have waged for liberation. The vast majority of the speeches deal with the problems of black Americans in a society in which racism is deeply imbedded, and methods of solving them. But one will also find here speeches which concern themselves with universal issues, such as women's rights, the efforts of people in all parts of the world to liberate themselves from tyranny, the activities of organized workers, black and white, and the movement toward socialism. In every case, however, the speaker related these universal issues to the special problems facing his own people.

Black orators provided leadership in the struggle against slavery before the Civil War and in the battle for equal rights and meaningful freedom that characterizes the black protest movement from emancipation to the current scene. All too often, however, white American historians do not adequately permit the Negro to speak for himself and usually justify this omission, if they bother to explain it, by asserting that there are simply no records of the viewpoints of black Americans on issues concerning them. This volume demonstrates that the records do exist and that the black American has never lacked his own voice in speaking out against injustice.

The first of the black orators were preachers who often turned the pulpit in Negro churches into social forums concerned with antislavery protest and general problems facing their people. Later there were the fugitive-slave lecturers, chief among them Frederick Douglass, of whom Harriet Beecher Stowe wrote, "Few orators among us surpass him." While slavery was the main target of most black speakers during these years, the local problems of the "nominally free" Negroes (to use Douglass' characterization) were not neglected. All of the speeches of this period were delivered in the North. The slaves in the South could not, of course, use the platform to voice their feelings, and even free blacks were forced to remain silent south of the Mason-Dixon line. When mere possession of a copy of *Uncle Tom's Cabin* by a free Negro in Maryland brought ten years in prison, it is clear that to voice public opposition to slavery was to risk being reenslaved. Indeed, the first public meeting of blacks in Baltimore took place on February 29, 1864.

But free blacks in the North would not and could not be silenced, even though their speeches were often interrupted by mobs and the speakers were stoned and driven from the platform. Still they spoke, and none more often than those who had experienced the bitterness of slavery. For they knew they had a special mission. Who else could refute so effectively the testimony of those who upheld slavery and argued that slaves actually benefited from their bondage and were happy to be human property? No white Abolitionist could meet this challenge; so it was not surprising that after 1840 the number of Negroes employed as Abolitionist speakers rose significantly. John A. Collins, an Abolitionist agent, pointed out in a letter to William Lloyd Garrison early in 1842, "The public have itching ears to hear a colored man speak, and particularly a *slave*. Multitudes will flock to hear one of this class speak."

During the Civil War, too, black orators made a special contribution. The United States entered the war with the avowed object of preserving the Union, and only that. Gradually a fundamental change occurred in the thinking of the American people. From a confused and somewhat timid hope that slavery might die of its own weight if only it were held to the South, the lessons of the war brought to the majority of the Northern population the realization that slavery had been the primary cause of the conflict, and that the end of slavery and the arming of the Negro people, free and slave, was the only key to victory and a stable peace. The shift in popular thought to an antislavery orientation during the course of the war was the result of patient and persistent education carried on by the Abolitionists; the contributions of black orators to this movement was of outstanding importance. From the outset of the conflict, they urged the government of the United States to arm the Negroes and abolish slavery. And in due time they were to see this program adopted as the policy of the Lincoln administration and to hear Lincoln himself admit that "the emancipation policy and the aid of the colored troops constituted the severest blow yet dealt to the rebellion."

In an article published in *Social Education* of February, 1954, Professor Harris L. Dante wrote of the role played by the Negro during the Reconstruction era, "He should have been the central figure in the story, but he had no voice." The truth is, as this collection makes abundantly clear, the Negro had many voices during these decisive years. These voices spoke out persistently, sharply and convincingly to the American people, reminding them that the Negro people, through direct participation in the American Revolution and the Civil War, contributed to the defense and maintenance of the Republic and were entitled to all the rights of citizenship in that government, and warning that anything less than full and complete freedom and equality for black Americans would endanger the life of the Republic.

Writing from Mobile, Alabama, in August, 1871, a black

correspondent of *The Christian Recorder*, official weekly of the African Methodist Episcopal Church, noted the special place lectures occupied among the freedmen of the South. "While we need some to diffuse literature in the form of journals and periodicals, we also need those who instruct the masses orally, especially those who cannot read, nor will not subscribe for a paper to be read to them." The same weekly carried in its issue of September 23, 1871, the following letter from Mobile under the heading, "A Female Lecturer":

It is with peculiar diffidence that I make any reference to Mrs. F. E. W. Harper's very instructive Lectures in this as well as many other portions of the South. Mrs. Harper has done an immeasurable amount of good, especially in bringing wholesome instructions to the very firesides of the lowly. She manifested a love of race, that would prompt any to say, she has the highest good of her people at heart. . . . When persons come among us, who will not, at the peril of their lives, compromise our race, nor injure our common cause, they should have our healthy support. Mrs. Harper is evidently devoted to the interest of our race. . . . She has impressed many who were averse to females entering the lecture field, that public speaking is her native element; the practical cast of her mind gives rare coloring and beauty to her lectures. Many more like Mrs. Harper are greatly needed, especially in the South, to remove the bad odor from the name "Negro" that it may be placed among the names most distinguished. . . .

Mrs. Harper was also one of a series of black orators whose lectures were sponsored by the Social, Cultural and Statistical Association of the Colored People of Pennsylvania, an organization located in Philadelphia. These speakers analyzed the significance of the issues of Reconstruction to an important body of Northern blacks.

When the thirteenth, fourteenth and fifteenth amendments to the Constitution were adopted, there were those who believed that the need for black orators who voiced the race's grievances no longer existed. But events soon demonstrated that this belief had no basis in reality. A new pattern of oppression, replacing the old slave system, grew up in the South; and in the North, the problems of prejudice and a caste society still prevailed. "Press, platform, pulpit," Frederick Douglass wrote in July, 1870, "should continue to direct their energies to the removal of the hardships and wrongs which continue to be the lot of the colored people of this country because they wear a complexion which two hundred and fifty years of slavery taught the great mass of the American people to hate and which the Fifteenth Amendment has not yet taught the American people to love."

Once again articulate black Americans mounted the platform to fight for civil and political equality for their people. Nor were the black speakers now confined to the North. Some of the greatest of the black speakers emerged in the South, a number of them former slaves, and their speeches, like those of the first black Congressmen, reminded the American people that while Constitutional amendments guaranteeing the Negro equality and rights as a citizen looked very fine in print, the practice of the nation was quite a different thing. What, they asked, were the fourteenth and fifteenth amendments worth to the victims of Ku Klux Klan terror? What did the ballot mean to men reduced to a state of peonage?

These voices were not heeded. The hopes and opportunities raised by the outlawing of slavery and the granting of citizenship and enfranchisement were relentlessly diminished by various kinds of legal and illegal acts. By 1900 nearly all the liberals in the North who had demanded equal rights for the Negro were silent. The Northern press had ceased to criticize Southern treatment of Negroes, federal courts were handing down decisions nullifying much of what was valuable in the fourteenth and fifteenth amendments and ruling that "separate but equal" facilities for Negroes were Constitutional. The South was thus left free to deal with the Negro as it saw fit. By the 1890's Negro disenfranchisement had begun in earnest, and by 1910 it was an established fact through most of the South. By that time, too, a Jim Crow society existed in the South.

In this period a new Negro leadership arose that advocated a policy of accommodation as the most realistic approach to a very difficult situation. Led by Booker T. Washington, these black spokesmen urged the acceptance of second-class citizenship as a prerequisite to obtaining any concessions from the dominant whites. Negroes were urged to learn trades and develop the attitude that hard work is the highest virtue. They were assured that only in this way could they achieve the rights of citizenship. "The time will come," declared Washington, "when the Negro in the South will be accorded all the political rights which his ability, character and material possessions entitle him to." In the meantime, he should cease all agitation and protest.

This approach did not go unopposed. The demand for immediate application of the thirteenth, fourteenth and fifteenth amendments, for full citizenship, was asserted by black men and women under the leadership of W. E. B. Du Bois: This group declared in speech after speech: "We shall not be satisfied with less than our full manhood rights. We claim for our-

selves every right that belongs to a free-born American, civil
and social, and until we get these rights we shall never cease
to protest and assail the ears of America with the stories of its
shameful deeds toward us." It is this militant theme that dominates the remaining part of this book from the era of the Niagara
Movement to that of Black Power.

There are enough masterpieces of Negro eloquence in this
collection to fill a volume of ordinary size. What all the speeches
present, regardless of style, is an important picture of conditions that faced black Americans at different stages in our
history and a determination to change these conditions, even
though many spoke with knowledge of a battle being waged
against tremendous odds. The sense of engagement, of the
speakers' passionate concern for the welfare of their people,
runs like fire through almost all of these speeches. This collection has the feel of life itself. For it is the expression of men
and women from all walks of life who for almost two centuries
knew the daily humiliation of having been born black in the
land that prided itself as the symbol of hope for the world's oppressed peoples.

Most of the speeches in this collection are understandably
polemical, for there never was a time when the black American
was not outraged at the conditions imposed upon him.

"The man that has a grievance is supposed to speak for himself," Dr. W. E. B. Du Bois declared in 1907. "No one can
speak for him—no one knows the thing as well as he does."
The men and women whose speeches are collected in this volume voiced not only their own grievances, but also, as Martin
Luther King, Jr., noted in 1967, those of "the voiceless." They
voiced the grievances of a whole people throughout most of our
nation's history. "The grievances of which we complain," said
Charles Lenox Remond in April, 1943, "are not imaginary but
real—not local, but universal; not occasional, but continual
. . . and have become, to the disgrace of our common country,
matter of history." The very last speech included in this volume
points up the fact that one hundred and twenty years later
many of these same grievances continue to "disgrace" our country.

Many of the speeches in this collection are in newspapers,
magazines, pamphlets and books located in libraries and historical societies throughout the country. I wish to express my
deep appreciation to the staffs of the Lincoln University Library,
the Schomburg Collection of the New York Public Library, the
Library of Howard University, the Library of the University of
California, Berkeley, Rutgers University Library, Princeton

University Library, the New York Public Library, the National Archives, Washington, D. C., the Library of Congress, the Library of Bowdoin College, the Library of Atlanta University, the Library of Fisk University, the Boston Public Library, the Nashville Public Library, the Wisconsin State Historical Society, the Abdel Wentz Library of the Lutheran Theological Seminary, the American Antiquarian Society, the Tamiment Institute Library of New York University, and the Historical Society of Pennsylvania for assistance in the use of materials in these repositories. I also wish to thank Bishop John D. Bright, Sr., of the African Methodist Episcopal Church, First Episcopal District, and the Reverend Mr. Harry J. White, Sr., of the Mother Bethel African Methodist Episcopal Church of Philadelphia, for permission to use the files of *The Christian Recorder* in the archives of the church. Mr. Arthur Bronson of the Church was of kind assistance throughout my research.

I wish to thank the Association for the Study of Negro Life and History for permission to reprint a number of speeches; Mrs. Martin Luther King, Jr., for permission to publish the speeches of Dr. Martin Luther King, Jr.; the *Journal of Negro Education*, the National Association for the Advancement of Colored People, the National Urban League, Merit Publishers, Golden Bell Press, *Jewish Currents, Freedomways*, the Harlem Labor Committee, E. P. Dutton and Company, the Citadel Press, International Publishers, Congresswoman Shirley Chisholm, Congressman Adam Clayton Powell, Jr., the Honorable Thurgood Marshall, the Honorable Ralph Bunche, the Honorable Richard Gordon Hatchett, the Honorable Charles Evers, the Honorable Julian Bond, Bayard Rustin, Ossie Davis, the A. Philip Randolph Institute, John Henrik Clarke, Dr. Ralph Abernathy, Paul Robeson, the Estate of Lorraine Hansberry, for permission to reprint speeches.

Finally, I wish to thank Mrs. Jane Wesson for typing and other assistance in preparing the manuscript for the printer.

Philip S. Foner

Lincoln University, Pennsylvania

SECTION I

The
Antebellum Period

1797–1860

PRAY GOD GIVE US THE STRENGTH TO BEAR UP UNDER ALL OUR TROUBLES

By Prince Hall

On June 24, 1797, Prince Hall delivered a Masonic sermon to the African Lodge at Menotomy (later West Cambridge), Massachusetts, in which he strongly denounced the African slave trade and the shameful abuse of people of color in Boston, and expressed faith that God would soon end these and other evils imposed upon black people. Prince Hall was born in Barbados in 1748, the son of an Englishman and a free African woman. He came to America in 1765 and settled in Boston, where, as a free Negro, he became a property owner. Hall went to school at night and became a Methodist preacher. Ten years after his arrival in Boston, he was the accepted leader of the black community. He displayed an early interest in the plight of the slaves and signed petitions for their emancipation. Hall served in the local militias and took part in the Battle of Bunker Hill.

Prejudice made Hall the father of African secret societies in the United States. He first sought initiation into the white Masonic lodge in Boston, but was turned down because of his color. His application to the Army Lodge of an Irish regiment was favorably received, and on March 6, 1775, Hall and fourteen other black Americans were initiated into Lodge Number 44. When the British were forced to evacuate Boston on March 17, the Army Lodge gave Prince Hall and his colleagues a license to meet and function as a Lodge. On July 3, 1776, African Lodge No. 1 came into being—the first Lodge in Masonry established in America for men of African descent. It was not, however, until 1787 that the Negro Masons were granted a charter by the Grand Lodge of England under the name of the African Lodge No. 459. Prince Hall became the first Grand Mason of the first Grand Lodge of Negro Masons.

(The address presented here is taken from William C. Nell, The Colored Patriots of the American Revolution, *Boston, 1855, pp. 61–64.)*

BELOVED BRETHREN of the African Lodge: It is now five years since I delivered a charge to you on some parts and points of Masonry. As one branch of superstructure of the foundation, I endeavored to show you the duty of a mason to a mason, and of charity and love to all mankind, as the work and image of the great God and the Father of the human race. I shall now attempt to show you that it is our duty to sympathize with our fellow men under their troubles, and with the families of our brethren who are gone, we hope, to the Grand Lodge above.

We are to have sympathy, but this, after all, is not to be confined to parties or colors, nor to towns or states, nor to a kingdom, but to the kingdoms of the whole earth, over whom Christ the King is head and Grand Master for all in distress.

Among these numerous sons and daughters of a distress, let us see our friends and brethren; and first let us see *them* dragged from their native country, by the iron hand of tyranny and oppression, from their dear friends and connections, with weeping eyes and aching hearts, to a strange land, and among a strange people, whose tender mercies are cruel, and there to bear the iron yoke of slavery and cruelty, till death, as a friend, shall relieve them. And must not the unhappy condition of these, our fellow men, draw forth our hearty prayers and wishes for their deliverance from those merchants and traders, whose characters you have described in Revelations 17:11–13? And who knows but these same sort of traders may, in a short time, in like manner bewail the loss of the African traffic to their shame and confusion? The day dawns now in some of the West Indies Islands.* God can and will change their condition and their hearts, too, and let Boston and the world know that He hath no respect of persons, and that that bulwark of envy, pride, scorn and contempt, which is so visible in some, shall fall.

Jethro, an Ethiopian, gave instructions to his son-in-law, Moses, in establishing government. Exodus 18:22–24. Thus, Moses was not ashamed to be instructed by a black man. Philip was not ashamed to take a seat beside the Ethiopian Eunuch and to instruct him in the gospel. The Grand Master Solomon was not ashamed to hold conference with the Queen of Sheba. Our Grand Master Solomon did not divide the living child, whatever he might do with the dead one; neither did he pretend to make a law to forbid the parties from having free intercourse

---

* The reference is to the insurrection of the slaves in the French island of Saint Domingue which began in August, 1791, and led to the establishment of the Republic of Haiti.

with one another, without the fear of censure, or be turned out
of the synagogue.

Now, my brethren, nothing is stable; all things are change-
able. Let us seek those things which are sure and steadfast, and
let us pray God that, while we remain here, he would give us
the grace of patience and strength to bear up under all our
troubles, which, at this day, God knows, we have our share of.
Patience, I say; for were we not possessed of a great measure
of it, we could not bear up under the daily insults we meet with
in the streets of Boston, much more on public days of recreation. How, at such times, are we shamefully abused, and that
to such a degree that we may truly be said to carry our lives in
our hands, and the arrows of death are flying about our heads.
Helpless women have their clothes torn from their backs. . . .
And by whom are these disgraceful and abusive actions committed? Not by the men born and bred in Boston—they are
better bred—but by a mob or horde of shameless, low-lived,
envious, spiteful persons, some of them not long since servants
in gentlemen's kitchens scouring knives, horse tenders, chaise
drivers. I was told by a gentleman who saw the filthy behavior
in the Common that, in all places he had been in, he never saw
so cruel behavior in all his life; and that a slave in the West
Indies on Sundays or holidays enjoys himself and friends without molestation. Not only this man, but many in town who have
seen their behavior to us, and that without provocation twenty
or thirty cowards have fallen upon one man. (Oh, the patience
of the blacks!) 'Tis not for want of courage in you, for they
know that they do not face you man for man; but in a mob,
which we despise, and would rather suffer wrong than to do
wrong, to the disturbance of the community, and the disgrace
of our reputation; for every good citizen doth honor to the laws
of the state where he resides.

My brethren, let us not be cast down under these and many
other abuses we at present are laboring under, for the darkest
hour is just before the break of day. My brethren, let us remember what a dark day it was with our African brethren, six
years ago, in the French West Indies. Nothing but the snap of
the whip was heard, from morning to evening. Hanging, breaking on the wheel, burning, and all manner of tortures were
inflicted upon those unhappy people. But, blessed be God, the
scene is changed. They now confess that God hath no respect
of persons and, therefore, receive them as their friends and
treat them as brothers. Thus doth Ethiopia stretch forth her
hand from slavery, to freedom and equality.

ADDRESS TO THE PEOPLE OF COLOR

By Abraham Johnstone

In 1745, a broadside was issued entitled The Declaration and Confession of Jeffrey, Negro, *who was executed in Worcester, October 17, 1745, for the Murder of his Mistress Tabitha Sanford, at Mendon, the 12th of September. A notice of the broadside was published in the* Boston Evening Post *of October 28, 1745, but there does not appear to be in existence any copy of the sheet itself or the "Declaration and Confession."*

Early in 1797, Abraham Johnstone, a free Negro who had been born a slave in Delaware and manumitted by his master, was convicted by a jury of having murdered Thomas Read, also a Negro. He was sentenced to be hanged. When asked by the court for a statement, Johnstone delivered a long address to "the people of color," much of it devoted to advice on how to conduct themselves in American society. Sections of the address, which are printed below, were evidently intended for white listeners. The speech was later published in Philadelphia as "The Address of Abraham Johnstone. . . . to the People of Colour," and there was added "The Dying Words of Abraham Johnstone," and his letter to his wife, both written in Woodbury jail, July 8, 1797. The anonymous printer of the pamphlet in an address "To the Public," which appeared as a foreword, questioned Johnstone's guilt and pointed out that he had been convicted on very flimsy evidence. "Juries," he warned, "ought to be extremely cautious how they admit evidence founded solely on presumption to affect the life of a fellow creature and deprive society of a member: Proof of so vague and indeterminable a nature, being too dangerous to be admitted in this country where I am sorry to say there is but too little regard paid to oaths; and the most glaring perjuries are suffered to pass with impunity."

(The excerpts here presented were taken from a pamphlet in Rutgers University Library—The Address of Abraham Johnstone, A Black Man, Who Was Hanged at Woodbury in the County of Glocester, and State of New Jersey, on Saturday the 8th day of July last; to the People of Colour . . . , Philadelphia, 1797.)

. . . I MOST EARNESTLY EXHORT and pray you to be upright and circumspect in your conduct; I must the more earnestly urge this particular from a combination of circumstances that at this juncture of time concur to make it of importance to our color for my unfortunate unhappy fate, however unmerited or undeserved, may by some ungenerous and illiberal-minded persons, but particularly by those who oppose the emancipation of those of our brethern who as yet are in slavery, be made a handle of in order to throw a shade over or cast a general reflection on all those of our color, and the keen shafts of prejudice be launched against us by the most active and virulent malevolence. But such general reflections or sarcasms will be only made by the low-minded illiberal and sordid persons who are the enemies of our color, and of freedom; and to them I shall simply answer that if the population throughout the United States be then taken, and then a list of all the executions therein be had, and compared therewith impartially, it will be found that as they claim a preeminence over us in every thing else, so we find they also have it in this particular, and that a vast majority of whites have died on the gallows when the population is accurately considered. A plain proof that there are some whites (with all due deference to them) capable of being equally as depraved and more generally so, than blacks or people of color. . . .

From the first bringing of our color into this country they have been constantly kept to the greatest toil and labor, to drudge incessantly yet without the smallest hopes of a reward, and oftentimes denied a sufficient portion of food to suffice the cravings of nature, or raiment sufficient to hide their nakedness or shield them from the inclemency of the weather. Yet, laboring under all those hardships and difficulties, the most unheard-of cruelties and punishments were daily inflicted on us. For what? For not performing impossibilities, for not doing what was impossible for human nature or strength to have done within the time allotted. And if the most pressing hunger should compel us to take from that master by stealth what were sure to be denied if we asked, to satisfy our craving appetites, the most wanton and dreadful punishments were immediately inflicted on us even to a degree of inhumanity and cruelty. That I do not exaggerate is, I dare say, known to many of ye that hear me, or that may hereafter read this address to you, and therefore I appeal to ye, as personal knowledge of the facts I have here stated, I declare myself that I speak from experience. . . .

And here, my dear brethren, I think it necessary to take

notice of the cavils raised by some against us, and the foolishly chimerical notion that prevails with such, to say because we are black, we are not to enjoy a future state, not to be admitted to inherit the kingdom of God, and that our Saviour did not die for us, therefore we cannot hope a redemption; while some other speaking idiots would have us to be the seed of Cain* all equally fallacious and ridiculous; and indeed is enough to make any unconcerned or disinterested person merry to hear such foolishly frivolous arguments adduced with such solemnity against us. However, that I should not be wanting in respect to the whites, nor in justice to my own color, I shall make such objections to those arguments as will, I pledge myself, fully and completely refute them.

As to the first, I shall content myself with making one general observation, namely, that God is neither a respecter of persons, nor colors, be they white, black or mulatto, but respects them merely from their deeds and observance of His divine commands, and I humbly but confidentially insist that no one living can produce a scriptural or even respectably rational authority in support of such a vague and nonsensical opinion, therefore that argument fails.

As to the second, that we shall not inherit the kingdom of God, or enjoy a future state, I wonder where such chimerical notion exists, except in their heated brains or childishly prejudiced imaginations; for Scripture tells us expressly, "That all that believe shall be saved," but to go a step farther and reason the matter candidly and without prejudice, I am confident that the odds will be considerably in our favor. And first, I will ask all those persons seriously, how the economy of divine providence with respect to us, can be made reconcilable with our conceptions of the nature of the divine Supreme Being and his attributes, upon the supposition of this being the first and final stage of our existence? That we are endowed with reason and reflection, and a sensibility of pain as well as pleasure, is acknowledged to be an incontestable truth, neither can it be denied by any one. Nor is it less evident and unquestionable that the latter is oftentimes more than overbalanced by the

---

* A racist justification for enslavement of Africans was that blacks were descendants of Cain, who had been cursed by God for having killed Abel. A poem entitled "Africa," published in the *Literary Digest* of March 5, 1904, contained the lines:
> "She to whom fell the dark disgrace,
>   Cain's evil brood to bear!"
In the Mormon Church blacks cannot gain priesthood because they are believed to be descended from Cain.

former. To instance only in our poor brethren at this moment in slavery in the Southern states, what exquisite, what affecting tortures do many of them endure (tho some few of them perhaps meet a more friendly fate) from some merciless callous-hearted monster of a master? How frequently to the pangs of hunger and a distempered body are there added the most cutting stripes and scourges most liberally and as wantonly dealt out to them by their inhuman masters or drivers, and all this merely for their not effecting perhaps impossibilities! But wherefore all these agonizing pains and miseries heaped on an offspring of divine Providence? And why because our color happens to be black? Are we not a living animated part of the creation? Are we not flesh and blood? Do we not as well as they know what sorrow means? Yes; and for them only, their use, or accidentally their pride, their wantonness, their cruelty were we brought into a sensible existence! Shall one being be created, but even under the bare possibility of being made miserable (more or less) solely for the use and service of another? Lord, what is man? Or rather what are not brutes? The unmerited sufferings among whites urged with are great strength of reasoning, in proof of a recompense reserved for them hereafter. And must a being that happens to move in low and humble sphere in society be at once pronounced unworthy of the like provision? But wherefore this partiality to their noble selves? Why must they plead a right to be dealt with on the part of justice by the Almighty, and yet think it no injury done to us, if our sufferings in a state we are forced into by our common Lord and Creator, meet not from him an hereafter some similar tokens of an universal and impartial goodness toward his creatures so necessary and essential to the divine nature. But to bring it more closely home to these our enemies. I will ask them, if they would think it just or equitable for the Moors in Algiers to deny a salvation or a recompense in an hereafter to those of this country who are there kept in slavery; and whose color is white?* Oh, they surely would not, they would laugh at the absurdity of the idea and treat it with all the ridicule it justly deserved. . . .

---

* American vessels were attacked by pirates from Tripoli and Algiers, and American seamen were enslaved, acts which led to a war with Tripoli and the signing of a treaty ending the practices.

ABOLITION OF THE SLAVE TRADE

By Peter Williams, Jr.

*At the Constitutional Convention in 1787, the delegates
agreed that no law could be passed prohibiting the African
slave trade until the first day of 1808. On December 2,
1806, President Thomas Jefferson, responding to the pressure of antislavery forces in the United States, among
whom free Negroes were especially active, urged Congress
to outlaw the external slave trade, and on March 2, 1807,
a bill to that end was passed, but the prohibition was to
become effective on January 1, 1808. (England abolished
its traffic in slaves on March 25, 1807.) Weak enforcement
of the law, however, prevented total abolition of the slave
trade in America for many years.*

*Negroes throughout the North celebrated the closing of
the African slave trade. In New York City, the Reverend
Peter Williams, Jr. (1800?–1840), son of one of the founders of the African Methodist Episcopal Zion Church, delivered an address in the New York African Church hailing
the abolition of the slave trade.*

*(The address, presented here in part, is taken from
Peter Williams—An Oration on the Abolition of the Slave
Trade; Delivered in the African Church, in the City of
New York, January 1, 1808, New York, 1808.)*

FATHERS, brethren, and fellow citizens: At this auspicious moment I felicitate you on the abolition of the slave trade.
This inhuman branch of commerce which, for some centuries
past, has been carried on to a considerable extent is, by the
singular interposition of divine providence, this day extinguished. An event so important, so pregnant with happy consequences, must be extremely consonant to every philanthropic
heart.

But to us, Africans and descendants of Africans, this period
is deeply interesting. We have felt, sensibly felt, the sad effects
of this abominable traffic. It has made, if not ourselves, our
forefathers and kinsmen its unhappy victims and pronounced
on them and their posterity, the sentence of perpetual slavery.
But benevolent men have voluntarily stepped forward to obviate
the consequences of this injustice and barbarity. They have
striven assiduously to restore our natural rights; to guaranty

them from fresh innovations; to furnish us with necessary information; and to stop the source from whence our evils have flowed.

The fruits of these laudable endeavors have long been visible; each moment they appear more conspicuous; and this day has produced an event which shall ever be memorable and glorious in the annals of history. We are now assembled to celebrate this momentous era; to recognize the beneficial influences of humane exertions; and by suitable demonstrations of joy, thanksgiving and gratitude, to return to our heavenly Father and to our earthly benefactors our sincere acknowledgments.

Review for a moment, my brethren, the history of the slave trade. Engendered in the foul recesses of the sordid mind, the unnatural monster inflicted gross evils on the human race. Its baneful footsteps are marked with blood; its infectious breath spreads war and desolation; and its train is composed of the complicated miseries of cruel and unceasing bondage.

Before the enterprising spirit of European genius explored the western coast of Africa, the state of our forefathers was a state of simplicity, innocence and contentment. Unskilled in the arts of dissimulation, their bosoms were the seats of confidence; and their lips were the organs of truth. Strangers to the refinements of civilized society, they followed with implicit obedience the (simple) dictates of nature. Peculiarly observant of hospitality, they offered a place of refreshment to the weary and an asylum to the unfortunate. Ardent in their affections, their minds were susceptible of the warmest emotions of love, friendship and gratitude.

Although unacquainted with the diversified luxuries and amusements of civilized nations, they enjoyed some singular advantages from the bountiful hand of nature and from their own innocent and amiable manners, which rendered them a happy people. But, alas, this delightful picture has long since vanished; the angel of bliss has deserted their dwelling; and the demon of indescribable misery has rioted uncontrolled on the fair fields of our ancestors. After Columbus unfolded to civilized man the vast treasures of this Western world, the desire of gain, which had chiefly induced the first colonists of America to cross the waters of the Atlantic, surpassing the bounds of reasonable acquisition, violated the sacred injunctions of the gospel, frustrated the designs of the pious and humane and, enslaving the harmless aborigines, compelled them to drudge in the mines.

The severities of this employment were so insupportable to

men who were unaccustomed to fatigue that, according to Robertson's *History of America*, upwards of nine hundred thousand were destroyed in the space of fifteen years on the island of Hispaniola. A consumption so rapid must, in a short period, have deprived them of the instruments of labor, had not the same genius which first produced it found out another method to obtain them. This was no other than the importation of slaves from the coast of Africa.

The Genoese made the first regular importation, in the year 1517, by virtue of a patent granted by Charles of Austria to a Flemish favorite, since which this commerce has increased to an astonishing and almost incredible degree.

After the manner of ancient piracy, descents were first made on the African coast; the towns bordering on the ocean were surprised, and a number of the inhabitants carried into slavery.

Alarmed at these depredations, the natives fled to the interior and there united to secure themselves from the common foe. But the subtle invaders were not easily deterred from their purpose. Their experience, corroborated by historical testimony, convinced them that this spirit of unity would baffle every violent attempt and that the most powerful method to dissolve it would be to diffuse in them the same avaricious disposition which they themselves possessed and to afford them the means of gratifying it by ruining each other. Fatal engine, fatal thou hast proved to man in all ages; where the greatest violence has proved ineffectual, their undermining principles have wrought destruction. By thy deadly power, the strong Grecian arm, which bid the world defiance, fell nerveless; by thy potent attacks, the solid pillars of Roman grandeur shook to their base; and, oh, Africans, by this parent of the slave trade, this grandsire of misery, the mortal blow was struck which crushed the peace and happiness of our country. Affairs now assumed a different aspect; the appearances of war were changed into the most amicable pretensions; presents apparently inestimable were made; and all the bewitching and alluring wiles of the seducer were practiced. The harmless African, taught to believe a friendly countenance, the sure token of a corresponding heart, soon disbanded his fears and evinced a favorable disposition toward his flattering enemies.

Thus the foe, obtaining an intercourse by a dazzling display of European finery, bewildered their simple understandings and corrupted their morals. Mutual agreements were then made; the Europeans were to supply the Africans with those gaudy trifles which so strongly affected them, and the Africans in return were to grant the Europeans their prisoners of war and convicts as slaves. These stipulations, naturally tending to delude the mind, answered the twofold purpose of enlarging their criminal code and of exciting incessant war at the same time that it furnished a specious pretext for the prosecution of this inhuman traffic. Bad as this may appear, had it prescribed the bounds of injustice, millions of unhappy victims might have still been spared. But, extending widely beyond measure and without control, large additions of slaves were made by kidnaping and the most unpalliated seizures.

Trace the past scenes of Africa and you will manifestly perceive these flagrant violations of human rights. The prince who once delighted in the happiness of his people, who felt himself bound by a sacred contract to defend their persons and property, was turned into their tyrant and scourge. He who once strove to preserve peace and good understanding with the different nations, who never unsheathed his sword but in the cause of justice, at the signal of a slave ship assembled his warriors and rushed furiously upon his unsuspecting friends. What a scene does that town now present, which a few moments past was the abode of tranquillity. At the approach of the foe, alarm and confusion pervade every part; horror and dismay are depicted on every countenance; the aged chief, starting from his couch, calls forth his men to repulse the hostile invader. All ages obey the summons; feeble youth and decrepit age join the standard; while the foe, to effect his purpose, fires the town.

Now, with unimaginable terror the battle commences: hear now the shrieks of the women, the cries of the children, the shouts of the warriors, and the groans of the dying. See with what desperation the inhabitants fight in defense of their darling joys. But alas overpowered by a superior foe, their force is broken; their ablest warriors fall; and the wretched remnant are taken captives.

Where are now those pleasant dwellings, where peace and harmony reigned incessant? Where those beautiful fields, whose smiling crops and enchanting verdure enlivened the heart of every beholder? Alas, those tenements are now enveloped in destructive flames; those fair fields are now bedewed with blood and covered with mangled carcasses. Where are now those sounds of mirth and gladness which loudly rang throughout the village? Where those darling youth, those venerable aged, who mutually animated the festive throng? Alas, those exhilarating pearls are now changed into the dismal groans of inconceivable distress; the survivors of those happy people are now carried into cruel captivity. Ah, driven from their native soil,

they cast their languishing eyes behind and with aching hearts
bid adieu to every prospect of joy and comfort.

A spectacle so truly distressing is sufficient to blow into a
blaze the most latent spark of humanity; but the adamantine
heart of avarice, dead to every sensation of pity, regards not
the voice of the sufferers, but hastily drives them to market
for sale.

Oh, Africa, Africa, to what horrid inhumanities have thy
shores been witness; thy shores, which were once the garden of
the world, the seal of almost paradisaical joys, have been transformed into regions of woe; thy sons, who were once the happiest of mortals, are reduced to slavery and, bound in weighty
shackles, now fill the trader's ship. But, though defeated in the
contest for liberty, their magnanimous souls scorn the gross
indignity and choose death in preference to slavery. Painful—
ah, painful—must be that existence which the rational mind
can deliberately doom to self-destruction. Thus the poor Africans, robbed of every joy, while they see not the saddened
hearts, sink into the abyss of consummate misery. Their lives,
embittered by reflection, anticipation and present sorrows, they
feel burthensome; and death (whose dreary mansions appal
the stoutest hearts) they view as their only shelter.

You, my brethren, beloved Africans, who had passed the days
of infancy when you left your country, you best can tell the aggravated sufferings of our unfortunate race; your memories can
bring to view these scenes of bitter grief. What, my brethren,
when dragged from your native land on board the slave ship,
what was the anguish which you saw, which you felt? What the
pain, what the dreadful forebodings which filled your throbbing
bosoms?

But you, my brethren, descendants of African forefathers, I
call upon you to view a scene of unfathomable distress. Let your
imagination carry you back to former days. Behold a vessel
bearing our forefathers and brethren from the place of their
nativity to a distant and inhospitable clime; behold their de-
jected countenances, their streaming eyes, their fettered limbs;
hear them, with piercing cries and pitiful moans, deploring their
wretched fate. After their arrival in port, see them separated
without regard to the ties of blood or friendship—husband
from wife; parent from child; brother from sister; friend from
friend. See the parting tear rolling down their fallen cheeks;
hear the parting sigh die on their quivering lips.

But let us no longer pursue a theme of boundless affliction.
An enchanting sound now demands your attention. Hail, hail,
glorious day, whose resplendent rising disperseth the clouds

which have hovered with destruction over the land of Africa and illumines it by the most brilliant rays of future prosperity. Rejoice, oh Africans! No longer shall tyranny, war and injustice, with irresistible sway, desolate your native country; no longer shall torrents of human blood deluge its delightful plains; no longer shall it witness your countrymen wielding among each other the instruments of death; nor the insidious kidnaper, darting from his midnight haunt, on the feeble and unprotected; no longer shall its shores resound with the awful howlings of infatuated warriors, the deathlike groans of vanquished innocents, nor the clanking fetters of woe-doomed captives. Rejoice, oh, ye descendants of Africans! No longer shall the United States of America or the extensive colonies of Great Britain admit the degrading commerce of the human species; no longer shall they swell the tide of African misery by the importation of slaves. Rejoice, my brethren, that the channels are obstructed through which slavery and its direful concomitants have been entailed on the African race. But let incessant strains of gratitude be mingled with your expressions of joy. Through the infinite mercy of the great Jehovah, this day announces the abolition of the slave trade. Let, therefore, the heart that is warmed by the smallest drop of African blood glow in grateful transports and cause the lofty arches of the sky to reverberate eternal praise to his boundless goodness.

O God, we thank Thee, that Thou didst condescend to listen to the cries of Africa's wretched sons and that Thou didst interfere in their behalf. At Thy call humanity sprang forth and espoused the cause of the oppressed; one hand she employed in drawing from their vitals the deadly arrows of injustice; and the other in holding a shield, to defend them from fresh assaults; and at that illustrious moment, when the sons of '76 pronounced these United States free and independent; when the spirit of patriotism erected a temple sacred to liberty; when the inspired voice of Americans first uttered those noble sentiments, "We hold these truths to be self-evident, that all men are created equal; that they are endowed by their Creator with certain unalienable rights; among which are life, liberty and the pursuit of happiness"; and when the bleeding African, lifting his fetters, exclaimed, "Am I not a man and a brother"; then, with redoubled efforts, the angel of humanity strove to restore to the African race the inherent rights of man. . . .

May the time speedily commence when Ethiopia shall stretch forth her hands; when the sun of liberty shall beam resplendent on the whole African race; and its genial influences promote the luxuriant growth of knowledge and virtue.

A DEFENSE OF THE NEGRO

By William Hamilton

In an address to the New York African Society for Mutual Relief on January 2, 1809, William Hamilton, a pioneer black Abolitionist and leader of the black community in New York, effectively defended his people against the charge that Negroes are racially inferior and the supposed proof in the absence of distinguished men and women in literature, arts and science.

(*Excerpts from that address are taken from William Hamilton,* An Address to the New York African Society for Mutual Relief, Delivered in the Universalist Church, January 2, 1809, *New York, 1809.*)

. . . BUT MY BRETHREN, however this may be, it is for us to rejoice that the cause or source from whence these miseries sprang are removing; it is for us to rejoice not only that the sources of slavery are drying away, but that our condition is fast ameliorating; it is for us to rejoice that science has begun to bud with our race and soon shall our tree of arts bear its full burthen of rich and nectarious fruit, soon shall that contumelious assertion of the proud be proved false, to wit, that Africans do not possess minds as ingenious as other men.

The proposition has been advanced by men who claim a preeminence in the learned world, that Africans are inferior to white men in the structure both of body and mind; the first member of this proposition is below our notice; the reasons assigned for the second are that we have not produced any poets, mathematicians, or any to excel in any science whatever —our being oppressed and held in slavery forms no excuse, because, say they, among the Romans their most excellent artists and greatest scientific characters were frequently their slaves and that these on account of their ascendant abilities arose to superior stations in the state; and they exultingly tell us that these slaves were white men.

My brethren, it does not require a complete master to solve this problem, nor is it necessary, in order like good logicians to meet this argument, that we should know which is the major and the minor proposition; and the middle and extreme terms of syllogism, he must be a willful novice and blind intentionally, who cannot unfold this enigma.

Among the Romans it was only necessary for the slave to be manumitted, in order to be eligible to all the offices of the state, together with the emoluments belonging thereto; no sooner was he free than there was open before him a wide field of employment for his ambition, and learning and abilities with merit were as sure to meet with their reward in him as in any other citizen. But what station above the common employment of craftsmen and laborers would we fill, did we possess both learning and abilities; is there aught to enkindle in us one spark of emulation; must not he who makes any considerable advances under present circumstance be almost a prodigy: although it may be true we have not produced any to excel in arts and sciences, yet if our station be properly considered and the allowances made which ought to be, it will soon be perceived that we do not fall far behind those who boast of a superior judgment, we have produced some who have claimed attention, and whose works have been admired, yes in despite of all our embarrassments our genius does sometimes burst forth from its encumbrance, although the productions of Phillis Wheatley* may not possess the requisitions necessary to stand the test of nice criticism, and she may be denied a stand in the rank of poets, yet she does possess some original ideas that would not disgrace the pen of the best poets. . . .

* Phillis Wheatley (c. 1753–1784) was a poet whose volume of collected verse, *Poems on Various Subjects, Religious and Moral* (1773), was the first volume known to have been written by a Negro woman. Kidnaped in her native Senegal when she was about seven, she was brought to Boston in 1761 and sold to John Wheatley, a tailor of that city. She learned to read the Bible and acquired a knowledge of English and Latin literature. Her first publication, "A Poem, by Phillis, a Negro Girl in Boston, on the Death of the Reverend George Whitefield," appeared in 1770.

It is strange that Hamilton did not mention Benjamin Banneker (1731–1806), the free Negro astronomer and mathematician, of Maryland. In 1791 Banneker began to publish a series of almanacs that won wide recognition.

A TRIBUTE TO CAPTAIN PAUL CUFFE

By Peter Williams, Jr.

*Paul Cuffe, one of the outstanding leaders of the Negro
community in the United States during the post-Revolu-
tionary period, died on September 19, 1817. Five weeks
later, on October 21, 1817, at the New York African Institution, a meeting in Cuffe's honor was held. Here Peter
Williams, a New York Negro who had known Cuffe and
was then studying for the Episcopal priesthood, delivered
this eulogy:*
*(The excerpts presented here were taken from Benjamin
Brawley,* Early American Negro Writers, *Chapel Hill,
N. C., 1935, pp. 101–9.)*

. . . WERE I REQUIRED to delineate a character of distinguished greatness, I would not seek as my original one whose
blood has been ennobled through a long line of ancestry, who
has had all the advantages of fortune, education, wealth and
friends to push him forward; but for one who, from a state of
poverty, ignorance and obscurity, through a host of difficulties
and with an unsullied conscience, by the native energy of his
mind has elevated himself to wealth, to influence, to respectability and honor, and being thus elevated, conducts himself
with meekness and moderation, and devotes his time and talents to pious and benevolent purposes. Such a one's character
deserves to be drawn by the ablest artist and to be placed up
on high for public imitation and esteem; nay, the portrait
should be placed in our bosoms and worn as a sacred treasure
ever near to the heart. Such a one was Paul Cuffe, the son of a
poor African, whom the hand of unfeeling avarice had dragged
from home and connections, and consigned to rigorous and
unlimited bondage; subjected to all the disadvantages which
unreasonable prejudice heaps upon that class of men, destitute
of the means of early education, and more frequently struggling under the frowns of fortune than basking in her smiles,
by perseverance, prudence and laudable enterprise he raised
himself to wealth and respectability, and having attained that
eminence, he so distinguished himself by his amiable and upright deportment and his zealous exertions in the cause of
humanity and religion that he became not only an object of

general notice and regard throughout the civilized world, but even the untutored tribes that inhabit the regions of Ethiopia learned to consider him as a father and a friend. . . .

He was born in the year 1759, on one of the Elizabeth Islands, near New Bedford. His parents had ten children—four sons and six daughters. He was the youngest of the sons. His father died when he was about fourteen years of age, at which time he had learned but little more than his alphabet; and having from thence, with his brothers, the care of his mother and sisters devolving upon him, he had but little opportunity for the acquisitions of literature. Indeed, he never had any schooling, but obtained what learning he had by his own indefatigable exertions and the scanty aids which he occasionally received from persons who were friendly toward him. By these means, however, he advanced to a considerable proficiency in arithmetic and skill in navigation. Of his talent for receiving learning we may form an estimate from the fact that he acquired such a knowledge of navigation in two weeks as enabled him to command his vessel in the voyages which he made to Russia, to England, to Africa, to the West India Islands, as well as to a number of different ports in the Southern section of the United States. His mind, it appears, was early inclined to the pursuits of commerce. Before he was grown to manhood, he made several voyages to the West Indies, and along the American coast. At the age of twenty, he commenced business for himself, in a small open boat. With this, he set out trading to the neighboring towns and settlements; and though Providence seemed rather unpropitious to him at first, by perseverance, prudence and industry, his resources were so blessed with an increase that after a while he was enabled to obtain a good-sized schooner. In this vessel he enlarged the sphere of his action, trading to more distant places, and in articles requiring a larger capital; and thus, in the process of time, he became owner of one brig, afterward of two, then he added a ship, and so on until 1806, at which time he was possessed of one ship, two brigs, and several smaller vessels, besides considerable property in houses and lands. . . .

In the year 1780, Captain C. being just then of age, was with his brother John called on by the collector to pay his personal tax. At that time the colored people of Massachusetts were not considered as entitled to the right of suffrage or to any of the privileges peculiar to citizens. A question immediately arose with them, whether it was Constitutional for them to pay taxes, while they were deprived of the rights enjoyed by others who paid them? They concluded, it was not; and, though the sum was small, yet considering it as an imposition affecting the interests of the people of color throughout the state, they refused to pay it. The consequence was a lawsuit, attended with so much trouble and vexatious delay, that they finally gave it up, by complying with the requisitions of the collector. They did not, however, abandon the pursuit of their rights, but at the next session of the legislature presented a petition, praying that they might have the rights, since they had to bear the burden of citizenship; and though there was much reason to doubt of its success, yet it was granted, and all the free colored people of the state, on paying their taxes, were considered, from thenceforth, as entitled to all the privileges of citizens. For this triumph of justice and humanity over prejudice and oppression, not only the colored people of Massachusetts, but every advocate of correct principle, owes a tribute of respect and gratitude to John and Paul Cuffe.

In 1797, Captain Cuffe, lamenting that the place in which he lived was destitute of a school for the instruction of youth, and anxious that his children should have a more favorable opportunity of obtaining education than he had had, proposed to his neighbors to unite with him in erecting a schoolhouse. This, though the utility of the object was undeniable, was made the cause of so much contention (probably on account of his color) that he resolved at length to build a schoolhouse on his own land and at his own expense. He did so and, when finished, gave them the use of it gratis, satisfying himself with seeing it occupied for the purposes contemplated. I would not draw a contrast, brethren. The neighbors, no doubt, have long since atoned for their conduct on this occasion in a generous sorrow. But let not prejudice denounce such a man as possessed of an inferior soul.

But it was in his active commiseration in behalf of his African brethren that be shone forth most conspicuously as a man of worth. Long had his bowels yearned over their degraded, destitute, miserable condition. He saw, it is true, many benevolent men engaging in releasing them from bondage and pouring into their minds the light of literature and religion, but he saw also the force of prejudice operating so powerfully against them as to give but little encouragement to hope that they could ever rise to respectability and usefulness, unless it were in a state of society where they would have greater incentives to improvement, and more favorable opportunities than would probably be ever afforded them where the bulk of the population are whites.

Under this impression, he turned his thoughts to the British settlement at Sierra Leone;* and in 1811, finding his property sufficient to warrant the undertaking and believing it to be his duty to appropriate part of what God had given him to the benefit of his and our unhappy race, he embarked on board of his own brig, manned entirely by persons of color, and sailed to the land of his forefathers in the hope of benefiting its natives and descendants.

Arrived at the colony, he made himself acquainted with its condition and held a number of conversations with the governor and principal inhabitants, in which he suggested a number of important improvements. Among other things, he recommended the formation of a society for the purposes of promoting the interests of its members and of the colonists in general; which measure was immediately adopted, and the society named The Friendly Society of Sierra Leone. From thence he sailed to England, where, meeting with every mark of attention and respect, he was favored with an opportunity of opening his views to the board of managers of the African Institution, who, cordially acquiescing in all his plans, gave him authority to carry over from the United States a few colored persons of good character, to instruct the colonists in agriculture and the mechanical arts. After this he returned to Sierra Leone, carrying with him some goods as a consignment to the Friendly Society, to encourage them in the way of trade, which having safely delivered, and given them some salutary instructions, he set sail and returned again to his native land.

Thus terminated his first mission to Africa, a mission fraught with the most happy consequences, undertaken from the purest motives of benevolence, and solely at his own expense and risk.

Returned to the bosom of his family and friends, where every comfort awaited his command, he could not think of enjoying repose while he reflected that he might, in any degree, administer to the relief of the multitudes of his brethren who were groaning under the yoke of bondage or groping in the dark and horrible night of heathenish superstition and ignorance. Scarcely had the first transports of rejoicing at his return time to subside, before he commenced his preparations for a second

---

* The Sierra Leone colony was established by the Sierra Leone Company, which was founded in 1791 to enable destitute Negroes in London to make a new start by settling them on the west coast of Africa. On its board of directors were William Wilberforce, Thomas Clarkson and Granville Sharp, leading British abolitionists. Among the Negroes who settled Sierra Leone were those who had fought alongside the British in the American Revolution and had been taken to Halifax, Nova Scotia, when the war was over. The site they settled was named Freetown.

voyage, not discouraged by the labors and dangers he had past and unmindful of the ease which the decline of life requires and to which his long continued and earnest exertions gave him a peculiar claim. In the hope of finding persons of the description given by the African Institution, he visited most of the large cities in the union, held frequent conferences with the most reputable men of color, and also with those among the whites who had distinguished themselves as the friends of the Africans, and recommended to the colored people to form associations for the furtherance of the benevolent work in which he was engaged. The results were the formation of two societies, one in Philadelphia and the other in New York, and the discovery of a number of proper persons who were willing to go with him and settle in Africa. But unfortunately, before he found himself in readiness for the voyage, the war commenced between this country and Great Britain.* This put a bar in the way of his operations, which he was so anxious to remove that he traveled from his home at Westport to the city of Washington, to solicit the government to favor his views and to let him depart and carry with him those persons and their effects whom he had engaged to go and settle in Sierra Leone. He was, however, unsuccessful in the attempt. His general plan was highly and universally approbated, but the policy of the government would not admit of such an intercourse with an enemy's colony.

He had now no alternative but to stay at home and wait the event of the war. But the delay, thus occasioned, instead of being suffered to damp his ardor, was improved by him to the maturing of his plans and extending his correspondence, which already embraced some of the first characters in Great Britain and America. After the termination of the war, he with all convenient speed prepared for his departure, and in December, 1815, he took on board his brig thirty-eight persons of the dispersed race of Africa and, after a voyage of fifty-five days, landed them safely on the soil of their progenitors.

It is proper here to remark that Captain C. in his zeal for the welfare of his brethren had exceeded the instructions of the institution at London. They had advised him not to carry over, in the first instance, more than six or eight persons; consequently, he had no claim on them for the passage and other expenses attending the removal of any over that number. But this he had previously considered, and generously resolved to bear the burden of the expense himself, rather than any of those whom he had engaged should be deprived of an oppor-

* The War of 1812 began in June, 1812.

tunity of going where they might be so usefully employed. He moreover foresaw that when these persons were landed at Sierra Leone it would be necessary to make such provision for the destitute as would support them until they were enabled to provide for themselves.

For this also he had to apply to his own resources, so that in this voyage he expended, out of his own private funds, between three and four thousand dollars for the benefit of the colony.

Such was his public character. Such was the warmth of his benevolence, the activity of his zeal and the extent of his labors, in behalf of the African race. Indeed his whole life may be said to have been spent in their service. To their benefit he devoted the acquisitions of his youth, the time of his later years, and even the thoughts of his dying pillow.

THE CONDITION AND PROSPECTS OF HAITI

By John Browne Russwurm

No event of the late eighteenth century so alarmed the slaveholders of the United States and so aroused the enthusiasm of black Americans, free and slaves, as did the insurrection of the slaves in the French island of Saint Domingue. The revolt began in August, 1791, and, after a decade of bloody conflict, ended with the expulsion of the French, the defeat of Napoleon's crack army of 25,000 soldiers under General Le Clerc, and the establishment on January 1, 1804, of the Republic of Haiti—the first black Republic in the world, the first independent country in Latin America, the second independent nation in the hemisphere, and the one land in which black slaves defeated their masters.

It is not surprising then, that when the second black college graduate in the United States delivered his commencement address, he should have chosen the Haitian revolution and the future of Haiti as his subject.* The graduate was John Browne Russwurm; the institution

* The first Negro college graduate was Edward Jones, who received his degree from Amherst College on August 23, 1826.

*Bowdoin College, in Brunswick, Maine, and the date
September 6, 1826. Russwurm was born in Port Antonio,
Jamaica, October 1, 1799, of a black mother and a white
father who was an English merchant in the West Indies.
At the age of eight, Russwurm was sent to school in Que-
bec; and when a few years later the elder Russwurm
moved into the District of Maine, he brought his son with
him. Russwurm entered Bowdoin College in the fall of
1824 and graduated in 1826. In March, 1827, he became
coeditor and copublisher with Samuel B. Cornish, of* Freedom's Journal, *the first black newspaper published in the
United States. But Russwurm soon became convinced that
because of the strength of racism here no black man could
really live a life of freedom and dignity in the United
States. He turned to colonization and in 1829 went to
Africa as superintendent of public schools in Liberia. In
1836 he was appointed governor of the Cape Palmas district of Liberia, and he continued in this position until his
death on June 17, 1851.*

*Russwurm's commencement address at Bowdoin College
aroused some interest at the time it was delivered. An extract from the speech was published in the Portland*
Eastern Argus *of September 12, 1826;* this was reprinted
two days later in the Boston* Courier, *and somewhat later
in the* National Philanthropist *and the* Genius of Universal
Emancipation. *The latter, an early antislavery journal
published in Baltimore by Benjamin Lundy, headed the
extract, "African Eloquence." The full text of Russwurm's*

---

* The *Eastern Argus* also published the following interesting report of
the commencement:

"The Commencement of the Bowdoin College took place on Wednesday
last, (September 6). Thirty-one gentlemen received the degree of Bachelor
of Arts, of whom twenty-four were selected to take parts in the exhibition. . . .

"One circumstance was peculiarly interesting and we believe it was a
perfect novelty in the history of our Colleges. Among the young gentlemen
who received the honors of the College, and who had parts assigned to
them, was a Mr. Russwurm, a person of African descent. He came on the
stage under an evident feeling of embarrassment, but finding the sympathies of the audience in his favor, he recovered his courage as he proceeded. He pronounced his part in a full and manly tone of voice, accompanied with appropriate gestures, and it was received by the audience
with hearty applause. Altogether it was one of the most interesting performances of the day. His subject was happily selected. It was the condition and prospects of *Hayti.* Believing our readers would feel an interest
in a literary performance so novel under all its circumstances, we have
obtained the extracts which we subjoin. . . ."

commencement address is presented here with the permission of the Library of Bowdoin College, where the original, in Russwurm's handwriting, is kept.

THE CHANGES which take place in the affairs of this world show the instability of sublunary things. Empires rise and fall, flourish and decay. Knowledge follows revolutions and travels over the globe. Man alone remains the same being, whether placed under the torrid suns of Africa or in the more congenial temperate zone. A principle of liberty is implanted in his breast, and all efforts to stifle it are as fruitless as would be the attempt to extinguish the fires of Etna.

It is in the irresistible course of events that all men who have been deprived of their liberty shall recover this precious portion of their indefeasible inheritance. It is in vain to stem the current; degraded man will rise in his native majesty and claim his rights. They may be withheld from him now, but the day will arrive when they must be surrended.

Among the many interesting events of the present day, and illustrative of this, the Revolution in Haiti holds a conspicuous place. The former political condition of Haiti we all doubtless know. After years of sanguinary struggle for freedom and a political existence, the Haitians on the auspicious day of January first, 1804, declared themselves a free and independent nation. Nothing can ever induce them to recede from this declaration. They know too well by their past misfortunes, by their wounds, which are yet bleeding, that security can be expected only from within themselves. Rather would they devote themselves to death than return to their former condition.

Can we conceive of anything which can cheer the desponding spirit, can reanimate and stimulate it to put everything to the hazard? Liberty can do this. Such were its effects upon the Haitians—men who in slavery showed neither spirit nor genius: but when Liberty, when once Freedom struck their astonished ears, they became new creatures, stepped forth as men, and showed to the world, that though slavery may benumb, it cannot entirely destroy our faculties. Such men were Toussaint L'Ouverture, Dessalines and Christophe!*

The Haitians have adopted the republican form of government; and so firmly is it established that in no country are the

---

* Toussaint L'Ouverture, a black former slave, was the great leader of the Haitian revolution, and Henri Christophe and Jean-Jacques Dessalines, also Negro former slaves, were his chief generals. Toussaint L'Ouverture was tricked by Napoleon into visiting France for negotiations; there he was imprisoned, and there he died in 1803.

rights and privileges of citizens and foreigners more respected, and crimes less frequent. They are a brave and generous people. If cruelties were inflicted during the revolutionary war, it was owing to the policy pursued by the French commanders, which compelled them to use retaliatory measures.

For who shall expostulate with men who have been hunted with bloodhounds, who have been threatened with an auto-da-fé, whose relations and friends have been hanged on gibbets before their eyes, have been sunk by hundreds in the sea—and tell them they ought to exercise kindness toward such mortal enemies? Remind me not of moral duties, of meekness and generosity. Show me the man who has exercised them under these trials, and you point to one who is more than human. It is an undisputed fact, that more than sixteen thousand Haitians perished in the modes above specified. The cruelties inflicted by the French on the children of Haiti have exceeded the crimes of Cortes and Pizarro.

Thirty-two years of their independence, so gloriously achieved, have effected wonders. No longer are they the same people. They had faculties, yet were these faculties oppressed under the load of servitude and ignorance. With a countenance erect and fixed upon Heaven, they can now contemplate the works of divine munificence. Restored to the dignity of man and to society, they have acquired a new existence; their powers have been developed; a career of glory and happiness unfolds itself before them.

The Haitian government has arisen in the neighborhood of European settlements. Do the public proceedings and details of its government bespeak any inferiority? Their state papers are distinguished from those of many European courts only by their superior energy and nonexalted sentiments; and while the manners and politics of Boyer emulate those of his republican neighbors, the court of Christophe had almost as much foppery, almost as many lords and ladies of the bedchamber, and almost as great a proportion of stars and ribbons and gilded chariots as those of his brother potentates in any part of the world.*

(Placed by divine providence amid circumstances more favorable than were their ancestors, the Haitians can more easily

---

* After the elimination of the French, Dessalines was assassinated by the followers of Alexandre Pétion. Thereafter the island was divided during fourteen years of civil war between Pétion and Christophe. The latter ruled the north almost like a feudal monarchy and Pétion ruled the south. In 1822, after the death of both Christophe and Pétion, the latter's protégé, Jean-Pierre Boyer, ruled the whole island for twenty-five years.

than they, make rapid strides in the career of civilization—
they can demonstrate that although the God of nature may have
given them a darker complexion, still they are men alike sensible to all the miseries of slavery and to all the blessings of
freedom.)

May we not indulge in the pleasing hope, that the independence of Haiti has laid the foundation of an empire that will
take a rank with the nations of the earth—that a country, the
local situation of which is favorable to trade and commercial
enterprise, possessing a free and well-regulated government,
which encourages the useful and liberal arts, a country containing an enterprising and growing population which is determined to live free or die gloriously will advance rapidly in
all the arts of civilization.

We look forward with peculiar satisfaction to the period when,
like Tyre of old, her vessels shall extend the fame of her
riches and glory, to the remotest borders of the globe—to the
time when Haiti treading in the footsteps of her sister republics, shall, like them, exhibit a picture of rapid and unprecedented advance in population, wealth and intelligence.

THE ABOLITION OF SLAVERY IN NEW YORK

By Nathaniel Paul

*New York passed a gradual-emancipation act in 1799. The
law did not free those then in slavery, but provided that
those of their children born after July 4, 1799, should
have the status of bonded servants, the males until twenty-
eight years of age and the females until twenty-five, at
which time they were to be free. By a law of 1817 slaves
born before July 4, 1799, were to be free after July 3,
1827. Although slavery as an institution did not cease in
New York until 1841, Emancipation Day, July 4, 1827—
the day when the law of 1817 went into effect—was celebrated by Negroes throughout the state. The following is
part of an address delivered on July 5, 1827, by Nathaniel
Paul (1775?–1839), pastor of the African Baptist Society,
Albany, New York.*

*(The passages presented below have been excerpted
from* Freedom's Journal, *August 10, 1827.)*

THROUGH THE LONG LAPSE of ages it has been common for nations to record whatever was peculiar or interesting in the course of their history. Thus when Heaven, provoked by the iniquities of man, has visited the earth with the pestilence which moves in darkness or destruction, that wasteth at noonday, and has swept from existence, by thousands, its numerous inhabitants, or when the milder terms of mercy have been dispensed in rich abundance and the goodness of God has crowned the efforts of any people with peace and prosperity, they have been placed upon their annals and handed to future ages, both for their amusement and profit. And as the nations which have already passed away have been careful to select the most important events, peculiar to themselves, and have recorded them for the good of the people that should succeed them, so will we place it upon our history; and we will tell the good story to our children and to our children's children, down to the latest posterity, that on the Fourth Day of July, in the year of our Lord 1827, slavery was abolished in the state of New York.

Seldom, if ever, was there an occasion which required a public acknowledgment, or that deserved to be retained with gratitude of heart to the all-wise disposer of events, more than the present on which we have assembled.

It is not the mere gratification of the pride of the heart, or any vain ambitious notion, that has influenced us to make our appearance in the public streets of our city or to assemble in the sanctuary of the Most High this morning; but we have met to offer our tribute of thanksgiving and praise to almighty God for His goodness, to retrace the acts and express our gratitude to our public benefactors, and to stimulate each other to the performance of every good and virtuous act, which now does, or hereafter may, devolve as a duty upon us as freemen and citizens, in common with the rest of the community.

And if ever it were necessary for me to offer an apology to an audience for my absolute inability to perform a task assigned me, I feel that the present is the period. However, relying for support on the hand of Him who has said, "I will never leave nor forsake," and confiding in your charity for every necessary allowance, I venture to engage in the arduous undertaking.

In contemplating the subject before us, in connection with the means by which so glorious an event has been accomplished, we find much which requires our deep humiliation and our most exalted praises. We are permitted to behold one of the most pernicious and abominable of all enterprises, in which the depravity of human nature ever led man to engage, entirely eradicated. The power of the tyrant is subdued, the heart of the oppressed is cheered, liberty is proclaimed to the captive, and the opening of the prison to those who were bound, and he who had long been the miserable victim of cruelty and degradation is elevated to the common rank in which our benevolent Creator first designed that man should move—all of which have been effected by means the most simple, yet perfectly efficient. Not by those fearful judgments of the Almighty, which have so often fallen upon the different parts of the earth, which have over-turned nations and kingdoms, scattered thrones and scepters; nor is the glory of the achievement tarnished with the horrors of the field of battle. We hear not the cries of the widow and the fatherless; nor are our hearts affected with the sight of garments rolled in blood; but all has been done by the diffusion and influence of the pure, yet powerful principles of benevo-lence, before which the pitiful impotency of tyranny and op-pression is scattered and dispersed like the chaff before the rage of the whirlwind.

I will not, on this occasion, attempt fully to detail the abomi-nable traffic to which we have already alluded. Slavery, with its concomitants and consequences, in the best attire in which it can possibly be presented, is but a hateful monster, the very demon of avarice and oppression, from its first introduction to the present time; it has been among all nations the scourge of heaven, and the curse of the earth. It is so contrary to the laws which the God of nature has laid down as the rule of action by which the conduct of man is to be regulated toward his fellow man, which binds him to love his neighbor as himself, that it ever has, and ever will, meet the decided disapprobation of heaven.

Strange, indeed, is the idea that such a system, fraught with such consummate wickedness, should ever have found a place in this the otherwise happiest of all countries—a country the very soil of which is said to be consecrated to liberty, and its fruits the equal rights of man. But strange as the idea may seem, or paradoxical as it may appear to those acquainted with the constitution of the government, or who have read the bold declaration of this nation's independence; yet it is a fact that can neither be denied nor controverted, that in the United States of America, at the expiration of fifty years after its be-coming a free and independent nation, there are no less than fifteen hundred thousand human beings still in a state of un-conditional vassalage.

Yet America is first in the profession of the love of liberty, and loudest in proclaiming liberal sentiments toward all other nations, and feels herself insulted to be branded with anything

bearing the appearance of tyranny or oppression. Such are the
palpable inconsistencies that abound among us and such is
the medley of contradictions which stain the national character
and render the American republic a byword, even among
despotic nations. . . .

Brethren, we have been called into liberty; only let us use
that liberty as not abusing it. This day commences a new era
in our history; new scenes, new prospects open before us, and
it follows as a necessary consequence that new duties devolve
upon us—duties which, if properly attended to, cannot fail to
improve our moral condition and elevate us to a rank of respectable standing with the community, or if neglected, we fall
at once into the abyss of contemptible wretchedness. It is
righteousness alone that exalteth a nation, and sin is a reproach to any people. "Our liberties," says Mr. Jefferson, "are
the gift of God, and they are not to be violated but with his
wrath." Nations and individuals have been blest of the Almighty in proportion to the manner in which they have
appreciated the mercies conferred upon them; an abuse of His
goodness has always incurred His righteous frown, while a
right improvement of his beneficence has secured and perpetuated His gracious smiles; an abuse of His goodness has
caused those fearful judgments which have destroyed cities,
demolished thrones, overturned empires, and humbled to the
dust the proudest and most exalted of nations. As a confirmation of which the ruinous heaps of Egypt, Tyre, Babylon
and Jerusalem stand as everlasting monuments. If we would
then answer the great design of our creation and glorify the God
who has made us; if we would avert the judgment of Heaven;
if we would honor our public benefactors; if we would counteract the designs of our enemies; if we would have our own blessings perpetuated, and secure the happiness of our children
and our children's children, let each come forward and act well
his part in whatever circle he may move, or in whatever station
he may fill; let the fear of God and the good of our fellow men
be the governing principles of the heart. We do well to remember, that every act of ours is more or less connected with the
general cause of the cultivation of their minds! Blessed be God,
we live in a day that our fathers desired to see, but died without
the sight, a day in which science, like the sun of the firmament,
rising, darting as he advances his beams to every quarter of
the globe. The mists and darkness scatter at his approach, and
all nations and people are blessed with his rays; so the glorious
light of science is spreading from east to west, and Afric's
sons are catching the glance of its beams as it passes; its en-

lightening rays scatter the mists of moral darkness and ignorance which have but too long overshadowed their minds; it en-
lightens the understanding, directs the thoughts of the heart,
and is calculated to influence the soul to the performance of
every good and virtuous act. The God of nature has endowed
our children with intellectual powers surpassed by none; nor
is there anything wanting but their careful cultivation in order
to fit them for stations the most honorable, sacred or useful.
And may we not, without becoming vain in our imaginations,
indulge the pleasing anticipation that within the little circle of
those connected with our families there may hereafter be found
the scholar, the statesman, or the herald of the cross of Christ.
Is it too much to say, that among that little number there shall
yet be one found like to the wise legislator of Israel, who shall
take his brethren by the hand and lead them forth from worse
than Egyptian bondage to the happy Canaan of civil and
religious liberty; or one whose devotedness toward the cause of
God and whose zeal for the salvation of Africa shall cause him
to leave the land which gave him birth and cross the Atlantic,
eager to plant the standard of the cross upon every hill of that
vast continent that has hitherto ignobly submitted to the baleful crescent or crouched under the iron bondage of the vilest
superstition. Our prospects brighten as we pursue the subject,
and we are encouraged to look forward to that period when the
moral desert of Africa shall submit to cultivation, and verdant
groves and fertile valleys, watered by the streams of Siloia,
shall meet the eye that has long surveyed only the widespread
desolations of slavery, despotism and death. How changed shall
then be the aspect of the moral and political world! Africa,
elevated to more than her original dignity, and redressed for
the many aggravated and complicated wrongs she has sustained,
with her emancipated sons, shall take her place among the
other nations of the earth. The iron manacles of slavery shall
give place to the people of color, and with the general cause of
emancipation. Our conduct has an important bearing not only
on those who are yet in bondage in this country, but its influence is extended to the isles of India and to every part of the
world where the abomination of slavery is known. Let us then
relieve ourselves from the odious stigma which some have long
since cast upon us, that we were incapacitated by the God of
nature for the enjoyment of the rights of freemen, and convince
them and the world that although our complexion may differ,
yet we have hearts susceptible of feeling, judgment capable of
discerning, and prudence sufficient to manage our affairs with
discretion, and by example prove ourselves worthy the blessings

we enjoy. That it is the duty of all rational creatures to consult
the interest of their species is a fact against which there can
be no reasonable objection. It is recorded to the honor of
Titus, who perhaps was the most benevolent of all the Roman
emperors, on recollecting one evening that he had done nothing
the day preceding beneficial to mankind, the monarch exclaimed, "I have lost a day." The wide field of usefulness is now
open before us, and we are called upon by every consideration
of duty which we owe to our God, to ourselves, to our children,
and to our fellow creatures generally, to enter with a fixed determination to act well our part and labor to promote the happiness and welfare of all.

There remains much to be done, and there is much to encourage us to action. The foundation for literary, moral and
religious improvement, we trust, is already laid in the formation of the public and private schools for the instruction of our
children, together with the churches of different denominations
already established. From these institutions we are encouraged
to expect the happiest results; and while many of us are passing
down the declivity of life and fast hastening to the grave, how
animating the thought that the rising generation is advancing
under more favorable auspices than we were permitted to enjoy, soon to fill the places we now occupy; and in relation to
them vast is the responsibility that rests upon us; much of their
future usefulness depends upon the discharge of the duties we
owe them. They are advancing, not to fill the place of slaves,
but of freemen; and in order to fill such a station with honor
to themselves and with good to the public, how necessary their
education, how important the moral and religious still stronger
bonds of brotherly love and affection, and justice and equity
shall be the governing principles that shall regulate the conduct
of men of every nation. Influenced by such motives, encouraged
by such prospects, let us enter the field with a fixed determination to live and to die in the holy cause.

SLAVERY AND COLONIZATION

By Peter Williams, Jr.

*On December 28, 1816, the American Society for Coloniz-
ing the Free People of Colour of the United States (popularly known as the American Colonization Society) was
organized. The Society, supported by influential groups,
aimed to colonize free Negroes in Africa and thus rid the
United States of a "troublesome presence." Although some
leading free Negroes supported colonization, believing
that black people could never achieve freedom and dignity
in the United States, most free Negroes opposed the
scheme from its inception. They were convinced that the
promoters of the Society wished to get rid of the free
Negro in order to make slavery secure, and they were repelled by the racist arguments directed by the Society
against free Negroes as an inferior, degraded class who
should be removed from the United States. They charged,
furthermore, that the Society, by encouraging anti-Negro
prejudice, was responsible for the deprivation of rights already enjoyed by free Negroes.*

*On July 4, 1830, the Reverend Peter Williams, Jr., de-
livered a sharp indictment of the Colonization Society in
an address at St. Philip's Protestant Episcopal Church, of
which he was pastor. Williams was a member of the Board
of Managers of the New York Anti-Slavery Society, but in
1834 was forced to resign under pressure from his white
bishop.*

*(Excerpts from the Reverend Williams' speech have
been taken from Carter G. Woodson, Negro Orators and
Their Orations, Washington, D. C., 1925, pp. 77–81.)*

ON THIS DAY the fathers of this nation declared, "We
hold these truths to be self-evident, that all men are created
equal, that they are endowed by their Creator with certain unalienable rights, among which are life, liberty, and the pursuit
of happiness."

These truly noble sentiments have secured to their author a
deathless fame. The sages and patriots of the Revolution subscribed them with enthusiasm and "pledged their lives, their
fortunes, and their sacred honor" in their support.

The result has been the freedom and happiness of millions, by whom the annual returns of this day are celebrated with the loudest and most lively expressions of joy.

But, although this anniversary affords occasion of rejoicing to the mass of the people of the United States, there is a class, a numerous class, consisting of nearly three millions, who participate but little in its joys and are deprived of their unalienable rights by the very men who so loudly rejoice in the declaration that "all men are born free and equal."

The festivities of this day serve but to impress upon the minds of reflecting men of color a deeper sense of the cruelty, the injustice and oppression of which they have been the victims. While others rejoice in their deliverance from a foreign yoke, they mourn that a yoke a thousandfold more grievous is fastened upon them. Alas, they are slaves in the midst of freedom; they are slaves to those who boast that freedom is the unalienable right of all; and the clanking of their fetters and the voice of their wrongs make a horrid discord in the songs of freedom which resound through the land.

No people in the world profess so high a respect for liberty and equality as the people of the United States, and yet no people hold so many slaves or make such great distinctions between man and man.

From various causes (among which we cheerfully admit a sense of justice to have held no inconsiderable rank) the work of emancipation has within a few years been rapidly advancing in a number of states. The state we live in, since the fourth of July, 1827, has been able to boast that she has no slaves, and other states where there still are slaves appear disposed to follow her example.

These things furnish us with cause of gratitude to God, and encourage us to hope that the time will speedily arrive when slavery will be universally abolished. Brethren, what a bright prospect would there be before us in this land had we no prejudices to contend against after being made free.

But, alas, the freedom to which we have attained is defective. Freedom and equality have been "put asunder." The rights of men are decided by the color of their skin; and there is as much difference made between the rights of a free white man and a free colored man as there is between a free colored man and a slave.

Though delivered from the fetters of slavery, we are oppressed by an unreasonable, unrighteous and cruel prejudice, which aims at nothing less than the forcing away of all the free colored people of the United States to the distant shores of Africa. Far be it from me to impeach the motives of every member of the

African Colonization Society. The civilizing and Christianizing of that vast continent and the extirpation of the abominable traffic in slaves (which notwithstanding all the laws passed for its suppression is still carried on in all its horrors) are no doubt the principal motives which induce many to give it their support.

But there are those, and those who are most active and most influential in its cause, who hesitate not to say that they wish to rid the country of the free colored population, and there is sufficient reason to believe that with many this is the principal motive for supporting that society; and that whether Africa is civilized or not, and whether the slave trade be suppressed or not, they would wish to see the free colored people removed from this country to Africa.

Africa could certainly be brought into a state of civil and religious improvement without sending all the free people of color in the United States there.

A few well-qualified missionaries, properly fitted out and supported, would do more for the instruction and improvement of the natives of that country than a host of colonists, the greatest part of whom would need to be instructed themselves, and all of whom for a long period would find enough to do to provide for themselves instead of instructing the natives.

How inconsistent are those who say that Africa will be benefited by the removal of the free people of color of the United States there, while they say they are the *most vile and degraded* people in the world. If we are as vile and degraded as they represent us, and they wish the Africans to be rendered a virtuous, enlightened and happy people, they should not *think* of sending *us* among them, lest we should make them worse instead of better.

The colonies planted by white men on the shores of America, so far from benefiting the aborigines, corrupted their morals and caused their ruin; and yet those who say *we* are the most vile people in the world would send us to Africa to improve the character and condition of the natives. Such arguments would not be listened to for a moment were not the minds of the community strangely warped by prejudice.

Those who wish that that vast continent should be *compensated* for the injuries done it, by sending thither the light of the gospel and the arts of civilized life, should aid in sending and supporting well-qualified missionaries who should be wholly devoted to the work of instruction, instead of sending colonists who would be apt to turn the ignorance of the natives to their own advantage and do them more harm than good.

Much has also been said by Colonizationists about improving the character and condition of the people of color of this country by sending them to Africa. This is more inconsistent still. We are to be improved by being sent far from civilized society. This is a novel mode of improvement. What is there in the burning sun, the arid plains, and barbarous customs of Africa, that is so peculiarly favorable to our improvement? What hinders our improving here, where schools and colleges abound, where the Gospel is preached at every corner, and where all the arts and sciences are verging fast to perfection? Nothing, nothing but prejudice. It requires no large expenditures, no hazardous enterprises to raise the people of color in the United States to as highly improved a state as any class of the community. All that is necessary is that those who profess to be anxious for it should lay aside their prejudices and act toward them as they do by others.

We are *natives* of this country, we ask only to be treated as well as *foreigners*. Not a few of our fathers suffered and bled to purchase its independence; we ask only to be treated as well as those who fought against it. We have toiled to cultivate it and to raise it to its present prosperous condition; we ask only to share equal privileges with those who come from distant lands, to enjoy the fruits of our labor. Let these moderate requests be granted, and we need not go to Africa nor anywhere else to be improved and happy. We cannot but doubt the purity of the motives of those persons who deny us these requests, and would send us to Africa to gain what they might give us at home.

But they say the prejudices of the country against us are invincible; and as they cannot be conquered, it is better that we should be removed beyond their influence. This plea should never proceed from the lips of any man who professes to believe that a just God rules in the heavens.

The African Colonization Society is a numerous and influential body. Would they lay aside their *own* prejudices, much of the burden would be at once removed; and their example (especially if they were as anxious to have *justice done us here* as to send us to Africa) would have such an influence upon the community at large as would soon cause prejudice to hide its deformed head.

But, alas, the course which they have pursued has an opposite tendency. By the *scandalous misrepresentations* which they are continually giving of our character and conduct we have sustained much injury and have reason to apprehend much more.

Without any charge of crime we have been denied all access to places to which we formerly had the most free intercourse; the colored citizens of other places, on leaving their homes, have been denied the privilege of returning; and others have been absolutely driven out.

Has the Colonization Society had no effect in producing these barbarous measures?

They profess to have no other object in view than the colonizing of the free people of color on the coast of Africa, with their *own consent;* but if our homes are made so uncomfortable that we cannot continue in them, or if, like our brethren of Ohio* and New Orleans, we are driven from them and no other door is open to receive us but Africa, our removal there will be anything but voluntary.

It is very certain that very few free people of color *wish* to go to that *land.* The Colonization Society *knows* this, and yet they do certainly calculate that in time they will have us all removed there.

How can this be effected but by making our situation worse here, and closing every other door against us? . . .

IT IS TIME FOR US TO BE UP AND DOING

By Peter Osborne

The contradiction between the existence of slavery and the principles enunciated in the Declaration of Independence caused many Negroes to refuse to celebrate the Fourth of July until after the Emancipation Proclamation. The Negro people held their observance on July 5, and the speeches generally dealt with the need to apply the Declaration of Independence to all men, regardless of color. The following address on this subject was delivered

---

* The township trustees in Cincinnati, Ohio, informed the Negro inhabitants that "they must leave Cincinnati in thirty days, or the law, which requires that they shall individually give bonds to the amount of $300 will be put in force against them." When the Negroes had not complied after thirty days, Cincinnati was torn by a riot which raged through the Negro section. Soon thereafter, two thousand free Negroes left Cincinnati and founded the colony of Wilberforce in Canada.

*by Peter Osborne, a leading Connecticut Negro, in the
New Haven African Church, on July 5, 1832.*
(*The address as presented here was taken from* The
Liberator, *December 1, 1832.*)

FELLOW CITIZENS, on account of the misfortune of our
color, our Fourth of July comes on the fifth. But I hope and
trust that when the Declaration of Independence is fully executed, which declares that all men, without respect to person,
were born free and equal, we may then have our Fourth of July
on the fourth. It is thought by many that this is as impossible to
take place, as it is for the leopard to change his spots; but I
anticipate that the time is approaching very fast. The signs in
the North, the signs in the South, in the East and West, are all
favorable to our cause. Why, then, should we forbear contending for the civil rights of free countrymen? What man of
national feeling would slumber in content under the yoke of
slavery and oppression, in his own country? Not the most
degraded barbarian in the interior of Africa.

If we desire to see our brethren relieved from the tyrannical
yoke of slavery and oppression in the South, if we would enjoy
the civil rights of free countrymen, it is high time for us to
be up and doing. It has been said that we have already done
well, but we can do better. What more can we do? Why, we must
unite with our brethren in the North, in the South, and in
the East and West, and then with the Declaration of Independence in one hand and the Holy Bible in the other, I think we
might courageously give battle to the most powerful enemy
to this cause. The Declaration of Independence has declared to
man, without speaking of color, that all men are born free and
equal. Has it not declared this freedom and equality to us too?

What man would content himself and say nothing of the
rights of man with two millions of his brethren in bondage?
Let us contend for the prize. Let us all unite and with one
accord declare that we will not leave our own country to emigrate to Liberia,* or elsewhere, to be civilized or Christianized.
Let us make it known to America that we are not barbarians;
that we are not inhuman beings; that this is our native country;
that our forefathers have planted trees in America for us, and
we intend to stay and eat the fruit. Our forefathers fought,

* In 1821, the American Colonization Society purchased land in Africa
for the establishment of a colony which was named Liberia from the
Latin word *liber*, meaning "free." Its capital, Monrovia, was named in
honor of President James Monroe (1758–1831), a member of the Society.

bled and died to achieve the independence of the United States. Why should we forbear contending for the prize? It becomes every colored citizen in the United States to step forward boldly and gallantly defend his rights. What has been done within a few years, since the union of the colored people? Are not the times more favorable to us now, than they were ten years ago? Are we not gaining ground? Yes—and had we begun this work forty years ago, I do not hesitate to say that there would not have been, at this day, a slave in the United States. Take, courage, then, ye Afric-Americans! Don't give up the conflict, for the glorious prize can be won.

EULOGY ON WILLIAM WILBERFORCE

By William Whipper

Upon the death of William Wilberforce, the great British opponent of the slave trade, in late July, 1833, black Americans exhibited profound grief. The members of the Phoenix Society of New York, a Negro self-improvement organization, wore badges of mourning for a month, and memorial services were held in several cities. In the 1850's one of the two colleges founded for Negroes before the Civil War was named in his honor.

On December 6, 1833, the people of color of the city of Philadelphia met in the Second African Presbyterian Church for the purpose "not only of commemorating the disinterested labors of that great and good man, William Wilberforce, Esq., but the noble and dignified course which he so eminently and availingly advocated,—viz., the glorious cause of Freedom." At the invitation of a committee representing the colored citizens of Philadelphia, William Whipper delivered the eulogy.

William Whipper was born about 1801 and was a leading figure in the national and state conventions of colored people of the 1830's. He was a founder, in 1835, of the short-lived American Moral Reform Society, which emerged from the convention movement, and he edited the National Reformer, *the Society's organ. In Columbia, Pennsylvania, where he was engaged in the lumber busi-*

ness, Whipper was a conductor on the Underground Railroad.

In his eulogy, Whipper traced the long and persistent struggle Wilberforce waged in Parliament to achieve abolition of the slave trade. Following are concluding portions of the address.

(The passages quoted here are taken from a pamphlet of the Historical Society of Pennsylvania, Eulogy on William Wilberforce, Esq., Delivered at the Request of the People of Colour of the City of Philadelphia, in the Second African Presbyterian Church, on the Sixth Day of December, 1833, by William Whipper, *Philadelphia, n.d.)*

. . . WE ARE now approaching a new period and a fruitful era in the history of this long-delayed, though important, question. While it promised to England and all Europe the greatest blessings, it presented to Africa an opening dawn that might radiate her whole realm with a bright refulgency, whose beaming rays seemed to speak in the language of the poet—

> O ye winds and waves,
> Waft the glad tidings to the land of slaves;
> Proclaim on Guinea's coast by Gambia's side,
> As far as Niger rolls his eastern tide,
> That thy sons shall no longer be driven
> So far from happiness and Heaven.

In this interval of space, Mr. Wilberforce, although so often defeated, had sufficiently learned the encampments and bulwarks of the enemy to understand what materials were necessary to be obtained to carry the citadel. He lost no time and prepared accordingly, having learned the fact (that ought to throw the whole world in amazement) that one point they meant to establish was the natural inferiority of the African —his incapability of holding and enjoying civil and religious liberty, and that they were not legitimate heirs to the rights of man. To defeat this point, Mr. Wilberforce and his friends that were in conjunction with him found it necessary to establish a college at Clapham, a village in Surrey, about four leagues south of London, for the education of African pupils.*

* In the course of his work to abolish the slave trade, Wilberforce contributed immensely to exposing the whole concept of Negro inferiority. In this connection, he hammered away with concrete evidence at the concept that Africa, before the coming of the Europeans, had been inhabited by a primitive, savage people. (*See* William J. Baker, "Wilberforce vs. Idea of Negro Inferiority," *Journal of the History of Ideas,* XXXI, July–Sept., 1970, 433–40.)

It may seem somewhat astonishing, yet it is not less true, that in so enlightened a period of the world such doctrines should have been either believed or advocated in England (at a time when she could challenge the world to produce as many eminent philosophers and statesmen), that the intellectual quality of mankind was regulated by the *laws* of lights and shades. Yet we may be somewhat awakened from our revery when we reflect that we so often find some men the dupes of measures, while others are borne forward by interested motives to complete the execution of some plan that may promote their evil designs. For such is the character of many politicians when they assume the doctrine of *expediency,* that they resort to dazzling speculations in defense of opinions which can never be sustained by reason or advocated by reasonable men, to give them the coloring of virtue and thus insure the execution of designs at once inhuman and impious. That this must have been the situation of the opponents to the "abolition of the slave trade" is so self-evident that it needs no illustration. To have established the fact that Africa was once the cradle of science—the seat of civilization—and her sons its early votaries and boasted cultivators, who in their search after wisdom had scanned the "azure pathway of the heavens" and laid the foundation of some of the most abstruse sciences, they might only have referred to the Ptolemaic age or to that *mammoth* receptacle of their collected wisdom, the Alexandrian Library, that by the decree of Omar was consumed by fire with all its philosophical treasures. The light of its conflagration was followed by an age of darkness; and its incensed smoke appears in its fall to have brought down barbarism and superstition. Let history mourn the event.

Or when we approach more modern times, we find that the National Institute of France have examined the ancient college of La Marche, where African pupils were educated, and declared that there existed no difference betwen them and the Europeans, except the color of their skins.

Europe, previous to that period, had been a nursery for the improvement of African intellect, yet it appears that the doctrine of African inferiority was so well grounded, that not only Mr. Wilberforce and his associates had to establish a college for their instruction, so that in advocating their cause they might plead for the rights of human beings, but the celebrated Abbé Grégoire felt called upon to write a work, entitled "An Inquiry Concerning the Intellectual and Moral Faculties of Negroes," to prove that they were not of the brute creation.

We now approach the year 1804, as fixed by Mr. Wilberforce for again bringing the question before the House. His reasons and prospects for now agitating the question were on the account of the union that had taken place between England and Ireland, and his knowledge that the Irish members were favorable to the abolition. Therefore he recorded it to the credit of the *Irish* name, and to the honor of their country, that they were four centuries in advance of England in that national purity which bestows on mankind the enjoyment of those rights and privileges granted by his Creator. As early as the reign of Henry VII they were engaged in a domestic traffic in human beings; but having experienced a general calamity, which they imputed as a judgment from heaven on account of its wickedness, they abolished it.

On the thirtieth of March, Mr. Wilberforce asked leave to renew his bill for the abolition of the slave trade within a limited time. The sublimity of his speech on this occasion surpassed all his former eloquence. A warm debate ensued, both sides having recruited in resources as well as members; it was truly animated, which terminated in favor of the abolitionists, by a majority of 124 to 49. The bill was now sent up to the House of Lords, but the discussion was postponed to the next year.

In 1805, Mr. Wilberforce again renewed his motion of the former year, but it met with the same vigorous opposition and was finally lost by a majority of seven.

Mr. Wilberforce never again introduced the question. He now found that it was necessary to prepare for the next session of Parliament, when, it was generally believed, the bill would become a law.

Mr. Wilberforce, having now like a towering eagle in its aerial flight been faithfully supported by Messrs. Pitt and Fox, for a period of nineteen years, their soaring spirits could in prospect see the most triumphant success. Amidst this scene of enjoyment they were interrupted by the death of Mr. Pitt, in January, 1806, who, like Moses of old, had ascended Pisgah's top, but was not permitted to enjoy the promised land, and in him fell not only a powerful advocate, but the right wing of the *E pluribus unum*.

On the death of Mr. Pitt, Lord Grenville and Mr. Fox were called to the ministry; the former was a fit substitute for Mr. Pitt, both as a minister of the Crown and the cause. Thus was Mr. Wilberforce again ready to take his flight, and after calculating on the effect of ministerial influence, he advised Mr. Fox to bring forward the question, which he did on the tenth of June, 1806, enforced by a very able speech, which after some considerable debate was finally carried by a majority of 114 to 15.

Mr. Wilberforce, immediately after the division, moved an address to His Majesty, which was carried without a division. The resolutions of the lower House, together with the address, were sent to the Lords, which with the efforts of Lord Grenville were carried by a majority of 100 to 36.

Thus passed both houses of the legislature a bill that for its value, whether we regard the interest of Africa, Europe, or the world, is unequaled in legislation, and one which Mr. Fox regarded as the highest glory of his administration. But how often are the "pleasures of life illusory." Before the bill had received the royal sanction, Mr. Fox was numbered with the dead, and in him fell a giant of abolition, and the left wing of the golden eagle, when he had barely reached the shores of victory, before a friend could greet him at the end of his pilgrimage, his spirit had fled to join that of its departed associate.

Although the bill had passed both houses of the legislature, a circumstance took place which threw great terror into the ranks of the abolitionists and caused them much to fear, that at the moment when they had expected that it would receive the royal sanction, they might have to perform the whole work over again. The reason of this was His Majesty, being displeased with the introduction of the Roman Catholic's bill into the House of Commons, had signified his intention of displacing the ministry; therefore all their exertions were put into requisition to have the bill adopted in detail, and to have it printed; accordingly, on the twenty-fourth of March, 1807, the whole was completed. And on the next day at 11 o'clock in the morning, His Majesty's message was delivered to the *ministers* of the Crown, that they were to wait upon him and deliver up the seals of their offices.

The commission for the royal assent to this bill, among others had been obtained. And Mr. Clarkson relates that "the commission was opened by Lord Chancellor Erskine, who was accompanied by Lords Holland and Auckland; and as the clock struck twelve, just when the sun was in its meridian splendor to witness this august act, of the establishment of Magna Charta for Africa in Britain, and to sanction it by its most glorious beams, it was completed."

It was indeed a time for England, for Africa, and the friends of humanity all over the world to rejoice, at one of the most glorious victories ever recorded in the history of legislation—a victory achieved without bloodstained banners. Unlike the revolution of France, it was not the "illegitimate offspring of a bloody night." It was the overthrow of public opinion by the triumph of reason. It was placed on a permanent basis, because a virtuous posterity would vindicate and sustain its adoption. It left the enemies of the measure without a temple to erect their hopes for further invasions on Africa. It marked for tyrants a moral and legislative boundary and left them no charter to protect them from the omnipotence of the law, and without a panoply to shield their degrading infamy from the curse of time.

To its friends all was hope and rejoicing. The valiant band who had so faithfully sustained this great cause could look with pride on Mr. Wilberforce, who was the leader of the mighty phalanx—the director of their mighty genius—the general who won the victory and wears its laurels.

As a government measure, the triumph might have been given to Lord Grenville, but it was fairly given to Mr. Wilberforce. He was hailed with enthusiastic acclamations on reentering the house after his success, and the country reechoed it from shore to shore. Thus, in the language of the poet—

> When Wilberforce, the minister of grace,
> The new Las Cassas of a ruined race,*
> With angel might opposed the rage of hell,
> And fought like Michael till the dragon fell.

We will now leave the shores of Britain, and review the history of our own country. She too has passed a law prohibiting the slave trade. She too has had her heroes for abolition, and at no period like the present have the boasted sons of humanity and justice more powerfully stood forward to advocate the rights of the oppressed descendants of Africa. The same glorious success awaits *us* as the inhabitants of the Old World. We too have had a Benezet, a Jay, a Rush, a Franklin, a Wistar, a Lay, a Tyson and a Livingston,† as well as many others that

---

* Bishop Bartolomé de Las Casas became known as the "Apostle of the Indians" because of his efforts in Hispaniola to prevent the extermination of the Indians by the Spanish Conquistadores. Ironically, in 1517, Las Casas appealed to the Spanish king to replace the Carib Indians in the plantations of Hispaniola with slaves from Africa. He soon changed his opinion, and in his *History of the Indies* he confessed his error and opposed Negro enslavement as well as Indian slavery.

† Anthony Benezet, Benjamin Lay (both Quakers), Benjamin Rush, Job Roberts Tyson, Benjamin Franklin, and Caspar Wistar were Philadelphians active in the antislavery movement before and after the American Revolution, while Robert Livingston and John Jay were involved in a similar crusade in New York. Of the group, Benezet, Lay and Rush were the most important in their contributions to the cause of the Negro.

time would fail us to enumerate—men who have shone in the most important situations of private as well as public life and may be justly considered the pride of the nation, and whom the history of the present generation points to as the *departed Fathers of the Republic.*

Of the living we can truly say they are as valiant a band as ever stood by a friend or met a foe.

When we speak of America, we do it with those feelings of respect that are due to it as our country—not as the land of our adoption, nor with the alienated breath of foreigners, but with the instinctive love of native-born citizens. We look upon her as favored by Providence above all others for the geniality of her climate and fruitfulness of her soil and, in the language of Dr. Rush, as possessing "a compound of most climates of the world"—a country said to be the "freest on the globe," where not only the liberty of the press is guaranteed, but the Christian and the infidel, the Mohammedan and pagan, the deist and the atheist, the Jew and Gentile are not only protected in their faith, but may propagate their doctrines unmolested—a country where the oppressed of all nations and castes seek shelter from oppression and become incorporated into the spirit of her laws and rally round her standard of liberty, *except those of African origin.*

We admire her declaration of rights, and worship it as our holy creed; but we mourn over its fallen spirit as we would over some ancient ruin whose splendor and magnificence had attracted the gaze of an admiring world. We point to the graves of our relatives and immediate ancestors as the graves not of departed Africans, but of American citizens; many of whom have *fallen in battle* with the revolutionary fathers in their arduous struggle for liberty; whose blood has moistened this sacred soil, and whose tombstones, if erected, would not only direct us to the depositories of departed heroes, but would light our path to a patriot's grave. There are yet many of our aged fathers who were scions of the British colonies that have survived the struggle and have been incorporated in that bond of union that forms the national standard and have grown up through American liberty, but who have never enjoyed the glorious privilege of citizenship. They have *weakened* with her *strength,* and their heads that are now blossomed for a future world, stand as evidence against American cruelty, the injustice of her policy, and the spirit of her laws. . . .

My friends, of the millions who sound forth his praises, probably there are only thousands who do him honor. Those who advocate slavery and perpetual servitude are unworthy of kneeling at his sacred shrine; those who are opposed to the natural elevation of the man of color to the rights and privileges of free citizens, are unworthy of paying him devotion; those who have not adopted for the line of their conduct toward their fellow men, the golden rule—"do unto others as you would they should do unto you"—are unfit to utter forth his name. As well might an angel of darkness bow down and worship the prince of light and glory, as for men possessing such a motley of inconsistencies to attempt to pay tribute to his memory. But his fame is fixed, the influence of his exertions is felt, and the news that *a great and good man is fallen* has been uttered in such pathetic strains that babes have caught the sound, and are beginning to lisp forth his name, which must be transmitted to posterity enrobed in the mantle of Christian virtue that nothing can tarnish but our degeneracy. If we should fail to render ourselves worthy of so powerful an advocate, we shall retard the influence of those virtues. If we shall fail to walk in those paths of elevation, marked out for us by the laws of our country and the achievements of philanthropy, we shall not only destroy the prospects of those who come after us, but will weaken the cause of those who come forward for our support. Let that not be our course. Let us march forward with a firm, unvarying step, not only occupying every inch of ground acquired by those philanthropists who are laboring in our behalf, but let the strength of our characters, by the influence of their examples, acquire for us new territory, and the name of William Wilberforce will not only burnish into brighter fame, but will serve as a lamp, the light of whose blaze will grow broader and higher, until it shall have not only warmed the most remote regions, by "encircling the globe we inhabit," but, by its revolutionary power, *we*, in our ascent upward, shall be lost in the regions of the skies.

WHY A NEGRO CONVENTION IS NECESSARY

By William Hamilton

Beginning in 1830, the National Negro Convention met annually for six years. At these gatherings, the free colored population asserted its demands for full rights in American society and for the abolition of slavery, which

*held millions of their brothers and sisters in chains. At
the fourth annual Convention of the Colored People, held
in New York City from June 2 to June 13, 1834, there
were fifty delegates and two visitors from Canada and
Haiti. Here is the chief address, delivered by William Hamilton of New York.*

(*The text of this address is taken from* A Documentary
History of the Negro People in the United States, *Herbert
Aptheker, ed., New York, 1951, pp. 154–57.*)

GENTLEMEN: It is with the most pleasing sensations,
that I, in behalf of my colored fellow citizens of New York,
tender you of the delegation to this convention, a hearty welcome to our city. And in behalf of the Conventional Board, I
repeat the welcome. And, gentlemen, with regard to myself, my
full heart vibrates the felicitation.

You have convened to take into consideration what may be
the best means for the promotion of the best interest of the people of color of these United States, particularly of the free
people thereof. And that such convention is highly necessary, I
think a few considerations will amply show.

First, the present form of society divides the interest of the
community into several parts. Of these, there is that of the
white man, that of the slave, and that of the free colored man.
How lamentable, how very lamentable, it is that there should
be, anywhere on earth, a community of castes, with separate
interests! That society must be the most happy, where the good
of one is the common good of the whole. Civilization is not
perfect, nor has reason full sway, until the community shall
see that a wrong done to one is a wrong done to the whole; that
the interest of one is or ought to be the common interest of the
whole. Surely that must be a happy state of society where the
sympathies of all are to all alike.

How pleasing, what a compliment to the nation, is the expression of Monsieur Vallier, a celebrated traveler in Africa,
where, speaking of the Hottentots, he says, "There none need
to offer themselves as objects of compassion, for all are compassionate." Whatever our early-tutored prejudice may say to
the contrary, such a people must be happy. Give me a residence
in such a society, and I shall fancy myself in a community the
most refined.

But alas for the people of color in this community! Their interest is not identified with that of other men. From them, white
men stand aloof. For them the eye of pity hath scarcely a tear.

To them the hand of kindness is palsied, to them the dregs

of mercy scarcely are given. To them the finger of scorn is pointed; contumely and reproach is continually theirs. They are a taunt, a hissing, and a byword. They must cringe and crouch and crawl and succumb to their peers. Long, long, long has the demon of prejudice and persecution beset their path. And must they make no effort to throw off the evils by which they are beset? Ought they not to meet to spread out their wrongs before one another? Ought they not to meet to consult on the best means of their relief? Ought they not to make one weak effort—nay, one strong, one mighty moral effort—to roll off the burden that crushes them?

Under present circumstances it is highly necessary the free people of color should combine and closely attend to their own particular interest. All kinds of jealousy should be swept away from among them and their whole eye fixed, intently fixed, on their own peculiar welfare. And can they do better than to meet thus, to take into consideration what are the best means to promote their elevation, and after having decided, to pursue those means with unabating zeal until their end is obtained?

Another reason why this convention is necessary is that there is formed a strong combination against the people of color, by some who are the master spirits of the day, by men whose influence is of the strongest character, to whom this nation bow in humble submission and submit to their superior judgment, who turn public sentiment whichever way they please.

You cannot but perceive that I allude to the Colonization Society. However pure the motives of some of the members of that society may be, yet the master spirits thereof are evil-minded toward us. They have put on the garb of angels of light. Fold back their covering, and you have in full array those of darkness.

I need not spread before you the proof of their evil purposes. Of that you have had a quantity sufficient; and were there no other good reason for this convention, the bare circumstance of the existence of such an institution would be a sufficient one. I do hope, confidently hope, that the time will arrive and is near at hand when we shall be in full possession of all the rights of men.

But as long at least as the Colonization Society exists, will a convention of colored people be highly necessary. This society is the great Dragon of the land, before whom the people bow and cry, Great Jehovah, and to whom they would sacrifice the free people of color. That society has spread itself over this whole land; it is artful, it suits itself to all places. It is one thing at the South, and another at the North; it blows hot and cold;

it sends forth bitter and sweet; it sometimes represents us as the most corrupt, vicious and abandoned of any class of men in the community. Then again we are kind, meek and gentle. Here we are ignorant, idle, a nuisance and a drawback on the resources of the country. But as abandoned as we are, in Africa we shall civilize and Christianize all that heathen country. And by thus preaching continually they have distilled into the minds of the community a desire to see us removed.

They have resorted to every artifice to effect their purposes— by exciting in the minds of the white community the fears of insurrection and amalgamation; by petitioning state legislatures to grant us no favors; by petitioning Congress to aid in sending us away; by using their influence to prevent the establishment of seminaries for our instruction in the higher branches of education.

And such are the men of that society that the community are blind to their absurdities; contradictions and paradoxes. They are well acquainted with the ground and the wiles by which to beguile the people.

It is therefore highly necessary we should meet, in order that we may confer on the best means to frustrate the purpose of so awful a foe.

I would beg leave to recommend an attentive consideration to this matter. Already you have done much toward the enervation of this giant: he begins to grow feeble; indeed he seems to be making his last struggle, if we may judge from his recent movements. Hang around him, assail him quickly. He is vulnerable. Well-pointed darts will fetch him down, and soon he breathes no more.

Cheer up my friends! Already has your protest against the Colonization Society shown to the world that the people of color are not willing to be expatriated. Cheer up. Already a right feeling begins to prevail. The friends of justice, of humanity, and of the rights of man are drawing rapidly together and are forming a moral phalanx in your defense.

That hitherto strong-footed, but sore-eyed vixen, prejudice, is limping off, seeking the shade. The Anti-Slavery Society and the friends of immediate abolition are taking a noble, bold and manly stand in the cause of universal liberty. It is true they are assailed on every quarter, but the more they are assailed the faster they recruit. From present appearances the prospect is cheering, in a high degree. Antislavery societies are forming in every direction. Next August proclaims the British dominions free from slaves.

These United States are her children, they will soon follow

so good an example. Slavery, that Satanic monster, that beast whose mark has been so long stamped on the forehead of the nations, shall be chained and cast down into blackness and darkness for ever.

Soon, my brethren, shall the judgment be set. Then shall rise in glory and triumph, reason, virtue, kindness and liberty, and take a high exalted stand among the sons of men. Then shall tyranny, cruelty, prejudice and slavery be cast down to the lowest depths of oblivion—yea, be banished from the presence of God and the glory of his power forever. Oh blessed consummation; and devoutly to be desired!

It is for you, my brethren, to help on in this work of moral improvement. Man is capable of high advances in his reasoning and moral faculties. Man is in the pursuit of happiness. And reason—or experience, which is the parent of reason—tells us that the highest state of morality is the highest state of happiness. Aside from a future day of judgment and retribution, there is always a day of retribution at hand. That society is most miserable that is most immoral; that most happy that is most virtuous. Let me therefore recommend earnestly that you press upon our people the necessity and advantage of a moral reformation. It may not produce an excess of riches, but it will produce a higher state of happiness and render our circumstances easier.

You, gentlemen, can begin here. By managing this conference in a spirit of good will and true politeness; by constantly keeping in view and cultivating a spirit of peace, order and harmony, rather than satire, wit and eloquence; by putting the best possible construction on each other's language, rather than charging each other with improper motives. These dispositions will bespeak our character more or less virtuous and refined, and render our setting more or less pleasant. I will only now add, that the report of the Conventional Board will be submitted at your call; and my earnest hope is that you may have a peaceful, pleasant sitting.

PREJUDICE AGAINST THE COLORED MAN

By Theodore S. Wright

At the convention of the New York State Anti-Slavery Society, held in Utica, September 20, 1837, the Reverend Theodore S. Wright, pastor of the First Presbyterian Church in New York City, made two dramatic speeches condemning prejudice against colored people. In the first he attacked racist thinking present within the Abolitionist movement and made it clear that to the black people, it was not enough just to be against slavery. The second speech followed the introduction of a resolution denouncing prejudice against colored people as "nefarious and wicked and should be practically reprobated and discountenanced." Below are an extract from the first speech and the complete text of the second.

(The extract from the first speech is taken from The Colored American *[New York], October 4, 1837; the second speech is taken from* The Liberator, *October 2, 1837.)*

. . . THREE YEARS AGO, when a man professed to be an Abolitionist we knew where he was. He was an individual who recognized the identity of the human family. Now a man may call himself an Abolitionist and we know not where to find him. Your tests are taken away. A rush is made into the Abolition ranks. Free discussion, petition Anti-Texas, and political favor converts are multiplying.* Many throw themselves in, without understanding the breadth and depth of the principles of emancipation. I fear not the annexation of Texas. I fear not all the machination, calumny and opposition of slaveholders, when contrasted with the annexation of men whose hearts have not been deeply imbued with these high and holy principles. Why, sir, unless men come out and take their stand on the principle

---

* The reference is to those who joined the antislavery cause primarily in opposition to the annexation of Texas and the assault on freedom of speech and press. The petition issue refers to the "gag rule" adopted by Congress in 1836 on the motion of John C. Calhoun. It provided that all antislavery petitions thenceforth to be submitted to Congress be laid on the table without action. The struggle against the rule, led by John Quincy Adams, forced its repeal in 1844. The rule was attacked during this eight-year period as an unconstitutional deprivation of the right of petition.

of recognizing man as man, I tremble for the ark, and I fear our society will become like the expatriation society—everybody an Abolitionist. These points which have lain in the dark must be brought out to view. The identity of the human family, the principle of recognizing all men as brethren—that is the doctrine, that is the point which touches the quick of the community. It is an easy thing to ask about the vileness of slavery at the South, but to call the dark man a brother, heartily to embrace the doctrine advanced in the second article of the Constitution, to treat all men according to their moral worth, to treat the man of color in all circumstances as a man and brother— that is the test.

Every man who comes into this society ought to be catechized. It should be ascertained whether he looks upon man as man, all of one blood and one family. A healthful atmosphere must be created in which the slave may live when rescued from the horrors of slavery. I am sensible I am detaining you, but I feel that this is an important point. I am alarmed sometimes when I look at the constitutions of our societies. I am afraid that brethren sometimes endeavor so to form the constitutions of societies that they will be popular. I have seen constitutions of abolition societies, where nothing was said about the improvement of the man of color! They have overlooked the giant sin of prejudice. They have passed by this foul monster, which is at once the parent and offspring of slavery. Whilst you are thinking about the annexation of Texas, whilst you are discussing the great principles involved in this noble cause, remember this prejudice must be killed or slavery will never be abolished. Abolitionists must annihilate in their own bosoms the cord of caste. We must be consistent—recognize the colored man in every respect as a man and brother. In doing this we shall have to encounter scorn; we shall have to breast the storm. This society would do well to spend a whole day in thinking about it and praying over it. Every Abolitionist would do well to spend a day in fasting and prayer over it and in looking at his own heart. Far be it from me to condemn Abolitionists. I rejoice and bless God for this first institution which has combined its energies for the overthrow of heaven-daring, this soul-crushing, prejudice.

The successors of Penn, Franklin and Woolman* have shown

---

* John Woolman, Quaker antislavery agitator, was the author of a popular *Journal* and a series of pamphlets exposing slavery and the slave trade. The inclusion of Penn is not clear, since William Penn owned slaves and did not manumit them on his death.

themselves the friends of the colored race. They have done more in this cause than any other church, and they are still doing great things both in Europe and America. I was taught in childhood to remember the man of the broad-brimmed hat and drab-colored coat and venerate him. No class have testified more to the truth on this subject. They lifted up their voices against slavery and the slave trade. But, ah, with but here and there a noble exception, they go but halfway. When they come to the grand doctrine, to lay the ax right down at the root of the tree and destroy the very spirit of slavery—there they are defective. Their doctrine is to set the slave free, and let him take care of himself. Hence, we hear nothing about their being brought into the Friends' church, or of their being viewed and treated according to their moral worth. Our hearts have recently been gladdened by an address of the annual meeting of the Friends' Society in the city of New York, in which they insist upon the doctrine of immediate emancipation. But that very good man who signed the document as the organ of that society within the past year, received a man of color, a Presbyterian minister, into his house, gave him his meals alone in the kitchen, and did not introduce him to his family. That shows how men can testify against slavery at the South, and not assail it at the North, where it is tangible. Here is something for Abolitionists to do. What can the friends of emancipation effect while the spirit of slavery is so fearfully prevalent? Let every man take his stand, burn out this prejudice, live it down, talk it down, everywhere consider the colored man as a man, in the church, the stage, the steamboat, the public house, in all places, and the death blow to slavery will be struck.

Mr. President, with much feeling do I rise to address the Society on this resolution, and I should hardly have been induced to have done it had I not been requested. I confess I am personally interested in this resolution. But were it not for the fact that none can feel the lash but those who have it upon them, that none know where the chain galls but those who wear it, I would not address you.

This is a serious business, sir. The prejudice which exists against the colored man, the freeman, is like the atmosphere, everywhere felt by him. It is true that in these United States and in this state, there are men like myself, colored with the skin like my own, who are not subjected to the lash, who are not liable to have their wives and their infants torn from them, from whose hand the Bible is not taken. It is true that we may walk abroad; we may enjoy our domestic comforts, our families;

retire to the closet; visit the sanctuary, and may be permitted
to urge on our children and our neighbors in well doing. But
sir, still we are slaves. Everywhere we feel the chain galling us.
It is by that prejudice which the resolution condemns, the spirit
of slavery, the law which has been enacted here, by a corrupt
public sentiment, through the influence of slavery which treats
moral agents different from the rule of God, which treats them
irrespective of their morals or intellectual cultivation. This spirit
is withering all our hopes, and ofttimes causes the colored parent as he looks upon his child to wish he had never been born.
Often is the heart of the colored mother, as she presses her child
to her bosom, filled with sorrow to think that, by reason of this
prejudice, it is cut off from all hopes of usefulness in this land.
Sir, this prejudice is wicked.

If the nation and Church understood this matter, I would not
speak a word about that killing influence that destroys the colored man's reputation. This influence cuts us off from everything; it follows us up from childhood to manhood; it excludes
us from all stations of profit, usefulness and honor; takes away
from us all motive for pressing forward in enterprises, useful
and important to the world and to ourselves.

In the first place, it cuts us off from the advantages of the
mechanic arts almost entirely. A colored man can hardly learn
a trade, and if he does it is difficult for him to find any one who
will employ him to work at the trade, in any part of the state.
In most of our large cities there are associations of mechanics
who legislate out of their society colored men. And in many
cases where our young men have learned trades, they have had
to come to low employments for want of encouragement in
those trades.

It must be a matter of rejoicing to know that in this vicinity
colored fathers and mothers have the privileges of education. It
must be a matter of rejoicing that in this vicinity colored parents can have their children trained up in schools; at present,
we find the colleges barred against them.

I will say nothing about the inconvenience which I have experienced myself, and which every man of color experiences,
though made in the image of God. I will say nothing about the
inconvenience of traveling—how are we frowned upon and despised. No matter how we may demean ourselves, we find embarrassments everywhere.

But, sir, this prejudice goes farther. It debars men from
heaven. While, sir, slavery cuts off the colored portion of the
community from religious privileges, men are made infidels.
What, they demand, is your Christianity? How do you regard

your brethren? How do you treat them at the Lord's table?
Where is your consistency in talking about the heathen, travers-
ing the ocean to circulate the Bible everywhere, while you frown
upon them at the door? These things meet us and weigh down
our spirits.

And, sir, the constitution of society, molded by this prejudice,
destroys souls. I have known extensively that in revivals which
have been blessed and enjoyed in this part of the country the
colored population were overlooked. I recollect an instance. The
Lord God was pouring out His Spirit. He was entering every
house, and sinners were converted. I asked, Where is the colored man? Where is my brother? Where is my sister? Who is
feeling for him or her? Who is weeping for them? Who is endeavoring to pull them out of the fire? No reply was made. I was
asked to go round with one of the elders and visit them. We
went and they humbled themselves. The Church commenced
efficient efforts, and God blessed them as soon as they began
to act for these people as though they had souls.

And, sir, the manner in which our churches are regulated
destroys souls. Whilst the Church is thrown open to everybody,
and one says come, come in and share the blessings of the sanctuary, this is the gate of heaven—he says to the colored man,
be careful where you take your stand. I know an efficient church
in this state, where a respectable colored man went to the house
of God and was going to take a seat in the gallery, and one of
the officers contended with him and said, "You cannot go there,
sir."

In one place the people had come together to the house of the
Lord. The sermon was preached—the emblems were about to be
administered—and all at once the person who managed the
church thought the value of the pews would be diminished if
the colored people sat in them. They objected to their sitting
there, and the colored people left and went into the gallery, and
that, too, when they were thinking of handling the memorials
of the broken body and shed blood of the Saviour! And, sir, this
prejudice follows the colored man everywhere and depresses his
spirits.

Thanks be to God, there is a buoyant principle which elevates
the poor downtrodden colored man above all this; it is that
there is a society which regards man according to his worth; it
is the fact, that when he looks up to Heaven he knows that God
treats him like a moral agent, irrespective of caste or the circumstances in which he may be placed. Amid the embarrassments which he has to meet and the scorn and contempt that is
heaped upon him, he is cheered by the hope that he will be dis-

enthralled, and soon, like a bird, set forth from its cage, wing
his flight to Jesus, where he can be happy and look down with
pity on the man who despises the poor slave for being what God
made him, and who despises him because he is identified with
the poor slave. Blessed be God for the principles of the Gospel.
Were it not for these, and for the fact that a better day is dawning, I would not wish to live. Blessed be God for the antislavery
movement. Blessed be God that there is a war waging with slavery, that the granite rock is about to be rolled from its base. But
as long as the colored man is to be looked upon as an inferior
caste, so long will they disregard his cries, his groans, his
shrieks.

I rejoice, sir, in this Society, and I deem the day when I joined
this Society as one of the proudest days of my life. And I know
I can die better, in more peace today, to know there are men
who will plead the cause of my children.

Let me, through you, sir, request this delegation to take hold
of this subject. This will silence the slaveholder, when he says
where is your love for the slave? Where is your love for the
colored man who is crushed at your feet? Talking to us about
emancipating our slaves when you are enslaving them by your
feelings, and doing more violence to them by your prejudice,
than we are to our slaves by our treatment. They call on us to
evince our love for the slave, by treating man as man, the colored man as a man, according to his worth.

SLAVERY BRUTALIZES MAN

By Daniel A. Payne

*One of the earliest militant speeches against slavery by a
black American was delivered in June, 1839, by Daniel A.
Payne (1811–1893) at Fordsboro, New York, on the occasion of his ordination by the Franckean Synod of the
Lutheran Church. The speech was delivered in support of
a synodical report to end slavery in America, and it was
influential in achieving the acceptance of that report.*

*Payne was born February 24, 1811, in Charleston, South
Carolina, the son of free Negroes. Educated at a local
school established by free colored men and by a private
tutor, he mastered mathematics, Greek, Latin and French.*

In 1826 he joined the Methodist Episcopal Church and three years later opened a school for Negro children, which he conducted until the South Carolina legislature passed a law, on December 17, 1834, imposing a fine and whipping on free persons of color who kept schools to teach slaves or free Negroes to read or write. Forced to abandon his school, Payne entered the Lutheran Theological Seminary at Gettysburg, Pennsylvania, and became a Lutheran preacher. Later, he left the Lutheran Church, joined the African Methodist Episcopal Church in 1841, and in May, 1852, was elected a Bishop. In 1863 he became president of Wilberforce University, an Ohio institution established for the education of black youths in 1856, and served in that office for thirteen years.

(The speech appeared in the Lutheran Herald and Journal of the Fort Plain, N. Y., Franckean Synod, *Vol. I, No. 15 [August 1, 1839]. It is published here with permission of the Lutheran Theological Seminary, Abdel Ross Wentz Library, Gettysburg, Pennsylvania, where the only existing file of the paper is stored.)*

MR. PRESIDENT: I move the adoption of the Report, because it is based upon the following propositions:

American Slavery brutalizes man —destroys his moral agency, and subverts the moral government of God.

Sir, I am opposed to slavery, not because it enslaves the black man, but because it enslaves *man*. And were all the slaveholders in this land men of color, and the slaves white men, I would be as thorough and uncompromising an abolitionist as I now am; for whatever and whenever I may see a being in the form of a man, enslaved by his fellow man, without respect to his complexion, I shall lift up my voice to plead his cause, against all the claims of his proud oppressor; and I shall do it not merely from the sympathy which man feels towards suffering man, but because *God, the living God,* whom I dare not disobey, has commanded me to open my mouth for the dumb, and to plead the cause of the oppressed.

Slavery brutalizes man. We know that the word *man*, in its primitive sense, signifies ——— —.* But the intellectual and moral structure of man, and the august relations which he sustains to the Deity, have thrown around the name, and being designated by it, a halo of glory, brightened by all the ideas, that are ennobling on earth, and blessed in eternity. This being

* The blank space is in the original report of the speech.

God created but a little lower than the angels, and crowned him
with glory and honor; but slavery hurls him down from his
elevated position, to the level of brutes, strikes this crown of
glory from his head and fastens upon his neck the galling yoke,
and compels him to labor like an ox, through summer's sun and
winter's snow, without remuneration. Does a man take the calf
from the cow and sell it to the butcher? So slavery tears the
child from the arms of the reluctant mother, and barters it to
the soul trader for a young colt, or some other commodity! Does
the bird catcher tear away the dove from his mate? So slavery
separates the groaning husband from the embraces of his dis-
tracted and weeping wife! And are the beasts of the forest
hunted, tortured and slain at the pleasure of the cruel hunter?
So are the slaves hunted, tortured and slain by the cruel monster
slavery! To treat a man like a brute is to brutalize him. We have
seen that slavery treats man like a brute, therefore slavery brutalizes man! But does slavery stop here? Is it content with
merely treating the external man like a brute? No, sir, it goes
further, and with a heart as brazen as that of Belshazzar and
hands still more sacrilegious, it lays hold of the *immortal mind,
seizes the will, and binds that which Jehovah did not bind—fetters that which the Eternal made as free to move and act as the
breath of Heaven. "It destroys moral agency!"* To destroy moral
agency is to fetter or obstruct the will of man. Now let us see if
slavery is innocent of this. The very moment that a man con-
ceives the diabolic design of enslaving his brother's body, that
very moment does he also conceive the still more heinous design of fettering his will, for well does he know that in order to
make his dominion supreme over the body, he must fetter the
living spring of all its motions. Hence, the first lesson the slave
is taught is to yield his will unreservedly and exclusively to the
dictates of his master. And if a slave desire to educate himself
or his children, in obedience to the dictates of reason or the
laws of God, he does not, he cannot do it without the consent of
his master. Does reason and circumstances and the Bible command a slave to preach the gospel to his brethren? Slavery
arises, and with a frown, an oath and a whip, fetters or obstructs the holy volition of his soul! I knew a pious slave in
Charleston who was a licensed exhorter in the Methodist Episcopal Church; this good man was in the habit of spending his
Saturday nights on the surrounding plantations, preaching to
the slaves. One night, as usual, he got into a canoe, sailed upon
James' Island. While in the very act of preaching the unsearch-
able riches of Christ to dying men, the patrols seized him and
whipped him in the most cruel manner, and compelled him to

promise that he would never return to preach again to those slaves. In the year 1834, several colored brethren, who were also exhorters in the Methodist Episcopal Church commenced preaching to several *destitute white families,* who gained a subsistence by cultivating some poor lands about three or four miles from Charleston. The first Sunday I was present; the house was nearly filled with these poor white farmers. The master of the house was awakened to a sense of his lost condition. During the following week he was converted. On the third Sunday from the day he was convinced of sin he died in the triumphs of faith, and went to heaven. On the fourth Sunday from the time the dear brethren began to preach, the patrols scented their track, and put them to chase. Thus, an end was put to their labors. Their willing souls were fettered, and the poor whites constrained to go without the preaching of the gospel. In a word, it is in view of man's moral agency that God commands him to shun vice, and practice virtue. But what female slave can do this? I lived twenty-four years in the midst of slavery and never knew but six female slaves who were reputedly virtuous! What profit is to the female slave that she is disposed to be virtuous? Her will, like her body, is not her own; they are both at the pleasure of her master; and he brands them at his will. *So it subverts the moral government of God.*

In view of the moral agency of man, God hath most wisely and graciously given him a code of laws, and certain positive precepts, to control and regulate moral actions. This code of laws, and these positive precepts, with the divine influence which they are naturally calculated to exert on the mind of man, constitutes his moral government.

Now, to nullify these laws—to weaken or destroy their legitimate influence on the human mind, or to hinder man from yielding universal and entire obedience to them is to subvert the moral government of God.

Now, slavery nullifies these laws and precepts—weakens and destroys their influence over the human mind, and hinders men from yielding universal and entire obedience to them; therefore slavery subverts the moral government of God. This is the climax of the sin of slavery! This is the blackest, foulest, and most horrid feature of the heaven-daring *Monster!* He stretcheth out his hand against God, and strengtheneth himself against the Almighty—he runneth on him, even on his neck, upon the thick bosses of his buckler. Thus saith the Lord, "Thou shalt not commit adultery." But does the man who owns a hundred females obey the law? Does he not nullify it and compel

the helpless woman to disobey God? Concerning the religious
instruction of children, thus saith the Lord, "Bring them up in
the nurture and admonition of the Lord." But what saith slavery? "They are my property, and shall be brought up to serve
me." They shall not *even learn to read his word,* in order that
they may be brought up in his nurture and admonition. If any
man doubts this, let him read the slave code of Louisiana and
see if it is not death to teach slaves. Thus saith the Lord, "Remember the Sabbath day, to keep it holy." Does not slavery nullify this law, and compel the slave to work on the Sabbath?
Thus saith the Lord, "Obey thy father and thy mother." Can the
slave children obey this command of God? Does not slavery
command the children to obey the master and let him alone?
Thus saith the Son of God, "What God hath joined together let
no man put asunder." Does not slavery nullify this law, by
breaking the sacred bands of wedlock, and separating the husband and wife forever? Thus saith the Son of God, "Search the
Scriptures." Does not slavery seal up the word of God and make
it criminal for the slave to read it? In 1834, the legislature of
South Carolina enacted a law prohibiting the instruction of any
slave; and Mr. Lawrence, in a pamphlet which he published in
1835, to defend this law, declared that if the slaves were permitted to read the Bible, ninety of them would become infidels,
like Voltaire, where ten would become Christians. "Go ye into
all the world, and preach the Gospel unto every creature," saith
the Son of God. Does slavery permit it? In 1835, a minister of
the Episcopal Church, in the city of Charleston, appealed to the
civil authority for permission to preach to the free population of
an evening, but they would not permit him.

The objector may reply, that at the present moment there are
four Methodist missionaries, and one Lutheran, laboring among
the slave population of South Carolina. We answer, that this is
true, and we are glad of it; but this fact does not overthrow our
proposition, nor falsify what we have stated, for although a few
planters have permitted the Gospel to be preached to their slaves,
the majority of them prohibit it, and this permission is extraneous to slavery and is no part of its creed or code. Slavery never
legislates for the religious instruction of slaves, but, on the contrary, legislates to perpetuate their ignorance; and there are
laws this very moment in the statute books of South Carolina
and other states, prohibiting the religious instruction of slaves.
But this is not all that slavery does to subvert the moral government of God. The slaves are sensible of the oppression exercised by their masters; and they see these masters on the Lord's
day worshiping in his holy Sanctuary. They hear their masters

professing Christianity; they see their masters preaching the Gospel; they hear these masters praying in their families, and they know that oppression and slavery are inconsistent with the Christian religion; therefore they scoff at religion itself—mock their masters, and distrust both the goodness and justice of God. Yes, I have known them even to question His existence. I speak not of what others have told me, but of what *I have both seen and heard from the slaves themselves*. I have heard the mistress ring the bell for family prayer, and I have seen the servants immediately begin to sneer and laugh; and have heard them declare they would not go in to prayers, adding, if I go in she will only just read, "Servants obey your masters"; but she will not read, "Break every yoke, and let the oppressed go free." I have seen colored men at the church door, *scoffing at the ministers,* while they were preaching, and saying, you had better go home, and set your slaves free. A few nights ago between ten and eleven o'clock a runaway slave came to the house where I live for safety and succor. I asked him if he was a Christian. "No sir," said he, "white men treat us so bad in Mississippi that we can't be Christians."

Sir, I taught school in Charleston five years. In 1834 the legislature of our state enacted a law to prohibit colored teachers. My school was filled with children and youth of the most promising talents; and when I looked upon them and remembered that in a few more weeks this school shall be closed and I be permitted no more to teach them, notwithstanding I had been a professor seven years, I began to question the existence of the Almighty and to say, if indeed there is a God, does he deal justly? Is he a just God? Is he a holy Being? If so, why does he permit a handful of dying men thus to oppress us? Why does he permit them to hinder me from teaching these children, when nature, reason and Revelation command me to teach them? Thus I began to question the divine government and to murmur at the administration of His providence. And could I do otherwise, while slavery's cruelties were pressing and grinding my soul in the dust, and robbing me and my people of those privileges which it was hugging to its breast, and giving thousands to perpetuate the blessing which it was tearing away from us? Sir, the very man who made the law alluded to, did that very year, increase the property of South Carolina College.

In a word, slavery tramples the laws of the living God under its unhallowed feet—weakens and destroys the influence which those laws are calculated to exert over the mind of man, and constrains the oppressed to blaspheme the name of the Almighty. For I have often heard them sneeringly say, that *"The*

Almighty made Charleston on Saturday night, when he was weary, and in a great hurry." O, *Brethren of the Franckean Synod! awake! Awake to the battle and hurl the hottest thunders of divine truth at the head of this cruel monster, until he shall fall to rise no more, and the groans of the enslaved are converted into the songs of the free!!*

THE RIGHTS OF COLORED CITIZENS IN TRAVELING

By Charles Lenox Remond

Charles Lenox Remond (1810–1873) was an active Abolitionist and served for many years as an agent of the American Anti-Slavery Society. Remond was the first black Abolitionist speaker to address large audiences. In 1840 he attended the World Anti-Slavery Convention in London. After spending two years lecturing in Great Britain and Ireland, he returned to the United States in 1842 and became involved in the campaign to end segregation on the railroads of Massachusetts. In February, 1842, he testified before a legislative committee of the Massachusetts House of Representatives that was then holding hearings on the issue. Segregation was finally abolished in April, 1843.

Following is the address Remond delivered before the legislative committee. It is taken from The Liberator, *February 25, 1842.*

MR. CHAIRMAN and gentlemen of the Committee: In rising at this time, and on this occasion, being the first person of color who has ever addressed either of the bodies assembling in this building, I should, perhaps, in the first place, observe that, in consequence of the many misconstructions of the principles and measures of which I am the humble advocate, I may in like manner be subject to similar misconceptions from the moment I open my lips in behalf of the prayer of the petitioners for whom I appear, and therefore feel I have the right at least to ask, at the hands of this intelligent Committee, an impartial hearing, and that whatever prejudices they may have imbibed be eradicated from their minds, if such exist. I have, however, too much confidence in their intelligence and too much faith in their determination to do their duty as the representatives of this Commonwealth, to presume they can be actuated by partial motives. Trusting, as I do, that the day is not distant, when, on all questions touching the rights of the citizens of this state, men shall be considered great only as they are good, and not that it shall be told and painfully experienced that, in this country, this state—aye, this city, the Athens of America—the rights, privileges and immunities of its citizens are measured by complexion or any other physical peculiarity or conformation, especially such as over which no man has any control. Complexion can in no sense be construed into crime, much less be rightfully made the criterion of rights. Should the people of color, through a revolution of Providence, become a majority, to the last I would oppose it upon the same principle; for in either case it would be equally reprehensible and unjustifiable, alike to be condemned and repudiated. It is justice I stand here to claim, and not favor for either complexion. . . .

Our right to citizenship in this state has been acknowledged and secured by the allowance of the elective franchise and consequent taxation;* and I know of no good reason, if admitted in this instance, why it should be denied in any other.

With reference to the wrongs inflicted and injuries received on railroads by persons of color, I need not say they do not end with the termination of the route, but in effect tend to discourage, disparage and depress this class of citizens. All hope of reward for upright conduct is cut off. Vice in them becomes a virtue. No distinction is made by the community in which we live. The most vicious is treated as well as the most respectable, both in public and private.

But it is said we all look alike. If this is true, it is not true that we all behave alike. There is a marked difference; and we claim a recognition of this difference.

In the present state of things, they find God's provisions interfered with in such a way, by these and kindred regulations, that virtue may not claim her divinely appointed rewards. Color is made to obscure the brightest endowments, to degrade the fairest character, and to check the highest and most praiseworthy aspirations. If the colored man is vicious, it makes but little difference; if besotted, it matters not; if vulgar, it is quite

---

* The right of Negroes in Massachusetts to vote was established in the case of Paul Cuffe in 1778 (*see* pages 29–30). It was fully settled in the Body of Liberties of 1790, which guaranteed manhood suffrage without regard to race.

as well; and he finds himself as well treated, and received as readily into society, as those of an opposite character. Nay, the higher our aspirations, the loftier our purposes and pursuits, does this iniquitous principle of prejudice fasten upon us and especial pains are taken to irritate, obstruct and injure. No reward of merit, no remuneration for services, no equivalent is rendered the deserving. And I submit, whether this unkind and unchristian policy is not well calculated to make every man disregardful of his conduct and every woman unmindful of her reputation.

The grievances of which we complain, be assured, sir, are not imaginary, but real—not local, but universal; not occasional, but continual, everyday matter-of-fact things—and have become, to the disgrace of our common country, matter of history.

Mr. Chairman, the treatment to which colored Americans are exposed in their own country finds a counterpart in no other; and I am free to declare that, in the course of nineteen months' traveling in England, Ireland and Scotland, I was received, treated and recognized, in public and private society, without any regard to my complexion. From the moment I left the American packet ship in Liverpool, up to the moment I came in contact with it again, I was never reminded of my complexion; and all that know anything of my usage in the American ship, will testify that it was unfit for a brute, and none but one could inflict it. But how unlike that afforded in the British steamer *Columbia!* Owing to my limited resources, I took a steerage passage. On the first day out, the second officer came to inquire after my health; and finding me the only passenger in that part of the ship, ordered the steward to give me a berth in the second cabin; and from that hour until my stepping on shore at Boston, every politeness was shown me by the officers, and every kindness and attention by the stewards; and I feel under deep and lasting obligations to them, individually and collectively.

In no instance was I insulted or treated in any way distinct or dissimilar from other passengers or travelers, either in coaches, railroads, steam packets, or hotels; and if the feeling was entertained, in no case did I discover its existence.

I may with propriety here relate an accident, illustrative of the subject now under consideration. I took a passage ticket at the steam-packet office in Glasgow, for Dublin; and on going into the cabin to retire, I found the berth I had engaged occupied by an Irish gentleman and merchant. I inquired if he had not mistaken the number of his berth. He thought not. On comparing tickets, we saw that the clerk had given two tickets of the same number; and it appeared I had received mine first.

The gentleman at once offered to vacate the berth, against which I remonstrated and took my berth in an opposite state-room. Here, sir, we discover treatment just, impartial, reasonable; and we ask nothing beside.

There is a marked difference between social and civil rights. It has been well and justly remarked by my friend Mr. Phillips* that we all claim the privilege of selecting our society and associations; but, in civil rights, one man has not the prerogative to define rights for another. For instance, sir, in public conveyances, for the rich man to usurp the privileges to himself, to the injury of the poor man, would be submitted to in no well-regulated society. And such is the position suffered by persons of color. On my arrival home from England, I went to the railway station, to go to Salem, being anxious to see my parents and sisters as soon as possible, asked for a ticket, paid fifty cents for it, and was pointed to the American designation car. Having previously received information of the regulations, I took my seat peaceably, believing it better to suffer wrong than do wrong. I felt then, as I felt on many occasions prior to leaving home, unwilling to descend so low as to bandy words with the superintendents or contest my rights with conductors or any others in the capacity of servants of any stage or steamboat company or railroad corporation, although I never, by any means, gave evidence that by my submission I intended to sanction usages which would derogate from uncivilized, much less long- and loud-professing and high-pretending America.

Bear with me while I relate an additional occurrence. On the morning after my return home, I was obliged to go to Boston again, and on going to the Salem station I met two friends, who inquired if I had any objection to their taking seats with me. I answered, I should be most happy. They took their seats accordingly, and soon afterward one of them remarked to me, "Charles, I don't know if they will allow us to ride with you." It was some time before I could understand what they meant, and, on doing so, I laughed, feeling it to be a climax to every absurdity I had heard attributed to Americans. To say nothing of the wrong done those friends, and the insult and indignity offered me by the appearance of the conductor, who ordered the friends from the car in a somewhat harsh manner. They immediately left the carriage.

* Wendell Phillips (1811–1884), Boston-bred and Harvard-educated, was one of the greatest of the Abolitionist leaders associated with William Lloyd Garrison. He fought against discrimination as well as against slavery.

On returning to Salem some few evenings afterward, Mr. Chase, the superintendent on this road, made himself known to me by recalling bygone days and scenes, and then inquired if I was not glad to get home after so long an absence in Europe. I told him I was glad to see my parents and family again, and this was the only object I could have, unless he thought I should be glad to take a hermit's life in the great pasture; inasmuch as I never felt to loathe my American name so much as since my arrival. He wished to know my reasons for the remark. I immediately gave them, and wished to know of him, if, in the event of his having a brother with red hair, he should find himself separated while traveling because of this difference, he should deem it just. He could make no reply. I then wished to know if the principle was not the same; and if so, there was an insult implied by his question.

In conclusion, I challenged him as the instrument inflicting the manifold injuries upon all not colored like himself to the presentation of an instance in any other Christian or unchristian country, tolerating usages at once so disgraceful, unjust and inhuman. What if some few of the West or East India planters and merchants should visit our liberty-loving country, with their colored wives—how would he manage? Or, if R. M. Johnson, the gentleman who has been elevated to the second office in the gift of the people, should be traveling from Boston to Salem, if he was prepared to separate him from his wife or daughters.

Sir, it happens to be my lot to have a sister a few shades lighter than myself; and who knows, if this state of things is encouraged, whether I may not on some future occasion be mobbed in Washington Street, on the supposition of walking with a white young lady!

Gentlemen of the Committee, these distinctions react in all their wickedness—to say nothing of their concocted and systematized odiousness and absurdity—upon those who instituted them; and particularly so upon those who are illiberal and mean enough to practice them.

Mr. Chairman, if colored people have abused any rights granted them, or failed to exhibit due appreciation of favors bestowed, or shrunk from dangers or responsibilities, let it be made to appear. Or if our country contains a population to compare with them in loyalty and patriotism, circumstances duly considered, I have it yet to learn. The history of our country must ever testify in their behalf. In view of these and many additional considerations, I unhesitatingly assert their claim, on the naked principle of merit, to every advantage set forth in the Constitution of this Commonwealth.

Finally, Mr. Chairman, there is in this and other states a large and growing colored population, whose residence in your midst has not been from choice (let this be understood and reflected upon), but by the force of circumstances over which they never had control. Upon the heads of their oppressors and calumniators be the censure and responsibility. If to ask at your hands redress for injuries and protection in our rights and immunities, as citizens, is reasonable and dictated alike by justice, humanity and religion, you will not reject, I trust, the prayer of your petitioners.

Before sitting down, I owe it to myself to remark, that I was not appraised of the wish of my friends to appear here until passing through Boston, a day or two since; and having been occupied with other matters, I have had no opportunity for preparation on this occasion. I feel much obliged to the Committee for their kind, patient, and attentive hearing.

WE MUST ASSERT OUR RIGHTFUL CLAIMS AND PLEAD OUR OWN CAUSE

By Samuel H. Davis

A National Convention of Colored Citizens met in Buffalo, New York, August 15 to 19, 1843. While the highlight of the convention was Henry Highland Garnet's militant appeal to the slaves, the opening address of the Chairman, Samuel H. Davis of Buffalo, was also noteworthy. Here are excerpts from that address, reprinted from Minutes of the National Convention of Colored Citizens held at Buffalo on the 15th, 16th, 17th, 18th, and 19th of August, 1843, Albany, New York, *pp. 4–7.*

GENTLEMEN: I consider this a most happy period in our history, when we as a people are in some degree awake to a sense of our condition and are determined no longer to submit tamely and silently to wear the galling yoke of oppression, under which we have so long suffered—oppression riveted upon us, as well by an unholy and cruel prejudice, as by unjust and un-equal legislation. More particularly do I consider it ominous of good, when I see here collected, so much of wisdom and talent, from different parts of this great nation, collected here to de-liberate upon the wisest and best methods by which we may seek a redress of those grievances which most sorely oppress us as a people.

Gentlemen, in behalf of my fellow citizens of Buffalo, I bid you welcome, from the East and West, the North and South, to our city. Among you are the men who are lately from that part of our country where they see our brethren bound and manacled, suffering and bleeding, under the hand of the tyrant, who holds in one hand the Constitution of the United States, which guarantees freedom and equal rights to every citizen, and in the other "the scourge dripping with gore," drawn from the veins of his fellow man. Here also are those who live in my native New England, among the "descendants of the pilgrims," whose laws are more in accordance with the principles of free-dom and equal rights, so that but few laws are found recorded on their statute books of which we need complain. But though their laws are not marked with such palpable and flagrant in-justice toward the colored man as those of the South, yet there we are proscribed, by a fixed and cruel prejudice little less op-pressive. Our grievances are many and great, but it is not my intention to enumerate or to enlarge upon them. I will simply say, however, that we wish to secure for ourselves, in common with other citizens, the privilege of seeking our own happiness in any part of the country we may choose, which right is now unjustly and, we believe, unconstitutionally denied us in a part of this Union. We wish also to secure the elective franchise in those states where it is denied us, where our rights are legis-lated away, and our voice neither heard nor regarded. We also wish to secure, for our children *especially*, the benefits of edu-cation, which in several States are entirely denied us, and in others are enjoyed only in name. These, and many other things, of which we justly complain, bear most heavily upon us as a people; and it is our right and our duty to seek for redress, in that way which will be most likely to secure the desired end.

In your wisdom, you will, I doubt not, take into consideration these and the many other grievances which we suffer, and form such organizations and recommend such measures as shall, in your wisdom, seem most likely to secure our enfranchisement, the benefits of education to our children, and all our rights in common with other citizens of this republic.

Two objects should distinctly and constantly be borne in

mind, in all our deliberations. One is the diffusion of truth, and the other the elevation of our own people. By the diffusion of truth I mean that we must take a bold and elevated stand for the truth. We must determine, in the strength of God, to do everything that will advance the great and holy cause of freedom, and nothing that will in the least retard its progress. We must, by every means in our power, strive to persuade the white people to act with more confidence in their own principles of liberty—to make laws just and equal for all the people.

But while the color of the skin is made the criterion of the law, it is our right, our duty and, I hope I may say, our fixed determination, to make known our wrongs to the world and to our oppressors; to cease not day nor night to "tell, in burning words, our tale of woe," and pour a flood of living light on the minds and consciences of the oppressor, till we change their thoughts, feelings, and actions toward us as men and citizens of this land. We must convince our fellow men that slavery is unprofitable; that it is for the well-being and prosperity of this nation, the peace and happiness of our common country, that slavery and oppression be abolished within its borders, and that laws be enacted equal and just for all its citizens.

Proscription is not in accordance with equal rights, no more than is oppression with holy freedom, or slavery with the spirit of free institutions. The present system of laws, in this our country, enacted in reference to us, the oppressed and downtrodden descendants of Africa, do, and will continue to, operate like the canker worm in the root of the tree of liberty, preventing its growth and ultimately destroying its vitality. We may well say, in the language of a distinguished statesman and patriot of our own land, "We tremble for our country when we reflect that God is just, and that his justice will not always sleep."* By the example of other nations, who have gone before, whose history should be a warning to this people, we learn that slavery and oppression has nowhere prospered long; it blasts a nation's glory and prosperity, divides her power, weakens her strength, and grows like a corroding consumption in her very vitals. "God's judgments will not sleep forever, but he will visit the nations of the earth in justice." We love our common country—"With all her faults, we love her still." This is the land where we all drew our first breath; where we have grown up to strength and manhood. "Here is deposited the ashes of our

* This is one of Thomas Jefferson's most famous statements regarding slavery. He wrote it at the time of the battle in Congress over the Missouri Compromise.

fathers"; here we have contracted the most sacred engagements, the dearest relations of life; here we have found the companions of our childhood, the friends of our youth, the gentle partners of our lives; here are the haunts of our infancy, the scenes of every endearing hour—in a word, this is our own native land. I repeat it, then: We love our country, we love our fellow citizens—but *we love liberty more.* . . .

It is time that we were more awake to our own interests, more united in our efforts, and more efficient in our measures. We must profit by the example of our oppressors. We must act on their principles in resisting tyranny. We must adopt their resolutions in favor of liberty. "They have taught us a lesson, in their struggle for independence, that should never be forgotten. They have taught the world emphatically that a people united in the cause of liberty are invincible to those who would enslave them, and that heaven will ever frown on the cause of injustice, and ultimately grant success to those who oppose it." Shall we, then, longer submit in silence to our accumulated wrongs? Forbid it, heaven, that we should longer stand in silence, "hugging the delusive phantom of hope," when every gale that sweeps from the South, bears on its wings, to our ears, the dismal sound of slavery's clanking chains, now riveted on three millions of our brethren, and we ourselves are aliens and outcasts in our native land.

Is the question asked, what shall we do? Shall we petition for our rights? I do not pretend to dictate the course that should be pursued; but I have very little hope in petitioning longer. We have petitioned again and again, and what has been the result? Our humblest prayers have not been permitted a hearing. We could not even state our grievances. Our petitions were disregarded, our applications slighted, and we spurned from the mercy seat, insulted, abused and slandered. And this day finds us in the same unhappy and hopeless condition in which we have been for our whole lives; no other hope is let us, but in our own exertions and an "appeal to the God of armies." From what other source can we expect that help will come? Shall we appeal to the Christian community—to the church of our own land? What is her position? Behold her gigantic form, with hands upraised to heaven! See her increased and made rich by the toil and sweat and blood of slaves! View her arrayed in her pontifical robes, screening the horrid monster, slavery, with her very bosom—within her most sacred enclosures, that the world may not gaze on its distorted visage or view its hellish form! Yes, throwing around this accursed system, the very drapery of heaven, to cover this damning sin and give it character and respectability in the eyes of the country and in the eyes of the world. We cannot, therefore, look to her for help, for she has taken sides against us and on the side of slavery. Shall we turn to either of the great political parties of the day? What are our prospects there? Is there any hope of help? No, they are but the slaves of slavery, too, contending which shall be most faithful in supporting the foul system of slavery, that they may secure the vote of the slaveholder himself, and of his scores of human cattle. Shall we, then, look to the abolitionists and wait for them to give us our rights? I would not say a word that would have a tendency to discourage them in their noble efforts in behalf of the poor slave, or their exertions to advance the cause of truth and humanity. Some of them have made great sacrifices and have labored with a zeal and fidelity that justly entitle them to our confidence and gratitude. But if we sit down in idleness and sloth, waiting for them—or any other class of men—to do our own work, I fear it will never be done. If we are not willing to rise up and assert our rightful claims, and plead our own cause, we have no reason to look for success. We ourselves must be willing to contend for the rich boon of freedom and equal rights, or we shall never enjoy that boon. It is found only of them that seek. . . .

AN ADDRESS TO THE SLAVES OF THE UNITED STATES OF AMERICA

By Henry Highland Garnet

Henry Highland Garnet (1815–1881) was born a slave in Maryland, the son of an African chief who had been kidnaped and sold into slavery. He escaped with his parents in 1824 and settled in New York City. Garnet was educated in the African Free School No. 1 and at Oneida Institute. A brief stay at the Canaan Academy in Canaan, New Hampshire, in 1835 was interrupted when the academy was destroyed by an infuriated mob opposed to the education of Negroes. Garnet prepared for the ministry, and in 1842 was licensed to preach. He became pastor of the Liberty Street Presbyterian Church in Troy, New York, and later of the Shiloh Presbyterian Church in New York City,

*a pastorate he held for more than forty years, during
which time he became the foremost Negro clergyman in
the city.*

*In August, 1843, Garnet attended the National Conven-
tion of Negro Citizens at Buffalo, New York, and delivered
a militant speech calling for slave rebellions as the surest
way to end slavery. It was the most radical speech by a
black American during the antebellum period. The proposal stirred the delegates and failed by one vote of being
adopted. After he had read the speech, John Brown, the
martyr of Harper's Ferry, had it published at his own expense.*

(*Garnet's Address is published in* A Memorial Discourse
by Rev. Henry Highland Garnet, Delivered in the Hall of
the House of Representatives, Washington, D. C., on Sabbath, February 12, 1865, *with an Introduction by James
McCune Smith, M.D., Philadelphia, 1865, pp. 44–51.*)

BRETHREN AND FELLOW CITIZENS: Your brethren of the
North, East and West have been accustomed to meet together
in national conventions, to sympathize with each other, and
to weep over your unhappy condition. In these meetings we
have addressed all classes of the free, but we have never, until
this time, sent a word of consolation and advice to you. We have
been contented in sitting still and mourning over your sorrows,
earnestly hoping that before this day your sacred liberties
would have been restored. But we have hoped in vain. Years
have rolled on, and tens of thousands have been borne on
streams of blood and tears to the shores of eternity. While you
have been oppressed, we have also been partakers with you;
nor can we be free while you are enslaved. We, therefore, write
to you as being bound with you.

Many of you are bound to us, not only by the ties of a common humanity, but we are connected by the more tender relations of parents, wives, husbands and sisters and friends. As
such we most affectionately address you.

Slavery has fixed a deep gulf between you and us, and while
it shuts out from you the relief and consolation which your
friends would willingly render, it afflicts and persecutes you
with a fierceness which we might not expect to see in the fiends
of hell. But still the Almighty Father of mercies has left to us a
glimmering ray of hope, which shines out like a lone star in a
cloudy sky. Mankind is becoming wiser, and better, the oppressor's power is fading, and you every day are becoming better
informed and more numerous. Your grievances, brethren, are

many. We shall not attempt in this short address to present to the world all the dark catalogue of the nation's sins which have been committed upon an innocent people. Nor is it indeed necessary, for you feel them from day to day, and all the civil-ized world looks upon them with amazement.

Two hundred and twenty-seven years ago the first of our in-jured race were brought to the shores of America. They came not with glad spirits to select their homes in the New World. They came not with their own consent, to find an unmolested enjoyment of the blessings of this fruitful soil. The first dealings they had with men calling themselves Christians exhibited to them the worst features of corrupt and sordid hearts, and con-vinced them that no cruelty is too great, no villainy and no robbery too abhorrent for even enlightened men to perform, when influenced by avarice and lust. Neither did they come flying upon the wings of Liberty to a land of freedom. But they came with broken hearts from their beloved native land and were doomed to unrequited toil and deep degradation. Nor did the evil of their bondage end at their emancipation by death. Succeeding generations inherited their chains, and millions have come from eternity into time, and have returned again to the world of spirits, cursed and ruined by American slavery.

The propagators of the system, or their immediate successors, very soon discovered its growing evil and its tremendous wickedness, and secret promises were made to destroy it. The gross inconsistency of a people holding slaves, who had them-selves "ferried o'er the wave" for freedom's sake, was too ap-parent to be entirely overlooked. The voice of Freedom cried, "Emancipate your slaves." Humanity supplicated with tears for the deliverance of the children of Africa. Wisdom urged her solemn plea. The bleeding captive pleaded his innocence and pointed to Christianity who stood weeping at the cross. Jehovah frowned upon the nefarious institution, and thunderbolts, red with vengeance, struggled to leap forth to blast the guilty wretches who maintained it. But all was vain. Slavery had stretched its dark wings of death over the land, the Church stood silently by, the priests prophesied falsely, and the people loved to have it so. Its throne is established, and now it reigns triumphant.

Nearly three millions of your fellow citizens are prohibited by law and public opinion (which in this country is stronger than law) from reading the Book of Life. Your intellect has been destroyed as much as possible, and every ray of light they have attempted to shut out from your minds. The oppressors themselves have become involved in the ruin. They have become weak, sensual and rapacious; they have cursed you; they have cursed themselves; they have cursed the earth which they have trod.

The colonies threw the blame upon England. They said that the mother country entailed the evil upon them, and they would rid themselves of it if they could. The world thought they were sincere, and the philanthropic pitied them. But time soon tested their sincerity. In a few years the colonists grew strong and severed themselves from the British government. Their independence was declared, and they took their station among the sovereign powers of the earth. The declaration was a glorious document. Sages admired it, and the patriotic of every nation reverenced the Godlike sentiments which it contained. When the power of government returned to their hands, did they emancipate the slaves? No; they rather added new links to our chains. Were they ignorant of the principles of Liberty? Certainly they were not. The sentiments of their revolutionary orators fell in burning eloquence upon their hearts, and with one voice they cried, "Liberty or death." Oh, what a sentence was that! It ran from soul to soul like electric fire and nerved the arms of thousands to fight in the holy cause of Freedom. Among the diversity of opinions that are entertained in regard to physical resistance, there are but a few found to gainsay the stern declaration. We are among those who do not.

Slavery! How much misery is comprehended in that single word. What mind is there that does not shrink from its direful effects? Unless the image of God be obliterated from the soul, all men cherish the love of liberty. The nice discerning political economist does not regard the sacred right more than the untutored African who roams in the wilds of Congo. Nor has the one more right to the full enjoyment of his freedom than the other. In every man's mind the good seeds of liberty are planted, and he who brings his fellow down so low as to make him contented with a condition of slavery commits the highest crime against God and man. Brethren, your oppressors aim to do this. They endeavor to make you as much like brutes as possible. When they have blinded the eyes of your mind; when they have embittered the sweet waters of life; when they have shut out the light which shines from the word of God—then, and not till then, has American slavery done its perfect work.

To such degradation it is sinful in the extreme for you to make voluntary submission. The divine commandments you are in duty bound to reverence and obey. If you do not obey them, you will surely meet with the displeasure of the Almighty. He requires you to love Him supremely, and your neighbor as yourself, to keep the Sabbath day holy, to search the Scriptures, and bring up your children with respect for His laws, and to worship no other God but Him. But slavery sets all these at nought and hurls defiance in the face of Jehovah. The forlorn condition in which you are placed does not destroy your obligation to God. You are not certain of heaven, because you allow yourselves to remain in a state of slavery, where you cannot obey the commandments of the Sovereign of the universe. If the ignorance of slavery is a passport to heaven, then it is a blessing, and no curse, and you should rather desire its perpetuity than its abolition. God will not receive slavery, nor ignorance, nor any other state of mind, for love and obedience to Him. Your condition does not absolve you from your moral obligation. The diabolical injustice by which your liberties are cloven down, neither God nor angels, nor just men command you to suffer for a single moment. Therefore it is your solemn and imperative duty to use every means, both moral, intellectual and physical, that promises success. If a band of heathen men should attempt to enslave a race of Christians, and to place their children under the influence of some false religion, surely Heaven would frown upon the men who would not resist such aggression, even to death. If, on the other hand, a band of Christians should attempt to enslave a race of heathen men, and to entail slavery upon them, and to keep them in heathenism in the midst of Christianity, the God of heaven would smile upon every effort which the injured might make to disenthral themselves.

Brethren, it is as wrong for your lordly oppressors to keep you in slavery as it was for the man thief to steal our ancestors from the coast of Africa. You should therefore now use the same manner of resistance as would have been just in our ancestors when the bloody footprints of the first remorseless soul thief was placed upon the shores of our fatherland. The humblest peasant is as free in the sight of God as the proudest monarch that ever swayed a scepter. Liberty is a spirit sent out from God and, like its great Author, is no respecter of persons.

Brethren, the time has come when you must act for yourselves. It is an old and true saying that, "if hereditary bondmen would be free, they must themselves strike the blow." You can plead your own cause and do the work of emancipation better than any others. The nations of the Old World are moving in the great cause of universal freedom, and some of them at least will, ere long, do you justice. The combined powers of Europe have placed their broad seal of disapprobation upon the African slave trade. But in the slaveholding parts of the United States the trade is as brisk as ever. They buy and sell you as though you were brute beasts. The North has done much; her opinion of slavery in the abstract is known. But in regard to the South, we adopt the opinion of the *New York Evangelist*—"We have advanced so far, that the cause apparently waits for a more effectual door to be thrown open than has been yet." We are about to point you to that more effectual door. Look around you and behold the bosoms of your loving wives heaving with untold agonies! Hear the cries of your poor children! Remember the stripes your fathers bore. Think of the torture and disgrace of your noble mothers. Think of your wretched sisters, loving virtue and purity, as they are driven into concubinage and are exposed to the unbridled lusts of incarnate devils. Think of the undying glory that hangs around the ancient name of Africa— and forget not that you are native-born American citizens, and as such you are justly entitled to all the rights that are granted to the freest. Think how many tears you have poured out upon the soil which you have cultivated with unrequited toil and enriched with your blood; and then go to your lordly enslavers and tell them plainly that you *are determined to be free*. Appeal to their sense of justice and tell them that they have no more right to oppress you than you have to enslave them. Entreat them to remove the grievous burdens which they have imposed upon you, and to remunerate you for your labor. Promise them renewed diligence in the cultivation of the soil, if they will render to you an equivalent for your services. Point them to the increase of happiness and prosperity in the British West Indies since the Act of Emancipation.* Tell them, in language which they cannot misunderstand, of the exceeding sinfulness of slavery and of a future judgment and of the righteous retributions of an indignant God. Inform them that all you desire is freedom, and that nothing else will suffice. Do this, and forever after cease to toil for the heartless tyrants, who give you no other reward but stripes and abuse. If they then commence work of death, they, and not you, will be responsible for the consequences. You had far better all die—*die immediately*—than live slaves and entail your wretchedness upon your posterity. If you would be free in this generation, here is your only hope. However much you and all of us may desire it, there is not much hope of redemption without the shedding of blood. If you must bleed, let it all come at once—rather *die freemen than live to be the slaves*. It is impossible, like the children of Israel, to make a grand exodus from the land of bondage. The Pharaohs

* Slavery was abolished in the British West Indies by an act of Parliament in 1833.

are on both sides of the blood-red waters! You cannot move *en masse* to the dominions of the British Queen, nor can you pass through Florida and overrun Texas and at last find peace in Mexico. The propagators of American slavery are spending their blood and treasure that they may plant the black flag in the heart of Mexico and riot in the halls of the Montezumas.* In the language of the Reverend Robert Hall, when addressing the volunteers of Bristol who were rushing forth to repel the invasion of Napoleon, who threatened to lay waste the fair homes of England, "Religion is too much interested in your behalf not to shed over you her most gracious influences."

You will not be compelled to spend much time in order to become inured to hardships. From the first moment that you breathed the air of heaven, you have been accustomed to nothing else but hardships. The heroes of the American Revolution were never put upon harder fare than a peck of corn and few herrings per week. You have not become enervated by the luxuries of life. Your sternest energies have been beaten out upon the anvil of severe trial. Slavery has done this to make you subservient to its own purposes. But it has done more than this; it has prepared you for any emergency. If you receive good treatment, it is what you can hardly expect; if you meet with pain, sorrow, and even death, these are the common lot of the slaves.

Fellow men, patient sufferers, behold your dearest rights crushed to the earth! See your sons murdered, and your wives, mothers and sisters doomed to prostitution. In the name of the merciful God, and by all that life is worth, let it no longer be a debatable question, whether it is better to choose liberty or death.

In 1822, Denmark Veazie, of South Carolina, formed a plan for the liberation of his fellow men.† In the whole history of

---

* American-Mexican relations deteriorated after the annexation of Texas in December, 1845. American troops had moved into territory claimed by Mexico in July, 1845, and when the Mexicans entered this territory, President Polk requested a declaration of war, which Congress made on May 12, 1846. The war was basically the result of the drive by the slave-owners to acquire new land for cotton.

† Denmark Vesey was a slave in Charleston, South Carolina, who bought his own liberty after he won a $1,500 raffle. Once free himself, he was determined to aid his people in gaining their freedom, and for four years he planned a vast slave plot. The slaves involved had hidden away weapons and ammunition. In 1822 the plot was uncovered when two house slaves turned informers, and the authorities arrested 131 suspects. Federal troops were present to protect Charleston against further revolts as the leaders of the revolt were hanged.

human efforts to overthrow slavery, a more complicated and
tremendous plan was never formed. He was betrayed by the
treachery of his own people, and died a martyr to freedom.
Many a brave hero fell, but history, faithful to her high trust,
will transcribe his name on the same monument with Moses,
Hampden, Tell, Bruce and Wallace, Toussaint L'Ouverture,
Lafayette and Washington. That tremendous movement shook
the whole empire of slavery. The guilty soul thieves were overwhelmed with fear. It is a matter of fact that at this time, and
in consequence of the threatened revolution, the slave states
talked strongly of emancipation. But they blew but one blast of
the trumpet of freedom, and then laid it aside. As these men became quiet, the slaveholders ceased to talk about emancipation; and now behold your condition to-day! Angels sigh over it,
and humanity has long since exhausted her tears in weeping on
your account!

The patriotic Nathaniel Turner* followed Denmark Veazie.
He was goaded to desperation by wrong and injustice. By
despotism, his name has been recorded on the list of infamy,
and future generations will remember him among the noble
and brave.

Next arose the immortal Joseph Cinque, the hero of the *Amistad*.† He was a native African, and by the help of God he
emancipated a whole shipload of his fellow men on the high
seas. And he now sings of liberty on the sunny hills of Africa
and beneath his native palm trees, where he hears the lion roar
and feels himself as free as the king of the forest.

Next arose Madison Washington, that bright star of freedom, and took his station in the constellation of true heroism.‡

---

* The Nat Turner revolt in Virginia in 1831 was the greatest slave revolt
in American history. At the head of a small band of slaves, Turner moved
from plantation to plantation, murdering slaveholding families. Some
sixty whites were killed, and in retaliation, more than one hundred
Negroes, innocent and guilty, were murdered before the rebellion was
crushed. Turner was later captured and executed.

† In 1839, Joseph Cinque, son of an African king, led fifty-four slaves in
a revolt aboard the *Amistad* off the coast of Cuba. Cinque and his men
seized the ship and attempted to sail it back to Africa, but the slave
dealers, whose lives had been spared, landed the vessel on the Connecticut
coast. Defended by Abolitionists, the case went all the way up to the
Supreme Court with ex-President John Quincy Adams acting as the
lawyer for the Africans. On March 9, 1841, the Supreme Court ordered
Cinque and his fellow Africans freed. They returned to Sierra Leone in
1842.

‡ In 1841 a mutiny broke out aboard the *Creole,* sailing from Virginia for
New Orleans. On the high seas 130 slaves, led by Madison Washington,

He was a slave on board the brig *Creole,* of Richmond, bound to New Orleans, that great slave mart, with a hundred and four others. Nineteen struck for liberty or death. But one life was taken, and the whole were emancipated, and the vessel was carried into Nassau, New Providence.

Noble men! Those who have fallen in freedom's conflict, their memories will be cherished by the true-hearted and the God-fearing in all future generations; those who are living, their names are surrounded by a halo of glory.

Brethren, arise, arise! Strike for your lives and liberties. Now is the day and the hour. Let every slave throughout the land do this, and the days of slavery are numbered. You cannot be more oppressed than you have been; you cannot suffer greater cruelties than you have already. *Rather die freemen than live to be slaves.* Remember that you are *four millions!*

It is in your power so to torment the God-cursed slaveholders that they will be glad to let you go free. If the scale was turned, and black men were the masters and white men the slaves, every destructive agent and element would be employed to lay the oppressor low. Danger and death would hang over their heads day and night. Yes, the tyrants would meet with plagues more terrible than those of Pharaoh. But you are a patient people. You act as though you were made for the special use of these devils. You act as though your daughters were born to pamper the lusts of your masters and overseers. And worse than all, you tamely submit while your lords tear your wives from your embraces and defile them before your eyes. In the name of God, we ask, are you men? Where is the blood of your fathers? Has it all run out of your veins? Awake, awake; millions of voices are calling you! Your dead fathers speak to you from their graves. Heaven, as with a voice of thunder, calls on you to arise from the dust.

Let your motto be Resistance! *Resistance!* RESISTANCE! No oppressed people have ever secured their liberty without resistance. What kind of resistance you had better make you must decide by the circumstances that surround you, and according to the suggestion of expediency. Brethren, adieu! Trust in the living God. Labor for the peace of the human race, and remember that you are *four millions!*

---

rebelled, killed a slaveowner and guided the ship into the harbor of Nassau, where, under British law, they would be free. Over the objections of the United States State Department, the British allowed the Negroes to go free, although the British government finally agreed to pay an indemnity for not returning the slaves.

SLAVERY AS IT IS, AND ITS INFLUENCE UPON THE AMERICAN PEOPLE

By William Wells Brown

William Wells Brown (1815–1884) was born a slave in Kentucky. He escaped to the North and became an effective antislavery speaker, novelist (author of Clotel, or The President's Daughter, the first novel published by an American Negro), playwright and historian. In 1854, years after he had escaped from slavery, his English friends, worried for his safety under the Fugitive Slave Act of 1850, purchased Brown's freedom for three hundred dollars. Besides being one of the most active Abolitionist lecturers, Brown was deeply involved in the temperance, woman-suffrage, prison-reform and peace movements.

On November 4, 1847, Brown delivered a lecture on slavery and its influence upon the morals and character of the American people before the Female Anti-Slavery Society of Salem, Massachusetts. The lecture was later published in pamphlet form by the Massachusetts Anti-Slavery Society.

(Parts of this lecture are presented here; they were taken from William Wells Brown, A Lecture Delivered before the Female Anti-Slavery Society of Salem, at Lyceum Hall, Nov. 4, 1847, by William W. Brown, a Fugitive Slave, Reported by Henry M. Parkhurst, Boston, 1847.)

. . . IT IS DEPLORABLE to look at the character of the American people, the character that has been given to them by the institution of slavery. The profession of the American people is far above the profession of the people of any other country. Here the people profess to carry out the principles of Christianity. The American people are a sympathizing people. They not only profess, but appear to be a sympathizing people to the inhabitants of the whole world. They sympathize with everything else but the American slave. When the Greeks were struggling for liberty, meetings were held to express sympathy.* Now

* During the Greek struggle for independence from Turkey, there was widespread sympathy for the Greek cause in the United States. Webster, Clay, and other leading Americans favored American acknowledgment of

they are sympathizing with the poor downtrodden serfs of Ireland, and are sending their sympathy across the ocean to them.*

But what will the people of the Old World think? Will they not look upon the American people as hypocrites? Do they not look upon your professed sympathy as nothing more than hypocrisy? You may hold your meetings and send your words across the ocean; you may ask Nicholas of Russia to take the chains from his poor downtrodden serfs, but they look upon it all as nothing but hypocrisy. Look at our twenty thousand fugitive slaves, running from under the stars and stripes, and taking refuge in the Canadas; *twenty thousand,* some leaving their wives, some their husbands, some leaving their children, some their brothers, and some their sisters—fleeing to take refuge in the Canadas. Wherever the stars and stripes are seen flying in the United States of America, they point him out as a slave.

If I wish to stand up and say, "I am a man," I must leave the land that gave me birth. If I wish to ask protection as a man, I must leave the American stars and stripes. Wherever the stars and stripes are seen flying upon American soil, I can receive no protection; I am a slave, a chattel, a thing. I see your liberty poles around in your cities. If tomorrow morning you are hoisting the stars and stripes upon one of your liberty poles, and I should see the man following me who claims my body and soul as his property, I might climb to the very top of your liberty pole, I might cut the cord that held your stars and stripes and bind myself with it as closely as I could to your liberty pole, I might talk of law and the Constitution, but nothing could save me unless there be public sentiment enough in Salem. I could not appeal to law or the Constitution; I could only appeal to public sentiment; and if public sentiment would not protect me, I must be carried back to the plantations of the South, there to be lacerated, there to drag the chains that I left upon the Southern soil a few years since.

This is deplorable. And yet the American slave *can* find a spot where he may be a man—but it is not under the American flag. Fellow citizens, I am the last to eulogize any country where they oppress the poor. I have nothing to say in behalf of England or any other country, any further than as they extend pro-

---

the independence of the Greeks, and in 1823 President James Monroe at first recommended this course, but was persuaded by Secretary of State John Quincy Adams to abandon it.
* During the famine in Ireland in 1847, relief supplies were sent from the United States to aid the starving.

tection to mankind. I say that I honor England for protecting
the black man. I honor every country that shall receive the
American slave, that shall protect him, and that shall recognize
him as a man.

I know that the United States will not do it; but I ask you to
look at the efforts of other countries. Even the Bey of Tunis, a
few years since, has decreed that there shall not be a slave in
his dominions; and we see that the subject of liberty is being
discussed throughout the world. People are looking at it; they
are examining it; and it seems as though every country and
every people and every government were doing something, excepting the United States. But Christian, democratic, republican
America is doing nothing at all. It seems as though she would
be the last. It seems as though she was determined to be the
last to knock the chain from the limbs of the slave. Shall the
American people be behind the people of the Old World? Shall
they be behind those who are represented as almost living in
the dark ages?

> Shall every flap of England's flag
> Proclaim that all around are free,
> From farthest Ind to each blue crag
> That beetles o'er the western sea?
> And shall we scoff at Europe's kings,
> When Freedom's fire is dimmed with us;
> And round our country's altar clings
> The damning shade of Slavery's curse?

Shall we, I ask, shall the American people be the last? I am
here, not for the purpose of condemning the character of the
American people, but for the purpose of trying to protect or
vindicate their character. I would to God that there were some
feature that I could vindicate. There is no liberty here for me;
there is no liberty for those with whom I am associated; there
is no liberty for the American slave; and yet we hear a great deal
about liberty! How do the people of the Old World regard the
American people? Only a short time since, an American gentleman, in traveling through Germany, passed the window of a
bookstore where he saw a number of pictures. One of them was
a cut representing an American slave on his knees, with chains
upon his limbs. Over him stood a white man, with a long whip;
and underneath was written, "the latest specimen of American
democracy." I ask my audience, Who placed that in the hands of
those that drew it? It was the people of the United States.
Slavery, as it is to be found in this country, has given the serfs

of the Old World an opportunity of branding the American people as the most tyrannical people upon God's footstool.

Only a short time since, an American man-of-war was anchored in the bay opposite Liverpool. The English came down by the hundreds and thousands. The stars and stripes were flying; and there stood those poor persons that had never seen an American man-of-war, but had heard a great deal of American democracy. Some were eulogizing the American people; some were calling it the "land of the free and the home of the brave." And while they stood there, one of their number rose up, and pointing his fingers to the American flag, said:

> United States, your banner wears
> Two emblems,—one of fame;
> Alas, the other that it bears,
> Reminds us of your shame.
> The white man's liberty entyped,
> Stands blazoned by your stars;
> But what's the meaning of your stripes?
> They mean your Negro scars.

What put that in the mouth of that individual? It was the system of American slavery; it was the action of the American people; the inconsistency of the American people; their profession of liberty, and their practice in opposition to their profession. . . .

THE FUGITIVE SLAVE BILL

By Samuel Ringgold Ward

One of the provisions of the Compromise of 1850 to settle the sectional controversy arising from the Mexican War called for the enactment of a stricter fugitive-slave law. The proposed bill was denounced by black and white Abolitionists, and by none more vigorously than by Samuel Ringgold Ward (1817–c.1864). Brought to New York at the age of three by his parents, who escaped from slavery in Maryland, Ward received an education, taught school, and became a preacher. A leading antislavery agent, he became famous as an orator. After the fugitive-slave bill became law, Ward spoke out so vehemently against it

*that he was forced to flee to Canada. He never returned
to the United States, but continued to lecture in Canada
and England. He died in Jamaica.*

*The following is a speech Ward delivered in Boston on
March 25, 1850, at an anti-Webster meeting in Faneuil
Hall. In his speech in the Senate on March 7, 1850, Daniel
Webster had indicated his support for stricter enforcement of the fugitive-slave law, and the Boston Abolitionists
gathered to condemn the Senator from Massachusetts.
Ward denounced Webster and James M. Mason, Senator
from Virginia and author of the bill. He concluded his
speech with a call for resistance by all means necessary.*

(The speech here presented is taken from The Liberator,
April 5, 1850.)

I AM HERE TONIGHT as a guest. You have met here to
speak of the sentiments of a Senator of your state whose remarks you have the honor to repudiate. In the course of the remarks of the gentlemen who preceded me, he has done us the
favor to make honorable mention of a Senator of my own
State—William H. Seward.*

I thank you for this manifestation of approbation of a man
who has always stood head and shoulders above his party and
who has never receded from his position on the question of
slavery. It was my happiness to receive a letter from him a
few days since, in which he said he never would swerve from
his position as the friend of freedom.

To be sure, I agree not with Senator Seward in politics, but
when an individual stands up for the rights of men against
slaveholders, I care not for party distinctions. He is my brother.

We have here much of common cause and interest in this
matter. That infamous bill of Mr. Mason of Virginia proves itself to be like all other propositions presented by Southern men.
It finds just enough of Northern doughfaces† who are willing
to pledge themselves, if you will pardon the uncouth language of
a backwoodsman, to lick up the spittle of the slavocrats, and
swear it is delicious.

You of the old Bay State—a state to which many of us are
accustomed to look as to our fatherland, just as we look back to
England as our mother country—you have a Daniel who has de-

* William H. Seward, Senator from New York, opposed the Compromise
of 1850 including the fugitive-slave bill. He upheld the principle of the
"Higher Law"—the law of God—under which slavery could never be
justified.

† "Doughfaces" referred to Northerners with Southern principles.

serted the cause of freedom. We, too, in New York, have a "Daniel who has come to judgment," only he don't come quite fast enough to the right kind of judgment. Daniel S. Dickinson* represents some one, I suppose, in the State of New York; God knows, he doesn't represent me. I can pledge you that our Daniel will stand cheek by jowl with your Daniel. He was never known to surrender slavery, but always to surrender liberty.

The bill of which you most justly complain, concerning the surrender of fugitive slaves, is to apply alike to your state and to our state, if it shall ever apply at all. But we have come here to make a common oath upon a common altar, that that bill shall never take effect. Honorable Senators may record their names in its behalf, and it may have the sanction of the House of Representatives; but we, the people, who are superior to both Houses and the Executive, too, we, the people, will never be human bipeds, to howl upon the track of the fugitive slave, even though led by the corrupt Daniel of your state, or the degraded one of ours.

Though there are many attempts to get up compromises— and there is no term which I detest more than this, it is always the term which makes right yield to wrong; it has always been accursed since Eve made the first compromise with the devil. I was saying, sir, that it is somewhat singular, and yet historically true, that whensoever these compromises are proposed, there are men of the North who seem to forsee that Northern men, who think their constituency will not look into these matters, will seek to do more than the South demands. They seek to prove to Northern men that all is right and all is fair; and this is the game Webster is attempting to play.

"Oh," says Webster, "the will of God has fixed that matter; we will not reenact the will of God." Sir, you remember the time in 1841, '42, '43 and '44, when it was said that Texas could never be annexed. The design of such dealing was that you should believe it, and then, when you thought yourselves secure, they would spring the trap upon you. And now it is their wish to seduce you into the belief that slavery never will go there, and then the slaveholders will drive slavery there as fast as possible. I think that this is the most contemptible proposition of the whole, except the support of that bill which would attempt to make the whole North the slave catchers of the South.

You will remember that that bill of Mr. Mason says nothing

* Daniel Stevens Dickinson (1800–1866) was a leader of the Democratic party in New York State and was elected United States Senator in 1844 after serving as Lieutenant Governor.

about color. Mr. Phillips, a man whom I always loved, a man
who taught me my hornbook on this subject of slavery, when I
was a poor boy, has referred to Marshfield. There is a man who
sometimes lives in Marshfield, and who has the reputation of
having an honorable dark skin. Who knows but that some postmaster may have to sit upon the very gentleman whose character you have been discussing to-night? "What is sauce for
the goose is sauce for the gander." If this bill is to relieve
grievances, why not make an application to the immortal
Daniel of Marshfield? There is no such thing as complexion
mentioned. It is not only true that the colored men of Massachusetts—it is not only true that the fifty thousand colored men
of New York may be taken—though I pledge you there is one,
whose name is Sam Ward, who will never be taken alive. Not
only is it true that the fifty thousand black men of New York
may be taken, but any one else also can be captured. My friend
Theodore Parker alluded to Ellen Craft.* I had the pleasure of
taking tea with her and accompanied her here tonight. She is
far whiter than many who come here slave-catching. This line
of distinction is so nice that you cannot tell who is white or
black. As Alexander Pope used to say, "White and black soften
and blend in so many thousand ways, that it is neither white nor
black."

This is the question. Whether a man has a right to himself
and his children, his hopes and his happiness, for this world
and the world to come. That is a question which, according to
this bill, may be decided by any backwoods postmaster in this
state or any other. Oh, this is a monstrous proposition; and I do
thank God that if the Slave Power has such demands to make on
us, that the proposition has come now—now, that the people
know what is being done; now that the public mind is turned
toward this subject; now that they are trying to find what is
the truth on this subject.

Sir, what must be the moral influence of this speech of Mr.
Webster on the minds of young men, lawyers and others, here
in the North? They turn their eyes toward Daniel Webster as
toward a superior mind, and a legal and Constitutional oracle.
If they shall catch the spirit of this speech, its influence upon
them and upon following generations will be so deeply corrupt-
ing that it never can be wiped out or purged.

* Ellen Craft and her husband, William Craft, escaped from slavery in
Georgia by disguising themselves. Ellen Craft posed as a white gentleman
and her husband as her slave. They traveled through the slave states and
gained freedom in the North.

I am thankful that this, my first entrance into Boston and my first introduction to Faneuil Hall, gives me the pleasure and privilege of uniting with you in uttering my humble voice against the two Daniels, and of declaring, in behalf of our people, that if the fugitive slave is traced to our part of New York State, he shall have the law of Almighty God to protect him, the law which says, "Thou shalt not return to the master the servant that is escaped unto thee, but he shall dwell with thee in thy gates, where it liketh him best." And if our post-masters cannot maintain their Constitutional oaths and cannot live without playing the pander to the slave hunter, they need not live at all. Such crises as these leave us the right of Revolution, and if need be, that right we will, at whatever cost, most sacredly maintain.

I WON'T OBEY THE FUGITIVE SLAVE LAW

By Rev. J. W. Loguen

A month after the infamous Fugitive Slave Act was passed, the eloquent voice of Reverend J. W. Loguen, thundering defiance of the law, influenced the city of Syracuse, New York, to declare that city a refuge for Negro slaves. On October 4, 1850, the people of Syracuse filled the City Hall to hear a discussion of the recently passed law. Samuel Ringgold Ward, the distinguished black orator, spoke in opposition to the act, and he was followed by Reverend J. W. Loguen. A fugitive slave himself, Loguen appealed to his fellow citizens to honor the Constitution by dishonoring the law that would reenslave him and his people. Following his plea that Syracuse be made an "open city" for fugitive slaves, the meeting voted 395 to 96 in favor of his proposal.

A prominent Abolitionist, leader of the Underground Railway, Loguen became a bishop of the African Methodist Episcopal Zion Church.

(The speech is reprinted from The Rev. J. W. Loguen, As a Slave and As a Freeman: A Narrative of Real Life, Syracuse, N. Y., 1859, pp. 391–94.)

I WAS A SLAVE; I knew the dangers I was exposed to. I had made up my mind as to the course I was to take. On that score I needed no counsel, nor did the colored citizens generally. They had taken their stand—they would not be taken back to slavery. If to shoot down their assailants should forfeit their lives, such result was the least of the evil. They will have their liberties or die in their defense. What is life to me if I am to be a slave in Tennessee? My neighbors! I have lived with you many years, and you know me. My home is here, and my children were born here. I am bound to Syracuse by pecuniary interests, and social and family bonds. And do you think I can be taken away from you and from my wife and children, and be a slave in Tennessee? Has the President and his Secretary sent this enactment up here, to you, Mr. Chairman, to enforce on me in Syracuse?—and will you obey him? Did I think so meanly of you— did I suppose the people of Syracuse, strong as they are in numbers and love of liberty—or did I believe their love of liberty was so selfish, unmanly and unchristian—did I believe them so sunken and servile and degraded as to remain at their homes and labors, or, with none of that spirit which smites a tyrant down, to surround a United States Marshal to see me torn from my home and family, and hurled back to bondage— I say did I think so meanly of you, I could never come to live with you. Nor should I have stopped, on my return from Troy, twenty-four hours since, but to take my family and moveables to a neighborhood which would take fire, and arms, too, to resist the least attempt to execute this diabolical law among them. Some kind and good friends advise me to quit my country, and stay in Canada, until this tempest is passed. I doubt not the sincerity of such counsellors. But my conviction is strong, that their advice comes from a lack of knowledge of themselves and the case in hand. I believe that their own bosoms are charged to the brim with qualities that will smite to the earth the villains who may interfere to enslave any man in Syracuse. I apprehend the advice is suggested by the perturbation of the moment, and not by the tranquil spirit that rules above the storm, in the eternal home of truth and wisdom. Therefore I have hesitated to adopt this advice, at least until I have the opinion of this meeting. Those friends have not canvassed this subject. I have. They are called suddenly to look at it. I have looked at it steadily, calmly, resolutely, and at length defiantly, for a long time. I tell you the people of Syracuse and of the whole North must meet this tyranny and crush it by force, or be crushed by it. This hellish enactment has precipitated the conclusion that white men must live in dishonorable submission, and colored men be slaves, or they must give their physical as well as intellectual powers to the defense of human rights. The time has come to change the tones of submission into tones of defiance,— and to tell Mr. Fillmore and Mr. Webster, if they propose to execute this measure upon us, to send on their bloodhounds. Mr. President, long ago I was beset by over-prudent and good men and women to purchase my freedom. Nay, I was frequently importuned to consent that they purchase it, and present it as evidence of their partiality to my person and character. Generous and kind as those friends were, my heart recoiled from the proposal. I owe my freedom to the God who made me, and who stirred me to claim it against all other beings in God's universe. I will not, nor will I consent, that anybody else shall countenance the claims of a vulgar despot to my soul and body. Were I in chains, and did these kind people come to buy me out of prison, I would acknowledge the boon with inexpressible thankfulness. But I feel no chains, and am in no prison. I received my freedom from Heaven, and with it came the command to defend my title to it. I have long since resolved to do nothing and suffer nothing that can, in any way, imply that I am indebted to any power but the Almighty for my manhood and personality.

Now, you are assembled here, the strength of this city is here to express their sense of this fugitive act, and to proclaim to the despots at Washington whether it shall be enforced here—whether you will permit the government to return me and other fugitives who have sought asylum among you, to the Hell of slavery. The question is with you. If you will give us up, say so, and we will shake the dust from our feet and leave you. But we believe better things. We know you are taken by surprise. The immensity of this meeting testifies to the general consternation that has brought it together, necessarily, precipitately, to decide the most stirring question that can be presented, to wit, whether, the government having transgressed Constitutional and natural limits, you will bravely resist its aggressions, and tell its soulless agents that no slaveholder shall make your city and county a hunting field for slaves.

Whatever may be your decision, my ground is taken. I have declared it everywhere. It is known over the state and out of the state—over the line in the North, and over the line in the South. I don't respect this law—I don't fear it—I won't obey it! It outlaws me, and I outlaw it, and the men who attempt to enforce it on me. I place the governmental officials on the ground that they place me. I will not live a slave, and if force is employed to reenslave me, I shall make preparations to meet the crisis as becomes a man. If you will stand by me— and I believe you will do it, for your freedom and honor are involved as well as mine—it requires no microscope to see that—I say if you will stand with us in resistance to this measure, you will be the saviors of your country. Your decision to-night in favor of resistance will give vent to the spirit of liberty, and it will break the bands of party, and shout for joy all over the North. Your example only is needed to be the type of popular action in Auburn, and Rochester, and Utica, and Buffalo, and all the West, and eventually in the Atlantic cities. Heaven knows that this act of noble daring will break out somewhere—and may God grant that Syracuse be the honored spot, whence it shall send an earthquake voice through the land!

WOMAN'S RIGHTS

By Sojourner Truth

Sojourner Truth (c.1797–1883) was born a slave in New York and freed in 1827 when the state liberated its slaves. She did domestic work, and, after a period of religious revivalism, became an active Abolitionist, exchanging her name Isabella for the name Sojourner Truth. Although she remained illiterate all her life, she did valiant service in the antislavery and woman's-rights cause. When she died in November, 1883, the New York Globe, a black weekly, declared (December 1): "Sojourner Truth stands preeminently as the only colored woman who gained a National reputation on the lecture platform in the days before the war."

The speech reproduced here in part was made at the Woman's Rights convention in Akron, Ohio, in 1851. Some of the delegates to the convention urged that she not be allowed to speak, fearing that the Abolitionists would harm their cause. But Francis Dana Gage, who was presiding, invited her to speak. Sojourner Truth directed her remarks against the previous speaker, a clergyman who had ridiculed the weakness and helplessness of women, who should, therefore, not be entrusted with the vote.

Her eloquence and wit captured the gathering and won over new converts to the woman's-rights movement.

(Sojourner Truth's speech is reproduced in the dialect in which it was recorded in E. C. Stanton, S. B. Anthony, and M. J. Gage, History of Woman Suffrage, *Rochester, N. Y., 1887, Vol. I, p. 116.)*

WALL, CHILERN, whar dar is so much racket dar must be somethin' out o' kilter. I tink dat 'twixt de niggers of de Souf and de womin at de Norf, all talkin' 'bout rights, de white men will be in a fix pretty soon. But what's all dis here talkin' 'bout?

Dat man ober dar say dat womin needs to be helped into carriages and lifted ober ditches, and to hab de best place everywhar. Nobody eber helps me into carriages, or ober mud puddles, or gibs me any best place! And a'n't I a woman? Look at my arm! I have ploughed, and planted and gathered into barns, and no man could head me! And a'n't I a woman? I could work as much and eat as much as a man—when I could get it—and bear de lash as well! And a'n't I a woman? I have borne thirteen chilern, and seen 'em mos' all sold off to slavery, and when I cried out with my mother's grief, none but Jesus heard me! And a'n't I a woman?

Den dey talks 'bout dis ting in de head; what dis dey call it? ('Intellect," whispered some one near.) Dat's it, honey. What dat got to do wid womin's rights or nigger's rights? If my cup won't hold but a pint, and yourn holds a quart, wouldn't ye be mean not to let me have my little half-measure full?

Den dat little man in black dar, he say women can't have as much rights as men, 'cause Christ wan't a woman! Whar did your Christ come from? Whar did your Christ come from? From God and a woman! Man had nothin' to do wid Him!

If de fust woman God ever made was strong enough to turn de world upside down all alone, dese women togedder (and she glanced her eye over the platform) ought to be able to turn it back, and get it right side up again! And now dey is asking to do it, de men better let 'em.

MAY HUNGARY BE FREE

By George T. Downing

Louis Kossuth, leader of the unsuccessful 1848 rebellion in Hungary, had been forced to flee to Turkey. In 1851 he was brought from his exile to the United States, where he began a nationwide tour to raise funds for renewal of the revolutionary struggle against the Hapsburgs. On December 9, 1851, five days after reaching New York, he was addressed by George T. Downing, a wealthy black restaurant owner in Rhode Island and an active figure in the antislavery movement. Downing spoke on behalf of a reception committee of the Negro people, including John J. Zuille, James McCune Smith and Philip A. Bell.

The same issue of The Liberator *which carried the text of Downing's address also featured a poem by William E. Channing, the "Apostle of Unitarianism," entitled "The American Slave to Kossuth" which went in part:*

> O Kossuth! Magyar! Man, at last!
>   Betray us not, nor let there be
> Our curses lingering on thy past,
>   Our hate a household thing for thee.

But Kossuth disappointed the Negro people by refusing to take a position on American slavery, and on February 26, 1852, Frederick Douglass published an open letter to the Hungarian patriot reminding him that on the issue of slavery "there is no neutral ground here for any man."

Downing's remarks at the reception for Kossuth follow. They are taken from The Liberator, *December 19, 1851.*

WE APPEAR before you to pay homage to a great principle, which you announce with so much distinctness and uphold with so much power, the principle that a man has a right to the full exercise of his faculties and powers in the land which gave him birth; and that it is his first duty to devote all the energies of his being to maintain that right for himself and his compatriots. Around this principle you have thrown a radiance which almost clothes it with the sacredness of a new Evangelist, and from your world's platform have called upon peoples and nations, however weak, to stand up and maintain it against whatever odds oppression and tyranny may have arrayed against it.

In the face of the distinguished example of the Pilgrim Fathers and the many eminent men who have made this their *exile* home, we have steadily maintained this birth-home right during the last third of a century in this our native land, and will continue to maintain it until its ultimate triumph, "for the first love of man is in his home."

We feel that this great principle is surely gaining ground, and we hail in your person its living Apostle, who has given it voice and expression. We would express the deep sympathy we feel in you, because of the relation you sustain to Liberty. We feel that your mission is a most happy and propitious one. We see in it a part of the special ordering of Providence. The landing of the Pilgrim Fathers; our Declaration of Independence; the Revolutionary struggle, led by Washington; and the later developments of the principles of Liberty, as seen in the struggles now going on in our own country for its further advancement and application to all men, are kindred efforts.

God speed you in your mission! May Hungary be free! And we earnestly pray that when the resurrection of your country shall indeed take place, she will clothe herself in the true vestment of democracy, fitly prepared for her when you abolished caste, so that pure republicanism will in her be vindicated and every man stand an equal in the eyes of the law. Yes! illustrious patriot, may Hungary be free! May the world rejoice in her speedy disenthrallment. May the joy be twofold in that Hungary shall be redeemed—and not Hungary alone, but with her the world, mankind.

The attention of nations is fixed upon you! At the mention of your name, tyrants tremble, the oppressed rejoice! There is not a principle advocated by you, not a word that escapes your lips, but that is caught up and wafted to every civilized nation. And deep and widespread is the joy felt through Europe, when you proclaim the thrilling and trumpet-toned annunciation, "Ye oppressed nations of Europe, be of good cheer and courage."

God moves in mysterious ways. The result of the late Hungarian struggle will be propitious to the general growth of freedom. But for your imprisonment, the world would not now be so electrified by your eloquence—by the spirit of freedom. Hungary suffers in the ordering of Providence, for the good of the whole, but her destiny is to be free.

Respected sir, your mission is too high to be allied with party or sect; it is the common cause of crushed, outraged humanity.

May you, when you leave our shores in furtherance of your heaven-high mission, carry with you the sympathy of *all*, the active countenance of *all*.

Be assured, that as you have now our prayers, so when the time comes, we shall give our own "liberty offering," though it may be but the "widow's mite."

THE MEANING OF JULY FOURTH FOR THE NEGRO

By Frederick Douglass

Frederick Douglass (1817–1895), the foremost Negro leader in nineteenth-century America, was born of a slave mother and a white father in Tuckahoe, Maryland, in February, 1817. He never knew his mother well, but lived with his grandparents until the age of eight, when he was raised by an "Aunt Katy," who was in charge of rearing slave children on the plantation of Colonel Edward Lloyd. Sent to Baltimore after a year to live with Mr. and Mrs. Hugh Auld, he began to study reading with Mrs. Auld. When Mr. Auld forbade any further instruction, Douglass managed, by various devices, to learn anyway. To compel him to submit more readily to slavery, he was sent to Edward Covey, a "slave breaker" who specialized in cracking the spirit of slaves too difficult to handle. Beaten daily with stick and whip for the slightest infraction of impossibly strict rules, he finally decided to fight back, and, in a hand-to-hand struggle which lasted two hours, forced Covey to give up his plan to beat him. Thus, at the age of seventeen, Douglass discovered that he was not afraid to die and that the only way to halt a tyrant was to fight back.

Returned to Hugh Auld in Baltimore, he was apprenticed to a shipyard to learn the trade of calker. He not only learned the trade, but also, by tracing the letters on the prows of ships, learned to write. On September 3, 1838, armed with seaman's papers supplied him by a free Negro, Douglass got on a train in Baltimore and escaped from slavery, via the Underground Railroad, to New Bedford,

Massachusetts. Five months later he first came in contact with William Lloyd Garrison's antislavery weekly, The Liberator, *and in 1841 delivered his first speech at a convention of the Massachusetts Anti-Slavery Society. He was immediately employed as an agent of the Society, and rapidly became the most famous of the black Abolitionists as well as one of the greatest orators of his day.*

At first Douglass confined his talks to accounts of his experiences as a slave, but soon he was denouncing slavery and calling for its immediate abolition. The more polished his speech became, the fewer people believed that he had ever been a slave. To dispel all doubts, he published his Narrative of the Life of Frederick Douglass *in 1845—in spite of the danger of reenslavement. Douglass resolved to go abroad, to England, and for two years he spoke against slavery in Ireland, Scotland and England. In 1847, his legal freedom purchased by his British friends for 150 pounds, he left London to take up the battle against slavery again in this country. He moved to Rochester, New York, to start his newspaper,* The North Star, *later called* Frederick Douglass' Paper. *Soon he became famous as an antislavery editor as well as an orator.*

In 1852 Frederick Douglass was invited to address the citizens of Rochester on the Fourth of July celebration. The speech, delivered on July 5, is one of the most famous of his orations. Reprinted as a pamphlet, it reached a wide audience.

Douglass' discussion of the Fourth of July was a logical development from a speech he had delivered on May 11, 1847, to a meeting of the American Anti-Slavery Society, following his return from England.* In introducing Douglass, Garrison sought to mollify some of his critics who had accused him of treason because of his attack on the United States while in England. Garrison assured the audience that Douglass really loved and was attached to his native land. Douglass, in the course of his speech, replied directly to Garrison as follows (quoting from the National Anti-Slavery Standard, *May 20, 1847):*

. . . I CANNOT AGREE with my friend Mr. Garrison, in relation to my love and attachment to this land. I have no love for America, as such; I have no patriotism; I have no country. What country have I? The institutions of this country do not

---

* In the second speech, however, Douglass no longer regarded the Constitution as a proslavery document.

know me, do not recognize me as a man. I am not thought of, spoken of, in any direction, out of the antislavery ranks as a man. I am not thought of, or spoken of, except as a piece of property belonging to some *Christian* slaveholder, and all the religious and political institutions of this country, alike pronounce me a slave and a chattel. Now, in such a country as this, I cannot have patriotism. The only thing that links me to this land is my family, and the painful consciousness that here there are three millions of my fellow creatures, groaning beneath the iron rod of the worst despotism that could be devised, even in Pandemonium; that here are men and brethren, who are identified with me by their complexion, identified with me by their hatred of slavery, identified with me by their love and aspirations for liberty, identified with me by the stripes upon their backs, their inhuman wrongs and cruel sufferings. This, and this only, attaches me to this land and brings me here to plead with you, and with this country at large, for the disenthrallment of my oppressed countrymen, and to overthrow this system of slavery which is crushing them to the earth. How can I love a country that dooms three millions of my brethren, some of them my own kindred, my own brothers, my own sisters, who are now clanking the chains of slavery upon the plains of the South, whose warm blood is now making fat the soil of Maryland and of Alabama, and over whose crushed spirits rolls the dark shadow of oppression, shutting out and extinguishing forever the cheering rays of that bright sun of Liberty lighted in the souls of all God's children by the Omnipotent hand of Deity itself? How can I, I say, love a country thus cursed, thus bedewed with the blood of my brethren? A country, the church of which, and the government of which, and the Constitution of which, is in favor of supporting and perpetuating this monstrous system of injustice and blood? I have not, I cannot have, any love for this country, as such, or for its Constitution. I desire to see it overthrown as speedily as possible, and its Constitution shivered in a thousand fragments, rather than this foul curse should continue to remain as now.

> *Here is the full text of Douglass' great speech on the meaning of the Fourth of July to the Negro, as quoted in the pamphlet* Oration Delivered in Corinthian Hall, Rochester, by Frederick Douglass, July 5, 1852, *Rochester, 1852.*

Mr. President, friends and fellow citizens: He who could address this audience without a quailing sensation, has stronger nerves than I have. I do not remember ever to have appeared as a speaker before any assembly more shrinkingly, nor with greater distrust of my ability, than I do this day. A feeling has crept over me quite unfavorable to the exercise of my limited powers of speech. The task before me is one which requires much previous thought and study for its proper performance. I know that apologies of this sort are generally considered flat and unmeaning. I trust, however, that mine will not be so considered. Should I seem at ease, my appearance would much misrepresent me. The little experience I have had in addressing public meetings, in country school houses, avails me nothing on the present occasion.

The papers and placards say that I am to deliver a Fourth of July oration. This certainly sounds large and out of the common way for me. It is true that I have often had the privilege to speak in this beautiful hall, and to address many who now honor me with their presence. But neither their familiar faces, nor the perfect gauge I think I have of Corinthian Hall seems to free me from embarrassment.

The fact is, ladies and gentlemen, the distance between this platform and the slave plantation, from which I escaped, is considerable, and the difficulties to be overcome in getting from the latter to the former are by no means slight. That I am here today is, to me, a matter of astonishment as well as of gratitude. You will not, therefore, be surprised, if in what I have to say I evince no elaborate preparation, nor grace my speech with any high-sounding exordium. With little experience and with less learning, I have been able to throw my thoughts hastily and imperfectly together; and trusting to your patient and generous indulgence, I will proceed to lay them before you.

This, for the purpose of this celebration, is the Fourth of July. It is the birthday of your national independence, and of your political freedom. This, to you, is what the Passover was to the emancipated people of God. It carries your minds back to the day, and to the act of your great deliverance, and to the signs and to the wonders associated with that act and that day. This celebration also marks the beginning of another year of your national life; and reminds you that the Republic of America is now seventy-six years old. I am glad, fellow citizens, that your nation is so young. Seventy-six years, though a good old age for a man, is but a mere speck in the life of a nation. Three score years and ten is the allotted time for individual men; but nations number their years by thousands. According to this fact, you are, even now, only in the beginning of your national career, still lingering in the period of childhood. I repeat, I am glad this is so. There is hope in the thought, and hope is much needed under the dark clouds which lower above the horizon. The eye of the reformer is met with angry flashes portending disastrous times; but his heart may well beat lighter at the thought that America is young, and that she is still in the impressible stage of her existence. May he not hope that high lessons of wisdom, of justice and of truth, will yet give direction to her destiny? Were the nation older, the patriot's heart might be sadder and the reformer's brow heavier. Its future might be shrouded in gloom and the hope of its prophets go out in sorrow. There is consolation in the thought that America is young. Great streams are not easily turned from channels worn deep in the course of ages. They may sometimes rise in quiet and stately majesty, and inundate the land, refreshing and fertilizing the earth with their mysterious properties. They may also rise in wrath and fury, and bear away on their angry waves the accumulated wealth of years of toil and hardship. They, however, gradually flow back to the same old channel and flow on as serenely as ever. But, while the river may not be turned aside, it may dry up and leave nothing behind but the withered branch and the unsightly rock, to howl in the abyss-sweeping wind, the sad tale of departed glory. As with rivers, so with nations.

Fellow citizens, I shall not presume to dwell at length on the associations that cluster about this day. The simple story of it is, that seventy-six years ago the people of this country were British subjects. The style and title of your "sovereign people" (in which you now glory) was not then born. You were under the British Crown. Your fathers esteemed the English government as the home government, and England as the fatherland. This home government, you know, although a considerable distance from your home, did, in the exercise of its parental prerogatives, impose upon its colonial children such restraints, burdens and limitations as, in its mature judgment, it deemed wise, right and proper.

But your fathers, who had not adopted the fashionable idea of this day, of the infallibility of government and the absolute character of its acts, presumed to differ from the home government in respect to the wisdom and the justice of some of those burdens and restraints. They went so far in their excitement as to pronounce the measures of government unjust, unreasonable and oppressive, and altogether such as ought not to be quietly submitted to. I scarcely need say, fellow citizens, that my opinion of those measures fully accords with that of your fathers. Such a declaration of agreement on my part would not be worth much to anybody. It would certainly prove nothing as to what part I might have taken had I lived during the great controversy of 1776. To say now that America was right and England wrong is exceedingly easy. Everybody can say it; the dastard, not less than the noble brave, can flippantly descant on the tyranny of England toward the American colonies. It is fashionable to do so; but there was a time when to pronounce against England and in favor of the cause of the colonies tried men's souls. They who did so were accounted in their day plotters of mischief, agitators and rebels, dangerous men. To side with the right against the wrong, with the weak against the strong, and with the oppressed against the oppressor—here lies the merit, and the one which, of all others, seems unfashionable in our day. The cause of liberty may be stabbed by the men who glory in the deeds of your fathers. But, to proceed.

Feeling themselves harshly and unjustly treated by the home government, your fathers, like men of honesty and men of spirit, earnestly sought redress. They petitioned and remonstrated; they did so in a decorous, respectful and loyal manner. Their conduct was wholly unexceptionable. This, however, did not answer the purpose. They saw themselves treated with sovereign indifference, coldness and scorn. Yet they persevered. They were not the men to look back.

As the sheet anchor takes a firmer hold when the ship is tossed by the storm, so did the cause of your fathers grow stronger as it breasted the chilling blasts of kingly displeasure. The greatest and best of British statesmen admitted its justice, and the loftiest eloquence of the British Senate came to its support. But, with that blindness which seems to be the unvarying characteristic of tyrants since Pharaoh and his hosts were drowned in the Red Sea, the British government persisted in the exactions complained of.

The madness of this course, we believe, is admitted now, even by England; but we fear the lesson is wholly lost on our present rulers.

Oppression makes a wise man mad. Your fathers were wise men, and if they did not go mad, they became restive under this treatment. They felt themselves the victims of grievous wrongs, wholly incurable in their colonial capacity. With brave men there is always a remedy for oppression. Just here, the idea of a total separation of the colonies from the Crown was born! It was a startling idea, much more so than we at this distance of time regard it. The timid and the prudent (as has been intimated) of that day were, of course, shocked and alarmed by it.

Such people lived then, had lived before and will, probably, ever have a place on this planet; and their course, in respect to any great change (no matter how great the good to be attained, or the wrong to be redressed by it), may be calculated with as much precision as can be the course of the stars. They hate all changes, but silver, gold and copper change! Of this sort of change they are always strongly in favor.

These people were called Tories in the days of your fathers; and the appellation probably conveyed the same idea that is meant by a more modern, though a somewhat less euphonious term, which we often find in our papers, applied to some of our old politicians.

Their opposition to the then dangerous thought was earnest and powerful; but, amid all their terror and affrighted vociferations against it, the alarming and revolutionary idea moved on, and the country with it.

On the second of July, 1776, the old Continental Congress, to the dismay of the lovers of ease, and the worshipers of property, clothed that dreadful idea with all the authority of national sanction. They did so in the form of a resolution; and as we seldom hit upon resolutions drawn up in our day whose transparency is at all equal to this, it may refresh your minds and help my story if I read it.

[We] solemnly publish and declare, That these United Colonies are, and of Right ought to be Free and Independent States; that they are Absolved from all Allegiance to the British Crown, and that all political connection between them and the State of Great Britain is and ought to be totally dissolved.

Citizens, your fathers made good that resolution. They succeeded; and today you reap the fruits of their success. The freedom gained is yours; and you, therefore, may properly celebrate this anniversary. The Fourth of July is the first great fact in your nation's history—the very ringbolt in the chain of your yet undeveloped destiny.

Pride and patriotism, not less than gratitude, prompt you to celebrate and to hold it in perpetual remembrance. I have said that the Declaration of Independence is the ringbolt to the chain of your nation's destiny; so, indeed, I regard it. The principles contained in that instrument are saving principles. Stand by those principles, be true to them on all occasions, in all places, against all foes, and at whatever cost.

From the round top of your ship of state, dark and threatening clouds may be seen. Heavy billows, like mountains in the distance, disclose to the leeward huge forms of flinty rocks! That bolt drawn, that chain broken, and all is lost. Cling to this day—cling to it, and to its principles, with the grasp of a storm-tossed mariner to a spar at midnight.

The coming into being of a nation, in any circumstances, is an interesting event. But, besides general considerations, there were peculiar circumstances which make the advent of this republic an event of special attractiveness.

The whole scene, as I look back to it, was simple, dignified and sublime. The population of the country, at the time, stood at the insignificant number of three millions. The country was poor in the munitions of war. The population was weak and scattered, and the country a wilderness unsubdued. There were then no means of concert and combination, such as exist now. Neither stream nor lightning had then been reduced to order and discipline. From the Potomac to the Delaware was a journey of many days. Under these and innumerable other disadvantages your fathers declared for liberty and independence and triumphed.

Fellow citizens, I am not wanting in respect for the fathers of this republic. The signers of the Declaration of Independence were brave men. They were great men, too—great enough to give frame to a great age. It does not often happen to a nation to raise, at one time, such a number of truly great men. The point from which I am compelled to view them is not, certainly, the most favorable; and yet I cannot contemplate their great deeds with less than admiration. They were statesmen, patriots and heroes, and for the good they did, and the principles they contended for, I will unite with you to honor their memory.

They loved their country better than their own private interests; and, though this is not the highest form of human excellence, all will concede that it is a rare virtue, and that when it is exhibited it ought to command respect. He who will intelligently lay down his life for his country is a man whom it is not in human nature to despise. Your fathers staked their lives, their fortunes and their sacred honor on the cause of their country. In their admiration of liberty, they lost sight of all other interests.

They were peace men; but they preferred revolution to peaceful submission to bondage. They were quiet men; but they did not shrink from agitating against oppression. They showed forbearance, but that they knew its limits. They believed in order, but not in the order of tyranny. With them, nothing was "settled" that was not right. With them, justice, liberty and humanity were "final," not slavery and oppression. You may well cherish the memory of such men. They were great in their day and generation. Their solid manhood stands out the more as we contrast it with these degenerate times.

How circumspect, exact and proportionate were all their movements! How unlike the politicians of an hour! Their statesmanship looked beyond the passing moment, and stretched away in strength into the distant future. They seized upon eternal principles and set a glorious example in their defense. Mark them!

Fully appreciating the hardships to be encountered, firmly believing in the right of their cause, honorably inviting the scrutiny of an on-looking world, reverently appealing to heaven to attest their sincerity, soundly comprehending the solemn responsibility they were about to assume, wisely measuring the terrible odds against them, your fathers, the fathers of this republic, did most deliberately, under the inspiration of a glorious patriotism and with a sublime faith in the great principles of justice and freedom, lay deep the cornerstone of the national superstructure, which has risen and still rises in grandeur around you.

Of this fundamental work, this day is the anniversary. Our eyes are met with demonstrations of joyous enthusiasm. Banners and pennants wave exultingly on the breeze. The din of business too is hushed. Even Mammon seems to have quitted his grasp on this day. The ear-piercing fife and the stirring drum unite their accents with the ascending peal of a thousand church bells. Prayers are made, hymns are sung and sermons are preached in honor of this day; while the quick martial tramp of a great and multitudinous nation, echoed back by all the hills, valleys and mountains of a vast continent, bespeak the occasion one of thrilling and universal interest—a nation's jubilee.

Friends and citizens, I need not enter further into the causes which led to this anniversary. Many of you understand them better than I do. You could instruct me in regard to them. That is a branch of knowledge in which you feel, perhaps, a much deeper interest than your speaker. The causes which led to the separation of the colonies from the British Crown have never lacked for a tongue. They have all been taught in your common schools, narrated at your firesides, unfolded from your pulpits, and thundered from your legislative halls, and are as familiar to you as household words. They form the staple of your national poetry and eloquence.

I remember also that as a people Americans are remarkably familiar with all facts which make in their own favor. This is esteemed by some as a national trait—perhaps a national weakness. It is a fact that whatever makes for the wealth or for the reputation of Americans and can be had cheap will be found by Americans. I shall not be charged with slandering Americans if I say I think the American side of any question may be safely left in American hands.

I leave, therefore, the great deeds of your fathers to other gentlemen whose claim to have been regularly descended will be less likely to be disputed than mine!

My business, if I have any here today, is with the present. The accepted time with God and His cause is the ever-living now.

> Trust no future, however pleasant,
> Let the dead past bury its dead;
> Act, act in the living present,
> Heart within, and God overhead.

We have to do with the past only as we can make it useful to the present and to the future. To all inspiring motives, to noble deeds which can be gained from the past, we are welcome. But now is the time, the important time. Your fathers have lived, died, and have done their work, and have done much of it well. You live and must die, and you must do your work. You have no right to enjoy a child's share in the labor of your fathers, unless your children are to be blest by your labors. You have no right to wear out and waste the hard-earned fame of your fathers to cover your indolence. Sydney Smith tells us that men seldom eulogize the wisdom and virtues of their fathers, but to excuse some folly or wickedness of their own. This truth is not a doubtful one. There are illustrations of it near and remote, ancient and modern. It was fashionable, hundreds of years ago, for the children of Jacob to boast, we have "Abraham to our father," when they had long lost Abraham's faith and spirit. That people contented themselves under the shadow of Abraham's great name, while they repudiated the deeds which made his name great. Need I remind you that a similar thing is being done all over this country today? Need I tell you that the Jews are not the only people who built the tombs of the prophets, and garnished the sepulchers of the righteous? Washington could not die till he had broken the chains of his slaves. Yet his monument is built up by the price of human blood, and the traders in the bodies and souls of men shout—"We have Washington to *our father*."—Alas! that it should be so; yet so it is.

> The evil that men do, lives after them,
> The good is oft interred with their bones.

Fellow citizens, pardon me, allow me to ask, why am I called upon to speak here today? What have I, or those I represent, to do with your national independence? Are the great principles of political freedom and of natural justice, embodied in that Declaration of Independence, extended to us? and am I, therefore, called upon to bring our humble offering to the national altar and to confess the benefits and express devout gratitude for the blessings resulting from your independence to us?

Would to God, both for your sakes and ours, that an affirmative answer could be truthfully returned to these questions! Then would my task be light and my burden easy and delightful. For *who* is there so cold that a nation's sympathy could not warm him? Who so obdurate and dead to the claims of gratitude that would not thankfully acknowledge such priceless benefits? Who so stolid and selfish that would not give his voice to swell the hallelujahs of a nation's jubilee, when the chains of servitude had been torn from his limbs? I am not that man. In a case like that, the dumb might eloquently speak, and the "lame man leap as an hart."

But such is not the state of the case. I say it with a sad sense of the disparity between us. I am not included within the pale of this glorious anniversary! Your high independence only reveals the immeasurable distance between us. The blessings in which you, this day, rejoice, are not enjoyed in common. The rich inheritance of justice, liberty, prosperity and independence, bequeathed by your fathers, is shared by you, not by me. The sunlight that brought light and healing to you, has brought stripes and death to me. This Fourth of July is *yours*, not *mine*. *You* may rejoice, *I* must mourn. To drag a man in fetters into the grand illuminated temple of liberty and call upon him to join you in joyous anthems were inhuman mockery and sacrilegious irony. Do you mean, citizens, to mock me, by asking me to speak today? If so, there is a parallel to your conduct. And let me warn you that it is dangerous to copy the example of a nation whose crimes, towering up to heaven, were thrown down by the breath of the Almighty, burying that nation in irrevocable ruin! I can today take up the plaintive lament of a peeled and woe-smitten people!

"By the rivers of Babylon, there we sat down. Yea! we wept when we remembered Zion. We hanged our harps upon the willows in the midst thereof. For there they that carried us away captive required of us a song; and they that wasted us required of us mirth, saying, Sing us one of the songs of Zion. How shall we sing the Lord's song in a strange land? If I forget thee, O Jerusalem, let my right hand forget her cunning. If I do not remember thee, let my tongue cleave to the roof of my mouth."

Fellow citizens, above your national, tumultuous joy I hear the mournful wail of millions, whose chains, heavy and grievous yesterday, are today rendered more intolerable by the jubilee shouts that reach them. If I do forget, if I do not faithfully remember those bleeding children of sorrow this day, "may my right hand forget her cunning, and may my tongue cleave to the roof of my mouth!" To forget them, to pass lightly over their wrongs and to chime in with the popular theme would be treason most scandalous and shocking and would make me a reproach before God and the world. My subject, then, fellow citizens, is American slavery. I shall see this day and its popular characteristics from the slave's point of view. Standing there identified with the American bondman, making his wrongs mine, I do not hesitate to declare, with all my soul, that the character and conduct of this nation never looked blacker to me than on this Fourth of July. Whether we turn to the declarations of the past or to the professions of the present, the conduct of the nation seems equally hideous and revolting. America is false to the past, false to the present, and solemnly binds herself to be false to the future. Standing with God and the crushed and bleeding slave on this occasion, I will, in the name of humanity which is outraged, in the name of liberty which is fettered, in the name of the Constitution and the Bible which are disregarded and trampled upon, dare to call in question and to denounce, with all the emphasis I can command, everything that serves to perpetuate slavery—the great sin and shame of America! "I will not equivocate; I will not excuse";* I will use the severest language I can command; and yet not one word shall escape me that any man, whose judgment is not blinded by prejudice, or who is not at heart a slaveholder, shall not confess to be right and just.

But I fancy I hear some one of my audience say, "It is just in this circumstance that you and your brother Abolitionists fail to make a favorable impression on the public mind. Would you argue more and denounce less, would you persuade more and rebuke less, your cause would be much more likely to succeed." But, I submit, where all is plain there is nothing to be argued. What point in the antislavery creed would you have me argue? On what branch of the subject do the people of this country need light? Must I undertake to prove that the slave is a man? That point is conceded already. Nobody doubts it. The slave-

---

* These words were used by William Lloyd Garrison in the first issue of *The Liberator.*

holders themselves acknowledge it in the enactments of laws
for their government. They acknowledge it when they punish
disobedience on the part of the slave. There are seventy-two
crimes in the state of Virginia which, if committed by a black
man (no matter how ignorant he be), subject him to the punishment of death; while only two of the same crimes will subject
a white man to the like punishment. What is this but the acknowledgment that the slave is a moral, intellectual and responsible being? The manhood of the slave is conceded. It is
admitted in the fact that Southern statute books are covered
with enactments forbidding, under severe fines and penalties,
the teaching of the slave to read or to write. When you can
point to any such laws in reference to the beasts of the field,
then I may consent to argue the manhood of the slave. When
the dogs in your streets, when the fowls of the air, when the
cattle on your hills, when the fish of the sea and the reptiles
that crawl shall be unable to distinguish the slave from a brute,
then will I argue with you that the slave is a man!

For the present, it is enough to affirm the equal manhood of
the Negro race. Is it not astonishing that, while we are plowing,
planting and reaping, using all kinds of mechanical tools, erecting houses, constructing bridges, building ships, working in
metals of brass, iron, copper, silver and gold; that, while we are
reading, writing and ciphering, acting as clerks, merchants and
secretaries, having among us lawyers, doctors, ministers, poets,
authors, editors, orators and teachers; that, while we are engaged in all manner of enterprises common to other men, digging gold in California, capturing the whale in the Pacific,
feeding sheep and cattle on the hillside, living, moving, acting,
thinking, planning, living in families as husbands, wives and
children, and, above all, confessing and worshiping the Christian's God and looking hopefully for life and immortality beyond the grave, we are called upon to prove that we are men!

Would you have me argue that man is entitled to liberty?
that he is the rightful owner of his own body? You have already
declared it. Must I argue the wrongfulness of slavery? Is that a
question for republicans? Is it to be settled by the rules of logic
and argumentation, as a matter beset with great difficulty, involving a doubtful application of the principle of justice, hard
to be understood? How should I look today, in the presence of
Americans, dividing and subdividing a discourse, to show that
men have a natural right to freedom, speaking of it relatively
and positively, negatively and affirmatively? To do so would be
to make myself ridiculous and to offer an insult to your under-

standing. There is not a man beneath the canopy of heaven that does not know that slavery is wrong *for him*.

What, am I to argue that it is wrong to make men brutes, to rob them of their liberty, to work them without wages, to keep them ignorant of their relations to their fellow men, to beat them with sticks, to flay their flesh with the lash, to load their limbs with irons, to hunt them with dogs, to sell them at auction, to sunder their families, to knock out their teeth, to burn their flesh, to starve them into obedience and submission to their masters? Must I argue that a system thus marked with blood and stained with pollution is *wrong*? No! I will not. I have better employment for my time and strength than such arguments would imply.

What, then, remains to be argued? Is it that slavery is not divine; that God did not establish it; that our doctors of divinity are mistaken? There is blasphemy in the thought. That which is inhuman, cannot be divine! *Who* can reason on such a proposition? They that can, may; I cannot. The time for such argument is passed.

At a time like this, scorching irony, not convincing argument, is needed. O! had I the ability, and could reach the nation's ear, I would, today, pour out a fiery stream of biting ridicule, blasting reproach, withering sarcasm and stern rebuke. For it is not light that is needed, but fire; it is not the gentle shower, but thunder. We need the storm, the whirlwind, and the earthquake. The feeling of the nation must be quickened; the conscience of the nation must be roused; the propriety of the nation must be startled; the hypocrisy of the nation must be exposed; and its crimes against God and man must be proclaimed and denounced.

What, to the American slave, is your Fourth of July? I answer: a day that reveals to him, more than all other days in the year, the gross injustice and cruelty to which he is the constant victim. To him, your celebration is a sham; your boasted liberty an unholy license; your national greatness swelling vanity; your sounds of rejoicing are empty and heartless; your denunciation of tyrants brass-fronted impudence; your shouts of liberty and equality hollow mockery; your prayers and hymns, your sermons and thanksgivings, with all your religious parade and solemnity, are to Him mere bombast, fraud, deception, impiety and hypocrisy—a thin veil to cover up crimes which would disgrace a nation of savages. There is not a nation on the earth guilty of practices more shocking and bloody than are the people of the United States at this very hour.

Go where you may, search where you will, roam through all the monarchies and despotisms of the Old World, travel through South America, search out every abuse, and when you have found the last, lay your facts by the side of the everyday practices of this nation, and you will say with me, that, for revolting barbarity and shameless hypocrisy, America reigns without a rival.

Take the American slave trade, which, we are told by the papers, is especially prosperous just now. Ex-Senator Benton tells us that the price of men was never higher than now. He mentions the fact to show that slavery is in no danger. This trade is one of the peculiarities of American institutions. It is carried on in all the large towns and cities in one half of this confederacy; and millions are pocketed every year by dealers in this horrid traffic. In several states this trade is a chief source of wealth. It is called (in contradistinction to the foreign slave trade) *"the internal slave trade."* It is probably called so, too, in order to divert from it the horror with which the foreign slave trade is contemplated. That trade has long since been denounced by this government as piracy. It has been denounced with burning words from the high places of the nation as an execrable traffic. To arrest it, to put an end to it, this nation keeps a squadron, at immense cost, on the coast of Africa. Everywhere in this country it is safe to speak of this foreign slave trade as a most inhuman traffic, opposed alike to the laws of God and of man. The duty to extirpate and destroy it is admitted even by our doctors of divinity. In order to put an end to it, some of these last have consented that their colored brethren (nominally free) should leave this country, and establish themselves on the western coast of Africa! It is, however, a notable fact that, while so much execration is poured out by Americans upon all those engaged in the foreign slave trade, the men engaged in the slave trade between the states pass without condemnation, and their business is deemed honorable.

Behold the practical operation of this internal slave trade, the American slave trade, sustained by American politics and American religion. Here you will see men and women reared like swine for the market. You know what is a swine drover? I will show you a man drover. They inhabit all our Southern states. They perambulate the country and crowd the highways of the nation with droves of human stock. You will see one of these human flesh jobbers, armed with pistol, whip and bowie knife, driving a company of a hundred men, women and children, from the Potomac to the slave market at New Orleans. These wretched people are to be sold singly or in lots, to suit purchasers. They are food for the cotton field and the deadly sugar mill. Mark the sad procession, as it moves wearily along, and the inhuman wretch who drives them. Hear his savage yells and his bloodcurdling oaths, as he hurries on his affrighted captives! There, see the old man with locks thinned and gray. Cast one glance, if you please, upon that young mother, whose shoulders are bare to the scorching sun, her briny tears falling on the brow of the babe in her arms. See, too, that girl of thirteen, weeping—*yes*, weeping—as she thinks of the mother from whom she has been torn! The drove moves tardily. Heat and sorrow have nearly consumed their strength; suddenly you hear a quick snap, like the discharge of a rifle; the fetters clank, and the chain rattles simultaneously; your ears are saluted with a scream, that seems to have torn its way to the center of your soul! The crack you heard was the sound of the slave whip; the scream you heard was from the woman you saw with the babe. Her speed had faltered under the weight of her child and her chains! That gash on her shoulder tells her to move on. Follow this drove to New Orleans. Attend the auction; see men examined like horses; see the forms of women rudely and brutally exposed to the shocking gaze of American slave buyers. See this drove sold and separated forever; and never forget the deep, sad sobs that arose from that scattered multitude. Tell me, citizens, where, under the sun, you can witness a spectacle more fiendish and shocking. Yet this is but a glance at the American slave trade, as it exists, at this moment, in the ruling part of the United States.

I was born amid such sights and scenes. To me the American slave trade is a terrible reality. When a child, my soul was often pierced with a sense of its horrors. I lived on Philpot Street, Fell's Point, Baltimore, and have watched from the wharves the slave ships in the Basin, anchored from the shore, with their cargoes of human flesh, waiting for favorable winds to waft them down the Chesapeake. There was at that time a grand slave mart kept at the head of Pratt Street by Austin Woldfolk. His agents were sent into every town and county in Maryland, announcing their arrival, through the papers, and on flaming *handbills* headed "Cash for Negroes." These men were generally well-dressed men, and very captivating in their manners; ever ready to drink, to treat and to gamble. The fate of many a slave has depended upon the turn of a single card; and many a child has been snatched from the arms of its mother by bargains arranged in a state of brutal drunkenness.

The fleshmongers gather up their victims by dozens, and drive them, chained, to the general depot at Baltimore. When a sufficient number has been collected here, a ship is chartered for the purpose of conveying the forlorn crew to Mobile, or to New Orleans. From the slave prison to the ship, they are usually driven in the darkness of night; for since the antislavery agitation a certain caution is observed.

In the deep, still darkness of midnight I have been often aroused by the dead, heavy footsteps and the piteous cries of the chained gangs that passed our door. The anguish of my boyish heart was intense; and I was often consoled, when speaking to my mistress in the morning, to hear her say that the custom was very wicked; that she hated to hear the rattle of the chains and the heart-rending cries. I was glad to find one who sympathized with me in my horror.

Fellow citizens, this murderous traffic is today in active operation in this boasted republic. In the solitude of my spirit I see clouds of dust raised on the highways of the South; I see the bleeding footsteps; I hear the doleful wail of fettered humanity on the way to the slave markets, where the victims are to be sold like *horses, sheep* and *swine*, knocked off to the highest bidder. There I see the tenderest ties ruthlessly broken, to gratify the lust, caprice and rapacity of the buyers and sellers of men. My soul sickens at the sight.

> Is this the land your Fathers loved,
>   The freedom which they toiled to win?
> Is this the earth whereon they moved?
>   Are these the graves they slumber in?

But a still more inhuman, disgraceful and scandalous state of things remains to be presented. By an act of the American Congress, not yet two years old, slavery has been nationalized in its most horrible and revolting form. By that act, Mason and Dixon's line has been obliterated; New York has become as Virginia; and the power to hold, hunt and sell men, women and children as slaves remains no longer a mere state institution, but is now an institution of the whole United States. The power is coextensive with the star-spangled banner and American Christianity. Where these go, may also go the merciless slave hunter. Where these are, man is not sacred. He is a bird for the sportsman's gun. By that most foul and fiendish of all human decrees, the liberty and person of every man are put in peril. Your broad republican domain is hunting ground for *men*. *Not* for thieves and robbers, enemies of society, merely, but for men guilty of no crime. Your lawmakers have commanded all good citizens to engage in this hellish sport. Your President, your Secretary of State, your *lords, nobles* and ecclesiastics enforce, as a duty you owe to your free and glorious country, and to your God, that you do this accursed thing. Not fewer than forty Americans have, within the past two years, been hunted down and, without a moment's warning, hurried away in chains and consigned to slavery and excruciating torture. Some of these have had wives and children, dependent on them for bread; but of this, no account was made. The right of the hunter to his prey stands superior to the right of marriage and to *all* rights in this republic, the rights of God included! For black men there is neither law nor justice, humanity nor religion. The Fugitive Slave *Law* makes mercy to them a crime; and bribes the judge who tries them. An American judge gets ten dollars for every victim he consigns to slavery, and five, when he fails to do so.* The oath of any two villains is sufficient, under this hell-black enactment, to send the most pious and exemplary black man into the remorseless jaws of slavery! His own testimony is nothing. He can bring no witnesses for himself. The minister of American justice is bound by the law to hear but *one* side; and *that* side is the side of the oppressor. Let this damning fact be perpetually told. Let it be thundered around the world that in tyrant-killing, king-hating, people-loving, democratic, Christian America the seats of justice are filled with judges who hold their offices under an open and palpable *bribe*, and are bound, in deciding the case of a man's liberty, *to hear only his accusers!*

In glaring violation of justice, in shameless disregard of the forms of administering law, in cunning arrangement to entrap the defenseless, and in diabolical intent this Fugitive Slave Law stands alone in the annals of tyrannical legislation. I doubt if there be another nation on the globe having the brass and the baseness to put such a law on the statute book. If any man in this assembly thinks differently from me in this matter and feels able to disprove my statements, I will gladly confront him at any suitable time and place he may select.

I take this law to be one of the grossest infringements of Christian liberty, and if the churches and ministers of our country were not stupidly blind or most wickedly indifferent, they too would so regard it.

At the very moment that they are thanking God for the enjoyment of civil and religious liberty, and for the right to worship God according to the dictates of their own consciences, they are utterly silent in respect to a law which robs religion of its chief

---

* Under the Fugitive Slave Act of 1850 the federal commissioner was awarded ten dollars if he directed the escaped slave's return, but only five dollars if he ordered the runaway's release.

significance and makes it utterly worthless to a world lying in wickedness. Did this law concern the *"mint, anise and cummin,"* abridge the right to sing psalms, to partake of the sacrament or to engage in any of the ceremonies of religion, it would be smitten by the thunder of a thousand pulpits. A general shout would go up from the church demanding *repeal, repeal, instant repeal!* And it would go hard with that politician who presumed to solicit the votes of the people without inscribing this motto on his banner. Further, if this demand were not complied with, another Scotland would be added to the history of religious liberty, and the stern old covenanters would be thrown into the shade. A John Knox would be seen at every church door and heard from every pulpit, and Fillmore would have no more quarter than was shown by Knox to the beautiful, but treacherous, Queen Mary of Scotland.* The fact that the church of our country (with fractional exceptions) does not esteem "the Fugitive Slave Law" as a declaration of war against religious liberty, implies that that church regards religion simply as a form of worship, an empty ceremony, and *not* a vital principle, requiring active benevolence, justice, love and good will toward man. It esteems sacrifice above mercy, psalm singing above right doing, solemn meetings above practical righteousness. A worship that can be conducted by persons who refuse to give shelter to the houseless, to give bread to the hungry, clothing to the naked, and who enjoin obedience to a law forbidding these acts of mercy is a curse, not a blessing to mankind. The Bible addresses all such persons as "scribes, pharisees, hypocrites, who pay tithe of *mint, anise* and *cummin,* and have omitted the weightier matters of the law, judgment, mercy and faith."

But the church of this country is not only indifferent to the wrongs of the slave, it actually takes sides with the oppressors. It has made itself the bulwark of American slavery and the shield of American slave hunters. Many of its most eloquent divines, who stand as the very lights of the church, have shamelessly given the sanction of religion and the Bible to the whole slave system. They have taught that man may, properly, be a slave; that the relation of master and slave is ordained of God; that to send back an escaped bondman to his master is clearly the duty of all the followers of the Lord Jesus Christ; and this horrible blasphemy is palmed off upon the world for Christianity.

For my part, I would say, Welcome infidelity! welcome athe-

---

* As President, Millard Fillmore (1800–1874) had signed the Fugitive Slave Law of 1850.

ism! welcome anything—in preference to the gospel, *as preached by those divines.* They convert the very name of religion into an engine of tyranny and barbarous cruelty, and serve to confirm more infidels, in this age, than all the infidel writings of Thomas Paine, Voltaire and Bolingbroke put together have done! These ministers make religion a cold and flinty-hearted thing, having neither principles of right action nor bowels of compassion. They strip the love of God of its beauty and leave the throne of religion a huge, horrible, repulsive form. It is a religion for oppressors, tyrants, man stealers, and *thugs.* It is not that *"pure and undefiled religion"* which is from above, and which is *"first pure, then peaceable, easy to be entreated,* full of mercy and good fruits, *without partiality and without hypocrisy,"* but a religion which favors the rich against the poor; which exalts the proud above the humble; which divides mankind into two classes, tyrants and slaves; which says to the man in chains, *stay there,* and to the oppressor, *oppress on;* it is a religion which may be professed and enjoyed by all the robbers and enslavers of mankind; it makes God a respecter of persons, denies his fatherhood of the race, and tramples in the dust the great truth of the brotherhood of man. All this we affirm to be true of the popular church, and the popular worship of our land and nation—a religion, a church, and a worship which, on the authority of inspired wisdom, we pronounce to be an abomination in the sight of God. In the language of Isaiah, the American church might be well addressed, "Bring no more vain oblations; incense is an abomination unto me: the new moons and Sabbaths, the calling of assemblies, I cannot away with; it is iniquity, even the solemn meeting. Your new moons, and your appointed feasts my soul hateth. They are a trouble to me; I am weary to bear them; and when ye spread forth your hands I will hide mine eyes from you. Yea! when ye make many prayers, I will not hear. Your hands are full of blood; cease to do evil, learn to do well; seek judgment; relieve the oppressed; judge for the fatherless; plead for the widow."

The American church is guilty, when viewed in connection with what it is doing to uphold slavery; but it is superlatively guilty when viewed in its connection with its ability to abolish slavery.

The sin of which it is guilty is one of omission as well as of commission. Albert Barnes but uttered what the common sense of every man at all observant of the actual state of the case will receive as truth, when he declared that "there is no power out of the church that could sustain slavery an hour, if it were not sustained in it."

Let the religious press, the pulpit, the Sunday school, the conference meeting, the great ecclesiastical, missionary, Bible and tract associations of the land array their immense powers against slavery and slaveholding; and the whole system of crime and blood would be scattered to the winds, and that they do not do this involves them in the most awful responsibility of which the mind can conceive.

In prosecuting the antislavery enterprise, we have been asked to spare the church, to spare the ministry; but *how,* we ask, could such a thing be done? We are met on the threshold of our efforts for the redemption of the slave, by the church and ministry of the country, in battle arrayed against us; and we are compelled to fight or flee. From *what* quarter, I beg to know, has proceeded a fire so deadly upon our ranks, during the last two years, as from the Northern pulpit? As the champions of oppressors, the chosen men of American theology have appeared —men honored for their so-called piety, and their real learning. The Lords of Buffalo, the Springs of New York, the Lathrops of Auburn, the Coxes and Spencers of Brooklyn, the Gannets and Sharps of Boston, the Deweys of Washington, and other great religious lights of the land have, in utter denial of the authority of *Him* by whom they professed to be called to the ministry, deliberately taught us, against the example of the Hebrews and against the remonstrance of the Apostles, *that we ought to obey man's law before the law of God.**

My spirit wearies of such blasphemy; and how such men can be supported as the "standing types and representatives of Jesus Christ" is a mystery which I leave others to penetrate. In speaking of the American church, however, let it be distinctly understood that I mean the *great mass* of the religious organizations of our land. There are exceptions, and I thank God that there are. Noble men may be found, scattered all over these Northern states, of whom Henry Ward Beecher, of Brooklyn; Samuel J. May, of Syracuse; and my esteemed friend (Rev. R. R. Raymond) on the platform, are shining examples; and let me say further, that upon these men lies the duty to inspire our ranks with high religious faith and zeal, and to cheer us on in the great mission of the slave's redemption from his chains.

One is struck with the difference between the attitude of the

* At the request of the Union Safety Committee of New York City, formed by conservative merchants, the clergymen of New York agreed to set aside December 12, 1850, as a day on which sermons would be delivered upholding the Compromise of 1850, especially the Fugitive Slave Act. Practically all the sermons advised acquiescence to the law and denounced the "higher law" doctrine.

American church toward the antislavery movement and that occupied by the churches in England toward a similar movement
in that country. There, the church, true to its mission of ameliorating, elevating and improving the condition of mankind,
came forward promptly, bound up the wounds of the West
Indian slave, and restored him to his liberty. There, the question
of emancipation was a high religious question. It was demanded
in the name of humanity and according to the law of the living
God. The Sharps, the Clarksons, the Wilberforces, the Buxtons,
the Burchells, and the Knibbs were alike famous for their piety
and for their philanthropy. The antislavery movement *there* was
not an antichurch movement, for the reason that the church
took its full share in prosecuting that movement: and the antislavery movement in this country will cease to be an antichurch
movement when the church of this country shall assume a
favorable instead of a hostile position toward that movement.

Americans! your republican politics, not less than your republican religion, are flagrantly inconsistent. You boast of your
love of liberty, your superior civilization and your pure Christianity, while the whole political power of the nation (as embodied in the two great political parties) is solemnly pledged to
support and perpetuate the enslavement of three millions of
your countrymen. You hurl your anathemas at the crowned-
headed tyrants of Russia and Austria and pride yourselves on
your democratic institutions, while you yourselves consent to be
the mere *tools* and *bodyguards* of the tyrants of Virginia and
Carolina. You invite to your shores fugitives of oppression from
abroad, honor them with banquets, greet them with ovations,
cheer them, toast them, salute them, protect them, and pour out
your money to them like water; but the fugitives from your own
land you advertise, hunt, arrest, shoot and kill. You glory in
your refinement and your universal education; yet you maintain
a system as barbarous and dreadful as ever stained the character of a nation—a system begun in avarice, supported in pride,
and perpetuated in cruelty. You shed tears over fallen Hungary,
and make the sad story of her wrongs the theme of your poets,
statesmen and orators, till your gallant sons are ready to fly to
arms to vindicate her cause against the oppressor; but, in regard
to the ten thousand wrongs of the American slave, you would
enforce the strictest silence and would hail him as an enemy of
the nation who dares to make those wrongs the subject of public
discourse! You are all on fire at the mention of liberty for France
or for Ireland, but are as cold as an iceberg at the thought of
liberty for the enslaved of America. You discourse eloquently on
the dignity of labor; yet, you sustain a system which, in its very

essence, casts a stigma upon labor. You can bare your bosom to the storm of British artillery to throw off a three-penny tax on tea, and yet wring the last hard-earned farthing from the grasp of the black laborers of your country. You profess to believe "that of one blood God made all nations of men to dwell on the face of all the earth" and hath commanded all men, everywhere, to love one another; yet you notoriously hate (and glory in your hatred) all men whose skins are not colored like your own. You declare before the world, and are understood by the world to declare, that you *"hold these truths to be self-evident, that all men are created equal; and are endowed by their Creator with certain unalienable rights; and that among these are, life, liberty and the pursuit of happiness";* and yet, you hold securely, in a bondage which, according to your own Thomas Jefferson, *"is worse than ages of that which your fathers rose in rebellion to oppose,"* a *seventh part* of the inhabitants of your country.

Fellow citizens, I will not enlarge further on your national inconsistencies. The existence of slavery in this country brands your republicanism as a sham, your humanity as a base pretense, and your Christianity as a lie. It destroys your moral power abroad; it corrupts your politicians at home. It saps the foundation of religion; it makes your name a hissing and a by-word to a mocking earth. It is the antagonistic force in your government, the only thing that seriously disturbs and endangers your union. It fetters your progress; it is the enemy of improvement; the deadly foe of education; it fosters pride; it breeds insolence; it promotes vice; it shelters crime; it is a curse to the earth that supports it; and yet you cling to it as if it were the sheet anchor of all your hopes. Oh, be warned! Be warned! A horrible reptile is coiled up in your nation's bosom; the venomous creature is nursing at the tender breast of your youthful republic; *for the love of God, tear away* and fling from you the hideous monster, and *let the weight of twenty millions crush and destroy it forever!*

But it is answered in reply to all this, that precisely what I have now denounced is, in fact, guaranteed and sanctioned by the Constitution of the United States, that the right to hold and to hunt slaves is a part of that Constitution framed by the illustrious Fathers of this Republic.

Then, I dare to affirm, notwithstanding all I have said before, your fathers stooped, basely stooped

> *To palter with us in a double sense:*
> *And keep the word of promise to the ear,*
> *But break it to the heart.*

And instead of being the honest men I have before declared them to be, they were the veriest impostors that ever practiced on mankind. This is the inevitable conclusion, and from it there is no escape; but I differ from those who charge this baseness on the framers of the Constitution of the United States. It is a slander upon their memory, at least, so I believe. There is not time now to argue the Constitutional question at length; nor have I the ability to discuss it as it ought to be discussed. The subject has been handled with masterly power by Lysander Spooner, Esq., by William Goodell, by Samuel E. Sewall, Esq., and last, though not least, by Gerrit Smith, Esq. These gentlemen have, as I think, fully and clearly vindicated the Constitution from any design to support slavery for an hour.

Fellow citizens, there is no matter in respect to which the people of the North have allowed themselves to be so ruinously imposed upon as that of the proslavery character of the Constitution. In that instrument, I hold, there is neither warrant, license nor sanction of the hateful thing; but, interpreted as it ought to be interpreted, the Constitution is a glorious liberty document. Read its preamble, consider its purposes. Is slavery among them? Is it at the gateway? Or is it in the temple? It is neither. While I do not intend to argue this question on the present occasion, let me ask, if it be not somewhat singular that, if the Constitution were intended to be, by its framers and adopters, a slaveholding instrument, why neither *slavery, slaveholding* nor *slave* can anywhere be found in it. What would be thought of an instrument, drawn up, legally drawn up, for the purpose of entitling the city of Rochester to a tract of land, in which no mention of land was made? Now, there are certain rules of interpretation for the proper understanding of all legal instruments. These rules are well established. They are plain, common-sense rules, such as you and I and all of us can understand and apply, without having passed years in the study of law. I scout the idea that the question of the constitutionality, or unconstitutionality of slavery, is not a question for the people. I hold that every American citizen has a right to form an opinion of the Constitution, and to propagate that opinion, and to use all honorable means to make his opinion the prevailing one. Without this right, the liberty of an American citizen would be as insecure as that of a Frenchman. Ex-Vice-President Dallas tells us that the Constitution is an object to which no American mind can be too attentive, and no American heart too devoted. He further says, the Constitution, in its words, is plain and intelligible, and is meant for the home-bred, unsophisticated understandings of our fellow citizens. Senator Berrien tells us that the Constitution is the fundamental law, that which controls all others. The charter of our liberties, which every citizen has a personal interest in understanding thoroughly. The testimony of Senator Breese, Lewis Cass, and many others that might be named, who are everywhere esteemed as sound lawyers, so regard the Constitution. I take it, therefore, that it is not presumption in a private citizen to form an opinion of that instrument.

Now, take the Constitution according to its plain reading, and I defy the presentation of a single proslavery clause in it. On the other hand, it will be found to contain principles and purposes, entirely hostile to the existence of slavery.

I have detained my audience entirely too long already. At some future period I will gladly avail myself of an opportunity to give this subject a full and fair discussion.

Allow me to say, in conclusion, notwithstanding the dark picture I have this day presented, of the state of the nation, I do not despair of this country. There are forces in operation which must inevitably work the downfall of slavery. "The arm of the Lord is not shortened," and the doom of slavery is certain. I, therefore, leave off where I began, with hope. While drawing encouragement from "the Declaration of Independence," the great principles it contains and the genius of American institutions, my spirit is also cheered by the obvious tendencies of the age. Nations do not now stand in the same relation to each other that they did ages ago. No nation can now shut itself up from the surrounding world and trot round in the same old path of its fathers without interference. The time was when such could be done. Long-established customs of hurtful character could formerly fence themselves in and do their evil work with social impunity. Knowledge was then confined and enjoyed by the privileged few, and the multitude walked on in mental darkness. But a change has now come over the affairs of mankind. Walled cities and empires have become unfashionable. The arm of commerce has borne away the gates of the strong city. Intelligence is penetrating the darkest corners of the globe. It makes its pathway over and under the sea, as well as on the earth. Wind, steam and lightning are its chartered agents. Oceans no longer divide, but link nations together. From Boston to London is now a holiday excursion. Space is comparatively annihilated. Thoughts expressed on one side of the Atlantic are distinctly heard on the other.

The far-off and almost fabulous Pacific rolls in grandeur at our feet. The Celestial Empire, the mystery of ages, is being solved. The fiat of the Almighty, "Let there be Light," has not yet spent its force. No abuse, no outrage, whether in taste, sport or avarice, can now hide itself from the all-pervading light. The iron shoe and crippled foot of China must be seen in contrast with nature. Africa must rise and put on her yet unwoven garment. "Ethiopia shall stretch out her hand unto God." In the fervent aspirations of William Lloyd Garrison, I say, and let every heart join in saying it,

> God speed the year of jubilee
>   The wide world o'er!
> When from their galling chains set free,
> Th' oppress'd shall vilely bend the knee,
> And wear the yoke of tyranny
>   Like brutes no more.
> That year will come, and freedom's reign,
> To man his plundered rights again
>   Restore.
>
> God speed the day when human blood
>   Shall cease to flow!
> In every clime be understood,
> The claims of human brotherhood,
> And each return for evil, good,
>   Not blow for blow;
> That day will come all feuds to end,
> And change into a faithful friend
>   Each foe.
>
> God speed the hour, the glorious hour,
>   When none on earth
> Shall exercise a lordly power,
> Nor in a tyrant's presence cower;
> But to all manhood's stature tower,
>   By equal birth!
> That hour will come, to each, to all,
> And from his prison-house, to thrall
>   Go forth.
>
> Until that year, day, hour, arrive
> With head, and heart, and hand I'll strive,
> To break the rod, and rend the gyve,
> The spoiler of his prey deprive—
> So witness Heaven!
> And never from my chosen post,
> Whate'er the peril or the cost,
> Be driven.

OUR RIGHTS AS MEN

By William J. Watkins

*Since Negroes were barred from state militias, they formed
military companies of their own. Still, without state or
federal support, Negro militia companies were at a disadvantage and could not obtain proper equipment. In May,
1852, Robert Morris and Charles Lenox Remond, bearing
petitions for the establishment of a Negro company, appeared before the Military Committee of the Massachusetts legislature. Ten months later Morris appeared again
before the legislature as did William J. Watkins, and they
presented petitions signed by sixty-five Negroes praying
for a charter to form an independent military company.
Watkins also delivered a brilliant speech before the legislative committee on the militia, February 24, 1853, in which
he recited the role played by the Negro in the American
Revolution and the War of 1812 and demolished the arguments advanced against granting the Negroes' request. But
his appeal brought no result. In 1859 a bill authorizing
Negroes to join the state militia was passed by the legislature, but was vetoed by Governor N. P. Banks as unconstitutional. His veto was sustained.*

*Here is the major portion of William J. Watkins' ad-
dress before the legislative committee. When the speech
was published as a pamphlet, Watkins wrote in the preface:* "The Author is not a man of war. He thinks the Apostolic injunction, 'Be at peace with all men,' should elicit
universal and implicit obedience. These pages are a vindication of our Rights as Citizens, not a discourse upon our
Duty as Christians. A military Hero is not his beau ideal of
a Christian, but vice versa. The vocation of Beelzebub is
to 'scatter, tear and slay'; that of Man, to 'deal justly, love
mercy, and walk humbly before God.' At least, so thinks
the Author."

(The speech here presented is taken from the pamphlet
Our Rights As Men—An Address Delivered in Boston, Be-
fore The Legislative Committee on the Militia, February
24, 1853, By William J. Watkins, in Behalf of Sixty-Five
Colored Petitioners, Praying For a Charter to Form an
Independent Military Company, *Boston, n.d.)*

Watkins' speech was followed by an appeal by the black

lawyer, Robert Morris, who in 1843, at the age of twenty-one, had been admitted to the Boston bar. Morris' speech was not published.

MR. CHAIRMAN AND GENTLEMEN: It is with unaffected diffidence and extreme reluctance that I appear before you in the present capacity; and my diffidence and reluctance are induced by a multiplicity of considerations. The arduous duties of my vocation, aside from others of an extraneous nature, have precluded the possibility of that due preparation I consider necessary for one of my youth and consequent inexperience to appear before your honorable body. Another consideration, gentlemen, is a consciousness of my inability to bring the subject before you with that force and perspicuity of style which would doubtless elicit in its behalf an intensity of interest commensurate with its nature and importance.

Laboring, gentlemen, under those crushing disabilities to which my complexion has made me liable, I have never dived very deeply into the artesian well of Science; I have never been able to "talk with the thunder as friend to friend, or weave my garland from the lightning's wing"; I have been denied those educational advantages of which the more favored race have been and still are the recipients. But although I cannot bring into requisition that profundity of thought, that logical acumen, that elegance of diction, of which you, gentlemen, are capable, this fact does not in the least derogate from the truthfulness of the sentiments I shall endeavor to advance, nor does it detract from their acceptability.

We have come here today, to deal not in rhyme and rhetoric, but in plain matter of fact, in sober reality. We have come, Mr. Chairman, to tell you what we want: why such a petition as this has been presented to the Honorable Body of whom you form a part, and why, in our opinion, such a petition should be granted. We have come before you, trusting in the inherent righteousness of our cause and the justice which should, and which doubtless will, characterize your honorable body; and we trust our prayer will be effectual.

Mr. Chairman, I shall endeavor today to argue the general merits of this question according to the measure of my ability. I would not, were I able, intrude upon the vocation of my learned friend by discussing the question in its legal bearings; I leave that for a wiser head and a tongue more eloquent. And while I stand up to represent those with whom I am proud to be identified, I respectfully solicit you, gentlemen, to regard us not as obsequious suppliants for favor, but as men proud of and conscious of the inherent dignity of manhood; as men who, knowing our rights, dare at all hazards to maintain them. You know, gentlemen, every one of you, that we as a people are the victims of a cruel and relentless spirit of caste. The Juggernaut of American Prejudice would feign crush the manhood out of us and place us in the category of the vilest of the vile; aye, with the brutes that perish; but we are, nevertheless, men— men, whether you regard our mental, moral or physical confor- mation—and all we demand of you is that we be treated as men, that we be dealt with as all law-abiding citizens; and God will take care of the consequences, let those consequences be what they may.

Mr. Chairman, in addressing you for a few moments, let us inquire,

First, into the nature of the Petition;

Secondly, into the character of the petitioners;

Thirdly, why should the Petition be granted?

Fourthly, we will notice briefly the happy results consequent upon granting it.

First, then, the nature of the Petition.

"To the Honorable Senate and House of Representatives, of the Commonwealth of Massachusetts.

"We, the undersigned, citizens of Boston and vicinity, respect- fully pray for a Charter to form an Independent Military Company."

Surely, gentlemen, there can be nothing unreasonable in the nature of this Petition. Nothing, absolutely nothing; nothing generally, nothing particularly. If there is, gentlemen, I am utterly unable to discern it. But, possibly, it is for the Scriptural reason that "the light shineth in the darkness, and the darkness comprehendeth it not." We merely ask for a Charter to form an Independent Military Company; such a one as has been granted to a company of white citizens. We ask, sir, that the old Bay State will throw around us its protecting arm. We know that by wishing to be treated as men, we shall elicit the vindictive anathemas of a few, who live daily and hourly on the pap of American prejudice; but none of these things move us, if Massa- chusetts but gather us together as a hen gathereth her brood under her wings. We might, with propriety, have petitioned your honorable body, that we be enrolled among the General Militia; that the same immunities be extended toward us that are extended toward other citizens of Massachusetts, irrespec- tive of complexional distinction and physical peculiarities.

But we do not wish you to understand us as acquiescing in the righteousness of the proscriptive principle, because we ask for your protection in the exercise and enjoyment of a *portion* of our rights as men; for we are entitled to *all* the rights and immunities of *citizens of Massachusetts.* Thank God, this is the Age of Progress, not Retrogression. We are content now, for certain reasons, to ask for a charter to form an independent company; a state company, if you please. You, gentlemen, certainly cannot consider this as presumption. If you grant us this Petition, there is nothing in the nature of it that will tend directly or indirectly to the dissolution of the federal union. For we are, *de facto,* a state company, an independent company, segregated from the rest of mankind, and not in a position to cause the hair of our loving brethren of the Georgia Fusileers, or the South Carolina Dragoons, to "stand on end like quills upon the fretful porcupine," because, like them, we are enrolled among the General Militia, and liable to be called upon, when they are summoned, to defend our lives, our fortunes and our sacred honors.

Having briefly noticed the nature of the Petition, and shown that there is nothing particularly dreadful and alarming about it, we will, in accordance with our arrangement, inquire into the character of the Petitioners.

And who are they, Mr. Chairman? What is their character, gentlemen? In a word, they are among the most respectable men in the community. They are law-abiding, tax-paying, liberty-loving, native-born, American citizens; men who love their country, despite its heinous iniquities—iniquities piled up in dreadful agony to the heavens. I see arrayed in the list of signers, men of affluence and education, of respectability and moral worth; men in possession of those great and good qualities the development of which exerts a healthy influence throughout the varied ramifications of society. They are men, sir, that do honor to the state; as respectable in every point of view, as any list ever appended to a Petition, since "the morning stars sang together, and all the sons of God shouted for joy." And more than this, some of them are the descendants of Revolution sires, and Revolution mothers; the descendants of those, who, in those times that tried men's souls, counted not their lives dear unto them, but their blood flowed freely in defense of their country; they fought, they bled, they conquered—aye, they died, that we might live as freemen. And shall we be excluded from the pale of humanity, denied those rights, left to us as a legacy by our fathers? Shall we be driven from the festive board, when all the world has been invited to come, and sit around the table? Yes, every nation, kindred, tongue and people! Forbid it Justice, forbid it Humanity, forbid it, ye spirits of our Fathers, now hovering over us, forbid it our country, forbid it Heaven!

Gentlemen, the very fact that some of these who have signed this Petition are descendants of those who faced the cannon's mouth, and quaked not when it bellowed forth its dreadful thunders; who quailed not beneath its lurid lightnings, and yet are denied rights and privileges accorded to the descendants of those who shot down the brave patriots of the Revolution, should be enough to cause the blood to boil within you and cause "horror upon horror's head accumulate."

In presenting these petitioners before you, Mr. Chairman, in describing their character, gentlemen, I have nothing extenuated, nor set down aught in hyperbolic phrase. They are just the men I represent them to be, and this being the case, your sense of right and your love of Justice forbid any other treatment of their Petition than one which can abide the test of manly criticism and stand out in the blazing sunlight, eliciting the approbation of God, the admiration of angels, the approval of your own consciences, the plaudits of the world of Truth and Justice and Humanity. We beseech you, by the exalted character of those whom we have the honor to represent, by all that is noble, just and true therein, *"Hear us for our cause."*

In the third place, gentlemen, Why should this Petition be granted?

It should be granted because the request is a reasonable one, and one emanating from a body of men who have an absolute right to demand it. We proceed, then, upon the assertion that we have an unrestricted right to the enjoyment of full civil privileges; a right to demand and receive everything which Massachusetts by her Bill of Rights grants to her citizens, irrespective of any accidental or fortuitous circumstance, the contingency of birth, education, fortune or complexion. We are men, and we wish to be treated as men in the land of the Pilgrims should be treated. Mr. Chairman, the laws of this Commonwealth know no man by the color of his skin, the texture of his hair, or the symmetrical development of his physical organism. It is too true, sir, that even here, American prejudice, the inseparable concomitant of American slavery, stands out in bold relief, the embodiment of death, hell, and the grave; the incarnation of a principle which had its origin in the council chamber of the lost, and one which is fostered only by those affiliated with the Prince of Darkness. But, thank God, in the eye of the law we all, sir, stand upon one common platform. What have the colored people of this country done that we should be treated as a hissing and a byword, a pest and a nuisance, the off-scouring of the earth?

When we cast our eyes abroad this vast Republic, a singular anomaly, a living paradox presents itself. Once every year in this land of the free, on Freedom's natal day, the people assemble in public convocation and, in intonations loud and long, proclaim to the despotism of the world, "We hold these truths to be self-evident; that all men are born free and created equal and are endowed by their Creator, with certain unalienable rights, and among these are life, liberty, and the pursuit of happiness." Yes. Our jubilatic anthems roll over the wide waste of waters, o'er hills and valleys, rivers, woods and plains; and the burden of our song is, "We are free, We are free."

But hark! For amid the rapturous symphonies of Freedom's song, I hear a low sepulchral voice; the voice of agony, of Rachel weeping for her children and refusing to be comforted; I also hear the voice of the nominally free, of men, women and children whose Freedom (?) gives the lie to your song of Jubilee. God grant the murmurings of the crushed of this *soi-disant* Republic, which roll toward heaven like the voice of many waters, descend not in curses upon the defenseless head of this great nation; that the lightnings that now sleep side by side, with the thunders of God Almighty's wrath, be not commissioned to strike the proud fabric of our glory, and humble us in the dust. Mr. Chairman, American republicanism, and its loving handmaid American Christianity (?) seem determined, if there is any manhood in us, to crush it out of us. We are hunted like the partridge upon the mountain, persecuted, afflicted, tormented. You are the Jews, the chosen people of the Lord, and we are the poor rejected Gentiles. But the times of refreshing are soon coming from the presence of the Lord, and we wait, with anxious expectation, the arrival of this auspicious era; for then, we trust, the fullness of the Gentiles will be brought in.

> Fly swiftly round, ye wheels of Time,
> And bring the welcome day.

You talk about the caste of the Hindu, et cetera. Why, the spirit of caste lives and breathes in this country, as though it were stamped with the impress of imperishable vitality.

Your laws are founded in caste, conceived in caste, born in caste. Caste is the God whom this great nation delights to honor. Caste is in your singing, your preaching, your praying; your *beau idéal* of Heaven is a place of unfading joy, and resplendent magnificence, where you shall play forever upon your

golden harps, and the colored people, if they, like Uncle Tom,*
submit to your indignities with Christian meekness and becoming resignation, shall be permitted from the Negro pew to *peep
into* the glory of your third heaven to all eternity!

Gentlemen, only look at the picture. Your schools and colleges and stores and pulpits are all closed against us; every
avenue to honor and renown is piled up with mountains to
obstruct our progress, and if we ever stand forth, a disenthralled
people, we must burst a chain as long and broad as the ever-
grasping arm of this great country, and ten thousand times
more solid than the compact which binds you together. *O
tempora! O mores!* And then, to add insult to injury, we are
gravely told that God has drawn a broad line of demarcation
between us; that we are innately inferior to the white man; that
we are in the language of a Reverend Colonizationist, "too low
in our debasement to be reached by the heavenly light." And
this precious divine *et id omne genus* tell us in the same breath
that we are the people to evangelize and Christianize Africa.
Yes, with all our ignorance and degradation, we only are the
people, the ordained people of the Lord. Truly "God moves in a
mysterious way His wonders to perform." How is it, that while
we remain in this enlightened land, we are buried so low in the
abyss of infamy that the arm of God's omnipotence cannot
resurrect us? But, just go across the water, and be landed upon
the shores of Africa, where, as the Honorable Edward Everett†
tells us, "Death sits portress at the undefended gateways of her
mud-built villages; yellow and intermittent fevers, blue plagues
and poisons, that you can see as well as feel, await your approach." Yes, if we land on these healthy shores, then, we become kings and priests unto God, and thrones and dominions
and principalities and powers dance before our vision like dew-
drops glittering before the king of day. Colonization does for
us in Africa what God cannot do for us in America. *Mirabile
dictu!*

* Harriet Beecher Stowe's *Uncle Tom's Cabin, or Life Among the Lowly*
was first published as a serial (June 5, 1851–April 1, 1852) in the *National Era,* an antislavery paper of Washington, D. C., and as a book in
two volumes on March 20, 1852. Actually, in the novel, Uncle Tom died
under the lash for refusing to reveal the whereabouts of a fugitive slave.
† Edward Everett (1794–1865), graduate of Harvard University and
Boston Divinity School, was a Unitarian clergyman, orator and statesman.
He was a member of Congress, governor of Massachusetts, United States
Minister to Great Britain, president of Harvard University, and Secretary
of State under President Millard Fillmore.

O wonderful efficacy of the Atlantic Ocean! What wonderful power of transformation!

The departed Webster in making a Colonization speech, once said, we (the whites) imitate the example of Abram and Lot; when a difficulty had arisen between their respective herdsmen, said the former, "Let there be no strife, I pray thee, between me and thee. If thou wilt take the left hand; then I will go to the right." But the distinguished statesman did not get more than halfway in his illustration. We are perfectly willing to accept from the United States a similar proposition to the one offered by Abram. Let us read the whole of it. "Let there be no strife between us, we pray thee; between thy herdsmen, et cetera, et cetera, for we be brethren. Is not the whole land before thee? Separate thyself from me, I pray thee: If thou wilt go to the left hand, then I will go to the right; but if thou wilt go to the right hand, then I will go to the left." But, as Mr. Webster related the interesting colloquy, the proposition is of a jug-handle character.

If *you* will go to Africa, then *we* will stay in America, says Mr. W., and there stops; but why not imitate the whole example, and say, "But if *you* will stay in America, then *we* will go to Africa." This reminds me of an anecdote you have doubtless heard before. A white man and an Indian once went in pursuit of game and agreed prior to starting that they would divide whatever game they might catch. When the expedition was over, they found that they had shot a wild goose and a buzzard. They then proceeded to divide, according to agreement. Said the white man, "Goose for me, and turkey buzzard for you, or turkey buzzard for you, and goose for me." "But," said the Indian, "you no say goose for me once."

Now, Mr. Chairman, we know who are our friends and who are our enemies. Yes, gentlemen, despite our innate inferiority, notwithstanding the obliquity of our mental vision, our perceptions are sufficiently acute to discern iniquity whether we behold it arrayed in the habiliments of legislative wisdom or enveloped beneath the garb of ministerial sanctity and missionary zeal, or stalking abroad the land unmasked, in all its native hideousness, its heart-appalling deformity.

We ask no favors, Mr. Chairman, at the hands of our country; all we demand is the unrestricted right to breathe, unmolested, the pure, unadulterated atmosphere of heaven. We are told we cannot rise! Take the millstone from off our necks. We are inferior to the white man! *Give us our rights*. We can't be elevated in the land of our birth! Give us our rights, we ask no more.

Treat us like men; carry out the principles of your immortal
declaration, "All men are born free, and created equal, and are
endowed by their Creator with certain unalienable rights, and
among these are life, liberty, and the pursuit of happiness,"
and *then,* if we do not equal you in every respect, let us be
the recipients of your intensified hate, your vituperative anathemas; *then* let your ponderous Juggernaut roll on, or like
Nebuchadnezzar, let us be driven beyond the pale of humanity,
to hcrd with the beasts of the field. But do not blame us for
occupying a position in which *you* have placed us. And all this
Petition demands is that you place us in a position that we may
command respect. You need not fear the consequences. Pull
down the barrier that obstructs our progress; hew down the
mountains; fill up the valleys; make the crooked paths straight,
and the rough places smooth, and then you may talk as long
and loudly as you please about the incapacity of the colored
race. What says the Honorable Edward Everett concerning our
intellectual inferiority?

It would, says he, "be unjust to urge, as a proof of the intellectual inferiority of the civilized men of color in this country,
that they have not made much intellectual progress. It appears
to me that they have done quite as much as could be expected
under the depressing circumstances in which they have been
placed. What branch of the European family, if held in the
same condition for three centuries, would not be subject to the
same reproach?" And now, Mr. Chairman, are we unworthy to
elicit the treatment due to man, man created in the image of
God and stamped with the impress of Immortality? In the
language of the Apostle, I would exhort you, whatsoever things
are true, whatsoever things are just, whatsoever things are
honest, whatsoever things are lovely and of good report, *think
on these things.* I know that the majority of the nation have
signed the deed which abrogates the right to *speak* on these
things, but, gentlemen, you are yet at liberty to "*drink* on these
things," the requisitions of the compromise, the edict of the
Baltimore Inquisition* to the contrary notwithstanding. Why,
gentlemen, should our Petition be granted? Or rather, why
should it not be granted? Gentlemen of the legislature may

* The reference is to the attack by mobs on the editor and press of the
Baltimore *Federal Republican* in June, 1812, because of the paper's opposition to the War of 1812. During the riot the mobs burned down the
house of a free colored man and was setting fire to an African church
when dispersed. A month later a mob broke into the jail where one of the
editors of the *Federal Republican* and a few of his friends were imprisoned and killed them.

advance what ostensible reasons they please; showing why, in their opinion, it should not be, but to this conclusion they must come at last: "You are colored men, and you must not be elevated, you must not stand on equality with white men."

But, sir, if colored men helped achieved *your* liberty as well as mine, if *your* fathers and my fathers found one common Revolutionary grave, we ask you in the name of crushed and bleeding humanity, why should you, in point of privileges, like Capernaum of old, be elevated to heaven, and we be cast down to hell? No wonder Jefferson "trembled for his country when he reflected that God is just, and his justice sleeps not forever." Why should *you* be a chosen people more than *we*? . . .*

This is professedly a republican government; we are an integral portion of this Republic. We claim the absolute right, the inalienable, God-given right of freemen. You, gentlemen, have no more right to say we shall not obtain a charter than you have to monopolize the winds of heaven or the rain which falls alike upon the just and the unjust. Because the sun hath looked more intensely upon me than on you, I as a colored man am doomed to degradation; "hitherto shalt thou come and no further, and here shall thy proud waves be stayed." This is the imperious *dictum* that emanates from the *sanctum sanctorum* of republican Christianity and Christian republicanism.

But you might as well command the morning star to leap from its azure home, or command us what we shall eat and drink or wherewithal we shall be clothed. It cannot be denied that if we are men, we are entitled to all the rights of men everywhere; and no one has a right, gentlemen, morally speaking, either natural or acquired, to dehumanize and segregate us from the rest of mankind. You may withhold our right, but you can't annihilate it. The very word *right* presupposes the idea of obligation. The words are, in fact, reciprocal. We then, gentlemen, have the right; where rests the obligation? It rests somewhere! Where, I ask with increased emphasis, rests the obligation? I pause that you may reflect. But I will merely touch on another point, a point upon which I suppose my learned friend Robert Morris, Esq., will dwell at full length.

It has been affirmed, sir, that colored men cannot legally be

* Here Watkins developed the argument that colored men fought for the Independence of the United States and during the War of 1812 by quoting lengthy extracts from Botta's *History of the Wars of the Independence of the United States of America*, William C. Nell's pamphlet, *Services of the Colored Americans in the Wars of 1776 and 1812*, and Andrew Jackson's famous address to the free people of color of Louisiana, December 18, 1814, praising them for their role in the Battle of New Orleans.

enrolled among the General Militia, that we are among the absolute exempts. But this is an egregious error. What is the language of the law, sir, relative to enrollment, exemption, et cetera? Let us read the third section:

Every able-bodied white male citizen, resident in the Common-wealth, who is, or shall be of the age 18, and under the age of 45 years, except persons enrolled in Volunteer Companies; persons be-longing to the religious denominations of Quakers, or Shakers, who shall procure to the assessors a certificate, as provided in the Second Section; idiots, lunatics, common drunkards, vagabonds, paupers, and persons convicted of any infamous crimes in this, or any other State, shall be enrolled in the General Militia.

Now, gentlemen, who are the absolute exempts? Are the sixty-five gentlemen who have signed this Petition, embraced in the category? No, for the simple yet conclusive reason that they are not Quakers nor Shakers (although the intonations of the thunder's voice, and the lurid lightnings of the wrath of man are sufficient to induce a general paralysis throughout our body politic, and compel us to be Quakers and Shakers against our will); we are not able to produce to the assessors a certificate, as provided in the second section, proving that we are idiots, or lunatics, or drunkards, common or uncommon, or vagabonds, or paupers, or persons convicted of any infamous crime. But, gentlemen, although you do not place us in this honorable company by name, yet you virtually "number us among the trangressors."

Gentlemen, do we deserve to be placed in this category? If we do, we should be taken care of; for lunatics and idiots are not able to take care of themselves, and criminals should be looked after especially. If we do not, we have a right to demand that you withdraw us from the company with whom we find ourselves involuntarily associated. You will perceive that we are not literally among the absolute exempts, although prejudice may so construe it. For although able-bodied white male citizens shall be enrolled among the General Militia, there is nothing here which says able-bodied colored citizens shall *not*. It seems to be left optional with us. Our fathers were not able-bodied white male citizens; but they were able enough to face British cannon in 1776 and 1812.

So, gentlemen, you perceive that we base our petition upon the grand, fundamental, eternal, heaven-approving principle of *Right; our absolute Right to enjoy full civil privileges*. If it can be proved we are not able-bodied *men;* if it can be proved we are incapable of performing every honorable duty, you should consider our petition as a gross insult to your body, but if not, there is no alternative but to treat us as citizens of this Commonwealth should be treated—as able-bodied, honorable men.

In the fourth and last place, Mr. Chairman, I will briefly notice some of the beneficial results which will accrue from the granting of this Petition.

And allow me to remark that these results will be reciprocally beneficial. I am conscious, gentlemen, there are some men in the country, foreigners especially, who would not sleep very soundly, unless your report were adverse to our Petition. There are some so peculiarly sensitive, that were they to behold an able-bodied colored company parading down State Street, where fell the noble Crispus Attucks,* they would be almost ready to proclaim the hour of God's judgment come; or, what is about the same thing in their estimation, we would be upon the eve of a dissolution of the Union. They would not shut their eyes, but to dream of miserable hobgoblins; and black regiments of soldiers would so harrow up their little, narrow, contracted souls, that with mournful and elongated visage they would feel called on to walk up and down our streets, and proclaim, "Woe, woe, woe" unto Massachusetts and to the inhabitants thereof, "for the great day of His wrath is come, and who shall be able to stand?"

Why, gentlemen, if you grant us a charter, the soap bubble gasconade and characteristic rhodomontade of Southern bullyism would be launched forth against you with fearful power. Think you South Carolina would then stay in the Union, if she could by any means exist out of it?

But, Mr. Chairman, to be serious; if any one dreams of any evil consequences inevitably flowing from the granting of this Petition, we should charitably attribute all to the hallucination of a moonstruck imagination. In the first place, grant our Petition and you evince to the world that Massachusetts careth for her colored citizens; that she does not repudiate them as vagrants or criminals, but is disposed to help those who help themselves. It shows forth to the world that Massachusetts knows no man by the color of his skin, but all, irrespective of accidental circumstances, stand upon one broad, common and ever-enduring platform, on which the whole world may stand and it will not fall.

We love Massachusetts; if she reciprocates that love, let her

* Crispus Attucks, a runaway slave, was the first American to die in the American Revolution. He was one of five men killed in the Boston Massacre and the first to die. He was canonized by black Americans of later generations.

show forth her love by her works. Let her throw around us the mantle of her protection, and then, O Massachusetts, if we forget thee, "may our right hand forget its cunning, and our tongue cleave to the roof of our mouth!" Yes! Let the old Bay State treat us as men, and she shall elicit our undying, indissoluble attachment. And neither height, nor depth, nor principalities, nor powers, nor things present, nor things to come, shall ever be able to alienate our affection from her. We will be with her in the sixth trouble, and in the seventh, we will neither leave nor forsake her. Amid the angry howling of the tempest, as well as in the cheering sunshine, we shall be ever found, a faithful few, indomitable, unterrified, who know their friends to love them with that affection which nought but the Destroying Angel can annihilate.

Again, grant this petition, and it will induce in us a determination to surmount every obstacle calculated to impede our progress; to rise higher and *higher*, and *higher*, until we scale the Mount of Heaven and look down from our lofty and commanding position upon our revilers and persecutors. Yes, sir; it will incite us to renewed diligence and cause our arid desert to rejoice and blossom as the rose. It will inspire us with confidence and encourage us to hope amid the almost tangible darkness that envelops us. We care not for the hoarse, rough thunder's voice, nor the lightning's lurid gleamings, if we are yet to be a people; if we are yet to behold the superstructure of our liberties, consummated amid paeans of thanksgiving, and shouts from millions, redeemed, regenerated and disenthralled.

You can today, gentlemen, either bid us hope on, hope ever, or contribute toward smothering those irrepressible aspirations after freedom which God has placed in our hearts and stamped with His own eternity. Again, grant us our Petition and you shall be consoled with the reflection that you have done your duty; you shall elicit the approbation of Heaven, the admiration of every lover of truth, justice and humanity. Yes, gentlemen, when Death, with his icy and attenuated fingers, shall begin to feel around your heart, your mind shall revert to the present hour, and the consciousness of having done your duty will send a thrill of joy through every avenue of your soul. It is needless, gentlemen, for me to exhort you to do your duty, regardless of the smiles and frowns of an ever-fluctuating public opinion. Finally, grant us our Petition and you perform a work upon which your children shall look with smiles of approval. I know a prophet has no honor in his own country. It is said, the evil that men do generally lives after them, while the good is often interred with their bones.

But I look down the vista of time, and I behold the faithful historian holding up to the gaze and admiration of the then living world as paragons of genuine philanthropy and pure patriotism those who now elicit on every hand the most virulent persecutions, the most vindictive anathemas; those who dare brave the storm; who smile when the storm cloud frowns; and who, amid lightning, tempest, earthquake, whirlwind, dare proclaim, *"Our Country is the World; our Countrymen all Mankind."*

Gentlemen, will you show this day that you are among the faithful few and cause the wheels of the car of freedom to revolve with accelerated impetus. Our cause is onward. Our enemies might as well attempt to mesmerize an earthquake or rock the whirlwind to sleep, or command the ocean, "Hitherto shalt thou come, and no farther," with the expectation of eliciting obedience to the mandate, as to attempt to crush the immortal aspirations of a people determined to be free.

Truth, Justice, Humanity, God, are on our side. They that are for us, are more than all that are against us. *"Magna est veritas, et praevalebit."* "Lift up your eye toward the heavens; look also upon the earth; the heavens shall vanish like smoke; the earth shall be removed, and they that dwell therein shall die; but my salvation shall be forever, and my righteousness shall not be abolished." Thus saith the Lord. "Let the rains descend and the winds blow and the floods come and beat upon this house; it shall stand, being founded upon a rock."

And now, Mr. Chairman, I have done. Pardon me for trespassing so long upon your kind indulgence. I hope I have not spoken in vain. May you discharge your duty to your God, to yourselves, and to bleeding humanity, and ultimately attain to light, life and immortality.

THE CLAIMS OF THE NEGRO ETHNOLOGI-
CALLY CONSIDERED

By Frederick Douglass

On July 12, 1854, Frederick Douglass delivered an address
at Western Reserve College in which he set out to refute
the theories of a number of ethnologists and anthropologists who served the interests of slavery by proclaiming
that the Negro was not a man. After expressing his gratitude that he who had never had a day's schooling in his
life had been called to speak in the halls of a university,
Douglass demolished the absurd theory that the Negro was
not a man; he demonstrated that he had a common origin
with all other men, and that black people had played a
prominent role in building the ancient civilizations of
Egypt and Ethiopia. This he proved by arguments in
which, as the Ohio Observer remarked, "he exhibited considerable knowledge and research." So wide was the interest aroused by the publication of the address in Douglass' paper, that it became necessary to reprint it as a
pamphlet. "It is one of the marvels of the age," commented the National Era, "that a fugitive from slavery,
reared to manhood under all the weight of its depressing
influences, should be the author of this able and learned
address. This fact alone is the best refutation of the atheis-
tical fanatics who would exclude the Negro from the pale
of manhood."

Here is the major part of that speech, taken from Frederick Douglass, The Claims of the Negro Ethnologically
Considered, Rochester, 1854.

. . . GENTLEMEN, in selecting the claims of the Negro
as the subject of my remarks today, I am animated by a desire
to bring before you a matter of living importance—a matter
upon which action as well as thought is required. The relation
subsisting between the white and black people of this country
is the vital question of the age. In the solution of this question,
the scholars of America will have to take an important and
controlling part. This is the moral battlefield to which their
country and their God now call them. In the eye of both, the
neutral scholar is an ignoble man. Here a man must be hot or

be accounted cold, or perchance something worse than hot or cold. The lukewarm and the cowardly will be rejected by earnest men on either side of the controversy. The cunning man who avoids it to gain the favor of both parties will be rewarded with scorn; and the timid man who shrinks from it for fear of offending either party will be despised. To the lawyer, the preacher, the politician, and to the man of letters, there is no neutral ground. He that is not for us is against us. Gentlemen, I assume at the start that wherever else I may be required to speak with bated breath, here at least I may speak with freedom the thought nearest my heart. This liberty is implied by the call I have received to be here; and yet I hope to present the subject so that no man can reasonably say that an outrage has been committed or that I have abused the privilege with which you have honored me. I shall aim to discuss the claims of the Negro, general and special, in a manner, though not scientific, still sufficiently clear and definite to enable my hearers to form an intelligent judgment respecting them.

The first general claim which may here be set up respects the manhood of the Negro. This is an elementary claim, simple enough, but not without question. It is fiercely opposed. A respectable public journal, published in Richmond, Virginia, bases its whole defense of the slave system upon a denial of the Negro's manhood.

The white peasant is free, and if he is a man of will and intellect, can rise in the scale of society; or at least his offspring may. He is not deprived by law of those "inalienable rights," "liberty and the pursuit of happiness," by the use of it. But here is the essence of slavery—that we do declare the Negro destitute of these powers. We bind him by law to the condition of the laboring peasant forever, without his consent, and we bind his posterity after him. Now, the true question is, have we a right to do this? If we have not, all discussions about his comfortable situation, and the actual condition of free laborers elsewhere, are quite beside the point. If the Negro has the same right to his liberty and the pursuit of his own happiness that the white man has, then we commit the greatest wrong and robbery to hold him a slave—an act at which the sentiment of justice must revolt in every heart—and Negro slavery is an institution which that sentiment must sooner or later blot from the face of the earth.—Richmond *Examiner*.

After stating the question thus, the *Examiner* boldly asserts that the Negro has no such right—*because he is not a man!*

There are three ways to anwer this denial. One is by ridicule; a second is by denunciation; and a third is by argument. I hardly know under which of these modes my answer today will fall. I feel myself somewhat on trial; and that this is just the point where there is hesitation, if not serious doubt. I cannot, however, argue; I must assert. To know whether a Negro is a man, it must first be known what constitutes a man. Here, as well as elsewhere, I take it, that the "coat must be cut according to the cloth." It is not necessary, in order to establish the manhood of any one making the claim, to prove that such an one equals Clay in eloquence, or Webster and Calhoun in logical force and directness; for, tried by such standards of mental power as these, it is apprehended that very few could claim the high designation of *man*. Yet something like this folly is seen in the arguments directed against the humanity of the Negro. His faculties and powers, uneducated and unimproved, have been contrasted with those of the highest cultivation; and the world has then been called upon to behold the immense and amazing difference between the man admitted and the man disputed. The fact that these intellects, so powerful and so controlling, are almost, if not quite, as exceptional to the general rule of humanity in one direction as the specimen Negroes are in the other, is quite overlooked.

Man is distinguished from all other animals, by the possession of certain definite faculties and powers, as well as by physical organization and proportions. He is the only two-handed animal on the earth—the only one that laughs, and nearly the only one that weeps. Men instinctively distinguish between men and brutes. Common sense itself is scarcely needed to detect the absence of manhood in a monkey, or to recognize its presence in a Negro. His speech, his reason, his power to acquire and to retain knowledge, his heaven-erected face, his habitudes, his hopes, his fears, his aspirations, his prophecies, plant between him and the brute creation a distinction as eternal as it is palpable. Away, therefore, with all the scientific moonshine that would connect men with monkeys; that would have the world believe that humanity, instead of resting on its own characteristic pedestal—gloriously independent—is a sort of sliding scale, making one extreme brother to the orangoutang and the other to angels, and all the rest intermediates! Tried by all the usual, and all the *un*usual tests, whether mental, moral, physical, or psychological, the Negro is a *man*—considering him as possessing knowledge, or needing knowledge, his elevation or his degradation, his virtues, or his vices—whichever road you take, you reach the same conclusion, the Negro is a *man*. His good and his bad, his innocence and his guilt, his joys and his sorrows, proclaim his manhood in speech that all mankind practically and readily understand.

A very recondite author says, that "man is distinguished from all other animals, in that he resists as well as adapts himself to his circumstances." He does not take things as he finds them, but goes to work to improve them. Tried by this test, too, the Negro is a man. You may see him yoke the oxen, harness the horse, and hold the plow. He can swim in the river; but he prefers to fling over it a bridge. The horse bears him on his back—admits his mastery and dominion. The barnyard fowl know his step and flock around to receive their morning meal from his sable hand. The dog dances when he comes home, and whines piteously when he is absent. All these know that the Negro is a *man*. Now, presuming that what is evident to beast and to bird cannot need elaborate argument to be made plain to men, I assume, with this brief statement, that the Negro is a man.

The first claim conceded and settled, let us attend to the second, which is beset with some difficulties, giving rise to many opinions, different from my own, and which opinions I propose to combat.

There was a time when, if you established the point that a particular being is a man, it was considered that such a being, of course, had a common ancestry with the rest of mankind. But it is not so now. This is, you know, an age of science, and science is favorable to division. It must explore and analyze, until all doubt is set at rest. There is, therefore, another proposition to be stated and maintained, separately, which in other days (the days before the Notts, the Gliddens, the Agassiz, and Mortons made their profound discoveries in ethnological science) might have been included in the first.

It is somewhat remarkable that, at a time when knowledge is so generally diffused, when the geography of the world is so well understood—when time and space, in the intercourse of nations, are almost annihilated—when oceans have become bridges—the earth a magnificent hall—the hollow sky a dome— under which a common humanity can meet in friendly conclave—when nationalities are being swallowed up—and the ends of the earth brought together—I say it is remarkable— nay, it is strange that there should arise a phalanx of learned men—speaking in the name of *science*—to forbid the magnificent reunion of mankind in one brotherhood. A mortifying proof is here given that the moral growth of a nation or an age does not always keep pace with the increase of knowledge and suggests the necessity of means to increase human love with human learning.

The proposition to which I allude, and which I mean next to assert, is this, that what are technically called the Negro race are a part of the human family, and are descended from a common ancestry with the rest of mankind. The discussion of this point opens a comprehensive field of inquiry. It involves the question of the unity of the human race. Much has and can be said on both sides of that question.

Looking out upon the surface of the globe, with its varieties of climate, soil and formations, its elevations and depressions, its rivers, lakes, oceans, islands, continents, and the vast and striking differences which mark and diversify its multitudinous inhabitants, the question has been raised and pressed with increasing ardor and pertinacity (especially in modern times): can all these various tribes, nations, tongues, kindreds, so widely separated and so strangely dissimilar, have descended from a common ancestry? That is the question, and it has been answered variously by men of learning. Different modes of reasoning have been adopted, but the conclusions reached may be divided into two—the one Yes, and the other No. *Which* of these answers is most in accordance with facts, with reason, with the welfare of the world, and reflects most glory upon the wisdom, power and goodness of the Author of all existence, is the question for consideration with us. On which side is the weight of the argument, rather than which side is absolutely proved?

It must be admitted at the beginning that, viewed apart from the authority of the Bible, neither the unity nor diversity of origin of the human family can be demonstrated. To use the terse expression of the Reverend Dr. Anderson, who, speaking on this point, says, "It is impossible to get far enough back for that." This much, however, can be done. The evidence on both sides, can be accurately weighed, and the truth arrived at with almost absolute certainty.

It would be interesting, did time permit, to give here some of the most striking features of the various theories which have of late gained attention and respect in many quarters of our country—touching the origin of mankind—but I must pass this by. The argument today is to the unity, as against that theory which affirms the diversity of human origin.

THE BEARINGS OF THE QUESTION

A moment's reflection must impress all that few questions have more important and solemn bearings than the one now under consideration. It is connected with eternal as well as with terrestrial interests. It covers the earth and reaches heaven. The unity of the human race—the brotherhood of man—the reciprocal duties of all to each and of each to all are too plainly taught in the Bible to admit of cavil. The credit of the Bible is at stake, and if it be too much to say that it must stand or fall by the decision of this question, *it is* proper to say that the value of that sacred Book—as a record of the early history of mankind—must be materially affected by the decision of the question.

For myself I can say my reason (not less than my feeling and my faith) welcomes with joy the declaration of the Inspired Apostle "that God has made of one blood all nations of men for to dwell upon all the face of the earth." But this grand affirmation of the unity of the human race, and many others like unto it, together with the whole account of the creation given in the early Scriptures, must all get a new interpretation or be overthrown altogether if a diversity of human origin can be maintained. Most evidently, this aspect of the question makes it important to those who rely upon the Bible as the sheet anchor of their hopes and the framework of all religious truth. The young minister must look into this subject and settle it for himself before he ascends the pulpit to preach redemption to a fallen race.

The bearing of the question upon Revelation is not more marked and decided than its relation to the situation of things in our country at this moment. *One seventh* part of the population of this country is of Negro descent. The land is peopled by what may be called the most dissimilar races on the globe. The black and white, the Negro and the European—these constitute the American people, and in all the likelihoods of the case, they will ever remain the principal inhabitants of the United States in some form or other. The European population are greatly in the ascendant in numbers, wealth and power. They are the rulers of the country, the masters—the Africans are the slaves, the proscribed portion of the people—and precisely in proportion as the truth of human brotherhood gets recognition will be the freedom and elevation in this country of persons of African descent. In truth, this question is at the bottom of the whole controversy now going on between the slaveholders on the *one* hand and the Abolitionists on the other. It is the same old question which has divided the selfish from the philanthropic part of mankind in all ages. It is the question whether the rights, privileges and immunities enjoyed by some ought not to be shared and enjoyed by all.

It is not quite two hundred years ago when such was the simplicity (I will not now say the pride and depravity) of the Anglo-Saxon inhabitants of the British West Indies that the learned and pious Godwin, a missionary to the West Indies, deemed it necessary to write a book to remove what he conceived to be the injurious belief that it was sinful in the sight of God to baptize Negroes and Indians. The West Indies have made progress since that time. God's emancipating angel has broken the fetters of slavery in those islands, and the praises of the Almighty are now sung by the sable lips of eight hundred thousand freemen, before deemed only fit for slaves, and to whom even baptismal and burial rights were denied.

The unassuming work of Godwin may have had some agency in producing this glorious result. One other remark before entering upon the argument. It may be said that views and opinions, favoring the unity of the human family, coming from one of lowly condition, are open to the suspicion that *"the wish is father to the thought,"* and so, indeed, it may be. But let it be also remembered, that this deduction from the weight of the argument on the one side, is more than counterbalanced by the pride of race and position arrayed on the other. Indeed, ninety-nine out of every hundred of the advocates of a diverse origin of the human family in this country, are among those who hold it to be the privilege of the Anglo-Saxon to enslave and oppress the African—and slaveholders, not a few, like the Richmond *Examiner* to which I have referred, have admitted that the whole argument in defense of slavery becomes utterly worthless the moment the African is proved to be equally a man with the Anglo-Saxon. The temptation therefore, to read the Negro out of the human family is exceedingly strong, and may account somewhat for the repeated attempts on the part of Southern pretenders to science, to cast a doubt over the Scriptural account of the origin of mankind. If the origin and motives of most works, opposing the doctrine of the unity of the human race, could be ascertained, it may be doubted whether *one* such work could boast an honest parentage. Pride and selfishness, combined with mental power, never want for a theory to justify them—and when men oppress their fellow men, the oppressor ever finds, in the character of the oppressed, a full justification for his oppression. Ignorance and depravity, and the inability to rise from degradation to civilization and respectability, are the most usual allegations against the oppressed. The evils most fostered by slavery and oppression are precisely those which slaveholders and oppressors would transfer from their system to the inherent character of their victims. Thus the very crimes of slavery become slavery's best defense. By making the enslaved a character fit only for slavery, they excuse themselves for refusing to make the slave a free man. A wholesale method of accomplishing this result is to overthrow the instinctive consciousness of the common brotherhood of man. For, let it be once granted that the human race are of multitudinous origin, naturally different in their moral, physical and intellectual capacities, and at once you make plausible a demand for classes, grades and conditions for different methods of culture, different moral, political and religious institutions, and a chance is left for slavery, as a necessary institution. The debates in Congress on the Nebraska Bill during the past winter* will show how slaveholders have availed themselves of this doctrine in support of slaveholding. There is no doubt that Messrs. Nott, Glidden, Morton, Smith and Agassiz were duly consulted by our slavery-propagating statesmen.

ETHNOLOGICAL UNFAIRNESS TOWARD THE NEGRO

The lawyers tell us that the credit of a witness is always in order. Ignorance, malice or prejudice may disqualify a witness, and why not an author? Now, the disposition everywhere evident, among the class of writers alluded to, to separate the Negro race from every intelligent nation and tribe in Africa, may fairly be regarded as one proof that they have staked out the ground beforehand and that they have aimed to construct a theory in support of a foregone conclusion. The desirableness of isolating the Negro race, and especially of separating them from the various peoples of Northern Africa, is too plain to need a remark. Such isolation would remove stupendous difficulties in the way of getting the Negro in a favorable attitude for the blows of scientific Christendom.

Dr. Samuel George Morton may be referred to as a fair sample of American ethnologists. His very able work *Crania Americana*, published in Philadelphia in 1839, is widely read in this country. In this great work his contempt for Negroes is ever conspicuous. I take him as an illustration of what had been alleged as true of his class.

The fact that Egypt was one of the earliest abodes of learning and civilization is as firmly established as are the everlasting

* On January 4, 1854, Stephen A. Douglas introduced his Nebraska Bill in the Senate. It would have permitted slavery in the Nebraska territory even though it was north of the 36°30′ line, thus repealing the Missouri Compromise, even though through "popular sovereignty" slavery might be kept out. It also provided that the Fugitive Slave Law of 1850 was to be applied in Nebraska.

hills, defying with a calm front the boasted mechanical and architectural skill of the nineteenth century—smiling serenely on the assaults and the mutations of time, there she stands in overshadowing grandeur, riveting the eye and the mind of the modern world—upon her, in silent and dreamy wonder— Greece and Rome—and through them Europe and America have received their civilization from the ancient Egyptians. This fact is not denied by anybody. But Egypt is in Africa. Pity that it had not been in Europe, or in Asia, or better still in America! Another unhappy circumstance is that the ancient Egyptians were not white people; but were, undoubtedly, just about as dark in complexion as many in this country who are considered genuine Negroes; and that is not all; their hair was far from being of that graceful lankness which adorns the fair Anglo-Saxon head. But the next best thing, after these defects, is a positive unlikeness to the Negro. Accordingly, our learned author enters into an elaborate argument to prove that the ancient Egyptians were totally distinct from the Negroes, and to deny all relationship between. Speaking of the "Copts and Fellahs," who everybody knows are descendants of the Egyptians, he says, *"The Copts, though now remarkably distinct from the people that surround them, derive from their remote ancestors some mixture of Greek, Arabian, and perhaps even Negro blood."* Now, mark the description given of the Egyptians in this same work: *"Complexion brown. The nose is straight, excepting the end, where it is rounded and wide; the lips are rather thick, and the hair black and curly."* This description would certainly seem to make it safe to suppose the presence of *"even* Negro blood." A man, in our day, with brown complexion, "nose rounded and wide, lips thick, hair black and curly," would, I think, have no difficulty in getting himself recognized as a Negro!!

The same authority tells us that the "Copts are supposed by Niebuhr, Denon and others, to be the descendants of the ancient Egyptians"; and Dr. Morton adds, that it has often been observed that a strong resemblance may be traced between the Coptic visage and that presented in the ancient mummies and statues. Again, he says, the *"Copts can be, at most, but the degenerate remains, both physically and intellectually, of that mighty people who have claimed the admiration of all ages."* Speaking of the Nubians, Dr. Morton says (page 26):

The hair of the Nubian is thick and black—often curled, either by nature or art, and sometimes *partially frizzled,* but *never woolly.*

Again:

Although the Nubians occasionally present their national characters unmixed, they generally show traces of their social intercourse
with the Arabs, and *even* with the Negroes.

The repetition of the adverb here, *"even,"* is important, as
showing the spirit in which our great American ethnologist
pursues his work, and what deductions may be justly made
from the value of his researches on that account. In everything touching the Negro, Dr. Morton, in his *Crania Americana,*
betrays the same spirit. He thinks that the Sphinx was not the
representative of an Egyptian deity, but was a shrine worshiped
at by the degraded *Negroes* of Egypt; and this fact he alleges as
the secret of the mistake made by Volney, in supposing that the
Egyptians were real Negroes. The absurdity of this assertion
will be very apparent, in view of the fact that the great Sphinx
in question was the chief of a series, full two miles in length.
Our author again repels the supposition that the Egyptians were
related to Negroes by saying there is no mention made of *color*
by the historian in relating the marriage of Solomon with
Pharaoh's daughter; and with genuine American feeling, he
says, such a circumstance as the marrying of an European
monarch with the daughter of a Negro would not have been
passed over in silence in our day. This is a sample of the reasoning of men who reason from *prejudice* rather than from *facts.*
It assumes that a *black skin* in the *East* excites the same prejudice which we see here in the West. Having denied all relationship of the Negro to the ancient Egyptians, with characteristic
American assumption, he says, "It is easy to prove that, whatever may have been the hue of their skin, they belong to the
same race with ourselves."

Of course, I do not find fault with Dr. Morton or any other
American for claiming affinity with Egyptians. All that goes in
that direction belongs to my side of the question and is really
right.

The leaning here indicated is natural enough and may be
explained by the fact that an educated man in Ireland ceases
to be an Irishman; and an intelligent black man is always supposed to have derived his intelligence from his connection with
the white race. To be intelligent is to have one's Negro blood
ignored.

There is, however, a very important physiological fact contra-
dicting this last assumption; and that fact is that intellect is
uniformly derived from the maternal side. Mulattoes, in this
country, may almost wholly boast of Anglo-Saxon male ancestry.

It is the province of prejudice to blind; and scientific writers, not less than others, write to please, as well as to instruct, and even unconsciously to themselves (sometimes) sacrifice what is true to what is popular. Fashion is not confined to dress; but extends to philosophy as well—and it is fashionable now, in our land, to exaggerate the differences between the Negro and the European. If, for instance, a phrenologist or naturalist undertakes to represent in portraits the differences between the two races—the Negro and the European—he will invariably present the *highest* type of the European, and the *lowest* type of the Negro.

The European face is drawn in harmony with the highest ideas of beauty, dignity and intellect. Features regular and brow after the Websterian mold. The Negro, on the other hand, appears with features distorted, lips exaggerated, forehead depressed—and the whole expression of the countenance made to harmonize with the popular idea of Negro imbecility and degradation. I have seen many pictures of Negroes and Europeans, in phrenological and ethnological works; and all, or nearly all, excepting the work of Dr. Prichard and that other great work Combs's *Constitution of Man,* have been more or less open to this objection. I think I have never seen a single picture in an American work designed to give an idea of the mental endowments of the Negro, which did anything like justice to the subject—nay, that was not infamously distorted. The heads of A. Crummel, Henry H. Garnet, Sam'l R. Ward, Chas. Lenox Remond, W. J. Wilson, J. W. Penington, J. I. Gaines, M. R. Delany, J. W. Loguen, J. M. Whitfield, J. C. Holly, and hundreds of others I could mention, are all better formed, and indicate the presence of intellect more than any pictures I have seen in such works; and while it must be admitted that there are Negroes answering the description given by the American ethnologists and others of the Negro race, I contend that there is every description of head among them, ranging from the highest Indo-Caucasian downward. If the very best type of the European is always presented, I insist that *justice* in all such works demands that the very best type of the Negro should also be taken. The importance of this criticism may not be apparent to all; to the *black* man it is very apparent. He sees the injustice and writhes under its sting.

But to return to Dr. Morton, or rather to the question of the affinity of the Negroes to the Egyptians: It seems to me that a man might as well deny the affinity of the American to the Englishman as to deny such affinity between the Negro and the Egyptian. He might make out as many points of difference in the case of the one as in that of the other. Especially could this

be done if, like ethnologists, in given cases, only typical specimens were resorted to. The lean, slender American, pale and
swarthy if exposed to the sun, wears a very different appearance
to the full, round Englishman, of clear, *blond* complexion. One
may trace the progress of this difference in the common portraits of the American Presidents. Just study those faces, beginning with Washington; and as you come through the Jeffersons,
the Adamses, and the Madisons, you will find an increasing
bony and wiry appearance about those portraits, and a greater
remove from that serene amplitude which characterizes the
countenances of the earlier Presidents. I may be mistaken, but I
think this is a correct index of the change going on in the
nation at large—converting Englishmen, Germans, Irishmen
and Frenchmen into Americans and causing them to lose, in
a common American character, all traces of their former
distinctive national peculiarities.

AUTHORITIES AS TO THE RESEMBLANCE
OF THE EGYPTIANS TO NEGROES

Now, let us see what the best authorities say as to the
personal appearance of the Egyptians. I think it will be at once
admitted that, while they differ very strongly from the Negro
debased and enslaved, that difference is not greater than may be
observed in other quarters of the globe, among people notoriously belonging to the same variety, the same original stock
—in a word, to the same family. If it shall be found that the
people of Africa have an African character, as general, as well
defined, and as distinct as have the people of Europe or the
people of Asia, the exceptional differences among them afford
no ground for supposing a difference of race; but, on the
contrary, it will be inferred that the people of Africa constitute
one great branch of the human family, whose origin may be as
properly referred to the families of Noah as can be any other
branch of the human family from whom they differ. Denon, in
his *Travels in Egypt*, describes the Egyptians as of full but
"delicate and voluptuous forms, countenances sedate and
placid, round and soft features, with eyes long and almond
shaped, half shut and languishing and turned up at the outer
angles, as if habitually fatigued by the light and heat of the
sun; cheeks round; thick lips, full and prominent; mouth
large, but cheerful and smiling; complexion dark, ruddy and
coppery, and the whole aspect displaying—as one of the most
graphic delineators among modern travelers has observed—
the genuine African character, of which the *Negro* is the exag-

gerated and extreme representation." Again, Prichard says
(page 152):

Herodotus traveled in Egypt and was, therefore, well acquainted
with the people from personal observation. He does not say anything directly, as to the descriptions of their persons, which were too
well known to the Greeks to need such an account, but his indirect
testimony is very strongly expressed. After mentioning a tradition,
that the people of Colchis were a colony from Egypt, Herodotus
says, that "there was one fact strongly in favor of this opinion—
the Colchians were *black* in complexion and *woolly* haired."

These are the words by which the complexion and hair of
Negroes are described. In another passage, he says that

The pigeon, said to have fled to Dodona, and to have founded the
Oracle, was declared to be *black*, and that the meaning of the story
was this: The Oracle was, in reality, founded by a female captive
from the Thebaid; she was *black*, being an Egyptian. Other Greek
writers . . . have expressed themselves in similar terms.

Those who have mentioned the Egyptians as a *swarthy* people,
according to Prichard, might as well have applied the term
black to them, since they were doubtless of a chocolate color.
The same author brings together the testimony of Aeschylus and
others as to the color of the ancient Egyptians, all corresponding,
more or less, with the foregoing. Among the most direct testimony educed by Prichard is first that of Volney, who, speaking
of the modern Copts, says: "They have a puffed visage, swollen
eyes, flat nose, and thick lips, and bear much resemblance to
mulattoes."

Baron Larrey says, in regard to the same people: "They have
projecting cheek bones, dilating nostrils, thick lips, and hair
and beard black and *crisp*."

Mr. Ledyard (whose testimony, says our learned authority,
is of the more value, as he had no theory to support) says:
"I suspect the *Copts* to have been the *origin* of the *Negro* race;
the nose and lips correspond with those of the Negro; the hair,
wherever I can see it among the people here, is curled, *not*
like that of the Negroes, but like the mulattoes."

Here I leave our learned authorities, as to the resemblance of
the Egyptians to Negroes.

It is not in my power, in a discourse of this sort, to adduce
more than a very small part of the testimony in support of a
near relationship between the present enslaved and degraded
Negroes and the ancient highly civilized and wonderfully endowed Egyptians. Sufficient has already been adduced to show

a marked similarity in regard to features, hair, color, and I doubt not that the philologist can find equal similarity in the structures of their languages. In view of the foregoing, while it may not be claimed that the ancient Egyptians were Negroes —viz, answering, in all respects, to the nations and tribes ranged under the general appellation *Negro*—still, it may safely be affirmed that a strong affinity and a direct relationship may be claimed by the Negro race, to that grandest of all the nations of antiquity, the builders of the pyramids.

But there are other evidences of this relationship, more decisive than those alleged in a general similarity of personal appearance. Language is held to be very important by the best ethnologists in tracing out the remotest affinities of nations, tribes, classes and families. The color of the skin has sometimes been less enduring than the speech of a people. I speak by authority and follow in the footsteps of some of the most learned writers on the natural and ethnological history of man when I affirm that one of the most direct and conclusive proofs of the general affinity of Northern African nations, with those of West, East and South Africa, is found in the general similarity of their language. The philologist easily discovers and is able to point out something like the original source of the multiplied tongues now in use in that yet mysterious quarter of the globe. Dr. R. G. Latham, F. R. S., corresponding member of the Ethnological Society, New York, in his admirable work entitled *Man and his Migrations,* says:

In the languages of Abyssinia, the Gheez and Tigre, admitted, as long as they have been known at all, to be *Semitic,* graduate through the Amharic, the Talasha, the Harargi, the Gafat and other languages, which may be well studied in Dr. Beke's valuable comparative tables, into the Agow tongue, unequivocally indigenous to Abyssinia, and through this into the true Negro classes. But, unequivocal as may be the Semitic elements of the Berber, Coptic and Galla, their affinities with the tongues of Western and Southern Africa are more so. I weigh my words when I say, not *equally,* but *more;* changing the expression, for every foot in advance which can be made towards the Semitic tongues in one direction, the African philologist can go a yard towards the Negro ones in the other.

In a note, just below this remarkable statement, Dr. Latham says:

A short table of the Berber and Coptic, as compared with the other African tongues, may be seen in the Classical Museum of the British Association, for 1846. In the Transactions of the Philological Society is a grammatical sketch of the Tumali language, by Dr. S.

Tutshek of Munich. The Tumali is a truly Negro language, of Kordufan; whilst, in respect to the extent to which its inflections are formed by internal changes of vowels and accents, it is fully equal to the Semitic tongues of Palestine and Arabia.

This testimony may not serve prejudice, but to me it seems quite sufficient.

SUPERFICIAL OBJECTIONS

Let us now glance again at the opposition. A volume on the Natural History of the Human Species, by Charles Hamilton Smith, quite false in many of its facts, and as mischievous as false, has been published recently in this country and will doubtless be widely circulated, especially by those to whom the thought of human brotherhood is abhorrent. This writer says, after mentioning sundry facts touching the dense and spherical structure of the Negro head:

This very structure may influence the erect gait which occasions the practice, common also to the Ethiopian or mixed nations, of carrying burdens and light weights, even to a tumbler full of water, upon the head.

No doubt this seemed a very sage remark to Mr. Smith, and quite important in fixing a character to the Negro skull, although different to that of Europeans. But if the learned Mr. Smith had stood, previous to writing it, at our door (a few days in succession), he might have seen hundreds of Germans and of Irish people, not bearing burdens of "*light* weight," but of *heavy* weight, upon the same vertical extremity. The carrying of burdens upon the head is as old as Oriental society; and the man writes himself a blockhead who attempts to find in the custom a proof of original difference. On page 227, the same writer says, "The voice of the Negroes is feeble and hoarse in the male sex."

The explanation of this mistake in our author, is found in the fact that an oppressed people, in addressing their superiors —perhaps I ought to say, their oppressors—usually assume a minor tone, as less likely to provoke the charge of intrusiveness. But it is ridiculous to pronounce the voice of the Negro feeble; and the learned ethnologist must be hard pushed, to establish differences, when he refers to this as one. Mr. Smith further declares, that "the typically woolly-haired races have never discovered an alphabet, framed a grammatical language, nor made the least step in science or art."

Now, the man is still living (or was but a few years since), among the Mandingoes of the western coast of Africa, who has framed an alphabet; and while Mr. Smith may be pardoned for his ignorance of that fact, as an ethnologist he is inexcusable for not knowing that the Mpongwe language, spoken on both sides of the Gaboon River, at Cape Lopez, Cape St. Catharine, and in the interior to the distance of two or three hundred miles, is as truly a grammatically framed language as any extant. I am indebted for this fact to Rev. Dr. M. B. Anderson, President of the Rochester University; and by his leave, here is the Grammar [holding up the Grammar]. Perhaps, of all the attempts ever made to disprove the unity of the human family and to brand the Negro with natural inferiority, the most compendious and barefaced is the book entitled *Types of Mankind,* by Nott and Glidden. One would be well employed in a series of lectures directed to an exposure of the unsoundness, if not the wickedness, of this work.

THE AFRICAN RACE BUT ONE PEOPLE

But I must hasten. Having shown that the people of Africa are probably one people; that each tribe bears an intimate relation to other tribes and nations in that quarter of the globe, and that the Egyptians may have flung off the different tribes seen there at different times, as implied by the evident relations of their language and by other similarities; it can hardly be deemed unreasonable to suppose that the African branch of the human species—from the once highly civilized Egyptian to the barbarians on the banks of the Niger—may claim brotherhood with the great family of Noah, spreading over the more northern and eastern parts of the globe. I will now proceed to consider those physical peculiarities of form, features, hair and color, which are supposed by some men to mark the African, not only as an inferior race, but as a distinct species, naturally and originally different from the rest of mankind and as really to place him nearer to the brute than to man.

THE EFFECT OF CIRCUMSTANCES UPON
THE PHYSICAL MAN

I may remark, just here, that it is impossible, even were it desirable, in a discourse like this, to attend to the anatomical and physiological argument connected with this part of the subject. I am not equal to that, and if I were, the occasion does not require it. The form of the *Negro*—I use the term *Negro,* precisely in the sense that you use the term Anglo-Saxon; and I believe, too, that the former will one day be as illustrious as the latter—has often been the subject of remark. His flat feet, long arms, high cheekbones and retreating forehead are especially dwelt upon, to his disparagement, and just as if there were no white people with precisely the same peculiarities. I think it will ever be found that the *well* or *ill* condition of any part of mankind will leave its mark on the physical as well as on the intellectual part of man. A hundred instances might be cited, of whole families who have degenerated, and others who have improved in personal appearance, by a change of circumstances. A man is worked upon by what *he* works on. He may carve out his circumstances, but his circumstances will carve him out as well. I told a bootmaker in New Castle upon Tyne that I had been a plantation slave. He said I must pardon him, but he could not believe it; no plantation laborer ever had a high instep. He said he had noticed that the coal heavers and work people in low condition had, for the most part, flat feet, and that he could tell by the shape of the feet whether a man's parents were in high or low condition. The thing was worth a thought, and I have thought of it and have looked around me for facts. There is some truth in it; though there are exceptions in individual cases.

The day I landed in Ireland nine years ago, I addressed (in company with Father Spratt and that good man who has been recently made the subject of bitter attack; I allude to the philanthropic James Haughton, of Dublin) a large meeting of the common people of Ireland on temperance. Never did human faces tell a sadder tale. More than five thousand were assembled; and I say, with no wish to wound the feelings of any Irishman, that these people lacked only a black skin and woolly hair, to complete their likeness to the plantation Negro. The open, uneducated mouth, the long, gaunt arm, the badly formed foot and ankle, the shuffling gait, the retreating forehead and vacant expression, and their petty quarrels and fights—all reminded me of the plantation, and my own cruelly abused people. Yet, *that* is the land of Grattan, of Curran, of O'Connell, and of Sheridan. Now, while what I have said is true of the common people, the fact is there are no more really handsome people in the world, than the educated Irish people. The Irishman educated is a model gentleman; the Irishman ignorant and degraded compares in form and feature with the Negro!

I am stating facts. If you go into southern Indiana, you will see what climate and habit can do, even in one generation. The man may have come from New England, but his hard features, sallow complexion, have left little of New England on his brow. The right arm of the blacksmith is said to be larger and stronger than his left. The ship carpenter is at forty round-shouldered. The shoemaker carries the marks of his trade. One locality becomes famous for one thing, another for another. Manchester and Lowell, in America, Manchester and Sheffield, in England, attest this. But what does it all prove? Why, nothing positively, as to the main point; still it raises the inquiry—May not the condition of men explain their various appearances? Need we go behind the vicissitudes of barbarism for an explanation of the gaunt, wiry, apelike appearance of some of the genuine Negroes? Need we look higher than a vertical sun, or lower than the damp, black soil of the Niger, the Gambia, the Senegal, with their heavy and enervating miasma, rising ever from the rank growing and decaying vegetation, for an explanation of the Negro's color? If a cause, full and adequate, can be found here, *why seek further?*

The eminent Dr. Latham, already quoted, says that nine tenths of the white population of the globe are found between 30 and 65 degrees North latitude. Only about one fifth of all the inhabitants of the globe are white; and they are as far from the Adamic complexion as is the Negro. The remainder are— *what?* Ranging all the way from the brunette to jet black. There are the red, the reddish-copper color, and yellowish, the dark brown, the chocolate color, and so on, to the jet black. On the mountains on the north of Africa, where water freezes in winter at times, branches of the same people who are *black* in the valley are *white* on the mountains. The Nubian, with his beautiful curly hair, finds it becoming frizzled, crisped, and even woolly, as he approaches the great Sahara. The Portuguese, white in Europe, is brown in Asia. The Jews, who are to be found in all countries, never intermarrying, are white in Europe, brown in Asia, and black in Africa. Again, what does it all prove? Nothing, absolutely; nothing which places the question beyond dispute; but it *does* justify the conjecture before referred to, that outward circumstances *may* have something to do with modifying the various phases of humanity; and that color itself is at the control of the world's climate and its various concomitants. It is the sun that paints the peach, and may it not be that he paints the *man* as well? My reading, on this point, however, as well as my own observation, has convinced me, that from the beginning the Almighty, within certain limits, endowed mankind with organizations capable of countless variations in form, feature and color, without having it necessary to begin a new creation for every new variety.

A powerful argument in the favor of the oneness of the human family, is afforded in the fact that nations, however dissimilar, may be united in one social state, not only without detriment to each other, but, most clearly, to the advancement of human welfare, happiness and perfection. While it is clearly proved, on the other hand, that those nations freest from foreign elements present the most evident marks of deterioration. Dr. James McCune Smith, himself a colored man, a gentleman and scholar, alleges—and not without excellent reason—that this, our own great nation, so distinguished for industry and enterprise, is largely indebted to its composite character. We all know, at any rate, that now what constitutes the very heart of the civilized world—I allude to England—has only risen from barbarism to its present lofty eminence, through successive invasions and alliances with her people. The Medes and Persians constituted one of the mightiest empires that ever rocked the globe. The most terrible nation which now threatens the peace of the world, to make its will the law of Europe, is a grand piece of Mosaic work, in which almost every nation has its characteristic feature, from the wild Tartar to the refined Pole.

But, gentlemen, the time fails me and I must bring these remarks to a close. My argument has swelled beyond its appointed measure. What I intended to make special, has become, in its progress, somewhat general. I meant to speak here today for the lonely and the despised ones with whom I was cradled, and with whom I have suffered; and now, gentlemen, in conclusion, what if all this reasoning be unsound? What if the Negro may not be able to prove his relationship to Nubians, Abyssinians and Egyptians? What if ingenious men are able to find plausible objections to all arguments maintaining the oneness of the human race? What, after all, if they are able to show very good reasons for believing the Negro to have been created precisely as we find him on the Gold Coast, along the Senegal and the Niger—I say, what of all this? "A man's a man for a' that." I sincerely believe that the weight of the argument is in favor of the unity of origin of the human race, or species, that the arguments on the other side are partial, superficial, utterly subversive of the happiness of man and insulting to the wisdom of God. Yet, what if we grant they are not so? What, if we grant that the case, on our part, is not made out? Does it follow that the Negro should be held in contempt? Does it follow that to enslave and imbrute him is either *just* or *wise*? I think not. Human rights stand upon a common basis; and by all the reason that they are supported, maintained and defended for one variety of the human family, they are supported, maintained and defended for *all* the human family; because all mankind have the same wants, arising out of a common nature. A diverse origin does not disprove a common nature, nor does it disprove a united destiny. The essential characteristics of humanity are everywhere the same. In the language of the eloquent Curran, "No matter what complexion, whether an Indian or an African sun has burnt upon him," his title deed to freedom, his claim to life and to liberty, to knowledge and to civilization, to society and to Christianity, are just and perfect. It is registered in the Courts of Heaven, and is enforced by the eloquence of the God of all the earth.

I have said that the Negro and white man are likely ever to remain the principal inhabitants of this country. I repeat the statement now, to submit the reasons that support it. The blacks can disappear from the face of the country by three ways. They may be colonized, they may be exterminated, or they may die out. Colonization is out of the question; for I know not what hardships the laws of the land can impose, which can induce the colored citizen to leave his native soil. He was here in its infancy; he is here in its age. Two hundred years have passed over him, his tears and blood have been mixed with the soil, and his attachment to the place of his birth is stronger than iron. It is not probable that he will be exterminated; two considerations must prevent a crime so stupendous as that—the influence of Christianity on the one hand, and the power of self-interest on the other. And, in regard to their dying out, the statistics of the country afford no encouragement for such a conjecture. The history of the Negro race proves them to be wonderfully adapted to all countries, all climates, and all conditions. Their tenacity of life, their powers of endurance, their malleable toughness, would almost imply especial interposition on their behalf. The ten thousand horrors of slavery, striking hard upon the sensitive soul, have bruised and battered and stung, but have not killed. The poor bondman lifts a smiling face above the surface of a sea of agonies, *hoping on, hoping ever*. His tawny brother, the Indian, dies under the flashing glance of the Anglo-Saxon. *Not* so the Negro; civilization cannot kill him. He accepts it—becomes a part of it. In the church, he is an Uncle Tom; in the state, he is the most abused and least offensive. All the facts in his history mark out for him a destiny united to America and Americans. Now, whether this population shall, by Freedom, Industry, Virtue and Intelligence, be made a blessing to the country and the world, or whether their multiplied wrongs shall kindle the vengeance of an offended God, will depend upon the conduct of no class of men so much as upon the scholars of the country. The future public opinion of the land, whether antislavery or proslavery, whether just or unjust, whether magnanimous or mean, must redound to the honor of the scholars of the country or cover them with shame. There is but one safe road for nations or for individuals. The fate of a wicked man and of a wicked nation is the same. The flaming sword of offended justice falls as certainly upon the nation as upon the man. God has no children whose rights may be safely trampled upon. The sparrow may not fall to the ground without the notice of His eye, and men are more than sparrows.

Now, gentlemen, I have done. The subject is before you. I shall not undertake to make the application. I speak as unto wise men. I stand in the presence of scholars. We have met here today from vastly different points in the world's condition. I have reached here—if you will pardon the egotism—by little short of a miracle; at any rate, by dint of some application and perseverance. Born, as I was, in obscurity, a stranger to the halls of learning, environed by ignorance, degradation and their concomitants, from birth to manhood, I do not feel at liberty to mark out, with any degree of confidence or dogmatism, what is the precise vocation of the scholar. Yet, this I *can* say, as a denizen of the world, and as a citizen of a country rolling in the sin and shame of slavery, the most flagrant and scandalous that ever saw the sun, "Whatsoever things are true, whatsoever things are honest, whatsoever things are just, whatsoever things are pure, whatsoever things are lovely, whatsoever things are of good report, if there be any virtue, and if there be any praise, think on these things."

THE TRIUMPH OF EQUAL SCHOOL RIGHTS IN BOSTON

By William C. Nell

During the 1820's and 1830's the public-school system was established for white children, with Negroes explicitly excluded, while separate schools for Negroes—almost always very inferior to those for whites—were provided at public expense. Negroes and their allies began a campaign during the 1840's and 1850's throughout the North to supplant separate schools with integrated schools. Agitation to this end was pressed most vigorously through convention appeals, petitions, refusal to pay taxes, and litigation, but usually without success. But in Boston, where the most notable desegregation campaign took place, the battle for equal school rights was successful, and in large measure this was due to the untiring efforts and labors of the black Abolitionist William Cooper Nell.

Connected with Garrison's Liberator *for many years, Nell won fame as an orator and also as one of the first black historians in the United States. He began collecting Negro historical data and produced in 1852 the study,* Services of Colored Americans in the Wars of 1776 and 1812, *followed four years later by the* Colored Patriots of the American Revolution. *But it was his leadership in the desegregation campaign in Boston's schools which won Nell his greatest fame. Under his direction, Negroes in Boston deluged the Massachusetts legislature with petitions demanding the abolition of separate schools and had them taught privately until in 1855 a law was enacted requiring public schools in the state to admit students without regard to color.*

On December 17, 1855, the black community of Boston sponsored a meeting in the Southac Street Church for the purpose of presenting a testimonial to Nell "for his disinterested and untiring exertions procuring the opening of the public schools of the city to all children and youth within its limits, irrespective of complexional differences." After the presentation, Nell delivered an address, the major portion of which follows; text is taken from Triumph of Equal School Rights in Boston: Proceedings of the Presentation Meeting Held in Boston, December 17, 1855, *Boston, 1856, pp. 5–11.*

. . . IN THE YEAR 1829, while a pupil in the basement story of the Belknap Street church, the Honorable Harrison Gray Otis, then mayor of the city, accompanied the Honorable Samuel T. Armstrong to an examination of the colored school. It chanced that Charles A. Battiste, Nancy Woodson and myself were pronounced entitled to the highest reward of merit. In lieu of Franklin Medals, legitimately our due, Mr. Armstrong gave each an order on Deacon James Loring's bookstore for the *Life of Benjamin Franklin.* This is the copy I received! The white medal scholars were invited guests to the Faneuil Hall dinner. Having a boy's curiosity to be spectator at the "feast of reason and the flow of soul," I made good my court with one of the waiters, who allowed me to seem to serve others as the fee for serving myself, the physical being then with me subordinate. Mr. Armstrong improved a prudent moment in whispering to me, "*You* ought to be here with the other *boys*." Of course, the same idea had more than once been mine, but his remark, while witnessing the honors awarded to white scholars, only augmented my sensitiveness all the more, by the intuitive inquiry which I eagerly desired to express: "If you think so, why have you not taken steps to bring it about?"

The impression made on my mind, by this day's experience, deepened into a solemn vow that, God helping me, I would do my best to hasten the day when the color of the skin would be no barrier to equal school rights. . . . While I would not in the smallest degree detract from the credit justly due the *men* for their conspicuous exertions in this reform, truth enjoins upon me the pleasing duty of acknowledging that to the *women,* and the *children* also, is the cause especially indebted for success.

In the dark hours of our struggle, when betrayed by traitors within and beset by foes without, while some men would become lukewarm and indifferent, despairing of victory, then did the women keep the flame alive; and as their hopes would weave bright visions for the future, their husbands and brothers would rally for a new attack upon the fortress of Colorphobia. Yes, sir, it was the *mothers* (God bless them!) of these little bright-eyed boys and girls, who, through every step of our progress, were executive and vigilant, even to that memorable Monday morning (September 3, 1855), the trial hour, when the colored children of Boston went up to occupy the long-promised land. It was these mothers who accompanied me to the various schoolhouses, to residences of teachers and committeemen, to see the laws of the old Bay State applied in good faith.

An omniconsciousness of my own experience when a schoolboy—and how my heart would have leaped in the enjoyment then of equal school rights—has proved a strong incentive to my interest for your boys and girls; for, having none of my own, I took the liberty of adopting them all as my children. And the smiles of approbation with which so many of them have greeted me in their homes and the highways and byways of life have imparted to me a wealth of inspiration and encouragement not obtainable from any other source. He that makes glad the heart of a child receives in return whole volumes of benedictions and is richer far than if upon his brow were entwined a monarch's diadem.

These mothers have also labored at home to instill into the minds of their children the necessity of striving to obtain, as also to appreciate, those rights—emulating that New England mother who was said to mingle instruction in her children's bread and milk and put good morals into their apple pies! With commendable zeal, the boys and girls have endeavored to profit by these counsels.

On the morning preceding their advent to the public schools, I saw from my window a boy passing the exclusive Smith School, where he had been a pupil, and raising his hands, he exultingly exclaimed to his companions, *"Goodbye forever, colored school! Tomorrow we are like other Boston boys."*

In my daily walks, I behold the companionship, in studies and healthful glee, of boys and girls of all colors and races in these temples of learning, so justly a theme of pride to every citizen —sights and sounds indeed to me chief among ten thousand, and altogether lovely.

And since the third of September to the present time, the sun, moon and stars are regular in their courses! No orb has proved so eccentric as to shoot madly from its sphere in consequence, and the State House on Beacon Hill, and old Faneuil Hall, remain as firm on their bases as ever. . . .

To the colored boys and girls of Boston it may now in truth be said, "The lines have fallen to you in pleasant places." Behold, you have a goodly heritage! May it stimulate you to heed the voice of Wisdom, as she sweetly offers the choicest treasures of her gathered stores:

> With eager hand the glowing page to turn,
> To scan the earth and cleave the distant sky,
> And find the force that holds the planets in their spheres.

Do not waste your spring of youth in idle dalliance, but plant rich seeds to blossom in your manhood and bear fruit when you are old. The public schools of Boston are the gateways to the pursuits of honor and usefulness, and if rightly improved by you, the imagination almost wearies as future prospects dawn upon its vision; for

> Hills peep o'er hills, and Alps on Alps arise.

In response to your floral tribute, so pleasing and acceptable, allow me to say that I need it not as an evidence of your satisfaction with the rights obtained, or my participancy therein, for the pleasure of the service has abundantly rewarded me.

Endeavor to retain the impressions made upon your memories by this meeting, for, after all, you children are the parties benefited. Your parents have labored to achieve this good for you, and to them you must ever render due honor. The three children of an Eastern lady were invited to furnish her with an expression of their love before she went on a long journey. One brought a marble tablet, with the inscription of her name; another presented her with a garland of flowers; the third entered her presence, and thus accosted her: "Mother, I have neither marble tablet nor fragrant nosegay, but I have a *heart*. *Here* your name is engraved; *here* your name is precious; and this *heart*, full of affection, will follow you wherever you travel, and remain with you wherever you repose." I know of no more appropriate advice to boys and girls than to commend their imitation of that child's example; and when a few short years shall have rolled away and all proscription shall have done its work in the land, may

> You love at times to pause, and strew the way
> With the wild flowers that luxuriant pend
> From spring's gay branches, that whene'er you send
> Your Memory to retrace your pilgrimage,
> She by those flowers her winding course may bend,
> Back through each twilight and each weary stage,
> And with those early flowers wreathe the white brow of age.

I could cull from my chapter of experience and observation many an unkind and insulting remark uttered against the rights of colored children in Boston, by school-committee men, editors and others occupying responsible positions; but, as they can be reserved for future use to "point a moral" if *not* to "adorn a tale," let us, in this hour of victory, be magnanimous enough to cover with the charity of our silence the names of *all* who have opposed us.

Madam, in accepting this elegant token from your hands, I am not vain enough to monopolize the honor and gratitude so eminently due to those I have mentioned and others who have promoted this great work. Let it be regarded as a joint offering to them all, to be held in trust by me only so long as I am faithful to the elevation of those with whom I am identified by complexion and condition—the cause of humanity. . . .

THE NEGRO RACE, SELF-GOVERNMENT AND THE HAITIAN REVOLUTION

By James T. Holly

Throughout the pre-Civil War years, the Haitian Revolution continued to serve as a theme for speeches by black Americans.* But no one so effectively discoursed on the events in Haiti before, during and after the first black Republic in the world was established as did James T. Holly, a former shoemaker, in the following speech. Holly (1829–1911) was a frequent visitor to Haiti. On his return from the island in the fall of 1855, he delivered this lecture on the history of Haiti as a vindication of the ability of the Negro people to establish self-government and achieve progress. During the summer of 1856 he repeated the lecture in Ohio, Michigan and Canada. As the foremost advocate of emigration to Haiti in the decade before the Civil War, Holly closed his lecture with a fervent appeal for Negroes to leave the United States and move to Haiti rather than to Africa. He himself finally settled in Haiti.

In 1857 the lecture was published† by the Afric American Printing Company of New Haven, Connecticut, an organization formed to publish Negro literature, especially writings and speeches favoring emigration. The pamphlet was dedicated by Holly to the Reverend William C. Munroe, Rector of St. Matthew's Church, Detroit, who had served as a missionary in Haiti.

Though some of Holly's interpretations of events during and after the Haitian Revolution would not pass the test of modern scholarship, they were important in their day for dispelling numerous falsehoods about the black Republic.

---

* See James McCune Smith, *A Lecture on the Haytian Revolution: with a Sketch of the Character of Toussaint L'Ouverture* (Delivered at the Stuyvesant Institute, for the benefit of the Colored Orphan Asylum, February 26, 1841), New York, 1841.

† James T. Holly, *A Vindication of the Capacity of the Negro Race for Self-Government and Civilized Progress as Demonstrated by Historical Events of the Haytian Revolution* (New Haven, 1857).

. . . THE TASK that I propose to myself in the present
lecture is an earnest attempt to defend the inherent capabilities
of the Negro race for self-government and civilized progress.
For this purpose I will examine the events of Haitian history
from the commencement of their revolution down to the
present period, so far as the same may contribute to illustrate
the points I propose to prove and defend. Permit me, however,
to add, in extenuation of this last comprehensive proposition,
that I must necessarily review these events hastily, in order
to crowd them within the compass of an ordinary lecture.

Reasons for Assuming Such a Task

Notwithstanding the remarkable progress of philanthropic
ideas and humanitarian feelings during the last half century,
among almost every nation and people throughout the habitable
globe, yet the great mass of the Causasian race will deem the
Negro as entirely destitute of those qualities on which they
selfishly predicate their own superiority.

And we may add to this overwhelming class that cherish
such self-complacent ideas of themselves—to the great prejudice of the Negro—a large quota also of that small portion of
the white race, who profess to believe the truths "that God is no
respecter of persons," and that "He has made of one blood all
the nations that dwell upon the face of the earth." Yes, I say,
we may add a large number of the noisy agitators of the present
day, who would persuade themselves and the world that they
are really Christian philanthropists, to that overwhelming
crowd who openly traduce the Negro; because too many of
those pseudo humanitarians have lurking in their heart of
hearts a secret infidelity in regard to the real equality of the
black man, which is ever ready to manifest its concealed sting,
when the full and unequivocal recognition of the Negro in all
respects is pressed home upon their hearts.

Hence, between this downright prejudice against this long-
abused race, which is flauntingly maintained by myriads of
their oppressors, on the one hand, and this woeful distrust of
his natural equality among those who claim to be his friends,
on the other, no earnest and fearless efforts are put forth to
vindicate their character by even the few who may really acknowledge this equality of the races. They are overawed by the
overpowering influence of the contrary sentiment. This sentiment unnerves their hands and palsies their tongue; and no pen
is wielded or voice heard among that race of men which fearlessly and boldly places the Negro side by side with the white
man as his equal in all respects. But to the contrary, everything

is done by the enemies of the Negro race to vilify and debase them. And the result is that many of the race themselves are almost persuaded that they are a brood of inferior beings.

It is, then, to attempt a fearless but truthful vindication of this race with which I am identified—however feeble and immature that effort may be—that I now proceed to set forth the following address:

I wish, by the undoubted facts of history, to cast back the vile aspersions and foul calumnies that have been heaped upon my race for the last four centuries by our unprincipled oppressors, whose base interest, at the expense of our blood and our bones, have made them reiterate from generation to generation during the long march of ages everything that would prop up the impious dogma of our natural and inherent inferiority.

An Additional Reason for the Present Task

But this is not all. I wish hereby to contribute my influence—however small that influence—to effect a grander and dearer object to our race than even this truthful vindication of them before the world. I wish to do all in my power to inflame the latent embers of self-respect that the cruelty and injustice of our oppressors have nearly extinguished in our bosoms during the midnight chill of centuries that we have clanked the galling chains of slavery. To this end, I wish to remind my oppressed brethren, that dark and dismal as this horrid night has been and sorrowful as the general reflections are, in regard to our race, yet, notwithstanding these discouraging considerations, there are still some proud historic recollections, linked indissolubly with the most important events of the past and present century, which break the general monotony and remove some of the gloom that hangs over the dark historic period of African slavery and the accursed traffic in which it was cradled.

The Revolutionary History of Haiti
THE BASIS OF THIS ARGUMENT

These recollections are to be found in the history of the heroic events of the Revolution of Haiti.

This revolution is one of the noblest, grandest, and most justifiable outbursts against tyrannical oppression that are recorded on the pages of the world's history.

A race of almost dehumanized men—made so by an oppressive slavery of three centuries—arose from their slumber of ages and redressed their own unparalleled wrongs with a terrible hand in the name of God and humanity.

In this terrible struggle for liberty, the Lord of Hosts directed their arms to be the instruments of His judgment on their oppressors, as the recompense of His violated law of love between man and his fellow, which these tyrants of the new world had been guilty of in the centuries of blood, wrong and oppression, which they had perpetrated on the Negro race in that isle of the Caribbean Sea.

But aside from this great providential and religious view of this great movement that we are always bound to seek for in all human affairs, to see how they square with the mind of God, more especially if they relate to the destinies of nations and people, the Haitian Revolution is also the grandest political event of this or any other age. In weighty causes and wondrous and momentous features, it surpasses the American Revolution, in an incomparable degree. The revolution of this country was only the revolt of a people already comparatively free, independent, and highly enlightened. Their greatest grievance was the imposition of three pence per pound tax on tea, by the mother country, without their consent. But the Haitian Revolution was a revolt of an uneducated and menial class of slaves against their tyrannical oppressors, who not only imposed an absolute tax on their unrequited labor, but also usurped their very bodies, and who would have been prompted by the brazen infidelity of the age then rampant to dispute with the Almighty the possession of the souls of these poor creatures, could such brazen effrontery have been of any avail, to have wrung more ill-gotten gain out of their victims to add to their worldly goods.

These oppressors, against whom the Negro insurgents of Haiti had to contend, were not only the government of a far-distant mother country, as in the case of the American revolution; but unlike and more fearful than this revolt, the colonial government of Haiti was also thrown in the balance against the Negro revolters. The American revolters had their colonial government in their own hands, as well as their individual liberty at the commencement of the revolution. The black insurgents of Haiti had yet to grasp both their personal liberty and the control of their colonial government, by the might of their own right hands, when their heroic struggle began.

The obstacles to surmount and the difficulties to contend against in the American Revolution, when compared to those of the Haitian, were (to use a homely but classic phrase) but a "tempest in a teapot" compared to the dark and lurid thunder-storm of the dissolving heavens.

Never before, in all the annals of the world's history, did a nation of abject and chattel slaves arise in the terrific might of their resuscitated manhood and regenerate, redeem and dis-enthral themselves by taking their station at one gigantic bound as an independent nation among the sovereignties of the world.

It is, therefore, the unparalleled incidents that led to this wonderful event that I now intend to review rapidly, in order to demonstrate thereby the capacity of the Negro race for self-government and civilized progress, to the fullest extent and in the highest sense of these terms.

Preliminary Incidents of the Revolution

I shall proceed to develop the first evidence of the compe-tency of the Negro race for self-government, amid the historical incidents that preceded their terrible and bloody revolution, and in the events of that heroic struggle itself.

When the cosmopolitan ideas of Liberty, Fraternity and Equality, which swayed the mighty minds of France toward the close of the eighteenth century, reached the colony of Santo Domingo, through the Massaic Club, composed of wealthy co-lonial planters, organized in the French capital, all classes in that island, except the black slave and the free colored man, were instantly wrought up to the greatest effervescence and swayed with the deepest emotions by the startling doctrines of the equal political rights of all men, which were then so boldly enunciated in the face of the tyrannical despotisms and the im-memorial assumptions of the feudal aristocracies of the old world.

The colonial dignitaries, the military officers, and other agents of the government of France then resident in Santo Do-mingo, the rich planters and the poor whites (these latter called in the parlance of that colony "Les petits blancs") were all from first to last swayed with the intensest and the most indescribable feelings at the promulgation of these bold and radical theories.

All were in a perfect fever to realize and enjoy the priceless boon of political and social privileges that these revolutionary ideas held out before them. And in their impatience to grasp these precious prerogatives, they momentarily forgot their co-lonial dependence on France and spontaneously came together in a general assembly at a small town of Santo Domingo called St. Marc, and proceeded to deliberate seriously about taking upon themselves all the attributes of national sovereignty and independence.

And when they had deliberately matured plans to suit themselves, they did not hesitate to send representatives to propose them to the national government of France for its acknowledgment and acquiescence in their desires.

Such was the radical consequence to which the various classes of white colonists in Santo Domingo seized upon and carried the cosmopolitan theories of the French philosophers and political agitators of the last century.

But from all this excitement and enthusiasm I have already excepted the black and colored inhabitants of that island.

The white colonists of Santo Domingo, like our *liberty-loving* and *democratic* fellow citizens of the United States, never meant to include this despised race in their glowing dreams of "Liberty, Equality and Fraternity."

Like our *model republicans*, they looked upon this hated race of beings as placed so far down the scale of humanity that when the Rights of Man were spoken of, they did not imagine that the most distant reference was thereby made to the Negro or anyone through whose veins his tainted blood sent its crimsoned tide.

And so blind were they to the fact that the Rights of Man could be so construed as to recognize the humanity of that oppressed race that when the National Assembly of France, swayed by the just representations of the "Friends of the Blacks," was led to extend equal political rights to the free men of color in Santo Domingo at the same time that this national body ratified the doings of the General Colonial Assembly of St. Marc, these same colonists who had been so loud in their hurrahs for the Rights of Man now ceased their clamors for liberty in the face of this just national decree and sullenly resolved "to die rather than share equal political rights with a bastard race." Such was the insulting term that this colonial assembly then applied to the free men of color, in whose veins coursed the blood of the proud planter, commingled with that of the lowly Negress.

The Self-Possession of the Blacks

AN EVIDENCE OF THEIR CAPACITY FOR SELF-GOVERNMENT

The exceptional part which the blacks played in the moving drama that was then being enacted in Santo Domingo, by their stern self-possession amid the furious excitement of the whites, is one of the strongest proofs that can be adduced to

substantiate the capabilities of the Negro race for self-government.

The *careless reserve* of the seemingly dehumanized black
slave, who continued to toil and delve on in the monotonous
round of plantation labor, under a cruel task master, in a manner so entirely heedless of the furious hurrahs for freedom and
independence, the planting of Liberty poles surmounted by the
cap of Liberty, and the erection of statues to the goddess of
Liberty, which was going on around him—this apparent indifference and carelessness to the surging waves of freedom
that were then awakening the despotisms of earth from their
slumber of ages, showed that the slave understood and appreciated the difficulties of his position. He felt that the hour of
destiny, appointed by the Almighty, had not yet tolled its summons for him to arise and avenge the wrong of ages.

He therefore remained heedless of the effervescence of liberty that bubbled over in the bosom of the white man, and continued at his sullen labors, biding his time for deliverance. And
in this judicious reserve on the part of the blacks we have one of
the strongest traits of self-government.

When we look upon this characteristic of cool self-possession,
we cannot but regard it as almost a miracle under the circumstances. We cannot see what magic power could keep such a
warm-blooded race of men in such an icebound spell of cold
indifference, when every other class of men in that colony was
flush with the excitement of *liberty* and the whole island was
rocked to its center with the deafening surges of "Equality" that
echoed from ten thousand throats.

One would have supposed, that at the very first sound of freedom, the 500,000 bondmen in that island, whose ancestry for
three centuries had worn the yoke of slavery, would have raised
up at once in their overwhelming numerical power and physical
stalwartness and cried out "Liberty!" with a voice so powerful
as to have cleft asunder the bowels of the earth and buried
slavery and every Negro hater and oppressor who might dare
oppose their just rights, in one common grave.

But, as I have said, they did no such thing; they had a conscious faith in the ultimate designs of God; and they silently
waited, trusting to the workings of His overruling Providence
to bring about the final day of their deliverance. In doing so, I
claim they have given an evidence of their ability to govern
themselves that ought to silence all proslavery calumniators of
my race at once, and forever, by its powerful and undying refutation of their slanders.

And let no one dare to rob them of this glorious trait of character, either by alleging that they remained thus indifferent, because they were too ignorant to appreciate the blessings of liberty or by saying that if they understood the import of these clamors for the Rights of Man, they were thus quiet, because they were too cowardly to strike for their disenthrallment.

The charge that they were thus ignorant of the priceless boon of freedom, is *refuted* by the antecedent history of the servile insurrections, which never ceased to rack that island from 1522 down to the era of Negro independence. The Negro insurgents, Polydore, Macandel* and Padrejan, who had at various times led on their enslaved brethren to daring deeds in order to regain their God-given liberty, brand that assertion as a libel on the Negro character, that says he was too cowardly to strike for the inheritance of its precious boon.

And the desperate resolution to be free that the Maroon Negroes† of the island maintained for eighty-five years, by their valorous struggles in their wild mountain fastnesses against the concentrated and combined operations of the French and Spanish authorities then in that colony, and which finally compelled these authorities to conclude a treaty with the intrepid Maroon chief, Santiago, and thereby acknowledge their freedom forever thereafter—this fact, I say, proves him to be a base calumniator who shall dare to say that a keen appreciation of liberty existed not in the bosom of the Negroes of Santo Domingo.

But again, as to the plea of cowardice, in order to account for the fact of their cool self-possession amidst the first convulsive throes of revolutionary liberty, permit me to add in refutation of this fallacy that, if the daring incidents of anteced-

---

* After he had run away from his master in 1740, François Macandal (or Macandel) waged a relentless war against the landowners of Saint Domingue and poisoned a number of white settlers, overseers, and even some slaves who refused to turn against their masters. In 1758, Macandal and his associates among the slaves made elaborate plans for an insurrection which would drive the whites off the island. But the plot, betrayed by a young black, was suppressed. Macandal was captured, condemned to death and burned alive at Cap Français.

† Maroons were runaway slaves who established their own communities in mountains, swamps and forests. They were numerous in the Caribbean and Brazil but also existed in the United States. Prior to the great Revolution of 1791 which led to the establishment of the black Republic of Haiti, Saint Domingue had a whole century of Maroon activity with bands of Negroes establishing hideouts in the woods and the more inaccessible plantations, maintaining themselves by night raids on neighboring plantations for food and weapons.

ent insurrections do not sufficiently refute this correlative charge also, then the daring deeds of dreadless heroism performed by a Toussaint, a Dessalines, a Rigaud, and a Christophe, in the subsequent terrible but necessary revolution of the Negroes in which black troops gathered from the plantations of slavery met the best-appointed armies of France, and at various times those of England and Spain also, and proved their equal valor and prowess with these best-disciplined armies of Europe—this dreadless heroism evinced by the blacks, I say, is sufficient to nail the infamous imputation of cowardice to the wall at once and forever.

Hence, nothing shall rob them of the immaculate glory of exhibiting a stern self-possession in that feverish hour of excitement, when everybody around them was crying out "Liberty." And in this judicious self-control at this critical juncture, when their destiny hung on the decision of the hour, we have a brilliant illustration of the capacity of the race for self-government.

Similar Evidence on the Part of the Free Men of Color

But additional and still stronger evidence of this fact crowds upon us, when we see that the free men of color remained entirely passive during the first stage of this revolutionary effervescence. This class of men, as a general thing, was educated and wealthy; and they were burthened with duties by the state, without being invested with corresponding political privileges. From such unjust exactions they had every reason to seek a speedy deliverance. And this great tumult that now swept over the island, offered them a propitious opportunity to agitate with the rest of the free men of the colony for the removal of their political disabilities.

They had greater cause to agitate than the whites, because they suffered under heavier burdens than that class. Nevertheless, in the first great outbreak of the waterfloods of liberty, tempting as the occasion was, and difficult as restraint must have been, yet the free men of color also possessed their souls in patience and awaited a more propitious opportunity. Certainly no one will attempt to stigmatize the calm judgment of these men in this awful crisis of suspense as the result of ignorance of the blessings of freedom, when it is known that many of this class were educated in the seminaries of France, under her most brilliant professors, and that they were also patrons of that prodigy of literature, the Encyclopedia of France.

Neither can they stigmatize this class of men as cowards, as it is also known that they were the voluntary compeers of the

Revolutionary heroes of the United States, and who, under the banners of France, mingled their sable blood with the Saxon and the French in the heroic battle of Savannah.

Then this calm indifference of the men of color in this crisis, notwithstanding the blood of three excitable races mingled in their veins with that of the African (viz., that of the French, the Spanish and the Indian) and notwithstanding they had glorious recollections of their services in the cause of American independence inciting them on—this calm indifference, on their part, I say, notwithstanding these exciting causes, is another grand and striking illustration of the conservative characteristics of the Negro race that demonstrate their capacity for self-government.

The Opportune Movement of the Free Colored Men

The tumultuous events of this excitement among the white colonists rolled onward and brought the auspicious hour of Negro destiny in that island nearer and nearer, when Providence designed that he should play his part in the great drama of freedom that was then being enacted. Of course, the propitious moment for the free men of color to begin to move would present itself prior to that for the movement of the Negro slaves.

The opportunity for the men of color presented itself when the General Colonial Assembly of St. Marc's (already referred to) sent deputies to France, to present the result of its deliberations to the National Assembly, and to ask that august body to confer on the colony the right of self-government.

At this time, therefore, when the affairs of the colony were about to undergo examination in the supreme legislature of the mother country, the free men of color seized upon the occasion to send deputies to France also, men of their own caste, to represent their grievances and make their wishes known to the National Assembly. This discreet discernment of such an opportune moment to make such a movement divested of every other consideration shows a people who understand themselves, what they want, and how to seek it.

But when we proceed to consider the most approved manner in which the representations were made to the National Assembly by the colored delegates in behalf of their caste in the colony of Santo Domingo, and the influences they brought to bear upon that body as exhibited hereafter, we shall perceive thereby that they showed such an intimate acquaintance with the secret springs of governmental machinery as demonstrated at once their capacity to govern themselves.

This deputation first drew up a statement in behalf of their caste in the colony, of such a stirring nature as would be certain to command the national sympathy in their cause, when presented to the National Assembly. But previously to presenting it to that assembly, they took the wise precaution to wait upon the honorable president of that august body, in order to enlist and commit him in their favor, as the first steppingstone to secure the success of their object before the supreme legislature.

They prevailed in their mission to the president of the Assembly and succeeded in obtaining this very emphatic assurance from him: "No part of the nation shall vainly reclaim their rights before the assembly of the representatives of the French people."

Having accomplished this important step, the colored deputies next began to operate through the Abolition Society of Paris, called "Les Amis des Noirs," upon such of the members of the Assembly as were affiliated with this society and thus already indirectly pledged to favor such a project as theirs, asking simple justice for their race. They were again successful, and Charles De Lameth, one of the zealous patrons of that society and an active member of the National Assembly, was engaged to argue their cause before the supreme legislature of the nation —although, strange to say, he was himself a colonial slaveholder at that time.

And at the appointed moment in the National Assembly, this remarkable man felt prompted to utter these astounding words in behalf of this oppressed and disfranchised class of the colony: "I am one of the greatest proprietors of Santo Domingo; yet I declare to you that, sooner than lose sight of principles so sacred to justice and humanity, I would prefer to lose all that I possess. I declare myself in favor of admitting the men of color to the rights of citizenship, and in favor of the freedom of the blacks."

Now let us for a moment stop and reflect on the measures resorted to by the colored deputies of Santo Domingo, in Paris, who, by their wise stratagems, had brought their cause step by step to such an eventful and auspicious crisis as this.

Could there have been surer measures concocted for the success of their plans than thus committing the president of the Assembly to their cause in the first place, and afterwards pressing a liberty-loving slaveholder into their service, to thunder their measures through the National Assembly by such a bold declaration?

Who among the old fogies of Tammany Hall*—that junta of

* Tammany Hall was the leading Democratic club in New York City.

scheming politicians who govern this country by pulling the wires of party and thereby making every official of the nation, from the President of the United States down to the Commissioners for Street Sweeping in the City of New York, dance as so many puppets at their bidding—I repeat it—who among these all powerful but venal politicians of old Tammany could have surpassed these tactics of those much-abused men of color who thus swayed the secret springs of the National Assembly of France? And who, after this convincing proof to the contrary, shall dare to say that the Negro race is not capable of self-government?

But to return to the thread of our narrative. When the secret springs had been thus secured in their behalf, they had nothing to fear from the popular heart of the nation, already keenly alive to the sentiments of Liberty, Equality and Fraternity, because the simple justice of their demands would commend them to the people as soon as they were publicly made known in France.

In order to make the very best impression on the popular heart of the nation, their petition demanding simple justice to their caste was accompanied with a statement very carefully drawn up.

In this statement they showed that their caste in the colony of Santo Domingo possessed one third of the real estate, and one fourth of the personal effects of the island. They also set forth the advantages of their position in the political and social affairs of Santo Domingo, as a balance of power in the hand of the imperial government of France, against the high pretensions of the haughty planters on the one hand and the seditious spirit of the poor whites on the other. And, as an additional consideration, by way of capping the climax, they offered, in the name and in behalf of the free men of color in the colony, six millions of francs as a loyal contribution to the wants and financial exigencies of the national treasury, to be employed in liquidating the debt of their common country.

Thus, if neither their wire-working maneuvers, the justice of their cause nor the conservative influence which their position gave them in the colony had been enough to secure the end which they sought, then the tempting glitter of so much cash could not be resisted when its ponderous weight was also thrown in the scale of justice. They succeeded, as a matter of course, in accomplishing their purpose; and the National Assembly of France promulgated a decree on the eighth of March, 1790, securing equal political rights to the men of color.

The very success of this movement and the means by which

its success was effected, the opportune moment when it was commenced and the immense odds that were against those that sought its accomplishment—all these things must hereafter be emblazoned on the historic page as an everlasting tribute to the genius of the Negro race and remain an ineffaceable evidence of their capacity for self-government, that may be triumphantly adduced and proudly pointed at in this and every succeeding generation of the world, until the latest syllable of recorded time.

The Crisis Produced in the Colony by This Decree

THE MEN OF COLOR ON THE SIDE OF LIBERTY, LAW AND ORDER

It was when this decree was made known in the colony of Santo Domingo, that the General Assembly of the colony, then sitting at St. Marc's, expressed the malignant sentiments of the white colonists in a resolution that I have already quoted—viz., they resolved that they would "rather die, than share equal political rights with a bastard race."

Vincent Oje, a man of color and one of the delegates to Paris in behalf of his caste, anticipated a venomous feeling of this kind against his race on the part of the white colonists, when these decrees should be made known to them. He, however, resolved to do whatever was within his power to allay this rancorous feeling. He did not, therefore, hasten home to the colony immediately after the decree was promulgated. He delayed, in order to allow time for their momentary excitement as expressed in the resolution above, to cool off by a more calm reflection on their sober second thought. He also tarried in France, to secure a higher political end, by which he would be personally prepared to return to Santo Domingo, to make the most favorable impression in behalf of his race and the objects of that decree on the minds of the white colonists.

To this end he succeeds in getting the appointment of Commissioner of France from the French government, to superintend the execution of the decree of the eighth of March, 1790, in the island of Santo Domingo.

Certainly, he might hope that, being invested with the sacred dignity of France, his person, his race (thus honored through him by that imperial government) and the national decree itself with which he was charged would now be respected.

But not content with accumulating the national honors of France, fearing lest the proslavery colonists would disregard these high prerogatives by looking upon them as having been obtained through the *fanatical* "Friends of the Blacks" at Paris, by those partisans exerting an undue influence on the national government, he further proceeds to gather additional honors, by ingratiating himself into the favor of a potentate of Holland, the Prince of Limbourg, from whom he received the rank of lieutenant colonel and the Order of the Lion. Thus he wished to demonstrate to the infatuated colonists, who regarded his race as beneath their consideration, that he could not only obtain titles and reputation in France, by means of ardent friends, but that over and above these, and beyond the boundaries of France, he could also command a European celebrity.

This was indeed a splendid course of conduct on his part; and by thus gathering around him and centering within himself these commanding prestiges of respect, he demonstrated his thorough knowledge of one of the most important secrets in the art of governing, and so far made another noble vindication of the capacity of the Negro race for self-government.

But as we proceed to consider the manner that he afterward undertook to prosecute his high national commission in promulgating in Santo Domingo the decree of the eighth of March, 1790, we shall see additional evidence of the same master skill crowd upon us.

He had now delayed his return from Europe in order to allow time for the allaying of hasty excitement, and for the purpose of making the most favorable advent to the island.

He comes a commissioned envoy of the French nation and an honored chevalier of Europe. Nevertheless, with that prudent foresight which anticipates all possible emergencies, he landed in Santo Domingo in a cautious and unostentatious manner, so as not to provoke any forcible demonstration against him. Having landed, he gathered around him a suite of two hundred men for his personal escort, which his station justified him in having as his cortege, and which might also serve the very convenient purpose of a bodyguard to defend him against any attempt at a cowardly assassination from any lawless or ruthless desperadoes of oppression in the colony.

At the head of this body of men, he at once proceeded to place himself in communication with the Colonial Assembly, then in session, to inform it officially of his commission and the national decree which he bore, and to require that assembly, as the legislative authority of the island, to enforce its observance by enacting an ordinance in accordance with the same.

In this communication of Oje, being aware of their proslavery prejudices, he endeavored to conciliate them by a peace offering. That peace offering was the sanctioning of Negro slavery, for he stated to the assembly that the decree did not refer to the blacks in servitude; neither did the men of color, said he, desire to acknowledge their equality.

This specific assurance on the part of Oje, although it does not speak much for his high sense of justice, when abstractly considered, yet shows as much wisdom and tact in the science of government as is evinced by the sapient or *sap*-headed legislators of this country who make similar compromises as a peace offering to the prejudice and injustice of the oligarchic despots of this nation.

Oje, however, failed to make the desired impression on the infatuated colonists, either by his national and European dignities or by his peace offering of 500,000 of his blacker brethren. He fell beneath the malignant hate of the slaveholding colonists, after defending himself with his little band of followers against the overwhelming odds of these sanguinary tigers with a manly heroism only equaled by the Spartans at the pass of Thermopylae, and thus has cut for himself an enduring niche among the heroes in the temple of fame.

He was captured; and after a mock trial, illustrative of pro-slavery justice—something similar, for instance, to our Fugitive Slave Law trials in Boston, Philadelphia and Cincinnati—(though more merciful in its penalty than these)—this mock court of Santo Domingo condemned Vincent Oje and his brave lieutenant, Jean Chevanne, with their surviving compatriots, to be broken alive on the wheel.

We forget the error of the head committed by this right-hearted, noble and generous man toward his more unfortunate brethren, in order to weep over his ignoble and unworthy fate, received at the hands of those monsters of cruelty in Santo Domingo.

I cannot better close this notice of Oje than by repeating the concluding lines from a poem dedicated to him, by that distinguished man of color, our own fellow countryman, Professor George B. Vashon, of McGrawville College: *

> Sad was your fate, heroic band,
> Yet mourn we not, for yours the stand
> Which will secure to you a fame,
> That never dieth, and a name
> That will, in coming ages be
> A signal word for Liberty.
> Upon the Slave's o'erclouded sky,

* George B. Vashon, a graduate of Oberlin College, lawyer and poet, held the professorship of belles lettres at Central College, in McGrawville, New York.

Your gallant actions traced the bow,
Which whispered of deliverance nigh—
The need of one decisive blow.
Thy coming fame, Oje! is sure;
Thy name with that of L'Ouverture,
And the noble souls that stood
With both of you, in times of blood,
Will live to be the tyrant's fear—
Will live, the sinking soul to cheer!

The Hour of Destiny for the Blacks

This untimely death of the great leader of the men of color served only to demonstrate how plentifully the race was supplied with sagacious characters, capable of performing daring deeds; it served to show how well the race was supplied with the material out of which great leaders are made, at any moment, and for any exigency.

Now came the hour for the patient, delving black slave to begin to move. He has manfully bided his time, whilst the white colonists were rampant in pursuit of high political prerogatives; and he has remained quiet, whilst his brother, the freed man of color, has carried his cause demanding equal political rights triumphantly through the National Assembly of France.

But, most intolerable of all, he has been perfectly still, whilst his more fortunate brethren have offered even to strike hands with the vile oppressor in keeping the iron yoke on his neck.

Nevertheless, he has lived to see both of these classes foiled by the overruling hand of Providence from interpreting the words "Liberty, Equality and Fraternity" to suit their own selfish and narrow notions. He finds these two parties now at open hostilities with one another. He sees, on one hand, the despicable colonists inviting foreign aid into the island, to resist the execution of the national decree and to prop up their unhallowed cause by the dread alternative of treason and rebellion, whilst on the other hand, he beholds the men of color fighting on the side of the nation, law and order, against the white colonists. Amid this general commotion his pulsations grow quick and he feels that the hour of destiny is coming for *even* him to strike.

Yet he still possesses his soul in patience until the destined moment. At last he hears that France now vacillates in carrying out the tardy measure of justice that her national legislature had enacted. The mother country that had so nobly commenced the work of justice, by the national decree enfranchising the free men of color, now begins to recede from the high position she had assumed in order to favor the frenzied prejudice of the infatuated colonists. The Negro slave had hoped that, by this national act of justice to the free man of color, a permanent step had been taken toward universal emancipation and consequently his own eventual disenthrallment. With this hope he was willing to continue quietly to wear his galling chains, rejoicing in the newly acquired boon of his more fortunate brethren as the earnest and pledge of his own future deliverance by a similar act of national justice. Thus the way seemed already paved for a peaceful termination of his servitude.

But, I repeat it again, the toiling black slave at last hears that the national government of France vacillates in her judgment, quails before the storm of proslavery invectives hurled by the insensate bigots of Santo Domingo against the men of color; and finally she recedes from her high position by the National Assembly repealing the decree of the eighth of March, 1790. Thus the slaves' dawning ray of hope and liberty is extinguished, and there is nothing ahead but the impenetrable gloom of eternal slavery.

This, then, is the ominous moment reserved for the chained bondmen to strike; and he rises now from his slumber of degradation in the terrific power of brute force. Bouckman (called by a Haitian historian the Spartacus of his race) was raised up as the leader of the insurgents, who directed their fury in the desperate struggle for liberty and revenge, until the work of devastation and death was spread throughout the island to the most frightful extent. He continued to ride on the storm of revolution in its hurricane march, with a fury that became intensified as it progressed, until the colonists, by some fortuitous circumstances, were enabled to wreak their vengeance on this Negro hero.

But when this first hero of the slaves was captured and executed by their oppressors, like Oje, the first hero of the free men of color, the capacity of the race to furnish leaders equal to any emergency was again demonstrated.

A triumvirate of Negro and mulatto chieftains now succeeded these two martyred heroes.

Jean François, Biassou and Jeannot now appeared upon the stage of action and directed the arms of the exasperated insurgents against a faithless nation, the cruel colonists and their English allies, whose aid these colonists had invited, in their treasonable resistance to the national decree which Oje came from France to promulgate in the name of the nation.

In order to contend against such overwhelming odds effectually, and for the purpose of obtaining the necessary supply of arms and ammunition, the insurgents went over, for a time, to the service of Spain. This government had always regarded the French as usurpers in the island; and the Spaniards were therefore glad of any prospect of expelling the French colonists entirely from Santo Domingo. Hence they gladly accepted the proffered service of the blacks as a means to effect this end.

However, we have no reason to regard the Spanish government as being more favorably disposed toward the blacks than that of France. We may rather conclude that Spain was willing to use the blacks to subserve her end, and afterward would doubtless have endeavored to reduce them to a state of slavery again.

Nevertheless, the black slaves and free men of color went over to the cause of Spain and used her to subserve their purpose in driving France not only to reenact her previous decree in relation to the men of color, but also to proclaim the immediate emancipation of the blacks and to invest them with equal political rights. For this purpose, three national commissioners of France were sent to the island, bearing these decrees of the supreme government.

When this glorious result was thus triumphantly effected, they left the service of Spain and returned to the cause of France again.

During the struggles that took place while the insurgents were in the cause of Spain, the three leaders who headed them when they united with the Spaniards, were shifted, by the fortunes of war, from their chieftainship and replaced by Toussaint and Rigaud, one a black and the other a mulatto, when they returned to the service of France.

These two leaders, at the head of their respective castes in the service of France, fighting on the side of liberty, law and order, compelled the turbulent and treasonable colonists to respect these last national decrees, drove their English allies from the colony and extinguished the Spanish dominion therein, and thus reduced the whole island to the subjection of France.

When we duly consider this shrewd movement of the blacks in thus pressing Spain in their service at that critical moment, when everything depended upon the decision of the hour, by which they were enabled to accomplish such a glorious result, we have thereby presented another strong and convincing proof of the capacity of the Negro to adopt suitable means to accomplish great ends; and it therefore demonstrates in the most powerful manner his ability for self-government.

The Auspicious Dawn of Negro Rule

Toussaint, by his acute genius and daring prowess, made himself the most efficient instrument in accomplishing these important results, contemplated by the three French commissioners, who brought the last decrees of the National Assembly of France, proclaiming liberty throughout the island to all the inhabitants thereof, and thus, like another Washington, proved himself the regenerator and savior of his country.

On this account, therefore, he was solemnly invested with the executive authority of the colony; and their labors having been thus brought to such a satisfactory and auspicious result, two of the commissioners returned home to France.

No man was more competent to sway the civil destinies of these enfranchised bondmen than he who had preserved such an unbounded control over them as their military chieftain and led them on to glorious deeds amid the fortunes of warfare recently waged in that island. And no one else could hold that responsible position of an official mediator between them and the government of France with so great a surety and pledge of their continued freedom as Toussaint L'Ouverture. And there was no other man, in fine, that these rightfully jealous freemen would have permitted to carry out such stringent measures in the island, so nearly verging to serfdom, which were so necessary at that time in order to restore industry, but one of their own caste whose unreserved devotion to the cause of their freedom placed him beyond the suspicion of any treacherous design to reenslave them.

Hence, by these eminent characteristics possessed by Toussaint in a superexcellent degree, he was the very man for the hour, and the only one fitted for the governorship of the colony calculated to preserve the interests of all concerned.

The leading commissioners of France then in the island duly recognized this fact and did not dispute with him the claim to this responsible position. Thus had the genius of Toussaint developed itself to meet an emergency that no other man in the world was so peculiarly prepared to fulfill; and thereby he has added another inextinguishable proof of the capacity of the Negro for self-government.

But if the combination of causes which thus pointed him out as the only man that could safely undertake the fulfillment of the gubernatorial duties are such manifest proofs of Negro capacity, then the manner in which we shall see that he afterward discharged the duties of that official station goes still further to magnify the self-evident fact of Negro capability.

The means that he adopted to heal the internecine dissensions that threatened civil turmoil, and the manner in which he successfully counteracted the machinations of the ambitious General Hedouville, a French commissioner that remained in the colony, who desired to overthrow Toussaint, showed that the Negro chieftain was no tyro in the secret of government.

He also established commercial relations between that island and foreign nations; and he is said to be the first statesman of modern times who promulgated the doctrine of free trade and reduced it to practice. He also desired to secure a constitutional government to Santo Domingo, and for this purpose he assembled around him a select council of the most eminent men in the colony, who drew up a form of constitution under his supervision and approval, and which he transmitted with a commendatory letter to Napoleon Bonaparte, then First Consul of France, in order to obtain the sanction of the imperial government.

But that great bad man did not even acknowledge its receipt to Toussaint; but in his mad ambition he silently meditated when he should safely dislodge the Negro chief from his responsible position, as the necessary prelude to the reenslavement of his sable brethren, whose freedom was secure against his nefarious designs so long as Toussaint stood at the helm of affairs in the colony.

But decidedly the crowning act of Toussaint L'Ouverture's statesmanship was the enactment of the Rural Code, by the operation of which he was successful in restoring industrial prosperity to the island, which had been sadly ruined by the late events of sanguinary warfare. He effectually solved the problem of immediate emancipation and unimpaired industry, by having the emancipated slaves produce thereafter as much of the usual staple productions of the country as was produced under the horrible regime of slavery; nevertheless, the lash was entirely abolished, and a system of wages adopted, instead of the uncompensated toil of the lacerated and delving bondman.

In fact, the island reached the highest degree of prosperity that it ever attained, under the Negro governorship of Toussaint.

The Rural Code, by which so much was accomplished, instead of being the horrible nightmare of despotism—worse than slavery, that some of the proslavery calumniators of Negro freedom and rule would have us believe—was, in fact, nothing more than a prudent government regulation of labor, a regulation which made labor the first necessity of a people in a state of freedom, a regulation which struck a death blow at idleness, the parent of poverty and all the vices, a regulation, in fine, which might be adopted with advantage in every civilized country in the world, and thereby extinguish two thirds of the pauperisms, vagrancy and crime that curse these nations of the earth, and thus lessen the need for poorhouses, police officers, and prisons, that are now sustained at such an enormous expense for the relief of the poor and the correction of felons.

This Haitian Code compelled every vagabond or loafer about the towns and cities, who had no visible means of an honest livelihood, to find an employer and work to do in the rural districts. And if no private employer could be found, then the government employed such on its rural estates, until they had found a private employer. The hours and days of labor were prescribed by this code, and the terms of agreement and compensation between employer and employed were also determined by its provisions. Thus, there could be no private imposition on the laborers; and, as a further security against such a spirit, the government maintained rural magistrates and a rural police, whose duty it was to see to the faithful execution of the law on both sides.

By the arrangement of this excellent and celebrated code, everybody in the commonwealth was sure of work and compensation for the same, either from private employers or from the government. Nobody need fear being starved for want of work to support themselves, as is often the case among the laborers of Europe, and is fast coming to pass in the densely populated communities of this country, where labor is left to take care of itself under the private exploitation of mercenary capitalists. Under this code nobody need fear being exploited by such unprincipled and usurious men, who willingly take advantage of the poor to pay them starvation prices for their labor, because, against such, the law of Toussaint secured to each laborer a living compensation.

By the operation of this code, towns and cities were cleared of all those idle persons who calculate to live by their wits and who commit nine tenths of all the crimes that afflict civilized society. All such were compelled to be engaged at active industrial labors, and thus rendered a help to themselves and a blessing to the community at large.

By this industrial regulation, everything flourished in the island in an unprecedented degree; and the Negro genius of Toussaint, by a bold and straightforward provision for the regulation and protection of his emancipated brethren, effected that high degree of prosperity in Haiti, which all the wisdom of the British nation has not been able to accomplish in her emancipated West India colonies, in consequence of her miserable

shuffling in establishing coolie and Chinese apprenticeship—
that semisystem of slavery—in order to gratify the prejudices of
her proslavery colonial planters, and because of the baneful influence of absentee landlordism, which seems to be an inseparable incident of the British system of property.

Thus did the Negro government of Santo Domingo show
more paternal solicitude for the well-being of her free citizens
than they ever could have enjoyed under the capricious despotism of individual masters who might pretend to care for them;
and thus did it more truly subserve the purposes of a government than any or all of the similar organizations of civilization,
whose only care and object seem to be the protection of the
feudal rights of property in the hands of the wealthy few, leaving the honest labor of the many unprotected, and the poor laborer left to starve or to become a criminal, to be punished
either by incarceration in the jails, prisons and dungeons provided for common felons, or executed on the gallows as the
greatest of malefactors.

The genius of Toussaint by towering so far above the common ideas of this age in relation to the true purposes of government and by carrying out his bold problem with such eminent
success, has thereby emblazoned on the historic page of the
world's statesmanship a fame more enduring than Pitt, who
laid the foundation of a perpetual fund to liquidate the national
debt of England.

I say Toussaint has carved for himself a more enduring fame,
because his scheme was more useful to mankind. The Negro
statesman devised a plan that comprehended in its scope the
well-being of the masses of humanity. But Pitt only laid a
scheme whereby the few hereditary paupers pensioned on a
whole nation, with the absurd right to govern it, might still
continue to plunge their country deeper and deeper into debt,
to subserve their own extravagant purposes, and then provide
for the payment of the same out of the blood and sweat and
bones of the delving operatives and colliers of Great Britain.
Thus, then, Toussaint by the evident superiority of his statesmanship has left on the pages of the world's statute book an
enduring and irrefutable testimony of the capacity of the Negro
for self-government and the loftiest achievements in national
statesmanship.

And Toussaint showed that he had not mistaken his position
by proving himself equal to that trying emergency when that
demigod of the historian Abbott, Napoleon Bonaparte, First
Consul of France, conceived the infernal design of reenslaving
the heroic blacks of Santo Domingo, and who for the execution

of this nefarious purpose sent the flower of the French Army and a naval fleet of fifty-six vessels under command of General Leclerc, the husband of Pauline, the voluptuous and abandoned sister of Napoleon.

When this formidable expedition arrived on the coast of Santo Domingo, the commander found Toussaint and his heroic compeers ready to defend their God-given liberty against even the terrors of the godless First Consul of France. Wheresoever these minions of slavery and despotism made their sacrilegous advances, devastation and death reigned under the exasperated genius of Toussaint.

He made that bold resolution and unalterable determination, which, in ancient times, would have entitled him to be deified among the gods; that resolution was to reduce the fair Eden-like Isle of Hispaniola to a desolate waste like Sahara and suffer every black to be immolated in a manly defense of his liberty, rather than the infernal and accursed system of Negro slavery should again be established on that soil. He considered it far better that his sable countrymen should be dead freemen than living slaves.

The French veterans grew pale at the terrible manner that the blacks set to work to execute this resolution. Leclerc found it impossible to execute his design by force; and he was only able to win the reconciliation of the exasperated blacks to the government of France by abandoning his hostilities and pledging himself to respect their freedom thereafter. It was then that the brave Negro generals of Toussaint went over in the service of Leclerc; and it was then that the Negro chieftain himself resigned his post to the Governor General appointed by Napoleon, and went into the shades of domestic retirement at his home in Ennery.

Thus did Toussaint, by his firm resolution to execute his purpose, by his devotion to liberty and the cause of his race, so consistently maintained under all circumstances, more than deify himself; he proved himself more than a patriot; he showed himself to be the unswerving friend and servant of God and humanity.

Now, with the illustrious traits of character of this brilliant Negro before us, who will dare to say that the race who can thus produce such a noble specimen of a hero and statesman is incapable of self-government? Let such a vile slanderer, if there any longer remains such, hide his diminutive head in the presence of his illustrious Negro superior!

I know it may be said that, after all, Toussaint was found wanting in the necessary qualities to meet and triumph in the last emergency, when he was finally beguiled and sent to perish in the dungeons of France, a victim of the perfidious machinations of the heartless Napoleon.

On this point I will frankly own that Toussaint was deficient in those qualities by which his antagonist finally succeeded in getting him in his power.

So long as manly skill and shrewdness, so long as bold and open tactics and honorable stratagems were resorted to, the black had proved himself, in every respect, the equal of the white man. But the Negro's heart had not yet descended to that infamous depth of subtle depravity that could justify him in solemnly and publicly taking an oath, with the concealed, jesuitical purpose of thereby gaining an opportunity to deliberately violate the same. He had no conception, therefore, that the white man from whom he had learned all that he knew of true religion—I repeat it, he had no conception that the white man, bad as he was, slaveholder as he was—that *even* he was really so debased, vile and depraved as to be capable of such a double-dyed act of villainy as breaking an oath solemnly sealed by invoking the name of the Eternal God of Ages.

Hence, when the Captain General Leclerc said to Toussaint, in presence of the French and black generals, uplifting his hand and jeweled sword to heaven, "I swear before the face of the Supreme Being to respect the liberty of the people of Santo Domingo," Toussaint believed in the sincerity of this solemn oath of the white man. He threw down his arms and went to end the remainder of his days in the bosom of his family. This was, indeed, a sad mistake for him, to place so much confidence in the word of the white man. As the result of this first error, he easily fell into another equally treacherous. He was invited by General Brunet, another minion of Napoleon in Santo Domingo, to partake of the social hospitalities of his home; but, Toussaint, instead of finding the domestic civilities that he expected, was bound in chains, sent on board the *Hero*, a vessel already held in readiness for the consummation of the vile deed, in which he was carried a prisoner to France.

The magnanimous man bitterly repented at his leisure his too-great confidence in the word of the white man, in the cold dark dungeons of the castle of Joux. And the depth of his repentance was intensified by a compulsory fast ordered by that would-be great and magnanimous man, Napoleon Bonaparte, who denied him food and starved him to death.

Great God! how the blood runs chill, in contemplating the ignoble end of the illustrious Negro chieftain and statesman, by such base and perfidious means! . . .

Having now arrived at the epoch when the banners of Negro independence waved triumphantly over the Queen of the Antilles, if we look back at the trials and tribulations through which they came up to this point of national regeneration, we have presented to us, in the hardy endurance and perseverance manifested by them, in the steady pursuit of liberty and independence, the overwhelming evidence of their ability to govern themselves. For fourteen long and soul-trying years—twice the period of the revolutionary struggle of this country—they battled manfully for freedom. It was on the eighth of March, 1790, as we have seen, that the immortal man of color, Vincent Oje, obtained a decree from the National Assembly guaranteeing equal political privileges to the free men of color in the island. And, after a continued sanguinary struggle dating from that time, the never-to-be-forgotten self-emancipated black slave, Jean Jacques Dessalines, on the first of January, 1804, proclaimed Negro freedom and independence throughout the island of Santo Domingo.

That freedom and independence are written in the world's history in the ineffaceable characters of blood; and its crimsoned letters will ever testify of the determination of the ability of the Negro to be free, throughout the everlasting succession of ages. . . .

There have been but eight rulers in Haiti since 1804, counting separately, Christophe and Petion, who ruled cotemporaneously. This is a period of fifty-three years down to the present time. And in the United States, since 1809, there have been ten different chief magistrates—a period of forty-eight years. Thus, this country has had two more rulers than Haiti, within a period five years less than the Haitian sovereignty.

The fact is, there is no nation in North America, but the United States, nor any in South America, except Brazil, that can pretend to compare with Haiti, in respect to general stability of government. The Spanish republics of America will have as many different rulers in eight years as Haiti has had in a half century.

And the colonial dependencies of European nations change governors at least three times as often as that Negro nation has done. This political stability, therefore, on the part of the Haitians indicates a vast remove from barbarism. It is far ahead of the anarchy of some so-called civilized nations. And it therefore indicates a high degree of civilization and progress. . . .

The overthrow of the government of Dessalines by the spontaneous uprising of the people in their majesty, when it had become a merciless and tyrannical despotism, may also be noted here as another evidence of progress in political freedom of thought that made the race scorn to be tyrannized over by an oppressive master, whether that master was a cruel white tyrant or a merciless Negro despot. . . .

The Haitian people when governed by the crowned and imperial Dessalines testified their love of liberty by destroying the tyrant when he violated the constitution and overstepped the laws of his country.

The American people under a republican form of government manifest their want of a love of true liberty when they permit a vagabond set of politicians, whose character for rowdyism disgraces the nation, to enact such an odious law as the Fugitive Slave bill, violating the writ of habeas corpus and other sacred guarantees of the Constitution, and then tamely submit to this high-handed outrage because such unprincipled scoundrels voted in their insane revelry that it must be the supreme law of the land.

If there was one half of the real love of liberty among even the people of the professedly free Northern states as there is among the Negroes of Haiti, every one of their national representatives who voted for that infamous bill, or who would not vote instantaneously for its repeal, would be tried for his life, condemned and publicly executed as accessory to man stealing. Thus would a free people, determined to preserve their liberties, rid themselves of a brood of petty tyrants who seek to impose their unhallowed partisan caprices upon the country, as the supreme law of the land, overriding even the Higher Law of God. And thus in time would they exhibit an equally jealous regard for their rights as the Haitians did when they rid themselves of the tyrant Dessalines.

If such was the real love of liberty among the Northern people of this vainglorious Republic, we should soon annihilate that morally spineless class of politicians who need decision of character, when they get to Washington, to legislate for freedom. All such as were thus morally destitute of spinal vertebrae to resist the aggressions of the slave power in the national halls of legislation would also soon be physically deficient in their cervical vertebrae, when they returned home, to meet the extreme penalty of an outraged and indignant constituency.

But such a determined spirit of liberty does not exist here, and honest men must submit, therefore, with lamblike patience to this republican despotism of irresponsible political partisans who violate every just principle of law, because these unrighteous decrees are perpetrated in the name of the sovereign people.

Hence there is far more security for personal liberty and the general welfare of the governed among the monarchical Negroes of Haiti, where the rulers are held individually responsible for their public acts, than exists in this bastard democracy.

The single-necked despot is soon reached by the keen avenging ax of liberty, for any acts of despotism among the Haitian blacks; but here its dull and blunted edge lies useless, for it might be hurled in vain and fall powerless among a nameless crowd of millions.

Conclusion

But our historical investigations are at an end, and we must hasten to bring our reflections to a conclusion. I have now fulfilled my design in vindicating the capacity of the Negro race for self-government and civilized progress against the unjust aspersions of our unprincipled oppressors, by boldly examining the facts of Haitian history and deducing legitimate conclusions therefrom. I have summoned the sable heroes and statesmen of that independent isle of the Caribbean Sea and tried them by the high standard of modern civilization, fearlessly comparing them with the most illustrious men of the most enlightened nations of the earth; and in this examination and comparison the Negro race has not fallen one whit behind their contemporaries. And in this investigation I have made no allowance for the Negroes just emerging from a barbarous condition and out of the brutish ignorance of West Indian slavery. I have been careful not to make such an allowance, for fear that instead of proving Negro equality only, I should prove Negro superiority. I shun the point of making this allowance to the Negro, as it might reverse the case of the question entirely that I have been combating and, instead of disproving his alleged inferiority only, would on the other hand, go farther, and establish his superiority. Therefore as it is my design to banish the words "superiority" and "inferiority" from the vocabulary of the world, when applied to the natural capacity of races of men, I claim no allowance for them on the score of their condition and circumstances.

Having now presented the preceding array of facts and arguments to establish, before the world, the Negro's equality with the white man in carrying forward the great principles of self-government and civilized progress, I would now have these facts exert their legitimate influence over the minds of my race in this country, in producing that most desirable object of arousing them to a full consciousness of their own inherent dignity, and thereby increasing among them that self-respect which shall urge them on to the performance of those great deeds which the age and the race now demand at their hands.

Our brethren of Haiti, who stand in the vanguard of the race, have already made a name and a fame for us that is as imperishable as the world's history. They exercise sovereign authority over an island that in natural advantages is the Eden of America and the garden spot of the world. Her rich resources invite the capacity of ten million human beings to adequately use them. It becomes, then, an important question for the Negro race in America to well consider the weighty responsibility that the present exigency devolves upon them, to contribute to the continued advancement of this Negro nationality of the New World until its glory and renown shall overspread and cover the whole earth and redeem and regenerate by its influence in the future the benighted fatherland of the race in Africa.

Here in this black nationality of the New World, erected under such glorious auspices, is the standpoint that must be occupied, and the lever that must be exerted, to regenerate and disenthrall the oppression and ignorance of the race throughout the world. We must not overlook this practical vantage ground which Providence has raised up for us out of the depths of the sea, for any man-made and utopian scheme that is prematurely forced upon us, to send us across the ocean, to rummage the graves of our ancestors, in fruitless and ill-directed efforts at the wrong end of human progress. Civilization and Christianity are passing from the East to the West; and their pristine splendor will only be rekindled in the ancient nations of the Old World after they have belted the globe in its westward course and revisited the Orient again. The Serpentine trial of civilization and Christianity, like the ancient philosophic symbol of eternity, must coil backward to its fountainhead. God, therefore, in permitting the accursed slave traffic to transplant so many millions of the race to the New World and educing therefrom such a Negro nationality as Haiti, indicates thereby that we have a work now to do here in the Western world, which in his own good time shall shed its Orient beams upon the fatherland of the race. Let us see to it that we meet the exigency now imposed upon us as nobly on our part at this time as the Haitians met theirs at the opening of the present century. And in seeking to perform this duty, it may well be a question with us whether it is not our duty to go and identify our destiny with our heroic brethren in that independent isle of the Caribbean Sea, carrying with us such of the arts, sciences and genius of modern civilization as we may gain from this hardy and enterprising Anglo-American race, in order to add to Haitian advancements, rather than to indolently remain here, asking for political rights which, if granted a social proscription stronger than conventional legislation, will ever render nugatory and of no avail the manly elevation and general well-being of the race. If one powerful and civilized Negro sovereignty can be developed to the summit of national grandeur in the West Indies, where the keys to the commerce of both hemispheres can be held, this fact will solve all questions respecting the Negro, whether they be those of slavery, prejudice or proscription, and wheresoever on the face of the globe such questions shall present themselves for a satisfactory solution.

A concentration and combination of the Negro race of the Western Hemisphere in Haiti, can produce just such a national development. The duty to do so is therefore incumbent on them. And the responsibility of leading off in this gigantic enterprise Providence seems to have made our peculiar task by the eligibility of our situation in this country as a point for gaining an easy access to that island. Then let us boldly enlist in this high pathway of duty, while the watchwords that shall cheer and inspire us in our noble and glorious undertaking shall be the soul-stirring anthem of God and Humanity.

IF THERE IS NO STRUGGLE THERE IS NO PROGRESS

By Frederick Douglass

In 1833, after years of pressure by antislavery crusaders, the British government passed a bill for the abolition of slavery in the British West Indies, to go into effect on August 1, 1834. Although a system of apprenticeship continued until the end of 1838, limiting for several years the effectiveness of the law, the emancipation of the slaves in the West Indies stimulated the struggle against the institution in this country and was annually celebrated by the Abolitionists. On August 4, 1857, the twenty-third anniversary, Frederick Douglass delivered a "West India Emancipation" speech at Canandaigua, New York. Most of the

*address was devoted to the significance of the British
legislation, but the closing portions are of great importance
as a presentation of Douglass' philosophy of militant abolitionism.*

*At first, Douglass, an avid disciple of William Lloyd
Garrison, was guided by the concept that "moral suasion"
was the chief weapon in the battle to end slavery. But new
associations and his studies and thinking caused him to
abandon faith in moral suasion and advance the doctrine
that the Negro would never get his freedom unless he
fought for it even at the cost of his life. The Negro, moreover, had to play a leading role in the fight against slavery
rather than serve as a subordinate to white Abolitionists.
Although the Garrisonians bitterly attacked Douglass for
breaking with their doctrines, accusing him of selfishly
placing his own interests above those of the antislavery
cause, the great Negro spokesman persisted in presenting
his own antislavery philosophy, and never more firmly and
eloquently than in the concluding section of this 1857
"West India Emancipation" speech. That section, presented here, is taken from the pamphlet* Two Speeches by
Frederick Douglass, One on West India Emancipation
. . . and the Other on the Dred Scott Decision . . . ,
Rochester, 1857.

. . . THE GENERAL SENTIMENT of mankind is that a
man who will not fight for himself, when he has the means of
doing so, is not worth being fought for by others, and this sentiment is just. For a man who does not value freedom for himself
will never value it for others, or put himself to any inconvenience to gain it for others. Such a man, the world says, may lie
down until he has sense enough to stand up. It is useless and
cruel to put a man on his legs, if the next moment his head
is to be brought against a curbstone.

A man of that type will never lay the world under any obligation to him, but will be a moral pauper, a drag on the wheels
of society, and if he too be identified with a peculiar variety of
the race he will entail disgrace upon his race as well as upon
himself. The world in which we live is very accommodating to
all sorts of people. It will cooperate with them in any measure
which they propose; it will help those who earnestly help themselves, and will hinder those who hinder themselves. It is very
polite, and never offers its services unasked. Its favors to individuals are measured by an unerring principle in this—viz.,
respect those who respect themselves, and despise those who

despise themselves. It is not within the power of unaided human nature to persevere in pitying a people who are insensible to their own wrongs and indifferent to the attainment of their own rights. The poet was as true to common sense as to poetry when he said,

Who would be free, themselves must strike the blow.

When O'Connell, with all Ireland at his back, was supposed to be contending for the just rights and liberties of Ireland, the sympathies of mankind were with him, and even his enemies were compelled to respect his patriotism. Kossuth, fighting for Hungary with his pen long after she had fallen by the sword, commanded the sympathy and support of the liberal world till his own hopes died out. The Turks, while they fought bravely for themselves and scourged and drove back the invading legions of Russia, shared the admiration of mankind. They were standing up for their own rights against an arrogant and powerful enemy; but as soon as they let out their fighting to the Allies, admiration gave way to contempt. These are not the maxims and teachings of a coldhearted world. Christianity itself teaches that a man shall provide for his own house. This covers the whole ground of nations as well as individuals. Nations no more than individuals can innocently be improvident. They should provide for all wants—mental, moral and religious —and against all evils to which they are liable as nations. In the great struggle now progressing for the freedom and elevation of our people, we should be found at work with all our might, resolved that no man or set of men shall be more abundant in labors, according to the measure of our ability, than ourselves.

I know, my friends, that in some quarters the efforts of colored people meet with very little encouragement. We may fight, but we must fight like the Sepoys of India, under white officers. This class of Abolitionists don't like colored celebrations, they don't like colored conventions, they don't like colored antislavery fairs for the support of colored newspapers. They don't like any demonstrations whatever in which colored men take a leading part. They talk of the proud Anglo-Saxon blood as flippantly as those who profess to believe in the natural inferiority of races. Your humble speaker has been branded as an ingrate, because he has ventured to stand up on his own right and to plead our common cause as a colored man, rather than as a Garrisonian. I hold it to be no part of gratitude to allow our white friends to do all the work, while we merely hold their coats. Opposition of the sort now referred to is partisan op-

position, and we need not mind it. The white people at large
will not largely be influenced by it. They will see and appreciate
all honest efforts on our part to improve our condition as a
people.

Let me give you a word of the philosophy of reform. The
whole history of the progress of human liberty shows that all
concessions yet made to her august claims have been born of
earnest struggle. The conflict has been exciting, agitating, all-
absorbing, and for the time being, putting all other tumults to
silence. It must do this or it does nothing. If there is no struggle
there is no progress. Those who profess to favor freedom and
yet deprecate agitation are men who want crops without plowing up the ground; they want rain without thunder and lightning. They want the ocean without the awful roar of its many
waters.

This struggle may be a moral one, or it may be a physical
one, and it may be both moral and physical, but it must be a
struggle. Power concedes nothing without a demand. It never
did and it never will. Find out just what any people will quietly
submit to and you have found out the exact measure of injustice and wrong which will be imposed upon them, and these
will continue till they are resisted with either words or blows,
or with both. The limits of tyrants are prescribed by the endurance of those whom they oppress. In the light of these ideas,
Negroes will be hunted at the North and held and flogged at
the South so long as they submit to those devilish outrages and
make no resistance, either moral or physical. Men may not get
all they pay for in this world, but they must certainly pay for
all they get. If we ever get free from the oppressions and wrongs
heaped upon us, we must pay for their removal. We must do
this by labor, by suffering, by sacrifice, and if needs be, by our
lives and the lives of others.

Hence, my friends, every mother who, like Margaret Garner,
plunges a knife into the bosom of her infant to save it from the
hell of our Christian slavery,* should be held and honored as a
benefactress. Every fugitive from slavery who, like the noble
William Thomas at Wilkes Barre, prefers to perish in a river
made red by his own blood to submission to the hell hounds who

* In January, 1856, the Garner family, slaves of Archibald K. Gaines of
Kentucky, escaped and found refuge in Cincinnati. They were pursued
and attacked. Before the group was captured, Margaret Garner killed
one of her children and severely wounded two others "to save them all
from slavery by death." She was tried on a murder charge in Cincinnati
and found guilty, but due to jurisdictional difficulties was returned to
slavery in Kentucky.

were hunting and shooting him should be esteemed as a glorious martyr, worthy to be held in grateful memory by our people. The fugitive Horace, at Mechanicsburgh, Ohio, the other day, who taught the slave catchers from Kentucky that it was safer to arrest white men than to arrest him, did a most excellent service to our cause. Parker and his noble band of fifteen at Christiana, who defended themselves from the kidnapers with prayers and pistols, are entitled to the honor of making the first successful resistance to the Fugitive Slave Bill.* But for that resistance, and the rescue of Jerry and Shadrack,† the man hunters would have hunted our hills and valleys here with the same freedom with which they now hunt their own dismal swamps.

There was an important lesson in the conduct of that noble Krooman in New York the other day, who, supposing that the American Christians were about to enslave him, betook himself to the masthead and with knife in hand said he would cut his throat before he would be made a slave. Joseph Cinque, on the deck of the *Amistad*, did that which should make his name dear to us. He bore nature's burning protest against slavery. Madison Washington who struck down his oppressor on the deck of the *Creole*, is more worthy to be remembered than the colored man who shot Pitcairn at Bunker Hill.‡

My friends, you will observe that I have taken a wide range,

* In the early dawn of September 11, 1851, an attack was made on the home of William Parker, of Christiana, Pennsylvania, to arrest some fugitive slaves said to be hidden there. The Negroes in the neighborhood came to their defense, and a battle took place in which Edward Gorsuch, a Maryland slaveowner, was killed by Parker and Gorsuch's son was wounded. Parker escaped to Canada, assisted from Rochester by Frederick Douglass. Thirty-eight of the men involved in the battle, thirty-six Negroes and two whites, were indicted for treason against the United States and brought to trial in Lancaster County Courthouse. Castner Hanway, a Quaker who had refused to assist in capturing the fugitives, was the first to be tried. The jury found Hanway not guilty, and the others were released.

† The Jerry Rescue occurred at Syracuse, New York, on October 1, 1851. Gerrit Smith and other Abolitionists forcibly rescued the fugitive slave Jerry McHenry, who had been seized and imprisoned by a deputy United States marshal, and helped him to escape to Canada and freedom.

In February, 1851, Shadrach, a Negro waiter in Boston, was arrested and charged with having escaped from the South. Before the case was decided, a body of Negroes led by Lewis Hayden broke into the prison, seized Shadrach, and dispatched him to Canada.

‡ British Major Pitcairn was killed, it is generally assumed, by a volley from the musket of Peter Salem, one of the Negroes who fought in the Battle of Bunker Hill.

and you think it is about time that I should answer the special objection to this celebration. I think so too. This, then, is the truth concerning the inauguration of freedom in the British West Indies. Abolition was the act of the British government. The motive which led the government to act no doubt was mainly a philanthropic one, entitled to our highest admiration and gratitude. The national religion, the justice and humanity cried out in thunderous indignation against the foul abomination, and the government yielded to the storm. Nevertheless a share of the credit of the result falls justly to the slaves themselves. "Though slaves, they were rebellious slaves." They bore themselves well. They did not hug their chains, but according to their opportunities, swelled the general protest against oppression. What Wilberforce was endeavoring to win from the British senate by his magic eloquence the slaves themselves were endeavoring to gain by outbreaks and violence. The combined action of one and the other wrought out the final result. While one showed that slavery was wrong, the other showed that it was dangerous as well as wrong. Mr. Wilberforce,* peace man though he was, and a model of piety, availed himself of this element to strengthen his case before the British Parliament, and warned the British government of the danger of continuing slavery in the West Indies. There is no doubt that the fear of the consequences, acting with a sense of the moral evil of slavery, led to its abolition. The spirit of freedom was abroad in the Islands. Insurrection for freedom kept the planters in a constant state of alarm and trepidation. A standing army was necessary to keep the slaves in their chains. This state of facts could not be without weight in deciding the question of freedom in these countries.

I am aware that the rebellious disposition of the slaves was said to arise out of the discussions which the Abolitionists were carrying on at home, and it is not necessary to refute this alleged explanation. All that I contend for is this: that the slaves of the West Indies did fight for their freedom, and that the fact of their discontent was known in England, and that it assisted in bringing about that state of public opinion which finally resulted in their emancipation. And if this be true, the objection is answered.

* Wilberforce was active in the battle against the slave system in the British West Indies, but the struggle was actually led by Thomas Fowell Buxton. However, as Eric Williams has emphasized, it was the activities of the slaves themselves in repeated uprisings that played a decisive role in West Indies emancipation. (See Eric Williams, *Capitalism and Slavery*, New York, 1961, p. 197.)

Again, I am aware that the insurrectionary movements of the slaves were held by many to be prejudicial to their cause. This is said now of such movements at the South. The answer is that abolition followed close on the heels of insurrection in the West Indies, and Virginia was never nearer emancipation than when General Turner kindled the fires of insurrection at Southampton.

Sir, I have now more than filled up the measure of my time. I thank you for the patient attention given to what I have had to say. I have aimed, as I said at the beginning, to express a few thoughts having some relation to the great interests of freedom both in this country and in the British West Indies, and I have said all that I meant to say, and the time will not permit me to say more.

I WILL SINK OR SWIM WITH MY RACE

By John S. Rock

Schoolteacher, dentist, physician, lawyer, graduate of the American Medical College in Philadelphia, member of the Massachusetts Bar, proficient in Greek and Latin, Dr. John S. Rock was one of the leaders of the movement for equal rights for black Americans in the North. Dr. Rock used the lecture platform effectively to challenge the racist concept that Negroes were inferior to whites. A good example is the following speech he delivered at Boston, March 5, 1858, at a meeting commemorating the Boston Massacre. Three years before the outbreak of the Civil War, Dr. Rock was predicting that black Americans were destined to play an important role in the impending military conflict over slavery.

John S. Rock was born in Salem, New Jersey, in 1825. He was a teacher in the public schools during 1844–48, and in the following year he finished studying dentistry under Dr. Harbert Hubbard. In 1850 he began practicing dentistry in Philadelphia, and in 1851 he received a silver medal for the creation of artificial teeth and another silver medal for a prize essay on temperance. In 1852 he graduated from the American Medical College in Philadelphia, and the following year began the practice of medicine and

dentistry in Boston. He was admitted to practice law in
Massachusetts in 1861 and on September 21 of that year
received a commission from the governor as justice of
peace for seven years for the city of Boston and the County
of Suffolk.

In February, 1865, presented by Charles Sumner as a
candidate to argue cases before the Supreme Court, Rock
was sworn in by Chief Justice Salmon P. Chase as the
first Negro to be accredited as a Supreme Court lawyer.
He died in Boston on December 3, 1866.

(Dr. Rock's Boston Massacre speech, presented here in
part, was published in The Liberator, *March 12, 1858.)*

WHITE AMERICANS have taken great pains to try to prove
that we are cowards. We are often insulted with the assertion
that, if we had had the courage of the Indians or the white man,
we would never have submitted to be slaves. I ask if Indians
and white men have never been slaves? The white man tested
the Indian's courage here when he had his organized armies,
his battlegrounds, his places of retreat, with everything to hope
for and everything to lose. The position of the African slave has
been very different. Seized a prisoner of war, unarmed, bound
hand and foot, and conveyed to a distant country among what
to him were worse than cannibals; brutally beaten, half-starved,
closely watched by armed men, with no means of knowing their
own strength or the strength of their enemies, with no weapons,
and without a probability of success. But if the white man will
take the trouble to fight the black man in Africa or in Haiti,
and fight him as fair as the black man will fight him there—if
the black man does not come off victor, I am deceived in his
prowess. But, take a man, armed or unarmed, from his home,
his country, or his friends, and place him among savages, and
who is he that would not make good his retreat? "Discretion is
the better part of valor," but for a man to resist where he knows
it will destroy him shows more foolhardiness than courage.
There have been many Anglo-Saxons and Anglo-Americans enslaved in Africa, but I have never heard that they successfully
resisted any government. They always resort to running indis-
pensables.

The courage of the Anglo-Saxon is best illustrated in his
treatment of the Negro. A score or two of them can pounce upon
a poor Negro, tie and beat him, and then call him a coward because he submits. Many of their most brilliant victories have
been achieved in the same manner. But the greatest battles
which they have fought have been upon paper. We can easily

account for this; their trumpeter is dead. He died when they used to be exposed for sale in the Roman market, about the time that Cicero cautioned his friend Atticus not to buy them, on account of their stupidity. A little more than half a century ago, this race, in connection with their Celtic neighbors, who have long been considered (by themselves, of course) the bravest soldiers in the world, so far forgot themselves as to attack a few cowardly, stupid Negro slaves, who, according to their accounts, had not sense enough to go to bed. And what was the result? Why, sir, the Negroes drove them out from the island like so many sheep, and they have never dared to show their faces, except with hat in hand.

Our true and tried friend Reverend Theodore Parker* said, in his speech at the State House a few weeks since, that "the stroke of the ax would have settled the question long ago, but the black man would not strike." Mr. Parker makes a very low estimate of the courage of his race if he means that one, two or three millions of these ignorant and cowardly black slaves could, without means, have brought to their knees five, ten or twenty millions of intelligent, brave white men, backed up by a rich oligarchy. But I know of no one who is more familiar with the true character of the Anglo-Saxon race than Mr. Parker. I will not dispute this point with him, but I will thank him or any one else to tell us how it could have been done. His remark calls to mind the day which is to come, when one shall chase a thousand, and two put ten thousand to flight. But when he says that "the black man *would not strike,*" I am prepared to say that he does us great injustice. The black man is not a coward. The history of the bloody struggles for freedom in Haiti, in which the blacks whipped the French and the English and gained their independence in spite of the perfidy of that villainous First Consul, will be a lasting refutation of the malicious aspersions of our enemies. The history of the struggles for the liberty of the United States ought to silence every American calumniator. . . .

The white man contradicts himself who says that if he were in our situation he would throw off the yoke. Thirty millions of white men of this proud Caucasian race are at this moment held as slaves, and bought and sold with horses and cattle. The iron heel of oppression grinds the masses of all the European races to the dust. They suffer every kind of oppression, and no one dares to open his mouth to protest against it. Even in the

---

* Theodore Parker (1810–1860), Unitarian clergyman and a leader in the antislavery movement, also addressed the Boston meeting.

Southern portion of this boasted land of liberty, no white man dares advocate so much of the Declaration of Independence as declares that all men are created free and equal, and have an unalienable right to life, liberty et cetera.

White men have no room to taunt us with tamely submitting. If they were black men, they would work wonders; but, as white men, they can do nothing. "O, Consistency, thou art a jewel!"

Now, it would not be surprising if the brutal treatment which we have received for the past two centuries should have crushed our spirits. But this is not the case. Nothing but a superior force keeps us down. And when I see the slaves rising up by hundreds annually, in the majesty of human nature, bidding defiance to every slave code and its penalties, making the issue Canada or death, and that too while they are closely watched by paid men armed with pistols, clubs, and bowie knives, with the army and navy of this great model Republic arrayed against them, I am disposed to ask if the charge of cowardice does not come with ill grace . . .

Our fathers fought nobly for freedom, but they were not victorious. They fought for liberty, but they got slavery. The white man was benefited, but the black man was injured. I do not envy the white American the little liberty which he enjoys. It is his right, and he ought to have it. I wish him success, though I do not think he deserves it. But I would have all men free. We have had much sad experience in this country, and it would be strange indeed if we do not profit by some of the lessons which we have so dearly paid for. Sooner or later, the clashing of arms will be heard in this country, and the black man's services will be needed: 150,000 freemen capable of bearing arms, and not all cowards and fools, and three quarters of a million slaves, wild with the enthusiasm caused by the dawn of the glorious opportunity of being able to strike a genuine blow for freedom, will be a power which white men will be "bound to respect." Will the blacks fight? Of course they will. The black man will never be neutral. He could not if he would and would not if he could. Will he fight for this country, right or wrong? This the common sense of every one answers; and when the time comes, and come it will, the black man will give an intelligent answer. Judge Taney may outlaw us;* Caleb

* The reference is to the Dred Scott decision rendered by the Supreme Court on March 6, 1857. Dred Scott, a slave, had been brought by his master into the Louisiana Territory north of the line above which slavery was prohibited by law. After he was returned to the slave state of Missouri, he sued for his freedom. Chief Justice Roger B. Taney, writing the majority opinion, held that Dred Scott could never be a citizen within

Cushing* may show the depravity of his heart by abusing us; and this wicked government may oppress us; but the black man will live when Judge Taney, Caleb Cushing and this wicked government are no more. White men may despise, ridicule, slander and abuse us; they may seek, as they always have done, to divide us and make us feel degraded; but no man shall cause me to turn my back upon my race. With it I will sink or swim.

The prejudice which some white men have, or affect to have, against my color gives me no pain. If any man does not fancy my color, that is his business, and I shall not meddle with it. I shall give myself no trouble because he lacks good taste. If he judges my intellectual capacity by my color, he certainly cannot expect much profundity, for it is only skin deep, and is really of no very great importance to anyone but myself. I will not deny that I admire the talents and noble characters of many white men. But I cannot say that I am particularly pleased with their physical appearance. If old mother nature had held out as well as she commenced, we should, probably, have had fewer varieties in the races. When I contrast the fine tough muscular system, the beautiful, rich color, the full broad features and the gracefully frizzled hair of the Negro with the delicate physical organization, wan color, sharp features and lank hair of the Caucasian, I am inclined to believe that when the white man was created, nature was pretty well exhausted. But, determined to keep up appearances, she pinched up his features and did the best she could under the circumstances.

I would have you understand that I not only love my race, but am pleased with my color; and while many colored persons may feel degraded by being called Negroes and wish to be classed among other races more favored, I shall feel it my duty, my pleasure and my pride to concentrate my feeble efforts in elevating to a fair position a race to which I am especially identified by feelings and by blood. . . .

In this country, where money is the great sympathetic nerve which ramifies society and has a ganglia in every man's pocket, a man is respected in proportion to his success in business. When the avenues to wealth are opened to us, we will then

the meaning of the Constitution and therefore had no right to sue in a federal court. The Negro, Taney insisted, possessed "no rights that a white man is bound to respect." Taney also went on to declare that the Missouri Compromise was unconstitutional when it forbade slavery above 36° 30′ north latitude.

* Caleb Cushing (1800–1879), a leading Massachusetts Democrat, was a member of Congress from 1835 to 1843 and Attorney General of the United States from 1853 to 1857.

become educated and wealthy, and then the roughest-looking colored man that you ever saw, or ever will see, will be pleasanter than the harmonies of Orpheus, and black will be a very pretty color. It will make our jargon wit, our words oracles; flattery will then take the place of slander, and you will find no prejudice in the Yankee whatever. We do not expect to occupy a much better position than we now do, until we shall have our educated and wealthy men, who can wield a power that cannot be misunderstood. Then, and not till then, will the tongue of slander be silenced and the lip of prejudice sealed. Then, and not till then, will we be able to enjoy true equality, which can exist only among peers.

SHOULD COLORED MEN BE SUBJECT TO THE PENALTIES OF THE FUGITIVE SLAVE LAW?

By Charles H. Langston

Charles H. Langston (1817–1892), a Negro leader in Ohio, was especially active in resisting the Fugitive Slave Act. In September, 1858, he joined with students of Oberlin College and citizens of the town in rescuing a recaptured fugitive slave, John Price, who was being held in the neighboring town of Wellington. Price was removed from custody and transported to Canada and freedom. Langston was the second to be tried for violating the law in the famous case, and he delivered a brilliant and moving speech in answer to the question of the judge why the sentence should not be pronounced. His speech struck the court so favorably that even though he was sentenced to twenty days' imprisonment and fined $100 and costs amounting to $872.72, it was a much lighter sentence than that given to his white predecessor, whose actions were judged equally "criminal." One aspect of Langston's defense that is especially interesting is his plea that he was not tried before a jury of peers.

John Mercer Langston, Charles Langston's famous brother, later professor of law at Howard University and Congressman from Virginia, wrote an account of the "Oberlin-Wellington Rescue" in The Anglo-African Maga-

*zine of June, 1859 (pp. 209–16), printing his brother's
speech to the court. He described Charles Langston as
follows: "He is widely known as a devoted and laborious
advocate of the claims of the Negro to liberty and its at-
tendant blessings. Discreet and far-seeing, uncompromising and able, he has labored most efficiently in behalf of
the slave and the disfranchised American."*

*The speech was reprinted in pamphlet form and in
leading newspapers throughout the North.*

I AM for the first time in my life before a court of justice,
charged with the violation of law, and am now about to be
sentenced. But before receiving that sentence, I propose to say
one or two words in regard to the mitigation of that sentence,
if it may be so construed. I cannot, of course, and do not expect
that which I may say will in any way change your pre-
determined line of action. I ask no such favor at your hands.

I know that the courts of this country, that the laws of this
country, that the governmental machinery of this country, are
so constituted as to oppress and outrage colored men, men of
my complexion. I cannot then, of course, expect, judging from
the past history of the country, any mercy from the laws, from
the Constitution, or from the courts of the country.

Some days prior to the thirteenth day of September, 1858,
happening to be in Oberlin on a visit, I found the country round
about there and the village itself filled with alarming rumors as
to the fact that slave catchers, kidnapers, Negro stealers were
lying hidden and skulking about, waiting some opportunity to
get their bloody hands on some helpless creature to drag him
back—or for the first time—into helpless and lifelong bondage.
These reports becoming current all over that neighborhood, old
men and innocent women and children became exceedingly
alarmed for their safety. It was not uncommon to hear mothers
say that they dare not send their children to school, for fear
they would be caught and carried off by the way. Some of these
people had become free by long and patient toil at night, after
working the long, long day for cruel masters, and thus at length
getting money enough to buy their liberty. Others had become
free by means of the good will of their masters. And there were
others who had become free by the intensest exercise of their
God-given powers—by escaping from the plantations of their
masters, eluding the bloodthirsty patrols and sentinels so thickly
scattered all along their path, outrunning bloodhounds and
horses, swimming rivers and fording swamps, and reaching at
last, through incredible difficulties, what they, in their delusion,

supposed to be free soil. These three classes were in Oberlin, trembling alike for their safety, because they well knew their fate should those men-hunters get their hands on them.

In the midst of such excitement the thirteenth day of September was ushered in—a day ever to be remembered in the history of that place, and I presume no less in the history of this court —on which those men, by lying devices, decoyed into a place where they could get their hands on him—I will not say a slave, for I do not know that, but a *man*, a *brother*—who had a right to his liberty under the laws of God, under the laws of nature and under the Declaration of American Independence.

In the midst of all this excitement, the news came to us like a flash of lightning that an actual seizure under and by means of fraudulent pretenses had been made!

Being identified with that man by color, by race, by manhood, by sympathies, such as God had implanted in us all, I felt it my duty to go and do what I could toward liberating him. I had been taught by my Revolutionary father—and I say this with all due respect to him—and by his honored associates that the fundamental doctrine of this government was that *all* men have a right, to life and liberty, and coming from the Old Dominion I brought into Ohio these sentiments, deeply impressed upon my heart; I went to Wellington, and hearing from the parties themselves by what authority the boy was held in custody, I conceived from what little knowledge I had of law that they had no right to hold him. And as your Honor has repeatedly laid down the law in this court, a man is free until he is proven to be legally restrained of his liberty, and I believed that upon the principle of law those men were bound to take their prisoner before the very first magistrate they found and there establish the facts set forth in their warrant, and that until they did this, every man should presume that their claim was unfounded, and to institute such proceedings for the purpose of securing an investigation as they might find warranted by the laws of this state. Now, sir, if that is not the plain, common sense and correct view of the law, then I have been misled by your Honor and by the prevalent received opinion.

It is said that they had a warrant. Why then should they not establish its validity before the proper officers? And I stand here today, sir, to say that with an exception of which I shall soon speak, *to procure such a lawful investigation of the authority under which they claimed to act was the part I took in that day's proceedings, and the only part*. I supposed it to be my duty as a citizen of Ohio—excuse me for saying that, sir—as an *outlaw of the United States*, to do what I could to secure at least this form of justice to my brother whose liberty was in peril. *Whatever more than that has been sworn to on this trial as an act of mine is false, ridiculously false.* When I found these men refusing to go, according to the law, as I apprehended it, and subject their claim to an official inspection, and that nothing short of a habeas corpus would oblige such an inspection, I was willing to go even thus far, supposing in that county a sheriff, might, perhaps, be found with nerve enough to serve it. In this I again failed. Nothing then was left me, nothing to the boy in custody, but the confirmation of my first belief that the pretended authority was worthless, and the employment of those means of liberation which belong to us. With regard to the part I took in the forcible rescue which followed, I have nothing to say further than I have already said. The evidence is before you. It is alleged that I said, "We will have him anyhow." *This I never said.* I did say to Mr. Lowe, what I honestly believed to be the truth, that the crowd were very much excited, many of them averse to longer delay, and bent upon a rescue at all hazards; and that, he being an old acquaintance and friend of mine, I was anxious to extricate him from the dangerous position he occupied and therefore advised that he urge Jennings to give the boy up. Further than this I did not say, either to him or any one else.

The law under which I am arraigned is an unjust one, one made to crush the colored man, and one that outrages every feeling of humanity, as well as every rule of right. I have nothing to do with its constitutionality; about that I care but little. I have often heard it said by learned and good men that it was unconstitutional; I remember the excitement that prevailed throughout all the free states when it was passed; and I remember how often it has been said by individuals, conventions, legislatures, and even *judges,** that it never could be, never should

* At this point in his report of the speech, John Mercer Langston appended the following footnote:

"The following resolutions were reported to and adopted by an indignation meeting held in Cleveland shortly after the passage of the Fugitive Slave Law, Judge Hiram V. Wilson being on the Committee on Resolutions:

"1. *Resolved*, That the passage of the Fugitive Slave Law was an act unauthorized by the Constitution, hostile to every principle of justice and humanity, and if persevered in, fatal to Human Freedom.

"2. *Resolved*, That the law strikes down some of the dearest principles upon which our fathers predicated their right to assert and maintain their independence, and is characterized by the most tyrannical exercise of be, and never was meant to be enforced. I had always believed, until contrary appeared in the actual institution of proceedings, that the provisions of this odious statute would never be enforced within the bounds of this state.

But I have another reason to offer why I should not be sentenced, and one that I think pertinent to the case. I have not had a trial before a jury of my peers. The common law of England—and you will excuse me for referring to that, since I am but a private citizen—was that every man should be tried before a jury of men occupying the same position in the social scale with himself. That lords should be tried before a jury of lords; that peers of the realm should be tried before peers of the realm; vassals before vassals, and *aliens before aliens;* and they must not come from the district where the crime was committed, lest the prejudices of either personal friends or foes should affect the accused. The Constitution of the United States guarantees, not merely to its citizens, but *to all persons,* a trial before an *impartial* jury. I have had no such trial.

The colored man is oppressed by certain universal and deeply fixed *prejudices.* Those jurors are well known to have shared largely in these prejudices, and I therefore consider that they were neither impartial, nor were they a jury of my peers. And the prejudices which white people have against colored men grow out of the facts that we have as a people *consented* for two hundred years to be *slaves* of the whites. We have been scourged, crushed and cruelly oppressed, and have submitted to it all tamely, meekly, peaceably—I mean as a people, and with rare individual exceptions—and today you see us thus, meekly submitting to the penalties of an infamous law. Now the Americans have this feeling, and it is an honorable one, that they will respect those who will rebel at oppression but despise

---

power; and that it cannot be sustained without repudiating the doctrines of the Declaration of Independence and the principles upon which all free governments rest.

"3. *Resolved,* That tyranny consists in the willfully violating, by those in power, of man's natural right to his personal security, personal liberty and private property; and it matters not whether the act is exercised by one man or a million men, it is equally unjust, unrighteous, and destrucive of the ends of all just governments.

"4. *Resolved,* That regarding some portions of the Fugitive Law as unconstitutional, and the whole of it as oppressive, unjust and unrighteous, we deem it the duty of every good citizen to *denounce, oppose* and *resist,* by all proper means, the execution of said law, and that we demand its immediate and unconditional repeal, and will not cease to agitate the question, and use all our powers to secure that object, until it is accomplished."

those who tamely submit to outrage and wrong; and while our people, as people, submit, they will as a people be despised. Why, they will hardly meet on terms of equality with us in a whisky shop, in a car, at a table, or even at the altar of God— so thorough and hearty a contempt have they for those who will meekly *lie still* under the heel of the oppressor. The jury came into the box with that feeling. They know they had that feeling, and so the court knows now and knew then. The gentleman who prosecuted me, the court itself, and even the counsel who defended me, have that feeling.

I was tried by a jury who were prejudiced, before a court that was prejudiced, prosecuted by an officer who was prejudiced, and defended, though ably, by counsel that was prejudiced. And therefore, it is, your Honor, that I urge by all that is good and great in manhood that I should not be subjected to the pains and penalties of this oppressive law, when I have *not* been tried, either by a jury of my peers or by a jury that were impartial.

One more word, sir, and I have done. I went to Wellington, knowing that colored men have no rights in the United States which white men are bound to respect; that the courts had so decided; that Congress had so enacted; that the people had so decreed.

There is not a spot in this wide country, not even by the altars of God nor in the shadow of the shafts that tell the imperishable fame and glory of the heroes of the Revolution; no, nor in the old Philadelphia Hall, where any colored man may dare to ask a mercy of a white man. Let me stand in that Hall and tell a United States marshal that my father was a Revolutionary soldier, that he served under Lafayette and fought through the whole war, and that he fought for *my* freedom as much as for his own, and he would sneer at me and clutch me with his bloody fingers and say he has a *right* to make me a slave! And when I appeal to Congress, they say he has a right to make me a slave; when I appeal to your Honor, *your Honor* says he has a right to make me a slave, and if any man, white or black, seeks an investigation of that claim, they make themselves amenable to the pains and penalties of the Fugitive Slave Act, for *black men have no rights which white men are bound to respect.* I, going to Wellington with the full knowledge of all this, knew that if that man was taken to Columbus, he was hopelessly gone, no matter whether he had ever been in slavery before or not. I knew that I was in the same situation myself, and that by the decision of your Honor, if any man whatever were to claim me as his slave and seize me, and my brother, being a

lawyer, should seek to get out a writ of habeas corpus to expose
the falsity of the claim, he would be thrust into prison under
one provision of the Fugitive Slave Law, for interfering with
the man claiming to be in pursuit of a fugitive, and I, by the
perjury of a solitary wretch, would by another of its provisions
be helplessly doomed to lifelong bondage, without the possibility of escape.

Some may say that there is no danger of free persons being
seized and carried off as slaves. No one need labor under such
a delusion. Sir, *four* of the eight persons who were first carried
back under the act of 1850 were afterwards proved to be *free
men*. They were free persons, but wholly at the mercy of the
oath of one man. And but last Sabbath afternoon, a letter came
to me from a gentleman in St. Louis, informing me that a young
lady who was formerly under my instructions at Columbus, a
free person, is now lying in the jail at that place, claimed as the
slave of some wretch who never saw her before and waiting for
testimony from relatives at Columbus to establish her freedom.
I could stand here by the hour and relate such instances. In the
very nature of the case they must be constantly occurring. A
letter was not long since found upon the person of a counter-
feiter when arrested, addressed to him by some Southern gentleman, in which the writer says:

"Go among the niggers: find out their marks and scars; make
good descriptions and send to me, and I'll find masters for 'em."

That is the way men are carried "back" to slavery.

But in view of all the facts, I say that if ever again a man is
seized near me and is about to be carried southward as a slave,
before any legal investigation has been had, I shall hold it to
be my duty, as I held it that day, to secure for him, if possible,
a legal inquiry into the character of the claim by which he is
held. And I go further: I say that if it is adjudged illegal to
procure even such an investigation, then we are thrown back
upon those last defenses of our rights which cannot be taken
from us, and which God gave us that we need not be slaves. I
ask your Honor, while I say this, to place yourself in my situation, and you will say with me that if your brother, if your
friend, if your wife, if your child, had been seized by men who
claimed them as fugitives, and the law of the land forbade you
to ask any investigation and precluded the possibility of any
legal protection or redress, then you will say with me that you
would not only demand the protection of the law, but you would
call in your neighbors and your friends and would ask them to
say with you that these, your friends, *could not* be taken into
slavery.

And now I thank you for this leniency, this indulgence, in giving a man unjustly condemned by a tribunal before which he is declared to have no rights, the privilege of speaking in his own behalf. I know that it will do nothing toward mitigating your sentence, but it is a privilege to be allowed to speak, and I thank you for it. I shall submit to the penalty, be it what it may. But I stand here to say, that if, for doing what I did on that day at Wellington, I am to go in jail six months and pay a fine of a thousand dollars, according to the Fugitive Slave Law—and such is the protection the laws of this country afford me—I must take upon myself the responsibility of self-protection; when I come to be claimed by some perjured wretch as his slave, I shall never be taken into slavery. And as in that trying hour I would have others do to me, as I would call upon my friends to help me, as I would call upon you, your Honor, to help me, as I would call upon you [to the District Attorney] to help me, and upon you [to Judge Bliss], and upon you [to his counsel], *so help me* God I stand here to say that I will do all I can for any man thus seized and held, though the inevitable penalty of six months' imprisonment and one thousand dollars fine for each offense hangs over me! We have all a common humanity, and you all would do that; your manhood would require it, and no matter what the laws might be, you would honor yourself for doing it, while your friends and your children to all generations would honor you for doing it, and every good and honest man would say you had done *right!*

ON THE FOURTEENTH QUERY OF THOMAS JEFFERSON'S *NOTES ON VIRGINIA*

By James McCune Smith

James McCune Smith (1813–1865), a leading black physician, writer and Abolitionist, was born in New York City, the "son of a slave, owing his liberty to the Emancipation Act of the State of New York and of a self-emancipated bondswoman." He was educated in the African Free School and entered the University of Glasgow in 1832, receiving the degrees of B.A. in 1835, M.A. in 1836, and M.D. in 1837. Following a short period in the clinics of

Paris, he returned to New York City and for twenty-five years was a noted doctor and surgeon. But his fame rested largely on his activities in the struggle of the black community of New York for equality and on his battle against slavery. Smith was a frequent lecturer and spoke often in support of the physical and moral equality of the black race. His most famous lecture was his discourse in 1859 on Thomas Jefferson's widely quoted claim that "the blacks, whether originally a distinct race, or made distinct by time and circumstances, are inferior to the whites in the endowments of both body and mind." The following is a major portion of Smith's analysis of Jefferson's thesis set forth in Notes on Virginia; *it is taken from* The Anglo-African Magazine, *August, 1859, pp. 225–38.*

"WHAT FURTHER is to be done with them?"* inquired Thomas Jefferson in 1787. "What, then, *is* to be done?"† is demanded of Dr. Dewey fifty-seven years afterward. These questions relate to the colored population of these United States. "What further is to be done with them?" "What is to be done with them?" Can they be elevated to the same rank with the white citizens of this great Republic? This question involves another, Is the standard occupied by the whites really elevated above that occupied by the black population? What is the standard of mind—of excellence? Is it ingenuity in constructing machinery? Is it in morals? Is it in physical courage? Or is it to be measured by the tone of a "shopkeeping gentility"? The standard of excellence is not fixed. The question of elevation must therefore be an undeterminate question. It is hard to say who is more elevated—the master, learned, acute, ingenious, the constructer of splendid machinery, the framer of laws, the successful financier, the acute philosopher—the one master of all this, with a slave whip in his hand—or the poor Christian slave, his breast heaving, his eyes raining tears, his flesh rooted up, quivering beneath the lash, whilst he prays God to soften the heart of the accomplished torturer. Who is the more elevated?

It is better to lay aside, then, this word *elevation*, because it is uncertain in its meaning. Let us put the same question in another form: Can the black and the white live together in harmony under American institutions, each contributing to the peace and prosperity of the country, and to the develop-

* Jefferson, Fourteenth Query, *Notes*, Philadelphia, 1801, p. 202.—J. M. S.
† Orville Dewey, *Discourse on Slavery and the Annexation of Texas,* New York, C. S. Francis, 1844.—J. M. S.

ment of the problem of self-government involved in American institutions?

If there be any reason why they cannot live together and contribute to the general advancement, this reason must be found either in the institutions of the country or in the nature of the people.

There is no such reason to be found in the institutions of the country, when those institutions are in accordance with the principles of democracy. In Maine, Massachusetts and Rhode Island, where the laws are made equal for all men, we find all men, including black and white, living in peace and harmony.* And these states are bright examples of progress. It is only where the institutions of the state make invidious distinctions, as in South Carolina, Mississippi and Georgia, that we find the whites and blacks living together, in peace indeed, but retrograding rather than advancing in civil and religious liberty, and in general prosperity.

There is nothing, therefore, in institutions, purely and equally democratic, which bars the mutual harmony and general progress of these races.

If there be no reason, founded upon democratic institutions, which prevents the harmonious dwelling together of these two races, is there anything in the races themselves which constitutes such a prohibition?

Mr. Jefferson contends that there are physical and mental distinctions between the Negro and the white man—distinctions which must ever prevent them from an equal and harmonious participation in the blessings of democratic freedom.

This constitutes the main proposition in his fourteenth query. In support of this proposition he produces certain views, speculations and reasonings, which many writers since his day, including de Tocqueville† and Dr. Dewey, have admitted without questioning and have urged as quite unanswerable. In fact, the only stain upon the literary merit of de Tocqueville's great work consists in this: he gives Mr. Jefferson's views as if they were de Tocqueville's views, and gives them in Mr. Jefferson's own words—thus, not only committing unpardonable plagiarism, but also adding the apparently independent and calm opinion of a foreign observer in favor of the perpetuation of American slavery.

* Smith here exaggerates the freedom and rights enjoyed by blacks in the New England states. See John S. Rock's discussion of this issue, pages 258–59.
† The reference is to Alexis de Tocqueville's classic work, *Democracy in America*.

Dr. Dewey pursues a different course; he states the result of Mr. Jefferson's views, refers to the book which contains them, and declines repeating the argument, saying that he feels a repugnance to these details arising from delicacy toward his brethren of the darker hue, which he cannot overcome.*

There are, certainly, in this world, various ways of fleeing from our own convictions. This mode of the reverend gentleman has the merit of novelty. He is too refined to brand with epithets of inferiority a class of men who have done him no harm, but he refers the world, men, women and children, to where they may find this brand affixed in what he deems an indelible manner. Had he been candid, he would have said that the testimony of Mr. Jefferson was unfit for him to repeat, as a Christian man—for this very testimony, mingled up with sneers at religion, contains statements in themselves revolting to any mind which has the slightest regard for the decencies and proprieties of life. . . .

On the 268th page of his *Notes on Virginia*, Mr. Jefferson asks: "Why not retain and incorporate the blacks into the state," et cetera? He answers, on the next page, "Deep-rooted prejudices entertained by the whites; ten thousand recollections by the blacks of the injuries they have sustained; new provocations; the real distinctions which nature has made; and many other circumstances, will divide us into parties and produce convulsions which will probably never end but in the extermination of the one or the other race. To these objections, which are political, may be added others which are physical and moral," et cetera.

Mr. Jefferson then states the physical and mental differences which exist, and which, in his opinion, will forever prevent the incorporation of the blacks into the state. His arrangement of these views is so mixed and confused that we must depart from it and consider, first the physical, secondly the mental, differences between the races.

First, In regard to the physical differences between the races.

In discussing this portion of the subject, we will not confine ourselves to the views announced by Thomas Jefferson, but will examine all the views and statements which have been urged since his work appeared, and which support his views.

The physical differences which are urged as existing between whites and blacks are, first, those which relate to the bones of the body; secondly, those which relate to the muscles;

* *Discourse on Slavery and the Annexation of Texas.* p. 11.—J. M. S.

thirdly, those which relate to the texture of the hair; and fourthly, the color of the skin. . . .

The color of their skin is, in the opinion of Thomas Jefferson and his followers, another objection to incorporating the blacks into the American Republic. This may be called the "physical distinction" upon which the question is made to rest by the opponents of the black man in this Republic.

Mr. Jefferson asks, with an air of triumph, "Is this difference of no importance? Is it not the foundation of a greater or less share of beauty in the two races? Are not the fine mixtures of red and white, the expressions of every passion by greater or less suffusions of color in the one, preferable to that eternal monotony which reigns in the countenances, that immovable veil of black which covers all the emotions of the other race?" We regret that a sense of propriety prohibits us from finishing this quotation, for the argument against the part which must be omitted is full and conclusive.

In reply to what has been quoted from Mr. Jefferson, it would be sufficient to give the testimony of Mr. Waddington, in regard to a race of black men whom he saw on the eastern coast of Africa. He says, "The general complexion of the Shegya is jet black—clear, glossy, jet black—which appeared to my then unprejudiced eyes to be the finest color that could be selected for a human being." Mr. Jefferson himself, if we may credit the statement of Dr. Bacon, in his account of the colored Virginians who are now living in Liberia—Mr. Jefferson himself has left living testimony against his own expressions above quoted—testimony whose close resemblance to himself, and partial inheritance of his talents, should forever close the mouths of men who refer to Jefferson's *Notes on Virginia* as proof of the impossibility of incorporating the colored race into the state. "That testimony," says Dr. Bacon, "is a colored granddaughter of Thomas Jefferson." Those who are anxious to examine this matter will find the statements alluded to in the *Wanderings on the Seas and Shores of Africa,* by Dr. F. R. Bacon.

Another witness against this view of Mr. Jefferson, is Bishop Heber. On his first entrance into the Hoogly river he described the crew of a vessel as *"extremely black,* but well made, with good countenances and fine features—certainly a handsome race.*

There is higher testimony than Mr. Waddington, or Thomas

* J. C. Prichard, *Physical History of Man,* Vol. 4, p. 236.—J. M. S.

Jefferson, or Bishop Heber, on this subject—testimony which
we can hold in regard, if the Apostle of Democracy did not—

I am black but comely, oh ye daughter of Jerusalem, as the
tents of Kedar, as the curtains of Solomon. Look not upon me, because I am black, because the sun hath looked upon me: my
mother's children were angry with me; they made me the keeper
of the vineyards . . .*

I am black but comely . . .
"For we are all His workmanship."†

Such testimony is enough to show that there is nothing essentially hideous or distinctly deformed in a black complexion.

Let us take a more general view of this matter, the complexion of the human skin. The fact is, that the term *white*
is an arbitrary one, when used in contradistinction to *black,*
the latter meaning the colored mixed race now enslaved in this
Republic.

A more accurate investigation of the subject has shown that
there are but three great varieties to the human complexion,
varieties under which all mankind may be classed: The Leucos,
or white, variety; the Xanthic, or yellow, variety; and the
Melanic, or black, variety.

First, in regard to the leucos, or white, complexion. The
word *white*, in physics, means a combination of all colors; a
reflection, from the white object, of all the rays of color, hence
the object itself is perfectly colorless. In the leucos, or white-
skinned, variety of mankind, therefore, there is an entire
absence of coloring matter in the skin, which is milk-white, in
the hair, which is also white, and in the iris, which suffers the
red blood to gleam through its colorless parietes. There is an
absence of the dark pigment in the colored coat. This color,
or rather colorless, skin is not confined to mankind. It occurs
frequently among domesticated animals, in rabbits, cats and
dogs, sheep, hogs, goats, et cetera. It has been found in many
wild species, as in monkeys, squirrels, rats and mice; several
species of birds, as crows, blackbirds, canary birds, partridges,
et cetera, exhibit similar phenomena, having their feathers of
a pure white color and their eyes red.

White has often been termed, from Lord Bacon's time, the
color of *defect*. The whiteness of the hair is owing to a defect of a peculiar secretion. It is in age, when the frame has

* Song of Solomon 1:5–6.—J. M. S.
† Ephesians 2:10.—J. M. S.

lost its vigor and the life has extended beyond its prime, that the hair of men—not albinos—turns white. A similar delicacy, or deficiency in strength, of constitution appears to accompany the leucos, or albino, variety of mankind from birth. It is congenital deficiency. Hence the pure white is a deformed variety of the human species. The leucos, or white, class of men are very few. But the most curious fact is that they may be children of either the Negro or the European, the Indian or the Asiatic. All have seen, in the museums, white children with black parents. These are leucos, or albino, children. Cases are recorded of albinos born of white parents. We saw one a few months ago. The complexion was the same milk-white with the albinos of African origin. The features were European, and the hair, also white, was straight. Horace Greeley is nearly an albino. Far from being the rule or distinctive type of any race, then, the albino, or white, is a variety, an exception, occurring in all races, whether African or Caucasian, Indian or Mongolian.

Second, the xanthous variety of complexion is marked by yellow hair and light eyes. The color of the skin is fair but not white, and is agreeaby relieved by that ruddy tint which characterizes the sanguine temperament. The xanthous variety of mankind appears to have a degree of the same delicacy which marks the leucoses. Medical writers from the time of Galen have remarked a certain degree of irritability and delicacy of constitution in what they term the sanguine temperament. Persons of very fair compexion are often less robust than those of more swarthy hue. The xanthous variety composes a much larger proportion of mankind than the leucos variety. The north of Europe, including the Danes, the Belgians, a portion of the Germans, and the northeastern part of Asia—to wit, Eastern Siberia—and even some of the Highlands of Africa, are principally inhabited by the xanthous variety of mankind.

Third, the melanocomous, or dark-haired, variety of mankind is distinguished by black hair, dark eyes, and a compexion, varying from a bright brunette of the Italian to jet black of the Negro. Men of the melanie variety are of the choleric or melancholic temperament, and have generally sounder and more vigorous constitutions, and are less susceptible of morbific impressions from external causes than the sanguine. This variety composes the greatest proportion of the human race. The south of Europe, nearly all Asia, all Africa and Australia, with a large portion of the American continent, are occupied by the melanic, or dark, variety of mankind. To this variety of mankind, says Dr. Prichard, the Negro belongs.

Hence it appears that the black comprises no special variety of the human race, no distinctive species of mankind, but is part and parcel of the great original stock of humanity—of the rule, and not of the exception. He also belongs to that variety which is endowed with the most powerful constitutions.

This black complexion does not constitute him a special or distinctive variety in the melanic race. Far from it. In America and in India are found men of the melanic race quite as black as the African Negro. It is stated by Dr. Forry that "even among the American [Indian] tribes, known the world over as the *red man*, the most remarkable diversities of complexion are presented, varying from a decidedly white to an unequivocally black skin. Of so deep a hue are the Californians that La Perouse compares them to the Negro of the West Indies. "The complexion of the Californians," he says, "very nearly resembles that of Negroes."

"Although the Americans," says Dr. Morton, "possess a pervading and characteristic complexion, there are occasional and very remarkable deviations, including all the tints, from a decided white to an unequivocally black skin."

In India there are not only many Hindus with complexion perfectly black, but what is more singular, the Brahmins, even of the highest caste, vary in complexion from nearly white to perfectly black.

Mr. Fraser, in his journey to the Himalaya, states that the Pavrias, or hill tribes, of Garbawal, Suinor and Bisabur vary in complexion from a dark brown or black to a tawny yellow. Mr. Traill (Prichard, Vol. 4, p. 205) states that the Doms, natives of Kuman, are extremely black, their hair inclining to wool.

Bishop Heber also says of the Hindus, "The great difference in color between the different natives struck me much. Of the crowd by whom we were surrounded, some were black as Negroes, others merely copper-colored, and others little darker, et cetera." Mr. Mill, the principal of Bishop's College, who has seen more of India than most men, tells me that he cannot account for this difference, which is general throughout the country and everywhere striking. It is not merely the difference of exposure, since this variety of tint is visible in the fish women who are naked all alike. Nor does it depend on caste, since very high-caste Brahmins are sometimes black, while Pariahs are comparatively fair.

From these facts, it is evident that the black complexion is not confined to the Negroes of Africa and their descendants in this country.

There is proof on another point—namely, that the black

complexion of the Negro is not peculiar to him as a variety of the melanic race, but arises from a climatic influence which produces the same color on men who are not Negroes. These climatic agencies are a low, flat soil, in a very hot climate. It is a popular opinion that all the natives of Negroland, or the slave region of Africa, are black. This is not true.

The Fulahs are a tribe of Africans living on the borders of the Senegal, between Podher and Galam. They have been generally termed blacks. But, according to Park and other travelers, they are not black. He says they have soft, silky hair, and are of a tawny color. These Fulahs, of a lighter complexion than other Africans, are natives of Fouta-Jallo in the high regions about Timbu.

Among the Abyssinians, on the eastern coast of Africa, there is every variety of complexion, from the pure black to the xanthic, or as it is called popularly, the white race. A question which here presents itself, says Dr. Prichard, "is whether differences in complexion exist among the Abyssinians, bearing any relation to climate or the elevation of countries.

"The low and hot tracts which extend round Abyssinia to the west and northwest, covered with forests and containing the plants and animals of tropical climates, are inhabited by the Shan-galla Negroes. To the eastward, the low countries are occupied by Ha-Forta or Shiho, who are almost equally black."

Dixan, although situated at a considerable elevation above the coast, is a comparatively low region. Mr. Salt informs us that the people here are of a very dark hue, few of them having claims to the term "copper-colored," which Mr. Bruce bestowed on them.

Mr. Bruce informs us that the natives of the high regions of Narea, or Enarea, of the high country, are lightest in complexion of any people of Abyssinia.

"The Fungi, a race of Negroes who two hundred years ago conquered the highlands of Nubia, are now no longer Negroes in appearance."

In India, the Hindus who dwell on low, flat lands have a pure-black complexion, whilst those of the same race, language and religion, who live in a higher and colder region, about Jumnotri and Gangotri, have the following appearance: — "Their complexions are frequently fair, though much sunburnt, their eyes often blue, their hair and beards curled, and of a light and even red color." (P. 209. See Vol. 4, p. 248.)

From these facts it is plain that the black complexion of the Negro race is not a distinctive mark, separating them from the rest of mankind, but is, on the contrary, a result of the combined influence of the hot climate and low, marshy soil, on which they or their ancestors resided in Africa.

From these facts it would appear that under climatic influences of a peculiar kind, the complexion of the dark races, even of the black, can be changed to a lighter, even a white hue. The Ethiopian can change his skin.

It is a familiar fact that the hue of a white man can be greatly changed by a residence in a torrid climate.

Hence it would seem that the color of the skin, be that color what it may, does not mark a distinct species in man.

A curious inquiry here suggests itself: What was the original complexion of mankind? Deeply interesting as is this inquiry, we cannot examine into it at present. Dr. Prichard (Vol. 1, p. 220) records his belief that the original complexion of the human race was the dark or melanic complexion.

The older anatomists held that the color of the skin, in the Negro, depended upon a specific membrane peculiar to him. Microscopic science has exploded this idea. Before quoting the highest authority on this point, it may be well to state that the skin of the human being is made up of cells of very minute size; by tearing open an orange, and examining one of the extremely small bags which contain the juice, an accurate idea of an anatomic cell is afforded, as to shape; if we imagine a dark central spot in one of these cells, we see what microscopists call a *nucleus;* and if within this dark spot we imagine one still smaller and darker, this is what microscopy terms a *nucleolus* or central *nucleus.*

Writing of the color of the human skin, Mr. Wilson says, "There is another feature in the history of the development of the epidermal cell which I regard as peculiarly interesting. This relates to an organic change taking place in the assimilative powers of the primitive granules by which the latter are altered in their color; in short, are converted into 'pigment granules.' Pigment granules appear to differ in no respect from the primitive granules, excepting in tint of color. They have the same globular form, the same size, and occupy the same position in the cell, being always accumulated around the nucleus and dispersed less numerously through the rest of the cell. The nucleus of the cell in the epidermis of the Negro appears to consist wholly of pigment granules, while in the European there is greater or less admixture of colored or uncolored granules. . . . When pigment granules are examined separately, they offer very little indication of the depth of color which is produced by their accumulation. We have observed some to have the hue of amber, while others scarcely exceeded the most delicate fawn. The depth of color of the deep stratum of the epidermis in the Negro is evidently due to the composition of that layer of these granules chiefly." (*Diseases of the Skin,* by Erasmus Wilson, F. R. S., fourth edition, London 1857, p. 12.)

The fact that the fairest women of the "white" races, during gestation, present an accumulation of these pigment granules, in other words, turn nearly black around the centres of the mammae, may afford a hint on the original complexion of the human race.

We have now arrived at a resting place in this tedious array of facts. We have carefully examined into the principal physical differences, which are alleged to constitute a bar in the way of incorporating the black men into the American state.

Do these differences in reality constitute such a bar? "Words," said Mirabeau, "are things." The history of words would be one of the most interesting of all histories. You may have observed that we use the word *black,* as distinguishing the class whom we have under consideration. This word *black* and the other word *Negro* were the common, the usual, term used for this class at the time Mr. Jefferson wrote. That is more than fifty years ago. The newspapers, sure indices of public opinion, now call this same class *"colored people."* The class is the same, the name is changed; they are no longer blacks, bordering on bestiality; they are "colored," and they are a "people." I will not stop to inquire whether the word *colored* be used as a euphony for *black,* nor whether it marks the fact of an already perceptible change in the hue of the skin of this class. It answers our argument if it show, and it does show, a lessening of the distance—a step toward harmony and reciprocal kindness between man and his fellow man—between the black and the white man in this Republic.

The question is already partly answered; the physical differences do not constitute a permanent bar, because the public voice has already softened the terms which denote those differences.

Then there is that other word, *people.* What does it mean? Tell us, poor, cringing sycophant, thou who art fearful that the two races can only live together as master and slave, what does this word *people* mean? In Thomas Jefferson's time, "we, the people" meant men endowed with certain unalienable rights; men exercising those rights, the noblest of which was the great, the Godlike right of governing themselves! There was, then, in that word *people* a profound, a sublime import. It meant men who were part and parcel of—were the great sires and the great inheritors of this

Fair broad Empire, State with State,

which their prowess in war had snatched from tyrannical
hands—which their wisdom in peace had erected into a magnificent fabric, capable of holding within its ample dome the
majestic presence of Liberty!

Hic currus fuit! hic illius arma! [*This was a chariot! This
its weapons!*]

Here were her arms, and here reposed her chariot. The same
import which the word *people* had then, the same import it
has now. Place before it what epithet you may, let the American
public but call men *people,* and those men, residing in this
Republic, are already raised by the public voice into the dignity
and privileges of citizenship. I care not if the fact be delayed
a few years; the principle is already established; the physical
distinctions of the black class in this country are not any longer
a bar against their being incorporated with the people of the
state.

The question asked by Mr. Jefferson in his fourteenth
query would never have been propounded had he been acquainted with the philosophy of human progress. Instead of
asking, How shall we get rid of them?—instead of affirming
that they could never be safely incorporated in the state—had
he possessed the insight or sagacity for which he is so celebrated, he would have welcomed their presence as one of the
positive elements of natural progress. . . .

Whilst Jefferson, Dewey, and last of all Doolittle, raise their
impotent voices to exclude the blacks from the United States,
Henry Ward Beecher* exclaims from his pulpit, with higher instincts and keener insight, "What! drive out the colored people
from among us? I would as soon, with these two hands, undertake to uproot and cast out every shrub, bush and tree that
grows between this and the Rocky Mountains!"

* Henry Ward Beecher (1813–1887), an antislavery clergyman, spoke out
against slavery regularly in sermons delivered in Plymouth Church of
Brooklyn, New York, where, on October 10, 1847, he began a public career
unequaled by any other American clergyman.

THE AMERICAN GOVERNMENT AND THE NEGRO

By Robert Purvis

Robert Purvis was born on November 4, 1810, in Charleston, South Carolina, the son of William Purvis, an English merchant, and a Jewish-Moorish mother, Harriet Judah. In 1819 William Purvis sent the entire family to Philadelphia, where his three sons could be educated. He died in 1825 leaving an inheritance of $125,000. Robert Purvis was educated in private schools in Philadelphia and spent some time at Pittsfield Academy and finished his education at Amherst College. But he left college to devote himself to the antislavery movement and at the age of seventeen made his first public speech against slavery. Purvis, a wealthy Negro who lived in a fine home in a suburb of Philadelphia, was one of a group of black Americans who gave Garrison money to help him launch The Liberator in 1831. Two years later Purvis became a charter member of the American Anti-Slavery Society. He was also a founder of the Pennsylvania Anti-Slavery Society, "president" of the Pennsylvania Underground Railroad, and a vigorous fighter against discrimination against Negroes until his death in 1898.

At the twenty-seventh anniversary of the American Anti-Slavery Society in New York City, May 8, 1860, Purvis, a leading figure on the antislavery lecture platform, delivered a brilliant denunciation of the American government for its treatment of the Negro.

Here is part of Purvis' speech, excerpted from The Liberator, *May 18, 1860.*

. . . SIR, I need not say here that I belong to the same class who at the South are bought and leased, mortgaged, and in all respects treated as absolute property; I belong to the class who, here at the North, are declared by the highest tribunal known to your government, to possess "no rights that a *white* man is bound to respect."*

I say *your* government; it is not mine. Thank God, I have

---

* The allusion is to the Dred Scott decision.

no willing share in a government that deliberately, before the world and without a blush, declares one part of its people —and that for no crime or pretext of crime—disfranchised and outlawed. For such a government, I as a man can have no feeling but of *contempt, loathing* and *unutterable abhorrence!* And, sir, I venture to affirm that there is no man in the audience who has a spark of manhood in him, who has a tittle of genuine self-respect in his bosom, who does not justify me in these feelings.

What are the facts in the case? What is the attitude of your boasting, braggart Republic toward the 600,000 free people of color who swell its population and add to its wealth? I have already alluded to the dictum of Judge Taney in the notorious Dred Scott decision. That dictum reveals the animus of the whole government; it is a fair example of the cowardly and malignant spirit that pervades the entire policy of the country. The end of that policy is, undoubtedly, to destroy the colored man as a man, to prevent him from having any existence in the land except as a "chattel personal to all intents, constructions and purposes whatsoever." With this view, it says a colored man shall not sue and recover his lawful property; he shall not bear arms and train in the militia; he shall not be a commander of a vessel, not even of the meanest craft that creeps along the creeks and bays of your Southern coast; he shall not carry a mailbag, or serve as a porter in a post office; and he shall not even put his face in a United States courtroom for any purpose, except by the sufferance of the white man.

I had occasion, a few days since, to go to the United States courtroom in the city of Philadelphia. My errand was a proper one; it was to go bail for one of the noble band of colored men who had so bravely risked their lives for the rescue of a brother man on his way to eternal bondage. As I was about entering the door, I was stopped, and ordered back. I demanded the reason. "I have my orders," was the reply. What orders? "To keep out all colored people." Now, sir, who was the man that offered me this indignity? It was Deputy Marshal Jenkins, the notorious slave catcher. And why did he do it? Because he had his orders from pious, praying, Christian Democrats, who hold and teach the damnable doctrine that the "black man has no rights that the white man is bound to respect." It is true that Marshal Yost, to whom I indignantly appealed, reversed this man's orders and apologized to me, assuring me that I could go in and out at my pleasure. But, sir, the apology made the matter worse; for, mark you, it was not me personally that was objected to, *but the race* with which I stand identified. Great God! who can think of such outrages, such meanness, such dastardly, cowardly cruelty, without burning with indignation, and choking for want of words with which to denounce it? And in the case of the noble little band referred to, the men who generously, heroically risked their lives to rescue the man who was about being carried back to slavery, look at their conduct; you know the circumstances. We recently had a slave trial in Philadelphia —no new thing in the City of *Brotherly Love.* A victim of Virginia tyranny, a fugitive from Southern injustice, had made good his escape from the land of whips and chains to Pennsylvania, and had taken up his abode near the capital of the state. The place of his retreat was discovered; the bloodhounds of the law scented him out, and caught him; they put him in chains and brought him before Judge Cadwallader, a man whose proslavery antecedents made him a fitting instrument for the execution of the accursed Fugitive Slave Law.

The sequel can easily be imagined. Brewster, a leading Democrat—the man who, like your O'Conor* of this city, has the unblushing hardihood to defend the enslavement of the black man upon principle—advocated his return. The man was sent into lifelong bondage. While the trial was going on, slaveholders, Southern students and proslavery Market Street salesmen were freely admitted; but the colored people, the class most interested, were carefully excluded. Prohibited from entering, they thronged around the door of the courthouse. At last the prisoner was brought out, handcuffed and guarded by his captors; he was put into a carriage which started off in the direction of the South. Some ten or twelve brave black men made a rush for the carriage, in hopes of effecting a rescue; they were overpowered, beaten, put under arrest and carried to prison, there to await their trial, before this same Judge Cadwallader, for violating the Fugitive Slave Law! Mark you, they may go into the courtroom as *prisoners,* but not as *spectators!* They may not have an opportunity of hearing the law expounded, but they may be punished if they make themselves chargeable with violating it!

Sir, people talk of the bloody code of Draco, but I venture to assert, without fear of intelligent contradiction, that, all things considered, that code was mild, that code was a law of love, compared with the hellish laws and precedents that disgrace the statute books of this modern democratic, Christian Republic! I said that a man of color might not be a commander

* Charles O'Conor, a Democratic party lawyer in New York, was a blatant supporter of slavery and the slaveowners.

of the humblest craft that sails in your American waters. There was a man in Philadelphia, the other day, who stated that he owned and sailed a schooner between that city and different ports in the state of Maryland—that his vessel had been seized in the town of Easton (I believe it was) or some other town on the Eastern Shore, on the allegation that, contrary to law, there was no white man on board. The vessel constituted his entire property and sole means of supporting his family. He was advised to sue for its recovery, which he did, and, after a long and expensive litigation, the case was decided in his favor. But by this time the vessel had rotted and gone to wreck, and the man found himself reduced to beggary. His business in Philadelphia was to raise fifty dollars with which to take himself and family out of this cursed land, to a country where liberty is not a mockery, and freedom a mere idle name! . . .

But, sir, narrow and proscriptive as, in my opinion, is the spirit of what is called native Americanism,* there is another thing I regard as tenfold more base and contemptible, and that is your American democracy—your piebald and rotten democracy—that talks loudly about equal rights and at the same time tramples one sixth of the population of the country in the dust and declares that they have "no rights which a white man is bound to respect." And, sir, while I repudiate your native Americanism and your bogus democracy, allow me to add, at the same time, that I am not a Republican. I could not be a member of the Republican party if I were so disposed; I am disfranchised; I have no vote; I am put out of the pale of political society. The time was in Pennsylvania, under the old Constitution, when I could go to the polls as other men do, but your modern democracy has taken away from me that right.† Your Reform Convention, your Pierce Butlers—the man who, a year ago, put up nearly four hundred human beings on the block in Georgia, and sold them to the highest bidder—your Pierce Butlers disfranchised me, and I am without any political rights whatever. I am taxed to support a government which takes my money and tramples on me. But, sir, I would not be a member of the Republican party if it were in my power. How could I,

* The native American movement opposed foreign immigration, especially of Irish Catholics. Its strength was reflected in the rise of the Know-Nothing Party in the 1850's.
† In 1838 the legislature of Pennsylvania passed legislation disfranchising the free people of color in the state. Robert Purvis was chairman of a protest meeting of Pennsylvania Negroes opposing the legislation, and one of the authors of an "Appeal of Forty Thousand Citizens Threatened with Disfranchisement to the People of Pennsylvania."

a colored man, join a party that styles itself emphatically the "white man's party"? How could I, an Abolitionist, belong to a party that is and must of necessity be a proslavery party? The Republicans may be, and doubtless are, opposed to the extension of slavery, but they are sworn to support, and they *will* support, slavery where it already exists. . . . No, sir, I am not a Republican. I can never join a party the leaders of which conspire to expel us from the country. . . .

Sir, in contrast with the feelings manifested by Greeley and other Republican leaders toward the colored man,* look at that noble martyr and saint, the innocent hero of Harpers Ferry! John Brown† believed what he professed, and practiced what he believed:

> He nobly acted what he nobly thought,
> And sealed by death the lessons which he taught.

He believed that the black man was a man, and he laid down his life to secure for him the rights of man. Who can look at the noble hero and see him stoop on the way to the scaffold to kiss the Negro child, and not be struck with admiration at his fidelity and sublime consistency? Sir, the antislavery cause is onward; its doctrines are destined to triumph in this country; and no party can succeed that refuses to acknowledge it. Slavery will be abolished in this land, and with it, that twin relic of barbarism, prejudice against color.

* In 1860 the Democrats charged that the Republicans, if they should win the Presidential election, would abolish slavery and extend civil rights to Negroes. Republican spokesmen, answering this charge, openly proclaimed the party as a "white man's party." Horace Greeley, editor of the New York *Tribune* and an influential Republican spokesman, declared publicly that the Republican party sought no more than to restrict slavery to the existing states, and did not aim to abolish slavery or to extend equal rights to free Negroes.

† Leading a group of nineteen men that included five Negroes and his own sons, John Brown (1800–1859) attacked the federal arsenal at Harpers Ferry, Virginia, October 16, 1859, with the aim of fomenting a slave revolt and eventually establishing a Negro republic in the mountains of Virginia. Brown and his men captured the arsenal, but the next day a company of United States Marines under Colonel Robert E. Lee assaulted the group, killed ten and took Brown prisoner. After a hurried trial, the wounded Brown was sentenced to be hanged. Brown's bravery and dignity during the trial and on the scaffold moved millions of people to regard him as a hero. Among the Negro people, he was considered a saint.

I DO NOT BELIEVE IN THE ANTISLAVERY OF ABRAHAM LINCOLN

By H. Ford Douglass

In the Presidental campaign of 1860, black Americans, even though few of them could vote, were confronted with the question of whom to support. There were four candidates for the Presidential office, and many Negroes preferred Abraham Lincoln, the Republican nominee, though few were enthusiastic about him. Some, however, regarded Lincoln as no better than the other candidates, an advocate of white supremacy and an opponent of equality for Negroes. The most outspoken black critic of Lincoln was H. Ford Douglass, of Illinois.

A runaway slave who became a leading Abolitionist orator in the Midwest, Douglass came east during the 1860 campaign and delivered a series of speeches attacking the Republican candidate. On July 4, he spoke at Framingham, Massachusetts, at a mass meeting sponsored by the Massachusetts Anti-Slavery Society, held to celebrate the day and, in the words of the call, "to consider the solemn and pregnant issues of the hour—how best to preserve the principles of the Revolution and carry them forward to a speedy and enduring triumph." The black orator not only catalogued the reasons why no friend of the slave could support Lincoln, but went on to challenge the advocates of Negro inferiority, among whom he listed the Republican Presidential candidate. His speech is especially interesting in view of the current controversy over the man hailed in history textbooks as the "Great Emancipator."

(The major part of Douglass' speech is presented here; it is taken from The Liberator, July 3, 1860.)

MR. PRESIDENT, LADIES AND GENTLEMEN: I hope that my friends will not do me the injustice to suppose for a single moment that I have any connection, either by blood or politically, with Stephen Arnold Douglas,* of Chicago. I am some-

* Stephen Arnold Dougles (1831–1861) was the Democratic Senator from Illinois. He infuriated all antislavery groups when he introduced the Kansas-Nebraska bill in 1854, with its provision permitting the existence of slavery in territories above the line delimiting it in the Missouri Com-

what proud of the name of Douglass. It was once, in the history of dear old Scotia, a tower of strength on the side of free principles;* and so firmly did they oppose the usurpations of royal power, that, on one of the kings of Scotland coming to the throne, he issued an edict, expelling from his realm every man who bore that hated name; and I cannot account for the signal departure from the ancient and hereditary principles by one who bears that name, upon any other theory than that of bastard blood.

There are a great many people in this country who seem to be in love with Stephen A. Douglas, and to regard him as a great statesman. It seems to me that there are certain elements necessary to true statesmanship. In the first place, a statesman must have a heart—that is one of the essential elements of statesmanship. Now, who supposes that Stephen A. Douglas has a heart? I cannot account for the existence of so mean a man as Douglas on any other theory than that of the transmigration of souls. It was held by one of the old philosophers of Greece that when a man died, somebody was born, and that the soul of the dead entered the body of the newborn; but when Douglas was born, nobody happened to die!

But, ladies and gentlemen, I had no intention of making these remarks. We are here for the purpose of celebrating the Fourth of July. Eighty-four years ago today, this nation had its birth. We stand, to-day, a governmental prodigy, surpassing, in our extraordinary growth, any of the states of ancient or modern times. But nations who seek success amid the possibilities of the future are not measured by the accumulation of wealth or by the breadth of territorial domain; for down beneath the glittering splendor which the jeweled hand of Croesus has lifted up to intoxicate the gaze of the unthinking multitude, there will be found a silent and resistless influence working its way beneath the surface of society and shaping the destiny of men.

When John Adams wrote that this would always be a day of bonfires and rejoicing, he did not foresee the evils which half a century would bring, when his own son, standing in his place amid the legislators of the Republic, would shame posterity into a brave indifference to its empty ceremonies. John

---

promise. Antislavery people also disliked Douglas' advocacy of the doctrine of popular sovereignty under which the people of a territory have the right to decide for themselves whether they wish the territory to be admitted to the Union as a slave or a free state.

* The Scottish hero Douglass was celebrated in Sir Walter Scott's poem "Lady of the Lake." Frederick Douglass, after he escaped from slavery, derived his name from Scott's hero.

Quincy Adams said, twenty years ago, that "the preservation, propagation and perpetuation of slavery is the vital and animating spirit of the national government,"* and this truth is no less apparent today. Every department of our national life— the President's chair, the Senate of the United States, the Supreme Court, and the American pulpit—is occupied and controlled by the dark spirit of American slavery. We have four parties in this country that have marshaled themselves on the highway of American politics, asking for the votes of the American people to place them in possession of the government. We have what is called the Union party, led by Mr. Bell of Tennessee;† we have what is called the Democratic party, led by Stephen A. Douglas, of Illinois; we have the party called the Seceders, or the Slave-Code Democrats, led by John C. Breckinridge, of Kentucky,‡ and then we have the Republican party, led by Abraham Lincoln, of Illinois.§ All of these parties ask for your support, because they profess to represent some principle. So far as the principles of freedom and the hopes of the black man are concerned, all these parties are barren and unfruitful; neither of them seeks to lift the Negro out of his fetters and rescue this day from odium and disgrace.

Take Abraham Lincoln. I want to know if any man can tell me the difference between the antislavery of Abraham Lincoln

* After serving as President of the United States from 1825 to 1829, John Quincy Adams (1767–1848) served as a Representative in Congress and played a leading role in the House in opposition to the extension of slavery and a champion of the right of petition for antislavery men and women. He made this statement during the Congressional debate over excluding abolition petitions. For the background of the statement, see Russel B. Nye, *Fettered Freedom: A Discussion of Civil Liberties and the Slavery Controversy in the United States, 1830 to 1860*, East Lansing, Michigan, 1949, pp. 35–49.
† John Bell (1797–1869), U. S. Senator from Tennessee, was the leader of the conservative elements in the South which supported both slavery and the Union. He was nominated for the Presidency in 1860 by the Constitutional Union party.
‡ In April, 1860, the Democratic national convention met at Charleston, but split over the question of federal protection of slavery in the territories. When this proposal by the delegates from the eight Southern states was rejected, they withdrew and the convention adjourned. On June 18 the Democrats reconvened at Baltimore, but this time when the Southern delegates again left, the convention nominated Stephen A. Douglas on a popular-sovereignty platform. On June 28, the Southern delegates who had bolted the convention met in Baltimore and chose John C. Breckinridge (1821–1875), of Kentucky, for President on a platform advocating federal protection of slavery in the territories.
§ The Republican party, meeting in Chicago, nominated Abraham Lincoln as their Presidential candidate on May 18, 1860.

and the antislavery of the old Whig party or the antislavery of Henry Clay? Why, there is no difference between them. Abraham Lincoln is simply a Henry Clay Whig, and he believes just as Henry Clay believed in regard to this question. And Henry Clay was just as odious to the antislavery cause and antislavery men as ever was John C. Calhoun.* In fact, he did as much to perpetuate Negro slavery in this country as any other man who has ever lived. Henry Clay once said, "That is property which the law declares to be property," and that "two hundred years of legislation have sanctioned and sanctified property in slaves." Wherever Henry Clay is today in the universe of God, that atheistic lie is with him, with all its tormenting memories.

I know Abraham Lincoln, and I know something about his antislavery. I know the Republicans do not like this kind of talk, because, while they are willing to steal our thunder, they are unwilling to submit to the conditions imposed upon that party that assumes to be antislavery. They say that they cannot go as fast as you antislavery men go in this matter; that they cannot afford to be uncompromisingly honest, or so radical as you Garrisonians; that they want to take time; that they want to do the work gradually. They say, "We must not be in too great a hurry to overthrow slavery; at least, we must take half a loaf, we cannot get the whole." Now, my friends, I believe that the very best way to overthrow slavery in this country is to occupy the highest possible antislavery ground. Washington Irving tells a story of a Dutchman who wanted to jump over a ditch, and he went back three miles in order to get a good start, and when he got up to the ditch he had to sit down on the wrong side to get his breath. So it is with these political parties; they are compelled, they say, when they get up to the ditch of slavery, to stop and take breath.

I do not believe in the antislavery of Abraham Lincoln, because he is on the side of this slave power of which I am speaking, that has possession of the federal government. What does he propose to do? Simply to let the people and the territories regulate their domestic institutions in their own way. In the great debate between Lincoln and Douglas in Illinois, when he was interrogated as to whether he was in favor of the admission of more slave states into the Union, he said, that so long as we owned the territories, he did not see any other way of doing than to admit those states when they made application, *with or*

* John C. Calhoun (1782–1850) was the outstanding champion of slavery in the U. S. Senate between 1832 and 1850.

*without slavery.** Now, that is Douglas' doctrine; it is stealing the thunder of Stephen A. Douglas.

In regard to the repeal of the Fugitive Slave Law, Abraham Lincoln occupies the same position that the old Whig party occupied in 1852. They asserted then, in their platform, that they were not in favor of the repeal of that law, and that they would do nothing to lessen its efficiency. What did he say at Freeport?† Why, that the South was entitled to a Fugitive Slave Law; and although he thought the law could be modified a little, yet, he said, if he was in Congress, he would have it done in such a way as *not to lessen its efficiency!* Here, then, is Abraham Lincoln in favor of carrying out that infamous Fugitive Slave Law, that not only strikes down the liberty of every black man in the United States, but virtually the liberty of every white man as well; for, under that law, there is not a man in this presence who might not be arrested today upon the simple testimony of one man, and, after an *ex parte* trial, hurried off to slavery and to chains. Habeas corpus, trial by jury—those great bulwarks of freedom, reared by the blood and unspeakable woe of your English ancestors, amidst the conflicts of a thousand years— are struck down by this law; and the man whose name is inscribed upon the Presidential banner of the Republican party is in favor of keeping it upon the statute book!

Not only would I arraign Mr. Lincoln in regard to that law, for his proslavery character and principles, but when he was a member of the House of Representatives, in 1849, on the tenth day of January, he went through the District of Columbia and consulted the prominent proslavery men and slaveholders of the District, and then went into the House of Representatives and introduced, on his own responsibility, a fugitive-slave law for the District of Columbia. It is well known that the law of 1793 did not apply to the District, and it was necessary, in order

* In the election for Senator from Illinois in 1858, Lincoln, the Republican candidate, and Douglas, the Democratic candidate, conducted a series of seven debates throughout the state. It is not clear what source H. Ford Douglass used to describe Lincoln's position during the debates on the question of slavery in the territories, since Lincoln made it clear that while neither he nor the Republican party wished to interfere with slavery where it already existed, both flatly opposed the further extension of slavery. Moreover, Lincoln was nominated for the Presidency in 1860 on a platform which denied "the authority of Congress, of a territorial legislature, or of any individuals to give legal existence to slavery in any territory of the United States."

† The second in the series of Lincoln-Douglas debates took place on August 27, 1858, at Freeport, Illinois.

that slaveholders might catch their slaves who sought safety under the shadow of the Capitol, that a special law should be passed for the District of Columbia; and so Mr. Lincoln went down deeper into the proslavery pool than even Mr. Mason of Virginia did in the Fugitive Slave Law of 1850. Here, then, is the man who asks for your votes and for the votes of the anti-slavery people of New England; who, on his own responsibility, without any temptation whatever, introduced into the District of Columbia a fugitive-slave law!* That is a fact for the consideration of antislavery men.

Then, there is another item which I want to bring out in this connection. I am a colored man; I am an American citizen, and I think that I am entitled to exercise the elective franchise. I am about twenty-eight years old, and I would like to vote very much. I think I am old enough to vote, and I think that, if I had a vote to give, I should know enough to place it on the side of freedom.† No party, it seems to me, is entitled to the sympathy of antislavery men, unless that party is willing to extend to the black man all the rights of a citizen. I care nothing about that antislavery which wants to make the territories free, while it is unwilling to extend to me, as a man, in the free states, all the rights of a man. In the state of Illinois, where I live—my adopted state—I have been laboring to make it a place fit for a decent man to live in. In that state, we have a code of black laws that would disgrace any Barbary State, or any uncivilized people in the far-off islands of the sea. Men of my complexion are not allowed to testify in a court of justice where a white man is a party. If a white man happens to owe me anything, unless I can prove it by the testimony of a white man, I cannot collect the debt. Now, two years ago, I went through the state of Illinois for the purpose of getting signers to a petition asking

---

* Douglass does not mention the fact that when Lincoln served in Congress in the years 1847–49, he voted against the Mexican War and on January 10, 1849, introduced a resolution proposing the abolition of slavery in the District of Columbia.

† After H. Ford Douglass had completed his speech, Frank B. Sanborn, an antislavery leader in New England and former associate of John Brown, declared: "When I reflect . . . that Mr. Douglass, with every power, with every talent, which, had he been of our own race, would have secured him a prominent position, not only among the citizens, but among the rulers of this country, and remember that instead of this, in his adopted state—a state which he earned by his heroic escape from slavery—he has not a single political right—when I reflect on this, it seems to me that our whole nation, our whole system of society, is not worth a straw. . . ." (*The Liberator,* July 3, 1860.)

the legislature to repeal the "Testimony Law," so as to permit colored men to testify against white men. I went to prominent Republicans, and among others, to Abraham Lincoln and Lyman Trumbull,* and neither of them dared to sign that petition, to give me the right to testify in a court of justice! In the state of Illinois, they tax the colored people for every conceivable purpose. They tax the Negro's property to support schools for the education of the white man's children, but the colored people are not permitted to enjoy any of the benefits resulting from that taxation. We are compelled to impose upon ourselves additional taxes in order to educate our children. The state lays its iron hand upon the Negro, holds him down, and puts the other hand into his pocket and steals his hard earnings, to educate the children of white men; and if we sent our children to school, Abraham Lincoln would kick them out, in the name of Republicanism and antislavery!

I have, then, something to say against the antislavery character of the Republican party. Not only are the Republicans of Illinois on the side of slavery, and against the rights of the Negro, but even some of the prominent Republicans of Massachusetts are not acceptable to antislavery men in that regard. In the Senate of the United States, some of your Senators from the New England states take special pains to make concessions to the slave power, by saying that they are not in favor of bringing about Negro equality; just as Abraham Lincoln did down in Ohio two years ago. When he went there to stump that state, the colored people were agitating the question of suffrage in that state. The *Ohio Statesman*, a paper published in Columbus, asserted, on the morning of the day that Mr. Lincoln made his speech, that he was in favor of Negro equality; and Mr. Lincoln took pains at that time to deny the allegation, by saying that he was not in favor of bringing about the equality of the Negro race; that he did not believe in making them voters, in placing them in the jury box, or in ever bringing about the political equality of the races. He said that so long as they lived here, there must be an inferior and superior position, and that he was, as much as anybody else, in favor of assigning to white men the superior position.†

* Lyman Trumbull (1813–1896) was United States Senator from Illinois between 1855 and 1873. A leader of the Republican party, he supported Lincoln in 1860.

† During Lincoln's early career in the Illinois legislature he voted in favor of a bill which, while eliminating real estate ownership as a prerequisite to the right to vote, restricted the vote to whites only. During the Lincoln-Douglas debates, Lincoln came out strongly against slavery, but also made

There is a good deal of talk in this country about the superiority of the white race. We often hear, from this very platform, praise of the Saxon race. Now, I want to put this question to those who deny the equal manhood of the Negro: What peculiar trait of character do the white men of this country possess, as a mark of superiority, either morally or mentally, that is not also manifested by the black man, under similar circumstances? You may take down the white and black part of the social and political structure, stone by stone, and in all the relations of life, where the exercise of his moral and intellectual functions is not restricted by positive law, or by the arbitrary restraints of society, you will find the Negro the equal of the white man in all the elements of head and heart. Of course, no one pretends that all men are mentally equal, or morally equal, any more than we do that all men are of the same weight, or equal in physical endowments. Here in this country, under the most favorable circumstances, we have idiots and fools, some in the lunatic asylum, and others, in the high places of government, who essay to be statesmen, who ought to be there. You say to the German, the Hungarian, the Irishman, as soon as he lands here, "Go out on the highway of the world's progress, and compete with me, if you can, in the race for empire and dominion." You throw no fetters upon that ever-restless sea of energies that chafes our shores, saying, "Thus far shalt thou go, but no further." No, with all that magnanimity which must be ever-present in the true soul, you say to the foreigner, whose liberty has been cloven down upon some disastrous European battlefield, whose fortune has been wrecked and lost amid the storms of adversity abroad, "Come here and better your condition, if you can!" I remember that a few years ago, when a Hungarian refugee—not an American citizen; he had only declared his intention to become one—was arrested in the harbor of Smyrna, for an offense against the Austrian government, Captain Ingraham, of the American warship *St. Louis*, demanded, in the name of the federal government, his instant release, and under the cover of her guns, the shackles of Austrian bondage melted from his limbs, and Martin Kozta walked the deck of that vessel a free man, as proud of his adopted country as we were of the gallant deed. That poor Hungarian, in the hour of his misfortune, could look at the American flag as it gleamed in the sunlight of the Austrian sky, and as he looked at its stars, that symbolized a constellation of republican states, he could feel all the poetic inspiration of Halleck when he sang,

it clear that he did not believe in the equality of the races and that the white race should be in a superior position.

Flag of the seas! on Ocean's wave
Thy stars shall glitter o'er the brave!
When death, careering on the gale,
Sweeps darkly 'round the bellied sail,
And frighted waves rush wildly back
Before the broadside's reeling rack,
The dying wanderer of the sea,
Shall look at once to heaven and thee,
And smile to see thy splendors fly,
In triumph o'er his closing eye.

But no colored man can feel any of this inspiration. We are denied all participation in the government; we remember that the flag only covers us as slaves, and that our liberties are only respected and our rights only secured to us, when, escaping from the beak of the American eagle, we can nestle in the shaggy mane of the British lion; and feeling this, we can feel no inspiration when we look at the American flag. . . .

Some three or four months ago a bill was under consideration in the Senate of the United States for the purpose of establishing a school for the education of free colored children in the District of Columbia. The matter created some discussion in the Senate, and, under the lash of Senator Mason, and other slave-drivers of the South, your own Senator, Mr. Wilson* "caved in" on this question and admitted, in the presence of the Senate, and with all Massachusetts to read his words, that the Negro was inferior. Now, I do not believe that the Negro is inferior. Man's ability wholly depends upon surrounding circumstances. You may take all of those races that have risen from the lowest estate of degradation to the highest eminence of intellectual and moral splendor, and you will discover that no race has ever yet been able, by any internal power and will of its own, to lift itself into respectability, without contact with other civilized tribes. Rome served as the scaffolding for the erection of the tribes of Western Europe into that huge political constellation whose drumbeats follow the sun round the world. When Julius Caesar landed in Britain, he found the ancestors of this boasted English race a miserable set of barbarians, bowing down to stocks and stones, and painting their bodies in fantastic colors. They were carried to Rome by the soldiers of Caesar and sold in the streets for five dollars; and so thoroughly brutalized were

---

* Henry Wilson (1812–1875) was U. S. Senator from Massachusetts between 1855 and 1873. A leading opponent of slavery, he was one of the founders of the Republican party. In 1872 he was elected Vice-President of the United States on the Republican ticket with Grant as President.

they that Cicero, the great Roman orator, said that the meanest slaves in Rome came from Great Britain; and, writing to his friend Atticus, he advised him not to buy the worthless wretches. Emerson says that it took many generations to trim and comb and perfume the first boatload of Norse pirates into royal highnesses and most noble knights of the garter; and yet, every spark and ornament of regal splendor dates back to the twenty thousand thieves that landed at Hastings. You will find, after that, I think, that there is no truth in the assertion that the Negro is inferior.

The men who justify slavery upon the assumed inferiority of the Negro race, are very slow to admit these facts. They are just as tardy in admitting that the remains of ancient grandeur, which have been exhumed from beneath the accumulated dust of forty centuries, were wrought by the ingenuity and skill of the Negro race, ere the Saxon was known in history. We are informed that the scepter of the world passed from the colored to the white race at the fall of Babylon. I know ethnological writers tell us we do not look like the Egyptian. They dig up an Egyptian mummy that has been dead and buried three thousand years, that once tripped "the light fantastic toe" amid the gilded halls of the Pharaohs, over whose grave the storms of thirty or forty centuries have swept, and because it doesn't look just like a Mississippi Negro of today, set it down that there is a difference in species between them!* I admit that centuries of oppression, under a vertical sun, may have worked marvelous changes not only in the physical, but in the intellectual characteristics of the race—I know it has. All other races are permitted to travel over the wide field of history and pluck the flowers that blossom there, to glean up the heroes, philosophers, sages and poets, and put them into a galaxy of brilliant genius and claim all the credit to themselves; but if a black man attempts to do so, he is met at the threshold by the objection, "You have no ancestry behind you."

Now, friends, I am proud of the Negro race, and I thank God today that there does not course in my veins a single drop of Saxon blood.† . . . I am proud of the Negro race. I think that *Negro* looks just as well on paper and sounds just as sweetly to

* For a more detailed discussion by a Negro on the relationship between the black American and the early Egyptians, see Frederick Douglass' speech "The Claims of the Negro Ethnologically Considered," pp. 152–155.

† Years later, W. E. B. Du Bois used almost the same language in his autobiography, writing: "I was born . . . with a flood of Negro blood, a strain of French, a bit of Dutch, but, thank God, no Anglo-Saxon."

the ear as *Saxon;* and I believe that by education, by wealth, by religion, the Negro may make that name as honorable as ever was that of *Saxon*, while the Saxon, by the practice of the opposite vices, may drag himself down as low as the Negro. . . .

Oh, no, friends; we colored men may well feel proud of our ancestors. Why, we were held in very high esteem by the ancient Greeks. There is a Grecian fable that we descended from the gods. Virgil says that Jupiter, in his aerial chariot, sailing through the skies, went so near the sun that it burnt his face black; and on that hypothesis they account for the existence of the colored race! The father of Grecian poetry, standing away back in the gray dawn of history, has struck some noble lines from his lyre, in praise of our ancestors of the sunny clime.*

> The sire of Gods, and all the ethereal train
> On the warm limits of the farthest main,
> Now mix with mortals, nor disdain to grace
> The feast of Ethiopia's blameless race.

Friends, I have no idea that those men who talk about the inferiority of the Negro race really believe it. They think it is absolutely necessary, for the success of their party, to cater to the dark spirit of slavery. But, after all, I say that the Negro is a man, and has all the elements of manhood, like other men; and by the way, I think that, in this country, he has the *highest* element of manhood. . . . You may dwarf his manhood by the iron of bondage, you may dry up the fountain of his intellectual life, but you can never destroy his faith in God, and the ultimate triumph of His almighty purpose. . . .

In view of the fact that the influence of slavery is dominant in every department of the government, I would rather curse than bless the hour that marked the fatal epoch in American history, when we threw off the yoke of a decent despotism, to become, in turn, the slaves of a mean and arrogant democracy. . . . Four million of my countrymen in chains today, ground between these two huge lies—like the upper and nether millstone—the Constitution of the United States and the Fourth of July, send me to the platform to bury the memory of that hour that witnessed the separation of these colonies from the mother country; for had we remained lined to her by political and social ties, we should inevitably have marched to freedom and equality, as she has done. . . . England . . . stands today, and has stood for a quarter of a century, upon the side of freedom; while

---

* Homer repeatedly praised the Ethiopians in his epic poems.

here in republican America we have, for the last eighty-three years, been constantly tending toward a despotism baser and blacker than anything that history has yet recorded. I say, then, I would rather curse than bless the day that marked the separation. . . . "Proclaim liberty throughout all the land, to all the inhabitants thereof" is the inscription upon the bell that hangs in "Independence Hall," in Philadelphia; but the old bell, more modest than the people, cracked the first time it was rung, because it had not *brass* enough to tell the lie again!

Hypocrisy is not a growth peculiar to American soil, but it has reached the most hateful development here. American slavery, the worst form of despotism ever imposed upon any people, is endorsed by Church and state as a great missionary institution. Eighty-four years ago today, your fathers . . . spoke this nation into existence, breathed into it the breath of life, by asserting the selfhood of every human being. . . . They declared that "all men are created equal"; and brave men from beyond the Rhine, and from the Rhine, and from the vine-clad hills of France, viewing from a distance that sublime struggle for the establishment of a free government, threw themselves at once into the conflict, and by their noble devotion to our cause, gave their names to history as a part of the glories of the Republic. But what did the fathers do to justify the expectations of these gallant strangers? Let four millions of slaves in our land answer the question! The liberty that Lafayette fought for, our fathers, in an hour of compromise, forgot, and went into a convention and sold the liberty of the black man, in order to form this guilty "covenant with death and agreement with hell";* and I say, that so long as that compromise exists, we are bound to stand outside the government and to commit ourselves to the dark spirit of slavery and to the political expediency of the hour. . . .

I know very well how imperfectly I have said my say. What can I say, then, as a black man, other than to thank the men and women of New England who have so nobly stood by the rights and liberties of my unfortunate race during the long years of suffering and sorrow, feeing, as their only compensation, that every wrong and every outrage which we suffer

> In the hot conflict of the right, shall be
> A token and a pledge of victory . . .

* The quotation is from William Lloyd Garrison, who described the Constitution, which guaranteed slavery, as "a covenant with death and an agreement with hell," and publicly burned copies of the document.

A PLEA FOR FREE SPEECH

By Frederick Douglass

At a meeting in Boston on December 3, 1860, to commemorate the anniversary of John Brown's execution, ruffians hired by merchants engaged in the Southern trade invaded the hall, disrupted the proceedings, and singled out Frederick Douglass, one of the speakers, for attack. Fighting "like a trained pugilist," the Negro Abolitionist was thrown "down the staircase to the floor of the hall."

The meeting was adjourned to a church on Joy Street. As the audience poured into the street, Negroes were seized, knocked down, trampled upon, and a number seriously injured. "The mob was howling with rage," Douglass recalled years later.

A few days later, Douglass spoke in Boston's Music Hall and presented one of the most stirring pleas for free speech in American history. He described at length the attack on the meeting by both respectable gentlemen and rowdies. The right of free speech, he emphasized, was basic to all other rights.

(The speech, here published in part, is taken from The Liberator, *December 14, 1860.)*

BOSTON IS a great city and Music Hall has a fame almost as extensive as Boston. Nowhere more than here have the principles of human freedom been expounded. But for the circumstances already mentioned, it would seem almost presumptuous for me to say anything here about these principles. And yet, even here, in Boston, the moral atmosphere is dark and heavy. The principles of human liberty, even if correctly apprehended, find but limited support in this hour of trial. The world moves slowly, and Boston is much like the world. We thought the principle of free speech was an accomplished fact. Here, if nowhere else, we thought, the right of the people to assemble and to express their opinion was secure. Dr. Channing had defended the right,* Mr. Garrison had practically asserted the right, and Theodore Parker had maintained it with steadiness and fidelity to the last.

* William Henry Channing (1810–1884), a Unitarian clergyman, was an ardent foe of slavery and a noted social reformer in the decades before the Civil War.

But here we are today contending for what we thought was gained years ago. The mortifying and disgraceful fact stares us in the face, that though Faneuil Hall and Bunker Hill monument stand, freedom of speech is struck down. No lengthy detail of facts is needed. They are already notorious; far more so than will be wished ten years hence.

The world knows that last Monday a meeting assembled to discuss the question, "How Shall Slavery Be Abolished?" The world also knows that that meeting was invaded, insulted, captured by a mob of gentlemen, and thereafter broken up and dispersed by the order of the mayor, who refused to protect it, though called upon to do so. If this had been a mere outbreak of passion and prejudice among the baser sort, maddened by rum and hounded on by some wily politician to serve some immediate purpose—a mere exceptional affair—it might be allowed to rest with what has already been said. But the leaders of the mob were gentlemen. They were men who pride themselves upon their respect for law and order.

These gentlemen brought their respect for the law with them and proclaimed it loudly while in the very act of breaking the law. Theirs was the law of slavery. The law of free speech and the law for the protection of public meetings they trampled underfoot, while they greatly magnified the law of slavery.

The scene was an instructive one. Men seldom see such a blending of the gentlemen with the rowdy, as was shown on that occasion. It proved that human nature is very much the same, whether in tarpaulin or broadcloth. Nevertheless, when gentlemen approach us in the character of lawless and abandoned loafers—assuming for the moment their manners and tempers—they have themselves to blame if they are estimated below their quality. No right was deemed by the fathers of the government more sacred than the right of speech. It was, in their eyes, as in the eyes of all thoughtful men, the great moral renovator of society and government. Daniel Webster called it a homebred right, a fireside privilege. Liberty was meaningless where the right to utter one's thoughts and opinions had ceased to exist. That, of all rights, is the dread of tyrants. It is the right which they first of all strike down. They know its power. Thrones, dominions, principalities, and powers, founded in injustice and wrong, are sure to tremble, if men are allowed to reason of righteousness, temperance, and of a judgment to come in their presence. Slavery cannot tolerate free speech. Five years of its exercise would banish the auction block and break every chain in the South. They will have none of it there, for they have the power. But shall it be so here?

Even here in Boston, and among the friends of freedom, we hear two voices: one denouncing the mob that broke up our meeting on Monday as a base and cowardly outrage; and another deprecating and regretting the holding of such a meeting, by such men, at such a time. We are told that the meeting was ill-timed, and the parties to it unwise.

Why, what is the matter with us? Are we going to palliate and excuse a palpable and flagrant outrage on the right of free speech, by implying that only a particular description of persons should exercise that right? Are we, at such a time, when a great principle has been struck down, to quench the moral indignation which the deed excites, by casting reflections upon those on whose persons the outrage has been committed? After all the arguments for liberty to which Boston has listened for more than a quarter of a century, has she yet to learn that the time to assert a right is the time when the right itself is called in question, and that the men of all others to assert it are the men to whom the right has been denied?

It would be no indication of the right of speech to prove that certain gentlemen of great distinction, eminent for their learning and ability, are allowed to freely express their opinions on all subjects, including the subject of slavery. Such a vindication would need, itself, to be vindicated. It would add insult to injury. Not even an old-fashioned Abolition meeting could vindicate that right in Boston just now. There can be no right of speech where any man, however lifted up, or however humble, however young, or however old, is overawed by force and compelled to suppress their honest sentiments.

Equally clear is the right to hear. To suppress free speech is a double wrong. It violates the right of the hearer as well as those of the speaker. It is just as criminal to rob a man of his right to speak and hear as it would be to rob him of his money. I have no doubt that Boston will vindicate this right. But in order to do so, there must be no concessions to the enemy. When a man is allowed to speak because he is rich and powerful, it aggravates the crime of denying the right to the poor and humble.

The principle must rest upon its own proper basis. And until the right is accorded to the humblest as freely as to the most exalted citizen, the government of Boston is but an empty name and its freedom a mockery. A man's right to speak does not depend upon where he was born or upon his color. The simple quality of manhood is the solid basis of the right—and there let it rest forever.

SECTION II

The Civil War
and Reconstruction

1861–1876

LET US TAKE UP THE SWORD

By Alfred M. Green

*Although black soldiers had fought in the American Rev-
olution and in the War of 1812, a federal law barred Negroes from serving in state militias, and there were no
Negroes in the regular United States Army. Despite this,
in the first weeks after the outbreak of the Civil War,
Northern Negroes offered their services to the government
to help suppress the rebellion. In the following speech delivered by Alfred M. Green, a Philadelphia schoolteacher,
at a meeting of Philadelphia Negroes on April 20, 1861,
barely a week after Fort Sumter, Negroes are called upon
to join the ranks of the Union Army and fight to destroy
slavery. Although these and other offers by blacks were
spurned by the federal and state governments, which responded that "this is a white man's war," Green continued
to urge Negroes to fight for the right to serve in the Union
Army. In a letter to* The Anglo-African *of October 12, 1861,
he wrote: "No nation has ever or ever will be emancipated
from slavery . . . but by the sword, wielded too by their
own strong arms. It is a foolish idea for us to still be nursing our past grievances to our own detriment, when we
should as one man grasp the sword. . . ."*

*(Green's speech, presented here, is taken from Alfred M.
Green,* Letters and Discussions on the Formation of Colored Regiments, *Philadelphia, 1862, pp. 3–4.)*

THE TIME HAS ARRIVED in the history of the great Republic when we may again give evidence to the world of the
bravery and patriotism of a race in whose hearts burns the love
of country, of freedom, and of civil and religious toleration. It is
these grand principles that enable men, however proscribed,
when possessed of true patriotism, to say, "My country, right or
wrong, I love thee still!"

It is true, the brave deeds of our fathers, sworn and subscribed to by the immortal Washington of the Revolution of
1776, and by Jackson and others in the War of 1812, have failed
to bring us into recognition as citizens, enjoying those rights
so dearly bought by those noble and patriotic sires.

It is true that our injuries in many respects are great; fugitive-slave laws, Dred Scott decisions, indictments for treason, and long and dreary months of imprisonment. The result of the most unfair rules of judicial investigation has been the pay we have received for our solicitude, sympathy and aid in the dangers and difficulties of those "days that tried men's souls."

Our duty, brethren, is not to cavil over past grievances. Let us not be derelict to duty in the time of need. While we remember the past and regret that our present position in the country is not such as to create within us that burning zeal and enthusiasm for the field of battle which inspires other men in the full enjoyment of every civil and religious emolument, yet let us endeavor to hope for the future and improve the present auspicious moment for creating anew our claims upon the justice and honor of the Republic; and, above all, let not the honor and glory achieved by our fathers be blasted or sullied by a want of true heroism among their sons.

Let us, then, take up the sword, trusting in God, who will defend the right, remembering that these are other days than those of yore; that the world today is on the side of freedom and universal political equality; that the war cry of the howling leaders of Secession and treason is: "Let us drive back the advance guard of civil and religious freedom; let us have more slave territory; let us build stronger the tyrant system of slavery in the great American Republic. Remember, too, that your very presence among the troops of the North would inspire your oppressed brethren of the South with zeal for the overthrow of the tyrant system, and confidence in the armies of the living God— the God of truth, justice and equality to all men.

WHAT IF THE SLAVES ARE EMANCIPATED?

By John S. Rock

When the Civil War began, in April, 1861, the sole Northern aim was restoration of the Union. But as the war continued, it became increasingly clear that to adhere to this position was to guarantee victory for the Confederacy. Thousands of slaves were doing the physical labor of the Confederate army—permitting the soldiers to conserve their strength for fighting, while millions of slaves were

*producing the sinews of war. Hence, black and white Aboli-
tionists argued soon after the outbreak of the war that the
struggle could not be won nor could the Union be restored
without the abolition of slavery. Repeatedly, however, they
were forced to answer the question, What should we do
with the slaves when they are emancipated? In a speech
delivered on January 23, 1862, before the Massachusetts
Anti-Slavery Society, John S. Rock came to grips with this
question. Rock not only dealt with the emancipation of the
slaves as a military necessity to guarantee a Union victory
over the Confederacy, but also discussed the future of the
free Negro in a white society.*

*Parts of Rock's speech are presented here; they are ex-
cerpted from* The Liberator, *February 4, 1862.*

LADIES AND GENTLEMEN: I am here not so much to make
a speech as to add a little more *color* to this occasion.

I do not know that it is right that I should speak, at this time,
for it is said that we have talked too much already; and it is being continually thundered in our ears that the time for speechmaking has ended, and the time for action has arrived. Perhaps
this is so. This may be the theory of the people, but we all know
that the active idea has found but little sympathy with either
of our great military commanders, or the national Executive;
for they have told us, again and again, that "patience is a cure
for all sores," and that we must wait for the "good time," which,
to us, has been long a-coming.

It is not my desire, neither is it the time for me to criticize
the government, even if I had the disposition so to do. The situation of the black man in this country is far from being an
enviable one. Today our heads are in the lion's mouth, and we
must get them out the best way we can. To contend against the
government is as difficult as it is to sit in Rome and fight with
the Pope. It is probable that, if we had the malice of the Anglo-
Saxon, we would watch our chances and seize the first opportunity to take our revenge. If we attempted this, the odds would
be against us, and the first thing we should know would be—
nothing! The most of us are capable of perceiving that the man
who spits against the wind, spits in his own face!

While Mr. Lincoln has been more conservative than I had
hoped to find him,* I recognize in him an honest man, striving

---

* Most Negroes were more critical of Lincoln, condemning the President
for failing to make emancipation the key issue of the war. This criticism
mounted after September 11, 1861, when Lincoln modified General John

to redeem the country from the degradation and shame into which Mr. Buchanan and his predecessors have plunged it.*

This nation is mad. In its devoted attachment to the Negro, it has run crazy after him and now, having caught him, hangs on with a deadly grasp, and says to him, with more earnestness and pathos than Ruth expressed to Naomi, "Where thou goest, I will go; where thou lodgest, I will lodge; thy people shall be my people, and thy God my God.". . .

The educated and wealthy class despise the Negro, because they have robbed him of his hard earnings, or, at least, have got rich off the fruits of his labor; and they believe if he gets his freedom, their fountain will be dried up and they will be obliged to seek business in a new channel. Their "occupation will be gone." The lowest class hate him because he is poor, as they are, and he is a competitor with them for the same labor. The poor ignorant white man, who does not understand that the interest of the laboring classes is mutual, argues in this wise: "Here is so much labor to be performed. That Negro does it. If he was gone, I should have his place." The rich and the poor are both prejudiced from interest, and not because they entertain vague notions of justice and humanity. While uttering my solemn protest against this American vice, which has done more than any other thing to degrade the American people in the eyes of the civilized world, I am happy to state that there are many who have never known this sin, and many others who have been converted to the truth by the "foolishness of antislavery preaching," and are deeply interested in the welfare of the race and never hesitate to use their means and their influence to help break off the yoke that has been so long crushing us. I thank them all, and hope the number may be multiplied, until we shall have a people who will know no man save by his virtues and his merits.

Now, it seems to me that a blind man can see that the present war is an effort to nationalize, perpetuate and extend slavery in this country. In short, slavery is the cause of the war: I might say, is *the* war itself. Had it not been for slavery, we should have had no war! Through two hundred and forty years of indescribable tortures, slavery has wrung out of the blood, bones and muscles of the Negro hundreds of millions of dollars and helped much to make this nation rich. At the same time, it has

C. Fremont's proclamation freeing the slaves of every rebel in the state of Missouri.

* James Buchanan (1791–1868), who was President when the secession movement took place, declared that secession was unconstitutional, but insisted that Congress had no power under the Constitution to prevent it.

developed a volcano which has burst forth, and, in a less number of days than years, has dissipated this wealth and rendered the government bankrupt! And, strange as it may appear, you still cling to this monstrous iniquity, notwithstanding it is daily sinking the country lower and lower! Some of our ablest and best men have been sacrificed to appease the wrath of this American god. . . .

There is a storm in that cloud which, today, though no larger than a man's hand, is destined to sweep over this country and wake up this guilty nation. Then we shall know where the fault is, and if these dry bones can live! The government wishes us to bring back the country to what it was before. This is possible; but what is to be gained by it? If we are fools enough to retain the cancer that is eating out our vitals when we can safely extirpate it, who will pity us if we see our mistake when we are past recovery? The Abolitionists saw this day of tribulation and reign of terror long ago and warned you of it; *but you would not hear!* You now say that it is their agitation, which has brought about this terrible civil war! That is to say, your friend sees a slow match set near a keg of gunpowder in your house and timely warns you of the danger which he sees is inevitable; you despise his warning and, after the explosion, say if he had not told you of it it would not have happened!

Now, when some leading men who hold with the policy of the President and yet pretend to be liberal argue that while they are willing to admit that the slave has an undoubted right to his liberty, the master has an equal right to his property; that to liberate the slave would be to injure the master, and a greater good would be accomplished to the country in these times by the loyal master's retaining his property than by giving to the slave his liberty—I do not understand it so. Slavery is treason against God, man and the nation. The master has no right to be a partner in a conspiracy which has shaken the very foundation of the government. Even to apologize for it, while in open rebellion, is to aid and abet in treason. The master's right to his property in human flesh cannot be equal to the slave's right to his liberty.

Today, when it is a military necessity and when the safety of the country is dependent upon emancipation, our humane political philosophers are puzzled to know what would become of the slaves if they were emancipated! The idea seems to prevail that the poor things would suffer if robbed of the glorious privileges they now enjoy! If they could not be flogged, half-starved, and work to support in ease and luxury those who have never waived an opportunity to outrage and wrong them, they would pine away and die! Do you imagine that the Negro can live out-side of slavery? Of course, now they can take care of themselves and their masters too; but if you give them their liberty, must they not suffer? Have you never been able to see through all this? Have you not observed that the location of this organ of sympathy is in the pocket of the slaveholder and the man who shares in the profits of slave labor? Of course you have; and pity those men who have lived upon their ill-gotten wealth. You know, if they do not have somebody to work for them, they must leave their gilded *salons* and take off their coats and roll up their sleeves and take their chances among the *live* men of the world. This, you are aware, these respectable gentlemen will not do, for they have been so long accustomed to live by robbing and cheating the Negro that they are sworn never to work while they can live by plunder.

Can the slaves take care of themselves? What do you suppose becomes of the thousands who fly ragged and penniless from the South every year, and scatter themselves throughout the free states of the North? Do they take care of themselves? I am neither ashamed nor afraid to meet this question. Assertions like this, long uncontradicted, seem to be admitted as established facts. I ask your attention for one moment to the fact that colored men at the North are shut out of almost every avenue to wealth, and yet, strange to say, the proportion of paupers is much less among us than among you! Are the beggars in the streets of Boston colored men? In Philadelphia, where there is a larger free colored population than is to be found in any other city in the free states, and where we are denied every social privilege and are not even permitted to send our children to the schools that we are taxed to support or to ride in the city horse-cars, yet even there we pay taxes enough to support our own poor, and have a balance of a few thousand in our favor, which goes to support those "poor whites" who "can't take care of themselves."

Many of those who advocate emancipation as a military necessity seem puzzled to know what is best to be done with the slave, if he is set at liberty. Colonization in Africa, Haiti, Florida and South America are favorite theories with many well-informed persons. This is really interesting! No wonder Europe does not sympathize with you. You are the only people, claiming to be civilized, who take away the rights of those whose color differs from your own. If you find that you cannot rob the Negro of his labor and of himself, you will banish him! What a sub-lime idea! You are certainly a great people! What is your plea? Why, that the slaveholders will not permit us to live among them as freemen, and that the air of Northern latitudes is not good for us! Let me tell you, my friends, *the slaveholders are not the men we dread!* They do not desire to have us removed. The Northern proslavery men have done the free people of color tenfold more injury than the Southern slaveholders. In the South, it is simply a question of dollars and cents. The slaveholder cares no more for you than he does for me. They enslave their own children and sell them, and they would as soon enslave white men as black men. The secret of the slaveholder's attachment to slavery is to be found in the dollar, and *that* he is determined to get without working for it. There is no prejudice against color among the slaveholders. Their social system and one million of mulattoes are facts which no arguments can demolish. If the slaves were emancipated, they would remain where they are. Black labor in the South is at a premium. The free man of color has always had the preference over the white laborer. Many of you are aware that Southerners will do a favor for a free colored man, when they will not do it for a white man in the same condition in life. They believe in their institution because it supports them. . . .

Other countries have been held out as homes for us. Why is this? Why is it that the people from all other countries are invited to come here and we are asked to go away? Is it to make room for the refuse population of Europe? Or why is it that the white people of this country desire to get rid of us? Does any one pretend to deny that this is our country? Or that much of the wealth and prosperity found here is the result of the labor of our hands? Or that our blood and bones have crimsoned and whitened every battlefield from Maine to Louisiana? Why this desire to get rid of us? Can it be possible that because the nation has robbed us for nearly two and a half centuries and, finding that she can no longer and preserve her character among nations, now, out of hatred, wishes to banish because she cannot continue to rob us? Or why is it? Be patient and I will tell you! The free people of color have succeeded, in spite of every effort to crush them, and we are today a living refutation of that shameless assertion that we "can't take care of ourselves." In a state of freedom, abject as our condition has been, our whole lives prove us superior to the influences that have been brought upon us to crush us. This could not have been said of your race when it was oppressed and enslaved! Another reason is, this nation has wronged us and for this reason many hate us. . . . When a man wrongs another, he not only hates him, but tries to make others dislike him. Strange as this may appear, it is nevertheless painfully true. You may help a

man during his lifetime, and you are a capital fellow; but your
first refusal brings down his ire, and shows you his ingratitude.
When he has got all he can from you, he has no further use for
you. When the orange is squeezed, we throw it aside. The black
man is a good fellow while he is a slave and toils for nothing;
but the moment he claims his own flesh and blood and bones
he is a most obnoxious creature, and there is a proposition to
get rid of him! He is happy while he remains a poor, degraded,
ignorant slave, without even the right to his own offspring.
While in this condition, the master can ride in the same carriage, sleep in the same bed, and nurse from the same bosom.
But give this same slave the right to use his own legs, his hands,
his body and his mind, and this happy and desirable creature
is instantly transformed into a miserable loathsome wretch, fit
only to be colonized somewhere near the mountains of the
moon, or eternally banished from the presence of all civilized
beings. You must not lose sight of the fact that it is the emancipated slave and the free colored man whom it is proposed to
remove—not the slave; this country and climate are perfectly
adapted to Negro slavery; it is the free black that the air is not
good for! What an idea! A country good for slavery, and not
good for freedom! . . .

I do not regard this trying hour as a darkness. The war that
has been waged on us for more than two centuries has opened
our eyes and caused us to form alliances, so that instead of
acting on the defensive we are now prepared to attack the enemy. This is simply a change of tactics. I think I see the finger
of God in all this. Yes, *there* is the handwriting on the wall: *I
come not to bring peace, but the sword. Break every yoke, and
let the oppressed go free. I have heard the groans of my people
and am come down to deliver them!* . . .

This rebellion for slavery means something! Out of it emancipation must spring. I do not agree with those men who see
no hope in this war. There is nothing in it but hope. Our cause
is onward. As it is with the sun, the clouds often obstruct his
vision, but in the end we find there has been no standing still.
It is true the government is but little more antislavery now than
it was at the commencement of the war; but while fighting for
its own existence, it has been obliged to take slavery by the
throat, and sooner or later *must* choke her to death. . . .

WE ASK FOR OUR RIGHTS

By John S. Rock

Addressing the West India Emancipation Day celebration, August 1, 1862, at Abington, Massachusetts, John S. Rock advanced what was probably the first demand for distribution of land to slaves emancipated during the Civil War. At the same time, he pointed out that the end of slavery was not the only issue confronting the nation, for the Negro in the free states was also oppressed. To emancipate the slaves and at the same time continue to deprive the black people of their full rights would be a hollow victory. Here are excerpts from Dr. Rock's speech, taken from The Liberator, *August 15, 1862.*

. . . THE ENGLISH GOVERNMENT instead of setting the planters to work to compensate the slaves for what they had plundered from them, paid the planters with British gold, the price of their blood to which they had not a shadow of a right, neither by the laws of God nor of nature. Robbed of everything but their liberty, and without any assistance, the new creatures sprang into a new life and have nobly vindicated their capacity to enjoy and appreciate their freedom. Why talk about compensating masters? Compensate them for what? What do you owe them? What does the slave owe them? What does society owe them? Compensate the master? No, never. It is the slave who ought to be compensated. The property of the South is by right the property of the slave. You talk of compensating the master who has stolen enough to sink ten generations, and yet you do not propose to restore even a part of that which has been plundered. This is rewarding the thief. Have you forgotten that the wealth of the South is the property of the slave? Will you keep back the price of his blood, which is upon you and upon your children? . . .

Emancipation will entirely revolutionize society. This system of free love must be abolished. This will be no child's play. When the government has been brought to the saving knowledge of emancipation, then the antislavery work will have but fairly commenced. I hope our friends will not stop here and think their work is done. The slaves have toiled for you for more than two centuries. It is but right that you should do something for them. They have a heavy claim against you—a long catalogue of outrage and oppression. You must not forsake them now. The slaves are to be educated for a higher civilization. They need your friendship and we ask you to cooperate with us, and help clear the way. All I ask for the black man is an unobstructed road and a fair chance.

The present position of the colored man is a trying one— trying because the whole nation seems to have entered into a conspiracy to crush him. But few seem to comprehend our position in the free states. The masses seem to think that we are oppressed only in the South. This is a mistake; we are oppressed everywhere in this slavery-cursed land. Massachusetts has a great name and deserves much credit for what she has done, but the position of the colored people in Massachusetts is far from being an enviable one. While colored men have many rights, they have few privileges here. To be sure, we are seldom insulted by passers-by, we have the right of suffrage, the free schools and colleges are open to our children, and from them have come forth young men capable of filling any post of profit or honor. But there is no field for these young men. Their education aggravates their suffering. The more highly educated the colored man is, the more keenly he suffers. The educated colored man meets, on the one hand, the embittered prejudices of the whites, and on the other, the jealousies of his own race. The colored man who educates his son, educates him to suffer. You can hardly imagine the humiliation and contempt a colored lad must feel by graduating first in his class and then being rejected everywhere else because of his color. To the credit of the nineteenth century, be it said, the United States is the only civilized country mean enough to make this invidious distinction. . . .

Nowhere in the United States is the colored man of talent appreciated. Even in Boston, which has a great reputation for being antislavery, he has no field for his talent. Some persons think that, because we have the right of suffrage and enjoy the privilege of riding in the cars, there is less prejudice here than there is farther South. In some respects this is true, and in others it is not true. We are colonized here in Boston. It is five times as difficult to get a house in a good location in Boston as it is in Philadelphia, and it is ten times more difficult for a colored mechanic to get employment than in Charleston. Colored men in business in Massachusetts receive more respect and less patronage than in any place that I know of. In Boston we are proscribed in some of the eating houses, many of the hotels, and all of the theaters but one. . . .

The friends of slavery are everywhere withdrawing their patronage from us and trying to starve us out by refusing to employ us even as menials. When our laboring men go to them for work, as heretofore, they reply "Go to the Abolitionists and Republicans who have turned the country upside down." The laboring men who could once be found all along the wharves of Boston, can now be found only about Central Wharf, with scarcely encouragement enough to keep soul and body together. You know that the colored man is proscribed in some of the churches, and that this proscription is carried even to the graveyards. This is Boston—by far the best, or at least the most liberal large city in the United States. . . .

We desire to take part in this contest, and when our government shall see the necessity of using the loyal blacks of the free states, I hope it will have the courage to recognize their manhood. It certainly will not be mean enough to force us to fight for your liberty . . . and then leave us when we go home to our respective states to be told that we cannot ride in the cars, that our children cannot go to the public schools, that we cannot vote; and if we don't like that state of things, there is an appropriation to colonize us. We ask for our rights. Hardships and dangers are household words with us. We are not afraid to dig or fight. A few black acclimated regiments would shake the Old Dominion. When will there be light enough in this cabinet to see this.

LINCOLN'S COLONIZATION PROPOSAL IS ANTI-CHRISTIAN

By Isaiah C. Wears

On August 14, 1862, President Lincoln met with five black men from the District of Columbia to enlist their support for his plan for colonizing the black population of America in Central America and other countries. He told the five Negroes that racial differences between Negro and white made it impossible for them to live as equals and promised them governmental assistance if they would recruit colored families to settle in Central America. Complete separation of the races was the only solution. "But for your race among us," he emphasized, "there could not be war,

although many men engaged on either side do not care for
you one way or the other. Nevertheless, I repeat, without
the institution of slavery, and the colored race as a basis,
the war could not have an existence. It is better for us both,
therefore, to be separated."

Accounts of this interview were widely publicized in
the Northern press and infuriated many Negroes. The
Statistical Association of the Colored People of Philadel-
phia met on August 15, and in a speech Isaiah C. Wears,
Association president, voiced the black community's op-
position to Lincoln's plan. The speech was then sent to the
committee of Negroes who had visited President Lincoln
to assist them in framing their reply to the Chief Execu-
tive. "No previous time, in our humble judgment," the
letter declared, "has ever presented itself for a committee
of colored men by a bold, judicious, manly and righteous
decision to make an impression on the enlightened and
civilized mind of the world as in this instance." The cor-
respondence was signed by Wears and William Still, Cor-
responding Secretary of the Association. Both Wears and
Still were prominent leaders of the Philadelphia black
community, and both were active in the city's Vigilance
Committee to aid fugitive slaves.

Here is Wears's answer to President Lincoln's proposal,
as excerpted from The Christian Recorder (*Philadelphia*),
August 23, 1862.

. . . TO BE ASKED, after so many years of oppression and
wrong have been inflicted in a land and by a people who have
been so largely enriched by the black man's toil, to pull up
stakes in a civilized and Christian nation and to go to an uncivilized and barbarous nation, simply to gratify an unnatural
wicked prejudice emanating from slavery, is unreasonable and
anti-Christian in the extreme.

How unaccountably strange it seems, that wise men familiar
with the history of this country, with the history of slavery,
with the rebellion and its merciless outrages, yet are apparently totally ignorant of the true cause of the war—or, if not
ignorant, afraid or ashamed to charge the guilt where it belongs.

Men profess to believe in God and the Bible, justice and humanity, but notwithstanding numerous examples in every age's
history vividly showing how cruel has been the oppressor's rule
and how invariably his heinous practices have brought on wars
and destruction, with God's sore displeasure and heavy judg-

ments—it is easy, nevertheless, to find excuses to ignore truth, to defy God's vengeance and trample on his creatures.

Says the President: The colored race are the cause of the war. So were the children of Israel the cause of the troubles in Egypt. So was Christ the cause of great commotions in Judea, in this same sense; and those identified with Him were considered of the baser sort, and really unfit for citizenship.

But surely the President did not mean to say that our race was the cause of the war, but the occasion thereof.

If black men are here in the way of white men, they did not come here of their own accord. Their presence is traceable to the white man's lust for power, love of oppression and disregard of the plain teachings of the Lord Jesus Christ, whose rule enjoins upon all men to "do unto others as they would be done by." Although a man may have had the misfortune to fall among thieves and become wounded and distressed by the wayside, the great Examplar would not recognize the right of either the Levite or priest to shield themselves behind their prejudices or selfishness and thus leave him to suffer.

But it is not the Negro that is the cause of the war; it is the unwillingness on the part of the American people to do the race simple justice. It is not social equality to be made the equal of the white man, to have kind masters to provide for him, or to find for him congenial homes in Africa or Central America that he needs, but he desires not to be robbed of his labor—to be deprived of his God-given rights.

The effect of this scheme of colonization, we fear, will be to arouse prejudice and to increase enmity against us, without bringing with it the remedy proposed or designed.

Repentance is more needed on the part of our oppressors than anything else. Could a policy that would lead to this wholesome course be adopted, some bright hope might be seen for the triumph of freedom and justice.

If the African race are not of a color most pleasing to their fairer-skinned brother, let the fault be charged upon the Creator, as the same hand that made the white man made the black man also. God has revealed no distinction in His word, touching the color of a man's skin.

But we are to leave this country on the score of selfishness to make room for our selfish white neighbor to sail smoothly, it was intimated.

True, enactments of terrible severity may be passed calculated to ostracize us—it will be strange if the President's suggestions do not directly invite persecutions of an aggravating character. But in our sober reflections, let us remember that Great Britain has got possessions adapted to our people, both of Southern and Northern birth in the Canadas and the West Indies, that are free for all colors—governed by laws that recognize no difference of a complexional character—admit all as equal citizens who will support the government. The humblest fugitive slave as well as those of noblest blood alike find protection on British soil.

The panting bondmen have always found a sure refuge in Canada, and yearly our labor has been sought by Englishmen for the West Indies. The doors, therefore, are wide open in these civilized lands, thank God. Under the laws of Great Britain, colored men are neither debarred from citizenship nor soldier's rights and duties when their services are required.

That it is hard for those who have all their lives been submitting to the wrongs heaped upon the black man, or identified with parties oppressing him, now in this fearful crisis to make the marvelous change that justice demands, none can question.

A very appropriate paragraph occurs in a letter from a friend, which came to hand months back, which I will here quote:

"Has slavery so paralyzed the arm of the nation, that there is no strength to grapple with it? Is there not a story told of a man who fell asleep in an arbor, to whose entrance came a snake so surcharged with venom that the man died poisoned by its breath? Does not the state of our country suggest a parallel case, poisoned to its heart's deep core by its guilty contact with slavery?"

In these remarks, though coming from one of the race considered to be inferior, lies in a nutshell the grand secret of all the nation's trouble. And it seems reasonable to infer that the nation shall not again have peace and prosperity until prejudice, selfishness and slavery are sorely punished in the nation.

FREEDOM'S JOYFUL DAY

By Rev. Jonathan C. Gibbs

Throughout the North, Negroes held meetings and church services on January 1, 1863, to commemorate and celebrate the issuance of the final Emancipation Proclamation. Unfortunately, nearly all of the speeches delivered by Ne-

*gro leaders at these celebrations were either not reported
in the press or have disappeared. One that has been preserved was delivered by Jonathan C. Gibbs, pastor of the
Colored Presbyterian Church of Philadelphia. The Reverend Mr. Gibbs did not confine himself to celebrating the
Proclamation, but called for meaningful freedom for his
people.*

*(Excerpts from the speech are presented here, taken
from* The Christian Recorder, *January 17, 1863.)*

THE MORNING DAWNS! The long night of sorrow and
gloom is past, rosy-fingered Aurora, early born of day, shows
the first faint flush of her coming glory, low down on the distant horizon of Freedom's joyful day. O day, thrice blessed, that
brings liberty to four million native-born Americans. O Liberty!
O sacred rights of every human soul! O source of knowledge, of
justice, of civilization, of Christianity, of strength, of power,
bless us with the inspiration of thy presence. Today, standing
on the broad platform of the common brotherhood of men, we
solemnly appeal to the God of justice, our common Father, to
aid us to meet manfully the new duties, the new obligations
that this memorable day will surely impose.

The Proclamation has gone forth, and God is saying to this
nation by its legitimate constitute head, Man must be free.

Scout, deride, malign this intimation, as the enemies of God
and man will and may, the American people must yield to His
inscrutable fiat, or the legacy of their fathers will be squandered 'midst poverty, ignorance, blood and shame. . . . The
people must support this Proclamation, heartily, earnestly,
strengthening the hands of our government by all the energies
and resources they possess, or in a short time the question will
not be whether black men are to be slaves, but whether white
men are to be free! You had better a thousand times let us into
the full light of liberty with yourselves, than that yourselves
come into a condition equal to that of the slave at the South.
We pray you this day, be just to yourselves, and then to us you
must be true.

The black people of this country are thoroughly loyal. We are
above disloyalty to the government. You may suspect a Garrisonian Abolitionist, but you cannot possibly suspect us. All
our hopes and interests lie in the success of our government. We
clearly discern that this is a contest between civilization and
barbarism, two antagonistic systems of government, two fundamental principles that oppose each other. The black man is only
a sort of accident connected with this struggle. The man who

stoops to malign or abuse us as the cause of this war is, in point of intelligence, away down among the apes; he must be given up as a hopeless blockhead. If the same state of things existed in any country in the world, that exists in this, and all parties were white, or were black, just such a contest must come between these two antagonistic systems as we witness this day in our country, and one or the other of these systems must prevail. Which shall it be?

O, God, we appeal to *Thee*. Let this strife be so decided that justice, truth, honor may not be put to shame. You, my country, entered into a solemn covenant with God in 1776 and declared before highest Heaven that your first and only purpose was to foster and cherish the equality and fraternity of man. How have you kept this covenant? Let Dred Scott decisions, fugitive-slave laws, the judicial murders of Denmark Vesey, Nat Turner, John Brown, Gabriel* and numerous others testify. . . .

Feeble-minded men are constantly asking what is to be done with the black, and the only alternative that presents itself to them is to send the bondman to the Torrid Zone where a civilization exists, if any at all, that is so nearly allied to barbarism that he may rationally expect that his posterity will relapse into the darkness of heathenism. And with such a solution they rest satisfied in one direction, but are highly dissatisfied in another, wondering, they say, at our singular obstinacy in refusing to leave our native land and go to Africa or some other hot country. It is our patriotism that prevents us, our strong love for America, our native land. . . .

Give unto us the same guarantee of life, liberty and protection in the pursuit of happiness that you so cheerfully award to others, and make the very same demands of us to support the government you make of others. In a word, enfranchise and arm the blacks North and South, and put them under the intelligent direction of a strong central government at New Orleans, or Charleston, South Carolina. Enfranchise and arm the black man. Let there be no half measures; half measures are dangerous measures in times like these. . . .

Many persons are asking, Will black men fight? That is not what they mean. The question they are asking is simply this: Have white men of the North the same moral courage, the pluck, the grit, to lay down their foolish prejudice against the colored

---

* In 1800, in Henrico County, Virginia, Gabriel Prosser led a slave insurrection, which was frustrated by informers. Scores of slaves were arrested, thirty-five were executed, and Gabriel, captured after having escaped, was executed.

man and place him in a position where he can bear his full share of the toils and dangers of this war? That is the question that all such persons are asking, and no other. . . . We, the colored men of the North, put the laboring oar in your hands; it is for white men to show that they are equal to the demands of these times, by putting away their stupid prejudices. We are not children, but men, and are in earnest about the matter. There is not a battlefield throughout the country, from the days of '76 until now, but what our bones lie bleaching with yours. I *know* whereof I affirm, and I challenge contradiction. In the very first resistance that was made to British aggression in the Revolution of '76 was a black man, Crispus Attucks, who led the attack and was one of the first slain.

Did not a regiment of Rhode Island's freed blacks on the river Delaware at Red Bank, withstand three successive bayonet charges of British soldiers and finally wipe out the minions of British thralldom? What is the testimony of Andrew Jackson on this subject (a man who knew how to deal with traitors)? What has made the name of Haiti a terror to tyrants and slaveholders throughout the world, but the terrible fourteen years' fight of black men against some of the best troops of Napoleon —and the black men wiped them out. There are some fights that the world will never forget, and among them is the fight of black men for liberty on the Island of Haiti. . . .

Your destiny as white men and ours as black men are one and the same; we are all marching on to the same goal. If you rise, we will rise in the scale of being. If you fall, we will fall; but you will have the worst of it. . . .

Finally, let us offer the homage of grateful hearts to the friends of liberty and human progress the world over, for the hopes and prospects now before us, confidently predicting that the future will show that no efforts made in behalf of the bondman in this country were in vain. The sum of human happiness in this country will be increased, and God honored by the utter destruction of the hideous system of American slavery. . . .

THE GOOD TIME IS AT HAND

By Robert Purvis

The thirtieth annual meeting of the American Anti-Slavery Society, held in New York City on May 12, 1863, was a joyous occasion. The Emancipation Proclamation had been issued four months earlier, and the war for the preservation of the Union had clearly become one for the total abolition of slavery. Negroes were being recruited in ever-increasing numbers in the Union Army, and black Americans were being granted rights long denied them. Negroes overjoyed at the change of heart of the Lincoln administration were willing to forgive its earlier hesitations and delays. In his speech to the American Anti-Slavery Society, Robert Purvis expressed the joy most Negroes felt at the turn the war had taken.

(Parts of this speech are presented here as excerpted from The Liberator, *May 22, 1863.)*

. . . MR. CHAIRMAN, this is a proud day for the "colored" man. For the first time since this society was organized, I stand before you a recognized citizen of the United States. And, let me add, for the first time since your government was a government, it is an honor to be a citizen of the United States! Sir, old things are passing away, all things are becoming new. Now a black man has rights, under this government, which every white man, here and everywhere, is bound to respect. The damnable doctrine of the detestable Taney is no longer the doctrine of the country. The slave power no longer rules at Washington. The slaveholders and their miserable allies are biting the dust. . . . The black man is a citizen; all honor to Secretary Bates, who has so pronounced him! The black man can take out a passport and travel to the uttermost parts of the earth protected by the broad aegis of the government; all honor to Secretary Seward, who was the first to recognize this right. The black man is a citizen soldier standing on an equality with the rank and file, with the white soldier; all honor to Secretary Stanton and the rest of the administration. Sir, I know very well that this government is not yet all that it ought to be. . . . But, sir, these gentlemen have in a signal manner recognized my rights and the rights of my oppressed countrymen. They have officially invested us with the prerogatives of which we have been basely robbed, and I would be false to my nature, false to my convictions, false to my best feelings, did I not thus publicly testify my sense of respect and heartfelt gratitude. . . . I have said that I consider it an honor to be a citizen of this Republic, and I repeat it. I am proud to be an American citizen. . . .

You know, Mr. Chairman, how bitterly I used to denounce the United States as the basest despotism the sun ever shone upon; and I take nothing back that I ever said. When this government was, as it used to be, a slaveholding oligarcy . . . I hated it with a wrath which words could not express, and I denounced it with all the bitterness of my indignant soul. . . . I was a victim, stricken, degraded, injured, insulted in my person, in my family, in my friends, in my estate; I returned bitterness for bitterness, and scorn for scorn. . . . But now I forget the past; joy fills my soul at the prospects of the future. . . .

The good time which has so long been coming is at hand. I feel it, I see it in the air. I read it in the signs of the times; I see it in the acts of Congress, in the abolition of slavery in the District of Columbia, in its exclusion from the territories, in solemn treaties for the effectual suppression of the infernal slave trade, in the acknowledgment of the black republics of Haiti and Liberia. I see it in the new spirit that is in the Army; I see it in the black regiment of South Carolina; I see it in the Fifty-fourth Regiment of Massachusetts; I see it in the order of Adjutant General Thomas, forming a black brigade at Memphis; I see it above all, and more than all, in the *glorious and immortal proclamation of Abraham Lincoln on the first of January,* 1863. By that imperishable instrument, the three million of slaves in the rebel states are legally and irrevocably free! By that immortal document, all the remaining slaves of the country are in effect promised their freedom. In *spirit* and in *purpose,* thanks to *Almighty God,* this is no longer a slaveholding republic. The fiat has gone forth which, when this rebellion is crushed . . . in the simple but beautiful language of the President, "will take all burdens from off all blacks, and make every man a freeman." Our country is not yet free, but thank God for those signs of the times that unmistakably indicate that it soon will be.

TRIBUTE TO A FALLEN BLACK SOLDIER

By J. Stanley

As the need for manpower for the war increased, Washington countenanced the policy of local recruiting of Southern Negro troops. But up to December, 1862, a national call for Negro volunteers had not been issued. The final Emancipation Proclamation, however, announced that freed slaves would be received into the armed forces of the United States "to garrison forts, positions, stations, and other places, and to man vessels of all sorts in said service." Early in 1863, a bill was passed in the House authorizing the President "to enroll, arm, equip and receive into the land and naval service of the United States such number of volunteers as he may deem useful to suppress the present rebellion." The Senate returned the bill to the House, deeming it unnecessary legislation, since the President had such power under previous acts of Congress such as the Confiscation Act and the Militia Act, both passed on July 17, 1862. Acting on this interpretation, Governor John A. Andrew of Massachusetts asked permission of the War Department to raise two regiments of Negro troops to serve for three years. Having received permission, Governor Andrew announced the formation of the Fifty-fourth Massachusetts Regiment, the first Negro regiment to be recruited in the North. Since Massachusetts' Negro population was too small to fill up a regiment, recruiting was done from all over the North.

Governor Andrew had said that his reputation would stand or fall with the success or failure of the Fifty-fourth Massachusetts. In the battle of Fort Wagner, July 18, 1863, the regiment covered itself with glory. "It made Fort Wagner such a name to the colored race as Bunker Hill has been for ninety years to the white Yankees," declared the New York Tribune.

On September 8, 1863, the Young Men's Literary Association together with the citizens of Chicago gathered at Bethel Church to pay respect to a former member, Sergeant Joseph Wilson, of the Fifty-fourth Massachusetts Regiment of Colored Volunteers, who had lost his life in the charge on Fort Wagner, "manfully fighting 'to uphold his country's banner.'" J. Stanley delivered a tribute to

Sergeant Wilson. The following excerpts from that tribute are taken from The Christian Recorder, *September 23, 1863.*

. . . THREE YEARS AGO, Joseph Wilson came among us an entire stranger, an obscure young man. At the formation of the Y.M.L. Association he became one of its first members. We found him modest and unpresuming. Wherever he was called upon to serve the Association, either as an officer or committee-man, he cheerfully assented. Feeling the want of early advantages, he ever manifested a strong desire for all useful information and instruction. The deceased, prior to the breaking-out of the rebellion, interested himself in a corps of citizen soldiery. Here the genius of the man developed itself; he excelled his companions in the healthy exercise of drilling; on this subject his mind was clear and comprehensive; in a word, he was a natural soldier.

When the Commonwealth of Massachusetts sent her agents to Illinois to recruit men for her colored regiments, Joseph Wilson was the first to enroll his name for the gallant Fifty-fourth. Need I tell you, fellow citizens, that the Fifty-fourth have won for themselves and their race imperishable honor? Need I tell you they have forever settled the question that colored men can and will fight? Yes, through God they have proved their fighting qualities, and have hurled into the teeth of their enemies the base and foul calumny that we are incapable of defending ourselves and the government which has so long oppressed us. If you ask for proof of this assertion, I shall with pride refer you to the victories achieved by colored troops in Kansas, at New Orleans, Milliken's Bend,* on the coast of Florida, Port Hudson,† and last, but not least, in South Carolina, where the brave and gallant Wilson fell in front of Fort Wagner. Imagine you see the commanding general placing to the right and advance of the column a regiment of colored men that has never seen service nor stood in front of an enemy? Why was such an honor conferred upon black men? And why were they selected from among the thousands of their white companions in

* On July 7, 1863, two regiments of newly recruited freedmen repulsed a Confederate attack on Milliken's Bend, a Union outpost on the Mississippi River, above Vicksburg.
† On May 27, 1863, two regiments of New Orleans free Negroes and Louisiana ex-slaves participated in an assault on Port Hudson, a Confederate stronghold on the lower Mississippi. The attack failed, but the Negroes fought heroically, advancing over open ground in the face of deadly artillery fire.

arms, who had fought on many a field of battle? What motive prompted General Gilmore to place Colonel Shaw's command where death and destruction awaited them? . . .*

He believed in the efficiency of the colored men whom he placed in front of his advancing columns; he knew well the danger to be met, the great labor to be performed; and it required men fearless of all consequences, whose souls were deeply imbued with the wrongs heaped upon them, to undertake this gigantic work. What has been the result?

We are told that upon that colored regiment was concentrated the fire of ten thousand rebels, from a battery impregnable—yet those men composing the Fifty-fourth Regiment, and in the face of a most deadly fire, attempted to storm the fort. The order was given to advance. On they went through a hail storm of shot and shell, trampling over the dead bodies of their comrades, until they reached the rebel parapets.

Their numbers being small, compared to their enemies, they were compelled to fall back; again and again they advanced to their work of death. Three successive times they mounted the parapet and called for reinforcements, but none came. Their only alternative was to give up the position won, which had cost so much labor, blood and sacrifice of life. Over six hundred of their number fell, to rise no more. Among them was the gallant Sergeant Wilson. But he met his fate like a hero and soldier. Singlehanded, he contended with four powerful cavalrymen until three of that number were made to bite the dust, and at his feet lay cold in death. But with strength exhausted, and no friend near to lend a helping hand, the fourth, demonlike, rushed upon him and took his life. Let the memory of Joseph Wilson be engraved on the heart of every colored man who has felt the strong arm of oppression.

Behold what a spectacle is presented to the world by the colored race of this country. It ought to excite the sympathy and compel the admiration of men and angels. Doomed through long centuries of barbarism to all the degradations of slavery, we find many of our people, with singular unanimity, forgetting their unnumbered wrongs and the powerful provocations to revenge, coming heartily to the support of the Union cause; and, by their fidelity, their courage and their Christian forgiveness of all they have suffered, trying to win some higher and better place, some recognition, however faint, in the estimation of those by whom they have been oppressed.

* Colonel Robert Shaw, the youthful white colonel of the Massachusetts Fifty-fourth Regiment, was killed in the assault on Fort Wagner.

They ask only a chance to prove their manhood. Ignorant and debased as we are by what we have endured and suffered, we still entreat them by all that is patriotic in government and sacred in religion to be the witnesses of what we will and can do, to establish our claims to be recognized as men worthy of a chance in the wide world to earn our bread, worthy of the enjoyment of the commonest right, the right to own ourselves.

On many a bloody field, at the head of many a desperate charge, in many a hazardous venture, their regiments have done deeds that white men, with all their boasting, might envy. Their true heroism is as much in their mercy and forgiveness of centuries of intolerable outrage and injury as in their readiness to encounter a new and more infernal slavery, the torture of the whip and faggot, and a lingering and cruel death in defense of the right. . . .

THE POSITION AND DUTIES OF THE COLORED PEOPLE

By J. W. C. Pennington

On July 11, 1863, the Provost Marshal's office opened for conscription in New York City. That same day wild mobs began to riot, and for five infamous days they stormed through the streets of New York City, unleashing their hatred against the National Conscription Act and committing unspeakable atrocities against the black community, murdering or maiming any Negro whom they came upon. The riots went unchecked until eleven Union regiments were released by the Secretary of War to quell the rioters.

The Draft Riots resulted from a combination of factors. New York City's poorer classes, sympathetic to the Democratic party, were not, in the main, sympathetic to the war's purposes and feared the emancipation of the slaves would be followed by an influx of black workers who would compete for their jobs. There was a huge criminal class in the city, and the riots gave an opportunity for looting. The Conscription Act passed by the government aroused

*indignation because it allowed richer members of the com-
munity to buy their way out of the draft.*

*After the riots had been crushed, the black community
in the North met to discuss its significance for their future. The most important speech arising out of these meetings was delivered by James W. C. Pennington in Pough-
keepsie, New York, on August 24, 1863. Pennington
(1809–1870) was born in slavery on the Eastern Shore of
Maryland, and was trained as a blacksmith, a trade he
followed until he was about twenty-one, when he decided
to run away. Befriended by a Pennsylvania Quaker, he
stayed with him for six months and began what was to be
an extensive education under his direction. After attending evening school in Long Island, he taught in colored
schools and, at the same time, studied theology. Pennington became a pastor in the African Congregational Church,
held pastorates in Hartford, Connecticut, and represented
that state at the World's Anti-Slavery Convention in London in 1843. He was also a delegate to the World's Peace
Society meeting in London that same year. He bought his
freedom in 1851 for $150. Pennington was the author of*
A Text Book of the Origin and History, &c., &c., of the
Colored People, *published in 1841, and* The Fugitive Blacksmith, *the story of his early life, published in London in
1849.) In 1855, together with Dr. James McCune Smith
and the Reverend Henry Highland Garnet, the Reverend
Pennington organized the Legal Rights Association for the
purpose of establishing the rights of Negroes to the public
conveyances in the city. The Association fought the cases
for Negroes kept off the streetcars.*

*(Pennington's speech as presented here has been ex-
cerpted from* The Principia *(New York), January 7, 14,
1864).*

. . . What shall we call the mob of July, 1863? Although I am
not now assuming the responsible task of giving it a full designation, yet I may remark in passing that intelligent colored
men of studious minds owe it to themselves to record this mob
in history by its right name. We should let no mere considerations of present relief deter us from bringing out all the facts
that will fasten the weight or responsibility where it belongs.

If it is an Irish Catholic mob prompted by American Protestant demagogues and Negro haters, let it be hereafter known
as such in history. If it was a desperate effort to resurrect the old
rabid and hateful spirit of colonization, so let it be known to be.

If it was an attempt of the Southern rebels to plant the black flag of the slavery propagandist on the banks of the Hudson, let future generations so read it. Ye living historians, record the truth, the whole truth and nothing but the truth.

The elements of this mob have been centering and gathering strength in New York for more than two years. And, as soon as the rebellion broke out, prominent colored men in passing the streets, were often hailed as "Old Abe," or "Jeff. Davis," evidently to feel their loyal pulse, and as it became evident that our sympathies were with the federal government, we became objects of more marked abuse and insult. From many of the grocery corners, stones, potatoes and pieces of coal would often be hurled by idle young loafers standing about, with the consent of the keepers of those places, and very often by persons in their employ. The language addressed to colored men, not seemly to record on paper, became the common language of the street, and even of some of the fashionable avenues. The streets were made to ring with words and sayings the most filthy, and yet no effort was made by magistrates, the press or authorities to suppress these ebullitions of barbarism. In no other country in the world would the streets of refined cities be allowed to be polluted, as those of New York have been, with foul and indecent language, without a word of rebuke from the press, the pulpit or the authorities. Every loafer, from the little rebel who could but just tussle over the curbstone, up to the lusty muttonfisted scamp who could throw a stone of half a pound's weight across the street at a colored man's head, might anywhere about the city, on any day and at any hour, salute colored persons with indecent language, using words surcharged with filth, malice and brutal insult. And what has been the result? Why, just what we might have expected—the engendering of a public feeling unfriendly toward colored people. This feeling, once created, might at any moment be intensified into an outbreak against its unoffending objects. We have, in this way, been made the victims of certain antagonisms.

I. The opposition to the draft comes largely from that class of men of foreign birth who have declared their intention to become citizens, but who have not done so. They have been duly notified that they could leave the country within sixty days, or submit to the draft. As soon as the President's proclamation containing this notice was made public, men of foreign birth, of this class, began to speak openly against the draft. And for obvious cause. They do not wish to leave the country, and they do not wish to fight. They came to make money, and so far as the war interferes with their schemes they oppose it.

Now, dishonest politicians aim to make these men believe that the war has been undertaken to abolish slavery; and, so far as they believe so, their feelings are against colored people, of course.

From this class there has been a very considerable mob element. Many of them are a little too shamefaced to be seen with a stone or brickbat in their hands in the streets; but they have in large numbers encouraged the mobbing of the colored people. It is known that they have allowed loafers to congregate in their places of business and concoct their plans. Yea, not a few of these men are among your grocerymen and others that you deal with, and are extremely malignant in their feelings. They are fair to your face, and will take your money, but behind your back, it is *"nigger."* These men know perfectly well that in the countries from which they come, conscription laws of a far more strict and severe character exist, and they also know that they would not dare to resist those laws if they were there; and hence their opposition to the draft is ungrateful and revolutionary. Many of this class of men are not so ignorant as to believe that the war is carried on by the President to abolish slavery. They have other objects in view. They fall in with the cry against the Negro only for effect.

II. The next point of antagonism which has developed itself in the recent attack upon us, is that between Catholicism and Protestantism.

Why have *Irish Catholics* led the way in the late murderous attack upon the *colored Protestants*? It is not known that a single colored Catholic family or individual suffered during the late riots at the hands of the Irish, except by mistake. If the colored people, as a body, were Roman Catholics, there would be no attacks made upon them by Irish Catholics. During the Sabbaths of the riots, while colored Protestant churches were closed, and colored Protestant ministers had to take shelter out of the city of New York, colored members of Catholic churches were quietly worshiping in Catholic churches without insult or molestation.

As to the color of the skin. Everybody knows that Catholics consist of all colors in the known world. In other countries, black priests, officials, and members are as common as the sun that shines.

As to the labor question. If colored mechanics and laborers, and all our women and youth who earn wages, were Catholics, we should hear no objection from the Irish Catholics about their employment, because the wages would be good Catholic money, and would go to extend that church.

The Irish objection to us is, then, not as colored laborers, but as *colored Protestant* laborers.

The American people may take a lesson from this and judge what may come next.

Let us look at the labor question a little more closely, and see what must be the greed of those who would have us believe that there is not room and labor enough in this country for the citizens of foreign birth and the colored people of native growth. The legitimate territory of these United States, is about 3,306,-863 acres. That is ten times larger than Great Britain and France together; three times larger than Britain, France, Austria, Prussia, Spain, Portugal and Denmark; and only one sixth less, in extent, than the fifty-nine or sixty republics and empires of Europe put together. And yet there are those who would teach the British and other foreigners the selfish and greedy idea that there is not room enough in this country for them and the colored man. Such a notion is ridiculous.

The foregoing state of fact suggests some lessons of duty.

First, we must study the use of arms, for *self-defense.* There is no principle of civil or religious obligation that requires us to live on in hazard and leave our persons, property and our wives and children at the mercy of barbarians. Self-defense is the first law of nature.*

Second, we must enter into a solemn free colored *Protestant industrial or labor league.*

Let the greedy foreigner know that a part of this country *belongs to us,* and that we assert the right to live and labor here, that in New York and other cities we claim the right to buy, hire, occupy and use houses and tenements, for legal considerations, to pass and repass on the streets, lanes, avenues and all public ways. Our fathers have fought for this country and helped to free it from the British yoke. We are now fighting to help to free it from the combined conspiracy of Jeff Davis and Company; we are doing so with the distinct understanding, that *we are to have all our rights as men and as citizens,* and that there are to be no side issues, no reservations, either political, civil or religious. In this struggle we know nothing but God, manhood and American nationality, full and unimpaired.

The right to labor, earn wages and dispose of our earnings for the support of our families, the education of our children

* In a lecture delivered in Hartford, Connecticut, entitled *The Reasonableness of the Abolition of Slavery,* Pennington had warned black Americans against resorting to force in the struggle to end slavery (Hartford, 1856, p. 13). Obviously, the experience of the Draft Riots had caused him to change his views.

and to support religious institutions of our free choice is inherent. No party or power in politics or religion can alienate this right.

No part of our influence has been used to prevent foreigners from coming to this country and enjoying its benefits. We have done them no wrong. What we ask in return is nonintervention. *Let us alone.*

Third, let us place our daughters and younger sons in industrial positions, however humble, and secure openings where they may be usefully employed. Every father and every mother may be of service, not only to their own children, but also to those of others. You will have many applications for "colored help." Be useful to applicants. Prepare your sons and daughters for usefulness in all the branches of domestic labor and service.

Fourth, let our able-bodied men go into the United States service. There is no better place for them. If I had a dozen sons, I would rather have them in the United States Army and Navy than to have them among our loose population. The Army of the United States must, hereafter, be the great bulwark of our life as a nation. The rebellion has rendered it necessary that we should have a powerful standing army. Colored men should enter the army in force, for the sake of the strength it will give them, the education they will obtain, the pay they will get, and the good service they will do for God, the country and the race.

There are some among us, who still doubt whether we are in duty bound to take up arms in support of the government, and whether the government has a right to draft colored men.

The answer is obvious. Nature and civil law have instituted a relation between colored men and the United States government, which is mutually binding. We are *bound* to support the government, and the government is *bound* to protect us. Neither party has a right to ignore this duty. The plain and safe course for colored men, is to *do service and claim their rights.*

Fifth, we should reconstruct our Union against the insidious influences of colonization. It is a fact that the time our present troubles began, colored men were very much divided on the question of our continuance in the country. Hardly any two of our leading men were agreed about the matter. Some had squarely gone over to colonization, adopting the views of those who hold that a black man can never be a man in this country. Many angry discussions had taken place. Old friendships were broken up, and a bitter spirit had been engendered among us. All this is to be traced to the insidious influences of colonizationists. It is a fact that for several years past any prominent colored man in the city of New York who would not cave in on the "colored car" system and go for some modified scheme of colonization was sure to be marked; and special effort was made to break him down. This influence has been most deadly. Years will not redeem us from its effects. At this moment, while the great and glorious Southern field of usefulness is spreading and widening before us, there is no adequate plan or movement on foot among us for raising up proper agents to occupy the field. Why is this the case? What are we, ministers and teachers, doing? Why is there not some great movement going on, to bring forward young men and women of color for the Southern field? These questions are to the point, and call for action on the part of our ministers and teachers who are in positions of influence. . . .

Lastly, we should remember that emancipation was resorted to as a purely military necessity imposed upon this government in the Providence of an all-wise God. The President has no alternative but to fall into the powerful current of events which God had put in motion.

This view of the subject is essential to the cultivation of a true and lofty spirit of patriotism. A true patriot must always feel that he owns and contends for property which God gave him, whether it be life, or liberty, or the pursuit of happiness. His greatest strength will be in the firm conviction that God is transacting his business, so to speak; even though he be called to pass through bitter waters of adversity, he feels that God has not undertaken for him in vain.

When the hand of God is with us, we are strong, and when he shows us his will, in regard to our duties, we should be in earnest to do it.

An intelligent view of the history of God's providential dealings with slavery leaves no room to doubt that its doom is sealed in this country; but let us not forget that there is yet a terrible contingency before us. We may have to face, in the field, an army of our own colored brethren of the South! Already it is known that the Southern commanders have made use of slaves in battle. And already it is rumored that the Confederate government thinks seriously of arming the slaves as a retaliative military necessity.* It is admitted, that from 1,750,000 to 2,000,000 out of the 4,000,000 of the slaves are yet in the possession of

* Although several plans to arm the slaves were projected by the Confederacy, none of them actually was adopted until March 13, 1865, when the Confederate Congress authorized President Davis to request state recruitment of black troops.

the rebels; of this number they can spare for arms at least 300,-
000 able-bodied men. These men armed and so used, certainly
cannot be expected to exercise any more liberty of choice than
the poor white Union men. So that if those men remain beyond
our reach and are armed and commanded by the Confederates
to fight us, they will be obliged to do so. If we take them prisoners, I suppose they will have to be exchanged as others. If they
desert and come to us, the case will be different. It is presumed
they will do so, when the opportunity presents itself—but how
much mischief they may be compelled to do, in the meantime,
it is impossible to foresee.

In my opinion, nothing is more likely to take place under
French influence than this arming of the slaves by the rebels
with the promise of freedom. It would be but a reproduction of
the French plan in Santo Domingo in 1794, to be followed by
the same treachery by the Confederates, should they use the
slaves successfully.

I have no doubt that Louis Napoleon is advising Jeff Davis
to this plan. Every week's delay in crushing out this rebellion
increases the danger that the slaves may be brought into the
field against us. I confess I am not of the number of those who
covet such an event, with the expectation that the slaves would
come to us *en masse*. It is not to be expected that, in the event
of the rebels arming the slaves they would neglect also to
present them with every possible allurement to fight hard and,
at the same time to surround them with every imaginable
obstacle to their desertion. On our side, the only wise and safe
course is to press rapidly into the heart of the slave country and
work out the problem of the Proclamation of freedom. We must
prove to the slaves that we have both the will and the power
to give effect to the Proclamation, and that it is not a mere
sound, reaching their ears, upon the wings of the wind. Here
is where our danger lies. The President is right. The Proclamation is the word of God's holy Providence, so to speak; but the
great North is slow to repent of slavery. There is yet a great
deal of wicked, angry and unrighteous feeling in the heart of
the Northern people. It may be that God intends to use the
sword as a lance to bleed the whole nation, until she begins to
faint for very loss of blood, and then to swathe up the opened
vein and apply restoratives.

Let us, then, not flatter ourselves that we shall escape. Let
us not be deceived by those who would persuade us that there
is any destiny for us as an integral part of this American nation
separate from the nation as a whole. If the slaves are brought

into the field by the Confederates, it will be a sad and awful day for us.

We conclude, then, that those who in the late riots undertook to expel, by murder, fire and persecution, the colored people for the accomplishment of either sham-democratic or Roman Catholic propagandism have undertaken a heavy and dangerous task, a task in which all the plans and purposes of a just God are against them. And it now remains to be seen whether intelligent colored men among us who have suffered in the late riots will allow the history of that outrageous scheme to pass unrecorded. Shall a few thousand dollars of relief money and a few words of good counsel and consolation be a sufficient inducement to neglect our own history? Remember that one of the great tests of civilization is that a people should be able to record their own annals by the pens of their own historians.

How does the matter sum up? It sums up thus: For more than a year the riot spirit had been culminating, before it burst forth. The police authorities were frequently applied to, by respectable colored persons, without being able to obtain any redress when assaulted and abused in the streets. We have sometimes pointed to the aggressors, but no arrests have been made. We have appealed to them for protection and apprised them of the fact that we had good reason to believe that a general attack was about to be made upon us under false pretenses. We have pointed to the street corners, and to the rowdies who stood at them and in open daylight assaulted colored persons, in passing. We have presented proof sufficient to indict houses where rioters assembled. We have named men who hired idle boys to throw stones at colored men, and offered to prove it. The hand of the ruffian has done its work in sending to the bar of God a number of swift witnesses against the perpetrators of the deeds of July, 1863. The better class of people of New York city would doubtless feel relief, could these departed spirits be called back to their earthly homes and their testimony, now recorded on the book of God against the bloody city, be erased. But as now, no power can restore those valuable members of society, so the full history of the riot must stand in all its painful bearings.

The loss of life and property makes only a small part of the damage. The breaking-up of families and business relations just beginning to prosper; the blasting of hopes just dawning; the loss of precious harvest time which will never again return; the feeling of insecurity engendered; the confidence destroyed; the reaction; and lastly, the gross insult offered to our character as a people, sum up a weight of injury which can only be realized by the most enlightened and sensitive minds among us.

The injury extends to our churches, schools, societies for mutual aid and improvement, as well as to the various branches of industry. And amidst the most honest, trustworthy, useful, laborious, pious and respected, none have suffered more than the sisters of the laundry. These excellent women are the support of our churches, ministers, and the encouragement of our schoolteachers. In these worthy women, New York landlords have found their best tenants. Many of them are the only support of orphan children. Many of them the wives of absent seamen, and some of coasting men and others who are absent during the week but spend their Sabbaths in the city. The nature of the business of these women is such that they are entrusted by their customers with large quantities of valuable clothing, from Monday morning until Saturday evening, when they are expected to return them, to a piece, in perfect order. The attack made upon the houses of the colored people has had the effect to render it extra hazardous to have valuable articles in their houses in trust, as anything found in their houses by rioters would be looked upon as common plunder.

The pretense, therefore, that there was no intention on the part of the rioters to injure our women is false. The severest blow was aimed at them.

There was not only an attempt to murder *en masse* their only male protectors, but it was the design of the rioters also to render their homes dangerous and insecure, both for life and business.

For all the purposes, therefore, of social, civil and religious enjoyment, and right, we hold New York solemnly bound to insure us, as citizens, permanent security in our homes. Relief and damage money are well enough. But it cannot atone fully for evils done by riots. It cannot bring back our murdered dead. It cannot remove the insults we feel; and finally, it gives no proof that the people have really changed their minds for the better toward us.

During the late riots, my wife and other lone females in the same tenement house were repeatedly annoyed and threatened with mob law and violence. When there was not a man about the house, by night or by day, the rioters prowled about, watching for the return of absent marked victims. Failing to secure those, the defenseless women were repeatedly ordered, or mobbishly advised to leave the house, and told that they *"must not be seen to carry a parcel away in their hands!"* Such was the treatment which our females received at the hands of the New

York mobbites, in the absence of their male protectors, which leaves no manner of doubt that a part of the hellish scheme was to mob and otherwise maltreat our women. Read this, and judge of its design:

"The mob will come to this house, soon. You nigger wenches must leave here, and you must not carry away a bundle, or anything, with you."

Such is a copy of a paper stuck under the door.*

DUTY OF COLORED MEN IN THE PRESENT NATIONAL CRISIS

By Francis Williams

Even black college students joined in the campaign urging colored men to enlist. At the close of the winter term (1863–64) Francis Williams, a student of Avery College, a Negro institution in Allegheny City, Pennsylvania, read the following speech, which he had written, to the students and faculty. It is presented as taken from The Christian Recorder, *April 23, 1864.*

FOR MORE THAN two hundred years the descendants of Africa have held, in this portion of the Western world, the position of an enslaved and degraded race. The same atrocity which caused them in the first place to be torn from their native shores has now plunged this country into all the horrors of a civil war. In this national crisis, how do colored Americans stand affected toward the country of their birth? Rebels in arms are striving to rend the Union asunder. Are colored men found in the ranks of those rebels? Traitors swarm through the land from the extreme North to farthest South. Are colored men to be classed among those traitors? No. White statesmen, Congressmen, and Cabinet officers, the once petted favorites of this government, are found in rebellion against it. Colored men, the descendants of those unhappy beings whom the ancestors of those very rebels tore from their land, brought here and en-

* The speech ends abruptly, as it appeared in print.

slaved—those colored men, I say, scorned and held in bondage, have shown themselves true to the country which oppressed them. They showed their fidelity and devotion by the eager desire which they manifested to be reckoned among the defenders of the nation at the outbreak of this war. But that fidelity and devotion was contemptuously spurned aside. "This was a white man's war—a war with which the Negro had nothing to do." Such was the language of the government and of the great majority of the people; and, accordingly, every effort was made to crush this slaveholder's rebellion without abolishing slavery; but, in spite of those efforts, the rebellion was growing stronger and stronger every day, until it became evident that the only way to cure this fearful disease of traitorous war was to remove slavery, the cause of it. Among other results of the antislavery sentiment, which then began to prevail, was this: that the repugnance to colored men as combatants gave place to a wiser policy. They were appealed to, they are still appealed to, to take up *arms;* to show their courage—their devotion—to their country by aiding to crush this rebellion.

Ought that appeal to be unheeded? Ought the remembrance of former wrongs to check the impulses of patriotism? Ought not colored men rather to see, in the antislavery progress of the last two years, in the abolition of slavery in the District of Columbia, in the prohibition of slavery in the territories, in the Proclamation of President Lincoln, evidences that a brighter day is dawning for them in the United States of America? Indeed, it accords with the highest probability that colored men, assuming the attitude of brave and daring soldiers, will soon be transformed into citizens, clothed in all the rights and immunities possessed by white men in this Republic. Let not the ungrateful conduct of Andrew Jackson in the War of 1812, toward black men who had helped drive British invaders from our Southern frontiers, be referred to in order to refute these expectations. A pair of shoes and a return to the overseer's lash on the cottonfield or on the sugar plantation, can no longer be the nation's reward for black valor and patriotism. Andrew Jackson was controlled by the same principle which now directs the course of Southern rebels. The hearts of such men as General Benjamin Butler are animated by a principle entirely different. Let colored men, then, heed the call of their country. Let colored regiments be raised, until they are raised by hundreds. Let colored soldiers, in every conflict with the minions of slavery, imitate the gallant achievements of their brothers at Port Hudson and Milliken's Bend, at Fort Wagner and Olustee. Then, as surely as the plans of the slave power are doomed to signal defeat, so surely will colored men in the land, preserved in part by their prowess, enjoy all the rights and immunities of citizens.

THE MISSION OF THE WAR

By Frederick Douglass

Chief among the issues which confronted the nation during the war, in Douglass' opinion, was the pressing problem of the Negro's status as a free man. In his speech "The Mission of the War," which he repeated week after week in different communities late in 1863 and early in 1864, he warned Abolitionists that "there never was a time when antislavery work was more needed than now," and impressed upon the nation the necessity of securing full freedom for the Negro people. On January 13, 1864, he was invited to deliver the speech at a meeting sponsored by the Women's Loyal League at Cooper Institute in New York City. This is the major portion of what was probably Douglass' most important speech during the Civil War. It is taken from the text which appeared in the New-York Tribune, *January 14, 1864.*

LADIES AND GENTLEMEN: By the mission of the war I mean nothing occult, arbitrary or difficult to be understood, but simply those great moral changes in the fundamental condition of the people, demanded by the situation of the country plainly involved in the nature of the war, and which, if the war is conducted in accordance with its true character, it is naturally and logically fitted to accomplish.

Speaking in the name of Providence, some men tell me that slavery is already dead, that it expired with the first shot at Sumter. This may be so, but I do not share the confidence with which it is asserted. In a grand crisis like this, we should all prefer to look facts sternly in the face and to accept their verdict whether it bless or blast us. I look for no miraculous destruction of slavery. The war looms before me simply as a great national opportunity, which may be improved to national salvation, or neglected to national ruin. I hope much from the bravery of our soldiers, but in vain is the might of armies if our rulers fail to profit by experience and refuse to listen to the suggestions of wisdom and justice. The most hopeful fact of the hour is that we are now in a salutary school—the school of affliction. If sharp and signal retribution, long protracted, wide-sweeping and overwhelming, can teach a great nation respect for the long-despised claims of justice, surely we shall be taught now and for all time to come. But if, on the other hand, this potent teacher, whose lessons are written in characters of blood and thundered to us from a hundred battlefields shall fail, we shall go down as we shall deserve to go down, as a warning to all other nations which shall come after us. It is not pleasant to contemplate the hour as one of doubt and danger. We naturally prefer the bright side, but when there is a dark side it is folly to shut our eyes to it or deny its existence.

I know that the acorn involves the oak, but I know also that the commonest accident may destroy its potential character and defeat its natural destiny. One wave brings its treasure from the briny deep, but another oftens sweeps it back to its primal depths. The saying that revolutions never go backward must be taken with limitations. The Revolution of 1848 was one of the grandest that ever dazzled a gazing world. It overturned the French throne, sent Louis Philippe into exile, shook every throne in Europe, and inaugurated a glorious Republic. Looking from a distance, the friends of democratic liberty saw in the convulsion the death of kingcraft in Europe and throughout the world. Great was their disappointment. Almost in the twinkling of an eye, the latent forces of despotism rallied. The Republic disappeared. Her noblest defenders were sent into exile, and the hopes of democratic liberty were blasted in the moment of their bloom. Politics and perfidy proved too strong for the principles of liberty and justice in that contest. I wish I could say that no such liabilities darken the horizon around us. But the same elements are plainly involved here as there. Though the portents are that we shall flourish, it is too much to say that we cannot fail and fall. Our destiny is to be taken out of our own hands. It is cowardly to shuffle our responsibilities upon the shoulders of Providence. I do not intend to argue but to state facts.

We are now wading into the third year of conflict with a fierce and sanguinary rebellion, one which, at the beginning of it, we were hopefully assured by one of our most sagacious and trusted political prophets would be ended in less than ninety days; a rebellion which, in its worst features, stands alone among rebellions a solitary and ghastly horror, without a parallel in the history of any nation, ancient or modern; a rebellion inspired by no love of liberty and by no hatred of oppression, as most other rebellions have been, and therefore utterly indefensible upon any moral or social grounds; a rebellion which openly and shamelessly sets at defiance the world's judgment of right and wrong, appeals from light to darkness, from intelligence to ignorance, from the ever-increasing prospects and blessings of a high and glorious civilization to the cold and withering blasts of a naked barbarism; a rebellion which even at this unfinished stage of it counts the number of its slain not by thousands nor by tens of thousands, but by hundreds of thousands; a rebellion which in the destruction of human life and property has rivaled the earthquake, the whirlwind and the pestilence that walketh in darkness and wasteth at noonday. It has planted agony at a million hearthstones, thronged our streets with the weeds of mourning, filled our land with mere stumps of men, ridged our soil with two hundred thousand rudely formed graves and mantled it all over with the shadow of death. A rebellion which, while it has arrested the wheels of peaceful industry and checked the flow of commerce, has piled up a debt heavier than a mountain of gold to weigh down the necks of our children's children. There is no end to the mischief wrought. It has brought ruin at home, contempt abroad, has cooled our friends, heated our enemies and endangered our existence as a nation.

Now, for what is all this desolation, ruin, shame, suffering and sorrow? Can anybody want the answer? Can anybody be ignorant of the answer? It has been given a thousand times from this and other platforms. We all know it is slavery. Less than a half a million of Southern slaveholders—holding in bondage four million slaves—finding themselves outvoted in the effort to get possession of the United States government, in order to serve the interests of slavery, have madly resorted to the sword—have undertaken to accomplish by bullets what they failed to accomplish by ballots. That is the answer.

It is worthy of remark that secession was an afterthought with the rebels. Their aim was higher; secession was only their second choice. Who was going to fight for slavery in the Union? It was not separation, but subversion. It was not Richmond, but Washington. It was not the Confederate rag, but the glorious Star-Spangled Banner.

Whence came the guilty ambition equal to this atrocious crime. A peculiar education was necessary to this bold wickedness. Here all is plain again. Slavery—the peculiar institution —is aptly fitted to produce just such patriots, who first plunder and then seek to destroy their country. A system which rewards labor with stripes and chains, which robs the slave of

his manhood and the master of all just consideration for the
rights of his fellow man—has prepared the characters, male
and female, that figure in this rebellion—and for all its cold-
blooded and hellish atrocities. In all the most horrid details of
torture, starvation and murder in the treatment of our prisoners, I behold the features of the monster in whose presence I
was born, and that is slavery. From no sources less foul and
wicked could such a rebellion come. I need not dwell here. The
country knows the story by heart. But I am one of those who
think this rebellion—inaugurated and carried on for a cause
so unspeakably guilty and distinguished by barbarities which
would extort a cry of shame from the painted savage—is quite
enough for the whole lifetime of any one nation, though the
lifetime should cover the space of a thousand years. We ought
not to want a repetition of it. Looking at the matter from no
higher ground than patriotism—setting aside the high considerations of justice, liberty, progress and civilization—the
American people should resolve that this shall be the last slaveholding rebellion that shall ever curse this continent. Let the
War cost more or cost little, let it be long or short, the work
now begun should suffer no pause, no abatement, until it is
done and done forever.

I know that many are appalled and disappointed by the apparently interminable character of this war. I am neither appalled nor disappointed without pretending to any higher
wisdom than other men. I knew well enough and often said it:
once let the North and South confront each other on the battlefield, and slavery and freedom be the inspiring motives of the
respective sections, the contest will be fierce, long and sanguinary. Governor Seymour* charges us with prolonging the war,
and I say the longer the better if it must be so—in order to
put an end to the hell-black cause out of which the rebellion has
risen.

Say not that I am indifferent to the horrors and hardships of
the war. I am not indifferent. In common with the American
people generally, I feel the prolongation of the war a heavy calamity, private as well as public. There are vacant spaces at my
hearthstone which I shall rejoice to see filled again by the boys
who once occupied them, but which cannot be thus filled while

---

* Horatio Seymour (1810–1886), Democratic governor of New York and
leader of the "Peace Democracy," opposed the Emancipation Proclamation, urged an early end to the war, and was labeled a "Copperhead" by
Horace Greeley. Seymour denounced the arrest of Clement L. Vallandigham, leader of the "Copperheads"—those in the North who favored the
South.

the war lasts, for they have enlisted "during the war."*

But even from the length of this struggle, we who mourn over it may well enough draw some consolation when we reflect upon the vastness and grandeur of its mission. The world has witnessed many wars—and history records and perpetuates their memory—but the world has not seen a nobler and grander war than that which the loyal people of this country are now waging against the slaveholding rebels. The blow we strike is not merely to free a country or continent, but the whole world, from slavery; for when slavery fails here, it will fall everywhere. We have no business to mourn over our mission. We are writing the statutes of eternal justice and liberty in the blood of the worst of tyrants as a warning to all aftercomers. We should rejoice that there was normal life and health enough in us to stand in our appointed place, and do this great service for mankind.

It is true that the war seems long. But this very slow progress is an essential element of its effectiveness. Like the slow convalescence of some patients the fault is less chargeable to the medicine than to the deep-seated character of the disease. We were in a very low condition before the remedy was applied. The whole head was sick and the whole heart faint. Dr. Buchanan and his Democratic friends had given us up and were preparing to celebrate the nation's funeral. We had been drugged nearly to death by proslavery compromises. A radical change was needed in our whole system. Nothing is better calculated to effect the desired change than the slow, steady and certain progress of the war.

I know that this view of the case is not very consoling to the peace Democracy. I was not sent and am not come to console this breach of our political church. They regard this grand moral revolution in the mind and heart of the nation as the most distressing attribute of the war, and howl over it like certain characters of whom we read—who thought themselves tormented before their time.

Upon the whole, I like their mode of characterizing the war. They charge that it is no longer conducted upon Constitutional principles. The same was said by Breckinridge and Vallandigham. They charge that it is not waged to establish the Union as it was. The same idea has occurred to Jefferson Davis. They charge that this is a war for the subjugation of the South. In a word, that it is an Abolition war.

For one, I am not careful to deny this charge. But it is in-

* Both of Douglass' sons, Charles and Lewis, enlisted in the Fifty-fourth Massachusetts Regiment.

structive to observe how this charge is brought and how it is met. Both warn us of danger. Why is this war fiercely denounced as an Abolition war? I answer, because the nation has long and bitterly hated Abolition and the enemies of the war confidently rely upon this hatred to serve the ends of treason. Why do the loyal people deny the charge? I answer, because they know that Abolition, though now a vast power, is still odious. Both the charge and the denial tell how the people hate and despise the only measure that can save the country.

An Abolition war! Well, let us thank the Democracy for teaching us this word. The charge in a comprehensive sense is most true, and it is a pity that it is true, but it would be a vast pity if it were not true. Would that it were more true than it is. When our government and people shall bravely avow this to be an Abolition war, then the country will be safe. Then our work will be fairly mapped out. Then the uplifted arm of the nation will swing unfettered to its work, and the spirit and power of the rebellion will be broken. Had slavery been abolished in the Border States at the very beginning of the war, as it ought to have been—had it been abolished in Missouri, as it would have been but for Presidential interference—there would now be no rebellion in the Southern states, for, instead of having to watch these Border States, as they have done, our armies would have marched in overpowering numbers directly upon the rebels and overwhelmed them. I now hold that a sacred regard for truth, as well as sound policy, makes it our duty to own and avow before heaven and earth that this war is, and of right ought to be, an Abolition war.

The abolition of slavery is the comprehensive and logical object of the war, for it includes everything else which the struggle involves. It is a war for the Union, a war for the Constitution, I admit; but it is logically such a war only in the sense that the greater includes the lesser. Slavery has proved itself the strong man of our national house. In every rebel state it proved itself stronger than the Union, stronger than the Constitution, and stronger than the Republican institutions. It overrode majorities, made no account of the ballot box, and had everything its own way. It is plain that this strong man must be bound and cast out of our house before Union, Constitution and Republican institutions can become possible. An Abolition war, therefore, includes Union, Constitution, Republican institutions, and all else that goes to make up the greatness and glory of our common country. On the other hand, exclude Abolition, and you exclude all else for which you are fighting.

The position of the Democratic party in relation to the war ought to surprise nobody. It is consistent with the history of the party for thirty years. Slavery, and only slavery, has been its recognized master during all that time. It early won for itself the title of being the natural ally of the South and of slavery. It has always been for peace or against peace, for war and against war, precisely as dictated by slavery. Ask why it was for the Florida War, and it answers, slavery. Ask why it was for the Mexican War, and it answers, slavery. Ask why it was for the annexation of Texas, and it answers, slavery. Ask why it was opposed to the habeas corpus when a Negro was the applicant, and it answers, slavery. Ask why it is now in favor of the habeas corpus, when rebels and traitors are the applicants for its benefits, and it answers, slavery. Ask why it was for mobbing down freedom of speech a few years ago, when that freedom was claimed by the Abolitionists, and it answers, slavery. Ask why it now asserts freedom of speech, when sympathizers with traitors claim that freedom, and again slavery is the answer. Ask why it denied the right of a state to protect itself against possible abuses of the Fugitive Slave Bill, and you have the same old answer. Ask why it now asserts the sovereignty of the states separately as against the states united, and again slavery is the answer. Ask why it was opposed to giving persons claimed as fugitive slaves a jury trial before returning them to slavery; ask why it is now in favor of giving jury trial to traitors before sending them to the forts for safekeeping; ask why it was for war at the beginning of the Rebellion; ask why it has attempted to embarrass and hinder the loyal government at every step of its progress, and you have but one answer, slavery.

The fact is, the party in question—I say nothing of individual men who were once members of it—has had but one vital and animating principle for thirty years, and that has been the same old horrible and hell-born principle of Negro slavery.

It has now assumed a saintly character. Its members would receive the benediction due to peacemakers. At one time they would stop bloodshed at the South by inaugurating bloody revolution at the North. The livery of peace is a beautiful livery, but in this case it is a stolen livery and sits badly on the wearer. These new apostles of peace call themselves Peace Democrats, and boast that they belong to the only party which can restore the country to peace. I neither dispute their title nor the pretensions founded upon it. The best that can be said of the peacemaking ability of this class of men is their bitterest condemnation. It consists in their known treachery to the loyal government. They have but to cross the rebel lines to be hailed by the traitors as countrymen, clansmen, kinsmen, and brothers beloved in a common conspiracy. . . .

Here is a part of the platform of principles upon which it seems to me every loyal man should take his stand at this hour:

First: That this war, which we are compelled to wage against slaveholding rebels and traitors, at untold cost of blood and treasure, shall be, and of right ought to be, an Abolition war.

Secondly: That we, the loyal people of the North and of the whole country, while determined to make this a short and final war, will offer no peace, accept no peace, consent to no peace, which shall not be to all intents and purposes an Abolition peace.

Thirdly: That we regard the whole colored population of the country, in the loyal as well as in the disloyal states, as our countrymen—valuable in peace as laborers, valuable in war as soldiers—entitled to all the rights, protection, and opportunities for achieving distinction enjoyed by any other class of our countrymen.

Fourthly: Believing that the white race has nothing to fear from fair competition with the black race, and that the freedom and elevation of one race are not to be purchased or in any manner rightfully subserved by the disfranchisement of another, we shall favor immediate and unconditional emancipation in all the states, invest the black man everywhere with the right to vote and to be voted for, and remove all discriminations against his rights on account of his color, whether as a citizen or as a soldier.

Ladies and gentlemen, there was a time when I hoped that events unaided by discussions would couple this rebellion and slavery in a common grave. But, as I have before intimated, the facts do still fall short of our hopes. The question as to what shall be done with slavery—and especially what shall be done with the Negro—threaten to remain open questions for some time yet.

It is true we have the Proclamation of January, 1863. It was a vast and glorious step in the right direction. But unhappily, excellent as that paper is—and much as it has accomplished temporarily—it settles nothing. It is still open to decision by courts, canons and Congresses. I have applauded that paper and do now applaud it, as a wise measure—while I detest the motive and principle upon which it is based. By it the holding and flogging of Negroes is the exclusive luxury of loyal men.

Our chief danger lies in the absence of all moral feeling in the utterances of our rulers. In his letter to Mr. Greeley the

President told the country virtually that the abolition or non-abolition of slavery was a matter of indifference to him.* He would save the Union with slavery or without slavery. In his last Message he shows the same moral indifference, by saying as he does say that he had hoped that the rebellion could be put down without the abolition of slavery.†

When the late Stephen A. Douglas uttered the sentiment that he did not care whether slavery were voted up or voted down in the territories, we thought him lost to all genuine feeling on the subject, and no man more than Mr. Lincoln denounced that sentiment as unworthy of the lips of any American statesman. But today, after nearly three years of a slaveholding rebellion, we find Mr. Lincoln uttering substantially the same heartless sentiments. Douglas wanted popular sovereignty; Mr. Lincoln wants the Union. Now did a warm heart and a high moral feeling control the utterance of the President, he would welcome, with joy unspeakable and full of glory, the opportunity afforded by the rebellion to free the country from the matchless crime and infamy. But policy, policy, everlasting policy, has robbed our statesmanship of all soul-moving utterances.

The great misfortune is and has been during all the progress of this war, that the government and loyal people have not understood and accepted its true mission. Hence we have been floundering in the depths of dead issues. Endeavoring to impose old and worn-out conditions upon new relations—putting new wines into old bottles, new cloth into old garments and thus making the rent worse than before.

Had we been wise we should have recognized the war at the outset as at once the signal and the necessity for a new order of social and political relations among the whole people.

* On August 19, 1862, Horace Greeley published in the New York *Tribune* an appeal to Lincoln entitled "The Prayer of Twenty Millions." Greeley demanded that Lincoln make emancipation one of the aims of the war. Although Lincoln had already determined to issue an emancipation proclamation, he did not reveal it in his public letter to Greeley. He wrote in part: "My paramount object in this struggle is to save the Union, and is not either to save or to destroy slavery. If I could save the Union without freeing any slave, I would do it; and if I could save it by freeing some and leaving others alone, I would also do that."

† Douglass is referring to the following sentence in Lincoln's annual message to Congress, December 8, 1863: "According to our political system, as a matter of civil administration, the general government had no lawful power to effect emancipation in any state, and for a long time it had been hoped that the rebellion could be suppressed without resorting to it as a military measure."

We could, like the ancients, discern the face of the sky, but not the signs of the times. Hence we have been talking of the importance of carrying on the war within the limits of a Constitution broken down by the very people in whose behalf the Constitution is pleaded! Hence we have from the first been deluding ourselves with the miserable dream that the old Union can be revived in the states where it has been abolished.

Now, we of the North have seen many strange things and may see many more; but that old Union, whose canonized bones we saw hearsed in death and inurned under the frowning battlements of Sumter, we shall never see again while the world standeth. The issue before us is a living issue. We are not fighting for the dead past, but for the living present and the glorious future. We are not fighting for the old Union, nor for anything like it, but for that which is ten thousand times more important; and that thing, crisply rendered, is national unity. Both sections have tried Union. It has failed.

The lesson for the statesmen at this hour is to discover and apply some principle of government which shall produce unity of sentiment, unity of idea, unity of object. Union without unity is, as we have seen, body without soul, marriage without love, a barrel without hoops, which falls at the first touch.

The statesmen of the South understood this matter earlier and better than the statesmen of the North. The dissolution of the Union on the old bases of compromise was plainly foreseen and predicted thirty years ago. Mr. Calhoun, and not Mr. Seward, is the original author of the doctrine of the irrepressible conflict. The South is logical and consistent. Under the teachings of their great leader they admit into their form of government no disturbing force. They have based their Confederacy squarely on their cornerstone. Their two great and all-commanding ideas are, first, that slavery is right, and second, that the slaveholders are a superior order or class. Around these two ideas their manners, morals, politics, religion and laws revolve. Slavery being right, all that is inconsistent with its entire security is necessarily wrong, and of course ought to be put down. There is no flaw in their logic.

They first endeavored to make the federal government stand upon their accursed cornerstone; and we but barely escaped, as you well know, that calamity. Fugitive-slave laws, slavery-extension laws, and Dred Scott decisions were among the steps to get the nation squarely upon the cornerstone now chosen by the Confederate states. The loyal North is less definite in regard to the necessity of principles of national unity. Yet, unconsciously to ourselves, and against our own protestations, we are in reality, like the South, fighting for national unity—a unity of which the great principles of liberty and equality, and not slavery and class superiority, are the cornerstone.

Long before this rude and terrible war came to tell us of a broken Constitution and a dead Union, the better portion of the loyal people had outlived and outgrown what they had been taught to believe were the requirements of the old Union. We had come to detest the principle by which slavery had a strong representation in Congress. We had come to abhor the idea of being called upon to suppress slave insurrections. We had come to be ashamed of slave hunting, and being made the watchdogs of slaveholders, who were too proud to scent out and hunt down their slaves for themselves. We had so far outlived the old Union four years ago that we thought the little finger of the hero of Harpers Ferry of more value to the world struggling for liberty than all the first families of old Virginia put together.

What business, then, have we to be pouring out our treasure and shedding our best blood like water for that old worn-out, dead and buried Union, which had already become a calamity and a curse? The fact is, we are not fighting for any such thing, and we ought to come out under our own true colors, and let the South and the whole world know that we don't want and will not have anything analogous to the old Union.

What we now want is a country—a free country—a country not saddened by the footprints of a single slave—and nowhere cursed by the presence of a slaveholder. We want a country which shall not brand the Declaration of Independence as a lie. We want a country whose fundamental institutions we can proudly defend before the highest intelligence and civilization of the age. Hitherto we have opposed European scorn of our slavery with a blush of shame as our best defense. We now want a country in which the obligations of patriotism shall not conflict with fidelity to justice and liberty. We want a country, and are fighting for a country, which shall be free from sectional political parties—free from sectional religious denominations— free from sectional benevolent associations—free from every kind and description of sect, party, and combination of a sectional character. We want a country where men may assemble from any part of it, without prejudice to their interests or peril to their persons. We are in fact, and from absolute necessity, transplanting the whole South with the higher civilization of the North. The New England schoolhouse is bound to take the place of the Southern whipping post. Not because we love the Negro, but the nation; not because we prefer to do this, because we must or give up the contest and give up the country. We want a country, and are fighting for a country, where social intercourse and commercial relations shall neither be embarrassed nor embittered by the imperious exactions of an insolent slaveholding oligarchy, which required Northern merchants to sell their souls as a condition precedent to selling their goods. We want a country, and are fighting for a country, through the length and breadth of which the literature and learning of any section of it may float to its extremities unimpaired, and thus become the common property of all the people—a country in which no man shall be fined for reading a book, or imprisoned for selling a book—a country where no man may be imprisoned or flogged or sold for learning to read, or teaching a fellow mortal how to read. We want a country, and are fighting for a country, in any part of which to be called an American citizen shall mean as much as it did to be called a Roman citizen in the palmiest days of the Roman Empire.

We have heard much in other days of manifest destiny.* I don't go all the lengths to which such theories are pressed, but I do believe that it is the manifest destiny of this war to unify and reorganize the institutions of the country, and that herein is the secret of the strength, the fortitude, the persistent energy —in a word, the sacred significance—of this war. Strike out the high ends and aims thus indicated, and the war would appear to the impartial eye of an onlooking world like better than a gigantic enterprise for shedding human blood.

A most interesting and gratifying confirmation of this theory of its mission is furnished in the varying fortunes of the struggle itself. Just in proportion to the progress made in taking upon itself the character I have ascribed to it has the war prospered and the rebellion lost ground.

Justice and humanity are often overpowered, but they are persistent and eternal forces, and fearful to contend against. Let but our rulers place the government fully within these trade winds of omnipotence, and the hand of death is upon the Confederate rebels. A war waged as ours seemed to be at first, merely for power and empire, repels sympathy though supported by legitimacy. If Ireland should strike for independence tomorrow, the sympathy of this country would be with her, and I doubt if American statesmen would be more discreet in the expression of their opinions of the merits of the contest than

* "Manifest Destiny," a phrase associated with expansionism, was based on the idea that God had set aside the American continents and their neighboring islands for the expansion of the system of government of the American people. In the late 1840's and 1850's, it was used to justify the expansion of slavery into new lands such as Mexico and Cuba.

British statesmen have been concerning the merits of ours. When we were merely fighting for the old Union the world looked coldly upon our government. But now the world begins to see something more than legitimacy, something more than national pride. It sees national wisdom aiming at national unity, and national justice breaking the chains of a long-enslaved people. It is this new complexion of our cause which warms our hearts and strengthens our hands at home, disarms our enemies and increases our friends abroad. It is this more than all else which has carried consternation into the bloodstained halls of the South. It has sealed the fiery and scornful lips of the Roebucks and Lindsays of England, and caused even the eloquent Mr. Gladstone to restrain the expression of his admiration for Jeff Davis and his rebel nation. It has placed the broad arrow of British suspicion on the prows of the rebel rams in the Mersey and performed a like service in France. It has driven Mason, the shameless man hunter, from London, where he never should have been allowed to stay for an hour, except as a bloodhound is tolerated in Regent Park for exhibition.*

We have had, from the first, warm friends in England. We owe a debt of respect and gratitude to William Edward Forster, John Bright, Richard Cobden, and other British statesmen, in that they outran us in comprehending the high character of our struggle. They saw that this must be a war for human nature, and walked by faith to its defense while all was darkness about us—while we were yet conducting it in profound reverence for slavery.

I know we are not to be praised for this changed character of the war. We did our very best to prevent it. We had but one object at the beginning, and that was, as I have said, the restoration of the old Union; and for the first two years the war was kept to that object strictly, and you know full well and bitterly with what results. I will not stop here to blame and denounce the past; but I will say that the most of the blunders and disasters of the earlier part of the war might have been avoided had our armies and generals not repelled the only true friends the Union cause had in the rebel states. The Army of the Potomac took up an anti-Negro position from the first and has not entirely renounced it yet. The colored people told me a

* James Murray Mason (1798–1871) was the Confederate diplomatic commissioner to England, when he and John Slidell were seized on board the *Trent* by Captain Wilkes of the United States Navy. Although he was well received when he arrived in England in 1862, the British government refused to receive him officially, and he was unable to achieve British recognition of the Confederacy or intervention in its behalf.

few days ago in Washington that they were the victims of the
most brutal treatment by these Northern soldiers when they
first came there. But let that pass. Few men, however great their
wisdom, are permitted to see the end from the beginning. Events
are mightier than our rulers, and these divine forces, with overpowering logic, have fixed upon this war, against the wishes of
our government, the comprehensive character and mission I
have ascribed to it. The collecting of revenue in the rebel ports,
the repossession of a few forts and arsenals and other public
property stolen by the rebels, have almost disappeared from
the recollection of the people. The war has been a growing war
in every sense of the word. It began weak and has risen strong.
It began low and has risen high. It began narrow and has become broad. It began with few and now, behold, the country is
full of armed men, ready, with courage and fortitude, to make
the wisest and best idea of American statesmanship the law of
the land.

Let, then, the war proceed in its strong, high and broad course
till the rebellion is put down and our country is saved beyond
the necessity of being saved again!

I have already hinted at our danger. Let me be a little more
direct and pronounced.

The Democratic party, though defeated in the elections last
fall, is still a power. It is the ready organized nucleus of a powerful proslavery and prorebel reaction. Though it has lost in members, it retains all the elements of its former power and malevolence.

That party has five very strong points in its favor, and its
public men and journals know well how to take advantage of
them.

First: There is the absence of any deep moral feeling among
the loyal people against slavery itself, their feeling against it
being on account of its rebellion against the government, and
not because it is a stupendous crime against human nature.

Secondly: The vast expense of the war and the heavy taxes in
money as well as men which the war requires for its prosecution. Loyalty has a strong back, but taxation has often broken it.

Thirdly: The earnest desire for peace which is shared by all
classes except government contractors who are making money
out of the war; a feeling which may be kindled to a flame by
any serious reverses to our arms. It is silent in victory but vehement and dangerous in defeat.

Fourthly: And superior to all others, is the national prejudice
and hatred toward all colored people of the country, a feeling

which has done more to encourage the hopes of the rebels than all other powers beside.

Fifthly: An Abolitionist is an object of popular dislike. The guilty rebel who with broad blades and bloody hands seeks the life of the nation, is at this hour more acceptable to the Northern Democracy than an Abolitionist guilty of no crime. Whatever may be a man's abilities, virtue or service, the fact that he is an Abolitionist makes him an object of popular hate.

Upon these five strings the Democracy still have hopes of playing themselves into power, and not without reason. While our government has the meanness to ask Northern colored men to give up the comfort of home, endure untold hardships, peril health, limbs and life itself, in its defense, and then degrades them in the eyes of other soldiers, by offering them the paltry sum of seven dollars per month, and refuses to reward their valor with even the hope of promotion—the Democratic party may well enough presume upon the strength of popular prejudice for support.

While our Republican government at Washington makes color and not character the criterion of promotion in the Army and degrades colored commissioned officers at New Orleans below the rank to which even the rebel government had elevated them, I think we are in danger of a compromise with slavery.

Our hopeful Republican friends tell me this is impossible— that the day of compromise with slavery is past. This may do for some men, but will not do for me.

The Northern people have always been remarkably confident of their own virtue. They are hopeful to the last. Twenty years ago we hoped that Texas could not be annexed; but if that could not be prevented we hoped that she would come in a free state. Thirteen years ago we were quite sure that no such abomination as the Fugitive Slave Bill could get itself on our national statute book; but when it got there we were equally sure that it never could be enforced. Four years ago we were sure that the slave states would not rebel, but if they did we were sure it would be a very short rebellion. I know that times have changed very rapidly, and that we have changed with them. Nevertheless, I know also we are the same old American people, and that what we have done once we may possibly do again. The leaven of compromise is among us. I repeat, while we have a Democratic party at the North trimming its sails to catch the Southern breeze in the next Presidential election, we are in danger of compromise. Tell me not of amnesties and oaths of allegiance. They are valueless in the presence of twenty hundred millions invested in human flesh. Let but the little finger of slavery get back into this Union, and in one year you shall see its whole body again upon our backs.

While a respectable colored man or woman can be kicked out of the commonest streetcar in New York where any white ruffian may ride unquestioned, we are in danger of a compromise with slavery. While the North is full of such papers as the New York *World, Express* and *Herald,* firing the nation's heart with hatred to Negroes and Abolitionists, we are in danger of a slaveholding peace. While the major part of antislavery profession is based upon devotion to the Union rather than hostility to slavery, there is danger of a slaveholding peace. Until we shall see the election of November next, and that it has resulted in the election of a sound antislavery man as President, we shall be in danger of a slaveholding compromise. Indeed, as long as slavery has any life in it anywhere in the country, we are in danger of such a compromise.

Then there is the danger arising from the impatience of the people on account of the prolongation of the war. I know the American people. They are an impulsive people, impatient of delay, clamorous for change, and often look for results out of all proportion to the means employed in attaining them.

You and I know that the mission of this war is national regeneration. We know and consider that a nation is not born in a day. We know that large bodies move slowly—and often seem to move thus when, could we perceive their actual velocity, we should be astonished at its greatness. A great battle lost or won is easily described, understood and appreciated, but the moral growth of a great nation requires reflection, as well as observation, to appreciate it. There are vast numbers of voters, who make no account of the moral growth of a great nation and who only look at the war as a calamity to be endured only so long as they have no power to arrest it. Now, this is just the sort of people whose votes may turn the scale against us in the last event.

Thoughts of this kind tell me that there never was a time when antislavery work was more needed than now. The day that shall see the rebels at our feet, their weapons flung away, will be the day of trial. We have need to prepare for that trial. We have long been saved a proslavery peace by the stubborn, unbending persistence of the rebels. Let them bend as they will bend, there will come the test of our sternest virtues.

I have now given, very briefly, some of the grounds of danger. A word as to the ground of hope. The best that can be offered is

that we have made progress—vast and striking progress—
within the last two years.

President Lincoln introduced his administration to the country as one which would faithfully catch, hold and return runaway slaves to their masters. He avowed his determination to
protect and defend the slaveholder's right to plunder the black
laborer of his hard earnings. Europe was assured by Mr. Seward
that no slave should gain his freedom by this war. Both the President and the Secretary of State have made progress since then.

Our generals, at the beginning of the war, were horribly proslavery. They took to slave catching and slave killing like ducks
to water. They are now very generally and very earnestly in
favor of putting an end to slavery. Some of them, like Hunter
and Butler, because they hate slavery on its own account, and
others, because slavery is in arms against the government.

The rebellion has been a rapid educator. Congress was the first
to respond to the instinctive judgment of the people, and fixed
the broad brand of its reprobation upon slave hunting in shoulder straps. Then came very temperate talk about confiscation,
which soon came to be pretty radical talk. Then came propositions for Border State, gradual, compensated, colonized emancipation. Then came the threat of a proclamation, and then came
the Proclamation. Meanwhile the Negro had passed along from
a loyal spade and pickax to a Springfield rifle.

Haiti and Liberia are recognized. Slavery is humbled in Maryland, threatened in Tennessee, stunned nearly to death in western Kentucky, and gradually melting away before our arms in
the rebellious states.

The hour is one of hope as well as danger. But whatever may
come to pass, one thing is clear: The principles involved in the
contest, the necessities of both sections of the country, the obvious requirements of the age, and every suggestion of enlightened policy demand the utter extirpation of slavery from every
foot of American soil, and the enfranchisement of the entire
colored population of the country. Elsewhere we may find peace,
but it will be a hollow and deceitful peace. Elsewhere we may
find prosperity, but it will be a transient prosperity. Elsewhere
we may find greatness and renown, but if these are based upon
anything less substantial than justice they will vanish, for
righteousness alone can permanently exalt a nation.

I end where I began—no war but an Abolition war; no peace
but an Abolition peace; liberty for all, chains for none; the black
man a soldier in war, a laborer in peace; a voter at the South as
well as at the North; America his permanent home, and all

Americans his fellow countrymen. Such, fellow citizens, is my idea of the mission of the war. If accomplished, our glory as a nation will be complete, our peace will flow like a river, and our foundations will be the everlasting rocks.

GIVE US EQUAL PAY AND WE WILL GO TO WAR

By Rev. J. P. Campbell

Although most of the outstanding Negro leaders in the North served as recruiting agents urging Negroes to join the Union Army, the response from black men was less enthusiastic than they had anticipated. In part, this was due to the fact that for the first time, owing to the booming war economy, Negroes enjoyed full employment. But the main reason was the fact that black soldiers did not enjoy equal rights with white soldiers and were discriminated against in such matters as pay, opportunities to become officers, and provisions and equipment. (Negroes were paid ten dollars per month, three dollars of which were deducted for clothing, while white privates received thirteen dollars per month plus a clothing allowance of $3.50.) When Maryland, which had recently abolished slavery, was called upon to fill its quota for the Union Army, a meeting of colored men was held in Baltimore, February 29, 1864, at the Methodist Episcopal Sharp Street Church, for the purpose of hearing addresses to encourage colored volunteering. ("This was the first meeting of the kind ever held in the city of Baltimore or in the State of Maryland," a reporter wrote.) The leading address was delivered by the Reverend J. P. Campbell, of Trenton, New Jersey, a high official of the African Methodist Episcopal Church. The Reverend Mr. Campbell used the opportunity to mobilize pressure upon Congress to achieve passage of a bill equalizing the pay of colored soldiers. (His speech, presented here in part, is taken from The Christian Recorder, *March 19, 1864.)*

. . . IF WE ARE ASKED the question why it is that black men have not more readily enlisted in the volunteer service of the United States government since the door has been opened to them, we answer, the door has not been fairly and sufficiently widely opened. It has been opened only in part, not the whole of the way. That it is not sufficiently and fairly opened will appear from the action of the present Congress upon the subject of the pay of colored soldiers. It shows a strong disposition not to equalize the pay of soldiers without distinction on account of color.

When the news of the first gun fired upon the flag of the Union at old Sumter reached the North, the friends of the Union were called upon to defend that flag. The heart of the black man at that hour responded to the call. He came forward at once and offered his services to the government, and failed to act immediately, because he was denied the opportunity of so doing. He was met with the cold, stern and chilling rebuke, that this was not the Negro's war, not a war upon slavery, and that in it the services of the Negro were not wanted; that slavery had nothing to do with the war, or the war with slavery; that it was purely a war for the safety of the Union and its preservation, without reference to the slavery question.

But the time came when it was thought that under very great restrictions, as by giving him unequal pay and restraining him from being an officer in the Army, the Negro might be allowed to bear arms. Afterward, the black man, saying nothing about officeholding for the time being, asked the government to acknowledge the justice of his claim to equal pay with the white soldier and to recommend the same to the then ensuing Congress, to be made law. The government pledged itself to this recommendation, and many colored men enlisted upon the faith which they had in the government and the future good legislation of Congress upon the subject of giving to black soldiers equal pay and equal bounties with white soldiers, and that all other necessary and needed provisions would be to both the same. Congress met, and the good President Lincoln, with the excellent Secretary of War, Mr. Stanton, proved faithful to their promise. They laid the matter before Congress in their Annual Message and Report. But, alas, that honorable body hesitates to act, and that, too, while the country and its liberties are in danger and calamity by armed rebellion against the government.

Now, we say to our honorable Senators and Representatives in Congress, gentlemen, don't be afraid to do the black man justice. He will not abuse your confidence in his fidelity to the

Constitution and the Union. He will never prove himself a traitor by his acts. He will never prove himself to be unworthy of receiving at your hands the rights and privileges which justice and equity demand.

Give to the black man those simple demands set forth in this bill of particulars, and he will rush to the defense of his country by thousands. His heart within him pants for the opportunity to show himself a man, capable of discharging all the duties of a common manhood, in whatever sphere that manhood may be called to act. Here we are, by thousands and ten thousands, standing ready to move at the nod of your august and mighty fiat. The state of Maryland wants to fill up her last quota of men demanded by the call of the President. This, with a little more time allowed, may be done, if she will do justice to the black citizens of her own soil. They are strong men, and true to the country which gave them birth. They will be ready, at the first sound of the bugle, to fill up the balance of Maryland's apportionment.

The law requires that black men shall pay as much commutation money as white men pay.* We ask, then, that the same pay, bounty, pensions, rights and privileges be given to black men that are given to white men, and they will go to the war, without paying the commutation money.

We want an equal chance to show our equal manhood and love for the Constitution and the Union. Under the above-named circumstances, we are standing ready to respond to the call of the government and go to defend our common country against the encroachments of an armed rebellion.

In conclusion, we ask the question, Will you have us? Will you accept of us upon equal terms with white men in the service of our country? We await, with deep solicitude and anxiety, the action of a government and people whom, with all their faults, we love, and whom we are willing to defend with our lives, liberty and sacred honor in common with white men. Will you have us so to do? That is the question. We ask for equal pay and bounty, not because we set a greater value upon money than we do upon human liberty, compared with which money is mere trash; but we contend for equal pay and bounty upon the principle that if we receive equal pay and bounty when we go into the war, we hope to receive equal rights and privileges when we come out of the war. If we go in equal in pay, we hope to come out equal in enfranchisement.

* Under this law a man drafted in the Union Army could pay for a substitute who would replace him.

Is that an unreasonable hope or an unjust claim? It takes as much to clothe and feed the black man's wife as it does the white man's wife. It takes as much money to go to market for the black man's little boys and girls as it does for the white man's little boys and girls. We have yet to learn why it is that the black soldier should not receive the same compensation for labor in the service of his country that the white soldier receives. There is no financial embarrassment, as in the case of Mr. Jefferson Davis' government at Richmond. Our great and good financier, Mr. Salmon P. Chase, Secretary of the Treasury, has money enough to carry on the war, and some millions of gold and silver to sell. Give us equal pay, and we will go to the war— not pay on mercenary principles, but pay upon the principles of justice and equity.

EVERY MAN SHOULD STAND EQUAL BEFORE THE LAW

By Arnold Bertonneau

The question of reconstruction of the Southern states arose during the war, and one of the first states where the issue developed was Louisiana. New Orleans Negroes called for the right to vote in the reconstructed state, but President Lincoln, in announcing his reconstruction policy on December 8, 1863, restricted the right to vote in Louisiana to whites. New Orleans Negroes refused to accept this exclusion from the ballot box, and on January 5, 1864, they drew up a petition for the franchise and addressed it to both President Lincoln and the Congress. The petition bore the signatures of more than one thousand men, and two of the signers, Jean Baptiste Roudanez and Arnold Bertonneau, were selected to take the petition to Washington. They presented it to Lincoln on March 12, and it was introduced into the Senate by Charles Sumner on March 15.

Before they returned to New Orleans, Roudanez and Bartonneau were invited by Republican leaders in Massachusetts to a dinner in their honor in Boston on April 12, 1864. After an introduction by Governor John A. Andrews

Arnold Bertonneau delivered the following speech to the diners. It is taken from the text published by The Liberator, *April 15, 1864.*

BEFORE THE OUTBREAK of the rebellion, Louisiana contained about forty thousand free colored people, and three hundred twelve thousand persons held in slavery. In the city of New Orleans, there were upwards of twenty thousand free persons of color. Nearly all the free persons of color read and write. The free people have always been on the side of law and good order, always peaceful and self-sustaining, always loyal. Taxed on an assessment of more than fifteen million dollars—among many other things, for the support of public-school education—debarred from the right of sending their children to the common schools which they have been and are compelled to aid in supporting, taxed on their property, and compelled to contribute toward the general expense of sustaining the state, they have always been and now are prohibited from exercising the elective franchise.

When the first fratricidal shot was fired at Sumter, and Louisiana had joined her fortunes with the other seceding states, surrounded by enemies educated in the belief that "Africans and their descendants had no rights that white men were bound to respect," without arms and ammunition, or any means of self-defense, the condition and position of our people were extremely perilous. When summoned to volunteer in the defense of the state and city against Northern invasion, situated as we were, could we do otherwise than heed the warning and volunteer in the defense of New Orleans? Could we have adopted a better policy? In the city of New Orleans, under the Confederate government, we raised one regiment of a thousand men, the line officers of which were colored.

When General Butler captured New Orleans,* and drove the rebel soldiers from the state, the colored people were the most truly loyal citizens to welcome his coming. Indeed, from the time that General Jackson, when Louisiana was threatened during the last war with Great Britain by an overwhelming British force, issued his famous appeal to the "noble-hearted, generous free men of color"—for so he called them in his proclamation,

---

* Benjamin F. Butler (1818–1893) commanded the land forces in the capture of New Orleans by the Union Army in 1862 and was military commander of the city until removed and transferred to the Department of East Virginia. While in New Orleans, Butler earned the hatred of Southern whites because of his use of black troops and his general policy that Negroes were entitled to equal rights.

censuring the "mistaken policy" before pursued, of exempting them from military service, and calling upon them as "Americans" and "sons of freedom" for aid and support—our fathers rallied to arms, and drove the red coats from the soil. I say, from that time to the present, the free colored people of Louisiana have always been loyal and ready and willing to defend the "Stars and Stripes." General Butler understood this. He knew instinctively who were loyal and who were not, on whom he could implicitly rely, in whose fidelity he could safely trust; and adopting the policy of that noble, brave and clear-sighted general who dared to take the responsibility, he received into the ranks of the Union Army, the colored volunteer soldiers of New Orleans.

Under General Butler, we had a foretaste of freedom. The colored people of Louisiana venerate his name; with us it is a household word. We bless his memory and shall always hold it in grateful remembrance. We felt that we were men and citizens, and were to be treated as such; we were animated by new hopes and new desires; we felt that there was a new life opened before us; so we gave our imagination full scope and play. The tyrant who was cruel to his slave was summoned before that general, and received proper punishment. The sympathizers with the rebellion, who wantonly insulted Union troops, were reminded that they could not do so with safety. Gentlemen and ladies of color were allowed to ride in public conveyances and were respectfully treated. Soon, however, the scene changed. General Butler was removed, and again a portentous cloud darkened the bright horizon of our future prospects. Our hope gave place to our fears; and with all true and loyal citizens of our state and city, we regretted the removal of a general who was determined to bring Louisiana back into the Union, free as in the state of Massachusetts.

While General Banks was at the siege of Port Hudson, again the city of New Orleans was threatened by the enemy, and fears were entertained that the rebel troops would take the city. At the call of General Shepley, the colored people again rallied under the banner of the Union, and in forty-eight hours raised the first regiment and were ready for duty. They were promised the same pay and rations as other soldiers. At the expiration of forty days' service, we were discharged; and when the time for payment arrived, each man being charged for his uniform, and his wages cut down to seven dollars per month, it was ascertained that each soldier was indebted to the government six dollars and ninety-seven cents. The soldiers composing this regiment are men of business and culture, mostly engaged in commercial and industrial pursuits, while some are artisans; and notwithstanding they closed their places of business, quit their various occupations, and joined in the defense of New Orleans, this sum stands charged against these soldiers in the books of the general government this day.

Some months ago, General Shepley, the military governor of Louisiana, issued an order, directing all Union male citizens over twenty-one years to register their names, that it might be ascertained who had a right to vote in the reorganization of civil government in the state of Louisiana. The free colored citizens applied for leave to register their names, but were refused the right to do so. They applied to the Military Governor and to General Banks, without success. An election took place, and no colored citizens were permitted to vote. In our struggle to gain the right to vote, we were aided and assisted by many of our most influential and truly loyal Union citizens. Their noble efforts in our behalf we shall never forget. To influence the action and to obtain the elective franchise for our people, we, as delegates of the free colored population of Louisiana, visited Washington to lay the matter before President Lincoln and the Congress of our country.* We ask that, in the reconstruction of the state government there, the right to vote shall not depend on the color of the citizen; that the colored citizen shall have and enjoy every civil, political and religious right that white citizens enjoy; in a word, that every man shall stand equal before the law. To secure these rights, which belong to every free citizen, we ask the aid and influence of every true loyal man all over the country. Slavery, the curse of our country, cannot exist in Louisiana again.

In order to make our state blossom and bloom as the rose, the character of the whole people must be changed. As slavery is abolished, with it must vanish every vestige of oppression. The right to vote must be secured; the doors of our public schools must be opened, that our children, side by side, may study from the same books, and imbibe the same principles and precepts from the Book of Books, learn the great truth that God "created one blood all nations of men to dwell on all the face of the earth"; so will caste, founded on prejudice against color, disappear.

Massachusetts has always been foremost in every good work.

---

* Lincoln was moved by the petition to write a private note to Governor Michael Hahn in Louisiana suggesting that in the forthcoming Constitutional convention "some of the colored people" might be granted the suffrage, "as, for instance, the very intelligent, and especially those who have fought gallantly in our ranks." But even this modest suggestion was rejected.

She, first of all the states, by positive law, struck the shackles from the limbs of every bondman within her limits. It was Massachusetts who first acknowledged the colored man as a citizen and gave him political equality. And today, by your enlightened legislation, no proscriptive laws remain on your statute book. In your state, color is no legal disqualification for any office of trust or power.

Mr. President, when we return to New Orleans, we shall tell our friends that in Massachusetts we could ride in every public vehicle; that the colored children not only were allowed to attend public schools with white children, but they were compelled by law to attend such schools; that we visited your courts of justice and saw colored lawyers defending their clients; and we shall tell them, too, of this most generous welcome extended to us by you. It will prove most grateful to their feeling, animate them with new hope and desires, and will prove a grand stimulus to renewed efforts for the acquisition of every right that can be guaranteed to them by law.

LET THE MONSTER PERISH

By Henry Highland Garnet

The Emancipation Proclamation had freed slaves only where the Federal troops were not in control to enforce the order—that is, those slaves living in areas still in rebellion against the government of the United States. It had specifically ruled out of the terms of emancipation all slave areas where federal troops were present, in Louisiana, Virginia and the Border States. Slavery was legally ended by the Thirteenth Amendment to the Constitution. In April, 1864, and January, 1865, the Senate and House respectively voted for the adoption of an amendment to the Constitution providing that neither slavery nor involuntary servitude, except as punishment for crime for which the party had been convicted, should exist within the United States or any place under its jurisdiction. The amendment was then sent to the state for ratification, which occurred in December, 1865 .

On February 12, 1865, in the hall of the House of Representatives, the Reverend Henry Highland Garnet preached a sermon commemorating the passage of the Thirteenth

*Amendment by Congress. At the time, Garnet was pastor
of the Fifteenth Street Presbyterian Church, in Washington, D. C. His sermon in the House of Representatives
made him the first Negro to speak in the halls of Congress.
In addition to praising the action of Congress, Garnet included an eloquent appeal for equal rights. (The Reverend
Mr. Garnet's sermon, reprinted here in part, is taken from*
A Memorial Discourse *by Rev. Henry Highland Garnet,
Delivered in the Hall of the House of Representatives,
Washington, D. C., on Sabbath, February 12, 1865, With
an Introduction by James McCune Smith, M.D., Phila-
delphia, 1865.)*

For they bind heavy burdens and grievous to be borne, and lay
them on men's shoulders, but they themselves will not move them
with one of their fingers.—Matthew 23:4.

IN THIS CHAPTER, of which my text is a sentence, the
Lord Jesus addressed his disciples, and the multitude that hung
spellbound upon the words that fell from his lips. He admonished them to beware of the religion of the Scribes and
Pharisees, which was distinguished for great professions, while
it succeeded in urging them to do but a little, or nothing that
accorded with the law of righteousness.

In theory they were right; but their practices were inconsistent and wrong. They were learned in the law of Moses and
in the traditions of their fathers, but the principles of righteousness failed to affect their hearts. They knew their duty but did
it not. The demands which they made upon others proved that
they themselves knew what things men ought to do. In condemning others they pronounced themselves guilty. They demanded that others should be just, merciful, pure, peaceable
and righteous. But they were unjust, impure, unmerciful—they
hated and wronged a portion of their fellowmen, and waged a
continual war against the government of God.

Such was their conduct in the Church and in the state. We
have modern Scribes and Pharisees, who are faithful to their
prototypes of ancient times.

With sincere respect and reverence for the instruction, and
the warning given by our Lord, and in humble dependence upon
him for his assistance, I shall speak this morning of the Scribes
and Pharisees of our times who rule the state. In discharging
this duty, I shall keep my eyes upon the picture which is painted
so faithfully and lifelike by the hand of the Saviour.

Allow me to describe them. They are intelligent and well-informed, and can never say, either before an earthly tribunal or at the bar of God, "We knew not of ourselves what was right." They are acquainted with the principles of the law of nations. They are proficient in the knowledge of Constitutional law. They are teachers of common law, and frame and execute statute law. They acknowledge that there is a just and impartial God, and are not altogether unacquainted with the law of Christian love and kindness. They claim for themselves the broadest freedom. Boastfully they tell us that they have received from the court of heaven the Magna Charta of human rights that was handed down through the clouds and amid the lightnings of Sinai, and given again by the Son of God on the Mount of Beatitudes while the glory of the Father shone around him. They tell us that from the Declaration of Independence and the Constitution they have obtained a guaranty of their political freedom, and from the Bible they derive their claim to all the blessings of religious liberty. With just pride they tell us that they are descended from the Pilgrims, who threw themselves upon the bosom of the treacherous sea and braved storms and tempests that they might find in a strange land and among savages free homes where they might build their altars that should blaze with acceptable sacrifice unto God. Yes! they boast that their fathers heroically turned away from the precious light of Eastern civilization and, taking their lamps with oil in their vessels, joyfully went forth to illuminate this land, that then dwelt in the darkness of the valley of the shadow of death. With hearts strengthened by faith they spread out their standard to the winds of heaven, near Plymouth Rock; and whether it was stiffened in the sleet and frosts of winter, or floated on the breeze of summer, it ever bore the motto, "Freedom to worship God."

But others, their fellow men, equal before the Almighty and made by Him of the same blood, and glowing with immortality, they doom to lifelong servitude and chains. Yes, they stand in the most sacred places on earth, and beneath the gaze of the piercing eye of Jehovah, the universal Father of all men, and declare that "the best possible condition of the Negro is slavery."

In the name of the Triune God I denounce the sentiment as unrighteous beyond measure, and the holy and the just of the whole earth say in regard to it, Anathema maranatha.

What is slavery? Too well do I know what it is. I will present to you a bird's-eye view of it; and it shall be no fancy picture, but one that is sketched by painful experience. I was born among the cherished institutions of slavery. My earliest recollections of parents, friends, and the home of my childhood are clouded with its wrongs. The first sight that met my eyes was a Christian mother enslaved by professed Christians, but, thank God, now a saint in heaven.* The first sounds that startled my ear and sent a shudder through my soul were the cracking of the whip and the clanking of chains. These sad memories mar the beauties of my native shores and darken all the slaveland, which, but for the reign of despotism, had been a paradise. But those shores are fairer now. The mists have left my native valleys, and the clouds have rolled away from the hills, and Maryland, the unhonored grave of my fathers, is now the free home of their liberated and happier children.

Let us view this demon, which the people have worshiped as a God. Come forth, thou grim monster, that thou mayest be critically examined! There he stands. Behold him, one and all. Its work is to chattelize man; to hold property in human beings. Great God! I would as soon attempt to enslave Gabriel or Michael as to enslave a man made in the image of God, and for whom Christ died. Slavery is snatching man from the high place to which he was lifted by the hand of God, and dragging him down to the level of the brute creation, where he is made to be the companion of the horse and the fellow of the ox.

It tears the crown of glory from his head and as far as possible obliterates the image of God that is in him. Slavery preys upon man, and man only. A brute cannot be made a slave. Why? Because a brute has not reason, faith, nor an undying spirit, nor conscience. It does not look forward to the future with joy or fear, nor reflect upon the past with satisfaction or regret. But who in this vast assembly, who in all this broad land, will say that the poorest and most unhappy brother in chains and servitude has not every one of these high endowments? Who denies it? Is there one? If so, let him speak. There is not one; no, not one.

But slavery attempts to make a man a brute. It treats him as a beast. Its terrible work is not finished until the ruined victim of its lusts and pride and avarice and hatred is reduced so low that with tearful eyes and feeble voice he faintly cries, "I am happy and contented. I love this condition."

> Proud Nimrod first the bloody chase began,
> A mighty hunter he; his prey was man.

The caged lion may cease to roar, and try no longer the strength of the bars of his prison, and lie with his head between his mighty paws and snuff the polluted air as though he heeded

---

* Garnet's mother was Henrietta Garnet. He was born a slave, at New Market, Kent County, Maryland, in 1815.

not. But is he contented? Does he not instinctively long for the freedom of the forest and the plain? Yes, he is a lion still. Our poor and forlorn brother whom thou hast labeled "slave," is also a man. He may be unfortunate, weak, helpless and despised and hated; nevertheless he is a man. His God and thine has stamped on his forehead his title to his inalienable rights in characters that can be read by every intelligent being. Pitiless storms of outrage may have beaten upon his defenseless head, and he may have descended through ages of oppression; yet he is a man. God made him such, and his brother cannot unmake him. Woe, woe to him who attempts to commit the accursed crime.

Slavery commenced its dreadful work in kidnaping unoffending men in a foreign and distant land, and in piracy on the seas. The plunderers were not the followers of Mahomet, nor the devotees of Hinduism, nor benighted pagans, nor idolaters, but people called Christians, and thus the ruthless traders in the souls and bodies of men fastened upon Christianity a crime and stain at the sight of which it shudders and shrieks.

It is guilty of the most heinous iniquities ever perpetrated upon helpless women and innocent children. Go to the shores of the land of my forefathers, poor bleeding Africa, which, although she has been bereaved and robbed for centuries, is nevertheless beloved by all her worthy descendants wherever dispersed. Behold a single scene that there meets your eyes. Turn not away either from shame, pity or indifference, but look and see the beginning of this cherished and petted institution. Behold a hundred youthful mothers seated on the ground, dropping their tears upon the hot sands, and filling the air with their lamentations.

Why do they weep? Ah, Lord God, thou knowest! Their babes have been torn from their bosoms and cast upon the plains to die of hunger, or to be devoured by hyenas or jackals. The little innocents would die on the "middle passage,"* or suffocate between the decks of the floating slave pen, freighted and packed with unparalleled human woe, and the slavers in mercy have cast them out to perish on their native shores. Such is the beginning, and no less wicked is the end of that system which Scribes and Pharisees in the Church and the state pronounce to be just, humane, benevolent and Christian. If such are the deeds of mercy wrought by angels, then tell me what works of iniquity there remain for devils to do? . . .

---

* During the African slave trade the voyage from Africa to the Americas was popularly referred to as the "middle passage." Overcrowding caused widespread deaths among the slaves.

It is the highly concentrated essence of all conceivable wickedness. Theft, robbery, pollution, unbridled passion, incest, cruelty, cold-blooded murder, blasphemy, and defiance of the laws of God. It teaches children to disregard parental authority. It tears down the marriage altar and tramples its sacred ashes under its feet. It creates and nourishes polygamy. It feeds and pampers its hateful handmaid, prejudice.

It has divided our national councils. It has engendered deadly strife between brethren. It has wasted the treasure of the Commonwealth and the lives of thousands of brave men, and driven troops of helpless women and children into yawning tombs. It has caused the bloodiest civil war recorded in the book of time. It has shorn this nation of its locks of strength that was rising as a young lion in the Western world. It has offered us as a sacrifice to the jealousy and cupidity of tyrants, despots, and adventurers of foreign countries. It has opened a door through which a usurper, a perjured but powerful prince, might stealthily enter and build an empire on the golden borders of our south-western frontier, and which is but a steppingstone to further and unlimited conquests on this continent. It has desolated the fairest portions of our land, "until the wolf long since driven back by the march of civilization returns after the lapse of a hundred years and howls amidst its ruins."

It seals up the Bible and mutilates its sacred truths, and flies into the face of the Almighty, and impiously asks, "Who art thou that I should obey thee?" Such are the outlines of this fearful national sin; and yet the condition to which it reduces man, it is affirmed, is the best that can possibly be devised for him.

When inconsistencies similar in character, and no more glaring, passed beneath the eye of the Son of God, no wonder he broke forth in language of vehement denunciation. Ye Scribes, Pharisees, and hypocrites! Ye blind guides! Ye compass sea and land to make one proselyte, and when he is made ye make him twofold more the child of hell than yourselves. Ye are like unto whited sepulchers, which indeed appear beautiful without, but within are full of dead men's bones and all uncleanness!

Let us here take up the golden rule, and adopt the self-application mode of reasoning to those who hold these erroneous views. Come, gird up thy loins and answer like a man, if thou canst. Is slavery, as it is seen in its origin, continuance and end, the best possible condition for thee? Oh, no! Wilt thou bear that burden on thy shoulders, which thou wouldst lay upon thy fellow man? No. Wilt thou bear a part of it, or remove a little of its weight with one of thy fingers? The sharp and indignant answer is no, no! Then how, and when, and where, shall we apply to thee the golden rule, which says, "Therefore all things that ye would that others should do to you, do ye even so unto them, for this is the law and the prophets.". . .

Every good principle and every great and noble power have been made the subject of the inspired verse and the songs of poets. But who of them has attempted to immortalize slavery? You will search in vain the annals of the world to find an instance. Should any attempt the sacrilegious work, his genius would fall to the earth as if smitten by the lightning of heaven. Should he lift his hand to write a line in its praise, or defense, the ink would freeze on the point of his pen.

Could we array in one line, representatives of all the families of men, beginning with those lowest in the scale of being, and should we put to them the question, Is it right and desirable that you should be reduced to the condition of slaves, to be registered with chattels, to have your persons and your lives and the products of your labor subjected to the will and the interests of others? Is it right and just that the persons of your wives and children should be at the disposal of others and be yielded to them for the purpose of pampering their lusts and greed of gain? Is it right to lay heavy burdens on other men's shoulders which you would not remove with one of your fingers? From the rude savage and barbarian the negative response would come, increasing in power and significance as it rolled up the line. And when those should reply, whose minds and hearts are illuminated with the highest civilization and with the spirit of Christianity, the answer deep-toned and prolonged would thunder forth, no, no!

With all the moral attributes of God on our side, cheered as we are by the voices of universal human nature—in view of the best interests of the present and future generations—animated with the noble desire to furnish the nations of the earth with a worthy example, let the verdict of death which has been brought in against slavery by the Thirty-eighth Congress be affirmed and executed by the people. Let the gigantic monster perish. Yes, perish now and perish forever!

It is often asked when and where will the demands of the reformers of this and coming ages end? It is a fair question, and I will answer.

When all unjust and heavy burdens shall be removed from every man in the land. When all invidious and proscriptive distinctions shall be blotted out from our laws, whether they be constitutional, statute or municipal laws. When emancipation shall be followed by enfranchisement, and all men holding allegiance to the government shall enjoy every right of American citizenship. When our brave and gallant soldiers shall have justice done unto them. When the men who endure the sufferings and perils of the battlefield in the defense of their country, and in order to keep our rulers in their places, shall enjoy the well-earned privilege of voting for them. When in the army and navy, and in every legitimate and honorable occupation, promotion shall smile upon merit without the slightest regard to the complexion of a man's face. When there shall be no more class legislation and no more trouble concerning the black man and his rights than there is in regard to other American citizens. When, in every respect, he shall be equal before the law, and shall be left to make his own way in the social walks of life.

We ask, and only ask, that when our poor, frail barks are launched on life's ocean,

> Bound on a voyage of awful length
> And dangers little known,

that, in common with others, we may be furnished with rudder, helm and sails and charts and compass. Give us good pilots to conduct us to the open seas; lift no false lights along the dangerous coasts, and if it shall please God to send us propitious winds or fearful gales, we shall survive or perish as our energies or neglect shall determine. We ask no special favors, but we plead for justice. While we scorn unmanly dependence; in the name of God, the universal Father, we demand the right to live and labor and enjoy the fruits of our toil. The good work which God has assigned for the ages to come will be finished when our national literature shall be so purified as to reflect a faithful and a just light upon the character and social habits of our race, and the brush and pencil and chisel and lyre of art shall refuse to lend their aid to scoff at the afflictions of the poor or to caricature or ridicule a long-suffering people. When caste and prejudice in Christian churches shall be utterly destroyed and shall be regarded as totally unworthy of Christians, and at variance with the principles of the Gospel. When the blessings of the Christian religion and of sound religious education shall be freely offered to all, then, and not till then, shall the effectual labors of God's people and God's instruments cease.

If slavery has been destroyed merely from *necessity*,* let every class be enfranchised at the dictation of *justice*. Then we

---

* In issuing the Emancipation Proclamation, January 1, 1863, President Lincoln described it "as a fit and necessary war measure for suppressing said rebellion."

shall have a Constitution that shall be reverenced by all, rulers who shall be honored and revered, and a Union that shall be sincerely loved by a brave and patriotic people, and which can never be severed.

Great sacrifices have been made by the people; yet, greater still are demanded ere atonement can be made for our national sins. Eternal justice holds heavy mortgages against us and will require the payment of the last farthing. We have involved ourselves in the sin of unrighteous gain, stimulated by luxury and pride and the love of power and oppression; and prosperity and peace can be purchased only by blood and with tears of repentance. We have paid some of the fearful installments, but there are other heavy obligations to be met.

The great day of the nation's judgment has come, and who shall be able to stand? Even we, whose ancestors have suffered the afflictions which are inseparable from a condition of slavery, for the period of two centuries and a half, now pity our land and weep with those who weep.

Upon the total and complete destruction of this accursed sin depends the safety and perpetuity of our Republic and its excellent institutions.

Let slavery die. It has had a long and fair trial. God himself has pleaded against it. The enlightened nations of the earth have condemned it. Its death warrant is signed by God and man. Do not commute its sentence. Give it no respite, but let it be ignominiously executed.

Honorable Senators and Representatives, illustrious rulers of this great nation, I cannot refrain this day from invoking upon you, in God's name, the blessings of millions who were ready to perish, but to whom a new and better life has been opened by your humanity, justice and patriotism. You have said, "Let the Constitution of the country be so amended that slavery and involuntary servitude shall no longer exist in the United States, except in punishment for crime." Surely, an act so sublime could not escape divine notice; and doubtless the deed has been recorded in the archives of heaven. Volumes may be appropriated to your praise and renown in the history of the world. Genius and art may perpetuate the glorious act on canvas and in marble, but certain and more lasting monuments in commemoration of your decision are already erected in the hearts and memories of a grateful people.

The nation has begun its exodus from worse than Egyptian bondage; and I beseech you that you say to the people that they go forward. With the assurance of God's favor in all things done in obedience to his righteous will, and guided by day and by night by the pillars of cloud and fire, let us not pause until we have reached the other and safe side of the stormy and crimson sea. Let freemen and patriots mete out complete and equal justice to all men and thus prove to mankind the superiority of our democratic, republican government.

Favored men, and honored of God as his instruments, speedily finish the work which he has given you to do. Emancipate, enfranchise, educate, and give the blessings of the gospel to every American citizen.

Then before us a path of prosperity will open, and upon us will descend the mercies and favors of God. Then shall the people of other countries, who are standing tiptoe on the shores of every ocean, earnestly looking to see the end of this amazing conflict, behold a Republic that is sufficiently strong to outlive the ruin and desolations of civil war, having the magnanimity to do justice to the poorest and weakest of her citizens. Thus shall we give to the world the form of a model Republic, founded on the principles of justice and humanity and Christianity, in which the burdens of war and the blessings of peace are equally borne and enjoyed by all.

COLORED MEN STANDING IN THE WAY OF THEIR OWN RACE

By James Lynch

At the May, 1865, meeting of the Young Men's Literary and Debating Society of Philadelphia, James Lynch delivered the following brief but significant speech. Lynch was born in Baltimore on January 8, 1839, and in his youth obtained a good education. In 1858 he joined the Presbyterian Church in New York, but soon thereafter was accepted by the African Methodist Episcopal Conference in Indiana. He transferred to Baltimore, and in 1863 went to South Carolina as a missionary to the freedmen from the A.M.E. Church. From 1866 to June 15, 1867, he was editor of The Christian Recorder in Philadelphia. Later he was with the Freedmen's Bureau in Mississippi and in 1871 was elected Secretary of State. He died on December 18, 1872.

(Lynch's speech as presented here has been taken from The Christian Recorder, *May 13, 1865.)*

IT IS STRANGE, but true, that we have such men among us. First on the list stand those who set no value on the ability of their race and adopt the opinions respecting them that prejudiced white men hold. Among these we find those who prefer white men as religious instructors, as teachers, physicians and lawyers, because they are white. They are studious in disparaging their own color, and paying homage to a supposed native superiority of the whites.

Then comes another class, who are always in the market for the white man's purchase. If they are flattered, feted or pecuniarily rewarded, they will kiss the hand of the oppressor and ally themselves with the enemies or disparagers of their race.

Another class is found in those who pride themselves on the color of their skins, feeling that a light complexion imparts superiority. It is questionable whether there is in existence a more contemptible feeling than this, for while it assumes superiority over the darker skin, it confesses inferiority to the lighter, or white, person. Certainly if A is superior to B because he has three fourths white blood in his veins, and B is his inferior, then a white man, who has nothing else but white blood in his veins must be superior to A, and A is the inferior.*

Those colored persons who hold this idea are holding to that which has been, and to some degree still is, the infamy of the nation, on which God is writing, with the iron pen of providence, in letters of blood, a death sentence. They are opposing themselves to God and the defenders of humanity.

Still another class are those who succumb to the prejudices of white men, and while they are loudmouthed for their right to ride in railroad cars and visit public places of instruction or amusement, they will not shave colored men in their barbershops nor accommodate them with a meal in their restaurants. The plea is that they will "lose custom." Well, white men can

---

* Lynch's discussion is reminiscent of Lincoln's attack on slavery in 1854 in which he said: "If A can prove, however conclusively, that he may of right enslave B, why may not B snatch the same argument and prove equally that he may enslave A? You say A is white and B is black. It is color, then; the lighter having the right to enslave the darker? Take care. By this rule you are to be slave to the first man you meet with a fairer skin than your own. . . ."

urge with equal force the same plea; and there is no reason why white men shall be expected to sacrifice more for colored men than colored men will for themselves.

It is cheering to think that the number of colored men who stand in the way of their race are in the minority by great odds. Still their existence is to be deplored, and if they be dragged forth into the burning sunlight of public opinion their baleful and miasmatic influence will soon be dried up by its heat. We echo Stanford's thrilling word, in reference to our people, "Action!" We want a healthy public sentiment among us, enlightened and energetic, that like an ever-flowing current, will sweep away the Tories and the Judases from their footings.

ADVICE TO EX-SLAVES

By Martin Robinson Delany

Martin Robinson Delany (1812–1885) was born in Charles Town, Virginia (now in West Virginia), the grandson of slaves and the son of free Negroes. His father's father was supposed to have been an African chieftain of the Golah tribe, captured with his family in battle, sold as a slave and brought to America. His mother's father was said to have been an African prince of the Mandingo line in the Niger Valley, also captured in war, enslaved, sold and transported to America.

Delany received his first instruction in reading from peddlers of books, continued his studies under the Reverend Louis Woodson in Pittsburgh, and went on to study medicine at Harvard, became a doctor, was one of seventy-five black officers in the Union Army, wrote a novel, ran for the office of lieutenant governor of South Carolina, and named his daughter Ethiopia. His little book The Condition, Elevation, Emigration, and Destiny of the Colored People of the United States, Politically Considered, *published in Philadelphia in 1852 at his own expense, is a remarkable source of information about the free black population in the antebellum North, and contains important suggestions for improvement of their conditions. One sen-*

tence in the Appendix of his book is the most quoted in the work: "We are a nation within a nation, as the Poles in Russia, the Hungarians in Austria, the Welsh, Irish and Scotch in the British dominions." Therefore Delany advocated founding a new Negro nation on the eastern coast of Africa "for the settlement of colored adventurers from the United States and elsewhere." In 1859 Delany traveled in Africa for about a year seeking places to which black Americans might emigrate. He signed treaties with eight kings of Abeokuta for grants of land to establish American Negro colonies in the Yoruba area. From Africa, Delany went on to London, and after stirring up an international incident at the International Statistical Congress in London with his assertion that "I am a Man"—a remark which caused all but one member of the American delegation to walk out of the Congress in protest—he continued to lecture on Africa in England and Scotland for almost seven months. He returned to the United States in 1861, six weeks after the Civil War had broken out.

In February, 1865, Martin R. Delany was commissioned a major of infantry and ordered to recruit an "armée d'Afrique" in South Carolina. But the end of the war cut short the project. Delany, however, continued to work in the South, serving for three years in the Freedmen's Bureau. In this capacity, he delivered a speech to a meeting of freedmen at St. Helena Island, South Carolina, in July, 1865. No report of the speech appeared in the contemporary press, but what appears to be an accurate account is in the files of the Freedmen's Bureau in the National Archives. Evidently the Bureau heads feared Delany's militancy and sent a lieutenant in the Union Army to report back what he had told the freedmen in his address. As the comments of the lieutenant reveal, Delany's advice to the ex-slaves to stand up for full freedom and resist reenslavement by arms if necessary, frightened the whites who were present and, indeed, the officer himself.

Delany's speech is published below as it was reported in the letter of Lieutenant Edward M. Stoeber. The entire letter is included to give the reader a picture of the setting and the reactions to the speech. I am indebted to William Loren Katz for calling this document to my attention.

Delany, who is acknowledged to be the father of American black nationalism, lectured frequently. But few of his speeches have been preserved.

Headquarters, Assistant Commissioner
Bureau Refugees, Freedmen and Abandoned Lands
South Carolina, Georgia and Florida.
Beaufort, S. C., July 24th, 1865.

Br[eve]t Maj. S. M. Taylor
   Asst. Adj't Gen'l.
Major:

In obedience to your request, I proceeded to St. Helena Island, yesterday morning, for the purpose of listening to the public delivery of a lecture by Major Delany 104th Ne[gro] S. C. Troops.

I was accompanied by Lieut. A. Whyte jr 128th Ne[gro] S. C. Troops, under Col. C. H. Howard 128th Ne[gro] S. C. Troops, Com[an]d'g Post.

The meeting was held near "Brick Church," the congregation numbering from 500 to 600.

As introduction Maj. Delany made them acquainted with the fact, that slavery is absolutely abolished, throwing thunders of damnations and maledictions on all the former slaveowners and people of the South, and almost condemned their souls to hell.

He says "It was only a War policy of the Government, to declare the slaves of the South free, knowing that the whole power of the South, laid in the possession of the Slaves. But I want you to understand, that we would not have become free, had we not armed ourselves and fought out our independence" (this he repeated twice). He further says, "If I had been a slave, I would have been most troublesome and not to be conquered by any threat or punishment. I would not have worked, and no one would have dared to come near me, I would have struggled for life or death, and would have thrown fire and sword between them.

"I know *you* have been good, only too good. I was told by a friend of mine that when owned by a man and put to work on the field, he laid quietly down, and just looked out for the overseer to come along, when he pretended to work very hard. But he confessed to me, that he never had done a fair day's work for his master. And so he was right, so I would have done the same, and all of you ought to have done the same.

"People say that you are too lazy to work, that you have no intelligence to get on for yourselves, without being guided and driven to the work by overseers. I say it is a lie, and a blasphemous lie, and I will prove it to be so.

"I am going to tell you now, *what* you are worth. As you know Christopher Columbus landed here in 1492. They came here only for the purpose to dig gold, gather precious pearls, diamonds and all sorts of jewels, only for the proud Aristocracy of the White Spaniards and Portuguese, to adorn their persons, to have brooches for their breasts, earrings for their ears, Bracelets for their ankles and rings for their limbs and fingers. They found here (red men) Indians whom they obliged to dig and work and slave for them—but they found out that they died away too fast and cannot stand the work. In course of time they had taken some blacks (Africans) along with them and put *them* to work—they could stand it—and yet the Whites say they are superior to our race, though they could not stand it. (At the present day in some of the Eastern parts of Spain, the Spaniard there (having been once conquered by the black race) have black eyes, black hair, black complexion. They have Negroe blood in them!!) The work was so profitable which those poor blacks did, that in the year 1502 Charles the V. gave permission to import into America yearly 4,000 blacks. The profit of these sales was so immense, that afterwards even the Virgin Queen of England and James the II. took part in the Slave trade and were accumulating great wealth for the Treasury of the Government. And so you *always* have been the means of riches.

"I tell you I have been all over Africa (I was born there)* and I tell you (as I told to the Geographical Faculty in London) that those people there, are a well-driving class of cultivators, and I never saw or heard of one of our brethern there to travel without taking seeds with him as much as he can carry and to sow it wherever he goes to, or to exchange it with his brethern.

"So you ought further to know, that all the spices, cotton, rice and coffee has only been brought over by *you*, from the land of our brethern.

"Your masters who lived in opulence, kept you to hard work by some contemptible being called overseer—who chastised and beat you whenever he pleased—while your master lived in some Northern town or in Europe to squander away the wealth only you acquired for him. He never earned a single Dollar in his life. You men and women, every one of you around me, made thousands and thousands of dollars for your master. Only you were the means for your masters to lead the idle and inglorious life, and to give his children the education, which he denied to you, for fear you may awake to conscience.† If I look around me, I tell you all the houses on this Island and in Beau-

---

* Delany was born in northern Virginia in 1812. He may have referred to his parents who traced their ancestry to African chieftains.
† The word was probably "consciousness."

fort, they are all familiar to my eye, they are the same structures which I have met with in Africa. They have all been made by the Negroes, you can see it by such exteriors.

"I tell you they (white man) cannot teach you anything, and they could not make them because they have not the brain to do it. (after a pause) At least I mean the Southern people; Oh the Yankees they are smart. Now tell me from all you have heard from me, are you not worth anything? Are you those men whom they think, God only created as a curse and for a slave? Whom they do not consider their equals? As I said before the Yankees are smart; there are good ones and bad ones. The good ones, if they are good they are very good, if they are bad, they are very bad. But the worst and most contemptible, and even worse than even your masters were, are those Yankees, who hired themselves as *overseers*.

"Believe not in these School teachers, Emissaries, Ministers, and agents, because they never tell you the truth, and I particularly warn you against those Cotton Agents, who come honey mouthed unto you, their only intent being to make profit by your inexperience.

"If there is a man who comes to you, who will meddle with your affairs, send him to one of your more enlightened brothers, who shall ask him who he is, what business he seeks with you, etc.

"Believe none but those Agents who are sent out by Government, to enlighten and guide you. I am an officer in the service of the U. S. Government, and ordered to aid Gen'l Saxton, who has been only lately appointed Asst Comr for South Carolina. So is Gen'l Wild Asst Comr for Georgia.

"When Chief Justice Chase* was down here to speak to you, some of those malicious and abominable New York papers derived from it that he only seeks to be elected by you as President. I have no such ambition, *I* let them have for a President a white or a black one. *I* don't care who it be—it may be who has a mind to. I shall not be intimidated whether by threats or imprisonment, and no power will keep me from telling you the truth. So I expressed myself even at Charleston, the hotbed of those scoundrels, your old masters, without fear or reluctance.

"So I will come to the main purpose for which I have come to see you. As before the whole South depended upon you, now

* Chief Justice of the Supreme Court Salmon Portland Chase (1808–1873) began an extended Southern tour in May 1865 to investigate conditions in the states lately in rebellion. At Charleston, South Carolina, and elsewhere he addressed audiences of blacks, advocating Negro suffrage.

the *whole country* will depend upon you. I give you an advice how to get along. Get up a community and get all the lands you can—if you cannot get any singly.

"Grow as much vegetables, etc, as you want for your families; on the other part of the land you cultivate Rice and Cotton. Now for instance 1. Acre will grow a crop of Cotton of $90— now a land with 10 Acres will bring $900 every year: if you cannot get the land all yourself,—the community can, and so you can divide the profit. There is Tobacco for instance (Virginia is the great place for Tobacco). There are whole squares at Dublin and Liverpool named after some place of Tobacco notoriety, so you see of what enormous value your labor was to the benefits of your masters. Now you understand that I want you to be the producers of this country. It is the wish of the Government for you to be so. We will send friends to you, who will further instruct you how to come to the end of our wishes. You see that by so adhering to our views, you will become a wealthy and powerful population.

"Now I look around me and notice a man, barefooted, covered with rags and dirt. Now I ask, what is that man doing, for whom is he working. I hear that he works for that and that farmer for 30 cents a day. I tell you that must not be. That would be cursed slavery over again. I will not have it, the Government will not have it, and the Government shall hear about it. I will tell the Government. I tell you slavery is over, and shall never return again. We have now 200,000 of our men well drilled in arms and used to War fare and I tell you it is with you and them that slavery shall not come back again, if you are determined it will not return again.

"Now go to work, and in a short time I will see you again, and other friends will come to show you how to begin. —Have your fields in good order and well tilled and planted, and when I pass the fields and see a land well planted and well cared for, then I may be sure from the look of it, that it belongs to a free Negro, and when I see a field thinly planted and little cared for, then I may think it belongs to some man who works it with slaves. The Government decided that you shall one third of the produce of the crops, from your employer, so if he makes $3— you will have to get $1.—out of it for your labor.

The other day some plantation owners in Virginia and Maryland offered $5.—a month for your labour, but it was indignantly rejected by Gen'l Howard, the Commissioner for the Government."*

* Oliver Otis Howard (1830–1909), brigadier general in the Union Army, was appointed on May 12, 1865, by President Johnson, commissioner of

These are the expressions, as far as I can remember, without having made notes at the time.

The excitement with the congregation was immense, groups were formed talking over what they have heard, and ever and anon cheers were given to some particular sentence of the speech.

I afterwards mingled with several groups, to hear their opinions. Some used violent language, "saying they would get rid of the Yankee employer." —"That is the only man who ever told them the truth." "That now those men have to work themselves or starve or leave the country, we will not work for them any more."

Some Whites were present, and listened with horror depicted in their faces to the whole performance. Some said, "What shall become of us now?" And if such a speech should be again given to those men, there will be open rebellion.

Major Delany was afterwards corrected by Mr Town the Superintendent at that place, to the effect, that the pay of labourers on this Island is not 30 cents a day, but 30 cents a task, and that a man can easily make from 75 to 90 cents a day. Major Delany then corrected himself accordingly, saying that he must have been misinformed.

My opinion of the whole affair is that Major Delany is a thorough hater of the white race and excites the colored people unnecessarily. He even tries to injure the magnanimous conduct of the Government towards them, either intentionally or through want of knowledge.

He tells them to remember "that they would not have become *free,* had they not *armed themselves* and *fought for their independence.* This is a falsehood and a misrepresentation. —Our President Abraham Lincoln declared the colored race free, before there was even an idea of arming colored men.* This is decidedly calculated to create bad feeling against the Government.

By giving them some historical facts and telling them that neither Indians nor Whites could stand the work, in this country, he wants to impress them (the colored men) with the idea that he in fact is not only superior, in a physical view, but also

---

the newly established Bureau of Refugees, Freedmen and Abandoned Lands (Freedmen's Bureau), for which position he had been selected by Lincoln.

* This, of course, is inaccurate. Negroes, as we have seen above, sought to enlist in the Union Army as soon as the war started, but were rejected. The enlistment of Negro troops in the Union Army began in late 1862 before Lincoln issued the Emancipation Proclamation.

in intelligence. —He says, "believe none of those ministers, schoolteachers, Emmisaries, because they never tell you the truth." It is only to bring distrust against all, and gives them to understand that they shall believe men of their own race. He openly acts and speaks contrary to the policy of the Government, advising them not to work for any man, but for themselves.

The intention of our Government, that all the men should be employed by their former masters, as far as possible, and contracts made between as superintended by some Officer empowered by the Government.

He says it would be old slavery over again, if a man should work for an employer, and *that* it must not be. Does he not give a hint of what they should do by his utterings "that if he had been a slave etc.?; or by giving narrative of the slave who did not work for his master?—further as he says: "that a field should show by its appearance by whom and for whom it is worked?"

The mention of having two hundred thousand men well drilled in arms:—does he not hint to them what to do?; if they should be compelled to work for employers?

In my opinion of this discourse he was trying to encourage them to break the peace of society and force their way by insurrection to a position he is ambitious they should attain to.

I am Major,

Very Respectfully,

Your obedient servant,

(Sgd) EDWARD M. STOEBER

1st Lieut 104th U.S.C.T.

A true Copy
(Sgd) EDWARD M. STOEBER
    1st Lieut 104th U.S.C.T.

THE ABILITIES AND POSSIBILITIES OF OUR RACE

By Frederick Douglass

*In the spring of 1865 forty Negroes in Baltimore formed
an association and purchased a building on Lexington
Street, near Davis, formerly occupied by Newton University, for the sum of $16,000. The association renamed the
building Douglass Institute in honor of Frederick Douglass, and dedicated it to "the intellectual advancement of
the colored portion of the community." On October 1,
1865, the Douglass Institute was formally opened with
Douglass himself as the featured speaker. Immediately
over the stand on which Douglass and the officers of the
Institute were seated was a full-length portrait of the late
President Abraham Lincoln.*

*The proceedings opened with a prayer by Bishop Alex-
ander W. Wayman of the African Methodist Episcopal
Church. Then Douglass was introduced and delivered his
address. He was followed by remarks by officers of the
Institute, after which Douglass again spoke briefly demanding "the equality of all men before the law." The
ceremonies closed with the reading of letters from Bishop
Daniel A. Payne of the African Methodist Episcopal
Church, Charles Sumner, and Major General W. B. Han-
cock in which they expressed their regrets at having been
unable to attend due to prior commitments. "I am glad,"
wrote Bishop Payne, "that you have named your Institute
after so eminent a man as Frederick Douglass. His merits
demand this honor." Sumner wrote: "I rejoice that you are
to listen to Frederick Douglass, who always speaks well,
and who knows how to portray the duties of the hour. His
presence—his voice—his example—each is a constant
protest against injustice to the colored race."*

*Douglass' speech was delivered at a time when the
Southern state legislatures, operating under the Reconstruction policies of President Andrew Johnson and dominated by former slaveholders, declined to confer citizenship upon ex-slaves, barred them from voting, and denied
them any place in the political life of the South. At the
same time, they adopted legislation such as the Black*

Codes, which bound Negroes to the land on which they worked and all but reenslaved them. In his address, Douglass refers to these events as furnishing sufficient proof of the value of the Institute.

(The address as here presented has been excerpted from the text that appeared in The Liberator, *October 13, 1865.)*

. . . LET ME at the outset put myself at ease by expressing to the founders of this institution my sincere and heartfelt thanks for assigning to me the high place I occupy on this occasion, and above all, for associating my name with the Institute here established. It is an honor. I look upon this proceeding on your part not merely as a compliment to me personally, but as an open avowal of the great principles of progress, liberty, justice and equality, which I have for years endeavored to advocate. When I left Maryland, twenty-seven years ago,* I did so with the firm resolve never to forget my brothers and sisters in bondage, and to do whatever might be in my power to accomplish their emancipation; and I have to say tonight, that in whatever else I may have failed, in this at least I have not failed. No man can truthfully say I ever deserted the post of duty.

The establishment of an Institute bearing my name by the colored people in the city of my boyhood, so soon after the act of emancipation in this state,† looms before me as a *first* grand indication of progress. I say it is a *first*, and first indications, whether observed in the silent, mysterious phenomena of physical nature, or in the moral or intellectual developments of human society, are always interesting in thoughtful men. . . .

A people hitherto pronounced by American learning as incapable of anything higher than the dull round of manly animal life—held to be originally and permanently inferior, fit only for the coarser and heavier labors of human society, deprived of the social incentives to excellence which everywhere act upon other men—dare here and now to establish an Institute, devoted to all the higher wants and aspirations of the human soul. It is a great fact. . . .

My friends, the present is a critical moment for the colored people of this country; our fate for weal or for woe, it may be yet for many generations, trembles now in the balance. No man can tell which way the scale will turn. There is not a breeze that

* On September 3, 1838, Douglass escaped from Baltimore and slavery.
† Slavery was abolished in Maryland by the adoption of the state constitution of 1864.

sweeps to us from the South, but comes laden with the wail of our suffering people. Heaven only knows what will be in store for our people in the South. But dismal as is the hour, troubled and convulsed as are the times, we may congratulate ourselves upon the establishment of this institution. It comes as a timely argument on the right side of the momentous questions which now agitate the nation. It comes at a time when the American people are once more being urged to do from necessity what they should have done from a sense of right and of sound statesmanship. It is the same old posture of affairs, wherein our rulers do wrong from choice and right from necessity. They gave us the bullet to save themselves; they will yet give the ballot to save themselves. My hope of the future is founded just where it was during all the war. I always said that I had much faith in the virtue of the great North, but that I had incomparably more in the villainy of the South. The South is now on its good behavior, we are told. They have been invested with powers merely to see how they will use them. If they do certain things, we are told, it will be well; but if they do certain other things—well, somebody will interfere. Very well. I expect to see the rebels consistent with their whole past. They are sworn now as at the beginning of the war, and with like results. They take the oath to support a government they hate. They are sure to abuse the power given them, and I believe there will be virtue enough in the country, when it shall see that the loyal whites can only be saved by giving the ballot to the Negro, to do the thing now called impossible.

This Institute comes to our help. It comes at a time when hesitation to extend suffrage to the colored people finds its best apology in our alleged incapacity. I deem it fortunate that, at such a time as this, in such a city as this, so near the capital of the nation as this, there has arisen here an institution in which we can confront ignorance and prejudice with the light and power of positive knowledge, and array against brazen falsehood the rightful influence of accomplished facts.

The very existence of this institution, established and sustained by colored men in this city, so recently a slaveholding city—in this state, so recently a slaveholding state; in this community, among whom freedom of speech was scarcely known by even the white citizens only a few months ago—is a most striking, cheering and instructive fact. It attests the progressive spirit, the sagacity, the courage, the faith, the intelligence and manly ambition of the colored people of this city and state, and reflects credit upon the colored people of the country generally. Its effects upon those who disparage us will be good, but its effects upon ourselves will, I trust, be far better. While to them it will be a standing contradiction, to us it will be happy concurrence with all our hopes, with all that is high, noble and desirable.

The colored boy and girl now, as they walk your streets, will hold themselves in higher estimation and assume a prouder and more elastic step as they look up to the fine proportions of this ample and elegant building and remember that from foundation to roof, from cornerstone to coping, in purpose and in value, in spirit and in aspiration, it is all the property of the colored citizens of Baltimore.

The establishment of this institution may be thought by some a thing of doubtful expediency. There was a time when I should have thought it so myself. In my enthusiasm, perhaps it was my simplicity (it is not material which), I once flattered myself that the day had happily gone by when it could be necessary for colored people in this country to combine and act together as a separate class, and in any representative character whatever. I would have had them infuse themselves and their works into the political, intellectual, artistic and mechanical activities and combinations of their white fellow countrymen. It seemed to me that colored conventions, colored exhibitions, colored associations and institutions of all kinds and descriptions had answered the ends of their existence and might properly be abandoned; that, in short, they were hindrances rather than helps in achieving a higher and better estimation in the public mind for ourselves as a race.

I may say that I still hold this opinion in a modified degree. The latent contempt and prejudice toward our race, which recent political doctrines with reference to our future in this country have developed, the persistent determination of the present Executive of the nation, and also the apparent determination of a portion of the people to hold and treat us in a degraded relation, not only justify for the present such associate effort on our part, but make it eminently necessary.

It is the misfortune of our class that it fails to derive due advantages from the achievements of its individual members, but never fails to suffer from the ignorance or crimes of a single individual with whom the class is identified. A Benjamin Franklin could redeem, in the eyes of scientific Europe, the mental mediocrity of our young white Republic, but the genius and learning of a Benjamin Banneker of your state of Maryland, the wisdom and heroism of Toussaint, are not permitted to do the same service for the colored race to which they belong. Wealth, learning and ability made an Irishman an Englishman. The same

metamorphosing power converts a Negro into a white man in
this country. When prejudice cannot deny the black man's ability, it denies his race and claims him as a white man. It affirms
that if he is not exactly white, he ought to be. If not what he
ought to be in this particular, he owes whatever intelligence he
possesses to the white race by contract or association. Great
actions, as shown by Robert Smalls,* the gallant captain of the
Planter, and by William Tilghman,† and other brave colored
men, which by the war slavery has tossed to the surface, have
not been sufficient to change the general estimate formed of
the colored race. The eloquence and learning of Doctor Smith,
Professors Vashon, Reason, Garnet, Remond, Martin, Rock,
Crummell,‡ and many others, have done us service; but they
leave us yet under a cloud. The public, with the mass of ignorance—notwithstanding that ignorance has been enforced and
compelled among our people, hitherto—has sternly denied the
representative character of our distinguished men. They are
treated as exceptions, individual cases, and the like. They contend that the race, as such, is destitute of the subjective original
elemental condition of a high self-originating and self-sustaining civilization.

Such is the sweeping and damaging judgment pronounced in
various high quarters against our race; and such is the current

* In May, 1862, Robert Smalls, the slave pilot of a Confederate gunboat,
the *Planter,* and the slave crew, sailed the ship out of Charleston harbor
and surrendered it to the Union fleet. Congress granted half of the prize
money for the *Planter* to Smalls and his men. Smalls later played a leading role in Reconstruction politics and served five terms as a South
Carolina Congressman.
† Douglass undoubtedly refers to William Tillman, the Negro steward
and cook of the schooner *S. J. Waring,* captured en route from New
York to South America in June, 1861, by a rebel privateer. Informed
that he was the property of the Confederate states and would be sold, on
his arrival at Charleston, as a slave, Tillman killed the Confederate captain and, seizing the revolver of the mate, whom he also killed, took
command of the vessel and sailed it back to New York. The Federal government awarded Tillman $6,000 as prize money for the capture of the
schooner.
‡ Charles L. Reason, of New York, became in 1852 head of the Institute
of Colored Youth in Philadelphia. J. Sella Martin, a slave who escaped
to the North in 1855, became pastor of the Joy Street Baptist Church,
in Boston, and was one of the best-known Negro ministers in the North.
Alexander Crummell, celebrated in a moving chapter in W. E. B. Du Bois'
The Souls of Black Folk, was a leading clergyman in the North. Between
1853 and 1873 he was active in Africa as an agent of the American
Colonization Society. After his return from Africa, he continued to play
a prominent role in the United States as a clergyman and political leader.

of opinion against which the colored people have to advance, if they advance at all. A few years ago, we met this unfavorable theory as best we could in three ways. We pointed our assailants and traducers to the ancient civilization of Northern Africa. We traced the entangled threads of history and of civilization back to their sources in Africa. We called attention to the somewhat disagreeable fact—agreeable to us, but not so to our Teutonic brethren—that the arts, appliances and blessings of civilization flourished in the very heart of Ethiopia, at a time when all Europe floundered in the depths of ignorance and barbarism. We dwelt on the grandeur, magnificence and stupendous dimensions of Egyptian architecture and held up the fact, now generally admitted, that that race was master of mechanical forces of which the present generations of men are ignorant.*

We pointed to the nautical skill, commercial enterprise and military prowess of Carthage, and justly claimed relationship with those great nations of antiquity. We are a dark people, and so were they. They stood between us and the Europeans in point of complexion as well as in point of geography. We have contended, and not illogically, that if the fact of color was no barrier of civilization in this case, it cannot be in ours.

Our second answer has been drawn from modern examples. These have not, I confess, been very numerous or striking, but enough to demonstrate the presence of highly progressive and civilizing elements in the colored race. We find them in Africa —we find them written down in the interesting travels of Barth, Livingstone and Wilson. We find them in Haiti, and we find them in our own country. Our third answer has been unfavorable influences under which our race has been placed by Christendom during the last three centuries. Where under the whole heavens was there ever a race so blasted and withered, so shorn and bereft of all opportunities for development as ourselves? It would seem that the whole Christian world had combined for the destruction of our race, and had summoned heaven and hell, philosophy and revelations, to assist in the work. Our history has been but a track of blood. Gaunt and hungry sharks have followed us on slave ships by sea, and the hungrier and greedier slave drivers have followed us during all these years with the bloody slave whip on land. The question forced upon us at

* For a detailed presentation by Douglass of African backgrounds and civilization, see his address, "The Claims of the Negro Ethnologically Considered," delivered at Western Reserve College, July 12, 1854 (see pp. 144–64).

every moment of our generation has not been, as with other races of men, how shall we adorn, beautify, exalt and ennoble life, but how shall we retain life itself. The struggle with us was not to do, but to be. Mankind lost sight of our human nature in the idea of our being property, and the whole machinery of society was planned, directed and operated to making us a stupid, spiritless, ignorant, besottcd, brutified, and utterly degraded race of men.

Thus far we have derived little advantage from any apologies we have made or from any explanations we have patiently given. Our relationship to the ancient Egyptians has been denied; the progress made by the emancipated people of the West Indies is not believed, and men still insist that the fault of our ignorance is not in slavery, but in ourselves. So stood the question concerning us up to the second year of the fierce and sanguinary rebellion now subsiding. Since then, the colored man has come before the country in a new light. He has illustrated the highest qualities of a patriot and a soldier. He has ranged himself on the side of government and country, and maintained both against rebels and traitors on the perilous edge of battle. They are now, many of them, sleeping side by side in bloody graves with the bravest and best of all our loyal white soldiers, and many of those who remain alive are scarred and battered veterans, mere stumps of men—armless, legless, maimed and mutilated ones are met with in the streets of every city. The veriest enemies of our race must now admit that we have at least one element of civilization. It is settled that we have manly courage, that we love our country, and that we will fight for an Idea. Both governments—the rebel as well as the federal—admitted the energy that slumbered in the black man's arm, and both, at last, endeavored to render that energy useful. But the charge still remains. Now, what are those elemental and original powers of civilization about which men speak and write so earnestly, and which white men claim for themselves and deny to the Negro? I answer that they are simply consciousness of wants and ability to gratify them. Here the whole machinery of civilization, whether moral, intellectual or physical, is set in motion.

Man is distinguished from all other animals, but in nothing is he distinguished more than in this: namely, resistance, active and constant resistance, to the forces of physical nature. All other animals submit to the same conditions and limitations from generation to generation. The bear today is as he was a thousand years ago. Nature provides him with food, clothing and shelter, and he is neither wiser nor better because of the experience of his bearish ancestors. Not so with man. He learns from the past and hands down his knowledge of the past to aftercoming generations of men, that they may carry their achievements to a still higher point. To lack this element of progress is to resemble the lower animals, and to possess it is to be men.

The mission of this institution and that of the colored race are identical. It is to develop manhood, to build up manly character among the colored people of this city and state. It is to teach them the true idea of manly independence and self-respect. It is to be a dispenser of knowledge, a radiator of light. In a word, we dedicate this institution to virtue, temperance, knowledge, truth, liberty and justice:

> In this fair hall, to Truth and Freedom given,
> Pledged to the right before all earth and heaven—
> A free arena for the strife of mind,
> No caste, or sect, or color are confined.

We who have been long debarred the privileges of culture may assemble and have our souls thrilled, with heavenly music, lifted to the skies on the wings of poetry and song. Here we can assemble and have our minds enlightened upon the whole circle of social, moral, political and educational duties. Here we can come and learn true politeness and refinement. Here the loftiest and best eloquence which the country has produced, whether of Anglo-Saxon or of African descent, shall flow as a river, enriching, ennobling, strengthening and purifying all who will lave in its waters. Here may come all who have a new and unpopular truth to unfold and enforce, against which old and respectable bars and bolts are iron gates. Here, from this broad hall, shall go forth an influence which shall at last change the current of public contempt for the oppressed, and lift the race into the popular consideration which justly belongs to their manly character and achievements.

DELIVER US FROM SUCH A MOSES

By Lewis Hayden

On October 24, 1864, Andrew Johnson addressing the Negro population of Nashville, denounced slavery and the "damnable aristocracy" which had profited from human bondage, and expressed the belief that only loyal men, white and Negro, should have a voice in the reconstruction of the seceded states. He ventured the hope that, "as in the days of old," a Moses might arise "to lead them safely to their Promised Land of freedom and happiness." The audience thereupon cried, "You are our Moses!" Johnson responded: "Humble and unworthy as I am, if no better shall be found, I will indeed be your Moses, and lead you through the Red Sea of war and bondage to a fairer future of liberty and peace." But when Lewis Hayden visited the South to encourage freedmen to join the Masonic Order, he found the man who had promised to become a new "Moses" was instrumental in assisting the former slaveowners to return the freedmen to a status resembling slavery. In a bitter attack on President Johnson before the Prince Hall Grand Lodge of Free and Accepted Masons in Boston of which he was Grand Master, on December 27, 1865, Hayden called for deliverance of his people from the policies of Andrew Johnson.

Born a slave, Lewis Hayden watched as the members of his family were separated and sold and his mother driven to madness. Sold twice at auction himself, Hayden was thirty-three years old and married by the time he managed to escape from slavery. He had taught himself to read by painfully struggling through discarded newspapers and the Bible. In a dramatic flight in a hack with his wife and son, he fled from Kentucky to Canada; later he moved to Detroit, where he built a church and school; finally he moved to Boston. Here he became a leading figure in the black community, established a clothing store in Boston, and when he died, he left an estate of five thousand dollars, which went to establish a scholarship fund for Black medical students at Harvard Medical School. During his life, Hayden put much of the profit from his clothing store into the abolition movement and also helped raise funds for John Brown's attack at Harpers Ferry.

The text below is from a lengthy speech by Hayden published as a pamphlet under the title, "Address before Prince Hall Grand Lodge of Free and Accepted Masons of the State of Massachusetts, at the Festival of St. John the Evangelist, December 27, 1865, by Lewis Hayden, Grand Master," *Boston, 1866, pp. 8–10.*

IN EACH OF THE PLACES I visited, there is evidently a deep and unalterable purpose in the hearts of the old oppressors to blast, or at least to crush out, the rising hopes and dawning prospects of their late bondmen. I rejoice, on the other hand, to be able to say that there is among our people that unwavering trust in God, and that abiding faith in the justice of their cause, which enable them to look to the future, not only with hope and confidence, but with exultation, feeling that

> Truth, crushed to earth, shall rise again;
> The eternal years of God are hers;
> But Error wounded, writhes in pain,
> And dies among his worshipers.

This, let me be understood, is the feeling of our people in the cities. With the dwellers in the country, it is different. Away from the cities and the seaboard, the condition of the colored man is deplorable enough today. Lacking the intelligence and opportunites of the freemen in the city—never having enjoyed the same advantages—he is still almost completely at the mercy of his old master. If the latter treats him kindly, it is well; but if ill-used and oppressed, in nine cases out of ten he has no remedy. There is no power under heaven to which he can appeal for redress. The United States Army can do nothing for him, for it has gone. If an agent of the Freedmen's Bureau happens along, no complaint can reach his ear till it has been forestalled by the story of the master and his interested attentions. The power of organized and concentrated effort, which may be available in the city, is denied to him. What, then, can he do? On what possible loop can he hang one solitary hope? God help him! For Andrew Johnson will not—although he was to be our Moses to lead us to liberty and equality; instead of which, I fear he will prove to be the Pharaoh of our day. In this we ought not to be deceived; for it is plain that he who undertakes to be the friend of

the black man in this land of Negro haters, will not have the
Negro haters all over the country singing praises to him, as
you see they are now doing to our said Moses; so much so,
that the astonished people stand off amazed, and know not
what to do or to say. First they look at him; then at Gettysburg;
then at Pittsburg Landing; then at Milliken's Bend; then at
Andersonville; and then at a murdered President. With all
these things before them, and ere they have had time for reflection, they are startled by the perpetration of some new act
of highhanded infidelity, which well serves his purpose to hide
some former wrong. As an evidence of some of his new acts of
infidelity, they beheld him, within three days after the murder
of our ever-to-be-lamented President, Abraham Lincoln, standing up before God and, in the presence of an outraged nation,
solemnly declaring that he would make treason a crime, and
punish the traitor. Has he done either? No. Then, what has
he done? you ask. My answer is that he has done much to make
treason a virtue, by elevating traitors to offices of honor and
trust, to be paid for their services in such offices by the taxing
of the widows and orphans, whose fathers and husbands their
own hands have slain. By these acts he has honored and given
new license to traitors to perpetuate outrages and crimes.
Humanity revolts and refuses to believe that man, made in the
image of God, could so debase and belie his nature as to be
guilty of such wrong against his fellow man. But did they not
murder their slaves with impunity while they had a moneyed
interest in them? If so, will they not slaughter the freedmen
in whom they have no such interest, with such an one at the
head of the nation fostering and honoring traitors? Were it
not that we are forbidden to speak against those in authority, I
should say, the Lord rebuke thee and deliver us from such a
Moses.

THE UNREASONABLE PREJUDICES AGAINST PEOPLE OF COLOR IN PHILADELPHIA

By Rev. B. F. Barrett

Although the major struggle for the rights of the Negro people centered in the South after the Civil War, an accelerated drive took place for civil rights and desegregation in the North. Nowhere was this campaign more needed than in Philadelphia, the City of Brotherly Love. Frederick Douglass visited Philadelphia early in 1862 and wrote: "There is not, perhaps, anywhere to be found a city in which prejudice against color is more rampant than in Philadelphia." Most of Philadelphia's streetcars allowed Negroes to ride only on the front platform, and some refused to admit colored people at all. Under the leadership of William Still, Philadelphia's Negroes launched an attack on streetcar segregation in 1859, and it increased in scope and intensity during and immediately after the Civil War. On Sunday morning, September 23, 1866, the Reverend B. F. Barrett preached a sermon on the subject in his church at the corner of Broad and Brandywine Streets. He bluntly condemned the entire community and called the outrages perpetrated against people of color a disgrace to the city. Above all, he declared, should the clergy be held responsible. It was a moving and militant protest in the name of Christianity, and it was an important factor in the final victory against streetcar discrimination in 1867.

(The sermon as presented here has been excerpted from the text which appeared in The Christian Recorder, *October 6, 1866.)*

Do JUSTICE to all men, but especially to the afflicted and needy—to the poor, the weak, the downtrodden, the despised. This is God's command. This is one of the grand requirements of Christianity. And that type of Christianity which ignores this requirement, or thinks lightly of the law of justice, must be pronounced a very poor type, must it not? . . .

Justice is impartial. It knows no distinctions of caste or color. It is perpendicular, straightforward, with an even surface, free from all crooks and sinuosities and subterfuges. . . . Justice

requires that all classes in the community should be equal before the law; that is, that no class be permitted, under legal
sanction, to enjoy rights, privileges and immunities that are
denied to another class, for this, obviously, would be unjust.
It would be unjust and, therefore, unchristian for your children
to have the privilege of the sidewalks, while your neighbor's
children may, with impunity and under legal sanction, be
pushed into the gutter. It is equally unjust that your children
and mine be admitted to the public schools and educated at the
public expense, while other children, for no fault of their own
or their parents, are shut out. It is unjust that one class of citizens be permitted to ride in the public conveyances and another
class be denied that privilege. It is unjust that one class of
children, whose fathers poured out their blood in defense of
their country, be watched over and cared for by the community
or state, while another class, reduced to orphanage in precisely
the same way, is passed by or forgotten. It is unjust that white
soldiers, disabled in the service of their country, be provided
with comfortable homes, while colored soldiers, disabled in the
same service, are thrust into miserable sheds, or left to shirk
for themselves. And to say that such things are unjust is to say
that they are unchristian. . . .

And now let us look for a moment at our Philadelphia type of
Christianity, as revealed especially in the popular feeling and
conduct toward that humble and despised race—the colored
people. Let us see how strong and pervading the love of justice
is in this professedly Christian city. And there is the more reason for doing this, because some, you know, are inclined to
boast of the Christianity of this city, as if its type were one of
peculiar excellence. They boast that it is *the* Christian city of
the land, because it does not, like heathenish Boston, Brooklyn,
New York and Chicago, tolerate that profane institution, the
Sunday passenger cars. Well, let us see if this claim be well
founded. Let us see if there be here a sense and a love of justice.
If not, then is our boasted Christianity a wretched counterfeit—
nothing more.

You all know that colored people are excluded from the passenger cars of this city simply on account of their color. A colored man or woman, however worthy or well-dressed, however
aged or infirm, or however wet and stormy the weather, is allowed no other place in our streetcars than a standing place on
the front platform. So, if these poor people desire to go, or have
to go, from one side of the city to the other in the most inclement weather, they must either submit to an indignity or walk the
whole distance; and they generally show a commendable self-

respect by choosing the latter. There is no need of showing how exceedingly unjust this is to the colored people, for everybody knows that already; and it is an injustice, I remark, peculiar to this city. No other Northern city where streetcars have been introduced, tolerates like injustice.

And not only are colored people denied admission to the streetcars, but if by chance one gets in, he is forcibly ejected, should he refuse to step out. This, as you know, has repeatedly been done.

But these, it will be said, are the acts of a few individuals only—the conductors on the railways, or the officers of the railway companies. I deny the assertion. It is the city of Philadelphia—the *people* of Philadelphia—who are the guilty party in all such outrages against the principles of justice. The city is just as guilty as if these acts had been ordered or committed by its own mayor or common council. For the railway companies know full well that, in ejecting colored people from their cars, they have the majority of the people on their side. They know that the popular sentiment of Philadelphia is with them and will sustain them in their wrongdoing. If the popular sentiment were against them, do you think such base acts could be repeated by the streetcar conductors? Suppose a white woman or a white man—Dr. Adams or Dr. Barnes, or the rector of St. Luke's or Holy Trinity—should be forcibly ejected from a streetcar on account of the color of his hair or his hat, would this community take it so quietly, think you? Would there be no public expression of the popular disapprobation? You know that the city would be all ablaze about it. You know that this community would be thrown into a tempest of wrath; that indignation meetings would be called, and that the press and the platform and the pulpit would ring with expressions of the popular condemnation. And if the officers of that street-railway company should attempt to justify or excuse the outrage, or the mayor should declare that it was committed with his "knowledge and approbation," as Mayor Henry did in one instance more than a year ago, you know it would be unsafe for any of these gentlemen to be seen in our streets.

And I ask if, in the eye of the Supreme Judge, or according to that standard of eternal rectitude which all Christians accept, it would be one whit more infamous to eject Dr. Adams or his wife from a streetcar without cause, than it is to eject the poorest colored man or woman if they be well-behaved? Would it be a whit more unjust or unchristian? Where lies the essential difference in the two cases? In the color of the skin, say you? But the Gospel, I take it, goes deeper than the skin. It knows no color—certainly none but the color of the heart. And you and I know that there may sometimes be very black hearts beneath white skins, and white hearts beneath black ones. And no one who reads his Bible needs to be told which it is that God looks at, the skin or the heart. Truth, honor, justice, courage, humility, love—what has the color of the skin to do with these? Nothing. Then what has the Gospel to do with the color of the skin? If our Lord had intended that we should discriminate between colors in the way that some of his professed followers do, then why has He given us no intimation of such intention? Why has He not told us that He had a peculiar regard for white people, and that his promised blessings were intended especially for them? . . .

I repeat that Christianity recognizes no color. Therefore, in the light of Christianity, it is as unjust and wicked to eject from a streetcar a colored man or a woman as a white one. Yet colored people have been repeatedly ejected, and no popular indignation has been excited by the outrage; no popular sympathy for the injured has been expressed; no popular rebuke been administered to the streetcar companies; no ministers' meetings been called to consider the subject and protest against such iniquity. . . .

It is the city of Philadelphia, then, that I arraign as the guilty party in this case. It is the community, and not merely the street-railway companies, that exclude or eject colored people from the cars; for it is the community that justify and uphold the companies in their wrong and unchristian conduct. . . . The city of Philadelphia generally has no sense of justice, where colored people's rights are concerned, or no disposition to do justly toward that despised race. And who, chiefly, are responsible for it—for the meager and eviscerated kind of Christianity that prevails here? I answer, with humiliation and sorrow, the men of my own profession, above all others. The two hundred and seventy clergymen of this city. Why? Because they and their predecessors have had more to do than all others in forming popular opinion upon questions of this kind. The prevailing popular sentiment on this subject is just what the ministers of Philadelphia have made it. It is they, more than all others, who have the molding of popular opinion on moral and religious questions. I say, then, that the ministers of Christ, above all others, are to be held responsible for that inveterate and unchristian prejudice and that cruel injustice toward the people of color, which is so prevalent here and so disgraceful to our city. Not that the ministers have deliberately advised or openly advocated any such wickedness. I presume they have not. Their sin has been the sin of silence, when they should have been spoken as with tongues of fire; the sin of indifference, when they should have been foremost to plead the cause and defend the rights of the helpless and oppressed; the sin of neutrality, when to be neutral was virtually to side with wrong; the sin of worldly prudence, when such prudence was disloyalty to God and cruelty to his despised little ones; the sin of timidly withholding remonstrance and warning, and counsel and reproof on this subject, with which they should have pricked the consciences of their people and made them feel how fearfully wicked it is to do injustice to the poor and weak.

I know it is said, in excuse for this unfaithfulness on the part of the clergy, that they cannot go against the prejudices of their people; they cannot proclaim unwelcome truths; they cannot be expected "to throttle each living, vigorous, but unconfessed, if not unconscious sin"; that it would not be wise or prudent to do so; it would cause disturbance; it would lessen the number of their hearers; it would gain for them hatred instead of love; it would expose them to persecution; it would result in their dismission and the loss of their living.

Disturbance, hatred, persecution, dismission, loss of living! Are these things worth considering when great principles are in question? Are these things to be thought of by the ministers of Him whose unswerving devotion to principle and fearless utterance of the truth disturbed the whole region round about, and subjected Him to hatred, persecution and an ignominious death? What right has a minister of Jesus Christ to keep back any truth which the people ought to hear, through a despicable fear of worldly loss or damage? What right has he to expect that fidelity to Christian principle will demand of him no sacrifice and excite no opposition? "If they have persecuted me, they will also persecute you." Is the disciple above the Master, or the servant above this Lord? Is it not enough for the disciple that he be as his Master, and the servant as his Lord? . . .

THESE ARE REVOLUTIONARY TIMES

By Rev. E. J. Adams

On March 2, 1867, Congress overrode President Johnson's vetoes and passed a series of Reconstruction acts. New governments were to be established in the South by delegates to conventions elected by universal-manhood (including Negro) suffrage, and these governments were to guarantee Negro voting and officeholding rights and to ratify the Fourteenth Amendment, which conferred state and national citizenship on "all persons born or naturalized in the United States," and prohibited the denial to any person of the equal protection of the law.

Although many freedmen were sorely disappointed that the legislation did not provide for the distribution of land, they hailed the action of Congress in a series of meetings. On March 19, 1867, a great mass meeting was held at Charleston, South Carolina, to voice approval of the Congressional legislation and to act upon the report of a committee of thirteen appointed to draft a platform for the organization of a Union Republican party. The meeting was called without regard to race or color, but, as might be expected, the gathering was mainly composed of blacks. At the conclusion of the reading of the resolutions, the Reverend E. J. Adams, a leader of the black community in Charleston, called for the adoption of the report, and delivered the address below.

The Reverend Mr. Adams correctly related events occurring in the United States to revolutionary changes taking place elsewhere in the world. A good portion of his address was directed toward defending the principle of universal suffrage. Many of the arguments he advanced were put forth by other speakers, but he was one of the few to justify the enfranchisement of the former slaves on the ground that it was a reparation "for the long years of slavery and disfranchisement of the now colored citizens of the United States." He closed his address amid "great cheering" with a keen sally at the bogey of social equality.

The text of the speech presented here is taken from the Charleston Courier, March 22, 1867.

FELLOW CITIZENS: These are revolutionary times. For many years a contest, terrible in its nature, has been waged between despotism and republican principles, between freedom and slavery, until finally we behold the genius of republican liberty bearing its escutcheon upon the threshold of the capitol of every nation, waving its banner in triumph over every continent, sea and ocean. The sacred fire pent up in the bosom of the Italian nation, like the fires of Vesuvius, hath recently burst forth in all its sublimity, scattering its enemies and unshackling itself from that despotism which trampled it under its feet for nearly two centuries. Russia hath given freedom to over thirty millions of serfs,* and Germany hath recently extricated itself from the despotism of Europe. We find today Canada struggling for liberty, and Ireland too is endeavoring to grasp the flag of liberty. So, too, with regard to our nation. The little leaven that was planted in this country when the government was founded has succeeded in permeating itself through every fiber of this great body politic, and now the flag that once floated over four millions of slaves, today waves in triumph over more than thirty millions of freemen. The bloody crimson stripes of that banner, once emblematic of the bloody furrows ploughed upon the quivering flesh of four million of slaves, today is emblematic of the bloody sacrifice offered upon the altars of American liberty.

We owe a debt of everlasting gratitude—first, to Almighty God; second, to the Congress of the United States—for the boon of freedom which both the white man and the black man today enjoy. We thank God because He has overruled the desires, the intentions and the will of men. When our war first broke out, it was the idea even of the Republican party, and even of the most radical of that party, that slavery should be confined to where it then existed; that it should have no further advancement, or be introduced into any of the territories shortly to become states. But the overruling hand of Providence, whose ways are in the whirlwind, brought good out of the wind, and today we can say, as Joseph said to his brethren, "As for you, ye meant evil unto me, but God meant it unto good to bring to pass that which has this day saved much people alive."

These resolutions vindicate universal suffrage, for which, thank God, we are in the enjoyment of today. I vindicate universal suffrage, first, because of a man's volition. I am in favor

---

* Serfdom was abolished in Russia by the act of emancipation of February 19, 1861.

of universal suffrage, upon the ground that every man is endowed with a certain degree of volition, having the right to choose or refuse that which is good or evil; that he has the right to choose the God whom he will serve, and if a man may choose the God he wishes to serve, has he not an equal right to choose the ruler that shall rule over him?

Some are opposed to universal suffrage on the ground that a black man is not capable of exercising that right with judgment. But let me tell you that all men may be led instinctively to do that which is right, or choose the wrong. Those men who are led instinctively to support the liberty of the country in the time of war by placing the ballot box in their hands, will also be led to support the right in the time and hour of peace. Universal suffrage is the only reward that can be given for the long years of slavery and disfranchisement of the now colored citizens of the United States.

Universal suffrage is compatible with the genius of our Republic. This could not be a republic in every sense of the word unless universal suffrage is accorded to all men alike. The meaning of republicanism is that all men alike have the right to enjoy the privilege of the ballot box.

Again, a perfect Union, justice, domestic tranquillity, the common defense, the general welfare, and the blessings of liberty cannot be secured without universal suffrage. It is the only means of defense for the illiterate and the poor. The educated, the rich and the wealthy have advantages over the poor, who must necessarily have some means by which their liberties and the blessings of republican institutions may be enjoyed.

Again, universal suffrage, universal education, an equal chance to acquire wealth, will fit the colored man for any position, social or political. I do not, however, wish to be understood that I advocate or wish for social equality. God forbid that. For some of my mean white drunken enemies may sneak into my house and marry my daughter.

WHEN WOMAN GETS HER RIGHTS MAN WILL BE RIGHT

By Sojourner Truth

Although she was already over eighty years of age, the great black fighter for human freedom, Sojourner Truth, was still engaged in the cause. A pioneer in the struggle for woman's rights as well as for the freedom of her people from slavery, Sojourner Truth made the rights of women a special feature of all her talks in the years following emancipation. She spoke twice at the first annual meeting of the American Equal Rights Association held in New York City on May 9 and 10, 1867. She closed her first speech by singing, "We are going home," and that evening again addressed the delegates of women engaged in the battle for equality with men and a few progressive men who also attended the session. Here is the major portion of Sojourner Truth's speeches in behalf of the rights of women. It is excerpted from the National Anti-Slavery Standard, *June 1, 1867.*

MY FRIENDS, I am rejoiced that you are glad, but I don't know how you will feel when I get through. I come from another field—the country of the slave. They have got their rights—so much good luck. Now what is to be done about it? I feel that I have got as much responsibility as anybody else. I have as good rights as anybody. There is a great stir about colored men getting their rights, but not a word about the colored women; and if colored men get their rights, and not colored women get theirs, there will be a bad time about it. So I am for keeping the thing going while things are stirring; because if we wait till it is still, it will take a great while to get it going again. White women are a great deal smarter, and know more than colored women, while colored women do not know scarcely anything. They go out washing, which is about as high as a colored woman gets, and their men go about idle, strutting up and down; and when the women come home, they ask for their money and take it all, and then scold because there is no food. I want you to consider on that, chil'n. I want women to have their rights. In the courts women have no right, no voice; nobody speaks for them. I wish woman to have her voice there among the pettifoggers. If it is not a fit place for women, it is unfit for men to be there. I am above eighty years old; it is about time for me to be going. But I suppose I am kept here because something remains for me to do; I suppose I am yet to help break the chain. I have done a great deal of work— as much as a man, but did not get so much pay. I used to work in the field and bind grain, keeping up with the cradler; but men never doing no more, got twice as much pay. So with the German women. They work in the field and do as much work, but do not get the pay. We do as much, we eat as much, we want as much. I suppose I am about the only colored woman that goes about to speak for the rights of the colored woman, I want to keep the thing stirring, now that the ice is broken. What we want is a little money. You men know that you get as much again as women when you write, or for what you do. When we get our rights, we shall not have to come to you for money, for then we shall have money enough of our own. It is a good consolation to know that when we have got this we shall not be coming to you any more. You have been having our right so long, that you think, like a slaveholder, that you own us. I know that it is hard for one who has held the reins for so long to give up; it cuts like a knife. It will feel all better when it closes up again. I have been in Washington about three years, seeing about those colored people. Now colored men have a right to vote; and what I want is to have colored women have the right to vote. There ought to be equal rights more than ever, since colored people have got their freedom. . . .

I know that it is hard for men to give up entirely. They must run in the old track. I was amused how men speak up for one another. They cannot bear that a woman should say anything about the man, but they will stand here and take up the time in man's cause. But we are going, tremble or no tremble. Men are trying to help us. I know that all—the spirit they have got; and they cannot help us much until some of the spirit is taken out of them that belongs among the women. Men have got their rights, and women has not got their rights. That is the trouble. When woman gets her rights man will be right. How beautiful that will be. Then it will be peace on earth and good will to men. But it cannot be until it be right. . . . It will come. . . . Yes, it will come quickly. It must come. And now when the waters is troubled, and now is the time to step into the pool. There is a great deal now with the minds, and now is the time to start forth. . . . The great fight was to keep the rights of the poor colored people. That made a great battle. And now I hope that this will be the last battle that will be in the

world. Let us finish up so that there be no more fighting. I have
faith in God and there is truth in humanity. Be strong women!
Blush not! Tremble not! I want you to keep a good faith and
good courage. And I am going round after I get my business
settled and get more equality. People in the North, I am going
round to lecture on human rights. I will shake every place
I go to.

TO MY WHITE FELLOW CITIZENS

By B. K. Sampson

*On Thanksgiving Day, 1867, the white citizens of Fair-
field, Ohio, invited B. K. Sampson, a young black orator
in the community, to be the speaker at the festivities that
had been planned. The invitation aroused considerable
comment in Ohio and other parts of the country, since
Fairfield had a reputation of having been exceedingly hostile to the presence of black people. But the white citizens
came "from far and near," and Sampson delivered a
speech, the major portion of which appears below; it is
taken from* The Christian Recorder, *January 13, 1868.*

MY WHITE FELLOW CITIZENS: Whatever may have been
your motives for elevating me with this profound honor, I
know not; but as a black man, fully appreciating the tokens of
this public regard, I make you my audience. With all veneration
we come to return thanks to Almighty God for the munificent
blessings which He has vouchsafed to the American people. I
understand that you have been an austere people; that you have
hated with a perfect hatred every likness of the Negro, and that
to the Southern lords you have long bowed. No proposition or
measure concerning justice to the black man ever met your
approval. Your reckless persistency in wrong has gained for
you much publicity. No man of somber complexion could tarry
in your midst and call his life his own. Even a dark-skinned
white man would find himself unsafe among you. You lapsed
from the doctrines of our fathers to a perverted idea of democracy, and through your apostacy your children deemed it right
to be called democratic. They become indoctrinated in the

faith, and slavery became the stone of the corner on which
was founded the Democratic party.

The American government has long been looked upon as the
purest and best under the sun; but the great obstruction in her
path to national glory, was the blasting system of human slavery.
To sanctify and make it right was arrayed the learning and
genius of some of our ablest men. Our popular institutions had
gained the envy of the world. None dared defend the poor;
none pleaded their cause. Thus, for over three fourths of a
century, we have lived, little expecting the terrible calamity
which has come upon us, though Henry had exclaimed, "Give
me liberty, or give me death!" and Jefferson had forewarned his
countrymen, that "God's justice would not sleep forever." The
voice of sublimest wisdom had long admonished us of the impending dangers; still the nation, with its blind infatuation,
moved on to almost inevitable disaster.

Again and again our national sky was lighted up by the
fierce flames of war, and in every contest in which our country
was involved, the colored man bounded forth to defend his
imperiled land. Still he was denied the sacred boon of liberty
and the blessings of political freedom, until the final overthrow
of the bloody conspiracy which threatened to destroy the government. Then the blacks took up arms for the defense of the
national cause . . . and in a short time thousands of thousands
of colored volunteers were in the field. O, glorious hour for
those who prayed for deliverance from captivity! Their prayers were heard in heaven. The old system of slavery was broken.
Brilliant victory followed victory in rapid succession; the
doomed are redeemed; the nation is free, and slavery is dead.

Let us solemnize this day with thanksgiving and gratula-
tion. Republican liberty is no longer an experiment. It has been
permanently established on these shores of the Western world,
and here it shall flourish forever. . . . Most perfidious, then,
is he who cannot unite with the beating hearts of the millions
in general gratitude for national unity and freedom. Not only
to you, then, but to every friend of civil liberty throughout the
world, I remark, that the offerings we make will avail nothing,
unless we pledge ourselves to make this liberty the liberty of
all men; unless we renounce our former predilections, abandon
every feeling of malignancy and repugnance to every species of
humanity, and swear hostility to every kind of injustice. . . .

Mr. Chairman, my heart swells with the most ardent hopes
for the future which awaits the rising generation. Sir, I am
aware that even at this time our colored brethren are bowed

down under the most depressing influences in the Southern states. They have been put to torture and to death by the fiendish traitors who plotted treason against the government. Still the dark mantle of oppression wraps itself about us. We have long been discarded as the ailing child in the great American family. But no longer must this be. We are the allies of the government against all foes, whether at home or abroad. We are the lawful heirs of the government and cannot be disinherited. We are a part and parcel of the government; we are with the government to all intents and purposes. Why, then, withhold the right of suffrage from the colored man? Why refuse to invest him with the power of protection and equality before the law? Is it that he is too ignorant to appreciate the intrinsic value of the power he wields through the ballot box? One fourth of the white population of this country know nothing about the Constitution and laws under which they vote, and among the more illiterate class votes have been used for speculation and gain. So far, the history of the black man has shown that he has sacredly guarded and preserved every personal and political right accorded him by the government. Far be it from me to make any right more or less than a natural right. When President Andrew Johnson told Major Stevens that the right of suffrage is a mere political and not a natural right, he said what a majority of the intelligent people of the country do not believe. I know that it is a natural right. It is the common heritage of all mankind, wherever protection and allegiance are implied. It is as ancient as the first-born of humanity, and no written document or constitution can justly withhold it. To do this would give to the monarchist undisputed sway; then would representative democracies lose their brightest gems. But truth is our strong ally. It is the same now as when it spoke through the thunders and smoke of Sinai, and though the whole world of political tricksters move against us with their false arguments, *magna est veritas, et praevalebit.* . . .

Do you desire then, my friends, to see the righteousness of God prevail? Commit yourselves, I exhort you, in His great name to His cause. Do you want to see the blacks elevated to the position of freemen? Then subdue all these passions of prejudice and injustice. Create within your midst a sentiment of purest philanthropy; a sentiment so radical in its nature that the hearts of the people shall become influenced with the spirit of equality and right. Then will the government of God and all men of all races become one grand mutuality of intellectual and moral design.

BREAK UP THE PLANTATION SYSTEM

By Francis L. Cardozo

The constitutional conventions elected under the Reconstruction acts of Congress were the first state assemblies in which Negroes participated as elected representatives of the people. In the South Carolina convention of 1868 there were 48 white delegates and 76 Negro, fully two thirds of whom had once been slaves. One of the most frequently discussed issues at the South Carolina convention was the land question, and the cry for partition of the large estates and distribution among the poorer black and white population. An extended debate raged around a proposed stay law designed to prevent the sale of large plantations for debt. Francis L. Cardozo, a leading Negro in the Reconstruction era, who was later Secretary of State and State Treasurer, delivered an important speech opposing the stay law on the grounds that nine tenths of the debts on the plantations were contracted for the sale of slaves. By taking this opportunity to throw the plantations upon the market, he insisted, they would be striking at the plantation system, "one of the greatest bulwarks of slavery," by breaking up the estates and selling them in small lots to the freedmen. Unfortunately, the convention did not take a stand in favor of breaking up the large plantations and distributing the land among the freedmen and poor whites—a failure generally recognized today to have been the most serious weakness of Radical Reconstruction.

Francis Louis Cardozo was a freeborn son of a Jewish economist in Charleston by a woman of mixed blood. After his elementary schooling, he became a journeyman carpenter. His savings, gained through summer employment and a one-thousand-dollar scholarship, enabled him to go to the University of Glasgow and then for two years to a theological school in London. At the outbreak of the Civil War he was a Presbyterian minister in New Haven, but when the conflict ended he went as principal to Avery Institute in Charleston and entered politics.

(Cardozo's speech, presented here, is taken from the Proceedings of the Constitutional Convention of South Carolina, 1868, *Charleston, 1868, Vol. I, pp. 115–18.)*

IN DISCUSSING this measure, I would say to the gentleman who preceded me, and those who will follow, that they will accomplish their object much sooner and with much more satisfaction by not impugning the motives of those with whom they differ. The gentleman who spoke last, made gratuitous assumptions and ascribed mercenary motives that, were it not for personal friendship, might be retorted upon him with perhaps worse effect than he made them. He asserted that the gentlemen who opposed him opposed his race. I intend to show that his race is not at all connected with the matter. In giving my view of the measure, I shall not resort to mere declamations or appeals to passion or prejudice. In the first place, I doubt its legality. It is true, it is said the Convention does not propose to legislate, but I contend that a request from this body carries a certain moral influence. It shows what it would do if it had the power. It is virtually legislation. I regard any stay law as unjust and unconstitutional. It is unjust to the creditors. Let every man who contracts a debt, pay it. If he is an honest man he will pay his debts at any sacrifice. In our country it is unfortunate, as Americans, that we have a character by no means enviable as repudiators. Look at the attempt to repudiate the national debt. As an American, I protest against any further repudiation whatever, either in the form of a stay law or illegal legislation. I deem it inappropriate for us to touch the matter at all. We are sent here to form a Constitution. To travel outside of our proper province, will probably be to incur odium, displeasure and dissatisfaction. I wish to confine the action of this Convention to its proper sphere. The first question that arises is, what claim have these debtors on our sympathies more than creditors? Are the debtors greater in number than creditors? If we legislate in favor of any, will it be doing the greatest good to the greatest number? I maintain it will not. It is a class measure. This will be but the beginning. We will be burdened with applications, and the burden will be upon those who introduced this measure, not upon those who refused to legislate for other special favorite classes. I ask not only what are the claims of the debtors, but also what are the nature of these sales? Was it the transfer of real estate? I think everyone here will say no. Nine tenths of the debts were contracted for the sale of slaves. I do not wish we should go one inch out of the way to legislate either for the buyer or seller. They dealt in that kind of property, they knew its precarious tenure, and therefore let them suffer. When the war commenced every rebel sold his property to give money to a common cause. And their slaves were sold for the same object, to maintain a war waged for the purpose of perpetually enslaving a people. That was the object. The ladies of the South stripped themselves of their jewels, and the men sold their lands and their slaves for that object. Now, let them suffer for it. As the gentleman from Charleston very ably said, "they have cast the die, let them take the chances."

There is also another reason, and one of the strongest, why the Convention should not take any action on the subject, but postpone it indefinitely. One of the greatest bulwarks of slavery was the infernal plantation system, one man owning his thousand, another his twenty, and another fifty thousand acres of land. This is the only way by which we will break up that system, and I maintain that our freedom will be of no effect if we allow it to continue. What is the main cause of the prosperity of the North? It is because every man has his own farm and is free and independent. Let the lands of the South be similarly divided. I would not say for one moment they should be confiscated, but if sold to maintain the war, now that slavery is destroyed, let the plantation system go with it. We will never have true freedom until we abolish the system of agriculture which existed in the Southern states. It is useless to have any schools while we maintain this stronghold of slavery as the agricultural system of the country. The gentleman has said that if these plantations were sold now, they would pass into the hands of a few mercenary speculators. I deny it and challenge a single proof to sustain the assertion. On the contrary I challenge proof to show that if the plantations are not sold, the old plantation masters will part with them. If they are sold, though a few mercenary speculators may purchase some, the chances are that the colored man and the poor man would be the purchasers. I will prove this, not by mere assertion, but by facts. About one hundred poor colored men of Charleston met together and formed themselves into a Charleston Land Company. They subscribed for a number of shares at $10 per share, one dollar payable monthly. They have been meeting for a year. Yesterday they purchased six hundred acres of land for $6,600 that would have sold for $25,000 or $50,000 in better times. They would not have been able to buy it had not the owner through necessity been compelled to sell. This is only one instance of thousands of others that have occurred in this city and state. I look upon it, therefore, as the natural result of the war that this system of large plantations, of no service to the owner or anybody else, should be abolished.

I think Providence has not only smiled upon every effort for abolishing this hideous form of slavery, but that since the war it has given unmistakable signs of disapprobation wherever continued, by blasting the cotton crops in that part of the country. Men are now beginning not to plant cotton but grain for food, and in doing so they are establishing a system of small farms, by which not only my race, but the poor whites and ninety-nine hundredths of the other thousands will be benefited. The real benefit from this legislation would inhere to not more than thirty thousand landholders against the seven hundred thousand poor people of the State. If we are to legislate in favor of a class at all, any honest man, any man who has the interest of the people at heart will legislate in favor of the greater number. In speaking against the landholders, and in taking this position I do not cherish one feeling of enmity against them as a class or individuals. But this question takes a larger range and is one in which the whole country is involved. I can never sacrifice the interests of nine or ten millions to the interests of three hundred thousand, more especially when the three hundred thousand initiated the war and were the very ones who established an infernal Negro code and want to keep their lands until better times. They do not want that a nigger or a Yankee shall ever own a foot of their land. Now is the time to take the advantage. Give them an opportunity, breathing time, and they will reorganize the same old system they had before the war. I say, then, just as General Grant said when he had Lee hemmed in around Petersburg, now is the time to strike, and in doing so we will strike for our people and posterity, and the truest interest of our country.

JUSTICE SHOULD RECOGNIZE NO COLOR

By William H. Gray

The Arkansas Constitutional Convention met in January and February, 1868, to frame a new constitution under the provisions of the Congressional Reconstruction Acts. During the debate over a new constitution, a white delegate spoke against Negro suffrage. He was effectively answered by William H. Gray, a black delegate from Phillips County, in the following speech, which is taken from The American Annual Cyclopedia, *Vol. VIII (1869), pp. 33–35.*

IT APPEARS to me the gentleman has read the history of his country to little purpose. When the Constitution was framed, in every state but South Carolina free Negroes were allowed to vote. Under British rule this class was free, and he interpreted that "we the people" in the preamble of the Constitution meant all the people of every color. The mistake of that period was that these free Negroes were not represented in *propria persona* in that constitutional convention, but by the Anglo-Saxon. Congress is now correcting that mistake. The right of franchise is due the Negroes bought by the blood of forty thousand of their race shed in three wars. The troubles now on the country are the result of the bad exercise of the elective franchise by unintelligent whites, the "poor whites" of the South. I could duplicate every Negro who cannot read and write, whose name is on the list of registered voters, with a white man equally ignorant. The gentleman can claim to be a friend of the Negro, but I do not desire to be looked upon in the light of a client. The government has made a solemn covenant with the Negro to vest him with the right of franchise if he would throw his weight in the balance in favor of the Union and bare his breast to the storm of bullets; and I am convinced that it would not go back on itself. There are thirty-two million whites to four million blacks in the country, and there need be no fear of Negro domination. The state laws do not protect the Negro in his rights, as they forbade their entrance into the state. I am not willing to trust the rights of my people with the white men, as they have not preserved those of their own race, in neglecting to provide them with the means of education. The Declaration of Independence declared all men born free and equal, and I demand the enforcement of that guarantee made to my forefathers, to every one of each race, who had fought for it. The constitution which this ordinance would reenact is not satisfactory, as it is blurred all over with the word *white*. Under it one hundred and eleven thousand beings who live in the state have no rights which white men are bound to respect. My people might be ignorant, but I believe with Jefferson that ignorance is no measure of a man's rights. Slavery has been abolished, but it left my people in a condition of peonage or caste worse than slavery, which had its humane masters. White people should look to their own ancestry; they should recollect that women were disposed of on James River, in the early settlement of the country, as wives, at the price of two hundred pounds of tobacco. When we have had eight hundred years as the whites to enlighten ourselves, it will be time enough to pronounce them incapable of civilization and enlightenment. The last election showed that they were intelligent enough to vote in a solid mass with the party that would give them their rights, and that too in face of the influence of the intelligence and wealth of the state, and in face of threats to take the bread from their very mouths. I have no antipathy toward the whites; I would drop the curtain of oblivion on the sod which contains the bones of my oppressed and wronged ancestors for two hundred and fifty years. Give us the franchise, and if we do not exercise it properly you have the numbers to take it away from us. It would be impossible for the Negro to get justice in a state whereof he was not a full citizen. The prejudices of the entire court would be against him. I do not expect the Negro to take possession of the government; I want the franchise given him as an incentive to work to educate his children. I do not desire to discuss the question of inferiority of races. Unpleasant truths must then be told; history tells us of your white ancestors who lived on the acorns which dropped from the oaks of Dodona, and then worshiped the tree as a God. I call upon all men who would see justice done, to meet this question fairly, and fear not to record their votes. . . . Justice should be like the Egyptian statue, blind and recognizing no color.

WE ASK AN EQUAL CHANCE IN THE RACE OF LIFE

By Oscar J. Dunn

Although history textbooks are filled with accounts of so-called "Negro domination" of the Southern governments established under Radical Reconstruction, few blacks actually held high positions in these governments. One of these few was Oscar J. Dunn, the first lieutenant governor of Louisiana elected under the provisions of the constitution of 1868. Dunn ran away from slavery and finally bought his freedom. In his Black Reconstruction in America, *W. E. B. Du Bois describes him as "a man of courage and firmness. He was admitted by the Democrats to be incorruptible. . . . His sudden death in November, 1871, was a severe loss."*

Below is the speech Dunn delivered on July 31, 1868,

after having been administered the oath of office as lieu-
tenant governor. He was introduced by Mr. Lynch, Presi-
dent of the Senate, who declared that Dunn's "prudence,
candor and ability . . . have won the admiration of all,
and augurs well for the future of the race he represents,
emerging from under the shadow of a great wrong into
the pure light of freedom and the privileges of a universal
franchise."

(*Dunn's speech is taken from the* Louisiana Senate
Journal, *July 13, 1868.*)

SENATORS OF LOUISIANA, the remarks of Senator Lynch
have caused me to feel sensibly the change that has been
brought about—a change which is apparent to all present. The
fact that the Senate of Louisiana is presided over by a man of
my race, one who has ever been kept in obscurity, shows the
progress which has taken place in the Southern states, a
progress more rapid than that of the Northern states, East or
West, and I hope that progress will continue until everywhere
throughout this land intelligence will be respected, whatever the
color of the skin. Not that I claim intelligence for myself, but I
hope that by your assistance and kindness toward me and my
race to prove worthy of every advantage bestowed upon us.
There is no one present more anxious than I am to see that the
state of Louisiana is restored to the Union—not as it was, but
as it is. Previously she was in the Union, and said to be a
free-state government; but her freedom was confined to one
class. Now she is going in under a republican form of government, granting civil and political rights to all men.

As to myself and my people we are not seeking social equality;
that is a thing no law can govern. We all have our preferences.
We all wish to select our associates, and no legislation can
select them for us. We ask nothing of the kind. We simply ask
to be allowed an equal chance in the race of life; an equal
opportunity of supporting our families, of educating our
children, and of becoming worthy citizens of this government.

I am truly happy that we are about to return into the Union,
for I as much as any of you object to military rule. I believe that
there is ability enough in the state to govern our own affairs and
I believe that harmony will exist among us, to such an extent
that no interference of military power will be necessary on
the part of the general government.

Gentlemen, I thank you for the kind courtesies and the
leniency you have extended toward me. If any action of mine
has been considered arbitrary, I hope that feeling will be re-

moved and that the Senate will believe I acted under my conscientious convictions of duty, for my sole object has been to act justly with all men. Certainly I shall use my utmost endeavors to preside impartially over this honorable body and to promote harmony and dignity in its deliberations.

I CLAIM THE RIGHTS OF A MAN

By Henry McNeal Turner

As each of the ten former Confederate states fulfilled the requirement set by the Reconstruction Acts of Congress, it was restored to the Union. On July 21, 1868, Georgia was restored. But the majority of the legislature, white Democrats, voted to unseat the two Republican state senators and twenty-five Republican state representatives on the ground that they were Negroes. On September 3, 1868, Henry McNeal Turner, one of the expelled members, stood before the assembled representatives and delivered a magnificent attack on the men who had refused to seat the Negro senators and representatives.

Turner (1834–1915) was born in Columbia, South Carolina, of free Negro parents, and in 1855 moved to Macon, where he joined the African Methodist Episcopal Church and became a preacher. "His eloquence," a church paper noted later, "attracted the attention of the white citizens, who considered him to be 'too smart a nigger' to remain in the South, and he was obliged to leave." Turner went to Baltimore and finally to Washington as pastor of Israel Bethel Church. Here he rapidly became a leader of the Negro community and an outstanding and militant fighter for racial justice in the capital. In 1863 he was appointed by President Lincoln as chaplain to the first United States Negro troops. After the war Turner moved to Georgia, where he continued preaching and played a prominent part in Reconstruction politics. "I was, on one occasion," he wrote in The Christian Recorder *of March 24, 1866, "lecturing to the young men on the political prospects of the colored people, when it was announced they were preparing outdoors to shoot me through the window. I cried out to let them shoot, and commenced speaking on*

*as I had been. . . . In a few moments the church was
picketed by brave young men, and everything went on
smoothly. This is the second time my life has been aimed
at through the window. But I am still alive." This fear-
lessness is reflected in his lengthy but militant speech in
defense of the rights of Georgia Negroes to sit in the legislature, excerpts from which follow.*

*Before he was declared ineligible for membership in
the Georgia House, Turner had introduced two bills of a
progressive nature, neither of which was passed. One
called for an eight-hour day for laborers and the other
sought to prevent common carriers "from distinguishing
between white and colored persons in the quality of accommodations furnished."*

*In 1880 Turner was ordained Bishop in the African
Methodist Episcopal Church. He died in Windsor, Canada,
in 1915.*

*(Turner's speech has been preserved in Ethel Maude
Christler's "Participation of Negroes in the Government of
Georgia, 1867–1870," unpublished Master's thesis, Atlanta University, June, 1932, pp. 82–96. Miss Christler
copied the speech from a pamphlet in which it was published and which she obtained from Bishop J. S. Flipper,
of Atlanta.)*

Mr. Speaker: Before proceeding to argue this question
upon its intrinsic merits, I wish the members of this House to
understand the position that I take. I hold that I am a member of
this body. Therefore, sir, I shall neither fawn nor cringe before
any party, nor stoop to beg them for my rights. Some of my
colored fellow members, in the course of their remarks, took occasion to appeal to the sympathies of members on the opposite
side, and to eulogize their character for magnanimity. It reminds
me very much, sir, of slaves begging under the lash. I am here
to demand my rights and to hurl thunderbolts at the men who
would dare to cross the threshold of my manhood. There is an
old aphorism which says, "Fight the devil with fire," and if I
should observe the rule in this instance, I wish gentlemen to
understand that it is but fighting them with their own weapon.

The scene presented in this House, today, is one unparalleled
in the history of the world. From this day, back to the day when
God breathed the breath of life into Adam, no analogy for it
can be found. Never, in the history of the world, has a man
been arraigned before a body clothed with legislative, judicial
or executive functions, charged with the offense of being a

darker hue than his fellow men. I know that questions have been before the courts of this country, and of other countries, involving topics not altogether dissimilar to that which is being discussed here today. But, sir, never in the history of the great nations of this world—never before—has a man been arraigned, charged with an offense committed by the God of Heaven Himself. Cases may be found where men have been deprived of their rights for crimes and misdemeanors; but it has remained for the state of Georgia, in the very heart of the nineteenth century, to call a man before the bar, and there charge him with an act for which he is no more responsible than for the head which he carries upon his shoulders. The Anglo-Saxon race, sir, is a most surprising one. No man has ever been more deceived in that race than I have been for the last three weeks. I was not aware that there was in the character of that race so much cowardice or so much pusillanimity. The treachery which has been exhibited in it by gentlemen belonging to that race has shaken my confidence in it more than anything that has come under my observation from the day of my birth.

What is the question at issue? Why, sir, this Assembly, today, is discussing and deliberating on a judgment; there is not a Cherub that sits around God's eternal throne today that would not tremble—even were an order issued by the Supreme God Himself—to come down here and sit in judgment on my manhood. Gentlemen may look at this question in whatever light they choose, and with just as much indifference as they may think proper to assume, but I tell you, sir, that this is a question which will not die today. This event shall be remembered by posterity for ages yet to come, and while the sun shall continue to climb the hills of heaven.

Whose legislature is this? Is it a white man's legislature, or is it a black man's legislature? Who voted for a constitutional convention, in obedience to the mandate of the Congress of the United States? Who first rallied around the standard of Reconstruction? Who set the ball of loyalty rolling in the state of Georgia? And whose voice was heard on the hills and in the valleys of this state? It was the voice of the brawny-armed Negro, with the few humanitarian-hearted white men who came to our assistance. I claim the honor, sir, of having been the instrument of convincing hundreds—yea, thousands—of white men, that to reconstruct under the measures of the United States Congress was the safest and the best course for the interest of the state.

Let us look at some facts in connection with this matter. Did half the white men of Georgia vote for this legislature? Did not the great bulk of them fight, with all their strength, the Constitution under which we are acting? And did they not fight against the organization of this legislature? And further, sir, did they not vote against it? Yes, sir! And there are persons in this legislature today who are ready to spit their poison in my face, while they themselves opposed, with all their power, the ratification of this Constitution. They question my right to a seat in this body, to represent the people whose legal votes elected me. This objection, sir, is an unheard-of monopoly of power. No analogy can be found for it, except it be the case of a man who should go into my house, take possession of my wife and children, and then tell me to walk out. I stand very much in the position of a criminal before your bar, because I dare to be the exponent of the views of those who sent me here. Or, in other words, we are told that if black men want to speak, they must speak through white trumpets; if black men want their sentiments expressed, they must be adulterated and sent through white messengers, who will quibble and equivocate and evade as rapidly as the pendulum of a clock. If this be not done, then the black men have committed an outrage, and their representatives must be denied the right to represent their constituents.

The great question, sir, is this: Am I a man? If I am such, I claim the rights of a man. Am I not a man because I happen to be of a darker hue than honorable gentlemen around me? Let me see whether I am or not. I want to convince the House today that I am entitled to my seat here. A certain gentleman has argued that the Negro was a mere development similar to the orangoutang or chimpanzee, but it so happens that, when a Negro is examined, physiologically, phrenologically and anatomically, and, I may say, physiognomically, he is found to be the same as persons of different color. I would like to ask any gentleman on this floor, where is the analogy? Do you find me a quadruped, or do you find me a man? Do you find three bones less in my back than in that of the white man? Do you find fewer organs in the brain? If you know nothing of this, I do; for I have helped to dissect fifty men, black and white, and I assert that by the time you take off the mucous pigment—the color of the skin—you cannot, to save your life, distinguish between the black man and the white. Am I a man? Have I a soul to save, as you have? Am I susceptible of eternal development, as you are? Can I learn all the arts and sciences that you can? Has it ever been demonstrated in the history of the world? Have black men ever exhibited bravery as white men have done?

Have they ever been in the professions? Have they not as good articulative organs as you? Some people argue that there is a very close similarity between the larynx of the Negro and that of the orangoutang. Why, sir, there is not so much similarity between them as there is between the larynx of the man and that of the dog, and this fact I dare any member of this House to dispute. God saw fit to vary everything in nature. There are no two men alike—no two voices alike—no two trees alike. God has weaved and tissued variety and versatility throughout the boundless space of His creation. Because God saw fit to make some red, and some white, and some black, and some brown, are we to sit here in judgment upon what God has seen fit to do? As well might one play with the thunderbolts of heaven as with that creature that bears God's image—God's photograph.

The question is asked, "What is it that the Negro race has done?" Well, Mr. Speaker, all I have to say upon the subject is this: If we are the class of people that we are generally represented to be, I hold that we are a very great people. It is generally considered that we are the children of Canaan, and the curse of a father rests upon our heads, and has rested, all through history. Sir, I deny that the curse of Noah had anything to do with the Negro.* We are not the Children of Canaan; and if we are, sir, where should we stand? Let us look a little into history. Melchizedek was a Canaanite; all the Phoenicians—all those inventors of the arts and sciences—were the posterity of Canaan; but, sir, the Negro is not. We are the children of Cush, and Canaan's curse has nothing whatever to do with the Negro. If we belong to that race, Ham belonged to it, under whose instructions Napoleon Bonaparte studied military tactics. If we belong to that race, Saint Augustine belonged to it. Who was it that laid the foundation of the great Reformation? Martin Luther, who lit the light of gospel truth—a light that will never go out until the sun shall rise to set no more; and, long ere then, Democratic principles will have found their level in the regions of Pluto and of Proserpine. . . .

The honorable gentleman from Whitfield (Mr. Shumate),

---

* The "Curse of Ham" (Genesis 9:25–27) was used from the beginning of the African slave trade in the fifteenth century to prove that the Bible justified Negro enslavement. Ham and his descendants—the black race—were to be slaves because he had seen Noah in his nakedness. Actually, it was on Canaan (the son of Noah) and his descendants that the curse was laid. The actual text reads: "Cursed be Canaan; a servant of servants shall he be unto his brethren." The misinterpretation probably occurred because the Hebrew words (B'no Hakatan) could be interpreted as "his young son" or "his grandson."

when arguing this question, a day or two ago, put forth the proposition that to be a representative was not to be an officer— "it was a privilege that citizens had a right to enjoy." These are his words. It was not an office; it was a "privilege." Every gentleman here knows that he denied that to be a representative was to be an officer. Now, he is recognized as a leader of the Democratic party in this House, and generally cooks victuals for them to eat; makes that remarkable declaration, and how are you, gentlemen on the other side of the House, because I am an officer, when one of your great lights says that I am *not* an officer? If you deny my right—the right of my constituents to have representation here—because it is a "privilege," then, sir, I will show you that I have as many privileges as the whitest man on this floor. If I am not permitted to occupy a seat here, for the purpose of representing my constituents, I want to know how white men can be permitted to do so. How can a white man represent a colored constituency, if a colored man cannot do it? The great argument is: "Oh, we have inherited" this, that and the other. Now, I want gentlemen to come down to cool, common sense. Is the created greater than the Creator? Is man greater than God? It is very strange, if a white man can occupy on this floor *a seat created by colored votes*, and a black man cannot do it. Why, gentlemen, it is the most shortsighted reasoning in the world. A man can see better than that with half an eye; and even if he had no eye at all, he could forge one, as the Cyclops did, or punch one with his finger, which would enable him to see through that.

It is said that Congress never gave us the right to hold office. I want to know, sir, if the Reconstruction measures did not base their action on the ground that no distinction should be made on account of race, color or previous condition? Was not that the grand fulcrum on which they rested? And did not every reconstructed state have to reconstruct on the idea that no discrimination, in any sense of the term, should be made? There is not a man here who will dare say No. If Congress has simply given me merely sufficient civil and political rights to make me a mere political slave for Democrats, or anybody else—giving them the opportunity of jumping on my back in order to leap into political power—I do not thank Congress for it. Never, so help me God, shall I be a political slave. I am not now speaking for those colored men who sit with me in this House, nor do I say that they endorse my sentiments [cries from the colored members, "We Do!"], but assisting Mr. Lincoln to take me out of servile slavery did not intend to put me and my race into *political* slavery. If they did, let them take away my ballot—I do not want it, and shall not have it. [Several colored members: "Nor we!"] I don't want to be a mere tool of that sort. I have been a slave long enough already.

I tell you what I would be willing to do: I am willing that the question should be submitted to Congress for an explanation as to what was meant in the passage of their Reconstruction measures, and of the Constitutional Amendment. Let the Democratic party in this House pass a resolution giving this subject that direction, and I shall be content. I dare you, gentlemen, to do it. Come up to the question openly, whether it meant that the Negro might hold office, or whether it meant that he should merely have the right to vote. If you are honest men, you will do it. If, however, you will not do that, I would make another proposition: Call together, again, the convention that framed the constitution under which we are acting; let them take a vote upon the subject, and I am willing to abide by their decision. . . .

These colored men, who are unable to express themselves with all the clearness and dignity and force of rhetorical eloquence, are laughed at in derision by the Democracy of the country. It reminds me very much of the man who looked at himself in a mirror and, imagining that he was addressing another person, exclaimed: "My God, how ugly you are!" These gentlemen do not consider for a moment the dreadful hardships which these people have endured, and especially those who in any way endeavored to acquire an education. For myself, sir, I was raised in the cotton field of South Carolina, and in order to prepare myself for usefulness, as well to myself as to my race, I determined to devote my spare hours to study. When the overseer retired at night to his comfortable couch, I sat and read and thought and studied, until I heard him blow his horn in the morning. He frequently told me, with an oath, that if he discovered me attempting to learn, that he would whip me to death, and I have no doubt he would have done so, if he had found an opportunity. I prayed to Almighty God to assist me, and He did, and I thank Him with my whole heart and soul. . . .

So far as I am personally concerned, no man in Georgia has been more conservative than I. "Anything to please the white folks" has been my motto; and so closely have I adhered to that course, that many among my own party have classed me as a Democrat. One of the leaders of the Republican party in Georgia has not been at all favorable to me for some time back, because he believed that I was too "conservative" for a Republican. I can assure you, however, Mr. Speaker, that I have had quite enough, and to spare, of such "conservatism.". . .

But, Mr. Speaker, I do not regard this movement as a thrust at me. It is a thrust at the Bible—a thrust at the God of the Universe, for making a man and not finishing him; it is simply calling the Great Jehovah a fool. Why, sir, though we are not white, we have accomplished much. We have pioneered civilization here; we have built up your country; we have worked in your fields and garnered your harvests for two hundred and fifty years! And what do we ask of you in return? Do we ask you for compensation for the sweat our fathers bore for you—for the tears you have caused, and the hearts you have broken, and the lives you have curtailed, and the blood you have spilled? Do we ask retaliation? We ask it not. We are willing to let the dead past bury its dead; but we ask you, now for our *rights*. You have all the elements of superiority upon your side; you have our money and your own; you have our education and your own; and you have our land and your own too. We, who number hundreds of thousands in Georgia, including our wives and families, with not a foot of land to call our own—strangers in the land of our birth; without money, without education, without aid, without a roof to cover us while we live, nor sufficient clay to cover us when we die! It is extraordinary that a race such as yours, professing gallantry and chivalry and education and superiority, living in a land where ringing chimes call child and sire to the church of God—a land where Bibles are read and Gospel truths are spoken, and where courts of justice are presumed to exist; it is extraordinary that, with all these advantages on your side, you can make war upon the poor defenseless black man. You know we have no money, no railroads, no telegraphs, no advantages of any sort, and yet all manner of injustice is placed upon us. You know that the black people of this country acknowledge you as their superiors, by virtue of your education and advantages. . . .

You may expel us, gentlemen, but I firmly believe that you will some day repent it. The black man cannot protect a country, if the country doesn't protect him; and if, tomorrow, a war should arise, I would not raise a musket to defend a country where my manhood is denied. The fashionable way in Georgia, when hard work is to be done, is for the white man to sit at his ease while the black man does the work; but, sir, I will say this much to the colored men of Georgia, as, if I should be killed in this campaign, I may have no opportunity of telling them at any other time: Never lift a finger nor raise a hand in defense of Georgia, unless Georgia acknowledges that you are men and invests you with the rights pertaining to manhood. Pay your taxes, however, obey all orders from your employers, take good counsel from friends, work faithfully, earn an honest living, and show, by your conduct, that you can be good citizens.

Go on with your oppressions. Babylon fell. Where is Greece? Where is Nineveh? And where is Rome, the Mistress Empire of the world? Why is it that she stands, today, in broken fragments throughout Europe? Because oppression killed her. Every act that we commit is like a bounding ball. If you curse a man, that curse rebounds upon you; and when you bless a man, the blessing returns to you; and when you oppress a man, the oppression also will rebound. Where have you ever heard of four millions of freemen being governed by laws, and yet have no hand in their making? Search the records of the world, and you will find no example. "Governments derive their just powers from the consent of the governed." How dare you to make laws by which to try me and my wife and children, and deny me a voice in the making of these laws? I know you can establish a monarchy, an autocracy, an oligarchy, or any other kind of *ocracy* that you please; and that you can declare whom you please to be sovereign; but tell me, sir, how you can clothe me with more power than another, where all are sovereigns alike? How can you say you have a republican form of government, when you make such distinction and enact such proscriptive laws?

Gentlemen talk a good deal about the Negroes "building no monuments." I can tell the gentlemen one thing: that is, that we could have built monuments of fire while the war was in progress. We could have fired your woods, your barns and fences, and called you home. Did we do it? No, sir! And God grant that the Negro may never do it, or do anything else that would destroy the good opinion of his friends. No epithet is sufficiently opprobrious for us now. I say, sir, that we have built a monument of docility, of obedience, of respect, and of self-control, that will endure longer than the Pyramids of Egypt.

We are a persecuted people. Luther was persecuted; Galileo was persecuted; good men in all nations have been persecuted; but the persecutors have been handed down to posterity with shame and ignominy. If you pass this bill, you will never get Congress to pardon or enfranchise another rebel in your lives. You are going to fix an everlasting disfranchisement upon Mr. Toombs* and the other leading men of Georgia. You may think

* Robert A. Toombs (1810–1885) had been Secretary of State in the Confederacy and as one of the Confederate leaders was disfranchised and barred from holding public office under the Radical Republican plan of Reconstruction.

you are doing yourselves honor by expelling us from this House; but when we go, we will do as Wickliffe* and as Latimer did. We will light a torch of truth that will never be extinguished— the impression that will run through the country, as people picture in their mind's eye these poor black men, in all parts of this Southern country, pleading for their rights. When you expel us, you make us forever your political foes, and you will never find a black man to vote a Democratic ticket again; for, so help me God, I will go through all the length and breadth of the land, where a man of my race is to be found, and advise him to beware of the Democratic party. Justice is the great doctrine taught in the Bible. God's Eternal Justice is founded upon Truth, and the man who steps from Justice steps from Truth, and cannot make his principles to prevail.

I have now, Mr. Speaker, said all that my physical condition will allow me to say. Weak and ill, though I am, I could not sit passively here and see the sacred rights of my race destroyed at one blow. We are in a position somewhat similar to that of the famous "Light Brigade," of which Tennyson says, they had

> Cannon to right of them,
> Cannon to left of them,
> Cannon in front of them,
> Volleyed and thundered.

I hope our poor, downtrodden race may act well and wisely through this period of trial, and that they will exercise patience and discretion under all circumstances.

You may expel us, gentlemen, by your votes, today; but, while you do it, remember that there is a just God in Heaven, whose All-Seeing Eye beholds alike the acts of the oppressor and the oppressed, and who, despite the machinations of the wicked, never fails to vindicate the cause of Justice, and the sanctity of His own handiwork.†

* John Wycliffe (c.1328–1384) was the English religious leader who stood up against the abuses of the Church, championed the cause of the poor, opposing serfdom, and laid the foundations of Lollard thought and practice in England. His influence spread to Bohemia and formed the basis of the Hussite movement.
† At the insistence of Congress, which refused to admit Georgia to the Union until it seated the black legislators, the expelled members of the Georgia legislature were readmitted in 1869 with pay for lost time.

FINISH THE GOOD WORK OF UNITING COLORED AND WHITE WORKINGMEN

By Isaac Myers

At the third national convention of the National Labor Union, held in Philadelphia, August, 1869, nine of the 142 delegates were Negroes. One of these delegates was Isaac Myers, representing the Colored Caulkers' Trades Union Society of Baltimore and the first important black labor leader in the United States. During the convention, Myers was commissioned by the black delegates to voice their thanks for the "unanimous recognition" of the Negro worker's right to representation in the gathering. The speech he delivered on August 18, 1869, is an historic appeal for unity of black and white workers, and probably the first published labor speech of a black union leader. The reporter for The New York Times, *where the speech appeared, wrote: "The whole Convention listened . . . with the most profound attention . . . and at its close delegates advanced and warmly congratulated him."*

Myers was born a free Negro in Baltimore in 1835 and at the age of sixteen was apprenticed to a prominent local Negro to learn the ship-calking trade. Four years later he was in charge of the calking of large clipper ships. In 1865 a strike of white workers against the presence of colored mechanics and longshoremen resulted in the dismissal of over a hundred Negroes from their jobs in the Baltimore shipyards. As a result of this crisis, Myers helped organize a union of colored workers in the shipyards, and established the Chesapeake Marine Railway and Dry Dock Company, a cooperative venture, owned entirely by Negroes.

(The speech presented here was excerpted from The New York Times, *August 19, 1869.)*

   . . . GENTLEMEN, silent but powerful and far-reaching is the revolution inaugurated by your act of taking the colored laborer by the hand and telling him that his interest is common with yours, and that he should have an equal chance in the race for life. These declarations of yours are ominous, and will not only be felt throughout the length and breadth of this great Republic, but will become another great problem in American poli-

tics for the kings and dynasties of Europe to solve. It is America
and it is only Americans that can work up and work out such
great revolutions in a day. God grant that it may be as lasting
as the eternal hills. I speak today for the colored men of the
whole country, from the Lakes to the Gulf—from the Atlantic
to the Pacific—from every hilltop, valley and plain throughout
our vast domain, when I tell you that all they ask for themselves is a fair chance; that you and they may make one steady
and strong pull until the laboring man of this country shall receive such pay for time made as will secure them a comfortable
living for their families, educate their children and leave a dollar for a rainy day and old age. Slavery, or slave labor, the main
cause of the degradation of white labor, is no more. And it is
the proud boast of my life that the slave himself had a large
share in the work of striking off the fetters that bound him by
the ankle, while the other end bound you by the neck.

The white laboring men of the country have nothing to fear
from the colored laboring man. We desire to see labor elevated
and made respectable; we desire to have the highest rate of
wages that our labor is worth; we desire to have the hours of
labor regulated, as well to the interest of the laborer and the
capitalist. And you, gentlemen, may rely on the support of the
colored laborers of this country in bringing about this result. If
they have not strictly observed these principles in the past, it
was because the doors of the workshops of the North, East and
West were firmly bolted against them, and it was written over
the doors: "No Negro admitted here." Thus barred out, thus
warned off, his only hope was to put his labor in the market to
be controlled by selfish and unscrupulous speculators who will
dare do any deed to advance their own ends.

Mr. President and gentlemen, American citizenship with the
black man is a complete failure if he is proscribed from the
workshops of this country, if any man cannot employ him who
chooses, and if he cannot work for any man whom he will. If
citizenship means anything at all, it means the freedom of
labor, as broad and as universal as the freedom of the ballot. I
cannot tell how far your action in admitting colored delegates
on this floor is going to influence the minor organizations
throughout the country. Shall they still proscribe the colored
labor, or will they feel bound to follow your noble example of
Monday? The question being today asked by the colored men of
this country is only to be answered by the white men of the
country. We mean in all sincerity a hearty cooperation. You cannot doubt us. Where we have had the chance, we have always

demonstrated it. We carry no prejudices. We are willing to forget the wrongs of yesterday and let the dead past bury its dead. An instance of this may be found in my own native Maryland. After we had been driven from shipyard to shipyard, until at last we were kicked completely out and cast upon the cold charity of the world, we formed a cooperative union, got it incorporated, raised $40,000, bought a shipyard,* gave employment to all of our men and now pay them, outside of their wages, fifty percent on their investment. And is that all? No. We give employment to a large number of the men of your race, without regard to their political creed, and to the very men who once sought to do us injury. So you see, gentlemen, we have no prejudice. We have issued a call for a National Labor Convention, to meet in the City of Washington the first Monday in December next.† Delegates will be admitted without regard to color, and I hope you will be well represented in that convention. Questions of the mightiest importance to the labor interest of the United States will be disposed of. We will be very glad to have your cooperation there, as you have ours now. The resolutions of this convention will have an important bearing on that convention. The more you do here, the less we will have to do there.

The colored men of this nation are entirely opposed to the repudiation of the national debt.‡ They go in for every honest dollar borrowed to be honestly paid back, and on the terms stipulated in the original agreement. Any other course is more ruinous to the laborer than to the capitalist. The permanence, not of this administration nor of any other, but of the govern-

---

* The Chesapeake Marine Railway and Dry Dock Company in Baltimore was organized by Isaac Myers in 1865. Within four months he raised $10,000 cash in shares sold to Negroes at $5 each, and purchased a yard and railway worth $40,000. It secured a number of government contracts, employed white mechanics as well as Negroes, and paid off its debt within five years. It remained in existence until 1876, when the shift to steel ships forced it to close down. But its very existence forced the white calkers' union to admit Negroes.
† In 1869 a call for a National Colored Labor Convention to meet in Washington was issued by the Maryland State Convention of Negro Workers. The convention met on December 5 and organized the National Colored Labor Union with Isaac Myers as president.
‡ During the Civil War, the government had issued greenbacks. The greenbacks had depreciated, but the bankers had used these greenbacks to buy government bonds, which were redeemable in gold and paid interest in gold. Many trade unions favored repudiating these public debts to force bankers who invested in U. S. Bonds to put their capital into industrial, commercial and manufacturing enterprises.

ment itself, depends on the honest paying of its debts. A dishonest government, like a dishonest individual, will be arrested, tried, convicted and punished.

The money borrowed was from individual pockets. The slaveholders of the South and their sympathizers in the North forced us to borrow that money. It was borrowed to put down the rebellion, not to put down slavery, for that was not in the contract. Liberty to the slave was a bird hatched by the eggs of the rebellion. And of all men in the United States, the laboring men of the North, East and West are most benefited by the money borrowed. You know that had you not whipped slavery, slavery would have whipped you. If the rebellion had succeeded, slavery would have soon spread over the entire country, and you white laboring men of the country would have been forced to work for what a man chose to give you, and that very often under the lash, as was the case in South Carolina. What has stopped this? The money that our government borrowed in good faith. Has the government paid too much for its use? We think you will find it is no fault of the government, but of those who rebelled against it. These are questions that require your weightiest consideration. The workingmen of this country are a vast power, can take care of themselves, and will not be hoodwinked by any political demagogue in or out of power. What we want is low prices for the necessaries of life, and honest administration of the government, reasonable hours of labor, and such a compensation for the time made as will afford us an independent living. We want no land monopolies, any more than money monopolies or labor monopolies. We want the same chance for the poor as is accorded to the rich—not to make the rich man poorer, but the poor man richer. We do not propose to wage a war on capital, and we do not intend to let capital wage a war on us. Capital and labor must work in harmony; reforms, to be made successful, must be founded on the soundest principles of political economy. We feel that in the person of President Grant the workingmen have a strong friend. After the quibbling of the Attorney General, and others in authority, whether Congress meant you should have a day's wages for eight hours' labor,* President Grant ordered, and it was declared, that eight hours

---

* On June 25, 1868, Congress passed a bill providing for an eight-hour day for laborers, mechanics and all other workmen in federal employ. However, wages were cut by government officials when the eight-hour law became effective. In 1869, responding to protests from organized labor, President Grant issued an executive order that "no reduction should be made in the wages by the day to such laborers . . . on account of such reduction in the hours of labor."

was a day's labor, for which there should be no reduction of pay. His is a type of Americanism as handed down by the Fathers. He cannot be an aristocrat, he cannot feel himself above the common people, and any measure looking to the elevation of the workingmen of this country, we believe, is sure to have his support. The colored men of the country, we believe, are sure to have his support. The colored men of the country thoroughly indorse him.*

Gentlemen, again thanking you for what you have done, and hoping you may finish the good work of uniting the colored and white workingmen of the country by some positive declaration of this convention,† I wish you a complete success.

A PLEA FOR DESEGREGATED SCHOOLS

By Hiram R. Revels

From 1869 to 1901, from the Forty-first Congress through the Fifty-sixth, twenty-two black Americans, all with the backing of the Republican party, were elected to Congress from the Southern states—twenty to the House of Representatives and two to the Senate. The first Negro to be seated in Congress was Hiram Rhodes Revels (1827–1901), who served as Senator from Mississippi from February 25, 1870, to March 3, 1871. He was born in Fayetteville, North Carolina, attended seminaries in Indiana and

---

* There was a strong movement in the National Labor Union to organize a Labor Reform party, and it was hoped that Negroes would support labor's drive for independent political action. But, as Myers indicated, Negroes in the vast majority supported the Republican party as the party of Lincoln and the one that had pushed through a radical program of Reconstruction. Hence his warm endorsement of President Grant.

† The convention of the National Labor Union did pass a resolution which read: "The National Labor Union knows no North, no South, no East, no West, neither color nor sex on the question of the rights of labor, and urges our colored fellow members to form organizations in all legitimate ways, and send their delegates from every state in the Union to the next congress." In addition, a special committee was appointed to "organize the colored men of Pennsylvania into labor unions." Unfortunately, few trade unions were willing to listen to this appeal, and when the committee reported on its work to the next convention, it stated that many unions would not accept Negro mechanics, and proposed that Negroes be organized into separate Jim Crow locals.

Ohio, was graduated from Knox College in Bloomington, Illinois, and was ordained a minister in the African Methodist Episcopal Church, at Baltimore, in 1845. At the outbreak of the Civil War, Revels assisted in organizing the first two colored regiments in Maryland, and he himself served as chaplain of a colored regiment at Vicksburg, Mississippi, in 1864. He settled in Natchez after the Civil War, was elected alderman of the city in 1868, and became a member of the state senate in 1870. Upon the readmission of Mississippi to representation in the Union, he was elected to the United States Senate.

On February 8, 1871, the Senate Committee on the District of Columbia brought in a report on the District's schools which contained the clause, "And no distinction on account of race, color, or previous condition of servitude shall be made in the admission of pupils to any of the schools under the control of the Board of Education, or in the mode of education or treatment of pupils in such schools." Immediately a move arose in the Senate to strike out the antisegregation clause, and an amendment was offered leaving the choice of segregation or desegregation to the Board of Education in the District. Against this amendment Revels delivered a powerful plea that dealt with discrimination not only in education but in travel and in all aspects of life. Revels argued that the deportment of the Negro people was in no way responsible for prejudice; that it was the duty of the federal government actively to resist the spread of segregation, and that people learned prejudice against color by living under Jim Crow restrictions. Unfortunately, neither Revels' plea nor those of Senator Charles Sumner and others prevailed, and school segregation remained legal in the District of Columbia until the Supreme Court decision of May 17, 1954.

(Senator Revels' speech is taken from the Congressional Globe, *41st Congress, 3rd Session, Part 2, pp. 1059–60.)*

MR. PRESIDENT, I rise to express a few thoughts on this subject. It is not often that I ask the attention of the Senate on any subject, but this is one on which I feel it is my duty to make a few brief remarks.

In regard to the wishes of the colored people of this city, I will simply say that the trustees of colored schools and some of the most intelligent colored men of this place have said to me that they would have before asked for a bill abolishing the separate colored schools and putting all children on an equality in the common schools if they had thought they could obtain it. They feared they could not; and this is the only reason why they did not ask for it before.

I find that the prejudice in this country to color is very great, and I sometimes fear that it is on the increase. For example, let me remark that it matters not how colored people act, it matters not how well they behave themselves, how well they deport themselves, how intelligent they may be, how refined they may be—for there are some colored persons who are persons of refinement; this must be admitted—the prejudice against them is equally as great as it is against the most low and degraded colored man you can find in the streets of this city or in any other place.

This, Mr. President, I do seriously regret. And is this prejudice right? Have the colored people done anything to justify the prejudice against them that does exist in the hearts of so many white persons, and generally of one great political party in this country? Have they done anything to justify it? No, sir. Can any reason be given why this prejudice should be fostered in so many hearts against them simply because they are not white? I make these remarks in all kindness, and from no bitterness of feeling at all.

Mr. President, if this prejudice has no cause to justify it, then we must admit that it is wicked, we must admit that it is wrong; we must admit that it has not the approval of Heaven. Therefore I hold it to be the duty of this nation to discourage it, simply because it is wicked, because it is wrong, because it is not approved of by Heaven. If the nation should take a step for the encouragement of this prejudice against the colored race, can they have any ground upon which to predicate a hope that Heaven will smile upon them and prosper them? It is evident that it is the belief of Christian people in this country and in all other enlightened portions of the world that as a nation we have passed through a severe ordeal, that severe judgments have been poured upon us on account of the manner in which a poor, oppressed race was treated in this country.

Sir, this prejudice should be resisted. Steps should be taken by which to discourage it. Shall we do so by taking a step in this direction, if the amendment now proposed to the bill before us is adopted? Not at all. That step will rather encourage, will rather increase this prejudice; and this is one reason why I am opposed to the adoption of the amendment.

Mr. President, let me here remark that if this amendment is rejected, so that the schools will be left open for all children to be entered into them, irrespective of race, color, previous condition, I do not believe the colored people will act imprudently. I know that in one or two of the late insurrectionary states the legislatures passed laws establishing mixed schools,* and the colored people did not hurriedly shove their children into those schools; they were very slow about it. In some localities where there was but little prejudice or opposition to it they entered them immediately; in others they did not do so. I do not believe that it is in the colored people to act rashly and unwisely in a manner of this kind.

But, sir, let me say that it is the wish of the colored people of this District, and of the colored people over this land, that this Congress shall not do anything which will increase that prejudice which is now fearfully great against them. If this amendment be adopted you will encourage that prejudice; you will increase that prejudice; and, perhaps, after the encouragement thus given, the next step may be to ask Congress to prevent them from riding in the streetcars, or something like that. I repeat, let no encouragement be given to a prejudice against those who have done nothing to justify it, who are poor and perfectly innocent, as innocent as infants. Let nothing be done to encourage that prejudice. I say the adoption of this amendment will do so.

Mr. President, I desire to say here that the white race has no better friend than I. The Southern people know this. It is known over the length and breadth of this land. I am true to my own race. I wish to see all done that can be done for their encouragement, to assist them in acquiring property, in becoming intelligent, enlightened, useful, valuable citizens. I wish to see this much done for them, and I believe God makes it the duty of this nation to do this much for them; but at the same time, I would not have anything done which would harm the white race.

Sir, during the canvass in the state of Mississippi I traveled into different parts of that state, and this is the doctrine that I everywhere uttered: That while I was in favor of building up the colored race I was not in favor of tearing down the white race. Sir, the white race need not be harmed in order to build up the colored race. The colored race can be built up and as-

---

* The two states were South Carolina and Louisiana. The South Carolina General Assembly of 1868 provided that all schools "supported in whole or in part by public funds shall be free and open to all the children and youths of the state without regard to race or color." Louisiana provided: "There shall be no separate schools or institutions of learning established exclusively for any race in the state of Louisiana."

sisted, as I before remarked, in acquiring property, in becoming intelligent, valuable, useful citizens, without one hair upon the head of any white man being harmed.

Let me ask, will establishing such schools as I am now advocating in this District harm our white friends? Let us consider this question for a few minutes. By some it is contended that if we establish mixed schools here a great insult will be given to the white citizens, and that the white schools will be seriously damaged. All that I ask those who assume this position to do is to go with me to Massachusetts, to go with me to some other New England states where they have mixed schools,* and there they will find schools in as prosperous and flourishing a condition as any to be found in any part of the world. They will find such schools there; and they will find between the white and colored citizens friendship, peace and harmony.

When I was on a lecturing tour in the state of Ohio, I went to a town, the name of which I forget. The question whether it would be proper or not to establish mixed schools had been raised there. One of the leading gentlemen connected with the schools in that town came to see me and conversed with me on the subject. He asked me, "Have you been to New England, where they have mixed schools?" I replied, "I have, sir." "Well," said he, "please tell me this: does not social equality result from mixed schools?" "No, sir; very far from it," I responded. "Why," said he, "how can it be otherwise?" I replied, "I will tell you how it can be otherwise, and how it is otherwise. Go to the schools and you see there white children and colored children seated side by side, studying their lessons, standing side by side and reciting their lessons, and perhaps in walking to school they may walk along together; but that is the last of it. The white children go to their homes; the colored children go to theirs;

* By the 1840's integrated schools existed in many Massachusetts communities, but Boston's schools were still segregated. In 1849 Benjamin Roberts, a Negro, sued the Primary School Committee of Boston for excluding his daughter from the school in her neighborhood. Roberts, who was represented by Charles Sumner and the Negro lawyer Robert Morris, lost in the courts. In his argument to the court, Sumner insisted that a separate school could never be equal, but the state Supreme Court upheld the legality of separate schools. However, led by William C. Nell, hundreds of Negroes and whites petitioned the Massachusetts legislature for a law abolishing separate schools, and Negroes of Boston also took their children out of separate schools and had them taught privately until the legislature gave in. In 1855 the Massachusetts legislature enacted a law requiring public schools to admit students without regard to color. See pp. 164–68.

and on the Lord's day you will see those colored children in
colored churches, and the white children in white churches; and
if an entertainment is given by a white family, you will see the
white children there, and the colored children at entertainments
given by persons of their color." I aver, sir, that mixed schools
are very far from bringing about social equality.

Then, Mr. President, I hold that establishing mixed schools
will not harm the white race. I am their friend. I said in Mississippi, and I say here, and I say everywhere, that I would
abandon the Republican party if it went into any measures of
legislation really damaging to any portion of the white race; but
it is not in the Republican party to do that.

In the next place, I desire to say that school boards and
school trustees and railroad companies and steamboat companies are to blame for the prejudice that exists against the
colored race, or to their disadvantage in those respects. Go to the
depot here, now, and what will you see? A well-dressed colored
lady with her little children by her side, whom she has brought
up intelligently and with refinement, as much so as white children, comes to the cars; and where is she shown to? Into the
smoking car, where men are cursing, swearing, spitting on the
floor; where she is miserable, and where her little children have
to listen to language not fitting for children who are brought
up as she has endeavored to bring them up to listen to.

Now, sir, let me ask, why is this? Is it because the white passengers in a decent, respectable car are unwilling for her to be
seated there? No, sir; not as a general thing. It is a rule that the
company has established, that she shall not go there.

Let me give you a proof of this. Some years ago I was in the
state of Kansas and wanted to go on a train of cars that ran
from the town where I lived to St. Louis, and this rule prevailed
there, that colored people should go into the smoking car. I had
my wife and children with me and was trying to bring up my
children properly, and I did not wish to take them into the
smoking car. So I went to see the superintendent who lived in
that town, and I addressed him thus: "Sir, I propose to start for
St. Louis tomorrow on your road, and wish to take my family
along; and I do not desire to go into the smoking car. It is all
that I can do to stand it myself, and I do not wish my wife and
children to be there and listen to such language as is uttered
there by men talking, smoking, spitting, and rendering the car
very foul; and I want to ask you now if I cannot obtain permission to take my family into a first-class car, as I have a first-
class ticket?" Said he: "Sir, you can do so; I will see the conductor and instruct him to admit you." And he did admit me,

and not a white passenger objected to it, not a white passenger gave any evidence of being displeased because I and my family were there.

Let me give you another instance. In New Orleans, and also in Baltimore, cities that I love and whose citizens I love, some trouble was raised some time ago because colored people were not allowed to ride in the streetcars. The question was taken to the courts; and what was the decision? That the companies should make provision for colored passengers to go inside of the cars. At first they had a car with a certain mark, signifying that colored people should enter. I think the words were, in Baltimore, "Colored people admitted into this car"; and in New Orleans they had a star upon the car. They commenced running. There would be a number of white ladies and white gentlemen who wanted to go in the direction that this car was going, and did not want to wait for another; and notwithstanding there was a number of colored persons in the car, they went in and seated themselves just as if there had not been a colored person there. The other day, in Baltimore, I saw one of these cars passing along with the words, "Colored persons admitted into this car." The car stopped, and I saw a number of white ladies and gentlemen getting in, and not one colored person there. It was the same way in New Orleans. Let me tell you how it worked in New Orleans. The company finally came to the conclusion that if white persons were willing to go into a car appropriated to colored persons and ride with them without a word of complaint, they could not consistently complain of colored persons going into cars that were intended for white persons; and so they repealed their rule and opened the cars for all to enter. And ever since that time all have been riding together in New Orleans,* and there has not been a word of complaint. So it will be I believe in regard to the school. Let lawmakers cease to make the difference, let school trustees and school boards cease to make the difference, and the people will soon forget it.

---

* Streetcar segregation was practiced as company policy from the time the cars were placed in service in New Orleans in the 1820's. A few of the omnibus lines excluded Negroes altogether, but others operated special cars for colored passengers, identified by large stars painted on the front, rear, and both sides. This practice continued until immediately following the Civil War. In May, 1867, a massive Negro demonstration led to the desegregation of streetcars. The evidence concerning segregated transportation in Baltimore, referred to by Senator Revels, is not clear. The first Jim Crow laws in Maryland were not passed until 1904 when the General Assembly enacted two laws imposing segregation of the races on all railroads and steamships in the state.

Mr. President, I have nothing more to say. What I have said I have said in kindness; and I hope it will be received in that spirit.

THE KU KLUX OF THE NORTH

By Isaiah C. Wears

In 1838 Pennsylvania removed the right of Negroes to vote and it was not until ratification of the Fifteenth Amendment that Pennsylvania Negroes regained that right. Several thousand Negroes appeared at the Philadelphia polls in the fall of 1870. In one ward all white men were allowed to vote first, and Negroes, formed into a separate waiting line, voted afterward. When it was reported that the waiting Negroes were not being allowed to vote, General E. M. Gregory, United States marshal for the eastern district of Pennsylvania, sent in a company of marines to keep order and see that the Negroes were permitted to vote. In the fall election of 1871 no federal troops were used in Philadelphia and violence ensued. Race hatred, stirred up before and during the election campaign, culminated in the murder of three Negroes and the injury of many others. Among those killed was Octavius V. Catto, who had been commissioned a major in the infantry during the Civil War, and after the war became a high-school principal and firm equal-rights advocate in Philadelphia. A large meeting of colored citizens was held "the object of which was to give expression of sorrow at the untimely death of Professor O. V. Catto, Messrs. Chase, Gordon, Boiden, and others." Isaiah C. Wears, a leading Philadelphia Negro, delivered the main address.

Catto received a hero's funeral and was buried with full military honors. But no one was ever brought to justice for his death.

(The address presented here is taken from The Christian Recorder, *November 18, 1871.)*

MR. CHAIRMAN, . . . To us these scenes are nothing new. Their horrible and community-disgracing record dates back a whole generation. At last we have gained the public ear;

at last, through the success of Republican principles, we are able to hold up to public execration the authors of our woes. The party that stands guilty of the crimes of today is the same class of merciless persecutors that have followed and dogged us as no other people in this country have been followed, and this, too, under the blazing sunlight of a Christian civilization. Whenever and wherever we have made any effort to lift ourselves, mobs were sent to burn our dwellings, our schoolhouses, our churches, and our orphan asylums, hanging us to lampposts and clubbing us to death on the highways. Indeed, this persecuting spirit has been so intense, the ostracism inflicted upon us so murderous, its appetite for such immeasurable cruelties so insatiate, that even death itself the common leveler of us all, could not intervene or withstand its potential sway. No; they followed us to the graveyard and barred there the gates of the cities of the dead against us. The men who aided in these things are the authors and instigators of these murders.

It is a disagreeable duty to speak about the unpleasant truths that stand out disgustingly conspicuous in this terrible affair, yet 'tis a duty nevertheless. . . . Proclamations offering thousands for the arrest of murderers may be seen everywhere. If you would find the murderers, come with me to the laudable places of amusement, to the situations of instruction and, in some cases, of devotion, and see there the prescription inflicted upon us. Arrest this blighting—this withering ostracism. Convict it before the country and the world, then these murders will cease, and the reward will be justly earned. As it is, let the most intelligent and respectable among us attempt to avail himself of the accommodations of even a third- or fourth-rate hotel, he will be driven away like a dog. There are men claiming position in the higher walks of life who have nothing but their color to recommend them, hence they fight for it in this way; they labor to keep alive public sentiment, the logical consequence of which is the murder of our people. Whenever you hear a man threaten or suggest a probable "war of races," be satisfied that you have before you a murderer, and though his instrument or agent may not be present he is willing to wait until some turbulent state of public feeling offers an opportune moment to hiss his kennel of savage hounds upon us. Low men often exhibit the instincts of brutes. We know that the commonest and most cowardly cur upon a door mat joins readily in chase of the pursued. We are inhumanly dealt with by the meanest and shabbiest of men only when they find grades of society above them banded against us. Let us then turn our attention to the real authors of these murders.

The Ku Klux of the South are not by any means the lower classes of society.* The same may be said of the Ku Klux of the North. Both are industriously engaged in trying to break us down into beggary and crime.

And even now the sad events that call us here tonight come at this juncture to give practical life to the very sentiment that they were intended to destroy—"they meant it for evil God meant it for good." Let us so accept it. Let no man think that we ask for people's pity or commiseration. What we do ask is fairness and equal opportunities in the battle of life. We are friends of our country; treat us as well as you do its enemies; we have fought to defend her, let us have the same chances as those who have fought against her; then if we gravitate to the bottom there is just where we belong.

> We're men and fear no rivals now;
> Freed from the shackles of the rod,
> We only ask with lifted brow,
> Justice from man and strength from God.

A PLEA IN BEHALF OF THE CUBAN REVOLUTION

By Henry Highland Garnet

The Cuban revolution to gain independence from Spain began on October 10, 1868. It was to last for ten years and to end in a shaky victory for Spain. During these ten years, many Americans voiced repeated support for the Cuban revolutionary cause and urged the government of the United States to recognize the belligerence of the Cuban rebels so that they could purchase arms in this country. Among the most vocal supporters of the Cuban revolution

---

* During Radical Reconstruction the advocates of white supremacy banded together in the South in secret organizations, of which the most important was the Ku Klux Klan. Disguised by hoods, the Klan roamed the countryside, shooting, flogging and terrorizing Negroes and their supporters, burning homes and public buildings, and perpetrating all sorts of acts of violence. Recent studies have confirmed Wears's statement that "respectable" white Southerners were influential in these terrorist organizations.

were black Americans, especially after the Constitutional Convention of Cuban revolutionists, meeting at Guaimaro on April 10, 1869, adopted the first Constitution of Free Cuba, the twenty-fourth article of which declared that "all the inhabitants of the Republic are absolutely free." A victory for the Cuban revolution meant the end of slavery in the island. Another reason for black Americans' support of the revolution was the important role played in the struggle against Spain by the Negroes of Cuba under the leadership of the great Cuban guerrilla fighter, Antonio Maceo. Unfortunately, all of the public pressure for recognition of Cuban belligerency did not bring about the desired results. In August, 1869, President Grant favored extending recognition to the Cuban revolutionists and actually ordered a proclamation written according them recognition. But Hamilton Fish, Secretary of State, succeeded in obtaining first a delay and then the complete suppression of the document. Thereafter, Grant moved consistently away from recognizing the belligerency of the revolutionists.

In December, 1872, a call was circulated in New York City by Negro citizens for a meeting to be held at Cooper Institute in behalf of the Cuban patriots, and to take proper action "to advance the cause of freedom." The key speech at the meeting, held on December 13, 1872, was delivered by the Reverend Henry Highland Garnet, secretary of the Cuban Anti-Slavery Committee. It is presented here as taken from Slavery in Cuba: A Report of the Proceedings of the Meeting Held at Cooper Institute, New York City, December 13, 1872, *New York, 1872, pp. 15–18. (Copy in Columbia University Library.)*

MR. CHAIRMAN, in the invitation that I received to attend this meeting and take part in the proceedings, I recognize the call of liberty and the groans of five hundred thousand of our enslaved fellow men. We who have passed through the terrible ordeal of the struggle for freedom and equal rights which in 1861 brought the two divisions of our country into deadly conflict and culminated in the complete overthrow of despotism in the United States, are in hearty sympathy with the patriots of Cuba, and we pray God that He will give strength to the arms of the defenders of freedom and cause the propitious winds to sweep over the fruitful island, that shall bear aloft in the skies the flag of the free. In the annals of poetry, in which glow the promises of the better days that are to dawn upon the earth and the prophecies that foretell the final reign of universal liberty, there is none that gives greater assurance to the struggling but invincible sons of freedom throughout the whole world than is found in this stanza:

> *Freedom's battle once begun,*
> *Bequeathed from bleeding sire to son,*
> *Though baffled oft is ever won.*

I see before me tonight many native Cubans, who, driven by the fierce fire of Spanish oppression, have sought and found shelter in our free land. Permit me to assure you, my exiled friends, that I know that I am justified in saying to you that this meeting, and millions of American citizens, bid you Godspeed in your noble cause; and in their behalf I extend to you my hand, pledging ourselves to stand united with you in your efforts for the promotion of the interests of liberty and the universal brotherhood of man. My sympathies were drawn to your cause when I saw the article in the constitution of the patriots: *"All the people of Cuba are absolutely free."* But not now, for the strong hand of tyranny is clutching the throat of liberty, and the government of the island is not yours. But Cuba must be free. God has decreed it, and the spirit of the age approves it. Slavery shall be blotted out from every island in the Western Sea, as it has been banished from the Western Continent. The shores of our Republic shall not be washed by the waves made bloody by Cuban slavery. When the new and free flag of Cuba shall be triumphantly unfurled to the breeze of heaven, bearing for its motto, "Impartial Liberty and Equality," then shall the spirit of that article of your constitution, to which I have referred, be carried out. We regret that we cannot give you that material aid we would wish to afford you, but we can do one thing—we can create a public sentiment in this land that will urge our government to acknowledge the belligerent rights of the patriots of Cuba. The sympathies of the government of the United States are strongly in favor of Cuban liberty, and when the time shall come when, in conformity with international law they can render Cuba the aid she needs, I believe it will not be withheld.* Aside from humanitarian considerations, I think I

---

* Garnet's faith in the Grant administration was not shared by most of those at the meeting. The Negro citizens present unanimously declared that the government had been remiss in not recognizing the belligerency of the Cuban revolutionists and resolved that "we, therefore, after four years' patient waiting, deem it our duty, and do hereby petition our government at Washington, the President and Congress of the United States,

may safely say that all the civilized nations that once maintained human slavery in the Western world, and have abolished it, are utterly opposed to giving Spain the monopoly of that diabolical system. Let slavery and involuntary servitude perish at once and forever from every inch of soil in the continent, and in Cuba and Porto Rico. I have twice visited Cuba and have witnessed the horrors of slavery as it exists there, and allow me to state that the slavery recently abolished in our country was mild when compared with the crime that Spain today upholds in Cuba. I have seen slave ships enter the port of Havana, and cargoes of miserable men and women, some dying and some of them dead, dragged and hurried from the decks of slavers and thrown upon the shores. You cannot forget, Cubans, the immortal mulatto poet of your country, the brave and heroic Plácido* Like yourselves, you know that he loved liberty and freely offered himself on her sacred altar. He was accused of being concerned in an attempted insurrection, and was condemned to die the death of a traitor. When he was led forth to death, he cried:

> O Liberty! I hear thy voice calling me
> Deep in the frozen regions of the North, afar,
> With voice like God's, and vision like a star.

God grant that liberty from her home in "the frozen regions of the North" may continue to call in trumpet tones until she shall arouse every patriotic son of Cuba to unconquerable resistance to slavery. As I have already said, we cannot give you the material aid we would wish to, for the reason that our government holds diplomatic relations with Spain. I wish that we had none. . . . If our relations with Spain retard the progress of liberty in Cuba and Porto Rico, I had almost said that I am sorry that we have any. Haiti has disenthralled herself, and

---

to accord to the Cuban patriots that favorable recognition that four years' gallant struggle for freedom justly entitles them to."
* Gabriel de la Concepción Valdés, known as "Plácido," was a free Cuban Negro who became famous for his poems written to celebrate anniversaries and birthdays. On the surface there was nothing revolutionary in these verses, but underneath there was always an affirmation of his hatred of tyrants and love for freedom. So great was the fear of slave rebellions in Cuba that his verses could no longer be tolerated. In 1844 "Plácido" was arrested on the trumped-up charge of being an agent for a British abolitionist and of having been selected as president of the Republic to be set up by a group of slave conspirators. Though the evidence against him was obtained by torture, he was executed.

with her own strong arm has broken the tyrant's power. All the nations on the American continent have done likewise, and when Cuba shall have succeeded the last foul blot of slavery will be removed from our portion of the globe.* Let us pray and work, and success will at last crown our efforts.

THE CIVIL RIGHTS BILL

By Robert Browne Elliott

The speeches of the first black Congressmen dealt with a wide variety of legislation, but many were appeals for the passage of a civil-rights bill introduced by Senator Charles Sumner in Congress in the fall of 1871. Sumner's bill proposed to secure equality of civil rights to Negroes all over the country, and prohibited discrimination in railroads, theaters, hotels, schools, cemeteries and churches, and on juries. In February, 1875, after Sumner's death, an emasculated version of his bill, omitting discrimination in schools and cemeteries, became a law. In 1883 the United States Supreme Court declared unconstitutional the Civil Rights Act of 1875.

Below are parts of a speech in favor of the civil-rights bill by Robert Browne Elliott (1842–1884), black Congressman from South Carolina, delivered in Congress on January 6, 1874. Elliott was born free in Boston, of West Indian descent. He was educated abroad, first in Jamaica and then in England, where he graduated from Eton with honors in 1859. While in England he also studied law, and was admitted to the bar and practiced in Columbia, South Carolina. After serving as a member of the South Carolina House of Representatives from July 6, 1868, to October 23, 1870, and as assistant adjutant general of South Carolina, 1869–71, he was elected as a Republican to the Forty-second Congress from the Third District of South Carolina. He was reelected, but resigned on November 1, 1874, and returned to the South Carolina House of Representatives, where he became speaker. Elliott spoke French, German, Spanish and Latin, and had the largest private library in

---

* Slavery was not abolished in Cuba until October 7, 1886.

*the state of South Carolina. He was considered one of the
greatest black orators up to that time in American history.
(The speech presented below is taken from the pamphlet* Civil Rights—Speech of Hon. Robert B. Elliott of
South Carolina, in the House of Representatives, January
6, 1874, *Washington(?), Beardsley & Snodgrass, n.d.)*

MR. SPEAKER: While I am sincerely grateful for this
high mark of courtesy that have been accorded to me by this
House, it is a matter of regret to me that it is necessary at this
day that I should rise in the presence of an American Congress
to advocate a bill which simply asserts equal rights and equal
public privileges for all classes of American citizens. I regret,
sir, that the dark hue of my skin may lend a color to the imputation that I am controlled by motives personal to myself in my
advocacy of this great measure of national justice. Sir, the motive that impels me is restricted by no such narrow boundary,
but is as broad as your Constitution. I advocate it, sir, because
it is right. The bill, however, not only appeals to your justice,
but it demands a response from your gratitude.

In the events that led to the achievement of American independence the Negro was not an inactive or unconcerned
spectator.* He bore his part bravely upon many battlefields, although uncheered by that certain hope of political elevation
which victory would secure to the white man. The tall granite
shaft, which a grateful State has reared above its sons who fell
in defending Fort Griswold against the attack of Benedict Arnold, bears the name of Jordan, Freeman, and other brave men
of the African race, who there cemented with their blood the
cornerstone of the Republic.† In the state which I have the
honor in part to represent (South Carolina) the rifle of the
black man rang out against the troops of the British Crown in
the darkest days of the American Revolution. Said General
Greene, who has been justly termed the "Washington of the
North," in a letter written by him to Alexander Hamilton, on the
tenth of January, 1781, from the vicinity of Camden, South
Carolina: "There is no such thing as national character or national sentiment. The inhabitants are numerous, but they would

* Some five thousand Negroes fought in the Revolutionary army, of whom
many were slaves.
† When the British, led by Benedict Arnold, stormed Fort Griswold on
September 6, 1781, and massacred the defenders, two Negroes, Jordan
Freeman and Lambert Latham, were among those killed. Before dying,
Freeman managed to kill a British major named Montgomery. Latham
had more than thirty wounds in his body.

be rather formidable abroad than at home. There is a great spirit of enterprise among the black people, and those that come out as volunteers are not a little formidable to the enemy."*

At the battle of New Orleans under the immortal Jackson, a colored regiment held the extreme right of the American line unflinchingly and drove back the British column that pressed upon them at the point of the bayonet. So marked was their valor on that occasion that it evoked from their great commander the warmest encomiums, as will be seen from his dispatch announcing the brilliant victory.

As the gentleman from Kentucky (Mr. Beck), who seems to be the leading exponent on this floor of the party that is arrayed against the principle of this bill, has been pleased, in season and out of season, to cast odium upon the Negro and to vaunt the chivalry of his state, I may be pardoned for calling attention to another portion of the same dispatch. Referring to the various regiments under his command, and their conduct on that field which terminated the second war of American Independence, General Jackson says, "At the very moment when the entire discomfiture of the enemy was looked for with a confidence amounting to certainty, the Kentucky reinforcements, in whom so much reliance had been placed, ingloriously fled."

In quoting this indisputable piece of history, I do so only by way of admonition and not to question the well-attested gallantry of the true Kentuckian, and to the gentleman that it would be well that he should not flaunt his heraldry so proudly while he bears this bar sinister on the military escutcheon of his state—a state which answered the call of the Republic in 1861, when treason thundered at the very gates of the Capital, by coldly declaring her neutrality in the impending struggle.†
The Negro, true to that patriotism and love of country that have ever marked and characterized his history on this continent, came to the aid of the government in its efforts to maintain the Constitution. To that government he now appeals; that Constitution he now invokes for protection against outrage and unjust prejudices founded upon caste.

But, sir, we are told by the distinguished gentleman from Georgia (Mr. Stephens)‡ that Congress has no power under the

---

* Both General Nathaniel Greene and Alexander Hamilton made strenuous efforts to persuade South Carolina and Georgia to permit the enrollment of Negroes as soldiers. Their effort, as well as one by Congress, failed.

† Kentucky maintained neutrality until September, 1861, when the legislature voted to remain loyal to the Union.

‡ Alexander Hamilton Stephens (1812–1883), member of Congress from Georgia from 1843 to 1859, became Vice-President of the Confederate

Constitution to pass such a law, and that the passage of such an act is in direct contravention of the rights of the states. I cannot assent to any such proposition. The Constitution of a free government ought always to be construed in favor of human rights. Indeed, the thirteenth, fourteenth, and fifteenth amendments, in positive words, invest Congress with the power to protect the citizen in his civil and political rights. Now, sir, what are civil rights? Rights natural, modified by civil society. Mr. Lieber* says: "By civil liberty is meant, not only the absence of individual restraint, but liberty within the social system and political organism—a combination of principles and laws which acknowledge, protect and favor the dignity of man . . . civil liberty is the result of man's twofold character as an individual and social being, so soon as both are equally respected."

Alexander Hamilton, the right-hand man of Washington in the perilous days of the then infant Republic; the great interpreter and expounder of the Constitution, says: "Natural liberty is the gift of a beneficent Creator to the whole human race; civil liberty is founded on it, civil liberty is only natural liberty modified and secured by civil society." . . .

Are we then, sir, with the amendments to our Constitution staring us in the face; with these grand truths of history before our eyes; with innumerable wrongs daily inflicted upon five million citizens demanding redress, to commit this question to the diversity of legislation? In the words of Hamilton, "Is it the interest of the government to sacrifice individual rights to the preservation of the rights of an artificial being called the states? There can be no truer principle than this, that every individual of the community at large has an equal right to the protection of government. Can this be a free government if partial distinctions are tolerated or maintained?"

The rights contended for in this bill are among "the sacred rights of mankind, which are not to be rummaged for among old parchments or musty records; they are written as with a sunbeam in the whole volume of human nature, by the hand

---

States of America. He was imprisoned at the end of the war, then was paroled and was elected U. S. Senator during the era of President Andrew Johnson's Reconstruction, but was refused his seat by Congress. From 1873 to 1882 he was a member of the House of Representatives.

* Francis Lieber (1800–1872), educator and political philosopher, was born in Germany and came to the United States in 1827. He was professor of history and political economy at Columbia University from 1857 to 1865, and at Columbia Law School from 1865 to 1872. He wrote many books on political science, including *On Civil Liberty and Self-Government* (2 volumes, 1853).

of the divinity itself, and can never be erased or obscured by mortal power."

But the Slaughterhouse cases!—The Slaughterhouse cases!*

The honorable gentleman from Kentucky, always swift to sustain the failing and dishonored cause of proscription, rushes forward and flaunts in our faces the decision of the Supreme Court of the United States in the Slaughterhouse cases, and in that act he has been willingly aided by the gentleman from Georgia. Hitherto, in the contests which have marked the progress of the cause of equal civil rights, our opponents have appealed sometimes to custom, sometimes to prejudice, more often to pride of race, but they have never sought to shield themselves behind the Supreme Court. But now, for the first time, we are told that we are barred by a decision of that court, from which there is no appeal. If this be true we must stay our hands. The cause of equal civil rights must pause at the command of a power whose edicts must be obeyed till the fundamental law of our country is changed.

Has the honorable gentleman from Kentucky considered well the claim he now advances? If it were not disrespectful I would ask, has he ever read the decision which he now tells us is an insuperable barrier to the adoption of this great measure of justice?

In the consideration of this subject, has not the judgment of the gentleman from Georgia been warped by the ghost of the dead doctrines of states' rights? Has he been altogether free from prejudices engendered by long training in that school of politics that well-nigh destroyed this government?

Mr. Speaker, I venture to say here in the presence of the gentleman from Kentucky and the gentleman from Georgia, and in the presence of the whole country, that there is not a line or word, not a thought or dictum even, in the decision of the Supreme Court in the great Slaughterhouse cases, which casts

---

* The Slaughterhouse Cases of 1873 did not directly involve rights of Negroes. But the Court frequently referred to these cases in later interpretations of those rights. The legislature of Louisiana had passed a statute which granted a monopoly of the slaughterhouse business within certain parishes of New Orleans in favor of one corporation and thus deprived more than a thousand persons of the right to engage in business. In the majority opinion, the Supreme Court said that the thirteenth, fourteenth and fifteenth amendments had no purpose except the protection of the freedom of the Negro. The business of slaughtering cattle in New Orleans, which the legislature had converted into a monopoly, could proceed in such manner as the state might dictate, without infringement of any right, privilege, or immunity conferred upon citizens of the United States by the Fourteenth Amendment.

a shadow of doubt on the right of Congress to pass the pending bill, or to adopt such other legislation as it may judge proper and necessary to secure perfect equality before the law to every citizen of the Republic. Sir, I protest against the dishonor now cast upon our Supreme Court by both the gentleman from Kentucky and the gentleman from Georgia. In other days, when the whole country was bowing beneath the yoke of slavery, when press, pulpit, platform, Congress and courts felt the fatal power of the slave oligarchy, I remember a decision of that court which no American now reads without shame and humiliation. But those days are past; the Supreme Court of today is a tribunal as true to freedom as any department of this government, and I am honored with the opportunity of repelling a deep disgrace which the gentleman from Kentucky, backed and sustained as he is by the gentleman from Georgia, seeks to put upon it. . . .

The amendments in the Slaughterhouse cases, one and all, are thus declared to have as their all-pervading design and ends the security of the recently enslaved race, not only their nominal freedom, but their complete protection from those who had formerly exercised unlimited dominion over them. It is in this broad light that all these amendments must be read, the purpose to secure the perfect equality before the law of all citizens of the United States. What you give to one class you must give to all, what you deny to one class you shall deny to all, unless in the exercise of the common and universal police power of the state, you find it needful to confer exclusive privileges on certain citizens, to be held and exercised still for the common good of all.

Such are the doctrines of the Slaughterhouse cases—doctrines worthy of the Republic, worthy of the age, worthy of the great tribunal which thus loftily and impressively enunciates them. Do they--I put it to any man, be he lawyer or not; I put it to the gentleman from Georgia—do they give color even to the claim that this Congress may not now legislate against a plain discrimination made by state laws or state customs against that very race for whose complete freedom and protection these great amendments were elaborated and adopted? Is it pretended, I ask the honorable gentleman from Kentucky or the honorable gentleman from Georgia—is it pretended anywhere that the evils of which we complain, our exclusion from the public inn, from the saloon and table of the steamboat, from the sleeping coach on the railway, from the right of sepulture in the public burial ground, are an exercise of the police power of the state? Is such oppression and injustice nothing but the exercise by the state of the right to make regulations for the health, comfort and security of all her citizens? Is it merely enacting that one man shall so use his own as not to injure another's? Is the colored race to be assimilated to an unwholesome trade or to combustible materials, to be interdicted, to be shut up within prescribed limits? Let the gentleman from Kentucky or the gentleman from Georgia answer. Let the country know to what extent even the audacious prejudice of the gentleman from Kentucky will drive him, and how far even the gentleman from Georgia will permit himself to be led captive by the unrighteous teachings of a false political faith.

If we are to be likened in legal view to "unwholesome trades," to "large and offensive collections of animals" to "noxious slaughterhouses," to "the offal and stench which attend on certain manufactures," let it be avowed. If that is still the doctrine of the political party, to which the gentleman belong, let it be put upon record. If state laws which deny us the common rights and privileges of other citizens, upon no possible or conceivable ground save one of prejudice, or of "taste" as the gentleman from Texas termed it, and as I suppose the gentlemen will prefer to call it, are to be placed under the protection of a decision which affirms the right of a state to regulate the police power of her great cities, then the decision is in conflict with the bill before us. No man will dare maintain such a doctrine. It is as shocking to the legal mind as it is offensive to the heart and conscience of all who love justice or respect manhood. I am astonished that the gentleman from Kentucky or the gentleman from Georgia should have been so grossly misled as to rise here and assert that the decision of the Supreme Court in these cases was a denial to Congress of the power to legislate against discriminations on account of race, color or previous conditions of servitude because that Court has decided that exclusive privileges conferred for the common protection of the lives and health of the whole community are not in violation of the recent amendments. The only ground upon which the grant of exclusive privileges to a portion of the community is ever defended is that the substantial good of all is promoted; that in truth it is for the welfare of the whole community that certain persons should alone pursue certain occupations. It is not the special benefit conferred on the few that moves the legislature, but the ultimate and real benefit of all, even of those who are denied the right to pursue those specified occupations. Does the gentleman from Kentucky say that my good is promoted when I am excluded from the public inn? Is the health or safety of the community promoted? Doubtless his prejudice is gratified. Doubtless his democratic instincts are pleased; but will he or

his able coadjutor say that such exclusion is a lawful exercise
of the police power of the state, or that it is not a denial to me
of the equal protection of the laws? They will not so say.

But each of these gentlemen quote at some length from the
decision of the court to show that the court recognizes a difference between citizenship of the United States and citizenship
of the states. That is true and no man here who supports this
bill questions or overlooks the difference. There are privileges
and immunities which belong to me as a citizen of the United
States, and there are other privileges and immunities which
belong to me as a citizen of my state. The former are under
the protection of the Constitution and laws of the United States,
and the latter are under the protection of the constitution and
laws of my state. But what of that? Are the rights which I now
claim—the right to enjoy the common public conveniences
of travel on public highways, of rest and refreshment at public
inns, of education in public schools, of burial in public cemeteries—rights which I hold as a citizen of the United States or
of my state? Or, to state the question more exactly, is not the
denial of such privileges to me a denial to me of the equal protection of the laws? For it is under this clause of the Fourteenth
Amendment that we place the present bill, no state shall "deny
to any person within its jurisdiction the equal protection of the
laws." No matter, therefore, whether his rights are held under
the United States or under his particular state, he is equally
protected by this amendment. He is always and everywhere
entitled to the equal protection of the laws. All discrimination
is forbidden; and while the rights of citizens of a state as such
are not defined or conferred by the Constitution of the United
States, yet all discrimination, all denial of equality before the
law, all denial of equal protection of the laws whether state or
national laws, is forbidden.

The distinction between the two kinds of citizenship is clear,
and the Supreme Court has clearly pointed out this distinction,
but it has nowhere written a word or line which denies to Congress the power to prevent a denial of equality of rights whether
those rights exist by virtue of citizenship of the United States
or of a state. Let honorable members mark well this distinction.
There are rights which are conferred on us by the United States.
There are other rights conferred on us by the states of which we
are individually the citizens. The Fourteenth Amendment does
not forbid a state to deny to all its citizens any of those rights
which the state itself has conferred with certain exceptions
which are pointed out in the decision which we are examining.
What it does forbid is inequality, is discrimination or, to use

the words of the amendment itself, is the denial "to any person within its jurisdiction, the equal protection of the laws." If a state denies to me rights which are common to all her other citizens, she violates this amendment, unless she can show, as was shown in the Slaughterhouse cases, that she does it in the legitimate exercise of her police power. If she abridges the rights of all her citizens equally, unless those rights are specifically guarded by the Constitution of the United States, she does not violate this amendment. This is not to put the rights which I hold by virtue of my citizenship of South Carolina under the protection of the national government; it is not to blot out or overlook in the slightest particular the distinction between rights held under the United States and rights held under the states; but it seeks to secure equality to prevent discrimination, to confer as complete and ample protection on the humblest as on the highest.

The gentleman from Kentucky, in the course of the speech to which I am now replying, made a reference to the state of Massachusetts which betrays again the confusion which exists in his mind on this precise point. He tells us that Massachusetts excludes from the ballot box all who cannot read and write, and points to that fact as the exercise of a right which this bill would abridge or impair. The honorable gentleman from Massachusetts (Mr. Dawes) answered him truly and well, but I submit that he did not make the best reply, why did he not ask the gentleman from Kentucky if Massachusetts had ever discriminated against any of her citizens on account of color or race or previous condition of servitude? When did Massachusetts sully her proud record by placing on her statute book any law which admitted to the ballot the white man and shut out the black man? She has never done it; she will not do it; she cannot do it so long as we have a Supreme Court which reads the Constitution of our country with the eyes of justice; nor can Massachusetts or Kentucky deny to any man on account of his race, color or previous condition of servitude, that perfect equality of protection under the laws so long as Congress shall exercise the power to enforce by appropriate legislation the great and unquestionable securities embodied in the Fourteenth Amendment to the Constitution. . . .

Now, sir, having spoken of the prohibition imposed by Massachusetts, I may be pardoned for a slight inquiry as to the effect of this prohibition. First, it did not in any way abridge or curtail the exercise of the suffrage by any person who enjoyed such right. Nor did it discriminate against the illiterate native and the illiterate foreigner. Being enacted for the good of the entire commonwealth, like all just laws, its obligations fell equally and impartially on all its citizens. And as a justification for such a measure, it is a fact too well known almost for mention here that Massachusetts had, from the beginning of her history, recognized the inestimable value of an educated ballot, by not only maintaining a system of free schools, but also enforcing an attendance thereupon, as one of the safeguards for the preservation of a real republican form of government. Recurring then, sir, to the possible contingency alluded to by the gentleman from Kentucky, should the state of Kentucky, having first established a system of common schools whose doors shall swing open freely to all, as contemplated by the provisions of this bill, adopt a provision similar to that of Massachusetts, no one would have cause justly to complain. And if in the coming years the result of such legislation should produce a constituency rivaling that of the old Bay State, no one would be more highly gratified than I. Mr. Speaker, I have neither the time nor the inclination to notice the many illogical and forced conclusions, the numerous transfers of terms, or the vulgar insinuations which further encumber the argument of the gentleman from Kentucky. Reason and argument are worse than wasted upon those who meet every demand for political and civil liberty by such ribaldry as this—extracted from the speech of the gentleman from Kentucky: "I suppose there are gentlemen on this floor who would arrest, imprison, and fine a young woman in any state of the South if she were to refuse to marry a Negro man on account of color, race or previous condition of servitude, in the event of his making her a proposal of marriage and her refusing on that ground. That would be depriving him of a right he had under the amendment, and Congress would be asked to take it up and say, 'This insolent white woman must be taught to know that it is a misdemeanor to deny a man marriage because of race, color or previous condition of servitude,' and Congress will be urged to say after a while that that sort of thing must be put a stop to, and your conventions of colored men will come here asking you to enforce that right."

Now, sir, recurring to the venerable and distinguished gentleman from Georgia (Mr. Stephens) who has added his remonstrance against the passage of this bill, permit me to say that I share in the feeling of high personal regard for that gentleman which pervades this House. His years, his ability, and his long experience in public affairs entitle him to the measure of consideration which has been accorded to him on this floor. But in this discussion I cannot and will not forget that the welfare and rights of my whole race in this country are involved. When, therefore, the honorable gentleman from Georgia lends his voice and influence to defeat this measure, I do not shrink from saying that it is not from him that the American House of Representatives should take lessons in matters touching human rights or the joint relations of the state and national governments. While the honorable gentleman contented himself with harmless speculations in his study, or in the columns of a newspaper, we might well smile at the impotence of his efforts to turn back the advancing tide of opinion and progress; but, when he comes again upon this national arena, and throws himself with all his power and influence across the path which leads to the full enfranchisement of my race, I meet him only as an adversary; nor shall age or any other consideration restrain me from saying that he now offers this government, which he has done his utmost to destroy, a very poor return for its magnanimous treatment, to come here and seek to continue, by the assertion of doctrines obnoxious to the true principles of our government, the burdens and oppressions which rest upon five millions of his countrymen who never failed to lift their earnest prayers for the success of this government when the gentleman was seeking to break up the union of these states and to blot the American Republic from the galaxy of nations.

Sir, it is scarcely twelve years since that gentleman shocked the civilized world by announcing the birth of a government which rested on human slavery as its cornerstone.* The progress of events has swept away that pseudo government which rested on greed, pride and tyranny; and the race whom he then ruthlessly spurned and trampled on is here to meet him in debate, and to demand that the rights which are enjoyed by its former oppressors—who vainly sought to overthrow a government which they could not prostitute to the base uses of slavery —shall be accorded to those who even in the darkness of slavery kept their allegiance true to freedom and the Union. Sir, the gentleman from Georgia has learned much since 1861; but he is still a laggard. Let him put away entirely the false and fatal theories which have so greatly marred an otherwise enviable record. Let him accept, in its fullness and beneficence, the great doctrine that American citizenship carries with it every civil and political right which manhood can confer. Let him lend his

---

* Alexander Stephens, Vice-President of the Confederacy, said of the Confederate States of America: ". . . its foundations are laid, its cornerstone rests upon the great truth that the Negro is not equal to the white man. That slavery-subordination to the superior race is his natural and normal condition."

influence with all his masterly ability, to complete the proud structure of legislation which makes this nation worthy of the great declaration which heralded its birth, and he will have done that which will most nearly redeem his reputation in the eyes of the world and best vindicate the wisdom of that policy which has permitted him to regain his seat upon this floor.

To the diatribe of the gentleman from Virginia (Mr. Harris) who spoke yesterday, and who so far transcended the limits of decency and propriety as to announce upon this floor that his remarks were addressed to white men alone, I shall have no word of reply. Let him feel that a Negro was not only too magnanimous to smite him in his weakness, but was even charitable enough to grant him the mercy of his silence. I shall, sir, leave to others less charitable the unenviable and fatiguing task of sifting out of that mass of chaff the few grains of sense that may, perchance deserve notice. Assuring the gentleman that the Negro in this country aims at a higher degree of intellect than that exhibited by him in this debate, I cheerfully commend him to the commiseration of all intelligent men the world over —black men as well as white men.

Sir, equality before the law is now the broad, universal, glorious rule and mandate of the Republic. No state can violate that. Kentucky and Georgia may crowd their statute books with retrograde and barbarous legislation; they may rejoice in the odious eminence of their consistent hostility to all the great steps of human progress which have marked our national history since slavery tore down the Stars and Stripes on Fort Sumter; but, if Congress shall do its duty, if Congress shall enforce the great guarantees which the Supreme Court has declared to be the one pervading purpose of all the recent amendments, then their unwise and unenlightened conduct will fall with the same weight upon the gentlemen from those states who now lend their influence to defeat this bill, as upon the poorest slave who once had no rights which the honorable gentlemen were bound to respect.

But, sir, not only does the decision in the Slaughterhouse cases contain nothing which suggests a doubt of the power of Congress to pass the pending bill, but it contains an express recognition and affirmance of such power. I quote from page 81 of the volume: "Nor shall any State deny to any person within its jurisdiction the equal protection of the laws."

In the light of the history of these amendments and the pervading purpose of them which we have already discussed, it is not difficult to give a meaning to this clause. The existence of laws in the states where the newly emancipated Negroes resided, which discriminated with gross injustice and hardship against them as a class, was the evil to be remedied by this clause, and by it such laws are forbidden.

If, however, the states did not conform their views to its requirements, then, by the fifth section of the article of amendment, Congress was authorized to enforce it by suitable legislation. We doubt very much whether any action of a state not directed by way of discrimination against the Negroes as a class, or on account of their race, will ever be held to come within the purview of this provision. It is so clearly a provision for that race and that emergency, that a strong case would be necessary for its application to any other. But as it is a state that is to be dealt with, and not alone the validity of its laws, we may safely leave that matter until Congress shall have exercised its power, or some case of state oppression, by denial of equal justice in its courts, shall have claimed a decision at our hands.

No language could convey a more complete assertion of the power of Congress over the subject embraced in the present bill than is here expressed. If the states do not conform to the requirements of this clause, if they continue to deny to any person within their jurisdiction the equal protection of the laws or, as the Supreme Court had said, "deny equal justice in it Courts" then Congress is here said to have power to enforce the Constitutional guarantee by appropriate legislation. That is the power which this bill now seeks to put in exercise.

It proposes to enforce the Constitutional guarantee against inequality and discrimination by appropriate legislation. It does not seek to confer new rights, nor to place rights conferred by state citizenship under the protection of the United States, but simply to prevent and forbid inequality and discrimination on account of race, color or previous condition of servitude. Never was there a bill which appealed for support more strongly to that sense of justice and fair play which has been said, and in the main with justice, to be a characteristic of the Anglo-Saxon race. The Constitution warrants it; the Supreme Court sanctions it; justice demands it.

Sir, I have replied to the extent of my ability to the arguments which have been presented by the opponents of this measure. I have replied also to some of the legal propositions advanced by gentlemen on the other side; and now that I am about to conclude, I am deeply sensible of the imperfect manner in which I have performed the task. Technically, this bill is to decide upon the civil status of the colored American citizen; a point disputed at the very formation of our present form of government, when by a short-sighted policy, a policy repugnant to true republican government, one Negro counted as three fifths of a man. The logical result of this mistake of the framers of the Constitution strengthened the cancer of slavery, which finally spread its poisonous tentacles over the Southern portion of the body politic. To arrest its growth and save the nation we have passed through the harrowing operation of intestine war, dreaded at all times, resorted to at the last extremity, like the surgeon's knife, but absolutely necessary to extirpate the disease which threatened with the life of the nation the overthrow of civil and political liberty on this continent. In that dire extremity the members of the race which I have the honor in part to represent—the race which pleads for justice at your hands to-day—forgetful of their inhuman and brutalizing servitude at the South, their degradation and ostracism at the North, flew willingly and gallantly to the support of the national government.

Their sufferings, assistance, privations and trials in the swamps and in the rice fields, their valor on the land and on the sea, form a part of the ever-glorious record which makes up the history of a nation preserved, and might, should I urge the claim, incline you to respect and guarantee their rights and privileges as citizens of our common Republic. But I remember that valor, devotion and loyalty are not always rewarded according to their just deserts, and that after the battle some who have borne the brunt of the fray may, through neglect or contempt, be assigned to a subordinate place, while the enemies in war may be preferred to the sufferers.

The results of the war, as seen in reconstruction, have settled forever the political status of my race. The passage of this bill will determine the civil status, not only of the Negro, but of any other class of citizens who may feel themselves discriminated against. It will form the capstone of that temple of liberty, begun on this continent under discouraging circumstances, carried on in spite of the sneers of monarchists and the cavils of pretended friends of freedom, until at last it stands, in all its beautiful symmetry and proportions, a building the grandest which the world has ever seen, realizing the most sanguine expectations and the highest hopes of those who, in the name of equal, impartial and universal liberty, laid the foundation stone.

The Holy Scriptures tell us of an humble handmaiden who long, faithfully and patiently gleaned in the rich fields of her wealthy kinsman, and we are told further that at last, in spite of her humble antecedents she found favor in his sight. For

over two centuries our race has "reaped down your fields," the
cries and woes which we have uttered have "entered into the
ears of the Lord of Sabaoth" and we are at last politically free.
The last vestiture only is needed—civil rights. Having gained
this, we may, with hearts overflowing with gratitude and thankful that our prayer has been answered, repeat the prayer of
Ruth: "Entreat me not to leave thee, or to return from following
after thee; for whither thou goest, I will go; and where thou
lodgest, I will lodge; thy people shall be my people, and thy
God my God; where thou diest I will die, and there will I be
buried; the Lord do so to me, and more also, if ought but death
part thee and me."

A DEFENSE OF INDEPENDENT VOTING

By William Still

*In the mayoralty election of 1874 in Philadelphia, William
Still, the distinguished black Abolitionist, Underground
Railroad worker and civil-rights advocate, announced that
he was joining Robert Purvis and other leading Negroes
in the city in opposing the local Republican machine and
supporting the People's Party candidate for mayor, Colonel
A. K. McClure. Still was subjected to such bitter attacks
from Negroes active in the Republican party that his
friends sponsored a public meeting at the Concert Hall,
March 10, 1874, at which Still delivered a speech defending his political independence.*

*The son of slaves, William Still rose to prominence in
the Philadelphia antislavery movement, became an active
agent of the Underground Railroad and secretary of the
city's Vigilance Committee, which aided fugitive slaves.
Later, he became a prosperous coal merchant. Still played
a prominent role in the campaign to end discrimination
against Negroes on Philadelphia's streetcars. His book,*
The Underground Railroad, *is one of the major sources
on the organization which helped slaves escape from the
South.*

*The following excerpts from Still's speech are reprinted
from* William Still, An Address on Voting and Laboring.

Delivered at Concert Hall, Tuesday Evening, March 10th, 1874, *Philadelphia, 1874, pp. 6–11. (Copy in Library Company of Philadelphia.)*

SINCE THE FACT of my having voted for the candidate for the mayoralty of the People's Party, in the recent Municipal election, has subjected me to the charge of having "deserted my principles," I propose briefly to refute the charge, and at the same time to give the reasons for my course. The friends of freedom may judge whether I have swerved from the old platform of equal rights.

I quote from my late article (published in the Philadelphia *Press*) as follows:

"If a colored voter chooses upon due consideration, to vote an independent or nonpartisan or even Democratic ticket, I think he should be free to do so; and, still further, I think that colored men, who have been so long bound down under the yoke and have been so long compelled to think and act only at the bidding of the dominant race, should be the last people on earth to institute or encourage this kind of political tyranny."

When penning this paragraph (the most offensive one, in the eye of one of our "distinguished colored leaders") contained in my late communication, I never thought that there would be the slightest room for alleging that I had undergone a change of sentiment with regard to voting, nor do I now see how such a view is in any sense whatever in conflict with the Fifteenth Amendment, or antagonistical to the avowed principles of the Republican party.

I am not forgetful of the fact that a good deal is claimed of the colored man on the score of "gratitude," and I must freely own that in view of the wonderful changes that have taken place in the condition of our race in this country within the last dozen years, our hearts cannot too often swell with gratitude to God and good men for what has been accomplished in the interest of freedom and humanity.

Indeed, I have thought a thousand times that there had been much less gratitude manifested than was really due to the friends of freedom.

From my boyhood (I was in my teens when I first commenced taking antislavery papers) I have intensely watched the movements of good men and women of all parties who openly espoused the cause of the slave when it was extremely unpopular and even dangerous to do so, some facing angry mobs, brickbats, prisons, enduring separations from friends and relatives where the ties were the strongest, expulsion from church and state, becoming a hissing and byword, sacrificing time and money with a liberal hand in the cause of the slave. Men and women for adhering to the "higher law," and the commands of Christ to help undo every burden and let the oppressed go free, were daily called upon to suffer in every conceivable way; but they never relaxed their efforts, never ceased to push on the glorious work of emancipation, until the "irrepressible conflict," thus waged, had its desired results and every fetter was broken and every bondman free as air.

Now, if when the claims for special gratitude are made they embrace these early, earnest, and self-sacrificing workers, I should only be too glad to be found at the "front." But I rather think those old workers have been overlooked and forgotten in the midst of political excitement—in the hurry of "counting in and counting out," which has become so common of late, in order to keep up party influences. . . .

Now, with regard to my vote for Colonel A. K. McClure: In this matter I did not act without due reflection. For some time before the election I had made up my mind that I could not consistently with my sense of duty vote for the "Ring." The numerous election frauds, high taxes, et cetera, together with the very strenuous efforts made by this power to defeat the New Constitution, determined me to withhold my vote therefrom, provided that a Republican from the thirty-four thousand majority in Philadelphia for the New Constitution should be selected as an Independent or People's Party candidate.

Colonel McClure having been thus nominated, I decided to vote for him. For a long while he had been a prominent leader in the Republican party, filling the highest positions in the state legislature; and also, for two years at least, he had been very actively co-operating with the Reformers of this city, a body of the most respectable and staid men of this city, largely made up from the Republican ranks. In the Senate he actively advocated the Constitutional Convention, and he was given the credit of having labored with success, and great force, in attacking many of the defects of the old constitution, and of advocating, with equal success, the important points of the new. Hence the fact of his running for mayor in this independent manner, as a non-partisan, appeared to afford an opportunity for all independent-thinking citizens, whether Republicans or Democrats, to vote according to honest convictions.

In order to free citizens from partisan trammels, especially with regard to municipal elections, the framers of the New Constitution had very wisely changed the municipal elections from October—the time of holding the state election (when

state or national issues might have weight in constraining
voters to follow party lines)—to February, when no state or
national issues need be considered, but when men could vote
in reference only to the city affairs, just as the stockholders of
the Pennsylvania Railroad vote in electing their officers. Probably I am not wise enough or politician enough to see that this
is a very "bad arrangement." I confess I like the change and
look for good results therefrom. So much for voting a nonpartisan ticket.

To come now to the most objectionable point—namely, the
right of a colored man to vote a Democratic ticket if he chooses
to do so upon due consideration.

This right seems so self-evident that under a Republican form
of government its denial, one might suppose, would subject a
man to the charge of being out of his mind or very ignorant. In
a government like ours, is this denial supportable? I think not
for a single moment. I am sure no sane white Republican takes
this extreme view held by some colored Republicans in Philadelphia. All private and public organizations, secular and religious, are directly at variance with this idea, and I presume I
can very readily convince any reasonable man of the absurdity
of the notion. For instance, the churches, colleges, and schools
all over the land are composed of and controlled by Republicans
and Democrats—railroads, banking institutions, insurance companies, and in short, all our great public or private corporations
are managed by boards made up in this way. Nothing is more
common and natural than to find Republicans and Democrats
members of the same business firms—partners in every trade
and profession; so indissolubly so that you might as well undertake to remove the Allegheny Mountains as to keep them separated. And even in politics we see the same intermingling
constantly going on, see the President of the United States, the
late Secretary of War, Edwin M. Stanton, Generals Butler, Sheridan and many others conspicuous in the Republican ranks today, who were once conspicuous in the Democratic ranks.

The slavery issues on which the two parties have so long been
contending are all, except Senator Sumner's Civil Rights Bill,
settled, and the way is now prepared for new issues, such as
tariff, currency, specie payments, railroads, government bonds,
the United States debt, the Granges movement, et cetera. It
needs but half an eye to see that these issues are soon to bring
about many political changes. It is deeply interesting to mark
how the signs are portending the near approach of these events.

Landless and without capital, even with the Civil Rights Bill
secured by the Congress of the nation, the condition of the col-

ored man would still be pitiable, unless he is wise. Of course he cannot vote the Democratic ticket when the Democratic party is arrayed against him; but it would not be unwise to carefully watch the changes in parties and movements, as there are many Democrats, doubtless, who still adhere to the party of their fathers, who are no longer in sympathy with old proslavery doctrines and ideas; and while they still hold on to their party they are anxious for a general change, in which the civil and political rights of the colored man shall be recognized. Now, which would be just the best way on the part of the colored man to help bring about this desirable change, I may not be able to point out. But I am sure the counsel that favors the wholesale denunciation of every Democrat and every colored man who might be disposed to vote a Democratic ticket, will never hasten that long-looked-for day of peace which should be desired by every American citizen.

Obvious changes have been going on in this city in the Democratic party all must admit—signs too palpable for a denial. For instance. I know full well, when laboring for years for the rights of the colored people in our city passenger cars, it was a common occurrence to meet men who would profess to be friendly, but would tell me that the Democrats would mob and kill the colored people the instant a change was made. Men would tell me that white people would not ride with us. However (thanks to a change in public opinion) our equal rights were secured. But no earthquake followed. No Democratic mobs have yet appeared. Colored people ride in the cars just as freely as they walk the streets, without the slightest molestation. I believed that it would be so, no less while I was getting signers to petitions than I do today with the fact verified before my eyes.

And here is another illustration:

The jury box in Philadelphia until within a few years had never been occupied under the late constitution, by a man of African descent. Doubtless many men with the old hate and prejudice against the Negro in their hearts, swore that they would never serve on a jury with one of this hated race. The first test came, and a Democrat, dyed in the wool, was on the bench.

You all remember how the Negro-hating juryman defiantly refused to serve with the black citizen, and I am sure you have not forgotten how promptly the Democratic judge, Ludlow, imposed imprisonment and fine upon this unwilling brother. Since that day, although colored men have frequently served, I am not aware that the slightest objection has been made. Democratic judges in Philadelphia are not fools, at least. Still another sign worthy of note in this city. During the exciting canvasses preceding the vote for the New Constitution and for mayor, I looked in vain to find in any of the Democratic papers any sneers against the colored man. Nor did it fall to my lot in passing and repassing through the streets to hear the insult and abuse that I had been accustomed to hear a few years prior to suffrage and riding in the cars. Now I regard these things as favorable signs, and as long as our people are under the necessity of seeking employment from Democrats, and as long as they choose to spend their money so freely with them in the localities where they live most numerously, I do not see the wisdom of reviving dead issues and thereby allowing ourselves to be needlessly frightened by "Ring" office seekers. Wrath kindleth wrath, and I am sure we have had enough of this baneful commodity to be willing to see it die out both in our own breasts and in the breasts of our nominal enemies.

"Let us have peace." . . .

EULOGY ON CHARLES SUMNER

By Joseph H. Rainey

Joseph Hayne Rainey (1832–1887) was the first Negro to serve in the House of Representatives. Born in Georgetown, South Carolina, he received a limited education and followed the trade of barber. In 1862 he was drafted to work on the Confederate fortifications in Charleston harbor, but he eventually escaped to the West Indies and did not return to South Carolina until the end of the Civil War. In 1868 Rainey became a delegate to the state constitutional convention, and a year later he was elected to the state senate. He resigned in 1870 and was elected to the Forty-first Congress from the First District of South Carolina.

On March 11, 1874, Senator Charles Sumner, the great foe of slavery and champion of equality for Negroes, died. Everywhere Negroes met in memorial meetings to pay tribute to the man regarded as the greatest friend of black Americans. In Congress, on April 27, 1874, Representative Rainey delivered the following eulogy in honor of the late

Senator from Massachusetts; it is taken from the Congressional Record, *43rd Congress, 1st Session, Vol. 2, Part 4, pp. 3412–14.*

MR. SPEAKER, not long since, we were called upon to lay aside our accustomed duties of legislation to participate in the mournful procession that signalized the departure of the distinguished statesman and philanthropist who has been summoned before the bar of our final Judge. We have again halted to pay further tribute to his memory and intrinsic worth.

The announcement of the death of Charles Sumner, late Senator from the state of Massachusetts, sent a thrill of sorrow and cast a shade of melancholy gloom over this country more pervading in its general effects than any similar event since the assassination of the lamented Lincoln. Language such as I have at my command is too imperfect and feeble to convey in adequate terms the high estimation in which he was held, or to express fully and feelingly the depth of grief his demise has occasioned. Men and women mourn his loss and shed the tear of regretful sadness, not only in large cities and the palatial dwellings occupied by the learned and wealthy, but in villages and hamlets, upon farms and the distant plantations of the South; into the cabins of the unlettered and the lowly, bereavement found its way, bowing the hearts of all in mournful lamentation for this irreparable loss. Mr. Sumner, in name and deeds, is known, revered and esteemed by all classes of our people. The remarkable and noble battles of argument and eloquence which he has fought in the Senate in behalf of the oppressed, have enshrined him in the hearts of the countrymen, millions of whom never beheld his majestic form, nor heard his deep and impressive voice—that which at no time indulged silence when the cause of the downtrodden and the enslaved was the issue.

Early in life Mr. Sumner espoused the cause of those who were not able to speak for themselves, and whose bondage made it hazardous for anyone else to venture a word in their behalf. No one knew the danger and magnitude of such an undertaking better than the deceased. Public sentiment at that time was opposed to his course; ostracism confronted him; friends forsook him; but undaunted and full of courage he pursued the right, sustained his convictions, and lived long enough to see the fruition of his earnest labors. He was among the first to arouse the Commonwealth of his beloved Massachusetts to consider the justice and equity of mixed schools.* The blows

* *See* pp. 164–68.

he gave were effectual; the separating walls could not withstand them; they consequently tottered and fell. The doors of
the schoolhouses flew open to all; prejudice was well-nigh consumed by the blaze of his ardent eloquence, and proscription
gave way to more liberal views. It was upon his motion that
the first colored man was admitted to practice before the
Supreme Court of the United States.*

These remarks are made to show that the cause of my race
was always foremost in his mind; indeed, he was a friend who
in many instances stuck closer than a brother. He was one of
those who never slumbered upon his lance, but stood ever
watchful for the opportunity to hurl the shaft of his forensic
powers against the institution of slavery. The forum, the platform and the legislative hall bear equal testimony to his untiring zeal and determined opposition thereto.

The barbarities and atrocities of slavery, through the aid of
his giant mind, were brought to the attention of the American
people and the world in a manner and style hitherto unknown.
He was God's chosen advocate of freedom and denouncer of the
crime of the "peculiar institution" which blurred the fair record
and threatened ultimately to destroy the growing fame of his
country. So attractive, so instructive and inviting was his mode
of argument, that even those who opposed him most strenuously
were constrained to "read, mark, learn and inwardly digest" his
utterances. This was doubtless owing in a great measure to his
rare talents and acquirements, and the splendid opportunity he
enjoyed of speaking to the country.

Mr. Sumner was a patriot of no ordinary rank. He was a lover
of his country, the whole country, in the broadest and the most
comprehensive signification of the term. Whatever he did to
hinder the extension of slavery or to hasten the day of its
final abolition, was based not upon hatred or antipathy to the
South, but upon a conviction that it was not only wrong to
humanity, but an accursed blot upon the escutcheon of the Republic. He knew full well that it would tarnish the beauty of its
history; therefore he felt the duty pressing to combat it. In a
word, he did not hate the South, not the slaveholders, but he
hated and detested *slavery*. His desire was that the South as
well as the North should share in the real grandeur of this
republican empire. He was aware that the impartial historian
could not complete his task so long as slavery existed, unless the
pen, as it were, was dipped in human blood; the thought of
which to him was revolting. Oh that the South had heeded his

* *See* page 204.

admonition and let the oppressed go free! As a statesman, Mr.
Sumner may have allowed his zeal to outrun his discretion,
and thus made mistakes.

"To err is human; to forgive, divine."

It was evident, however, that his errors ever leaned to the
side of justice and humanity. He could not comprehend any
fundamental law that did not embrace in its provisions the
cause of the poor and the needy; consequently his construction
of the Constitution differed in many essential particulars from
that put upon it by other statesmen, who were less liberal in
their opinions and more partial and biased in their judgment.
He was strong to his convictions, faithful to duty, and true to
his country. How appropriate are the following lines in tracing his active and useful life:

> Staunch at thy post, to meet life's common doom,
> It scarce seems death to die as thou hast died;
> Thy duty done, thy truth, strength, courage tried,
> And all things ripe for the fulfilling tomb!
> A crown would mock thy hearse's sable gloom,
> Whose virtues raised thee higher than a throne,
> Whose faults were erring Nature's, not his own—
> Such be thy sentence, writ with Fame's bright plume,
> Amongst the good and great, for thou wert great,
> In thought, word, deed—like mightiest ones of old—
> Full of the honest truth, which makes men bold,
> Wise, pure, firm, just; the noblest Roman's state
> Became not more a ruler of the free
> Than thy plain life, high thoughts, and matchless constancy.

Compared to his admirers, Mr. Sumner's circle of intimate
friends was not very numerous. Only a few genial spirits imparted to him social pleasure and mental enjoyment. He found
his chief delight in the companionship of books and the study
of the fine arts. But with this rare appreciation for the classic
and the artistic, he possessed in an astonishing degree the
faculty of adapting himself to social intercourse with those
whose attainments were not commensurate with his own. He
was always willing to receive such as visited him, seeking counsel or advice, without regard to present circumstances or
former condition. His friendship, when formed, was sincere
and advantageous. I did myself the honor to call upon him
occasionally; not as often, however, as I felt inclined, for I
knew that his time was valuable, not only to himself, but to
his country. Never did I call but I found him glad to see me
and ready to lay aside constantly exacting duties, and engage

in such conversation as invariably resulted in my being benefited. It was very perceptible that the aim and bent of his mastermind was to elevate to true manhood the race with which I am particularly identified. I can never forget so long as I have the faculty of recollection the warm and friendly grasp he gave my hand soon after I was admitted a member of this House. On my first visit to the Senate he said, "I welcome you to this chamber. Come over frequently; you have rights here as well as others."

During his Senatorial career, embracing a period of twenty-three years, he has contended for a moral principle against enemies more daring and intrepid, perhaps, than any other man has encountered in life itself. His conscientious conviction that slavery was a national crime and moral sin could not endure tamely assertions to the contrary. He heeded not the menacing denunciations of those "who eat the bread of wickedness, and drink the wine of violence." Their execrations could not move nor intimidate him. Finding these instruments of wickedness could not deter him or turn the keen edge of his argument, he was brutally and cowardly assaulted in the Senate chamber, in 1856, by Preston S. Brooks, a Representative from South Carolina. This occurred a few days after his masterly effort setting forth the "Crime Against Kansas."*

Mr. Speaker, that unprovoked assault declared to the country the threatening attitude of the two sections, one against the other, and awakened a determination on the part of the North to resist the encroachments of slavery. The unexpressed sympathy that was felt for him among the slaves of the South, when they heard of this unwarranted attack, was only known to those whose situations at the time made them confidants. Their prayers and secret importunities were ever uttered in the interest of him who was their constant friend and untiring advocate and defender before the high court of the nation.

Mr. Speaker, it is said that "the blood of the martyrs is the seed of the Church." With equal truthfulness and force, I think it may be said that the blood of Charles Sumner, spilled

* On May 19–20, 1856, Sumner delivered a major speech in the Senate, "The Crime Against Kansas," in the course of which he attacked Senator Butler of South Carolina as serving his mistress "the harlot, Slavery." On May 22, United States Congressman Preston Brooks of South Carolina, a relative of Butler, found Sumner at his desk in the Senate after adjournment and beat him until he fell unconscious to the floor. It required three years for Sumner to regain his health. During this period Massachusetts reelected him on the ground that his vacant seat was itself an eloquent plea for abolition.

upon the floor of the Senate because he dared to oppose the slave power of the South and to interpose in the path of its progress, was the seed that produced general emancipation; the result of which is too well known to need comment. It spoke silently, but effectively, of the cruelty and inquities of that abominable institution.

Notwithstanding that dastardly assault, his valor was not cooled, neither was his determination abated to resist the advancing steps of that *power* which was the source of so much distraction to the Republic and disgrace to the nineteenth century. Sir, I believe in a Providence that shapes events and controls circumstances. His hand is most conspicuously seen in the life and death of the lamented Senator. Though he was a martyr to the cause of freedom and universal liberty, he nevertheless lived long enough to see the struggles of his eventful public life crowned with victory, and the broken shackles of the slave scattered at his feet, before he was gathered to his fathers. The emancipated and enfranchised will pay grateful homage to his memory in life, and dying bequeath the name of him who was their benefactor as a befitting one for the reverence and adoration of posterity.

> Farewell! if ever fondest prayer
> For others' weal availed on high
> *Ours* will not be lost in air,
> But waft thy name beyond the sky.

Mr. Speaker, the intentness of his thought on the subject of his mission, for which apparently he was born, clung to him to the closing moments of his life. When weary and longing for rest, having his eyes fixed upon that "mansion not made with hands, eternal in the heavens," and just preceding his final step over the threshold of time into the boundless space of eternity, he uttered in dying accents, yet with an eloquence more persuasive and impressive than ever, these words: "Do not let the civil-rights bill fail!"

How remarkable the connecting incidents of his history! This is particularly apparent when we recall the fact that he began as an advocate of human rights, continued through an eventful career the same, and closing his last hours on earth, facing the judgment seat of the very God, he looked back for a moment and repeated these words, which will ever be memorable, *"Do not let the civil-rights bill fail!"**

* As he lay on his deathbed, too sick to recognize anyone, Sumner kept entreating, "You must take care of the civil-rights bill—my bill, the civil-rights bill—don't let it fail." This was his last public message.

This sentence, we trust, will prove more potent and availing in securing equality before the law for all men than any of his former efforts. This is not the proper time—neither is the occasion propitious—for further comment on that dying appeal. I therefore with trembling hands and a grateful heart lay it gently in the lap of the Muses, that it may be wrought into imperishable history as an additional evidence of his sincerity in life and his devotion to the grand principle of equal rights even in the embrace of death. He can never be repaid for the services he has rendered the Republic. No libation, adoration or sacrifice can equal the beneficence and magnitude of the service he has rendered his country and mankind.

As for my race and me, his memory will ever be precious to us. We will embalm it among the choicest gems of our recollection. Yes;

> Let laurels, drench'd in pure Parnassian dews,
> Reward his memory, dear to every muse,
> Who, with a courage of unshaken root,
> In honor's field advancing his firm foot,
> Plants it upon the line that Justice draws,
> And will prevail or perish in her cause.
> 'Tis to the virtues of such men man owes
> His portion in the good that Heaven bestows.

Now, sir, my grateful task is done. This humble but heartfelt tribute I lay at the base of the broken column in token of him who was an eminent statesman, renowned philanthropist, and devoted friend to the friendless. "May he rest in peace."

EQUALITY BEFORE THE LAW

By John Mercer Langston

The battle for an effective and meaningful civil-rights law was waged by Negroes outside Congress as well as in the halls of the legislative body. On May 17, 1874, in a speech at Oberlin College, of which he was a graduate, John Mercer Langston (1829–1897) brilliantly depicted the prevailing prejudices against the enjoyment of civil liberties by Black Americans and analyzed the reasons for the enactment of the bill proposed by Senator Sumner. At the

end of his address, he urged black Americans to rally in
support of the Cuban people then engaged in the long and
bitter war for independence from Spain.

Born a slave in Virginia, Langston was emancipated
after the death of his father and owner, and sent to Ohio
where he attended school. He graduated from the literary
department of Oberlin College in 1849 and from the
theological department in 1852. He studied law and was
admitted to the bar in 1854. In 1855 he became the first
Negro elected to public office in the United States when he
won the post of township clerk in Brownhelm, Ohio. Dur-
ing the Civil War he was a recruiter for the famed Negro
regiments of the Fifty-fourth and Fifty-fifth of Massa-
chusetts and the Fifth Ohio. He was dean of the law de-
partment of Howard University from 1869 to 1876. Lang-
ston served in Congress from September 23, 1890, to
March 3, 1891, representing the Fourth District of
Virginia.

(The Oberlin speech presented here was excerpted from
John M. Langston, Freedom and Citizenship: Selected
Lectures and Addresses of John M. Langston, with an
introductory sketch by Rev. J. E. Rankin, *Washington,*
D. C., 1883, pp. 141–61.)

MR. PRESIDENT AND FRIENDS: I thank you for the invitation which brings me before you at this time, to address you
upon this most interesting occasion. I am not unmindful of the
fact that I stand in the presence of instructors, eminently distinguished for the work which they have done in the cause of
truth and humanity. Oberlin was a pioneer in the labor of
abolition.* It is foremost in the work of bringing about equality
of the Negro before the law. Thirty years ago on the first day
of last March, it was my good fortune, a boy seeking an education, to see Oberlin for the first time. Here I discovered at once
that I breathed a new atmosphere. Though poor, and a colored
boy, I found no distinction made against me in your hotel, in
your institution of learning, in your family circle. I come here
today with a heart full of gratitude, to say to you in this public
way that I not only thank you for what you did for me individually, but for what you did for the cause whose success

* Oberlin College was a center of Abolitionism before the Civil War, and
a station on the Underground Railroad. Oberlin students and professors
were involved in the Oberlin-Wellington Rescue of 1858, in which Langston's brother, Charles, played a leading role in defying the Fugitive Slave
Act of 1850. (See pp. 208–15.)

makes this day the colored American a citizen sustained in all the rights, privileges and immunities of American citizenship by law.

As our country advances in civilization, prosperity and happiness, cultivating things which appertain to literature, science and law, may your Oberlin, as in the past, so in all the future, go forward, cultivating a noble, patriotic, Christian leadership. In the name of the Negro, so largely blest and benefited by your institution, I bid you a hearty Godspeed.

Mr. President, within less than a quarter of a century, within the last fifteen years, the colored American has been raised from the condition of four-footed beasts and creeping things to the level of enfranchised manhood. Within this period the slave oligarchy of the land has been overthrown, and the nation itself emancipated from its barbarous rule. The compromise measures of 1850, including the Fugitive Slave law, together with the whole body of law enacted in the interest of slavery, then accepted as finalities, and the power of leading political parties pledged to their maintenance have, with those parties, been utterly nullified and destroyed. In their stead we have a purified Constitution and legislation no longer construed and enforced to sanction and support inhumanity and crime, but to sustain and perpetuate the freedom and the rights of us all.

Indeed, two nations have been born in a day. For in the death of slavery, and through the change indicated, the colored American has been spoken into the new life of liberty and law; while new, other and better purposes, aspirations and feelings have possessed and moved the soul of his fellow countrymen. The moral atmosphere of the land is no longer that of slavery and hate; as far as the late slave, even, is concerned, it is largely that of freedom and fraternal appreciation. . . .

Great as the change has been with regard to the legal status of the colored American, in his freedom, his enfranchisement and the exercise of political powers, he is not yet given the full exercise and enjoyment of all the rights which appertain by law to American citizenship. Such as are still denied him are withheld on the plea that their recognition would result in social equality, and his demand for them is met by considerations derived from individual and domestic opposition. Such reasoning is no more destitute of logic than law. While I hold that opinion sound which does not accept mere prejudice and caprice instead of the promptings of nature, guided by cultivated taste and wise judgment as the true basis of social recognition; and believing, too, that in a Christian community, social recognition may justly be pronounced a duty, I would not deal in this discussion with matters of society. I would justify the claim of the colored American to complete equality of rights and privileges upon well considered and accepted principles of law.

As showing the condition and treatment of the colored citizens of this country, anterior to the introduction of the Civil Rights Bill, so called, into the United States Senate by the late Honorable Charles Sumner, I ask your attention to the following words from a letter written by him:

"I wish a bill carefully drawn, supplementary to the existing Civil Rights Law, by which all citizens shall be protected in equal rights:

"1. On railroads, steamboats and public conveyances, being public carriers.

"2. At all houses in the nature of 'inns.'

"3. All licensed houses of public amusement.

"4. At all common schools.

"Can you do this? I would follow as much as possible the language of the existing Civil Rights Law, and make the new bill supplementary."

It will be seen from this very clear and definite statement of the Senator that in his judgment, in spite of and contrary to common-law rules applied in the case, certainly of all others, and recognized as fully settled, the colored citizen was denied those accommodations, facilities, advantages and privileges furnished ordinarily by common carriers, innkeepers, at public places of amusement and common schools, and which are so indispensable to rational and useful enjoyment of life that without them citizenship itself loses much of its value and liberty seems little more than a crime.

The judicial axiom, *omnes homines aequales sunt,* is said to have been given the world by the jurisconsults of the Antonine era. From the Roman, the French people inherited this legal sentiment; and, through the learning, the wisdom and patriotism of Thomas Jefferson and his Revolutionary compatriots, it was made the chief cornerstone of jurisprudence and politics. In considering the injustice done the colored American, denying him common-school advantages on general and equal terms with all others, impartial treatment in the conveyances of common carriers by sea and land, and the enjoyment of the usual accommodations afforded travelers at public inns, and in vindicating his claim to the same, it is well to bear in mind this fundamental and immutable principle upon which the Fathers built, and in the light of which our law ought to be construed and enforced. This observation has especial significance as regards the obligations and liabilities of common carriers and innkeepers; for from the civil law we have borrowed those principles largely which have controlling force in respect to these subjects. It is manifest, in view of this statement, that the law with regard to these topics is neither novel nor unsettled; and when the colored American asks its due enforcement in his behalf, he makes no unnatural and strange demand.

Denied, generally, equal school advantages, the colored citizen demands them in the name of that equality of rights and privileges which is the vital element of American law. Equal in freedom, sustained by law; equal in citizenship, defined and supported by the law; equal in the exercise of political powers, regulated and sanctioned by law; by what refinement of reasoning, or tenet of law, can the denial of common-school and other educational advantages be justified? To answer that so readeth the statute, is only to drive us back of the letter to the reasonableness, the soul of the law, in the name of which we would, as we do, demand the repeal of that enactment which is not only not law, but contrary to its simplest requirements. It may be true that that which ought to be law is not always so written; but, in this matter, that only ought to remain upon the statute book, to be enforced as to citizens and voters, which is law in the truest and best sense.

Without dwelling upon the advantages of a thorough common-school education, I will content myself by offering several considerations against the proscriptive, and in favor of the common school. A common school should be one to which all citizens may send their children, not by favor, but by right. It is established and supported by the government; its criterion is a public foundation; and one citizen has as rightful claim upon its privileges and advantages as any other. The money set apart to its organization and support, whatever the sources whence it is drawn, whether from taxation or appropriation, having been dedicated to the public use, belongs as much to one as to another citizen; and no principle of law can be adduced to justify any arbitrary classification which excludes the child of any citizen or class of citizens from equal enjoyment of the advantages purchased by such fund, it being the common property of every citizen equally, by reason of its public dedication.

Schools which tend to separate the children of the country in their feelings, aspirations and purposes, which foster and perpetuate sentiments of caste, hatred and ill will, which breed a sense of degradation on the one part and of superiority on the other, which beget clannish notions rather than teach and impress an omnipresent and living principle and faith that we are all Americans, in no wise realize our ideal of common schools, while they are contrary to the spirit of our laws and institutions.

Two separate school systems, tolerating discriminations in favor of one class against another, inflating on the one part, degrading on the other; two separate school systems, I say, tolerating such state of feeling and sentiment on the part of the classes instructed respectively in accordance therewith, cannot educate these classes to live harmoniously together, meeting the responsibilities and discharging the duties imposed by a common government in the interest of a common country.

The object of the common school is twofold. In the first place it should bring to every child, especially the poor child, a reasonable degree of elementary education. In the second place it should furnish a common education, one similar and equal to all pupils attending it. Thus furnished, our sons enter upon business or professional walks with an equal start in life. Such education the government owes to all classes of the people.

The obligations and liabilities of the common carrier of passengers can, in no sense, be made dependent upon the nationality or color of those with whom he deals. He may not, according to law, answer his engagements to one class and justify nonperformance or neglect as to another by considerations drawn from race. His contract is originally and fundamentally with the entire community, and with all its members he is held to equal and impartial obligation. On this subject the rules of law are definite, clear and satisfactory. These rules may be stated concisely as follows: It is the duty of the common carrier of passengers to receive all persons applying and who do not refuse to obey any reasonable regulations imposed, who are not guilty of gross and vulgar habits of conduct, whose characters are not doubtful, dissolute or suspicious or unequivocally bad, and whose object in seeking conveyance is not to interfere with the interests or patronage of the carrier so as to make his business less lucrative.

And, in the second place, common carriers may not impose upon passengers oppressive and grossly unreasonable orders and regulations. Were there doubt in regard to the obligation of common carriers as indicated, the authorities are abundant and might be quoted at large. Here, however, I need not make quotations. The only question which can arise as between myself and any intelligent lawyer, is as to whether the regulation made by common carriers of passengers generally in this country, by which white passengers and colored ones are separated on steamboats, railroad cars, and stage coaches, greatly to the disadvantage, inconvenience and dissatisfaction of the latter class, is reasonable. As to this question, I leave such lawyer to the books and his own conscience. We have advanced so far on this subject, in thought, feeling and purpose that the day cannot be distant when there will be found among us no one to justify such regulations by common carriers, and when they will be made to adjust themselves, in their orders and regulations with regard thereto, to the rules of the common law. The grievance of the citizen in this particular is neither imaginary nor sentimental. His experience of sadness and pain attests its reality, and the awakening sense of the people generally, as discovered in their expressions, the decisions of several of our courts, and the recent legislation of a few states, shows that this particular discrimination, inequitable as it is illegal, cannot long be tolerated in any section of our country.

The law with regard to innkeepers is not less explicit and rigid. They are not allowed to accommodate or refuse to accommodate wayfaring persons according to their own foolish prejudices or the senseless and cruel hatred of their guests.

Their duties are defined in the following language, the very words of the law:

"Inns were allowed for the benefit of travelers, who have certain privileges whilst they are in their journeys, and are in a more peculiar manner protected by law.

"If one who keeps a common inn refuses to receive a traveler as a guest into his house, or to find him victuals or lodging upon his tendering a reasonable price for the same, the innkeeper is liable to render damages in an action at the suit of the party grieved and may also be indicted and fined at the suit of the King.

"An innkeeper is not, if he has suitable room, at liberty to refuse to receive a guest who is ready and able to pay him a suitable compensation. On the contrary, he is bound to receive him, and if, upon false pretenses, he refuses, he is liable to an action."

These are doctrines as old as the common law itself; indeed, older, for they come down to us from Gaius and Papinian. All discriminations made, therefore, by the keepers of public houses in the nature of inns, to the disadvantage of the colored citizen, and contrary to the usual treatment accorded travelers, is not only wrong morally, but utterly illegal. To this judgment the public mind must soon come.

Had I the time, and were it not too great a trespass upon your patience, I should be glad to speak of the injustice and illegality, as well as inhumanity, of our exclusion, in some localities, from jury, public places of learning and amusement, the church and the cemetery. I will only say, however (and in this statement I claim the instincts, not less than the well-formed judgment of mankind, in our behalf), that such exclusion at least seems remarkable and is difficult of defense upon any considerations of humanity, law or Christianity. Such exclusion is the more remarkable and indefensible since we are fellow citizens, wielding like political powers, eligible to the same high official positions, responsible to the same degree and in the same manner for the discharge of the duties they impose; interested in the progress and civilization of a common country, and anxious, like all others, that its destiny be glorious and matchless. It is strange, indeed, that the colored American may find place in the Senate, but is denied access and welcome to the public place of learning, the theater, the church and the graveyard, upon terms accorded to all others.

But, Mr. President and friends, it ill becomes us to complain; we may not tarry to find fault. The change in public sentiment, the reform in our national legislation and jurisprudence which we this day commemorate, transcendent and admirable, augurs and guarantees to all American citizens complete equality before the law, in the protection and enjoyment of all those rights and privileges which pertain to manhood, enfranchised and dignified. To us the Thirteenth Amendment of our Constitution, abolishing slavery and perpetuating freedom; the Fourteenth Amendment establishing citizenship and prohibiting the enactment of any law which shall abridge the privileges or immunities of citizens of the United States, or which shall deny the equal protection of the laws to all American citizens; and the Fifteenth Amendment, which declares that the *right* of citizens of the United States to vote shall not be denied or abridged by the United States or by any state, on account of race, color or previous condition of servitude, are national utterances which not only recognize, but sustain and perpetuate our freedom and rights.

To the colored American, more than to all others, the language of these amendments is not vain. To use the language of the late Honorable Charles Sumner, "within the sphere of their influence no person can be created, no person can be born, with civil or political privileges not enjoyed equally by all his fellow citizens; nor can any institution be established recognizing distinction of birth. Here is the great charter of every human being, drawing vital breath upon this soil, whatever may be his condition and whoever may be his parents. He may be poor, weak, humble or black; he may be of Caucasian, Jewish, Indian or Ethiopian race; he may be of French, German, English or Irish extraction; but before the Constitution all these distinctions disappear. He is not poor, weak, humble or black; nor is he Caucasian, Jew, Indian or Ethiopian; nor is he French, German, English or Irish—he is a man, the equal of all his fellow men. He is one of the children of the state, which like an impartial parent regards all its offspring with an equal care. To some it may justly allot higher duties according to higher capacities; but it welcomes all to its equal hospitable board. The state, imitating the Divine Justice, is no respecter of persons."

With freedom established in our own country, and equality before the law promised in early federal, if not state legislation, we may well consider our duty with regard to the abolition of slavery, the establishment of freedom and free institutions upon the American continent, especially in the island of the seas, where slavery is maintained by despotic Spanish rule, and where the people declaring slavery abolished,* and appealing to the civilized world for sympathy and justification of their course, have staked all upon "the dread arbitrament of war." There can be no peace on our continent, there can be no harmony among its people, till slavery is everywhere abolished and freedom established and protected by law; the people themselves making for themselves and supporting their own government. Every nation, whether its home be an island or upon a continent, if oppressed, ought to have, like our own, a "new birth of freedom," and its "government of the people, by the people, and for the people" shall prove at once its strength and support.

Our sympathies especially go toward the struggling patriots of Cuba. We would see the "Queen of the Antilles" free from Spanish rule; her slaves all freemen, and herself advancing in her freedom, across the way of national greatness and renown. Or if her million and a half inhabitants, with their thousands of rich and fertile fields, are unable to support national independence and unity, let her not look for protection from, or annexation to, a country and government despotic and oppressive in its policy. By its proximity to our shores, by the ties of blood which connect its population and ours; by the examples

---

* At the constitutional convention at Guaimaro, April 10, 1869, six months after the Ten Years' War for independence started, the Cuban revolutionists adopted the first constitution of Free Cuba. The Twenty-fourth Article declared that "all the inhabitants of the Republic are absolutely free."

presented in our Revolutionary conflict, when France furnished succor and aid to our struggling but heroic fathers; by the lessons and examples of international law and history; by all the pledges made by our nation in favor of freedom and equal rights, the oppressed and suffering people of Cuba may justly expect, demand our sympathies and support in their struggle for freedom and independence. Especially let the colored American realize that where battle is made against despotism and oppression, wherever humanity struggles for national existence and recognition, there his sympathies should be felt, his word and succor inspiriting, encouraging and supporting. Today let us send over our word of sympathy to the struggling thousands of Cuba, among whom, as well as among the people of Porto Rico, we hope soon to see slavery, indeed, abolished,* free institutions firmly established, and good order, prosperity and happiness secured. This accomplished, our continent is dedicated to freedom and free institutions; and the nations which compose its population will enjoy sure promise of national greatness and glory. Freedom and free institutions should be as broad as our continent. Among no nations here should there be found any enslaved or oppressed. "Compromises between right and wrong, under pretense of expediency," should disappear forever; our house should be no longer divided against itself; a new cornerstone should be built into the edifice of our national, continental liberty, and those who "guard and support the structure" should accept, in all its comprehensiveness, the sentiment that all men are created equal, and that governments are established among men to defend and protect their inalienable rights to life, liberty and the pursuit of happiness.

CIVIL RIGHTS BILL

By James T. Rapier

One of the most effective speeches in Congress in support of the Civil Rights Bill was delivered on February 4, 1875, by the black Congressman from Alabama, James T. Rapier. No one better described how a black man felt as an alien in

---

* As we have seen above, Spain emerged victorious from the Ten Years' War, and slavery was not abolished in Cuba until October 7, 1886.

his own native land or more brilliantly posed the question why the black man who had given so much to save the nation was still denied his basic rights.

Rapier was born in Florence, Alabama, in 1839, of a white father and black mother. His father acknowledged him as a "natural son" and sent him to Montreal College in Canada and the University of Glasgow in Scotland. Returning to Alabama after the Civil War, Rapier was successively a delegate to the Reconstruction constitutional convention, newspaper editor, labor organizer and secretary of the Alabama Equal Rights League. In 1872 he was elected to Congress from the Second Congressional District of Alabama. He served one term, during which he fought repeatedly for civil rights. Rapier died in 1883.

(Rapier's civil-rights speech, presented here in part, is taken from the text which appeared in the Congressional Record, *43rd Congress, 1st Session, Vol. II, Part 1, pp. 565–67.)*

. . . I MUST CONFESS it is somewhat embarrassing for a colored man to urge the passage of this bill, because if he exhibits an earnestness in the matter and expresses a desire for its immediate passage, straightway he is charged with a desire for social equality, as explained by the demagogue and understood by the ignorant white man. But then it is just as embarrassing for him not to do so, for, if he remains silent while the struggle is being carried on around, and for him, he is liable to be charged with a want of interest in a matter that concerns him more than any one else, which is enough to make his friends desert his cause. So in steering away from Scylla I may run upon Charybdis. But the anomalous and, I may add, the supremely ridiculous position of the Negro at this time, in this country, compels me to say something. Here his condition is without comparison, parallel alone to itself. Just that the law recognizes my right upon his floor as a lawmaker, but that there is no law to secure to me any accommodations whatever while traveling here to discharge my duties as a Representative of a large and wealthy constituency. Here I am the peer of the proudest, but on a steamboat or car I am not equal to the most degraded. Is not this most anomalous and ridiculous? . . .

I wish to say in justice to myself that no one regrets more than I do the necessity that compels one to the manner born to come in these halls with hat in hand (so to speak) to ask at the hands of his political peers the same public rights they enjoy. And I shall feel ashamed for my country if there be any foreigners present who have been lured to our shores by the popular but untruthful declaration that this land is the asylum of the oppressed, to hear a member of the highest legislative body in the world declare from his place, upon his responsibility as a Representative, that, notwithstanding his political position, he has no civil rights that another class is bound to respect.

Here a foreigner can learn what he cannot learn in any other country, that it is possible for a man to be half free and half slave, or, in other words, he will see that it is possible for a man to enjoy political rights while he is denied civil ones; here he will see a man legislating for a free people, while his own chains of civil slavery hang about him and are far more galling than any the foreigner left behind him; here he will see what is not to be seen elsewhere, that position is no mantle of protection in our "land of the free and home of the brave"; for I am subjected to far more outrages and indignities in coming to and going from this capital in discharge of my public duties than any criminal in the country provided he be white. Instead of my position shielding me from insult, it too often invites it.

Let me cite a case. Not many months ago Mr. Cardozo, treasurer of the state of South Carolina, was on his way home from the West. His route lay through Atlanta. There he made request for a sleeping berth. Not only was he refused this, but he was denied a seat in a first-class carriage, and the parties went so far as to threaten to take his life because he insisted upon his rights as a traveler. He was compelled, a most elegant and accomplished gentleman, to take a seat in the dirty smoking car, along with the traveling rabble, or else be left, to the detriment of his public duties.

I affirm, without the fear of contradiction, that any white ex-convict (I care not what may have been his crime, nor whether the hair on the shaven side of his head has had time to grow out or not) may start with me today to Montgomery, that all the way down he will be treated as a gentleman, while I will be treated as the convict. He will be allowed a berth in a sleeping car with all its comforts, while I will be forced into a dirty, rough box with the drunkards, apple sellers, railroad hands, and next to any dead that be in transit, regardless of how far decomposition may have progressed. Sentinels are placed at the doors of the better coaches, with positive instructions to keep persons of color out; and I must do them the justice to say that they guard these sacred portals with a vigilance that would have done credit to the flaming swords at the gates of Eden. Tender, pure, intelligent young ladies are forced to travel in this way if they are guilty of the crime of color, the only unpardonable sin known in our Christian and Bible lands, where sinning against the Holy Ghost (whatever that may be) sinks into insignificance when compared with the sin of color. If from any cause we are compelled to lay over, the best bed in the hotel is his if he can pay for it, while I am invariably turned away, hungry and cold, to stand around the railroad station until the departure of the next train, it matters not how long, thereby endangering my health, while my life and property are at the mercy of any highwayman who may wish to murder and rob me.

And I state without the fear of being gainsaid, the statement of the gentleman from Tennessee to the contrary notwithstanding, that there is not an inn between Washington and Montgomery, a distance of more than a thousand miles, that will accommodate me to a bed or meal. Now, then, is there a man upon this floor who is so heartless, whose breast is so void of the better feelings, as to say that this brutal custom needs no regulation? I hold that it does and that Congress is the body to regulate it. Authority for its action is found not only in the Fourteenth Amendment to the Constitution, but by virtue of that amendment (which makes all persons born here citizens) authority is found in Article 4, Section 2, of the federal Constitution, which declares in positive language that "the citizens of each state shall have the same rights as the citizens of the several states." Let me read Mr. Brightly's comment upon this clause; he is considered good authority, I believe. In describing the several rights he says they may be all comprehended under the following general heads: "Protection by the government; the enjoyment of life and liberty, with the right to acquire and possess property of every kind, and to pursue and obtain happiness and safety; the right of a citizen of one state to pass through or to reside in any other state for purposes of trade, agriculture, professional pursuits, or otherwise."

It is very clear that the right of locomotion without hindrance and everything pertaining thereto is embraced in this clause; and every lawyer knows if any white man in antebellum times had been refused first-class passage in a steamboat or car, who was free from any contagious disease, and was compelled to go on deck of a boat or into a baggage car, and any accident had happened to him while he occupied that place, a lawsuit would have followed and damages would have been given by any jury to the plaintiff; and whether any accident had happened or not in the case I have referred to, a suit would have been brought for a denial of rights, and no one doubts what would have been the verdict. White men had rights then that common carriers were compelled to respect, and I demand the same for the colored men now.

Mr. Speaker, whether this deduction from the clause of the Constitution just read was applicable to the Negro prior to the adoption of the several late amendments to our organic law is now a question, but that it does apply to him in his new relations no intelligent man will dispute. Therefore I come to the national, instead of going to the local legislatures for relief, as has been suggested, because the grievance is national and not local; because Congress is the lawmaking power of the general government, whose duty it is to see that there be no unjust and odious discriminations made between its citizens. I look to the government in the place of the several states, because it claims my first allegiance, exacts at my hands strict obedience to its laws, and because it promises in the implied contract between every citizen and the government to protect my life and property. I have fulfilled my part of the contract to the extent I have been called upon, and I demand that the government, through Congress, do likewise. Every day my life and property are exposed, are left to the mercy of others, and will be so as long as every hotelkeeper, railroad conductor and steamboat captain can refuse me with impunity the accommodations common to other travelers. I hold further, if the government cannot secure to a citizen his guaranteed rights it ought not to call upon him to perform the same duties that are performed by another class of citizens who are in the free and full enjoyment of every civil and political right.

Sir, I submit that I am degraded as long as I am denied the public privileges common to other men, and that the members of this House are correspondingly degraded by recognizing my political equality while I occupy such humiliating position. What a singular attitude for lawmakers of this great nation to assume, rather come down to me than allow me to go up to them. Sir, did you ever reflect that this is the only Christian country where poor, finite man is held responsible for the crimes of the infinite God whom you profess to worship? But it is; I am held to answer for the crime of color, when I was not consulted in the matter. Had I been consulted, and my future fully described, I think I should have objected to being born in this Gospel land. The excuse offered for all this inhuman treatment is that they consider the Negro inferior to the white man, intellectually and morally. This reason might have been offered and probably accepted as truth some years ago, but not one now

believes him incapable of a high order of culture, except someone who is himself below the average of mankind in natural
endowments. This is not the reason, as I shall show before I
have done.

Sir, there is a cowardly propensity in the human heart that
delights in oppressing somebody else, and in the gratification
of this base desire we always select a victim that can be outraged with safety. As a general thing, the Jew has been the
subject in most parts of the world; but here the Negro is the
most available for this purpose; for this reason in part he was
seized upon, and not because he is naturally inferior to anyone
else. Instead of his enemies believing him to be incapable of a
high order of mental culture, they have shown that they believe
the reverse to be true, by taking the most elaborate pains to
prevent his development. And the smaller the caliber of the
white man the more frantically has he fought to prevent the
intellectual and moral progress of the Negro, for a simple but
good reason that he has most to fear from such a result. He does
not wish to see the Negro approach the high moral standard of
a man and gentleman.

Let me call your attention to a case in point. Some time since,
a well-dressed colored man was traveling from Augusta to Montgomery. The train on which he was stopped at a dinner house.
The crowd around the depot, seeing him well dressed, fine-
looking, and polite, concluded he must be a gentleman (which
was more than their righteous souls could stand), and straightway they commenced to abuse him. And, sir, he had to go into
the baggage car, open his trunks, show his cards, faro bank,
dice, et cetera, before they would give him any peace; or, in
other words, he was forced to give satisfactory evidence that he
was not a man who was working to elevate the moral and intellectual standards of the Negro before they would respect him.
I have always found more prejudice existing in the breast of
men who have feeble minds and are conscious of it, than in the
breast of those who have towering intellects and are aware of it.
Henry Ward Beecher reflected the feelings of the latter class
when on a certain occasion he said: "Turn the Negro loose; I am
not afraid to run the race of life with him." He could afford to
say this, all white men cannot; but what does the other class
say? "Build a Chinese wall between the Negro and the schoolhouse, discourage in him pride of character and honest ambition, cut him off from every avenue that leads to the higher
grounds of intelligence and usefulness, and then challenge
him to a contest upon the highway of life to decide the question
of superiority of race." By their acts, not by their words, the

civilized world can and will judge how honest my opponents are in their declarations that I am naturally inferior to them. No one is surprised that this class opposes the passage of the civil-rights bill, for if the Negro were allowed the same opportunities, the same rights of locomotion, the same rights to comfort in travel, how could they prove themselves better than the Negro? . . .

Mr. Speaker, time will not allow me to review the history of the American Negro, but I must pause here long enough to say that he has not been properly treated by this nation; he has purchased and paid for all, and for more than, he has yet received. Whatever liberty he enjoys has been paid for over and over again by more than two hundred years of forced toil; and for such citizenship as is allowed him he paid the full measure of his blood, the dearest price required at the hands of any citizen. In every contest, from the beginning of the Revolutionary struggle down to the War Between the States, has he been prominent. But we all remember in our late war when the government was so hard pressed for troops to sustain the cause of the Union, when it was so difficult to fill up the ranks that had been so fearfully decimated by disease and the bullet; when every train that carried to the front a number of fresh soldiers brought back a corresponding number of wounded and sick ones; when grave doubts as to the success of the Union arms had seized upon the minds of some of the most sanguine friends of the government; when strong men took counsel of their fears; when those who had all their lives received the fostering care of the nation were hesitating as to their duty in that trying hour, and others questioning if it were not better to allow the star of this Republic to go down and thus be blotted out from the great map of nations than to continue the bloodshed; when gloom and despair were widespread; when the last ray of hope had nearly sunk below our political horizon, how the Negro then came forward and offered himself as a sacrifice in the place of the nation, made bare his breast to the steel, and in it received the thrusts of the bayonet that were aimed at the life of the nation by the soldiers of that government in which the gentleman from Georgia figured as second officer.

Sir, the valor of the colored soldier was tested on many a battlefield, and today his bones lie bleaching beside every hill and in every valley from the Potomac to the Gulf; whole mute eloquence in behalf of equal rights for all before the law, is and ought to be far more persuasive than any poor language I can command.

Mr. Speaker, nothing short of a complete acknowledgement

of my manhood will satisfy me. I have no compromises to make, and shall unwillingly accept any. If I were to say that I would be content with less than any other member upon this floor I would forfeit whatever respect any one here might entertain for me, and would thereby furnish the best possible evidence that I do not and cannot appreciate the rights of a freeman— just what I am charged with by my political enemies. I cannot willingly accept anything less than my full measure of rights as a man, because I am unwilling to present myself as a candidate for the brand of inferiority, which will be as plain and lasting as the mark of Cain. If I am to be thus branded, the country must do it against my solemn protest.

Sir, in order that I might know something of the feelings of a freeman, a privilege denied me in the land of my birth, I left home last year and traveled six months in foreign lands, and the moment I put my foot upon the deck of a ship that unfurled a foreign flag from its masthead, distinctions on account of my color ceased. I am not aware that my presence on board the steamer put her off her course. I believe we made the trip in the usual time. It was in other countries than my own that I was not a stranger, that I could approach a hotel without the fear that the door would be slammed in my face. Sir, I feel this humiliation very keenly; it dwarfs my manhood, and certainly it impairs my usefulness as a citizen.

The other day when the centennial bill was under discussion I would have been glad to say a word in its favor, but how could I? How would I appear at the centennial celebration of our national freedom, with my own galling chains of slavery hanging about me? I could no more rejoice on that occasion in my present condition than the Jews could sing in their wonted style as they sat as captives beside the Babylonish streams; but I look forward to the day when I shall be in the full enjoyment of the rights of a freeman, with the same hope they indulged, that they would again return to their native land. I can no more forget my manhood, than they could forget Jerusalem.

After all, this question resolves itself to this: either I am a man or I am not a man. If one, I am entitled to all the rights, privileges and immunities common to any other class in this country; if not a man, I have no right to vote, no right to a seat here; if no right to vote, then 20 percent of the members on this floor have no right here, but, on the contrary, hold their seats in violation of the law. If the Negro has no right to vote, then one eighth of your Senate consists of members who have no shadow of a claim to the places they occupy; and if no right to vote, a half-dozen governors in the South figure as usurpers.

This is the legitimate conclusion of the argument, that the Negro is not a man and is not entitled to all the public rights common to other men, and you cannot escape it. But when I press my claims I am asked, "Is it good policy?" My answer is, "Policy is out of the question; it has nothing to do with it; that you can have no policy in dealing with your citizens; that there must be one law for all; that in this case justice is the only standard to be used, and you can no more divide justice than you can divide Deity." On the other hand, I am told that I must respect the prejudices of others. Now, sir, no one respects reasonable and intelligent prejudice more than I. I respect religious prejudices, for example; these I can comprehend. But how can I have respect for the prejudices that prompt a man to turn up his nose at the males of a certain race, while at the same time he has a fondness for the females of the same race to the extent of cohabitation? Out of four poor unfortunate colored women, who from poverty were forced to go to the lying-in branch of the Freedman's Hospital here in the District last year, three gave birth to children whose fathers were white men, and I venture to say that if they were members of this body, would vote against the civil-rights bill. Do you, can you wonder at my want of respect for this kind of prejudice? To make me feel uncomfortable appears to be the highest ambition of many white men. It is to them a positive luxury, which they seek to indulge at every opportunity.

I have never sought to compel any one, white or black, to associate with me, and never shall; nor do I wish to be compelled to associate with any one. If a man does not wish to ride with me in the streetcar, I shall not object to his hiring a private conveyance; if he does not wish to ride with me from here to Baltimore, who shall complain if he charter a special train? For a man to carry out his prejudices in this way would be manly and would leave no cause for complaint, but to crowd me out of the usual conveyance into an uncomfortable place with persons for whose manners I have a dislike, whose language is not fit for ears polite, is decidedly unmanly and cannot be submitted to tamely by anyone who has a particle of self-respect. . . .

Mr. Speaker, though there is not a line in this bill the Democracy approve of, yet they made the most noise about the school clause. Dispatches are freely sent over the wires as to what will be done with the common-school system in the several Southern states in the event this bill becomes a law. I am not surprised at this, but, on the other hand, I looked for it. Now what is the force of that school clause? It simply provides that all the children in every state where there is a school system supported in whole or in part by general taxation shall have equal advantages of school privileges. So that if perfect and ample accommodations are not made convenient for all the children, then any child has the right to go to any school where they do exist. And that is all there is in this school clause. I want some one to tell me of any measure that was intended to benefit the Negro that they have approved of. Of which one did they fail to predict evil? They declared if the Negroes were emancipated that the country would be laid waste, and that in the end he would starve, because he could not take care of himself. But this was a mistake. When the Reconstruction acts were passed and the colored men in my state were called upon to express through the ballot whether Alabama should return to the Union or not, white men threw up their hands in holy horror and declared if the Negro voted that never again would they deposit another ballot. But how does the matter stand now? Some of those very men are in the Republican ranks, and I have known them to grow hoarse in shouting for our platforms and candidates. They hurrah for our principles with all the enthusiasm of a newborn soul, and, sir, so zealous have they become that in looking at them I am amazed and am often led to doubt my faith and feel ashamed for my lukewarmness. And those who have not joined our party are doing their utmost to have the Negro vote with them. I have met them in the cabins night and day where they were imploring him, for the sake of old times, to come up and vote with them.

I submit, Mr. Speaker, that political prejudices prompt the Democracy to oppose this bill as much as anything else. In the campaign of 1868 Joe Williams, an uncouth and rather notorious colored man, was employed as a general Democratic canvasser in the South. He was invited to Montgomery to enlighten us, and while there he stopped at one of the best hotels in the city, one that would not dare entertain me. He was introduced at the meeting by the chairman of the Democratic executive committee as a learned and elegant, as well as eloquent, gentleman. In North Alabama he was invited to speak at the Seymour and Blair barbecue,* and did address one of the largest audiences, composed largely of ladies, that ever assembled in that part of the state. This I can prove by my simon-pure Democratic colleague, Mr. Sloss, for he was chairman of the com-

* The reference is to the Presidential campaign of 1868, when Horatio Seymour and Francis P. Blair were respectively the Presidential and Vice-Presidential candidates of the Democratic Party. Ulysses S. Grant, the Republican Presidential candidate, was elected.

mittee of arrangements on that occasion, and I never saw him
so radiant with good humor in all my life as when he had the
honor of introducing "his friend," Mr. Williams. In that case
they were extending their courtesies to a coarse, vulgar stranger,
because he was a Democrat, while at the same time they were
hunting me down as a partridge on the mount, night and day,
with their Ku Klux Klan, simply because I was a Republican and
refused to bow at the foot of their Baal. I might enumerate
many instances of this kind, but I forbear. But to come down
to a later period, the Greeley campaign.* The colored men who
were employed to canvass North Carolina in the interest of the
Democratic party were received at all the hotels as other men
and treated, I am informed, with marked distinction. And in the
state of Louisiana a very prominent colored gentleman saw
proper to espouse the Greeley cause, and when the fight was
over and the McEnery government saw fit to send on a committee to Washington to present their case to the President,
this colored gentleman was selected as one of that committee.
On arriving in the city of New Orleans prior to his departure he
was taken to the St. Charles, the most aristocratic hotel in the
South. When they started he occupied a berth in the sleeping
car; at every eating house he was treated like the rest of them,
no distinction whatever. And when they arrived at Montgomery,
I was at the depot, just starting for New York. Not only did the
conductor refuse to allow me a berth in the sleeping-car, but I
was also denied a seat in the first-class carriage. Now, what
was the difference between us? Nothing but our political faith.
To prove this I have only to say that just a few months before
this happened, he, along with Frederick Douglass and others,
was denied the same privileges he enjoyed in coming here. And
now that he has returned to the right party again I can tell him
that never more will he ride in another sleeping car in the
South unless this bill becomes law. There never was a truer
saying than that circumstances alter cases.

Mr. Speaker, to call this land the asylum of the oppressed is
a misnomer, for upon all sides I am treated as a pariah. I hold
that the solution of this whole matter is to enact such laws and
prescribe such penalties for their violation as will prevent any
person from discriminating against another in public places on
account of color. No one asks, no one seeks the passage of a law
that will interfere with any one's private affairs. But I do ask

* In the Presidential election of 1872, Horace Greeley was the candidate
of the Liberal Republican Party and of the Democratic Party. Grant, the
Republican candidate, was reelected.

the enactment of a law to secure me in the enjoyment of public privileges. But when I ask this I am told that I must wait for public opinion; that it is a matter that cannot be forced by law. While I admit that public opinion is a power, and in many cases is a law of itself, yet I cannot lose sight of the fact that both statute law and the law of necessity manufacture public opinion. I remember it was unpopular to enlist Negro soldiers in our late war, and after they enlisted it was equally unpopular to have them fight in the same battles; but when it became a necessity in both cases, public opinion soon came around to that point. No white father objected to the Negro's becoming food for powder if thereby his son could be saved. No white woman objected to the Negro marching in the same ranks and fighting in the same battles if by that her husband could escape burial in our savannas and return to her and her little ones.

Suppose there had been no Reconstruction Acts nor amendments to the Constitution, when would public opinion in the South have suggested the propriety of giving me the ballot? Unaided by law when would public opinion have prompted the administration to appoint members of my race to represent this government at foreign courts? It is said by some well-meaning men that the colored man has now every right under the common law; in reply I wish to say that that kind of law commands very little respect when applied to the rights of colored men in my portion of the country; the only law that we have any regard for is uncommon law of the most positive character. And I repeat, if you will place upon your statute books laws that will protect me in my rights, that public opinion will speedily follow.

Mr. Speaker, I trust this bill will become law, because it is a necessity, and because it will put an end to all legislation on this subject. It does not and cannot contemplate any such ideas as social equality; nor is there any man upon this floor so silly as to believe that there can be any law enacted or enforced that would compel one man to recognize another as his equal socially; if there be, he ought not to be here, and I have only to say that they have sent him to the wrong public building. I would oppose such a bill as earnestly as the gentleman from North Carolina, whose associations and cultivations have been of such a nature as to lead him to select the crow as his standard of grandeur and excellence in the place of the eagle, the hero of all birds and our national emblem of pride and power. I will tell him that I have seen many of his race to whose level I should object to being dragged.

Sir, it matters not how much men may differ upon the question of state and national rights; here is one class of rights, however, that we all agree upon, namely, individual rights, which include the right of every man to select associates for himself and family, and to say who shall and who shall not visit at his house. This right is God-given and custom-sanctioned, and there is, and there can be, no power overruling your decision in this matter. Let this bill become law, and not only will it do much toward giving rest to this weary country on this subject, completing the manhood of my race and perfecting his citizenship, but it will take him from the political arena as a topic of discussion where he has done duty for the last fifty years, and thus freed from anxiety respecting his political standing, hundreds of us will abandon the political fields who are there from necessity, and not from choice, and seek other and more pleasant ones; and thus relieved, it will be the aim of the colored man as well as his duty and interest, to become a good citizen, and to do all in his power to advance the interests of a common country.

THE GREAT PROBLEM TO BE SOLVED

By Frances Ellen Watkins Harper

Frances Ellen Watkins Harper (1825–1911), distinguished poet, novelist, antislavery lecturer and agent, was born in Baltimore of free parents. She was educated at her uncle's school for colored children, moved to Ohio in 1850 and taught domestic science at Union Seminary, at Columbia. In 1853 she went to Little York, Pennsylvania, to work with the Underground Railroad. She was engaged as a full-time lecturer in 1854 by the Anti-Slavery Society of Maine. Her first book, Poems on Various Subjects, *was published the same year. Her books of antislavery and religious verse sold widely, but her novel,* Iola Leroy, or The Shadows Uplifted, *is her best-known work. After the Civil War, Mrs. Harper worked as a representative of the Women's Christian Temperance Union, specializing in work among Negroes.*

On April 14, 1875, Mrs. Harper delivered an address at the Centennial Anniversary of the Pennsylvania Society for Promoting the Abolition of Slavery, held in Philadelphia. She spoke at a time when Negroes in the South

were being massacred and otherwise intimidated by il-
legal organizations like the Ku Klux Klan and the White
Leagues.

(Her speech, as presented here, is taken from Alice
Moore Dunbar, ed., Masterpieces of Negro Eloquence, *New*
York, 1914, pp. 101–6.)

LADIES AND GENTLEMEN: The great problem to be solved by the American people, if I understand it, is this: Whether or not there is strength enough in democracy, virtue enough in our civilization, and power enough in our religion to have mercy and deal justly with four millions of people but lately translated from the old oligarchy of slavery to the new commonwealth of freedom; and upon the right solution of this question depends in a large measure the future strength, progress and durability of our nation. The most important question before us colored people is not simply what the Democratic party may do against us or the Republican party do for us; but what are we going to do for ourselves? What shall we do toward developing our character, adding our quota to the civilization and strength of the country, diversifying our industry, and practicing those lordly virtues that conquer success and turn the world's dread laugh into admiring recognition? The white race has yet work to do in making practical the political axiom of equal rights and the Christian idea of human brotherhood; but while I lift mine eyes to the future I would not ungratefully ignore the past. One hundred years ago and Africa was the privileged hunting ground of Europe and America, and the flag of different nations hung a sign of death on the coasts of Congo and Guinea, and for years unbroken silence had hung around the horrors of the African slave trade. Since then Great Britain and other nations have wiped the bloody traffic from their hands and shaken the gory merchandise from their fingers, and the brand of piracy has been placed upon the African slave trade. Less than fifty years ago mob violence belched out its wrath against the men who dared to arraign the slaveholder before the bar of conscience and Christendom. Instead of golden showers upon his head, he who garrisoned the front had a halter around his neck.* Since, if I may borrow the idea, the nation has caught the old inspiration from his lips and written it in the new organic world. Less than twenty-five years ago slavery clasped

---

* In 1835, William Lloyd Garrison was dragged by an antiabolitionist mob through the streets of Boston with a rope around his neck. In order to prevent a lynching, the authorities placed him in the local prison.

hands with King Cotton, and said slavery fights and cotton conquers for American slavery. Since then slavery is dead, the
colored man has exchanged the fetters on his wrist for the ballot
in his hand. Freedom is king, and Cotton a subject.

It may not seem to be a gracious thing to mingle complaint
in a season of general rejoicing. It may appear like the ancient
Egyptians seating a corpse at their festal board to avenge the
Americans for their shortcomings when so much has been accomplished. And yet, with all the victories and triumphs which
freedom and justice have won in this country, I do not believe
there is another civilized nation under heaven where there are
half so many people who have been brutally and shamefully
murdered, with or without impunity, as in this Republic within
the last ten years. And who cares? Where is the public opinion
that has scorched with red-hot indignation the cowardly murderers of Vicksburg and Louisiana?* Sheridan lifts up the veil
from Southern society, and behind it is the smell of blood and
our bones scattered at the grave's mouth; murdered people; a
White League with its "covenant of death and agreement with
hell." And who cares? What city pauses one hour to drop a pitying tear over these mangled corpses, or has forged against the
perpetrator one thunderbolt of furious protest? But let there be
a supposed or real invasion of Southern rights by our soldiers,
and our great commercial emporium will rally its forces from
the old man in his classic shades, to clasp hands with "dead
rabbits" and "plug-uglies" in protesting against military interference. What we need today in the onward march of humanity
is a public sentiment in favor of common justice and simple
mercy. We have a civilization which has produced grand and
magnificent results, diffused knowledge, overthrown slavery,
made constant conquests over nature, and built up a wonderful
material prosperity. But two things are wanting in American
civilization—a keener and deeper, broader and tenderer sense
of justice; a sense of humanity, which shall crystallize into the
life of the nation the sentiment that justice, simple justice, is
the right, not simply of the strong and powerful, but of the
weakest and feeblest of all God's children; a deeper and broader
humanity, which will teach men to look upon their feeble brethren not as vermin to be crushed out, or beasts of burden to be
bridled and bitted, but as the children of the living God; of that
God who we may earnestly hope is in perfect wisdom and in

* The reference is to terrorist campaigns against Negroes by the White
Leagues in Mississippi and Louisiana, which resulted in the slaying of
many blacks.

perfect love working for the best good of all. Ethnologists may differ about the origin of the human race. Huxley may search for it in protoplasms, and Darwin send for the missing links,* but there is one thing of which we may rest assured—that we all come from the living God and that He is the common Father. The nation that has no reverence for man is also lacking in reverence for God and needs to be instructed.

As fellow citizens, leaving out all humanitarian views—as a mere matter of political economy—it is better to have the colored race a living force animated and strengthened by self-reliance and self-respect, than a stagnant mass, degraded and self-condemned. Instead of the North relaxing its efforts to diffuse education in the South, it behooves us for our national life to throw into the South all the healthful reconstructing influences we can command. Our work in this country is grandly constructive. Some races have come into this world and overthrown and destroyed. But if it is glory to destroy, it is happiness to save; and oh, what a noble work there is before our nation! Where is there a young man who would consent to lead an aimless life when there are such glorious opportunities before him? Before our young men is another battle—not a battle of flashing swords and clashing steel, but a moral warfare, a battle against ignorance, poverty and low social condition. In physical warfare the keenest swords may be blunted and the loudest batteries hushed; but in the great conflict of moral and spiritual progress your weapons shall be brighter for their service and better for their use. In fighting truly and nobly for others you win the victory for yourselves.

Give power and significance to your own life, and in the great work of upbuilding there is room for woman's work and woman's heart. Oh, that our hearts were alive and our vision quickened, to see the grandeur of the work that lies before. We have some culture among us, but I think our culture lacks enthusiasm. We need a deep earnestness and a lofty unselfishness to round out our lives. It is the inner life that develops the outer, and if we are in earnest the precious things lie all around our feet, and we need not waste our strength in striving after the dim and unattainable. Women, in your golden youth; mother, binding around your heart all the precious ties of life,—let no magnificence of culture, or amplitude of fortune, or refinement of sensibilities, repel you from helping the weaker and less favored. If

* Thomas Henry Huxley was the author of *Man's Place in Nature* (1863), and Charles Darwin published his famous *Origin of Species by Means of Natural Selection* in 1859.

you have ampler gifts, hold them as larger opportunities with which you can benefit others. Oh, it is better to feel that the weaker and feebler our race the closer we will cling to them, than it is to isolate ourselves from them in selfish, or careless unconcern, saying there is a lion without. Inviting you to this work I do not promise you fair sailing and unclouded skies. You may meet with coolness where you expect sympathy; disappointment where you feel sure of success; isolation and loneliness instead of heart support and cooperation. But if your lives are based and built upon these divine certitudes, which are the only enduring strength of humanity, then whatever defeat and discomfiture may overshadow your plans or frustrate your schemes, for a life that is in harmony with God and sympathy for man there is no such word as *fail*. And in conclusion, permit me to say, let no misfortunes crush you, no hostility of enemies or failure of friends discourage you. Apparent failure may hold in its rough shell the germs of a success that will blossom in time, and bear fruit throughout eternity. What seemed to be a failure around the Cross of Calvary and in the garden has been the grandest recorded success.

ORATION IN MEMORY OF ABRAHAM LINCOLN

By Frederick Douglass

On April 14, 1876, the anniversary of Lincoln's assassination and of the emancipation of the slaves in the District of Columbia, the Freedmen's Memorial Monument to Abraham Lincoln was unveiled in Lincoln Park, Washington, D. C. (The idea of the monument originated with Charlotte Scott, an ex-slave, on the day following Lincoln's assassination; Negroes contributed $16,242 toward its completion.) By a joint resolution, Congress declared the day a holiday. President Ulysses S. Grant and his Cabinet, Supreme Court Justices, and many Senators and Congressmen were present. Frederick Douglass delivered the main address on the occasion. While mainly laudatory of Lincoln, he also noted that he "was preeminently the white man's President, entirely devoted to the welfare of white men." Here is a major portion of this speech, one of the most balanced interpretations of Lincoln's attitude toward slav-

ery and the Negro. It is excerpted from Inaugural Ceremonies of the Freedmen's Memorial Monument to Abraham Lincoln, Washington City, April 14, 1876, *St. Louis, 1876, pp. 16–26.*

. . . FELLOW CITIZENS, in what we have said and done today, and in what we may say and do hereafter, we disclaim everything like arrogance and assumption. We claim for ourselves no superior devotion to the character, history and memory of the illustrious name whose monument we have here dedicated today. We fully comprehend the relation of Abraham Lincoln both to ourselves and to the white people of the United States. Truth is proper and beautiful at all times and in all places, and it is never more proper and beautiful in any case than when speaking of a great public man whose example is likely to be commended for honor and imitation long after his departure to the solemn shades, the silent continents of eternity. It must be admitted—truth compels me to admit—even here in the presence of the monument we have erected to his memory, Abraham Lincoln was not, in the fullest sense of the word, either our man or our model. In his interests, in his associations, in his habits of thought, and in his prejudices, he was a white man.

He was preeminently the white man's President, entirely devoted to the welfare of white men. He was ready and willing at any time during the first years of his administration to deny, postpone and sacrifice the rights of humanity in the colored people to promote the welfare of the white people of this country. In all his education and feeling he was an American of the Americans. He came into the Presidential chair upon one principle alone, namely, opposition to the extension of slavery. His arguments in furtherance of this policy had their motive and mainspring in his patriotic devotion to the interests of his own race. To protect, defend and perpetuate slavery in the states where it existed Abraham Lincoln was not less ready than any other President to draw the sword of the nation. He was ready to execute all the supposed guarantees of the United States Constitution in favor of the slave system anywhere inside the slave states. He was willing to pursue, recapture and send back the fugitive slave to his master, and to suppress a slave rising for liberty, though his guilty master was already in arms against the government. The race to which we belong were not the special objects of his consideration. Knowing this, I concede to you, my white fellow citizens, a preeminence in this worship at once full and supreme. First, midst and last, you and yours were the objects of his deepest affection and his most earnest solicitude. You are the children of Abraham Lincoln. We are at best only his stepchildren; children by adoption, children by forces of circumstances and necessity. To you it especially belongs to sound his praises, to preserve and perpetuate his memory, to multiply his statues, to hang his pictures high upon your walls, and commend his example, for to you he was a great and glorious friend and benefactor. Instead of supplanting you at his altar, we would exhort you to build high his monuments; let them be of the most costly material, of the most cunning workmanship; let their forms be symmetrical, beautiful and perfect; let their bases be upon solid rocks, and their summits lean against the unchanging blue, overhanging sky, and let them endure forever! But while in the abundance of your wealth, and in the fullness of your just and patriotic devotion, you do all this, we entreat you to despise not the humble offering we this day unveil to view; for while Abraham Lincoln saved for you a country, he delivered us from a bondage, according to Jefferson, one hour of which was worse than ages of the oppression your fathers rose in rebellion to oppose.

Fellow citizens, ours is no newborn zeal and devotion—merely a thing of this moment. The name of Abraham Lincoln was near and dear to our hearts in the darkest and most perilous hours of the Republic. We were no more ashamed of him when shrouded in clouds of darkness, of doubt and defeat than when we saw him crowned with victory, honor and glory. Our faith in him was often taxed and strained to the uttermost, but it never failed. When he tarried long in the mountain; when he strangely told us that we were the cause of the war; when he still more strangely told us that we were to leave the land in which we were born; when he refused to employ our arms in defense of the Union; when, after accepting our services as colored soldiers, he refused to retaliate our murder and torture as colored prisoners; when he told us he would save the Union if he could with slavery; when he revoked the Proclamation of Emancipation of General Fremont; when he refused to remove the popular commander of the Army of the Potomac, in the days of its inaction and defeat, who was more zealous in his efforts to protect slavery than to suppress rebellion; when we saw all this, and more, we were at times grieved, stunned and greatly bewildered; but our hearts believed while they ached and bled. Nor was this, even at that time, a blind and unreasoning superstition. Despite the mist and haze that surrounded him; despite the tumult, the hurry and confusion of the hour, we were able to take

a comprehensive view of Abraham Lincoln and to make reasonable allowance for the circumstances of his position. We saw
him, measured him and estimated him—not by stray utterances
to injudicious and tedious delegations, who often tried his patience; not by isolated facts torn from their connection; not by
any partial and imperfect glimpses, caught at inopportune
moments; but by a broad survey in the light of the stern logic
of great events and view of that divinity which shapes our ends,
rough hew them how we will, we came to the conclusion that
the hour and the man of our redemption had somehow met in
the person of Abraham Lincoln. It mattered little to us what
language he might employ on special occasions; it mattered
little to us, when we fully knew him, whether he was swift or
slow in his movements; it was enough for us that Abraham
Lincoln was at the head of a great movement, and was in living
and earnest sympathy with that movement, which, in the nature
of things, must go on until slavery should be utterly and forever
abolished in the United States.

When, therefore, it shall be asked what we have to do with
the memory of Abraham Lincoln, or what Abraham Lincoln had
to do with us, the answer is ready, full and complete. Though
he loved Caesar less than Rome, though the Union was more to
him than our freedom or our future, under his wise and beneficent rule we saw ourselves gradually lifted from the depths of
slavery to the heights of liberty and manhood; under his wise
and beneficent rule, and by measures approved and vigorously
pressed by him, we saw that the handwriting of ages, in the
form of prejudice and proscription, was rapidly fading away
from the face of our whole country; under his rule, and in due
time, about as soon after all as the country could tolerate the
strange spectacle, we saw our brave sons and brothers laying off
the rags of bondage and being clothed all over in the blue uni-
forms of the soldiers of the United States; under his rule we
saw two hundred thousand of our dark and dusky people responding to the call of Abraham Lincoln and, with muskets on
their shoulders and eagles on their buttons, timing their high
footsteps to liberty and union under the national flag; under his
rule we saw the independence of the black republic of Haiti, the
special object of slaveholding aversion and horror, fully recognized, and her minister, a colored gentleman, duly received here
in the city of Washington;* under his rule we saw the internal

---

* The United States government extended diplomatic recognition to
Haiti and Liberia in 1862.

slave trade, which so long disgraced the nation, abolished, and slavery abolished in the District of Columbia;* under his rule we saw for the first time the law enforced against the foreign slave trade, and the first slave trader hanged like any other pirate or murderer;† under his rule, assisted by the greatest captain of our age, and his inspiration, we saw the Confederate states, based upon the idea that our race must be slaves and slaves forever, battered to pieces and scattered to the four winds; under his rule, and in the fullness of time, we saw Abraham Lincoln, after giving the slaveholders three months' grace in which to save their hateful slave system, penning the immortal paper, which, though special in its language, was general in its principles and effect, making slavery forever impossible in the United States. Though we waited long, we saw all this and more.

Can any colored man, or any white man friendly to the freedom of all men, ever forget the night which followed the first day of January, 1863, when the world was to see if Abraham Lincoln would prove to be as good as his word? I shall never forget that memorable night, when in a distant city I waited and watched at a public meeting, with three thousand others not less anxious than myself, for the word of deliverance which we have heard read today. Nor shall I ever forget the outburst of joy and thanksgiving that rent the air when the lightning brought to us the Emancipation Proclamation. In that happy hour we forgot all delay and forgot all tardiness, forgot that the President had bribed the rebels to lay down their arms by a promise to withhold the bolt which would smite the slave system with destruction; and we were thenceforward willing to allow the President all the latitude of time, phraseology, and every honorable device that statesmanship might require for the achievement of a great and beneficent measure of liberty and progress.

Fellow citizens, there is little necessity on this occasion to speak at length and critically of this great and good man, and of his high mission in the world. That ground has been fully occupied and completely covered both here and elsewhere. The whole field of fact and fancy has been gleaned and garnered. Any man can say things that are true of Abraham Lincoln, but no man can say anything that is new of Abraham Lincoln. His

* Slavery was abolished in the District of Columbia by act of Congress in April, 1862.
† Nathaniel P. Gordon was captured with his ship *Erie*, with 893 slaves aboard, off the African coast by a United States war vessel. He was hanged on February 7, 1862.

personal traits and public acts are better known to the American people than are those of any other man of his age. He was a mystery to no man who saw him and heard him. Though high in position, the humblest could approach him and feel at home in his presence. Though deep, he was transparent; though strong, he was gentle; though decided and pronounced in his convictions, he was tolerant toward those who differed from him, and patient under reproaches. Even those who only knew him through his public utterance obtained a tolerably clear idea of his character and personality. The image of the man went out with his words, and those who read them knew him.

I have said that President Lincoln was a white man and shared the prejudices common to his countrymen toward the colored race. Looking back to his times and to the condition of his country, we are compelled to admit that this unfriendly feeling on his part may be safely set down as one element of his wonderful success in organizing the loyal American people for the tremendous conflict before them, and bringing them safely through that conflict. His great mission was to accomplish two things: first, to save his country from dismemberment and ruin; and, second, to free his country from the great crime of slavery. To do one or the other, or both, he must have the earnest sympathy and the powerful cooperation of his loyal fellow countrymen. Without this primary and essential condition to success his efforts must have been vain and utterly fruitless. Had he put the abolition of slavery before the salvation of the Union, he would have inevitably driven from him a powerful class of the American people and rendered resistance to rebellion impossible. Viewed from the genuine abolition ground, Mr. Lincoln seemed tardy, cold, dull and indifferent; but measuring him by the sentiment of his country, a sentiment he was bound as a statesman to consult, he was swift, zealous, radical and determined.

Though Mr. Lincoln shared the prejudices of his white fellow countrymen against the Negro, it is hardly necessary to say that in his heart of hearts he loathed and hated slavery. . . .* The man who could say, "Fondly do we hope, fervently do we pray, that this mighty scourge of war shall soon pass away, yet if God wills it continue till all the wealth piled by two hundred years of bondage shall have been wasted, and each drop of blood drawn by the lash shall have been paid for by one drawn by the sword,

---

* "I am naturally anti-slavery. If slavery is not wrong, nothing is wrong. I cannot remember when I did not so think and feel."—Letter of Mr. Lincoln to Mr. Hodges, of Kentucky, April 4, 1864.—F.D.

the judgments of the Lord are true and righteous altogether,"
gives all needed proof of his feeling on the subject of slavery.
He was willing, while the South was loyal, that it should have
its pound of flesh, because he thought that it was so nominated
in the bond; but farther than this no earthly power could make
him go.

Fellow citizens, whatever else in this world may be partial,
unjust and uncertain, time—time!—is impartial, just and certain in its action. In the realm of mind, as well as in the realm
of matter, it is a great worker, and often works wonders. The
honest and comprehensive statesman, clearly discerning the
needs of his country and earnestly endeavoring to do his whole
duty, though covered and blistered with reproaches, may safely
leave his course to the silent judgment of time. Few great public
men have ever been the victims of fiercer denunciation than
Abraham Lincoln was during his administration. He was often
wounded in the house of his friends. Reproaches came thick and
fast upon him from within and from without, and from opposite
quarters. He was assailed by Abolitionists; he was assailed by
slaveholders; he was assailed by the men who were for peace at
any price; he was assailed by those who were for a more vigorous prosecution of the war; he was assailed for not making the
war an abolition war; and he was bitterly assailed for making
the war an abolition war.

But now behold the change: the judgment of the present hour
is that, taking him for all in all, measuring the tremendous
magnitude of the work before him, considering the necessary
means to ends, and surveying the end from the beginning, infinite wisdom has seldom sent any man into the world better
fitted for his mission than Abraham Lincoln. His birth, his
training and his natural endowments, both mental and physical,
were strongly in his favor. Born and reared among the lowly,
a stranger to wealth and luxury, compelled to grapple singlehanded with the flintiest hardships of life, from tender youth
to sturdy manhood, he grew strong in the manly and heroic
qualities demanded by the great mission to which he was called
by the votes of his countrymen. The hard condition of his early
life, which would have depressed and broken down weaker men,
only gave greater life, vigor and buoyancy to the heroic spirit of
Abraham Lincoln. He was ready for any kind and any quality
of work. What other young men dreaded in the shape of toil, he
took hold of with the utmost cheerfulness.

> A spade, a rake, a hoe,
> A pick-axe, or a bill;

A hook to reap, a scythe to mow,
A flail, or what you will.

All day long he could split heavy rails in the woods, and half the night long he could study his English grammar by the uncertain flare and glare of the light made by a pine knot. He was at home on the land with his ax, with his maul, with gluts and his wedges; and he was equally at home on water, with his oars, with his poles, with his planks, and with his boat hooks. And whether in his flatboat on the Mississippi River, or at the fireside of his frontier cabin, he was a man of work. A son of toil himself, he was linked in brotherly sympathy with the sons of toil in every loyal part of the Republic. This very fact gave him tremendous power with the American people, and materially contributed not only to selecting him to the Presidency, but in sustaining his administration of the government.

Upon his inauguration as President of the United States, an office, even when assumed under the most favorable conditions, fitted to tax and strain the largest abilities, Abraham Lincoln was met by a tremendous crisis. He was called upon not merely to administer the government, but to decide, in the face of terrible odds, the fate of the Republic.

A formidable rebellion rose in his path before him; the Union was already practically dissolved; his country was torn and rent asunder at the center. Hostile armies were already organized against the Republic, armed with the munitions of war which the Republic had provided for its own defense. The tremendous question for him to decide was whether his country should survive the crisis and flourish, or be dismembered and perish. His predecessor in office had already decided the question in favor of national dismemberment, by denying to it the right of self-defense and self-preservation—a right which belongs to the meanest insect.

Happily for the country, happily for you and for me, the judgment of James Buchanan, the patrician, was not the judgment of Abraham Lincoln, the plebeian. He brought his strong common sense, sharpened in the school of adversity, to bear upon the question. He did not hesitate, he did not doubt, he did not falter; but at once resolved that at whatever peril, at whatever cost, the union of the states should be preserved. A patriot himself, his faith was strong and unwavering in the patriotism of his countrymen. Timid men said before Mr. Lincoln's inauguration, that we had seen the last President of the United States. A voice in influential quarters said, "Let the Union slide." Some said that a Union maintained by the sword was worthless. Others said a rebellion of eight million cannot be suppressed; but in the midst of all this tumult and timidity, and against all this, Abraham Lincoln was clear in his duty and had an oath in heaven. He calmly and bravely heard the voice of doubt and fear all around him; but he had an oath in heaven, and there was not power enough on earth to make this honest boatman, backwoodsman, and broad-handed splitter of rails evade or violate that sacred oath. He had not been schooled in the ethics of slavery; his plain life had favored his love of truth. He had not been taught that treason and perjury were the proof of honor and honesty. His moral training was against his saying one thing when he meant another. The trust that Abraham Lincoln had in himself and in the people was surprising and grand, but it was also enlightened and well founded. He knew the American people better than they knew themselves, and his truth was based upon this knowledge.

Fellow citizens, the fourteenth day of April, 1865, of which this is the eleventh anniversary, is now and will ever remain a memorable day in the annals of this Republic. It was on the evening of this day, while a fierce and sanguinary rebellion was in the last stages of its desolating power; while its armies were broken and scattered before the invincible armies of Grant and Sherman; while a great nation, torn and rent by war, was already beginning to raise to the skies loud anthems of joy at the dawn of peace, it was startled, amazed, and overwhelmed by the crowning crime of slavery—the assassination of Abraham Lincoln. It was a new crime, a pure act of malice. No purpose of the rebellion was to be served by it. It was the simple gratification of a hell-black spirit of revenge. But it has done good after all. It has filled the country with a deeper abhorrence of slavery and a deeper love for the great liberator.

Had Abraham Lincoln died from any of the numerous ills to which flesh is heir; had he reached that good old age of which his vigorous constitution and his temperate habits gave promise; had he been permitted to see the end of his great work; had the solemn curtain of death come down but gradually, we should still have been smitten with a heavy grief, and treasured his name lovingly. But dying as he did die, by the red hand of violence, killed, assassinated, taken off without warning, not because of personal hate—for no man who knew Abraham Lincoln could hate him—but because of his fidelity to union and liberty, he is doubly dear to us, and his memory will be precious forever.

Fellow citizens, I end, as I began, with congratulations. We have done a good work for our race today. In doing honor to the memory of our friend and liberator, we have been doing highest honors to ourselves and those who come after us; we have been fastening ourselves to a name and fame imperishable and immortal; we have also been defending ourselves from a blighting scandal. When now it shall be said that the colored man is soulless, that he has no appreciation of benefits or benefactors; when the foul reproach of ingratitude is hurled at us, and it is attempted to scourge us beyond the range of human brotherhood, we may calmly point to the monument we have this day erected to the memory of Abraham Lincoln.

THE SIOUX'S REVENGE

By B. T. Tanner

On June 25, 1876, Colonel George A. Custer and his army were annihilated in the Battle of the Little Big Horn. Custer's "last stand" against Crazy Horse and Sitting Bull made him a hero to most white Americans, but black Americans did not mourn his death. At the Sabbath service at Bethel Church in Philadelphia, July 13, 1876, two black speakers discussed the fatal outcome of Custer's war against the Sioux Indians in Dakota. One was Dr. Henry McNeal Turner, who, in the course of his remarks about the retributive justice of God, said: "I am sorry for the General,* as I would be for any other man, but I could not forget that the General has been an apologist, and a defender of those who have been murdering Republicans in the South, and that hundreds of black men greater than General Custer ever was are sleeping in bloody graves, with the sanction and approval of this same picayune General. . . . Thousands of our race have been murdered for nothing except to gratify the ungodly spleen of such men as Custer, and no tears were shed for them." Dr. Turner was followed by the Reverend B. T. Tanner, editor of The Christian Recorder. *Here are Tanner's remarks, taken from the text which appeared in* The Christian Recorder, *July 20, 1876.*

* Custer had been a major general during the Civil War, but he had lost his title when the volunteer army was disbanded following Appomattox.

I CAN ALMOST SEE the grim visage of the terrible Sioux light up with joy at the idea of having at last got revenge of the "long-haired chief"; almost hear the unearthy laughter, if a Sioux ever laughs, as around his campfire he tells of the slaughter of the fatal June twenty-fifth. Say what you will, the Sioux has a human soul within him—a soul that is conscious of wrongs perpetrated upon his tribe, until it has become as an outcast in its own land. And, taught by a Christian government that the proper thing to do in the case of wrongs perpetrated is to seek revenge, he has acted upon it, to the grief of the whole nation. But why should the nation grieve other than it is human to grieve for friends stricken down. Surely it cannot expect other than that they may perish by the sword, who take the sword. Of all our military captains, Custer was the one who took pleasure in the sword. He was the *beau sabreur* of our Army and with joy did he unsheathe it to strike down the "red nagurs" of the Far West—the "red nagurs," as the men of his command felt free to call the Indians in his presence. Custer hated the Indians, as he hated any man of color. Upon the morning of his fatal departure from the main body of his troops, his insisting upon having his command "homogeneous" occasioned the absence of comrades that might possibly have saved him and his brave Seventh. But alas, the offer was rejected.*

Of course, we gathered here today do not feel as the nation feels, nor can we—nor can any Negro. Does one say he does? He is either a fool or a hypocrite. Our blood has flowed and is flowing too freely for us to go into any hysterics of grief for the loss of this commander and his command; however gallant he, however patriotic they were. Have we tears to shed—and we have—we shed them for the scores and hundreds of our people who die violently every day in the South. Have we a heart to bleed, it is rather for our brothers cowardly assaulted and more cowardly riddled with Southern bullets. It cannot be that all the blood shedding is to be on one side.

Far be it from me to have had one so eagle-like as George A. Custer slain by warlike savages. Neither would I have had him fighting them. By the sacred obligations of treaty, no white man

* Black soldiers had volunteered to assist Custer's army, but had been rejected. However, Isaiah Dorman, who had served as a courier for the War Department in the Dakota territory, and may have been part Sioux, was assigned to Custer's command at the Colonel's request for an interpreter, and was the only black man in the expedition. Dorman was among the 264 men who fought and died with Custer. For reasons never made clear, the Sioux did not scalp and mutilate Dorman as they did the white soldiers.

had any right or business to the Black Hill country. It belongs to the Sioux, and is guaranteed him by the nation. As well might the President allow men to come and put me out of my own house, as allow settlers to possess themselves of that region. If, therefore, the Sioux make war for his rights he does no more than the common law sanctions and the thing to do is not to fight him, but to secure him his right.

HOW LONG? HOW LONG, O HEAVEN?

By Rev. Henry McNeal Turner

The wave of brutal assaults on defenseless Negroes in the South by the Ku Klux Klan and other extralegal organizations reached its climax on July 9, 1876, in Hamburg, South Carolina. The Negro militia of the city was attacked by three hundred armed whites and ordered to give up their arms. When they refused, the whites opened fire on the building in which the militia were assembled. A piece of artillery was used to attack the building, and as they were captured, five of the black militiamen were marched out, one by one, and shot to death in the presence of a large body of their captors. Others were wounded, several mortally. Governor D. H. Chamberlain of South Carolina wrote that the Hamburg massacre "presents a darker picture of human cruelty than the slaughter of Custer and his soldiers, for they were shot in open battle. The victims at Hamburg were murdered in cold blood after they had surrendered and were utterly defenseless."

Bitterly denouncing the merciless attacks upon his people in the South, Henry McLean Turner delivered a stinging sermon at Union Church in Philadelphia, August 5, 1876. It is interesting that Turner's suggestion that black Americans appeal to European nations for assistance in their struggle for survival anticipated such appeals to the Paris Peace Conference at Versailles and to the United Nations.

Following are some of Turner's remarks, taken from the printed text, which appeared in The Christian Recorder, *August 10, 1876.*

In 1822 the authorities of South Carolina hanged twenty-eight colored men because they were suspicioned of conspiring to assert and take their freedom—six at one time, twenty-two at another—and yet the blood of a mouse was not shed, throughout the whole so-called conspiracy.* Nevertheless, upon this trumped-up charge, they hanged several colored men, who, for Christian integrity and loyalty to law and order, were as far ahead of the Calhouns, Rhetts, Brookses, Adamses, et cetera, as Gabriel is ahead of the devil. Yet, when a disloyal white general and his diabolical crew, incarnate fiends, brutally murder and maim for life nearly or quite a dozen of the colored defenders of that state and of the nation, scores of newspapers loom up with wicked apologies, and thousands of pretended church members openly endorse the act. Still we talk about this being a Christian country. Did you ever read the history of the Dark Ages? I have, and I have read of nothing being perpetrated during that long night of dissipation and cruelty, which surpassed the deeds of horror that have been committed in Louisiana, Georgia, Mississippi, South Carolina, and other states, where not only men pretend to be civilized, but Christianized.

The acts of blood and carnage which have disgraced this nation for the last half-dozen years and are justified by a whole party that even essays to make a President are so revolting to the very instincts of a savage that I should not be surprised to see Hottentots coming as missionaries to this country. The cold-blooded murders that have been perpetrated in this country with impunity and silent approval could not have gone on in any European country without causing a war and arousing the whole continent.

And if we colored people were not so blind and stupid, we would hold a convention somewhere and send a delegation to England, Germany, France, or to all the civilized countries in the Old World, and ask them to interfere in our behalf and save us from mad frenzy of infuriated mobs, before whom the national government, with its immense army and navy, quails and sinks in the dust. I had rather live under a monarch, autocrat,

* In Charleston, South Carolina, in 1822, a huge slave plot was uncovered. Its leader was a free black carpenter, Denmark Vesey, who had bought his own liberty when he won a $1,500 raffle. The conspiracy had been planned for four years and the slaves involved had hidden away weapons and ammunition. The authorities, alerted by two house slaves, arrested 131 suspects. Federal troops stood by to protect the city as the 28 blacks found guilty and sentenced to death were led to the gallows.

despot, or under any impartial authority than pretend to live under a mobocracy, with no power in the state or nation to quell and bid them stop. How long? How long, O Heaven, before this condition of things will change? When will thy justice, O God, avenge our wrongs?

SECTION III

The Post-Reconstruction Period

1877–1915

SOCIALISM: THE REMEDY FOR THE EVILS OF SOCIETY

By Peter H. Clark

Peter H. Clark, principal of the Colored High School in Cincinnati, Ohio, was probably the first American Negro Socialist. He was a Republican until 1877, when, disillusioned with the Republican party's indifference to the problems of Negroes in the South and concerned about the growing power of industrial capitalists, he joined the Socialist movement, becoming a member of the Workingmen's Party of the United States (founded in Philadelphia in 1876), and publicly proclaimed himself in favor of Socialism. Following is the speech Clark delivered at Cincinnati on July 22, 1877, to a huge crowd of striking railroad workers. The great railroad strike of 1877 began in July when the principal railroads instituted a third ten-percent wage cut since the beginning of the depression in 1873. At Martinsburg, West Virginia, a strike broke out, and spontaneously, without united leadership, it spread to a dozen railroad centers, including Cincinnati. Scores were killed during the strike, millions of dollars' worth of property burned, and hundreds of factories closed by strikers. President Rutherford B. Hayes used federal troops against strikers—the second time the United States Army was sent in to break a strike. This was the setting for Clark's speech. The Cincinnati Commercial *(July 23, 1877), which published the speech in full,* commented: "The intelligent colored teacher and speaker was introduced . . . as the first speaker, and was well received. His calm face had a soothing effect upon the excited multitude." Here, so far as is known, is the first speech of a black American Socialist.*

* Extracts from this speech can be found in Herbert G. Gutman, "Peter H. Clark: Pioneer Negro Socialist, 1877," *Journal of Negro Education,* Fall, 1965, pp. 413–18.

GENTLEMEN: If I had the choosing of a motto for this meeting, I should select the words of the patriotic and humane Abraham Lincoln, "With malice toward none, with charity for all, with firmness in the right as God gives us to see the right." These words, so full of that charity which we should exercise toward each other, are especially suited to this day and time, when wrongs long condemned have at last been resisted and men are bleeding and dying in the busy centers of our population, and all over the land other men, with heated passions, are assembling to denounce the needless slaughter of innocent men who, driven by want, have appealed to force for that justice which was otherwise refused to them. . . .

I sympathize in this struggle with the strikers, and I feel sure that in this I have the cooperation of nine tenths of my fellow citizens. The poor man's lot is at best a hard one. His hand-to-hand struggle with the wolf of poverty leaves him no leisure for any of the amenities of life, his utmost rewards are a scanty supply of food, scanty clothing, scanty shelter, and if perchance he escapes a pauper's grave [he] is fortunate. Such a man deserves the aid and sympathy of all good people, especially when, in the struggle for life, he is pitted against a powerful organization such as the Baltimore and Ohio Railroad or Pennsylvania Central. The Baltimore and Ohio Railroad was taken possession of by the government during the war, and was rebuilt in a manner, from end to end. Such a firm roadway, such tunnels and bridges, are rarely seen as are possessed by that road, and at the end the road was turned over to its owners in a better condition than it had ever been, so that much of the outlay which other roads are compelled to make was saved to this. They were paid for the use of the road many millions of dollars and the managers have lately declared a dividend of ten percent, and if their stock was watered, as I have no doubt it is, this ten percent is equivalent to fifteen or twenty percent upon the capital actually invested in it. Yet this road, so built, so subsidized, so prosperous, if we may judge from its dividend, declares itself compelled to put the wages of its employees down to starvation rates. Either they were not honestly able to declare that dividend or they are able to pay living wages to the men whom they employ. The blood of those men murdered at Baltimore cries from the ground against these men who by their greed have forced their men to the desperate measure of a strike, and then invoked the strong arm of the government to slaughter them in their misery.

The too-ready consent of the state and national governments to lend themselves to the demand of these wealthy corporations cannot be too severely condemned. Has it come to this, that the President of a private corporation can, by the click of a telegraphic instrument, bring state and national troops into the field to shoot down American citizens guilty of no act of violence? For you observe that neither at Grafton, Baltimore or Pittsburgh was there violence offered to persons or property until the troops were deployed upon the scene. At Grafton it is noticeable that women, wives and mothers, were the chief forces employed by the strikers to keep others from taking their places.

The sight of the soldiery fired the hot blood of the wronged men, and they met force with force. Whether they are put down or not, we are thankful that the American citizen, as represented by these men, was not slave enough to surrender without resistance the right to appeal for a redress of grievances. When that day comes that a mere display of force is sufficient to awe a throng of Americans into submission, the people will have sunk too low to be entrusted with self-government.

Those men will be avenged—nobly avenged. Capital has been challenged to the contest; and in the arena of debate, to which in a few days the question will be remanded, the American people will sit as judges, and just as surely as we stand here, their decision will be against monopolists and in favor of the workingmen. In twenty years from today there will not be a railroad in the land belonging to a private corporation; all will be owned by the government and worked in the interests of the people. Machinery and land will, in time, take the same course, and cooperation instead of competition will be the law of society. The miserable condition into which society has fallen has but one remedy, and that is to be found in Socialism.

Observe how all civilized communities pass from a condition of what is called prosperity to one of depression and distress. Observe how continually these fluctuations occur; how the intervals between them grow shorter; how each one is more violent than the last, the distress produced more widespread. Observe, too, that after each the number of capitalists decrease, while those who remain grow more wealthy and more powerful, while those who have failed join the great army of workers who hang forever on the ragged edge of pauperism.

The so-called periods of prosperity are more properly periods of unrestrained speculation. Money accumulates in the hands of the capitalists, [through (?)] some governmental device as a tariff or the issue of greenbacks. This abundance tempts men to embark in business enterprises which seem to promise rich returns. For a time all goes well, shops are crowded with busy

men, and all [are] ready to say, "Behold how prosperous we are!"
But there comes a check to all this. The manufacturers begin to
talk about a glutted market. There has been overproduction.
There comes the period of sharp competition. Prices are reduced, goods are sold at cost—below cost—then comes the
crash, bosses fail, shops are closed, men are idle, and the
miserable workmen stand forth, underbidding each other in the
labor market. If the competition be too sharp, they resort to
strikes as in the present instance. Then comes violence, lawlessness, bloodshed and death.

People who talk of the anarchy of socialism surely cannot
have considered these facts. If they had, they would have discovered not a little of anarchy on their side of the question.

It is folly to say that a condition of poverty is a favorable
one, and to point to men who have risen to affluence from that
condition. For one man who is strong through the hindrances
of poverty, there are ten thousand who fail. If you take ten
thousand men and weigh them with lead and cast them into
the midst of Lake Erie, a few may swim out but the majority
will be drowned.

This condition of poverty is not a favorable one either for
the individual or for the nation. Especially is it an unfavorable
condition for a nation whose government lies in the hands of
all its citizens. A monarchy or an aristocracy can afford to have
the mass of its citizens steeped in poverty and ignorance. Not
so in a republic. Here every man should be the owner of wealth
enough to render him independent of the threats or bribes of
the demagogue. He should be the owner of wealth enough to
give leisure for that study which will qualify him to study and
understand the deep questions of public policy which are
continually demanding solution. The more men there are who
have this independence, this leisure, the safer we are as a
nation; reduce the number, and the fewer there are, the more
dangerous the situation. So alarming has been the spread of
ignorance and poverty in the past generation, that whole cities
in our land—whole states, indeed—are at the mercy of an
ignorant rabble who have no political principle except to vote
for the men who pay the most on election days and who promise
to make the biggest dividend of public stealing. This is sadly
true, nor is the Negro, scarcely ten years from slavery, the
chief sinner in this respect.

That this evil of poverty is partially curable, at least, I am
justified in thinking, because I find each of the great political
parties offering remedies for the hard times and the consequent
poverty. Many wise men, learned in political economy, assure

us that their doctrines, faithfully followed, will result in a greater production of wealth and a more equal division of the same. But as I have said before, there is but one efficacious remedy proposed, and that is found in Socialism.

The present industrial organization of society has been faithfully tried and has proven a failure. We get rid of the king, we get rid of the aristocracy, but the capitalist comes in their place, and in the industrial organization and guidance of society his little finger is heavier than their loins. Whatever Socialism may bring about, it can present nothing more anarchical than is found in Grafton, Baltimore and Pittsburgh today. . . .

To increase the volume of the currency, which is the remedy proposed by some, means simply that money shall be made so abundant that the capitalist, in despair of any legitimate returns in the way of interest, shall embark in any and all enterprises which promise returns for the idle cash in his coffers. It means a stimulation of production in a community already suffering from excess of production; it means speculation, competition, finally a reduction of values, bankruptcy, ruin. The American people have traveled that path so frequently in the past fifty years that it requires no prophetic powers to map out the certain course which will be pursued. Already our capitalists rush to invest their money at four and a half percent in markets which a short time since gave readily two percent a month. Increase your volume—let it be either greenbacks or silver—and we enter on the career I have described with a certainty that the gulf at the end is deeper and more hopeless than the one in which we now wallow.

Trades-unions, Grangers, Sovereigns of Industry, cooperative stores and factories are alike futile.* They are simply combina-

---

* During the depression years many radicals grew to believe that trade-unions and strikes were useless in solving the problems of workers under capitalism.

Grangers, or Patrons of Husbandry, were farmers' organizations formed in the Midwest after the Civil War. Although they concerned themselves with educational and social activities, their principal objective was the furtherance of state legislation designed to protect farmers against the economic abuses of railroads, storage warehouses and grain elevators.

The Order of the Sovereigns of Industry grew out of the Grangers and was mainly concerned with establishing consumers' cooperatives for the distribution of necessaries of life among wage earners. The Sovereigns cooperated in several cases with the Patrons of Husbandry, and even united with the Grangers to maintain a cooperative store. The total membership of the Sovereigns of Industry in 1875–76 was said to be 40,000, of whom 75 percent were in New England and 43 percent in Massachusetts. Its decline started in 1875, and by 1878 it was passing out of existence.

tions of laborers who seek to assume toward their more unfortunate fellows who are not members the attitude that the
capitalist assumes toward them. They incorporate into their
constitutions all the evil principles which afflict society.
Competition, overproduction mark their stores and factories as
much as do those of individual enterprises, and when the periodic crash comes, they succumb as readily as any.

All these plans merely poultice the ulcer in the body politic
which needs Constitutional treatment. The momentary improvement they produce is always succeeded by a corresponding depression. The old fable of Sisyphus is realized, and the heavy
stone rolled to the top of the mountain with infinite labor rolls
back again.

The government must control capital with a strong hand. It is
merely the accumulated results of industry, and there would
be no justice should a few score bees in the hive take possession
of the store of honey and dole it out to the workers in return
for services which added to their superabundant store. Yet
such is the custom of society.

Future accumulations of capital should be held sacredly for
the benefit of the whole community. Past accumulations may be
permitted to remain in private hands until, from their very use-
lessness, they will become a burden which their owners will
gladly surrender.

Machinery too, which ought to be a blessing but is proving to
be a curse to the people should be taken in hand by the government and its advantages distributed to all. Captain Cutter wrote
in his song of steam:

> Soon I intend ye may go and play,
> While I manage this world myself.

Had he written, ye may go and starve, it would have been
nearer the truth. Machinery controlled in the interests of labor
would afford that leisure for thought, for self-culture, for
giving and receiving refining influences, which are so essential
to the full development of character. "The ministry of wealth"
would not be confined to a few, but would be a benefit to all.

Every railroad in the land should be owned or controlled by
the government. The title of private owners should be extinguished, and the ownership vested in the people. All a road will
need to meet will be a running expense and enough to replace
waste. The people can then enjoy the benefit of travel, and where
one man travels now, a thousand will travel then. There will
be no strikes, for the men who operate the road will be the
recipient of its profits.

Finally, we want governmental organization of labor so that ruinous competition and ruinous overproduction shall equally be avoided, and these commercial panics which sweep over and engulf the world will be forever prevented.

It will be objected that this is making our government a machine for doing for the citizen everything which can be more conveniently done by combined than by individual effort. Society has already made strides in the direction of Socialism. Every drop of water we draw from hydrants, the gas that illumines our streets at night, the paved streets upon which we walk, our parks, our schools, our libraries, are all outgrowths of the Socialistic principle. In that direction lies safety.

Choose ye this day which course ye shall pursue.

Let us, finally, not forget that we are American citizens, that the right of free speech and of a free press is enjoyed by us. We are exercising today the right to assemble and complain of our grievances. The courts of the land are open to us, and we hold in our hands the all-compelling ballot.

There is no need for violent counsels or violent deeds. If we are patient and wise, the future is ours.

I PROTEST AGAINST HAYES'S SOUTHERN POLICY

By Jesse Lawson

On March 4, 1877, Rutherford B. Hayes was elected President of the United States, the victor in the disputed election of 1876. The victory of the Republican Presidential candidate had been achieved as a result of a bargain with the Southern Democrats in which he agreed to remove the federal troops from the last remaining Southern states and permit the people of South Carolina and Louisiana the right to control their own affairs in their own way, "subject to the Constitution of the United States and the laws made in pursuance hereof." The Southern white-supremacists were not disturbed by the allusion to the Constitution and the laws, for once the federal troops were removed, they would deal with the Constitution as they saw fit. Soon after his inauguration, Hayes withdrew federal troops from

Columbia, South Carolina, and New Orleans—a step which assured the complete triumph of the white-supremacists in the South.

In August, 1877, the black citizens of New Jersey met in convention at Princeton to discuss "the President's Southern policy, the faltering of the Northern Republicans, and the wrongs and sufferings which so many of our brethren (if we are not) are made now to sustain." At the gathering, Jesse Lawson of Plainfield delivered an address attacking Hayes's Southern policy of which the following excerpt was published by The Christian Recorder, *August 30, 1877.*

ALTHOUGH constitutionally free and entitled to the elective franchise, the colored people in most parts of the country have been deprived of rights that belong to American citizens. In the past election, cunning and designing politicians have urged the black man to hazard life and property in behalf of Republican interests, and what has been the result?

The question of the hour is, Can black men trust the Republican party? On the seventh of November last, his Excellency the Honorable Rutherford B. Hayes was elected President of the United States. In the Electoral College of 369 votes it was agreed by the Returning Boards of the several states that Mr. Hayes was elected by one vote. The same Returning Boards that declared the states of South Carolina and Louisiana for Hayes and Wheeler, declared them in favor of Chamberlain and Packard respectively.* The same persons who voted for Hayes and Wheeler in those states, voted for Chamberlain and Packard. On the fifth of last March Mr. Hayes was inaugurated and inducted into office. But how was it with Chamberlain and Packard?

"O liberty, how many wrongs are indicted in thy name."

"Left out in the cold," somebody says.

Yes, left out in the cold.

I do not question at all the President's purpose to do what is right by our brethren in the South, but I have no confidence in the means employed. To barter away the liberties of a people to appease implacable rebels is not just the right thing. I do not encourage an attitude that would embarrass the President in his conciliatory measures toward the South, but must enter

* Chamberlain and Packard were the Republican candidates for governor and lieutenant governor of South Carolina. They were defeated in the election of 1876.

my most solemn protest against his Southern policy. This is done from the honest conviction that this policy is not calculated to subserve the end of good and lawful government in the South, and this is the opinion of ninety-nine one-hundredths of the colored people of the United States.

REASONS WHY THE COLORED AMERICAN SHOULD GO TO AFRICA

By John E. Bruce

With the outbreak of the Civil War, the emigration move-ment to Africa among black Americans took second place to the struggle to achieve emancipation and political and civil rights. But as the promise of Reconstruction turned into a nightmare for the Negro, the back-to-Africa move-ment once again emerged. In October, 1877, John E. Bruce delivered a speech in Philadelphia urging a return to Africa as the only real solution for his people. The Negro journalist outlined a series of reasons why black Americans should return to the homeland, emphasizing especially the fact that even after the Constitutional amendments adopted since the Civil War they were only "nominally free." Here is the major portion of Bruce's speech, as excerpted from The Christian Recorder, *November 1, 1877.*

. . . I SHALL ENDEAVOR to show tonight why the colored American should emigrate to Africa—*first,* because Africa is his fatherland; *secondly,* because, before the war, in the South he was a slave, and in the North a victim of prejudice and ostra-cism; and *thirdly,* because, since the close of the war, although he has been freed by emancipation and invested with en-franchisement, he is only nominally free; and lastly, because he is still a victim of prejudice, and practically proscribed socially, religiously, politically, educationally, and in the various in-dustrial pursuits.

First, then, he should emigrate to Africa because it is his fatherland. Africa is a country rich in its productions, offering untold treasures to the adventurer who may go there. It has a peculiar claim upon the colored American in this country, and that claim is as just and as equitable as any could be. One hundred and fifty millions of our people are on the other side of the broad Atlantic, groveling in darkness and superstition; five millions are on this side surrounded by all the advantages that could be desired in the march toward civilization. It is our duty to carry to those benighted, darkened minds a light to guide them in the march toward civilization. For centuries the colored race has not been highly educated. This has not always been the fact, and history, which shows what has been done, proves what may yet be. The Africans held possession of southern Egypt when Isaiah wrote, "Ethiopia shall soon stretch out her hands unto God." When the Queen of Sheba brought added wealth to the treasures of Solomon, and when a princely and learned Ethiopian became a herald of Christ before Paul the Hebrew, Cornelius, or the European soldiers were converted. The race to whom had been given the wonderful continent of Africa, can be educated and elevated to wealth, power and station among the nations of the earth.

Secondly, why the colored American should emigrate to Africa is because, before the war, in the South he was a slave and in the North a victim of prejudice and ostracism. During the cruel days of slavery the colored American had no right which the white American was bound to respect; he was a nonentity before the law—an automaton with an immortal soul. "Old Massa" had full power and control over him and his posterity. His relatives, his children and friends who were dear to him were snatched up any time by "Old Massa" and sold into slavery, driven into misery everlasting, woe and discontentment. So much for slavery.

Thirdly, Why the colored American should emigrate to Africa is because, since the war, although he has been freed by emancipation and invested with enfranchisement, he is only nominally free. His rights are abridged; he is an American only in name. The doors of the public schools are closed against his children, notwithstanding the fact that he is taxed to support them. The common carriers, hotels and places of amusement, refuse to recognize him as a free man; no matter what his rank or station may be, he cannot enjoy the privileges which the Constitution (the supreme law of the land) guarantees to the humblest citizen. The atrocious massacre of unoffending colored men during the past five years in the states of Mississippi, South Carolina and Louisiana have blackened the page of American history and cast a gloom over the whole civilized world. Innocent men and women were butchered in cold blood by the inhuman wretches who glory in the name "American citizen." These brutal murders were committed in defiance of all law and justice. Men can never forget them. The blood of thousands of our race cries aloud unto the God of justice, and the day of retribution is not far distant.

And lastly, why the colored American should emigrate to Africa is because he is still a victim of prejudice, and practically proscribed socially, religiously and politically. He cannot enter a hotel and obtain accommodations without paying a double price, should he be successful in entering at all. If he go to the church of God in this Christian land, he is thrust into the gallery. If he wants to go South, he is packed in the car nearest the engine so that he will be the first killed in case of a collision. Politically he is a failure and cannot begin to compete with his white brother. He is used by him in all dirty jobs to advance his interests—to fill his pockets with ill-gotten gains; he is virtually a tool and a scapegoat in this respect, and he is regarded as an indispensable auxiliary in time of elections by these unscrupulous and unprincipled demagogues, who are a disgrace and a curse to such a republic as this claims to be.

And now Mr. President, I think I have shown why the colored American should emigrate to Africa. It is to his interest and his gain to do so. He is surrounded on every hand by prejudice and opposition, and it remains for him to carve out for himself a destiny among the nations of the earth.

RACE UNITY

By Ferdinand L. Barnett

On May 6–9, 1879, a national conference of colored men met in Nashville, Tennessee. Most of those present came from all sections of the South, but five Midwestern states and one in the Far West, Oregon, sent delegates. (Other than the District of Columbia, one Northern state, Pennsylvania, was represented.) Most of the discussion dealt with the problems of poverty and insecurity of the black people of the South, but one delegate from Chicago discussed the general problem of race unity. He was Ferdinand L. Barnett, and his speech carried the full title,

*"Racial Unity—Its Importance and Neccessity—Causes
Which Retard Its Development—How It May Be Secured
—Our Plain Duty."*

Ferdinand Lee Barnett, graduate of Chicago's College
of Law, was founder and editor of the Chicago **Conservator**,
which began publication in 1878. Later, he was the first
Negro assistant state's attorney of Illinois, and in 1906 he
was defeated by 304 votes for Judge of the Municipal
Court. In 1895 Barnett married Ida B. Wells, the militant
fighter against lynching.

(Barnett's speech is presented here as excerpted from
the text in Proceedings of the National Conference of
Colored Men of the United States, Held in the State Capitol
at Nashville, Tennessee, May 6, 7, 8, and 9, 1879, *Washington, D. C., 1879, pp. 83–86.*)

. . . RACE ELEVATION can be attained only through race
unity. Pious precepts, business integrity, and moral stamina of
the most exalted stamp may win the admiration for a noble few,
but unless the moral code, by the grandeur of its teachings,
actuates every individual and incites us as a race to nobler
aspirations and quickens us to the realization of our moral
shortcomings, the distinction accorded to the few will avail us
nothing. The wealth of the Indies may crown the efforts of
fortune's few favored ones. They may receive all the homage
wealth invariably brings, but unless we as a race check the
spirit of pomp and display and, by patiently practicing the most
rigid economy, secure homes for ourselves and children, the
preferment won by a few wealthy ones will prove short-lived
and unsatisfactory. We may have our educational lights here
and there, and by the brilliancy of their achievements they may
be living witnesses to the falsity of the doctrine of our inherited
inferiority, but this alone will not suffice. It is a general enlightenment of the race which must engage our noblest powers. One
vicious, ignorant Negro is readily conceded to be a type of all
the rest, but a Negro educated and refined is said to be an exception. We must labor to reverse this rule; education and moral
excellence must become general and characteristic, with ignorance and depravity the exception.

Seeing, then, the necessity of united action and universal
worth rather than individual brilliancy, we sorrowfully admit
that race unity with us is a blessing not yet enjoyed, but to be
possessed. We are united only in the conditions which degrade
and actions which paralyze the efforts of the worthy, who labor
for the benefit of the multitude. We are a race of leaders, every

one presuming that his neighbor and not himself was decreed to be a follower. Today, if any one of you should go home and announce yourself candidate for a certain position, the following day would find a dozen men in the field, each well prepared to prove that he alone is capable of obtaining and filling the position. Failing to convince the people, he would drop out of the race entirely or do all in his power to jeopardize the interest of a more successful brother.

Why this nonfraternal feeling? Why such a spirit of dissension? We attribute it, first, to lessons taught in bygone days by those whose security rested in our disunion. If the same spirit of race unity had actuated the Negro which has always characterized the Indian, this government would have trembled under the blow of that immortal hero, John Brown, and the first drop of fratricidal blood would have been shed, not at Fort Sumter, but at Harpers Ferry. Another cause may be found in our partial enlightenment. The ignorant man is always narrow-minded in politics, business or religion. Unfold to him a plan, and if he cannot see some interest resulting to self, however great the resulting good to the multitude, it meets only his partial approbation and fails entirely to secure his active co-operation. A third reason applies, not to the unlearned, but to the learned. Too many of our learned men are afflicted with a mental and moral aberration, termed in common parlance "big-headed." Having reached a commendable degree of eminence, they seem to stand and say, "Lord, we thank Thee we are not as other men are." They view with perfect unconcern the struggles of a worthy brother; they proffer him no aid, but deem it presumption in him to expect it. They may see a needed step but fail to take it. Others may see the necessity, take steps to meet it, and call it, and call them to aid. But, no; they did not lead; they will not follow, and half of their influence for good is sacrificed by an insane jealousy that is a consuming fire in every bosom wherein it finds lodgment.

A few of the prominent causes which retard race unity having been noticed, let us look for the remedy. First, our natural jealousy must be overcome. The task is no easy one. We must look for fruits of our labor in the next generation. With us our faults are confirmed. An old slave once lay dying, friends and relatives were gathered around. The minister sat at the bedside endeavoring to prepare the soul for the great change. The old man was willing to forgive every one except a certain particularly obstreperous African who had caused him much injury. But being overpersuaded, he yielded and said, "Well, if I dies I forgives him, but if I lives—dat darkey better take care." It is much the same with us; when we die our natures will change, but while we live our neighbors must take care. Upon the young generation our instruction may be effective. They must be taught that in helping one another they help themselves; and that in the race of life, when a favored one excels and leads the rest, their powers must be employcd, not in retarding his progress, but in urging him on and inciting others to emulate his example.

We must dissipate the gloom of ignorance which hangs like a pall over us. In former days we were trained in ignorance, and many of my distinguished hearers will remember when they dare not be caught cultivating an intimate acquaintance with the spelling book. But the time is passed when the seeker-after-knowledge is reviled and persecuted. Throughout the country the public-school system largely obtains; books without number and papers without price lend their enlightenment; while high schools, colleges and universities all over our broad domain throw open their inviting doors and say, "Whosoever will may come."

We must not fail to notice any dereliction of our educated people. They must learn that their duty is to elevate their less favored brethren, and this cannot be done while pride and conceit prevent them from entering heartily into the work. A spirit of missionary zeal must actuate them to go down among the lowly and by word and action say, "Come with me, and I will do you good."

We must help one another. Our industries must be patronized, and our laborers encouraged. There seems to be a natural disinclination on our part to patronize our own workmen. We are easily pleased with the labor of the white hands, but when the same is known to be the product of our own skill and energy, we become extremely exacting and hard to please. From colored men we expect better work, we pay them less, and usually take our own good time for payment. We will patronize a colored merchant as long as he will credit us, but when on the verge of bankruptcy he is obliged to stop the credit system, we pass by him and pay our money to the white rival. For these reasons our industries are rarely remunerative. We must lay aside these "besetting sins" and become united in our appreciation and practical encouragement of our own laborers.

Our societies should wield their influence to secure colored apprentices and mechanics. By a judicious disposition of their custom, they might place colored apprentices in vocations at present entirely unpracticed by us. Our labor is generally menial. We have hitherto had a monopoly of America's menial occupations, but thanks to a progressive Caucasian element, we no longer *suffer* from that monopoly. The white man enters the vocations hitherto exclusively ours, and we must enter and become proficient in professions hitherto exclusively practiced by him.

Our communities must be united. By concerted action great results can be accomplished. We must not only act upon the defensive, but when necessary we should take the offensive. We should jealously guard our every interest, public and private. Let us here speak of our schools. They furnish the surest and swiftest means in our power of obtaining knowledge, confidence and respect. There is no satisfactory reason why all children who seek instruction should not have full and equal privileges, but law has been so perverted in many places, North and South, that sanction is given to separate schools, a pernicious system of discrimination which invariably operates to the disadvantage of the colored race. If we are separate, let it be from "turret to foundation stone." It is unjust to draw the color line in schools, and our communities should resent the added insult of forcing the colored pupils to receive instructions from the refuse material of white educational institutions. White teachers take colored schools from necessity, not from choice. We except, of course, those who act from a missionary spirit.

White teachers in colored schools are nearly always mentally, morally or financially bankrupts, and no colored community should tolerate the imposition. High schools and colleges are sending learned colored teachers in the field constantly, and it is manifestly unjust to make them stand idle and see their people taught by those whose only interest lies in securing their monthly compensation in dollars and cents. Again, colored schools thrive better under colored teachers. The St. Louis schools furnish an excellent example. According to the report of Superintendent Harris, during the past two years the schools have increased under colored teachers more than fifty percent, and similar results always follow the introduction of colored teachers. In cases of mixed schools our teachers should be eligible to positions. They invariably prove equal to their requirements. In Detroit and Chicago they have been admitted and proved themselves unquestionably capable. In Chicago their white pupils outnumber the colored ten to one, and yet they have met with decided success. Such gratifying results must be won by energetic, united action on the part of the interested communities. White people grant us few privileges voluntarily. We must wage continued warfare for our rights, or they will be disregarded and abridged.

Mr. President, we might begin to enumerate the rich results of race unity at sunrise and continue to sunset, and half would not be told. In behalf of the people we are here to represent, we ask for some intelligent action of this conference, some organized movement whereby concerted action may be had by our race all over the land. Let us decide upon some intelligent, united system of operation, and go home and engage the time and talent of our constituents in prosperous labor. We are laboring for race elevation, and race unity is the all-important factor in the work. It must be secured at whatever cost. Individual action, however insignificant, becomes powerful when united and exerted in a common channel. Many thousand years ago, a tiny coral began a reef upon the ocean's bed. Years passed and others came. Their fortunes were united and the structure grew. Generations came and went, and corals by the million came, lived and died, each adding his mite to the work, till at last the waters of the grand old ocean broke in ripples around their tireless heads, and now, as the traveler gazes upon the reef, hundreds of miles in extent, he can faintly realize what great results will follow united action.

So we must labor, with the full assurance that we will reap our reward in due season. Though deeply submerged by the wave of popular opinion, which deems natural inferiority inseparably associated with a black skin, though weighted down by an accursed prejudice that seeks every opportunity to crush us, still we must labor and despair not—patiently, ceaselessly, and unitedly. The time will come when our heads will rise above the troubled waters. Though generations come and go, the result of our labors will yet be manifest, and an impartial world will accord us that rank among other races which all may aspire to, but only the worthy can win.

THE EMIGRATION OF COLORED CITIZENS FROM THE SOUTHERN STATES

By Richard T. Greener

In 1877 Republican President Rutherford B. Hayes withdrew the last federal troops from the South and announced that local government would be left to "the honorable and influential Southern whites." The hopes of the Negro

people raised by enfranchisement during the Radical Re-
construction were soon relentlessly put down by varying
kinds of disfranchisement. Although it was not until the
1890's that legal disfranchisement got under way, pre-
liminary disfranchising techniques, ranging from out-
right violence and intimidation to the more subtle devices
of a poll tax and highly complex ballot procedures, orgi-
nated in some Southern states as early as the withdrawal
of federal troops. Conditions for Negroes, now mostly
second-class citizens, rapidly became intolerable. Peonage,
inadequate educational opportunities, mob law and vio-
lence, and loss of political rights made life in the South
increasingly unattractive to many Negroes. The first major
Negro exodus occurred in January and February, 1879,
and was centered in, though not confined to, southern
Louisiana. A bad crop, a devastating yellow-fever epidemic,
an unsuccessful effort on the part of Negro tenants to
force a reduction in rent, caused something like fifty
thousand Negroes to move from the South. Many of them
headed for Kansas. Most, however, were unprepared for
the bitter cold of Missouri and Kansas and had hardly
enough funds to keep them alive when they reached the
Kansas plains. Gradually, the emigration fever subsided.

There was sharp difference among Negro leaders as to
the wisdom of the "great exodus." Frederick Douglass op-
posed the exodus, since "it leaves the whole question of
equal rights on the soil of the South open and still to be
settled." Continued migration, Douglass argued, "would
make freedom and free institutions depend upon migra-
tion rather than protection."

Douglass' position was challenged by Richard T.
Greener, the first Negro graduate of Harvard College and
dean of Howard University's law school from 1879 to
1880. Greener supported migration as one of several solu-
tions to the problems of Southern Negroes. On September
12, 1879, Greener read a paper before the American Social
Science Association at Saratoga, New York, in which he
outlined the reasons for his support of emigration. Here
are parts of this speech, excerpted from the text published
in the Journal of Social Science, *Vol. XI, May, 1880, pp.*
303–15.

. . . WITH THE DOWNFALL of Reconstruction a new
lease of life was given to Southern barbarity and lawlessness.
As usual, the Negro was the principal sufferer. Negro represent-

ation went first;* next the educational system, which the
carpetbagger had brought to the South, was crippled by insufficient appropriations.† Majorities were overcome by shotgun intimidation, or secretly by the tissue ballot. Radical officeholders were forced to resign, robbed of their property by "due
process of law," and driven North. The jury box and representation the Negro was forced to give up; but after enduring all
this, he found himself charged exorbitantly for the most necessary articles of food. His land was rented to him at fabulous
prices. His cabin was likely to be raided at any time, whenever
capricious lust or a dreadful thirst for blood was roused. He
saw his crop dwindling day by day; he saw himself growing
poorer and getting into debt; his labor squandered between exacting landlords and rapacious storekeepers. It was then the
Negro resolved to give up the fruitless contest so long and hopelessly waged, and try his fortune in the great West, of which
he had heard and read so much during the past ten years. . . .

This emigration will benefit the Negro, who is now too much
inclined to stay where he is put. At the South he never knows his
own possibilities. Then again, the South is a wretched place
for any people to develop in, and this is especially true of the
Negro, because, like all subject races, he imitates the life
about him. The Negro at the South is in a demoralized condition, and no jury will convict for political offenses committed
against him. Chief Justice Waite, at Charleston, in the case
of the Ellenton rioters,‡ could not charge the jury in favor of
liberty and protection. District attorneys are appointed at the
recommendation of known rebels and sympathizers and assassins. Of course, they will not do their duty; hence, the Negro
dares not look for justice in the courts—once proudly called

---

* Although the Negro voter was often deprived of his vote by threats and
fraudulent counts, the black electorate was still a political factor in the
South until the late 1890's. Negro officeholding also survived in parts of
the South even after the restoration of white supremacy. Negroes in
Virginia were elected to every session of the state legislature from 1869
to 1890, and in South Carolina to every legislative session from 1868
through 1900. Negroes were elected to Congress up to 1901.
† During Congressional Reconstruction the first public-school systems
were established in the South.
"Carpetbaggers" referred usually to Northerners who hastened, with
little more than a carpetbag of personal effects, into the South following
the adoption of Congressional Reconstruction. Many went for self-seeking
purposes, but quite a few were interested in helping build a more democratic society in the South.
‡ On September 17, 1876, a serious race riot erupted in Ellenton, South
Carolina, which led to the death of two white men and fifteen Negroes.

the palladium of English liberty. The use of the military power to enforce any right is repudiated at the North. But I remember it was employed quite efficaciously to return Anthony Burns and Simms,* fugitive slaves, some years ago. I need not enumerate the demoralizing features of Southern life, the reckless disregard for human life, the lack of thrift, drinking customs, gaming, horse racing, et cetera. The Negro needs contact with all that is healthful and developing in modern civilization, and by emigration the Negro will learn to love thrift and unlearn many bad habits and improvident notions acquired from preceding generations.

The exclusive devotion of the Negro to the culture of cotton and rice is demoralizing to him. They drag women and children into the field, with no commissioner of labor to look out for outraged childhood and impaired maternity. I do not expect this argument to find favor with those who think the Negro has no other future before him than to cultivate sugar, cotton and rice. On the politico-economic side a partial exodus will benefit those who remain, by raising the wage fund, increasing the demand, and insuring better treatment to those who are left; the fact of the exodus being a preventive check, if I may borrow a phrase from Mr. Malthus. It will remove the Negro from the incessant whirl of politics, in which, like all dark races, he is governed more by feeling than selfish interest.

At present the Negro stands in the way of his own advancement, by reason of political fidelity and the very excess of population, not diminished since the war, and yet not so systematically diffused and employed. Even Senator Butler, of South Carolina, says, "We have too much cheap Negro labor in the South." As to wages, the average Negro can earn higher wages and live more comfortably at the North, even if confined to humble employments, than he can at the South. When we add such trifles as protection, school privileges, free suffrage and Christian influences, we transcend the limits of legitimate comparison. That the departure of the few will benefit the many might be abundantly illustrated by the condition of Ireland after the famine of 1848, or England after the Lancashire distress, when Canon Girdlestone, Mr. Froude and Goldwin Smith counseled emigration.

---

* Anthony Burns, a fugitive slave from Richmond, Virginia, who was hiding in Boston, was returned to slavery in May, 1854, with the assistance of the United States Army sent for that purpose by President Franklin Pierce. Franklin Sims, a fugitive slave, was arrested in Boston in 1851 and, with the police of the city and the militia of the state for an escort, was taken on shipboard and returned to Savannah.

I assume that the predominance of the Negro in politics at the South is gone for a generation at least. The South will not have it and the North has exhibited no very marked disposition to enforce it. If it be ever desirable again, let it come when the children of the present black colonists go back to the mother land, improved in all that makes good citizens by a sojourn in the West. . . .

The Western lands are waiting for settlers, and are being rapidly filled up by Swedes, Norwegians, Mennonites, Icelanders and Poles. Why should not the Negro participate? Six hundred thousand acres of public land have been taken up since June 30, 1878; fifty thousand families have gone westward under the Homestead law,* exclusive of those who have small sums to invest. Why shall we debar the Negro? Irish Catholics have raised a fund of $100,000 to assist their poor from the large cities. The Hebrews have also an excellent association for the same purpose. These aid societies hold meetings and solicit funds. No one denounces them or impugns the motives of their advocates. What will benefit Irish, Hebrew, Swede and Norwegian cannot be decidedly injurious to the colored race alone. . . .

No view of the movement would be complete which did not notice the relation of the colored people of the country to this flight from oppression. The first stage is passed, the appeal to white philanthropists. My notion is the second is here, the appeal to ourselves. We must organize societies, contribute our dimes, and form a network of communication between the South and every principal point North and West. We should raise $200,000 to form a company; we should have a national executive committee, and have agents to buy land, procure cheap transportation, disseminate accurate information, and see to it that they are neither deluded nor defrauded. Such an organization, working through our churches and benevolent societies, would do more to develop our race than all the philanthropic measures designed to aid us since the war.

The little rill has started on its course toward the great sea of humanity. It moves slowly on by virtue of the eternal law of gravitation, which leads peoples and individuals toward peace, protection and happiness. Today it is a slender thread and makes way with difficulty amid the rocks and tangled growth; but it has already burst through serious impediments, showing

---

* The Homestead Act enacted in 1862 made available to adult citizens and to those who declared their intention of becoming citizens 160 acres of the public domain. Only men who had borne arms against the United States were excluded.

itself possessed of a mighty current. It started in Mississippi, but it is even now being rapidly fed by other rills and streams from the territory through which it flows. Believing that it comes from God, and feeling convinced that it bears only blessings in its course for that race so long tossed, so ill-treated, so sadly misunderstood, I greet its tiny line, and almost see in the near future its magnificent broad bosom, bearing proudly onward, until at last, like the travel-worn and battle-scarred Greeks of old, there bursts upon its sight the sea, the broad sea of universal freedom and protection.

A CALL FOR A CHANGE IN OUR INDIAN POLICY

By Blanche K. Bruce

The traditional Indian policy of the United States government, as pursued by the Army and the Interior Department, was one of extermination. As a result, by 1880 there were hardly two hundred thousand Indians remaining in the United States, whereas, when Columbus discovered America, probably a million Indians lived on the continent to the north of Mexico. As a result of widespread opposition to the extermination policy, bills were introduced in Congress which proposed breaking up tribal autonomy even on the reservation, to divide up reservation land and give each family head 160 acres to cultivate, and after a probation period of twenty-five years, he was to be granted full rights of ownership and full citizenship in the United States. In support of such a bill, Blanche Kelso Bruce (1841–1898), the first Negro to serve a full term as a United States Senator, spoke in the Senate on April 7, 1880. Bruce was born a slave in Virginia on March 1, 1841. He escaped from slavery during the Civil War, taught school in Missouri, attended Oberlin College, Ohio, and moved to Mississippi during Reconstruction. There he became a successful planter, was elected Senator from Mississippi in 1874, and served from March 4, 1875, to March 3, 1881.

Here is the speech Bruce delivered in which he de-

nounced the American Indian policy "that has kept the Indian a fugitive and a vagabond, that has bred discontent, suspicion, and hatred in the mind of the red man. . . ." It is taken from the Congressional Record, *46th Congress, 2d Session, Part 3, pp. 2195–96.*

MR. PRESIDENT, I shall support the pending bill, and without attempting a discussion of the specific features of the measure, I desire to submit a few remarks upon the general subject suggested by it.

Our Indian policy and administration seem to me to have been inspired and controlled by a stern selfishness, with a few honorable exceptions. Indian treaties have generally been made as the condition and instrument of acquiring the valuable territory occupied by the several Indian nations and have been changed and revised from time to time as it became desirable that the steadily growing, irrepressible white races should secure more room for their growth and more lands for their occupancy; and wars, bounties and beads have been used as auxiliaries for the purpose of temporary peace and security for the whites, and as the preliminary to further aggressions upon the red man's lands, with the ultimate view of his expulsion and extinction from the continent.

No set purpose has been evinced in adequate, sufficient measure to build him up, to civilize him, and to make him part of the great community of states. Whatever of occasional and spasmodic effort has been made for his redemption from savagery and his perpetuity as a race, has been only sufficient to supply that class of exceptions to the rule necessary to prove the selfishness of the policy that we allege to have been practiced toward him.

The political or governmental idea underlying the Indian policy is to maintain the paramount authority of the United States over the Indian Territory and over the Indian tribes, yet recognizing tribal independence and autonomy and a local government, un-American in structure and having no reference to the Constitution or laws of the United States, so far as the tribal governments affect the persons, lives and rights of the members of the tribe alone. Currently with the maintenance of a policy thus based, under treaty obligations, the government of the United States contributes to the support, equipments and comforts of these Indians, not only by making appropriations for food and raiment but by sustaining blacksmiths, mechanics, farmers, millers and schools in the midst of the Indian reservations. This government also, in its treaties and its enforcement thereof, encourages and facilitates the missionary enterprises of the different churches which look to the Christianization and education of the Indians distributed throughout the public domain. The effort, under these circumstances, to preserve peace among the Indian tribes in their relations to each other and in their relations to the citizens of the United States becomes a very onerous and difficult endeavor, and has not heretofore produced results that have either satisfied the expectations and public sentiment of the country, vindicated the wisdom of the policy practiced toward this people, or honored the Christian institutions and civilizations of our great country.

We have in the effort to realize a somewhat intangible ideal —to wit, the preservation of Indian liberty and the administration and exercise of national authority—complicated an essentially difficult problem by surrounding it with needless and equivocal adjuncts; we have rendered a questionable policy more difficult of successful execution by basing it upon a political theory which is un-American in character, and which, in its very structure, breeds and perpetuates the difficulties sought to be avoided and overcome.

Our system of government is complex in that it recognizes a general and local jurisdiction, and seeks to subserve and protect the rights of the individual and of the different political communities and the great aggregates of society making up the nation, by a division of authority distributed among general and local agencies, which are required like "the wheels within wheels" of Ezekiel's vision, to so move in their several appropriate spheres as shall not only prevent attrition and collision, but as shall secure unity in the system, in its fullest integrity, currently with the enjoyment of the largest liberty by the citizen.

Our system, I repeat, is complex, but it is nevertheless homogeneous. It is not incongruous; the general and local organisms belong to the same great class; they are both American, and they are moved by and respond to the same great impulse —the popular will of the American people.

Now, the political system that underlies our Indian policy is not only complex but it is incongruous, and one of the governments embraced in the system, ostensibly to secure the largest license and independence to the red race affected by the subject of this nondescript policy, is foreign in its character; the individuals and the system of laws are neither American. All the contradictions, the absurdities, and impossibilities developed and cropping out on the surface of our administration of Indian affairs are referable to this singular philosophy upon which, as a political theory, the Indian policy of the United States rests.

Now, sir, there must be a change in the Indian policy if beneficent practical results are expected, and any change that gives promise of solving this red-race problem must be a change based upon an idea in harmony, and not at war, with our free institutions. If the Indian is expected and required to respond to federal authority; if this people are expected to grow up into organized and well-ordered society; if they are to be civilized, in that the best elements of their natures are to be developed in the exercise of their best functions, so as to produce individual character and social groups characteristic of enlightened people; if this is to be done under our system, its ultimate realization requires an adoption of a political philosophy that shall make the Indians, as an individual and as a tribe, subjects of American law and beneficiaries of American institutions, by making them first American citizens, and clothing them, as rapidly as their advancement and location will permit, with the protective and ennobling prerogatives of such citizenship.

I favor the measure pending, because it is a step in the direction that I have indicated. You propose to give the Indian not temporary but permanent residence as a tribe, and not tribal location, but by a division of lands in severalty you secure to him the individual property rights which, utilized, will sustain life for himself and family better than his nomadic career. By this location you lay the foundation for that love of country essential to the patriotism and growth of a people, and by the distribution of lands to the individual, in severalty, you appeal to and develop that essential constitutional quality of humanity, the disposition to accumulate, upon which, when healthily and justly developed, depends the wealth, the growth, the power, the comfort, the refinement and the glory of the nations of the earth.

The measure also, with less directness, but as a necessary sequence to the provisions that I have just characterized, proposes, as preliminary to bringing the red race under the operation of our laws, to present the best phases of civilized life. Having given the red man a habitat, having identified the individual as well as the tribe with his new home, by securing his individual interests and rights therein, having placed these people where law can reach them, govern them and protect them, you purpose a system of administration that shall bring them in contact not with the adventurer of the border, not a speculative Indian agent, not an armed blue-coated soldier, but with the American people, in the guise and fashion in which trade, commerce, arts—useful and attractive—in the panoply that loving peace supplies, and with the plenty and comforts that follow in the footsteps of peace, and for the first time in the Indian's history, he will see the industrial, commercial, comfortable side of the character of the American people, will find his contact and form his associations with the citizens of the great Republic, and not simply and exclusively its armed men—its instruments of justice and destruction. So much this measure, if it should be a type of the new policy, will do for the Indian; and the Indian problem—heretofore rendered difficult of solution because of the false philosophy underlying it and the unjust administration too frequently based upon it, a policy that has kept the Indian a fugitive and a vagabond, that has bred discontent, suspicion and hatred in the mind of the red man—will be settled, not immediately, in a day or a year, but it will be put in course of settlement, and the question will be placed where a successful issue will be secured beyond a peradventure.

Mr. President, the red race are not a numerous people in our land, not equaling probably a half million souls, but they are the remnants of a great and multitudinous nation, and their hapless fortunes heretofore not only appeal to sympathy and to justice in any measures that we may take affecting them, but the vigor, energy, bravery and integrity of this remnant entitle them to consideration on the merits of the question.

Our age has been signalized by the grand scientific and mechanical discoveries and inventions which have multiplied the productive forces of the world. The power of nature has been harnessed to do the work of man, and every hour some new discovery contributes to swell the volume of the physical energies and its utilization, human ingenuity and thought have already been directed to the conservation, to the economy against the waste, of the physical forces. The man is considered a public benefactor who can utilize waste fuel, who can convert to some practical end some physical energy still lost, to a percent at least, through the imperfection of the machinery employed.

Now, sir, the Indian is a physical force; a half million vigorous, physical, intellectual agents ready for the plastic hand of Christian civilization, living in a country possessing empires of untilled and uninhabited lands. The Indian tribes, viewed from this utilitarian standpoint, are worth preservation, conservation, utilization and civilization, and I believe that we have reached a period when the public sentiment of the country demands such a modification in the Indian policy, in its purposes and in its methods, as shall save and not destroy these people.

There is nothing in the matter of obstructions, as suggested by the opponents of this measure, to convince me that the new policy is either impracticable or visionary. As a people, our history is full of surmounted obstacles; we have been solving difficult problems for more than a hundred years; we have been settling material, moral and great political questions that, before our era, had been unsolved, and the possible solution of which, even among the timid in our midst, was questioned.

The Indian is human, and no matter what his traditions or his habits, if you will locate him and put him in contact, and hold him in contact, with the forces of our civilization, his fresh, rugged nature will respond, and the fruit of his endeavor, in his civilization and development, will be the more permanent and enduring because his nature is so strong and obdurate. When you have no longer made it necessary for him to be a vagabond and fugitive; when you have allowed him to see the lovable and attractive side of our civilization as well as the stern military phase; when you have made the law apply to him as it does to others, so that the ministers of the law shall not only be the executors of its penalties but the administrators of its saving, shielding, protecting provisions, he will become trustful and reliable; and when he is placed in position in which not only to become an industrial force—to multiply his comforts and those of his people—but the honest, full sharer of the things he produces, savage life will lose its attractions, and the hunter will become the herdsman, the herdsman in his turn the farmer, and the farmer the mechanic, and out of the industries and growth of the Indian homes will spring up commercial interests and men competent to foster and handle them.

The American people are beginning to reach the conscientious conviction that redemption and civilization are due to the Indian tribes of the United States, and the present popular purpose is not to exterminate them but to perpetuate them on this continent.

The Indian policy has never attracted so much attention as at the present time,* and the public sentiment demands that the new departure on this question shall ultimate in measures, toward the wild tribes of America, that shall be Christian and righteous in their character. The destruction of this vigorous race, rather than their preservation and development, is coming

---

* During the 1870's wars between the Indians and the U. S. Army occurred frequently, as Indians reacted in anger to encroachments on their reservations. In 1876, four years before Bruce delivered his speech, the Sioux had annihilated Colonel Custer in the Battle of the Little Big Horn. A year after Bruce spoke, in 1881, even greater attention was paid to the Indian question by the publication of Helen Hunt Jackson's *A Century of Dishonor*, a scorching indictment of traditional governmental policy toward the Indians.

to be considered not only an outrage against Christian civilization, but an economic wrong to the people of the United States; and the people of America demand that the measures and administration of government relative to these people shall proceed upon the wise and equitable principles that regulate the conduct of public affairs relative to every other race in the Republic, and when rightful conceptions obtain in the treatment of the red race, the Indian question, with its cost, anxieties and wars, will disappear.*

A PLEA FOR UNIVERSAL EDUCATION IN THE SOUTH

By Robert McElwee

On January 23, 1883, Robert McElwee, a black member of the Tennessee legislature, delivered a speech to that body in support of a bill to "provide for Normal Education of white and colored youth." His chief argument was that it was the duty of the state to extend the benefits of education to all its people alike, and that Tennessee owed it to its citizens to place ample educational facilities within the reach of all its citizens.

The bill was recommitted to the Committee on Education, which had already recommended its rejection. On February 13, 1883, the bill was voted on in the legislature and defeated.

Here is a part of McElwee's speech, excerpted from the Nashville Daily American, *January 24, 1883.*

* The proposals Bruce favored were finally enacted in 1887 in the Dawes Act, although it was not until 1924 that the United States granted full citizenship to all the Indians in the country. However, the program Bruce advocated, although he was not aware of this at the time, did the Indians more harm than good. When the land was divided under the Dawes Act, the poorest territory was usually given to the Indians, and the best was sold to white settlers. Even where he gained good land, inexperience with ownership and with legal matters left the individual Indian vulnerable to the same kind of deceitful practice that had marked the making of tribal treaties.

. . . In my judgment there is no question among the many living and vital issues which we now as a nation are called upon to consider of greater importance to the South than the question of education. The time is auspicious in the South for a more exalted position on the question. Cannot the legislature of Tennessee assembled in Nashville, our capital city, the boasted Athens of the South, sound the keynote and give the signal for the onward march in the great cause of normal education? . . . Let Tennessee take a high stand on this question and other Southern states will follow, and ere long, before another decade, the voice of our people from Old Virginia, the Mother of Presidents, to Texas, the Lone Star State, will greet with joy the dawn of a better day in our Southland. Then with dead issues of the past buried in the sea of oblivion, and our homes, formerly devastated and laid waste by war, built up, with the mineral resources of our country developed, with the color line obliterated, and with our many manufacturing industries, the South will move on to a grand and noble future. The voice of her sons will again be heard in the national halls of the Congress of the United States, and no longer will the people of this great nation look to one section of our country for our chief ruler. I ask this appropriation, because we are worthy of it. I ask it because we are poor. I ask it because there are many worthy young men and women of African descent in our state, who would make good and efficient teachers, if they had the aid which this bill will give them. I ask it because the happiness and prosperity of any state depends upon the intelligence of its citizens. . . . I ask it in order that my people may be aided on the road to thrift, intelligence, culture, virtue and every other element of the highest civilization. . . .

In closing my argument on this question, I wish to call your attention to some very important facts in regard to the educational status of the South.

The last census discloses some very alarming facts in regard to the educational condition in the South. . . . According to the last census report, five million of our population are unable to read; six million are unable to write. Think of it. In a country like ours such a large number of people unable to read and write! A great country like ours, in which the people are sovereigns, can ill afford to have the education of a part of its citizens neglected. When we study carefully our form of government, we can at once realize that the very first principle upon which it is founded is the intelligence of its citizens. Hence the imperative necessity of universal education in order that not only the state of Tennessee, but the entire South may keep pace with other parts of the country in literary progress and general education. The education of the youth must be carefully provided for. It is a question of paramount importance and ought to receive due consideration. As the state of Tennessee has thus far failed to meet the adequate demands of a growing and prospering people, it is nothing more than the part of wisdom, to say nothing of the prosperity of the act, that the present legislature should take the matter in hand. When we contemplate the condition of affairs in the South and the low ebb of educational interest manifested by some of the states, we tremble for our free institutions. We are led to ask ourselves these questions: What is to be the future of this great country with over fifty million inhabitants? What is to be the future of the form of government transmitted to us by the fathers and protected by the invincible genius of the land? This fear is even augmented when we know that men of every clime and race are daily coming to our shores; our portals are open alike to all—the English, the German, the Frenchman, the Italian, the Scandinavian, the Asiatic—all find in America a hearty welcome. Then let us as servants of the people of a great country act wisely the part assigned to us by encouraging education.

Mr. Speaker and gentlemen of the House, if you desire to enshrine your names in the hearts of a great and noble people, if you desire your names to live in the memory of Christian hearts and that your deeds may shine as bright and imperishable stars in the diadem of our republic when you have filled your graves, show by your votes on this question that you are in favor of more and better and higher education.

THE BLACK WOMAN OF THE SOUTH: HER NEGLECTS AND HER NEEDS

By Alexander Crummell

Alexander Crummell (1819–1898), a graduate of Oxford University, England, was a leading clergyman in the North before the Civil War. Between 1853 and 1873 he was active in Africa as an agent of the American Colonization Society. After his return from Africa, he continued to play a prominent role in the United States as a clergyman, political leader, and lecturer. Here are portions of an address Crummell delivered before the Freedman's Aid Society, Methodist Episcopal Church, Ocean Grove, New Jersey, August 15, 1883.

(The address is presented here as excerpted from Africa and America: Addresses and Discourses by Alex. Crummell, *Springfield, Mass., 1891, pp. 61–82, The full text has also been published as a pamphlet*—The Black Woman of the South; Her Neglects and Her Needs, Washington, *D. C., 1883.)*

It is an age clamorous everywhere for the dignities, the grand prerogatives and the glory of woman. There is not a country in Europe where she has not risen somewhat above the degradation of centuries and pleaded successfully for a new position and a higher vocation. As the result of this new reformation, we see her, in our day, seated in the lecture rooms of ancient universities, rivaling her brothers in the fields of literature, the grand creators of ethereal art, the participants in noble civil franchises, the moving spirit in grand reformations, and the guide, agent, or assistant in all the noblest movements for the civilization and regeneration of man.

In these several lines of progress the American woman has run on in advance of her sisters in every other quarter of the globe. The advantage she has received, the rights and prerogatives she has secured for herself are unequaled by any other class of women in the world. It will not be thought amiss, then, that I come here today to present to your consideration the one grand exception to this general superiority of women—viz., *the black woman of the South.* . . .

The rural or plantation population of the South was made up almost entirely of people of pure Negro blood. And this brings out also the other disastrous fact, namely, that this large black population has been living from the time of their introduction into America, a period of more than two hundred years, in a state of unlettered rudeness. The Negro all this time has been an intellectual starveling. This has been more especially the condition of the black woman of the South. Now and then a black man has risen above the debased condition of his people. Various causes would contribute to the advantage of the *men:* the relation of servants to superior masters; attendance at courts with them; their presence at political meetings; listening to table talk behind their chairs; traveling as valets; the privilege of books and reading in great houses, and with indulgent masters—all these served to lift up a black *man* here and there to something like superiority. But no such fortune fell to the lot of the plantation woman. The black woman of the South was left perpetually in a state of hereditary darkness and rudeness. . . . The lot of the black *man* on the plantation has been sad and desolate enough; but the fate of the black woman has been awful! Her entire existence from the day she first landed, a naked victim of the slave trade, has been degradation in its extremest forms.

In her girlhood all the delicate tendencies of her sex have been rudely outraged. In the field, in the rude cabin, in the press room, in the factory, she was thrown into the companionship of coarse and ignorant men. No chance was given her for delicate reserve or tender modesty. From her childhood she was the doomed victim of the grossest passions. All the virtues of her sex were utterly ignored. If the instinct of chastity asserted itself, then she had to fight like a tigress for the ownership and possession of her own person, and ofttimes had to suffer pains and lacerations for her virtuous self-assertion. When she reached maturity all the tender instincts of her womanhood were ruthlessly violated. At the age of marriage—always prematurely anticipated under slavery—she was mated, as the stock of the plantation were mated, *not* to be the companion of a loved and chosen husband, but to be the breeder of human cattle, for the field or the auction block. With that mate she went out, morning after morning to toil, as a common field hand. As it was *his*, so likewise was it her lot to wield the heavy hoe or to follow the plow or to gather in the crops. She was a "hewer of wood and a drawer of water." She was a common field hand. She had to keep her place in the gang from morn till eve, under the burden of a heavy task, or under the stimulus or the fear of a cruel lash. She was a picker of cotton. She labored at the sugar mill and in the tobacco factory. When, through weariness or sickness, she has fallen behind her allotted task, there came, as punishment, the fearful stripes upon her shrinking, lacerated flesh.

Her home life was of the most degrading nature. She lived in the rudest huts, and partook of the coarsest food, and dressed in the scantiest garb, and slept, in multitudinous cabins, upon the hardest boards.

Thus she continued a beast of burden down to the period of those maternal anxieties which, in ordinary civilized life, give repose, quiet, and care to expectant mothers. But, under the slave system, few such relaxations were allowed. And so it came to pass that little children were ushered into this world under conditions which many cattle raisers would not suffer for their flocks or herds. Thus she became the mother of children. But even then there was for her no suretyship of motherhood or training or control. Her own offspring were *not* her own. She and husband and children were all the property of others. All these sacred ties were constantly snapped and cruelly sundered. *This* year she had one husband; and next year, through some auction sale, she might be separated from him and mated to another. There was no sanctity of family, no binding tie of marriage, none of the fine felicities and the endearing affections of home. None of these things was the lot of Southern black women. Instead thereof, a gross barbarism which tended to blunt the tender sensibilities, to obliterate feminine delicacy and womanly shame, came down as her heritage from generation to generation; and it seems a miracle of providence and grace that, notwithstanding these terrible circumstances, so much struggling virtue lingered amid these rude cabins, that so much womanly worth and sweetness abided in their bosoms, as slaveholders themselves have borne witness to.

But some of you will ask: "Why bring up these sad memories of the past? Why distress us with these dead and departed cruelties?" Alas, my friends, these are not dead things. Remember that

> The evil that men do lives after them.

The evil of gross and monstrous abominations, the evil of great organic institutions crop out long after the departure of the institutions themselves. If you go to Europe you will find not only the roots, but likewise many of the deadly fruits of the old feudal system still surviving in several of its old states and kingdoms. So, too, with slavery. The eighteen years of freedom have not obliterated all its deadly marks from either the souls or bodies of the black woman. The conditions of life, indeed, have been modified since emancipation; but it still maintains that the black woman is the Pariah woman of this land! We have, indeed, degraded women, immigrants, from foreign lands. In their own countries some of them were so low in the social scale that they were yoked with the cattle to plow the fields. They were rude, unlettered, coarse and benighted. But when they reach *this* land there comes an end to their degraded condition.

> They touch our country and their shackles fall.

As soon as they become grafted into the stock of American life they partake at once of all its large gifts and its noble resources.

Not so with the black woman of the South. Freed legally she has been; but the act of emancipation had no talismanic influence to reach to and alter and transform her degrading social life.

When that proclamation was issued she might have heard the whispered words in her every hut, "Open, Sesame"; but, so far as her humble domicile and her degraded person were concerned, there was no invisible but gracious jinni, who on the instant could transmute the rudeness of her hut into instant elegance and change the crude surroundings of her home into neatness, taste and beauty.

The truth is, Emancipation Day found her a prostrate and degraded being; and, although it has brought numerous advantages to her sons, it has produced but the simplest changes in her social and domestic condition. She is still the crude, rude, ignorant mother. Remote from cities, the dweller still in the old plantation hut, neighboring to the sulky, disaffected master class, who still think her freedom was a personal robbery of themselves, none of the "fair humanities" have visited her humble home. The light of knowledge has not fallen upon her eyes. The fine domesticities which give the charm to family life, and which, by the refinement and delicacy of womanhood, preserve the civilization of nations, have not come to *her*. She has still the rude, coarse labor of men. With her rude husband she still shares the hard service of a field hand. Her house, which shelters, perhaps, some six or eight children, embraces but two rooms. Her furniture is of the rudest kind. The clothing of the household is scant and of the coarsest material, has ofttimes the garniture of rags, and for herself and offspring is marked, not seldom, by the absence of both hats and shoes. She has rarely been taught to sew, and the field labor of slavery times has kept her ignorant of the habitudes of neatness and the requirements of order. Indeed, coarse food, coarse clothes, coarse living, coarse manners, coarse companions, coarse surroundings, coarse neighbors, both black and white, yea, everything coarse, down to the coarse, ignorant, senseless religion, which excites her sensibilities and starts her passions, go to make up the life of the masses of black women in the hamlets and villages of the rural South.

This is the state of black womanhood. Take the girlhood of this same region, and it presents the same aspect, save that in large districts the white man has not forgotten the olden times of slavery and with indeed the deepest sentimental abhorrence of "amalgamation," still thinks that the black girl is to be perpetually the victim of his lust! In the larger towns and in cities our girls in common schools and academies are receiving superior culture. Of the 15,000 colored schoolteachers in the South, more than half are colored young women, educated since emancipation. But even these girls, as well as their more ignorant sisters in rude huts, are followed and tempted and insulted by the ruffianly element of Southern society, who think that black *men* have no rights which white men should regard, and black *women* no virtue which white men should respect!

And now look at the *vastness* of this degradation. If I had been speaking of the population of a city, or a town, or even a village, the tale would be a sad and melancholy one. But I have brought you the condition of millions of women. According to the census of 1880 there were, in the Southern states 3,327,678 females of all ages of the African race. Of these there were 674,365 girls between twelve and twenty, 1,522,696 between twenty and eighty. "These figures," remarks an observing friend of mine, "are startling!" And when you think that the masses of these women live in the rural districts; that they grow up in rudeness and ignorance; that their former masters are using few means to break up their hereditary degradation, you can easily take in the pitiful condition of this population and forecast the inevitable future to multitudes of females unless a mighty special effort is made for the improvement of the black womanhood of the South.

I know the practical nature of the American mind, I know how the question of values intrudes itself into even the domain of philanthropy; and, hence, I shall not be astonished if the query suggests itself, whether special interest in the black woman will bring any special advantage to the American nation.

Let me dwell for a few moments upon this phase of the subject. Possibly the view I am about suggesting has never before been presented to the American mind. But, Negro as I am, I shall make no apology for venturing the claim that the Negress is one of the most interesting of all the classes of women on the globe. I am speaking of her, not as a perverted and degraded creature, but in her natural state, with her native instincts and peculiarities.

Let me repeat just here the words of a wise, observing, tenderhearted philanthropist, whose name and worth and words have attained celebrity. It is fully forty years ago since the celebrated Dr. Channing* said: "We are holding in bondage one of

---

* William Ellery Channing (1740–1842), clergyman and author, often referred to as the "Apostle of Unitarianism," was the founder of the

the best races of the human family. The Negro is among the mildest, gentlest of men. He is singularly susceptible of improvement from abroad. . . . His nature is affectionate, easily touched, and hence he is more open to religious improvement than the white man. . . . The African carries with him much more than *we* the genius of a meek, long-suffering, loving virtue."

I should feel ashamed to allow these words to fall from my lips if it were not necessary to the lustration of the character of my black sisters of the South. I do not stand here today to plead for the black *man*. He is a man; and if he is weak he must go to the wall. He is a man; he must fight his own way, and if he is strong in mind and body, he can take care of himself. But for the mothers, sisters and daughters of my race I have a right to speak. And when I think of their sad condition down South—think, too, that since the day of emancipation hardly any one has lifted up a voice in their behalf—I feel it a duty and a privilege to set forth their praises and to extol their excellencies. For, humble and benighted as she is, the black woman of the South is one of the queens of womanhood. If there is any other woman on this earth who in native aboriginal qualities is her superior, I know not where she is to be found; for, I do say, that in tenderness of feeling, in genuine native modesty, in large disinterestedness, in sweetness of disposition and deep humility, in unselfish devotedness, and in warm, motherly assiduities, the Negro woman is unsurpassed by any other woman on this earth. . . .

Perhaps I may be pardoned the intrusion, just here, of my own personal experience. During a residence of nigh twenty years in West Africa, I saw the beauty and felt the charm of the native female character. I saw the native woman in her *heathen* state, and was delighted to see, in numerous tribes, that extraordinary sweetness, gentleness, docility, modesty, and especially those maternal solicitudes which make every African boy both gallant and defender of his mother.

I saw her in her *civilized* state, in Sierra Leone; saw precisely the same characteristics, but heightened, dignified, refined and sanctified by the training of the schools, the refinements of civilization and the graces of Christian sentiment and feeling. Of all the memories of foreign travel there are none more delightful then those of the families and the female friends of Freetown.

American Unitarian Association. He was the author of numerous essays, including "Negro Slavery" (1835) and "Self Culture" (1838). Although he was not an Abolitionist, his writings on slavery were important.

A French traveler speaks with great admiration of the black ladies of Haiti. "In the towns," he says, "I met all the charms of civilized life. The graces of the ladies of Port-au-Prince will never be effaced from my recollections."

It was, without doubt, the instant discernment of these fine and tender qualities which prompted the touching sonnet of Wordsworth, written in 1802, on the occasion of the cruel exile of Negroes from France by the French government:

> Driven from the soil of France, a female came
>> From Calais with us, brilliant in array,
>> A Negro woman like a lady gay,
> Yet downcast as a woman fearing blame;
>> Meek, destitute, as seemed, of hope or aim
>> She sat, from notice turning not away,
> But on all proffered intercourse did lay
>> A weight of languid speech—or at the same
> Was silent, motionless in eyes and face.
>> Meanwhile those eyes retained their tropic fire
> Which burning independent of the mind,
>> Joined with the luster of her rich attire
> To mock the outcast—O ye heavens, be kind!
> And feel, thou earth, for this afflicted race!

But I must remember that I am to speak not only of the neglects of the black woman, but also of her needs. And the consideration of her needs suggests the remedy which should be used for the uplifting of this woman from a state of brutality and degradation.

I have two or three plans to offer, which, I feel assured, if faithfully used will introduce widespread and ameliorating influences amid this large population.

a. The *first* of these is specially adapted to the adult female population of the South and is designed for more immediate effect. I ask for the equipment and the mission of "sisterhoods" to the black women of the South. I wish to see large numbers of practical Christian women, women of intelligence and piety; women well trained in domestic economy; women who combine delicate sensibility and refinement with industrial acquaintance —scores of such women to go South; to enter every Southern state; to visit Uncle Tom's Cabin; to sit down with "Aunt Chloe" and her daughters; to show and teach them the ways and habits of thrift, economy, neatness and order; to gather them into mothers' meetings and sewing schools; and by both lectures and talks guide these women and their daughters into the modes and habits of clean and orderly housekeeping.

There is no other way, it seems to me, to bring about this domestic revolution. We cannot postpone this reformation to another generation. Postponement is the reproduction of the same evils in numberless daughters now coming up into life, imitators of the crude and untidy habits of their neglected mothers, and the perpetuation of plantation life to another generation. No, the effect must be made immediately, in *this* generation, with the rude, rough, neglected women of the times.

And it is to be done at their own homes, in their own huts. In this work all theories are useless. This is a practical need, and personal as practical. It is emphatically a personal work. It is to be done by example. The "Sister of Mercy," putting aside all fastidiousness, is to enter the humble and, perchance, repulsive cabin of her black sister, and gaining her confidence, is to lead her out of the crude, disordered and miserable ways of her plantation life into neatness, cleanliness, thrift and self-respect. In every community women could be found who would gladly welcome such gracious visitations and instructors, and seize with eagerness their lessons and teachings. Soon their neighbors would seek the visitations which had lifted up friends and kinsfolk from inferiority and wretchedness. And then, erelong, whole communities would crave the benediction of these inspiring sisterhoods, and thousands and tens of thousands would hail the advent of these missionaries in their humble cabins. And then, the seed of a new and orderly life planted in a few huts and localities, it would soon spread abroad, through the principle of imitation, and erelong, like the Banyan tree, the beneficent work would spread far and wide through large populations. Doubtless they would be received, first of all, with surprise, for neither they nor their mothers, for two hundred years, have known the solicitudes of the great and cultivated for their domestic comfort. But surprise would soon give way to joy and exultation. Mrs. Fanny Kemble Butler, in her work, *Journal of a Residence on a Georgian Plantation in 1838–39*, tells us of the amazement of the wretched slave woman on her husband's plantation when she went among them and tried to improve their quarters and to raise them above squalor; and then of their immediate joy and gratitude.*

* Frances Anne "Fanny" Kemble was a famous English actress. She came to the United States in 1833, toured the country, and married Pierce Butler, a member of an aristocratic Southern family. Before leaving for the South, she promised to write her friend Elizabeth Sedgwick, who was an opponent of slavery, of her experiences on Butler's cotton and rice plantations. In a series of letters Fanny Kemble described the conditions of the slaves and her reaction to slavery, and later she re-

There is nothing original in the suggestion I make for the "Sisters of Mercy." It is no idealistic and impractical scheme I am proposing, no newfangled notion that I put before you. The Roman Catholic Church has for centuries been employing the agency of women in the propagation of her faith and as dispensers of charity. The Protestants of Germany are noted for the effective labors of holy women, not only in the Fatherland but in some of the most successful missions among the heathen in modern times. The Church of England, in that remarkable revival which has lifted her up as by a tidal wave, from the dead passivity of the last century to an apostolic zeal and fervor never before known in her history, has shown, as one of her main characteristics, the wonderful power of "Sisterhoods," not only in the conversion of reprobates, but in the reformation of whole districts of abandoned men and women. This agency has been one of the most effective instrumentalities in the hands of that special school of devoted men called Ritualists. Women of every class in that church, many of humble birth, and as many more from the ranks of the noble, have left home and friends and the choicest circles of society, and given up their lives to the lowliest service of the poor and miserable. They have gone down into the very slums of her great cities, among thieves and murderers and harlots; amid filth and disease and pestilence; and for Christ's sake served and washed and nursed the most repulsive wretches; and then have willingly laid down and died, either exhausted by their labors or poisoned by infectious disease. Any one who will read the life of "Sister Dora" and of Charles Lowder, will see the glorious illustrations of my suggestion. Why cannot this be done for the black women of the South?

b. My second suggestion is as follows, and it reaches over to the future. I am anxious for a permanent and uplifting civilization to be engrafted in the Negro race in this land. And this can only be secured through the womanhood of a race. If you want the civilization of a people to reach the very best elements of their being and then, having reached them, there to abide as an indigenous principle, you must imbue the *womanhood* of that people with all its elements and qualities. Any movement which passes by the female sex is an ephemeral thing. Without them, no true nationality, patriotism, religion, cultiva-

leased her letters for book publication, hoping that her description of slavery would influence Great Britain to support the Union rather than the Confederacy. Her *Journal of a Residence on a Georgian Plantation* was published in New York, 1863.

tion, family life or true social status is a possibility. In *this* matter it takes *two* to make one—mankind is a duality. The *male* may bring, as an exotic, a foreign graft, say of a civilization, to a new people. But what then? Can a graft live or thrive of itself? By no manner of means. It must get vitality from the *stock* into which it is put; and it is the woman who gives the sap to every human organization which thrives and flourishes on earth.

I plead, therefore, for the establishment of at least one large *industrial school* in every Southern state for the black girls of the South. I ask for the establishment of schools which may serve especially the *home* life of the rising womanhood of my race. I am not soliciting for these girls scholastic institutions, seminaries for the cultivation of elegance, conservatories of music, and schools of classical and artistic training. I want such schools and seminaries for the women of my race as much as any other race; and I am glad that there are such schools and colleges, and that scores of colored women are students within their walls.

But this higher style of culture is not what I am aiming after for *this* great need. I am seeking something humbler, more homelike and practical, in which the education of the land and the use of the body shall be the specialties, and where the intellectual training will be the incident.

Let me state just here definitely what I want for the black girls of the South:

1. I want boarding schools for the *industrial training* of one hundred and fifty or two hundred of the poorest girls, of the ages of twelve to eighteen years.

2. I wish the *intellectual* training to be limited to reading, writing, arithmetic and geography.

3. I would have these girls taught to do accurately all domestic work, such as sweeping floors, dusting rooms, scrubbing, bedmaking, washing and ironing, sewing, mending and knitting.

4. I would have the trades of dressmaking, millinery, strawplaiting, tailoring for men, and suchlike, taught them.

5. The art of cooking should be made a specialty, and every girl should be instructed in it.

6. In connection with these schools, garden plots should be cultivated, and every girl should be required, daily, to spend at least an hour in learning the cultivation of small fruits, vegetables and flowers.

I am satisfied that the expense of establishing such schools would be insignificant. As to their maintenance, there can be no doubt that, rightly managed, they would in a brief time be self-supporting. Each school would soon become a hive of industry, and a source of income. But the *good* they would do is the main consideration. Suppose that the time of a girl's schooling be limited to *three*, or perchance to *two* years. It is hardly possible to exaggerate either the personal family or society influence which would flow from these schools. Every class, yea, every girl in an outgoing class, would be a missionary of thrift, industry, common sense and practicality. They would go forth, year by year, a leavening power into the houses, towns and villages of the Southern black population—girls fit to be thrifty wives of the honest peasantry of the South, the worthy matrons of their numerous households.

I am looking after the domestic training of the *masses;* for raising up women meet to be the helpers of *poor* men, the rank and file of black society, all through the rural districts of the South. The city people and the wealthy can seek more ambitious schools, and should pay for them.

Ladies and gentlemen, since the day of emancipation millions of dollars have been given by the generous Christian people of the North for the intellectual training of the black race in this land. Colleges and universities have been built in the South, and hundreds of youth have been gathered within their walls. The work of your own church in this regard has been magnificent and unrivaled, and the results which have been attained have been grand and elevating to the entire Negro race in America. The complement to all this generous and ennobling effort is the elevation of the black woman. Up to this day and time your noble philanthropy has touched, for the most part, the male population of the South, given them superiority and stimulated them to higher aspirations. But a true civilization can only then be attained when the life of woman is reached, her whole being permeated by noble ideas, her fine taste enriched by culture, her tendencies to the beautiful gratified and developed, her singular and delicate nature lifted up to its full capacity; and then, when all these qualities are fully matured, cultivated and sanctified, all their sacred influences shall circle around ten thousand firesides, and the cabins of the humblest freedmen shall become the homes of Christian refinement and of domestic elegance through the influence and the charm of the uplifted and cultivated black woman of the South!

THE COLOR LINE IN AMERICA

By Frederick Douglass

By the 1880's the Constitutional provisions of the four-teenth and fifteenth amendments with regard to the Negro were being rendered valueless by state legislation and Su-preme Court decisions. Most Negroes in the South were either sharecroppers or tenants, and for them this was simply another form of slavery; they were held on the land by a combination of heavy debt to their white landlords and a total lack of monetary reimbursement for their services. Prejudice was barring Negroes from participation in almost all phases of American life, and most avenues of social and economic improvement remained closed to them. The federal government, controlled by the Republi-can party, adopted a "hands off" policy and permitted white supremacy to emerge in the South unchallenged. In a speech at a Convention of Colored Men, Louisville, Ken-tucky, September 24, 1883, Frederick Douglass analyzed this situation and offered a solution. Here are parts of this speech, excerpted from the text in Three Addresses on the Relations Subsisting Between the White and Colored Peo-ple of the United States *by Frederick Douglass,* Washing-ton, 1886, p. 3–23.*

. . . WITH APPARENT SURPRISE, astonishment and im-patience we have been asked, "What more can the colored peo-ple of this country want than they now have, and what more is possible to them?" It is said they were once slaves, they are now free; they were once subjects, they are now sovereigns; they were once outside of all American institutions, they are now in-side of all and are a recognized part of the whole American peo-ple. Why, then, do they hold Colored National Conventions and thus insist upon keeping up the color line between themselves and their white fellow countrymen? We do not deny the perti-nence and plausibility of these questions, nor do we shrink from a candid answer to the argument which they are supposed to contain. For we do not forget that they are not only put to us by those who have no sympathy with us, but by many who wish us well, and that in any case they deserve an answer.

Before, however, we proceed to answer them, we digress here

to say that there is only one element associated with them which excites the least bitterness of feeling in us or that calls for special rebuke, and that is when they fall from the lips and pens of colored men who suffer with us and ought to know better. A few such men, well known to us and the country, happening to be more fortunate in the possession of wealth, education and position than their humbler brethren, have found it convenient to chime in with the popular cry against our assembling, on the ground that we have no valid reason for this measure or for any other separate from the whites; that we ought to be satisfied with things as they are. With white men who thus object the case is different and less painful. For them there is a chance for charity. Educated as they are and have been for centuries, taught to look upon colored people as a lower order of humanity than themselves and as having few rights, if any, above domestic animals, regarding them also through the medium of their beneficent religious creeds and just laws—as if law and practice were identical—some allowance can, and perhaps ought to, be made when they misapprehend our real situation and deny our wants and assume a virtue they do not possess. But no such excuse or apology can be properly framed for men who are in any way identified with us. What may be erroneous in others implies either baseness or imbecility in them. Such men, it seems to us, are either deficient in self-respect or too mean, servile and cowardly to assert the true dignity of their manhood and that of their race. To admit that there are such men among us is a disagreeable and humiliating confession. But in this respect, as in others, we are not without the consolation of company: we are neither alone nor singular in the production of just such characters. All oppressed people have been thus afflicted.

It is one of the most conspicuous evils of caste and oppression that they inevitably tend to make cowards and serviles of their victims, men ever ready to bend the knee to pride and power that thrift may follow fawning, willing to betray the cause of the many to serve the ends of the few; men who never hesitate to sell a friend when they think they can thereby purchase an enemy. Specimens of this sort may be found everywhere and at all times. There were Northern men with Southern principles in the time of slavery, and Tories in the revolution for independence. There are betrayers and informers today in Ireland, ready to kiss the hand that smites them and strike down the arm reached out to save them. Considering our long subjection to servitude and caste, and the many temptations to which we are exposed to betray our race into the hands of their enemies, the wonder is not that we have so many traitors among us as that we have so few.

The most of our people, to their honor be it said, are remarkably sound and true to each other. . . .

If liberty, with us, is yet but a name, our citizenship is but a sham, and our suffrage thus far only a cruel mockery, we may yet congratulate ourselves upon the fact, that the laws and institutions of the country are sound, just and liberal. There is hope for a people when their laws are righteous, whether for the moment they conform to their requirements or not. But until this nation shall make its practice accord with its Constitution and its righteous laws, it will not do to reproach the colored people of this country with keeping up the color line—for that people would prove themselves scarcely worthy of even theoretical freedom, to say nothing of practical freedom, if they settled down in silent, servile and cowardly submission to their wrongs, from fear of making their color visible. They are bound by every element of manhood to hold conventions, in their own name and on their own behalf, to keep their grievances before the people and make every organized protest against the wrongs inflicted upon them within their power. They should scorn the counsels of cowards and hang their banner on the outer wall.

Who would be free, themselves must strike the blow. We do not believe, as we are often told, that the Negro is the ugly child of the national family, and the more he is kept out of sight the better it will be for him. You know that liberty given is never so precious as liberty sought for and fought for. The man outraged is the man to make the outcry. Depend upon it, men will not care much for a people who do not care for themselves. Our meeting here was opposed by some of our members, because it would disturb the peace of the Republican party. The suggestion came from coward lips and misapprehended the character of that party. If the Republican party cannot stand a demand for justice and fair play, it ought to go down. We were men before that party was born, and our manhood is more sacred than any party can be. Parties were made for men, not men for parties.

If the six millions of colored people of this country, armed with the Constitution of the United States, with a million votes of their own to lean upon, and millions of white men at their back, whose hearts are responsive to the claims of humanity, have not sufficient spirit and wisdom to organize and combine to defend themselves from outrage, discrimination and oppression, it will be idle for them to expect that the Republican party or any other political party will organize and combine for them or care what becomes of them. Men may combine to prevent cruelty to animals, for they are dumb and cannot speak for themselves; but we are men and must speak for ourselves, or we shall not be spoken for at all. We have conventions in America for Ireland, but we should have none if Ireland did not speak for herself. It is because she makes a noise and keeps her cause before the people that other people go to her help. It was the sword of Washington that gave independence the sword of Lafayette. In conclusion upon this color objection, we have to say that we meet here in open daylight. There is nothing sinister about us. The eyes of the nation are upon us. Ten thousand newspapers may tell if they choose of whatever is said and done here. They may commend our wisdom or condemn our folly, precisely as we shall be wise or foolish.

We put ourselves before them as honest men, and ask their judgment upon our work.

THE LABOR QUESTION

Not the least important among the subjects to which we invite your earnest attention is the condition of the laboring class at the South. Their cause is one with the laboring classes all over the world. The labor unions of the country should not throw away this colored element of strength. Everywhere there is dissatisfaction with the present relation of labor and capital, and today no subject wears an aspect more threatening to civilization than the respective claims of capital and labor, landlords and tenants. In what we have to say for our laboring class we expect to have and ought to have the sympathy and support of laboring men everywhere and of every color.

It is a great mistake for any class of laborers to isolate itself and thus weaken the bond of brotherhood between those on whom the burden and hardships of labor fall. The fortunate ones of the earth, who are abundant in land and money know nothing of the anxious care and pinching poverty of the laboring classes, may be indifferent to the appeal for justice at this point, but the laboring classes cannot afford to be indifferent. What labor everywhere wants, what it ought to have and will some day demand and receive, is an honest day's pay for an honest day's work. As the laborer becomes more intelligent he will develop what capital already possesses—that is, the power to organize and combine for its own protection. Experience demonstrates that there may be a wages of slavery only a little less

galling and crushing in its effects than chattel slavery, and that
this slavery of wages must go down with the other. . . .

THE ORDER SYSTEM*

No more crafty and effective device for defrauding the
Southern laborer could be adopted than the one that substitutes
orders upon shopkeepers for currency in payment of wages. It
has the merit of a show of honesty, while it puts the laborer
completely at the mercy of the landowner and the shopkeeper.
He is between the upper and the nether millstones and is hence
ground to dust. It gives the shopkeeper a customer who can
trade with no other storekeeper, and thus leaves the latter no
motive for fair dealing except his own moral sense, which is
never too strong. While the laborer holding the orders is tempted,
by their worthlessness as a circulating medium, to get rid of
them at any sacrifice, and hence is led into extravagance and
consequent destitution.

The merchant puts him off with his poorest commodities at
highest prices, and can say to him take those or nothing. Worse
still, by this means the laborer is brought into debt, and hence
is kept always in the power of the landowner. When this system
is not pursued and land is rented to the freedman, he is charged
more for the use of an acre of land for a single year than the
land would bring in the market if offered for sale. On such a
system of fraud and wrong one might well invoke a bolt from
heaven—red with uncommon wrath.

It is said if the colored people do not like the conditions upon
which their labor is demanded and secured, let them leave and
go elsewhere. A more heartless suggestion never emanated
from an oppressor—having for years paid them in shop orders,
utterly worthless outside the shop to which they are directed,
without a dollar in their pockets, brought by this crafty process
into bondage to the landowners, who can and would arrest them
if they should attempt to leave them when they are told to go.

We commend the whole subject to the Senate Committee of
Labor and Education, and urge upon that Committee the duty
to call before it not only the landowners, but the landless laborers of the South, and thus get at the whole truth concerning
the labor question of that section.

* Under the Order System, Negro sharecroppers and laborers were paid
not in legal currency but in scrip, which was redeemable at face value
only at the store of the planter or merchant who issued it. A somewhat
similar system was used in the company stores of the coal mines.

EDUCATION

On the subject of equal education and educational facilities, mentioned in the call for this convention, we expect little resistance from any quarter. It is everywhere an accepted truth that in a country governed by the people, like ours, education of the youth of all classes is vital to its welfare, prosperity, and to its existence.

In the light of this unquestioned proposition, the patriot cannot but view with a shudder the widespread and truly alarming illiteracy as revealed by the census of 1880.*

The question as to how this evil is to be remedied is an important one. Certain it is that it will not do to trust to the philanthropy of wealthy individuals or benevolent societies to remove it. The states in which this illiteracy prevails either cannot or will not provide adequate systems of education for their own youth. But, however this may be, the fact remains that the whole country is directly interested in the education of every child that lives within its borders. The ignorance of any part of the American people so deeply concerns all the rest that there can be no doubt of the right to pass laws compelling the attendance of every child at school. Believing that such is now required and ought to be enacted, we hereby put ourselves on record in favor of stringent laws to this end.

In the presence of this appalling picture presented by the last census, we hold it to be the imperative duty of Congress to take hold of this important subject and, without waiting for the states to adopt liberal school systems within their respective jurisdictions, to enter vigorously upon the work of universal education.

The national government, with its immense resources, can carry the benefits of a sound common-school education to the door of every poor man from Maine to Texas, and to withhold this boon is to neglect the greatest assurance it has of its own perpetuity. As a part of the American people we unite most emphatically with others who have already spoken on this subject, in urging Congress to lay the foundation for a great national system of aid to education at its next session. . . .

POLITICAL EQUALITY

Flagrant as have been the outrages committed upon colored citizens in respect to their civil rights, more flagrant, shock-

* In the census of 1880, seventy percent of the Negro population were recorded as illiterate.

ing and scandalous still have been the outrages committed upon our political rights, by means of bulldozing and Kukluxing, Mississippi plans, fraudulent counts, tissue ballots and the like devices. Three states in which the colored people outnumber the white population are without colored representation and their political voice suppressed. The colored citizens in those states are virtually disfranchised, the Constitution held in utter contempt and its provisions nullified. This has been done in the face of the Republican party and successive Republican administrations.

It was once said by the great O'Connell that the history of Ireland might be traced like a wounded man through a crowd by the blood, and the same may be truly said of the history of the colored voters of the South.

They have marched to the ballot box in face of gleaming weapons, wounds and death. They have been abandoned by the government and left to the laws of nature. So far as they are concerned, there is no government or Constitution of the United States.

They are under control of a foul, haggard and damning conspiracy against reason, law and Constitution. How you can be indifferent, how any leading colored men can allow themselves to be silent in presence of this state of things, we cannot see.

"Should tongues be mute while deeds are wrought which well might shame extremest hell?" And yet they are mute, and condemn our assembling here to speak out in manly tones against the continuance of this infernal reign of terror.

This is no question of party. It is a question of law and government. It is a question whether men shall be protected by law or be left to the mercy of cyclones of anarchy and bloodshed. It is whether the government or the mob shall rule this land; whether the promises solemnly made to us in the Constitution be manfully kept or meanly and flagrantly broken. Upon this vital point we ask the whole people of the United States to take notice that whatever of political power we have shall be exerted for no man of any party who will not in advance of election promise to use every power given him by the government, state or national, to make the black man's path to the ballot box as straight, smooth and safe as that of any other American citizen.

POLITICAL AMBITION

We are as a people often reproached with ambition for political offices and honors. We are not ashamed of this alleged ambition. Our destitution of such ambition would be our real shame. If the six millions and a half of people whom we represent could develop no aspirants to political office and honor under this government, their mental indifference, barrenness and stolidity might well enough be taken as proof of their unfitness for American citizenship.

It is no crime to seek or hold office. If it were it would take a larger space than that of Noah's Ark to hold the white criminals.

One of the charges against this convention is that it seeks for the colored people a larger share than they now possess in the offices and emoluments of the government.

We are now significantly reminded by even one of our own members that we are only twenty years out of slavery, and we ought therefore to be modest in our aspirations. Such leaders should remember that men will not be religious when the devil turns preacher . . .

We are far from affirming that there may not be too much zeal among colored men in pursuit of political preferment; but the fault is not wholly theirs. They have young men among them noble and true, who are educated and intelligent—fit to engage in enterprise of "pith and moment"—who find themselves shut out from nearly all the avenues of wealth and respectability, and hence they turn their attention to politics. They do so because they can find nothing else. The best cure for the evil is to throw open other avenues and activities to them.

We shall never cease to be a despised and persecuted class while we are known to be excluded by our color from all important positions under the government.

While we do not make office the one thing important, nor the one condition of our alliance with any party, and hold that the welfare, prosperity and happiness of our whole country is the true criterion of political action for ourselves and for all men, we cannot disguise from ourselves the fact that our persistent exclusion from office as a class is a great wrong, fraught with injury, and ought to be resented and opposed by all reasonable and effective means in our power.

We hold it to be self-evident that no class or color should be the exclusive rulers of this country. If there is such a ruling class, there must of course be a subject class, and when this condition is once established this government of the people, by the people and for the people, will have perished from the earth.

THESE EVILS CALL LOUDLY FOR REDRESS

By John P. Green

In May, 1884, seventy-five delegates from twelve states, nearly all located in the North, convened in Pittsburgh to examine the problems of the black American and apply pressure on the Republican party to deal with them. The leading address was delivered by John P. Green, a member of the Ohio state legislature. Green was born in North Carolina in 1845 and moved to Cleveland at the age of twelve. After graduation from high school he studied law, spent a few years in South Carolina during Reconstruction, and upon his return to Cleveland was elected Justice of the Peace for three successive terms and, in 1881, to the lower house of the state legislature. Green was the first Negro to serve in the state senate. In the legislature he championed civil rights and introduced the state Labor Day bill, which became law in 1890 and made him known as the "Daddy of Labor Day." He served in the Post Office Department in Washington under Presidents William McKinley and Theodore Roosevelt.

Green's speech to the Pittsburgh convention combined an indictment of the treatment of his people in American society, a plea to the Republican party to live up to its platforms, and an optimistic prediction of what the future held in store for the Negro. The speech, presented here in part, appeared in the New York Globe, *May 3, 1884.*

MR. CHAIRMAN AND GENTLEMEN: The Negro-hating class of the United States, not satisfied that they robbed us of our liberties and for two hundred and fifty years subjected us to bondage worse than death, which prostituted our manhood and denied us all the essentials to the pursuit of happiness, have today, like their Attic prototype, prepared for us a Procrustean bed, to which we must conform or lie in torture on it. If too short, they would stretch us to its dimensions, and if we overreach, curtail our fair proportions. Such an emergency as this, my friends, we are here to ponder over, and how we best may meet it.

It is a sad reflection for the young colored men of this day and generation that, although they are nominally free, they are as a matter of fact so proscribed and hampered by class legislation, unjust decisions and caste distinctions, as almost to produce in their mind the conviction that the term *citizen* is a delusion and a snare, meaning one thing in the North and another in the South, everywhere varying in its signification, according to the color of the person to whom it is applied. Turn where he may, he is confronted with a discouraging paradox. In Ohio, Indiana, and other states of the North, for instance, the colored man is a citizen and by implication the equal of every other citizen; yet if he has in his veins "a distinct and visible admixture of African blood," he is not, according to law, the equal of the white citizen. In South Carolina, Georgia, and all Southern states, he has the right of suffrage, nominally, but he finds that custom has made "a scarecrow of the law" and he has neither a "free ballot nor a fair count." At every point, although to the manor born, at home, and in the midst of friends (?) he is none the less an alien and an outcast—hated, shunned and despised. . . .

What can be more hateful than a law like the following, found upon the pages of the revised statutes of Ohio, and to the same effect in other Northern states: "A person of pure white blood who intermarries, or has illicit carnal intercourse with any Negro, or person having a distinct and visible admixture of African blood; or any Negro, or person having a distinct and visible admixture of African blood, who intermarries, or has illicit carnal intercourse with any person of pure white blood, shall be fined not less than one hundred dollars, or imprisoned not more than three months, or both" (R. S. 6987). Here, then, is a statute that prescribes and limits our social status, and makes criminal in us an act which is permitted to every other race under the sun, and today, unless he has been pardoned, a colored man languishes in prison in the city of Toledo, Ohio, for marrying a white woman, an act which is not denied to any man in the state of Ohio, except to those of African descent. Far be it from me—or any other colored man, so far as my knowledge goes—to entertain a desire to trespass on the society of any person, or force our company on one who does not desire it, be she white or colored; for our social domain is sufficiently broad and varied to satisfy the most exacting, embracing, as it does, ladies of all shades of color to be found on the habitable globe. But to sit still, in this progressive age, with an obnoxious law, which discriminates against us on account of our racial affinity, staring us in the face, and menacing our future welfare, would be not only unwise, but criminal. . . . Again, in the revised statutes of Ohio (4008), we find the following: "When in the judgment of the Board [of Education] it will be for the advantage of the district to do so, it may organize separate schools for colored children." You will note the fact that the organization of these separate schools for colored children depends, not on what may be considered for the best good of the children, but upon what the Board may judge "for the advantage of the district." And so, with poor schoolhouses and in many instances ignorant teachers, we are, for the greater part, compelled to be contented; and our delicate little children trudge their weary way through mud and slush, and rain and snow, for miles and miles; even though a well-appointed schoolhouse may be situated within a rod of their father's house. If this be justice, then away with it! Give us one law for all, as equal in its application as it is universal in its operation, and which will not give to one famishing child bread, while it cast to another a stone. If the foregoing statements surprise and humiliate well-meaning American citizens, what shall be said of the ineffable crimes which stain the records of Southern events during the past decade, while the perpetrators of them stalk through the land unmolested? By the lurid glare of the incendiary torch, and the cruel hiss of the Ku Klux lash, liberty has been led captive and trembles in chains. Upon the escutcheons of three proud states the names Hamburg, Danville* and Copiah are written in deep-dyed characters.

> Here's the smell of blood still, (that)
> All the perfumes of Arabia will not sweeten . . .

Laws passed ostensibly for the punishment and suppression of crime, but in reality to entrap and enslave the ignorant and too-confiding freedmen, are seized upon as a sure and never-failing source for the supply of labor for the coal mines of Alabama, and the construction of public works in most of the Southern states.† Speaking of this system, a committee of the

* A massacre of Negroes occurred on July 8, 1876, in Hamburg, South Carolina. On November 4, 1883, a major race riot broke out in Danville, Virginia. It began after a Negro accidently jostled a white man in the streets, and ended with four Negroes and one white killed.

† The reference is to the convict-lease system, under which Negroes, in the main, were arrested for petty offenses and leased out by the state to private corporations and contractors, with the payment going to the state. Basically, it was a system for the recruitment of cheap labor for the benefit of corporations and individuals and a source of revenue for the state.

In January, 1888, the Tennessee Coal, Iron & Railroad Company in Birmingham, Alabama, was given an exclusive contract for ten years to use all state convicts as laborers in its coal mines. The company promised to compensate the state at a rate ranging from $9 to $18 a month, depending on the classification of the convict.

Mississippi legislature says: "Crimes have been committed under the guise of law, more cruel and offensive than in the Fleet and Marshalsea under the English system." And in regard to the subletting system the report says: "It is so horrible that the committee deems it improper to make public its horrors." . . . Some one may say, "These laws are of a general nature, and hence bear equally upon persons of both races." There might be some ground on which to base such a statement, were it not for the glaring facts that in those states where these systems are in vogue, the laboring and lower classes are composed almost exclusively of colored people, and the juries, judges and witnesses are nearly all white men who believe that the natural estate of the Negro is to labor for them and for the additional reason that the convicts so sentenced and ill-treated are almost exclusively colored. . . .

These evils call loudly for redress, and woe betide us if we heed not the cry! But listen, my friends, and I will speak to you of another monster of evil, whose gargantuan proportions, restricted to no particular section of this country, cast a baleful shadow, to dwarf and blight the energies of every colored American. I refer to caste prejudice; an influence as widespread as it is obnoxious to its victims; which defies all statutory enactments, yields to no physical pressure and will, I fear, succumb only to the stern logic of events. It is so thoroughly woven in the texture of our social fabric that it confronts a colored man wheresoever he may turn. Is there a youth of African descent born in this land of liberty, in the full blaze of our boasted civilization, whose hopes beat high and whose aspirations would lead him up the mount of fame? Then let him not imagine that any laudable ambition, profound learning, suavity of manner, or correctness of deportment can open for him the doors which caste has closed against him, or make for him a place at the fireside of the dominant race. If he would keep alive the precious germ and make it bear perennial fruit, let him stop this bane as he would the deadly simoon and seek for strength and encouragement from that source from which all blessings flow. However, the worst phase of this iniquity does not consist in the fact that the colored American is, at home, a social pariah, whose very touch is shunned; it lies deeper than this, and becomes oppressive, when met in the commercial world, obstructing our progress and keeping us poor. The road to clerical positions is nearly blocked by it; the doors of schoolhouses are closed against us asking positions as teachers, unless it be in schools for colored children exclusively, and our ministers are remanded to the pulpits of colored organizations. The doors to

lodges and benevolent associations refuse to open to us knocking, while barbershops, restaurants, hotels and common carriers either refuse flatly to accommodate us, or else make us
feel that we are of the despised race by insulting us. Recognizing
the fact that matters of a strictly social nature will regulate
themselves, and that every man has a right to select his own
company, no gentleman or lady of color demands or expects
any legislation in this behalf, for to do so would be superlative
nonsense. But while the foregoing is true, it is none the less a
fact that, where this prejudice intervenes to rob us of the means
necessary to the enjoyment of our civil rights, we do complain,
and look to the government to protect and shield us by direct
legal enactment. And here again we are confronted by another
paradox, as enunciated by our model Supreme Court;* that is
to say, the Constitution has created us citizens, but, except in
the territories, has conferred upon us no rights which Congress
can protect us in. . . .

It will hardly be disputed that in the past, when we were
bowed down in grief and sorrow, that grand organization known
as the Republican party, like a white-winged angel of mercy,
came to our rescue and pulled us out of the slough of despond,
placed our feet upon the rock of liberty, threw about our
shoulders the mantle of citizenship and, placing in our hands
improved arms and the ballot as our shield of defense, if properly used, bade us advance and protect ourselves in the rights
of life, liberty and the pursuit of happiness. For all this we are
grateful, and say "God bless the Grand Old Party!" But this is
not sufficient; it must do more ere its noble mission will be fulfilled. In its platforms, and by the utterances of some of its most
conspicuous standard-bearers, it has declared in favor of the
equality of all men before the law. Nay, more; we have been
taught to believe by the platforms and declarations of that
party in the past, that it stood for just such a centralized form
of government as could and would protect the humblest citizen
in all the fundamental rights implied in the term, and would
merit and gain the dignified term *nation*. Will it longer stand
by in silence, while good men and true are denied their citizenship in sections of this country, and murdered while quietly
attempting to maintain them? Is it ready now to admit that this
government has not the power under the law to protect the
humblest citizen in the enjoyment of his civil liberties, that its

* Green is referring to the decision of the Supreme Court in 1883 declaring unconstitutional most of the provisions of the Civil Rights Act of
1875.

only power is to tax and draft for war, giving nothing in return? Or will it stand by the doctrine that this government is of the people and for the people, having in its organism those essential inherent qualities which will perpetuate its own existence, and gain the respect and love of the citizen? If the former, we would none of it; but if the latter, then we are willing to once again rally to its support and contribute of our votes and influence, and of our blood if need be, as we have done many other times in the past, to the end that it may maintain its position of proud eminence. There is one danger, however, incident to this age of magic that we must guard against. I refer to the danger of being too easily discouraged. Our progress during the last two decades has been of such a phenomenal nature that we are apt to become discouraged if we do not see the results of our labor speedily appear. This should not be; for though the picture disclosed to our view is a sad one in many respects, when compared with that which confronted us twenty years ago it is full of encouragement. From every section of this glorious land come encouraging reports as to the progress of the colored Americans. In the South, where his name is legion, he only needs protection and a little encouragement, to enable him to become a strong tower of defense. Thoroughly American in all his feeling and sympathies, with a willing heart and strong arm, the United States may well be proud of him as a reliable source of strength in time of need. He is accumulating wealth and heaping up stores of knowledge, and his influence is destined to be felt for good for all time to come.

REASONS FOR A NEW POLITICAL PARTY

By Rev. Henry McNeal Turner

The abandonment of Radical Reconstruction by the Republican party caused a number of black Americans to question the wisdom of supporting the party of Abraham Lincoln, but it was not until the Supreme Court decision of 1883 nullifying the Civil Rights Act of 1875 that disenchantment with the Republican party made considerable headway in the Negro community. Henry McNeal Turner broke with the Republican party soon after the decision, and publicly advised his people to do likewise. In a speech in Atlanta, Georgia, February 12, 1886, Turner spoke out in favor of a new political party to fulfill the promise of the Civil War and Reconstruction. As a strict temperance man, he favored unity of all nondrinking Americans regardless of color to achieve this goal. Here is a major extract from this speech, taken from the text published in The Christian Recorder, *April 1, 1886.*

. . . I HAVE NOT DESERTED the Republican party, the Republican party has deserted me and seven millions of my race—under circumstances, too, of the most dastardly character known in human events. . . . We know what the Republican party has done. But, unfortunately, we know too much. We know that after it freed the Negro and pretended to clothe him with the aegis of citizenship, by making him a voter, officeholder, juror, et cetera, that it was a hard task to get an enactment through Congress that contemplated anything like civil rights; and that after the Negro held conventions, wrote petitions, whined and howled in ghastly refrains all over the land from year to year, until a feeble civil rights act was passed, that a Republican Supreme Court (really a conclave of human donkeys) there in Washington City declared the whole thing null and void, thus leaving the Negro, both those freed and who were free before, in a condition compared with which the serfs of Russia are lords. Never was a people left in such a degraded situation since time began, under a status of pretended citizenship, yet the Republican party gives that infamous decision a virtual acquiescence by such a dead silence that cannot be interpreted other than as an approval of it. . . .

The sequence of that decision and the reticence of the Republican party, amounting to a virtual approval, has entailed upon the Negro of the South a species of degradation almost indescribable. Our ladies are robbed daily and insulted upon the public highways by railroad roughs brought here from the ends of the earth, even down to Swedes who can scarcely utter the language of their insults. We are put in front of baggage cars in many instances, so that, if an accident should happen, the trunks and other baggage would fare better than the Negro in the smashup. We must either starve along the highways or travel or go to the kitchen and buy scraps, not being allowed even to enter the dining room to eat at a separate table, when in many instances the boardinghouse itself does not compare with my kitchen. Right here at our depot in Atlanta, I cannot enter the lunch stand and drink a cup of tea at the counter much less at a table. If I get the tea at all, it must be sent out-

doors. These and a hundred other reasons which I cannot enumerate prompt a desire in me for a new party.

A great moral temperance party, a party that will take up
the work of reform and equity where the Republican party laid
it down, and carry it to successful completion. Between the
Democratic party and the Republican party there is no difference at present, so far as it affects the Negro; one holds and the
other throttles, one robs and the other looks with a smile, one
steals and the other conceals, one lampoons and the other says
well done. Therefore, as a man, a free man, a free-born man
though a Negro, I cannot support either one of these parties as
such. I mean upon their respective merits, nor will I ever do so
while both ignore my civil rights. Thus my reasons for clamoring for a third party or a new party, a great moral-reform party,
a party that good men of all parties, shades and complexions
can join and finish the work of humanity.

A civilization that does not comprehend humanity is rotten,
corrupt and evanescent. Our country cannot stand with seven
millions of enemies in it, and every Negro who has any of the
nobler instincts in his nature will loathe this country as long
as his humanity is proscribed, insulted and outraged. These are
only a few of my reasons for wanting a third party. Let us have
a great party made up of sober men, no liquor-drinking men,
men of high moral sentiments, a party whose policy will be
right and not anything for success, and my word for it, millions
of sober Republicans and sober Democrats and nonpartisans
and ministers of the gospel and philanthropists and humanitarians North and South will rally to its support. . . .

THE PRESENT RELATIONS OF LABOR AND CAPITAL

By T. Thomas Fortune

*The year 1886 was one of intense struggle between labor
and capital in the United States. In cities and towns the
armies of labor organized and gave expression to the pent-
up bitterness of years of exploitation in a series of strikes
which shook the nation to its foundation. On May 1, 1886,*

about 350,000 workers in 11,562 establishments in the country at large went on strike for an eight-hour day.

This was the setting for the speech delivered on April 20, 1886, by T. Thomas Fortune before the Brooklyn (New York) Literary Union. Born a slave in 1856 in Florida, Fortune saw the Ku Klux Klan in action as a boy. With little formal education, but with practical knowledge of the printer's trade, Fortune came to New York in 1879 and rose to become the most able black journalist of his day. He became part owner and editor of his own newspaper, the Globe, *which later became the* Freeman, *and finally the New York* Age. *Fortune was influenced by Karl Marx and Henry George and he demonstrated this in his remarkable book,* Black and White: Land, Labor and Politics in the South, *published in New York in 1884.*

(The speech presented here is taken from the New York Freeman, *May 1, 1886.)*

I DO NOT EXAGGERATE the gravity of the subject when I say that it is now the very first in importance not only in the United States but in every country in Europe. Indeed the wall of industrial discontent encircles the civilized globe.

The iniquity of privileged class and concentrated wealth has become so glaring and grievous to be borne that a thorough agitation and an early readjustment of the relation which they sustain to labor can no longer be delayed with safety to society.

It does not admit of argument that every man born into the world is justly entitled to so much of the produce of nature as will satisfy his physical necessities; it does not admit of argument that every man, by reason of his being, is justly entitled to the air he must breathe, the water he must drink, the food he must eat and the covering he must have to shield him from the inclemency of the weather. These are self-evident propositions, not disputed by the most orthodox advocate of excessive wealth on the one hand and excessive poverty on the other. That nature intended these as the necessary correlations of physical being is abundantly proved in the primitive history of mankind and in the freedom and commonality of possession which now obtain everywhere among savage people. The moment you deny to a man the unrestricted enjoyment of all the elements upon which the breath he draws is dependent, that moment you deny to him the inheritance to which he was born.

I maintain that organized society, as it obtains today, based as it is upon feudal conditions, is an outrageous engine of torture and an odious tyranny; that it places in the hands of a few the prime elements of human existence, regardless of the great mass of mankind; that the whole aim and necessity of the extensive and costly machinery of the law we are compelled to maintain grows out of the fact that this fortunate or favored minority would otherwise be powerless to practice upon the masses of society the gross injustice which everywhere prevails.

For centuries the aim and scope of all law have been to more securely hedge about the capitalist and the landowner and to repress labor within a condition wherein bare subsistence was the point aimed at.

From the institution of feudalism to the present time the inspiration of all conflict has been that of capitalist, landowner and hereditary aristocracy against the larger masses of society —the untitled, the disinherited proletariat of the world.

This species of oppression received its most memorable check in the great French Revolution, wherein a new doctrine became firmly rooted in the philosophy of civil government—that is, that the toiling masses of society possessed certain inherent rights which kingcraft, hereditary aristocracy, landlordism and usury mongers must respect. As a result of the doctrine studiously inculcated by the philosophers of the French Revolution we had the revolt of the blacks of Haiti, under the heroic Touissaint L'Ouverture, the bloody Dessalines and the suave, diplomatic and courtly Christophe, by which the blacks secured forever their freedom as free men and their independence as a people; and our own great Revolution, wherein the leading complaint was taxation by the British government of the American colonies without conceding them proportionate representation. At bottom in each case, bread and butter was the main issue. So it has always been. So it will continue to be, until the scales of justice are made to strike a true balance between labor on the one hand and the interest on capital invested and the wages of superintendence on the other. Heretofore the interest on capital and the wages of superintendence have absorbed so much of the wealth produced as to leave barely nothing to the share of labor.

It should be borne in mind that of this trinity labor is the supreme potentiality. Capital, in the first instance, is the product of labor. If there had never been any labor there would not now be any capital to invest. Again, if a bonfire were made of all the so-called wealth of the world it would only require a few years for labor to reproduce it; but destroy the brawn and muscle of the world and it could not be reproduced by all the gold ever delved from the mines of California and Australia and the fabulous gems from the diamond fields of Africa. In short, labor has been and is the producing agency, while capital has been and is the absorbing or parasitical agency.

Should we, therefore, be surprised that with the constantly growing intelligence and democratization of mankind labor should have grown discontented at the systematic robbery practiced upon it for centuries, and should now clamor for a more equitable basis of adjustment of the wealth it produces?

I could name you a dozen men who have in the last forty or fifty years amassed among them a billion dollars, so that a millionaire has become as common a thing almost as a pauper. How came they by their millions? Is it possible for a man in his lifetime, under the most favorable circumstances, to amass a million dollars? Not at all! The constitution of our laws must be such that they favor one as against the other to permit of such a glaring disparity.

I have outlined for you the past and present relations of capital and labor. The widespread discontent of the labor classes in our own country and in Europe gives emphasis to the position here taken.

I abhor injustice and oppression wherever they are to be found, and my best sympathies go out freely to the struggling poor and the tyranny-ridden of all races and lands. I believe in the divine right of man, not of caste or class, and I believe that any law made to perpetuate or to give immunity to these as against the masses of mankind is an infamous and not-to-be-borne infringement of the just laws of the Creator, who sends each of us into the world as naked as a newly fledged jay bird and crumbles us back into the elements of Mother Earth by the same processes of mutation and final dissolution.

The social and material differences which obtain in the relations of mankind are the creations of man, not of God. God never made such a spook as a king or a duke; he never made such an economic monstrosity as a millionaire; he never gave John Jones the right to own a thousand or a hundred thousand acres of land, with their complement of air and water. These are the conditions of man, who has sold his birthright to the Shylocks of the world and received not even a mess of pottage for his inheritance. The thing would really be laughable, if countless millions from the rice swamps of the Carolinas to the delvers in the mines of Russian Siberia, were not ground to powder to make a holiday for some selfish idler.

Everywhere labor and capital are in deadly conflict. The battle has been raging for centuries, but the opposing forces are just now in a position for that death struggle which it was inevitable must come before the end was. Nor is it within the scope of finite intelligence to forecast the lines upon which the settlement will be made. Capital is entrenched behind ten centuries of law and conservatism, and controlled withal by the wisest and coolest heads in the world. The inequality of the forces joined will appear very obvious. Yet the potentiality of labor will be able to force concessions from time to time, even as the commoners of England have through centurics been able to force from royalty relinquishment of prerogative after prerogative, until, from having been among the most despotic of governments under Elizabeth, the England of today under Queen Victoria is but a royal shadow. So the time may come when the forces of labor will stand upon absolute equality with those of capital, and that harmony between them obtain which has been sought for by wise men and fools for a thousand years.

HOW SHALL WE GET OUR RIGHTS?

By Rev. M. Edward Bryant

On December 4, 1887, the black citizens of Selma, Alabama, celebrated the anniversary of the Emancipation Proclamation and the Thirteenth Amendment. The Reverend M. Edward Bryant, an editor and minister of that city, delivered an address which militantly advocated uniting the entire black community of the United States in favor of complete freedom. His speech is noteworthy for its emphasis on the need for unity of the oppressed people, regardless of color, against their exploiters, for its support of labor unions, and for its call for resistance to violence and for the building of black economic and political power.

(The address presented here in part has been taken from the text which appeared in The Christian Recorder, *January 19, 1888.)*

IT BELONGS to us and to our children with strong propriety to celebrate this day. We see around us thousands of blessings which force emotions inexpressible in words and actions, which call upon us in the still small voice of gratitude and in the thunder tones of race pride and race appreciation to celebrate the day with songs, music, marches, acclamations, prayers and sermons. . . . But when we revisit the old plantation and the "nigger quarters" and in imagination hear the baying of the "nigger hounds," the low, brutal cursings of the overseer, and see the "nigger lash"; when we again pass through and by the swamps where we used to hide as "runaway niggers"; when we behold the fields fertilized with, and since cursed, by our spilled blood and that of our fathers and mothers—these things call upon us to do more than rejoice. They call upon us to bring our children to the altar, as Hamilcar did his son Hannibal, and make them swear never to rest contented night nor day until the tyrannical spirit of oppression which yet lingers in this land and the sprouts of the deadly upas tree of slavery shall be plucked up by root and branch, and a man and a woman shall be known, by the way they conduct themselves, without regard to color.

Let the world know that we prefer death by assassination, by drowning, by fire, by wild beasts, as the martyrs in the Middle Ages, as the Haitians under Toussaint, as the Americans under the British, to such liberty as we have today. The white fathers died that their children might be free. Does the Negro love *his* children?

Against that honest class of whites who are in favor of giving us our rights I have nothing to say but praise. Neither do I plead for war or resort to force, but a fixed, unyielding, unalterable determination to defend ourselves when attacked and to petition, persuade and demand our rights whatever may be the consequences. They would die before they would endure what we are enduring. History proves this. . . .

This is a day of great rejoicing and thanksgiving with us, and rightly so. But the Negro is yet to create his own national thanksgiving and celebration day by some mighty achievements of his own. He is yet to march his own army across the Red Sea and erect his own monuments, and his own poets are yet to compose and sing his own triumphal songs. . . .

What kind of government is this under which we live today? . . . The fathers of this country who wrote and laid down their lives for the grand, godlike proposition, "All men are created equal," were martyrs to the freedom of the earth. Today we honor them. But descendants of these almost-inspired men have disgraced their fathers and have followed in the track of the ancient doctrines that "might makes right," until they plunged this country into the cursed system of slavery which has brought the curse of almighty God upon this land—plunged it into civil internecine war and nearly destroyed the government of the fathers. Not yet satisfied, these descendants are still trying to perpetuate a system worse than slavery upon the colored and poor whites of this country which threatens the curse of God again upon this land. The laborers of this country are oppressed and downtrodden. In the North, the Goulds, Vanderbilts, are the oppressors and tyrants. In the South, the legislatures, social system, landowners, advance houses and in fact two thirds of the whites are the usurpers, tyrants, oppressors. . . .

The Negro is so treated today in regard to his civil, political and social rights in many parts that any condition would be preferable to his present condition. That in this country and under this government all men are created equal, is especially in the South a lie. It is a lie in our courts, it is a lie on railroads and steamboats; it is a lie in hotels; it is a lie in the streets, woods; it is a lie as it flaunts to the breezes on sea and in foreign parts; it is a lie in church; it is a lie at the sacrament table; it is a lie at the dying bed; a lie with the dead; a lie in the graveyard; it is a lie everywhere.

We are robbed, swindled, cheated, assassinated, falsely imprisoned, lynched, told to stand back and every indignity heaped upon us. The future will tell a sad story if this is continued. . . .

The dominant race up to this very moment insist upon describing the limits, prescribing the prerogatives of colored Americans. They say, you can't enter this car, you can't vote here, you can't work here, you shall not publish newspapers to stir up niggers concerning their rights, you can't hold office. Your wives and children and property shall not have the same protection we have. I do not advocate force. The logic of peace should be exhausted before any appeal is made to force. But we should have an intelligent understanding of what are our rights, and then we should have the courage to maintain and defend those rights. We should contend for our rights on every ground and protect them against outrage. The man or the party who attempts to abridge our rights, crush our manhood and womanhood because of our color, must be looked upon as robbers, villains, usurpers, tyrants.

A lot of fools have advanced the theory that "if we give the Negro his civil and political rights this will bring about social equality." What are civil rights? "All such as affect the whole people are regulated by them in their collective capacity as a government." "Social rights" are regulated wholly by individual tastes and inclinations. Social equality can never arise except by the consent of the parties themselves. We want civil and political rights. We helped to develop this country and are doing so now. We pay taxes and it is one of your laws that taxation without representation is tyranny. What should the Negro be advised to do under the circumstances?

1. Join the Knights of Labor and every other organization which promises to struggle to bring about a revolution and reformation in our affairs.

2. Organize leagues to raise money to prosecute railroads, steamboats, stores, hotels, and every one who tries to abridge our rights.

3. Organize leagues, not to create confusion, but to defend ourselves when attacked, just as the whites have always done.

4. Trade with your own business houses and those white men only who treat us right.

5. Never work any man's land who in any way abridges or helps to abridge our rights.

6. Support your own newspapers and never those who seek every opportunity to throw mud at us. No one can tell what and how much good our newspapers are doing to uplift the race.

7. Build schools everywhere, controlled and taught by yourselves, where true manhood and womanhood are taught. You need never expect a Negro child to be properly taught in a school which Southern white people control. His education and training and avarice disqualify him for the work.

Do you say you are afraid to try these things? Every true man despises a coward. His own children learn to hate him. His wife ought to leave him. "Eternal vigilance is the price of liberty." . . . We want honest, intelligent, temperance, level-headed, common-sense leaders who cannot be bought, and these leaders want followers who cannot be bought.

The colored people are waking up. A new race is coming on the stage. These persons are realizing that they must, through actual acquirements, succeed to their places in the affairs of this nation. We must take our cause in our hands very largely. We must press it in the social, civil, literary, artistic and business circles. Yes, we must press it everywhere. Congress, United States Commissioners, Supreme Court, President, have virtually said they cannot enforce the laws in the states. The Negro must stop whining and crying because the powers will not protect him. Wipe away tears, hush crying, be a man, protect himself, then go to law.

Has the Negro the power to carry out the above measures? The Negro has great latent power. He only needs to learn how to use this power wisely. The Negro is the laborer, the producer of this country. All professions, and business enterprises depend to a large extent upon agriculture. Let the Negro own his own homes, stock, control all products which are made by the race. . . . Then let race unite into one solid compact, and then ally itself with other suffering peoples as opportunities offer, and join the parties needing and bidding for his votes. Let him do away with political demagogues and select his best men as leaders and there will be a mighty revolution in this land. . . . The result will be that the great business houses which directly and indirectly are supported by us will go down and their owners must go to work or go somewhere else. In either case they will grow weaker and we stronger and stronger. . . . We can and must undermine our oppressors by controlling our own moneys until "All men are created equal" becomes a truth in this land.

Let me state here that some white people may think my remarks are severe. But let me state: all such must remember that I am a Southerner by birth and education and have inherited from my ancestors as much of the chivalric blood as they have. Secondly, I have read their histories and learned how to act and what to advise from them themselves. If they want to understand me let them take their wife and children and put them in the place of mine and let them take my place. . . .

Colored men of America, we have made great advances, but we have not reached Canaan. We must still contend against the Amalekites, Hittites, Hivites and Philistines. May the God who presides over the destinies of nations help us to work out our destiny. Physical slavery has fallen. Let us unite to break the chains of prejudice, ostracism, deprivation of civil, political and social rights, and the sins that are worse than physical slavery. . . .

IMPORTANCE OF RACE PRIDE

By Edward Everett Brown

Edward Everett Brown, a distinguished black lawyer, delivered an address on the importance of race pride before the National League of Boston, March 5, 1888. Here is the major portion of the address, taken from the New York Age, *March 24, 1888.*

. . . WHY SHOULD any man of African descent be ashamed of his race? Why should he consider himself inferior to a man of Anglo-Saxon descent? Why should he play the part of a coward and bow down and cringe and tamely submit to every indignity and outrageous insult that are constantly being heaped upon him? We have much to be proud of, as we calmly stop and consider what has been accomplished. It has been said that it is impossible to civilize us. Is it impossible to civilize man in one port of the earth more than in another? Turn back the pages of history and see if Rome, Greece, France, Germany or England was the cradle of civilization. The answer is no. For as far back as the lamp of tradition reaches, Africa was the cradle of science while Rome and Greece were clothed in darkness. As far back as the first rudiments of improvement can be traced they came from the very headwaters of the Nile, far in the interior of Africa, and it is an undisputed fact that there have been found, in shapeless ruins, the monuments of this primeval civilization. While the northern and western parts of Europe were yet barbarous, the Mediterranean coast of Africa was filled with cities, museums and churches. Every colored man who is interested in the progress of his race, ought to be proud of the glorious achievements of the race, especially when he thinks of the courage, the bravery displayed by black men when the black clouds of war burst upon this great nation from the time of the Revolution when that noble, heroic, immortal black patriot, Crispus Attucks, fired with the love of liberty and freedom, fell dead in King Street, Boston, fighting with that noble band against British tyranny and oppression. And in every great contest that has taken place in this country, black men were always in the front ranks, notwithstanding the fact that they were not recognized as men. They always fought with Spartan bravery and heroism to defend the institutions of America from the ruthless hand of the invader.

Since the ancient temples of slavery, rendered venerable alone by their antiquity, have crumbled into dust, the Negro has made rapid strides in this country, in spite of all the obstacles he has had to contend with. His influence today is being felt as never before in this great republic. In every department of industry, in its higher scientific branches, the Negro is proving to the world beyond any question that he is the equal and in many cases the superior of his Anglo-Saxon brother, if an equal opportunity be given him. The time has come now when the Negro asks no favors because he is colored, but he is willing to stand or fall upon his merits in the great battle of life and prove by his brains, his ambition, his pluck, his perseverance, his integrity, his patriotism, that he is a man created in the image of God with all the attributes of true manhood. In education the advancement of the Negro has been marvelous, when we consider that he was ground down so many years under that damnable accursed system of slave oligarchy that will always stain the fair fame of this great republic. Schools and colleges have sprung up as if by magic, which are sending forth an army of competent, well-trained, young colored men and women full of ambition, pride, enthusiasm, pluck, push and determination, bound to climb up the dizzy heights of the Alps and then cross over, understanding that beyond the Alps lies Italy, which means that their honest efforts have been crowned with success. In politics today the Negro is a very important factor. This is acknowledged by distinguished statesmen and politicians, for he is fast learning to think and act for himself. He has made up his mind that he will no longer bow down and be the slave of any party, that he will no longer support any man for public office who is an enemy of the race. It is a source of congratulation that in Boston and all over this country colored men see the necessity of banding themselves together in solid organization, firmly resolved to wage never-ceasing warfare against American prejudice, to secure equal rights and equal privileges.

What we need is more confidence in each other. Laying aside the petty jealousy, making a contribution of our best powers of mind and soul to benefit our race. A great many movements that have been started honestly and in good faith by noble, unselfish, courageous, intelligent colored men to promote and advance the interests of the race, have been killed by the mean, contemptible, designing treachery of other colored men, who, false to themselves and to their race, prove traitors and stab the movement in the back with their cruel daggers, as the Roman conspirators did Caesar in the senate chamber. There is a mighty work to be done in this country to elevate the race, and we need men of courage and principle who will contend for equal rights and never rest until those rights are guaranteed us. It is outrageous to know at this late day there is so much mean, contemptible prejudice and discrimination shown toward our race in this country in restaurants, schools, railroads and public places of amusement. It is a disgrace to American civilization that in Washington, the capitol of the nation, where the colored population is so extensive, that black children are prohibited from attending the same schools with the whites. And it is more disgraceful still that the colored people themselves are in part responsible for this state of affairs; because they fear that colored principals and schoolteachers would lose their situations, they submit to this galling state of serfdom, degrade their manhood and stifle conscience. . . . We often have exhibitions of the degrading influences that have come down to us as a result of the terrible system of slavery that the race has been under until within a very short time. So terrible has been its effects upon some of our people, that even now there are those who are even recognized by a large number of colored people, who have the effrontery to stand up and say that the Negro has no capacity for any position in which he can display qualifications like those exhibited by white men.

The hour is come when a courageous stand must be taken against the ruthless oppressors of our race. We owe it to the thousands who are wearing out a miserable existence under the galling yoke of prejudice and oppression. We owe it to ourselves if we would be true men and not the menials of tyrants. Let us have more self-respect, to be proud of our color and boast of our nationality, at all times to love better than all things colored men and things of our own race. . . . Let us use every effort to hurl men, whether they be black or white, from place or power when they fail to subserve our interests and see that we get fair play and equal chance in all the walks of life. . . .

WOMAN SUFFRAGE

By Frederick Douglass

Next to Abolition and the battle for equal rights for the Negro people, the cause closest to the heart of Frederick Douglass was woman's rights. The masthead of his paper, The North Star, featured the slogan, "Right is of no sex." Douglass was one of the few men present at the pioneer woman's-rights convention held at Seneca Falls, New York, in July, 1848, and it was he who seconded the resolution proposed by Elizabeth Cady Stanton, which asserted that it was "the duty of the women of this country to secure to themselves their sacred right to the elective franchise." Thereafter, Douglass was a constant champion of the right of women to vote. In April, 1888, in a speech before the International Council of Women, in Washington, D. C., Douglass recalled his role at the Seneca Falls convention,

and once again came out strongly for woman suffrage.
Here is a major portion of this address, excerpted from the
text that appeared in the Woman's Journal, *April 14, 1888.*

. . . THERE ARE FEW FACTS in my humble history to
which I look back with more satisfaction than to the fact, recorded in the history of the woman-suffrage movement, that I
was sufficiently enlightened at that early day, and when only
a few years from slavery, to support your resolution for woman
suffrage. I have done very little in this world in which to glory
except this one act—and I certainly glory in that. When I ran
away from slavery, it was for myself; when I advocated emancipation, it was for my people; but when I stood up for the rights
of woman, self was out of the question, and I found a little no-
bility in the act.

In estimating the forces with which this suffrage cause has
had to contend during these forty years, the fact should be remembered that relations of long standing beget a character in
the parties to them in favor of their continuance. Time itself is
a conservative power—a very conservative power. One shake of
his hoary locks will sometimes paralyze the hand and palsy the
tongue of the reformer. The relation of man to woman has the
advantage of all the ages behind it. Those who oppose a readjustment of this relation tell us that what is always was and
always will be, world without end. But we have heard this old
argument before, and if we live very long we shall hear it again.
When any aged error shall be assailed, and any old abuse is to
be removed, we shall meet this same old argument. Man has
been so long the king and woman the subject—man has been
so long accustomed to command and woman to obey—that both
parties to the relation have been hardened into their respective
places, and thus has been piled up a mountain of iron against
woman's enfranchisement.

The same thing confronted us in our conflicts with slavery.
Long years ago Henry Clay said, on the floor of the American
Senate, "I know there is a visionary dogma that man cannot
hold property in man," and, with a brow of defiance, he said,
"That is property which the law makes property. Two hundred
years of legislation has sanctioned and sanctified Negro slaves
as property." But neither the power of time nor the might of
legislation has been able to keep life in that stupendous barbarism.

The universality of man's rule over woman is another factor
in the resistance to the woman-suffrage movement. We are
pointed to the fact that men have not only always ruled over

women, but that they do so rule everywhere, and they easily think that a thing that is done everywhere must be right. Though the fallacy of this reasoning is too transparent to need refutation, it still exerts a powerful influence. Even our good Brother Jasper yet believes, with the ancient Church, that the sun "do move," notwithstanding all the astronomers of the world are against him. One year ago I stood on the Pincio in Rome and witnessed the unveiling of the statue of Galileo. It was an imposing sight. At no time before had Rome been free enough to permit such a statue to be placed within her walls. It is now there, not with the approval of the Vatican. No priest took part in the ceremonies. It was all the work of laymen. One or two priests passed the statue with averted eyes, but the great truths of the solar system were not angry at the sight, and the same will be true when woman shall be clothed, as she will yet be, with all the rights of American citizenship.

All good causes are mutually helpful. The benefits accruing from this movement for the equal rights of woman are not confined or limited to woman only. They will be shared by every effort to promote the progress and welfare of mankind everywhere and in all ages. It was an example and a prophecy of what can be accomplished against strongly opposing forces, against time-hollowed abuses, against deeply intrenched error, against worldwide usage, and against the settled judgment of mankind, by a few earnest women, clad only in the panoply of truth, and determined to live and die in what they considered a righteous cause.

I do not forget the thoughtful remark of our president in the opening address to this International Council, reminding us of the incompleteness of our work. The remark was wise and timely. Nevertheless, no man can compare the present with the past, the obstacles that then opposed us, and the influences that now favor us, the meeting in the little Methodist chapel forty years ago, and the Council in this vast theater today, without admitting that woman's cause is already a brilliant success. But, however this may be and whatever the future may have in store for us, one thing is certain—this new revolution in human thought will never go backward. When a great truth once gets abroad in the world, no power on earth can imprison it, or prescribe its limits, or suppress it. It is bound to go on till it becomes the thought of the world. Such a truth is woman's right to equal liberty with man. She was born with it. It was hers before she comprehended it. It is inscribed upon all the powers and faculties of her soul, and no custom, law or usage can ever destroy it. Now that it has got fairly fixed in the minds of the few, it is bound to become fixed in the minds of the many, and be supported at last by a great cloud of witnesses, which no man can number and no power can withstand.

The women who have thus far carried on this agitation have already embodied and illustrated Theodore Parker's three grades of human greatness. The first is greatness in executive and administrative ability; second, greatness in the ability to organize; and, thirdly, in the ability to discover truth. Wherever these three elements of power are combined in any movement, there is a reasonable ground to believe in its final success; and these elements of power have been manifest in the women who have had the movement in hand from the beginning. They are seen in the order which has characterized the proceedings of this Council. They are seen in the depth and comprehensiveness of the discussions had upon them in this Council. They are seen in the fervid eloquence and downright earnestness with which women advocate their cause. They are seen in the profound attention with which woman is heard in her own behalf. They are seen in the steady growth and onward march of the movement, and they will be seen in the final triumph of woman's cause, not only in this country, but throughout the world.

I DENOUNCE THE SO-CALLED EMANCIPATION AS A STUPENDOUS FRAUD

By Frederick Douglass

In the winter of 1888 Frederick Douglass visited South Carolina and Georgia to obtain a firsthand picture of the conditions of his people in the South during the post-Reconstruction era. He was deeply shocked by what he discovered. On April 10, soon after his return, he wrote to one of the leaders of a movement for encouraging the emigration of Southern Negroes to the Northwest: "I had hoped that the relations subsisting between the former slaves and the old master class would gradually improve; but while I believed this, and still have some such weak faith, I have of late seen enough, heard enough and learned enough of the condition of these people in South Carolina and Georgia to make me welcome any movement which will take them out of the wretched condition in which I now know them to be. While I shall continue to labor for increased justice to those who stay in the South, I give you my hearty 'Godspeed' your emigration scheme. I believe you are doing a good work."

A few days later, April 16, 1888, he spoke in Washington at the celebration of the twenty-sixth anniversary of emancipation in the District of Columbia. His address, one of the most effective he ever delivered, revealed how deeply he had been moved by his Southern tour. His voice quivered with rage as he described how the Negro was "nominally free" but actually a slave. In earnest tones, he told the nation: "I here and now denounce his so-called emancipation as a stupendous fraud—a fraud upon him, a fraud upon the world." He drew a terrifying picture of the exploitation of the Southern Negro, and he denounced the national government for having abandoned the black man, ignored his rights as an American citizen, and left him "a deserted, a defrauded, a swindled, and an outcast man—in law, free; in fact, a slave."

Douglass' speech created a sensation. Senator George B. Edmonds called it "the greatest political speech that I have read or heard in perhaps twenty years," and urged that it "be printed broadcast throughout our land." Here is Douglass' great and searing indictment of the treatment of the black American in the years following the overthrow of Reconstruction. The text is reprinted from the Washington National Republican, *April 17, 1888.*

FRIENDS AND FELLOW CITIZENS: it has been my privilege to assist in several anniversary celebrations of the abolition of slavery in the District of Columbia, but I remember no occasion of this kind when I felt a deeper solicitude for the future welfare of our emancipated people than now.

The chief cause of anxiety is not in the condition of the colored people of the District of Columbia, though there is much that is wrong and unsatisfactory here, but the deplorable condition of the Negro in the Southern states. At no time since the abolition of slavery has there been more cause for alarm on this account than at this juncture in our history.

I have recently been in two of the Southern states—South Carolina and Georgia—and my impression from what I saw, heard and learned there is not favorable to my hopes for the race. I know this is a sad message to bring you on this twenty-sixth anniversary of freedom in the District of Columbia, but I know, too, that I have a duty to perform and that duty is to tell the truth, the whole truth, and nothing but the truth, and I should be unworthy to stand here, unworthy of the confidence of the colored people of this country, if I should from any considerations of policy withhold any fact or feature of the condition of the freedmen which the people of this country ought to know.

The temptation on anniversary occasions like this is to prophesy smooth things, to be joyful and glad, to indulge in the illusions of hope—to bring glad tidings on our tongues, and words of peace reveal. But while I know it is always easier to be the bearer of glad tidings than sad ones, while I know that hope is a powerful motive to exertion and high endeavor, while I know that people generally would rather look upon the bright side of their condition than to know the worst; there comes a time when it is best that the worst should be made known, and in my judgment that time, in respect to the condition of the colored people of the South, is now. There are times when neither hope nor fear shoud be allowed to control our speech. Cry aloud and spare not, is the word of wisdom as well as of Scripture. "Ye shall know the truth, and the truth shall make you free," applies to the body not less than the soul, to this world not less than the world to come. Outside the truth there is no solid foundation for any of us, and I assume that you who have invited me to speak, and you who have come to hear me speak, expect me to speak the truth as I understand the truth.

The truth at which we should get on this occasion respects the precise relation subsisting between the white and colored people of the South, or, in other words, between the colored people and the old master class of the South. We have need to know this and to take it to heart.

It is well said that "a people may lose its liberty in a day and not miss it in half a century," and that "the price of liberty is eternal vigilance." In my judgment, with my knowledge of what has already taken place in the South, these wise and wide-awake sentiments were never more apt and timely than now.

I have assisted in fighting one battle for the abolition of slavery, and the American people have shed their blood in defense of the Union and the Constitution, and neither I nor they should wish to fight this battle over again; and in order that we may not, we should look the facts in the face today and, if possible, nip the evil in the bud.

I have no taste for the role of an alarmist. If my wishes could be allowed to dictate my speech I would tell you something quite the reverse of what I now intend. I would tell you that everything is lovely with the Negro in the South; I would tell you that the rights of the Negro are respected, and that he has no wrongs to redress; I would tell you that he is honestly paid for his labor; that he is secure in his liberty; that he is tried by a jury of his peers when accused of crime; that he is no longer subject to lynch law; that he has freedom of speech; that the gates of knowledge are open to him; that he goes to the ballot box unmolested; that his vote is duly counted and given its proper weight in determining result; I would tell you that he is making splendid progress in the acquisition of knowledge, wealth and influence; I would tell you that his bitterest enemies have become his warmest friends; that the desire to make him a slave no longer exists anywhere in the South; that the Democratic party is a better friend to him than the Republican party, and that each party is competing with the other to see which can do the most to make his liberty a blessing to himself and to the country and the world. But in telling you all this I should be telling you what is absolutely false, and what you know to be false, and the only thing which would save such a story from being a lie would be its utter inability to deceive.

What is the condition of the Negro at the South at this moment? Let us look at it both in the light of facts and in the light of reason. To understand it we must consult nature as well as circumstances, the past as well as the present. No fact is more obvious than the fact that there is a perpetual tendency of power to encroach upon weakness, and of the crafty to take advantage of the simple. This is as natural as for smoke to ascend or water to run down. The love of power is one of the strongest traits in the Anglo-Saxon race. This love of power common to the white race has been nursed and strengthened at the South by slavery: accustomed during two hundred years to the unlimited possession and exercise of irresponsible power, the love of it has become stronger by habit. To assume that this feeling of pride and power has died out and disappeared from the South is to assume a miracle. Any man who tells you that it has died out or has ceased to be exercised and made effective, tells you that which is untrue and in the nature of things could not be true. Not only is the love of power there, but a talent for its exercise has been fully developed. This talent makes the old master class of the South not only the masters of the Negro, but the masters of Congress and, if not checked, will make them the masters of the nation.

It was something more than an empty boast in the old times, when it was said that one slave master was equal to three Northern men. Though this did not turn out to be true on the battlefield, it does seem to be true in the councils of the nation. In sight of all the nation these ambitious men of the South have dared to take possession of the government which they, with broad blades and bloody hands, sought to destroy; in sight of all the nation they have disregarded and trampled upon the Constitution, and organized parties on sectional lines. From the ramparts of the Solid South, with their 153 electoral votes in the Electoral College, they have dared to defy the nation to put a Republican in the Presidential chair for the next four years, as they once threatened the nation with civil war if it elected Abraham Lincoln. With this grip on the Presidential chair, with the House of Representatives in their hands, with the Supreme Court deciding every question in favor of the states, as against the powers of the federal government, denying to the government the right to protect the elective franchise of its own citizens, they may well feel themselves masters, not only of their former slaves, but of the whole situation. With these facts before us, tell me not that the Negro is safe in the possession of his liberty. Tell me not that power will not assert itself. Tell me not that they who despise the Constitution they have sworn to support will respect the rights of the Negro, whom they already despise. Tell me not that men who thus break faith with God will be scrupulous in keeping faith with the poor Negro laborer of the South. Tell me not that a people who have lived by the sweat of other men's faces, and thought themselves Christian gentlemen while doing it, will feel themselves bound by principles of justice to their former victims in their weakness. Such a pretense in face of facts is shameful, shocking and sickening. Yet there are men at the North who believe all this.

Well may it be said that Americans have no memories. We look over the House of Representatives and see the Solid South enthroned there. We listen with calmness to eulogies of the South and of the traitors, and forget Andersonville.* We look over the Senate and see the Senator from South Carolina, and we forget Hamburg. We see Robert Smalls cheated out of his seat in Congress,† and forget the *Planter,* and the service rendered by the colored troops in the late war for the Union.

Well, the nation may forget; it may shut its eyes to the past

---

* Andersonville was the notorious Confederate prison in southwestern Georgia for Union prisoners, who were packed together with little food and hardly any medicine. From June to September, 1864, 8,589 prisoners died in Andersonville.

† In 1886 Robert Smalls was not seated in Congress as representative from South Carolina, even though he spoke for his right to his seat.

and frown upon any who may do otherwise, but the colored people of this country are bound to keep fresh a memory of the past till justice shall be done them in the present. When this shall be done we shall as readily as any other part of our respected citizens plead for an act of oblivion.

We are often confronted of late in the press and on the platform with the discouraging statement that the problem of the Negro as a free man and a citizen is not yet solved; that since his emancipation he has disappointed the best hopes of his friends and fulfilled the worst predictions of his enemies, and that he has shown himself unfit for the position assigned him by the mistaken statesmanship of the nation. It is said that physically, morally, socially and religiously he is in a condition vastly more deplorable than was his condition as a slave; that he has not proved himself so good a master to himself as his old master was to him; that he is gradually, but surely, sinking below the point of industry, good manners and civilization to which he attained in a state of slavery; that his industry is fitful; that his economy is wasteful; that his honesty is deceitful; that his morals are impure; that his domestic life is beastly; that his religion is fetichism, and his worship is simply emotional; and that, in a word, he is falling into a state of barbarism.

Such is the distressing description of the emancipated Negro as drawn by his enemies and as it is found reported in the journals of the South. Unhappily, however, it is a description not confined to the South. It has gone forth to the North. It has crossed the ocean; I met with it in Europe. And it has gone as far as the wings of the press and the power of speech can carry it. There is no measuring the injury inflicted upon the Negro by it. It cools our friends, heats our enemies, and turns away from us much of the sympathy and aid which we need and deserve to receive at the hands of our fellow men.

But now comes the question, Is this description of the emancipated Negro true? In answer to this question I must say, Yes and no. It is not true in all its lines and specifications and to the full extent of the ground it covers, but it certainly is true in many of its important features, and there is no race under heaven of which the same would not be equally true with the same antecedents and the same treatment which the Negro is receiving at the hands of this nation and the old master class, to which the Negro is still a subject.

I admit that the Negro, and especially the plantation Negro, the tiller of the soil, has made little progress from barbarism to civilization, and that he is in a deplorable condition since his emancipation. That he is worse off, in many respects, than when he was a slave, I am compelled to admit, but I contend that the fault is not his, but that of his heartless accusers. He is the victim of a cunningly devised swindle, one which paralyzes his energies, suppresses his ambition, and blasts all his hopes; and though he is nominally free he is actually a slave. I here and now denounce his so-called emancipation as a stupendous fraud—a fraud upon him, a fraud upon the world. It was not so meant by Abraham Lincoln; it was not so meant by the Republican party; but whether so meant or not, it is practically a lie, keeping the word of promise to the ear and breaking it to the heart.

Do you ask me why the Negro of the plantation has made so little progress, why his cupboard is empty, why he flutters in rags, why his children run naked, and why his wife hides herself behind the hut when a stranger is passing? I will tell you. It is because he is systematically and universally cheated out of his hard earnings. The same class that once extorted his labor under the lash now gets his labor by a mean, sneaking, and fraudulent device. That device is a trucking system which never permits him to see or to save a dollar of his hard earnings. He struggles and struggles, but, like a man in a morass, the more he struggles the deeper he sinks. The highest wages paid him is eight dollars a month, and this he receives only in orders on the store, which, in many cases, is owned by his employer. The scrip has purchasing power on that one store, and that one only. A blind man can see that the laborer is by this arrangement bound hand and foot, and is completely in the power of his employer. He can charge the poor fellow what he pleases and give what kind of goods he pleases, and he does both. His victim cannot go to another store and buy, and this the store-keeper knows. The only security the wretched Negro has under this arrangement is the conscience of the storekeeper—a conscience educated in the school of slavery, where the idea prevailed in theory and practice that the Negro had no rights which white men were bound to respect, an arrangement in which everything in the way of food or clothing, whether tainted meat or damaged cloth, is deemed good enough for the Negro. For these he is often made to pay a double price.

But this is not all, or the worst result of the system. It puts it out of the power of the Negro to save anything of what he earns. If a man gets an honest dollar for his day's work, he has a motive for laying it by and saving it for future emergency. It will be as good for use in the future and perhaps better a year hence than now, but this miserable scrip has in no sense the quality of a dollar. It is only good at one store and for a limited period. Thus the man who has it is tempted to get rid of it as soon as possible. It may be out of date before he knows it, or the storekeeper may move away and it may be left worthless on his hands.

But this is not the only evil involved in this satanic arrangement. It promotes dishonesty. The Negro sees himself paid but limited wages—far too limited to support himself and family, and that in worthless scrip—and he is tempted to fight the devil with fire. Finding himself systematically robbed he goes to stealing and as a result finds his liberty—such as it is— taken from him, and himself put to work for a master in a chain gang, and he comes out, if he ever gets out, a ruined man.

Every Northern man who visits the old master class, the landowners and landlords of the South, is told by the old slaveholders with a great show of virtue that they are glad that they are rid of slavery and would not have the slave system back if they could; that they are better off than they ever were before, and much more of the same tenor. Thus Northern men come home duped and go on a mission of duping others by telling the same pleasing story.

There are very good reasons why these people would not have slavery back if they could—reasons far more creditable to their cunning than to their conscience. With slavery they had some care and responsibility for the physical well-being of their slaves. Now they have as firm a grip on the freedman's labor as when he was a slave and without any burden of caring for his children or himself. The whole arrangement is stamped with fraud and is supported by hypocrisy, and I here and now, on this Emancipation Day: denounce it as a villainous swindle, and invoke the press, the pulpit and the lawmaker to assist in exposing it and blotting it out forever.

We denounce the imposition upon the working classes of England, and we do well, but in England this trucking system is abolished by law. It is a penal offense there, and it should be made so here. It should be made a crime to pay any man for his honest labor in any other than honest money. Until this is done in the Southern states the laborer of the South will be ground to the earth, and progress with him will be impossible. It is the duty of the Negro press to take up the subject. The Negro, where he may have a vote, should vote for no man who is not in favor of making this scrip and truck system unlawful.

I come now to another feature of Southern policy which bears hard and heavily on the Negro laborer and land renter. It is found in the landlord-and-tenant laws. I will read an extract to you from these laws that you may see how completely and rigidly the rights of the landlord are guarded and how entirely the tenant is in the clutches of the landlord:

REVISED CODE OF MISSISSIPPI

SEC. 1301. Every lessor of land shall have a lien on all the agricultural products of the leased premises, however and by whomsoever produced, to secure the payment of the rent and the market value of all advances made by him to his tenant for supplies for the tenant and others for whom he may contract.

SEC. 1304. When any landlord or lessor shall have just cause to suspect and shall verily believe that his tenant will remove his effects from the leased premises to any other place within or without the county before the rent or claims for supplies will fall due, so that no distress can be made, such landlord or lessor on making oath thereof, and of the amount the tenant is to pay, and at what time the same will fall due, and giving a bond as required in the preceding section, may, in like manner obtain an attachment against the goods and chattels of such tenant, and the officers making the distress shall give notice thereof and advertise the property distrained for sale, in the manner directed in the last preceding section, and if such tenant shall not, before the time appointed for such sale, give bond with sufficient security in double the amount of the rent, or other demand payable to the plaintiff, conditioned for the payment of said rent or other thing at the time it shall be due, with all cost, the goods distrained, or so much thereof as shall be necessary, shall be sold by the said officer at public sale to the highest bidder for cash, and out of the proceeds of the sale he shall pay to the plaintiff the amount due him, deducting interest for the time until the same shall become payable.

SEC. 1361. Said lien shall exist by virtue of the relation of the parties as employer and employee, and without any writing or recording.

SEC. 1362. Provides that any person who aids or assists in removing anything subject to these liens; without the consent of the landlord, shall, upon conviction, be punished by a fine of not more than $500, and be imprisoned in the county jail not more than six months, or by either such fine and imprisonment.

VOORHEE'S REVISED LAWS OF LA. 2D

SEC. 2165. Article 287 shall be so amended that a lessor may obtain a writ of provisional seizure even before the rent is due, and it shall be sufficient to entitle the lessor to the writ to swear to the amount which he claims, whether due or not due, and that he has good reasons to believe that the lessee will remove the furniture or property upon which he has a lien or privilege out of the premises, and that he may be, therefore, deprived of his lien.

LAWS OF FLORIDA—M'CLELLAN'S DIGEST

SEC. I, chapter 137. All claims for rent shall be a lien on agricultural products raised on the land rented, and shall be superior to all other liens and claims, though of older date, and also a superior lien on all other property of the lessee or his sublessee, or assigns usually kept on the premises, over any lien acquired subsequently to such property having been bought on the premises leased.

CODE OF ALABAMA

SEC. 3055, chapter 6. Lien continues and attaches to crop of succeeding years. When the tenant fails to pay any part of such rent or advances, and continues his tenancy under the same landlord for the next succeeding year for which the original lien for advances, if any remain unpaid, shall continue on the articles advanced or property purchased with money advanced or obtained by barter in exchange for articles advanced, and for which a lien shall also attach to the crop of such succeeding year.

You have thus seen a specimen, and a fair specimen, of the landlord-and-tenant laws of several of the old slave states; you have thus seen how scrupulously and rigidly the rights of the landlords are guarded and protected by these laws; you have thus seen how completely the tenant is put at the mercy of the landlord; you have thus seen the bias, the motive, and intention of the legislators by whom these laws have been enacted, and by whom they have been administered; and now you are only to remember the sentiment in regard to the Negro, peculiar to the people of the South, and the character of the people against whom these laws are to be enforced, and the fact that no people are better than their laws, to have a perfectly just view of the whole situation.

To my mind these landlord-and-tenant laws are a disgrace and a scandal to American civilization. A more skillfully contrived device than these laws to crush out all aspiration, all hope of progress in the landless Negro could not well be devised. They sound to me like the grating hinges of a slave prison. They read like the inhuman bond of Shylock, stipulating for his pound of flesh. They environ the helpless Negro like the devilfish of Victor Hugo, and draw the blood from every pore. He may writhe and twist, and strain every muscle, but he is held and firmly bound in a strong, remorseless and deadly grasp, a grasp from which only death can free him. Floods may rise, droughts may scorch, the elements may destroy his crops, famine may come, but whatever else may happen, the greedy landlord must have from his tenant the uttermost farthing. Like the den of the lion, all toes in its path turn inward.

The case is aggravated when you think of the illiteracy and ignorance of the people who sign land leases. They are ignorant of the terms of the contract, ignorant of the requirements of the law, and are thus absolutely in the power of the land-holder.

You have heard much, read much, and thought much of the flagrant injustice, the monstrous cruelty and oppression inflicted on the tenant class in Ireland. I have no disposition to underrate the hardships of that class. On the contrary, I deplore them. But knowing them as I do* and deploring them as I do, I declare to you that the condition of the Irish tenant is merciful, tender and just, as compared with the American freedman. There are thousands in Ireland today who fix the price of their own rent, and thousands more for whom the government itself measures the amount of rent to be paid, not by the greed of the landlord, but by the actual value of the land and its productions, and by the ability of the tenant to pay.

But how is it with us? The tenant is left in the clutches of the landlord. No third party intervenes between the greed and power of one and the helplessness of the other. The landholder imposes his price, exacts his conditions, and the landless Negro must comply or starve. It is impossible to conceive of conditions more unfavorable to the welfare and prosperity of the laborer. It is often said that the law is merciful, but there is no mercy in this law.

Now let us sum up some of the points in the situation of the freedman. You will have seen how he is paid for his labor, how a full-grown man gets only eight dollars a month for his labor, out of which he has to feed, clothe and educate his children. You have seen how even this sum is reduced by the infamous truck system of payment. You have seen how easily he may be charged with one third more than the value of the goods that he buys. You have seen how easily he may be compelled to receive the poorest commodities at the highest prices. You have seen how he is never allowed to see or handle a dollar. You have seen how impossible it is for him to accumulate money or property. You have seen how completely he is chained to the

* During his first trip abroad in 1845–46, Douglass toured all over Ireland and delivered more than fifty lectures there.

locality in which he lives. You have seen, therefore, that having no money, he cannot travel or go anywhere to better his condition. You have seen by these laws that even on the premises which he rents he can own nothing, possess nothing. You have seen that he cannot sell a sheep, or a pig, or even a chicken without the consent of the landlord, whose claim to all he has is superior and paramount to all other claims whatsoever. You have seen all this and more, and I ask, in view of it all, How, in the name of human reason, could the Negro be expected to rise higher in the scale of morals, manner, religion and civilization than he has done during the twenty years of his freedom. Shame, eternal shame, on those writers and speakers who taunt, denounce and disparage the Negro because he is today found in poverty, rags and wretchedness.

But again, let us see what are the relations subsisting between the Negro and the state and national governments—what support, what assistance he has received from either of them. Take his relation to the national government and we shall find him a deserted, a defrauded, a swindled, and an outcast man— in law free, in fact a slave; in law a citizen, in fact an alien; in law a voter, in fact, a disfranchised man. In law, his color is no crime; in fact, his color exposes him to be treated as a criminal. Toward him every attribute of a just government is contradicted. For him, it is not a government of the people, by the people, and for the people. Toward him, it abandons the beneficent character of a government, and all that gives a government the right to exist. The true object for which governments are ordained among men is to protect the weak against the encroachments of the strong, to hold its strong arm of justice over all the civil relations of its citizens and to see that all have an equal chance in the race of life. Now, in the case of the Negro citizen, our national government does precisely the reverse of all this. Instead of protecting the weak against the encroachments of the strong, it tacitly protects the strong in its encroachments upon the weak. When the colored citizens of the South point to the fourteenth and fifteenth amendments of the Constitution for the protection of their civil and political rights, the Supreme Court of the United States turns them out of court and tells them they must look for justice at the hands of the states, well knowing that those states are, in effect, the very parties that deny them justice. Thus is the Negro citizen swindled. The government professes to give him citizenship and silently permits him to be divested of every attribute of citizenship. It demands allegiance, but denies protection. It taxes him as a citizen in peace, and compels him to bear arms and meet bullets in war. It imposes upon him all the burdens of citizenship and withholds from him all its benefits.

I know it is said that the general government is a government of limited powers. It was also once said that the national government could not coerce a state and it is generally said that this and that public measure is unconstitutional. But whenever an administration has had the will to do anything, it has generally found Constitutional power to do it. If the general government had the power to make black men citizens, it has the power to protect them in that citizenship. If it had the right to make them voters it has the right to protect them in the exercise of the elective franchise. If it has this right, and refuses to exercise it, it is a traitor to the citizen. If it has not this right, it is destitute of the fundamental quality of a government and ought to be hissed and hurried out of the sisterhood of government, a usurper, a sham, a delusion and a snare.

On the other hand, if the fault is not in the structure of the government, but in the treachery and indifference of those who administer it, the American people owe it to themselves, owe it to the world, and to the Negro, to sweep from place and power those who are thus derelict in the discharge of their place in the government who will not enforce the Constitutional right of every class of American citizen.

I am a Republican. I believe in the Republican party. My political hopes for the future of the colored people are enforced in the character and composition, in the wisdom and justice, in the courage and fidelity of the Republican party. I am unable to see how any honest and intelligent colored man can be a Democrat or play fast and loose between the two parties. But while I am a Republican and believe in the party, I dare to tell that party the truth. In my judgment it can no longer repose on the history of its grand and magnificent achievements. It must not only stand abreast with the times, but must create the times. Its power and greatness consisted in this at the beginning. It was in advance of the times and made the times when it abolished the slave trade between the states, when it emancipated the slaves of the District of Columbia, when it stemmed the bloody tide of disunion, when it abolished slavery in all the states, when it made the Negro a soldier and a citizen, when it conceded to him the elective franchise; and now, in my judgment, the strength, success and glory of the Republican party will be found in its holding this advanced position. It must not stand still or take any step backward. Its mission is to lead, not to follow; to make circumstances, not to be made by them. It is held and firmly bound by every sentiment of justice and honor to make a living fact out of the dead letter of the Constitutional amendments. It must make the path of the black citizen to the ballot box as safe and smooth as that of the white citizen. It must make it impossible for a man like James Russell Lowell* to say he sees no difference between the Democratic party and the Republican party. If it fails to do all this, I for one shall welcome the bolt which shall scatter it into a thousand fragments.

The supreme movement in the life of the Republican party is at hand. The question, to be or not to be, will be decided at Chicago, and I reverently trust in God that it may be decided rightly. If the platform it shall adopt shall be in accordance with its earlier antecedents; if the party shall have the courage in its maturity which it possessed and displayed in its infancy; if it shall express its determination to vindicate the honor and integrity of the Republic by stamping out the fraud, injustice and violence which make elections in the South a disgrace and scandal to the Republic, and place a man on that platform with a clear head, a clean hand and a heroic heart, the country will triumphantly elect him. If it, however, should fail to elect him, we shall have done our duty and shall still have under us a grand party of the future, certain of success.

I do not forget that there are other great interests beside the Negro to be thought of. The civil service is a great interest, protection to American industry is a great interest, the proper management of our finances so as to promote the business and prosperity of the country is a great interest; but the national honor—the redemption of our national pledge to the freedmen, the supremacy of the Constitution in the fullness of its spirit and in the completeness of its letter over all the states of the Union alike—is an incomparably greater interest than all others. It touches the soul of the nation, which against all things else should be preserved. Should all be lost but this, the nation would be like Chicago after the fire—more prosperous and beautiful than ever. But what I ask of the Republican party requires no sacrifice or postponement of the material interest of the country. I simply say to the Republican party: Those things ye ought to have done and not to have left the others undone, and the present is the time to enforce this lesson.

The time has come for a new departure as to the kind of

---

* James Russell Lowell (1819–1891), poet, essayist, editor and diplomat, frequently wrote against slavery in his poetry. In his *Bigelow Papers* (1848) he had opposed the Mexican War.

man who is to be the standard-bearer of the Republican party. Events are our instructors. We have had enough of names, we now want things. We have had enough of good feeling, enough of shaking hands over the bloody chasm, enough of conciliation, enough of laudation of the bravery of our Southern brethren. We tried all that with President Hayes, of the purity of whose motives I have no shadow of doubt. His mistake was that he confided in the honor of the Confederates, who were without honor. He supposed that if left to themselves and thrown upon their honor they would obey the Constitution they had sworn to support and treat the colored citizens with justice and fairness at the ballot box.* Time has proved the reverse of all this, and this fact should cure the Republican party of adopting in its platform any such soft policy or any such candidate. Let us have a candidate this time of pronounced opinions and, above all, a backbone. . . .

There has been no show of federal power in the borders of the South for a dozen years. Its people have been left to themselves. Northern men have even refrained from going among them in election times to discuss the claims of public men, or the wisdom of public measures. They have had the field all to themselves, and we all now know just what has come of it, and the eyes of the leaders of the Republican party are, I trust, wide open. Mr. James G. Blaine, after, as well as before, he failed of his election,† pointed out the evil which now besets us as a party and a nation. Senator John Sherman‡ knows full well that the Solid South must be broken, that the colored citizen must not be cheated out of his vote any longer and that

* When Rutherford B. Hayes removed the troops from Louisiana and South Carolina, he wrote in his diary that the governors and legislatures of these two states had pledged to observe the thirteenth, fourteenth and fifteenth amendments. He concluded: "I am confident this is a good work. Time will tell." Eighteen months later he was deeply shocked that Louisiana and South Carolina were not keeping their promises. Gravely, he wrote: "By State legislation, by frauds, by intimidation and by violence of the most atrocious character, colored citizens have been deprived of the right of suffrage—a right guaranteed by the Constitution, and to the protection of which the people of those States have been solemnly pledged." (T. Harry Williams, editor, *Hayes: The Diary of a President, 1875–1881*, Philadelphia, 1964, pp. 122, 196).

† James Gillespie Blaine (1830–1893) was the Republican candidate for President in 1884 against Grover Cleveland, the victorious Democratic candidate.

‡ John Sherman (1823–1900), author of the Sherman Anti-Trust Act of 1890, was a leading Republican Senator and U. S. Secretary of State (1897–98).

the Constitution must be obeyed in all parts of the country alike; that individual states are great, but that the United States are greater. He has said the right word, and said it calmly but firmly, in the face of the South itself, and I thank him and honor him for it. I am naming no candidate for the presidency. Any one of the dozen statesmen whose names are in the air, and many whose names are not, would suit me and gain my best word and vote. There is one who has not been named and not likely to be named, who would suit me and who would fulfill the supreme demand of the hour; and that man is a Southern man. I refer to the Honorable John M. Harlan, Justice of the Supreme Court of the United States, who, true to his convictions, stood by the plain intention of the Fourteenth Amendment of the Constitution of the United States in opposition to all his brothers on the bench.* The man who could do that in the circumstances in which he was placed, if made President of the United States, could be depended upon in any emergency to do the right thing.

But, as I have said, I am not naming candidates. The candidate of the Republican party will, in all the likelihoods of the case, be my candidate. I am no partisan. I have no ambition to be the first to name any man or make any man obliged to me for naming him for the high office of President. Other men may do this, and I have no disposition to find fault with them for doing it. If, however, John A. Logan were living I might name him.† I am sure he would not allow himself to be trifled with, or allow the Constitution to be defied or trampled in the dust. I have faith also, in Roscoe Conkling,‡ whose dangerous illness we all deplore and whose recovery we profoundly and anxiously desire. With such a man in the Presidential chair, the red shirt and rifle, horseback and tissue-ballot plan of South

---

* John Marshall Harlan (1833–1911), born in Kentucky, served on the U. S. Supreme Court from 1877 to 1911, during which time he consistently supported rights of black Americans. He dissented in the Civil Rights Case of 1883 and the *Plessy v. Ferguson* decision of 1896, in both cases denouncing the deprivation of the Constitutional rights of Negroes under the Fourteenth Amendment.
† John A. Logan (1826–1886), a Union general and frequent supporter of Negro rights, was U. S. Senator from Illinois (1871–77; 1879–86).
‡ Roscoe Conkling (1829–1888), leader of the Republican party in New York and Senator from that state between 1867 and 1881, was a stanch opponent of reconciliation with the South. He headed the so-called Stalwart faction in the Republican party, which stood for upholding the rights of the Negroes under the Constitutional amendments adopted during Reconstruction.

Carolina and the Mississippi bulldozing plan would receive no encouragement.* I am, however, not here to name men. My mission now, as all along during nearly fifty years, is to plead the cause of the dumb millions of our countrymen against injustice, oppression, meanness and cruelty, and to hasten the day when the principles of liberty and humanity expressed in the Declaration of Independence and the Constitution of the United States shall be the law and the practice of every section, and of all the people of this great country without regard to race, sex, color or religion.

ORGANIZED RESISTANCE IS OUR BEST REMEDY

By John E. Bruce

Among the many proposals made during the post-Reconstruction period as to how best to meet the violence experienced daily by black Americans was one advanced by John E. Bruce, a leading Negro journalist, calling for "a resort to force under wise and discreet leaders." Basing his advice on the ancient principle of self-defense, Bruce called upon his people to meet force with force. His speech was delivered on October 5, 1889, but the occasion and place where it was made are not indicated in the manuscript in Bruce's papers.

John E. Bruce, better known to the public as "Bruce Grit," was born in Piscataway, Maryland, February 22, 1856. In The Colored American *of February 16, 1901, he was described as "the prince of Negro newspaper correspondents, having for the past twenty-six years represented papers in the West Indies, Africa and various sections of America." Bruce was the author of many pamphlets dealing with the problems of his people, in-*

* In states where Negroes were a majority or nearly so, virtual disfranchisement of the blacks was accomplished without legal action, after the overthrow of Reconstruction, by such devices as the Mississippi Plan, which used violence to force Negroes to desist from political action. "Red Shirts" were armed vigilantes on horseback in South Carolina.

cluding The Blood Record, *a review of lynchings in the United States "by civilized white men." His papers are available in the Schomburg Library in New York City. The text of the address presented here is in manuscript, dated October 5, 1889, Folder No. 7, John E. Bruce Collection, Schomburg Collection, New York Public Library.*

I FULLY REALIZE the delicacy of the position I occupy in this discussion and know too well that those who are to follow me will largely benefit by what I shall have to say in respect to the application of force as one of the means to the solution of the problem known as the Negro problem. I am not unmindful of that fact that there are those living who have faith in the efficacy of submission, who are impregnated with the slavish fear which had its origin in oppression and the peculiar environments of the slave period. Those who are thus minded will advise a pacific policy in order, as they believe, to effect a settlement of this question, with which the statesmanship of a century has grappled without any particularly gratifying results. Agitation is a good thing, organization is a better thing. The million Negro voters of Georgia, and the undiscovered millions in other Southern states—undiscovered so far as our knowledge of their number exists—could with proper organization and intelligent leadership meet force with force with most beneficial results. The issue upon us cannot be misunderstood by those who are watching current events . . . The man who will not fight for the protection of his wife and children is a *coward* and deserves to be ill treated. The man who takes his life in his hand and stands up for what he knows to be right will always command the respect of his enemy.

Submission to the *dicta* of the Southern bulldozers is the basest cowardice, and there is no just reason why manly men of any race should allow themselves to be continually outraged and oppressed by their equals before the law. . . .

Under the present conditions of affairs the only hope, the only salvation for the Negro is to be found in a resort to force under wise and discreet leaders. He must sooner or later come to this in order to set at rest for all time to come the charge that he is a moral coward. . . .

The Negro must not be rash and indiscreet either in action or in words but he must be very determined and terribly in earnest, and of one mind to bring order out of chaos and to convince Southern rowdies and cutthroats that more than two can play at the game with which they have amused their fellow conspirators in crime for nearly a quarter of a century. Under the Mosaic dispensation it was the custom to require an eye for an eye and a tooth for a tooth under a no less barbarous civilization than that which existed at that period of the world's history; let the Negro require at the hands of every white murderer in the South or elsewhere a life for a life. If they burn our houses, burn theirs, if they kill our wives and children kill theirs, pursue them relentlessly, meet force with force everywhere it is offered. If they demand blood, exchange it with them, until they are satiated. By a vigorous adherence to this course the shedding of human blood by white men will soon become a thing of the past. Wherever and whenever the Negro shows himself to be a man he can always command the respect even of a cutthroat. Organized resistance to organized resistance is the best remedy for the solution of the vexed problem of the century, which to me seems practical and feasible, and I submit this view of the question, ladies and gentlemen, for your careful consideration.

NAT TURNER

By Arthur W. Handy

In its issue of December 28, 1889, the New York Age featured on its first page under the heading "Nat Turner" the news that a young black student at New York City College, Arthur W. Handy, a graduate of Grammar School No. 81, of which Professor Charles L. Reason, a black educator, was principal, had chosen for his senior oration in a contest for the post of class orator the topic of the slave who led the great rebellion in Virginia in 1831. The rest of the article reprinted the oration that Mr. Handy was to deliver. We do not know whether this oration won the contest, but it is truly a remarkable analysis by a black college undergraduate of the significance of Nat Turner, and the point made of the similarity between Turner and John Brown was certainly far ahead of its time. Here is the text of the senior oration by a black student at New York City College. It was originally entitled "The Hero." For a definitive account of the revolt led by Turner, see Herbert Aptheker, Nat Turner's Slave Rebellion, New York, 1968.

IN EVERY AGE, in every clime, heroes have arisen. Men who have laid down family ties, honor, and even life itself for the maintenance of a principle. Men whose courage and devotion under the most trying circumstances have caused mankind to wonder in silent admiration. The world knows nothing of some of its greatest heroes, for there are forms of greatness which die and make no sign. There are martyrs that miss the palm, but not the stake. Heroes without the laurels and conquerors without the triumph. It has been said, and said truly, that the times make the man. Greece had her Leonidas, Rome her Horatius, and England her Cromwell. Nathaniel Turner was a hero! Characterized from the rest of his downtrodden brethren by natural aptitude, by dint of hard work in secret places, Turner learned to read and write.

Exercising his knowledge by reading such documents as the Right to Petition, Turner's eyes were opened. He saw that all men were created free and equal. Immediately, like a flash of lightning, his whole being was suffused with a noble idea. Like Joan of Arc, he saw his mission in the flash of meteors, he heard his summons in the roaring of the wind. Collecting about him those whom he could trust, he planned a formidable uprising stretching from the land of Dixie to the palmetto groves of South Carolina. Slowly but surely the movement progressed. The time at last arrived when the slave with sword in hand was to strike one blow for liberty. Was it done? Your histories do not record it. Nathaniel Turner was betrayed and by one of his own number. And yet how history repeats itself. How many such causes have lost through treachery! Yet he died like a hero. No murmur escaped his lips. No sigh of regret for the failure of his plans.

With his death ceased all such attempts for freedom until the immortal John Brown took up the cause. And yet how different were the surroundings of these two men, and still both aimed at the same result. Turner alone, friendless, with nothing but his ignorant companions to cheer him in the mighty struggle, worked with undaunted fortitude. Brown was watched and encouraged by a host of admiring friends. Thousands of dollars were appropriated for his scheme, and some of the noblest spirits on this continent bade him Godspeed. How strange is it that these two men, brought up under such different influences, should have been animated by the same desire. The crime for which Brown died at Harpers Ferry was identical with the one for which Turner died in South Carolina, the means by which it was to have been accomplished the same. And yet all the world unites in giving glory and honor to Brown while Turner is forgotten.

Let those of us in whom the love of humanity responds to the spirit of the Bard Burns, who in his "Honest Poverty," declares that "a man's a man for a' that," lift the veil of obscurity shrouds the deeds of black men at the South. When the Nation's history shall be written in the days to come, Nathan Hale and Crispus Attucks will be accorded places side by side. May we not hope that John Brown and Nathaniel Turner will be surrounded with an equal halo of glory? Then rest in peace, thou more than hero, in other ages, in distant climes, when truth shall get a hearing, thy name shall be mentioned with reverence and with honor.

THE AFRICAN PROBLEM AND THE METHODS OF ITS SOLUTION

By Edward W. Blyden

Born in St. Thomas, then a Danish island, in the West Indies in 1832, Edward Blyden came to the United States in 1850, but finding the treatment of his people unendurable, he emigrated to Liberia in 1851. A learned man, he became a leading figure in Liberia, but concerned himself with the plight of African people the world over. He was convinced that the only way to bring respect and dignity to the people of African descent was by building progressive new "empires" in Africa which, while remaining basically African, would incorporate useful elements of Western culture. He spent his life in educational and missionary work in Liberia and in the encouragement of emigration to Liberia. In 1880, he became president of Liberia College. Blyden made several trips to the United States, and on January 19, 1890, he delivered the following speech as the annual discourse at the seventy-third anniversary of the American Colonization Society in Washington, D. C. Blyden died in 1912.

(The text of this speech is taken from Blyden's pamphlet The African Problem and the Methods of Its Solution, *Washington, D. C., 1890.)*

I AM SERIOUSLY IMPRESSED with a sense of the responsibility of my position tonight. I stand in the presence of the representatives of that great organization which seems first of all the associations in this country to have distinctly recognized the hand of God in the history of the Negro race in America— to have caught something of the meaning of the divine purpose in permitting their exile to and bondage in this land. I stand also in the presence of what, for the time being at least, must be considered the foremost congregation of the land—the religious home of the President of the United States. There are present, also, I learn, on this occasion, some of the statesmen and lawmakers of the land.

My position, then, is one of honor as well as of responsibility, and the message I have to deliver, I venture to think, concerns directly or indirectly the whole human race. I come from that ancient country, the home of one of the great original races, occupied by the descendants of one of the three sons to whom, according to Biblical history, the whole world was assigned—a country which is now engaging the active attention of all Europe. I come, also, from the ancestral home of at least five millions in this land. Two hundred millions of people have sent me on an errand of invitation to their blood relations here. Their cry is, "Come over and help us." And I find among hundreds of thousands of the invited an eager and enthusiastic response. They tell me to wave the answer across the deep to the anxious and expectant hearts, which, during the long and weary night of separation, have been constantly watching and praying for the return—to the Rachels weeping for their children, and refusing to be comforted because they are not— they tell me, "Wave the answer back to our brethren to hold the fort for we are coming." They have for the last seventy years been returning through the agency of the Society whose anniversary we celebrate to-night. Some have gone every year during that period, but they have been few compared to the vast necessity. They have gone as they have been able to go, and are making an impression for good upon that continent. My subject to-night will be "The African Problem and the Method of Its Solution."

This is no new problem. It is nearly as old as recorded history. It has interested thinking men in Europe and Asia in all ages. The imagination of the ancients peopled the interior of that country with a race of beings shut out from and needing no intercourse with the rest of mankind, lifted by their purity and simplicity of character above the necessity of intercourse with other mortals—leading a blameless and protracted existence and producing in their sequestered, beautiful and fertile home, from which flowed the wonderful Nile, the food of the Gods. Not milk and honey but nectar and ambrosia were supposed to abound there. The Greeks especially had very high conceptions of the sanctity and spirituality of the interior Africans. The greatest of their poets picture the Gods as vacating Olympus every year and proceeding to Ethiopia to be feasted by its inhabitants. Indeed, the religion of some portion of Greece is supposed to have been introduced from Africa. But leaving the region of mythology, we know that the three highest religions known to mankind—if they had not their origin in Africa—were domiciled there in the days of their feeble beginnings, Judaism, Christianity and Mohammedanism.

A sacred mystery hung over that continent, and many were the aspirations of philosophers and poets for some definite knowledge of what was beyond the narrow fringe they saw. Julius Caesar, fascinated while listening to a tale of the Nile, lost the vision of military glory. The philosopher overcame the soldier and he declared himself ready to abandon for a time the alluring fields of politics in order to trace out the sources of that mysterious river which gave to mankind Egypt with her magnificent conceptions and splendid achievements.

The mystery still remains. The problem continues unsolved. The conquering races of the world stand perplexed and worried before the difficulties which beset their enterprise of reducing that continent to subjection. They have overcome the whole of the Western Hemisphere. From the Bering Strait to Cape Horn, America has submitted to their sway. The native races have almost disappeared from the mainland and the islands of the sea. Europe has extended her conquests to Australia, New Zealand, and the Archipelagos of the Pacific. But, for hundreds of years, their ships have passed by those tempting regions, where "Afric's sunny fountains roll down their golden sands," and though touching at different points on the coast, they have been able to acquire no extensive foothold in that country. Notwithstanding the reports we receive on every breeze that blows from the East, of vast "spheres of influence" and large European possessions, the points actually occupied by white men in the boundless equatorial regions of that immense continent may be accurately represented on the map only by microscopic dots. I wish that the announcements we receive from time to time with such a flourish of trumpets, that a genuine civilization is being carried into the heart of the Dark Continent, were true. But the fact is, that the bulk of Central Africa is being rapidly subjected to Mohammedanism. That system will soon be—or rather is now—knitting together the conquerors and the conquered into a harmonious whole; and unless Europe gets a thorough understanding of the situation, the gates of missionary enterprise will be closed, because, from all we can learn of the proceedings of some, especially in East Africa, the industrial regime is being stamped out to foster the militant. The current number of the *Fortnightly*, near the close of an interesting article on "Stanley's Expedition," has this striking sentence: "Stanley has triumphed, but Central Africa is darker than ever!"*

It would appear that the world outside of Africa has not yet stopped to consider the peculiar conditions which lift that continent out of the range of the ordinary agencies by which Europe has been able to occupy other countries and subjugate or exterminate their inhabitants.

They have not stopped to ponder the providential lessons on this subject scattered through the pages of history, both past and contemporary.

First. Let us take the most obvious lesson as indicated in the climatic conditions. Perhaps in no country in the world is it so necessary (as in Africa) that the stranger or newcomer should possess the *mens sana in corpore sano*—the sound mind in sound body—for the climate is most searching, bringing to the surface any and every latent physical or mental defect. If a man has any chronic or hereditary disease it is sure to be developed, and if wrong medical treatment is applied it is very apt to be exaggerated and often to prove fatal to the patient. And as with the body so with the mind. Persons of weak minds, either inherited or brought on by excessive mental application or troubles of any kind, are almost sure to develop an impatience or irritability, to the surprise and annoyance of their friends who knew them at home. The Negro immigrant from a temperate region sometimes suffers from these climatic inconveniences; only in his case, after a brief process of acclimatization, he becomes himself again, while the white man never regains his soundness in that climate, and can retain his mental equilibrium only by periodical visits to his native climate. The regulation of the British government for West Africa is that their officials

---

* Henry Morton Stanley (1841–1904) led an expedition to Africa in 1869 to find David Livingstone, the Scottish missionary. On November 10, 1871, the celebrated meeting of Stanley and Livingstone occurred. Thereafter, Stanley made several further expeditions to Africa, exploring the continent and paving the way for British and Belgian imperialistic domination.

are allowed six months' leave of absence to return to Europe after fifteen months' residence at Sierra Leone and twelve months on the Gold Coast or Lagos; and for every three days during which they are kept on the coast after the time for their leave arrives, they are allowed one day in Europe. The neglect of this regulation is often attended with most serious consequences.

Second. When we come into the moral and intellectual world it would seem as if the Almighty several times attempted to introduce the foreigner and a foreign civilization into Africa and then changed his purpose. The Scriptures seem to warrant the idea that in some way inexplicable to us, and incompatible with our conception of the character of the Sovereign of the Universe, the unchangeable Being sometimes reverses His apparent plans. We read that "it repented God," et cetera. For thousands of years the northeastern portion of Africa witnessed a wonderful development of civilization. The arts and sciences flourished in Egypt for generations, and that country was the center of almost universal influence; but there was no effect produced upon the interior of Africa. So North Africa became the seat of a great military and commercial power which flourished for seven hundred years. After this the Roman Catholic Church constructed a mighty influence in the same region, but the interior of the continent received no impression from it.

In the fifteenth century the Congo country, of which we now hear so much, was the scene of extensive operations of the Roman Catholic Church. Just a little before the discovery of America thousands of the natives of the Congo, including the most influential families, were baptized by Catholic missionaries; and the Portuguese, for a hundred years, devoted themselves to the work of African evangelization and exploration. It would appear that they knew just as much of interior Africa as is known now after the great exploits of Speke and Grant and Livingstone, Baker and Cameron and Stanley. It is said that there is a map in the Vatican, three hundred years old, which gives all the general physical relief and the river and lake systems of Africa with more or less accuracy; but the Arab geographers of a century before had described the mountain system, the great lakes, and the course of the Nile.

Just about the time that Portugal was on the way to establish a great empire on that continent, based upon the religious system of Rome, America was discovered, and, instead of the Congo, the Amazon became the seat of Portuguese power. Neither Egyptian, Carthaginian, Persian nor Roman influence was allowed to establish itself on that continent. It would seem that in the providential purpose no solution of the African problem was to come from alien sources. Africans were not doomed to share the fate of some other dark races who have come in contact with the aggressive European. Europe was diverted to the Western Hemisphere. The energies of that conquering race, it was decreed, should be spent in building up a home for themselves on this side. Africa followed in chains.

The Negro race was to be preserved for a special and important work in the future. Of the precise nature of that work no one can form any definite conception. It is probable that if foreign races had been allowed to enter their country they would have been destroyed. So they were brought over to be helpers in this country and at the same time to be preserved. It was not the first time in the history of the world that a people have been preserved by subjection to another people. We know that God promised Abraham that his seed should inherit the land of Canaan; but when He saw that in their numerically weak condition they would have been destroyed in conflicts with the indigenous inhabitants, he took them down to Egypt and kept them there in bondage four hundred years that they might be fitted, both by discipline and numerical increase, for the work that would devolve upon them. Slavery would seem to be a strange school in which to preserve a people; but God has a way of salting as well as purifying by fire.

The Europeans, who were fleeing from their own country in search of wider areas of freedom and larger scope for development, found here an aboriginal race unable to cooperate with them in the labors required for the construction of the material framework of the new civilization. The Indians would not work, and they have suffered the consequences of that indisposition. They have passed away.* To take their place as accessories in the work to be done God suffered the African to be brought hither, who could work and would work, and could endure the climatic conditions of a new southern country, which Europeans could not. Two currents set across the Atlantic toward the west for nigh three hundred years—the one from Europe, the other from Africa. The one from Africa had a crimson color. From that stream of human beings millions fell victims to the cruelties of the middle passage, and otherwise suffered from the brutal instincts of their kidnapers and enslavers. I do not know whether Africa has been invited to the celebration of the fourth centenary of the discovery of America; but she has quite as

* Blyden later states that the Indians were exterminated by the white colonizers of the New World.

much reason, if not as much right, to participate in the demonstration of that occasion as the European nations. Englishman, Hollander, and Huguenot, Nigritian and Congo came together. If Europe brought the head, Africa furnished the hands for a great portion of the work which has been achieved here, though it was the opinion of an African chief that the man who discovered America ought to have been imprisoned for having uncovered one people for destruction and opened a field for the oppression and suffering of another.

But when the new continent was opened Africa was closed. The veil, which was being drawn aside, was replaced, and darkness once more enveloped the land, for then not the *country* but the *people* were needed. They were to do a work elsewhere, and meanwhile their country was to be shut out from the view of the outside world.

The first Africans landed in this country in the state of Virginia in the year 1619.* Then began the first phase of what is called the *Negro problem*. These people did not come hither of their own accord. Theirs was not a voluntary but a compulsory expatriation. The problem, then, on their arrival in this country, which confronted the white people was how to reduce to effective and profitable servitude an alien race which it was neither possible nor desirable to assimilate. This gave birth to that peculiar institution, established in a country whose *raison d'être* was that all men might enjoy the "right to life, liberty and the pursuit of happiness." Laws had to be enacted by Puritans, Cavaliers and Roundheads for slaves, and every contrivance had to be devised for the safety of the institution. It was a difficult problem, in the effort to solve which both master and slave suffered.

It would seem, however, that in the first years of African slavery in this country, the masters upon many of whom the relationship was forced, understood its providential origin and purpose, until after a while, avarice and greed darkened their perceptions, and they began to invent reasons, drawn even from the Word of God, to justify their holding these people in perpetual bondage for the advantage of themselves and their children forever.† But even after a blinding cupidity had captured the generality by its bewitching spell, there were those (farsighted men, especially after the yoke of Great Britain had been

* There is evidence that the first Negro slaves arrived in 1526 with Lucas Vasquez de Ayllon, a Spanish colonizer, who founded a town in what is now South Carolina, at the mouth of the Pedee River.
† Blyden is referring to the Curse of Ham and the Curse of Cain to justify enslavement of Africans.

thrown off) who saw that the abnormal relation could not be permanent under the democratic conditions established by the fundamental law of the land. It was Thomas Jefferson, the writer of the Declaration of Independence, who made the celebrated utterance: "Nothing is more clearly written in the Book of Destiny than the emancipation of the blacks; and it is equally certain that the two races will never live in a state of equal freedom under the same government, so insurmountable are the barriers which nature, habit and opinion have established between them."

For many years, especially in the long and weary period of the antislavery conflict, the latter part of this dictum of Jefferson was denounced by many good and earnest men. The most intelligent of the colored people resented it as a prejudiced and anti-Christian conception. But as the years go by and the Negroes rise in education and culture, and therefore in love and pride of race, and in proper conception of race gifts, race work and race destiny, the latter clause of that famous sentence is not only being shorn of its obscurity and repulsiveness, but is being welcomed as embodying a truth indispensable to the preservation and prosperity of both races, and as pointing to the regeneration of the African Fatherland. There are some others of the race who, recognizing Jefferson's principle, would make the races one by amalgamation.

It was under the conviction of the truth expressed by that statesman that certain gentlemen of all political shades and differing religious views, met together in this city in the winter of 1816–17, and organized the American Colonization Society. Though friendly to the antislavery idea, and anxious for the extinction of the abnormal institution, these men did not make their views on that subject prominent in their published utterances. They were not Abolitionists in the political or technical sense of that phrase. But their labors furnished an outlet and encouragement for persons desiring to free their slaves, giving them the assurance that their freedmen would be returned to their Fatherland, carrying thither what light of Christianity and civilization they had received. It seems a pity that this humane, philanthropic, and farseeing work should have met with organized opposition from another band of philanthropists, who, anxious for a speedy deliverance of the captives, thought they saw in the Colonization Society an agency for riveting instead of breaking the fetters of the slave, and they denounced it with all the earnestness and eloquence they could command, and they commanded, both among whites and blacks, some of the finest orators the country has ever produced. And they did a grand work, both directly and indirectly, for the Negro and for Africa. They did their work and dissolved their organization. But when their work was done the work of the Colonization Society really began.

In the development of the Negro question in this country the colonizationists might be called the prophets and philosophers; the abolitionists, the warriors and politicians. Colonizationists saw what was coming and patiently prepared for its advent. Abolitionists attacked the first phase of the Negro problem and labored for its immediate solution; colonizationists looked to the last phase of the problem and labored to get both the whites and blacks ready for it. They labored on two continents, in America and in Africa. Had they not begun as early as they did to take up lands in Africa for the exiles, had they waited for the abolition of slavery, it would now have been impossible to obtain a foothold in their fatherland for the returning hosts. The colonizationist, as prophet, looked at the state as it would be; the abolitionist, as politician, looked at the state as it was. The politician sees the present and is possessed by it. The prophet sees the future and gathers inspiration from it. The politician may influence legislation; the prophet, although exercising great moral influence, seldom has any legislative power. The agitation of the politician may soon culminate in legal enactments; the teachings of the prophet may require generations before they find embodiment in action. The politician has today; the prophet, tomorrow. The politician deals with facts, the prophet with ideas, and ideas take root very slowly. Though nearly three generations have passed away since Jefferson made his utterance, and more than two since the organization of the Colonization Society, yet the conceptions they put forward can scarcely be said to have gained maturity, much less currency, in the public mind. But the recent discussions in the halls of Congress show that the teachings of the prophet are now beginning to take hold of the politician. It may take many years yet before the people come up to these views, and, therefore, before legislation upon them may be possible, but there is evidently movement in that direction.

The first phase of the Negro problem was solved at Appomattox, after the battle of the warrior, with confused noise and garments rolled in blood. The institution of slavery, for which so many sacrifices had been made, so many of the principles of humanity had been violated, so many of the finer sentiments of the heart had been stifled, was at last destroyed by violence.

Now the nation confronts the second phase, the educational, and millions are being poured out by state governments and by individual philanthropy for the education of the freedmen, preparing them for the third and last phase of the problem, viz., Emigration.

In this second phase, we have that organization, which might be called the successor of the old Anti-Slavery Society, taking most active and effective part. I mean the American Missionary Association. I have watched with constant gratitude and admiration the course and operations of that Society, especially when I remember that, organized in the dark days of slavery, twenty years before emancipation, it held aloft courageously the banner on which was inscribed freedom for the Negro and no fellowship with his oppressors. And they, among the first, went South to lift the freedmen from the mental thralldom and moral degradation in which slavery had left him. They triumphed largely over the spirit of their opponents. They braved the dislike, the contempt, the apprehension with which their work was at first regarded, until they succeeded by demonstrating the advantages of knowledge over ignorance, to bring about that state of things to which Mr. Henry Grady,* in his last utterances, was able to refer with such satisfaction—viz., that since the war the South has spent $122,000,000 in the cause of public education, and this year it is pledged to spend $37,000,-000, in the benefits of which the Negro is a large participant.

It is not surprising that some of those who, after having been engaged in the noble labors of solving the first phase of the problem—in the great antislavery war—and are now confronting the second phase, should be unable to receive with patience the suggestion of the third, which is the emigration phase, when the Negro, freed in body and in mind, shall bid farewell to these scenes of his bondage and discipline and betake himself to the land of his fathers, the scene of larger opportunities and loftier achievements. I say it is not surprising that the veterans of the past and the present should be unable to give much enthusiasm to the work of the future. It is not often given to man to labor successfully in the land of Egypt, in the wilderness and across the Jordan. Some of the most effective workers, must often, with eyes undimmed and natural force unabated, lie down and die on the borders of full freedom, and if they live, life to them is like a dream. The young must take up the work. To old men the indications of the future are like a dream. Old men are like

* Henry W. Grady (1850–1889) was editor and part owner of the Atlanta *Constitution* and an advocate of the "New South," a South of industrial development in which, however, there would be no real place for the Negro. Grady was a stanch advocate of the "Solid South" and "white supremacy."

them that dream. Young men see visions. They catch the spirit of the future and are able to place themselves in accord with it.

But things are not yet ready for the solution of the third and last phase of the problem. Things are not ready in this country among whites or blacks. The industrial condition of the South is not prepared for it. Things are not yet ready in Africa for a complete exodus. Europe is not yet ready; she still thinks that she can take and utilize Africa for her own purposes. She does not yet understand that Africa is to be for the African or for nobody. Therefore she is taking up with renewed vigor, and confronting again, with determination, the African problem. Englishmen, Germans, Italians, Belgians, are taking up territory and trying to wring from the gray-haired mother of civilization the secret of the ages. Nothing has come down from Egypt so grand and impressive as the Sphinxes that look at you with calm and emotionless faces, guarding their secret today as they formerly guarded the holy temples. They are a symbol of Africa. She will not be forced. She only can reveal her secret. Her children trained in the house of bondage will show it to the world. Some have already returned and have constructed an independent nation as a beginning of this work on her western borders.

It is a significant fact that Africa was completely shut up until the time arrived for the emancipation of her children in the Western world. When Jefferson and Washington and Hamilton and Patrick Henry were predicting and urging the freedom of the slave, Mungo Park* was beginning that series of explorations by English enterprise which has just ended in the expedition of Stanley. Just about the time that England proclaimed freedom throughout her colonies, the brothers Lander made the great discovery of the mouth of the Niger; and when Lincoln issued the immortal proclamation, Livingstone was unfolding to the world that wonderful region which Stanley has more fully revealed and which is becoming now the scene of the secular and religious activities of Christendom. The King of the Belgians has expended fortunes recently in opening the Congo and in introducing the appliances of civilization, and by a singular coincidence a bill has been brought forward in the U. S. Senate to assist the emigration of Negroes to the Fatherland just at the time when that philanthropic monarch has despatched

---

* Mungo Park visited Africa in the late eighteenth century and explored large parts of the continent. His book *Travels in the Interior Districts of Africa,* describing his experiences, was the most popular of all African travel books.

an agent to this country to invite the co-operation in his great work of qualified freedmen. This is significant.*

What the King of the Belgians has just done is an indication of what other European powers will do when they have exhausted themselves in costly experiments to utilize white men as colonists in Africa. They will then understand the purpose of the Almighty in having permitted the exile and bondage of the Africans, and they will see that for Africa's redemption the Negro is the chosen instrument. They will encourage the establishment and building up of such states as Liberia. They will recognize the scheme of the Colonization Society as the providential one.

The little nation which has grown up on that coast as a result of the efforts of this Society, is now taking hold upon that continent in a manner which, owing to inexperience, it could not do in the past. The Liberians have introduced a new article into the commerce of the world—the Liberian coffee. They are pushing to the interior, clearing up the forests, extending the culture of coffee, sugar, cocoa and other tropical articles, and are training the aborigines in the arts of civilization and in the principles of Christianity. The Republic occupies five hundred miles of coast with an elastic interior. It has a growing commerce with various countries of Europe and America. No one who has visited that country and has seen the farms on the banks of the rivers and in the interior, the workshops, the schools, the churches, and other elements and instruments of progress will say that the United States, through Liberia, is not making a wholesome impression upon Africa—an impression which, if the members of the American Congress understood, they would not begrudge the money required to assist a few hundred thousand to carry on in that country the work so well begun. They would gladly spare them from the laboring element of this great nation to push forward the enterprises of civilization in their Fatherland, and to build themselves up on the basis of their race manhood.

If there is an intelligent Negro here tonight I will say to him, let me take you with me in imagination to witness the new creation or development on that distant shore; I will not paint you an imaginary picture, but will describe an historical fact; I will tell you of reality. Going from the coast, through those depressing alluvial plains which fringe the eastern and western borders

* Blyden seems to have been ignorant of the fact that the "appliances of civilization" introduced into the Congo by Leopold II, King of the Belgians, included wholesale massacre and dismemberment of the people in the Congo. Leopold's objective in the Congo was not to "civilize" the Congolese but to force them to produce rubber and ivory.

of the continent, you reach, after a few miles' travel, the first
high or undulating country, which, rising abruptly from the
swamps, enchants you with its solidity, its fertility, its verdure,
its refreshing and healthful breezes. You go further, and you
stand upon a higher elevation, where the wind sings more
freshly in your ears and your heart beats fast as you survey the
continuous and unbroken forests that stretch away from your
feet to the distant horizon. The melancholy cooing of the pi-
geons in some unseen retreat or the more entrancing music of
livelier and picturesque songsters alone disturb the solemn and
almost oppressive solitude. You hear no human sound and see
the traces of no human presence. You decline to pursue your
adventurous journey. You refuse to penetrate the lonely forest
that confronts you. You return to the coast, thinking of the long
ages which have elapsed, the seasons which, in their onward
course, have come and gone, leaving those solitudes undisturbed. You wonder when and how are those vast wildernesses
to be made the scene of human activity and to contribute to
human wants and happiness. Finding no answer to your perplexing question you drop the subject from your thoughts. After
a few years—a very few it may be—you return to those scenes.
To your surprise and gratification your progress is no longer
interrupted by the inconvenience of bridle paths and tangled
vines. The roads are open and clear. You miss the troublesome
creeks and drains which, on your previous journey, harassed
and fatigued you. Bridges have been constructed, and without
any of the former weariness you find yourself again on the summit, where in loneliness you had stood sometime before. What
do you now see? The gigantic trees have disappeared, houses
have sprung up on every side. As far as the eye can see the roofs
of comfortable and homelike cottages peep through the wood.
The waving corn and rice and sugar cane, the graceful and
fragrant coffee tree, the umbrageous cocoa, orange, and mango
plum have taken the place of the former sturdy denizens of the
forest. What has brought about the change? The Negro emi-
grant has arrived from America, and, slender though his facilities have been, has produced these wonderful revolutions. You
look beyond and take in the forests that now appear on the distant horizon. You catch glimpses of native villages embowered
in plantain trees, and you say these also shall be brought under
civilized influences, and you feel yourself lifted into manhood,
the spirit of the teacher and guide and missionary comes upon
you, and you say, "There, below me and beyond lies the world
into which I must go. There must I cast my lot. I feel I have a
message to it, or a work in it"; and the sense that there are

thousands dwelling there, some of whom you may touch, some of whom you may influence, some of whom may love you or be loved by you, thrills you with a strange joy and expectation, and it is a thrill which you can never forget; for ever and anon it comes upon you with increased intensity. In that hour you are born again. You hear forevermore the call ringing in your ears, "Come over and help us."

These are the visions that rise before the Liberian settler who has turned away from the coast. This is the view that exercises such an influence upon his imagination and gives such tone to his character, making him an independent and productive man on the continent of his fathers.

As I have said, this is no imaginary picture, but the embodiment of sober history. Liberia, then, is a fact, an aggressive and progressive fact, with a great deal in its past and everything in its future that is inspiring and uplifting.

It occupies one of the most charming countries in the western portion of that continent. It has been called by qualified judges the garden spot of West Africa. I love to dwell upon the memories of scenes which I have passed through in the interior of that land. I have read of countries which I have not visited—the grandeur of the Rocky Mountains and the charms of the Yosemite Valley, and my imagination adds to the written description and becomes a gallery of delightful pictures. But of African scenes my memory is a treasure house in which I delight to revel. I have distinctly before me the days and dates when I came into contact with their inexhaustible beauties. Leaving the coast line, the seat of malaria, and where are often seen the remains of the slaver's barracoons, which always give an impression of the deepest melancholy, I come to the high tablelands with their mountain scenery and lovely valleys, their meadow streams and mountain rivulets, and there, amid the glories of a changeless and unchanging nature, I have taken off my shoes and on that consecrated ground adored the God and Father of the Africans.

This is the country and this is the work to which the American Negro is invited. This is the opening for him which, through the labors of the American Colonization Society, has been effected. This organization is more than a *colonization* society, more than an emigration society. It might with equal propriety and perhaps with greater accuracy be called the African *Repatriation* Society; or since the idea of planting towns and introducing extensive cultivation of the soil is included in its work, it might be called the African Repatriation and Colonization Society, for then you bring in a somewhat higher idea than mere

colonization—the mere settling of a new country by strangers
—you bring in the idea of restoration, of compensation to a race
and country much and long wronged.

Colonizationists, notwithstanding all that has been said
against them, have always recognized the manhood of the Negro
and been willing to trust him to take care of himself. They have
always recognized the inscrutable providence by which the African was brought to these shores. They have always taught
that he was brought hither to be trained out of his sense of irresponsibility to a knowledge of his place as a factor in the
great work of humanity; and that after having been thus trained
he could find his proper sphere of action only in the land of his
origin to make a way for himself. They have believed that it has
not been given to the white man to fix the intellectual or spiritual status of this race. They have recognized that the universe
is wide enough and God's gifts are varied enough to allow the
man of Africa to find out a path of his own within the circle of
genuine human interests, and to contribute from the field of his
particular enterprise to the resources—material, intellectual and
moral—of the great human family.

But will the Negro go to do this work?

Is he willing to separate himself from a settled civilization
which he has helped to build up to betake himself to the wilderness of his ancestral home and begin anew a career on his own
responsibility?

I believe that he is. And if suitable provision were made for
their departure tomorrow, hundreds of thousands would avail
themselves of it. The African question, or the Negro problem, is
upon the country, and it can no more be ignored than any other
vital interest. The chief reason, it appears to me, why it is not
more seriously dealt with is because the pressure of commercial
and political exigencies does not allow time and leisure to the
stronger and richer elements of the nation to study it. It is not a
question of color simply—that is a superficial accident. It lies
deeper than color. It is a question of race, which is the outcome
not only of climate, but of generations subjected to environments which have formed the mental and moral constitution.

It is a question in which two distinct races are concerned.
This is not a question then purely of reason. It is a question also
of instinct. Races feel; observers theorize.

The work to be done beyond the seas is not to be a reproduction of what we see in this country. It requires, therefore, distinct race perception and entire race devotion. It is not to be the
healing up of an old sore, but the unfolding of a new bud, an
evolution; the development of a new side of God's character and

a new phase of humanity. God said to Moses, "I am that I am"; or, more exactly, "I shall be that I shall be." Each race sees from its own standpoint a different side of the Almighty. The Hebrews could not see or serve God in the land of the Egyptians; no more can the Negro under the Anglo-Saxon. He can serve *man* here. He can furnish the labor of the country, but to the inspiration of the country he must ever be an alien.

In that wonderful sermon of Saint Paul on Mars Hill in which he declared that God hath made of one blood all nations of men to dwell on all the face of the earth and hath determined the bounds of their habitation, he also said, "In Him we live and move and have our being." Now it cannot be supposed that in the types and races which have already displayed themselves God has exhausted himself. It is by God in us, where we have freedom to act out ourselves, that we do each our several work and live out into action, through our work, whatever we have within us of noble and wise and true. What we do is, if we are able to be true to our nature, the representation of some phase of the Infinite Being. If we live and move and have our being in Him, God also lives and moves and has His being in us. This is why slavery of any kind is an outrage. It spoils the image of God as it strives to express itself through the individual or the race. As in the Kingdom of Nature, we see in her great organic types of being, in the movement, changes and order of the elements, those vast thoughts of God, so in the great types of man, in the various races of the world, as distinct in character as in work, in the great divisions of character, we see the will and character and consciousness of God disclosed to us. According to this truth a distinct phase of God's character is set forth to be wrought out into perfection in every separate character. As in every form of the inorganic universe we see some noble variation of God's thought and beauty, so in each separate man, in each separate race, something of the absolute is incarnated. The whole of mankind is a vast representation of the Deity. Therefore we cannot extinguish any race either by conflict or amalgamation without serious responsibility.

You can easily see, then, why one race overshadowed by another should long to express itself—should yearn for the opportunity to let out the divinity that stirs within it. This is why the Hebrews cried to God from the depths of their affliction in Egypt, and this is why thousands and thousands of Negroes in the South are longing to go to the land of their fathers. They are not content to remain where everything has been done on the line of another race. They long for the scenes where everything is to be done under the influence of a new racial spirit, under the impulse of new skies and the inspiration of a fresh development. Only those are fit for this new work who believe in the race— have faith in its future—a prophetic insight into its destiny from a consciousness of its possibilities. The inspiration of the race is in the race.

Only one race has furnished the prophets for humanity—the Hebrew race; and before they were qualified to do this they had to go down to the depths of servile degradation. Only to them were revealed those broad and pregnant principles upon which every race can stand and work and grow; but for the special work of each race the prophets arise among the people themselves.

What is pathetic about the situation is that numbers among whites and blacks are disposed to ignore the seriousness and importance of the question. They seem to think it a question for political manipulation and to be dealt with by partisan statesmanship, not recognizing the fact that the whole country is concerned. I freely admit the fact, to which attention has been recently called, that there are many Afro-Americans who have no more to do with Africa than with Iceland, but this does not destroy the truth that there are millions whose life is bound up with that continent. It is to them that the message comes from their brethren across the deep, "Come over and help us."

IT IS TIME TO CALL A HALT

By T. Thomas Fortune

The first Negro protest organization after the Reconstruction period was the National Afro-American League. The League was initiated by T. Thomas Fortune, the militant editor of the New York Age. In 1887 Fortune called upon Negroes to form an organization to fight for the rights denied them. At the founding convention of the League held in Chicago in January, 1890, one hundred and forty-one delegates from twenty-three states assembled to form a permanent organization. As temporary chairman of the convention, Fortune delivered a long, stirring address. This address is presented here in part, excerpted from the New York Age, January 25, 1890.

LADIES AND GENTLEMEN of the Afro-American League: We are met here today, representatives of eight million free men who know our rights and have the courage to defend them. We have met here today to emphasize the fact that the past condition of dependence and helplessness upon men who have used us for selfish and unholy purposes, who have murdered and robbed and outraged us, must be reversed. . . . Ladies and gentlemen, we have been robbed of the honest wages of our toil, we have been robbed of the substance of our citizenship by murder and intimidation; we have been outraged by enemies and deserted by friends; and because in a society governed by law, we have been true to the law, true to treacherous friends, and as true in distrust of our enemies, it has been charged upon us that we are not made of the stern stuff which makes the Anglo-Saxon race the most consummate masters of hypocrisy, of roguery, of insolence, of arrogance, and of cowardice, in the history of races.

Was ever race more unjustly maligned than ours? Was ever race more shamelessly robbed than ours? Was ever race used to advance the political and pecuniary fortunes of others as ours? Was ever race so patient, so law-abiding, so uncomplaining as ours?

Ladies and gentlemen, it is time to call a halt. It is time to begin to fight fire with fire. It is time to stand shoulder to shoulder as men. It is time to rebuke the treachery of friends in the only way that treachery should be rebuked. It is time to face the enemy and fight him inch by inch for every right he denies us.

We have been patient so long that many believe that we are incapable of resenting insult, outrage and wrong; we have so long accepted uncomplainingly all that injustice and cowardice and insolence heaped upon us, that many imagine that we are compelled to submit and have not the manhood necessary to resent such conduct. When matters assume this complexion, when oppressors presume too far upon the forbearance and the helplessness of the oppressed, the condition of the people affected is critical indeed. Such is our condition today. Because it is true; because we feel that something must be done to change the condition; because we are tired of being kicked and cuffed by individuals, made the scapegoats of the law, used by one party as an issue and by another as a steppingstone to place and power, and elbowed at pleasure by insolent corporations and their minions, corporations which derive their valuable franchises in part by consent of these very people they insult and outrage—it is because of the existence of these things that we are assembled here today, determined to perfect an organization whose one mission shall be to labor by every reasonable and legal means to right the wrongs complained of, until not one right justly ours under the Constitution is denied us.

Ladies and gentlemen, I stand here today and assert in all soberness that we shall no longer accept in silence a condition which degrades our manhood and makes a mockery of our citizenship. I believe I voice the sentiments of each member of the League here assembled when I assert that from now and hence we shall labor as one man, inspired with one holy purpose, to wage relentless opposition to all men who would degrade our manhood and who would defraud us of the benefit of citizenship, guaranteed alike to all born upon this soil or naturalized by the Constitution, which has been cemented and made indestructible by our blood in every war, foreign or domestic, waged by this grand Republic. And it is our proud boast that never in the history of this government has an Afro-American raised the hand of treason against the Star-Spangled Banner. Loyal in every condition to the flag of the Union—as a slave, as contraband of war, as soldier and as citizen—we feel that we have a right to demand of the government we have served so faithfully the measure of protection guaranteed to us and freely granted the vilest traitor who followed Robert E. Lee. There are Afro-American veterans in every state in the Union, of whom it may be said:

> If you ask from whence they came,
> Our answer it should be,
> They came from Appomattox
> And its famous apple tree.

In the name of these veterans, who like their white comrades went back to their homes after the toils of war and mingled in the pursuits of peace, aiding by their industry to pay the enormous debt contracted to vindicate the right of every man born on this soil to be free indeed—in the name of these veterans who wore the blue, we appeal here today to the loyal people of the nation, to frown upon the manifold wrongs practiced upon us and to give their sympathy and their support to the movement we have met to inaugurate to combat these wrongs. It is a reproach to this nation that one man entitled to the protection of the laws should be outraged in his person or in his property, and be unable to get redress. It is a shame and disgrace to the entire people that the arm of the government, which is long enough to reach the naturalized Irishman in British dungeons, to ward off the conscriptions of the German government when it would lay unholy hands upon a naturalized German—I say it is a shame and a disgrace that the government has the power to protect the humblest of its citizens in foreign lands and has not the power to protect its citizens at home—if we have a black face. Venerable prelates of the Church have been insulted and outraged by corporations; refined and delicate women have been submitted to the grossest indignity on the public highway; men and women are lynched and flogged every day, and a million voters are practically disfranchised, have no representation in federal or state legislature; and we are told by the supreme court of the land that the government which made the citizen and conferred coequal rights upon him has no power to protect him in the vital matters here recited. If this be true, if it be true that the power which can create has no power to protect the creature, then it is high time that it secure to itself the necessary power.

We appeal to the nation, which fears a righteous God and loves justice, to judge if our contention here is unreasonable, and we here demand of the party now in power, which has promised so much and which enjoyed our best confidence and our support in the past, that it make good the promises made, that it pay us for our confidence and support in the past, or abide the consequences. We are weary of the empty promises of politicians and the platitudes of national conventions, and we demand a fulfillment of the stipulation in the bond as a condition of our further confidence and support. We do not mince our words here. For the constitutional opponents of our rights we have no faith, no confidence and no support, and of professed friends we here demand that they perform their part of the contract, which alone can justify the sacrifices we have been called upon to make. If it cannot do this, then it has ceased to be the party of Lincoln, of Sumner, of Wilson, and of Logan, and deserves to die, and will die, that another party may rise to finish the uncompleted work, even as the Whig party died that the Republican party might triumph in the nation. . . .

I am now and I have always been a race man and not a party man. Let this League be a race League. To make it anything else is to sow the seed of discord, disunion and disaster at the very beginning of our important work. We stand for the race, and not for this party or that party, and we should know a friend from a foe when we see him. . . .

I now give in consecutive order the reasons which, in my opinion, justify the organization of the National Afro-American League, to wit:

1. The almost universal suppression of our ballot in the South, and consequent taxation without representation, which in the cities, counties and states where we have undisputed preponderating majorities of the voting population we have, in the main, no representation, and therefore no voice in the making and enforcing the laws under which we live.

2. The universal and lamentable reign of lynch and mob law, of which we are made the victims, especially in the South, all the more aggravating because all the machinery of the lawmaking and enforcing power is in the hands of those who resort to such outrageous, heinous and murderous violations of the law.

3. The unequal distribution of school funds, collected from all taxpayers equally and to the equal and undivided benefit of which all are alike entitled.

4. The odious and demoralizing penitentiary system of the South, with its chain gangs, convict leases and indiscriminate mixing of males and females.

5. The almost universal tyranny of common-carrier corporations in the South—railroad, steamboat and other—in which the common rights of men and women are outraged and denied by the minions of these corporations.

6. The discrimination practiced by those who conduct places of public accommodation and are granted a license for this purpose, such as keepers of inns, hotels, and conductors of theaters and kindred places of amusement.

7. The serious question of wages, caused in the main by the vicious industrial system in the South, by the general contempt employers feel for employees, and by the overcrowded nature of the labor market. . . .

I have pondered long and seriously on the evils which beset us, and I have sought, as light was given me, for an antidote to them, if such there be. I lay them before you, and you are here to adopt or reject them.* I propose, then,

1. The adoption by this league of an Afro-American Bank, with central offices in some one of the great commercial centers of the Republic and branches all over the country. We need to concentrate our earnings . . .

I propose (2) the establishment of a Bureau of Emigration. We need to scatter ourselves more generously throughout the Republic.

I propose (3) the establishment of a committee on legislation. We need to have a sharp eye upon the measures annually proposed in the federal and state legislatures affecting us and our

* These proposals were not adopted by the convention.

interests, and there are laws everywhere in the Republic the repeal of which must engage our best thought and effort.

I propose (4) the establishment of a bureau of technical industrial education. We need trained artisans, educated farmers and laborers more than we need educated lawyers, doctors and loafers on the street corners. The learned professions are overcrowded. There is not near so much room at the top as there was in the days of Daniel Webster.

And I propose (5) lastly the establishment of a bureau of cooperative industry. We need to buy the necessaries of life cheaper than we can command them in many states. We need to stimulate the business instinct, the commercial predisposition of the race. We not only want a market for the products of our industry, but we want and must have a fair, and a living return for them. . . .

As the agitation which culminated in the abolition of African slavery in this country covered a period of fifty years, so may we expect that before the rights conferred upon us by the war amendments are fully conceded, a full century will have passed away. We have undertaken no child's play. We have undertaken a serious work which will tax and exhaust the best intelligence and energy of the race for the next century. . . .

JUSTICE OR EMIGRATION SHOULD BE OUR WATCHWORD

By Bishop Henry McNeal Turner

In the years between Reconstruction and World War I the chief advocate of emigration of black Americans to Africa was Bishop Henry McNeal Turner of the African Methodist Episcopal Church. Turner was convinced that there was no future for the Negro in the United States, dominated as it was by white racism, and his conviction was fully fixed in 1883, when the Supreme Court nullified the Civil Rights Act of 1875 in a decision which declared that the federal government could not prevent racial discrimination by private parties. During the next decade, Turner was further convinced of the necessity for emigration to Africa by the increasing tempo of lynching and racist violence. In 1893,

Turner summoned a representative gathering of "the friends of African repatriation or Negro nationalism elsewhere," but not the "stay-at-home portion" of the race. Many Negro leaders agreed to attend, but they opposed mass emigration, and in the face of strong opposition, Turner shifted the emphasis of the meeting from emigration to general protest. To the National Council of Colored Men, which met in Cincinnati in November, 1893, Turner delivered an eloquent opening address, outlining the terrible plight of the Negro people in the United States and pleading for action to alleviate their condition. His speech is also significant for the fact that it is one of the earliest, carefully outlined plans for reparations for the unpaid labor of black Americans during the years of their enslavement.

The more than six hundred delegates voted against emigration, but agreed to step up the fight for justice at home. They sent memorials to Congress, to the state governors, and to the American people; and they formed an Equal Rights Council with Turner as chancellor.

(Turner's speech, presented here in part, is taken from the text which appeared in the Voice of Missions, Atlanta, *December, 1893.)*

GENTLEMEN OF THE NATIONAL COUNCIL: In pursuance of a call issued September 30th,* by the solicitation and endorsement of over three hundred prominent and distinguished members of our race, from every section of the United States, we have assembled in a national convention today. The circumstances that bring us together are of the most grave, serious and solemn character that could command attention and sober consideration. Our anomalous condition as a race and the increasing evils under which we exist have impressed me for the last four years that a national convention or council of our people should assemble and speak to the country, at least, or sue in some other respects for better conditions. . . .

* The call declared in part that, "owing to the dreadful, horrible, anomalous and unprecedented conditions of our people in the United States, it would seem that some common action, move or expression on our part as a race is demanded. The revolting, hideous, monstrous, unnatural, brutal and shocking crimes charged upon us daily on the one hand, and the reign of mobs, lynchers, and fire fiends, and midnight and midday assassins on the other, necessitated a national convention upon our part, for the purpose of crystallizing our sentiments and unifying our endeavors for better conditions in this country, or a change of base for existence." (*Voice of Missions,* October, 1893).

Let us, by way of premises itemize a few facts, connected with our career in this country, deserving more than a transient notice. We have been inhabitants of this continent for 273 years, and a very limited part of the time we were citizens—I mean from the ratification of the Fourteenth Amendment of the national Constitution, until the Supreme Court of the United States, October 15, 1883, declared that provision of the Constitution null and void, and decitizenized us. . . . Singular and strange as it may appear to some present, a black man completed the Goddess of Liberty which ornaments the dome of our national capitol;* and it will stand there, heaven high, as a monument to his genius and industry for ages to come. Yet, this same Goddess of Liberty has been transformed into a lying strumpet so far as she symbolizes the civil liberties of the black man. . . .

I am willing to accord to the white man every meed of honor that ability, grit, backbone, sagacity, tact and invincibility entitle him to. For this Anglo-Saxon, I grant, is a powerful race; but put him in our stead, enslave him for 250 years, emancipate him and turn him loose upon the world, without education, without money, without horse or mule or a foot of land, when passion engendered by war was most intense, to eke out a subsistence from nothing beyond the charity of an indignant people on the one hand, and cold-shouldering and proscriptive people on the other; and I do not believe he would have equaled us in respect, obedience, fidelity and accomplished results and maintained the pacific equilibrium we have. Our nation freed the black man as a war measure, I grant, but that freedom entailed and left upon us a mendicancy that the unborn will ask the reason why. Even the usufruct claim, guaranteed to the serfs of Russia†—a nation at that time regarded as semicivilized—was denied the freedmen by this so-called enlightened and Christian nation.

The mule and forty acres of land, which has been so often ridiculed for being expected by the black man, was a just and righteous expectation,‡ and had this nation been one-fiftieth

* The reference is to Stephen Fortune, a black craftsman.
† The Russian emancipation act was promulgated in 1861, but the Russian peasant was given some opportunity to acquire land, even though at an exorbitant price, and was left undisturbed as an independent tiller of the soil.
‡ "Forty acres and a mule" was the slogan popularized among the freedmen during and after the Civil War. It aroused their hope that they would obtain land and a mule from the federal government so as not to be at the mercy of the white planters.

part as loyal to the black man, as he has been to it, such a bestowment would have been made, and the cost would have been a mere bagatelle, compared with the infinite resources of this Republic, which has given countless millions to foreigners, to come into the country and destroy respect for the Sabbath, flood the land with every vice known to the ends of the earth, and form themselves into anarchal bands for the overthrow of its institutions and venerated customs. . . .

The United States Congress and Supreme Court both have dumped the Negro. Our supposed Constitutional rights have been nullified, and the President of the United States can do nothing but give us few secondhand positions, and those of us who are not dead are simply living by the grace of our respective communities, and we had as well realize our situation and pander to no sentimentality, but that which involves our honor and manhood. . . .

Unless this nation, north and south, east and west, awakes from its slumber and calls a halt to the reign of blood and carnage in this land, its dissolution and utter extermination is only a question of a short time . . . and the United States will never celebrate another centennial of undivided states, without a change of program. A Negro is a very small item in the body politic of this country, but his groans, prayers and innocent blood will speak to God day and night, and the God of the poor and helpless will come to his relief sooner or later, and another fratricidal war will be the sequence, though it may grow out of an issue as far from the Negro as midday is from midnight. For this is either a nation or a travesty. If it is a nation, every man east and west, north and south, is bound to the protection of human life, and the institutions of the country; but if it is a burlesque or a national sham, then the world ought to know it. The North is responsible for every outrage perpetrated in the South, and the South is responsible for every outrage perpetrated in the North, and so of the East and West, and it is no use to blame the South and excuse the North, or blame the North and excuse the South. For every species of injustice perpetrated upon the Negro, every man in every portion of this nation, if it is a nation, is responsible.

The truth is, the nation as such has no disposition to give us manhood protection anyway. Congress had the Constitutional power to pursue a runaway slave, by legislation, into any state and punish the man who would dare conceal him, and the Supreme Court of the United States sustained its legislation so long as slavery existed. Now the same Supreme Court has the power to declare, that the Negro has no civil rights under the

general government that will protect his citizenship and author-
izes the states to legislate upon and for us, as they may like;
and they are passing special acts to degrade the Negro, by authority of the said high tribunal, and Congress proposes no remedy by legislation or by such a Constitutional amendment as
will give us the status of citizenship in the nation that it is presumed we are to love and to sacrifice our lives, if need be, in
defense of. Yet Congress can legislate for the protection of the
fish in the sea and the seals that gambol in our waters, and obli-
gate its men, its money, its navy, its army and its flag to protect, but the eight million or ten million of its black men and
women, made in the image of God, possessing $265,000,000
worth of taxable property, with all their culture, refinement in
many instances, and noble bearing, must be turned off to become the prey of violence, and when we appeal to the general
government for recognition and protection, Justice, so called,
drops her scales and says, Away with you.

I am abused as no other man in this nation, because I am an
African Emigrationist, and while we are not here assembled to
consider that question, nor do I mention it at the present time
to impose it upon you, but if the present condition of things is
to continue, I had, not only rather see my people in the heart of
Africa, but in icebound, ice-covered, and ice-fettered Greenland.

"Give me liberty, or give me death!"
Other American Negroes may sing—

> My country, 'tis of thee,
> Sweet land of liberty,
> Of thee we sing.

But here is one Negro, whose tongue grows palsied, whenever he is invited to put music to these lines. . . .

As one, I feel grateful for many things that have been done
for us within the last thirty years. I am thankful for Mr. Lincoln's manumitting Proclamation, for its ratification by Congress, for the thirteenth, fourteenth and fifteenth amendments
to the Constitution, which were placed there by the American
people for the benefit of our race, even if the United States
Supreme Court has destroyed the Fourteenth Amendment by its
revolting decision.

I am thankful to our generous-hearted friends of the North
who have given voluntarily millions upon millions to aid in our
education. I am thankful to the South for the school laws they
have enacted and for the generous manner they have taxed
themselves in building and sustaining schools for our enlighten-

ment and intellectual and moral elevation. But, if this country is to be our home, the Negro must be a self-controlling, automatic factor of the body politic or collective life of the nation. In other words, we must be full-fledged men. Otherwise we will not be worth existence itself.

To passively remain here and occupy our present ignoble status, with the possibility of being shot, hung or burnt, not only when we perpetrate deeds of violence ourselves, but whenever some bad white man wishes to dark his face and outrage a female, as I am told is often done, is a matter of serious reflection. To do so would be to declare ourselves unfit to be free men or to assume the responsibilities which involve fatherhood and existence. For God hates the submission of cowardice. But on the other hand to talk about physical resistance is literal madness. Nobody but an idiot would give it a moment's thought. The idea of eight or ten million ex-slaves contending with sixty million people of the most powerful race under heaven. Think of two hundred and sixty-five millions of dollars battling with one hundred billion of dollars! Why, we would not be a drop in the bucket. It is folly to indulge such a thought for a moment.

Since I have called this convention, hundreds of letters have been written to me, but I will only refer to two, which were evidently written by men of prominence. One from New York says: "The colored people are such cowards is the reason they have so many things to complain of and until they fight and die a little it will continue to be the case." But another letter from Philadelphia says: "You Negroes had better not provoke a conflict with the white people at your convention in Cincinnati, for if you do the whites, North and South, will join together and exterminate the last one of you from the face of the land. Take warning now, for I know the sentiment of the North, and the South justly hates you." Of the two letters referred to, the latter, I fear, deserves more attention than the former; for the white people of the United States, to provoke some kind of race war as in every instance when a race war is spoken of, it comes from some white quarter. The black man never thinks about it, much less speaks about it, for where individual conflicts take place between white and colored men, in a thousand cases to one they are provoked by the former. I know the Negro as well as any man that breathes the breath of life, and I affirm before earth and heaven today, that no such project has ever been contemplated, nor do I believe it ever will be. We have been reared in this country to revere, honor and love the whites, and we delight to do it when they will give us half a chance.

I know that thousands of our people hope and expect better

times for the Negro in this country, but as one I see no signs of a reformation in our condition; to the contrary, we are being more and more degraded by legislative enactments and judicial decisions. Not a thing has been said or done that contemplates our elevation or the promotion of our manhood in twelve or fifteen years, outside of promoting our education in erecting schools for our general enlightenment; but a hundred things have been done to crush out the last vestige of self-respect and avalanche us with contempt. My remedy, without a change, is, as it would be folly to attempt resistance and our appeals for better conditions are being unheeded, for that portion of us, at least, who feel we are self-reliant, to seek other quarters. There are many propositions before the colored people of this country. Some favor a partial African emigration, and I am one of that number; others favor Mexican emigration, Canadian emigration, Central and South American emigration, while the Honorable John Temple Graves, one of the profoundest thinkers, most brilliant orators and broadest humanitarians in the country,* advocates the setting-apart of a portion of the public domain as a separate and distinct state, where we can have our own governors, United States Senators, members of the lower house of Congress, and all the machinery of state, and thereby have a chance to speak for ourselves, where we can be heard, and give evidence of statesmanship to show to the world that we are capable of self-government, and where our educated sons and daughters can practicalize the benefits of their culture. The position of Mr. Graves may not commend itself to the favorable consideration of all present, any more than my African sentiments or the Mexican, Canadian, or Central American theories, but we must do something. We must agree upon some project. We must offer some plan of action to our people or admit that we are too ignorant and worthless to do anything. This nation justly, righteously and divinely owes us for work and services rendered, billions of dollars, and if we cannot be treated as American people, we should ask for five hundred million dollars, at least, to begin an emigration somewhere, if we cannot receive manhood recognition here at home, for it will cost sooner or later *far more than* that amount to keep the Negro down unless they reestablish slavery itself. Freedom and perpetual deg-

---

* John Temple Graves (1856–1925) was a Southern editor and political spokesman in Florida and Georgia during the 1880's and a prominent lecturer in the early 1900's. Although he supported the plan for a separate Negro state, he was also a white-supremacist who fanned the flames of racial animosity in the South, particularly as editor of the Atlanta *News* and Atlanta *Georgian* during 1906–7.

radation are not in the economy of human events. It is against reason, against nature, against precedent and against God. A people who read, attend schools, receive the instruction of the pulpits, write for the public press, think and furnish famous orators, cannot be chained to degradation forever. They will be a menace to the land, and God himself, with all the laws of nature, will help them to fight the injustice, and no pomp or boast of heraldry can prevent it, yet it may involve horror to both races. Money to leave and build up a nation of our own, where we can respect ourselves at least, or *justice* at the hands of the American nation, should be the watchword of every Negro in the land. . . .

The Negro, at best in this country, occupies a very low plane. Look at the Greek, Latin and mathematical scholars employed as Pullman-car porters and other college-bred young man, restricted by the sphere of a scullion, because color prejudice bars them from employment, in harmony with their culture. Yet the Negro is the nearest competitor in aptitude, physical endurance, industrial application and punctuality to business, the white man has on the face of the globe; and because this fact is well known, the moment some ignorant white man gets into some legislature, he is offering a bill to increase the degradation of the Negro. For you never find such bills or resolutions emanating from first-class white gentlemen. All of these discriminating and proscribing laws that have been enacted against the colored people on these railroads have originated with what we used to call, in slave time, "poor white trash." True, some of them since freedom have climbed up a little and have got to be Congressmen and even governors of states, but it is the same old second-class roughs, who can find nothing else to think or talk about but the ghost of the Negro. Yet the first-class white men and the entire nation North and South are responsible, and the God of nations will so hold them. I refer to these facts merely to show you that degradation or extermination appears to hold a prominent place in the minds of the ruling powers of this country, and I cannot believe that our freedom which cost so much blood and treasure was intended for any such ultimatum.

But some of you may think that I am overgloomy, too despondent, that I have reached the plane of despair; and should any one present so presume, you will be not much at fault. For I confess that I have seen so much and know so much about American prejudice, that I have no hope in the future success of my race in our present situation.

But you will discover that in this address, I have largely

spoken for myself. You will have time enough, and I know you have the ability to speak for yourselves. Should we differ, as we naturally will, let us defend our respective positions and sentiments with the best logical arguments we are able to advance. Slurs, philippics, witty utterances, light anecdotes, innuendoes, cutting remarks, sarcasm, tirades and bitter invectives should not be indulged in in this convention. Men of ability will not do it; they will have too many other things to say. Moreover, if we cannot now, surrounded as we are by mobs, lynchers, ropes, bullets, fire, proscription, color prejudice, decitizenship, blood, carnage, death and extermination, present a united front of action, although we may differ in opinions, then there is no unity of action in us and our destiny is a hopeless one.

You evidently see from the points I have endeavored to raise, and many more that I have not touched, that our condition in this country inferiorates us, and no amount of booklearning, divested of manhood respect and manhood promptings, will ever make us a great people, for, underlying all school culture, must exist the consciousness that I am somebody, that I am a man, that I am as much as anybody else, that I have rights, that I am the creature of law and order, that I am entitled to respect, and that every avenue to distinction is mine. For where this consciousness does not form the substratum of any people, inferioration, retrogression and ultimate degradation will be the result. And seeing that this is our status in the United States today, it devolves upon us to project a remedy for our condition, if such a remedy is obtainable, or demand of this nation, which owes us billions of dollars for work done and services rendered, five hundred million dollars to commence leaving it; or endorse the petition of the colored lawyers' convention, which was held in Chattanooga, Tennessee, asking Congress for a billion dollars for the same purpose. For I can prove, by mathematical calculation, that this nation owes us forty billion dollars for daily work performed.

The one great desideratum of the American Negro is manhood impetus. We may educate and acquire general intelligence, but our sons and daughters will come out of college with all their years of training and drift to the plane of the scullion, as long as they are restricted, limited and circumbounded by colorphobia. For abstract education elevates no man, nor will it elevate a race. What we call the heathen African will strut around in his native land, three fourths naked, and you can see by the way he stands, talks and acts, that he possesses more manhood than fifty of some of our people in this country, and any ten of our most distinguished colored men here; and until we are free from menace by lynchers, hotels, railroads, stores, factories, restaurants, barbershops, courthouses and other places, where merit and worth are respected, we are destined to be a dwarfed people. Our sons and daughters will grow up with it in their very flesh and bones.

Gentlemen of the National Council, I leave the grave, solemn and awful subject with you.

THE ETHICS OF THE HAWAIIAN QUESTION

By William Saunders Scarborough

William Saunders Scarborough was born near Macon, Georgia, February 16, 1852, the son of a free Negro and a slave mother. He took his mother's status, as the law required. After the Civil War, he studied at schools established by the Freedmen's Bureau and was the first graduate of Atlanta University. He continued his studies at Oberlin College, from which he graduated in 1875, and though only twenty-three, became professor of Latin and Greek at Wilberforce University, a Negro institution in Ohio. To help his students, Scarborough wrote a textbook, First Lessons in Greek, which was published by a New York publisher and was widely used as a textbook in both black and white institutions, including Yale University. The book was frequently cited to refute the myth that the Negro was incapable of mastering the complications of Greek conjugation. In 1882, a year after his book was published, Scarborough was elected a member of the American Philological Association. In 1908 he was appointed President of Wilberforce and served until 1920, while continuing his scholarly activities in the field of linguistics and writing and speaking on race relations.

In March, 1894, Scarborough, then professor at Wilberforce University, delivered a scorching attack on the move to annex Hawaii in a speech delivered to students, faculty and guests at the university. The speech was notable for its exposure of the imperialist forces behind annexation

and the role that racial issues played in the determination
of American businessmen in Hawaii to control the island
in their own interests. Scarborough also indicted the mis-
sionaries for their role in the island.

(Scarborough's address presented here is taken from
The Christian Recorder, *March 15, 1894.)*

NOT LONG AGO there was a prize fight in the city of Jacksonville, Florida, between two well-known pugilists, James Corbett and Charles Mitchell. The contest was to decide which of the two should have the honor (?) of being the champion of the world. The victor was to receive in addition, a purse of twenty thousand dollars or more. Strenuous efforts are said to have been put forth by the governor of the state to prevent the contest from taking place. Even state militia were assembled in considerable numbers to assist the governor in carrying out his purposes. "There shall be no fight in the state of Florida" was the edict that came forth from the executive mansion; and the Christian world gladly gave its approval of the governor's veto. There was a fight, however, as all well know, and large crowds assembled to witness the gladiatorial combat. The *"hoc habet" "hoc habet"* differed in no respect from that of similar gatherings of ancient Rome and even now of Spanish bullfights, where each party shouts for his especial favorite in the words quoted or something similar.

Prize fighting is objected to on the ground that it is not only brutal and demoralizing, but a curse to civilization and destructive of our moral and social interests, while it fosters gambling and a spirit of hatred and murder—exerting a bad influence generally. Taking up this strain, the pulpits throughout the land assailed and abused the participants, while they invoked the vengeance of God upon their heads. The clergy were unsparing in their denunciations of prize fighting and prize fighters. The religious press united with the pulpit and the best class of the secular newspapers did likewise. It was clear that public sentiment was against it, as it ought to have been, and that there was a determination to prevent it at all events.

While all must approve of the efforts put forth to check such inhuman contests and consign them to oblivion, it is our opinion that prize fighting is a very small thing as compared with the wrong inflicted upon a weak and defenseless people like the Hawaiians by a strong power like our own. The annexationists, so called, are at the bottom of the Hawaiian imbroglio, and the assistance rendered them by the United States minister in his official capacity, makes our government equally culpable and ought to cause the whole nation to bow its head in shame.*

The sin of prize fighting is subjective rather than objective and affects those taking part directly or indirectly more than anyone else. The purloining of a kingdom, great or small, is infinitely more disastrous to all parties concerned than the Corbett-Mitchell contest could possibly be. The consequences are far more reaching than it is possible for those to be which attend a prize fight where two men meet by common consent and agree to bruise and batter one another up for their own amusement and the greatest purse offered the victor. If the former has an ethical phase, certainly the latter has also, and it is upon this I wish to offer some observations. In regard to the Hawaiian question, we find that almost the entire clergy favor the scheme of the annexationists and the *modus operandi* adopted by the supporters of the so-called Provisional Government to wrest a throne from the hands of those to whom it rightly belongs. The religious press as a whole has joined the *hoi polloi* and united its voice with the rest of annexation sympathizers in the *"hoc habet"* cry, not that Corbett has won or that Mitchell is the winner, but that the *Provisional Government is the head of the Hawaiian affairs and it should be let alone.*

The secular press as a whole is divided by party lines, with truth left out. There are some exceptions of course. The De-

---

* In 1890, 99 percent of Hawaiian exports consisted of sugar for the American mainland. In that year Congress admitted other foreign sugars (as well as Hawaii's) duty-free; but the Louisiana planters persuaded Congress to give United States growers a bounty of two cents a pound. Hawaii's single-crop economy, controlled by white—mainly American-descended—planters, who had displaced the native Hawaiians from their land, was severely wounded. At the same time, native Hawaiians were becoming more and more dissatisfied with a constitution they had been forced to accept, under which control of the government was in the hands of white foreigners, while property qualifications disfranchised most native citizens. Hawaiian discontent spread after 1891, when Queen Liliuokalani, a "strong and resolute" opponent of white rule, became head of the government. In 1893 the white businessmen, aided by the American minister to Hawaii, John L. Stevens, who had secured for them the protection of American troops landed from a cruiser, rose up in rebellion. Stevens immediately recognized the provisional government set up by the rebels, who lost no time in dispatching a five-man commission to Washington to negotiate a treaty of annexation. This treaty, sent to the Senate by the retiring President Benjamin Harrison, who favored it, was held up by Democratic opposition, and was still under discussion when Grover Cleveland became President. Cleveland rejected the treaty of annexation.

Hawaii was annexed during the Spanish-American War in the wave of imperialist expansion which featured that conflict.

mocracy as a rule supports the administration, while the Republican press takes up the gauntlet for Mr. Harrison. Both the President and ex-President committed blunders from beginning to end, but the former's are much less serious than the latter's. The former's were rather in practice than in theory, while the latter's were both in practice and theory. Mr. Cleveland is to be commended for the courage of his convictions. The issues involved in the Hawaiian problem should be calmly considered and calmly discussed and weighed without reference to party or party lines. It is not a party question, but a question of rights and duties—the rights of the Hawaiians and the duty of the United States. The annexation scheme has fallen to the ground. "The stolen kingdom" presented by missionaries or missionaries' sons to the United States failed to carry, as it deserved to do. It has been denied that it is a "stolen kingdom" and we are challenged and called upon to prove it. Here is our proof. In the language of the objector* himself:

The missionaries' sons in Hawaii comprise, first, about four hundred persons from age to infancy, who are directly sprung from the sixty original missionaries and who still continue to reside. A majority live in America. Added to this number by marriage are perhaps a hundred others, perhaps, mostly American-born. Numbering probably five hundred more are a body of people closely connected with the former in business and church relations and who are in active sympathy with them. This thousand people of all ages constitute the nucleus of our strong and progressive American colony of over three thousand persons. There are also the leading and influential element shaping political and social opinions among the great majority of 22,000 whites of the country. Until last May railed at as missionaries, it is now the order of the day to term them missionaries' children and no credit to their parents.

This strong little community of one thousand souls has recently built and paid for a church costing a hundred and thirty thousand dollars and said to surpass any church edifice on the Pacific coast in beauty outside and within. They stately contribute thirty thousand dollars per annum for church and missionary purposes, besides numberless local and irregular benefactions for schools and other causes. By force of character and culture they occupy a majority of the highest public positions. Two out of three of the supreme judges are sons of missionaries; three out of the four ministers of state are the same. Of the Hawaiian legation at Washington, Thurston was grandson and Alexander a son of missionaries, men who would have distinction in any community. Three sons of missionaries by most honorable exertions are among the wealthiest of sugar planters and

* Rev. Sereno Bishop in the New York *Independent.*—W.S.S.

men of great beneficence. For presumable good reasons this large
and reputable body of white natives and old residents of Hawaii are
practically unanimous for the overthrow of the monarchy and for
annexation to the United States. In accord with them are the great
majority of the right-living and intelligent class of the native
Hawaiians. Now as to the charge of tendering the stolen kingdom,
the only right Liliuokalani or Kaiualani can claim in the matter
is that the welfare of the kingdom calls for their rule. It cannot be
stolen from them. They may have some claim for support as being
put out of place. No one will refuse them such support when they
are ready to make terms for it.

This is a strained view to take of the question and lacks the
element of sincerity. In the first place, where did the foreigners
get an island to tender to America? How did they get into
power? What legal right can they lay to the possession they now
claim? Certainly not by right of conquest nor by series of wars
did they triumph, for, as they are in the minority, being hardly
a handful they could make but slight resistance to the powers
that be. The Hawaiian authorities certainly did not make them
a present of the country, nor did they voluntarily relinquish
their claims to it. No such irregular method of doing business
as this is anywhere referred to. No, it was a systematic scheme
laid long and deep to cheat these people out of their own, and
they have succeeded admirably. It was by the grace of the
Hawaiians that our first missionaries were allowed to land upon their territory, and this is the reward the islanders are receiving in return. Of course, it is taken for granted that the
sole purpose of these missionaries was to educate and Christianize the natives and make them better men and women, or else
foreigners would never have been allowed the freedom of the
soil. Subsequent events however would indicate that these people had another object in view. The charges against the character of the queen amount to but little. Examples are not
wanting at the present day of plenty other monarchs whose
character could vie in this especial respect with that of the ex-
queen. But these still hold their scepters with right unquestioned
by other nations on this account.

The annexation movement was the consummation of one of
the most gigantic schemes to steal from a poor helpless people
what was as much theirs as America was the Indians' before
the days of Columbus. What is most peculiar about the matter
is that the Christian world seems to sanction on a big scale
what it condemns on a small one. If the United States fails to
right the wrong it committed by its agents, it will deserve the
condemnation of all Christendom. It cannot afford to pass over

the matter lightly whatever be the attitude of the adherents to the Provisional Government. It is a question of ethics and upon ethical grounds it must be settled—if rightly settled at all— everything else to the contrary.

We have strong evidence of the fact that it is not so much an immoral and dissolute queen as it is a question of color and nationality. It is an ethnological question as well. A proof of this is seen in the nature and character of the caricatures of the deposed ruler that have filled the daily papers. These journals have taken especial pains to enlarge the racial phases of the question that they regard decidedly objectionable in order that they might stir up the prejudices of the people to the extent that they would look over the ethical phase and prevent justice from being done. By way of illustration we note the following:

"I think," says a prominent Buffalo contractor and one who has spent some time on the island, "that President Cleveland has been misinformed about what the people on the Island really want. The temper of the white inhabitants is strongly in favor of the Provisional Government, although they are in the minority—being about one fifth of the entire population. It would be a vain injustice to the whites to force royalty upon them. They do not want to be ruled by a dissolute *negress any more than would the people of Alabama.* They have established such a government as they desire and now simply want to be let alone."

If the good people, whether missionaries or sons of missionaries, find the moral atmosphere out of harmony with their own, let them unite and attempt to cancel the evil of which they complain by raising the moral standard of these islanders, by raising their aspirations making them better citizens. The end sought will come in time, and the example set will be worth all the time spent in bringing about the change.

It is said on good authority that Queen Liliuokalani is no better and no worse than many other women of her race. "Her devotion to religion has induced her to do many praiseworthy acts. She has always been generous to the poor and an active worker in the hospitals and homes for the destitute or unfortunate. She is at times exceedingly fervent in her devotion, attending prayer meetings regularly and lifting her voice in loud and earnest supplications. Now and then she exhorts her followers to repentance."

Whatever may be said to the contrary, it seems to be a fact that at the time of the landing of the *Boston* with her men the queen's troops were the only organized armed forces and were in control of the city; that the United States Marine forces were stationed opposite the government building across the streets with Gatling guns ready for action at a moment's notice; that these troops were landed by request of the United States' minister and those who were the instigators of the riotous movement; that these troops were landed twenty-four hours before the Provisional Government was proclaimed and that the government *de facto* and *de jure* asked the protection of the United States' troops but was refused by order of the United States' Minister Stevens, who was in sympathy with the revolutionists and was their abettor and accomplice in overturning the queen's government.

Again, the evidence seems to be conclusive that the palace was not seized by a mob of thirty armed men until twenty-four hours after the landing of our Marine forces, and that the presence of the latter was designed to intimidate the rightful ruler, "a menace against her" if she attempted to resist the revolutionists. That it was a success goes without saying; that the United States through its minister was a party to the deal is equally true. We have further evidence that the queen was given to understand that she must vacate; that it was the desire of the United States' minister that she should surrender her authority at least until the authorities at Washington should pass upon the situation.

Liliuokalani would naturally infer from this, that she would be restored, if she should peacefully abdicate and leave the matter to the United States for arbitration. To emphasize this perfidious action we need only to add that the Provisional Government declared that its existence would be determined by annexation or union with the United States or whatever the latter should agree upon. The revolutionist could not have maintained their own a fraction of the day if the United States troops had not been employed as a menace and an intimidation, which is evidently in violation of our neutrality laws and places us in a very humiliating position before the world.

The adherents of the Provisional Government declare after they had become firmly established in power that it was their intention to disfranchise a large percentage of the natives and supporters of the royal government, that they might perpetuate their ill-gotten lease of power. Well may these men fear for their heads, after the conception and execution of such a scheme. Who would not? Minister Thurston has not only been outspoken, but defiant on more occasions than one, and the very government against which he has spoken in terms not the most complimentary, for not adopting the annexation scheme, receives him as the accredited minister from a government whose right to exist is more than questionable in the minds of many.

Right the wrong at whatever cost, and if there is to be a Provisional or any other form of government aside from a monarchy, let it come in the regular order and legitimately. Only this will satisfy the demands of justice.

The Christian Church, the religious and secular press, and every American citizen that has in any way sympathized with or given encouragement to a sort of men whose purpose has been all along to throttle justice and enthrone a sham government under the false name of a Provisional Government or a Republic to further their own selfish ends, should *blush with shame and veil their faces, sitting in sackcloth and ashes.*

ATLANTA EXPOSITION ADDRESS

By Booker T. Washington

Booker T. Washington (1856–1915) was born a slave on a plantation in Virginia. Soon after emancipation, the family moved near Charleston, West Virginia, where he mastered the alphabet from Webster's spelling book, which his mother secured. He attended elementary school for colored children, working five hours before school in a salt furnace and mine. In 1872, at the age of seventeen, he set out for Hampton Institute, about five hundred miles away, with a few dollars. Earning his board and expenses as a janitor, he spent three years at Hampton and was greatly influenced by the ideas of industrial education for Negroes espoused by General Samuel C. Armstrong, the principal. In 1881 he was chosen by General Armstrong to head a Negro normal school being started at Tuskegee, Alabama. Emphasizing industrial education and the acquisition of manual skills, Washington built Tuskegee from a dilapidated shanty with forty students to a world-famous institution, which at the time of his death had more than a hundred buildings, owned 2,000 acres of local land, and boasted an endowment of nearly $2,000,000 with an annual budget of $290,000; its 197 faculty members taught 1,537 students, all Negroes. The male students stressed farming, carpentry, blacksmithing, and similar vocations, and the girls learned sewing, flower gardening

*and practical housekeeping. A good part of the funds for
Tuskegee came from Northern capitalists who responded
favorably to Washington's emphasis on industrial education for Negroes and his assurance that, once employed
in industry, they would prove to be faithful workers who
avoided trade unions and strikes.*

*Washington was frequently called upon as a public
speaker, but it was his speech at the Cotton States and
International Exposition at Atlanta, Georgia, September
18, 1895, which gained him acclaim and recognition as
the leading Negro in the country, successor to Frederick
Douglass, who had just died. He spoke at a time when Negroes in the South were being denied the ballot in deliberate defiance of the Fourteenth and Fifteenth Amendments
and were being forced to live under a system of strict racial
segregation. Washington proposed a compromise by which
the Negro would not ask for social or political equality in
return for a pledge that he would be provided with industrial training and the opportunity to take a place in the
economic development of the New South. He stressed that
the Negro must win dignity and respect by self-help and
emphasized Negro responsibilities rather than rights.*

*Washington's proposal was welcomed with relief by the
South and with enthusiasm by the North as evidence of
the Negro's acceptance of the order of white supremacy.
His influence soon extended far beyond Tuskegee. Presidents of the United States asked his advice when appointing Negroes to federal offices, and he exercised powerful
influence over Negro publications. He supported Negro
business enterprises and in 1900 organized the National
Negro Business League.*

*Scholars differ sharply over the necessity for and value
of Washington's policies, and some have pointed out that
he did not entirely neglect the struggle for equal rights and
contributed secretly to protest activities. (See Louis R.
Harlaw, "The Secret Life of Booker T. Washington,"* Journal of Southern History, *vol. XXXVII, August, 1971, pp.
393–416.) Essentially, however, he urged Negroes to learn
trades and develop an attitude that hard work is the highest virtue, and assured them that only in this way could
they achieve the rights of citizenship. In the meantime,
they should cease agitation and protest.*

*Here is the text of Washington's Atlanta Exposition Ad-
dress, taken from his* Up From Slavery, *N.Y., 1965, pp.
154–9.*

MR. PRESIDENT and gentlemen of the Board of Directors and citizens: One third of the population of the South is of the Negro race. No enterprise seeking the material, civil or moral welfare of this section can disregard this element of our population and reach the highest success. I but convey to you, Mr. President and Directors, the sentiment of the masses of my race when I say that in no way have the value and manhood of the American Negro been more fittingly and generously recognized than by the managers of this magnificent exposition at every stage of its progress. It is a recognition that will do more to cement the friendship of the two races than any occurrence since the dawn of our freedom.

Not only this, but the opportunity here afforded will awaken among us a new era of industrial progress. Ignorant and inexperienced, it is not strange that in the first years of our new life we began at the top instead of at the bottom; that a seat in Congress or the state legislature was more sought than real estate or industrial skill; that the political convention or stump speaking had more attractions than starting a dairy farm or truck garden.

A ship lost at sea for many days suddenly sighted a friendly vessel. From the mast of the unfortunate vessel was seen a signal, "Water, water; we die of thirst!" The answer from the friendly vessel at once came back, "Cast down your bucket where you are." A second time the signal, "Water, water; send us water!" ran up from the distressed vessel, and was answered, "Cast down your bucket where you are." And a third and fourth signal for water was answered, "Cast down your bucket where you are." The captain of the distressed vessel, at last heeding the injunction, cast down his bucket, and it came up full of fresh, sparkling water from the mouth of the Amazon River. To those of my race who depend on bettering their condition in a foreign land or who underestimate the importance of cultivating friendly relations with the Southern white man, who is their next-door neighbor, I would say, "Cast down your bucket where you are"—cast it down in making friends in every manly way of the people of all races by whom we are surrounded.

Cast it down in agriculture, mechanics, in commerce, in domestic service, and in the professions. And in this connection it is well to bear in mind that whatever other sins the South may be called to bear, when it comes to business, pure and simple, it is in the South that the Negro is given a man's chance in the commercial world, and in nothing is this exposition more eloquent than in emphasizing this chance. Our greatest danger is that in the great leap from slavery to freedom we may over-

look the fact that the masses of us are to live by the productions
of our hands, and fail to keep in mind that we shall prosper in
proportion as we learn to dignify and glorify common labor
and put brains and skill into the common occupations of life;
shall prosper in proportion as we learn to draw the line between
the superficial and the substantial, the ornamental gewgaws of
life and the useful. No race can prosper till it learns that there
is as much dignity in tilling a field as in writing a poem. It is
at the bottom of life we must begin, and not at the top. Nor
should we permit our grievances to overshadow our opportunities.

To those of the white race who look to the incoming of those
of foreign birth and strange tongue and habits for the prosperity of the South, were I permitted I would repeat what I say
to my own race, "Cast down your bucket where you are." Cast
it down among the eight millions of Negroes whose habits you
know, we shall contribute one third to the business and industrial prosperity of the South, or we shall prove a veritable body
of death, stagnating, depressing, retarding every effort to advance the body politic.

Gentlemen of the exposition, as we present to you our humble
effort at an exhibition of our progress, you must not expect
overmuch. Starting thirty years ago with ownership here and
there in a few quilts and pumpkins and chickens (gathered
from miscellaneous sources), remember the path that has led
from these to the inventions and production of agricultural implements, buggies, steam engines, newspapers, books, statuary,
carving, paintings, the management of drugstores and banks,
has not been trodden without contact with thorns and thistles.
While we take pride in what we exhibit as a result of our independent efforts, we do not for a moment forget that our part
in this exhibition would fall far short of your expectations but
for the constant help that has come to our educational life, not
only from the Southern states, but especially from Northern
philanthropists, who have made their gifts a constant stream
of blessing and encouragement.

The wisest among my race understand that the agitation of
questions of social quality is the extremest folly, and that progress in the enjoyment of all the privileges that will come to us
must be the result of severe and constant struggle rather than
of artificial forcing. No race that has anything to contribute to
the markets of the world is long in any degree ostracized. It is
important and right that all privileges of the law be ours, but
it is vastly more important that we be prepared for the exercises
of these privileges. The opportunity to earn a dollar in a factory

just now is worth infinitely more than the opportunity to spend a dollar in an opera house.

In conclusion, may I repeat that nothing in thirty years has given us more hope and encouragement, and drawn us so near to you of the white race, as this opportunity offered by the exposition; and here bending, as it were, over the altar that represents the results of the struggles of your race and mine, both starting whose fidelity and love you have tested in days when to have proved treacherous meant the ruin of your firesides. Cast down your bucket among these people who have, without strikes and labor wars, tilled your fields, cleared your forests, built your railroads and cities, and brought forth treasures from the bowels of the earth, and helped make possible this magnificent representation of the progress of the South. Casting down your bucket among my people, helping and encouraging them as you are doing on these grounds, and to education of head, hand and heart, you will find that they will buy your surplus land, make blossom the waste places in your fields, and run your factories. While doing this, you can be sure in the future, as in the past, that you and your families will be surrounded by the most patient, faithful, law-abiding and unresentful people that the world has seen. As we have proved our loyalty to you in the past, in nursing your children, watching by the sickbed of your mothers and fathers, and often following them with tear-dimmed eyes to their graves, so in the future, in our humble way, we shall stand by you with a devotion that no foreigner can approach, ready to lay down our lives, if need be, in defense of yours, interlacing our industrial, commercial, civil and religious life with yours in a way that shall make the interests of both races one. In all things that are purely social we can be as separate as the fingers, yet one as the hand in all things essential to mutual progress.

There is no defense or security for any of us except in the highest intelligence and development of all. If anywhere there are efforts tending to curtail the fullest growth of the Negro, let these efforts be turned into stimulating, encouraging, and making him the most useful and intelligent citizen. Effort or means so invested will pay a thousand per cent interest. These efforts will be twice blessed—"blessing him that gives and him that takes." . . .

Nearly sixteen millions of hands will aid you in pulling the load upward, or they will pull against you the load downward. We shall constitute one third and more of the ignorance and crime of the South, or one third its intelligence and progress; practically empty-handed three decades ago, I pledge that in

your effort to work out the great and intricate problem which
God has laid at the doors of the South, you shall have at all
times the patient, sympathetic help of my race; only let this
be constantly in mind, that, while from representations in these
buildings of the product of field, of forest, of mine, of factory,
letters and art, much good will come, yet far above and beyond
material benefits will be that higher good, that, let us pray God,
will come in a blotting-out of sectional differences and racial
animosities and suspicions, in a determination to administer
absolute justice, in a willing obedience among all classes to
the mandates of law. This, this, coupled with our material prosperity, will bring into our beloved South a new heaven and a
new earth.

A PLEA AGAINST THE DISFRANCHISEMENT
OF THE NEGRO

By Thomas E. Miller

*After the overthrow of Radical Reconstruction in South
Carolina, the conservative white element continued to
govern the state under the constitution of 1868 adopted
by black and white delegates. In 1892, however, the extreme white-supremacists, led by United States Senator
Benjamin R. "Pitchfork" Tillman, gained control of the
legislature and by a small majority in 1894 carried the
referendum for a new convention on the issue of restrict-
ing the Negro vote and delivering South Carolina from
the "shame" of being governed under the "Radical rag" of
1868.*

*Representation in the 1895 Constitutional Convention
included 112 Tillmanite Democrats, 42 Conservative Democrats, and 6 Negro Republicans. Dominated by the Till-
manites, the Committee on the Rights of Suffrage reported
a new amendment to the constitution which provided suffrage for male citizens over twenty-one who could meet
the qualifications of residence in the state for two years,
county for one year, precinct for four months, and payment of the poll tax at least six months before the elections. These were calculated to eliminate many Negroes*

because of their tendency to move about and their inability to pay their poll taxes in May, a time when ready cash was least available to sharecroppers and farmers. But the chief proposal to disfranchise the Negro was the literary requirement, a provision that each registrant prove to the satisfaction of the board that he could read and write any section of the constitution; if he failed to meet this test he might register if he owned and paid taxes on property assessed at three hundred dollars or more. The board, of course, would be able to overlook any number of white illiterates and paupers.

Even though they knew it was futile, the Negro delegates to the convention fought the white-supremacists and made appeals for the maintenance of unrestricted suffrage. The first and most eloquent of the six speeches was made on October 26, 1895, by Thomas Ezekiel Miller. He reviewed the history of the Negro people in America, citing the martyrdom of Crispus Attucks and the favorable comments of Charles Pinckney and Henry Laurens, South Carolina leaders during the American Revolution, on the contributions of black soldiers in the War for Independence. He made an appeal to those who feared the disfranchisement of the poor whites, pointing out that the three-hundred-dollar property qualification would not be a sufficient alternative for those who were poor as well as illiterate. Miller openly challenged the upholders of the lost-cause tradition to face the truth.

So effective was Miller's speech that Tillman was forced to reply, and he dragged out the issue of Negro domination and fraud during the era of Reconstruction as justification for disfranchising the black voters. Miller then spoke again, fearlessly defending the record of the Negro during Reconstruction. Even the white-supremacist Columbia Register *was impressed, and it commented on October 27: "Miller's speech Friday was an eloquent appeal on behalf of the Negro. While listening to his soaring flights, many of the delegates regretted that they felt an inexorable determination not to accede to his plea, a determination born of stern necessity." As predicted, the convention proceeded to disfranchise the Negroes of South Carolina.*

Miller's speeches were not published in the official journal of the convention. They appeared (along with briefer speeches of the other Negro delegates) in a pamphlet published at her own expense by Mary J. Miller, who wrote in a preface: "That the country may read these speeches

*and learn to know these brave and true men, I have edited
a few of their arguments and prepared this pamphlet. I
regard them as gems of Negro eloquence."*

*Thomas E. Miller was born a free Negro in Ferebeeville,
South Carolina, on June 17, 1849. He moved with his parents to Charleston in 1851 and attended the public schools
in Charleston and in Hudson, New York. During this time
he worked as a newsboy on a railroad. He was graduated
from Lincoln University, Pennsylvania, in 1872, and
moved to Grahamville, South Carolina, where he served
as school commissioner of Beaufort County. In 1888 he
was elected to Congress and served one term (September
24, 1889, to March 3, 1891) during which he spoke out
vigorously against the lynching and exploitation of his
people in the South. In 1894 he was returned to the state
House of Representatives. In 1896 he was elected president
of the State Colored College in Orangeburg. He died in
Charleston on April 8, 1938.*

*Here are significant excerpts from Miller's speeches in
the Constitutional Convention of 1895. They are taken
from Mary J. Miller,* The Suffrage. Speeches by Negroes
in the Constitutional Convention. The Part Taken by Colored Orators in Their Fight for a Fair and Impartial Ballot,
*n.p., n.d., pp. 5–16. (Copy in the Schomburg Branch of the
New York Public Library.)*

MR. PRESIDENT: As an American citizen, as one who
yields to no man in respect for the laws of the United States
and South Carolina, as one who loves the past history of our
nation and the dear old state when that history has been for the
good and benefit of mankind, as one who has never by word or
vote committed an act that in any way tended to destroy the
rights of any citizen, white or black, as one who wishes to see
every male citizen—and woman too—who is not disqualified
on account of crime or mental condition the equal of every
other citizen in the enjoyment of inalienable rights, the chief
of which is to have a voice in the government, I approach the
discussion of the proposed disfranchisement of the common
people of South Carolina, white and black.

Mr. President, the conservative force in our state is the common people, the burden-bearing people, and, sir, when you say
that three hundred dollars and the capacity to read and write
are the requirements to be possessed by voters, you are striking
at the root of the tree of universal government. I ask in the name

of the brotherhood of man and equal citizenship of the American people that I should not be trammeled by rules making my say a short one. I ask forbearance and the necessary time to discuss this all-important question, and I do hope and believe that, although I am in a feeble minority, this all-powerful majority will hear me, because I approach the discussion with malice toward none, but with a loving hope for the final settlement of this very vexed question. May the spirits of departed patriots, who have shed their blood for the rights of man on this soil bear witness of our condition and in some way hover over us and guide us to the right. . . .

Hand in hand with a united effort, the white man and the black reclaimed this country and made it the asylum of the oppressed from every clime. And here today, Mr. President, after a residence of more than 250 years, with love and affection for the government, after having borne our part in every struggle and answered to every call, after having proven to the world that we are conservative in thought and action, lovable in our natures, forbearing toward our oppressor, living under and by the laws at all times, we are confronted at this hour, the noonday of peace and unity in the nation, the noonday of prosperity and hope, the noonday of this magnificent existence of ours with this proposition to disfranchise the common people; to take from them the dearest right, the right to vote. Oh, Mr. President, why is this to be done? Is there anybody here who can or dare deny that the sole purpose for which this convention was called is for the disfranchisement of the common people, and the Negro more especially? If there is such a person I ask him to read the speeches of the leaders who forced this convention upon us against the will of the people, and they will all be convinced that the only thing for which this convention was called is for the disfranchisement of that class of people, whose chief lot has been to toil, toil, toil. With no hopes but to toil! Then if the speeches leave any reasonable doubt I ask him to read this article of disfranchisement, the article that has been pronounced by Senator Irby as a political monstrosity, and he will be thoroughly convinced that the purpose for which this convention was called is to disfranchise the Negro in the rice fields and his poor, uneducated white brother, who plows the bobtail ox or mule on the sandhills. He will be convinced that this convention was called to disfranchise the Negro in every walk of life and the poor white boy who edits a newspaper in which he speaks fulsomely for the greatest of all misnomers and Southern bugbears—white supremacy. There is no hope for

him, though he wields an eloquent pen, if he is poor. His forefathers may have come here, and, like the Negro, spilt his
blood, shed his tear, and toiled to plant this magnificent tree
of liberty, but if this monstrosity becomes the law, there is no
hope for him but to toil and grovel in poverty, because for the
want of three hundred dollars, though an educated Caucasian,
he is no better off than his ignorant brother in black skin.
Trickery is not legislation. These little innocent "ifs" and "ors"
may in the hands of skilled manipulators of fraudulent registration enable the poor, illiterate white men to vote at one or
two succeeding elections, but in less than six years, under the
part of this law saying that a man cannot vote who cannot read
and write a section of the Constitution, that a man cannot vote
who does not own three hundred dollars' worth of property, a
governor will be elected who will turn the machinery over to
the wealthy, to the managers of corporate rights, to the gold-
bugs, to the whisky trust, and we will have a spectacle like
this: The poor, ignorant white man, the poor, educated white
man, the poor, ignorant Negro, and the poor, educated Negro
will be nonentities in the government, with no voice to say who
shall rule, with no representation in the legislative halls, with
no representation in the courts; it will be turning back the
wheel of progress, and revolutions should never go backward. . . .

Why do they say that the Negro must be disfranchised? Is it
because he is lawless? No! Is it because he is riotous in the discharge of the right of suffrage? No! They answer, "Because
his skin is black, he should not vote. Because his skin is black,
he is inferior. Because he did not fight for the ballot, he should
not have it. Because we are a conquered people and were conquered by the national government, in the name of the Negro,
he shall not vote."

Mr. President, these are some of the reasons given by those
who swear by the altar of liberty that we shall not be citizens.
Why have they thus sworn? Mr. President, this country and its
institutions are as much the common birthright and heritage
of the American Negro as it is the possession of you and yours.
We have fought in every Indian war, in every foreign war, in
every domestic struggle by the side of the white soldiers from
Boston Common and Lake Erie to the Mississippi Valley and
the banks of the Rio Grande. . . .

But, Mr. President, although we have purchased this land of
our birth by our past deeds, you and yours say that we must
not vote, because we are an alien race. Aliens, say you, because
our skins are black. But oh! Mr. President,

'Tis neither birth, race, clime or clan,
'Tis brain, not skin, nor hair, that makes the man.

Call us aliens? We, *aliens*? The people who were the foundation of the American civilization, *aliens*? A people who, by their
sweat, assisted in clothing the barren rocks of the Northeast
in verdure, who drained the swamps of the South, and made
them to mimic gold in the harvest time; who by their endurance, toil and suffering made it possible for our white neighbors
to establish this government, the asylum of us all; who by
their toil developed the canal and railroad systems of this country—call us *aliens*? Then to whom can the term *citizens* be
applied? A residence of our foreparents of near three hundred
years; birth and rearage here; our adaptation to the wants of
the country; our labor and forbearance; our loyalty to the government—are all these elements indices of an alien race? If
we are aliens, then who are the citizens? It is true that we did
not come here of our own volition, nor is the epoch of our coming one to be remembered with delight. There was no Castle
Garden open to us; no merchant princes with a philanthropic
hand extended to us; no Christian mission inviting us to come;
but against our will, in chains, we were dragged from our native land to assist in converting the wilds of America into homes
of freemen; to assist in establishing this government, the best
that has ever been given to man. Its foundations were laid by our
toil and sufferings; its growth and development have been matured by our blood. Whether on the farms, in the workshops,
the canals, the railroads, or in your homes—wherever work
was to be done, obstacles overcome, and barren hills to be fertilized—there, at all times, the white man could rely upon the
Negro, and he has never failed him. The Negro has borne the
burden of toil, and for what? To plan a civilization from which
he is to be forever excluded. No, no, no! We have purchased
it with labor; we have purchased it with afflictions; we have
purchased it with loyalty; we have purchased it with blood
drawn at the point of the lash of the taskmaster; we have purchased it with blood spilt upon the fields of battle; it is ours by
all the laws of right and justice. Right, under the watchful care
of God, makes might. It is ours; absolutely ours. We are no more
aliens to this country or to its institutions than our brothers in
white. We have instituted it; our forefathers paid dearly for it.
The broken hearts of those who first landed here is the first
price that was paid for the blessings for which we now contend.
By the God of right, by the God of justice, by the God of love,
we will stay here and enjoy it, share and share alike with those

who call us aliens and invite us to go. Together we planted the tree of liberty and watered its roots with our tears and blood, and under its branches we will stay and be sheltered.

Mr. President, those of you who seek to deny us this boon of citizenship tell the North a tale of woe and say that good government and white supremacy are in danger, and to protect the sweets of domestic happiness that were bequeathed us by our fallen sires, white and black, it is necessary to disfranchise the Negro. Shades of those departed heroes, bear witness to what I here say: The Negro does not by his presence retard the wheels of progress. The Negro will never by his vote overthrow good government. The Negro will never by any act of his seek to destroy white supremacy. He is nonobstructive; he is the best element of conservative citizenship in the South. Into his hands is the keeping of peace and happiness of the Southern people. But the Honorable George D. Tillman says that the South is a conquered province. The majority of you blame the poor Negro for the humility inflicted upon you during that conflict, but he had nothing to do with it. It was your love of power and your supreme arrogance that brought it upon yourselves. You are too feeble to settle up with the government for that old grudge. This hatred has been centered upon the Negro; and he is the innocent sufferer of your spleen. But, sirs, we are here. We intend to obey every phase of law that you may legislate against us. We intend to continue to love and forgive you for what you are doing to us. We intend to remain here and cause the South to blossom anew by our toil and suffering. We intend to place our case in the hands of God and the American white people, and while we are waiting for the full enjoyment of the blessings about which Jefferson wrote, for which Washington fought, and Attucks died, let me remind you of the truism that the part is not greater than the whole, and we know that we are compelled to move along within our circumscribed limits until the majority of the white sons and daughters of the South, yea, the entire nation, shall cease to be fooled into the belief that by reason of the Negro's presence, white supremacy is in danger. This is a white man's country, it is claimed, and I will not discuss it, but let me recall to you the words of the sainted Lincoln: "You can fool all of the people sometimes, you can fool some of the people all the time, but you can't fool all the people all the time."

The flame of education in this nation is ablaze and sheds its rays from every hilltop and amid the dales, and through and by means of education the scales of prejudice and false impressions will drop from the eyes of every white man, high and low. And they, right here in the South, will in time accord us every right and shed blood by our sides to maintain it. But to say that we are not fitted to enjoy the rights of a voter at this time is false, absolutely false, for we are the conservative element of Southern citizenship.

Senator Tillman, in an interview a few days ago, said that the Southern white man is the true friend of the Negro, and he asked the North to keep out of this discussion and deliver the rights of Negro citizenship to his proffered, tender mercy. I would not deny that the Southern white man is friendly to the Negro and will and does assist him as long as he does not attempt to don the habiliments of American citizenship, but if he attempts to clothe himself in the garb of citizenship and claim equal rights before the law and under the Stars and Stripes, the average white man becomes cantankerous and he imagines things that are impossible, and if he chances to be a leader, he flaunts into the face of the American nation the false flag of the fear of Negro domination. The Negroes do not want to dominate. They do not want and would not have social equality, but they do want to cast a ballot for the men who make their laws and administer the laws. Is there anything new in this plaintive appeal to the nation, asking in the name of friendship for and to the Negro to be left with the Negro and his rights in their hands? Why, sirs, it is not, for it was the cry of the feudal lords when they were grinding the white slaves of Europe between the millstones of misery and poverty. It was the cry of the school of slavery when the chains of servitude were riveted around the necks of the slaves on this continent, and the thoughtful are always reminded that when the lords of the soil ask the common people to surrender to them their rights, whether their intention is so to do or not, they are building barriers between people who surrender to them their rights. . . .

In the image of God, made He man, all equal, in the possession of inalienable rights, but at all times it has been the property-owning class who have sought to grind down, impoverish and brutalize their own blood if that blood was in the body of the poor and the weak. It is against class legislation that I stand here and raise my voice, and in the name of the poor, struggling white man and the peaceful, toiling, loving Negro. I ask that this act of feudal barbarism against the poor and common people do not be engrafted into and become a part of the Magna Charta of free white and black South Carolinians.

Mr. President, it is the boast that no illiterate white man shall be disfranchised. It is the boast that the illiterate and educated poor Negro shall be disfranchised. Pass this law and you disfranchise them both, unless trickery and fraud are to be enthroned at our election booths. Pass this law, and you disfranchise all the laboring people, white and black, unless you so administer this law, which is the avowed intention of your leaders, as to discriminate against the Negro. Such a discrimination, Mr. President, will be a nullification of the Fifteenth Amendment. In the thirties our statesmen played at the game of nullification,* and ever thereafter they taught nullification until their teachings culminated in secession and secession led to war, and a brother's hand was imbued in a brother's blood in that fight which was the struggle of the common people against the slaveholding class; the common people won that fight, and hence, by reason of false teaching, and by South Carolina placing her interests in the hands of selfish and ambitious men in the past, we are in this deplorable condition. Right is right, because God is God. Let us, as sons of South Carolina, dare to do right to all our citizens, for it is the only safe course of our citizens or state to follow. Therefore, I do hope that the enacting words of the articles of disfranchisement will be stricken out. It is hard to kick against the pricks. The majority of the white people of this nation are the common laboring class, and they will not sit down idly and see South Carolina again nullify any law that secures to the common people rights that are sacred to every freeman. . . .

Oh! countrymen, there is no good to come of this state out of this proposed act. Let us kill it and return to the constitutional provisions that we now have relating to the subject. I would that you could see the future as I see it. I would that our statesmen would use their energies and their great brain development in a better cause. I would that they would formulate plans by which our waste places could be reclaimed. Labor to bring immigrants into the confines of the dear old state. Strive to induce capital to come into our midst. Strive to teach the masses the lessons to forbear and stand the ills we have and ask God to assist us in a united effort, with the one purpose, and

---

* In his "South Carolina Exposition" (1828), John C. Calhoun of South Carolina preached states' rights and the right of a state to nullify an unjust federal law, the state itself being the judge of what constituted injustice. On November 24, 1832, the legislature of South Carolina passed an Ordinance of Nullification, defining the tariff acts of 1828 and 1832, as passed by the Congress of the United States, illegal in South Carolina. President Andrew Jackson received Congressional authority to carry out the revenue acts involved, in the "Force Bill" of March 2, 1833, but a compromise tariff was finally adopted.

that purpose to make South Carolina the home of free, loving, prosperous humanity. Labor, let us all, to banish from our state caste prejudice and hatred of one man toward another. Let us cease to legislate in favor or against any class of people. Let us tell our people that this is the common heritage of whites and blacks, and it is our duty as free men to live in peace and assist in the government of the state.

Let us labor to prove that we are all a part of this nation, that we love her and intend to make this part of our common country the most glorious and certain place for peace and happiness of any portion of our great domain.

The gentleman from Edgefield (Mr. Tillman) has read from the "Book of Fraud" to prove that my race is not qualified to vote, and why so? Is he ignorant of the way in which the book was made up? If he from experience knew so much about it as I do, he would not quote from it so freely. It was prepared by a partisan committee, and it is greatly colored.

But, Mr. President, I will not discuss that thread-worn tale so eloquently rehashed by the two gentlemen from Edgefield (Messrs. Tillman and Sheppard), but I do remind them and this convention that the white people of South Carolina themselves are more responsible for the state of affairs which existed during what they call "the dark period of their struggle," than is the Negro or carpetbagger. Though they had been in rebellion, seeking to destroy the very foundation of the greatest government ever planned and maintained, Congress by humane and charitable acts made it possible for them and the Negroes as co-heirs to reconstruct their own state governments; but with a haughtiness that showed their contempt for favors bestowed, they stood aloof, refused to vote or assist in reconstructing what in mad folly they had destroyed. A new class of rulers called carpetbaggers came among the ignorant Negroes, some of them honest and with patriotic motives. The country had been desolated by five years of war. County jails and courthouses had been destroyed, bridges burned, ferries broken up and roads cut to pieces—all of which had to be reconstructed. Charitable and penal institutions had to be rebuilt and maintained, and city, village and town governments reestablished, making this a period peculiarly adapted to peculation, jobbery and plunder. Is it to be wondered at that right on the heels of a great war, with so much to be done anew, there was jobbery and peculation? There were many avenues to be traversed, great and diversified work to be done, and it was therefore impossible to keep out of the administration of affairs men who came among us for plunder. Why continue to hold that picture up to prove the worthlessness of a race? Removed so far as we are from it why continue to say that by reason of such acts we should not be entrusted with the right to vote?

Strange as it may appear, I plead specially for the Negro; during the three years he was the major factor in making and sustaining the government in South Carolina, that is from 1873 to 1876, he displayed greater conservative force, appreciation for good laws, knowledge of the worth of honest financial legislation, regard for the rights of his fellow citizens in relation to property and aptitude for honest financial state legislation than has ever been shown by any other people. "Fresh from the auction block and the slave pen," in the words of Professor Bryce, "ten-year-old children were more fitted to exercise the right of franchise." They first elected whom they supposed to be their friends, but in the short period of less than five years we who participated in that government learned that though they were our friends, any act on their part predicated upon plunder meant universal destruction, and from 1873 to 1876, inclusive, the record made by Negro legislators and Negroes charged with fiduciary trusts in the management of the government for certain reforms, has never been surpassed in any of the conservative states of New England. It is but too true, "the evil one does lives after him—the good is oft interred with his bones." . . .

We were eight years in power. We had built schoolhouses, established charitable institutions, built and maintained the penitentiary system, provided for the education of the deaf and dumb, rebuilt the jails and courthouses, rebuilt the bridges and reestablished the ferries. In short, we had reconstructed the state and placed it upon the road to prosperity and, at the same time, by our acts of financial reform transmitted to the Hampton government an indebtedness not greater by more than $2,500,000 than was the bonded debt of the state in 1868, before the Republican Negroes and their white allies came into power.*

I stand here pleading for justice to a people whose rights are about to be taken away with one fell swoop, and I don't stand here answering any personal allusions, but representing the

* In his evaluation of the benefits of Reconstruction, Miller was pointing out facts that were to be ignored by most historians until very recently. In the *American Historical Review* of July, 1910, Dr. W. E. B. Du Bois published an article entitled "Reconstruction and Its Benefits" which supported in detail the thesis Miller had advanced fifteen years earlier. Du Bois' point of view, however, was dismissed by contemporary historians.

interests of the most conservative element of the Southern citizenship.

What is the trouble? The trouble comes from this, Mr. President. One white faction in South Carolina has been arrayed against another, and to prevent us from standing up in a representative capacity in a minority as representatives of the majority, they have rehashed this stale tale that has been written and read by the North, East and West until judgment has been passed upon it.

Because there had been robbery and fraud and perjury during a part of the time of Negro domination as it is called, it must not be thought that all Negroes were dishonest, any more than that all white men in New York were dishonest because Tweed and his gang had been corrupt.* That did not signify that all of the men who put Tweed into office were corrupt.

Because white Democrats voted solidly for, and by their votes elected, the most corrupt judge (Thomas J. Mackey) that has ever disgraced the judicial ermine in South Carolina, why should the white people of our state be pronounced as venal as that arch scoundrel?

Oh, Mr. President, peace! Peace! Peace is the thing that I ask. But can we hope for peace and good feeling between the two races when such exhibitions as that made here by the gentleman from Edgefield is repeated?

Peace! Peace! Peace, happiness and prosperity, and the hope for a brighter day seems withered!

What right would I have to recall the scenes of Hamburg and Ellenton, where the helpless Negroes were murdered in cold blood? What right would I have to refer to the fact that a gentleman on this floor treasures as a parlor ornament a rifle which he claims he used at those riots?

Peace! Peace to all men! Judge these educated white people by what they are doing, and ask them if the poor ignorant Negro should be thus judged. . . .

I want a united people. Let us forever bury all the bad deeds of both races of the past. Let us try to bear and forbear. Let us strive to bind up the wounds, old wounds of long, long ago, with bandages of loving kindness toward the two races. God has placed your race and my race here on this continent; together it is our lot to dwell. Oh, countrymen, of this Southland, one and

* The Tweed Ring was a political organization in New York City from 1860 to 1871, ruled by a "Boss" Tweed; it was notorious for graft and corruption. After the Ring was overthrown in 1871, it was discovered that the city debt had been increased from $20,000,000 to $101,000,000. Tweed was ultimately arrested, and he died in prison.

594 THE VOICE OF BLACK AMERICA

all, white and black, let us be just, one to another; let us at all
times speak only the truth about our people and the old state;
let us labor to unite our people for the good of the people in
common; let us secure to our children prosperity and happiness
founded upon the rock of justice and peace, justice and peace,
justice and peace!

WE ARE STRUGGLING FOR EQUALITY

By John Hope

*Five months after Booker T. Washington had announced
his policy of accommodation at the Atlanta Exposition, an
important attack on this ideology by a black American was
delivered. It came from John Hope (1868–1936), one of
the outstanding Negro college presidents in American history. Hope delivered the blast at Washington in a speech
before the colored debating society of Nashville on George
Washington's birthday, 1896.**

*Hope was the son of James Hope, a Scot who came to
America and established a cotton mill in Augusta, Georgia,
in 1845. He moved to New York after selling his mill and
became a wine importer. Here he met a beautiful young
quadroon, a former slave named Fannie, and after the
Civil War, the couple returned to Augusta, where John
Hope was born, the third of the couple's children. Until
his father's death, John had a secure childhood, but when
he was only eight years old, he witnessed the 1876 Hamburg, South Carolina, massacre in which the Negro militiamen of that city were attacked and overwhelmed by an
armed white mob, three hundred strong, who summarily
executed a number of their captives. The massacre was
followed by an armed assault upon Negro houses and a
reign of terror against the black community.*

*Hope attended school in the North, and after his father's
death worked for five years in a restaurant. With a loan
from his brother, he studied at Worcester Academy, in*

* For criticism of Washington's Atlanta Exposition speech by black
Americans even before Hope expressed these views, see Philip S. Foner,
editor, "Early Opposition to Washington's Ideas," *Journal of Negro History,* Vol. LV, October, 1970, pp. 343–47.

*Massachusetts, earning his way by serving meals and
working in the summer as a waiter at hotels and resorts.
From Worcester he went to Brown University, where he
also faced financial hardships, and then taught at Atlanta
Baptist College. Eventually Hope became president of
Atlanta Baptist (later Morehouse College), and at Atlanta
he became a close associate of W. E. B. Du Bois and other
foes of Booker T. Washington.*

*Here is the concluding part of John Hope's speech (from
the text presented in Ridgley Torrence,* The Story of
John Hope, *New York, 1948, pp. 114–15).*

IF WE ARE NOT STRIVING for equality, in heaven's name
for what are we living? I regard it as cowardly and dishonest
for any of our colored men to tell white people or colored people
that we are not struggling for equality. If money, education, and
honesty will not bring to me as much privilege, as much equality
as they bring to any American citizen, then they are to me a
curse, and not a blessing. God forbid that we should get the implements with which to fashion our freedom, and then be too
lazy or pusillanimous to fashion it. Let us not fool ourselves
nor be fooled by others. If we cannot do what other free men
do, then we are not free. Yes, my friends, I want equality.
Nothing less. I want all that my God-given powers will enable
me to get, then why not equality? Now, catch your breath, for
I am going to use an adjective: I am going to say we demand
social equality. In this republic we shall be less than free
men, if we have a whit less than that which thrift, education
and honor afford other free men. If equality, political, economic
and social, is the boon of other men in this great country of
ours, of *ours*, then equality, political, economic and social, is
what we demand. Why build a wall to keep me out? I am no
wild beast, nor am I an unclean thing.

Rise, Brothers! Come, let us possess this land. Never say,
"Let well enough alone." Cease to console yourselves with adages
that numb the moral sense. Be discontented. Be dissatisfied.
"Sweat and grunt" under present conditions. Be as restless as
the tempestuous billows on the boundless sea. Let your discontent break mountain-high against the wall of prejudice, and
swamp it to the very foundation. Then we shall not have to
plead for justice nor on bended knee crave mercy; for we shall
be men. Then and not until then will liberty in its highest sense
be the boast of our Republic. . . .

THE WHOLE RACE MUST PROTEST

By Pinckney B. S. Pinchback

While Booker T. Washington urged his people not to be concerned by the mounting pace of disfranchisement of Negro citizens in the South and the spread of Jim Crow laws, other Negro leaders warned of the dangers of indifference to this development. Louisiana ex-Governor Pinckney B. S. Pinchback spoke for this group in a speech at a testimonial. The exact date of the event is not known, but the reference to the "late national campaign" in which William McKinley was elected President, would indicate that it took place sometime in 1897. Although Pinchback appears to have more confidence in the Supreme Court—especially after the decisions in the Civil Rights Act and the case of Plessy v. Ferguson—than most black Americans at the time, it is an important note of protest in an era of rising accommodation.

Pinckney B. S. Pinchback was born May 10, 1851, near Macon, Georgia, of a slave mother, Eliza Stewart, and a white Mississippi planter father, William Pinchback. His father subsequently manumitted the mother of his children and moved his family to the North. Pinchback was educated, first at home, and then at school in Cincinnati. After the death of his father, he was forced to make his own living, and followed steamboating on the Ohio, Missouri, Red and Mississippi rivers, becoming a steward, the highest position a man of his race could then attain in this line of employment. In 1862, he recruited a company of black soldiers (Corps d'Afrique) in response to a call of Maj.-Gen. Benjamin F. Butler that free colored men take up arms in defense of the Union. Pinchback became the captain of the company; but practically white in appearance, he refused to pass as a white man and was forced by indignant whites to resign the captaincy. He was active in Louisiana politics during Reconstruction, succeeded Oscar J. Dunn as lieutenant governor, and when Governor H. C. Warmoth was impeached, Pinchback became acting governor of the state for a month. Following Reconstruction, he held the posts of Internal Revenue agent, and Surveyor of Customs for the Port of Orleans. He was admitted to the bars of federal and state courts in Louisiana and practiced law until his death in Washington, D. C., in 1921.

(The speech referred to above follows in part, as taken from the text in Pinckney B. S. Pinchback, "Speech at Testimonial on State Constitutions which Disenfranchise Black People," P. B. S. Pinchback Papers, Moorland Collection, Howard University. It is published with permission of the library of Howard University.)

. . . I FEEL compelled to . . . submit for your consideration a few facts which seem to be of vital interest to us and to our people.

Numbering quite ten millions, of every shade of color, from jet black to the complexion of the fairest Caucasian, counting those who by reason of their fair complexion are not identified with the race, they constitute at least one sixth of the entire population, and guaranteed by the organic law of the land every right and privilege of citizenship and equality before the law, the race is subjected to the most odious proscription and humiliation in several of the Southern states by class legislation, which enforces their separation from all the other classes of citizens, in railroad stations and coaches and places of public resort.

In my Cooper Union speech in the late national campaign, when we were all doing yeoman service for the national Republican party and endeavoring to aid it in its effort to reelect that typical American and ideal President, William McKinley, and continue his illustrious and successful administration four years more, I called attention to this monstrous wrong and quoted Article 4, Section 2, of the Constitution of the United States to show that the action of those states was a flagrant violation of the provisions of that document. That section says: "The citizens of each state shall be entitled to all privileges and immunities of citizens in the several states." If it is conceded— which I do not concede—that a state has the right to make obnoxious regulations to govern any particular nationality within its jurisdiction, even then I emphatically deny its right to abridge the "privileges and immunities" of the citizens of the other states when they temporarily enter or are passing through it. There can be but one interpretation of the section quoted. It was put in the Constitution for the express purpose of preventing any state from doing just what Mississippi, South Carolina, Louisiana and North Carolina have done by their Jim Crow laws. Those laws not only deprive the colored citizens of "privileges and immunities" enjoyed by all other citizens in those states, of every nationality and condition, but they impose a humiliating and degrading separation of the colored from every other element of the people in the places designated in those laws. It is an odious discrimination against, and a brand of inferiority upon, not only the colored people residing in said states, but upon every member of the entire race if they should have occasion to visit or pass through one of those states. It is an insult and a wrong which should be resisted by the whole race with every lawful means at its command. The first and most important step in that direction, in my opinion, is to secure a decision on the merits of the case from the Supreme Court of the United States as to the constitutionality of the so-called constitutions recently arbitrarily and fraudulently adopted in several Southern states, under which wholesale disfranchisement is imposed upon the race solely on account of color.

The ballot, in a government such as ours, is the palladium of the rights of the citizens. A voteless class has no rights that anybody is bound to respect. They are sure to become the footballs of demagogues and ambitious politicians to be kicked about hither and thither, and made the objects of contempt or ridicule, just as the exigencies of the case may require.

It is noticeable that wherever colored men have been deprived of the ballot, unjust class legislation has speedily followed, race antagonism has been intensified, and lawlessness and outrage against the race increased.

This is a very grave condition of affairs. If it is not remedied or halted, it will menace, if it does not destroy, our rights, privileges and immunities in every state in the Union. It is truly said that eternal vigilance is the price of liberty. It will not do for you and me and others of the race who are not now under the immediate shadow of these unjust laws to be indifferent. It is the whole race that is assailed, and the whole race should protest against and oppose these wrongs to the last extremity. The colored citizens of the great Eastern and Western states, like New York, Pennsylvania, Massachusetts, Illinois, Ohio and the others, must invoke the power of their respective states to prevent their humiliation and degradation on account of color if they should visit or pass through any of those Southern states; thus making the matter an issue between the states and of national import, instead of a mere race issue.

Thousands of white men in the North, in the East, in the West, and even in the South, do not approve of these unjust discriminations against our people, and are ready and willing to aid us.* Our cause is just and must prevail if we manfully, earnestly and judiciously appeal to the heart and conscience of the American people for redress of our grievances. Justice is not dead in the Republic. The great Jehovah still lives, watches over the destinies of nations, and rules the universe. He will not be deaf to the cries of the afflicted.

THE FUNCTIONS OF THE NEGRO SCHOLAR

By G. N. Grisham

In its issue of March 26, 1898, The Colored American, published in Washington, D. C., carried the following notice in its leading article: "Prof. G. N. Grisham, principal of the high school at Kansas City, Mo., one of the ablest educators and most practical philosophers in the country, delivered an address in this city during the recent session of the Negro Academy, which was a valuable contribution to modern literature. The occasion was a reception to the Graduates Club at the residence of Prof. Kelly Miller, on College Street, December 28th, 1897."

Professor Grisham's address was subtitled, "The Interpreter and Guide of Civilization—A Hostage to the Race's Future Greatness." It was delivered at a time of the growing influence of the conception popularized by Booker T. Washington, that Negroes should be educated in industrial colleges to be farmers, domestics, artisans and craftsmen to do the more menial work in society and should leave the field of scholarship to whites. Professor Grisham, on the other hand, felt strongly that there was an important place in society for the Negro scholar, and he urged "the thinking Negro" to "contribute to magazines, write books and cooperate with learned societies . . . investigate and discover truth . . . attack evils, devise remedies and advocate reforms . . . " He also rejected the view that the scholar should stand "aloof from the practical

---

* Originally Pinchback had written "Millions of white men . . ." for delivery in his speech, but evidently he thought better of it and changed it to "Thousands."

world," and he emphasized that "even in his own interest the Negro scholar must do something for his race."

(*The speech follows, taken from the text published in* The Colored American, Washington, D. C., *March 26, 1898.*)

IN THE SOCIAL ORGANISM, every kind of human power has its special place, and every grade of intelligence has its function. Men of will trace with their swords the bounds of empire, or as statesmen enter the affairs of nations; men of feeling fashion the cults of picture with pen or brush half-uttered yearnings of races; men of scholarship have likewise their functions of leadership in the higher sense of the word. The scholar is the interpreter of civilization, as well as its guide. In him is renewed the spirit of the past; in him are the aspirations of the future, which color the best deeds of the present. The great schools of the world are supposed to be engaged in the task of producing men of this higher type. But, in spite of their efforts, mental maturity is rarer than physical maturity. On every hand we meet with intellectual dwarfs, collegiate runts standing in sorry contrast with the great giants of intellect, whose scholarship dominates the world. The true scholar may be a college graduate, but the college graduate is not necessarily a scholar. He is at best, but a promise. The city of Washington is to be congratulated on having formed the first general organization of college-trained Negroes in this country. In this graduates' club are men and women holding degrees from the leading universities of America, men and women who recognize the fact that the power of a man in the modern world is measured not so much by what he does in school as by what he can do and does after he leaves school. The test of scholarship is the ability of the individual when turned loose by his instructors to further extend his mental horizon by his own exertions; but there is a higher scholarship which extends the world's horizon. These two types of men have in common an unsatisfied mental curiosity, but while one ascends on ladders constructed by other men, the other adds new rounds to the ladder of knowledge. In some ages of the world the scholar was the man who knew books, but today the true scholar is he who, in addition to knowing books, knows men, whose studies have led him to comprehend the relation of man to his kind, the relation of man to the universe of matter and mind.

The Negro graduate is here. If any one questions whether the Negro scholar has yet been discovered we will not debate the

question of fact, but we want to insist that the function of the
Negro scholar is the same as the function of any other scholar
in whom mankind thinks its highest thoughts, preparatory to
doing the grandest deed. But the Negro who today ought to be
a scholar is in peculiar danger by virtue of the novelty of his
situation. He, therefore, needs to be warned in advance, lest
his claims to real scholarship prove baseless. In almost every
community the general grade of scholarship is so low that
it takes far less knowledge to make a Negro conspicuous than
would give prominence to a man of another race. "He is a
smart man for a Negro," is a compliment that has stunted the
growth of many a smart person. The cheap compliments of the
press and a yearning for prominence leads men to overlook
the claims of genuine merit, and resort to the familar tricks
of charlatanry. The plagiarism of Chatterton;* the scientific
hoax of the age, the Cardiff giant;† and now, recently, the
visionary claims of young Edison, who pretends to be able to
photograph a man's thoughts‡—these are samples of the things
to be avoided by the Negro who would be a scholar; remembering the words of Goethe:

> What glitters, of the moment,
>   As with the moment passed,
> Ages to come will know true worth,
>   For it alone can last.

It is no less important that he avoid the error of attempting
too much. Many a young man leaves college with the honest
intention of attempting to keep up his studies. The sooner he
learns it cannot be done the better for him. For much of the

---

* The reference is to the "Thomas Rowley" poems, which Thomas Chatterton, a young British poet, attempted to pass off as a work of a medieval
cleric. It was actually a case of literary forgery rather than one of
plagiarism.
† The "Cardiff giant" was the famous hoax of the nineteenth century.
In 1868 George Hall, of Binghamton, New York, obtained a block of
gypsum from the deposits in Fort Dodge, hauled it overland to Chicago,
had it carved in the shape of a human figure, and buried it near Cardiff,
Onondaga County, in New York, where it was discovered by men digging
a well in 1869. The "Cardiff giant" was exhibited in various parts of the
country, as a petrified man or a statue dating from prehistoric times.
The hoax was exposed by Othniel C. Marsh, of Yale, and the perpetrator
confessed his part in it.
‡ It is interesting that at a time when the press was busily engaged in
the creation of a wide number of fantasies associated with Thomas A.
Edison, Grisham expressed a skeptical attitude toward one of these
claims.

university work served no purpose in generating a certain amount of power, in giving the student mental perspective, in coordinating his faculties, in supplying material for reflection, in creating habits of thought, in refining the taste and biasing the individual in favor of the work he can best do for the world. These purposes served, he would be by no means poor if he forgets, as he certainly will, the major portion of all that his professors thought. Let him single out one great task and do it. Bacon took all knowledge for his province, but no man of our age can hope to do more than reach excellence in some one department. The medieval scholar undertook to know and discuss all questions of culture. The modern scholar is content to be ignorant of much. The young aspirant for fame often feels conscious of enormous powers of acquisition, but he will not have gone far before discovering the evil of sacrificing depth to extent of research. Said Goethe to Eckerman: "It is a great thing to be able to do one thing well." He who attempts more may illustrate the sad picture drawn by Schiller: "With a thousand sails spread to the winds, the youth embarks upon the ocean; calmly the old man enters the harbor in a lifeboat."

There was a time when the scholar stood aloof from the practical world, as if he formed no part of it. Scholarship cannot create and breathe an atmosphere all its own. It is commendable to search for truth as the thing best worth knowing, but not much is justified in directing his energies altogether without reference to the needs of the great world in which he lives. Man and society eventually condition each other. The maximum of individual power is attained only in the best social organization, and society is best only when the individual has a chance to become his best. No man can well refuse to raise the platform on which he, himself, must stand. There is a charge today that the better-favored Negro is disposed to desert his kind and dwell apart from the masses, but even in his own interest the Negro scholar must do something for his race. He can and should offer defense against unjust criticism and wrong. He should in his exalted personality, furnish a standard for budding aspiration, and his superior intelligence and keen foresight should offer guidance over the thousands of moral, social and political difficulties that throng the dark and devious pathway of the people. The race has a right to look to him for helpful suggestions, for kindly, sympathetic criticism, for a clear outline of policy and for the inspiration which can come alone from those whose lofty reaches of thought enable them to contemplate the depths from the standpoint of the heights.

This is no mean or narrow task, for it can be best performed only by those who clearly recognize the fact that the Negro scholar must form the connection between his race and civilization. In him they breathe its spirit, think its thought, grapple with its difficulties, and aid in the solution of its problems. The Negro scholar must not confine himself to Negro questions. He must, in action, manifest the breadth of Terence, who, in one famous utterance, identified himself with mankind—"I am a man and deem nothing that concerns humanity foreign to me." The greatest unifying social principle is intelligence that lifts men above littleness and fixes attention upon those intrinsic qualities of soul which make a man valuable to another. If Dante and Tasso in Italy united ancient and modern scholarship, the new nationalities of Europe—France, England, Spain, Germany and America—vitally connected themselves with that common center of thought in the persons of their thinkers, who saw world problems in their own national embarrassments. The commission of international scholarship has removed the harshness of national boundaries and softened the asperities of native prejudices. Erasmus and Moore, Newton and Descartes, Galileo and Kepler, Tennyson and Victor Hugo, Carlyle and Emerson are but examples of the unifying principles of modern scholarship. Let the thinking Negro join them. Let him contribute to magazines, write books and cooperate with learned societies, let him investigate and discover truth, let him attack evils, devise remedies and advocate reforms, let him withal manifest that sympathetic approach leading him to sacrifice no realized good for any imaginary excellence. The world's work is increasingly great. It calls for brain power, and men stand ready to crown with distinction any one of whatever race, who with ability and courage will address himself successfully to the task of settling questions that arise from age to age. The Negro scholar, untrammeled by traditional modes of thought and undazzled by glittering errors of the past, may be peculiarly fitted for that clear thinking and intellectual daring now demanded in the solution of the great problems of civilization.

THE WILMINGTON MASSACRE

By Rev. Charles S. Morris

In 1894 a coalition of Populists and Negro Republican groups gained control of North Carolina. During the next four years, legislation was passed aiding education, eliminating restrictions upon the suffrage, granting Negroes a number of public offices, reducing interest charges, and equalizing the taxation system.

In 1898 the Democrats, assisted by defections from Fusionists, regained control in a campaign characterized by Professor James W. Bassett, of Trinity College, who witnessed the events, as "a great deal of intimidation and a great deal of fraud." The high point in the intimidation came in Wilmington and resulted in a riot in which between nine and eleven Negroes were killed and twenty-five wounded. (Charles W. Chesnutt's novel, The Marrow of Tradition, includes a vivid description of the Wilmington massacre.) Justification for the massacre by white-supremacists was that it was necessary to end "Negro domination," but this was effectively answered by Rev. Charles S. Morris, a Negro refugee from Wilmington, in a speech delivered in January, 1899, before the International Association of Colored Clergymen in Boston. The Reverend Mr. Morris also pointed out the inconsistency of the United States' imperialist venture supposedly to establish a republican government in the Philippines, while unwilling to maintain it in Wilmington, North Carolina.

The speech, which is presented here, is preserved in a printed leaflet in "Writing of Charles H. Williams," Wisconsin State Historical Society Library, Madison, Wisconsin. The three-page leaflet is entitled, "The Race Problem: A Story of Cruel Wrongs Suffered by Colored People of the South, Told by One of That People." It was issued by Charles H. Williams, Baraboo, Jan. 21, 1899. Williams appended to Morris' speech his own comment, which concluded: "When will this people, this nation, take up this grave question, as they did the Spanish barbarities against the Cubans, as they do those of the Turks against the Armenians? Here is a call that should come home to every justice-loving man and woman in the land, North and South, causing them to act promptly, act at once, demand-

ing of the national government that these long-oppressed people should be protected and secured in all rights as citizens."

NINE NEGROES massacred outright; a score wounded and hunted like partridges on the mountain; one man, brave enough to fight against such odds would be hailed as a hero anywhere else, was given the privilege of running the gauntlet up a broad street, where he sank ankle-deep in the sand, while crowds of men lined the sidewalks and riddled him with a pint of bullets as he ran bleeding past their doors; another Negro shot twenty times in the back as he scrambled empty-handed over a fence; thousands of women and children fleeing in terror from their humble homes in the darkness of the night, out under a gray and angry sky, from which falls a cold and bone-chilling rain, out to the dark and tangled ooze of the swamp amid the crawling things of night, fearing to light a fire, startled at every footstep, cowering, shivering, shuddering, trembling, praying in gloom and terror; half-clad and barefooted mothers, with their babies wrapped only in a shawl, whimpering with cold and hunger at their icy breasts, crouched in terror from the vengeance of those who, in the name of civilization, and with the benediction of the ministers of the Prince of Peace, inaugurated the reformation of the city of Wilmington the day after the election by driving out one set of white officeholders and filling their places with another set of white officers—the one being Republican and the other Democrat. All this happened, not in Turkey, nor in Russia, nor in Spain, not in the gardens of Nero, nor in the dungeons of Torquemada, but within three hundred miles of the White House, in the best state in the South, within a year of the twentieth century, while the nation was on its knees thanking God for having enabled it to break the Spanish yoke from the neck of Cuba. This is our civilization. This is Cuba's kindergarten of ethics and good government. This is Protestant religion in the United States that is planning a wholesale missionary crusade against Catholic Cuba. This is the golden rule as interpreted by the white pulpit of Wilmington.

Over this drunken and bloodthirsty mob they stretch their hands and invoke the blessing of a just God. We have waited two hundred and fifty years for liberty, and this is what it is when it comes. O Liberty, what crimes are committed in thy name! A rent and bloody mantle of citizenship that has covered as with a garment of fire, wrapped in which as in a shroud, forty thousand of my people have fallen around Southern ballot boxes. A carload of workingmen, whose only crime is their color, halted at the border of the state of Lincoln and Grant by a governor who ought to be in a penitentiary.* A score of intelligent colored men, able to pass even a South Carolina election officer, shot down at Phoenix, South Carolina, for no reason whatever, except, as the Charleston *News and Courier* said, because the baser elements of the community loved to kill and destroy. The pitiful privilege of dying like cattle in the red gutters of Wilmington, or crouching waist-deep in the icy waters of neighboring swamps, where terrified women gave birth to a dozen infants, most of whom died of exposure and cold. This is Negro citizenship! This is what the nation fought for from Bull Run to Appomattox!

What caused all this bitterness, strife, arson, murder, revolution and anarchy at Wilmington? We hear the answer on all sides—"Negro domination." I deny the charge. It is utterly false, and no one knows it better than the men who use it to justify crimes that threaten the very foundation of republican government; crimes that make the South red with blood, white with bones and gray with ashes; crimes no other civilized government would tolerate for a single day. The colored people comprise one third of the population of the state of North Carolina; in the legislature there are one hundred and twenty representatives, seven of whom are colored, there are fifty senators, two of whom are colored—nine in all out of a hundred and seventy. Can nine Negroes dominate one hundred and sixty white men? That would be a fair sample of the tail wagging the dog. Not a colored man holds a state office in North Carolina; the whole race has less than five percent of all the offices in the state. In the city of Wilmington, the mayor was white, seven out of ten members of the board of aldermen, and sixteen out of twenty-six members of the police force were white; the city attorney was white, the city clerk was white, the city treasurer was white, the superintendent of streets was white, the superintendent of garbage was white, the superintendent of health was

---

* The reference is to the attacks on Negro strikebreakers by white miners in the Pana and Virden area of Illinois in 1898. The miners were supported by Governor John B. Tanner. Although the Afro-American Labor and Protective Association of Alabama denounced "the action of the colored miners in going to Pana, remaining at Pana or participating in any manner in carrying out their tyrannical design against labor," many black papers and speakers attacked Governor Tanner for not condemning the murder of blacks during antiscab riots. Since Negroes were excluded from most trade unions, they argued, they had a right to obtain work as strikebreakers.

white, the superintendent of city hospitals was white, and all the nurses in the white wards were white; the superintendent of the public schools was white, the chief and assistant chief of the fire department, and three out of five fire companies were white; the school committee has always been composed of two white men and one colored; the board of audit and finance is composed of five members, four of whom were white, and the one Negro was reported to be worth more than any of his white associates. The tax rate under this miscalled Negro regime was less than under its predecessors. This is Negro domination in Wilmington. This is a fair sample of that Southern scarecrow— conjured by these masters of the black art everywhere.

The Good Samaritan did not leave his own eldest son robbed and bleeding at his own threshold, while he went 'way off down the road between Jerusalem and Jericho to hunt for a man that had fallen among thieves. Nor can America afford to go eight thousand miles from home to set up a republican government in the Philippines while the blood of citizens whose ancestors came here before the Mayflower is crying out to God against her from the gutters of Wilmington.

THE FALLACY OF INDUSTRIAL EDUCATION AS THE SOLUTION OF THE RACE PROBLEM

By Rev. C. S. Smith

The vast majority of the opponents of Booker T. Washington were centered in the North and the strongest critics were black intellectuals, for the most part graduates of leading Northern universities. Yet Washington did not entirely lack black critics in the South. Bishop Henry M. Turner was one of these critics, and another was the Reverend C. S. Smith, of Tennessee. In a speech delivered in Nashville to a meeting of blacks on January 28, 1899, the Reverend Mr. Smith criticized Washington's thesis that Negroes should be educated in industrial institutions and that industrial training which would produce black craftsmen and scientific farmers was the only real solution of the race problem in the United States. By making themselves useful to white Southerners, Washington insisted,

*blacks would in time gain from them their civil and po-
litical rights; hence they should concentrate on industrial
education until that time came sometime in the future.
Without specifically mentioning Washington by name, the
Reverend Mr. Smith tore into his fundamental concept
of Negro education and pronounced it unsound.*

*The Reverend Mr. Smith's speech, presented here, is
taken from the text that appeared in the Nashville American, January 29, 1899.*

I AM heartily in favor of the industrial and mechanical
training for such Negroes as may feel that their calling is on
the farm or in the factory, but I challenge the assertion of
those who claim that the only solution of the so-called race
problem lies in the direction of the industrial and mechanical
training of the Negro.

Surprisingly strange, perhaps, but nevertheless true, slavery
itself furnished the race with valuable lessons in industrial and
mechanical training, and produced a race of high-class mechanics, skilled workers in wood and iron and metals of all kinds,
many of whom remain until this day, and, I regret to say, far
more than can obtain employment, caused by the unreasonable
and unfriendly attitude of the trade-unions toward colored
mechanics.* How, then, can the multiplication of Negro mechanics help to solve the so-called race problem, when those
who are already skilled cannot obtain employment? In this
city, to my personal knowledge, there are a score or more of
skilled Negro mechanics who are subject to enforced idleness
by reason of the colorphobia which dominates the trade-unions.
Those who are disposed to advance the Negro's best interests
can render him invaluable services by demanding, in tones of
thunder loud and long, that the trade-unions shall cease to
draw the color line, and that fitness and character shall be the
only passport to their fellowship. When this barrier shall have
been removed, the time for the multiplication of Negro mechanics, on anything like a large scale, will have become opportune,
but not until then.

I know full well the argument of the contra-contendents—

---

* By the late 1890's most of the unions affiliated with the American
Federation of Labor and all of the Railroad Brotherhoods barred Negroes
from membership either through constitutional barriers or specific
restrictive clauses in their rituals. Negro mechanics in the South were
organized in a few unions affiliated with the A.F. of L. into separate Jim
Crow locals, but their conditions were inferior to the white members of
the unions and their numbers were limited.

how that an appreciable increase in the present number of Negro mechanics would make a white contractor independent of white mechanics when his interests might warrant the employment of Negro tradesmen. But it cannot be justly claimed that this argument rises to the force and dignity of an argument. It is at the very best but a mere theory, and one shorn of plausibility for the reason that it apparently overlooks the fact that the trade-unions, by the power of the boycott, could influence the dealers both in raw and manufactured material not to sell to said contractor, and thus abort his designs to defy them by the employment of Negro artisans. The trade-unions constitute a most potent organization, and it is very difficult to thwart its will. Therefore, the primal and essential accomplishment is to influence its directors to abandon the cruel and frigid color line.

But, then, it can be answered that if the Negro mechanic cannot find employment for his skilled hands, let him go to the farm and engage in agricultural pursuits—learn how to scientifically raise sweet potatoes, as the present chief revivalist of the industrial training for the Negro is wont to urge.

When in the unregistered aeons of the genesis of creative development—when prehistoric man roamed at will, and before God had fixed the bounds of man's habitation—in what recorded cycle of time was it written on the tablet of divine fiat that the universal position of the Negro should be that of a tiller of the soil? It may not be a self-evident truth that all men are created free and equal, but it is an axiomatic verity that all men, other than imbeciles and idiots, are endowed with mental and spiritual capacities capable of varied and illimitable expansion; and the Negro, being a man, is irremovably within the sphere of this axiomatic verity. Hence, unless it can be established that the Negro is not an integral and component part of the original plan of man's creation, but the increment of a mere accident, the crystallization of the particles of the surplus dust that marked the creative place of generic man, it must be accepted as the corollary of the axiomatic verity that the Negro, in common with all the other race varieties, is endowed with mental and spiritual capacities, capable of varied and illimitable expansion; and that, as a whole, his sphere of operation cannot be limited to the tilling of the soil; but that his development will be marked by variety of attainments and accomplishments, thus proving himself to be an originator as well as an imitator.

Moreover, the acquisition of scientific agriculture cannot possibly profit the masses of the Negroes to any great extent, seeing that they are not the owners of the soil. By this I refer to the diversification of crops as the result of a knowledge of scientific agriculture. The diversification of crops is not dictated and controlled by the tillers of the soil, but by the owners. The plantation hand in the South exercises no choice whatever as to the number of acres he shall plant in cotton or the number he shall plant in corn or wheat or any other cereal. In this regard he must obey the mandate of his employer. In view of this, is the suggestion valueless that so far as the utility of a diversification of crops is concerned, that this advice should be pressed upon the owner of the soil rather than upon the tiller? It is the owner alone who can change the existing conditions of things. The advice which Secretary of Agriculture Wilson gave to the young white men of the South, in his address at the McKinley banquet in Savannah, Georgia, was most opportune and should impress the present chief revivalist of industrial training for the Negro with the fact that in insisting on the study of scientific agriculture by the masses of the Negroes, he is building a cage for a bird that is yet to be caught; unless, perchance, the Negroes should become the owners of the soil. There can be no doubt that the practical application of the principles of scientific agriculture will increase the yield of a given crop in a stated area; but if by this it is meant that a knowledge of scientific agriculture is essential to teach the Negro how to hoe cotton and plant corn, such is as far from the reality as the east is from the west; as the Negro has long since graduated in the accomplishment of hoeing cotton and planting corn, and his diploma was stamped on the great majority of the ten million bales of cotton which were marketed in this country last year. Therefore aspire to add to the Negro's present limited fund of knowledge by teaching him how to do something which he does not now know how to do.

The necessity of the Negro's training in industrial pursuits, either as a theory or a dictum, did not originate with this generation, but is coeval with his existence on the American continent. With equal propriety might one term John Wesley the apostle of Christianity as to term the Master of Tuskegee the apostle of industrial training for the Negro. The former was simply the revivalist of a long-existing doctrine; the latter is merely the revivalist of an ancient dictum, "Teach the Negro how to work,"* and in reechoing this dictum has struck a popu-

* For evidence that industrial education had a long history in this country prior to the appearance of Booker T. Washington as its leading exponent, see August Meier, "The Beginning of Industrial Education in Negro Schools," *Midwest Journal*, Vol. VII (Spring, 1955), pp. 23–44.

lar chord in the minds, if not the hearts, of a large element of the American people, some of whom emphasize their approval by throwing dollars into his open hands. . . .

When the present chief advocate of industrial training for the Negro as the speediest and most effective solution of the so-called race problem shall have gone outside of his own bailiwick, as I have; when he shall have placed himself in a position to observe the present status of the various elements of mankind, notably in Europe, West and Southwest Africa, South America, and the Caribbean Archipelago; when he shall have seen a woman and a dog hitched together and drawing a loaded cart through the streets of Antwerp, Belgium; when he shall have seen Hungarian women digging coal in the mines of their own native land; when he shall have looked upon the peasantry of Europe, so poorly fed, poorly clad, poorly housed, and poorly paid; when his attention shall have been directed to the fact that three fifths of the inhabitants of the earth live in a one-room hut, that scientific agriculture is as little known to the peasantry of Europe as it is to the plantation hands of the Southland, and that the farmer has no more to do with the diversification of the crops than do the latter, he may at least find some of his views modified thereby, come to realize that the doctrine of the survival of the fittest will shape and govern the destiny of the Negro as it does that of all other race societies, that the Negro cannot be limited to any one sphere of physical or mental operation, but will ramify every nook and corner of Americanism and add his quota to its strength, perpetuity and adornment.

TWO CONTRASTING BLACK VOICES

Bishop Alexander Walters and
Booker T. Washington

On March 16, 1899, the white citizens of Palmetto, Georgia, broke into the town jail and killed four Negroes and seriously wounded another four, all of whom had been accused of having set fires in the town. During the next few weeks the outrage was discussed at meetings of black people all over the country. The contrasting reactions of two of America's Negro leaders were presented in speeches during the last week of April, 1899—one by Bishop Alexander Walters of the African Methodist Episcopal Church, who spoke at Jersey City, and the other by Booker T. Washington, who spoke at Philadelphia.

Bishop Walters was one of the signers of the call for the formation of a National Afro-American League issued in 1889. In 1898 the League was merged into the National Afro-American Council under the presidency of Bishop Walters, and it was in this capacity that he spoke. Later, Bishop Walters joined the Niagara Movement and in 1909 was one of the founders of the National Negro Committee, which a year later changed its name to National Association for the Advancement of Colored People.

Following are excerpts from these speeches, taken from the texts published in Public Opinion, *May 4, 1899, p. 553.*

BISHOP ALEXANDER WALTERS

The real cause of our trouble is race hatred. Some years ago it was thought that as the Negroes became intelligent and cultured this race prejudice would disappear; but in some sections of the country it has only intensified this feeling. The passing of the Jim-Crow-car laws in several of the Southern states; the disfranchisement of Negroes, regardless of qualification; the shutting-out of them from hotels, restaurants, and places of amusement, are all manifestations of race hatred. We are censured as a race for not exhibiting manly qualities and are considered "impudent niggers" if we presume to assert our manhood. We are truly between the upper and nether millstone. I have come to the conclusion that nothing but manly resistance on the part of the Afro-Americans themselves will stop these outrages. President McKinley and the federal government have shown themselves impotent to convict the murderers of federal officials.* The governors of certain states in the South have acknowledged their inability to protect their colored citizens. In the name of almighty God, what are we to do but fight and die?

* The reference is to the murder on February 22, 1898, at Lake City, South Carolina, of the black Postmaster Baker and his baby, the shooting and maiming for life of his wife and three daughters, and the wounding of his son. The post office and his house were burned to the ground by the armed mob of whites. The Cleveland *Gazette* of February 26, 1898, called it "the most revolting crime ever perpetrated," but the federal government did nothing to bring the murderers to justice.

BOOKER T. WASHINGTON

As a rule, the men guilty of these outrages are ignorant individuals who have had no opportunity to secure an education and moral restraint. The only permanent remedy for such crimes as have been recently perpetrated in Georgia, and the only permanent remedy for the mob violence, is in the thorough education of all the people in the South—education that shall reach the head, the hand, the heart, so that, in discussing the educational needs of my people this evening, after all, we are considering the problem which is fundamental in the salvation of the whole South.

SOME FACTS ABOUT SOUTHERN LYNCHINGS

By Rev. D. A. Graham

In May, 1899, the National Afro-American Council issued a proclamation calling upon the Negro people to set apart Friday, June 2, "as a day of fasting and prayer," and special exercises were to be held in all Negro churches the following Sunday, as a protest against oppression and, especially, lynching. On June 4, the Reverend D. A. Graham delivered the following sermon at the Bethel A.M.E. Church in Indianapolis. The statistics on lynching in his sermon were obtained from the Chicago Record, a white daily paper, and the Richmond Planet, a black weekly.

Here is the Reverend Mr. Graham's sermon reprinted from The Recorder, *a Negro weekly published in Indianapolis, of June 10, 1899.*

THE AMERICAN NEGRO is afflicted, and the cause of his affliction is a most unreasonable and silly prejudice in the white Americans. If the hatred were reversed it would seem more reasonable, since the Caucasian has suffered nothing from the Negro, while the latter has suffered everything at the hands of the Caucasian. While this prejudice is greatest in the South, it also manifests itself greatly to the affliction of the colored man in the North.

When he wants to buy property or rent a house he is often

turned away because of his color. When he seeks employment where help is advertised for, he is told that "Negroes need not apply." Our girls cannot get employment in shops, stores or factories, no matter how well educated, refined and good-looking. Naturally, this causes many to fall into evil ways and makes dishonest men of youth who with a man's chance would have become honorable and industrious citizens.

But when we cross Mason and Dixon's line the evil shows itself at every turn. Separate waiting rooms, separate ticket windows, separate cars, nothing to eat at any lunch counter. Refused admission to churches, cemeteries and even parks. Parks and cemeteries are placarded "Negroes and dogs not admitted." The effect of such proscription is most baneful as well as inconvenient. How can the colored youth ever learn to look upon himself as a man when he is constantly treated as a brute? This is one of the greatest causes of vice and drunkenness among the Negroes.

To the Southern whites the manly, refined Negro is the most despicable because "he tries to act white," while the ignorant, servile fellow who dances jigs and acts the monkey on the streets is the "good old darkey of antebellum days." The disfranchisement of the Negroes in the South is not the worst evil. If they would require an educational qualification for all voters, we would see no evil in it whatever.

The greatest affliction we have to suffer is the lack of trial by jury when accused of crime. Lynching of Negroes is growing to be a Southern pastime. When reproved for their barbarity they say, "The only way to stop lynching is to stop the crime which leads to lynching." Many Northern people are influenced by this cry and talk about lynching as if it were always for crimes against women. Even some colored people up here have fallen into this error. You will pardon me, therefore, while I give you some plain facts to set you right about this. Since January 1, 1892, 1,226 people have been lynched in this country, principally Negroes. Not one third of these persons were accused of assaulting women.

In 1892, out of 241 lynched, only 46 had such charge against them. In 1893, out of 159 lynched, 39 were so charged. Last year, out of 131 lynched, 24 were charged either with assault or attempted assault. In the face of these figures who can say that we can stop lynching by stopping one crime? The very next day after Sam Hose was roasted and his charred remains divided among the white savages of Georgia for souvenirs, a Negro, Willis Sees, at Osceola, Arkansas, was hung on suspicion of barn burning. In 1894, 10 were lynched for barn burning.

Three women were lynched the same year in three different states. Again, I beg you to consider carefully these charges of assault. How many of them are guilty? What is the proof against them?

One year ago yesterday in the town of Dorcyville, Louisiana, a man named Will Steak was burned alive upon the charge of assault of one Mrs. Parrish. The *Times Democrat* of New Orleans in its account of the affair said: "Mrs. Parrish identified the Negro almost positively." He died protesting his innocence, but because he was almost identified he was burned alive.

William Offet, of Elyria, Ohio, was fortunate because he was in a Northern state. Being identified by Mrs. J. C. Underwood, the wife of a minister, he was sent to the penitentiary for fifteen years. When he had been in prison four years, this "respectable white lady," conscience smitten, confessed to her husband that she was equally guilty with the Negro. The husband had the prisoner pardoned, and secured a divorce from his depraved wife. There are many such cases.

Ed Coy, who was burned at Texarkana, Arkansas, was another instance exactly similar to that of Offet, and Judge Tourgee* obtained the proof that the relatives and husband of the woman who made the charge were fully cognizant of the fact that she was equally guilty with Coy. They compelled her to make the charge and then to set fire to her paramour. Again, white men often black themselves and commit crime, then lead a mob to lynch some Negro who may happen to be in the neighborhood. In Atlanta, Georgia, about four years ago a black man was discovered in the room of a young white girl of high standing. While attempting to escape he was shot and captured. The black man was found to be the son of a prominent white neighbor with his face and hands blacked. Had he not been captured some poor Negro would have been seized, identified "almost positively" and hung to the nearest tree. A similar case happened in Tennessee a few years ago. Many innocent men are thus hanged or burned alive just because American prejudice refuses them a trial by their peers.

And some court trials are little better than mob trials. The present governor of Georgia, Mr. Candler, while district judge

* Albion W. Tourgée, a reformist judge in North Carolina during Reconstruction and author of two Reconstruction novels, *A Fool's Errand* (1879) and *Bricks Without Straw* (1880), was the leading white champion of Negro equality in the post-Reconstruction era. In October, 1891, Tourgée founded the National Citizens' Rights Association, an interracial organization, to combat lynching and disfranchisement and uphold Negro rights.

three years ago, sent Ed Aikin, a boy of nineteen years, to the chain gang for ten years on the charge of attempted assault. The only evidence the girl offered against him was that she met him coming down a path and as he did not get out of the path she was afraid and ran. She swore that he was not within ten feet of her, did not speak to her, and did not follow her, but she was afraid of him and ran. Judge Candler told him that he would make an example of him so that young darkies would get out of the path when they saw white girls coming. Thereupon he sentenced him to ten years in the chain gang. This is an example of attempted assault.

Now, we want it distinctly understood that we are not trying to excuse crime. We contend that the death penalty should be inflicted upon every man who assaults a woman, without regard to the color of the victim or the criminal. This is more than the whites ask or will allow. In fact, there are twenty colored women assaulted by white men for every white woman assaulted by Negroes. Such cases are countless in every community in the South, but there is no redress for the colored women, either by law or by custom. Colored women are absolutely at the mercy of white men in the South, and a man does not lose social prestige or church relationship for ruining colored girls. I compelled a white Southern minister to acknowledge this fact before the ministers' meeting of Minneapolis a few years ago. And yet they talk about the immorality of the Negroes!

Under all these afflictions we have a great work to perform. We must not allow the injustice and cruelty of the whites to divert our attention from our own weaknesses and shortcomings. More attention must be given to the cultivation of Christian character. The morals of the race must be improved. Our women must spend more time in mothers' meetings and clubs for intellectual and moral culture and less on parties, receptions and balls. More money should be spent for good literature and in support of Christian Endeavor, Y.M.C.A., and kindred organizations instead of on Sunday excursions and theaters.

If American justice and Christianity have decreed that we must lift ourselves by our own bootstraps let us set ourselves heroically to the task. Measured by the depth from which we have come, we have much to encourage us; casting our eyes to the summits yet to be gained, let us thank God and press on.

THE STATE OF THE COUNTRY FROM A
BLACK MAN'S POINT OF VIEW

By Rev. D. P. Brown

The annual sessions of the conference of the African Methodist Episcopal Church usually featured the presentation of an address on the state of the country. In August, 1899, at the height of white-supremacist crimes against the Negro people, the Reverend D. P. Brown delivered a lengthy, moving and extremely effective analysis of the state of the country as seen by a black man, in an address to the New England Conference of the African Methodist Episcopal Church. No keener summing-up of the status of black Americans at this time was presented, and few more effective indictments of the indifference of the national administration to the plight of the black citizens had been set forth. The closing portion of the address included a scorching attack on American imperialist policy in the Philippine Islands.

The speech of the Reverend Mr. Brown is presented here as excerpted from the text published in The Christian Recorder, *August 17, 1899.*

WHEN THIS annual conference was in session about one year ago, our country was just entering upon a war, the purpose of which was declared to be the independence of Cuba, to assist that people struggling for freedom to throw off the Spanish yoke of oppression and to assist them in driving from their borders the last trace of Spanish tyranny and misrule from their fair land, made red with the blood of their fathers fighting for their independence.

This on the part of the Americans was a most laudable purpose, for it was in the cause of humanity, in behalf of a brave people who deserved, and ought, to be free; and yet we cannot yield the fact that there were many persons who believed then, as many do now, that the war on the part of the Americans was not so much in the interest of humanity as it was for territorial expansion—a war to open up to this country greater commercial interest and advantages. It was difficult to make many believe that a government which had shown so little concern for the lives and liberties of ten millions of its most loyal citizens should so suddenly become interested in and imbued with a love of liberty for our brothers in black in another country. I believe I express the wish of this conference that only good should come to this people and that this war should be the indirect means for wiping out the prejudice and bitterness that has become so firmly rooted against the black man in this country. That we have emerged from this war a greater and more powerful nation in the eyes of the civilized world, no one will deny. Our wonderful resources have been shown in that we were in a day able to man a navy from nothing, that astonished the civilized nations of the earth and compelled us to wonder at our own powers.

Our formidable position among the great nations has, as never before, become recognized. This much at least has been accomplished. When the bugle sounded "to arms," white men were not the only men to answer and obey that call, but men of our race, whose ancestors have felt the wrongs of human slavery, were most eager to shoulder the musket, that they might, if need be, give their lives to the cause, if thereby freedom should come to brave Maceo and his devoted followers.*

Strange as it may appear, it was not difficult to convince those in authority that men of our race should be permitted to bare their breasts to Spanish shot and shell, to give their lives in the cause of humanity.

This war was felt to be the "white man's burden," freeing this dark-hued race, a war in which the black man was not wanted. A strange thing! The bravery which our ancestors had shown at Fort Wagner, Fisher, Port Hudson, Nashville, and a hundred other battlefields where they fought and shed their blood for the preservation of the Union, was, it would seem, no guarantee that in this war for humanity they would make fit soldiers. It seemed to have been the policy, even after they were accepted, not to permit them to go to the front and take an active part in the conflict. But for the black heroes of the 9th and 10th Cavalry and of the 24th and 25th Infantry, who immortalized themselves when they marched up San Juan Hill, even over the bodies of our own white troops who could not stand the Spanish bullets and who fought as soldiers had never before in their gallant charge at El Caney, virtually and forever crushing Spanish rule in Cuba, winning for themselves the plaudits of the civilized world, the black soldiers would not have been known in the

---

* Antonio Maceo, "the Bronze Titan," was the black leader of the guerrilla independence fighters in Cuba during the Ten Years' War (1868–1878) and the Second War for Independence, which began in 1895. He was killed in battle by the Spaniards in 1896.

American-Spanish war.* This gallant charge has left the impression that he has no superior and few equals as a soldier, and yet for this daring bravery in saving the day rescuing the Rough Riders from certain death, how many of these immortal heroes have received commissions in the regular Army? Not a man. On the other hand, how many hundred white men have been commissioned for bravery with a life term in the regular Army, who have never been in a battle? Why this discrimination against these heroes? Has the war wiped out the color line as we had hoped it would? On the contrary has it not more clearly drawn the lines? Has not the bravery of these black heroes opened the eyes of the white man to the fact that there is in his midst a race of people capable of furnishing soldiers equal to, if not in many respects superior to, his own? Even if, before his election as Governor of New York, Roosevelt called our soldiers brave men, and spoke in the highest terms of them, yet since his election he calls these same soldiers cowards; shame on such a man who would contradict himself, which shows to the world his only desire was to secure the black man's vote.†

The picture we have seen fit to paint may not be such a one as many would like to gaze upon. It is far better that we should deal with the facts as we see them, than to cover them up. No wrong was ever righted that was not at first exposed. To discuss the "State of the Country" in the usual way might indicate a

* One Southern white officer said: "If it had not been for the Negro cavalry the Rough Riders would have been exterminated. I am not a Negro lover. My father fought with Mosby's Rangers, and I was born in the South, but the Negroes saved the fight, and the day will come when General Shafter will give them credit for their bravery." (*Literary Digest*, August 27, 1898, p. 248.)

† When campaigning for the governorship of New York in October, 1898, Roosevelt said, "As I heard one of the Rough Riders say after the charge at San Juan, 'Well, the Ninth and Tenth men [the Negroes in the Ninth and Tenth Cavalry] are all right. They can drink out of our canteens.'" He expressed the highest praise for the Negroes who charged up San Juan with his Rough Riders and concluded, "I don't think that any Rough Rider will ever forget the tie that binds us to the Ninth and Tenth Cavalry." But writing in *Scribner's Magazine* in April of the following year, months after he had been elected Governor, Roosevelt said that the Negroes behaved well, *but* "they are, of course, peculiarly dependent on their white officers. . . . None of the white regulars of Rough Riders showed the slightest sign of weakening; but under the strain the colored infantrymen began to get a little uneasy and to drift to the rear. . . ." Roosevelt added that he could not permit this and drew his revolver in order to halt the retreating Negroes, and threatened that he would shoot any man who went to the rear under any pretense whatever.

different line from the one I have seen fit to follow. I go out of the beaten track because I believe it is right to do so. Our prosperity, our commercial relations, our wonderful resources, our material growth might seem proper, but imbued with and impelled by a love of humanity broader than mere material wealth and prosperity and filled with a race pride for our fellow man, we are under the circumstances compelled to speak out in "open meeting" and discuss "The State of the Country" from a black man's point of view, as I think I see it, to cry down from the house tops and spare not, until righteousness shall prevail in all parts of this country and man shall do justice to his fellow man. What does the greatness or prosperity of our country amount to, to us as a race, if at the same time it shows to the civilized world either its weakness or unwillingness to protect ten millions of its most loyal citizens in the enjoyment of the simplest rights set forth in the Declaration of Independence that gave birth to this country and is supposed to be the fundamental principles and cornerstone upon which this fabric rests? What is it to us if the wages of the factory employees are increased, if over the door of each of them the sign hangs out, "No Black Man Wanted Here," no black boy or girl shall enter here that they may become skilled artisans? Why should we shout for prosperity that means much to the white man and but little to his brother in black, when we know that it is the fixed purpose and determination to drive us from every favored avenue where we may earn our daily bread? What is all this to us if the courts in many sections are closed against us, meting out to us only injustice and cruelty? Why should we shout for a seeming prosperity,* when those high in authority sit silently by and see us murdered without cause, and robbed of every right guaranteed in the Constitution and laws, and utter not a single protest against these outrages? I am not a pessimist, my whole nature is the opposite, but the better part of me rebels, and all else is forgotten when I know the wrongs and injustices meted out to us as a race. A condition of things that makes me quake with fear for the safety of my country, when I remember that God is just. As a nation we are sowing to the wind, and we must certainly, ultimately reap the whirlwind and the question is, And what shall that harvest be?

Where shall we seek for relief? Shall we seek it in the com-

---

* The Republican party boasted that it had restored prosperity after the economic depression of 1893 to 1897, and McKinley campaigned for reelection in 1900 on the "full dinner pail" platform as well as in favor of overseas expansion.

mercial or industrial avenues? Shall we hope to find it in the ordinary walks of life? Are we not being excluded almost wholly from each and all of these?

At one time it was said "get wealth and education and all else will follow." Have we not in a single generation, beginning without capital, gathered in material wealth and landed possessions, more than four hundred million and sent forth from our best colleges hundreds of cultured men and women, and given more than three millions of our boys and girls the rudiments of a common-school education such as is enjoyed by the masses of the whites? And yet, equipped along these lines as we are, instead of these solving the problem in our favor they seem to operate against us, and but add fuel to the flames and have made the white man more determined to oppress us in all the avenues. What is the cause of this? Some say that it is prejudice, but I cannot lead myself to so believe. Better call it friction or competition. The greater our attainments the greater the desire to enter the more favored avenues and the more we like to compete with our white brother in these.

Does not this grow out of the fact that we have demonstrated to the white man that under the same favorable conditions we are capable of the same development along the favored lines that he treads? We are competing and, handicapped as we are, winning; and in this lies the secret of the oppression which is daily being heaped upon the race. Is it not to crush out the manhood in us, well knowing if that can be accomplished all else they wish to our detriment will follow? If in one generation these wonderful strides have been made, is it probable that with a capital of culture and wealth to the credit side of the ledger, that this will be greatly increased? Is not this wonderful progress the real cause underlying this antagonism? In short, have we not become too great competitors? Is not this the secret? Shall we, however, become less ambitious? Shall we cease to gather wealth and culture to our stock already in hand? On the contrary, should we not redouble our efforts as never before? Wealth and education will not lessen the friction of the oppression heaped upon us—not for the present at least. The wealthiest among the race, who may count his thousands by the hundreds, receives the same treatment as the most ordinary black man who represents no material wealth, when the question arises as to his enjoyment of his rights as a man, to which he is entitled. He must be driven into the same Jim Crow car with the most degraded, however cultured he may be. After all, there is but one thing needed by the Negro in this country, and that is absolute liberty. Grant him that and there will be no so-called Negro problem to solve. Grant him all the rights enjoyed by the most degraded Anglo-Saxon and we would ask for nothing more. Give us an even chance along these lines is all we ask. How shall this be accomplished, do you ask? By molding sound, healthy public sentiment against these outrages and injustices. By whom, do you ask? The churches of the Anglo-Saxon are dumb, just as they were when the slave trade made and held public sentiment for their peculiar institution, American slavery. We can, therefore, hope for but little from that source. Our own churches cannot do it alone. Would I venture too far to say that there is no more powerful factor for this, than the head of this nation, the Chief Executive?

We do not forget certain limitations contained in the Constitution, which may, in some instances, hamper him; and yet one word from him condemning these outrages, lynchings, burnings, and the denial of our rights as American citizens, would do more to further this end and correct these evils than anything else. One word, said officially to these wrongdoers, would do more to mold this public sentiment than any other. A word to Congress condemning this wholesale slaughter of our race, and pointing out to that body wherein we are denied our civil and political rights, would compel that body to take judicial notice of them. A word in his message to Congress, last December, touching upon the slaughter of our people in North and South Carolina, for no other reason than that the black man wished to exercise his right of suffrage, would have done much good. But, like the Anglo-Saxon church, he was silent upon *this* class of American citizens. He *must* be aroused, and it is the duty of *our* church, with more than a half million of members, who are marching up the hill of progress, to remind him that we are not asleep and that he must see to it that the laws are faithfully executed in all sections of this country, in protecting the lives and property of the citizens. This very silence on his part has encouraged these Southern murderers in their cruelty. As an evidence of this, only a short while ago he was visiting in Georgia, virtually for the time the guest of the state; a score of colored men were lynched in Georgia and Mississippi, not for the usual crime with which they are accused, rape, but in the former state only accused of house burning, with evidence that was not conclusive of their guilt; and yet not a word condemning them for these outrages. His very silence is taken as a license to continue this dastardly work.

Let us as Christian brethren, arouse the head of the nation. The politicians, the officeholders among us, dare not speak out for fear of offending the appointing power. We can no longer look to them for a protest. Let us say to the country that we are opposed to any expansion or extension of territory, extending the power to rule over other dark-hued people, so long as this government demonstrates either its weakness or unwillingness to protect our people in this country in the enjoyment of their civil and political rights. Governments are created for this purpose, and when it does not perform this sacred duty, it should not be permitted to extend its weakness and dominion over other people. Let us speak out, in no uncertain language, and enter our protest against this further murdering of an inoffensive people in the Philippines, struggling for their independence. Let us protest against this sham of taking to these people the Christian religion and civilization, with the Bible in one hand, and the bayonet and torch in the other. Until this government shall have demonstrated its ability or willingness to protect the humblest of its citizens at home, in all the enjoyment of all his rights under the law, it is the duty of every black man to protest, even with his vote, against any further expansion or extending its weakness over other black people beyond the seas. We can do this by properly organizing.

We cannot disguise the fact that the Anglo-Saxon cares but little for appeals or protests unless there is something behind them. He cares more for the power contained in the little bit of white paper called the ballot, when it is judiciously handled than all the conventions and resolutions we can hold or send forth. Let every colored man make up his mind to withhold his vote from any man who is named for Congressional honors, until he shall pledge them that he will do all in his power in the lawmaking body, to see that laws are enacted to correct these evils, if they are not already upon the statute books, and to refuse to seat any man who comes with his certificates of election, bringing with it the blood of his fellow man. I repeat, let colored men so organize as to compel the Chief Executive and Congress, to see that every American citizen shall enjoy all the rights guaranteed to him in the Constitution, however humble he may be, whether his face be black or white. . . .

Let us, then, send forth from this conference in no uncertain sounds our grievances, and continue to do so from year to year, until the blackest and humblest citizen shall stand forth a man, enjoying all the rights to which every American citizen is entitled. Until we shall have done this, we shall have failed in our duty to ourselves and our fellow man, and shall fail to receive from God the righteous judge, "Well done thou good and faithful servant." And as we go to our respective fields of labor let us pray:

God give us men. A time like this demands
Strong minds, great hearts, true faith and ready hands;
Men whom the lust of office does not kill;
Men whom the spoils of office cannot buy;
Men who possess opinions and a will;
Men who have honor, men who will not lie;
Men who can stand before a demagogue,
And scorn his treacherous flatteries without winking,
Tall men, sun-crowned, who live above the fog
In public duty and private thinking.

I RAISE MY VOICE AGAINST ONE OF THE MOST DANGEROUS EVILS IN OUR COUNTRY

By George H. White

Three thousand seven hundred and twenty-four people were lynched in the United States from 1889 through 1930; four fifths of them were Negroes. Although the usual defense of the lynchers was that the victims of this most bestial of crimes were guilty of raping white women, fewer than one sixth of them were even accused of rape. With lynchings mounting after 1889 as a weapon of Southern racists in maintaining white supremacy, Negro spokesmen fought to make it a crime. The most important move in this direction came from Congressman George Henry White (1852–1918). On January 20, 1900, he introduced the first Congressional bill to make lynchings a federal crime, and delivered a speech exposing the fallacy of the charge that rape of white women was the cause of lynchings.

White was born a slave in North Carolina, attended public schools after the Civil War and graduated from Howard University in 1877. He served six years in the North Carolina legislature and eight years in as a state prosecuting attorney. In 1896 and 1898 he was elected to Congress by Negro and white voters of his state on a Fusion ticket of Populists and Republicans. In Congress, White was an outstanding champion of the rights of his people. Here are parts of his speech in behalf of his bill, which un-

*fortunately never came to a vote. (The excerpts are taken
from the text published in the* Congressional Record, *56th
Congress, 1st Session, pp. 2151–54.)*

MR. CHAIRMAN, it would be a great pleasure to me to
know that fairness and justice would be meted out to all the
constituent parts of our beloved country alike in such a way as
to leave no necessity for a defense of my race in this House
against the attacks and unfair charges from any source. The
very intimation of this fact with reference to the surroundings
of the colored people of this country at this time, naturally
causes the inquiry, Should not a nation be just to all of her
citizens, protect them alike in all their rights, on every foot of
her soil—in a word, show herself capable of governing all
within her domain before she undertakes to exercise sovereign
authority over those of a foreign land*—with foreign notions
and habits not at all in harmony with our American system of
government? Or, to be more explicit, should not charity first
begin at home?

There can be but one candid and fair answer to this inquiry,
and that is in the affirmative. But, unfortunately for us, what
should have been done has not been done, and to substantiate
this assertion we have but to pause for a moment and make a
brief survey of the manumitted Afro-American during the last
thirty-five years. We have struggled on as best we could with
the odds against us at every turn. Our Constitutional rights have
been trodden under foot; our right of franchise in most every
one of the original slave states has been virtually taken away
from us, and during the time of our freedom fully fifty thousand
of my race have been ignominiously murdered by mobs, not one
percent of whom have been made to answer for their crimes in
the courts of justice, and even here in the nation's Capitol—in
the Senate and House—Senators and Representatives have undertaken the unholy task of extenuating and excusing these
foul deeds, and in some instances, they have gone so far as to
justify them. . . .

It is easy for these gentlemen to taunt us with our inferiority,
at the same time not mentioning the causes of this inferiority.
It is rather hard to be accused of shiftlessness and idleness
when the accuser of his own motion closes the avenues for labor
and industrial pursuits to us. It is hardly fair to accuse us of ignorance when it was made a crime under the former order of

---

* The reference is to the acquisition by the United States of Puerto Rico
and the Philippine Islands following the Spanish-American War.

things to learn enough about letters to read even the Word of
God.

While I offer no extenuation for any immorality that may
exist among my people, it comes with rather poor grace from
those who forced it upon us for two hundred and fifty years, to
taunt us with that shortcoming.

We are trying hard to relieve ourselves of the bonds with
which we were bound and over which we had no control, nothing daunted, however, like the skilled mariner who, having been
overtaken by the winds and storms and thrown off his bearings,
stops to examine the chart, the compass, and all implements of
navigation, that he may be sure of the proper course to travel
to reach his destination.

In our voyage of life struggle for a place whereon we can
stand, speak, think and act as unrestricted American citizens,
we have been and are now passing through political gales,
storms of ostracism, torrents of proscription, waves and inunda-
tions of caste prejudice and hatred; and, like the mariner, it is
proper that we should examine our surroundings, take our
bearings, and devise ways and means by which we may pursue
our struggle for a place as men and women as a part of this
body politic.

Possibly at no time in the history of our freedom has the effort
been made to mold public sentiment against us and our progress
so strongly as it is now being done. The forces have been set in
motion and we must have sufficient manhood and courage to
overcome all resistance that obstructs our progress.

A race of people with the forbearance, physical development,
and Christian manhood and womanhood which has characterized us during the past two hundred and eighty-five years will
not down at the bidding of any man or set of men, and it would
be well that all should learn this lesson now.

As slaves we were true to our rulers; true to every trust reposed in us. While the white fathers and sons went forth to
battle against us and the nation to perpetuate our bonds, the
strong, brawny arms of the black man produced the food to
sustain the wives, children and aged parents of the Confederate
soldier, and kept inviolable the virtue and care of those entrusted to his keeping, and nowhere will anyone dare say that
he was unfaithful to the helpless and unprotected over whom
he kept a guardian watch.*

---

* While White understandably emphasized the loyalty of slaves to their
masters during the Civil War to meet the arguments advanced by the
defenders of lynching, the fact is that thousands upon thousands of

How does this statement of facts compare with the frequent charges made against colored men for outraging white females? Is it a futile attempt to prove that an ignorant slave was a better man and more to be trusted than an intelligent free man? But of these brutal murders, let us revert to a few facts and figures.

Since January 1, 1898, to April 25, 1899, there were lynched in the United States 166 persons, and of this number 155 occurred in the South. Of the whole number lynched, there were 10 white and 156 colored. The thin disguise usually employed as an excuse for these inhuman outrages is the protection of the virtue among white women.

I have taken the pains to make some little investigation as to the charges against the 166 persons killed, and find as a result of my efforts that 32 were charged with murder, 17 were charged with assault, criminal or otherwise, 10 with arson, 2 with stealing, 1 with being impudent to white women, and I am ashamed to acknowledge it, but this latter took place in North Carolina. Seventy-two of the victims were murdered without any specific charge being preferred against them whatever. . . .

These facts and figures which I have detailed are reliable; still the same old, oft-repeated slander, like Banquo's ghost, will not down, but is always in evidence. . . .

I tremble with horror for the future of our nation when I think what must be the inevitable result if mob violence is not stamped out of existence and law once permitted to reign supreme.

If state laws are inadequate or indisposed to check this species of crime, then the duty of the national government is plain. . . . To the end that the national government may have jurisdiction over this species of crime, I have prepared and introduced the following bill, now pending before the Committee on the Judiciary, to wit:

"A bill for the protection of all citizens of the United States against mob violence, and the penalty for breaking such laws.

"*Be it enacted by the Senate and House of Representatives of the United States of America in Congress assembled.* That

---

slaves fled the plantations to the ranks of the Union Army and freedom. "The question as to approximately how many slaves ran away to the Federals during the war cannot be answered," writes Bell I. Wiley. "But it can be said with safety that the arrival of Union soldiers in any part of the South marked the beginning of a flow of black humanity toward the Federal camp; and that, in many cases, the flow was so great that it carried away the bulk of the male slave population" (*Southern Negroes, 1861–1865*, New Haven, Connecticut, 1938, p. 8).

all persons born or naturalized in the United States, and subject to the jurisdiction thereof, and being citizens of the United
States, are entitled to and shall receive protection in their lives
from being murdered, tortured, burned to death by any and all
organized mobs commonly known as 'lynching bees,' whether
said mob be spontaneously assembled or organized by pre-
meditation for the purpose of taking the life or lives of any
citizen or citizens in the United States aforesaid; and that
whenever any citizen or citizens of the United States shall be
murdered by mob violence in the manner hereinabove described, all parties participating, aiding, and abetting in such
murder and lynching shall be guilty of treason against the
Government of the United States, and shall be tried for that
offense in the United States courts; full power and jurisdiction
being hereby given to said United States courts and all its
officers to issue process, arrest, try, and in all respects deal
with such cases in the same manner now prescribed under
existing laws for the trial of felonies in the United States
courts.

"Sec. 2. That any person or persons duly tried and convicted
in any United States court as principal or principals, aiders,
abettors, accessories before or after the fact, for the murder
of any citizen or citizens of the United States by mob violence
or lynching as described in Section 1 hereof, shall be punished
as is now prescribed by law for the punishment of persons
convicted of treason against the United States Government.

"Sec. 3. That all laws and parts of laws in conflict with this
statute are hereby repealed."

I do not pretend to claim for this bill perfection, but I have
prepared and introduced it to moot the question before the
Congress of the United States with the hope that expedience
will be set aside and justice allowed to prevail. . . .

In concluding these remarks, Mr. Chairman, I wish to disclaim any intention of harshness or the production of any friction between the races or the sections of this country. I have
simply raised my voice against a growing and, as I regard it, one
of the most dangerous evils in our country. I have simply
raised my voice in behalf of a people who have no one else to
speak for them here from a racial point of view; in behalf of a
patient and, in the main, inoffensive race which has often been
wronged but seldom retaliated; in behalf of the people who—

Like birds, for others we have built the downy nest;
Like sheep, for others we have worn the fleecy vest;
Like bees, for others we have collected the honeyed food;
Like the patient ox, we have labored for others' good.

THE NEGRO'S PART IN NEW NATIONAL PROBLEMS

By Frank Putnam

In April, 1898, the United States declared war against Spain, ostensibly for the purpose of helping the Cubans to secure their independence, and after defeating Spain, seized Puerto Rico, the Philippines and Guam, and maintained a military occupation in Cuba until 1902. War lasted in the Philippines for several years, until the Filipinos were subjugated. The majority of the Negro people opposed the imperialist wars and openly sided with the masses in Puerto Rico, Cuba and the Philippines who were being deprived of their freedom and independence. A leading Negro paper of the period, the Richmond Planet, warned in 1898 that "the American Negro cannot become the ally of imperialism without enslaving his own race." A mass organization, the Colored National League, the next year issued an "Open Letter to President McKinley," and called upon the President to "pause in pursuit of your national policy of criminal aggression abroad to consider the criminal aggression at home against humanity and American citizenship, which is in full tide of successful conquest of the South." But, as a result of a coalition of Republicans and Southern Democrats the treaty annexing the Philippines was passed in the Senate by one vote. This left the final disposition of the issue to the Presidential campaign of 1900 with the Republican party standard-bearer, William McKinley, openly supporting an imperialist policy and the Democratic party leader, William Jennings Bryan, opposing it.

In May, 1900, before the two parties met in convention, drew up their platforms, and nominated their candidates, Frank Putnam, a Negro worker in Chicago who spoke frequently on public issues, delivered an address in which he announced his opposition to the imperialist policies of the Republican administration. He declared he could no longer support the Republican party and called upon the Negro people to vote for Bryan if he were nominated by the Democrats. His speech, while inaccurate in its estimate of Lin-

*coln's policy at the outbreak of the Civil War and kinder
to McKinley than he merited, was an excellent presentation of the link between imperialism and racism. It aroused
such interest in the Negro community that it was published
in* The Colored American. *In submitting his speech to the
magazine at its request, Putnam wrote that he stood for
the principle of democracy, "the principle of protest, continually forcing concessions from the intrenched-in-office
aristocracy of money."*

*(The speech as presented here has been excerpted from
the text that appeared in* The Colored American, *June,
1900, pp. 69–76.)*

No OTHER American citizen is so vitally interested in the
right settlement of the problems growing out of the Spanish-
American War as the colored man. He is today thirty-five years
out of bondage. Not quite two score years ago he was declared
free by an incident of a war to preserve the Union. Doubtless,
most of you will say that his emancipation was the primary purpose of that war; and, in a broad general sense it was. But men
do not always see the end when they begin; finite minds do not
read the purposes of infinite wisdom until after the fact. Slavery
made the war necessary, because it debauched the moral character of the Southern people, destroyed their ideals of abstract
justice and liberty, and led them to jeopardize the life of the
Republic by attempting to divide it. Yet the best information that
I can get from history and hearsay is that most of the leaders of
the North and the great conservative masses of the North did
not foresee that the war for the preservation of the Union would
result in the enfranchisement of the slaves. As I understand it,
the people of the North generally hoped to do no more than preserve the Union and to limit slavery to the Southern states in
which it was implanted, maintaining universal freedom in all
new states.

I have no doubt—who that has read his speeches delivered
years before the war can doubt?—that Abraham Lincoln foresaw the necessity of abolition, and that he entered upon the war
determined to bring it to pass. So also with Whittier, Garrison,
Phillips, and the other great Abolitionists. But not so the masses
of the Northern people. . . .

Thirty-five years of freedom. So very short a span of preparation, backed by two hundred years of slavery here, and by six
thousand years of isolation from the rest of the world in Africa.
Isolation that forbade the mingling of bloods that alone builds
up the highest powers of any race; slavery that bred helpless-

ness and melancholy, and stifled aspiration in the souls of the bondmen.

Thirty-five years of freedom—with such a heritage to carry through up the heights of progress! . . .

Today we see that war-won freedom challenged. Challenged in the South by the old reactionary spirit which enacts amendments to state constitutions embodying defiance to the national Constitution, disfranchising the colored citizen. Challenged at the North by the powers of plutocracy.

The federal Supreme Court acquiesces, for expediency's sake, in the infamous ruling of a Southern court, a ruling that repudiates the sacrifice of half a million lives on Southern battlefields, that gives the lie to the doctrine of Lincoln, and back of him to the sacred Declaration of Independence, and that would hurl into the face of the Almighty a denial of the divine law of human progress. The administration of the national government by its enactments denies the fitness of the colored men of Porto Rico, of Cuba and of the Philippines for self government; asserts by its actions its belief that self-government is the right of only the white race. Through its press it hurls the dastardly epithet of traitor at men who dare demand equal and exact justice for the younger and less fully developed peoples. Its press is silent upon, for the most part, or flippantly accepts, the intention of the Southern states to set the colored man back into political bondage—to strip from him the one instrument by which he can maintain his rights as a human being.

What is the significance of these conditions for the colored man? What do they mean for him? How shall he act in this crisis?

They mean nothing new. They mean that an aristocracy based upon the possession of material wealth is in the saddle in this country; that this aristocracy, in the way of all aristocracies of all lands and in all ages, is blindly and in greed trying to corner the opportunities of life and to limit power to the few.

The acquiescence of the federal Supreme Court in a ruling that aims covertly at Negro disfranchisement, the enactment of a white-supremacy policy in the newly acquired islands, and the silence of the Northern press—a money-controlled press in the main, with some splendid exceptions—on the reactionary work of the Southern states; these things mean that the hosts of plutocracy are now better organized than ever before in this country, and more daring.

They gain money by exploiting opportunity; they gain opportunity by controlling the government. Seated in power, they levy toll upon the masses, white and black, for the ostensible benefit of the masses, for the real benefit of themselves. They make the government a machine for extracting money from the toil of the people. They do this by levying protective tariffs, by granting subsidies to favored corporations, by protecting these creatures of their favor in the pursuit of their aims. . . .

Money has no soul, no conscience; an aristocracy founded upon money, like the thing it typifies, has no bowels of compassion, no sympathy for the clod struggling to rise from the earth. Such an aristocracy, finding the masses contemptible— finding them too ignorant to protect themselves and too slavish by nature to dare assert and maintain, except in rare instances and at long intervals, such rights as they do see to be naturally their own—comes naturally to regard the masses as inferior beings, divinely ordained to eternal toil for the benefit of their masters. Such an aristocracy loses sight of eternal laws in contemplation of present conditions; it becomes proud and cruel, while flattering itself it is kind and charitable. It lives by the toil of the masses and "generously" doles back a part of its plunder in the form of colleges (which usually teach the science of selfishness), of hospitals (made necessary mainly because the greed of the givers has denied culture to their inmates), and the like.

Today this aristocracy of money is enslaving the white masses at the North, is preparing to enslave the patriots of Cuba, Porto Rico and the Philippines, and is aiding by consent the reenslavement of the colored men of the Southern states. Its operations are as automatic as human nature. It is not a deliberate plan, but a glacial tendency; it is not human, but inhuman.

It represents the doctrine that ruled mankind before Jesus Christ gave the world the doctrine of the equality of men. It stands for the survival of the fittest—that law of the jungle that ruled before men existed, and it works in the way it then worked in the jungle, ignoring all that the world has learned in the long cycles that have intervened, all that Christ taught.

We cannot escape the operations of the law of the survival of the fittest,* but we can and will give it new meaning: we shall cease to slaughter the unfit and shall strengthen them, so that they and their descendants *shall* be fit, as fit as any.

* The reference is to "Social Darwinism," a pseudo-scientific principle popularized by Herbert Spencer and his many American disciples to justify the dominance of the wealthy classes in society. Among other things, the "Social Darwinists" argued that the Nordic race is superior to all other peoples, particularly Negroes and other colored people, and that the principle of the "survival of the fittest" should apply in business and in politics as well as in nature.

In the ranks of the aristocracy of money are many noble men and women, born to the purple, or raised to it by their own efforts, who retain their passionate democratic love for the principles of abstract liberty and equality; who do all that lies in their power to offset the wrongs inflicted by the system of which they find themselves a part; who follow the teachings of Christ, the great democrat, in all but the final sacrifice of self—they will not give up their property, but hold it for their sons. To give it up would invite the charge of insanity alike from the people of their own class, and from the lower classes of society, as at present organized. So they hold it, and it sets their sons and daughters apart from the toilers; in their sons and daughters it becomes mere money, without bowels, without compassion.

Let no man censure another; let all remember that each is the product of conditions shaped before he was born; and so let our judgments be tempered with charity and patience. But, while we may not censure, it is not denied us to oppose that which we forbear to censure. Charity does not mean submission; whether we would or not, we cannot submit. An impulse higher than man bids him aspire and he does it through infinite pain and labor. Charity for our opponents is but the oil that eases the wheels of progress.

These gentle and truly generous men in the ranks of the aristocracy of money are the rare exceptions, and they still more rarely reproduce their kind; and though we may rejoice in them we must not cease trying to educate ourselves and others away from the system that makes it possible even for them to acquire the power of life and death over their fellow men.

Since the forces of plutocracy are united for selfish ends, shall the forces of labor—of democracy in the broad sense—remain disunited? Shall our forces be split up on the eve of the greatest battle for human liberty ever fought on the continent? Shall our main army, in which rests our sole hope of staying the advances of plutocracy, be depleted and weakened to the losing point by the desertion of many detachments, forlorn hopes far out in front crying after desires not yet attainable? Shall some of us still follow a name, when that name—the name of the Republican party—has ceased to mean the things it once meant, and has come to mean their exact antithesis? Shall the men Lincoln freed continue to vote with the party that he once honored and made his instrument, now that that party is giving the lie to the great truths for which Lincoln contended and for which he died? Shall the men freed vote the chains back upon their ankles?

Let no man believe that the white men who in the South are

denying the Negro's right to citizenship, and who wear the name of democracy, are really democrats. They are not; they are of the plutocracy; they are of the Middle Ages; they are at war with the most vital tenets of the true democracy—the democracy of the ages in all lands; the democracy of universal brotherhood and of equal opportunities; the democracy that survives and shall survive forever; the democracy that today animates the utterances of that greathearted Christian gentleman, William Jennings Bryan.

The white leaders of the South who are—by their own defiant declarations—voting the Negro back into political bondage, are at heart plutocrats; if they have not material wealth, they desire it and strive for it. Their hope and their purpose is that, once they have taken the ballot from the Negro and have so become free to divide on economic questions, they may carry several of the Southern states for the plutocratic doctrines of the protective tariff, subsidies, special privileges. It is the hope that the South can be so divided that it silences the lips of the administration leaders at the North. In this way the forces of the aristocracy of money are working together. By this token it behooves the colored man in the North, where he is still permitted to vote, to cast his ballot next November for the candidate who stands for equal freedom in our newly acquired islands of the sea, and who opposes every effort made to limit the national rights and opportunities of the toiling masses here at home.

I make no interested plea. I am a laboring man, and expect always to be a laboring man; I know of nothing saner and more satisfying than labor, lit by enthusiasm, rewarded with simple plenty, and so limited as to allow in each day some hours for self-education.

I am not more interested in the success of one party than of another, except as one party represents, today, certain principles which I believe in, and the other party, drifted far from the standards that made its early history glorious, represents propositions—I cannot call them principles—which are abhorrent alike to my native instincts and to the teachings of our patriot fathers.

In my boyhood, I had no prouder utterance than, "I am a Republican." The Republican party freed the slaves: my heart thrilled with the beauty of it. My father fought in the Union Army; I fought on the school ground to prove he was right. The flag then seemed to be peculiarly the symbol of the Republican party; to assail one was to assail the other.

I voted for William McKinley. I believed in the genuine goodness of his heart, in the sturdiness of his Americanism. I still believe in him, but I see that he is, like the exceptional democratically minded member of the aristocracy of money, powerless to guide the course of his party. I see that when he recognized and declared, in effect, that forcible conquest of the Philippines would be "criminal aggression," and that "our plain duty" to the Porto Ricans was to take them into full citizenship, the power of plutocracy overruled him, and committed the party to a course of "criminal aggression" in the Philippines, and to a violation of our "plain duty" in Porto Rico.

For these reasons, and because the study of the last four years has given me more light and a broader view of the forces at work in our civilization, I shall this year vote for William Jennings Bryan if he be the candidate of the Democracy, as doubtless he will be.

A DEFENSE OF THE NEGRO RACE

By George H. White

On January 29, 1901, George Henry White stood in the House of Representatives for the last time. It was not until twenty-eight years later that Congress was to greet its next Negro member. In his farewell speech, the last Negro Congressman from the South summarized the Negro's accomplishments in the first thirty-five years of freedom and predicted that the occasion was "perhaps the Negroes' temporary farewell to the American Congress."

The Washington Star carried White's speech and introduced it as follows: "With the close of this session, Mr. White of North Carolina, the only colored man in the House of Representatives, goes out of Congress, January 29th, in the House. Mr. White pronounced 'the Negro's temporary farewell to the American Congress' in an impassioned speech, which brought forth applause on the floor and in the galleries."

(The speech as presented here has been excerpted from the Congressional Record, 56th Congress, 2d Session, pp. 1636–38.)

Mr. Chairman: I want to enter a plea for the colored man, the colored woman, the colored boy, and the colored girl of this country. I would not thus digress from the question at issue and detain the House in a discussion of the interests of this particular people at this time but for the constant and the persistent efforts of certain gentlemen upon this floor to mold and rivet public sentiment against us as a people, and to lose no opportunity to hold up the unfortunate few, who commit crimes and depredations and lead lives of infamy and shame, as other races do, as fair specimens of representatives of the entire colored race.* And at no time, perhaps, during the 56th Congress were these charges and countercharges, containing, as they do, slanderous statements, more persistently magnified and pressed upon the attention of the nation than during the consideration of the recent reapportionment bill, which is now a law.† As stated some days ago on this floor by me, I then sought diligently to obtain an opportunity to answer some of the statements made by gentlemen from different states, but the privilege was denied me; and I therefore must embrace this opportunity to say, out of season perhaps, that which I was not permitted to say in season.

I would like to advance the statement that the musty records of 1868, filed away in the archives of Southern capitols, as to what the Negro was thirty years ago, is not a proper standard by which the Negro living on the threshold of the twentieth century should be measured. Since that time we have reduced the illiteracy of the race at least 45 percent. We have written and published nearly five hundred books. We have nearly eight

* Rayford W. Logan writes: "During White's two terms, Negroes were subjected to vilification in Congress the like of which has rarely been equaled except in the early days of Nazi struggle for power in Germany and some recent attacks upon eminent Americans by an irresponsible Senator" (*The Negro in American Life and Thought, the Nadir, 1877–1901*, New York, 1954, p. 90). The Senator referred to was Senator Joseph R. McCarthy.

† The reference is to the debates on the reapportionment of the House of Representatives after the census of 1900. Bills were introduced dealing only with the size of the House, but Republican Representatives Marlin E. Olmsted of Pennsylvania and Edgar D. Crumpacker of Indiana sought to direct attention to the second section of the Fourteenth Amendment, because of the disfranchisement of Negroes in Southern states. (The second section of the Amendment required the reduction of representation in the House in the same proportion as the number deprived of the right to vote.) Crumpacker's amendment to the bill of Edwin C. Burleigh of Maine, January 7, 1901, provided for the loss of three seats each by Mississippi, South Carolina, Louisiana and North Carolina. No vote was taken on Crumpacker's amendment.

hundred newspapers, three of which are dailies. We have now in practice over two thousand lawyers, and a corresponding number of doctors. We have accumulated over $12,000,000 worth of school property and about $40,000,000 worth of church property. We have about 140,000 farms and homes, valued in the neighborhood of $750,000,000, and personal property valued about $170,000,000. We have raised about $11,000,000 for educational purposes, and the property per capita for every colored man, woman and child in the United States is estimated at $75.

We are operating successfully several banks, commercial enterprises among our people in the Southland, including one silk mill and one cotton factory. We have 32,000 teachers in the schools of the country; we have built, with the aid of our friends about 20,000 churches, and support seven colleges, seventeen academies, fifty high schools, five law schools, five medical schools and twenty-five theological seminaries. We have over 600,000 acres of land in the South alone. The cotton produced, mainly by black labor, has increased from 4,669,770 bales in 1860 to 11,235,000 in 1899. All this was done under the most adverse circumstances. We have done it in the face of lynching, burning at the stake, with the humiliation of Jim Crow cars, the disfranchisement of our male citizens, slander and degradation of our women, with the factories closed against us, no Negro permitted to be conductor on the railway cars, whether run through the streets of our cities or across the prairies of our great country, no Negro permitted to run as engineer on a locomotive, most of the mines closed against us.

Labor unions—carpenters, painters, brick masons, machinists, hackmen and those supplying nearly every conceivable avocation for livelihood—have banded themselves together to better their condition, but, with few exceptions, the black man has been left out. The Negroes are seldom employed in our mercantile stores. At this we do not wonder. Some day we hope to have them employed in our own stores. With all these odds against us we are forging our way ahead, slowly perhaps, but surely. You may tie us and then taunt us for a lack of bravery, but some day we will break the bonds. You may use our labor for two and a half centuries and then taunt us for poverty, but let me remind you we will not always remain poor. You may withhold even the knowledge of how to read God's word and learn the way from earth to glory and then taunt us for our ignorance, but we will remind you that there is plenty of room at the top, and we are climbing.

After enforced debauchery with many kindred horrors incident to slavery, it comes with ill grace from the perpetrators of these deeds to hold up the shortcomings of some of our race to ridicule and scorn.

The new man, the slave who has grown out of the ashes of thirty-five years ago, is inducted into the political and social system, cast into the arena of manhood, where he constitutes a new element and becomes a competitor for all its emoluments. He is put upon trial to test his ability to be counted worthy of freedom, worthy of the elective franchise; and after thirty-five years of struggling against almost insurmountable odds, under conditions but little removed from slavery itself, he makes a fair and just judgment, not of those whose prejudice has endeavored to forestall, to frustrate, his every forward movement, rather those who have lent a helping hand, that he might demonstrate the truth of the "fatherhood of God and the brotherhood of man."

Now, Mr. Chairman, before concluding my remarks I want to submit a brief recipe for the solution of the so-called American Negro problem. He asks no special favors, but simply demands that he be given the same chance for existence, for earning a livelihood, for raising himself in the scales of manhood and womanhood, that are accorded to kindred nationalities. Treat him as a man; go into his home and learn of his social conditions; learn of his cares, his troubles and his hope for the future; gain his confidence; open the doors of industry to him; let the word "Negro," "colored," and "black" be stricken from all the organizations enumerated in the Federation of Labor.

Help him to overcome his weaknesses, punish the crime-committing class by the courts of the land, measure the standard of the race by its best material, cease to mold prejudicial and unjust public sentiment against him, and—my word for it—he will learn to support, hold up the hands of, and join in with that political party, that institution, whether secular or religious, in every community where he lives, which is destined to do the greatest good for the greatest number. Obliterate race hatred, party prejudice, and help us to achieve nobler ends, greater results and become satisfactory citizens to our brother in white.

This, Mr. Chairman, is perhaps the Negro's temporary farewell to the American Congress; but let me say, pheonixlike he will rise up some day and come again. These parting words are in behalf of an outraged, heartbroken, bruised and bleeding, but God-fearing, people, faithful, industrious, loyal people, rising people, full of potential force.

Mr. Chairman, in the trial of Lord Bacon, when the court

disturbed the counsel for the defendants, Sir Walter Raleigh raised himself up to his full height and addressing the court, said, "Sir, I am pleading for the life of a human being."

The only apology that I have to make for the earnestness with which I have spoken is that I am pleading for the life, the liberty, the future happiness, and manhood suffrage for one eighth of the entire population of the United States.

THE REMEDY FOR ANARCHY

By Jesse Lawson

On February 5, 1902, Professor Jesse Lawson, a leader of the black community of New Jersey and one of the leaders of the National Afro-American Council, delivered an address before the Bethel Literary and Historical Association of Washington, D. C. Part of the speech dealt with the issue of anarchy and was widely discussed in the nation following the assassination of President McKinley. That part is presented here as taken from The Colored American, *February 8, 1902.*

SINCE PRESIDENT MCKINLEY was shot down by a dastardly assassin amid the festivities of the Pan-American Exposition, in the city of Buffalo, on the sixth of last September, this nation has been keened up to the highest pitch on the subject "How Best to Rid Ourselves of the Anarchists." Many bills have been introduced in Congress with a view to punishing any attempt on the life of the President. These measures are manifestations of the righteous indignation of the people against a growing evil in our midst. The time is now ripe for action, and something will be done. The bills introduced are good as far as they go, but they do not go far enough. The way to cure anarchy is to strike at the very root of the evil. Anarchy in this country began with the surrender of the governments of the Southern states in 1877, and it has been taking root in our soil ever since that time. The right of the majority to rule is a well-established principle in our system of government, and when we fail to adhere to that principle then we fail to maintain a government according to the Constitution. Where there is no government according to the Constitution, there anarchy abounds.

Can any one say that there has been a Constitutional election held at the South since Grant shook hands with Hayes on the east front of the Capitol, March 4, 1877? Has anybody heard of such an election being held? I pause for an answer.

The only way to cure anarchy is to live up to the Constitution and enforce the law, and the only way to make the life of the President safe in this country is to make it safe for the life of every man in the Republic.

If Congress has power—and I think it has—to pass a law against anarchy in one form, it also has the power to pass laws against anarchy in any other form; and if this nation can punish the anarchists it can also punish the persons who are guilty of mob violence in every part of the United States.

A PLAN FOR A DEFENSE MOVEMENT

By William Costley

In September, 1902, William Costley, Socialist candidate for Congress from the Fourth Congressional District of California, delivered the following speech in San Francisco, appealing for assistance of all black San Franciscans in his campaign for Congress. The speech was later published as a pamphlet and addressed to the Negroes of the United States. In his plea for financial support to help him win election, Costley outlined a defense program which he would push, once he was in Congress, in order to put an end to the outrages against his people. Here, too, it is interesting to note that part of the plan called for an appeal to heads of European governments and even the Pope to win their aid in this campaign.

Costley was one of three Negro delegates to the Socialist Unity Convention in 1901 which led to the formation of the Socialist Party of the United States.

(Costley's speech is taken from The Christian Recorder, *September 30, 1902.)*

TO THE NEGROES OF THE UNITED STATES

BROTHERS, in giving my consent to the circulation of this subscription list to a campaign fund, I do so with the firm conviction that I am best serving the interest of my race. The reasons I have for doing so are these:

Born in the sixties in Maryland, and raised in Washington, D. C., it was no unusual sight for my boyish eyes to see Negro Congressmen, Senators and high state officials in the halls of Congress at Washington. One by one they have dwindled away until today the ten million Negroes in this country have not one representative there. I remember that this decline of our race as political factors in the halls of Congress took place in inverse ratio to the advancement of the Republican party to influence and power. I remember the first rumors and faint whisperings that some of the Southern states were about to take measures to disfranchise our people in a so-called *legal* way; not being quite satisfied with the shotgun method. I said to myself, surely the all-powerful Republican party will not allow this crime to be committed against our people who have given it their undivided support and long years of service. The party will throw the strong arm of protector around them. But, unfortunately the rumors were only too true; we were disfranchised. I say *we*, for the blow struck at our Southern brothers is a blow at every Negro in the Union.

I remember hearing and reading of the many cruelties inflicted upon our people: denial of civil rights; beating defenseless men, women and children; false imprisonment, and sold on the auction block to cruel contractors; thousands upon thousands of cold-blooded murders that are unrecorded; thousands upon thousands of lynchings, of men and women and children. And I remember the day that the world was horrified with the news that the people of Paris, Texas, had burnt a Negro alive at the stake. Now, I thought to myself, this will surely open the eyes of the Republican party, they will act and act quickly, if not in the defense of the Negro they will at least take some action in defense of the good name and honor of the country.

But since that time burning has grown in fashion until now they are mentioned in six-line news items in the press dispatches. And so today I am compelled to admit the facts that the crimes committed against our people are committed by Democrats with the tacit, if not the open, consent of the Republican party of the country. They have the Congress, the Senate, the President. They control the Army and Navy, and the only reasons for the existence of these forces are for the protection of life and property. Now I ask every Negro to ask himself this question: Suppose the situation were reversed and the Negroes were committing these crimes upon the whites? Would the Republican Congress *act*? Would the Republican Senate *act*? Would the Republican President *act*? But no—they *will not act*.

But *we* must *act,* and this is the time. If given the required aid in this matter and elected, I will devote the best part of the salary of the office to forming a defense movement among our people on novel and original lines that I am confident will be successful. For instance, the circulation of a petition of protest in the name of God, humanity and civilization, that these crimes be stopped, getting it signed by every Negro in the Union and sending this petition, in charge of a good committee, to the Pope of Rome and the other religious and government heads of Europe. This would serve to publish to the world the infamy and criminal indifference of the white people of America who are fond of posing as champions of liberty. We can hold them up to scorn and ridicule of the civilized world by these means.

Another method is to set a day apart, on that day placing in the hands of every white churchgoer and many others, a short history of the atrocious crimes that have been committed against us; for instance, the official report of the prison investigation of the state of Texas that declared that "the life of a human was not considered of as much value as a dog's and that the condition in the prisons was a disgrace to the state of Texas." These are mostly innocent Negroes who are suffering in these shambles in all states of the South. Have these pamphlets printed on paper with deep mourning bands. By such methods we can arouse much sympathy that will enable us to have the best legal talent in the land for the purpose of suing for heavy damages every county wherein crimes are committed against our people by organized mobs. Have them appeal these cases, if necessary, to the Supreme Court of the land and make them go on record that human life shall or shall not have the same protection as the private property of the whites, for if private property is destroyed by a mob the county is responsible for full damages. These are some of the lines of battle that I have thought of and with your assistance the fight for our rights will begin right now, and if elected or not, I will start the fight on the lines outlined.

THE PROGRESS OF COLORED WOMEN

By Mary Church Terrell

In her autobiography, A Colored Woman in a White World, *published in 1940, Mary Church Terrell wrote: "I was invited to speak to the Congregational Association of Maryland and the District of Columbia, which was holding a meeting in the First Congregational Church. . . . Contrary to a custom observed all my life when speaking in public, I used a manuscript and spoke on 'The Progress of Colored Women.'" This speech, the only one of many delivered by Mrs. Terrell that was preserved, was fortunately published in* The Voice of the Negro *in July, 1904 (pp. 292–94).*

Mary Church Terrell was born in Memphis at the end of the Civil War. Her mother had been educated in slavery and her father, Robert R. Church, Sr., was the son of a pro-Union slaveowner, who made a fortune in real estate. Mary was sent to the North for schooling at six. After being graduated from Oberlin College, she taught at Wilberforce University and at a colored high school in Washington, D. C. She married Robert J. Terrell, a black graduate of Harvard University, who became a municipal judge in Washington, a position he occupied for twenty years. Active in work among Negro women, Mrs. Terrell was elected the first president of the National Association of Colored Women. Mrs. Terrell was still actively fighting Jim Crow in Washington at the age of eighty-nine.

In its issue of November 25, 1899, The Colored American, *of Washington, D. C., said of Mary Church Terrell: "As a platform orator and champion of the rights and privileges of the race, she has no superior among her sex in all the land."*

. . . WHEN ONE CONSIDERS the obstacles encountered by colored women in their effort to educate and cultivate themselves, since they became free, the work they have accomplished and the progress they have made will bear favorable comparison, at least with that of their more fortunate sisters, from whom the opportunity of acquiring knowledge and the means of self-culture have never been entirely withheld. Not only are colored women with ambition and aspiration handicapped on account of their sex, but they are almost everywhere baffled and mocked because of their race. Not only because they are women, but because they are colored women are discouragement and disappointment meeting them at every turn. But in spite of the obstacles encountered, the progress made by colored women along many lines appears like a veritable miracle of modern times. Forty years ago for the great masses of colored women there was no such thing as home. Today in each and every section of the country there are hundreds of homes among colored people, the mental and moral tone of which is as high and as pure as can be found among the best people of any land.

To the women of the race may be attributed in large measure the refinement and purity of the colored home. The immorality of colored women is a theme upon which those who know little about them or those who maliciously misrepresent them love to descant. Foul aspersions upon the character of colored women are assiduously circulated by the press of certain sections and especially by the direct descendants of those who in years past were responsible for the moral degradation of their female slaves. And yet, in spite of the fateful heritage of slavery, even though the safeguards usually thrown around maidenly youth and innocence are in some sections entirely withheld from colored girls, statistics compiled by men not inclined to falsify in favor of my race show that immorality among the colored women of the United States is not so great as among women with similar environment and temptations in Italy, Germany, Sweden and France.

Scandals in the best colored society are exceedingly rare, while the progressive game of divorce and remarriage is practically unknown.

The intellectual progress of colored women has been marvelous. So great has been their thirst for knowledge and so Herculean their efforts to acquire it that there are few colleges, universities, high and normal schools in the North, East and West from which colored girls have not graduated with honor. In Wellesley, Vassar, Ann Arbor, Cornell and in Oberlin, my dear alma mater, whose name will always be loved and whose praise will always be sung as the first college in the country broad, just and generous enough to extend a cordial welcome to the Negro and to open its doors to women on an equal footing with the men, colored girls by their splendid records have forever settled the question of their capacity and worth. The instructors in these and other institutions cheerfully bear testimony to their intelligence, their diligence and their success.

As the brains of colored women expanded, their hearts began

to grow. No sooner had the heads of a favored few been filled with knowledge than their hearts yearned to dispense blessings to the less fortunate of their race. With tireless energy and eager zeal, colored women have worked in every conceivable way to elevate their race. Of the colored teachers engaged in instructing our youth it is probably no exaggeration to say that fully eighty percent are women. In the backwoods, remote from the civilization and comforts of the city and town colored women may be found courageously battling with those evils which such conditions always entail. Many a heroine of whom the world will never hear has thus sacrificed her life to her race amid surroundings and in the face of privations which only martyrs can bear.

Through the medium of their societies in the church, beneficial organizations out of it and clubs of various kinds, colored women are doing a vast amount of good. It is almost impossible to ascertain exactly what the Negro is doing in any field, for the records are so poorly kept. This is particularly true in the case of the women of the race. During the past forty years there is no doubt that colored women in their poverty have contributed large sums of money to charitable and educational institutions as well as to the foreign and home missionary work. Within the twenty-five years in which the educational work of the African Methodist Episcopal Church has been systematized, the women of that organization have contributed at least five hundred thousand dollars to the cause of education. Dotted all over the country are charitable institutions for the aged, orphaned and poor which have been established by colored women. Just how many it is difficult to state, owing to the lack of statistics bearing on the progress, possessions and prowess of colored women.

Among the charitable institutions either founded, conducted or supported by colored women, may be mentioned the Hale Infirmary of Montgomery, Alabama, the Carrie Steel Orphanage of Atlanta, the Reed Orphan Home of Covington, and the Hains Industrial School of Augusta, all three in the state of Georgia; a home for the aged of both races in New Bedford, and St. Monica's Home of Boston, in Massachusetts, Old Folks Home of Memphis, Tennessee, and the Colored Orphan's Home of Lexington, Kentucky, together with others which lack of space forbids me to mention. Mt. Meigs Institute is an excellent example of a work originated and carried into successful execution by a colored woman. The school was established for the benefit of colored people on the plantations in the black belt of Alabama. In the township of Mt. Meigs the population is practically all colored. Instruction given in this school is of the kind best suited to the needs of the people for whom it was established. Along with some scholastic training, girls are taught everything pertaining to the management of the home, while boys are taught practical farming, wheelwrighting, blacksmithing, and have some military training. Having started with almost nothing, at the end of eight years the trustees of the school owned nine acres of land and five buildings in which several thousand pupils had received instructions, all through the energy, the courage and the sacrifice of one little woman.

Up to date, politics have been religiously eschewed by colored women, although questions affecting our legal status as a race is sometimes agitated by the most progressive class. In Louisiana and Tennessee colored women have several times petitioned the legislatures of their respective states to repel the obnoxious Jim-Crow-car laws. Against the convict-lease system, whose atrocities have been so frequently exposed of late, colored women here and there in the South are waging a ceaseless war. So long as hundreds of their brothers and sisters, many of whom have committed no crime or misdemeanor whatever, are thrown into cells whose cubic contents are less than those of a good-size grave, to be overworked, underfed and only partially covered with vermin-infested rags, and so long as children are born to the women in these camps who breathe the polluted atmosphere of these dens of horror and vice from the time they utter their first cry in the world till they are released from their suffering by death, colored women who are working for the emancipation and elevation of their race know where their duty lies. By constant agitation of this painful and hideous subject they hope to touch the conscience of the country, so that this stain upon its escutcheon shall be forever wiped away.

Alarmed at the rapidity with which the Negro is losing ground in the world of trade, some of the farsighted women are trying to solve the labor question, so far as it concerns the women at least, by urging the establishment of schools of domestic science wherever means therefor can be secured. Those who are interested in this particular work hope and believe that if colored women and girls are thoroughly trained in domestic service, the boycott which has undoubtedly been placed upon them in many sections of the country will be removed. With so few vocations open to the Negro and with the labor organizations increasingly hostile to him, the future of the boys and girls of the race appears to some of our women very foreboding and dark.

The cause of temperance has been eloquently espoused by

two women, each of whom has been appointed national superintendent of work among colored people by the Woman's Christian Temperance Union. In business, colored women have had signal success. There is in Alabama a large milling and cotton business belonging to and controlled by a colored woman, who has sometimes as many as seventy-five men in her employ. Until a few years ago the principal ice plant of Nova Scotia was owned and managed by a colored woman, who sold it for a large amount. In the professions there are dentists and doctors whose practice is lucrative and large. Ever since a book was published in 1773 entitled "Poems on Various Subjects, Religious and Moral by Phillis Wheatley, Negro Servant of Mr. John Wheatley," of Boston, colored women have given abundant evidence of literary ability. In sculpture we are represented by a woman upon whose chisel Italy has set her seal of approval; in painting by one of Bouguereau's pupils and in music by young women holding diplomas from the best conservatories in the land.

In short, to use a thought of the illustrious Frederick Douglass, if judged by the depths from which they have come, rather than by the heights to which those blessed with centuries of opportunities have attained, colored women need not hang their heads in shame. They are slowly but surely making their way up to the heights, wherever they can be scaled. In spite of handicaps and discouragements they are not losing heart. In a variety of ways they are rendering valiant service to their race. Lifting as they climb, onward and upward they go struggling and striving and hoping that the buds and blossoms of their desires may burst into glorious fruition ere long. Seeking no favors because of their color nor charity because of their needs they knock at the door of Justice and ask for an equal chance.

REVOLUTION BY THE BALLOT

By George Edwin Taylor

George Edwin Taylor, of Ottumwa, Iowa, was the first Negro to be nominated for the Presidency of the United States. Taylor was selected by a convention of the National Liberty Party held at St. Louis, July 5–6, 1904, and attended by delegates from thirty-six states. Born a free Negro in 1857 in Little Rock, Arkansas, Taylor was active in

*journalism and politics, editing a local Knights of Labor
paper in La Crosse, Wisconsin, in the 1880's. For a time
Taylor worked within the Republican party, but in 1892
he broke with it. He was president of the Negro National
Democratic League from 1900 to 1904. By then he had
become convinced that the Negro people must undertake
independent political action.*

*Here is Taylor's keynote address following his nomina-
tion for President by the National Liberty Party. It was
published in* The Voice of the Negro *(October, 1904, pp.
479–81), which described Taylor as "The Only Colored
Man Ever Nominated for the Presidency."*

THE NATIONAL LIBERTY PARTY now confronts the people
of the United States, claiming their consideration for the first
time, but though the organization is in its infancy, the principles for which it stands are fundamental to our republican
form of government. In fact, we are struggling to revive the
well-nigh deserted principles of the grand old Whig party (the
mother of the Republican party), which declared for "popular
rights," government of all the people, for all the people, and by
all the people.

When the founders of this republic were called upon to
frame the Declaration of Independence and a Constitution for
the future guidance, protection and foundation rock of the government, through their inspired wisdom they drafted ordinances
declaring their independence, and guaranteeing protection,
equal privileges, equal opportunity and equal rights to all citizens of the government. It was at that time clear to them that
upon no other premises could the American people hope to
secure their freedom and independence, and maintain a popular
government. And the history of the past one hundred and
twenty-seven years proves the correctness of their judgment,
that to depart from these fundamental principles is to endanger
the very perpetuity of our government.

The National Liberty Party calls the attention of the people
of the United States to the bold fact that these fundamental
principles are fast being covered up, ignored, disregarded, and
practically nullified by the administrative powers, the national
governing forces of both the Republican and Democratic parties,
and the controlling political forces of at least six states of the
Union which have recently by state constitutional amendment
actually disfranchised over two million American-born citizens.

Practically all of these disfranchised people are Negroes, and
it is also a fact that, under the federal Constitution and laws,

we are as emphatically recognized as citizens as are the most aristocratic Caucasians. If not, why not?

The history of the National Liberty Party is very brief. It is the direct outgrowth of the Civil and Personal Liberty Leagues, which for years have thrived among the Negroes of the South, and portions of the East. Through the efforts of Stanley P. Mitchell (the head of the Liberty Leagues) of Memphis, Tennessee, and his associates, the first national convention of the National Liberty Party was held in the auditorium of the Douglas Hotel in the city of St. Louis, on the fifth and sixth of July last, when a permanent and complete organization of the party was effected. Thirty-six states were represented in the convention.

We religiously adhere to the sacredness of our form of government, and subscribe to its every tenet, law and claim. We believe that the tendency of the dominant parties is to dissipate these tenets, laws and demands and that it is our duty and the duty of every sober-minded citizen to join us in the arrest of this wholesale dissipation, in the interests of good government, the maintenance of federal power and the perpetuity of our system of government, which the popular sentiment of the world pronounces the most beneficent the world has ever known.

It must be clear to all unprejudiced students of history that whenever a government fails to secure for all its subjects or citizens at home, as well as abroad, that which it guarantees, that such government is nearing dangerous ground—it matters not whether said neglected citizens belong to or represent a popular or unpopular class. For, in such neglect, a fundamental principle of government is abused, distorted, abandoned; and like a cancer, it will continue to grow and spread until finally it gnaws in twain the very vital cords. The Negro who now suffers most directly by reason of this neglect (disfranchisement) is not in fact the only sufferer, for his immediate calamity is the beginning of the end of the downfall of the producing element of the races who comprise the vast common working classes of this great republic. The Negro of the United States is distinctively an important factor in the great and grand army of American workingmen, and whatever enhances, strengthens, retards or impedes his progress, happiness, manhood or citizenship rights proportionately affects all the citizens of his class and standing. Hence, the interest that all common people of every race or nationality in the United States should have in this government. Does the question, "Am I my black brother's keeper?" arise in the minds of the common (white) people? If so, I refer to the history of the world from the days of Cain and Abel for your answer. Judas betrayed the Christ only to earn for himself eternal reproach and an ignominious death. Napoleon, through intrigue, captured and starved to the death in a dungeon that gallant statesman and warrior, Toussaint l'Ouverture, and as a reward, died the death of an exile; the Spaniards, through deception and cunning, assassinated General Maceo, the greatest Negro soldier and general of modern times, and soon afterward were subjected to banishment and disgraceful defeat as their reward. In short, the history of the world proves the ultimate defeat of wrong and the establishment of right.

It is the purpose of the National Liberty Party to point out some of the dangerous errors in our present system of government and work for their correction, and we shall not cease until this end shall have been accomplished, for it appears to us to be patriotically obligatory.

As to the independence of the National Liberty Party, I do not hesitate to state that, in every sense of the word, we are, and propose to remain, purely independent, for the principles for which we stand are not now germane to the platform of principles of any other political party. If they were, there would be no room or occasion for the existence of this party. The National Liberty Party is purely a creature of necessity.

Never before in the history of American Negro citizenship has the time been so opportune for an independent political movement on the part of the race. And never before has there been a time when such a movement could draw materially from the race. But now in the light of the history of the past four years, with a Republican President in the executive chair, and both branches of Congress and a majority of the Supreme Court of the same political faith, we are confronted with the amazing fact that more than one fifth of the race are actually disfranchised, robbed of all the rights, powers and benefits of true citizenship, we are forced to lay aside our prejudices, indeed, our personal wishes, and consult the higher demands of our manhood, the true interests of the country and our posterity, and act while we yet live, ere the time when it shall be too late. No other race of our strength would have quietly submitted to what we have during the past four years without a rebellion, a revolution, or an uprising.

We, too, propose a rebellion, a revolution, an uprising, not by physical force, but by the ballot, through the promulgation of the National Liberty Party. Our education, our civilization and our natural disposition, all incline us to this course as the only rational, consistent, effective method of attaining the desired end—viz., representation as well as taxation; the full exercise of our Constitutional rights as citizens. The only truly effective way for the common people to correct a national evil lies in their power at the ballot box, if they will but exercise it judiciously.

Whenever the race and their colaborers shall array themselves in one grand independent political phalanx, the very foundations of the two dominant political parties will be shaken and the leaders of both will be brought to a realization of the danger which threatens their organization, and *"the rights of the people"* will again be considered by them instead of that of special classes, as is the present rule.

It is the intention of the committee of the National Liberty Party to perfect all necessary arrangements to have placed upon the ballots of the several states, Presidential electors, and in many instances to nominate by petition or otherwise, Congressional candidates. Should we fail to complete the organization in all the states this year, we shall continue the work after the election. Our greatest strength, of course, lies in the Southern states which have not as yet adopted disfranchisement amendments. We expect to make a good showing in Kansas, Indiana, Illinois, Ohio, Pennsylvania, West Virginia, Tennessee, Iowa, Texas, and many other states.* It is conservative to estimate that at least sixty percent of the Negroes of the states in which we secure a place upon the ballot for our candidates, will vote with us. It is also fair to presume that a goodly number of the white independents in these states will support the movement. Why not? We stand for the text and the spirit of the Declaration of Independence, and the federal Constitution, for universal suffrage; for the pensioning of all veterans of the war of the rebellion; for the establishment of a National Arbitration Board with power to adjust all differences that may arise between employer and employee; for the abolition of polygamy; for the nullification and repeal of all class legislation; for unsubsidized competition in all lines of commerce, and industry, which means the abolishment of all trusts and combines; for the pensioning of ex-slaves, according to the terms of the "Hanna Bill";† and for a reduction of the tariff. We do not con-

* There is no way of learning just how many votes were cast for Taylor in the Presidential election of 1904.
† On February 4, 1903, Senator Mark Hanna of Ohio introduced a bill in the Senate (by request) proposing a pension for every ex-slave (male and female alike). Although the ex-slave pension plan was denounced as a fraud by many black papers, it did have the support of a number of them. Nothing, however, came of the proposal.

sider the money standard an issue of any merit in this campaign.

Every Negro who is loyal to his race and the powers that made him a free man, must join with us in heart, if not in action, in this effort to emphasize the fact that the Constitution of the United States is no respector of persons, but that all American citizens are entitled to exercise all the rights of citizenship, regardless of race or color.

WE MUST BE A LAW-ABIDING AND LAW-RESPECTING PEOPLE

By Booker T. Washington

On September 22, 1906, climaxing a local political campaign with Negro disfranchisement as an issue and featured by the whipping-up by the press of anti-Negro sentiment, the Atlanta Riot began. Attacks on Negroes got under way on that day, and when, on September 24, Negroes organized to defend themselves, the police joined the white mobs. At least ten Negroes (including two women) and two whites were killed, sixty Negroes and ten whites were seriously injured, and scores of Negro homes were looted and burned. Numerous Negroes sold their property and left Atlanta.

All over the North black Americans called for mobilization of self-defense groups to protect their people against rioters and urged their brothers and sisters to act at once in their defense. But Booker T. Washington condemned this advice and urged calmness and self-control. He also excoriated the Negroes of the North for inflaming blacks in the South. In a speech before the Afro-American Council in New York, October 11, 1906, Washington summed up his position. Negroes should devote their energies to getting rid of agitators in their ranks and become law-abiding citizens. (Nothing was said about the law-breaking whites who murdered blacks.) It is an important speech, since it fully highlighted the kind of advice Washington gave to

*his people and which made him so admired and supported
by whites North and South.*
    (*The text presented here is taken from* The Public, *October 20, 1906.*)

IN THE SEASON of disturbances and excitement if others
yield to the temptation of losing control of their judgment and
give way to passion and prejudice, let us, as a race, teach the
world that we have learned the great lesson of calmness and
self-control; that we are determined to be governed by reason
rather than by feeling. Our victories in the past have come to
us through our ability to be calm and patient, often while enduring great wrong.

Again, I am most anxious—and I know that in this I speak
the sentiment of every conservative member of our race—that
our race everywhere bears the reputation of a law-abiding and
law-respecting people. If others would break the law and trample
it underfoot, let us keep and respect it, and teach our children
to follow our example. In this connection I repeat what I have
uttered on a recent occasion: that every iota of influence that
we possess should be used to get rid of the criminal and loaf-
ing element of our people and to make decent, law-abiding
citizens.

To the members of my race who reside in the Northern states
let me utter the caution that in your enthusiastic desire to be of
service to your brethren in the South you do not make their
path more thorny and difficult by rash and intemperate utterances. Before giving advice to the Negro in the South, the
Negro in the North should be very sure that what he advises is
that which he himself would be willing to take into the heart
of the South and put into practice. Be careful not to assist in
lighting a fire which you will have no ability to put out.

Some may think that the problems with which we are grappling will be better solved by inducing millions of our people
to leave the South for residence in the North, but I warn you
that instead of this being a solution it will but add to the complications of the problem.

While condemning the giving of prominence to the work of
the mob in the South, we should not fail to give due credit to
those of the white race who stood manfully and courageously
on the side of law and order during the recent trying ordeals
through which this section of our country has been passing.
During the racial disturbances the country very seldom hears
of the brave and heroic acts of a certain element of Southern

white people whose deeds are seldom heralded through the press.

The indiscriminate condemnation of all white people on the part of any member of our race is a suicidal and dangerous policy. We must learn to discriminate. We have strong friends, both in the South and in the North, and we should emphasize and magnify the efforts of our friends more than those of them who wish us evil.

I have said we must differentiate between white people at the South. We cannot afford to class all as our enemies, for there are many who are our friends. The country must also learn to differentiate among black people. It is a mistake to place all in the same class when referring to labor, morality or general conduct. There is a vicious class that disgraces us; there is also a worthy class which should always receive commendation. Further, we must frankly face the fact that the great body of our people are to dwell in the South, and any policy that does not seek to harmonize the two races and cement them is unwise and dangerous.

Creation—construction, in the material, civic, educational, moral and religious world—is what makes races great. Any child can cry and fret, but it requires a full-grown man to create, to construct. Let me implore you to teach the members of our race everywhere that they must become, in an increasing degree, creators of their own careers.

THE BROWNSVILLE AFFAIR

By Kelly Miller

In 1907, Professor Kelly Miller, of Howard University, delivered a paper before the American Negro Academy, on President Theodore Roosevelt and the Negro. An important section dealt with the Brownsville Affair, a key issue in the Negro community at that time. Below is Miller's analysis of this incident. For a basic study of the Brownsville affair, see John D. Weaver, The Brownsville Raid *(New York, 1970)*

Born of ex-slave parents, Miller came to Howard at seventeen with a few dollars in his pockets, the gift of a missionary society interested in training boys for the ministry. But Miller decided upon a teaching career, and a job in the Pension Office enabled him to complete his degree requirements at Howard, take graduate work in mathematics by extension from the Johns Hopkins University, and study sociology. Miller taught at Howard and became dean of the university. He was one of the best-known Negro spokesmen of the opening decade of the twentieth century.

(The speech as presented here has been excerpted from Kelly Miller, Roosevelt and the Negro, *Washington, D. C., 1907, pp. 13–21.)*

. . . THE CHIEF IRRITATING ISSUE between the President and the Negro race is the outcome of a most deplorable incident. The Negro soldier has ever been an object of detestation to the Southern whites. The soldierly spirit is incompatible with the status to which the black man is assigned in their political and social scheme. Every Southern state has disbanded its colored militia. The feeling was accentuated by the Spanish War, where Negro and Southern white troops were placed on a footing of soldierly equality, and where the black troops gained the higher meed of glory. Occasional friction between local authorities and Negro troops passing through the South to and from the front but added fuel to the flame.

In the face of this feeling a Negro battalion was quartered in an obscure town on the remote frontier of Texas. The air about Brownsville became tense with trouble. Citizens goaded soldiers to the point of acute irritation. One dark night some shooting was done in the streets, resulting in the death of a barkeeper and the wounding of an officer of the law. The alarm was sounded that the Negro soldiers have "shot up the town." Race passion was stirred to the utmost. Brownsville would have been drenched in blood had it not been for the firm attitude of the gallant commander of the fort. The local grand jury could not find sufficient regular evidence for indictment of the hated troops quartered among them. Word was flashed to the Commander in Chief at Washington, who forthwith proceeded to deal with the matter out of hand. The Army inspector was dispatched to the scene to investigate and report. Unfortunately, the inspector was a man of Southern birth and bias. The distress cry of the city through the undercurrent of communication made its subconscious appeal with Masonic secrecy and force. Every thoughtful student knows that where race passion is aroused the judicial temperament takes flight. Suspicion or even suggestion of wrongdoing on the part of the Negro, if reiterated with loud outcry and demand for blood, is assumed to be confirmation strong as Holy Writ. Instantaneously every white man aligns himself on the side of his race. Where racial instinct is appealed to, the laws of evidence have little weight. "Lynch the brutes!" was on the lips of every citizen, and the execution was stayed only by the too fearful aspect of Uncle Sam's bayonets. In the midst of this inflammable state of things a son of Georgia as inspector general repaired to Brownsville. Instantly he assumed the feeling of the community. The investigator acted the role of prosecutor with preconceived conviction of guilt. He accepted the representation of the citizens of Brownsville and propounded a few shrewdly calculated questions to the suspected soldiers, whose answers were designed to confirm their guilt. No opportunity was afforded them to prove their innocence. Assuming the existence of a criminal conspiracy, he demanded of the noncommissioned officers the names of their guilty companions. Compliance with this request would inevitably have been self-incriminatory, convicting the respondent of murder if personally involved or of guilty knowledge if a nonparticipant. Following the method of the mob in dealing with a black culprit, he declared them guilty, and graciously offered them the opportunity to confess. Affirming their innocence, they refused to confess; and declaring their ignorance, they declined to inform on their fellows. The inspector hastened to Washington and reported to the President that some fifteen or twenty men out of a total of one hundred and sixty-seven had shot up the town, murdered and maimed its citizens, while the rest had guilty knowledge of the deed, but were disposed to shield their companions in crime. The city of Brownsville had worked out the case with such circumstantial confirmation of detail as to deceive even the commanding colonel, who reluctantly assented to the findings of the inspector general. On fuller investigation, however, Colonel Penrose changed this opinion and now stoutly affirms his belief in the innocence of his men.

When this report was presented to President Roosevelt he was bound to accept in good faith the findings of the inspector general, the regularly authorized agent for such service, and especially so when concurred in by the chief officers of the command.

A flood of righteous indignation welled up within him at this outrage upon the national arm. He would teach the wrongdoers a lesson which would never be forgotten. The color of the offenders, he stoutly avers, neither mitigated nor magnified the character of the offense in his mind. The discipline of the Army must be upheld. It is easy to believe that the President's conduct at this stage was not based upon consideration of color. He is himself of a military mold of mind. In military matters, as elsewhere, he is a law unto himself and has little reverence for those above, around or beneath him. He shatters a military idol with as little hesitancy as he would reprimand a common soldier. Did he not criticize and discredit the sagacity of his own commanding general with a little round robin? The man who spoke disparagingly of the troops who saved his life on the battlefield, who unceremoniously reprimanded General Miles, the gallant head of the Army and hero of many battles, who imputed cowardice to Admiral Schley, our only naval hero who has triumphed with modern guns over modern armor, might naturally be supposed to act vigorously in case of reported wrongdoers at Brownsville.

Basing his action on General Garlington's report, the President with ruthless hand, though righteous purpose, ignored all forms and precedents of military, judicial or executive procedure and proceeded to mete out drastic punishment. Although there was no pretense at determination of individual guilt, and although not more than ten percent of the battalion could possibly have participated in the outrage, the whole number was dismissed without honor, and in the hot indignation of his wrath he imposed upon them serious civil disability by executive fiat. The disqualifying feature of his order was flagrantly *ultra vires* and void by virtue of its own nullity. It was afterward rescinded, but its original issuance stands as a memorial of the state of mind actuating the President at the time.

This order of the President violates every principle of our jurisprudence. It assumed that the men were guilty and imposed upon them the onus of proving their innocence; it condemned them without even the formality of a trial; it imposed punishment without proof of individual culpableness; by it one hundred and fifty probably innocent men were made to suffer in order that fifteen possibly guilty ones might not escape.

The President must have foreseen or forefelt the tumult which the issuance of this order was calculated to excite, for with prudent political sagacity he held it up till the day after the election, in which the Negro vote might prove a determining factor, and especially in the Congressional district where the political fate of his son-in-law was involved. In the meantime he had betaken himself to the high seas, planning to return, it would seem, after the clouds had rolled by.

But instead of rolling by to accommodate the return of the President, the clouds continued to gather in density and ominousness. The whole Negro race was dazed. Theodore Roosevelt had for the second time struck at the Negro soldier, the pride and idol of the race.* Protest, indignation, cries of outrage flew thick and fast from the Negro press, pulpit and platform. The great papers of the country with practical unanimity condemned the order as one of unusual and unnecessary severity. Those versed in Constitutional lore declared that the President had set a precedent which might prove dangerous to the principle of American liberty. It was reserved for Senator Tillman to describe the act as executive lynching, a description which characterizes the deed with his wonted picturesque aptness of language. It possesses the essential characteristics of mob vengeance. It inflicts punishment on demand of the rabble rather than by judicial process. It furnishes victims to appease popular vengeance without nice regard to the identity of the perpetrator. The punishment of the possibly innocent effectually destroys the evidence by which the guilty might subsequently be apprehended. The Secretary of War, with political forethought, sought to have the order suspended until further investigation, but to no avail. What was written was written.

From a racial point of view it was doubly unfortunate that the President should have selected the weak and helpless Negro, the increasing object of the nation's contumely and despite, upon whom to make this drastic departure from the usual procedure. The disciplinary value of the example would doubtless have been more effective had he applied it in the first instance to the white troops guilty of the offense charged against the colored troops in Ohio some months previous. Coming, too, as it did, swiftly upon the heels of the Atlanta riot, it added the color of justification to that awful slaughter. Indeed, John Temple Graves,† the justifier of this atrocious murder of innocent men, employs the same line of justificatory argument as that used to defend the President's position. But the most unjust cut of all is when the President, acridly assuming a defensive attitude, holds the race up to the world, by executive decree, as fostering a criminal fellowship.

In the meantime, the session of Congress was approaching. In his annual message the President undertook to discuss the subject of lynching. In this document he imputed to the colored race a lecherous tendency, which is not justified by the infrequent occurrence of clearly proved cases of assault. He placed

* Years before, Theodore Roosevelt had spoken with contempt of the role of the Negro soldier during the Spanish-American War. See pages 618–19.
† John Temple Graves, editor of the Atlanta News, was accused of fanning the racial animosity which exploded in the Atlanta riots of September, 1906.

upon the whole race the responsibility of restraining and controlling the wild passion of the dastardly few. In his eagerness to effect the wished-for consummation, he overlooked the absurdity of imposing upon a race studiously deprived of governmental power and authority, without the means of inflicting punishment, the obligation of reaching, correcting and coercing the criminally disposed. This vicarious burden is imposed upon no other class of citizens. The alleged infirmities of the Negro race are thus set forth and embalmed in an official document and held up to the gaze of all the world. However holy and righteous may have been the President's intentions, this message is calculated to do the Negro more harm than any other state paper ever issued from the White House. Construed as it was in connection with the Brownsville order and the recent Atlanta barbarities, this message seemed to accentuate the Negroes' rapidly culminating ills.

With the opening of Congress the Brownsville order assumed the character of political discussion. It threatened to split in twain the triumphant Republican party. The President's closest personal and political friends felt forced to uphold his contentions, though not without apology. The Southern Democrats, with a single and grotesquely singular exception, reversed the tenor of their teachings and traditions and upheld the President in the unwarranted exercise of executive power. The aroused passion of race has twisted their immemorial political doctrine. Then came Senator Foraker,* like a gallant knight of old, and stepped into the arena as the champion of the helpless and overborne. The voice of ten million Americans, unheard and unheeded in the conduct of the nation's affairs, found expression in this eloquent and fearless Ohioan. And yet not so much he proclaimed because the victims were black, but because the method employed was violative of the principles of American jurisprudence and liberty. He assumed neither the innocence nor guilt of the accused, but planted himself firmly on the bedrock principle of the law, that a full and fair trial should precede conviction and punishment. The country and the Senate sided with Mr. Foraker, although by the nice amenities of legislative verbiage they refrained from wounding the Presidential pride. An inquiry by the Senate was ordered. In the meantime the President had dispatched a law officer to Brownsville in quest of

* John B. Foraker (1846–1917), Governor of Ohio and United States Senator from that state, led the battle against President Roosevelt for his dismissal of the entire company of Negro soldiers after the Brownsville incident.

confirmatory evidence. He found what he was sent for. By a prudential intuition these government agents seem to divine the conclusion of the Presidential mind. His method was of the same ex parte character as that of the Army inspector, and of course the foregone conclusion was confirmed. The President became incensed at the persistent attitude of the colored race, and in several special messages reiterated his innuendoes with redoubled vim and emphasis. Senator Foraker became the principal object of his wrath. It was rumored that at a social function, where secrecy was imposed upon all present, a personal colloquy between the two was sharp and bitter. All of this served to make Senator Foraker the hero and idol of the Negro heart. Roosevelt lost what Foraker gained. The Ohio Senator is the only commanding statesman of our day who has risked his public career on an issue involving the Negro's cause. Whatever may be the immediate outcome of the issue,* he has and will have, his reward, for no one who devotes his powers to the defense of the helpless will fail to receive the highest meed of praise when the rancor and heat of the conflict have passed away.

Under the guidance of Senator Foraker the Senate inquiry has now proceeded for several months. At the instance of the President several eminent Republican Senators reluctantly consented to reinforce the Democrats in upholding his hand. The accused soldiers have been given a hearing. Their straightforward, manly, unwavering testimony in their own behalf has raised in the public mind a reasonable doubt of their guilt. That one hundred and sixty-seven men, ignorant and unlettered, unskilled in the art of double-tongued dialectics, should unite and persist in one straightforward tale and suffer loss of livelihood and honor without one confessing or informing voice would be the most remarkable psychological phenomenon in the history of criminal procedure.

On the other hand the citizens of Brownsville have given the most positive and circumstantial evidence of guilt. These

---

* In 1909 Senator Foraker pushed through Congress an act establishing a court of inquiry to pass on the cases of the discharged soldiers. It provided that all the discharged soldiers who were found to be qualified for reenlistment were to be judged eligible, and that if they reenlisted they were to be considered as having enlisted immediately after their discharge. Any such soldier was to receive back pay and all other rights and benefits that he would have been entitled to "if he had been honorably discharged . . . and had reenlisted immediately." The court of inquiry resulted in the return to service of a large number of the discharged men with back pay.

farsighted witnesses have testified under oath that they saw these men in the act and distinguished their uniform, color and visage at a distance of a hundred yards on a dark night, when the trained eyesight of Army officers could not recognize a brother officer ten feet away. The weight of this testimony is weakened by the prepossessions of the witness as well as by its inherent incredibility. Aroused race passion is as heedless of fact as it is of reason and logic. It blunts the physical as well as the moral sense. For any white citizen of Brownsville to say one word contradictory of the popular prejudice means permanent banishment or sure and sudden death. The wealthiest man of the town was assassinated because he had the temerity to question the accuracy of certain of this testimony. Had these Springfield rifles in the hands of men who have never failed to use them when ordered by their commanders proved less dissuasive from violence, and had half dozen Negro soldiers been lynched on the broadest street of Brownsville in broad daylight, neither the Army inspector, nor the President's law officer, nor the Senate committee could have found a single citizen who was able to see such happenings under the bright sunlight of a Texas sky. These same citizens with farsighted vision in the gloom of night would have developed suddenly a case of myopia that could not distinguish objects of their own handling in open day. The rule works both ways. A witness who will not see that which he does not want to see can easily compound for the failure by seeing things which do not exist, in obedience to the demand of prejudice or passion.

As the matter now stands before the bar of public opinion, this black battalion is at least entitled to a Scotch verdict—"not proven." There is all but a universal concurrence in this verdict except among those whose racial sentiment renders them incapable of considering the case with judicial calmness and poise. But whatever may finally be proved as to the guilt or innocence of some or all of these men, they have not received a "square deal"* at the hands of its author, who borrowed the phrase from the gaming table and consecrated it to a higher and worthier ideal.

This affair has shaken the prestige of the President as has no other occurrence in his public career. It gives him no end of keen concern. There is every reason to believe that he could wish the deed undone. He has sought to conciliate the Negro

* The "Square Deal" was Theodore Roosevelt's program on assuming the Presidency. He announced he intended neither to harass industry nor to pamper it, but to carry out the law.

with the blandishment of office, but to no avail. With the double view of disconcerting Foraker and reconciling the colored brother, at the psychological moment, when the Ohio Senator was booked to make a strategic move in the Brownsville affair, announcement was made of the intention to appoint a colored citizen to the leading federal office in the Senator's own state and home city. But as this move seemed to embarrass the President's own friends, including his son-in-law, as much as it did the offending Senator, it was abandoned. But not to be outdone, on the day of the evening that Senator Foraker was announced to sound the keynote of his position in a speech to his constituents, the Associated Press announced to the country that Ralph W. Tyler, a worthy colored citizen of Ohio, had been appointed Auditor of the Treasury Department at Washington. But this conspicuous appointment had not the slightest effect upon racial sentiment, except to intensify it against the the President. A nice young man got a nice fat office without changing the attitude of a single Negro in or out of Ohio. The whole race is wounded and sore. There is no division of sentiment. Never before has there been such unanimity. The balm of office cannot heal it. Even the colored members of the President's official household can only preserve a prudent and salutary silence.

There has recently appeared a cartoon by a clever Negro artist representing the "Black Man's Burden." It is in the form of a cross, not a crown of thorns, but a cross of skulls. At the top of the vertical upright is the head of Roosevelt; Hoke Smith and Tom Watson are arranged underneath; on the left of the crosspiece are Thomas Dixon* and John Temple Graves; on the right Tillman and Vardaman.† An athletic Negro with broken body is bowed beneath this awful load. Theodore Roosevelt, America's most passionate civil patriot, whose every impulse beats in sympathetic resonance with the welfare and betterment of the nation, who had stood firmly by the Negro at Charleston and Indianola,‡ and who had proclaimed to the race the gospel

* Thomas Dixon was the author of numerous violently anti-Negro writings, one of which, *The Clansman*, became the basis for the racist motion picture *The Birth of a Nation*.
† Hoke Smith, Tom Watson, Benjamin R. Tillman and J. K. Vardaman were outstanding Southern white racists and open advocates of Negro disfranchisement and segregation.
‡ Roosevelt appointed William D. Crum, a leading Negro citizen, to the Collectorship of the Port of Charleston, South Carolina, and when Southerners objected, he declared that unless some valid reason other than color could be brought forward against Crum, the appointment would stand.
When the Negro postmistress at Indianola, Mississippi, resigned be-

of a "square deal" and an open door is placed as chief among those who breathe out hatred and slaughter against the Negro with every vital breath. It is the law of human passion that friendship which lapses or seems to lapse begets the bitterest hate. The good deeds are forgotten; the hurtful act rankles in the soul. A deliberate and candid judgment would declare this attitude unjust; but it would be equally uncandid to deny that it is real.

President Roosevelt is easily the most popular man in America. The whites who join issue with him on the Brownsville incident regard it as a thing apart. With the Negro it overshadows all else. With a consenting nod he can be reelected President almost by acclamation. Not only so, but he is easily the foremost man of all the world today. Should the Peace Congress now sitting at the Hague usher in Tennyson's prophesied "Parliament of man, the Federation of the world," Roosevelt, by unanimous consent of the participating nations, would be chosen speaker of this world-controlling body. And yet he has so wounded his colored fellow citizens that today they stand apart from this world acclaim. As he treads the dizzy highway of universal fame, he must feel a certain sad, unsatisfied something prompting him to become reconciled to his black brother who may justly have aught against him.

THE VALUE OF AGITATION

By W. E. B. Du Bois

Scholar and educator, Dr. W. E. B. Du Bois was the most prominent figure in the Negro struggle for equal rights in the first part of the twentieth century and the leading opponent of Booker T. Washington's ideology of accommodation. Dr. Du Bois was born in Great Barrington, Massachusetts, February 23, 1868. He grew up in an environment almost free of racial prejudice. He attended the local high school and at his graduation delivered an oration on

---

cause of pressure of the white citizens of the town, Roosevelt ordered the Post Office Department to refuse to accept her resignation, and when she would not serve, the post office was closed. Even though the office was later reopened with a white postmaster in charge, Negroes hailed Roosevelt for his action in the Indianola affair.

*the great Abolitionist Wendell Phillips. His one ambition
was to go to Harvard College, but his family's funds could
only provide enough for him to attend Fisk, a Negro university in Nashville, Tennessee. He spent his summers
teaching in a rural school in Tennessee, where he learned
at first hand the shocking conditions of the Southern Negro. Obtaining a grant from Harvard, Du Bois went to
Cambridge for two years, received his bachelor's degree
from Harvard College, and then spent two more years in
the Graduate School as a Fellow in History and Political
Science. Another grant took him to the University of Berlin, and on his return to the United States, he taught
Latin, Greek, German, and English and Sociology at Wilberforce College. In 1896 the University of Pennsylvania
offered him an appointment to conduct a one-year study of
Negro life in the city of Philadelphia.* The Philadelphia
Negro—*as the completed report was titled*—*was the first
work in urban sociology in the United States. It was published by the University of Pennsylvania Press. Simultaneously, Harvard University honored Du Bois by publishing his doctoral dissertation,* The Suppression of the
African Slave Trade to America, *as the first volume in a
projected series of Harvard Historical Studies.*

*Invited by Atlanta University to teach in its new soci-
ology department, Dr. Du Bois went to Georgia, developed at the university a body of trained black sociologists,
and launched the publication of the Atlanta University
studies of problems of the Negro. In 1903 Dr. Du Bois published his great work,* The Souls of Black Folk. *Among the
essays was one dealing with Booker T. Washington. While
avoiding a direct attack upon the leading Negro figure in
the country, Du Bois wrote that the long-range results of
Washington's philosophy of education and accommodation were proving disastrous to the Negro people. On July
9, 1905, to reverse this trend, Du Bois issued a call to a
select list of black Americans to a meeting that led to the
formation of the Niagara Movement, the first important
Negro protest movement since the rise of Washington to
prominence.*

*"We claim for ourselves every single right that belongs
to a freeborn American, political, civil and social; and until we get these rights we will never cease to protest and
assail the ears of America," Dr. Du Bois wrote in the Niagara Address of 1906. The militant tone of the statement
alarmed large sections of the press accustomed to the ac-*

commodating language of Booker T. Washington, and Du Bois was denounced as "an agitator." His reply came a year later in a speech which was published in The Voice of the Negro *(Vol. IV, March, 1907). It is as valid today as when it was first delivered.*

THERE ARE those people in the world who object to agitation and one cannot wholly blame them. Agitation, after all, is unpleasant. It means that while you are going peaceably and joyfully on your way some half-mad person insists upon saying things that you do not like to hear. They may be true, but you do not like to hear them. You would rather wait till some convenient season; or you take up your newspaper and instead of finding pleasant notices about your friends and the present progress of the world, you read of some restless folks who insist on talking about wrong and crime and unpleasant things. It would be much better if we did not have to have agitation; if we had a world where everything was going so well and it was unnecessary often to protest strongly, even wildly, of the evil and the wrong of the universe. As a matter of fact, however, no matter how unpleasant the agitator is, and no matter how inconvenient and unreasonable his talk, yet we must ever have him with us. And why? Because this is a world where things are not all right. We are gifted with human nature, which does not do the right or even desire the right always. So long as these things are true, then we are faced by this dilemma: either we must let the evil alone and refuse to hear of it or listen to it or we must try and right it. Now, very often it happens that the evil is there, the wrong has been done, and yet we do not hear of it—we do not know about it. Here then comes the agitator. He is the herald—he is the prophet—he is the man that says to the world: "There are evils which you do not know; but which I know, and you must listen to them." Now, of course, there may be agitators who are telling the truth and there may be agitators who are telling untruths. Those who are not telling the truth may be lying or they may be mistaken. So that agitation in itself does not necessarily mean always the right and always reform.

Here, then, is some one who thinks that he has discovered some dangerous evil and wants to call the attention of good men of the world to it. If he does not persevere, we may perhaps pass him by. If he is easily discouraged, we may perhaps think that the evil which he thought he saw has been cured. But if he is sincere and if he is persistent, then there is but one thing for a person to do who wants to live in a world worth living in; that is, listen to him carefully, prove his tale and then try and right the wrong.

If we remember the history of all great reform movements, we remember that they have been preceded by agitation. Take, for instance, the suppression of the slave trade. It was in a day when slavery could not be successfully attacked. But there was no doubt of the horrors of the slave trade. The best and worst of people alike admitted that. Here came a young man just graduated from college. By writing a prize essay he found himself interested in this great evil. He began to know and learn of things which other people did not know. Not that they knew nothing about them, but they had not brought together all the facts. One isolated person knew that fact and one knew this fact, but no one person knew both facts in juxtaposition. When they did become acquainted with all the facts he was sure that they must be moved to act. What then must he do? He must agitate. It was not pleasant—it was putting himself in jeopardy; he was called upon to lose friends in some cases, and in all cases to make himself unpleasant, insistent, persistent, telling of things that people did not want to hear about, because they were not interested in them. He must interest people in things in which they were not interested before, which is a hard task in this busy world; and yet, nevertheless, if Clarkson* had not persisted, we would have much less than a chance to agitate for human rights today.

So it is with all great movements. They must be preceded by agitation. In the present status of the Negro it is particularly necessary that we today make the world realize what his position is—make them realize that he is not merely insisting on ornamental rights, and neglecting plain duties, but that the rights we want are the rights that are necessary, inevitable before we can rightly do our duties.

Mrs. Gilman† has a poem somewhere, where she speaks of that rule which is to be laid down in the great future state, "Un-

---

* Thomas Clarkson (1760–1846), pioneer British abolitionist, was active for over sixty years with William Wilberforce in the battle against slavery and the slave trade. Clarkson's interest in abolition was aroused during his student days at St. John's College, Cambridge. His Latin essay, "Is it right to make men slaves against their will?" brought him into contact with Granville Sharp and Wilberforce, and into the ranks of the movement for the universal abolition of the slave trade and the universal freeing of slaves.

† Mrs. Charlotte P. Gilman (1860–1955), an influential woman suffragist and reformer, was the author of Women and Economics (1898), Concerning Children (1900), and The Man-Made World (1910).

less a man works, he may not eat," and she says very aptly that "the cart is before the horse," because "unless a man eats he cannot work." So to those people who are saying to black men today, "Do your duties first, and then clamor for rights," we have a right to answer and to answer insistently, that the rights we are clamoring for are those that will enable us to do our duties. That we cannot possibly be asked to do any partial measure of our duty even, unless we can have those rights and have them now. We realize this. The great mass of people in the United States do not realize it. What then are we to do? We may sit in courteous and dumb self-forgetting silence until other people are interested and come to our rescue. But is it reasonable to suppose that this is going to happen before degeneration and destruction overtake us? This is a busy world. People are attending to their own affairs as they ought to. The man that has a grievance is supposed to speak for himself. No one can speak for him—no one knows the thing as well as he does. Therefore it is reasonable to say that if the man does not complain that it is because he has no complaint. If a man does not express his needs, then it is because his needs are filled. And it has been our great mistake in the last decade that we have been silent and still and have not complained when it was our duty not merely to ourselves but to our country and to humanity in general to complain and to complain loudly. It is, then, high time that the Negro agitator should be heard in the land.

It is not a pleasant role to play. It is not always pleasant to nice ears to hear a man ever coming with his dark facts and unpleasant conditions. Nevertheless it is the highest optimism to bring forward the dark side of any human picture. When a man does this he says to the world, "Things are bad, but it is worthwhile to let the world know that things are bad in order that they may become better." The real crushing pessimism takes hold of the world when people say things are so bad that they are not worth complaining of, because they cannot be made better.

It is manifest that within the last year the whole race in the United States has awakened to the fact that they have lost ground and must start complaining and complain loudly. It is their business to complain.

This complaint should be made with reason and with strict regard to the truth, but nevertheless it should be made. And it is interesting to find even those persons who were deriding complaint a few years ago joining in the agitation today.

We of Niagara Movement welcome them. We are glad of help from all sources. We are confirmed in our belief that if a man stand up and tell the thing he wants and point out the evil around him, that this is the best way to get rid of it. May we not hope, then, that we are going to have in the next century a solid front on the part of colored people in the United States saying we want education for our children and we do not have it today in any large measure; we want full political rights, and we never have had that; we want to be treated as human beings; and we want those of our race who stand on the threshold and within the veil of crime to be treated not as beasts, but as men who can be reformed or as children who can be prevented from going further in their career.

If we all stand and demand this insistently, the nation must listen to the voice of ten millions.

EQUALITY OF RIGHTS FOR ALL CITIZENS, BLACK AND WHITE ALIKE

By Francis J. Grimké

Francis James Grimké (1850–1937) was a famous Negro clergyman of the early twentieth century. Like his equally famous brother, Archibald H. Grimké, he was born near Charleston, the son of Henry Grimké, a South Carolina planter, and Nancy Weston, a beautiful slave. With his brother he attended a school conducted for children of free colored people of Charleston and, after the Civil War, a school for colored children opened by Gilbert Pillsbury, a Northern Abolitionist, who became Charleston's Reconstruction mayor. He and his brother then went North to attend Lincoln University, at Oxford, Pennsylvania. After graduation from Lincoln University, Francis J. Grimké went on to become a leading clergyman in Washington, D. C.

In a fiery sermon delivered on November 20, 1898, Reverend Mr. Grimké had denounced black spokesmen who advocated acquiescence to the "shot-gun policy" of the white South, and predicted that as long as there was a single Negro alive in the United States, the struggle against white supremacy would continue. "As long as there is one manly, self-respecting Negro in this country, the agitation will go on, will never cease until right is triumphant" (*Richmond [Virginia]* Planet, *November 26, 1898*). Here is an excerpt from a discourse delivered by the Reverend Mr. Grimké in 1909. It is taken from Francis James Grimké, Equality of Rights for All Citizens, Black and White Alike. A Discourse Delivered in the Fifteenth Presbyterian Church, Washington, D. C., Sunday, March 7th, 1909, *Washington, 1909*.

. . . IN THE SCHEME of citizenship of our country for years following the close of the war the Negro had no part; and he had no part because he was looked upon as an inferior. "Subordination to the superior race is declared to be his natural and moral condition." His inferiority was asserted to be a "great physical, philosophical and moral truth."

And this is exactly the Southern view today and is exactly the program to which it is committed. Its whole attitude today is in harmony with the great principle upon which the Southern Confederacy was founded—the non-recognition of the Negro as an equal in any respect—socially, civilly, politically. The South holds to this view just as tenaciously today as it did when Mr. Stephens made his Great Cornerstone Speech in 1861. The Ku Klux Klan, the White Caps, the Red Shirt Brigade, tissue ballots,* the revised constitutions with their grandfather clauses,† Jim-Crow-car legislation,‡ the persistent effort of the South to

* The Ku Klux Klan, White Caps, Red Shirts Brigade were all set up in the South during Reconstruction to reestablish white supremacy. The Ku Klux Klan operated all over the South. The White Caps functioned in Louisiana and Mississippi; and the Red Shirts, led by Wade Hampton in South Carolina, advocated "force without violence," but actually used terror and fraud.

Tissue ballots were ballots printed upon thin tissue paper which were given to a voter for the Democratic ticket and which enabled him to cast more than one vote. They were invariably used to defeat candidates friendly to the blacks.

† The grandfather clause was a device developed in the Southern states in the late 1890's and early 1900's to deprive the Negro of the suffrage, despite the guarantees given him by the Fifteenth Amendment to the Constitution. Voters who were unable to prove that they were descendants of persons who voted prior to the Civil War or prior to 1867, when Congressional Reconstruction went into operation, thus including the bulk of Southern Negroes, were required to pay poll and property taxes and meet educational provisions before being allowed to vote. The grandfather clause was declared unconstitutional by the Supreme Court in 1915.

‡ The system of racial segregation was established legally through the passage of Jim Crow laws by one Southern state after another between

disfranchise the Negro—all these things have grown out of the idea that the rightful place of the Negro is that of subordination to the white man, that he has no rightful place in the body politic.

But I cannot believe that the nation is always going to leave its loyal black citizens to be despoiled of their civil and political rights by the men who sought to destroy the Union. A better day is coming, and coming soon, I trust.

While we are waiting, however, for the nation to come to its senses—waiting for a revival of the spirit of justice and of true democracy in the land—it is important for us to remember that much, very much, will depend upon ourselves. In the passage of Scripture read in our hearing at the beginning of this discourse, three things we are exhorted to do, and must do, if we are ever to secure our rights in this land:

1. We are exhorted to be watchful. "Watch ye," is the exhortation. We are to be on our guard. "Eternal vigilance is the price of liberty." There are enemies ever about us and are ever plotting our ruin—enemies within the race and without it. We have got to live in the consciousness of this fact. If we assume that all is well, that there is nothing to fear, and so relax our vigilance, so cease to be watchful, we need not be surprised if our enemies get the better of us, if we are worsted in the conflict.

2. We are exhorted to stand fast in the faith—in the faith we feel that, as American citizens, we are entitled to the same rights and privileges as other citizens of the Republic. In this faith we are to stand, and stand fast. We are not to give it up; we are not to allow anyone, white or black, friend or foe, to induce us to retreat a single inch from this position.

3. We are exhorted to quit ourselves like men, to be strong. And by this, I understand, is meant that we are to stand up in a manly way for our rights; that we are to seek by every honorable means the full enjoyment of our rights. It is still true—

Who would be free himself must strike the blow.

And, if we are ever to be free from invidious distinctions in this country, based upon race, color, previous condition, we have got to be alive, wide-awake to our own interest. If we are not, we have no right to expect others to be; we have no right to expect anything but failure, but defeat. And we deserve defeat if ours

1870 and 1917. Under these laws the color line marked off restaurants, theaters, beaches, saloons, schools, courts and cemeteries. There were Jim Crow Bibles to swear on in Atlanta courts, Jim Crow cemeteries for dogs in Washington, Jim Crow textbooks in Florida.

is the spirit of indifference, of unconcern. We are not going to secure our rights in this land without a struggle. We have got to contend, and contend earnestly, for what belongs to us. Victory isn't coming in any other way. No silent acquiescence on our part in the wrongs from which we are suffering, contrary to law; no giving of ourselves merely to the work of improving our condition, materially, intellectually, morally, spiritually, however zealously pursued, is going to bring relief. We have got, in addition to the effort we are making to improve ourselves, to keep up the agitation, and keep it up until right triumphs and wrong is put down. A program of silence on the part of the race is a fool's program. Reforms, changes in public sentiment, the righting of wrongs, are never effected in that way; and our wrongs will never be. A race that sits quietly down and rests in sweet content in the midst of the wrongs from which it is suffering is not worth contending for, is not worth saving.

This is not true of this race, however. We are not sitting down in sweet content, let it be said to our credit. I thank God from the bottom of my heart for these mutterings of discontent that are heard in all parts of the land. The fact that we are dissatisfied with present conditions, and that we are becoming more and more so, shows that we are growing in manhood, in self-respect, in the qualities that will enable us to win out in the end. It is our duty to keep up the agitation for our rights, not only for our sakes, but also for the sake of the nation at large. It would not only be against our own interest not to do so, but it would be unpatriotic for us quietly to acquiesce in the present condition of things, for it is a wrong condition of things. If justice sleeps in this land, let it not be because we have helped to lull it to sleep by our silence, our indifference; let it not be from lack of effort on our part to arouse it from its slumbers. Elijah said to the prophets of Baal, while they were crying to their god, "Peradventure he sleepeth." And it may be that he was asleep; but it was not their fault that he continued asleep, for they kept up a continual uproar about his altar. And so here, sleeping Justice in this land may go on slumbering, but let us see to it that it is due to no fault of ours. Even Balaam's ass cried out in protest when smitten by his brutal master, and God gave him the power to cry out, endowed him miraculously with speech in which to voice his protest.

It is not necessary for God to work a miracle to enable us to protest against our wrong; He has already given us the power. Let us see to it that we use it. If we are wise we will be able to take care of ourselves. If we are not wise, however, if we adopt the policy of silence, and if we continue to feel that it is our duty to follow blindly, slavishly, any one political party, we will receive only such treatment as is accorded to slaves, and will go on pleading for our rights in vain. The only wise course for us to pursue is to keep on agitating, and to cast our votes where they will tell most for the race. As to what party we affiliate with is a matter of no importance whatever; the important thing is our rights. And until we recognize that fact, and act upon it, we will be the football of all political parties. John Boyle O'Reilly,* in speaking on the race question years ago, said: "If I were a colored man I should use parties as I would a club —to break down prejudice against my people. I shouldn't talk about being true to any party, except so far as that party was true to me. Parties care nothing for you, only to use you. You should use parties; the highest party you have in this country is your own manhood. That is the thing in danger from all parties; that is the thing that every colored man is bound in duty to himself and his children to defend and protect." And that is good advice. It embodies the highest political wisdom for us as a people.

The exhortation of the text is, "Watch ye, stand fast in the faith, quit you like men, be strong." And this is the message that I bring to you who are here this morning, and to the members of our race all over the country. We must be watchful; we must hold firmly to our faith in our citizenship, and in our rights as citizens; and we must act the part of men in the maintenance of those rights. In the end the victory is sure to be ours. The right is bound, sooner or later, to triumph.

> Before the monstrous wrong he sits him down—.
> One man against a stone-walled city of sin.
> For centuries those walls have been a-building;
> Smooth porphyry, they slope and coldly glass
> The flying storm and wheeling sun.
>
> No chinks, no crevice, lets the thinnest arrow in.
> He fights alone, and from the cloudy ramparts
> A thousand evil faces gibe and jeer him.
> Let him lie down and die; what is the right
> And where is justice in a world like this?

* John Boyle O'Reilly, a Boston Irish nationalist and Roman Catholic, was a champion of the rights of workers, immigrants, Jews, Indians and Negroes. His paper, the Boston *Pilot*, spoke out repeatedly in behalf of black Americans from Reconstruction through the 1880's.

But by and by earth shakes herself, impatient;
And down, in one great roar of ruin, crash
Watch-tower and citadel and battlements.
When the red dust has cleared, the lonely soldier
Stands with strange thoughts beneath the friendly stars.

And so, in the end, will it be with this great evil of race prejudice against which we are contending in this country, if, like the lonely soldier, we show the same earnestness, the same patient determination, the same invincible courage. A better day is coming; but we have got to help bring it about. It isn't coming independently of our efforts, and it isn't coming by quietly, timidly, cowardly acquiescing in our wrongs.

POLITICS AND INDUSTRY

By W. E. B. Du Bois

A race riot in Springfield, Illinois, home and burial place of Abraham Lincoln, in August, 1908, set in motion the issuance of a call by fifty-three people, including six black Americans, for a national conference on the Negro question to be held in New York City on May 31 and June 1, 1909. This was the initial public meeting that led a year later to the formation of the National Association for the Advancement of Colored People. Dr. Du Bois signed the call for the conference and read two papers at the sessions. Here is the first of these papers. (Text is from the Proceedings of the National Negro Conference, New York, May 31 and June 1, 1909, pp. 79–86.)

IN DISCUSSING NEGRO SUFFRAGE we must remember that in the three hundred years between the settlement of this country and the present, there never has been a time when it was not legal for a Negro to vote in some considerable part of this land. From 1700 to 1909 Negroes have probably cast their ballots at some time in every single state of the Union, and all the time in some states, and there has been no period in the history of the land when all Negroes were disfranchised. The early movement for disfranchisement came in two waves: the first, early in the eighteenth century, when Negro freedmen first appeared with required qualifications for voting. In this case Negroes, along with Jews and Catholics, were deprived of a vote. This initial movement was persisted in only in South Carolina and Georgia. In all other states, South and North, it subsided, and Negroes regularly voted in nearly every other state. Then came a second wave of disfranchisement in the North, about the beginning of the nineteenth century, which had the same object as the disfranchisement clauses in the Western states early in the next century—namely, to discourage and drive out free Negroes. The third wave of disfranchisement came in the South about 1830 and marked the end of the abolition movement there, and the beginning of the cotton kingdom. The population of free Negroes began to decrease and the complete subjection of the black race was in sight.

The last wave of disfranchisement began in 1890 in Mississippi and now embraces Virginia, North Carolina and the Gulf States excepting Florida and Texas. These states have adopted four kinds of qualifications: 1. educational qualifications; 2. property qualifications; 3. qualifications of birth; 4. other miscellaneous qualifications the effect of which depends entirely on local election officials. These qualifications have been proposed with two reasons: (a) to keep the Negroes from voting; (b) to eliminate the ignorant electorate.

Against both these excuses there were strong arguments, but at the time they were gathering force and momentum there came a counter argument that practically stopped all effective opposition to the disfranchisement laws. This argument was that the economic development of the Negro in right lines demanded his exclusion from the right of suffrage at least for the present. This proposition his been insisted on so strenuously and advocated by Negroes of such prominence that it simply took the wind out of the sails of those who had proposed defending his rights, and today so deeply has this idea been driven that to most readers' minds the Negroes of the land are divided into two great parties—one asking no political rights but giving all attention to economic growth; and the other wanting votes, higher education and all rights. Moreover, the phrase "take the Negro out of politics" has come to be regarded as synonymous with industrial training and property-getting by the black men.

I want in this short paper to show that, in my opinion, both these propositions are wrong and mischievous. In the first place, there is no such division of opinion among Negroes as is assumed. They are practically a unit in their demand for the ballot. The real difference of opinion comes as to how the ballot is to be gained. One set of opinions favors open, frank agitation. The other favors influence and diplomacy; and the result, curious to say, is that the latter party has today an organized political machine which dictates the distribution of offices among black men and sometimes among Southern whites. It is not too much to say that today the political power of the black race in America is in certain restricted lines very considerable. But those of us who oppose this party hold that this kind of political development by secrecy and machine methods is both dangerous and unwholesome and is not leading toward real democracy. It may, and undoubtedly does, put a large number of black men in office and it lessens momentary friction, but it is encouraging a coming economic conflict which will threaten the South and the Negro race.

And this brings me to the second proposition: that political power in the hands of the Negro would hinder economic development. It is untrue that any appreciable number of black men today forget or slur over the tremendous importance of economic uplift among Negroes. Every intelligent person knows that the most pressing problem of any people suddenly emancipated from slavery is the problem of regular work and accumulated property. But this problem of work and property is no simple thing—it is complicated of many elements. It is not simply a matter of manual dexterity but includes the spirit and the ideal back of that dexterity.

We who have to build firmly the strong foundations of a racial economy believe in vocational training, but we also believe that the vocation of a man in a modern civilized land includes not only the technique of his actual work but intelligent comprehension of his elementary duties as a father, citizen, and maker of public opinion, as a possible voter, a conserver of the public health, an intelligent follower of moral customs, and one who can at least appreciate if not partake something of the higher spiritual life of the world. We do not pretend that all of this can be taught each individual in school but it can be put into his social environment, and the more that environment is curtailed and restricted the more emphatic is the demand that some part at least of the group shall be trained and trained thoroughly in these higher matters of human development, if—and here is the crucial question—if they are going to be able to share the surrounding civilization.

This brings us to the matter of voting. It is possible—easily possible—to train a working class who shall have no right to participate in the government. Most of the manual workers in the history of the world have been so trained. It is also possible, and the modern world thinks desirable, to train a working class who shall also have the right to vote—both these things are possible although the overwhelming trend of modern thought is toward making workers voters. But the one thing that is impossible, and proven so again and again, is to train two sets of workers side by side in economic competition and make one set voters and deprive the other set of all participation in government. To attempt this is madness. It invites conflict and oppression. A nation cannot exist half slave and half free. Either the slave will rise through blood or the freeman will sink.

So far, tremendous effort in the South has been put forth to keep down economic competition between the races by confining the Negroes by law and custom to certain vocations. But, for two reasons, this effort is bound to break down: first, there is no caste of ability corresponding with the caste of color; and secondly, because if every Negro in the South worked twenty-four hours a day at the kinds of work which are tacitly assigned him, he could not fill the demand for that kind of labor. Economic competition is therefore inevitable as facts like these show: In Alabama there are 94,000 Negro farm laborers and 82,000 whites. In Georgia there are 1,100 Negro barbers and 275 white barbers. In Florida there are 2,100 Negroes employed on railroads and 1,500 whites. In Tennessee there are 1,000 white masons and 1,200 black masons. And so on we might go through endless figures showing that economic competition among whites and blacks was not only existent but growing.

Moreover the schools that increase the competition are the industrial schools and this is both natural and proper. Negro professional men, teachers, physicians and artists come very seldom in competition with the whites. But farmers, masons, painters, carpenters, seamstresses and shoe repairers work at the same work as whites and largely under like conditions. This competition accentuates race prejudice; when a whole community, a whole nation, pours contempt on a fellow man it seems a personal insult for that man to work beside me or at the same kind of work. Thus, one of the first results of the denial of civil rights is industrial jealousy and hatred. Here is a man who, all my companions say, is unworthy and dangerous as a companion on the streetcar or steam car, as a fellow listener at a concert, theater or lecture, as a table companion in the same house or restaurant, often as a dweller in the same street or same neighborhood and always as a worshiper in the same church or occupant of the same graveyard. If all this is so—and this the Southern white workingman is industriously taught from the cradle to the grave—if this is so, then why should I be forced to work at the same job or be engaged in similar kinds of work, or receive the same wages? If we cannot play together why should we work together?

Not only is there this feeling, but there is also power to act. After the Atlanta riot* the police and militia searched the houses of colored people and took away guns and ammunition; while the sheriff almost gave away guns to some of the very men who had composed the mob. We think this monstrous, but it is but a parallel of the action of the whole nation. They have put the ballot in the hands of the white workingmen of the South and taken it away from the black fellow workmen. The result is that the white workman can enforce his feelings of prejudice and repulsion. Other things being equal the employer is forced to discharge the black man and hire the white man— public opinion demands it, the administrators of government, including police, magistrates, et cetera, render it easier, since by preferring the white many intricate questions of social contact are avoided and political influence is vastly increased.

Under such circumstances there is nothing for the Negro to do but to bribe the employer by underbidding his white fellow; to work not only for less money wages, but for longer hours and under worse conditions. No sooner does he do this than he is mocked as a "scab" from Mexico to Canada, and visited with all the consequent penalties. He is said to be taking bread from others' mouths, and he may be, but his excuse is tremendous: he is dragging others down to keep himself from complete submergence and he is taking some of the bread from others' mouths lest his children starve. Does he *want* to do this? Does he like long hours? Ignorant as he is as a mass, has he not intelligence enough to perceive the value of the labor unions and the meaning of the labor movement? No, it is not because the black man is a fool but because he is a victim that he drags labor down.

Faced by this situation, the next step of the white workmen is to enforce by law and administration that which they cannot gain by competition. In the past these laws have been laws to separate and humiliate the blacks, but more aggressive laws are demanded today and will be in the future. The Alabama child-labor law excepts from its operation children in domestic service and in agriculture—that is, Negro children. *They* may grow up in absolute ignorance, so far as the law is concerned.

* Dr. Du Bois was in Alabama when the riot broke out, and he hastened home to his family in Atlanta. En route, he wrote his magnificent "Litany at Atlanta."

The Alabama law makes the breaking of a contract to work by a farm laborer a felony punishable by a penitentiary sentence. Such a breaking of law in other industries is a misdemeanor punishable by a fine. Certain oppressive labor regulations in many Southern states are only applicable to such counties as vote their enforcement. Counties with white workmen vote it down. Counties with disfranchised black workmen vote it in. In the state civil service no Negro can be employed at any job which any white man wants, for obvious reasons. More than that, no white man whose business depends on public approbation or political concession can dare to hire Negroes or, if he hires them, promote them as they deserve. He must often be content with a distinctly inferior grade of white help.

Judges and juries in the South are at the absolute mercy of the white voters. Few ordinary judges would dare oppose the momentary whim of the white mob and practically only now and then will a jury convict a white man for aggression on a Negro. This is true not only in criminal but also in civil suits— so much so that it is a widespread custom among Negroes of property never to take a civil suit to court but to let the white complainant settle it. In all public benefits like schools and parks and gatherings and institutions, Negroes are regularly taxed for what they cannot enjoy. I am taxed for the Carnegie Public Library of Atlanta where I cannot enter to draw my own books. The Negroes of Memphis are taxed for public parks where they cannot sit down. . . .

Even in serving his own people and organizing his own business the Negro is at the absolute mercy of the white voters. It is often said grandiloquently: let the Negroes organize their own theaters, transport their own passengers, organize their own industrial companies; but such kinds of businesses are almost absolutely dependent on public license and taxation requirements. A theater built and equipped could by a single vote be refused a license, a transportation company could get no franchise, and an industrial enterprise could be taxed out of existence. This is not always done, but it is done just as soon as any white man or group of white men begin to feel the competition. Then the voters proceed to put the industrial screws on the disfranchised. Witness the strike of the white locomotive firemen in Georgia today. Negro firemen get from fifty cents to one dollar a day less than the white firemen and have to do menial work and cannot become engineers. They can, however, by good service and behavior, be promoted to the best runs by the rule of seniority. Even this the white firemen now object to and say in a manifesto: the "white people of this state refuse to accept Negro equality. This is worse than that." The other day the white automobile drivers of Atlanta made a frantic appeal in the papers for persons to stop hiring black drivers. The black drivers replied, "We have had fewer accidents than you and get less wages," but the whites simply said, "This ought to be a white man's job."

This sort of thing is destined to grow and develop. The fear of Negro competition in all lines is increasing in the South. The demand of tomorrow is going to be increasingly not to protect white people from ignorance and degradation, but from knowledge and efficiency—that is, to so arrange the matter by law and custom as to make it possible for the inefficient and lazy white workman to be able to crush and keep down his black competitor at all hazards, and so that no black man shall be allowed to do his best if his success lifts him to any degree out of the place in which millions of Americans are being taught he ought to stay.

This is bad enough, but this is not all. The voteless Negro is a provocation, an invitation to oppression, a plaything for mobs and a bonanza for demagogues. They serve always to distract attention from real issues and to ride fools and rascals into political power. The political campaign in Georgia before the last was avowedly and openly a campaign not against Negro crime and ignorance, but against Negro intelligence and property owning and industrial competition as shown by an 83 percent increase in their property in ten years.

It swept the state and if it had not culminated in riot and bloodshed and thus scared capital, it would still be triumphant. As it is, the end is not yet. The political power of a mass of active working people thus without votes is greater for harm, manipulation and riot than the power of the same people with votes could possibly be, with the additional fact that voters would learn to vote intelligently by voting. Fourteen years ago Mississippi began disfranchising Negroes. You were promised that the result would be to settle the Negro problem. Is it settled? No, and it never will be until you give black men the power to be men, until you give them the power to defend that manhood. When the Negro casts a free and intelligent vote in the South, then, and not until then, will the Negro problem be settled.

RACE PREJUDICE AS VIEWED FROM AN ECONOMIC STANDPOINT

By William L. Bulkley

Dr. William Lewis Bulkley, the leading Negro educator in New York City in the early twentieth century, was born a slave in Greenville, South Carolina, in 1861. As a boy he attended the local log-cabin school and was graduated from Claflin University, in his home state, in 1882. He attended Wesleyan University, in Connecticut, and continued his studies in France and Germany. In 1893 he received his Ph.D. degree at Syracuse University. For a time he taught as professor of Latin and Greek at Claflin University, but moved to New York City in the 1890's and was appointed seventh-grade teacher in a lower-Manhattan public school. In 1899 he became principal of Public School 80, on West Forty-first Street in the heart of the Negro district, and in 1909, despite protest meetings and petitions from the teachers of Public School 126, Bulkley became the first Negro principal of a predominantly white school in the history of American cities. Bulkley supported the program of W. E. B. Du Bois and became a founder of the N.A.A.C.P. Together with Mary White Ovington, a white Socialist interested in the Negro cause, in 1906 he founded the Committee for Improving the Industrial Condition of the Negro in New York, which later became one of the organizations that merged to form the National Urban League.

Here is Dr. Bulkley's speech at the 1909 National Negro Conference. The text is taken from the Proceedings of the Conference, *pp. 89–97.*

I WISH to preface my argument with the following indictment: Race prejudice in the South (1) does not recognize the value of an intelligent, contented laboring class; (2) closes the door to occupations requiring skill and responsibility; (3) drives out of the South, by humiliating and oppressive laws and practices, many of its most desirable citizens; (4) forces across the line thousands of mixed-blood; (5) forces into the ranks of unskilled labor in the North and West many who are skilled.

Considering the race question from a purely economic stand-point, no part of this country, North, South, East or West, ought to continue the unjust industrial restrictions upon us as a people. In the North these restrictions act as an injustice to the weaker race, but do not cause any perceptible economic loss to the community. In the South, on the contrary, any limitation put upon the development of the Negro in any line of manual labor or skill seriously affects its economic development. Already is this loss to its industrial life evident in the desperate efforts to induce European immigration. But the suggestion that this need of more and better labor is caused by her sins of omission or commission would doubtless meet from the South the most robust denials. And yet, any thoughtful student of economics would readily see that this lack of reliable labor is, at least in part, due to the absence of effort on the part of the South to enlighten, to encourage and to render contented its laboring classes. With the exception of a makeshift of a school lasting for a few weeks each year, the South offers its farming masses absolutely no other inducement to a larger and better life. Little wonder is it that there are hundreds of thousands of acres cultivated in the same sort of indifferent way year after year.

And again, from the ranks of skilled labor, race oppression is driving out of the South a host of the best Negroes, best in culture of mind, best in sturdiness of character, best in skill of hand. A census of the Negroes in any city in the North would show that the majority of the most progressive of them, whether in the professions, in business, or in the trades, were more or less recent arrivals from the South. Can the South afford to lose this class? Can any country afford to drive out its best? Does not the South need the influence of such men and women over the ignorant, the idle, or the depraved of our race? Is it wise to make living conditions so unbearable that only the most ignorant or the most unworthy are contented to remain and endure with the characteristic grin of a sycophant?

The desirable, the progressive, the intelligent Negroes who remain South are there for one of two reasons: because they can't get away; or because they feel they ought to stay and suffer with their own. And all these heave from the depths of their hearts the despairing cry, "How long, O Lord, how long?"

If only a small part of the time that is devoted to schemes to restrict, to humiliate and to oppress the Negroes were spent in an effort to study means by which they might be made more intelligent, more thrifty as laborers, more skillful as artisans, more content as citizens, there are few spots on the globe that would show so great an industrial awakening during the twentieth century.

Wise legislators in any community would endeavor to enact such laws or establish such customs as would develop a contented middle and a hopeful laboring class. Indeed, the North and West, with their attractive wages, with their excellent schools, libraries, reading rooms, clubs, and settlement houses, with a cordial welcome to full American citizenship, have beckoned invitingly the millions of Europeans that make the wealth of these great sections of our nation. During these same years another part of our land has spent its time in devising plans to keep down in dependence and hopelessness its millions of laborers, millions native to the soil, ready and willing to do whatever they are able for the development of the only land they know and the only land they care to know.

In the second place, there is a decided economic loss in keeping within the bounds of unskilled labor those who might do credit in the ranks of skilled labor; and yet that is what the South or any part of the country does when it inhibits and circumscribes the vocations of a part of its people. There are certain classes of skilled labor which it is not permitted a Negro to enter. In fact, my observation convinces me that even certain vocations which belonged almost exclusively to the Negroes ever since the days of slavery are fast being closed against them. The present railroad strike in Georgia illustrates this point.* Parenthetically I may say that due credit should be given to the papers, North and South, that have rung out with no uncertain sound about this strike; and yet it would seem impossible to counteract in one day in the year all the evil that these same papers do us in the other 364 days in written words or insinuations against us as a people. And so down the line there seems to be a purpose to restrict the Negroes within the limits of unskilled labor, to reduce them to a state which, while not nineteenth-century slavery may be twentieth-century peonage.

Thirdly, as was suggested previously, the humiliating laws and practices are forcing out of the South thousands of its best Negroes, Negroes who love their birthplace, love its balmy air, its sunny skies, its fertile fields, its luxuriant forests, the com-

---

* The strike on the Georgia railroads was caused by the refusal of white members of the Brotherhood of Firemen and the Brotherhood of Engineers to work with Negroes, and by their determination to force all black workers out of skilled jobs on the railroads.

radeship of their kith and kin. To us there never cease to come times of yearning to revisit the old spots of our childhood and of our youth, to meet our brethren, to hear their tale of woe, to weep with them over their distresses, to rejoice with them in their successes, to share with them the soul refreshings that only a Negro revival can give. How near they seem to get to the great loving heart of God in their deep, religious fervor, and childlike trustfulness! But when our yearning seizes us, there appears before us the spectral hand of blighting prejudice, inviting uninvitingly.

I never cease to wonder whether farsighted white men of the South see the loss in letting so many of their best Negroes leave; whether they ever think that it would be wise to abate their prejudices to the extent of consulting with us for some ground of mutual understanding and sympathy. It is too high a compliment to be credible that we have developed such a large class of desirables that the thousands who leave are easily spared. If a community seeks to acquire and to retain the largest possible number of upright, cultured, property-holding, progressive people, it should inquire into the causes that drive out and keep out this very class. But has there been a single act of a Southern legislature in thirty-five years aimed to render more comfortable the lot of that class of Negroes who, out of great tribulation, have struggled up and are still struggling up, and rearing their families into clean and commendable manhood and womanhood?

We are needed in the South, needed to help our brethren up, needed to give our white neighbors the assurance of our confidence, needed to join with all honest and earnest men for the regeneration of the land of our birth, scarred by slavery, blighted by the ravages of war, crippled by years of post-bellum misrule, hampered by narrow, nearsighted, selfish prejudice. There is not one of us who would not gladly go back home if we did not know that every right dear to any full man has been ruthlessly torn from our grasp. Gladly would we rush to the embrace of our loved ones in bonds, but we cannot, we cannot.*

In the fourth place, we do not get the full economic credit due to us, because of the loss of a host of mixed-bloods who cross the line. Even in the South this crossing occasionally happens. Sometimes the whites know it and wink at it, as was evidenced some time ago in the South Carolina State Consti-

* Bulkley was obviously referring to himself, too, since he considered himself a Southerner driven from his home by racism.

tutional Convention in a speech by Mr. Tillman, brother of Senator Tillman. There is scarcely a colored man who could not tell of some friend or relative who has crossed the line North or South, now prominent in business, professors in institutions of learning, married into good society, and rearing families that have no dreams of the depths that their parent has escaped. We could tell the story, if we would—but who would be the knave to disturb their peace?

Lastly, intolerance drives the ambitious, competent, skilled laborer out of the South, but in coming into the North, he meets an industrial competition which he had not figured on. Here he finds the field of skilled labor preempted by the native white man and the foreigner. They guard jealously all approaches to it, whether threatened by Negro or Japanese or Chinaman, or what not. The new arrival attributes to prejudice the difficulties he encounters. I can hardly believe that it is prejudice that keeps Negroes out of the industrial fields in the North as much as other reasons. Only today I was talking with a young man, a graduate of Hampton, who has worked his way up to a successful upholstery business in this city. He said, "I had a hard time at first, because people didn't believe a colored man could do upholstery work satisfactorily. Now that I have made good, I get plenty of work." I could weary you with numerous instances of this kind.

There are, as I see it, three chief reasons why we are not working easily into the skilled trades in the North: (1) skepticism as to our ability; (2) the already crowded labor market, that looks with disfavor upon inroads from any source; (3) a feeling, which I think is human—viz., the pleasure found in knocking the weaker fellow. Joseph Bernstein and Max Robinsky would not likely have any feeling against Jim Smith as a man; but as Joseph and Max have just come from a kicking themselves there may be some comfort in finding the chance to try the dose on another fellow. So Pat O'Flannagan does not have the least thing in the world against Jim from Dixie, but it didn't take Pat long after passing the Statue of Liberty to learn that it is popular to give Jim a whack. He would be a little more than human if he did not want to try on Jim what his English lord had so long tried on him. These people who have escaped the persecutions and the class proscriptions of Europe feel a newly awakened consciousness that they are not after all at the bottom of the heap. They would strike in like manner against any other individual, or religion, or language, or race, provided that they were prompted to it by prevailing custom.

Labor discriminations in the North are not deep-seated and

ineradicable.* It is impossible to educate the youth of a land in the same schools, in the same classes, side by side in their recitations, united in their sports, shouting the same yell, feeling the same thrill at the success of their colleagues, whether white or yellow or brown or black, without at the same time developing a better understanding with each other, a kindlier feeling toward each other. The thing we call race prejudice in the North differs from race prejudice in the South as a skin affection differs from scrofula. The latter is organic, in the very blood, drawn in with the mother's milk, and fed by the virus of public sentiment. The other is superficial, readily subject to treatment, and not difficult to cure.

But whatever may be the outcome of the people who leave the South, there is one thing certain—the South is losing a class of citizens which it should wish to retain. Men and women of culture and of character are needed in every community, and in no place more than in the South; but when the Southern whites, by every conceivable means, humiliate, proscribe and hamper the best of us, there should be no surprise if we seek more congenial climes, where we can at least protect our wives and daughters from the contumely that the lowest white man can heap upon them with absolute impunity.

Whither are we tending? Are we drifting with a sort of fatalistic indifference? Or is there a purpose behind all these restrictions, all these proscriptions?

If there be a purpose what can it be? Is the purpose to go back to slavery? I had hoped that it had been settled, forever settled, that this country cannot exist part slave and part free. If there be no purpose behind it all, there is lacking that far-seeing statesmanship which every government should have. It is difficult to believe that the problem of ten million citizen-aliens does not merit the wisest statesmanship. We are forty-six years from the Emancipation Proclamation, and yet today so widespread is this race oppression that a gathering of this kind is imperative. At the same rate of retrogression, in forty-six more years the then twenty millions of colored people will be veritable serfs.

What would that mean to the country at large? A tuberculosis bacillus from a black man's lung is as contagious as a bacillus from a white man's lung. Black men of vicious lives cannot fail to affect to a greater or less degree the communities

---

* How overoptimistic Bulkley was about labor discrimination in the North was to be revealed again and again in race riots in the years following the 1909 conference.

where they live. You cannot circumscribe vice; it is contagious. Leave these millions of Negroes to battle alone with this terrible weight with which they are now burdened and they would prove themselves little better than mortals if they did not follow the lines of least resistance and sink lower and lower into indolence, vagrancy and criminality. You may deprive a man of the right to vote, but you cannot deprive him of the right to steal.

Give them encouragement. Offer them incentives for intelligence, for skill, for sobriety, for character. Let them feel that as they push themselves out of the quagmire, they will be recognized on their merits. Reward industry. Recognize proved ability. But, if for the sake of argument, it be granted that they are all that their most virulent enemies charge them with being, so much greater is the need of sparing no efforts for their uplift, not so much for their sakes as for your sakes. If it were only one man or a hundred men, there might be some hope of their dying or some way might be suggested to get rid of them; but here is a race of ten million, as many people as are in all British America and all Central America; they are not dying out; they are not going to die out. As I see it, there are only four things possible: (1) expatriate them; (2) annihilate them; (3) degrade them; (4) elevate them. If they remain here and are allowed no incentives to pull upward, it must follow as the night the day, they will surely run downward.

To work in any way that one has the ability should be the inalienable right of every American citizen. A clean, attractive, honest-looking young man came to my office last week to see if I could help him. He stated that he is a junior in the pharmaceutical course at Columbia. He desires to spend his vacation in a wholesale drug concern for the sake of needed information and experience. He had written to several drug establishments in this city. He received replies to call, intimating that there were opportunities for work. He stated that he had just come from a useless round of visits to the stores, for the proprietors had suddenly changed their minds on seeing him. Now, that young man is good enough to sit by the side of and work with the best in Columbia University; is it not presumable that he is good enough to work out in the world by the side of those who are no better than his mates in college?

We do not ask for charity; all we ask is opportunity. We do not beg for alms; we beg only for a chance. The right to work; opportunity to work; encouragement to work; reward for work; this is all we ask; less than this should not be given.

LYNCHING, OUR NATIONAL CRIME

By Ida M. Wells-Barnett

One of the most militant opponents of Booker T. Washington's philosophy of accommodation, a heroic fighter against discrimination, and the person who had more to do with originating and carrying out a crusade against lynching than any other was Ida May Wells. At the early age of nineteen, as editor of the Memphis Free Press, *she began her campaign against lynching. Threatened by white-supremacists if she continued her exposure of lynching, she defied them but took care always to carry two pistols for protection. In 1892 she published an article revealing that the lynching of three successful Negro grocers was the work of their white competitors. Her press was destroyed and she would have been lynched had she not been in Philadelphia covering a convention. Miss Wells went to Chicago, where she joined the Chicago* Conservator *and then lectured throughout the Northern part of the United States and in Europe on lynching. She was among the first to point out the falsity of the charge of rape as "explaining" lynching. In 1894 she published* A Red Record, *the first book to document the crime of lynching. A year later, she married Ferdinand Lee Barnett, of Chicago, lawyer and later the first Negro assistant state's attorney of Illinois. In 1898 she was the spokesman for a delegation of women and Congressmen to President McKinley to protest the lynching of a Negro postmaster. An active member of the Niagara Movement, she was also one of the signers of the call for the National Negro Conference in 1909 and later a founder of the N.A.A.C.P. Mrs. Wells-Barnett delivered the following address at the 1909 Conference. (Text is taken from the* Proceedings of the Conference, *pp. 174–79.)*

THE LYNCHING RECORD for a quarter of a century merits the thoughtful study of the American people. It presents three salient facts:

First: Lynching is color-line murder.

Second: Crimes against women is the excuse, not the cause.

Third: It is a national crime and requires a national remedy.

Proof that lynching follows the color line is to be found in the statistics which have been kept for the past twenty-five years. During the few years preceding this period and while frontier lynch law existed, the executions showed a majority of white victims. Later, however, as law courts and authorized judiciary extended into the far West, lynch law rapidly abated, and its white victims became few and far between.

Just as the lynch-law regime came to a close in the West, a new mob movement started in the South. This was wholly political, its purpose being to suppress the colored vote by intimidation and murder. Thousands of assassins banded together under the name of Ku Klux Klans, "Midnight Raiders," "Knights of the Golden Circle," et cetera, et cetera, spread a reign of terror, by beating, shooting and killing colored people by the thousands. In a few years, the purpose was accomplished, and the black vote was suppressed. But mob murder continued.

From 1882, in which year fifty-two were lynched, down to the present, lynching has been along the color line. Mob murder increased yearly until in 1892 more than two hundred victims were lynched and statistics show that 3,284 men, women and children have been put to death in this quarter of a century. During the last ten years from 1899 to 1908 inclusive the number lynched was 959. Of this number 102 were white, while the colored victims numbered 857. No other nation, civilized or savage, burns its criminals; only under the Stars and Stripes is the human holocaust possible. Twenty-eight human beings burned at the stake, one of them a woman and two of them children, is the awful indictment against American civilization—the gruesome tribute which the nation pays to the color line.

Why is mob murder permitted by a Christian nation? What is the cause of this awful slaughter? This question is answered almost daily—always the same shameless falsehood that "Negroes are lynched to protect womanhood." Standing before a Chautauqua assemblage, John Temple Graves, at once champion of lynching and apologist for lynchers, said: "The mob stands today as the most potential bulwark between the women of the South and such a carnival of crime as would infuriate the world and precipitate the annihilation of the Negro race." This is the never-varying answer of lynchers and their apologists. All know that it is untrue. The cowardly lyncher revels in murder, then seeks to shield himself from public execration by claiming devotion to woman. But truth is mighty and the lynching record discloses the hypocrisy of the lyncher as well as his crime.

The Springfield, Illinois, mob rioted for two days, the militia of the entire state was called out, two men were lynched, hundreds of people driven from their homes, all because a white woman said a Negro assaulted her. A mad mob went to the jail, tried to lynch the victim of her charge and, not being able to find him, proceeded to pillage and burn the town and to lynch two innocent men. Later, after the police had found that the woman's charge was false, she published a retraction, the indictment was dismissed and the intended victim discharged. But the lynched victims were dead. Hundreds were homeless and Illinois was disgraced.

As a final and complete refutation of the charge that lynching is occasioned by crimes against women, a partial record of lynchings is cited; 285 persons were lynched for causes as follows:

Unknown cause, 92; no cause, 10; race prejudice, 49; miscegenation, 7; informing, 12; making threats, 11; keeping saloon, 3; practicing fraud, 5; practicing voodooism, 2; bad reputation, 8; unpopularity, 3; mistaken identity, 5; using improper language, 3; violation of contract, 1; writing insulting letter, 2; eloping, 2; poisoning horse, 1; poisoning well, 2; by white caps, 9; vigilantes, 14; Indians, 1; moonshining, 1; refusing evidence, 2; political causes, 5; disputing, 1; disobeying quarantine regulations, 2; slapping a child, 1; turning state's evidence, 3; protecting a Negro, 1; to prevent giving evidence, 1; knowledge of larceny, 1; writing letter to white woman, 1; asking white woman to marry, 1; jilting girl, 1; having smallpox, 1; concealing criminal, 2; threatening political exposure, 1; self-defense, 6; cruelty, 1; insulting language to woman, 5; quarreling with white man, 2; colonizing Negroes, 1; throwing stones, 1; quarreling, 1; gambling, 1.

Is there a remedy, or will the nation confess that it cannot protect its protectors at home as well as abroad? Various remedies have been suggested to abolish the lynching infamy, but year after year, the butchery of men, women and children continues in spite of plea and protest. Education is suggested as a preventive, but it is as grave a crime to murder an ignorant man as it is a scholar. True, few educated men have been lynched, but the hue and cry once started stops at no bounds, as was clearly shown by the lynchings in Atlanta, and in Springfield, Illinois.

Agitation, though helpful, will not alone stop the crime. Year after year statistics are published, meetings are held, resolutions are adopted and yet lynchings go on. Public sentiment does measurably decrease the sway of mob law, but the irresponsible bloodthirsty criminals who swept through the streets of Springfield, beating an inoffensive law-abiding citizen to death in one part of the town, and in another torturing and shooting to death a man who for threescore years had made a reputation for honesty, integrity and sobriety, had raised a family and had accumulated property, were not deterred from their heinous crimes by either education or agitation.

The only certain remedy is an appeal to law. Lawbreakers must be made to know that human life is sacred and that every citizen of this country is first a citizen of the United States and secondly a citizen of the state in which he belongs. This nation must assert itself and defend its federal citizenship at home as well as abroad. The strong arm of the government must reach across state lines whenever unbridled lawlessness defies state laws and must give to the individual citizen under the Stars and Stripes the same measure of protection which it gives to him when he travels in foreign lands.

Federal protection of American citizenship is the remedy for lynching. Foreigners are rarely lynched in America. If, by mistake, one is lynched, the national government quickly pays the damages.* The recent agitation in California against the Japanese compelled this nation to recognize that federal power must yet assert itself to protect the nation from the treason of sovereign states. Thousands of American citizens have been put to death and no President has yet raised his hand in effective protest, but a simple insult to a native of Japan was quite sufficient to stir the government at Washington to prevent the threatened wrong. If the government has power to protect a foreigner from insult, certainly it has power to save a citizen's life.

The practical remedy has been more than once suggested in Congress. Senator Gallinger, of New Hampshire, in a resolution introduced in Congress called for an investigation "with the view of ascertaining whether there is a remedy for lynching which Congress may apply." The Senate Committee has under consideration a bill drawn by A. E. Pillsbury, formerly Attorney General of Massachusetts, providing for federal prosecution of lynchers in cases where the state fails to protect citizens or foreigners. Both of these resolutions indicate that the attention of the nation has been called to this phase of the lynching question.

As a final word, it would be a beginning in the right direction

---

* In 1899 five Italians were lynched in Tallulah, Louisiana. Following the protest of the Italian minister to the United States, the American government hastened to make necessary amends in the form of compensation to the families of the victims.

if this conference can see its way clear to establish a bureau for the investigation and publication of the details of every lynching, so that the public could know that an influential body of citizens has made it a duty to give the widest publicity to the facts in each case; that it will make an effort to secure expressions of opinion all over the country against lynching for the sake of the country's fair name; and lastly, but by no means least, to try to influence the daily papers of the country to refuse to become accessory to mobs either before or after the fact.* Several of the greatest riots and most brutal burnt offerings of the mobs have been suggested and incited by the daily papers of the offending community. If the newspaper which suggests lynching in its accounts of an alleged crime, could be held legally as well as morally responsible for reporting that "threats of lynching were heard"; or, "it is feared that if the guilty one is caught, he will be lynched"; or, "there were cries of 'lynch him,' and the only reason the threat was not carried out was because no leader appeared," a long step toward a remedy will have been taken.

In a multitude of counsel there is wisdom. Upon the grave question presented by the slaughter of innocent men, women and children there should be an honest, courageous conference of patriotic, law-abiding citizens anxious to punish crime promptly, impartially and by due process of law, also to make life, liberty and property secure against mob rule.

Time was when lynching appeared to be sectional, but now it is national—a blight upon our nation, mocking our laws and disgracing our Christianity. "With malice toward none but with charity for all" let us undertake the work of making the "law of the land" effective and supreme upon every foot of American soil—a shield to the innocent; and to the guilty, punishment swift and sure.

* Through its Legal Committee (and other committees) as well as its official organ, The Crisis, edited by W. E. B. Du Bois, the N.A.A.C.P. did precisely what Ida May Wells-Barnett called for.

SOME ELEMENTS NECESSARY TO RACE DEVELOPMENT

By Robert Russa Moton

Booker T. Washington's leadership and philosophy was challenged by W. E. B. Du Bois, Kelly Miller, William Monroe Trotter, Francis J. Grimké, William Ferris, and other black spokesmen. Still there were many accommodationists. The most prominent Negro to follow in Washington's tradition after the latter's death was Robert Russa Moton (1867–1940), Washington's successor as principal of Tuskegee Institute. He was born on a plantation in Prince Edward County, Virginia, where he was secretly taught by his mother to read. When the mistress of the plantation learned of these lessons, she instructed her daughter to teach the young boy an hour a day and supply him with books. This experience helped shape Moton's belief that most Southern whites were really interested in the Negro's advancement. Moton was educated at Hampton Institute, where he was commandant of cadets from 1890 to 1915, when he went to Tuskegee. In May, 1912, in an address delivered at a Tuskegee commencement, Moton sounded the keynote that he was to strike in many of his future speeches. He emphasized that the Negro's inferior background and lack of education and moral character underlay his rejection by white society, and indicated his strong belief in Washington's theory of industrial education.

Here is a major portion of this speech, excerpted from the text in Alice Moore Dunbar, Masterpieces of Negro Eloquence, *pp. 367–76.*

STUDENTS, FRIENDS: Among the most highly developed races we observe certain dominant characteristics, certain very essential elements of character, by which they have so influenced mankind and helped the world that they were enabled to write their names in history so indelibly as to withstand and endure the test of time.

Your education, your observation, your occupation, have brought you into close touch and into personal and vital relations with the fundamental problems of life. We may call it the truth problem, the labor problem, the Indian problem, or perhaps the Negro problem. I like to call it the "human-race problem."

The dawn of history breaks upon a world at strife, a universal conflict of man at war with his brother. The very face of the earth has been dyed in blood and its surface whitened with human bones in an endeavor to establish a harmonious and helpful adjustment between man and man. There can be no interest more fundamental or of greater concern to the human family than the proper adjustment of man's relations to his brother.

You and I belong to an undeveloped, backward race that is rarely for its own sake taken into account in the adjustment of man's relation to man, but is considered largely with reference to the impression which it makes upon the dominant Anglo-Saxon. The Negro's very existence is itself somewhat satellitious, and secondary only to the great white orb around which he revolves. If by chance any light does appear in the black man's sphere of operations, it is usually assumed that it is reflected from his association with his white brother. The black is generally projected against the white and usually to the disadvantage and embarrassment of the former. It becomes very easy, therefore, to see in our minds and hearts what is so apparent in our faces, "Darkness there and nothing more."

But you must keep in mind that the Negro is a tenth part of a great cosmopolitan commonwealth; he is a part of a nation to which God has given many very intricate probems to work out. Who knows but that this nation is God's great laboratory which is being used by the Creator to show the rest of the world what it does not seem thoroughly to understand, that it is possible for all God's people, even the two most extreme types, the black and the white, to live together harmoniously and helpfully?

The question that the American nation must face, and which the Negro as a part of the nation should soberly and dispassionately consider, is the mutual, social, civic and industrial adjustment upon common ground of two races, differing widely in characteristics and diverse in physical peculiarities, but alike suspicious and alike jealous, and alike more or less biased and prejudiced each toward the other. Without doubt the physical peculiarities of the Negro, which are perhaps the most superficial of all the distinctions, are nevertheless the most difficult of adjustment. While I do not believe that a man's color is ever a disadvantage to him, he is very likely to find it an inconvenience sometimes, in some places.

We might as well be perfectly frank and perfectly honest

with ourselves; it is not an easy task to adjust the relations of ten millions of people who, while they may be mature in passion and perhaps in prejudice, are yet to a large extent children in judgment and in experience, to a race of people not only mature in civilization, but the principles of whose government were based upon more or less mature judgment and experience at the beginning of this nation; and when we take into account also the wide difference in ethnic types of the two races that are here brought together, the problem becomes one of the gravest intricacy that has ever taxed human wisdom and human patience for solution. This situation makes it necessary for the Negro as a race to grasp firmly two or three fundamental elements.

The first is *race consciousness*.

The Negro must play essentially the primary part in the solution of this problem. Since his emancipation he has conclusively demonstrated to most people that he possesses the same faculties and susceptibilities as the rest of human mankind; this is the greatest victory the race has achieved during its years of freedom. Having demonstrated that his faculties and susceptibilities are capable of the highest development, it must be true of the black race as it has been true of other races, that it must go through the same process and work out the same problem in about the same way as other races have done.

We can and we have profited very much by the examples of progressive races. This is a wonderful advantage, and we have not been slow to grasp it. But we must remember that we are subject to the same natural factor in the solution of this problem, and that it cannot be solved without considering this factor. The Negro must first of all have a conscientious pride and absolute faith and belief in himself. He must not unduly depreciate race distinctions and allow himself to think that, because out of one blood God created all nations of the earth, brotherhood is already an accomplished reality. Let us not deceive ourselves, blighted as we are with a heritage of moral leprosy from our past history and hard pressed as we are in the economic world by foreign immigrants and by native prejudice; our one surest haven of refuge is in ourselves; our one safest means of advance is our belief in and implicit trust in our own ability and worth. No race that despises itself, that laughs at and ridicules itself, that wishes to God it were anything else but itself, can ever be a great people. There is no power under heaven that can stop the onward march of ten millions of earnest, honest, inspired, God-fearing, race-loving and united people.

Secondly, we must have *a high moral ideal.*

With a strong race consciousness and reasonable prudence, a people with a low, vacillating, and uncertain moral ideal may, for a time, be able to stem the tide of outraged virtue, but this is merely transitory. Ultimate destruction and ruin follow absolutely in the wake of moral degeneracy; this, all history shows; this, experience teaches. God visits the iniquities of the fathers upon the children unto the third and fourth generations. "The judgments of the Lord are true and righteous all together."

Not long ago I stood in the city of Rome amid its ruined fountains, crumbling walls, falling aqueducts, ancient palaces, and amphitheaters, today mere relics of ancient history. One is struck with wonder and amazement at the magnificent civilization which that people was able to evolve. It does not seem possible that the Roman people, who could so perfect society in its organic and civic relations and leave to the world the organic principles which must always lie at the base of all subsequent social development—it does not seem possible that such a people should so decay as to leave hardly a vestige of its original stock, and that such cities as the Romans erected should so fall as to leave scarcely one stone upon another. Neither does it seem credible that a people who could so work out in its philosophical aspect man's relation to the eternal mystery, and come as near a perfect solution as is perhaps possible for the human mind to reach, that a people who could give to the world such literature, such art, such ideals of physical and intellectual beauty, as did the Greeks, could so utterly perish from the face of the earth; yet this is the case not only with Rome and Greece, but with a score or more of nations which were once masters of the world. The Greeks, Romans, Persians, Egyptians, and even God's chosen people, allowed corruption and vice to so dwarf their moral sense that there was, according to the universal law of civilization, nothing left for them but death and destruction.

It is no reproach to the Negro to say that his history and environment in this country have well-nigh placed him at the bottom of the moral scale. This must be remedied, if the Negro is ever to reach his full status of civilized manhood and womanhood. It must come through the united efforts of the educated among us. We must be united to stop the ravages of disease among our people; united to keep black boys from idleness, vice, gambling and crime; united to guard the purity of black womanhood and, I might add, black manhood also. It is not enough to simply protest that ninety-five out of every hundred

Negroes are orderly and law-abiding. The ninety-five must be banded together to restrain and suppress the vicious five.

The people must be impressed with the idea that a high moral character is absolutely essential to the highest development of every race, white quite as much as black. There is no creature so low and contemptible as he who does not seek first the approval of his own conscience and his God; for, after all, how poor is human recognition when you and your God are aware of your inward integrity of soul! If the Negro will keep clean hands and a pure heart, he can stand up before all the world and say, "Doubtless Thou, O Lord, art our Father, though Abraham be ignorant of us and Israel acknowledge us not."

Thirdly, and lastly, *the Negro needs intelligent industry.*

Slavery taught the Negro many things for which he should be profoundly thankful—the Christian religion, the English language, and, in a measure, civilization, which in many aspects may be crude in form, but these have placed him a thousand years ahead of his African ancestors.

Slavery taught the Negro to work by rule and rote but not by principle and method. It did not and, perhaps, could not teach him to love and respect labor, but left him, on the contrary, with the idea that manual industry was a thing to be despised and gotten rid of, if possible; that to work with one's hands was a badge of inferiority. A tropical climate is not conducive to the development of practical energy. Add to the Negro's natural tendency his unfortunate heritage from slavery, and we see at once that the race needs especially to be rooted and grounded in the underlying scientific principles of concrete things. The time when the world bowed before merely abstract, impractical knowledge has well-nigh passed; the demand of this age and hour is not so much what a man knows—though the world respects and reveres knowledge and always will, I hope—what the world wants to know is what a man can do and how well he can do it.

We must not be misled by high-sounding phrases as to the kind of education the race should receive, but we should remember that the education of a people should be conditioned upon their capacity, social environment, and the probable life which they will lead in the immediate future. We fully realize that the ignorant must be taught, the poor must have the Gospel, and the vicious must be restrained, but we also realize that these do not strike the "bedrock" of a permanent, lasting citizenship.

If the Negro will add his proportionate contribution to the economic aspect of the world's civilization, it must be done through intelligent, well-directed, conscientious, skilled industry. Indeed, the feasible forms of civilization are nothing but the concrete actualization of intelligent thought applied to what are sometimes called common things.

The primary sources of wealth are agriculture, mining, manufacturing and commerce. These are the lines along which the thoughtful energy of the black race must be directed. I mean by agriculture, *farming*—the raising of corn, cotton, peas and potatoes, pigs, chickens, horses and cows.

Land may be bought practically anywhere in the South almost at our own price.* Twenty years hence, with the rapidly developing Southern country and the strenuous efforts to fill it up with foreign immigrants, it will be difficult, if not impossible, for us to buy land. God gave the children of Israel the "Land of Canaan" but, oh, what a life-and-death struggle they had to take possession of it and hold on to it. God has given to the Negro here in this Southern country two of the most fundamental necessities in his development—*land* and *labor*. If you don't possess this land and hold this labor, God will tell you, as He has often told other races, "to move on."

The Creator never meant that this beautiful land should be forever kept as a great hunting ground for the Indian to roam in savage bliss, but he intended that it should be used. The Indian, having for scores of generations failed to develop this land, God asked the Anglo-Saxon to take possession and dig out the treasures of wheat, corn, cotton, gold and silver, coal and iron, and the poor Indian was told "to move on."

The Negro in Africa sits listlessly in the sunshine of barbarous idleness while the same progressive, indomitable, persevering, white man is taking possession; the same edict has gone forth to the native African—he is being told "to move on."

The same God will tell the white man in America and in Africa, if he does not mete out absolute justice and absolute fairness to his weaker and less-advantaged brother, black or red or brown, if he cannot do justly and love mercy, just as he told the patricians of Rome, he will tell the white man "to move on."

Whatever question there may be about the white man's part in this situation, there is no doubt about ours. Don't let us delude ourselves, but keep in mind the fact that the man who

---

* Moton ignored widespread evidence that white owners of land in the South generally refused to sell land to Negroes. Moreover, most Negro farmers lacked the capital to buy land and tools, and were therefore landless tenants or sharecroppers.

owns his home and cultivates his land and lives a decent,
self-respecting, useful, and helpful life is no problem anywhere.
We talk about the "color line," but you know and I know that
the blackest Negro in Alabama or Mississippi or Africa or anywhere else who puts the same amount of skill and energy into
his farming gets as large returns for his labor as the whitest
Anglo-Saxon. The earth yields up her increase as willingly to
the skill and persuasions of the black as of the white husband-
man. Wind, wave, heat, steam and electricity are absolutely
blind forces and see no race distinction and draw no "color
line." The world's market does not care and it asks no question
about the shade of the hand that produces the commodity, but it
does insist that it shall be up to the world's requirements.

I thank God for the excellent chance to work that my race
had in this Southern country; the Negro in America has a real,
good, healthy job, and I hope he may always keep it. I am not
particular what he does or where he does it, so he is engaged
in honest, useful work.

Remember always that building a house is quite as important
as building a poem; that the science of cooking is as useful to
humanity as the science of music; that the thing most to be
desired is a harmonious and helpful adaptation of all the arts
and sciences to the glory of God and the good of humanity;
that whether we labor with muscle or with brain, both need
divine inspiration. Let us consecrate our brain and muscle to
the highest and noblest service, to God and humanity. . . .

WHAT SOCIALISM MEANS TO US

By Hubert H. Harrison

*Born in the Virgin Islands, self-educated, author, lecturer,
journalist and critic, staff lecturer for the New York City
Board of Education, Hubert Henry Harrison was one of the
great Socialist orators of the first decade of the twentieth
century. Between 1909 and 1912, he was a regular speaker
on Socialism at indoor and outdoor meetings in New York's
black community. His soapbox in Madison Square was a
common sight, and he addressed both blacks and whites
on the meaning and importance of Socialism. Henry
Miller, who heard Harrison speak in Madison Square, described him in* Plexus *as a remarkable orator. "There was*

no one in those days . . . who could hold a candle to Hubert Harrison. With a few well-directed words he had the ability to demolish any opponent. He did it neatly and smoothly too—'with kid gloves,' so to speak. . . . Beside him the other speakers, the white ones, looked like pygmies, not only physically, but culturally, spiritually." Unfortunately, most of Harrison's speeches were delivered extemporaneously, and few have been published. But the following is a major portion of one of Harrison's speeches to black Americans urging them to join the Socialist party, of which he was a member until he resigned in 1916. The speech was delivered around 1912 and was published in Harrison's book, The Negro and the Nation *(New York, 1917[?], pp. 48–58).*

. . . TODAY, fellow sufferers, they tell us that we are free. But are we? If you will think for a moment you will see that we are not free at all. We have simply changed one form of slavery for another. Then it was chattel slavery, now it is wage slavery. For that which was the essence of chattel slavery is the essence of wage slavery. It is only a difference in form. The chattel slave was compelled to work by physical force; the wage slave is compelled to work by starvation. The product of the chattel slave's labor was taken by his master; the product of the wage slave's labor is taken by the employer.

The United States government has made a study of the wealth-producing power of the wage slaves and has shown that the average worker *produces* $2,451 a year. The government has also made a study of wages in the United States, and that study shows that the average worker gets $437 a year. This means that the average employer takes away from the average wage slave $2,014 a year. In the good old days the master took away the wealth produced by the slave in the simplest form; today he takes it away in the form of profits. But in one respect the wage slave is worse off than the chattel slave. Under chattel slavery the master owned the man and the land; he had to feed and clothe the man. Under wage slavery the man feeds and clothes himself. Under chattel slavery it was to the interest of the owner to give the slave work and to keep him from starving to death. Under wage slavery, if the man is out of work the employer doesn't care; that is no loss to him; and if the man dies, there are millions of others eager to take his place, because, as I said before, they must either work for him or starve. There is one very striking parallel between the two cases. Today there are many people who say that this system is divinely

appointed—is a law of nature—just as they said the same thing
of chattel slavery. Well, there are millions of workers who say
it is wrong. Under chattel slavery black workers were robbed;
under wage slavery all the workers are robbed. The Socialist
party says that this robbing shall cease; that no worker black
or white shall be exploited for profit. And it says, further, that
there is one sure and certain way of putting an end to the system, and that is by working for the success of Socialism. . . .

Under the old system, the capitalist owned the man; today
he owns the tools with which the man must work. These tools
are the factories, the mines, and the machines. The system that
owns them owns you and me and all the rest of us, black, white,
brown, red and yellow. We can't live unless we have access to
these tools, and our masters the capitalists see to it that we
are separated from what we make by using these things, except
so much as is necessary to keep us alive that we may be able
to make more—for them. This little bit is called wages. They
wouldn't give us even that if they thought that we could live
without it. In the good old days the chattel slave would be
fastened with a chain if they thought that he might escape.
Today no chain is necessary to bind us to the tools. We are as
free as air. Of course. We are free to starve. And that chain of
the fear of starvation binds us to the tools owned by the capitalist as firmly as any iron chain ever did. And this system doesn't
care whether the slaves who are bound in this new way are
white or black. To the capitalist system all workers are equal—
in so far as they have a stomach.

Now the one great fact for the Negro in America today is
race prejudice. The great labor problem with which all working
people are faced is made harder for black working people by
the addition of a race problem. I want to show you how one
grows out of the other and how, at bottom, they are both the
same thing. In other words, I want you to see the economic
reason for race prejudice.

In the first place, do you know that the most rabid, Negro-
hating, Southern aristocrat has not the slightest objection to
sleeping in the same house with a Negro—if that Negro sleeps
there as his servant? He doesn't care if his food is prepared by
a Negro cook and handled by a Negro waiter before it gets to
him; he will eat it. But if a Negro comes into the same public
restaurant to buy and eat food, then—oh my!—he gets all het
up about it. But why? What's the differences? I will tell you.
The aristocrat wants the black man to feel that he is on a lower
level. When he is "in his place," he is liked. But he must not be
allowed to do anything to make him forget that he is on this

lower level; he must be kept "in his place," which means the place which the aristocrat wants him to keep. You see, the black man carries the memory of slavery with him. Everybody knows that the slaves were the exploited working class of the South. That put them in a class by themselves, down at the bottom, downtrodden, despised, "inferior."

Do you begin to see now that race prejudice is only another name for *caste prejudice*? If our people had never been slaves; had never been exploited workers, and so, at the bottom of the ladder, there would be no prejudice against them now. In every case where there has been a downtrodden class of workers at the bottom, that class has been despised by the class that lived by their labor. Do you doubt it? Then look at the facts. If you had picked up a daily paper in New York in 1848 you would have found at the end of many an advertisement for butler, coachman, lady's maid, clerk or bookkeeper these words: "No Irish need apply." There was a race prejudice against the Irish then, because most of the manual unskilled laborers were Irish. They were at the bottom, exploited and despised. But they have changed things since then. Beginning in the seventies, when Jewish laborers began to come here from Russia, Austria and Germany, and lasting even to our own day, there has been race prejudice against the Jews. And today, when the Italian has taken the place which the Irish laborer vacated—at the bottom —he too comes in for his share of prejudice. In every one of these cases it was the condition of the people at the bottom— as despised, exploited, wage slaves—that was responsible for the race prejudice. And it is just so in the black man's case— with this difference: his color marks what he once was, and even though he should wear a dress suit every evening and own an automobile or a farm, he can always be picked out and reminded.

Now, under the present system, exploiting the wage slave is respectable. I have already shown you that wherever the worker is exploited he is despised. So you will see that despising the wage slave is quite fashionable. . . . As long as the present system continues, the workers will be despised; as long as the workers are despised, the black man will be despised, robbed and murdered, because they are least able to defend themselves. Now ask yourself whether you haven't a very special interest in changing the present system.

Of course, you will ask: "But haven't white working people race prejudice too?" Sure, they have. Do you know why? It pays the capitalist to keep the workers divided. So he creates and keeps alive these prejudices. He gets them to believe that their interests are different. Then he uses one half of them to club the other half with. In Russia when the working men demand reform, the capitalists sick them on the Jews. In America they sick them on the Negroes. That makes them forget their own condition; as long as they can be made to look down upon another class. "But then," you will say, "the average wage slave must be a chump." Sure, he is. That's what the capitalist counts on. And Socialism is working to educate the workers to see this and to unite them in doing away with the present system.

Socialism stands for the emancipation of the wage slaves. Are you a wage slave? Do you want to be emancipated? Then join hands with the Socialists. Hear what they have to say. Read some of their literature. Get a Socialist leaflet, a pamphlet, or, better still, a book. You will be convinced of two things: that Socialism is right, and that it is inevitable. It is right because any order of things in which those who work have least while those who work them have most, is wrong. It is inevitable because a system under which the wealth produced by the labor of human hands amounts to more than two hundred and twenty billions a year while many millions live on the verge of starvation, is bound to break down. Therefore, if you wish to join with the other class-conscious, intelligent wage earners— in putting an end to such a system; if you want to better living conditions for black men as well as for white men; to make this woeful world of ours a little better for your children and your children's children, study Socialism—and think and work your way out. . . .

SEGREGATION DESTROYS FELLOWSHIP AND CITIZENSHIP

By William Monroe Trotter

During the Presidential campaign of 1912, Woodrow Wilson, the Democratic candidate, to win Negro support, came out with a statement that should he become President, the Negroes could count on him for absolute fair dealing and for help in advancing the interests of their race in the United States. He promised the Negroes "fair dealing," and asserted he would be President of all the people. With this statement, W. E. B. Du Bois resigned from the Socialist party and announced his support of Wilson, and together with Bishop Waldron and William Monroe Trotter, appealed to Negroes to vote for him. It has been estimated that as many as a hundred thousand black Americans heeded the appeal.

Negroes' hopes were soon dashed. President Wilson replaced many Negro officeholders with whites and sent white ministers to Haiti and Santo Domingo in place of blacks. But the most disappointing development was the institution of segregation in government lunchrooms, toilets and other facilities. As early as 1913, Negroes began the protest against Wilson's policies. In November, 1914, a delegation of black Americans, headed by William Monroe Trotter, visited the White House to protest segregation in the federal government under President Wilson. The visit aroused wide attention when the press reported that the President had been insulted by Trotter's "offensive manner," and had refused to discuss any issues with the delegation so long as Trotter was a member. At a mass meeting in Washington, Trotter declared, "I emphatically deny that in language, manner, tone—in any respect, or to the slightest degree—I was impudent, insolent or insulting to the President" (Washington Evening Star, November 13, 1914).

William Monroe Trotter was the editor and publisher of the Boston Guardian, which the Broad Ax, a black newspaper in Chicago, described as "the best newspaper published in the interest of the Afro-American race in any part of this country." He was a graduate of Harvard College and the first Negro to be elected to Phi Beta Kappa there. A militant and outspoken opponent of Booker T. Washington, Trotter had worked closely with Du Bois in the Niagara Movement, but had refused to follow him into the N.A.A.C.P. because he charged it was dominated by whites. He continued the fight for full equality for black Americans through the Equal Rights Leagues.

Here is the text of Trotter's remarks to President Wilson, as derived from reports of Trotter's speech in the Washington Evening Star, November 12, 1914, and the Chicago Defender, November 21, 1914.

ONE YEAR AGO we presented a national petition, signed by Afro-Americans in thirty-eight states, protesting against the segregation of employees of the national government whose ancestry could be traced in whole or in part to Africa, as instituted under your administration in the Treasury and Post Office departments. We then appealed to you to undo this race segregation in accord with your duty as President and with your preelection pledges. We stated that there could be no freedom, no respect from others, and no equality of citizenship under segregation for races, especially when applied to but one of the many racial elements in the government employ. For such placement of employees means a charge by the government of physical indecency or infection, or of being a lower order of beings, or a subjection to the prejudices of other citizens, which constitutes inferiority of status. We protested such segregation as to working positions, eating tables, dressing rooms, rest rooms, lockers, and especially public toilets in government buildings. We stated that such segregation was a public humiliation and degradation, entirely unmerited and far-reaching in its injurious effects, a gratuitous blow against ever-loyal citizens and against those many of whom aided and supported your elevation to the Presidency of our common country.

At that time you stated you would investigate conditions for yourself. Now, after the lapse of a year, we have come back, having found that all the forms of segregation of government employees of African extraction are still practiced in the Treasury and Post Office department buildings, and to a certain extent have spread into other government buildings.

Under the Treasury Department, in the Bureau of Engraving and Printing, there is segregation not only in dressing rooms, but in working positions, Afro-American employees being herded at separate tables, in eating, and in toilets. In the Navy Department there is herding at desks and separation in lavatories; in the Post Office Department there is separation in work for Afro-American women in the alcove on the eighth floor, of Afro-American men in rooms on the seventh floor, with forbidding even of entrance into an adjoining room occupied by white clerks on the seventh floor, and of Afro-American men in separate rooms just instituted on the sixth floor, with separate lavatories for Afro-American men on the eighth floor; in the main Treasury Building in separate lavatories in the basement; in the Interior Department separate lavatories, which were specifically pointed out to you at our first hearing; in the State and other departments in separate lavatories, though there is but one Afro-American clerk to use it; in the War Department in separate lavatories; in the Post Office Department Building separate lavatories; in the sewing and bindery divisions of the Government Printing Office on the fifth floor there is herding at

working positions of Afro-American women and separation in
lavatories, and new segregation instituted by the division chief
since our first audience with you. This lavatory segregation is
the most degrading, most insulting of all. Afro-American employees who use the regular public lavatories on the floors where
they work are cautioned and then warned by superior officers
against insubordination.

We have come by vote of this league to set before you this
definite continuance of race segregation and to renew the protest and to ask you to abolish segregation of Afro-American
employees in the Executive Department.

Because we cannot believe you capable of any disregard of
your pledges, we have been sent by the alarmed American citizens of color. They realize that if they can be segregated and
thus humiliated by the national government at the national
capital, the beginning is made for the spread of that persecution and prosecution which makes property and life itself insecure in the South; the foundation of the whole fabric of this
citizenship is unsettled.

They have made plain enough to you their opposition to
segregation last year by a national antisegregation petition,
this year by a protest registered at the polls, voting against every
Democratic candidate save those outspoken against segregation.
The only Democrat elected governor in the Eastern states was
Governor Walsh of Massachusetts, who appealed to you by
letter to stop segregation. Thus have the Afro-Americans shown
how they detest segregation.

In fact, so intense is their resentment that the movement to
divide this solid race vote and make peace with the national
Democracy, so suspiciously revived when you ran for the Presidency, and which some of our families for two generations have
been risking all to promote, bids fair to be undone.

Only two years ago you were heralded as perhaps the second
Lincoln, and now the Afro-American leaders who supported you
are hounded as false leaders and traitors to their race. What a
change segregation has wrought!

You said that your "colored fellow citizens could depend upon
you for everything which would assist in advancing the interests
of their race in the United States." Consider that pledge in the
face of the continued color segregation! Fellow citizenship
means congregation. Segregation destroys fellowship and citizenship. Consider that any passerby on the streets of the national capital, whether he be black or white, can enter and use
the public lavatories in government buildings, while citizens of
color who do the work of the government are excluded.

As equal citizens and by virtue of your public promises we are entitled at your hands to freedom from discrimination, restriction, imputation and insult in government employ. Have you a "new freedom" for white Americans and a new slavery for your "Afro-American fellow citizens"? God forbid!

The colored people object to the government undertaking to interpret this treatment of them in the way of sympathy and help and charity for the benefit of dependent wards. The colored American is a full-fledged, absolutely equal citizen under the law.

Segregation is in itself an injury and denial of the equality of citizenship. It is unfair to separate the Afro-American when there is no similar segregation of the Semitic, Teutonic, Latin, Celtic or Slavic government employees.

It is entirely contrary to the facts to say that segregation was instituted because of racial friction. White and colored employees have been working together in peace and harmony and friendship for years, even under a former Democratic President.* Segregation was drastically introduced as soon as this administration came into being by John Skelton Williams, Secretary McAdoo and Postmaster General Burleson, because of their own racial prejudices.

It would be impossible for us, were we willing, to make the colored people of the United States to regard segregation as anything other than humiliating and degrading. We have been delegated to ask you to issue an executive order against any and all segregation of government employees because of race and color, and to ask whether you will do so. We await your reply, that we may give it to the waiting citizens of the United States of African extraction.

* The reference is to Grover Cleveland, Democratic President 1885–1889 and 1893–1897.

THERE IS STILL MUCH TO BE DONE

By Booker T. Washington

Booker T. Washington died on November 14, 1915. A little over two weeks before his death, he delivered his last address before the American Missionary Association and National Council of Congregational Churches, New Haven, Connecticut, October 25, 1915. While noting the progress made by his people since the abolition of slavery, he stressed that the need for educational facilities for the Negro was as great as it had ever been. The speech portrayed the nature of the problems facing the Negro more realistically than was usual in Washington's addresses. Here is Booker T. Washington's last speech, taken from the text in E. Davidson Washington, editor, Selected Speeches of Booker T. Washington, New York, 1932, pp. 277–83.

MR. CHAIRMAN, ladies and gentlemen: A few days ago I visited a little colony of black people near Mobile, Alabama, several of whom were born in Africa and came here on the last slave ship to reach America. Several of the older people still survive and tell interesting stories about their early and varied experiences. A little way from the colony may be seen the hulk of the slave ship on which they were brought to this country.

This has occurred practically within a single generation. What a transformation has been wrought to my race since the landing of the first slaves at Jamestown and the landing of the last slaves at Mobile! This transformation involves growth in number, mental awakening, self-support, securing of property, moral and religious development, and adjustment of relations between the races. To what in a single generation are we more indebted for this transformation in the direction of a higher civilization than the American Missionary Association?

I have said we have grown in numbers. Do you realize that today there are as many Negroes in the United States as there are persons in the whole of Minnesota, Iowa, Missouri, North Dakota, South Dakota, Nebraska and Kansas? And do you know (as of course you do) that the American Missionary Association was the pioneer factor in the educational work of Negroes? Your association established on September 16, 1861, at Fortress

Monroe, Virginia, the first school for freedmen.* In this school the first experiment among the freedmen in industrial education was made. Out of this school the Hampton Institute grew. I am, therefore, in a way the product of your association.

No one of the religious organizations which have engaged in the work of educating the Negro has done a more useful work than your association. You are maintaining more schools for the higher and secondary education of the Negro than any other board or association. I have had opportunity to visit practically every Negro institution in the country. In so doing I have been very favorably impressed with the good work which the educational institutions under the auspices of your association are doing. I have in mind not only the larger and more prominent schools, such as Fisk and Talladega, but also the smaller and less well-known institutions.

Fifty years ago the education of the Negro in the South had just begun. There were fewer than one hundred schools devoted to this purpose. In 1867 there were only 1,938 schools for the freedmen, with 2,087 teachers, of whom 699 were colored. There were 111,442 pupils. Of these, 13,758 pupils were studying the alphabet, 55,163 were in the spelling and easy-reading classes, 42,879 were learning to write, 40,454 were studying arithmetic, 4,611 were studying the higher branches. Thirty-five industrial schools were reported in which there were 2,624 students who were taught sewing, knitting, straw-braiding, repairing and making garments. In 1915 there are almost 2,000,-000 Negro children enrolled in the public schools of the South, and over 100,000 in the normal schools and colleges. The 699 colored teachers have increased to over 34,000, of whom 3,000 are teachers in colleges and normal and industrial schools.

When the American Missionary Association began its work among the freedmen there were in the South no institutions for higher and secondary education of the Negro. There were only 4 in the entire United States. In 1915 there are in the South 50 colleges devoted to their training. There are 13 institutions for the education of Negro women. There are 26 theological schools and departments. There are 3 schools of law, 4 of medicine, 2 of dentistry, 3 of pharmacy, 17 state agricultural and mechanical colleges, and over 200 normal and industrial schools.

Fifty years ago the value of the school property used in the

* The American Missionary Association was founded in 1846 and was supported by many wealthy Abolitionists. In September, 1861, the Association began its work among the "contrabands" at Fortress Monroe. Although nondenominational, the Association received a good deal of its support from the Congregationalists.

education of the freedmen was small. The value of the property now owned by institutions for their secondary and higher training is over $17,000,000. Fifty years ago only a few thousand dollars was being expended for the education of the Negroes. In 1914 over $4,100,000 was expended for their higher and industrial training, and $9,700,000 in their public schools.

Although there has been great progress in Negro education during the past fifty years, the equipments and facilities in Negro schools are, on the whole, far below those in white schools. The majority of the rural schools in the South are still without school buildings, and the average length of their terms is from three to five months. The Negroes constitute about 11 percent of the total population of the country. A little less than 2 percent of the expenditures of over $700,000,000 expended annually for education is spent upon them. Of the $600,000,000 spent on public schools the Negroes receive about 1½ percent. More money is spent on special schools for Indians, about $4,800,000 annually, than is expended for higher and industrial training for the Negro, a little more than $4,100,000.

I find that in some instances there is a belief that Negro education has advanced far enough for the various philanthropic and religious associations to gradually withdraw their support and use their resources in other directions. The truth of the matter, however, is that after fifty years there is still as great a need for the work of the American Missionary Association and similar organizations to assist in Negro education as there was immediately following Emancipation.

There are about 1,800,000 Negro children in the South enrolled in the public schools. This is a large number but not as large, however, as the number not in school. According to the United States census reports, 52 percent of the Negro children in the South of school age are not attending school. There are yet in the South over 2,000,000 Negroes who are unable to read or write. Almost 1,000,000 of these are of school age.

Although there are perhaps 100,000 Negro students enrolled in normal schools and colleges, statistics show that only about one fourth of these are doing work above the elementary grades, and only about one third are receiving industrial education. In the fifty colleges devoted to Negro education there are, according to statistics, fewer than 3,000 students who are doing work of the collegiate grade.

In the North the Jew, the Slav, the Italian, many of whom are such recent arrivals that they have not yet become citizens and voters, even under the easy terms granted them by the federal naturalization laws, have all the advantages of education that are granted to every other portion of the population. In several states an effort is now being made to give immigrant people special opportunities for education over and above those given to the average citizen. In some instances night schools are started for their special benefit. Frequently schools which run nine months in the winter are continued throughout the summer, whenever a sufficient number of people can be induced to attend them. Sometimes, for example, as in New York state, where a large number of men were employed in digging the Erie Canal and in excavating the Croton Aqueduct, camp schools were started where the men employed on these public works in the day might have an opportunity to learn the English language at night. In some cases a special kind of textbook, written in two or three different languages, was prepared for use in these immigrant schools, and frequently teachers were specially employed who could teach in the native languages if necessary.

While in the North all this effort is being made to provide education for these foreign peoples, many of whom are sojourners in this country and will return in a few months to their homes in Europe, the Negro in the South has, as is often true in the country districts, no school at all, or one with a term of no more than four or five months, taught in the wreck of a log cabin and by a teacher who is paid about half the price received for the hire of a first-class convict.

There is sometimes much talk about the inferiority of the Negro. In practice, however, the idea appears to be that he is a sort of superman. He is expected, with about one fifth of what the whites receive for their education, to make as much progress as they are making. Taking the Southern states as a whole, about $10.23 per capita is spent in educating the average white boy or girl, and the sum of $2.82 per capita in educating the average black child.

In order to furnish the Negro with educational facilities so that the two million children of school age now out of school and the one million who are unable to read or write can have the proper chance in life, it will be necessary to increase the nine million dollars now being expended annually for Negro public-school education in the South to about twenty-five or fifty million dollars.

I find that the total value of all the property owned by institutions devoted to the industrial, secondary and higher training of Negroes amounts to about twenty million dollars, which is less than the combined values of the property owned by the two institutions alone—the University of Chicago and Columbia

University. The total value of the property owned by institutions for whites in the United States for secondary, higher and industrial training amounts to almost one billion dollars. The value of the manual-training and industrial schools for whites is almost fifty million dollars. If the amount of property devoted to Negro higher education were at all proportionate to the number of Negroes in the population of the country, they would have for their higher training about one hundred million dollars invested in property instead of the twenty million dollars which they now have.

In order to give the Negro youth in the South adequate facilities for obtaining thorough training in normal and college courses, it will be necessary to increase the little more than four million dollars now being expended annually for Negro higher and secondary education to ten million dollars or more. In other words Negro higher and secondary education needs about six million dollars more annually than it is now receiving.

At the present rate it is taking, not a few days or a few years, but a century or more to get Negro education on a plane at all similar to that on which the education of the whites is. To bring Negro education up where it ought to be, it will take the combined and increased efforts of all the agencies now engaged in this work. The North, the South, the religious associations, the educational boards, white people and black people, all will have to cooperate in a great effort to this common end.

SECTION IV

World War I to World War II

1917–1942

THE KIND OF DEMOCRACY THE NEGRO RACE EXPECTS

By William Pickens

When the United States entered World War I in 1917, to make the world safe for democracy, Negroes flocked to the armed forces, and by the time the war ended, more than 360,000 black Americans had served in the armed services. They hoped that they would now at last enjoy the fruits of democracy. In the speech below, delivered at various times in the course of America's participation in World War I, William Pickens outlined the type of democracy the Negro was fighting for and expressed optimism that this goal would be achieved.

Pickens was born in Pendleton, South Carolina, on January 15, 1881. At an early age his ex-slave parents moved near Little Rock, Arkansas, where he attended elementary and high school. He graduated from Yale with high honors, taught at Talladega and Wiley Colleges, and became dean of Morgan College. Pickens left Morgan to become field secretary for the N.A.A.C.P.

(The text of the speech presented here is taken from Carter G. Woodson, Negro Orators and Their Orations, pp. 654–58.)

DEMOCRACY is the most used term in the world today. But some of its uses are abuses. Everybody says "Democracy"! But everybody has his own definition. By the extraordinary weight of the Presidency of the United States many undemocratic people have had this word forced upon their lips but have not yet had the right ideal forced upon their hearts. I have heard of one woman who wondered with alarm whether "democracy" would mean that colored women would have the right to take any vacant seat or space on a streetcar, even if they had paid for it. That such a question should be asked, shows how many different meanings men may attach to the one word *democracy*. This woman doubtless believes in a democracy of me-and-my-kind, which is no democracy. The most autocratic and the worst caste systems could call themselves democratic by that definition. Even the Prussian *Junker* believes in that type of democracy: he has no doubt that he and the other *Junkers* should be free and equal in rights and privileges.

Many have accepted the word *democracy* merely as the current password to respectability in political thinking. The spirit of the times is demanding democracy; it is the tune of the age; it is the song to sing. But some are like that man who belonged to one of our greater political parties: after hearing convincing arguments by the stump speaker of the opposite party, he exclaimed: "Wa-al, that fellow has convinced my judgment, but I'll be *d——d* if he can *change my vote!*"

It is in order, therefore, for the Negro to state clearly what he means by *democracy* and what he is fighting for.

First. Democracy in Education. This is fundamental. No other democracy is practicable unless all of the people have equal right and opportunity to develop according to their individual endowments. There can be no real democracy between two natural groups, if one represents the extreme of ignorance and the other the best intelligence. The common public school and the state university should be the foundation stones of democracy. If men are artificially differentiated at the beginning, if we try to educate a "working class" and a "ruling class," forcing different race groups into different lines without regard to individual fitness, how can we ever hope for democracy in the other relations of these groups? Individuals will differ, but in democracy of education peoples living on the same soil should not be widely diverged in their training on mere racial lines. This would be illogical, since they are to be measured by the same standards of life. Of course, a group that is to live in Florida should be differently trained from a group that is to live in Alaska; but that is geography and general environment, and not color or caste. The Negro believes in democracy of education as first and fundamental; that the distinction should be made between individual talents and not between colors and castes.

Second. Democracy in Industry. The right to work in any line for which the individual is best prepared, and to be paid the standard wage. This is also fundamental. In the last analysis there could be very little democracy between multimillionaires and the abject poor. There must be a more just and fair distribution of wealth in a democracy. And certainly this is not possible unless men work at the occupations for which they are endowed and best prepared. There should be no "colored" wages and no "white" wages; no "man's" wage and no "woman's" wage.

Wages should be paid for the work done, measured as much as possible by its productiveness. No door of opportunity should be closed to a man on any other ground than that of his individual unfitness. The cruelest and most undemocratic thing in the world is to require of the individual man that his whole race be fit before he can be regarded as fit for a certain privilege or responsibility. That rule, strictly applied, would exclude any man of any race from any position. For every man to serve where he is most able to serve is public economy and is to the best interest of the state. This lamentable war that was forced upon us should make that plain to the dullest of us. Suppose that, when this war broke out, our whole country had been like Mississippi (and I refer to geography uninvidiously)—suppose our whole country had been like Mississippi, where a caste system was holding the majority of the population in the triple chains of ignorance, semiserfdom and poverty. Our nation would be now either the unwilling prey or the golden goose for the Prussian. The long-headed thing for any state is to let every man do his best all of the time. But some people are so shortsighted that they only see what is thrust against their noses. The Negro asks American labor in the name of democracy to get rid of its color caste and industrial *Junkerism*.

Third. Democracy in State. A political democracy in which all are equal before the laws; where there is one standard of justice, written and unwritten; where all men and women may be citizens by the same qualifications, agreed upon and specified. We believe in this as much for South Africa as for South Carolina, and we hope that our American nation will not agree with any government, ally or enemy, that is willing to make a peace that will bind the African Negro to political slavery and exploitation.

Many other evils grow out of political inequality. Discriminating laws are the mother of the mob spirit. The political philosopher in Washington, after publishing his opinion that a Negro by the fault of being a Negro is unfit to be a member of Congress, cannot expect an ignorant white man in Tennessee to believe that the same Negro is, nevertheless, fit to have a fair and impartial trial in a Tennessee court. Ignorance is too logical for that. I disagree with the premises but I agree with the reasoning of the Tennesseean: that if being a Negro unfits a man for holding a government office for which he is otherwise fit, it unfits the same man for claiming a "white man's" chance in the courts. The first move therefore against mob violence and injustice in the petty courts is to wipe out discriminating laws and practices in the higher circles of government. The ignorant man in Tennessee will not rise in ideal above the intelligent man in Washington.

Fourth. Democracy without Sex Preferment. The Negro cannot consistently oppose color discrimination and support sex discrimination in democratic government. This happened to be the opinion also of the First Man of the Negro race in America —Frederick Douglass.* The handicap is nothing more nor less than a presumption in the mind of the physically dominant element of the universal inferiority of the weaker or subject element. It is so easy to prove that the man who is down and under, deserves to be down and under. In the first place, he is down there, isn't he? And that is three fourths of the argument to the ordinary mind; for the ordinary mind does not seek ultimate causes. The argument against the participation of colored men and of women in self-government is practically one argument. Somebody spoke to the Creator about both of these classes and learned that they were "created" for inferior roles. Enfranchisement would spoil a good field hand or a good cook. Black men were once ignorant, women were once ignorant. Negroes had no political experience, women had no such experience. The argument forgets that people do not get experience on the outside. But the American Negro expects a democracy that will accord the right to vote to a sensible industrious woman rather than to a male tramp.

Fifth. Democracy in Church. The preachings and the practices of Jesus of Nazareth are perhaps the greatest influence in the production of modern democratic ideas. The Christian church is, therefore, no place for the caste spirit or for snobs. And the colored races the world over will have even more doubt in the future than they have had in the past of the real Christianity of any church which holds out to them the prospect of being united in heaven after being separated on earth.

Finally. The great colored races will in the future not be kinder to a sham democracy than to a "scrap-of-paper" autocracy. The private home, private right and private opinion must remain inviolate; but the commonwealth, the public places and public property must not be appropriated to the better use of any group by "Jim-Crowing" and segregating any other group. By the endowments of God and nature there are individual "spheres"; but there are no such widely different racial "spheres." Jesus' estimate of the individual soul is the taproot

* See pp. 517–20 above for Frederick Douglass' speech on Woman Suffrage.

of democracy, and any system which discourages the men of any race from individual achievement, is no democracy. To fix the status of a human soul on earth according to the physical group in which it was born, is the gang spirit of the savage which protects its own members and outlaws all others.

For real democracy the American Negro will live and die. His loyalty is always above suspicion, but his extraordinary spirit in the present war is born of his faith that on the side of his country and her allies is the best hope for such democracy. And he welcomes, too, the opportunity to lift the "Negro question" out of the narrow confines of the Southern United States and make it a world question. Like many other questions our domestic race question, instead of being settled by Mississippi and South Carolina, will now seek its settlement largely on the battlefields of Europe.

THEY ARE ALL HEROES

By Rev. Dr. George F. Miller

Negro soldiers training in the South were subject to constant goading and insults by white Southerners. Police brutality against blacks in uniform was a common complaint of the Negro soldiers. In several communities these practices caused indignant outbursts from black soldiers, and in Houston, Texas, it led to a riot. In September, 1917, the men of the Twenty-fourth Infantry, fed up with police harassment and insults by white civilians, beat up a few whites. The Negro soldiers were disarmed when it was feared that they would use their weapons in defending themselves. But the soldiers seized arms and in a battle with whites killed seventeen of them. With the merest pretense of a trial, thirteen black soldiers were hanged for murder and mutiny, forty-one were imprisoned for life, and forty others were held pending further investigation.

The Northern press joined the Southern papers in justifying the execution of the thirteen Negroes, but black Americans were furious. In a speech delivered on May 14, 1918, in St. Augustine's Episcopal Church (Colored) in Brooklyn, Rev. Dr. George F. Miller voiced black America's protest against the "legal lynching" of the black soldiers.

> Dr. Miller, one of the outstanding champions in the
> twentieth century of equal rights for Negroes, was born in
> Aiken, South Carolina, in 1873. He received his A. B. de-
> gree from Howard University in 1888 and the honorary
> degree of Doctor of Divinity in 1912. He was active in the
> founding of the N.A.A.C.P. in 1909 and in the Socialist
> party of New York both as a speaker and a candidate for
> office on the Socialist ticket. From 1901 to his death in
> 1948 Dr. Miller was rector of St. Augustine's Episcopal
> Church.
>
> (Dr. Miller's speech, presented here in part, is taken
> from the Brooklyn Daily Eagle, May 15, 1918.)

I AM NOT like the man who is fearful of what he may say
lest somebody take exception to him. The killing of these thirteen men we must deeply consider, as it comes close to us. I
here today charge that the commanding officer was guilty of a
military lynching, done for the purpose of appeasing the people
of the South, who had to be avenged. I wish to say to the Brooklyn *Eagle* that it is sadly mistaken when it says "the crime at
Houston will never be repeated." Give man the same provocation, and the same thing will happen fifty times again.

Lynching has never deterred the things that led up to it, and
this kind of thing will not make cowards of the black man.
Despite the court martial which is supreme at the present time,
the killing was done to appease the people of the South. The
war is not raging here in America as it is in Europe, and an opportunity should have been granted those men to have friends
make a plea for executive clemency.

If it had been reported in Washington, we would have been
able to make a plea for clemency. But those men were denied
their rights. They were soldiers and greater was their crime.
This is one phase. The people of the entire country should realize that it is a soldier's duty to hold his life cheap. The authority
that sent them there should have guarded them against the
brutality of the police.

I ask if this is calculated to increase our patriotism. There are
many of us who are not bound by ties of blood to these men
who consider that a deep wrong was done them. They were offered as a sacrifice upon the altar of infamous Southern prejudice. But still we are supposed to be glorying in patriotism and
are always proclaiming our patriotism. . . .

These men went to their death singing, that is something for
us to consider, something to be prouder about. These men did
not go to their deaths like dogs. Some people have predicted

that I will be in jail today. Anybody can be courageous when
there is no danger around. I feel that I have been called upon
to speak and we must trust God. I believe that in this world of
democracy the black man is going over the top with the rest of
them. It may be that we are in our darkest hour now, but they
can't shoot you for supplicating God. There are thousands today whose thoughts are the same as mine.

We should get the names of all these men. They are all heroes. They were men and only fought the wrongs of the police.
We should copy their example of courage and fortitude.

THE GREAT MIGRATION NORTH

By W. E. B. Du Bois

*During the years from 1910–1914, an average of over
900,000 Europeans migrated to this country each year. In
the following five years, the average fell to about 100,000
per year, due to World War I. In spite of the drop in immigration, the number of workers in manufacturing rose,
as did the output of the manufacturing sector. One of the
main sources of additional workers for Northern industries
was Southern Negroes. Many firms sent labor recruiters to
Southern areas and paid the transportation costs of Negroes, who would move to such cities as Chicago, New
York and Philadelphia. From 1910 to 1920 over half a million Negroes left the South for Northern cities.*

*Dr. W. E. B. Du Bois spoke frequently on the causes and
significance of the great migration north, and the following is an extract from one of these speeches, reprinted
from Philip S. Foner, editor, W. E. B. Du Bois Speaks:
Speeches and Addresses, 1890–1919 (New York, 1970),
pp. 268–71.*

SINCE 1910, the most significant economic development
among Negroes has been a large migration from the South.
This has been estimated to have involved at least 250,000 and
is still going on.

As to the reasons of the migration, undoubtedly the immediate cause was economic, and the movement began because of
floods in middle Alabama and Mississippi and because the lat-

est devastation of the boll weevil came in these same districts.

A second economic cause was the cutting off of immigration from Europe to the North and consequently widespread demand for common labor. The United States Department of Labor writes: "A representative to this department has made an investigation in regard thereto, but a report has not been printed for general distribution. It may be stated, however, that most of the help imported from the South has been employed by railroad companies, packinghouses, foundries, factories, automobile plants in northern states as far west as Nebraska. At the present time, the United States Employment Service is not cooperating in the direction of Negro help to the North."

The third reason has been outbreaks of mob violence in northern and southwestern Georgia and in western South Carolina.

These have been the three immediate causes, but back of them is, undoubtedly, the general dissatisfaction with the conditions in the South.

A colored man of Sumter, South Carolina, says: "The immediate occasion of the migration is, of course, the opportunity in the North, now at last open to us, for industrial betterment. The real causes are the conditions which we have had to bear because there was no escape."

These conditions he sums up as the destruction of the Negro's political rights, the curtailment of his civil rights, the lack of the protection of life, liberty and property, low wages, the Jim Crow car, residential and labor segregation laws and poor educational facilities.

The full economic result of this migration and its extent in the future cannot be forecast at the present writing, but the chances are that the demand for labor caused by the European war will result in a large rearrangement of Negro laborers and accelerate all tendencies in the distribution of that labor along lines already noted.

Figures like these are beginning to place the so-called Negro problem beyond the realm of mere opinion and prejudice. Here we see a social evolution working itself out before our eyes. The mass of freedmen are changing rapidly the economic basis of their social development. They have not given up their close connection with the soil, but they are changing its character tremendously, so that today a fourth of them are peasant proprietors. They are forcing themselves into the trades despite the long opposition of white labor unions. As small businessmen, purveying principally to their own group, they are gaining a foothold in trade. As more or less skilled employees, they form a considerable part of our transportation system and they are rapidly developing a professional class which serves its own group and also serves the nation at large.

Many indications of the effect of this new development are seen in the peculiar incidence of racial prejudice. We hear to-day less argument about Negro education and more about sumptuary laws to control Negro expenditure, freedom of movement and initiative and residence. Politically handicapped as the colored man is, he is learning to wield economic power, which shows that his political rights cannot long be held back. And finally, in the division of his occupations, there is evidence of forethought and calculation within the group which fore-shadows greater cooperation for the future.

Since the above was written, there has been a series of important economic happenings involving the American Negro which ought to be noted.

Severe floods and the cotton boll weevil reduced Negro tenants in many parts of the lower South to great distress during the winter following the declaration of war. They sold their cotton at a low figure or had none to sell. When the price of cotton rose, the plantation owners reaped the benefit and immediately began plans for the next season, calculating on labor at an unusually low price.

Meantime, a great foreign immigration of common laborers was cut off by the war, and there arose in the North an unusual demand for common labor. The Negroes began to migrate. In eighteen months 250,000 left the South and moved into the North. They were chiefly attracted by wages which were from 50 to 200 percent above what they had been used to receiving. And they saw also a chance to escape the lynching and discrimination of the South.

Every effort was made by the South to retain them. They were arrested wholesale, labor agents were taxed $500 to $1,000 or more, for licenses, and the daily press of the South began to take on a more conciliatory tone. A slow rise in wages has begun. The migration of Negroes, however, continues, since the demand continues. It is probable that not for a generation after the close of the war will there be any great immigration to the United States from Europe. In that case, the American Negro will have a chance to establish himself in large numbers in the North. We may look for migration of two or even three million.

To offset this, the labor unions have used every effort. The argument was that these blacks kept down the rate of wages. Undoubtedly they did keep wages from rising as high as they otherwise would have risen, but if Negroes had been received into the unions and trained into the philosophy of the labor cause (which for obvious reasons most of them did not know), they would have made as stanch union men as any. They are not working for low wages because they prefer to, but because they have to. Nine tenths of the unions, however, are closed absolutely against them, either by constitutional provision or by action of the local unions. It is probable, therefore, that the friction will go on in the North. East St. Louis has already been echoed at Chester, Pennsylvania,* and in other industrial centers.

Thus, in his effort to escape industrial slavery, murder, riot the unbelievable cruelty have met the Negro—and this not at the hands of the employers but at the hands of his fellow laborers who have in reality common cause with him.

"WORK OR FIGHT" IN THE SOUTH

By Walter F. White

One of the chief grievances of black Americans during World War I involved the "Work-or-Fight" rule promulgated by the federal government and the compulsory work legislation this rule gave rise to in state and local communities during the last year of the war. On May 24, 1918, the Provost Marshal of the United States Army, General Enoch E. Crowder, announced a work-or-fight order which

* In East St. Louis, Illinois, in 1917, at least forty Negroes lost their lives in a riot that grew out of the employment of Negroes in a factory holding government contracts. Negroes were stabbed, clubbed, and hanged. On July 28, 1917, Dr. Du Bois headed the great "Silent Protest Parade" on Fifth Avenue in New York staged by the N.A.A.C.P. in protest of the East St. Louis riots and other violence to Negroes. Some of the banners carried in the parade read: "Mr. President, why not make America safe for democracy?" and "Pray for the Lady Macbeths of East St. Louis."

On July 26, 1917, a race riot broke out in Chester, Pennsylvania, and continued on the twenty-seventh. It began when a mob of whites attacked two Negroes, one of whom shot someone in the mob in self-defense. On the twenty-seventh the mob overcame the local and state police and, before it could be suppressed by the arrival of additional guards, had killed three Negroes.

*stipulated that all able-bodied persons within the draft
ages must be employed in some necessary employment.
Soon Southern states, cities and small towns enacted compulsory-work laws that compelled all able-bodied men to
work under penalty of law. Blacks, including black women,
under these laws, were forced to work long hours for low
wages.*

*The N.A.A.C.P. led a protest movement against the com-
pulsory-work laws, and Walter F. White, who became assistant secretary of the organization in 1918, delivered
many speeches against these measures. His main speech
on the subject was published in* The New Republic *of
March 1, 1919, and is reprinted below.*

*Walter F. White was born in Atlanta, Georgia, on July
1, 1893. While his family was spared in the race riot of
1906, he always remembered the scenes of brutality
against the blacks. After graduation from Atlanta University, White did postgraduate study in economics and sociology at the College of the City of New York. After he became assistant secretary of the N.A.A.C.P., White played
a leading role in investigating lynchings. Posing as a white
man, he mingled freely with whites and exposed the lynchers. When James Weldon Johnson resigned his post as
executive secretary of the N.A.A.C.P. in 1930, White replaced him and remained in the post until his death in
1955.*

IN A SMALL TOWN in Alabama, sixteen miles from Montgomery, the state capital, the mayor of the town had a colored
cook. This cook one Saturday night asked her employer for a
higher wage. The mayor refused, stating that he had never paid
any more for a cook and wasn't going to do so now. The woman
thereupon quit, and, as the law provided, the mayor took up
her employment card, which he himself had issued to her. The
following morning a deputy sheriff appeared at her door and
demanded that she show her work card. Despite her explanation
of the reason why she had no card, she was arrested and on
Monday morning was brought up for trial *in the Mayor's Court,*
before the *mayor* himself. She was found guilty, and fined fourteen dollars, which fine was paid by the mayor, who then said
to her, "Go on up to my house, work out the fine and stop your
foolishness."

This is a striking example of the method by which certain
sections of the South have been able to improve on the Work-or-
Fight order of Provost Marshal General Crowder. This order

provided that every able-bodied male person between the draft
ages, must be engaged in some necessary employment. At first
this only included males of a maximum of thirty-one years of
age. Later the Selective Service Act was amended to include
males up to forty-five years of age. But it was not sufficient for
the many employers who found that the war took from them
workers they had used in civilian forms of labor, and, North
and South, compulsory-work laws were passed by various states.
Southern states whose legislatures were in session, Louisiana
and Kentucky, made a maximum working age for males of fifty-
five, and Georgia a maximum of sixty years. The Mississippi
legislature was also in session but passed no compulsory-work
legislation.

These federal and state laws, however, referred only to men.
But women's labor was also greatly in demand. The shortage of
domestic servants had been felt throughout the whole of the
United States, but it remained for the South to meet it in the
extraordinary manner exemplified by the mayor in Alabama.
Cities and towns and rural communities passed compulsory-
labor ordinances and by this means met with partial success in
keeping the population at its former work and sometimes at
prewar low wages. An effort to include women's labor within
the provisions of the Georgia state law was given up when determined opposition was voiced by leading Atlanta Negroes.

An example of the sort of local ordinance referred to is the
one passed in the little Georgia town of Wrightsville. This provided that "it shall be unlawful for any person from the ages of
sixteen to fifty inclusive to reside in or be upon the streets of
Wrightsville" unless this person can show that he "is actively
and assiduously engaged in useful employment fifty hours or
more per week." The law further provided that each person
must carry an employment card signed by his or her employer
showing that he or she had worked as the law provided. It can
easily be seen what a powerful weapon such a law would be in
the hands of those who would be unscrupulous enough to use
it. In Macon, Georgia, a colored woman was arrested for not
working. She told the court at her trial that she was married,
that her husband earned enough to enable her to stay at home
and take care of the home and her children, and these duties
kept her too busy to do any other work. Despite this statement,
she was fined $25.75 and told by the court that if she remained
in Macon she "would either work in service or on the public
works," as being married did not exempt her from the provisions
of the law.

In Birmingham, due to the shortage of domestic labor, an

article appeared on June 19 in local papers stating that all women must work. The white women immediately protested and on the twenty-first another article appeared headed "Negro Women Here Ordered to Work." About the same time the Municipal Employment Agency issued an order stating that "all *Negro* women . . . must either go to work or to jail." Twenty women were arrested, all colored, on the first day the order went into effect. The following morning the Birmingham *News* carried an ironical article headed: "United States Employment Bureau Calls Bluff of Ebony Hued Workers."

Some days later, the wife of a respectable colored man was sitting on her porch one afternoon paring potatoes for supper, waiting for her husband to come home from his work. An officer saw her, asked her if she was working, and on being told that her duties at home required all of her time and that her husband earned enough to allow her to stay at home, he arrested her for "vagrancy," taking her to the county jail. When her husband came home and was told of the arrest, he immediately went to the jail to provide bail for his wife. This he could not do as all of the officials had gone home. His wife was forced to remain in jail all night, and was released on bail the following morning. This case was dismissed when brought to trial.

In Bainbridge, Decatur County, Georgia, in July, the city council passed an ordinance forcing all women (which meant all *colored* women), whether married or not, whose duties were only those of their homes, to work at some particular job. An officer was sent to the homes of colored people who summoned the wives of a number of colored men to appear in court. There they were charged with vagrancy and fined fifteen dollars each and told that taking care of their homes was not enough work for them to be doing. On the following night an indignation meeting of the colored citizens was held and the city authorities were told that unless this unjust and discriminatory law were repealed, the colored people would resist "to the last drop of blood in their bodies." No further arrests were made.

No record could be found of any able-bodied white woman being molested.

These are some of the cases among colored women. The impulse to secure colored male labor and to hold it for such purposes as the white man felt most important to his own welfare was also in evidence. Among a number of instances the following are worthy of note:

In Pelham, Georgia, Rufus G. McCrary, colored, Agency Director for the Standard Life Insurance Company (Negro), a man who had under his direction twenty-five agents, the group having produced during 1917 over $900,000 worth of paid-for business, was informed by the town marshal that he must get a job as he (the town marshal) did not consider the selling of life insurance an essential occupation for a Negro. This was done in spite of the fact that Provost Marshal General Crowder had expressly stated that the selling of life insurance was essential. McCrary received a monthly salary of $225 and personally cleared over $3,000 annually through the bank at Pelham. The town marshal delivered this ultimatum to McCrary as he was lying in bed dangerously ill with influenza. McCrary died the following night. The marshal stated that he was acting under the orders of the county sheriff.

In the same town, Frank McCoy, a laborer at the Pelham Fertilizer Works, becoming dissatisfied with this work because of the lack of opportunity for advancement, and feeling that he had some ability in salesmanship, applied for and secured a part-time contract with the insurance company. He made an unusual success in this effort, producing between $15,000 and $20,000 of paid-for business each month, on which his commissions amounted to between $150 and $175 per month. This work was done on a part-time basis, the balance of his time being spent at the fertilizer works. The same town marshal ordered him to stop selling life insurance and to put in all of his time at the plant.

In Columbia County, in the western part of the state, no Negro can work for another Negro. If he wishes to work for an employer, he must work for a white employer.

In Lake County, Florida, eight colored men who were working as pickers in an orange grove where the scale of wages was much below the standard of $3.50 per day set by the Florida Citrus Exchange, like the mayor's cook, quit in order to go to work at another grove, where the wages were higher. Their employer notified the sheriff, upon finding that he could not secure other laborers to take their places, and the officer of the law called the men together and told them that they would either have "to go back to work at the former price, to war or to jail." This case, however, was so flagrant that it came to the attention of the State Labor Bureau. An adjuster was sent to the place and he settled the matter by allowing the men to continue at that grove where the wages were highest.

Enough has been said to show that many employers of Negro labor in the South utilized the national emergency to force Negroes into a condition which bordered virtually on peonage. No one can tell how far the system extended, as most of the offenses occurred in the smaller towns and communities where

Negroes dare not reveal the true conditions for fear of punishment, a fear which is well founded, as the lynching record of 1918 will testify.* In the larger cities the opposition of the Negroes themselves checked too-great abuses. The complaint of many reputable colored citizens in the cities is that the police authorities did not molest the criminal type of Negroes, the "blind tigers," gamblers, runners for immoral houses and the inmates of these houses, but only those who did work, even though they were of the casual labor group. If the campaign had been devoted solely to the former class, there would have been no opposition on the part of the better element of colored people, but in many cities there seems to be a reciprocal arrangement between the police and this class of community parasites.

The crux of the whole situation is found in the fact that domestic and farm labor has been affected by the new wartime conditions, and the South, in large measure, was unable to adjust itself to a condition where its former plethora of cheap labor was wiped out. It has the opportunity now to clean house and prevent further migration by wiping out the abuses which exist. If it is attempted through the courts to hammer down wages and persecute laborers, the South may expect increasingly to lose its Negro labor. Since 1914, it is variously estimated that between 500,000 and 1,500,000 Negroes have gone North. Without Negro labor, the South will be bankrupt. With it and its great natural resources, it can become one of the richest sections of the country. It remains to be seen whether the better element among the whites can (and will) gain the ascendancy over the larger element of those who practice the policy laid down by the Dred Scott decision of regarding the Negro as "having no rights which a white man is bound to respect."

* See pp. 737–39.

AFRICA AT THE PEACE TABLE AND THE DESCENDANTS OF AFRICANS IN OUR AMERICAN DEMOCRACY

By James Weldon Johnson

On January 6, 1919, the N.A.A.C.P. sponsored a mass meeting in New York's Carnegie Hall to voice the organization's program for the postwar world being shaped at the Congress of Versailles, and particularly to deal with the place of Africa at the peace conference. W. E. B. Du Bois had left for Europe on a mission for the N.A.A.C.P. to investigate the treatment of Negro soldiers abroad and to do what he could to see that the interests of Africa were represented during the peace negotiations. In his absence, "The Future of Africa—A Platform," drawn up by Dr. Du Bois and representing the point of view of the N.A.A.C.P., was read to the meeting. Preceding this was the main speech of the evening delivered by James Weldon Johnson, then the Field Secretary of the N.A.A.C.P.

James Weldon Johnson (1871–1938), distinguished poet, novelist, government official and secretary of the N.A.A.C.P., was born in Jacksonville, Florida, and received his early education there. He subsequently went to college at Atlanta University and was admitted to the Florida bar. In 1901, he and his brother, Rosamond, went to New York and entered the field of musical comedy with great success. From 1906 to 1913, Johnson was United States consul, first in Venezuela and later in Nicaragua. While he was in the consular service, he wrote his well-known novel, The Autobiography of an Ex-Colored Man, *dealing with the theme of passing into the white community. It was published in 1912. Upon his return to the United States, Johnson did newspaper work in New York and then became associated with the N.A.A.C.P., serving from 1916 to 1920 as field secretary, and from 1920 to 1930 as general secretary, during which he led the unsuccessful battle for the passage of the Dyer antilynching bill and exposed the conduct of United States Marines in Haiti. Johnson was a leading figure of the Harlem Renaissance, and his poetry and his anthology of Negro poetry,* Book of Amer-

ican Negro Poetry, *published in 1922, were very popular.
One of his earlier poems, "Lift Every Voice and Sing," was
set to music by his brother Rosamond; it was widely known
as the Negro national anthem.*
*Johnson's speech at the 1919 N.A.A.C.P. mass meeting
is presented here as excerpted from the text in* Africa in
the World Democracy *(New York: National Association
for the Advancement of Colored People, 1919), pp. 13–20.*

THERE HAS BEEN some slight criticism of the Advancement Association for the steps it has taken to bring Africa to
the attention of the Peace Conference and the civilized world.
There are those who profess to see in such a move a danger to
the cause of the American Negro. I wish to say that these steps
have not been the result of any passing flash of enthusiasm;
they were taken after careful thought and deliberation.

As long ago as the spring of 1915, Dr. Du Bois published in
the *Atlantic Monthly* an article entitled, "The African Roots of
War," in which he showed that when we cut down through the
layers of international rivalries and jealousies we found that
the roots of the Great War were in Africa.*

As soon as the Armistice was signed, the Association received
a large number of letters from organizations and individuals all
over the country and even from Canada, asking that some step
be taken to influence world opinion regarding the disposition
of the former German colonies in Africa. . . .

When the opportunity arose, the Advancement Association
sent Dr. Du Bois to France. He went in a threefold capacity: as
the special correspondent of *The Crisis* at the Peace Conference;
also to collect firsthand material to go into a history of the Negro in the Great War;† and as a representative of the Association for the purpose of bringing to bear all pressure possible on
the delegates at the peace table in the interest of the colored
people of the United States and of the world.

In the latter capacity it is the intention of Dr. Du Bois to call

---

* The article was published in the *Atlantic Monthly*, Vol. CXV, May,
1915, pp. 707–14. It is reprinted in Philip S. Foner, editor, *W. E. B. Du
Bois Speaks: Speeches and Addresses, 1890–1919*. New York, 1970, pp.
244–57.
† Although Dr. Du Bois never completed a full history of the Negro's
participation in the First World War, he did publish an essay on this
subject. See W. E. B. Du Bois, "An Essay Toward a History of the Black
Man in the Great War," *The Crisis*, June, 1919, pp. 63–87.

a Pan-African congress to meet in Paris and press the question of the internationalization of the former German colonies.*

The question will arise in the minds of some as to why the demand for self-determination is not included in this program for the future of these colonies. It is omitted not because of doubt in either the right of the natives to self-government or their ability for it, but because of the very practical reason that the question of the former German colonies will come up before the Peace Conference in only three forms: their return to Germany, their division among the Allies, or their internationalization.

It is idle to hope, even in this era of making the world safe for democracy, that any people will secure self-determination by merely petitioning for it or even as a matter of plain justice. Self-determination will be secured only by those who are in a position to force it. The natives of all the colonies in Africa may have self-determination whenever they are in a position to force it from their overlords. The internationalization of Central Africa holds the promise of being the quickest and least costly step by which the natives can reach that position.

And there is no man more preeminently fitted to press this matter than Dr. Du Bois—not only on account of his individual ability, but on account of the experience he gained and the connections he formed at the great Races Congress which met in London in 1911, to which he was a delegate.†

There are several reasons that justify the National Association in taking up the question of Africa, and I will give them to you briefly:

In the first place, the race question in the United States is a national question; the peace delegations neither of England, France nor Italy, would dare to broach it at the table; and it is hardly probable that the American delegation will voluntarily bring it up. Japan and China may possibly protest against discrimination against Asiatics. But not even these two great colored nations would so far violate international precedent and courtesy as to bring up to the peace table a matter which will

* The Pan-African Congress met in February, 1919, at the Grand Hotel in Paris and was attended by 57 delegetes including 16 American Negroes, 20 West Indians and 12 Africans. France, Belgium and Portugal were represented by officials.

† Dr. Du Bois delivered a paper at the Universal Races Congress held in London in July, 1911, entitled "The Negro Race in the United States." See G. Spiller, editor, Papers on Inter-Racial Problems, London, 1911, pp. 348–64.

be regarded as a domestic question with which only the United States is concerned.

I am not now speaking of what is right and of what ought to be done; I am speaking of what, according to all the probabilities and in accordance with international law, precedent, courtesy and *international red tape*, will and will not be done. I am facing the cold, hard facts.

On the other hand, the question of Africa is an international question; it belongs at the peace table; every nation represented there, from England to Liberia, can freely discuss it. Africa, as I have said, is at the bottom of this war, and I tell you we may form all the leagues of nations that can be formed, but if the African question is not settled justly, we will have wars and wars. Therefore, the African question being an international question, we had sense enough to know that we could bring it before this international body, and perhaps by that step pursue the very wisest and best means of focusing the attention of the peace delegates and the entire civilized world on the question of the just claims of the Negro everywhere.

There is another reason that justifies our interest in Africa, which is not so practical or material as the one I have just stated, but which is nevertheless vital in its effects. It will be a lamentable condition when the American Negro grows so narrow and so self-centered in his own wrongs and sufferings that he has no sympathy for the wrongs and sufferings of others, not even his blood brothers in Africa. When he reaches the state where he wants everybody to be interested in his condition, but has no interest in the condition of others, he will have forfeited the right to demand that others be interested in him.

Still another valid reason for taking up the cause of Africa is the dense ignorance about that land; not only dense ignorance, but criminal ignorance. There has been and still is a historical conspiracy against Africa which has successfully stripped the entire Negro race of all credit for what it contributed in past ages to the birth and growth of civilization.

Makers of history have taught the world that from the beginning of time the Negro has never been anything but a race of savages and slaves. Anyone who is willing to dig out the truth can learn that civilization was born in the upper valley of the River Nile; that in the misty ages of the past pure black men in Africa were observing the stars, were turning human speech into song, were discovering religious truths and laying the foundations of government, were utilizing the metals, developing agriculture and inventing the primitive tools—in fact, giving the impulse which started man on his upward climb; while the progenitors of present-day Anglo-Saxons and Teutons and Slavs were hairy savages living in dark caves and crunching on raw bones; savages that had not yet the faintest glimmer of a knowledge either of religion or letters or government.

Of course, the makers of history take cognizance of Egyptian civilization; but at the same time they claim that the ancient Egyptians were white people. This claim is made for obvious reasons, but it is made in spite of the fact that the features of the Sphinx and other early Egyptian monuments are as Negroid as the features of the typical deck hand of a Mississippi River steamboat.*

And in the same manner these makers of history have claimed as white other black and dark races who have accomplished something. The Arabs and the Hindus and the Moors are "white people." Efforts have been made to prove even that the Zulus on account of their bravery and prowess in battle are not really Negroes. We can all remember how, shortly after the close of the Russo-Japanese war, a number of scientifics and pseudo-scientifics sought to show that the Japanese people, after all, were a branch of the white race. It is a wonder that somebody didn't try to prove, after he licked Jim Jefferies, that Jack Johnson was a white man. Perhaps in the far future, when pugilism is a lost and forgotten art, some writer on the subject will try to prove it.

By these methods and means the Negro has been raped of all credit that is due him as a contributor to civilization. The truth is: the torch of civilization was lighted on the banks of the Nile, and we can trace the course of that torch, sometimes flaming, sometimes flickering, and at times all but extinguished—we can trace it from Egypt around the borders of the Mediterranean, through Greece and Italy and Spain, on into Northern Europe. In the hands of each people that held it, the torch of civilization has grown brighter and brighter, and then died down until it was passed on to other hands.

The fact that dark ages fell upon Africa and her people is no more of a discredit than the fact that dark ages fell upon the buried empires of Asia Minor, of Asia, and of ancient Greece. Races and peoples have in their turn carried this torch of civilization to a certain height, and then sunk back under the weight of their own exertions.

It seems that there is more truth than mythology in the story

* See Frederick Douglass, "The Claims of the Negro Ethnologically Considered," 1854, pp. 152–54.

of Antaeus and Hercules. Hercules in wrestling with Antaeus found that each time the giant was thrown he arose stronger. The secret lay in the fact that the earth was his mother, and each time he came in contact with her he gained renewed strength. Hercules then resorted to the stratagem of holding him off the earth until his strength was exhausted. So with races and peoples; it seems that after they have climbed to a certain height, they must fall back and lie close to the earth.

And this reminds us of the truth that all things in the universe move in cycles; so who knows but that in the whirl of God's great wheel the torch may not again flame in the upper valley of the Nile?

We ought to know about Africa, and if we did we would not be ashamed of it but proud of it. A knowledge of its history would give the background which would enable the Negro to hold up his head among the peoples of the world.

And it is only just that in the settlement to follow the war provisions should be made to secure the soil of Africa and the resources thereof for the benefit primarily of the natives; and for the establishment of governments that may insure them self-determination as rapidly as possible.

But the main interest of the Advancement Association, notwithstanding its broad sympathies for all oppressed peoples, is not in Africa and Africans, but in America and colored Americans. And the Advancement Association knows enough to realize that the problem of the Negro in the United States is not going to be settled around the peace table at Versailles. It knows that the powers of Europe are not going to do very much, even if they could, to change the laws and the disregard of laws in Georgia and Alabama and Mississippi.

And so, although the Advancement Association is willing to accomplish as much as is possible by bringing Africa, which is an international question, before this international body, it realizes that the fight for the democratic rights of the American Negro must be fought at close quarters right here at home.

In fact, the fight for democracy for native Africans and the fight for democracy for people of African descent in the United States are not on the same plane. The truth of the matter is, the question of the democratic rights of the American Negro has no recognized place at the peace table. The Negro in the United States is not a subject race and does not accept the status of a subject race. He is a citizen of the United States, with all the rights of American citizenship guaranteed him by the Constitution. Subject races all over the world are today struggling to have certain rights of citizenship written for them in the laws of the nations to which they bear allegiance; therefore, their cases naturally go for consideration before the international tribunal which is now assembling. But the American Negro is contending for the fulfillment of rights already guaranteed him by the Constitution and for the impartial interpretation and application of existing laws.

In other words, the American Negro is not asking a favor; he is not asking for something that belongs to somebody else; he is demanding only that which is legally his; he is laying claim to that of which he is being wrongfully deprived. The question as to the wisdom of writing the Negro down in the Constitution as a citizen is aside from the point; what is written is written, and these laws are law. And the righteousness, the morality, the self-respect and the common decency of the nation are involved in seeing that these laws are carried out.

This is the battleground on which the forces of the Advancement Association are entrenched, and it is on this front that we intend to fight it out without hesitation, without fear and without compromise, until the end is achieved.

The National Association realizes that our fight is here at home and must be fought at close quarters—not over there, but right here. And that is the big job before us; that is the job which we have been tackling for ten years, with increasing force and increasing earnestness. It is a big job. There are many phases of it; it is complicated; it is complex. There is an economic side. A great many people hold that all of this question is economic; that it is simply a question of exploitation, just as the European countries exploit natives in Africa. That is good as far as it goes, but it does not entirely cover this problem of ours in the United States.

I cannot take up this whole question, but there are two phases of which I shall speak. There is a bitter race hatred and there is a national apathy and indifference with which we have to contend. I hardly know which is the more dangerous and which works the greater damage. Bitter race hatred is limited, but makes up in activity for its limitation. But the apathy on this question of human rights as it concerns the American Negro is general, it is widespread. It is a sort of inertia, it is a thing difficult to move. But that is one of the jobs this Association believes it has before it, and that is a job we are tackling.

To do this, we are using every rightful means that we can command. This nation is indifferent; it is not thinking about us as it should be made to think and as it was made to think sixty years ago. The country is very much concerned about democracy abroad, but not very much interested in democracy at home, so far as it applies to more than ten million Negro citizens. But I will tell you what we are going to do—and this Association has mapped it out as one of its lines of attack. It is our intention to carry on an intelligent, persistent and aggressive agitation until we educate this nation—*more* than educate it, until we whip and sting its conscience, until we awaken it, until we startle it into a realization that we know what we want, we know what we are entitled to, and that we are determined by all that is sacred to have it and be satisfied with nothing else.

We have just finished the great war for democracy. There were those in my own race who thought and taught that all we needed to do while black boys were fighting over there was to buy Liberty Bonds and Thrift Stamps, to assist in Red Cross drives and other activities, keep our mouths shut, and the war would do the rest. I did not suffer from any such hallucination. The war is over, and no miracle has happened. And no miracle is going to happen. Miracles of that kind never happen. If loyalty to the nation and fighting its battles could give the American Negro his full rights he would have had them long ago.

Only a couple of weeks ago the newspapers recorded the lynching of an honorably discharged Negro soldier in Kentucky. And what was the crime for which he was lynched? He had resisted arrest by a constable. He did not even kill the constable; he merely knocked him down and walked off, claiming that a civil officer had no right to arrest a man in uniform. That is an idea about the law which is common among soldiers and sailors. But the mob got him and lynched him.

I want to say to my own people that the main thing we have thus far gotten out of this war was not the chance to fight in France, but the right to fight more effectively here at home for the things in the name of which this war was waged.

I can never forget what I felt on the day that I saw New York's own black regiment, the Buffaloes, march up Fifth Avenue to receive a stand of colors to be presented by the Union League Club. I remember how I thrilled at the sight of them as they swung out of Madison Square into the finest street in the world; how New York looked on, perhaps, with some wonder that these men could march away so bravely to die to gain for others a thing which they themselves were yet denied. I saw them stop in front of the Union League Club, and heard a thousand voices sing "The Star-Spangled Banner" as New York had never heard it sung. Then from the balcony of the club the governor of the state came down and presented the colors. And as he gave the flag into their keeping he raised his voice, trembling with emotion, and cried out, "Bring it back! Bring it back, boys!

Bring it back!" and the answer welled up in my heart: Never
you fear, Mr. Governor, never you fear, gentlemen of the Union
League Club, they will bring it back; perhaps tattered and torn,
but they will bring it back. And they will bring it back as they
have always done, whenever it has been entrusted to their
hands, without once letting it trail in the dust, without putting
a single stain of dishonor upon it. Then it will be for you, Mr.
Governor, for you, gentlemen of the Union League Club, for
you, people of America, to remove the only stains that are upon
it, stains that are upon it as these men carry it into battle, the
stains of lynching, of disfranchisement, of Jim-Crowism, of injustice and oppression. The record of black men on the fields of
France and Flanders give us the greater right to point to that
flag and say to the nation, "Those stains are still upon it; they
dim its stars and soil its stripes. Wash them out! Wash them
out!"

A great deal has been said about the atrocities committed
during this terrible war by Huns and Turks; but there are millions of intelligent Americans who do not know, who are not
concerned with the fact that every year atrocities are committed in this enlightened land that would cause envy in the heart
of the most benighted Turk.

Only a few days ago four Negroes were lynched in Mississippi, accused of having killed a white physician. Two of them
were young men in their early twenties, and the other two were
girls still in their teens, sisters they were, one of them only sixteen. And this younger sister was about to become a mother.
That fact I learned from the account of the lynching given in
the principal white newspaper of Mississippi. I believe when the
truth about this case is known it will show that the white man
who was killed was the father of the unborn babe that was
lynched.

There is the case of Jim McIlheron less than a year ago in
Tennessee, accused of killing two white men in a street fight,
and tortured with red-hot irons, then burned alive at the stake.
Jim McIlheron was one of three Negroes who within nine
months were tortured and burned alive in the single state of
Tennessee.

The records as kept by the department of research at Tuskegee Institute show that during 1918, while white and black
Americans were fighting side by side to make the world safe for
democracy, white mobs here at home were lynching 58 Negroes,
five of them being women. These records also show that in only
one fourth of these cases was there even a charge of assault or
attempted assault on women. Eighteen of these lynchings occurred in the state of Georgia.

I ask not only black Americans, but white Americans, Are you not ashamed of lynching? Do you not hang your head in humiliation to think that this is the only civilized country in the world—no, more than that, the only spot on earth—where a human being may be tortured with hot irons and then burned alive? The nation is today striving to lead the moral forces of the world in the support of the weak against the strong; well, I'll tell you it can't do it until it conquers and crushes out this monster in its own midst.

When I had the honor of going before the President of the United States to plead for those colored soldiers who were concerned in the Houston affair, I told him of the case of Jim McIlheron, describing it in detail to him, and when I had finished my recital the President said to me, "I had not heard about it," and he had not heard about it. But that is the sad commentary —that in this great, free, enlightened democracy a human being could be burned alive at the stake and the head of the nation not even hear about it. But we are going to make them hear about it, not only the head of the nation, but we are going to put the raw, naked, brutal facts of this question before the conscience of the whole nation until we make it sick.*

Our President is in Europe endeavoring to establish his lofty ideals and principles:† The guarantee of peace, the spread of democracy, the safeguarding of liberty and the protection of the weak; we are praying that he will succeed, for our own welfare is involved in his success. But if he does not succeed in bringing the whole world around to his enlightened views, we hope he will not feel absolutely discouraged; he still has a vast field in the nation over which he presides.

Talk about democracy, and human brotherhood and the protection of the weak, it will all result in sheer hypocrisy, in what Saint Paul calls a sounding brass and a tinkling cymbal, unless we apply those principles here at home.

* The N.A.A.C.P. did exactly that. In 1919 the Association published and widely distributed *Thirty Years of Lynching in the United States*, and, at the same time, began a series of public meetings to protest lynchings. (More than 200 were held in 1921 alone.) On November 23, 1922, the N.A.A.C.P. published full-page advertisements in leading newspapers headed, "The Shame of America," which began: "Do you know that the United States is the *Only Land On Earth* where human beings are *Burned At The Stake!* In four years, 1918–1921, Twenty-Eight People Were *Burned By American Mobs*. 3,436 People Lynched 1889 to 1922." The remedy, the advertisement continued, was passage of the Dyer Anti-Lynching Bill before the U. S. Senate. But the bill was held up by a filibuster staged by Southern Democrats and was finally, with Republican assistance, abandoned.

† President Wilson left the United States on December 4, 1918, to attend the Peace Conference at Versailles.

And now, if you are ashamed of these things, there is something that you can do and that is join and support this great movement. I claim that the National Association for the Advancement of Colored People is the only absolutely democratic movement in the United States. It is a great American movement. This is not a race movement. If anyone has the idea that the plan of this organization is merely a race movement, he is mistaken. The platform of this organization is so broad that every man, woman and child who loves justice, who loves liberty, can stand upon it, regardless of race or color. And so I appeal to white men and white women everywhere, North and South; to my own people everywhere; to all white people who love justice and to all black people who love liberty, to join the ranks, the fighting ranks of this Association and help to make America a democracy in deeds as well as in words.

HOW I MANAGED TO REACH THE PEACE CONFERENCE

By William Monroe Trotter

Eleven delegates were chosen by black Americans to appear for the estimated fourteen million Negroes in the United States at the Peace Conference in Paris. They applied for passports, but failed to receive them, and so stayed at home. But William Monroe Trotter was made of sterner stuff. He disguised himself as a cook, and crossed the ocean in that capacity on a small steamer. While he did not succeed in securing an audience with any of the important personages meeting at the Conference to establish the "democracy of the world, the brotherhood of man, and the rights of oppressed people," he did send them protests against the denial of passports to black Americans and against the failure to insert in the Peace Treaty a clause guaranteeing them life and liberty. He also sent various stories to the Paris papers, describing the plight of his people in the United States. Upon his return to Boston, his home city, in mid-July, 1919, Trotter addressed a meeting in Tremont Temple telling of his experiences. Following is that address as published in the Christian Science Monitor, *July 25, 1919.*

I WAS THE only one of eleven delegates chosen by American Negroes to represent them at the Paris Peace Conference who actually reached France. The eleven delegates, as you know, were chosen at a national assembly of the Negro people of the country held under the auspices of the National Equal Rights League, in Washington last December. We were all instructed to place before the Peace Conference the claims of the 14,000,-000 Negroes in the United States for equal rights and no discrimination. As you know, all the eleven delegates applied for passports and failed to receive them. We Negroes felt that the State Department had wronged us in refusing to grant passports, because, when soldiers were needed to win the war, the promise of world democracy was held out and was accepted as genuine by the Negro people. The Negroes are practically the only element in this country who are denied complete democracy, and therefore we need it. To deny even the right of petition we felt was extraordinary tyranny, flagrant enough to justify us in seeking to overcome it.

I took the money raised for my trip to Paris, and after arranging my own affairs, I went to a seaport city, disguised, where I tried to obtain passage without a passport. This failed, but to avoid violating any laws, I obtained a seaman's passport. I had considerable difficulty in getting a job on a ship, but after a course in cooking in a lodginghouse, I finally gained the sympathy of a Negro cook on a small steamship and was signed as second cook. The job hunt took six weeks.

On reaching Havre, the ship did not dock for several days, but at last the opportunity came to go ashore. I found that all members of the crew were prohibited from landing, but I got a chance to go on the wharf to mail a letter written by the cook. Then, although I was in my working clothes, I continued into Havre and found that no train was available until morning. I had been obliged to leave all my belongings on shipboard, but I had a small sum of money with me. I boarded an early train to Paris, where I learned that the peace terms had just been handed Germany. I also found at about this time that the State Department had ruled against granting any passports to American Negroes, and I was convinced that the course I had followed was thereby justified.

The next day I began my work of telling the world that the Negro race wants full liberty and equality of rights, as the fruit of the World War. *Le Journal des Débats, L'Intransigeant* and *Le Petit Journal* used the communications I sent them. I sent the protest to every peace delegate and received sympathetic acknowledgment from many of them.

The Jews had received everything they asked from the Peace Conference. But here, in the United States, is an ethnical minority denied equal rights, and we are asking that we be accorded only what everyone else has. After the Memorial Day speech of President Wilson, I prepared a statement recalling that many of the American troops were Negroes and, in view of a lynching that had just occurred in Missouri, demanding that in justice to them he ask Congress for a federal law against lynching. This statement was widely published in the French press and was cabled to this country by the Associated Press.

The colored soldiers in France charged that they had been discriminated against in France. Leave was regulated by the color line, and Negro troops were restricted from visiting large cities, certain streets, and certain cafés. The white soldiers spread damaging stories about the colored men, in order to make the French people fear them.* All menial tasks were shouldered upon colored soldiers. I prepared a protest to President Wilson in behalf of the colored soldiers, which was also widely printed in France. I also gave to the French press the facts about a particularly atrocious lynching in the South.

I was unable to obtain an audience with President Wilson or Premier Clemenceau. On the day that the Germans signed the Peace Treaty I felt that my work had been completed, and on July 4 I sent to Sir Eric Drummond, of the League of Nations, suggestions for amendment of the Covenant in the interest of American Negroes. I then returned to America as a passenger.

THE FAITH OF THE AMERICAN NEGRO

By Mordecai Wyatt Johnson

Negro hopes that by their service in the war they might achieve some greater democracy at home were frustrated. Negro soldiers were organized in separate regiments and faced prejudice and discrimination throughout the war. The American government was extremely reluctant to establish officers' training schools for Negroes, and did so

---

* The reference is to rumors spread by the U.S. Army that black soldiers would rape French women if they were allowed the privilege of social relations with them.

*only after prodding by the N.A.A.C.P. On the home front,
Southern Negroes moved by the hundreds of thousands to
the North as World War I shut off European immigration
and increased the demand for industrial workers in the
North. While they did find conditions in some ways better
than those they had left in the South, they also encountered discrimination and in many cases ran into savage violence and race hatred. After the war, returning Negro
soldiers encountered great hostility, and the most serious
outbreak of race riots in American history followed. In
1919 alone there were more than twenty-five riots; that
summer and fall have been referred to as the "Red Summer," because of the blood shed in racial violence. The
postwar years also witnessed the rise in radicalism among
the Negro people and a renewed movement to return to
Africa. The consequences of these developments are discussed in a speech by Mordecai Wyatt Johnson at a Harvard University Commencement, June 22, 1922.*

*Born in Paris, Tennessee, January 12, 1890, Johnson
was educated at various academies and colleges and universities, including Morehouse College, University of Chicago, and Harvard University. He became Professor of Social Science at Morehouse, Pastor of the First Baptist
Church, Charleston, West Virginia, and for many years,
beginning in 1926, was president of Howard University.*

*Johnson's speech, presented here, is taken from the text
in Carter G. Woodson,* Negro Orators and Their Orations,
pp. 658–63.

SINCE THEIR EMANCIPATION from slavery the masses of
American Negroes have lived by the strength of a simple but
deeply moving faith. They have believed in the love and providence of a just and holy God; they have believed in the principles of democracy and in the righteous purpose of the federal
government; and they have believed in the disposition of the
American people as a whole and in the long run to be fair in all
their dealings.

In spite of disfranchisement and peonage, mob violence and
public contempt, they have kept this faith and have allowed
themselves to hope with the optimism of Booker T. Washington
that in proportion as they grew in intelligence, wealth and self-
respect they should win the confidence and esteem of their fellow white Americans and should gradually acquire the responsibilities and privileges of full American citizenship.

In recent years, and especially since the Great War, this sim-

ple faith has suffered a widespread disintegration. When the
United States government set forth its war aims, called upon
Negro soldiers to stand by the colors and Negro civilians, men,
women and children, to devote their labor and earnings to the
cause, and when the war shortage of labor permitted a quarter
million Negroes to leave the former slave states for the better
conditions of the North, the entire Negro people experienced
a profound sense of spiritual release. For the first time since
emancipation they found themselves comparatively free to sell
their labor on the open market for a living wage, found themselves launched on a great world enterprise with a chance to
vote in a real and decisive way, and, best of all, in the heat of
the struggle they found themselves bound with other Americans
in the spiritual fellowship of a common cause.

When they stood on the height of this exalted experience and
looked down on their prewar poverty, impotence and spiritual
isolation, they realized as never before the depth of the harm
they had suffered, and there arose in them a mighty hope that
in some way the war would work a change in their situation.
For a time indeed it seemed that their hope would be realized.
For when the former slave states saw their labor leaving for
the North, they began to reflect upon the treatment they had
been accustomed to give the Negro, and they decided that it was
radically wrong. Newspapers and public orators everywhere expressed this change of sentiment, set forth the wrongs in detail, and urged immediate improvement. And immediate improvement came. Better educational facilities were provided
here and there, words of appreciation for the worth and spirit of
the Negro as a citizen began to be uttered, and public committees arose to inquire into his grievances and to lay out programs
for setting these grievances right. The colored people in these
states had never experienced such collective good will, and
many of them were so grateful and happy that they actually
prayed for the prolongation of the war.

At the close of the war, however, the Negro's hopes were suddenly dashed to the ground. Southern newspapers began at once
to tell the Negro soldiers that the war was over and the sooner
they forgot it the better. "Pull off your uniform," they said, "find
the place you had before the war, and stay in it." "Act like a
Negro should act," said one newspaper, "work like a Negro
should work, talk like a Negro should talk, study like a Negro
should study. Dismiss all ideas of independency or of being
lifted up to the plane of the white man. Understand the necessity of keeping a Negro's place." In connection with such ad-
monitions there came the great collective attacks on Negro life

and property in Washington, Chicago, Omaha, Elaine and Tulsa.* There came also the increasing boldness of lynchers who advertised their purposes in advance and had their photographs taken around the burning bodies of their victims. There came vain appeals by the colored people to the President of the United States and to the houses of Congress. And finally there came the reorganization and rapid growth of the Ku Klux Klan.†

The swift succession and frank brutality of all this was more than the Negro people could bear. Their simple faith and hope broke down. Multitudes took weapons in their hands and fought back violence with bloody resistance. "If we must die," they said, "it is well that we die fighting."‡ And the Negro American world, looking on their deed with no light of hope to see by, said, "It is self-defense; it is the law of nature, of man, and of God; and it is well."

From those terrible days until this day the Negro's faith in the righteous purpose of the federal government has sagged. Some have laid the blame on the parties in power. Some have laid it

* For three days during the summer of 1919, mobs, made up mainly of white sailors, soldiers, and marines, ran through the streets of Washington, D. C., killing several Negroes and injuring scores of others. The Negroes fought back, killing whites who attempted to invade and burn the Negro section of the city.

The Chicago riot started on July 27, 1919, and lasted thirteen days. Thirty-eight persons were killed—23 Negroes and 15 whites.

The riot in Omaha, Nebraska, resulted in the lynching of one Negro and the severe beating of several others.

In 1919 Negro farmers and sharecroppers in and around Elaine, Arkansas, attempted to organize to secure improvements in their conditions and end peonage. They were attacked by a sheriff's posse, and when a deputy was killed, a reign of terror spread throughout the area during which over two hundred Negroes were murdered. In a trial which lasted less than an hour, 12 Negro farmers were sentenced to death and 67 others were given long prison terms. In a case brought by the N.A.A.C.P., *Moore v. Dempsey* (1923), the Supreme Court reversed the convictions.

The Tulsa riot occurred in June, 1921. Twenty-one Negroes and nine whites were killed.

† The Invisible Empire of the Ku Klux Klan was reorganized in 1915 and, during the decade between 1920 and 1930, had almost two million members. It exercised political control over such diverse states as Texas, Oregon, Indiana, Colorado and Georgia.

‡ Negroes resisted and fought back against white mobs in all of the riots that took place following World War I. Claude McKay, the black poet, expressed the feelings of many Negroes in his poem, "If We Must Die," the last two lines of which went:

> Like men we'll face the murderous, cowardly pack,
> Pressed to the wall, dying but fighting back!

elsewhere. But all the colored people, in every section of the United States, believe that there is something wrong, and not accidentally wrong, at the very heart of the government.

Some of our young men are giving up the Christian religion, thinking that their fathers were fools to have believed it so long. One group among us repudiates entirely the simple faith of former days. It would put no trust in God, no trust in democracy, and would entertain no hope for betterment under the present form of government. It believes that the United States government is through and through controlled by selfish capitalists who have no fundamental good will for Negroes or for any sort of laborers whatever. In their publications and on the platform the members of this group urge the colored man to seek his salvation by alliance with the revolutionary labor movement of America and the world.

Another and larger group among us believes in religion and believes in the principles of democracy, but not in the white man's religion and not in the white man's democracy. It believes that the creed of the former slave states is the tacit creed of the whole nation, and that the Negro may never expect to acquire economic, political and spiritual liberty in America. This group has held congresses with representatives from the entire Negro world, to lay the foundations of a black empire, a black religion and a black culture; it has organized the provisional Republic of Africa, set going a multitude of economic enterprises, instituted branches of its organization wherever Negroes are to be found, and binds them together with a newspaper ably edited in two languages.

Whatever one may think of these radical movements and their destiny, one thing is certain: they are home-grown fruits, with roots deep sprung in a world of black American suffering. Their power lies in the appeal which they make to the Negro to find a way out of his trouble by new and self-reliant paths. The larger masses of the colored people do not belong to these more radical movements. They retain their belief in the Christian God, they love their country, and hope to work out their salvation within its bounds. But they are completely disillusioned. They see themselves surrounded on every hand by a sentiment of antagonism which does not intend to be fair. They see themselves partly reduced to peonage, shut out from labor unions, forced to an inferior status before the courts, made subjects of public contempt, lynched and mobbed with impunity, and deprived of the ballot, their only means of social defense. They see this antagonistic sentiment consolidated in the places of power in the former slave states and growing by leaps and bounds in the North and West. They know that it is gradually reducing them to an economic, political and social caste. And they are now no longer able to believe with Dr. Booker T. Washington, or with any other man, that their own efforts after intelligence, wealth and self-respect can in any wise avail to deliver them from these conditions unless they have the protection of a just and beneficent public policy in keeping with American ideals. With one voice, therefore, from pulpit and from press, and from the humblest walks of life, they are sending up a cry of pain and petition such as is heard today among the citizens of no other civilized nation in the world. They are asking for the protection of life, for the security of property, for the liberation of their peons, for the freedom to sell their labor on the open market, for a human being's chance in the courts, for a better system of public education, and for the boon of the ballot. They ask, in short, for public equality under the protection of the federal government.

Their request is sustained by every sentiment of humanity and by every holy ideal for which this nation stands. The time has come when the elemental justice called for in this petition should be embodied in a public policy initiated by the federal government and continuously supervised by a commission of that government representing the faith and will of the whole American people.

The Negro people of America have been with us here for three hundred years. They have cut our forests, tilled our fields, built our railroads, fought our battles, and in all of their trials until now they have manifested a simple faith, a grateful heart, a cheerful spirit, and an undivided loyalty to the nation that has been a thing of beauty to behold. Now they have come to the place where their faith can no longer feed on the bread of repression and violence. They ask for the bread of liberty, of public equality, and public responsibility. It must not be denied them.

We are now sufficiently far removed from the Civil War and its animosities to see that such elemental justice may be given to the Negro with entire good will and helpfulness toward the former slave states. We have already had one long attempt to build a wealth and culture on the backs of slaves. We found that it was a costly experiment, paid for at last with the blood of our best sons. There are some among our citizens who would turn their backs on history and repeat that experiment, and to their terrible heresy they would convert our entire great community. By every sacred bond of love for them we must not yield, and we must no longer leave them alone with their experiment. The faith of our whole nation must be brought to their support until such time as it is clear to them that their former slaves can be made both fully free and yet their faithful friends.

Across the seas the darker peoples of the earth are rising from their long sleep and are searching this Western world for light. Our Christian missionaries are among them. They are asking these missionaries: Can the Christian religion bind this multi-colored world in bonds of brotherhood? We of all nations are best prepared to answer that question, and to be their moral inspiration and their friend. For we have the world's problem of race relationships here in crucible, and by strength of our American faith we have made some encouraging progress in its solution. If the fires of this faith are kept burning around that crucible, what comes out of it is able to place these United States in the spiritual leadership of all humanity. When the Negro cries with pain from his deep hurt and lays his petition for elemental justice before the nation, he is calling upon the American people to kindle anew about the crucible of race relationships the fires of American faith.

THE PRINCIPLES OF THE UNIVERSAL NEGRO IMPROVEMENT ASSOCIATION

By Marcus Garvey

In the bitter, tension-ridden years after World War I, Marcus Garvey's Universal Negro Improvement Association won millions of followers, particularly among the black masses of the Northern cities. Garvey was born on August 17, 1887, in Jamaica, British West Indies, and apprenticed to learn the printer's trade. After trips to England and Central America, he came to the United States in 1916 and established his movement in Harlem. The goals of the Universal Negro Improvement Association were to instill race pride, develop an independent black nation in Africa, and gain economic and political control of black communities in the United States. Garvey started all-black business enterprises and launched the Black Star Line, a shipping enterprise financed by the sale of stock to blacks only. The movement began to disintegrate when it was discovered that only one of the vessels of the Black Star Line was sea-worthy, and further declined after Garvey was jailed in At-lanta in 1925 on the charge of using the mails to defraud. President Calvin Coolidge commuted his sentence in 1927, and Garvey was deported.

Garvey led the greatest black-nationalist movement in American history, and appealed to the black masses as no leader had ever done before. While scholars disagree over the actual number of members Garvey recruited for the U.N.I.A.—estimates range from five hundred thousand to three million—there is no question that Garvey launched the first mass movement among black Americans, and that his influence has continued down to the present day.

Here is the text of a speech Garvey delivered at Liberty Hall, New York City, November 25, 1922. The closing por-tion is among Garvey's most famous statements. (Text is taken from Philosophy and Opinions of Marcus Garvey, or Africa for the Africans, *Amy Jacques Garvey, compiler, New York, 1967, pp. 93–100.)*

OVER FIVE YEARS AGO the Universal Negro Improvement Association placed itself before the world as the movement through which the new and rising Negro would give expression of his feelings. This Association adopts an attitude not of hos-tility to other races and peoples of the world, but an attitude of self-respect, of manhood rights on behalf of four hundred mil-lion Negroes of the world.

We represent peace, harmony, love, human sympathy, human rights and human justice, and that is why we fight so much. Wheresoever human rights are denied to any group, whereso-ever justice is denied to any group, there the U.N.I.A. finds a cause. And at this time among all the peoples of the world, the group that suffers most from injustice, the group that is denied most of those rights that belong to all humanity, is the black group of four hundred million. Because of that injustice, be-cause of that denial of our rights, we go forth under the leader-ship of the One who is always on the side of right to fight the common cause of humanity; to fight as we fought in the Revo-lutionary War, as we fought in the Civil War, as we fought in the Spanish-American War, and as we fought in the war be-tween 1914 and '18 on the battle plains of France and Flanders. As we fought on the heights of Mesopotamia; even so under the leadership of the U.N.I.A., we are marshaling the four hun-dred million Negroes of the world to fight for the emancipation of the race and for the redemption of the country of our fathers.

We represent a new line of thought among Negroes. Whether you call it advanced thought or reactionary thought, I do not care. If it is reactionary for people to seek independence in government, then we are reactionary. If it is advanced thought for people to seek liberty and freedom, then we represent the advanced school of thought among the Negroes of this country. We of the U.N.I.A. believe that what is good for the other folks is good for us. If government is something that is worth while; if government is something that is appreciable and helpful and protective to others, then we also want to experiment in government. We do not mean a government that will make us citizens without rights or subjects without consideration. We mean a kind of government that will place our race in control even as other races are in control of their own governments.

That does not suggest anything that is unreasonable. It was not unreasonable for George Washington, the great hero and father of the country, to have fought for the freedom of America, giving to us this great republic and this great democracy; it was not unreasonable for the liberals of France to have fought against the monarchy to give to the world French democracy and French republicanism; it was no unrighteous cause that led Tolstoy to sound the call of liberty in Russia, which has ended in giving to the world the social democracy of Russia, an experiment that will probably prove to be a boon and a blessing to mankind.* If it was not an unrighteous cause that led Washington to fight for the independence of this country, and led the liberals of France to establish the Republic, it is therefore not an unrighteous cause for the U.N.I.A. to lead four hundred million Negroes all over the world to fight for the liberation of our country.

Therefore the U.N.I.A. is not advocating the cause of church building, because we have a sufficiently large number of churches among us to minister to the spiritual needs of the people, and we are not going to compete with those who are engaged in so splendid a work; we are not engaged in building any new social institutions, and Y.M.C.A. or Y.W.C.A., because there are enough social workers engaged in those praiseworthy efforts. We are not engaged in politics, because we have enough local politicians—Democrats, Socialists, Soviets, et cetera—and the political situation is well taken care of. We are not engaged in domestic politics, in church building or in social-uplift work, but we are engaged in nation building.

* The reference is to the Bolshevik Revolution of November, 1917, and the establishment of the Soviet Union, the first Socialist state in history.

MISREPRESENTATIONS

In advocating the principles of this Association we find we have been very much misunderstood and very much misrepresented by men from within our own race, as well as others from without. Any reform movement that seeks to bring about changes for the benefit of humanity is bound to be misrepresented by those who have always taken it upon themselves to administer to, and lead the unfortunate, and to direct those who may be placed under temporary disadvantages. It has been so in all other movements whether social or political; hence those of us in the Universal Negro Improvement Association who lead, do not feel in any way embarrassed about this misrepresentation, about this misunderstanding as far as the aims and objects of the Universal Negro Improvement Association go. But those who probably would have taken kindly notice of this great movement, have been led to believe that this movement seeks, not to develop the good within the race, but to give expression to that which is most destructive and most harmful to society and to government.

I desire to remove the misunderstanding that has been created in the minds of millions of peoples throughout the world in their relationship to the organization. The Universal Negro Improvement Association stands for the *bigger brotherhood;* the Universal Negro Improvement Association stands for human rights, not only for Negroes, but for all races. The Universal Negro Improvement Association believes in the rights of not only the black race, but the white race, the yellow race and the brown race. The Universal Negro Improvement Association believes that the white man has as much right to be considered, the yellow man has as much right to be considered, the brown man has as much right to be considered as well as the black man of Africa. In view of the fact that the black man of Africa has contributed as much to the world as the white man of Europe and the brown man and yellow man of Asia, we of the Universal Negro Improvement Association demand that the white, yellow and brown races give to the black man his place in the civilization of the world. We ask for nothing more than the rights of four hundred million Negroes. We are not seeking, as I said before, to destroy or disrupt the society or the government of other races, but we are determined that four hundred million of us shall unite ourselves to free our motherland from the grasp of the invader. We of the Universal Negro Improvement Association are determined to unite four hundred million

Negroes for their own industrial, political, social and religious emancipation.

We of the Universal Negro Improvement Association are determined to unite the four hundred million Negroes of the world to give expression to their own feeling; we are determined to unite the four hundred million Negroes of the world for the purpose of building a civilization of their own. And in that effort we desire to bring together the fifteen million of the United States, the one hundred and eighty million in Asia, the West Indies and Central and South America, and the two hundred million in Africa. We are looking toward political freedom on the continent of Africa, the land of our fathers.

NOT SEEKING A GOVERNMENT WITHIN A GOVERNMENT

The Universal Negro Improvement Association is not seeking to build up another government within the bounds or borders of the United States of America. The Universal Negro Improvement Association is not seeking to disrupt any organized system of government, but the Association is determined to bring Negroes together for the building-up of a nation of their own. And why? Because we have been forced to it. We have been forced to it throughout the world; not only in America, not only in Europe, not only in the British Empire, but wheresoever the black man happens to find himself, he has been forced to do for himself.

To talk about government is a little more than some of our people can appreciate just at this time. The average man does not think that way, just because he finds himself a citizen or a subject of some country. He seems to say, "Why should there be need for any other government?" We are French, English or American. But we of the U.N.I.A. have studied seriously this question of nationality among Negroes—this American nationality, this British nationality, this French, Italian or Spanish nationality—and have discovered that it counts for nought when that nationality comes in conflict with the racial idealism of the group that rules. When our interests clash with those of the ruling faction, then we find that we have absolutely no rights. In times of peace, when everything is all right, Negroes have a hard time, wherever we go, wheresoever we find ourselves, getting those rights that belong to us, in common with others whom we claim as fellow citizens; getting that consideration that should be ours by right of the constitution, by right of the law; but in the time of trouble they make us all partners in the cause, as happened in the last war, when we were partners, whether British, French or American Negroes. And we were told that we must forget everything in an effort to save the nation.

We have saved many nations in this manner, and we have lost our lives doing that before. Hundreds of thousands—nay, millions of black men, lie buried under the ground due to that old-time camouflage of saving the nation. We saved the British Empire; we saved the French Empire; we saved this glorious country more than once; and all that we have received for our sacrifices, all that we have received for what we have done, even in giving up our lives, is just what you are receiving now, just what I am receiving now.

You and I fare no better in America, in the British Empire, or in any other part of the white world; we fare no better than any black man wheresoever he shows his head. And why? Because we have been satisfied to allow ourselves to be led, educated, to be directed by the other fellow, who has always sought to lead in the world in that direction that would satisfy him and strengthen his position. We have allowed ourselves for the last five hundred years to be a race of followers, following every race that has led in the direction that would make them more secure.

The U.N.I.A. is reversing the old-time order of things. We refuse to be followers any more. We are leading ourselves. That means, if any saving is to be done, later on, whether it is saving this one nation or that one government, we are going to seek a method of saving Africa first. Why? And why Africa? Because Africa has become the grand prize of the nations. Africa has become the big game of the nation hunters. Today Africa looms as the greatest commercial, industrial and political prize in the world.

THE DIFFERENCE BETWEEN THE U.N.I.A. AND OTHER OR-
GANIZATIONS

The difference between the Universal Negro Improvement Association and the other movements of this country, and probably the world, is that the Universal Negro Improvement Association seeks independence of government, while the other organizations seek to make the Negro a secondary part of existing governments. We differ from the organizations in America because they seek to subordinate the Negro as a secondary consideration in a great civilization, knowing that in America the Negro will never reach his highest ambition, knowing that the Negro in America will never get his Constitutional rights. All those organizations which are fostering the improvement of

Negroes in the British Empire know that the Negro in the British Empire will never reach the height of his Constitutional rights. What do I mean by Constitutional rights in America? If the black man is to reach the height of his ambition in this country—if the black man is to get all of his Constitutional rights in America—then the black man should have the same chance in the nation as any other man to become president of the nation, or a street cleaner in New York. If the black man in the British Empire is to have all his constitutional rights it means that the Negro in the British Empire should have at least the same right to become premier of Great Britain as he has to become street cleaner in the city of London. Are they prepared to give us such political equality? You and I can live in the United States of America for a hundred more years, and our generations may live for two hundred years or for five thousand more years, and so long as there is a black and white population, when the majority is on the side of the white race, you and I will never get political justice or get political equality in this country. Then why should a black man with rising ambition, after preparing himself in every possible way to give expression to that highest ambition, allow himself to be kept down by racial prejudice within a country? If I am as educated as the next man, if I am as prepared as the next man, if I have passed through the best schools and colleges and universities as the other fellow, why should I not have a fair chance to compete with the other fellow for the biggest position in the nation? I have feelings, I have blood, I have senses like the other fellow; I have ambition, I have hope. Why should he, because of some racial prejudice, keep me down and why should I concede to him the right to rise above me and to establish himself as my permanent master? That is where the U.N.I.A. differs from other organizations. I refuse to stultify my ambition, and every true Negro refuses to stultify his ambition to suit any one, and therefore the U.N.I.A. decides if America is not big enough for two presidents, if England is not big enough for two kings, then we are not going to quarrel over the matter; we will leave one president in America, we will leave one king in England, we will leave one president in France and we will have one president in Africa. Hence, the Universal Negro Improvement Association does not seek to interfere with the social and political systems of France, but by the arrangement of things today the U.N.I.A. refuses to recognize any political or social system in Africa except that which we are about to establish for ourselves.

NOT PREACHING HATE

We are not preaching a propaganda of hate against anybody. We love the white man; we love all humanity, because we feel that we cannot live without the other. The white man is as necessary to the existence of the Negro as the Negro is necessary to his existence. There is a common relationship that we cannot escape. Africa has certain things that Europe wants, and Europe has certain things that Africa wants, and if a fair and square deal must bring white and black with each other, it is impossible for us to escape it. Africa has oil, diamonds, copper, gold and rubber and all the minerals that Europe wants, and there must be some kind of relationship between Africa and Europe for a fair exchange. So we cannot afford to hate anybody.

NEGROES EVER READY TO ASSIST HUMANITY'S CAUSE

The question often asked is, what does it require to redeem a race and free a country? If it takes manpower, if it takes scientific intelligence, if it takes education of any kind, or if it takes blood, then the four hundred million Negroes of the world have it.

It took the combined manpower of the Allies to put down the mad determination of the Kaiser to impose German will upon the world and upon humanity. Among those who suppressed his mad ambition were two million Negroes who have not yet forgotten how to drive men across the firing line. Surely those of us who faced German shot and shell at the Marne, at Verdun, have not forgotten the order of our Commander in Chief. The cry that caused us to leave America in such mad haste, when white fellow citizens of America refused to fight and said, "We do not believe in war and therefore, even though we are American citizens, and even though the nation is in danger, we will not go to war." When many of them cried out and said, "We are German-Americans and we cannot fight," when so many white men refused to answer to the call and dodged behind all kinds of excuses, four hundred million black men were ready without a question. It was because we were told it was a war of democracy; it was a war for the liberation of the weaker peoples of the world. We heard the cry of Woodrow Wilson, not because we liked him so, but because the things he said were of such a nature that they appealed to us as men. Wheresoever the cause of humanity stands in need of assistance, there you will find the Negro ever ready to serve.

He has done it from the time of Christ up to now. When the whole world turned its back upon the Christ, the man who was said to be the Son of God, when the world cried out "Crucify Him," when the world spurned Him and spat upon Him, it was a black man, Simon, the Cyrenian, who took up the cross. Why? Because the cause of humanity appealed to him. When the black man saw the suffering Jew, struggling under the heavy cross, he was willing to go to His assistance, and he bore that cross up to the heights of Calvary. In the spirit of Simon, the Cyrenian, nineteen hundred years ago, we answered the call of Woodrow Wilson, the call of a larger humanity, and it was for that that we willingly rushed into the war from America, from the West Indies, over one hundred thousand; it was for that that we rushed into the war from Africa, two million of us. We met in France, Flanders and in Mesopotamia. We fought unfalteringly. When the white men faltered and fell back on their battle lines, at the Marne and at Verdun, when they ran away from the charge of the German hordes, the black hell fighters stood before the cannonade, stood before the charge, and again they shouted, "There will be a hot time in the old town tonight."

We made it so hot a few months after our appearance in France and on the various battle fronts, we succeeded in driving the German hordes across the Rhine, and driving the Kaiser out of Germany, and out of Potsdam into Holland.* We have not forgotten the prowess of war. If we have been liberal-minded enough to give our life's blood in France, in Mesopotamia and elsewhere, fighting for the white man, whom we have always assisted, surely we have not forgotten to fight for ourselves, and when the time comes that the world will again give Africa an opportunity for freedom, surely four hundred million black men will march out on the battle plains of Africa, under the colors of the red, the black and the green.

We shall march out, yes, as black American citizens, as black British subjects, as black French citizens, as black Italians or as black Spaniards, but we shall march out with a greater loyalty, the loyalty of race. We shall march out in answer to the cry of our fathers, who cry out to us for the redemption of our own country, our motherland, Africa.

We shall march out, not forgetting the blessings of America. We shall march out, not forgetting the blessings of civilization.

* Early in November, 1918, Wilhelm I, Emperor of Germany, abdicated his throne and went into exile in Holland.

We shall march out with a history of peace before and behind us, and surely that history shall be our breastplate, for how can man fight better than knowing that the cause for which he fights is righteous? How can man fight more gloriously than by knowing that behind him is a history of slavery, a history of bloody carnage and massacre inflicted upon a race because of its inability to protect itself and fight? Shall we not fight for the glorious opportunity of protecting and forever more establishing ourselves as a mighty race and nation, never more to be disrespected by men. Glorious shall be the battle when the time comes to fight for our people and our race.

We should say to the millions who are in Africa to hold the fort, for we are coming, four hundred million strong.

OUR DEMOCRACY AND THE BALLOT

By James Weldon Johnson

Below is an address James Weldon Johnson delivered at a dinner to Congressman (later New York Mayor) Fiorello H. La Guardia at the Hotel Pennsylvania, New York City, March 10, 1923. In it, Johnson speaks out strongly against the disfranchisement of the Negro in the South, and calls for steps to be taken to force compliance with the Fourteenth Amendment. The speech as presented here is excerpted from the text in Carter G. Woodson, Negro Orators and Their Orations, *pp. 663–71.*

. . . IT IS one of the commonplaces of American thought that we have a democracy based upon the free will of the governed. The popular idea of the strength of this democracy is that it is founded upon the fact that every American citizen, through the ballot, is a ruler in his own right; that every citizen of age and outside of jail or the insane asylum has the undisputed right to determine through his vote by what laws he shall be governed and by whom these laws shall be enforced.

I could be cynical or flippant and illustrate in how many ways this popular idea is a fiction, but it is not my purpose to deal in *cleverisms*. I wish to bring to your attention seriously a situation, a condition, which not only runs counter to the popular conception of democracy in America but which runs counter to the fundamental law upon which that democracy rests and which, in addition, is a negation of our principles of government and a menace to our institutions.

Without any waste of words, I come directly to a condition which exists in that section of our country which we call "the South," where millions of American citizens are denied both the right to vote and the privilege of qualifying themselves to vote. I refer to the wholesale disfranchisement of Negro citizens. There is no need at this time of going minutely into the methods employed to bring about this condition or into the reasons given as justification for those methods. Neither am I called upon to give proof of my general statement that millions of Negro citizens in the South are disfranchised. It is no secret. There are the published records of state constitutional conventions in which the whole subject is set forth with brutal frankness. The purpose of these state constitutional conventions is stated over and over again, that purpose being to exclude from the right of franchise the Negro, however literate, and to include the white man, however illiterate.

The press of the South, public men in public utterances, and representatives of those states in Congress, have not only admitted these facts but have boasted of them. And so we have it as an admitted and undisputed fact that there are upwards of four million Negroes in the South who are denied the right to vote but who in any of the great Northern, Midwestern or Western states would be allowed to vote or would at least have the privilege of qualifying themselves to vote.

Now, nothing is further from me than the intention to discuss this question either from an anti-South point of view or from a pro-Negro point of view. It is my intention to put it before you purely as an American question, a question in which is involved the political life of the whole country.

Let us first consider this situation as a violation, not merely a violation but a defiance, of the Constitution of the United States. The fourteenth and fifteenth amendments to the Constitution taken together express so plainly that a grammar-school boy can understand it that the Negro is created a citizen of the United States and that as such he is entitled to all the rights of every other citizen and that those rights, specifically among them the right to vote, shall not be denied or abridged by the United States or by any state. This is the expressed meaning of these amendments in spite of all the sophistry and fallacious pretense which have been invoked by the courts to overcome it.

There are some, perhaps even here, who feel that it is no

more serious a matter to violate or defy one amendment to the Constitution than another. Such persons will have in mind the Eighteenth Amendment.* This is true in a strictly legal sense, but any sort of analysis will show that violation of the two Civil War amendments strikes deeper. As important as the Eighteenth Amendment may be, it is not fundamental; it contains no grant of rights to the citizen nor any requirement of service from him. It is rather a sort of welfare regulation for his personal conduct and for his general moral uplift.

But the two Civil War amendments are grants of citizenship rights and a guarantee of protection in those rights, and therefore their observation is fundamental and vital not only to the citizen but to the integrity of the government.

We may next consider it as a question of political franchise equality between the states. We need not here go into a list of figures. A few examples will strike the difference:

In the elections of 1920 it took 82,492 votes in Mississippi to elect two Senators and eight Representatives. In Kansas it took 570,220 votes to elect exactly the same representation. Another illustration from the statistics of the same election shows that one vote in Louisiana has fifteen times the political power of one vote in Kansas.

In the Congressional elections of 1918 the total vote for the ten Representatives from the state of Alabama was 62,345, while the total vote for ten Representatives in Congress from Minnesota was 229,127, and the total vote in Iowa, which has ten Representatives, was 316,377.

In the Presidential election of 1916 the states of Alabama, Arkansas, Georgia, Louisiana, Mississippi, North Carolina, South Carolina, Tennessee, Texas and Virginia cast a total vote for the Presidential candidates of 1,870,209. In Congress these states have a total of 104 Representatives and 126 votes in the Electoral College. The state of New York alone cast a total vote for Presidential candidates of 1,706,354, a vote within 170,000 of all the votes cast by the above states, and yet New York has only 43 Representatives and 45 votes in the Electoral College.

What becomes of our democracy when such conditions of inequality as these can be brought about through chicanery, the open violation of the law and defiance of the Constitution?

But the question naturally arises, What if there is violation of certain clauses of the Constitution; what if there is an in-

* The Eighteenth Amendment prohibited the sale and shipment of intoxicating liquors. It passed Congress in December, 1917, was ratified in January, 1919, and went into effect in January, 1920.

equality of political power among the states? All this may be justified by necessity.

In fact, the justification is constantly offered. The justification goes back and makes a long story. It is grounded in memories of the Reconstruction period. Although most of those who were actors during that period have long since died, and although there is a new South and a new Negro, the argument is still made that the Negro is ignorant, the Negro is illiterate, the Negro is venal, the Negro is inferior; and, therefore, for the preservation of civilized government in the South, he must be debarred from the polls. This argument does not take into account the fact that the restrictions are not against ignorance, illiteracy and venality, because by the very practices by which intelligent, decent Negroes are debarred, ignorant and illiterate white men are included.

Is this pronounced desire on the part of the South for an enlightened franchise sincere, and what has been the result of these practices during the past forty years? What has been the effect socially, intellectually and politically, on the South? In all three of these vital phases of life the South is, of all sections of the country, at the bottom. Socially, it is that section of the country where public opinion allows it to remain the only spot in the civilized world—no, more than that, we may count in the blackest spots of Africa and the most unfrequented islands of the sea—it is a section where public opinion allows it to remain the only spot on the earth where a human being may be publicly burned at the stake.

And what about its intellectual and political life? As to intellectual life I can do nothing better than quote from Mr. H. L. Mencken, himself a Southerner.* In speaking of the intellectual life of the South, Mr. Mencken says:

It is, indeed, amazing to contemplate so vast a vacuity. One thinks of the interstellar spaces, of the colossal reaches of the now mythical ether. One could throw into the South France, Germany and Italy, and still have room for the British Isles. And yet, for all its size and all its wealth and all the "progress" it babbles of, it is almost as sterile, artistically, intellectually, culturally, as the Sahara Desert. . . . If the whole of the late Confederacy were to be engulfed by a tidal wave tomorrow, the effect on the civilized

---

* H. L. Mencken (1880–1956), famous literary and social iconoclast, was born and operated in Baltimore, Maryland. He was the editor of the *American Mercury* and author of a series of annual volumes, beginning in 1919, under the title *Prejudices*.

minority of men in the world would be but little greater than that
of a flood on the Yang-tse-kiang. It would be impossible in all history to match so complete a drying-up of a civilization. In all that
section there is not a single poet, not a serious historian, not a
creditable composer, not a critic good or bad, not a dramatist dead
or alive.

In a word, it may be said that this whole section where, at
the cost of the defiance of the Constitution, the perversion of
law, the stultification of men's consciousness, injustice and
violence upon a weaker group, the "purity" of the ballot has
been preserved and the right to vote restricted to only lineal
survivors of Lothrop Stoddard's mystical Nordic supermen—
that intellectually it is dead and politically it is rotten.

If this experiment in superdemocracy had resulted in one-
hundredth of what was promised, there might be justification
for it, but the result has been to make the South a section
not only in which Negroes are denied the right to vote, but one
in which white men dare not express their honest political
opinions. Talk about political corruption through the buying
of votes, here is political corruption which makes a white man
fear to express a divergent political opinion. The actual and
total result of this practice has been not only the disfranchisement of the Negro but the disfranchisement of the white man.
The figures which I quoted a few moments ago prove that not
only Negroes are denied the right to vote but that white men
fail to exercise it; and the latter condition is directly dependent
upon the former.

The whole condition is intolerable and should be abolished. It
has failed to justify itself even upon the grounds which it is
claimed made it necessary. Its results and its tendencies make
it more dangerous and more damaging than anything which
might result from an ignorant and illiterate electorate. How this
iniquity might be abolished is, however, another story.

I said that I did not intend to present this subject either as
anti-South or pro-Negro, and I repeat that I have not wished to
speak with anything that approached bitterness toward the
South. Indeed, I consider the condition of the South unfortunate—more than unfortunate. The South is in a state of superstition which makes it see ghosts and bogeymen, ghosts which
are the creation of its own mental processes.

With a free vote in the South the specter of Negro domination would vanish into thin air. There would naturally follow
a breaking-up of the South into two parties. There would be
political light, political discussion, the right to differences of

opinion, and the Negro vote would naturally divide itself. No other procedure would be probable. The idea of a solid party, a minority party at that, is inconceivable. But perhaps the South will not see the light.

Then, I believe, in the interest of the whole country, steps should be taken to compel compliance with the Constitution, and that should be done through the enforcement of the Fourteenth Amendment, which calls for a reduction in representation in proportion to the number of citizens in any state denied the right to vote.

And now I cannot sit down after all without saying one word for the group of which I am a member.

The Negro in the matter of the ballot demands only that he should be given the right as an American citizen to vote under the identical qualifications required of other citizens. He cares not how high those qualifications are made—whether they include the ability to read and write, or the possession of five hundred dollars, or a knowledge of the Einstein Theory—just so long as these qualifications are impartially demanded of white men and black men.

In this controversy over which have been waged battles of words and battles of blood, where does the Negro himself stand?

The Negro in the matter of the ballot demands only that he be given his right as an American citizen. He is justified in making this demand because of his undoubted Americanism, an Americanism which began when he first set foot on the shores of this country more than three hundred years ago, antedating even the Pilgrim Fathers; an Americanism which has woven him into the woof and warp of the country and which has impelled him to play his part in every war in which the country has been engaged, from the Revolution down to the late World War.

Through his whole history in this country he has worked with patience, and in spite of discouragement he has never turned his back on the light. Whatever may be his shortcomings, however slow may have been his progress, however disappointing may have been his achievements, he has never consciously sought the backward path. He has always kept his face to the light and continued to struggle forward and upward in spite of obstacles, making his humble contributions to the common prosperity and glory of our land. And it is his land. With conscious pride the Negro can say:

> This land is ours by right of birth,
> This land is ours by right of toil;

We helped to turn its virgin earth,
Our sweat is in its fruitful soil.

Where once the tangled forest stood,
Where flourished once rank weed and thorn,
Behold the path-traced, peaceful wood,
The cotton white, the yellow corn.

To gain these fruits that have been earned,
To hold these fields that have been won,
Our arms have strained, our backs have burned
Bent bare beneath a ruthless sun.

That banner which is now the type
Of victory on field and flood—
Remember, its first crimson stripe
Was dyed by Attucks' willing blood.

And never yet has come the cry—
When that fair flag has been assailed—
For men to do, for men to die,
That we have faltered or have failed.

The Negro stands as the supreme test of the civilization, the Christianity and the common decency of the American people. It is upon the answer demanded of America today by the Negro that there depends the fulfillment or the failure of democracy in America. I believe that that answer will be the right and just answer. I believe that the spirit in which American democracy was founded, though often turned aside and often thwarted, can never be defeated or destroyed but that ultimately it will triumph.

If American democracy cannot stand the test of giving to any citizen who measures up to the qualifications required of others the full rights and privileges of American citizenship, then we had just as well abandon that democracy in name as in deed. If the Constitution of the United States cannot extend the arm of protection around the weakest and humblest of American citizens as around the strongest and proudest, then it is not worth the paper it is written on.

THE SHAME OF AMERICA, OR THE NEGRO'S CASE AGAINST THE REPUBLIC

By Archibald H. Grimké

The long and shameful story of discrimination against black Americans throughout the history of the United States was never more clearly and forcefully presented than in the speech Archibald H. Grimké delivered in 1924 before the American Negro Academy. Grimké (1849–1930) received his collegiate education at Lincoln University, Pennsylvania, was graduated from Harvard Law School in 1874, and became a successful lawyer in Boston. An independent in politics, Grimké was appointed by President Grover Cleveland as consul in Santo Domingo from 1894 to 1898. He spent his later years in Washington, D. C., where he was active in the N.A.A.C.P. and spoke frequently on the Negro question. Grimké was president of the American Negro Academy from 1903 to 1916.

Below is a section of Grimké's great speech that begins with the era following the Civil War; in an earlier part of the speech he had dealt with the Negro's immense contributions to the Union victory.

(The speech as presented here has been excerpted from the text in The Shame of America; or, The Negro's Case Against the Republic *by Archibald H. Grimké,* American Negro Academy Occasional Papers, No. 21, Washington, D. C., The Academy, 1924.*)*

. . . AMID WIDESPREAD REJOICING on the return of peace and the restoration of the Union, the Negro rejoiced among the gladdest, for his slave fetters were broken, he was no longer a chattel. He imagined in his simple heart, in his ignorance and poverty, that he had not only won freedom, but the lasting affection and gratitude of the powerful people for whom he had entered hell, to quench for them its raging fires with his blood. Yes, although black and despised, he, the slave, the hated one, had risen above his centuries of wrongs, above their bitter memories and bitterer sufferings to the love of enemies, to the forgiveness of those who had despitefully used him, ay, to those moral heights where heroes are throned and martyrs crowned. Surely, surely, he, who had been so unmindful of self in the

service of country, would not be left by that country at the mercy
of those who hated him then with the most terrible hatred for
that very cause. He who had been mighty to save others would
surely, now in his need, be saved by those whom he had saved.
"Oh! Justice, thou hast fled to brutish beasts, and men have lost
their gratitude."

I would gladly seal forever the dark chapter of our history,
which followed the close of the war. Gladly would I forget that
record of national shame and selfishness. But as it is better to
turn on light than to shut it off, I will, with your forbearance,
turn it on for our illumination and guidance, in the lowering
present.

The chapter opened with an introduction of characteristic
indifference on the part of the country in respect to the fate of
the Negro. With his shackles lying close beside him, he was left
in the hands of his old master who, seizing the opportunity,
proceeded straightway to refit them on the disenthralled limbs
of the former slave. State after state did so with such prompti-
tude and to such effect that within a few months a formidable
system of Negro serfdom had actually been constructed, and
cunningly substituted in place of the system of Negro slavery,
which the war had destroyed. An African serf power, phoenix-
like, was rising out of the ashes of the old slave power into
national politics. At sight of this truly appalling apparition, the
apparition of a returning slave power in thin disguise, all the
old sectional fear and hatred which had existed against it in
the free states before the Rebellion, awoke suddenly and hotly
in the breast of the North. Thinking mainly, if not wholly, of
its own safety in the emergency which confronted it, and how
best to avert the fresh perils which impended in consequence
over its ascendancy, the North prepared to make, and did in
fact make, for the time being, short shrift of this boldly retro-
active scheme of the South to recover within the Union all that
it had lost by its defeated attempt to land itself outside of the
Union.

Having tested to its entire satisfaction the Negro's value as a
soldier in its war for the preservation of the Union, the North
determined at this juncture to enlist his aid as a citizen in its
further conflicts with the South, for the preservation of its sectional domination in the newly restored Union. To this end the
fourteenth and fifteenth amendments to the Constitution were,
in the progress of events, incorporated into that instrument. By
these two great acts, the North had secured itself against the
danger of an immediate return of the South to anything like
political equality with it in the Republic. Between its supremacy

and the attacks of its old rival, it had erected a solid wall of
Negro votes. But immensely important as was the ballot to its
black contingent, it was not enough to meet all of his tremendous needs. Nevertheless, as the North was considering mainly
its own and not the Negro's necessities at this crisis, and as the
elective franchise in his hands was deemed by it adequate to
satisfy its own pressing needs, it gave the peculiar wants of the
Negro beyond that of the ballot but scant attention.

Homeless, landless, illiterate, just emerging from the blackness of two centuries of slavery, this simple and faithful folk
had surely other sacred claims on the North and the national
government than this right to the ballot. They had in truth a
strong claim to unselfish friendship and statesmanship, to un-
faltering care and guardianship, during the whole of their
transition from slavery to citizenship. They needed the organized hands, the wise heads, the warm hearts, the piled-up
wealth, the sleepless eyes, the faith, hope and charity of a
Christian people and a Christian government to teach them to
walk and to save them from industrial exploitation by their
old masters, as well as to vote. Did they receive from the Republic what the Republic owed them by every consideration of
justice, gratitude and humanity, as of enlightened self-interest?
Alas, not a tithe of this immense debt has the Republic ever
undertaken to pay to those who should have been, under all
circumstances, its sacredly preferred creditors. On the contrary
they were left to themselves by the government in the outer
darkness of that social state which had been their sad lot for
more than two centuries. They were left in that darkest night
of moral and civil anarchy to fight not alone their own terrible
battle with poverty, ignorance, and untutored appetites and passions, but also the unequal, the cruel battle for the preservation
of Northern political domination in the Union. For ten awful
years they fought that battle for the North, for the Republican
party, in the face of persecutions and oppressions, terrors and
atrocities, at the glare of which the country and the civilized
world shrank aghast.

Aghast shrank the North, but not for the poor Negro, faithful
unto death to it. For itself rather it shrank from the threatening
shadows which such a carnival of horrors was casting athwart
its vast and spreading network of trade and production. The
clamor of all its million-wheeled industry and prosperity was
for peace. "Let us have peace," said Grant, and "Let us have
peace" blew forthwith and in deafening unison, all the big and
little whistles of all the big and little factories and locomotives,
and steamships from Maine to California. Every pen of mer-

chant and editor scratched paper to the same mad tune. The pulpit and the platform of the land cooed their Cuckoo song in honor of those piping times of peace. The loud noise of chinking coin pouring into vaults like coal into bins, drowned the agonized cry of the forgotten and long-suffering Negro. Deserting him in 1876,* the North, stretching across the bloody chasm its two greedy, commercial hands, grasped the ensanguined ones of the South, and repeated, "Let us have peace." Little did the Northern people and the government reck then or now that at the bottom of that bloody chasm lay their faithful black friends. Little did they care that the blood on those Southern hands had been wrung drop by drop from the loyal heart of the Negro. But enough.

Years of struggle and oppression follow and we come to another chapter of American history; namely, the Spanish-American War. In the Spanish-American War the Negro attracted the attention of the world by his dashing valor. He attracted the attention of his country also. His fighting quality was of the highest, unsurpassed, and perhaps unequaled in brilliancy by the rest of the American army that invaded Cuba. He elicited applause and grudging justice from his countrymen, dashed with envy and race prejudice. Still it seemed for a brief time that his conspicuous service had given his case against the Republic a little better standing in court—a little better chance for a fair hearing at the Bar of Public Opinion. But our characteristic national emotionalism was too shallow and insincere to last. In fact, it died aborning. The national habit of a century and a half reasserted itself. There was no attempt made to square national profession and national practice, national promise and national performance. The Negro again had given his all to his country and had got in return at the hands of that country wrong and injustice. Southern propaganda presently renewed all of its vicious and relentless activity against the Negro. He was different, he was alien, he was unassimilable, he was inferior, and he must be kept so, and in the scheme of things he must be made forever subordinate to the white race. In this scheme of things white domination could best be preserved by the establishment of a caste system based on race and color. And so, following the Spanish-American War the North and the South put their heads together to complete their

---

* In the disputed election of 1876, the Democrats agreed to give Rutherford B. Hayes, the Republican candidate, the Presidency in return for his agreement to remove the last federal troops from the Southern states. This permitted the reestablishment of white supremacy in the South.

caste system. Everywhere throughout the Republic race prejudice, color proscription grew apace. One by one rights and
privileges which the Negroes had enjoyed for a brief space were
withdrawn, and the wall of caste rose higher and higher. He
was slowly and surely being shut out from all the things which
white men enjoyed by virture of their citizenship, and shut
within narrowing limits of freedom. Everywhere within his
prison house he read in large and sinister letters, "Thus far and
no farther." He was trapped, and about to be caged. In spite of
the Emancipation Proclamation and the three war amendments
he found that white men were becoming bolder in ignoring or
violating his freedom and citizenship under them. The walls
of the new bondage were closing about his right to life, liberty
and the pursuit of happiness in this boasted Land of the Free
and Christian Home of Democratic Hypocrisy and Cruelty.

Then Mr. Taft appeared upon the scene and became famous,
or infamous, as a builder on the walls of the Temple of the
New American Jerusalem, where profession is High Priest to the
God of Broken Promises. He proved himself a master workman
in following the lines of caste, in putting into place a new stone
in the edifice when he announced as his policy at the beginning
of his administration that he would not appoint any colored
man to office in the South where the whites objected. Caste had
won and the Negro's status was fixed, as far as this bourgeois
apostle of American democracy was able to fix it. His adds but
another illustrious name to the long list of those architects of
national dishonor who sought to build the Temple of American
Liberty upon a basis of caste.

Then in the fullness of time came Woodrow Wilson, the ripe,
consummate fruit of all this national contradiction between
profession and practice, promise and performance. He can give
Messrs. Washington, Jefferson, Jackson and Company odds
and beat them in the subtle art of saying sonorously, grandi-
osely, what in action he does not hesitate to flout and spurn.
When seeking the Negro's vote in 1912 he was the most profuse
and generous in eloquent profession, in iridescent promises, but
when he was elected he forgot straightway those fair professions and promises,* and began within a week after he entered
the White House to put into office men filled with colorphobia,
the better to finish the work of undoing in the government the

* During Wilson's administration segregation was established in government departments. See Harold Blumenthal, "Woodrow Wilson and
Federal Segregation," *Journal of Negro History,* Vol. XLVI, January, 1963,
pp. 302–28.

citizenship of the Negro, to whom he had promised not grudging justice but the highly sympathetic article, heaping up and running over. Mr. Taft had established the principle that no Negro was to be appointed to office in the South where the whites objected; Mr. Wilson carried the principle logically one step farther, namely, no Negro was to be put to work in any department of the government with white men and women if these white men and women objected to his presence. Segregation along the color line in Federal employment became forthwith the fixed policy of the Wilson administration.

There sprang up under the malign influence of this false prophet of the New Freedom* all sorts of movements in the District of Columbia and in the federal government hostile to the Negro—movements to exclude him from all positions under the Civil Service above that of laborer and messenger and charwoman, to Jim-Crow him on the street cars, to prohibit him from intermarrying with the whites, to establish for him a residential pale in the District; in short, to fix forever his status as a permanently inferior caste in the land for which he had toiled in peace and bled and died in war. The evil influence of this false apostle of freedom spread far and wide and spurred the enemies of the Negro to unwonted activity. The movement of residential segregation and for rural segregation grew in volume and momentum in widely separated parts of the country until it was finally checked by the decision of the Supreme Court in 1917.†

The condition of the Negro was at its worst and his outlook in America at its darkest, when the government declared war against Germany. Then was revived the Republic's program of false promises and hypocritical professions in order to bring this black man with his brawn and brains, with his horny hands and lion heart, with his unquenchable loyalty and enthusiasm to its aid. No class of its citizens surpassed him in the swiftness and self-forgetfulness of his response to the call of country. What he had to give he brought to the altar and laid it there— labor and wealth, wounds and death—with unsurpassed devotion and patriotism. But what he received in return was the same old treatment, evil for his good, ingratitude and treachery for his loyalty and service. He was discriminated against everywhere—was used and abused, shut out from equal recognition

* The "New Freedom" was Woodrow Wilson's slogan in the Presidential campaign of 1912.
† In 1917 in the case of *Buchanan v. Warley*, the Supreme Court declared unconstitutional the Louisville ordinance requiring Negroes to live in certain sections of the city.

and promotion with white men and women. Then when he went overseas he found American colorphobia more deadly than the gun and poison gas of the Germans. In the American army there was operated a ceaseless propaganda of meanness and malice, of jealousy and detraction against him. If our Expeditionary Force had given itself with a tithe of the zeal and industry to fighting the Germans, which a large section of it devoted to fighting the black soldier, it would have come out of the war with more honor and credit, and left behind in France a keener sense of gratitude and regard than exists for them in that country today. But, alas, thousands of them were more interested in watching the Negro and his reception by the French, in concocting villainous plots to degrade him in the eyes of that people,* in segregating him from all social contact with them, and in keeping him in his place, within the hard and fast lines of caste which they had laid for him in America.

But the Negro went and saw—saw the incredible meanness and malice of his own country by the side of the immense genius for Liberty and Brotherhood of France. There he found himself a man and brother regardless of his race and color. But if he has seen these things in France he has also conquered certain other things in himself, and has come back not as he went, but a New Negro.† He has come back to challenge injustice in his own land and to fight wrong with a courage that will not fail him in the bitter and perhaps bloody years to come. For he knows now as he has never known before that he is an American citizen with the title deeds of his citizenship written in a century and a half of labor and suffering and blood. From his brave black lips I hear the ringing challenge, "This is my right and by the Eternal I have come back to claim all that belongs to me of industrial and political equality and liberty." And let us answer his high resolve with a courage and will to match his own, and so help to redeem our country from its shame of a century and a half of broken promises and dishonored ideals.

But be not deceived, friends. Let us, like brave men and women, face the stern reality of our situation. We are where we are. We are in the midst of a bitter and hitherto an invincible race prejudice, which beats down into the dust all of our rights,

---

* Dismayed by the fact that the French people treated Negroes as social equals, American leaders, including those in the U. S. Army, warned that black Americans would take advantage of these liberties by raping French women.

† The New Negro movement got under way in the early 1920's. One of its aspects was what came to be known as the "Harlem Renaissance."

all of our attainments, all of our aspirations after freedom and excellence. The North and the South are in substantial accord in respect to us and in respect to the position which we are to occupy in this land. We are to be forever exploited, forever treated as an alien race, allowed to live here in strict subordination and subjection to the white race. We are to hew for it wood, draw for it water, till for it the earth, drive for it coaches, wait for it at tables, black for it boots, run for it errands, receive from it crumbs and kicks, to be for it, in short, social mudsills on which shall rest the foundations of the vast fabric of its industrial democracy and civilization.

No one can save us from such a fate but God, but ourselves. You think, I know, that the North is more friendly to you than the South, that the Republican party does more for the solution of this problem than the Democratic. Friends, you are mistaken. A white man is a white man on this question, whether he lives in the North or in the South. Of course, there are splendid exceptions. Scratch the skin of Republican or Democrat, of Northern white men or Southern white men, and you will find close to the surface race prejudice, American colorphobia. The difference, did you but know it, is not even epidermal, is not skindeep. The hair is Democratic Esau's, and the voice is Republican Jacob's. That is all. Make no mistake here, for a true understanding of our actual position at this point is vital.

On Boston Common stands a masterpiece in bronze, erected to commemorate the heroism and patriotism of Colonel Robert Gould Shaw and his black regiment. There day and night, through summer and winter, storm and shine, are to march forever those brave men by the side of their valiant young leader. Into the unknown they are hurrying to front and to fight their enemies and the enemies of their country. They are not afraid. A high courage looks from their faces, lives in the martial motion of their bodies, flashes from the barrels of their guns. On and yet ever on they are marching, grim bolts of war, across the Common, through State Street, past the old State House, over ground consecrated by the martyr's blood of Crispus Attucks, and the martyr's feet of William Lloyd Garrison. Farther and farther they are pressing forward into the unknown, into the South, to Wagner and immortal deeds, to death and an immortal crown.

Friends, we too are marching through a living and lowering present into the unknown, through an enemy's land, at the summons of duty. We are to face great labors, great dangers, to fight like men our passions and American caste prejudice and oppression, and God helping us, to conquer them.

SHALL THE NEGRO BE ENCOURAGED TO SEEK CULTURAL EQUALITY?

By W. E. B. Du Bois

On March 17, 1929, the Chicago Forum sponsored a debate on the topic, "Shall the Negro Be Encouraged to Seek Cultural Equality?" Dr. Du Bois spoke for the affirmative and Lothrop Stoddard, the racist, white-supremacist, pro-Nordic ideologist and author of the fear-inspiring The Rising Tide of Color, *upheld the negative.*

(The speech presented here has been taken from the pamphlet Report of Debate Conducted by the Chicago Forum, *March 17, 1929, n,p., n.d., pp. 3–9.)*

WE MAY WELL ASK in the beginning, Just what does one mean by "equality"? And what is "cultural" equality? We might even ask, Just what are "Negroes"? And how are you going to "encourage" anyone to seek this sort of equality?

I am going to take the broad common-sense view of what these words mean. By equality, I do not mean absolute identity or similarity of gift, but gifts of essentially equal values to human culture. By culture, I mean that organized tide which men call civilization. And persons are encouraged to seek cultural equality by the taking-down of bars and doing away with discriminations—by abolishing all efforts that directly or indirectly impede people in attaining a certain goal.

If you were not familiar with the race problem in the United States or in the modern world, you would ask, Why should you not encourage Negroes or anybody else in the wide world to seek cultural equality? Is not this the aim of civilization? Is it not the ideal for which all men yearn? What could you conceive as better than a world in which all citizens not only were encouraged to cultural equality but accomplished their aim? Would not this be the best conceivable sort of world?

And yet, you who know America, know perfectly well that large numbers of people have always denied to the Negro even the chance to try to reach such a goal. This denial has taken two forms, or perhaps two degrees, of emphasis on the same thesis. In early days Americans said frankly: The Negro should not be encouraged to seek cultural equality, because he cannot reach it; he is not really human in the sense that other people are human. One does not encourage dogs to do the things that men do, not because one has anything against dogs, but because dogs are not men and cannot act like men. And the same way (although perhaps the analogy is overdrawn), Americans do not encourage Negroes to share modern culture, because they cannot share it; we would simply make them unhappy if we let them try to reach to things which they can never reach.

Some years ago that was a logical statement and a statement difficult to answer. But in the last generation things have happened, and they have happened fast. We have had since Emancipation a bounding-forward of these millions of dark people in America. It does not make any difference how far you may wish to minimize what Negroes have done or what judgment you have as to its lasting value, there is no doubt about the work that has been done by these millions of emancipated slaves and their descendants in America. It is one of the wonderful accomplishments of this generation. It has few parallels in human history.

Some people might assume that this rise of the American Negro from slavery to freedom, from squalor, poverty and ignorance to thrift and intelligence and the beginnings of wealth, would bring unstinted applause. Negroes themselves expected this. They looked eagerly forward to this day when you cannot write a history or statement of American civilization and leave the black man out, as proof of their equality and manhood and they expected their advance, incomplete or imperfect though it remains, nevertheless to be greeted with applause.

On the contrary, all Negroes know that with all the generous praise given us there has been no phase of the advance that has not been looked on with a strong undercurrent of apprehension. America has feared the coming-forward of these black men; it has looked upon it as a sort of threat. And if you should ask just why that is so, white Americans would state the thesis which they have stated before but with some modification; they would say that the coming-forward of these people does not prove that they can make as great a gift to culture as the white people have made, but whether they can or not, they must not be allowed to come forward, because it threatens civilization! If you ask how this can possibly be—how the advance of one tenth of a nation can be a threat to the rest—you have various kinds of answers.

In the first place some seem to regard culture as a quantitative sort of thing; there is a certain amount of culture in the world; if you divide it up among all people, you have that much less for other people. Of course, everybody knows that the quantitative theory of civilization does not hold, that the analogy is not perfect, and yet the reason we use it is because we do regard civilization today in terms of the number of our physical possessions. We are buried beneath our material wealth, and if we think, say, of motorcars, we conclude that if black people have motorcars, there are so many less for the white people to occupy. And so on. We go through the whole catalogue of what a material age calls civilization, and think that if it is distributed to certain people, other people are not going to have as much.

Discarding this quantitative analogy, we fall back to the other argument. After all, it is not the things which people have that makes the major part of civilization, the real civilization; real culture depends on quality and not quantity; it is not, therefore, so much a matter of distribution of goods—of distribution of quantity—as of contamination of quality in goods and deeds.

And there we have brought back into the modern world the theory which the world has held and heard again and again— a few people have the chance to get unusual advancement; they have the chance to learn; they have leisure to think; they have food and shelter and encouragement; they push forward in the world, and then, after they have reached certain heights, suddenly they are overcome with admiration for themselves; suddenly it is suggested to them that they are wonderful and unusual people; that the universe was made particularly and especially for them; that never before have human beings attained such height and mastery—and finally we have the theory of the Chosen People!

The theory is as old as human culture is old, and yet today it comes back to us in the new dress of the belief that everything that has been done in modern times has been done by the Nordic people; that they are the people who are the salt of the earth; that if anything is done to change their type of civilization, then civilization fails and falls; that what we have got to be afraid of is the coming-forward of a mass of black people without real gift, without real knowledge of what culture is, who are going to spoil the divine gifts of the Nordics.

To a theory of this sort, the world—the overwhelming majority of human beings who are not Nordic—have a right to two replies:

First, your theory is unproven. There is no scientific proof that modern culture is of Nordic origin or that Nordic brains and physique are of better intrinsic quality than Mediterranean, Indian, Chinese or Negro. In fact, the proofs of essential human equality of gift are overwhelming.

But, if Nordics believe in their own superiority, if they wish voluntarily to work by themselves and for the development and encouragement of their own gifts, if they prefer not to mingle their blood with other races, or contaminate their culture with foreign strains, nothing is to hinder them from carrying out this program except themselves.

Nobody is going to make Nordics marry outside of their own group unless they want to marry outside. They can keep their group closed if they wish. Of course, civilization is, by the definition of the term, civilization for all mankind; but nobody is going to withhold applause if you make your contribution to the world.

Of course, civilization is the rightful heritage of all and cannot be monopolized and confined to one group. A group organization to increase and forward culture is legitimate and will bring its reward in universal recognition and applause.

But this has never been the Nordic program. Their program is the subjection and rulership of the world for the benefit of the Nordics. They have overrun the earth and brought not simply modern civilization and technique, but with it exploitation, slavery and degradation to the majority of men. They have broken down native family life, desecrated homes of weaker peoples and spread their bastards over every corner of land and sea. They have been responsible for more intermixture of races than any other people, ancient or modern, and they have inflicted this miscegenation on helpless, unwilling slaves by force, fraud and insult; and this is the folk that today has the impudence to turn on the darker races when they demand a share of civilization, and cry: "You shall not marry our daughters!"

The blunt, crude reply is: Who in hell asked to marry your daughters? If this race problem must be reduced to a matter of sex, what we demand is the right to protect the decency of our own daughters.

But the insistent demand of the Darker World is far wider and deeper than this. The black and brown and yellow men demand the right to be men. They demand the right to have the artificial barriers placed in their path torn down and destroyed; they demand a voice in their own government; the organization of industry for the benefit of colored workers and not merely for white owners and masters; they demand education on the broadest and highest lines and they demand as human beings social contact with other human beings as a basis of perfect equality.

That is what they call civilization. That is what we American

Negroes demand, and the demand is so reasonable and logical that to deny it is not simply to hurt and hinder them, it is to fly in the face of your own white civilization.

Think of what has been done in the name of "white supremacy" right here in the United States; the Middle West today is politically helpless, because, in order to deprive black Americans of the right to vote, they allowed the South to cast two votes—the vote of the white man and of the disfranchised Negro. The double political power of these rotten boroughs of the South makes democratic government in the United States a farce.

You decry lawlessness. Where do you get the lawlessness of Chicago and of the United States? You began it when as a nation you disregarded the thirteenth, fourteenth and fifteenth amendments, and then are vastly surprised when you cannot enforce the eighteenth. You have organized your life so as not to carry out the laws which you yourselves made and you have the heritage of lawlessness to pay for it.

You have created here in the United States, which today pretends to the moral leadership of the world, a situation where on the last night of the old year you can slowly and publicly burn a human being alive for the amusement of Americans who represent some of the purest strains of Nordic blood in that great place, Mississippi, which has done so much for the civilization of the world!

Not simply in these things have you attacked your own civilization. You have made it almost impossible for America to think logically.

I said to you a while ago that I might ask you what Negroes were. I come back to that question. I stand here gladly as the representative of the Negro race, and yet I know and you know that I can equally stand here as a representative of the Nordic race. Wherever it seems necessary to deny me any privilege, then I am a Negro, and whenever I do anything that is worth doing, suddenly I become preponderantly white. The United States measured soldiers in the Great War and came to wonderful conclusions concerning their intelligence, but the conclusions they came to were conclusions for the Negro race, and they knew perfectly well the men they were measuring were not Negroes, but that perhaps 70 percent of them had white blood. It is impossible by any scientific measurement to divide men into races, and even to prove there are separate races; and yet we talk about races and prescribe races and measure races; and because we are not talking logically when we talk about races, so we cannot talk logically about anything else—the tariff, farm relief, unemployment, credit, wages or capital.

The matter of our logic is not nearly so important as that of our ethics and religion. Here you are, a great white nation with a magnificent plan of salvation. You have an ethical code far beyond anything the world ever knew—if you do not believe it, listen to what you preach to the darker peoples. You are followers of the Golden Rule and of the meek and lowly Jesus. Yet you do not try to follow out your own religion because you know when your religion comes up against the race problem that religion has nothing absolutely to do with your attitude toward Negroes. The attacks that white people themselves have made upon their own moral structure are worse for civilization than anything that any body of Negroes could ever do.

Therefore, you stand today before the Great Alternative. Are you going to allow the colored people in the United States and the colored races in the world to go forward toward the goals of civilization free and unhampered, or are you going to organize to see that these people are kept in the places where you think they ought to stay? Here is a great decision, a decision which the white world has got to face.

The temptation to hold these colored people back is tremendous, because it is not merely a matter of academic wish or of wanton prejudice, but it is the kernel of the organization of modern life. You have got the colored people working for you all through the world. You have got your investments so made that they depend upon colored labor in Asia, Africa, in the Southern states of the United States, and in the islands of the sea. Your income and your power depend upon that organization being kept intact. If it is overthrown, if these black laborers get higher wages, if they begin to understand what life may be, if they increase in knowledge, self-assertion and power, it means the overthrow of the whole system of exploitation which is at the bottom of modern white civilization. What now is your decision?

Suppose you turn to the other side. Suppose you say, despite anything that the darker races, including the Negroes in the United States, may ask, we are going to sit tight and keep them where they belong. Then the question is, Can you do it?

In the first place, have you the ability to do it? It is going to call for ability. It is going to call for brains and genius of the highest order, and looking back upon the history of what you have done with the colored world, you have no right to preen yourselves on what you are going to do in the future. A few

years ago you fell out among yourselves, not because of any
quarrel you had with each other, but on the question as to how
you are going to divide among yourselves territory and raw
materials belonging to colored people. The World War was a
matter of jealousy in the division of the spoils of Asia and
Africa, and by it you nearly ruined civilization. Have you the
genius and the brains to carry out further an organization of
men by which the white people of the world are going to sit
on top of it, using it mainly for their own advantage and make
the rest of the world serve?

If you have the ability to do this, there then comes the next
question: Have you the force? Have you the physical force and
the machines to do it? Oh, you can do it in the United States.
You outnumber us ten to one. You can sweep us off the face of
the earth. You can starve us to death or make us wish we had
starved to death in the face of your insults. But, remember, you
are standing before the whole world, with hundreds of darker
millions watching. No matter what happens to us, these colored
people of the world are not going to take forever the kind of
treatment they have been taking. They have got beyond that.
They have come to the place where they know what civilization is, and if you are going to keep them in their place, you are
going to do it by brute force. Have you got the force, and is it
likely that you are going to get it?

A MESSAGE TO YOUTH

By Robert S. Abbott

*On August 15, 1931, ten thousand black children and
parents marched along South Parkway in Chicago en route
to a picnic at Washington Park. The marchers halted outside the residence of Robert S. Abbott, editor and publisher
of the* Chicago Defender, *the leading Negro weekly in the
nation. Abbott spoke briefly to the young marchers.*

Robert S. Abbott started the Chicago Defender *in 1910,
and quickly revolutionized Negro journalism. The Defender repeatedly urged Negroes in the South to flee the
area and come North, and these appeals and other features
converted the paper into a national weekly for black Americans. Abbott became a millionaire and shocked white
Chicagoans by riding about the city in a Rolls-Royce. He*

was bitterly criticized by black militants for his opposition to the Garvey movement, but the Defender *built its main circulation among lower-class Negroes.*

(Abbott's speech to the picnickers, presented here, is taken from the Chicago Defender, *August 22, 1931.)*

I AM HAPPY to see you youthful and healthy children who are to take on the burdens of the future. You are the foundation of, and represent what the race is to be tomorrow. You must be obedient, industrious, honest and brave. You must learn early to understand what your rights are and fight for them; and fight for the rights of all mankind. Fight with your pen, fight with your speech, fight with your conduct, and fight with your prayers. You will never obtain the goal for which you seek in this country without fighting for all of the rights and immunities that are guaranteed to you under and by the Constitution of the United States, and the constitutions of the several states made in conformity with the Constitution of the United States. As citizens you should fight for your place to live and for a voice in the government. Fight for your right to earn a legitimate living in the municipalities, the states and the country. Fight for your rights as firemen, policemen, motormen on the street-cars in the cities in which you live, train conductors and clerks in the various departments of the municipalities, states and nation. Fight for your rights in all professions and industries. Believe that God is right and right is might, and that you are equal to any man, anywhere, any time. Fight, fight, fight for what is right and for your status in the government as made and guaranteed by the federal and state constitutions of this country.

GIVE THE PEOPLE BREAD

By Angelo Herndon

On July 11, 1932, Angelo Herndon, a young Negro Communist organizer, was arrested in Atlanta, Georgia, where he had been active in organizing demonstrations of black and white unemployed for relief. When arrested he carried under his arm a box of membership blanks and pamphlets. The authorities dug up a Georgia statute enacted before

the Civil War which punished with death anybody who at-
tempted by speech or writing to excite an insurrection of
slaves, and imposed the same penalty on anybody who
brought in printed matter calculated to excite a slave in-
surrection. After the Civil War, the legislature dropped out
the references to slaves, but the law stayed on the statute
books and was never enforced until the Herndon case.
Herndon was indicted on the section which read: "Any at-
tempt, by persuasion or otherwise, to induce others to join
in any combined resistance to the lawful authority of the
State shall constitute an attempt to incite insurrection."
Despite a vigorous defense by Benjamin J. Davis, Jr., a
Negro lawyer who was appointed by the International
Labor Defense to defend him, Herndon was convicted and
sentenced to prison for eighteen to twenty years. After a
five-year struggle, the Supreme Court, by a vote of 5 to 4,
released Herndon.

Here is Herndon's speech to the jury. It is excerpted
from Angelo Herndon, Let Me Live, New York, 1935, pp.
342–48.

GENTLEMEN OF THE JURY: I would like to explain in
detail the nature of my case and the reason why I was locked
up. I recall back about the middle of June, 1932, when the Relief Agencies of the City of Atlanta, the County Commission and
the city government as a whole, were cutting both Negro and
white workers off relief. We all know that there were citizens
who suffered from unemployment. There were hundreds and
thousands of Negroes and whites who were each day looking
for work, but in those days there was no work to be found.

The Unemployment Council, which has connection with the
Unemployed Committees of the United States, after 23,000
families had been dropped from the relief rolls, started to organize the Negro and white workers of Atlanta on the same
basis, because we know that their interests are the same. The
Unemployment Council understood that in order to get relief,
both races would have to organize together and forget about
the question whether those born with a white skin are "superior"and those born with a black skin are "inferior." They both
were starving, and the capitalist class would continue to use this
weapon to keep them further divided. The policy of the Unemployment Council is to organize Negroes and whites together
on the basis of fighting for unemployment relief and unemployment insurance at the expense of the state. The Unemployment
Council of Atlanta issued those leaflets after the relief had been

cut off, which meant starvation for thousands of people here in Atlanta. The leaflets called upon the Negro and white workers to attend a meeting at the courthouse building on a Thursday morning. I forget the exact date. This action was initiated as the result of statements handed out to the local press by County Commissioners who said that there was nobody in the city of Atlanta starving, and if there were, those in need should come to the offices of the Commissioners and the matter would be looked into. That statement was made by Commissioner Hendrix.

The Unemployment Council pointed out in its circulars that there were thousands of unemployed workers in the city of Atlanta who faced hunger and starvation. Therefore, they were called upon to demonstrate in this courthouse building, about the middle part of June. When the Committee came down to the courthouse, it so happened that Commissioner Hendrix was not present that morning. There were unemployed white women with their babies almost naked and without shoes to go on their feet, and there were also Negro women with their little babies actually starving for the need of proper nourishment, which had been denied them by the county of Fulton and state of Georgia and city of Atlanta as well.

Well, the Negro and white workers came down to the Commissioners' office to show that there was starvation in the city of Atlanta and that they were in actual need of food and proper nourishment for their kids, which they never did receive. I think Commissioner Stewart was in the office at that time. The white workers were taken into his room and the Negroes had the door shut in their faces. This was done with the hope of creating racial animosity in order that they would be able to block the fight that the Negro and white workers were carrying on—a determined fight to get relief. The white workers were told: "Well, the county hasn't any money, and of course, you realize the depression and all that, but we haven't got the money." We knew that the county did have money, but were using it for their own interest, and not for the interest of the Negro workers or white workers, either way. They talked to the white workers some considerable time, but when the white workers came out, they had just about as much results as the Negroes did—only a lot of hot air blown over them by the Commissioners, which didn't put any shoes on their little babies' feet and milk in their stomachs to give them proper nourishment. No one disputed the fact they did keep the Negroes on the outside, but the white workers were in the same condition that their Negro brothers were in. In spite of the fact that the County

Commissioners had published statements to the effect that there was no money in the county treasury to provide unemployment relief for the Negro and white workers, still the next day after the demonstration the County Commissioners voted $6,000 for relief, mainly because it was shown that for the first time in the history of Atlanta and the state of Georgia, Negro and white workers did join together and did go to the Commissioners and demand unemployment insurance. Have not they worked in the city of Atlanta, in different industries, different shops and other industrial concerns located in Atlanta for all their years, doing this work, building up the city where it is at the present time? And now, when they were in actual need of food to hold their bodies together, and when they came before the state and county officials to demand something to hold their bodies together, they were denied it. The policy of the Unemployment Council is to organize these workers and demand those things that are denied them. They have worked as slaves, and are entitled to a decent living standard. And, of course, the workers will get it if you ever organize them.

After the successful demonstration, the solicitor's office had two detectives stationed at the post office to arrest anyone who came to take mail out of Box 339. On Monday, July 11, 1932, I went to the post office to get mail from this box and was arrested by detectives, Mr. Watson and Mr. Chester. I had organized unemployed workers, Negro and white, of Atlanta, and forced the County Commissioners to kick in $6,000 for unemployment relief. For this I was locked up in the station house and held eleven days without even any kind of charges booked against me. I was told at the station house that I was being held on "suspicion." Of course, they knew what the charges were going to be, but in order to hold me in jail and give me the dirtiest kind of inhuman treatment that one could describe, they held me there eleven days without any charge whatsoever until my attorney filed a writ of habeas corpus demanding that they place charges against me or turn me loose. It was about the twenty-second of July, and I still hadn't been indicted; there had been three sessions of the grand jury, and my case had been up before them each time, but still there was no indictment. This was a deliberate plot to hold me in jail. At the habeas corpus hearing, the judge ordered that if I wasn't indicted the next day by two-thirty, I should be released. Solicitor Hudson assured the judge that there would be an indictment, which, of course, there was. Ever since then I have been cooped up in Fulton County Tower, where I have spent close to six months— I think the exact time was five months and three weeks. But I want to describe some of the horrible experiences that I had in Fulton Tower. I was placed in a little cell there with a dead body and forced to live there with the dead body because I couldn't get out of the place. The man's name was William Wilson, who fought in the Spanish-American War for the American principles, as we usually call it. He was there on a charge of alimony. His death came as a result of the rotten food given to all prisoners, and for the want of medical attention. The county physician simply refused to give this man any kind of attention whatsoever. After three days of illness, he died, and I was forced to live there with him until the undertaker came and got him. These are just some of the things I experienced in jail. I was also sick myself. I could not eat the food they gave me as well as hundreds of other prisoners. For instance, they give you peas and beans for one dinner, and at times you probably get the same thing three times a week. You will find rocks in it, and when you crack down on it with your teeth, you don't know what it is, and you spit it out and there it is. They have turnip greens, and just as they are pulled up out of the ground and put in the pot, with sand, rocks and everything else. But that's what you have to eat, otherwise you don't live. For breakfast they feed grits that look as if they were baked instead of boiled, a little streak of grease running through them, about two strips of greasy fatback. That is the main prison fare, and you eat it or else die from starvation. I was forced to go through all this for five months without a trial. My lawyers demanded a trial time after time, but somehow the state would always find a reason to postpone it.

They knew that the workers of Atlanta were starving, and by arresting Angelo Herndon on a charge of attempting to incite insurrection the unity of Negro and white workers that was displayed in the demonstration that forced the County Commissioners to kick in with $6,000, would be crushed forever. They locked Angelo Herndon up on such charges. But I can say this quite clearly, if the state of Georgia and the city of Atlanta think that by locking up Angelo Herndon, the question of unemployment will be solved, I say you are deadly wrong. If you really want to do anything about the case, you must go out and indict the social system. I am sure that if you would do this, Angelo Herndon would not be on trial here today, but those who are really guilty of insurrection would be here in my stead. But this you will not do, for your role is to defend the system under which the toiling masses are robbed and oppressed. There are thousands of Negro and white workers who, because of unemployment and hunger, are organizing. If the

state wants to break up this organization, it cannot do it by arresting people and placing them on trial for insurrection; insurrection laws will not fill empty stomachs. Give the people bread.
The officials knew then that the workers were in need of relief,
and they know now that the workers are going to organize and
get relief. . . .

On Christmas Eve I was released. My bail was once $3,000
but they raised it to $5,000 and from that up to $25,000, just
in order to hold me in jail, but you can hold this Angelo Herndon and hundreds of others, but it will never stop these demonstrations on the part of Negro and white workers, who demand a decent place to live in and proper food for their kids
to eat.

I want to say also that the policy of the Unemployment
Council is to carry on a constant fight for the rights of the
Negro people. We realize that unless Negro and white workers
are united together, they cannot get relief. The capitalist class
teaches race hatred to Negro and white workers and keep it
going all the time, tit for tat, the white worker running after
the Negro worker and the Negro worker running after the
white worker, and the capitalist becomes the exploiter and the
robber of them both. We of the Unemployment Council are out
to expose such things. If there were not any Negroes in the
United States, somebody would have to be used as the scapegoat. There would still be a racial question, probably the Jews,
or the Greeks, or somebody. It is in the interest of the capitalist to play one race against the other, so greater profits can
be realized from the working people of all races. It so happens
that the Negro's skin is black, therefore making it much easier
for him to be singled out and used as the scapegoat.

I don't have to go so far into my case, no doubt some of
you jurymen sitting over there in that box right now are unemployed and realize what it means to be without a job, when
you tramp the streets day in and day out looking for work
and can't find it. You know it is a very serious problem and
the future looks so dim that you sometimes don't know what
to do, you go nuts and want to commit suicide or something.
But the Unemployment Council points out to the Negro and
white workers that the solution is not in committing suicide,
that the solution can only be found in the unity and organization of black and white workers. In organization the workers
have strength. Now, why do I say this? I say it because it is
to the interest of the capitalist class that the workers be kept
down all of the time so they can make as much profit as they
possibly can. So, on the other hand, it is to the interest of

Negro and white workers to get as much for their work as they can—that is, if they happen to have any work. Unfortunately, at the present time there are millions of workers in the United States without work, and the capitalist class, the state government, city government and all other governments, have taken no steps to provide relief for those unemployed. And it seems that this question is left up to the Negro and white workers to solve, and they will solve it by organizing and demanding the right to live, a right that they are entitled to. They have built up this country, and are therefore entitled to some of the things that they have produced. Not only are they entitled to such things, but it is their right to demand them. When the state of Georgia and the city of Atlanta raised the question of inciting to insurrection and attempting to incite to insurrection, or attempting to overthrow the government, all I can say is, that no matter what you do with Angelo Herndon, no matter what you do with the Angelo Herndons in the future, this question of unemployment, the question of unity between Negro and white workers cannot be solved with hands that are stained with the blood of an innocent individual. You may send me to my death, as far as I know. I expect you to do that anyway, so that's beside the point. But no one can deny these facts. The present system under which we are living today is on the verge of collapse; it has developed to its highest point and now it is beginning to shake. For instance, you can take a balloon and blow so much air in it, and when you blow too much it bursts; so with the system we are living under. Of course, I don't know if that is insurrection or not!

WHY NEGROES SHOULD SUPPORT THE COMMUNISTS

By William N. Jones

In May, 1932, the Communist party nominated James W. Ford, black leader of the party, as its candidate for Vice-President of the United States and its running mate with William Z. Foster, the Presidential candidate. William N. Jones, managing editor of the Baltimore Afro-American, one of the leading Negro weeklies in the United States,

*became chairman of the Foster-Ford Committee for Equal
Rights, and at a meeting held under the Committee's auspices on October 2, 1932, at the Renaissance Casino, Harlem, called upon all black Americans to join the ranks of
the Communists. Here is part of the speech, excerpted
from* The Liberator, *November 19, 1932.*

I BRING you greetings of fourteen million potential
colored Communists. I say this, because in my work I am able
to fathom somewhat what is going on in the minds of the
Negroes of this country.

My parents were born in slavery. Although the enormous
majority of the slaves struck boldly for their freedom whenever opportunity offered, there were a handful who were so
warped in mind that they preferred their chains. I had a maternal grandfather who felt that way. And today, whenever I
hear Negro "leaders" say that it is better to go on under the
aegis of the Republicans, the Democrats and the Socialists, I
think of that maternal grandfather.

Under the present economic system, Negroes are at the very
bottom of the economic ladder. Where the struggles of white
workers end, there the struggles of Negroes begin. The schools,
the press, philanthropy, all are used to keep us in subjection.
Such philanthropies as those of Rosenwald* do nothing more
than put a little salve on our sores.

What does any decent colored man or woman want in this
country? The right to work at the same jobs, to get the same
pay, to have recourse to the same cultural institutions, to walk
the streets as a free man.

A few weeks ago I went with some Negro leaders to visit
President Hoover. I went in my capacity as a newspaperman.
Hoover said to us, "When I help a bank, a railroad, an industrial
institution, I help a Negro the same as I help a white man." I
said to him, "President Hoover, when you put a bank on its
feet, you put into it a white president and a colored janitor. Do
you call that helping the colored man as you help the white
man?"

I have no faith in the Socialists, for I have dealt with them.†

---

* In 1910 Julius Rosenwald, Chicago millionaire, became interested in
the improvement of conditions among Negroes and established a fund
for the improvement of the educational facilities for Southern Negroes.
He also contributed to the Y.M.C.A. movement among Negroes.
† For a clear, trenchant criticism of the Socialist party's position on the
Negro question, *see* the speech of W. E. B. Du Bois "Socialism and the

Four years ago I worked with them in Maryland. From the day the campaign ended to the next election period, I never saw a Socialist. Socialists represent a group of people who, had they lived at the time of slavery, would have tried to *persuade* the slaveowners to give up their slaves.

We Negroes have got to join hands with a group of men and women who will begin a struggle that will not end until we have uprooted the whole system of inequality. I say this even though I know that our path may lead through terrible struggles.

Not only during an election campaign, but every day in the year, we Negroes have the opportunity to take part in the front ranks in a movement to liberate mankind—the Communist movement. I for one accept the challenge.

NEGROES SPEAK OF WAR

By Langston Hughes

Often called the Poet Laureate of the Negro people, Langston Hughes was born in Joplin, Missouri, in 1902. Because of the separation of his parents, his childhood was spent in several places. He finished high school in Cleveland when he was fourteen; he had been a member of the staff of the school magazine and an editor of the yearbook. After moving about a great deal, working on freight steamers, as doorman and cook, at the same time publishing poems, Hughes completed his formal education at Lincoln University, Pennsylvania, graduating in 1929. While at Lincoln he won the Witter Bynner Prize for undergraduate poetry and wrote his novel Not Without Laughter. *(His alma mater conferred upon him the degree of Litt. D. in 1943.) After Lincoln University, Hughes continued to write, publishing poetry, stories, novels, plays, articles and humorous sketches, as well as an autobiography. He won the Harmon Award in 1931 and a Guggenheim Fellowship in 1934. His books have been translated into many languages. He died in 1968.*

In July, 1934, an international conference of writers

Negro Problem," in Philip S. Foner, editor, W. E. B. Du Bois Speaks: Speeches and Addresses, 1890–1919, pp. 239–43.

*and artists was held in Paris to discuss war and peace.
During the sessions, Langston Hughes delivered a stinging attack on conditions of his people in the United States,
and warned that black Americans would not repeat the
mistakes of World War I of fighting to save the world for
democracy while they enjoyed none of it in their own
country.*

*Hughes's speech at the conference is presented here as
taken from* The Negro Worker, *August, 1934.*

When the time comes for the next war, I'm asking you,
remember the last war. I'm asking you, what you fought for,
and what you would be fighting for again. I'm asking, how
many of the lies you were told do you still believe? Does any
Negro believe, for instance, that the world was actually saved
for democracy? Does any Negro believe, any more, in closing
ranks with the war makers?* Maybe a few soldiers believed
Dr. Moton when he came over to France talking about "Be
nice and fight for the nice white folks."† Be meek and shoot
some Germans. But do any Negroes believe him now, with
lynched black workers hanging on trees all around Tuskegee?
I'm asking you.

And after the Chicago riots and the Washington riots and the
East St. Louis riots, and more recently the Bonus March,‡ is it
some foreign army needs to be fought?

And listen, I'm asking you, with all the warships and Marines
and officers and Secretary of the Navy going to Cuba, can't they
send even one sergeant after Shamblin in Alabama?§

And with all the money they got to buy bombing planes,

---

* This is a reference to the editorial W. E. B. Du Bois wrote in *The
Crisis* of July, 1918, entitled, "Close Ranks," which went in part: "Let
us not hesitate. Let us, while this war lasts, forget our special grievances
and close our ranks shoulder to shoulder with our white citizens and the
allied nations that are fighting for democracy."
† During World War I the U. S. War Department sent Robert R. Moton,
who had succeeded Booker T. Washington as head of Tuskegee, to
France to study conditions of Negro soldiers in the Army. Moton infuriated the black soldiers by telling them not to push their grievances
and not to expect that they would enjoy rights which they were accorded
in France when they returned to the United States.
‡ The reference is to the march of 15,000 to 20,000 veterans of World
War I, black and white, on Washington in the spring of 1932, demanding
a bonus. The bonus marchers were driven out of Washington by federal
troops led by General Douglas MacArthur.
§ The reference is to John Shamblin, head of the Ku Klux Klan in Alabama, who boasted of lynching Negroes.

why the hell can't they pay the teachers for my kids to go to school?

And even if I was studying fighting (which I ain't) why couldn't I do a little killing in the Navy without wrassling with pots and pans, or join the Marines (the lily white Marines) and see the world or go in the Air Force where you never admitted Negroes yet? I'd like to be above the battle too. Or do you think you gonna use me for stevedoring again?

And speaking of France, our once beloved ally, where Negroes can still eat in the restaurants in spite of Woodrow Wilson— don't let that fool you. Somebody ought to put the French black Africans wise to the fact that they *ought* to treat them well in Paris when they are drilling them by the hundreds of thousands to stop bullets with their breasts and bombs with their heads and fill the frontline trenches for dear old France (that only a handful of them have ever seen) in the next war. Or have they got a French Dr. Moton to lie to black Africans, too? I'm asking you.

And when the next war comes, I want to know whose war and why. For instance, if it's the Japanese you're speaking of, there's plenty of perils for me right here at home that need attending to—what about those labor unions that won't admit Negroes? And what about all of them factories where I can't work even if there was work? And what about the schools I can't go to, and the states I can't vote in, and the juries I can't sit on? And what about all them sheriffs that can never find out who did the lynching? And what about something to eat without putting on a uniform and going out to killing folks I never saw to get it? And what about them separate colored codes in the N.R.A.?* And what about a voice in who's running this country and why —before I even think about crossing the water and fighting again?

Who said I want to go to war? If I do, it ain't the same war the President wants to go to. No, sir, I been hanging on a rope in Alabama too long.

* Under the National Recovery Administration (N.R.A.) instituted by the New Deal of President Franklin D. Roosevelt, businesses were encouraged to establish "codes" which would include prices and wages. In some cases, separate codes for black workers were established.

WE ARE MOSTLY SUBJECT PEOPLES ALL OVER THE WORLD

By Marcus Garvey

Following his confinement in Atlanta Penitentiary and his deportation from the United States in 1927, Marcus Garvey continued the effort to build his Universal Negro Improvement Association, and many Negroes continued to celebrate August 17, Garvey's birthday, as an international Negro holiday. In 1928 he established a European headquarters in London. Gradually, however, his movement disintegrated and Garvey sank into obscurity. In August, 1935, the Seventh International Convention of the Negro Peoples of the World was held in St. Andrew, Jamaica. Garvey presided over the sessions, and though the convention was poorly attended, Garvey, undaunted, delivered a lengthy speech to the gathering. Following the convention, Garvey moved the headquarters of his movement to London, where he continued to agitate for the rebirth of a Negro nationalism until his death in 1940.

The excerpts presented below are taken from The Blackman, *September, 1935, pp. 4–12.*

. . . MY DUTY as President-General of the Universal Negro Improvement Association is to set before you for the month, as accurately as I can, the real situation affecting us as a people all over the world. None of us is ignorant of the fact that we are now living under changed conditions of life, not only as a group, but so is it with all other groups. Ever since the cessation of the war in Europe there has been a desperate effort on the part of all nations, representing all nationals and peoples and subjects and citizens, to readjust themselves to a new order of things. In the effort some of the countries have had to pass through terrible stress of revolution, such as Russia, Germany and Spain.

The old imperial Russia has had to reorganize herself into a social democracy; Italy herself which was an established monarchic empire has had to modify her political constitution. In England the most stable of the empires, there have had to be great changes to meet the new economic and social conditions forced upon them by postwar conditions. The great republic of the United States has had to undergo great changes in re-adjusting her economic life, and we had good evidence of how upset the American nation was when at the last election for President of that country the people almost revolted from the system that governed them for many years—the republican system.

All this tends to show how anxious the world is to measure up to the new order of things. Unfortunately, our race represents no constituted national force. We are mostly subject peoples all over the world. In America we are citizens of limitation, within the Empire we are subjects, more as wards of a higher culture than otherwise. Those who live under other countries or other nations fare no better than those who live under British and American rule. It is said that the highest type of Negro citizenship is supposed to be in France. This is also questionable, because as far as we know, from our political knowledge, it is only a few of the many millions of Negroes controlled by France who enjoy anything like real equality of rights and privileges, because like all other Negroes, the Negroes of France are more wards than citizens of equal rights. This is due to the fact that civilization as a whole looks upon us as a people not sufficiently competent, not sufficiently able to be on our own responsibility. The purpose of this convention is to intelligently impress the world of all nationalities that in some way we are entitled to much better consideration than we are receiving at the present time; but the mere statement of that will not be sufficient to convince, we will have to act it and live up to it, and have to prove it, so that this convention is far more serious to us than any convention we have held before, and I take pride in being a part of it and leader of it, for the nobleness of the aims and the purposes that we have in view. . . .

There isn't a morning that we take up our newspapers that we do not read of something threatening. The whole world is nervous, and the best of minds of the world are anticipating something unseemly and unusual, but the world is so afraid of itself that no one is able and bold enough or competent enough to even suggest a way through which this unseemly thing will happen. We have had most from Hitler within the last few months, as an indication of the disturbed forces now operating, but even the bellicose Hitler has had to reflect, because he finds himself hemmed in by the organized suspicion of a world not willing to take a chance again in anything that may lead to a confusion similar to that which was experienced between 1914 and 1918.

Men have become more sober, more reasonable, in the adjustment of their differences; and it is that soberness that we are going to depend upon. When we first started the Universal Negro Improvement Association, in the urge toward Negro nationalism, we had to adapt ourselves to the sentiment of the time, because all peoples and all nations and all men were then aggressive, they repudiated the rights of other peoples competitively, and they did much to trample upon those rights that led to the bloody war, which taught all men a lesson; and so, whether men are white or yellow or black, today they are compelled, under the new order of man, to adopt a new method of settling human differences, and if nations have been doing this, we as a weak group in this present age of civilization must also adopt new principles and new methods to treat with mankind at large, with whom we have to deal, and so this convention is quite different from others we have held.

Others are learning that they cannot gain much today by being too aggressive, we have to be very compromising, and if we have to be more compromising than other peoples, it is because of our peculiar position—a position that we have invited ourselves. We are a very weak economic group. The basis of living of the individual and of the group is organized economy. If you cannot control your own economic existence you cannot live for long, except with the tolerance of others, who control your very existence, and that is the unfortunate position of the Negro today. In the opportunities since Creation that he has had in common with other men whom God placed here, the Negro studiously or otherwise ignored the human essentials toward a greater life, and a more protected and useful life, and so he has never prepared himself, he has never felt himself as a racial entity, whilst others paid careful attention to that; therefore others have been able to build up strong structures of economic independence, they have become the employers of the world, they have become the producers of the world, they have become the controllers of the activities of civilization, and because of our lack of preparation and initiative up to this hour, we find ourselves a dependent people, dependent upon that creative intelligence of other races who were more thoughtful than we were.

It is unfortunate to admit all this, but we can only handle mankind with truth, if we are to prevail in the righteousness that is to be the conduct of all men, in keeping with the will and disposition of our Creator. The point is set, but I have to admit we have existed within our recent civilization merely on charity, merely on sympathy. I want you delegates to realize that we in America have existed on charity and on sympathy; within the British Empire we have existed on charity and sympathy. Under all the governments of the world, our contact with all the peoples of the world, we have existed on and through charity and through sympathy. Isn't it sad for a race and a people as old as the world, as old as any other group of mankind, to live on charity? If we want employment in America, we have to go to the sympathy and charity of the white man, if we want employment in the British Empire we have to go to the same charity and sympathy of the white man, and so the white man has been the producer, he has been the organizer, he has been the great commercial magnate, the industrial captain; he starts the factory going, he establishes the bank, he organizes the industries, and all we have done up to now has been to go to him wherever we find him and ask of his sympathy and depend upon his sympathy and his charity that we may live.

I do hope you realize the situation, and so in readjusting ourselves to the new order, as a leader, I could not encourage you in the sentiment and the feeling most of us had up to a few years ago, when we were living in a different world, because you would have nothing to gain but so much more to lose. If you live on the sympathy and charity of a man you cannot very well insult him, because, being human and sinful like all creatures, he may reserve that charity and sympathy for somebody else. I wonder if you realize the position in America. The white man could starve fifteen million Negroes to death in two years if he wants to, because the American Negro lost his opportunity in the old order of things to permanently establish himself as an economic factor in a country where he was emancipated to full citizenship, to which he had ample claim following periods of his service in the building of that great Republic. I tried my best, therefore, for nearly thirteen years, to arouse the American Negro to his sense of duty and responsibility of economically establishing himself and entrenching himself industrially. Those of you who have followed me, will know that in America I was very much pronounced in the industrialism and commercial expansion and independence of the Negro. I fought terrible battles there to get the Negro to become his own industrial master. He lost the opportunity and has perpetuated his social slavery and his economic slavery.

Sad it is today to reveal the fact that there are millions of American Negroes, centless, dimeless, dollarless, with no hope of occupation so that they may be able to take care of their individual or their family needs. They have had to resort to a more sympathetic charity, not of somebody giving them employment, but they have had to depend upon other men for feeding them—the worst form of charity that any race could depend on, to be fed by another without contributing to that food. It deprives a man of his manhood, it deprives him of his character and his independence. He cannot speak, he must have fears, and that is the condition of things that fifteen million people have brought upon themselves in a grand and glorious country where they had the most splendid opportunity—an opportunity that was given to them as it was given to the Jew and to the Greeks, to the Irish, to the Italians, to the Russians; which the Jews took advantage of, the Greeks took advantage of, the Italians took advantage of, the Russians took advantage of, the Irish took advantage of, and which the Negroes ignored. And what happened when the change came in the social, economic and political orders? The Jews went back to Palestine, the Greeks went back to Greece, to strengthen the foundation of Greece; the Irish went back to Ireland to strengthen the foundation of Ireland, the Italians went back to Italy to strengthen the foundation of Italy, and every other national group post haste went back to the original Fatherland to strengthen the Fatherland in the new order, in the preparation for the new anticipated crisis, but the Negro could not move from where he was. Do you see how we are playing with our lives and have played with the destiny and integrity of our race? That is America.

As far as we are affected within the British Empire, you will realize that we have just celebrated our Centenary, the first hundred years of our emancipation, and if you were to look throughout this country which is an index to all other West Indian islands where this emancipation took place one hundred years ago, you will find that the Jamaican Negro is no better off than the American Negro. In the march they are hungry, they are hopeless, they are unemployed, and if they do get employment it is chiefly the employment given to us by other peoples who have created for themselves, who are proprietors in their own rights; therefore, the situation remains the same in the West Indies as it is in America. The Negro is not a proprietor to any extent, the Negro is dependent still in our civilization. In Africa the condition is beyond description. The unfortunate condition of the race is such as to make any proud man of the race hang his head in shame, and for his heart to bleed. There are sections of Africa more progressive than others, such as the West Coast, the Nigerias, the Gold

Coast, but the progress of these sections under British rule is infinitesimal compared with the gross suffering of the hundreds of millions in Central Africa, in East Africa, in South Africa, in South West Africa, where they are virtual slaves, where they are virtual dogs instead of being considered as human beings.

Now, whom are we going to blame? Our past propaganda, because of the then order of things, led us to blame someone else, but studiously in this order, can we honestly blame anyone but ourselves, because we realize that out of the war (if we never lived in a period as inhuman as that before) that man is a cruel creature, not only against another race, but against himself. We are only in a generation at most of threescore years and ten, and so we did not live in the time of Alexander or Constantine, we did not even live in the time of Napoleon; we live in the modern Christian age, and what did we experience between 1914 and 1918? We saw men of one original stock fight on the battlefields of France, we saw them slaying themselves to the extent of millions. When I went to the battlefields of France and Flanders, I saw buried there, underneath an ocean of white tombstones, tens of thousands of dead, all traced back to one original racial stock, where men of one family slaughtered each other, as I said, to the extent of ten million.

Now, if your civilization and your religion is of that nature, that men will do that to their own kind and kin, what can you expect? The sin of man seems to be eternal until the Judgment, and so do not expect too much of man, because if he can so murder those of his own household, what sympathy can other men, not of the same household, have for you; so we must perforce adopt a policy of friendship, of tolerance, in an age as difficult as this. We cannot provoke, because we cannot maintain the provocation. I feel sure you understand what I mean by that. If you provoke me, I become angry, and I am disposed to knock you down. You will be safe from being knocked down only if you are strong enough. Are you strong enough? How can you be strong enough when you are hungry, when you are unemployed, when you are dining at the soup kitchen of charity, so that you can get from charity that which will keep you for twenty-four hours?

My American co-workers and wholehearted supporters wondered why for nearly three years I remained quiet, why I did not send to them fiery messages, why I did not attempt to continue stirring them up in enthusiasm. I could not have done that to their good and benefit, because of the peculiarity of the new order. I knew they would have been hungry, I knew they did not

follow my advice in the thirteen years prior, that of economically entrenching themselves so that they could be their own
producers and masters. I realized that in the new order they
were still seeking the good will of the man who still controlled
them. This is my explanation, my friends. I have reserved the
explanation for this convention, and the leader in America
who would provoke the white man in America today is only
trying to bring down the house upon the head of the poor
Negro who is not sufficiently strong to hold up, who is not strong
enough to hold out against the vexed man. It is no wonder Du
Bois has resigned from the National Association for the Advancement of Colored People. He can go no farther.* Can he
continue abusing the white man when the American Negro is
at the white man's soup kitchen? And so the unthinking
Negro thinks that Dr. Du Bois has changed, but he has only
had to keep clear and quiet, because he was so treacherous to
his race and so ignorant of his race's interest that when the
Universal Negro Improvement Association taught in the United
States and suggested a program of economic independence for
the race, he was one of the principal men who were against it.†
When we went as far as Liberia, where we could have advanced
colonization and when we still had a part of the substance that
we gathered during the war, to do it with, he opposed us, which
has caused the Negro to be in the soup kitchen today. The
ignorance of Du Bois and the treachery of Du Bois sabotaged
the one thing that would have saved the American Negro; but
now, naturally, he is ashamed of himself and he has gracefully,
as far as he sees himself, withdrawn from the active line, because he has nothing to give. And who is there that can do
better? All the leaders have been fools like Du Bois.

---

* In 1934 Dr. Du Bois resigned from the editorship of *The Crisis* and
from the Board of the N.A.A.C.P.
† This is not an entirely accurate description of Du Bois' atttude toward the program of the Universal Negro Improvement Association.
In 1921 Dr. Du Bois wrote that Garvey was "a sincere, hard-working
idealist," but also a "stubborn, domineering leader of the mass." He had,
Du Bois granted, "worthy industrial and commercial schemes," but was
"an inexperienced businessman." While Garvey's "dream of Negro
industry, commerce and the ultimate freedom of Africa were feasible,"
his "methods are bombastic, wasteful, illogical and ineffective and almost
illegal." Du Bois also opposed Garvey on the question of social equality,
criticizing him for being willing to accept the position that the United
States belonged to the white race and the Negro should not fight for
equality in American society. His most telling criticism consisted of a
detailed recitation of the financing of the Black Star Line. Garvey denounced Du Bois as a "traitor" to the Negro people.

The peculiar situation is this: the people in America have now lost confidence in their leaders, and even if they never intended it, they are compelled to, because they haven't as much now to contribute to leaders as when they were able to, and the leadership has led them nowhere but into the wilderness. If I had confidence in a man when I had ten pounds and gave him nine to prosecute that leadership, and I had but one pound left, what do you think would be my view toward that leader after he had deceived me? Wouldn't I be very conservative and very suspicious? And that is the position of the American Negro today—a position brought upon us first by the dishonesty of leadership, by the ignorance of leadership and by the insincerity of leadership. You will ask me to explain it. I explain it thus, probably very sympathetically toward the Negro leader, because I am against no Negro in the world. The policy of the Universal Negro Improvement Association is to unite all Negroes. No chain is stronger than its weakest link. The principle of the organization is to be in keeping with all Negroes, because we would still be unfinished in our work, and probably that is why you see old men coming back in service. The policy is not to put any man permanently out. The policy is to change him from one responsibility to another according to his ability. If I should find that my associates have no confidence in me, I would not expect them to put me permanently out of the Universal Negro Improvement Association, but I could be a member of the Universal Negro Improvement Association without being President-General, and probably I could do better work as a member than as President-General. If I could not be trusted as President-General of the Universal Negro Improvement Association I probably could be trusted as a member, and so when a man has kept an executive post and he has been removed, it is not that he is not a member; the only difference is that some are active members and some are not; so I hate no Negro, and when I talk about Dr. Du Bois or Pickens, it is not that I hate the men, but I am dealing with principles, and those men have never had any.

Now, what program do you expect the man opposing you to endorse as coming from you? Would you expect him to just freely and unreservedly say to you: Yes, compete with me, take away my banks, take away my railroads, take away my steamships, take away my tramway lines, take away my utilities; have them, because you are black and compete with me. Do you expect anybody in the world to do that? The relationship, therefore, of the American Negro and the American white man must be competitive, and if it is competition based upon all human principles, you must expect the white man to protect himself against the Negro as far as self-interest goes. The white man's attitude in getting his ends, and everything, is fair; for the black man is getting his ends also. White men are the guardians of the interests of their race. Their first interest is to their family group. Charity begins at home. My friends, this is the plight of the American Negro, he has not realized this.

You open a grocery store across the street and I open one here, and I try to trick you, we may be brothers, but I want my business to succeed more than yours, and so when you are not giving away matches to catch customers I may be giving away molasses to put over a bigger sale than you. It is human nature. Everything is fair in love and war. I spot a good-looking girl, and I would like to be her companion, and the other fellow spots her the same time. I give her presents the other fellow cannot give her, and tell her things about the other fellow that may not be true—everything is fair in love and war. Therefore, it is the duty of man, the individual, to protect himself; it is the duty of man in his clan to protect that clan against other clans and against other tribes; and if the white man protects himself do not blame him. The fault is yours not to protect yourself in a similar way. Now, if you get that, you get the policy of this convention and the program that we are to work on for our salvation.

We will never be able to convert the world on righteousness, and that is what the Negro churches are trying to do, by just appealing to the Christian fellowship and love of humanity. It is a right thing to do, but it is not the absolute thing to do for the salvation of the race. Living in an age as corrupt as this, you have to do something in addition to this, you have to just play human and that is what the U.N.I.A. and this convention intends to do—to just play human. Do not expect more than you will give in human conduct. Do not expect that the other fellow is Christ; if anything, he has more of the devil in him. Deal with him as a human being. You want a glass of water from him, put a sane proposition up to him, why you should have it, but do not say in the name of the Lord give me the glass of water. Find out what is more important and valuable to him at that particular minute than the glass of water. If the water is worth a shilling to him, give him the shilling. That is sound business. Don't go praying for it with the hope of getting it in the name of the Lord.

I hope to do nothing without the blessing of God Almighty. You will never win without Him; you will always lose. The position is too serious for you to treat it with levity, and I feel

sure that you who have come from America and other places
will spend a good time for us to soberly and intelligently devise
a scheme to extricate the suffering race in America, and this
suffering race in the West Indies and elsewhere. Not to go on
antagonizing other men, because it will take you nowhere. You
know there are periods of tension in the life of individuals and
in the life of movements. . . .

When I speak of the white man in America, I do not mean
to infer that all the white people of America are bad, otherwise
you would have been dead already. Our race exists in America
because a few men like Abraham Lincoln linger in American
civilization, but their influence is being nullified by the economic pressure. Today they are compelled to choose between
you in the bread line, and those who look like them, and if they
dare to send one of those who look like you to the jobs and
keep their own out, the rest look upon them as traitors.

We have been idling here ever since God sent us here. I want
to adopt a fair attitude toward the situation. I am blaming no
man for this condition but myself. I got into lots of trouble
since I have been in the organization, but I blame myself, and
when I suffer, the sensible man says he brought it upon himself, and that is my position, because if I go to jail tomorrow I
have no one to thank but myself and that is my responsibility.
Whatever you do, you are responsible for it. Do not go crying
and wiping your eyes. It isn't going to help you, my friends.
The law is there, the law of God and the law of man, and He
doesn't say we are to abolish the law because man sheds tears.
Show me in the Book of Life where it is said that breaking the
Commandments you shall be forgiven because you come shedding tears every time. You stand and fall by your own acts, so
do not blame anybody for your racial condition. Why go to the
white man weeping? Why, if you cannot go to God weeping,
how can you go to man weeping? What kind of a place you
think heaven would be if everybody who went there started to
cry? Why, nobody would want to be there. Heaven is a place of
joy, heaven is a place of happiness, of eternal bliss, where the
Master of all joy and happiness resides. He wants no crying
there. If you are to cry you go where? You go to hell! Negroes,
stop crying and be men and save yourselves. Crying is not going
to help, except into hell. It is no use teaching you envy and
covetousness, and as far as my country is concerned, it prevails
here, hence our universal condition. None of us can help the
other, because we envy each other.

If the American Negro had the proper leadership, as they
made Rockefeller succeed and Carnegie succeed, they would

make the black Rockefeller succeed from whom they could get
ten million dollars and from the black Carnegie ten million
dollars to help send the good work on, but the other Negroes
would not help the good Negro to succeed. If I die, you will
have to know that I am going to tell you the plain truth during
this convention. I do not care who wants to be vexed. I am going
to give you salvation as I see it. I am not going to tell you anything that is going to embarrass my children, because if I tell
you wrong my children will get into the same stew your children
will be in, in the next twenty years. Now is the time for intelligent anticipation. We will have to build up a strong, worldwide
Universal Negro Improvement Association that will put over a
program of salvation that will meet the intelligence of the world
on an equal plane and match men against men, in the survival
of the fittest.

THE RIGHT OF REVOLUTION FOR THE NEGRO
PEOPLE

By James W. Ford

*In August, 1935, James W. Ford, Secretary of the Harlem
Section of the Communist party, spoke before the Harlem
Section on the right of revolution for the Negro people.
Ford denounced organizations such as the N.A.A.C.P. and
the National Urban League as betrayers of the Negro people. The party was soon to establish the Popular Front,
which would seek to build alliances with these organizations.*

*Ford was born near Birmingham, Alabama, in Decem-
ber, 1893, and was forced to go to work at the age of fourteen. In 1917, after three years at Fisk University, he
joined the Army and, while in France, took an active part
in the struggle against the Jim-Crowing of Negro troops.
He entered the trade-union movement in Chicago in 1919,
and became a leader in the Chicago Federation of Labor.
Ford joined the Communist party in 1926, was active in
organizing Negro workers in left-wing unions, and became
a member of the Central Committee of the Communist
party.*

His speech to the Harlem Section, presented here in part,
is excerpted from a pamphlet written by him, The Right
to Revolution for the Negro People, *New York, n.d., issued*
by the Harlem Section of the Communist party.

DURING RECENT YEARS, especially since the economic
crisis of capitalism, there has been a rapid growth of Communist influence among Negroes, and undisguised alarm and concern on the part of the capitalists and petty-bourgeois Negro
reformists over this undeniable fact.

The Negro petty-bourgeois reformists all admit the oppressive
nature of the capitalist system. They admit that the Negro people are brutally oppressed and robbed under the capitalist system. But, admitting all this, they openly support the very capitalist system whose oppressive nature they are forced to admit.

They are under the influence of the various imperialist theories, including that of the "inherent inferiority" of Negroes and
the supposed "superiority" of the so-called white race. They all
look upon capitalism, and especially Jim-Crowism under capitalism, as offering them careers, chance to build personal fortunes at the expense of the Negro masses. These factors in a
measure determine the role of the Negro bourgeois reformists.

The top leadership of the National Association for the Advancement of Colored People, a petty-bourgeois reformist Negro
organization, is notoriously composed of bourgeois Negroes and
white agents of capitalism, like Major Spingarn and others.*
The National Association for the Advancement of Colored People leadership represents the highest expression of the united
front of the Negro bourgeoisie with the white imperialist enemies of the Negro masses. Its leaders have completely exposed
themselves in the Scottsboro case as well as the Crawford case.†

* Arthur B. Spingarn and his brother Joel were members of the
N.A.A.C.P.'s board of directors.
† The Scottsboro case began in 1931, when nine Negro youths, one barely
twelve years old, were accused of raping two white girls while "hoboing"
out of Alabama and into Tennessee. When the state sentenced the nine
youths to death in the electric chair, a defense campaign was instituted
and it grew to international proportions. The Negroes, as a result of the
campaign, escaped execution, but they remained in prison for years,
despite the clear evidence that the rape charge was a hoax.
    The Crawford case, in Virginia, involved a Negro accused of murder-
ing two white women. He was brought to trial and was convicted, even
though there was not the slightest evidence connecting him with the
slayings.
    During the defense movement for the Scottsboro boys, the N.A.A.C.P.
attacked the Communist-dominated International Labor Defense and the

The issues that face the Negro masses in America today are the fight against starvation, for unemployment and social insurance, emergency relief for small farmers, exemption of poor farmers, sharecroppers and tenant farmers from taxes and forced collection of debts, equal rights for the Negro masses, and the right of self-determination for the Negroes in the Black Belt of the South.* In the fight for these demands it is necessary to build a firm working-class unity in resistance against the capitalist hunger and war offensives, against the wage-slashing campaign, against terror, against all forms of suppression of the political rights of the workers, against imperialist war, and for the defense of the Chinese people and the Soviet Union. . . .

The bourgeois and Negro reformist mind cannot understand the tremendously progressive and ennobling role of revolution in the lives of millions of people, including millions of oppressed and degraded Negroes, who have been degraded, warped with superstition and race prejudice. The revolutionary activity of the masses, inspired by a Communist goal, will not only change their conditions, but will also change their natures as the gigantic achievements of the Soviet Union abundantly prove.

Precisely because of their revolutionary methods and revolutionary aims, the Communists are feared and hated by the Jim Crow rulers and exhorters of the United States.

Of course, it is true that the more the capitalists build up their bloody instruments of mass destruction and intensify their brutal terror against the masses, the more their agents declaim about the "violence" of the revolutionary workers. The crimes of all the slaveowners from ancient Rome down to pre-Civil War days in our own South pale into insignificance beside the bloody violence of modern capitalists against the exploited and oppressed of all lands. Capitalist wealth began with the plunder, pillage and murder of colonial peoples, and it continues

Communist party, and finally withdrew from the case. Its role in the case aroused resentment against the N.A.A.C.P. not only among the Communists but even among those black Americans who usually took a conservative stand.

* In 1930 the Communist party advanced the position that the Negro people were an oppressed nation and were entitled to the right of self-determination. This was regarded as especially true in the Black Belt in the South, where Negroes formed the majority of the people. While this policy did not call for setting up a "Negro republic" in the South, it did mean that the Negroes in the South should have the right of self-determination, to be exercised by the Negro nation whenever and however it saw fit to use this right. The position was later abandoned by the Communist party.

to drip with the lifeblood of millions of toilers at home and in the colonies. American history might easily be described as a story of capitalist violence, directed at all times particularly against the Negroes. Violence, the violent suppression of the exploited workers and poor farmers and of the Negro people, is of the very essence of capitalism. Over five thousand Negro toilers have been lynched since the Civil War. Is not this the most dastardly act of violence against an oppressed people? Indeed, what else is it but violence, when fifty million people throughout the capitalist world are forced to starve amidst plenty?

The history of capitalism has been the history of violence against the working class, and it is only by the revolutionary struggles of the majority of the working class, supported by the oppressed Negro workers and poor farmers, that the masses will finally be able to rid the country of the plague of capitalism. . . .

A ruling class that did not hesitate to murder thirteen million people in a war for profits will not peacefully relinquish its hold on the industries and wealth of a nation produced by the toil of the workers and poor farmers. Wherein is the essence of the revolutionary method? It consists, first, in developing a real struggle against every form of oppression and exploitation, against every wrong and grievance of the workers and poor toilers, against every case of police persecution, against every assault on the lives of the working classes, whether it be evictions or wage cuts or unemployment, et cetera. It consists of a thousand and one little daily struggles which are gathered up and accumulated and directed not only against one wrong or one grievance, but also against the entire system of economic, political and national oppression and exploitation of the majority of the population by a small group of parasitic landlords, bankers, capitalists and speculators. The essence of the revolutionary method consists in the fact that every action is inspired by a fundamental aim not merely to make the slavery of the masses more bearable under capitalism (this is what we call the reformist method), but to destroy the entire system of slavery, which breeds and exists only at the expense of the lifeblood of all the toilers.

In the second place, the revolutionary method consists in rousing ever larger masses to economic and political struggles against the capitalist system and the capitalist government. It seeks to awaken all the masses to political consciousness and to draw them into the arena of historical struggle for the establishment of a new social system.

For only their struggle can achieve this. Precisely because it is not merely a question of correcting one wrong, but of eliminating the very system that continually reproduces these wrongs, do the Communists seek to raise every struggle to a fundamental, revolutionary struggle aimed at the entire political and social system.

The revolutionary tradition of Negroes, of course, differs from the false bourgeois theory (and hope!) that slaves will never dare to strike for their freedom, that liberation is something that is handed down, or denied, from above. This nonsensical theory completely ignores the heroic slave insurrections in the United States under the leadership of Nat Turner, Denmark Vesey, Gabriel Prosser and scores of other Negro revolutionary leaders. It ignores the revolution of the Haitian Negro slaves who not only dared to strike for their freedom but overthrew the slave-holders and successively defeated the veteran troops of England and Spain.* These insurrectionary struggles of the Negro masses were also constantly lambasted in the press of the ruling class. This attitude represents the conscious policy of the Negro petty bourgeoisie of attempting to hide and destroy the revolutionary traditions of the Negro masses and to support the imperialist slander of the Negro people as servile and cowardly as accepting any conditions imposed upon them by the master class. From this position, the Negro petty bourgeoisie quite naturally proceeds to the advocacy of a boot-licking diplomacy for the Negro people.

It is the boot-licking diplomacy of the Negro petty bourgeoisie and its traitorous betrayal of the struggle of the Negro masses which retards the Negro liberation struggle and prevents the winning of greater victories. The slave insurrections in the United States had a tremendous effect in exposing the horrible nature of chattel slavery, in crystallizing abolitionist sentiment and in accelerating the armed conflict between feudal and capitalist economy for the domination of the country. The recent struggles of the Negro sharecroppers at Camp Hill, Alabama, forced the rich landowners to abandon their threat to cut off the food supply of the croppers during certain seasons.†

* The Haitian Negro slaves also defeated the crack armies of Napoleon.
† In June, 1931, the Communists organized the Negro sharecroppers of Camp Hill, Alabama, into the "Society for the Advancement of Colored People," a name designed to conceal the fact that it was in reality a sharecroppers' union. In July, a meeting of the members of the union was attacked by the sheriff and his deputies, aided by vigilantes, and these fired into the assembly and a battle ensued. One Negro was killed and several were wounded. The authorities started a reign of terror to

On one hand, the Negro bourgeoisie seeks to block the growth of the revolutionary movement. On the other, they engage in an opportunist exploitation of the fact of the growing radicalization of the Negro masses in order to bring petty concessions for themselves from the white ruling class. They use the radicalization of the Negro masses to scare the white ruling class into conceding them a greater share in the bitter exploitation of the Negro masses. In other words, they offer themselves as betrayers of the struggles of the Negro masses, as hangmen of the Negro workers, *for a price!*

Their Judas-bid for a few additional crumbs from the white ruling class is accompanied by an intensive campaign directed at confusing the Negro masses. Illusions are shamelessly peddled such as the "possibility" of liberation without a struggle against imperialism, of real democracy under robber capitalism, of emancipation from the skies—that is, by supernatural means—et cetera, et cetera.

These developments among the Negro masses are being rapidly hastened at the present time by the sharpening crisis of dying world capitalism, the growth of terror against the Negro masses and the increase in lynching.

The Negro workers suffer all the miseries of the working class as a whole. Their interests are, therefore, one with all the workers. But the Negro workers suffer special national oppression. Therefore, they have an important part in the leadership of the movement for the overthrow of American imperialism, and consequently, a leading role in the future dictatorship of the working class in this country.

Just as Communism is not the theory of the workers of any particular race or nation, but is the theory of the international working class, so is the Communist party not a party of white workers alone. It is the party of the workers, Negro and white. It represents the interests of the entire working class, independent of race or nationality.

Therefore, the Communist party points out and raises to the front the necessity of international solidarity of the working class as the prime condition for a successful struggle against the common enemy, the capitalists. It is to the interests of the

---

destroy the union, and Negroes were forced to leave their homes and take to the woods. Sixty Negroes were arrested, and five were charged with assault with intent to commit murder, seven with carrying concealed weapons, and twenty with conspiring to commit a felony. Charges were dropped against all but seven of the defendants, and eventually the remaining cases were postponed indefinitely. But the sharecroppers' union was destroyed.

white workers to support the struggles of the Negro masses for
freedom, because the white workers cannot be successful even
in their everyday struggles against capitalism without the fullest support of the struggles of the Negroes. Precisely in these
places where one hundred percent white chauvinism (race hatred) reigns supreme, and where oppression of the Negroes is
the sharpest (in the South), it is also found that the conditions
of the white workers are the most degrading.

Only the Communist party is leading the struggle of Negro
and white workers. Only the Communist party can lead such a
struggle. The imperialists and their agents, black and white,
therefore consider it necessary to intensify their offensive
against the Communist party.

The ruling class has by every means in its power instilled in
the white working class the racial hatred which has operated to
keep it apart from the Negro working class. The white bosses
sow seeds of race hatred as a means of keeping Negro and
white workers divided, or arousing suspicion and mistrust
among whites against Negroes. The Negro reformists likewise
sow distrust among the Negro workers against the white workers.

The trend of the present day, however, thanks to the leadership of the Communists, is the increasing emancipation of the
white workers from the poison of boss-class racial prejudice.
Hundreds of American workers have braved the bosses' policy
of terror to protest the frame-up and lynch verdicts handed
down by the boss lynch courts to the innocent Scottsboro boys.
The Negro and white workers are being solidly welded together
in the fires of the struggle for their common emancipation. Two
hundred thousand white workers on May first, 1934, in New
York, under the leadership of the Communist party, took the
Scottsboro mothers to their bosoms, showing their solidarity
with the Negro people for equal rights and national liberation.*

The growth of Communism, as the theory of the international
working class, could only take place in proportion to the development of the working class. The Negro masses did not embrace
Communism, say twenty years ago, for the simple reason that
the American working class in general and the Negro workers
in particular, had not accumulated sufficient experience; had

* This is a reference to the May Day parade. Actually, about 100,000
paraded, with the Scottsboro mothers in the lead. That evening 17,000
met in Madison Square Garden and were addressed by Jane Patterson,
mother of Heywood Patterson, and Mother Norris, mother of Clarence
Norris, both Scottsboro boys. The meeting passed a resolution demanding unconditional liberty for the Scottsboro boys.

not at that time reached the stage of development in which it was able to throw up from its midst an advanced detachment, capable of understanding the struggle and leading the masses of toilers, Negro and white, in struggle against the ruling class oppressors.

The explanation, therefore, for the growth of Communism among Negroes today is to be found, on the one hand, in the maturing of a Negro working class as a component part of that movement. This growth of a Negro working class is a most important phenomenon of recent years. This working class, through the experience of sharpening class struggles, is rapidly liberating itself from the reactionary influence of the Negro misleaders. This group, together with the white workers, is embracing Communism as its weapon in the struggle against American imperialism. Thus there has at last appeared among Negroes that class which, as an organic part of the whole working class, is the only force capable of rallying and leading the oppressed Negro masses in the struggle for national liberation—a struggle which, inspired largely by the example of the freedom won by the oppressed people in the Soviet Union, has gained a powerful impetus in recent years.

THE TASK OF THE NEGRO PEOPLE

By A. Philip Randolph

At the beginning of the New Deal in 1933, the Roosevelt administration encouraged Negro organizations to form a top group among themselves which could be relied upon by federal officials for expert advice on Negro affairs. Twenty-two black organizations responded and set up the Joint Committee on National Recovery. In May, 1935, the Joint Committee, in cooperation with the Division of Social Sciences of Howard University, sponsored a meeting at Howard for the purpose of discussing the new problems of the Negro arising out of the depression and formulating some general program of action. Out of this meeting emerged the National Negro Congress as a super-Negro protest organization. John P. Davis was the moving spirit behind the Congress and secretary of the National Sponsoring Committee. At the first Congress in February, 1936,

*the organization elected A. Philip Randolph as president.
Randolph was not present at the convention in Chicago,
but his address was read to the delegates.*

*Born April 15, 1889, in Crescent City, Florida, Randolph
finished high school in Florida, worked his way North and
subsisted on odd jobs while attending City College of New
York. (He never earned a college degree, and was mostly
self-taught.) Together with Chandler Owen, a young black
law student at Columbia University, Randolph became active in the Socialist party, and both edited* The Messenger,
*a radical black journal of opinion which endorsed Social-
ism and was a leading voice of the "New Negro" in the post-
World War I period. Randolph was asked by the Pullman
porters to help them organize, and in 1935, after twelve
years of hard struggle, the Brotherhood of Sleeping Car
Porters, with Randolph as president, forced the Pullman
company to recognize it.*

*Randolph's address to the National Negro Congress, pre-
sented here, is taken from* Resolutions of the National Negro Congress Held in Chicago, Ill., February 14, 15, 16,
1936, *a pamphlet, a copy of which is in the Schomburg Library.*

Mr. Chairman, officers of the National Sponsoring Committee
of the National Negro Congress, fellow delegates, fellow workers and friends: Greetings and felicitations upon this great
congress. Though absent in the flesh, I am with you in the
spirit of the deathless courage of the eighteenth- and nineteenth-
century black rebels and martyrs for human justice, in the spirit
of Frederick Douglass and Nat Turner, of Gabriel and Denmark
Vesey, of Harriet Tubman* and Sojourner Truth—those noble
rebels who struck out in the dark days of slavery that Negro
men and women might be free.

We have met in times of worldwide storm and stress, of social confusion, economic chaos, political disorder and intellectual uncertainty. Social institution, from the church to the
family, evince change and instability.

Unemployment falls like a deadening pall upon every great
power and machine nation. Democracies and dictatorships vie

* Harriet Tubman (1821–1913) was the Negro leader of fugitive slaves
who herself escaped from slavery in Maryland to lead flights of her
people from the South into the North. She made nineteen expeditions
into the South and was regarded as the most famous conductor of the
Underground Railroad. During the Civil War, she operated with a
guerrilla band behind the Confederate lines.

for supremacy. Witness the march of Fascist Italy and Nazi Germany along their imperialistic paths of manifest destiny.

Note their utter and flagrant abolition of democratic institutions, claiming that democracy is not only futile, but a menace to progress. Observe, too, tendencies toward fascist growth and development in existing countries with democratic governments, such as America, France and England. These are signs of grave and sinister portent to the world of workers, lovers of liberty and minority groups.

In threatening and disturbing significance, another world war looms upon the horizon. Many danger spots of conflict between great world powers stand out. Japan is restive in the face of the constant growth and power of Soviet Russia and is steadily resorting to provocative acts of war. Hitler seeks to serve as a spearhead of modern monopoly capitalism against the workers' republic.

Already Fascist Italy is on the march to subjugate the ancient kingdom of Ethiopia,* while France and Germany are in a state of truce, still at bay, awaiting the hour to strike for another conflict. England and Italy are in competition for place and prestige in the Mediterranean and darkest Africa, while Japan threatens to close the open door to American investigation and advance her claim to the adoption of a Monroe Doctrine over the Pacific which may bring Uncle Sam and Nippon to grips. Meanwhile, Tokyo proceeds on its long conquering trek to China.

With the collapse of the Naval Conference, a frenzied armament race swings into a high pace, and a war of world currencies, credits and trade is renewed. Thus the world is pregnant with the seeds of war, another war, a war in the air, on and under the water, with poison gases and high explosives, which may put an end to civilization as we know it.

Now, what of the American scene? It is no less forbidding and full of contradictions, unsettlement and cross currents in our social, economic and political life.

Of the outstanding problems that confront us following the collapse of capitalist prosperity and seeming stabilization of 1929, unemployment, trenching hard upon fifteen million, is one of the most perplexing. It has been attacked by the New Deal with its myriad legions of alphabets, but to little avail. Nor is there any solution offered either by the rugged individualists, despite their cry for the restoration of the grand era of Coolidge and Hoover, with a mythical "chicken in every pot" and a "flivver for every family."

---

* Italian troops invaded Ethiopia early in October, 1935.

With the economic affliction of nationwide joblessness stand the liquidation of the farmers, the small shopowners, the middle class and the poor share-crop and farm laborers, and the foreclosure of hundreds of thousands of mortgages upon the homes of the workers and the lower strata of the middle class, with no prospects of permanent rehabilitation by the hectic, sketchy, patchy and makeshift capitalist program.

But economic security, though baffling, is not the only challenge to the American workers, black and white, and the middle classes. There is also political and civil insecurity. Even the most credulous can sense an existing grave danger to our democratic institutions and constitutional liberties.

This danger is fascism—fascism which seeks the complete abrogation of all civil and political liberties in the manner and method of Nazi Germany and Fascist Italy. It is a menace to America. It is a world menace. It is a menace to black workers. It is a menace to religious tolerance and to the freedom and security of all minority groups.

And war is the twin evil sister of fascism. Its coming is not now improbable. It is a danger, an immediate danger, a danger to the American workers, black and white, who fight and pay for all wars in blood and taxes, while the bankers and munition makers, such as the Morgans and Du Ponts, reap huge and fabulous profits.

But this congress is called to attempt to meet the problems of black America, the submerged tenth of the population. While this is true, it is also true that the problems of the Negro peoples are the problems of the workers, for practically ninety-nine percent of the Negro peoples win their bread by selling their labor power in the labor market from day to day. They cannot escape the dangers and penalties of the depression, war or fascism.

However, our contemporary history is a witness to the stark fact that black America is a victim of both class and race prejudice and oppression. Because Negroes are black, they are hated, maligned and spat upon, lynched, mobbed and murdered. Because Negroes are workers, they are browbeaten, bullied, intimidated, robbed, exploited, jailed and shot down. Because they are black they are caught between the nether millstones of discrimination when seeking a job or seeking to join a union.

Thus, voteless in thirteen states; politically disregarded and discounted in the others; victims of the lynch terror in Dixie, with a Scottsboro frame-up of notorious memory; faced with the label of the white man's job and the white man's union; unequal before the law; Jim-Crowed in schools and colleges throughout the nation; segregated in the slums and ghettos of

the urban centers; landless peons of a merciless white landlordism; hunted down, harassed and hounded as vagrants in the
Southern cities, the Negro peoples face a hard, deceptive and
brutal capitalist order, despite its preachments of Christian
love and brotherhood.

What has brought us to this? is the insistent question. The
answer in brief lies in the World War, the sharpening and deepening of capitalist exploitation of the workers of hand and
brain, the acceleration of a technological revolution creating a
standing army of unemployed, the ripening and maturing of
monopoly capitalism thru trustification, rationalization and the
rapid march of financial imperialism, and the intensification of
racial and religious hatreds, together with increasingly blatant
and provocative nationalism.

But the war itself was the effect of a deeper cause, and that
cause was the profit system, which provides and permits the
enrichment of the few at the expense of the many, allowing two
percent of the people to own ninety percent of the wealth of
these United States, a condition not much different in other
capitalist countries, and also makes for the robbery and oppression of the darker and weaker colonial peoples of the world.

But the diagnosis of the causes of social problems such as
wars, economic depressions and fascism is only designed to enable the victims to seek and find a remedy. Before dealing with
some of the remedies, however, let me speak briefly of what are
not remedies:

First, the New Deal is no remedy. It does not seek to change
the profit system. It does not place human rights above property
rights, but gives the business interests the support of the state.
It is no insurance against the coming of fascism or the prevention of war or a recurrent depression, though it be more liberal
than the Republican Tories.

Second, the restoration of Republican rule is no solution. It
was the rule of the Grand Old Party under which the depression
came. Negroes have watched themselves disfranchised and
lynched under both regimes, Republican and Democratic.

Third, the Townsend Plan* is no panacea. While an adequate
old-age pension should be fought for, a pension far greater
than that offered by the New Deal Security legislation, the

---

* Early in January, 1935, Dr. Francis E. Townsend, an elderly California
physician, announced the "Townsend Plan," by which the government
would give $200 a month to every citizen sixty years old or older, the
cost to be paid by a sales tax. Each pensioner would be required to spend
his allowance within the month, thereby, according to the Plan, starting
a consumer boom which would end the depression.

Townsend Plan is well-nigh impossible of execution, and if executed would not achieve its aim.

Moreover, its aim is not designed to modify the structure of organized, profit-making private property, and any old-age-pension law will be so manipulated as to nullify its meritorious features so long as the workers have no effective voice in the councils of government.

Fourth, the "Share the Wealth" plan of the Huey Long* movement is fantastic and superficial, since it pretends to seek to share wealth while also seeking to maintain inviolate the profit system of exploitation.

Fifth, the currency cant of the Radio Priest† is a glittering mirage and not a remedy, for it would merely effect inflation, thereby creating more money, which has no magic power to reapportion or reallocate goods or wealth among the people.

Money is merely the measure of value and has no casual power of effecting the distribution of values. This can only be done by the organized might of the workers. Practically every government of the world has at one time or another tried the experiment of inflation, only to its sorrow and the sharper victimization of the workers.

Nor is deflation or reflation of any basic value. The mere existence of varying amounts of money does not affect the empty pockets of unemployed workers.

But back to remedies. At the top of the list of remedies I wish to suggest the struggle of the workers against exploitation of the employers. Next the struggle of the workers against fascism and for the preservation of democratic institutions, the arena in which alone their economic power may be built.

Third, the struggle to build powerful Negro civil-rights organizations. Fourth, the struggle against war, which wrecks the organizations of the workers and stifles and suppresses freedom of speech, the press and assembly. Fifth, the struggle to strengthen the forces of the exploited sharecroppers and tenant farmers. Sixth, the struggle to build mass consumers' movements to protect the housewives against price manipulation.

But the struggle to apply the aforementioned remedies can only be achieved through definite social, economic and political instrumentalities. Thus, the fight against the economic exploita-

---

* Senator Huey Long, the "Kingfish" of Louisiana, built up a national following on the strength of his vague plan to "share the wealth."

† Father Charles E. Coughlin, the "Radio Priest," broadcast weekly from Royal Oak, Michigan, and combined admiration for fascism, racism and anti-Semitism with attacks on Wall Street and international bankers.

tion of the workers can only be effectively carried on through industrial and craft unions, with the emphasis on the former.

The industrial union is important in this stage of economic development because modern business has changed in structure and assumed the form of giant trust and holding companies, with which the craft union can no longer effectively grapple.

Moreover, the craft union invariably has a color bar against the Negro worker, but the industrial union in structure renders race discrimination less possible, since it embraces all the workers included in the industry, regardless of race, creed, color or craft, skilled or unskilled.

Thus, this congress should seek to broaden and intensify the movement to draw Negro workers into labor organizations and break down the color bar in the trade-unions that now have it.*

The next instrumentality which the workers must build and employ for their protection against economic exploitation, war and fascism, is an independent working-class political party. It should take the form of a farmer-labor political organization. This is indispensable in view of the bankruptcy in principles, courage and vision of the old-line parties, Republican and Democratic.

They are the political committees of Wall Street and are constructed to serve the profit-making agencies and therefore can no more protect or advance the interests of the workers than can a sewing machine grind corn. It is poor working-class wisdom to fight big business for economic justice on the industrial field and vote for it on the political.

With these two major instrumentalities, there should also be built up great consumers' cooperatives, which, while less fundamental, nonetheless provide the basis for mass collective action on the part of the workers and lower middle classes.

They have stood the workers in good stead wherever they have been constructed, providing they are shaped and directed by working-class and not bourgeois interests.

The fight for civil and political rights of the Negro peoples can effectively be carried on if only those organizations that are pushing the struggles are broadened and built with a wider mass base. Those organizations that are serving on the civil-

* In the fall of 1935 the Committee for Industrial Organization was formed to help organize the mass-production industries through industrial unionism. The A. F. of L. unions founding the Committee were expelled from the Federation in 1936. The National Negro Congress was a major agency in aiding the C.I.O. to promote unionization among Negro workers.

rights front effectively for the Negro are the National Association for the Advancement of Colored People and the International Labor Defense.

It needs to be definitely understood, however, that the fight in the courts for civil and political rights cannot be effective except when backed by a broad nationwide, if not international, mass protest through demonstrations in the form of parades, mass meetings and publicity.

But the fight for civil and political liberties for the Negro peoples, while it has been brilliantly waged by the N.A.A.C.P. and the I.L.D., the gravity and complexity of the problems of civil and political liberties, accentuated and widened by the evil of fascist trends in America, demands that new tactics and strategy be employed to meet the situation.

The maneuvering and disposing of the forces of Negro peoples and their sympathetic allies against their enemies can only be effectively worked out through the tactics and strategy of the united front. The task of overcoming the enemies of democratic institutions and constitutional liberties is too big for any single organization. It requires the united and formal integrating and coordinating of the various Negro organizations— church, fraternal, civil, trade-union, farmer, professional, college and what not—into the framework of a united front, together with the white groups of workers, lovers of liberty and those whose liberties are similarly menaced for a common attack upon the forces of reaction, backed by the embattled masses of black and white workers.

The united-front strategy and tactics should be executed through methods of mass demonstration, such as parades, picketing, boycotting, mass protests, the mass distribution of propaganda literature, as well as legal action.

The united front does not provide an excuse for weakness or timidity, or reliance by any one organization upon the others who comprise it, but, on the contrary, it affords an opportunity for the contribution of strength by each organization to the common pool of organizational power for a common attack or a common defense against the enemy. Thus, the Negro peoples should not place their problems for solution down at the feet of their white sympathetic allies, which has been and is the common fashion of the old-school Negro leadership, for, in the final analysis, the salvation of the Negro, like the workers, must come from within.

The power and effectiveness of the united front will be developed by waging the struggles around definite, vital and immediate issues of life and living.

These issues should be obvious, clear and simple, such as prevention of stoppage of relief, cuts in relief allotments, layoffs of relief workers or workers in any industry, discrimination in the giving of relief, exorbitant rents, evictions, rent increases, police brutality, denial of free assembly, freedom of the press, freedom of speech to unpopular groups, denial of civil rights to Negroes, such as the right to be served in hotels and restaurants, to have access to public utilities and forms of transportation, such as the Pullman car.

Wage struggles around war upon Ethiopia by the fascist dictator Mussolini, strikes and lockouts of black and white workers, the amendment to the federal Constitution or the adoption of social legislation such as the Retirement Pension Act for railroad workers, fight for the freedom of Angelo Herndon, the Scottsboro boys, the Wagner-Costigan antilynching bill, the violations of the Wagner Labor Disputes bill, the forcing of teachers to take the oath, the goose-stepping of the students in the school system thru the R.O.T.C., the abolition of the color bar in trade-unions, the murder of Shoemaker in Tampa, Florida, exposing the menace of the American Liberty League, William Randolph Hearst and the Ku Klux Klan, and supporting the movement of John L. Lewis for industrial unionism.

Such is the task of Negro peoples. This task comes as a sharp and decisive challenge at a time when new atrocities and nameless terrorism are directed against black America and when the workers, black and white, are being goaded by oppression and intimidation, to resort to general strikes such as took place in San Francisco and in Pekin, Illinois, as well as national strikes such as the textile workers', the miners' and the workers' revolts in Minnesota and Toledo.

To meet this task, the Negro peoples, pressed with their backs against the wall, must face the future with heads erect, hearts undaunted and undismayed, ready and willing and determined to pay the price in struggle, sacrifices and suffering that freedom, justice and peace shall share and enjoy a more abundant life.

Forward to complete economic, political and social equality for Negro peoples. Forward to the abolition of this sinister system of Jim-Crowism in these United States! The united front points the way. More power to the National Negro Congress! The future belongs to the people!

THE CRISIS OF THE NEGRO AND THE CONSTITUTION

By A. Philip Randolph

The second annual meeting of the National Negro Congress was held in Philadelphia in 1937 and was attended by 1,149 delegates. Randolph's address to the conference outlined the key issues facing the Negro people at the beginning of the second Roosevelt administration. The text presented here is excerpted from Randolph, "The Crisis of the Negro and the Constitution," Official Proceedings, National Negro Congress, 1937.

. . . IN THIS HOUR of crisis in the nation, in the whole wide world, in governments, in industry, in trade-union movements and among oppressed minorities everywhere, the Second National Negro Congress, representing hundreds of thousands of Negroes in America, hails the Constitution on its 150th birthday. We hail it as a Magna Charta of human rights. The Negro people, oppressed and persecuted, especially look to the Constitution as an impregnable citadel of their liberties. . . .

In very truth, the Constitution is a means to an end. The end is the attainment of an enlightened and humane government, and an economic order that will invest the people with the right and the power to live the good life, the more abundant life.

And today, in a world of storm and stress, of confusion and uncertainty, of arrogant cynicism and deadly pessimism, of war and fascism, the American Constitution proudly reveals its deeper moorings of stability, assurance and hope for democracy.

While the Negro people, under the Constitution, because of nullification by the spirit of the Lost Cause, are still without the full measure of citizenship in the former Confederate States, the Constitution, at least, vouchsafes complete citizenship rights and provides the grounds of principle and promises to secure it.

Albeit, it is more and more becoming correctly understood that the task of realizing full citizenship for the Negro people is largely in the hands of the Negro people themselves. Assuring full citizenship rights to [the] Afro-American is the duty and responsibility of the state, but securing them is the task of the Negro; it is the task of labor and the progressive and liberal forces of the nation. Freedom is never given; it is won. And the

Negro people must win their freedom. They must achieve justice. This involves struggle, continuous struggle.

True liberation can be acquired and maintained only when the Negro people possess power; and power is the product and flower of organization—organization of the masses, the masses in the mills and mines, on the farms, in the factories, in churches, in fraternal organizations, in homes, colleges, women's clubs, student groups, trade-unions, tenants' leagues, in cooperative guilds, political organizations and civil-rights associations.

Organization is the purpose and aim of the Second National Negro Congress. While it does not seek, as its primary program, to organize the Negro people into trade-unions and civil-rights movements, it does plan to integrate and coordinate the existing Negro organizations into one federated and collective agency so as to develop greater and more effective power. The Congress does not stress or espouse any political faith or religious creed, but seeks to formulate a minimum political, economic and social program which all Negro groups can endorse and for which they can work and fight.

The Congress supports the fight of the National Association for the Advancement of Colored People for a federal antilynching bill, for around this issue there is no basic difference of opinion among Negroes. All Negro people desire and seek fair opportunities for work and the right to join trade-unions. No one can object to a proposal for more and better jobs, the abolition of Jim Crow labor unions, and for equal educational chances in public schools and universities.

It may not be amiss to add also, in this connection, that the Congress is not Communist or Republican, Democratic or Socialist. It is not Methodist, Baptist or Christian Scientist. It avoids control by any single religion or political party. It shuns the Scylla and Charybdis of the extreme left and the extreme right. But, in the true spirit of the united front, and in the pattern and purpose of integration and coordination, for mass strength, [it] embraces all sections of opinion among the Negro people. It does not seek to impose any issue of philosophy upon any organization or group, but rather to unite varying and various organizations, with various and varying philosophies, left, center, and right among the Negro people upon a simple, minimum program so as to mobilize and rally power and mass support behind vital issues affecting the life and destiny of the race.

Be it also known that the Congress does not seek to change the American form of government, but rather to implement it with new and rugged morals and spiritual sinews to make its democratic traditions, forms and ideals more permanent and abiding and a living force.

Startling changes, economic, political and social, have come upon the world. The empire of the Kaiser, apparently rock-ribbed and as steadfast as the sun, has been replaced by the totalitarian Third Reich. The Italian democratic state has given way to a corporate, fascist system. And the Czar of all the Russias has been relegated to oblivion by the Soviets of the workers.

And even if the honored democracies of the United States, England and France haven't succumbed and capitulated to the drastic and dangerous pattern of the dictator, they are under constant, menacing stress and strain of tendencies toward the rule of fascist force. Deadlocked, withal, in a mighty struggle for supremacy are the governments by the rule of "The man on horseback" and governments by rule of a free people.

Add to our existing political disorder reflected in the amazing and rapid transformation of the structure and direction of modern governments, economic maladjustments as seen in worldwide chronic and permanent unemployment, monetary fluctuations and industrial instability, the ever rising threat of a widening sweep of the wave of war, then optimism and hope are shattered and replaced by pessimism and fear.

Already, large areas of the world are in the flames of war. The "little brown men" of militaristic Nippon are raining fire and destruction upon the land of Confucius, but the Chinese people, proud in their noble heritage, are defending their country with matchless courage and resolve, yielding no single inch of territory except under the imperative of superior force.

And when we turn our eyes to the West, to the Mediterranean, we witness the vile and vicious efforts of Mussolini and Hitler, in accordance with the terms of a Berlin-Rome axis seeking to encompass by open murder the destruction of democracy. Lulled and solaced in conscience by the nonintervention sham, the democratic nations, England, France and the United States, are observing defenseless women and children of the legitimate Loyalists government of Spain massacred in shocking barbarism by the hordes of Franco, backed by the money and men in Italy and Germany.* Whither doth it lead, comes the query?

It is well-nigh accepted quite generally by the thoughtful

* During the Spanish Civil War (1936–39), the Loyalist government of Spain, composed of liberals and radicals, fought against the attacks of the fascist columns of Generalissimo Francisco Franco. A group of Americans, black and white, fought with the Spanish Loyalists in the Abraham Lincoln Brigade.

peoples everywhere that if the dikes of democracy break in the land of the little Iberian peninsula, a world flood of fascism may not be far behind, and [may] imperil free peoples everywhere.

This may be the tragic price that mankind must pay for its complacent and timid spirit before the brutal and ruthless aggression by Japan upon China in creating the puppet kingdom of Manchukuo, and the cruel and savage invasion of the ancient kingdom of Ethiopia by the Fascist legions of Italy. The independence of Ethiopia has been sold down the river by the League of Nations, while winked at by England and France.*

And when we return to our shores, we find closer at home that all is not well. Despite signs of some recovery from the depression, unemployment trenches hard upon eight million. Unemployment has taken on the picture of permanency. Production in certain industries increases while the workers decrease. The development of the machine, the refinements in management and the concentration and centralization of economic power in trusts and holding companies make this possible. With grave warning, President Roosevelt has declared that one third of the population is in ill health, underfed, underhoused and underclothed. Relief needs have not appreciably lessened, for jobs are still scarce for the workers.

Civil rights in industrial areas, where conflict between labor and capital is on, are arrogantly disregarded and broken down by pliant municipal representatives, and extragovernmental organizations such as the Ku Klux Klan, the Black Legion and other vigilante movements. . . .

But not only are the rights of the workers assailed by vigilante mobs at the behest of the Liberty League and the organized open-shop business interests of America, but in state legislatures and Congress, die-hard tories, such as Senator Vandenberg† and others, are seeking to enact legislation, forcing upon trade-unions and corporations, compulsory arbitration and the elimination of strikes. . . .

And as we look to labor we find its house divided. Thus it is obvious that the great problem of the workers in America today is the problem of unity. . . . Craft and industrial unionism can and must go side by side in the struggle of the workers for industrial democracy. These forms of organization must develop and function in one house of labor. Now, what of the Negro in relation to these problems?

* During the Ethiopian War launched by Benito Mussolini in 1935, Emperor Haile Selassie futilely appealed to the League of Nations for aid.
† Senator Arthur H. Vandenberg was a leading Republican conservative.

The Negro people are an integral part of the American commonwealth. They, like our white brothers, bleed and die in war. They suffer and hunger in the depression. Thus, theirs is the task of consolidating their interests with the interest of the progressive forces of the nation. Collective bargaining brings power to black as well as to white workers. The abolition of the company union frees the Negro workers from economic bondage and enables them to express their voice in the determination of wage rates, hours and working conditions the same as it does for white workers. Thus, the strengthening of the labor movement, the improvement of labor standards, brings comfort, health and decency to black as well as to white workers.

But there are other problems that the Negro people face. In the South there is a blight of Jim-Crowism, segregation, disfranchisement through grandfather clauses and lily-white primaries and the terror of the Ku Klux Klan.

Peonage, a form of involuntary servitude, in utter nullification of the Thirteenth Amendment, holds the Negro in many Southern states in a condition of virtual slavery. Negro tenant farmers are browbeaten, persecuted and driven, when they evince any semblance of independence, out of their miserable and squalid shacks onto the highway. Civil and political rights for them are virtually unknown. Differentials in wages and hours of work are a common practice. Relief, though given by the federal government is administered by whim of Southern prejudice in the mood of arrogant superiority. What can be done about this? The answer is:

Let us build a united front of all Negro organizations, of varying strata, purpose and outlook. Let us build a united front in cooperation with the progressive and liberal agencies of the nation whose interests are common with Black America.

With the spirit and strategy of the united front, the five remaining Scottsboro Boys can be released from their dark dungeon in Alabama. With it peonage in the South can be wiped out and the sharecropper and tenant farmers, black and white, can organize and improve their economic status through collective bargaining. With it the horror of lynching in America may be eliminated and mob terror relegated to oblivion.

Thus, on the occasion of the 150th Anniversary of the American Constitution, and the Second Anniversary of the National Negro Congress, the Negro peoples face the future, with heads erect and souls uncurbed, resolved to march forward in the van of progress, with hope and faith in the creation of a new and better world. And the Congress shall help to guide them, to lead them on!

What now of the stewardship of the Congress since its memorable bow to black and white America?

Can more be said than that it has fought a good fight? It has kept the faith. It has worked and not grown weary for a happier humanity.

On the far-flung battle lines of steel, it marshalled militant black men to march in the van with the C.I.O. to chalk up an enviable record in bringing workers into the field of industrial organization.* And it has worked with the American Federation of Labor. Our men did not fail or faint before blood or bullets—in South Chicago, Detroit, Michigan, Ohio and Pennsylvania.

The Congress has brought eager and aggressive black youth to grapple with the problem of the organization of the tobacco workers in Virginia. And these youth are winning their spurs.

To the laundry workers in Washington, D. C., the Congress is carrying the message of trade-union organization. And it enlisted Negro organizers to join C.I.O. forces to organize the automobile industry.

On the civil and political rights' front, the Congress joined the fighting forces of the National Association for the Advancement of Colored People, to battle for the Wagner-Gavagan federal antilynching bill.

And to the rescue of Herndon and the Scottsboro Boys, the Congress has carried its unflagging fighting spirit.

But not only has it fought in the front for the defense of the rights of the Negro people, the Congress has also thrown its might with the progressive forces in the land to aid in the cause of Spanish democracy, the independence of China from the domination of Japan, and the restoration of Haile Selassie to an independent Kingdom of Ethiopia.

Yes, it has joined the great demonstration of the nation against war and fascism. And, too, it is stirring the women and youth of the Negro people to join and struggle with the national and world agencies of their groups for a better world.

Therefore, with humble pride we cry out of the depths of our souls to mankind everywhere: Forward with the destruction of the imperialist domination and oppression of the great peoples of Africa! Forward to the abolition of the fascist rule of Italy over the noble, independent and unconquerable men of Ethiopia! Forward to the creation of a united, free and independent China! Forward to victory of the valiant loyalist armies over

* The National Negro Congress cooperated with the Steel Workers' Organizing Committee in that group's initiation of the conference of Negro and white steelworkers in Pittsburgh, January 9, 1937.

the fascist brigands of Franco! Long live the cause of world peace! Long live the spirit of world democracy! Long live the memory and love of the black revolutionist of the eighteenth century, led by Denmark Vesey, Nat Turner, Gabriel, Harriet Tubman, Sojourner Truth, and Frederick Douglass! Long live the valor of those black regiments of slaves and freedom* whose blood and courage made of Lincoln's Emancipation Proclamation a living reality!

Forward to the unity of the workers! Forward to democracy and freedom, progress and plenty! Forward with the torch of education, the instrument of agitation, the weapon of organization to a day of peace on earth and toward men, good will!

A CALL FOR MASS ACTION

By A. Philip Randolph

As America became increasingly involved in the war already raging in Europe, Negroes resented bitterly their exclusion from the nation's defense industries and the continuation of segregation in the armed forces. In 1940, A. Philip Randolph called for a march on Washington, D. C., to demand government action against this discrimination. Randolph's appeal led to the formation of the March on Washington Movement, which announced in June, 1941, that it would rally fifty thousand Negroes on July first in the nation's capital to demand that the federal government stop discrimination in the defense industries and the armed forces. Randolph refused to call off the march until President Roosevelt issued his famous Executive Order 8802 on June 25, 1941, forbidding discrimination in war industries and government training programs, and establishing a President's Committee on Fair Employment Practices.

Below is the major part of a speech Randolph delivered to the Policy Conference of the March on Washington Movement held in Detroit, September 26–27, 1942. On the cover of the pamphlet in which Randolph's speech is published are the words: "Winning democracy for the Negro

---

* The word obviously is *freedmen*.

*is winning the war for democracy." The speech clearly
shows that the March on Washington Movement was the
forerunner of the protest movement by black Americans in
the 1960's.*

The speech is excerpted from the booklet March on
Washington Movement: Proceedings of Conference Held
in Detroit, September 26-27, 1942 *(pp. 4-11), a copy of
which is in the Schomburg Library.*

FELLOW MARCHERS and delegates to the Policy Conference of the March on Washington Movement and friends: We
have met at an hour when the sinister shadows of war are
lengthening and becoming more threatening. As one of the sections of the oppressed darker races, and representing a part of
the exploited millions of the workers of the world, we are deeply
concerned that the totalitarian legions of Hitler, Hirohito and
Mussolini do not batter the last bastions of democracy. We know
that our fate is tied up with the fate of the democratic way of
life. And so, out of the depth of our hearts, a cry goes up for the
triumph of the United Nations. But we would not be honest with
ourselves were we to stop with a call for a victory of arms alone.
We know this is not enough. We fight that the democratic faiths,
values, heritages and ideals may prevail.

Unless this war sounds the death knell to the old Anglo-
American empire systems, the hapless story of which is one of
exploitation for the profit and power of a monopoly-capitalist
economy, it will have been fought in vain. Our aim, then, must
not only be to defeat Nazism, fascism and militarism on the
battlefield but to win the peace, for democracy, for freedom and
the Brotherhood of Man without regard to his pigmentation,
land of his birth or the God of his fathers.

We therefore sharply score the Atlantic Charter* as expressing
a vile and hateful racism and a manifestation of the tragic and
utter collapse of an old, decadent democratic political liberalism which worshiped at the shrine of a world-conquering monopoly capitalism. This system grew fat and waxed powerful off
the flesh, blood, sweat and tears of the tireless toilers of the
human race and the sons and daughters of color in the underdeveloped lands of the world.

* In the Atlantic Charter of 1941, Franklin D. Roosevelt and Winston
Churchill endorsed the goals in the war against the fascist Axis powers.
Among the principles enunciated were: no territorial aggrandizement; no
changes of territory against the wishes of the people concerned; and self-
government for all peoples. Nothing, however, was said about the
African or Asian colonies held by the Allied Powers.

When this war ends, the people want something more than the dispersal of equality and power among individual citizens in a liberal, political, democratic system. They demand with striking comparability the dispersal of equality and power among the citizen-workers in an economic democracy that will make certain the assurance of the good life—the more abundant life—in a warless world.

But, withal this condition of freedom, equality and democracy is not the gift of the Gods. It is the task of men—yes, men —brave men, honest men, determined men. . . .

Thus our feet are set in the path toward equality—economic, political and social and racial. Equality is the heart and essence of democracy, freedom and justice. Without equality of opportunity in industry, in labor unions, schools and colleges, government, politics and before the law, without equality in social relations and in all phases of human endeavor, the Negro is certain to be consigned to an inferior status. There must be no dual standards of justice, no dual rights, privileges, duties or responsibilities of citizenship. No dual forms of freedom. . . .

But our nearer goals include the abolition of discrimination, segregation and Jim Crow in the government, the Army, Navy, Air Corps, U. S. Marine, Coast Guard, Women's Auxiliary Army Corps and the Waves, and defense industries; the elimination of discrimination in hotels, restaurants, on public transportation conveyances, in educational, recreational, cultural, and amusement and entertainment places such as theaters, beaches and so forth.

We want the full works of citizenship with no reservations. We will accept nothing less.

But goals must be achieved. They are not secured because it is just and right that they be possessed by Negro or white people. Slavery was not abolished because it was bad and unjust. It was abolished because men fought, bled and died on the battlefield.

Therefore, if Negroes secure their goals, immediate and remote, they must win them and to win them they must fight, sacrifice, suffer, go to jail and, if need be, die for them. These rights will not be given. They must be taken.

Democracy was fought for and taken from political royalists —the kings. Industrial democracy, the rights of the workers to organize and designate the representatives of their own choosing to bargain collectively is being won and taken from the economic royalists—big business.

Now, the realization of goals and rights by a nation, race or class requires belief in and loyalty to principles and policies.

. . . Policies rest upon principles. Concretely, a policy sets forth one's position on vital public questions such as political affiliations, religious alliances. The March on Washington Movement must be opposed to partisan political commitments, religious or denominational alliances. We cannot sup with the Communists, for they rule or ruin any movement. This is their policy. Our policy must be to shun them. This does not mean that Negro Communists may not join the March on Washington Movement.

As to the composition of our movement. Our policy is that it be all-Negro, and pro-Negro but not anti-white, or anti-Semitic or antilabor, or anti-Catholic. The reason for this policy is that all oppressed people must assume the responsibility and take the initiative to free themselves. Jews must wage their battle to abolish anti-Semitism. Catholics must wage their battle to abolish anti-Catholicism. The workers must wage their battle to advance and protect their interests and rights.

The essential value of an all-Negro movement such as the March on Washington is that it helps to create faith by Negroes in Negroes. It develops a sense of self-reliance with Negroes depending on Negroes in vital matters. It helps to break down the slave psychology and inferiority complex in Negroes which comes and is nourished with Negroes relying on white people for direction and support. This inevitably happens in mixed organizations that are supposed to be in the interest of the Negro. . . .

Therefore, while the March on Washington Movement is interested in the general problems of every community and will lend its aid to help solve them, it has as its major interest and task the liberation of the Negro people, and this is sound social economy. It is in conformity with the principle of the division of labor. No organization can do everything. Every organization can do something, and each organization is charged with the social responsibility to do that which it can do, is built to do.

I have given quite some time to the discussion of this question of organizational structure and function and composition, because the March on Washington Movement is a mass movement of Negroes which is being built to achieve a definite objective, and is a departure from the usual pattern of Negro efforts and thinking. As a rule, Negroes do not choose to be to themselves in anything, they are only to themselves as a result of compulsive segregation. Negroes are together voluntarily for the same reason the workers join voluntarily into a trade-union. But because workers only join trade-unions, does not mean that the very same workers may not join organizations composed of some nonworkers, such as art museums or churches or fraternal

lodges that have varying purposes. This same thing is true of
Negroes. Because Negroes only can join the March on Washington Movement, does not indicate that Negroes in the M.O.W.M.
may not join an interracial golf club or church or Elks Lodge
or debating society or trade-union.

No one would claim that a society of Filipinos is undemocratic because it does not take in Japanese members, or that
Catholics are anti-Jewish because the Jesuits won't accept Jews
as members or that trade-unions are illiberal because they deny
membership to employers. Neither is the March on Washington
Movement undemocratic because it confines its members to
Negroes. Now this reasoning would not apply to a public school
or a Pullman car, because these agencies are public in nature
and provide a service which is necessary to all of the people of
a community.

Now, the question of policy which I have been discussing
involves, for example, the March on Washington Movement's
position on the war. We say that the Negro must fight for his
democratic rights now, for after the war it may be too late. This
is our policy on the Negro and the war. But this policy raises
the question of method, programs, strategy and tactics—namely,
how is this to be done. It is not sufficient to say that Negroes
must fight for their rights now, during the war. Some methods
must be devised, program set up, and strategy outlined.

This Policy Conference is designed to do this very thing. The
first requirement to executing the policies of the March on
Washington Movement is to have something to execute them
with. This brings me to the consideration of organization. Organization supplies the power. The formulation of policies and
the planning process furnish direction. Now, there is organization and organization. Some people say, for instance, Negroes
are already organized, and they cite The Sisters of the Mysterious Ten, The Sons and Daughters of I Will Arise, the Holy
Rollers, the social clubs, and so forth. But these organizations
are concerned about the individual interest of helping the sick
and funeralizing the dead or providing amusement and recreation. They deal with no social or racial problem which concerns
the entire people. The Negro people as a whole is not interested
in whether Miss A. plays Contract Bridge on Friday or not, or
whether the deacon of the Methodist Church has a 200- or 500-
dollar casket when he dies. These are personal questions. But
the Negro race is concerned about Negroes being refused jobs
in defense plants, or whether a Negro can purchase a lower in
a Pullman car, or whether the United States Treasury segregates Negro girls. Thus, while it is true Negroes are highly

organized, the organizations are not built to deal with and manipulate the mechanics of power. Nobody cares how many Whist Clubs or churches or secret lodges Negroes establish, because they are not compulsive or coercive. They don't seek to transform the socioeconomic racial milieu. They accept and do not challenge conditions with an action program.

Hence, it is apparent that the Negro needs more than organization. He needs mass organization with an action program, aggressive, bold and challenging in spirit. Such a movement is our March on Washington.

Our first job, then, is actually to organize millions of Negroes, and build them into block systems, with captains, so that they may be summoned to action overnight and thrown into physical motion. Without this type of organization, Negroes will never develop mass power, which is the most effective weapon a minority people can wield. Witness the strategy and maneuver of the people of India with mass civil disobedience and noncooperation and the marches to the sea to make salt.* It may be said that the Indian people have not won their freedom. This is so, but they will win it. The central principle of the struggle of oppressed minorities like the Negro, labor, Jews, and others is not only to develop mass-demonstration maneuvers, but to repeat and continue them. The workers don't picket firms today and quit. They don't strike today and fold up. They practice the principle of repetition. . . .

We must develop huge demonstrations, because the world is used to big dramatic affairs. . . . Besides, the unusual attracts. We must develop a series of marches of Negroes at a given time in a hundred or more cities throughout the country, or stage a big march of a hundred thousand Negroes on Washington to put our cause into the mainstream of public opinion and focus the attention of world interests. This is why India is in the news.

Therefore, our program is in part as follows:

1. A national conference for the integration and expression of the collective mind and will of the Negro masses.

2. The mobilization and proclamation of a nationwide series of mass marches on the city halls and city councils to awaken the Negro masses and center public attention upon the grievances and goals of the Negro people and serve as training and discipline of the Negro masses for the more strenuous struggle of a March on Washington, if, as, and when an affirmative de-

* The reference is to the struggles in India for independence from Great Britain under the leadership of Ghandi.

cision is made thereon by the Negro masses of the country through our national conference.

3. A march on Washington as an evidence to white America that black America is on the march for its rights and means business.

4. The picketing of the White House following the March on Washington and maintaining the said picket line until the country and the world recognize the Negro has become of age and will sacrifice his all to be counted as men, free men.

This program is drastic and exacting. It will test our best mettle and stamina and courage. Let me warn you that in these times of storm and stress, this program will be opposed. Our Movement, therefore, must be well knit together. It must have moral and spiritual vision, understanding, and wisdom.

How can we achieve this?

Our Movement must be blueprinted. Our forces must be marshaled, with block captains to provide immediate and constant contact. Our block captains must hold periodic meetings for their blocks to develop initiative and the capacity to make decisions and move in relation to direction from the central organization of the division.

Our educational program must be developed around the struggle of the Negro masses.

This can be done by developing mass plans to secure mass registration of the Negro people for the primaries and elections. Through this program the Negro masses can be given a practical and pragmatic view of the mechanics and function of our government and the significance of mass political pressure.

Plans should be mapped by the various divisions to fight for Negro integration in the public utilities as motormen and conductors. During the war women may be placed on these jobs. We must make a drive now to see to it that Negro men and women receive their appropriate consideration in every important field of American industry from which Negroes are now generally barred.

Our day-to-day exercise of our civil rights is a constant challenge. In theaters, hotels, restaurants, amusement places, even in the North, now there is discrimination against Negroes. This is true in every large city. Negroes have the moral obligation to demand the right to enjoy and make use of their civil and political privileges. If we don't, we will lose the will to fight for our citizenship rights, and the public will consider that we don't want them and should not have them. This fight to break down these barriers in every city should be carefully and painstakingly organized. By fighting for these civil rights the Negro masses will be disciplined in struggle. Some of us will be put in jail, and court battles may ensue, but this will give the Negro masses a sense of their importance and value as citizens and as fighters in the Negro liberation movement and the cause for democracy as a whole. It will make white people in high places and the ordinary white man understand that Negroes have rights that they are bound to respect.

The giant public protest meetings must continue. They are educative and give moral strength to our movement and the Negro masses.

For this task we need men and women who will dedicate and consecrate their life, spirit, mind and soul to the great adventure of Negro freedom and justice.

Our divisions must serve as Negro mass parliaments where the entire community may debate the day-to-day issues such as police brutality, high rents, and other questions and make judgments and take action in the interest of the community. These divisions should hold meetings at least twice a month. In them every Negro should be made to feel his importance as a factor in the Negro liberation movement. We must have every Negro realize his leadership ability, the educated and uneducated, the poor and wealthy. In the March on Washington Movement the highest is as low as the lowest and the lowest is as high as the highest. Numbers in mass formation is our key, directed, of course, by the collective intelligence of the people.

Let us put our weight behind the fight to abolish the poll tax.* This will give the black and white workers of the South new hope. But the Negro people are not the only oppressed section of mankind. India is now waging a world-shaking, history-making fight for independence. India's fight is the Negro's fight.

Now, let us be unafraid. We are fighting for big stakes. Our stakes are liberty, justice and democracy. Every Negro should hang his head in shame who fails to do his part now for freedom. This is the hour of the Negro. It is the hour of the common man. May we rise to the challenge to struggle for our rights. Come what will or may, let us never falter.†

* The poll tax, a tax which usually had to be paid in May when Negroes and poor whites had little or no cash, was a device used in the South to deny suffrage to blacks and poor whites.
† The March on Washington Movement held its last national conference on October 19, 1946, in Chicago, and officially passed away late in 1947.

SECTION V

Post–
World War II

1945–1963

ANTI-IMPERIALISTS MUST DEFEND AFRICA

By Paul Robeson

*Born in Princeton, New Jersey, April 9, 1898, Paul Robe-
son gained early fame as a scholar and athlete at Rutgers
University, where he was an "All-American" football player
and was elected to Phi Beta Kappa in his junior year. After
graduating from Columbia Law School with honors, he
went on to gain renown in the theater and in the concert
hall as a baritone. He spent considerable time in Europe,
but returned to the United States in 1939, interspersing
his concert performances with militant speeches for Negro
freedom.*

*As early as 1939 Robeson planned to set up an organi-
zation to assist the liberation struggles in Africa and raise
funds for the victims of imperialist persecution on that
continent. Together with Max Yergan, a Negro Y.M.C.A.
secretary, Robeson founded the Council of African Affairs
in New York City. They were joined by Alphaeus Hunton,
a professor of English at Howard University. A monthly
publication was issued devoted to developments in new
Africa, money was raised for starving people in South
Africa and striking miners in West Africa, African visitors
were welcomed, and public meetings were sponsored. One
such meeting was held at Madison Square Garden in New
York City on June 6, 1946, and was addressed by Paul
Robeson. Here is the text of Robeson's speech, a mimeo-
graphed copy of which is in the editor's possession.*

I HAVE SPOKEN for other causes on other occasions in
this great hall. And while they were all important causes about
which I was keenly concerned, I think I can say that never before have I faced such an audience as this with the sense of responsibility, of urgency, of intimacy with you that I now feel.

The Negro—and I mean American Negroes as well as West
Indians and Africans—has a direct and firsthand understanding, which most other people lack, of what imperialist exploitation and oppression is. With him it is no far-off theoretical
problem. In his daily life he experiences the same system of job
discrimination, segregation and denial of democratic rights

whereby the imperialist overlords keep hundreds of millions of people in colonial subjection throughout the world.

The one basic difference is that here in America the Negro has the law—at least partially, and in some sections of the country—on his side, and he has powerful allies in the ranks of white organized labor directly involved in his daily fight for justice. In Africa, in the West Indies, and in Asia, the colonial peoples wage a desperate struggle for recognition simply as human beings—as human beings to whom human rights are due. And these colonial peoples fight alone in each country— alone except for the help which reaches them from afar, from world-conscious labor in free countries and from other anti-fascist, anti-imperialist forces.

And that is why we are gathered here tonight. Because our own rights and liberties—even though limited—are far, far greater than those of our brothers in colonial bondage. Because we must exercise the greater strength which we have to help win freedom for them. And also because in that very process of helping others, we add to our own strength and bring nearer full freedom for ourselves.

Besides people like those of us who are here tonight, there is another category of Americans, quite few in number, but extremely powerful, who are interested in Africa. They are concerned, however, *not* with the *people* of the continent of Africa, but with the wealth that they can extract from it and from the labor of the people there. These American financiers and corporation heads have their own ideas about the future of Africa, and they *don't* include the idea of freedom. You can be sure of that. And another thing you can be sure of is that they're not losing any time in putting their ideas into action.

Our government, reports indicate, is getting uranium from the Belgian Congo for atomic bombs. American companies are prospecting for oil in Ethiopia and for minerals in Liberia. Mr. Firestone now has competitors in the latter country. These manifestations of a new and heightened interest in Africa on the part of American Big Business represent a challenge to the rest of us.

The race is on—in Africa as in every other part of the world —the race between the forces of progress and democracy on the one side and the forces of imperialism and reaction on the other. And Africa, with its immense undeveloped and unmeasured wealth of resources, is a major prize which the imperialists covet and which we, the anti-imperialists, must defend.

We on the anti-imperialist side are handicapped by lack of

money, lack of powerful organization, lack of influence in state and international affairs. But, although the enemy has all the advantage and has a head start in the race, it is yet possible for us to catch up and win. It is possible to win if the majority of the American people can be brought to see and understand in the fullest sense the fact that the struggle in which we are engaged is not a matter of mere humanitarian sentiment, but of life and death. The only alternative to world freedom is world annihilation—another bloody holocaust—which will dwarf the two world wars through which we have passed.

We have been hearing a lot of talk about a coming war. It has been defined by some of the bolder reactionaries in brutally clear terms as a war of the United States and Great Britain against the Soviet Union. This warmongering is the logical consequence of the get-tough-with-Russia policy preached and practiced by those who direct American and British foreign policy.

"Stop Russia!" the brass voices cry in chorus, and the men behind the voices hope that the people will be afraid and will turn against their wartime ally. Their frantic cries mask the program of imperialist aggression which these men themselves are seeking to impose upon the world.

The "Stop Russia" cry really means Stop the advance of the colonial peoples of Asia and Africa toward independence; stop the forces of the new democracy developing in Europe; stop the organized workers of America from trying to hold their ground against their profit-greedy employers; stop the Negro people from voting and joining trade-unions in the South. "Stop Russia" means Stop progress; maintain the status quo. It means Let the privileged few continue to rule and thrive at the expense of the masses.

A day or two ago Mr. Bevin, the British Foreign Minister, said, and I quote, "If we do not want to have total war, we must have total peace." For once I agree with him. But Mr. Bevin must be totally blind if he cannot see that the absence of peace in the world today is due precisely to the efforts of the British, American and other imperialist powers to retain their control over the peoples of Asia, the Middle East, Europe and Africa.

We must indeed win the peace—a total peace—but we can do it only by using methods exactly the opposite of those pursued at present by the British Foreign Office and our own State Department. To win total peace there must be total freedom.

At San Francisco, a year ago, it was the Soviet Foreign minister, Mr. Molotov, who said, "From the viewpoint of the in-

terests of international security, we must first of all see to it
that dependent countries are enabled as soon as possible to take
the path of national independence."*

But we are still waiting for the first European power in Africa
to declare that its African subjects may exercise the right of
self-determination and achieve self-government in the next ten
years, the next twenty years, or even the next hundred years.

The colonial rulers will tell you that the Africans will not be
ready for self-government in any foreseeable future. They lie.
They would delude you into believing that the African peoples
had no governments, no culture before the European came to
Africa. They would delude you into believing that Africans are
content to remain under European tutelage, and that this tutelage must continue indefinitely.

You have heard from other speakers tonight what sort of
tutelage the rulers of Africa provide. How can they dare pose
as so-called guardians of the Africans? How can they dare claim
the right to continue in that role? The Soviet Union has demonstrated how it is possible to wipe out colonialism and all that
that word connotes within a single generation. No wonder the
imperialists cry "Stop Russia!"

That cry must be drowned out by the voice of the American
people demanding Big Three unity for colonial freedom:

To arouse all sections of our population to the urgency of that
demand has been the purpose of this meeting. But we do not
in any sense regard our job as finished with the close of this
great rally. On the contrary, my friends, the Council on African
Affairs regards this job as having just begun. With your help,
with the cooperation of the organizations with which you are
associated and with the support of millions of like-minded peoples throughout our country and in other countries, we *shall
win the fight* against the forces of imperialism.

Tomorrow is *our* day, the day of the common people. By God's
grace and our united strength we *shall* win freedom and peace
for ourselves and for all the oppressed peoples of the earth.

* The reference is to the speech delivered at the founding of the United
Nations at San Francisco, May, 1945.

BEHOLD THE LAND

By W. E. B. Du Bois

In May, 1934, Dr. Du Bois resigned from the N.A.A.C.P.
Board and from editorship of its official organ, The Crisis.
He had become increasingly disillusioned with the slow,
gradual process of attacking discrimination through the
courts, and was more and more convinced that the Negro
should build his own economic and political power along
the path of socialism. Du Bois went back to Atlanta Uni-
versity as chairman of the Department of Sociology. In
1944, at the request of the organization, he returned to
the N.A.A.C.P. as Director of Special Research.

Du Bois delivered the speech below in Columbia, South
Carolina, October 20, 1946, at the closing session of the
Southern Youth Legislature, sponsored by the Southern
Negro Youth Congress, and attended by 861 black and
white delegates. In it, he calls on his audience to struggle
to remake the South. (The text is taken from Freedom-
ways, First Quarter, 1964, pp. 8–15.)

THE FUTURE of American Negroes is in the South. Here three hundred and twenty-seven years ago, they began to enter what is now the United States of America; here they have made their greatest contribution to American culture; and here they have suffered the damnation of slavery, the frustration of reconstruction and the lynching of emancipation. I trust, then, that an organization like yours is going to regard the South as the battleground of a great crusade. Here is the magnificent climate; here is the fruitful earth under the beauty of the Southern sun; and here, if anywhere on earth, is the need of the thinker, the worker and the dreamer. This is the firing line not simply for the emancipation of the American Negro, but for the emancipation of the African Negro and the Negroes of the West Indies; for the emancipation of the colored races; and for the emancipation of the white slaves of modern capitalistic monopoly.

Remember here, too, that you do not stand alone. It may seem like a failing fight when the newspapers ignore you; when every effort is made by white people in the South to count you out of citizenship and to act as though you did not exist as human beings, while all the time they are profiting by your labor, gleaning wealth from your sacrifices, and trying to build a nation and a civilization upon your degradation. You must remember that despite all this, you have allies, and allies even in the white South. First and greatest of these possible allies are the white working classes about you—the poor whites whom you have been taught to despise and who in turn have learned to fear and hate you. This must not deter you from efforts to make them understand, because in the past in your ignorance and suffering they have been led foolishly to look upon you as the cause of most of their distress. You must remember that this attitude is hereditary from slavery and that it has been deliberately cultivated ever since emancipation.

Slowly but surely the working people of the South, white and black, must come to remember that their emancipation depends upon their mutual cooperation; upon their acquaintanceship with each other; upon their friendship; upon their social intermingling. Unless this happens, each is going to be made the football to break the heads and hearts of the other.

White youth in the South is peculiarly frustrated. There is not a single great ideal which they can express or aspire to, that does not bring them into flat contradiction with the Negro problem. The more they try to escape it, the more they land into hypocrisy, lying and double-dealing; the more they become, what they least wish to become, the oppressors and despisers of human beings. Some of them, in larger and larger numbers, are bound to turn toward the truth and to recognize you as brothers and sisters, as fellow travelers toward the dawn.

There has always been in the South that intellectual elite who saw the Negro problem clearly. They have always lacked, and some still lack, the courage to stand up for what they know is right. Nevertheless they can be depended on in the long run to follow their own clear thinking and their own decent choice. Finally, even the politicians must eventually recognize the trend in the world, in this country, and in the South. James Byrnes, that favorite son of this commonwealth, and Secretary of State of the United States, is today occupying an indefensible and impossible position; and if he survives in the memory of men, he must begin to help establish in his own South Carolina something of that democracy which he has been recently so loudly preaching to Russia. He is the end of a long series of men whose eternal damnation is the fact that they looked *truth* in the face and did not see it; John C. Calhoun, Wade Hampton, Ben Tillman* are men whose names must ever be besmirched by the fact that they fought against freedom and democracy in a land which was founded upon democracy and freedom. Eventually this class of men must yield to the writing in the stars. That great hypocrite, Jan Smuts,† who today is talking of humanity and standing beside Byrnes for a United Nations, is at the same time oppressing the black people of Africa to an extent which makes their two countries, South Africa and the American South, the most reactionary peoples on earth. Peoples whose exploitation of the poor and helpless reaches the last degree of shame. They must in the long run yield to the forward march of civilization or die.

If, now, you young people, instead of running away from the battle here in Carolina, Georgia, Alabama, Louisiana and Mississippi, instead of seeking freedom and opportunity in Chicago and New York—which do spell opportunity—nevertheless grit your teeth and make up your minds to fight it out right here if it takes every day of your lives and the lives of your children's children; if you do this, you must in meetings like this ask yourselves what does the fight mean? How can it be carried on? What are the best tools, arms and methods? And where does it lead?

I should be the last to insist that the uplift of mankind never calls for force and death. There are times, as both you and I know, when

> Tho' love repine and reason chafe,
> There came a voice without reply,
> "Tis man's perdition to be safe
> When for truth he ought to die."

At the same time and even more clearly in a day like this, after the millions of mass murders that have been done in the world since 1914, we ought to be the last to believe that force is ever the final word. We cannot escape the clear fact that what is going to win in this world is reason if this ever becomes a

---

* Wade Hampton (1818–1902), Confederate general and South Carolina political leader, led the forces which overthrew Congressional Reconstruction in South Carolina and instituted the era of white supremacy. Benjamin R. Tillman (1847–1918), South Carolina Governor and U. S. Senator, was a leading foe of Negro rights and a champion of white supremacy.

† Jan Smuts was the leader of the racist forces in South Africa and head of its government. He was the originator of the policy which developed into apartheid.

reasonable world. The careful reasoning of the human mind backed by the facts of science is the one salvation of man. The world, if it resumes its march toward civilization, cannot ignore reason. This has been the tragedy of the South in the past; it is still its awful and unforgivable sin that it has set its face against reason and against the fact. It tried to build slavery upon freedom; it tried to build tyranny upon democracy; it tried to build mob violence on law and law on lynching and in all that despicable endeavor, the state of South Carolina has led the South for a century. It began not the Civil War, not the War between the States, but the War to Preserve Slavery; it began mob violence and lynching, and today it stands in the front rank of those defying the Supreme Court on disfranchisement.

Nevertheless, reason can and will prevail; but of course it can only prevail with publicity—pitiless, blatant publicity. You have got to make the people of the United States and of the world know what is going on in the South. You have got to use every field of publicity to force the truth into their ears, and before their eyes. You have got to make it impossible for any human being to live in the South and not realize the barbarities that prevail here. You may be condemned for flamboyant methods; for calling a congress like this; for waving your grievances under the noses and in the faces of men. That makes no difference; it is your duty to do it. It is your duty to do more of this sort of thing than you have done in the past. As a result of this you are going to be called upon for sacrifice. It is no easy thing for a young black man or a young black woman to live in the South today and to plan to continue to live here; to marry and raise children; to establish a home. They are in the midst of legal caste and customary insults; they are in continuous danger of mob violence; they are mistreated by the officers of the law and they have no hearing before the courts and the churches and public opinion commensurate with the attention which they ought to receive. But that sacrifice is only the beginning of battle; you must rebuild this South.

There are enormous opportunities here for a new nation, a new economy, a new culture in a South really new and not a mere renewal of an old South of slavery, monopoly and race hate. There is a chance for a new cooperative agriculture on renewed land owned by the state with capital furnished by the state, mechanized and coordinated with city life. There is chance for strong, virile trade-unions without race discrimination, with high wage, closed shop and decent conditions of work, to beat back and hold in check the swarm of landlords, monopolists and profiteers who are today sucking the blood out of this land. There is chance for cooperative industry, built on the cheap power of T.V.A. and its future extensions. There is opportunity to organize and mechanize domestic service with decent hours, and high wage and dignified training.

There is a vast field for consumers cooperation, building business on public service and not on private profit as the mainspring of industry. There is chance for a broad, sunny, healthy home life, shorn of the fear of mobs and liquor, and rescued from lying, stealing politicians, who build their deviltry on race prejudice.

Here in this South is the gateway to the colored millions of the West Indies, Central and South America. Here is the straight path to Africa, the Indies, China and the South Seas. Here is the path to the greater, freer, truer world. It would be shame and cowardice to surrender this glorious land and its opportunities for civilization and humanity to the thugs and lynchers, the mobs and profiteers, the monopolists and gamblers who today choke its soul and steal its resources. The oil and sulphur; the coal and iron; the cotton and corn; the lumber and cattle belong to you the workers, black and white, and not to the thieves who hold them and use them to enslave you. They can be rescued and restored to the people if you have the guts to strive for the real right to vote, the right to real education, the right to happiness and health, and the total abolition of the father of these scourges of mankind, *poverty*.

"Behold the beautiful land which the Lord thy God hath given thee." Behold the land, the rich and resourceful land, from which for a hundred years its best elements have been running away, its youth and hope, black and white, scurrying North because they are afraid of each other, and dare not face a future of equal, independent, upstanding human beings, in a real and not a sham democracy.

To rescue this land, in this way, calls for the *Great Sacrifice;* This is the thing that you are called upon to do because it is the right thing to do. Because you are embarked upon a great and holy crusade, the emancipation of mankind, black and white; the upbuilding of democracy; the breaking-down, particularly here in the South, of forces of evil represented by race prejudice in South Carolina, by lynching in Georgia, by disfranchisement in Mississippi, by ignorance in Louisiana, and by all these and monopoly of wealth in the whole South.

There could be no more splendid vocation beckoning to the youth of the twentieth century, after the flat failures of white civilization, after the flamboyant establishment of an industrial system which creates poverty and the children of poverty which are ignorance and disease and crime; after the crazy boasting of a white culture that finally ended in wars which ruined civilization in the whole world; in the midst of allied peoples who have yelled about democracy and never practiced it either in the British Empire or in the American Commonwealth or in South Carolina.

Here is the chance for young women and young men of devotion to lift again the banner of humanity and to walk toward a civilization which will be free and intelligent, which will be healthy and unafraid, and build in the world a culture led by black folk and joined by peoples of all colors and all races— without poverty, ignorance and disease!

Once, a great German poet cried: *"Selig der den Er in Sieges Glanze findet.* Happy man whom Death shall find in Victory's splendor."

But I know a happier one: he who fights in despair, and in defeat still fights. Singing with Arna Bontemps* the quiet, determined philosophy of undefeatable men:

I thought I saw an angel flying low,
I thought I saw the flicker of a wing
Above the mulberry trees; but not again,
Bethesda sleeps. This ancient pool that healed
A Host of bearded Jews does not awake.
This pool that once the angels troubled does not move.
No angel stirs it now, no Saviour comes
With healing in His hands to raise the sick
And bid the lame man leap upon the ground.

The golden days are gone. Why do we wait
So long upon the marble steps, blood
Falling from our open wounds? And why
Do our black faces search the empty sky?
Is there something we have forgotten? Some precious thing
We have lost, wandering in strange lands?

There was a day, I remember now,
I beat my breast and cried, "Wash me, God,"
Wash me with a wave of wind upon
The barley; O quiet one, draw near, draw near!
Walk upon the hills with lovely feet
And in the waterfall stand and speak!

* Arna Bontemps is a renowned black poet and novelist.

UNCLE TOM IS DEAD!

By William R. Hood

On October 27, 1951, at Cincinnati, Ohio, the founding convention of the National Negro Labor Council was held. The delegates, who came from shops and plants all across America, had helped to build the industrial unions of the C.I.O. But they were meeting to launch a struggle for jobs for blacks and for equality of black trade-unionists in the labor movement. They met under the shadow of the attack launched against the N.N.L.C. by Attorney General Herbert Brownell, the House Un-American Activities Committee, some white trade-union leaders, and conservative black spokesmen. The keynote address at the convention was delivered by William R. Hood, Secretary of Local 600, United Auto Workers, and first president of the N.N.L.C. Following the address, the founding convention adopted a program of fighting for 100,000 jobs, with special emphasis on the right of Negro women to work anywhere and everywhere, for fair-employment-practice laws, and for full freedom.

William R. Hood was born September 29, 1910, in Whitesville, Georgia. He came to Detroit in 1942 after attending Tuskegee Institute, started work at the Chevrolet Gear and Axle Plant, and later continued at the Ford River Rouge Plant in Dearborn, Michigan. He was elected Recording Secretary of Local 600 of the United Auto Workers in 1947. Here is Hood's address at the Founding Convention of the National Negro Labor Council, excerpted from the pamphlet, For These Things We Fight, *Detroit, 1951.*

BROTHERS AND SISTERS: This is a historic day. On this day we, the delegated representatives of thousands of workers, black and white, dedicate ourselves to the search for a new North Star, the same star that Sojourner Truth, Nat Turner and John Brown saw rise over the city of Cincinnati over a century ago.

We come conscious of the new stage in the Negro people's surge toward freedom. We come to announce to all America and to the world, that Uncle Tom is dead. "Old Massa" lies in the cold, cold grave. Something new is cooking on the Freedom Train.

We come here today because we are conscious at this hour of a confronting world crisis. We are here because many of our liberties are disappearing in the face of a powerful war economy and grave economic problems face working men and women everywhere. No meeting held anywhere in America at this mid-century point in world history can be more important nor hold more promise for the bright future toward which humanity strives than this convention of our National Negro Labor Council. For here we have gathered the basic forces of human progress; the proud black sons and daughters of labor and our democratic white brothers and sisters whose increasing concern for democracy, equality and peace is America's bright hope for tomorrow.

We, the Negro working sons and daughters, have come here to Cincinnati to keep faith with our forefathers and mothers who landed right here from the banks of the Ohio River in their dash for freedom from chattel slavery through the Underground Railroad. We come here to pledge ourselves that the fight for economic, political and social freedom which they began shall not have been in vain.

Yes, we are here as proud black American working men and women; proud of the right to live, not humiliated any. We are proud, too, because of our democratic white brothers and sisters who have come here; proud because these stanch allies are not afraid to stand shoulder to shoulder with us to fight for that which is right.

The Negro Labor Council is our symbol, the medium of expression of our aims and aspirations. It is the expression of our desire and determination to bring to bear our full weight to help win first-class citizenship for every black man, woman and child in America. We say that these are legitimate aims. We say that these aspirations burn fiercely in the breast of every Negro in America. And we further say that millions of white workers echo our demands for freedom. These white workers recognize in their struggle for Negro rights, the prerequisites of their own aspirations for a full life and a guarantee that the rising tide of fascism will not engulf America.

And we say that those whites who call the National Negro Labor Council "subversive" have an ulterior motive. We know them for what they are—the common oppressors of both people, Negro and white. We charge that their false cry of "subversive" is calculated to maintain and extend that condition of common oppression. We say to those whites: "You have never seen your mothers, sisters and daughters turned away from thousands of factory gates, from the air lines, the offices, stores and other places of desirable employment, insulted and driven into the streets many times when they tried to eat in public places— simply because of their color. You have never been terrorized by the mob, shot in cold blood by the police; you have never had your home burned when you moved out of the ghetto into another neighborhood—simply because you were black. You are not denied the franchise; you are not denied credit in banks, denied insurance, jobs and upgrading—because of the pigmentation of your skin. You are not denied union membership and representation; you do not die ten years before most of the people because of these many denials of basic rights.

"Therefore, you who call this National Negro Labor Council 'subversive' cannot understand the burning anger of the Negro people, our desire to share the good things our labor has produced for America. You do not understand this. So you sit like Walter Winchell, one of our attackers, in the Stork Club in New York and see that great Negro woman artist, Josephine Baker, humiliated and not raise a finger.

"The Negro Labor Council is dedicated to the proposition that these evils shall end and end soon. The world must understand that we intend to build a stronger bond of unity between black and white workers everywhere to strengthen American democracy for all. If this be subversion—make the most of it!"

A most significant event took place in Chicago in June of 1950. Over nine hundred delegates, Negro and white, gathered there to chart a course in the fight for Negro rights. They came from the mines, mills, farms and factories of America. Many of them were leaders in the organized-labor movement: seasoned, militant fighters. They voiced the complaints of Negro America.

The delegates were told that as you looked throughout the land you could see Negro men and women standing in long lines before the gates of the industrial plants for jobs, only to be told that no help was wanted—while at the same time white workers were hired. Negro women are denied the right to work in the basic sections of American industry, on the airlines, in the stores and other places. Those who were hired into industry during World War II have for the most part been systematically driven out—often in violation of union contracts. Vast unemployment since the war has struck the Negro community a severe blow.

In thousands of factories throughout the land Negroes were

denied upgrading and better job opportunities. Too often the
unions did not defend or fight for the right of the Negro workers to be upgraded.

We heard there in Chicago that Negro workers were denied
any opportunity to participate in the great number of appren-
ticeship-training programs either in industry or in government,
in such fields as the building trades, machine tools, printing
and engraving, and other skilled fields.

We found out there that thousands of lily-white shops exist
throughout the land, where no Negro has ever worked.

We discovered that federal, state and city governments maintain a severe policy of Jim Crow discrimination, beginning with
the White House and moving on down to the lowest level of
municipal government.

Our black brothers and sisters from the South told of unemployment, low wages, wage differentials, Jim Crow unions, peonage, sharecrop robbery and miserable destitution. They described the perpetuation of conditions in twentieth-century
Amercia that are cruelly reminiscent of slavery.

Black firemen and brakemen came to tell of the collusive
agreements between railroads and the railroad brotherhoods to
throw Negroes out of the railroad industry after a hundred
years or more, and of the denial of union membership in these
unions and no representation. A number of A.F. of L. unions
were singled out for their policy of exclusion and job "monkey
business" as regards black workers. We also learned that the
C.I.O. had joined the war crowd of colonial oppression and
exploitation and was running fast from its early position of the
thirties, when with John L. Lewis at its head it really fought
for Negro rights.

Many of the delegates were stunned to hear of the thousands
of denials of civil rights in public places in every state in the
union. We were saddened and angered when we heard about
the frameups of the Martinsville Seven, Willie McGhee, the
Trenton Six, and countless other Negroes because they were
black and for no other reason. We were horrified to hear of the
many police killings of Negroes from New York City to Birmingham, Alabama.

Negro families were still hemmed into the ghettos, charged
higher rents, chained by restrictive covenants, mob terror and
finally even bombed if they were not lucky or able to move out
in time. The rats are given ample opportunity to wreak their
damage upon human beings, their destruction through disease
and death.

Our delegates made it clear in that 1950 convention that

inferior Jim Crow schools are still the policy in the South and Jim Crow quotas in the colleges of the North. The desire of black children for education and a full, useful life is yet a dream unrealized.

Is there any wonder then that this great Chicago gathering of the black working sons and daughters of our land said that this oppression can no longer exist in our America? Or is it any wonder that we received the full support of these stalwart democratic white workers present there who truly love democracy and recognize our common, basic unity of interests? So it was that they, in all righteous indignation, gave unto us, the continuators' organization, a mandate. They said to us: "Go out and build strong the Negro Labor Councils throughout the land. Build them into instruments of democracy, equality and unity."

They gave unto us the main task of fighting on that front which we knew best—the economic front for jobs, upgrading, for an end to the lily-white shops, for apprenticeship training, government jobs, local and state fair-employment-practices legislation, the nondiscrimination clause in union contracts and finally, with emphasis, the right of Negro women to work anywhere and everywhere.

They gave unto us the mandate to build an organization composed in the main of Negro workers, united and determined to wage an uncompromising struggle against Jim Crow—to build an organization which can unite with white workers who are willing to accept and support our program—to exclude no freedom fighter!

That mandate commissioned us to cooperate with those existing organizations, community and trade-union, which have undertaken genuine campaigns for the full citizenship of the Negro people.

We were directed to build a new type of organization—not an organization to compete with those existing organizations of the Negro people already at work on many civil rights struggles. The delegates who met at Chicago demanded an organization of Negro workers from a wide variety of industries, organized and unorganized, from the great industrial centers of the North, the urban communities of the South and the farm workers from the great rural areas. Such an organization will encourage Negroes to join unions and urge unions to organize Negroes. It will call upon the entire Negro people to support labor's fight. . . .

During the course of our Council building there has been opposition from some of the trade-union leaders, particularly to this convention. They have accused us of attempting dual unionism, and some of them have gone so far as to advise Negro workers not to participate in this convention. To them we say: "Look at the Bill of Particulars, then tell us if it is not true that we are second-class citizens in this land. Negro are still barred from many trade-unions in this country, denied apprenticeship training, upgrading, and refused jobs in many, many places."

We are not represented in the policy-making bodies of most international unions. We say when the mobs came to Emerald Street in Chicago and to Cicero, Illinois, we did not see the great trade-unions move. Yet, the basic right to live in Cicero was denied, not only to the family of Harvey Clark, but to the Negro people as a whole. We say that we will no longer permit the denial of these basic rights in our country, and are pooling our strength for that purpose. We intend to do it on the basis of cooperation and unity, wherever possible, with the organized labor movement.

We wish to say further that the day has ended when white trade-union leaders or white leaders in any organization may presume to tell Negroes on what basis they shall come together to fight for their rights. Three hundred years has been enough of that. We ask for your cooperation—but we do not ask your permission!

We believe it to be the solemn duty of trade-unions everywhere, as a matter of vital self-interest, to support the Negro workers in their efforts to unite and to play a more powerful role in the fight of the Negro people for first-class citizenship based upon economic, political and social equality. We believe, further, that it is the trade-unions' duty and right to encourage the white workers to join with and support their Negro brothers and sisters in the achievement of these objectives. . . .

Brothers and sisters! Eloquence is a mighty weapon in the struggle for our just demands. But what is more eloquent than the struggle itself? The big white bosses, the men in Washington, will move far more rapidly when they see millions of us in struggle than when they hear speeches alone.

The Negro Labor Councils are, above all, organizations of struggle. We stand for the unity of all Negro workers, irrespective of union affiliation, organized and unorganized; for the unity of Negro and white workers together; for the unity of Negro workers with the whole Negro people in the common fight for Negro liberation; and for the alliance of the whole Negro people with the organized labor movement—the keystone combination for any kind of democratic progress in our country. . . .

POST-WORLD WAR II: 1945-1963

We face a number of grave tasks. We are called upon to chart a course that will win thousands of new job opportunities for Negro men and women, that will convince the organized-labor movement to complete the organization of the South on the basis of equality and nonsegregation, that will help bring the franchise to all the peoples in the South.

We are on the high road to a more democratic America. We are on the way toward breaking the grip of the Dixiecrats and the Northern reactionaries on our national life. I know that as you hammer out a program in these two days you will speed up the Freedom Train; you will give greater spirit and meaning to the Negro Labor Councils; you will adopt the battle cry of the great Frederick Douglass—"Without struggle there is no progress."

We move on, united—and neither man nor beast will turn us back. We will achieve, in our time, for ourselves and for our children, a world of no Jim Crow, of no more "white men's jobs" and "colored only" schools, a world of freedom, full equality, security and peace. Our task is clearly set forth. Brother and sisters, we move on to struggle and to victory!

THE NEGRO ARTIST LOOKS AHEAD

By Paul Robeson

Below, slightly abridged, is the text of Paul Robeson's address to the opening session of the Conference for Equal Rights for Negroes in the Arts, Sciences and Professions, held in New York City, December, 1951, under the auspices of the New York Council of the Arts, Sciences and Professions. The text is taken from Masses and Mainstream, *January, 1952, pp. 7–14.*

WE ARE here today to work out ways and means of finding jobs for colored actors and colored musicians, to see that the pictures and statues made by colored painters and sculptors are sold, to see that the creations of Negro writers are made available to the vast American public. We are here to see that colored scientists and professionals are placed in leading schools and universities, to open up opportunities for Negro technicians, to see that the way is open for colored lawyers to advance to judgeships—yes, to the Supreme Court of these United States, if you please.

It is not just a question of jobs, of positions, of commercial sales. No—the questions at hand cannot be resolved without the resolution of deeper problems involved here. We are dealing with the position in this society of a great people—of fifteen million closely bound human beings, of whom ten millions in the cotton and agricultural belt of the South form a kind of nation based upon common oppression, upon a magnificent common heritage, upon unified aspiration for full freedom and full equality in the larger democratic society.

The Negro people today are saying all up and down this nation (when you get on the streets, into the churches, into the bars to talk to them): "We will not suffer the genocide that might be visited upon us. We are prepared to fight to the death for our rights."

Yes, we are dealing with a great people. Their mere survival testifies to that. One hundred millions sacrificed and wasted in the slave ships, on the cotton plantations, in order that there might be built the basic wealth of this great land. It must have been a tremendously strong people, a people of tremendous stamina, of the finest character, merely to have survived. Not only have the Negro people survived in this America, they have given to these United States almost a new language, given it ways of speech, given it perhaps the only indigenous music.

One great creation, modern popular music—whether it be in theater, film, radio, records; wherever it may be—is almost completely based upon the Negro idiom. There is no leading American singer, performer of popular songs, whether it be a Crosby, a Sinatra, a Shore, a Judy Garland, an Ella Logan, who has not listened (and learned) by the hour to Holliday, Waters, Florence Mills, to Bert Williams, to Fitzgerald, and to the greatest of all, Bessie Smith. Without these models, who would ever have heard of a Tucker, a Jolson, a Cantor?

Go into the field of the dance. Where could there have come an Astaire, an Eleanor Powell and a James Barton without a Bill Robinson, a Bert Williams, an Eddie Rector, a Florence Mills? How could Artie Shaw and Bennie Goodman have appeared but for a Teddy Wilson, Turner Latan, Johnny Dunn, Hall Johnson, Will Marion Cook? Whence stems even Gershwin? From the music of Negro America joined with the ancient Hebrew idiom. Go and listen to some of the great melodies. Here again is a great American composer, deeply rooted, whether he knew it or not, in an African tradition, a tradition very close to his own heritage.

I speak very particularly of this popular form. This is very important to the Negro artists, because billions, literally billions of dollars, have been earned and are being earned from their creation, and the Negro people have received almost nothing.

At another stage of the arts there is no question, as one goes about the world, of the contribution of the Negro folk songs, of the music that sprang from my forefathers in their struggle for freedom—not songs of contentment, but songs like "Go Down, Moses" that inspired Harriet Tubman, John Brown, and Sojourner Truth to the fight for emancipation.

I think of Larry Brown who went abroad, heard Moussorgsky, heard the great folk music of other lands and dedicated himself, as did Harry Burleigh before him, to showing that this was a great music, not just "plantation songs."

One perhaps forgets my own career, and that for five years I would sing nothing but the music of my people. Later, when it was established as a fine folk music, I began to learn of the folk music of other peoples. This has been one of the bonds that have drawn me so close to the peoples of the world, bonds through this likeness in music that made me understand the political growth of many peoples, the struggles of many peoples, and brought me back to you to fight here in this land, as I shall continue to do.

I remember in England in the old days (incidentally, I just heard from Kingsley Martin, of the *New Statesman and Nation,* who is concerned about my inability to travel and to function as an artist in this land, and who is beginning a campaign in England on this basis)*—I remember writing several articles for the *New Statesman and Nation,* going to the whole root of this matter. I think back now—the deep pride that I had and still have in the creations of my people and in seeing the links here with Africa, and with the other peoples of Asia, and taking issue with the view that Western music was the only great music in the world and that everything else was so backward.

I remember writing: "Mr. Beethoven, yes, he is a great composer, but he deals with themes. He has to develop them a bit, but he starts with a very simple theme. . . ." And I was interested in reading a book the other day on the thematic process

* Paul Robeson's passport was taken away by the U. S. State Department because he was a champion of black militancy and the cause of oppressed people the world over, and a fervent advocate of peace and friendship with the Socialist countries. In addition, concert halls and the airways were closed to him. Worldwide protests, much of it organized in England, finally forced the State Department to remove the ban on his right to travel.

which takes the whole Ninth Symphony and proves that in every movement it begins and stems from a kernel that really in the end is a few bars. In those days I didn't quite know it technically, but had a feeling, and I listened to all the music and I still am looking to find anywhere greater themes to start with than "Deep River" or "Go Down, Moses," or "I'm a Poor Wayfaring Stranger."

So we are dealing with a people who come from great roots. There is no need to quote the names of an Anderson or a Hayes and many more; or of the great scientists—of a Julian, of a Carver. No need today for the Negro people to prove any more that they have a right to full equality. They have proven it again and again.

The roots of this great outpouring we are talking about today in the cultural expression of my people, is a great culture from a vast continent. If these origins are somewhat blurred in this America of ours, they are clear in Brazil, where Villa-Lobos joins Bach with African rhythms and melodies; in Cuba and Haiti a whole culture, musical and poetic, is very deep in the Africa of its origins—an African culture quite comparable to the ancient culture of the Chinese; similar in religious concepts, in language, in poetry, in its sculpture, in its whole esthetic; a culture which has deeply influenced the great artists of our time—a Picasso, a Modigliani, a Brancusi, an Epstein, a de Falla, a Milhaud. So we are today discussing the problems of a proud people, rich in tradition, a people torn from its ancient homeland but who in three hundred years have built anew, have enriched this new continent with its physical power, with its intellect, with its deep, inexhaustible spirit and courage.

As I have said, in spite of all these contributions to our culture, the fruits have been taken from us. Think of Handy, one of the creators of the blues; think of Count Basie, playing to half-filled houses at the Apollo; colored arrangers receiving a pittance while white bands reap harvests. What heartbreak for every Negro composer! Publishing houses taking his songs for nothing and making fortunes. Theaters in the heart of the Negro communities dictating to Negro performers what they shall act . . . arrogantly telling Negro audiences what they shall see. . . .

Let us touch for a moment on radio and television. We all know the difficulties—no major hours with Negro talent, an occasional guest appearance eagerly awaited by the Negro audience. Why this discrimination? Well, these mass media are based on advertising, commercialism at its worst, and the final answer is very simple. It goes to the root of all that has been said. The final answer is: "The South won't take it."

Now, I had a program myself in the forties, all set up by one of the biggest advertising agencies, a very fine program, a dignified program in which I would have been doing Othello and many other things. One morning they said, "We made some inquiries and the South just won't have it. You can come on once in a while and sing with Mr. Voorhees, and so forth, but no possibility of a Negro artist having his own program." Not *that* dignity. And so we have allowed the South with its patterns to determine for all America how, when and where the Negro will be denied an opportunity.

I think that public opinion could be aroused on this issue. This is a matter of national protest, of national pressure. These media happen to be under the control of Federal Communications. We are dealing here with matters as serious as the passage of an Anti-Lynch Bill, Anti-Poll Tax and Free Voting Legislation, of F.E.P.C., of the whole issue of federal and states' rights. We can demand a change in the public interest in the pursuance of democratic procedures. Added to this, of course, can be pressure on the advertisers who wax fat today from the purchases of Negro customers. These latter, plus their allies, could have very decisive influence.

The films today are of vast significance and influence. Here, too, the South determines the attempts to camouflage, to pass off so-called progressive films, to find new approaches to the treatment of the Negro. They have been very thoroughly analyzed and exposed for what they are by V. J. Jerome in his exhaustive pamphlet on "The Negro in Hollywood Films."* Here, too, the mounting of the right kind of campaign could shake Hollywood to its foundations, and help would be forthcoming from all over the world. Their markets everywhere in the world could be seriously affected, if the lead came from here.

The struggle on this front could have been waged with some real measure of success at any time, but today conditions insure the careful heeding of the collective wrath of the Negro people and their allies. For today, in the struggle extending all over the world, all pronouncements of our wonderful democracy ring hollow and clearly false as soon as one points the finger at the oppression of fifteen million second- and third-class citizens of this land.

---

* Victor J. Jerome's *The Negro in Hollywood Films* was published by *Masses & Mainstream* in 1950.

There is no way to cover that up. One day, Willie McGee; the next, Martinsville;* the next, Cicero; the next, Groveland, Florida. Behind these horrors is the mounting anger of a long-suffering people, of a people that has its Denmark Veseys, its Frederick Douglasses, its Sojourner Truths, its Harriet Tubmans, its Du Boises, its Benjamin Davises—a people that fought for its freedom in the great Civil War and buried the hated Confederate flags in the dust.

Behind these people and their allies here in the United States are the tens and tens of millions of advanced workers through the world, West and East, bulwarked by the overwhelming millions of a fast-emerging colonial world hastening to final and complete control of their destinies, inspired by the events of a November seventh, thirty-four years ago,† by the victories of many new people's democracies, by the world-shattering creation of the new People's Republic of China. This world in change makes possible here new levels of action, insures victories hitherto unsuspected. The millions of India watch and Mr. Bowles‡ will have his hands and his mouth full to convince these people that the civilization extolled by Byrnes of South Carolina, Smith of Georgia, Connally of Texas, is just the thing to bring new vistas of freedom and individual liberty to that ancient continent. I often get letters from India. They seem to be somewhat doubtful.

The government can be pressured in this time and it certainly can be pressured on this issue. Most important for us here is the recognition of the Negro's rights to all kinds of jobs in the arts, not only the rights of the artists, but technical jobs for engineers, all sorts of opportunities in production, in scenic design, at all levels. I am very much interested in that; I've got a son, Paul, who studied engineering at Cornell, majored in Communications. I'd like to see him get a good job in television.

And so in the case of Actors Equity—we who are members of Equity must fight not only for the rights of Negro actors, we must see that the stagehands are there. We must fight within the A. F. of L., Equity's parent organization, for the right of Negroes to work in *every* field. And so, in the American Guild of Musical Artists and in the American Federation of Radio Artists, they are shouting an awful lot these days about how democratic and American they are. Let them show it!

* The "Martinsville Seven" were seven Negroes of Martinsville, Virginia, who were executed for the alleged rape of a white woman in 1947.
† The reference is to the Bolshevik Revolution in Russia, November 7, 1917.
‡ Chester Bowles was the U. S. Ambassador to India.

The final problem concerns new ways, new opportunities based upon a deep sense of responsibility in approaching the problem of the Negro people in its totality. There are despoilers abroad in our land, akin to these who attempted to throttle our Republic at its birth. Despoilers who would have kept my beloved people in unending serfdom, a powerful few who blessed Hitler as he destroyed a large segment of a great people. Today they would recreate the image of Hitler, stifle millions of the hitherto oppressed as they struggle forth for their emancipation, destroy the people's republics, where life has been created anew, where the forces of nature have been turned to man's prosperity and good.

All these millions of the world stand aghast at the sight and the very name of *that* America. But they love *us;* they look to *us* to help create a world where we can all live in peace and friendship, where we can exchange the excellences of our various arts and crafts, the manifold wonders of our mutual scientific creations, a world where we can rejoice at the unleashed powers of our innermost selves, of the potential of great masses of people. To them *we* are the real America. Let us remember that.

And let us learn how to bring to the great masses of the American people *our* culture and *our* art. For in the end, what are we talking about when we talk about American culture today? We are talking about a culture that is restricted to the very, very few. How many workers ever get to the theater? I was in concerts for twenty years, subscription concerts, the two thousands seats gone before any Negro in the community, any worker, could even hear about a seat. Even then, the price was twelve dollars for six concerts. How could working people ever hear these concerts? Only by my going into the trade-unions and singing on the streets and on the picket lines and in the struggles for the freedom of our people—only in this way could the workers of this land hear me.

We are talking about a culture which as yet has no relationship to the great masses of the American people. I remember an experience in England. I sang not only in Albert Hall, the concert halls, but also in the picture theaters, and one night I came out and a young woman was standing there with her mother, an aged lady. "My grandmother wants to thank you very much. She always wanted to hear you in person. She heard you tonight and she's going home. She just had sixpence above her bus fare." So she was able to hear me. Later, that was so in the Unity Theater in London—now in a theater which has stretched all over England. Here in America, in 1948 in the Deep South, I remember standing singing to white workers in Memphis,

workers who had come out on strike that Negro workers might
get equal wages.

In the theater I felt this years ago and it would interest you to
know that the opening night of *Othello* in New York, in Chicago,
in San Francisco (I never told this to the Guild), I told Langner
he could have just one third of the house for the elite. I played
the opening night of *Othello* to the workers from Fur, from
Maritime, from Local 65.

Just the other night I sang at the Rockland Palace in the
Bronx, to this people's audience. We speak to them every night.
To thousands. Somewhere, with the impetus coming from the
arts, sciences and professions, there are literally millions of
people in America who would come to hear us, the Negro
artists. This can be very important. Marian Anderson, Roland
Hayes, all of us started in the Baptist churches. I'm going right
back there very soon. If you want to talk about audiences, I
defy any opera singer to take those ball parks like Sister Tharpe
or Mahalia Jackson. It is so in the Hungarian communities (I
was singing to the Hungarian-Americans yesterday), the
Russian-Americans, the Czech-Americans . . . all of them have
their audiences stretching throughout this land.

The progressive core of these audiences could provide a
tremendous base for the future, a tremendous base for our
common activity and a necessary base in the struggle for peace.
These people must be won. We can win them through our
cultural contributions. We could involve millions of people in
the struggle for peace and for a decent world.

But, the final point. This cannot be done unless we as artists
have the deepest respect for these people. When we say that we
are people's artists, we must mean that. I mean it very deeply.
Because, you know, the people created our art in the first place.

Haydn with his folk songs—the people made it up in the
first place. The language of Shakespeare—this was the creation of the English-speaking people; the language of Pushkin,
the creation of the Russian people, of the Russian peasants. That
is where it came from—a little dressed up with some big words
now and then which can be broken down into very simple
images.

So, in the end, the culture with which we deal comes from the
people. We have an obligation to take it back to the people, to
make them understand that in fighting for their cultural
heritage they fight for peace. They fight for their own rights, for
the rights of the Negro people, for the rights of all in this great
land. All of this is dependent so much upon our understanding

the power of this people, the power of the Negro people, the power of the masses of America, of a world where we can all walk in complete dignity.

THE NEGRO LABOR COMMITTEE

By Frank R. Crosswaith

In 1935 the Negro Labor Committee was organized by Frank R. Crosswaith, with the objective of organizing black workers into trade-unions and assisting the newly formed Committee for Industrial Organization to recruit Negro membership in the mass-production industries.

Crosswaith was born in St. Croix, Virgin Islands, in 1892. After coming to this country and serving in the United States Navy, he obtained a scholarship to the Rand School of Social Science, a Socialist educational center, where he taught for many years. An excellent orator, he was active in the Socialist party and was known as "the Negro Debs." A firm believer in trade-unionism and the integration of black workers into the labor movement, Crosswaith established the Trade Union Committee for Organizing Negro Workers in 1925, which ten years later was succeeded by the Negro Labor Committee. Crosswaith served as chairman of the Committee for thirty years.

In a speech delivered to delegates of a Committee conference, March 6, 1952, Crosswaith discussed the history and aims of the organization. It is clear that little remained of Crosswaith's earlier belief in Socialism. Part of the speech is presented here; it is excerpted from a copy of the text furnished by the Negro Labor Committee and published with the Committee's permission.

IN 1935, at a delegated conference similar to this, the Negro Labor Committee was born. At that time the organized labor movement of the United States faced one of the most disturbing problems of its life. Our country was then in the midst of that never-to-be-forgotten unemployment period with millions of workers moving through the streets of their cities

poorly clad and poorly shod, while garment workers and shoe-
makers were looking for work; millions of workers were sleeping along roadways and on river banks, while millions of carpenters, bricklayers, steelworkers and other construction workers were unable to find employment. Hunger, poverty, want and
misery were the daily diet of the average worker. I repeat, this
was a most disturbing condition facing the working class and
our democratic form of government.

It was then that three things of historic importance occurred.
The first was the passage of the immortal Wagner-LaGuardia
labor law which gave to labor the right to organize*—a right
which the Manufacturers' Association and the Chamber of
Commerce had always enjoyed. The second occurrence of
historic importance was the organization of the unemployed,
which compelled both federal and local governments to become
a little more socially enlightened and thus make relief provisions for the unemployed millions of the nation. The third
event to occur at that time was the birth of the Negro Labor
Committee. Of the three events thus listed, I consider the birth
of the Negro Labor Committee to be most significant and fundamental—as its history, when it is written some day by some
unbiased historian, will prove.

With labor now enjoying the right to organize, a campaign
was started to organize workers, reduce the work day and thus
open the door of employment to the unemployed. As this
campaign got under way, the responsible leaders of labor soon
discovered that in addition to facing the natural hostility of
employers they also had to face the antagonism of the millions
of Negro workers. This antagonism was the product of experience. Negroes in the world of toil always had to face
ignorance, prejudice and discrimination. The Negro was always the last to be hired and the first to be fired. A large number
of labor organizations had early established in their constitutions and bylaws provisions which relegated the Negro to the
status of an auxiliary worker or denied him membership in
their union. This experience drove the masses of Negro workers into the oasis of domestic service and agricultural labor; it
made the average Negro workers unsympathetic to the claims

---

* On February 21, 1935 Senator Robert F. Wagner introduced the "national labor relations bill" which outlawed unfair labor practices by employers, affirmed the right of workers to join unions of their own
choosing, and extended the provisions of the Norris-LaGuardia Act outlawing the yellow-dog contract, under which workers agreed as a condition of employment not to join a union.

and appeals of organized labor, and friendly to the employer's interests, for it was the employer—in his efforts to meet and overcome the increasingly loud demands of labor for "more pay and less work"—it was the employer who became the friend of the Negro by giving him a job outside a kitchen, a dining room, or operating an elevator. It was the employer who gave him a chance to move out upon the broad industrial plains of the nation and away from those low menial confines of service which the Negro inherited from 245 years of chattel slavery. In addition to the apathy of the Negro worker, we had to face two other obstacles. One was the opposition of the extreme leftists, whose main objective, as we all know, is to use the Negro to advance the ungodly, unmoral and barbaric objectives of Communism.

This then, in brief, was the world in which the Negro Labor Committee was born in 1935. Fortunately for the Negro and fortunately for labor, those of us who were privileged to shape and direct the course of the Committee understood and appreciated our responsibility, thus enabling the Committee to render the Negro and labor a service the value of which only a united and economically emancipated working class can adequately appraise. This duty we modestly place in the lap of the working class of the future.

For the present it is sufficient to state, that as a result of the work and influence of the Negro Labor Committee millions of Negro workers are today an integral part of the organized labor movement of the United States and the world. In many instances, many Negroes today occupy important and responsible posts in their unions, having been chosen for such posts not because of their color, but rather because of their demonstrated ability and devotion to the lofty ideals of labor and labor's inseparable destiny with the fate of democracy, freedom and justice.

Today, we face a problem equal in importance to those faced by organized labor in 1935, when the Negro Labor Committee was born. The Negro is now a part of the organized labor movement, but many of the problems which have haunted him down through the ages, during and after chattel slavery are still to be met and solved. He can only meet and solve such problems as lynching, segregation, race prejudice, inadequate educational facilities and opportunities, et cetera, if and when organized labor recognizes its common interest with the Negro and through education and organization joins with him to meet and solve them.

Out of this conference can come the machinery and the move-

ment that spell victory for all of us as workers in our desire
to justify our birth, justify our common divine origin and common destiny. . . .

STOP THE FOES OF NEGRO FREEDOM

By Rev. Edward D. McGowan

*Senator Joseph McCarthy of Wisconsin headed the post-
World War II witch-hunt against Communists and all
Americans of progressive thought, black and white, and
gave the word McCarthyism to the language as an expression for wild charges of disloyalty. McCarthyism began
in 1950 and reached its climax in 1953 and 1954. In
December, 1954, McCarthy was censured by the Senate
for "conduct unbecoming a member."*

*In 1953, as the intensity of the McCarthy era mounted
and more and more black Americans came under attacks
as "subversives" because they dared to speak up for freedom, the Committee to Defend Negro Leadership was
established. In a stirring address before the National
Fraternal Council of Churches, U.S.A., Inc., delivered in
Detroit, April 30, 1953, the Reverend Edward D. McGowan
made an appeal in behalf of the Committee, of which he
was chairman. Unlike leaders of long-established Negro
organizations like the N.A.A.C.P. and the National Urban
League, who either condemned radical black militants of
the period or remained silent while they were under attack
by the press and the House Un-American Activities Committee, McGowan defended them for their militancy and
courage. He linked persecution of black leadership in the
United States with that against leaders of the African peoples in their struggles for freedom and independence.*

*McGowan was for many years minister of the Ep-
worth Methodist Church, Bronx, New York, and then assumed the pastorate of the Asbury Methodist Church,
Frederick, Maryland. He was long a champion of the
needs of Negro youth, and in the late 1940's traveled
abroad to take part in a world peace conference.*

His Detroit speech, presented here in part, is taken from
Freedom *(New York), July, 1953.*

. . . ON BEHALF of the National Committee to Defend Negro Leadership, I want to thank you for permitting me, its chairman, to present the urgent cause of that Committee to such a distinguished assembly—yes, to you who are the core of leadership as well as the makers of leaders for the Negro people. There are some among you who have been the victims of the forces of reaction and oppression. Attempts have been made to discredit your distinguished leadership by name-calling and other smear tactics, your abilities to think and to arrive at decisions and courses of action that result in a better way of life for your people have been slandered by such false accusations as that other individuals or groups do your thinking for you; that you who are leaders because you do have these abilities are so weak that you can be easily "used" to "front" for other individuals or groups.

These attacks by the forces of reaction and enemies of the freedom of the Negro people have reached such alarming proportions that you and I must rise up in some concerted action to call a halt to these forces who would dictate to fifteen million American citizens who their leaders must be, how they must think and what they may speak.

I stand here this evening, a representative and a product of three movements in religion that were champions of the rights of the individual to freedom of thought, speech and action.

Nearly two thousand years ago the founder of the Christian Community gave His life for the right to think, to speak and to believe according to the dictates of His own conscience rather than be told by a religious hierarchy what He must think, speak, believe.

He believed that His sacrifice would vouchsafe that same freedom to generations following.

I would be a traitor to Him and to thousands of martyrs and saints—traitor to a movement whose influence has made crooked lives straight, whose power has caused the blind to see and the lame to walk, made bad men good, made somebodies out of nobodies—a traitor indeed, if I remained silent in my generation when these freedoms of the spirit were in jeopardy.

If at this crucial moment in history His ways are too hard for me I must renounce my claim to be a part of His movement.

I am also a Protestant—a movement whose leader, Martin Luther, nearly four centuries ago made a bold stroke for the right of the individual Christian to freedom of conscience, thought and speech in the area of religion, rather than to be dictated to by a religious hierarchy.

As a good Protestant I must protest every act that threatens the gains made by a movement whose followers in these nearly four hundred years have wrought righteousness, quenched the violence of fire, escaped the edge of the sword, and out of weakness were made strong.

I am a Methodist—a movement whose leader, John Wesley, exercised his freedom to think, speak and believe, according to the dictates of his own conscience, rather than conform to the decadent religious atmosphere of his age.

As a representative and a product of three great religious movements that have championed freedom of conscience, thought and speech, I must be vigilant lest these hard-won gains of two thousand years be lost to this and succeeding generations.

I must with every ounce of my being vouchsafe these same freedoms to every individual and group in society. Even to those with whom I disagree—I must oppose every instrument that threatens these freedoms to any group, because I know that that same instrument in the hands of those who disagree with me will deprive me of the freedoms which have nourished and sustained me these thirty-eight years.

And so I must protest the attempt of the Un-American Activities Committee to impugn the leadership of Bishop W. J. Walls* by calling the great leader of a great denomination "subversive"; . . . the insults and abuse to which the Reverend Charles A. Hill of this city† was subjected by the same committee; . . . the attempt of the U. S. State Department to deny passport rights to the Reverend James H. Robinson,‡ of New York City, because he insisted on voicing the Negro and colonial peoples' demands against racism as practiced at home and exported abroad; . . . the refusal of the neofascist Malan government in South Africa to permit Bishop Frederick Jordan and Bishop Primm to administer the work of the African Methodist Episcopal Zion Church in South Africa, the reasons for this denial being that the A.M.E. Church has cooperated in the resistance of the African people to the unjust laws.

The accusation against the A.M.E. Church is correct, be-

---

* Bishop William J. Walls was chairman of the Board of Religious Education of the African Methodist Episcopal Zion Church and a member of the National Board of Directors of the N.A.A.C.P.

† The Reverend Charles A. Hill was a Baptist clergyman in Detroit.

‡ The Reverend James H. Robinson was a New York clergyman, leader of many Harlem organizations, a member of the National Board of Directors of the N.A.A.C.P., and a champion of close relations between American Negroes and Africa.

cause the A.M.E. Church has been preaching the Gospel—a Gospel that emphasized the dignity of the human personality and wherever the Gospel is preached, men rise up to walk in freedom and in dignity.

The drums of freedom have begun to sound across Africa, and it is the rhythm of justice, equal opportunity and a decent life for its millions who have known this land as home for many centuries. The rhythm of those drums will not be silenced.

And so I must protest—yes, find ways in which to make effective protest—against the persecution of those leaders in South and East Africa—Dr. Dadoo, Dr. Z. K. Matthews, Jomo Kenyatta and the five other leaders who were sentenced to seven years' hard labor—because they oppose the exclusion of the African people from the political and economic life in a country which belongs to them.

I refuse to be engulfed by the hysteria and fear of our times, because I firmly believe that given a chance democracy will stem the tide as it has in every age. Only those who daily try to retard the full flowering of the democratic way of life become hysterical in the face of the world situation.

I know, too, that every denial of freedom weakens democracy.

I say these things in the face of the fact that I too am a victim of attack in another form, though for similar reasons. You and I must be on guard for the more subtle forms of attack that would silence those who speak and act for a more abundant life for the people.

Though my voice is not especially loud or strong, it seems that when I have spoken in behalf of peace and first-class status for fifteen million American citizens, too many people hear me (possibly the F.B.I. also) when I would be in New York. And so my superiors possibly feel that not so many people will hear me, and it will be much safer, down in Maryland, where I am being transferred as of May 24.

If in hysteria and fear we continue the course we are on, we will awake on tomorrow to discover that the house of Democracy has fallen. Not because of the attack of some enemy without; rather it will have fallen because of weakness from within by the denial of freedom—freedom to print and publish the truth as in the case of John H. McCray, Negro editor of *Lighthouse* and *Informer*, who was sentenced to sixty days on the chain gang, because he championed the rights of Negroes to vote in South Carolina; freedom to speak the truth, as in the case of J. Minor Sullivan, who was indicted and put on one thousand dollars bail because he dared give testimony in court showing that defendants in the Trenton Six case were drugged at the time of their so-called confessions.*

Negro Americans believe in our democratic way of life, and their fight for first-class status is motivated by the belief that when they really are first-class citizens democracy will be impregnable against every foe. They know also that the longer these rights and freedoms are denied, the weaker becomes the house of democracy and the greater becomes the despair and the hopelessness of 6 millions who await some sure word of hope.

And so they are insisting that *now* is the time. This is the hour, not tomorrow or the day after. They are saying to America, "Let us *this* day make this a government of the people, *by* the people, *for* the people. With liberty and justice not only for whites, Democrats, Republicans, Socialists, but liberty and justice for all the people."

The attacks against the leaders of the Negro people by the forces of reaction are an attempt to halt the mounting struggle of our people for dignity and full citizenship.

And so we must, by concerted action, foil the attempt of all those forces that would discredit the real leaders of the Negro people and substitute those who dare speak only as their masters please.

What could be more fitting than that I should be given the opportunity of presenting the cause of the Committee to Defend Negro Leadership to the National Fraternal Council of Churches? Bishop A. W. Womack,† when you speak you represent four million Negroes and some thirteen denominations. We made you our leader. We did not ask anyone whether or not we could make you our leader. We made you our leader because we saw in you qualities that we liked. We believed that you would represent the aspirations of our people for dignity and first-class status. And as the leader of the National Fraternal Council of Churches, when you speak you not only represent four million church members but fifteen million Negro Americans. And we will protest with every ounce of our being any attempt by the forces of reaction to silence you.

Dr. W. H. Hernigan, though there are thousands who do not know you personally, whenever your name is called a feeling of pride wells up in the breasts of our people, because we

---

* The "Trenton Six" involved six black youths charged with murder. The case aroused nationwide attention. The six were sentenced to life imprisonment.

† Bishop Arthur W. Womack was elected a bishop of the Colored Methodist Episcopal Church in 1950.

recognize you as our leader. We are grateful for the tremendous contribution which you have made in the interest of the Negro people and to the cause of religion in your eighty-eight years. We have made you our leader and we did not consult anyone to find out if we could or could not make you our leader. And we will protest any effort to silence you when you speak in our interest. The Negro church had its beginning at this point of the right of the individual to dignity and first-class status. Believing that all men are equal at the foot of the cross, the Negro established a church in which he could worship God in dignity and with a healthy sense of self-respect and not as a servant. He remembered that Jesus said, "I have not called you servant but friend."

And to the Negro church has been entrusted the responsibility of translating the hopes and aspirations of the Negro for dignity and freedom into reality. When my grandparents sang the spiritual "I Am Going to Eat at the Table One of These Days," it is true that they meant eternity. But they also meant that they were looking forward to a day in time when they would no longer have to eat in the kitchen of white folks but would eat at a table of their own in their own dining room at which they could sit in freedom and dignity.

The Committee to Defend Leadership, which represents such outstanding leaders of the Negro people as Bishop C. C. Alleyne* and Bishop R. C. Ransom,† Mrs. Mary Church Terrell, Rev. Charles A. Hill‡ and Mr. Coleman A. Young, of Detroit, Rev. Joseph Evans, of Chicago, and Mrs. Andrew W. Sinkins, of South Carolina, invites your cooperation and participation in its efforts in this direction.

We are convinced that we must come do the defense of all Negro leaders who are attacked. We will not succumb to the enemies of the Negro people who would divide us by name-calling and smear tactics. For we know that a better life for our people will not be achieved by a divided people. And so I must defend a Paul Robeson, the greatest artist of this century. Paul Robeson has interpreted the classics for me in a way that no other person could. When he sings I am thrilled as no other person can thrill me. I know Paul Robeson personally, and he has talked to me from the depths of his heart and I will come to my own conclusions about Paul Robeson. No one else can

* Bishop Cameron C. Alleyne was consecrated Bishop of the A.M.E. Zion Church in 1924.
† Bishop Reverdy C. Ransom was elected Bishop of the A.M.E. Zion Church and ordained in 1924.
‡ Rev. Charles A. Hill was a Baptist minister in Detroit, Michigan.

tell me what I must think or believe about this great leader of the Negro people.

And so I must defend Dr. W. E. B. Du Bois, who, when he speaks, reveals a vast knowledge—a knowledge of the universe.* Dr. Du Bois is the greatest scholar of this century, yet he has placed his vast knowledge and his skill as a scholar at the service of his people. He has spent more than fifty years in fighting for the dignity and first-class status of fifteen million Negro citizens, and because of this the Negro people have made him their leader.

I must defend Ben Davis. There are some who tell me he is a Communist. In New York City more than 75,000 Negroes and whites elected him to City Council on two occasions. They did not seem to question his politics. They knew that he was fighting for a better way of life for the Negro people and so they made him their leader. They did not ask permission as to whether they could or could not make him their leader.

In the struggle for full citizenship rights many different kinds of forces must unite for victory!

> In the shouting-out times
> In the stand-up-and-be-counted days
> When the roll is called
> Where will you be?

> In the shouting-out times
> In the stand-up-and-be-counted days
> Do you close your eyes?
> Do you turn your head?
> Are you afraid?

SEGREGATION AND DESEGREGATION

By Thurgood Marshall

Thurgood Marshall was born in Baltimore in 1915 and, after working his way through Lincoln University, entered Harvard Law School. In 1938 he joined the N.A.A.C.P.'s staff, soon becoming special counsel to the organization

---

* In 1951, Dr. Du Bois had been indicted, tried and acquitted on the charge of "unregistered foreign agent" in connection with his leadership of the Peace Information Center.

*and director of its Legal Defense and Educational Fund.
In this position he won a whole series of Supreme Court
victories and became known as "Mr. Civil Rights." In
December, 1953, he pleaded the cause of desegregation
before the Court in the famous school desegregation case,*
Brown v. Board of Education of Topeka, et al. *On the eve
of his victory in this case, Marshall delivered a lecture in
the Edwin Rogers Embree Memorial Lectures series at
Dillard University in New Orleans. The lecture in the
spring of 1954, optimistic in tone, summed up the achievements in desegregation, much of it accomplished by the
N.A.A.C.P.*

*Following his victory in the school desegregation cases
before the Supreme Court, Marshall went on to become a
judge in the federal circuit court, Solicitor General of the
United States, and the first Negro Supreme Court Justice.*

Here is Marshall's lecture, as excerpted from The Edwin
R. Embree Memorial Lectures, *New Orleans, Dillard University, n.d., pp. 33–44.*

. . . THERE HAS BEEN much discussion during recent
years concerning the question of the removal in this country of
dual citizenship based solely on race and color. The primary
emphasis has been on the elimination of racial segregation. No
one denies that progress is being made. There are, however,
some who say that the progress is too slow and others who say
that the progress is too rapid. The important thing to remember
is that progress is being made. We are moving ahead. We have
passed the crossroads. We are moving toward a completely integrated society, North and South.

Those who doubt this and those who are afraid of complete
integration are victims of a background based upon long indoctrination of only one side of the controversy in this country.
They know only of one side of the controversy in this country.
They know only of one side of slavery. They know only the
biased reports about Reconstruction and the long-standing
theory which seems to support the "legality" of the separate-
but-equal doctrine.

In order to adequately appraise the situation, we must first
understand the problem in relation to our history—legal and
political. Secondly, we must give proper weight to progress that
has been made with and without legal pressure, and thirdly, we
must look to the future.

Our government is based on the principle of the equality of
man the individual, not the group. All of us can quote the

principle that "All men are created equal." Our basic legal document, the Constitution of the United States, guarantees equal protection of the laws to all of us. Many state constitutions have similar provisions. We even have a "Bill of Rights" in the Constitution of Louisiana. These high-sounding principles we preach and teach. However, in the eyes of the world we stand convicted of violating these principles day in and day out.

Today, one hundred and seventy-seven years after the signing of the Declaration of Independence and eighty-six years after the Fourteenth Amendment was adopted, we have a society where, in varying degrees throughout the country, but especially in the South, Negroes, solely because they are Negroes, are segregated, ostracized and set apart from all other Americans. This discrimination extends from the cradle to the graveyard. (And I emphasize grave*yard*, rather than grave.) Or, to put it even more bluntly, in many areas of this country, a white paroled murderer would be welcome in places which would at the same time exclude such people as Ralph Bunche, Marian Anderson, Jackie Robinson, and many others. Constitutionally protected individual rights have been effectively destroyed by outmoded theories of racial or group inferiority. Why is this true? How long can we afford the luxury of segregation and discrimination?

One reason this condition of dual citizenship exists is because we have been conditioned to an acceptance of this theory as a fact. We are the products of a misunderstanding of history. As a matter of fact, only in recent years have accurate studies of the pre-Civil War period and the Reconstruction period of our history been published.

Our position today is tied up with our past history—at least as far back as the 1820's. At that time the antislavery movement was beginning to take permanent form. It should be borne in mind that those people in New England, Ohio and other areas, who started this movement became dedicated to a principle which has become known as the Judaeo-Christian ethic. This principle was carried forth in their determination to remove slavery from our society, and to remove the badges of caste and inferiority whereby an American could be ostracized or set apart from fellow Americans solely because of race. Of course, slavery per se was the immediate objective—the abolition of slavery—but the ultimate goal was the same as the unfinished business we have before us today, namely, to remove race and caste from the American life.

These people in the 1820 period—1820 to 1865—sought to translate their moral theories and principles into law. They started by pamphleteering and speechmaking. They recognized that equal protection of the laws must always be, in part, an ethical and moral concept, rather than a law. They sought to constitutionalize this moral argument or ideal. Slavery—with its theories of racial damnation, racial inferiority and racial discrimination—was inherently repugnant to the American creed and Christian ethics. They sought to support their moral theories by use of the Declaration of Independence and certain sections of the Constitution as it existed at that time. In so far as public meetings were concerned, speakers were barred from such meetings in the South—brutally beaten or killed, and many were run out of similar meetings in Northern cities and towns.* It was, therefore, impossible to get behind the original iron curtain to get public support for much of the program.

In their legal attack they were thwarted by the decision of the United States Supreme Court in the Dred Scott case, which held that no person of African descent, slave or free, had any rights that a white man was bound to respect. The important thing to remember throughout this period is that the opponents of slavery were seeking a Constitutional basis—a legal platform— for the democratic principle of the equality of man.

After the Emancipation Proclamation was signed, many states passed Black Codes and other infamous statutes, effectively returning the emancipated slaves to their inferior status. Consequently, the same people who fought to abolish slavery had to take the lead in Congress in writing the thirteenth, fourteenth and fifteenth amendments.

This short period of intense legislation was followed by the Reconstruction period. Much of that which we have read concerning this period has emphasized, overstated and exaggerated the errors of judgment made in trying to work out the "Negro problem" in such fashion as to give real meaning to these Civil War amendments [but these amendments] were actually thwarted by the conspiracy between Northern capitalists and others to bring "harmony" by leaving the Negro and his problem to the tender mercies of the South. This brought about the separate-but-equal pattern, which spread not only throughout the South but extended and now exists in many Northern and Western areas.

Despite the distortion of this historical background, which has become firmly embedded in our minds, is the "understanding" that racial segregation is legal and valid even if in violation of

* See in this connection Frederick Douglass' defense of freedom of speech, pp. 244–46.

our moral principles. The fallacy of this reasoning is that the equal protection of the laws was intended to be the constitutionalization of the ethic and moral principle of the absolute equality of man—the right of an individual neither to be circumscribed or conditioned by group, race or color.

It should, therefore, be remembered that our society is the victim of the following periods of history: the period of slavery, when the slaveholders defended slavery by repeating over and over again the myth that slavery was not only a positive good for the nation but was absolutely beneficial and necessary for the Negroes themselves. Consequently, even free Negroes were denied the right of citizenship and subjected to all manner of abuse without legal redress. Immediately following the Civil War, and indeed up to the 1930's, is the period when Negroes were no longer slaves but were certainly not yet full citizens. Having passed through this laissez-faire period in so far as asserting our Constitutional rights is concerned, Negroes began in the thirties the all-out fight to secure the right to vote and at the same time to break down discrimination and segregation.

In so far as securing the right to vote, beginning with the registration cases and the white-primary cases and others, much progress has been made to the end that as of the 1948 national elections, at least 1,300,000 Negroes voted in the deep South. We have seen Negroes elected to the city council in Richmond, Virginia, Nashville, Tennessee, and many cities in North Carolina. We have seen Negroes elected to the governing board of the Democratic party in Atlanta, Georgia. We have also seen Negroes elected to school boards in cities such as Atlanta, Georgia, Lynchburg, Virginia, and Winston-Salem, North Carolina. There are still, however, several small areas in Alabama, Mississippi, and at least four parishes in Louisiana where Negroes are still prevented from registering as qualified voters. (But these are distinctly local problems, which are being attended to and can be pushed aside on that basis.)

In the North we have seen the drive for protection of the right to work without regard to race and color—the drive for F.E.P.C. legislation. We have seen such legislation passed in at least eight states in the North, leaving forty states and the District of Columbia to go, before we have the necessary safeguards to protect man's right not to be deprived of an opportunity to earn a livelihood because of race, religion or ancestry.

We have also seen the breaking-down of the legal barriers to owning and occupying real property without regard to race or color. Today, as a result of several Supreme Court decisions, any American any place in the United States, regardless of race or color, may own and occupy property wherever he can find a willing seller, has the money to purchase the property and courage to live on it. We still, however, have residential segregation throughout the country, not by law, not by the courts, but by a combination of circumstances, such as, the reactionary policies of mortgage companies and real-estate boards, public-housing agencies, including F.H.A., and other governmental agencies. We also find an unwillingness on the part of many Negroes to exercise their rights in this field. In recent years instead of progress toward an integrated community, we find that the Negro ghetto is merely expanding into a larger and more glorified and gilded ghetto. This unwillingness to exercise our own rights is due in part to the long indoctrination that we are different from or inferior to others and therefore should voluntarily segregate ourselves.

As of the present time, the paramount issue in so far as Americanism is concerned is the ending of all racial distinctions in American life. The reasons for this are many. A weighty factor, of course, is the recognition by more and more people in high places that the world situation in regard to the sensitive areas throughout the world depends on how well we can handle our race problem in this country. Our country can no longer tolerate an Achilles heel of discriminatory practices toward its darker citizens. Even more important is the realization that the equality of man as a principle and the equal protection of the laws as a Constitutional concept are both based upon the moral principle of individual responsibility rather than racial identity.

Racial segregation in our country is immoral, costly, and damaging to the nation's prestige. Segregation and discrimination violate the Judaeo-Christian ethic, and the democratic creed on which our national morality is based is soundly established in the minds of most men. But in addition, it has been shown that the costs of segregation and discrimination to the nation are staggering. Elmo Roper, social scientist and pollster of American public opinion, has stated, "The resultant total of the cost of discrimination comes to roughly $10 out of every $75 paycheck, or, in total, $30 billion lost every year." This figure alone would amount to a cost of $2,000 per year to every individual in America. But perhaps even more damaging to the nation is the current effect of America's racial practices on America's role in international affairs and world leadership. According to a recent statement by our State Department experts, nearly half of the recent Russian propaganda about

America has been concentrated on race, linking Communist germ-warfare charges with alleged racial brutality in this country. In addition, Americans returning from abroad consistently report having been questioned over and over about racial problems in this country.

This concern about American racial practices seems especially strong among the two thirds of the world that is darker-skinned. Our former ambassador to India, Chester Bowles, wrote the following statement, after attending an Indian press conference: "As I later discovered is almost invariably the case in any Asian press conference or forum, the Number One question was, 'What about America's treatment of the Negro?'"

Shortly after returning from a tour of Asian and Pacific areas, Vice-President Nixon made this statement:

Americans must create a better understanding of American ideals abroad by practicing and thinking tolerance and respect for human rights every day of the year. Every act of racial discrimination or prejudice in the United States hurts Americans as much as an espionage agent who turns over a weapon to a foreign enemy.

Historically, we have to ask whether or not, even as we stand today, our country can afford to continue in practicing *not* what they preach. Historically, the segregation patterns in the United States are carry-overs from the principles of slavery. They are based on the exploded theory of the inferiority of the minority group. Segregation is recognized as resulting from the decision of the majority group without even consulting, less known in seeking, the consent of the segregated group. All of us know that segregation traditionally results in unequal facilities for the segregated group. Duplication of facilities is expensive, diverts funds from the economy which could be utilized to improve facilities for all groups. Finally, segregation leads to the blockage of real communication between the two groups. In turn, this blockage increases mutual suspicion, distrust, hostility, stereotypes and prejudice; and these, all together, result in a social climate of tension favorable to aggressive behavior and social disorganization which sometimes culminate in race riots. Even where we do not have race riots, the seeds of tension are ever present in a segregated system.

The harm done to the individual begins with the child's earliest years, when he becomes aware of status differences among groups in society and begins to react to patterns of segregation. Prejudice and discrimination are potentially damaging to the personalities of all children. The children of the

majority group are affected differently from those of the
minority group. This potential psychological damage is crystal-
lized by segregation practices sanctioned by public law—and it
is the same whether in the North, the East, the West, or the
South. Damage to the immediate community is inevitable. This
is followed by damage to the state, our federal government and,
finally, the world today. The only answer is the complete removal of all racial distinctions that lay at the basis of all this.

And now for the future. Everyone in and out of government
must understand that the future of our government and indeed
the world depends on the recognition of the equality of man—
the principle which is inherent in the theory of our government
and protected by our Constitution.

Of course, we have made progress, but instead of gloating
over this progress, we should get renewed courage to tackle the
next job. Let us not listen to the rantings of politicians like
Governors Byrnes and Talmadge. Governor Byrnes has declared:

Should the Supreme Court decide this case against our position,
we will face a serious problem. Of only one thing can we be certain.
South Carolina will not now, nor for some years to come, mix
white and colored children in our schools . . . If the Court
changes what is now the law of the land, we will, if it is possible,
live within the law, preserve the public-school system, and at the
same time maintain segregation. If that is not possible, reluctantly
we will abandon the public-school system.

That statement is made by a governor who was formerly a
member of the Supreme Court which he is now talking about.
Governor Herman Talmadge announces that if the decision
comes down opposed to what he thinks it should be, that *he*,
Governor Talmadge, will get together as much of his militia
as he can find and challenge the whole United States Army.

Instead of listening to people like this, why not listen to people
who speak for the South like Ralph McGill of the Atlanta *Constitution* who writes:

An end to segregation—when it comes—will not, of course, force
people to associate socially. That will remain, as now, personal
choice. But it will bring on change—and this is what state legislatures in South Carolina, Georgia, Mississippi, Virginia and
Alabama are, or will be, considering. They consider not how to
retain legal segregation—which they see soon ending—but how to
effect it without legal compulsion . . . Segregation is on the way
out and he who tries to tell the people otherwise does them great

disservice. The problem of the future is how to live with the change.

There are still those who will continue to tell us that law is one thing and ethics another. However, I prefer to follow what one legal historian has stated—"Laws and ethics, some men bluntly tell us are separate fields. So indeed they are. But spare America the day when both together do not determine the meaning of equal protection of the laws."

We must understand the slavery background of segregation and we must understand the complete lack of any scientific support for racial superiority or inferiority. We must understand that racial segregation is violative of every religious principle, as I said before. We must never forget what racial segregation did to our parents and is doing to us, and how it will affect our children. We must turn from misunderstanding and fear to intelligent planning, courage and determination.

Psychologists acknowledge that to achieve a well-balanced, well-adjusted personality, all human beings require a sense of personal dignity and worth, acknowledged not only within themselves but by the society in which they live—the total society. Not every child reacts to personality conflict in the same way. Behavior patterns depend on such interrelated factors as family relations, social and economic class, general personality patterns and other factors. In the final analysis, however, each segregated child is forced to adjust to conflicts not faced by members of the majority group.

Studies published in the *Journal of Social Psychology* indicate that members of the lower economic class may react to racial frustrations by overaggressive behavior, hostility toward the minority group and/or the majority group, and by anti-social behavior. These reactions are self-destructive inasmuch as society not only punishes the offenders but often interprets such behavior as justification for continuing segregation practices against all members of the group. These studies further indicate that members of the middle upper class may react by withdrawal, submissive behavior or rigid conformity to the expected pattern of segregation. Psychologically, this is equally bad.

Generally, however, children of all classes react by adopting an over-all defeatist attitude, a lowering of personal ambitions, hypersensitivity and anxiety about relations in a larger society, and a tendency to see hostility or rejection even where it might not exist. This may result in the development and perpetuation of generally sensitive, conflicting personalities.

Although the range of individual reaction in terms of behavior and personality patterns is very wide, there is no question that all minority children are necessarily affected adversely by enforced segregation—and there is not a single scientific study to the contrary.

While the effects of enforced segregation on majority-group children are more obscure, they are, nevertheless, real. Children who are taught prejudice, directly or indirectly, are also taught to gain and evaluate themselves on a totally unrealistic basis. Perceiving minority-group members as inferior does not permit a member of the majority group to evaluate himself in terms of actual ability or achievement but permits and encourages self-deception—that is, "I am at least better than a Negro."

A culture which permits and encourages enforced segregation motivates feelings of guilt and necessitates an adjustment to protect against recognizing the injustice of racial fears and hatreds.

The contradiction between moral, religious, democratic principles of the brotherhood of man, the importance of justice or fair play and the actuality of the prejudiced, discriminatory practices of individuals and institutions inevitably results in confusion, conflict, moral cynicism and guilt feelings in the majority group. This conflict, supported by pressure to conform to existing patterns, may result in disrespect for authority, unwholesomeness of ideals of all authorities (parents, political leaders) and a determination to run roughshod over everyone not in the conforming group. Some persons may attempt to resolve this conflict by intensifying hostility toward the minority group or to express self-hatred in aggressive behavior.

Of the large number of social scientists who replied to a questionnaire concerning the probable effect of enforced segregation under conditions of equal facilities, ninety percent replied that, regardless of the equality of the facilities provided, enforced segregation is psychologically harmful to the *minority* group members; eighty percent stated it was their opinion that enforced segregation would have damaging effects also on the *majority*-group members. (M. Deutscher and I. Chein, "The Psychological Effects of Enforced Segregation: A Survey of Social Science Opinion," *Journal of Psychology*, 1948, Vol. 26, pp. 259–87.)

Enforced segregation appears to have the same general and psychological effect regardless of the quality of facilities available. (That is to answer any of you who believe that the building of a new Jim Crow high school will solve the problem.)

Enforced-segregation public schools offer official recognition, sanction and perpetuation to the assumption of inferiority, a myth which has already been exploded.

The results of an effort to get a full picture of desegregation in American communities are now available. And it is hoped that these results can be passed on to every American and to our friends and critics overseas. For these results clearly show that in the past ten years, America has undergone a startling, dramatic and completely unprecedented change in race relations—and all for the better. Racial desegregation has been attempted successfully in literally hundreds of instances, in all regions, and in all walks of life. In addition to the more noticeable areas of schools and the armed forces, complete success has been reported in desegregating public-housing projects, labor unions, Catholic and Protestant churches, public and private swimming pools, professional organizations, some Y.M.C.A.'s and many Y.W.C.A.'s, Southern industries, notably the Southern plants of International Harvester Company, officers' and enlisted men's clubs and housing areas on Army posts, hospitals, summer camps, and many other areas—even cemeteries.

An impressive part of these great changes is the way that the "unthinkables" of ten years ago have become the "taken-for-granteds" of today. Ten years back, it was unthinkable that Negroes would participate in the white professional-baseball leagues. Today, Negroes are on the teams in Dallas, Texas, Atlanta, Georgia, Savannah, Georgia, and other areas. During World War II, it was unthinkable that Negro and white children would ever attend the same schools on Southern Army posts. As of 1953, the last federally operated Army school on a Southern military post was desegregated; and a recent announcement from the office of the Secretary of Defense states that segregation will be abolished in all schools of every Southern military post by September, 1955, in all states, including Mississippi. Before the war, Negroes traveling by train in Southern regions had great difficulty in getting Pullman berths, and risked embarrassment every time they sought to use the dining car. Since that time, legal action and voluntary adjustments made by some railroads have resulted in a shifting pattern in dining cars in the South—from complete exclusion, to being put behind a curtain, to seating at separate tables without a curtain, and, finally to a completely integrated seating pattern. Interstate travel patterns have been liberalized on railroads, buses and planes, but this has just barely dented the surface. Southern airports are not progressive.

One of the most impressive signs of change may be seen in

the area of schools. In 1943, as far as is known, no Negroes were attending Southern white institutions of higher learning. But today, the Sweatt and McLaurin cases* have opened the doors of previously all-white graduate schools in every Southern state except five—Mississippi, Alabama, Georgia, Florida, and South Carolina. It is now estimated that around two thousand Negroes are now attending Southern white institutions of higher learning. As of September, 1953, Negroes were attending the graduate or professional schools of twenty-three Southern white state-supported institutions, attending the undergraduate levels of ten Southern white state and municipal schools, and attending forty-two Southern white private schools. And, according to *The Journal of Negro Education*, "what is more important, there has not been reported a single untoward incident of any kind as a result of this change."

Private institutions of higher learning have admitted Negro students in eight Southern states, and, in one school, there are now two hundred fifty-one Negro students and five Negro teachers. Several Southern Negro colleges have admitted white students, and in Northern areas there are now over one hundred professors and instructors teaching in predominantly white schools.

Some specific incidents stand out. School authorities in Louisville, Kentucky, closed its Negro Municipal College, admitted Negro students to the white college, and hired one Negro teacher. In that same city, a young female Negro doctor is now teaching pediatrics in the previously all-white medical school. In St. Louis, Missouri, Washington, D. C., and Wilmington, Delaware, the Catholic parochial schools have admitted Negro students. In Tennessee, all but one member of a white theological seminary turned in their resignations to the president when the Board of Trustees refused to admit a Negro student. The Town Council of Oak Ridge, Tennessee, has asked the Atomic Energy Commission to end segregation in the public-school system. The Council passed a resolution to that effect by a 4–2 vote, and sent a copy of it to President Eisenhower.

In elementary and secondary schools outside the South, successful desegregation has been effected in fifty-nine separate communities in such states as Arizona (2 communities), California (1), Delaware (3), Illinois (12), Kansas (3), Indiana

---

* On four separate occasions between 1938 and 1950, a Negro sought admittance to a white graduate school, and four times the Supreme Court ordered the admission. Two of the cases were *Sweatt v. Painter* and *McLaurin v. Oklahoma State Regents* (1950).

(4), Maryland (1), New Jersey (16), New Mexico (2), New York (3), Ohio (7), and Pennsylvania (5)—fifty-nine known instances in the past four years of the breaking-down of segregation. Researchers suspect that there are many other instances of desegregation.

A special and informative example of successful school desegregation is found in the state of New Jersey. In 1947, the people of New Jersey adopted a new constitution, containing a provision that no person in the state shall be segregated in the public schools "because of religious scruples, race, color, ancestry or national origin." One year later a survey revealed that there were fifty-three New Jersey school districts containing one or more all-Negro schools, and that in forty-three of these, the all-Negro facilities were the result of deliberate segregation rather than geographical factors.

As a result of efforts by the state Commissioner of Education, it was announced in late August, 1948, that thirty of these forty-three school districts would open school in September on a completely integrated basis. Of the remaining thirteen, eight had taken partial steps, aiming for integration by September, 1949. In the other five districts, the situation remained unsettled. As of September, 1951, forty of the forty-three districts had undertaken complete elimination of the racially separated schools. Racial segregation still remained in the other three schools, though "progress was being made."

An especially interesting aspect of New Jersey school desegregation was what happened to the Negro teachers. In many circles, great fears have been expressed that Negro teachers will lose their jobs if the schools are desegregated. New Jersey offers an interesting testing ground for this fear. In 1945, New Jersey had 479 Negro teachers, and 415 of them were employed in the nine counties that maintained separate schools. A recent study of this situation shows that in these nine formerly segregated counties, there are 425 Negro teachers, and in the whole state, a total of 645 Negro teachers, a statewide gain of 166 Negro teachers. One community reported to have desegregated its Negro school, placed one Negro teacher in the high school and placed the Negro principal in charge of five white teachers.

Perhaps the most noticeable and the most complete example of desegregation involving millions of persons is found in the armed forces. At the beginning of World War II, the Army policy was one of almost complete segregation of Negro troops, the Air Force was just beginning an "experiment" in the training of Negro flyers in the face of a widespread belief that Negroes could not be taught to fly airplanes, the Navy confined

Negroes almost exclusively to the Messmen's Branch, and the Marines excluded Negroes entirely. But soon cracks began to appear in the wall. The Army's Officers Candidate School and a few other service schools became integrated; the Air Forces regarded its experiment with a Negro pursuit squadron as a success and expanded it to a fighter group; the Navy in 1942 allowed Negroes to enlist in branches other than the Messmen's service (although they were still segregated and barred from seagoing vessels); and, in 1942, the Marine Corps admitted its first Negroes, in strictly segregated units, as laborers, antiaircraft gunners and ammunition handlers.

Subsequently, the pressures for integration increased. The armed forces found that they had serious morale problems in some of the segregated Negro units. They also found that the picture of a segregated American Army of Occupation, attempting to teach democracy to the people of Germany and Japan, was a ridiculous experiment. So, in a series of careful and unpublicized moves, the armed forces began a gradual program of racial desegregation. In 1953, the Secretary of the Army reported that at least ninety percent of the Negroes in the Army were serving in nonsegregated units (the number continues to increase), and added: "The Army policy is one of complete integration, and it is to be accomplished as soon as possible."

In the European Army Command, a battalion commander from the deep South is quoted as saying: "We got the order. We got detailed instructions for carrying it out and a time limit to do it in. And that was it."

And in our armed forces all over the globe, Negro servicemen were brought into previously all-white units rapidly and with no trouble by officers who gave white servicemen such terse instructions as these: "Some Negro men are joining our unit. These men are soldiers. Treat them as such."

This is the problem that everybody says is such a "horrible" thing to face up to.

What is the picture today? According to Lee Nichols' exciting new book *Breakthrough on the Color Front*,* the Army reports that less than 10,000 Negroes are still serving in all-Negro units out of some 200,000 Negroes in the Army. Assistant Defense Secretary John A. Hannah estimates that by June, 1954, there will be no remaining segregated Army units. The Air Force, which had moved more rapidly, stated that Negro servicemen who were in the Air Force in August, 1953, had been integrated into all of its units throughout the world. Of the

* New York, Random House, 1954.

23,000 Negroes serving in the Navy in 1953, about half were still in the Messmen's or Steward's Branch. The rest were integrated and scattered through nearly every job classification that the Navy has. The Marine Corps, last of all the services to take Negroes, reports that its last two all-Negro units were integrated "some time" before the summer of 1952.

Today, Negro and white draftees from the most poverty-stricken parts of the deep South, as well as the rest of the nation, are inducted into a completely integrated command, and the typical report from commanders who had previously held fears was that "the frictions and antagonisms that lay behind previous race conflicts have been substantially reduced, and that so far there has not been a single major incident traceable to integration."

What about segregation in the nation's capital? Many Americans have expressed disgust, and foreign visitors have stated their amazement, at the fact that public and private facilities in the capital of our democracy were almost completely segregated—restaurants, schools, housing projects, theaters, and so forth. Though there is still much to be done in Washington, there have been several recent examples of progress. On June 3, 1953, the National Capital Housing Authority announced the adoption of a policy of opening all present and future public low-rent housing properties in the District of Columbia to low-income families, without regard to race. Around that same time, the Supreme Court handed down a decision preventing discrimination in Washington restaurants. All the restaurants have abided by the decision, and no incident of any kind has been reported. Hotel accommodations now are available to Negroes in most of the larger hotels, although the policy of many smaller hotels is still uncertain. Negroes are now admitted to the three legitimate theaters of Washington, and to at least four —and probably more—of the downtown movie theaters. The majority of the city's private schools have opened their doors to Negroes, and the Catholic parochial schools have also become integrated. A recent bulletin reports that the nation's capital has even agreed to desegregate the jails. Washington is slowly moving toward a position where it can command the respect of the world where race relations are involved.

Why have people decided to desegregate? Members of American communities have tried to integrate their institutions for an extremely varied number of reasons. The pressures to desegregate have come from several forces—sometimes from an aroused Negro community, sometimes from administrative rulings of local authorities, sometimes from rulings by a national body, sometimes from voluntary decision by a majority of concerned community members. It now appears that the success or failure of the desegregation effort is not related to the reason for desegregating, since the reasons are so varied.

The success of racial desegregation has been shown to be related not so much to the type of community that is involved or the prejudice of its members as to the close adherence to a set of specific principles. We have reached the stage where scientists, sociologists and others, have agreed upon rules which when followed bring about smooth desegregation whether in Illinois or Louisiana. The main point is that once the state law preventing intergroup communication in institutional life is removed, it is then up to the local community to work out its own salvation, with the understanding that it must be done within the American framework.

The accomplishment of effective and efficient desegregation with a minimum of social disturbance depends on the following five things:

1. There must be a clear and unequivocal statement of policy by leaders with prestige, and by authority officials.
2. There must be firm enforcement and persistent execution of the nonsegregation policy in the face of initial resistance.
3. Authorities and law enforcement officials must show a willingness to deal with violations, attempted violations or incitement to violations, by applying the law and backing it up with strong enforcement action.
4. Authorities must refuse to employ, engage in or tolerate subterfuges, gerrymandering or other devices for evading the principle and the fact of desegregation.
5. The accomplishment of desegregation must be accompanied by continual interpretation of the reasons for the action, and appealing to the democratic and moral values of all persons involved.

In conclusion, racial segregation is grounded upon the myth of inherent racial superiority. This myth has been completely exploded by all scientific studies. It now stands exposed as a theory which can only be explained as a vehicle for perpetuating racial prejudice. History reveals that racial segregation is a badge of slavery, is just as unscientifically supported, immoral and un-American as slavery. Recent history shows that it can be removed, and that it can be done effectively when approached intelligently.

There is no longer any justification for segregation. There is no longer any excuse for it. There is no longer any reason under

the sun why intelligent people should continue to find excuses
for not ending segregation in their own community, in the
South as well as in the North.

HUMAN RELATIONS IN WORLD PERSPECTIVE

By Ralph J. Bunche

The second lecture in the spring 1954 Edwin Rogers Em-
bree Memorial Lectures at Dillard University was delivered
by Ralph J. Bunche. Bunche was born in 1904 in Detroit,
Michigan. He was graduated from the University of Cali-
fornia in 1927 and received his Ph.D. from Harvard Uni-
versity in 1936. He taught at Howard University and was
a member of the "Black Cabinet" formed under President
Franklin D. Roosevelt. Bunche was an important member
of the team of researchers who worked with Gunnar Myr-
dal in the preparation of The American Dilemma. *In 1945*
Bunche became the first Negro division head in the State
Department and in the following year was appointed di-
rector of the Trusteeship Division of the United Nations.
As special mediator for the U.N. in the Palestine crisis, he
was able to restore peace in that country, and in 1950 re-
ceived the Nobel Peace Prize for this work.
    Here is Bunche's lecture, as excerpted from The Edwin
R. Embree Memorial Lectures, *New Orleans, Dillard Uni-*
versity, n.d., pp. 45–57.

. . . As I SEE IT, serious attention to the problem of
prejudice, or to put it more broadly, the bad state of human relations, which is to be found almost everywhere in the world
today, aims at the fundamental situation in the world in which
we live. Basically, relations among peoples of the world are bad.
They are characterized by blind prejudices—racial, religious,
national and cultural—by suspicions and fears, by attitudes of
arrogance and superiority on the part of one people toward
other people, by hatred and enmity.
    Now the causes for these bad attitudes are varied. There are
historical circumstances, varying in particular countries and
regions. There has been the exploitation of race and religion by
political demagogues. There is the poison which is constantly

spread by professional bigots. There is the loose acceptance of stereotypes by so many people, not maliciously, but quite casually and often unthinkingly. There is the reaction of many people to what appears to be "different." And there is basically, of course, ignorance about peoples. These are certainly some, but not all, of the causes.

The world's peoples—and we must underscore this—cannot hope to live together in amity and peace so long as bad relationships—these bad attitudes—prevail.

National and group prejudices against other peoples, in the final analysis, stem from attitudes of individuals. One has to learn to be prejudiced. One is not born prejudiced. That, we know, is an elemental fact. We know, also, that prejudice and discrimination are used by individuals and groups in varying situations to their own advantage. In many places, we need only to look at the power arrangements in the immediate society to determine the root of prejudices and discriminatory attitudes. One may find other situations in which it is convenient to have a scapegoat.

We know, also, that prejudice is a part of the cultural heritage and takes the form of practices and beliefs. It worms its way into the folkways of people and therefore we must emphasize that it is in the thinking and feeling of the individual that the source of evil is to be sought.

We know that improving group attitudes can come only as individuals purge themselves of false, unjust, dangerous and unchristian (if I may say so on this Sunday afternoon) feelings toward others among their fellow men. That is why we say in the United Nations that it is in the minds and hearts of men and women that wars are born and it is only through the minds and hearts of men and women that peace can ever be won.

I am always optimistic, and I believe that the most firm source of hope for improved relations and better community relationships, domestic and international, is to be found in the knowledge—knowledge based upon abundant evidence—that prejudiced attitudes of individuals and, therefore, of groups can and do change, and often quite easily and with little disruption or disturbance.

I apologize for making any personal reference, but being here in New Orleans on this beautiful afternoon, I cannot help thinking back to an experience I had in my first year of college which relates to what I have just been saying. I had just entered U.C.L.A., which, as you know, is Jackie Robinson's school —the school Jackie made famous—and I was out for the freshman basketball team. Out that same afternoon was another freshman, a white boy from New Orleans, whose family had just moved to Los Angeles. When this new arrival in Los Angeles from New Orleans saw me out for the team, he was perturbed, and saying nothing to me, went to the coach. He told the coach that he was disturbed about going out for the freshman team, having seen this "colored fellow" out there. He mentioned that he had just come to Los Angeles from the South and that his parents simply could not tolerate the idea of his being on a team with a "colored player." The coach was very sympathetic. He listened attentively to all he had to say and told him that he understood his problem exactly and that there was a very simple solution to it. Expectantly, the young fellow waited for the solution and heard the coach say, "Just turn in your suit over there."

It developed that this young man wanted to play basketball more than he wanted to cultivate his own prejudices or satisfy those of his parents, so he did not turn in his suit. But to drive the lesson home to him, the coach assigned him to play with me at guard, so we had to play together in very close teamwork. In a surprisingly short time, we became very good friends and have remained such to this day. Within a month after that day, I was at his home for meals, accepted by his parents, and he had visited my home. If the coach had coddled him or tried to uphold him in unthinking prejudice, this man might today still be a warped person. Having once got over this hump, he has taken a broad view of race and color ever since. . . .

Habitually, as an American Negro, I am confronted with questions about the racial situation in the United States. People of the press, people in governments, people in the streets, always ask about it, and trying to answer the questions becomes quite a burden and a chore. But last summer, for a welcome change, I found that practically no one was asking me about the status of the Negro in the United States. That was because everyone was asking me about Senator McCarthy.

With your indulgence, I would like to recite just a few experiences—and I do this quite deliberately—covering most of the forty-nine years of my life, more than half of the time that has elapsed since the Emancipation Proclamation in 1863. I do this only because it may be revealing, because it will explain my own deep and continuing concern with this problem, and because perhaps it will throw some light on my thinking about the problem, which, in a nutshell, is that it is a sore burden to the entire nation and costly to every American whatever his color, wherever he resides, whether in New Orleans or in New York.

We may start with Detroit, my birthplace, where I spent the first ten years of my life. I came up as a child in Detroit with prejudice against another group—ironical, to be sure, but also typical in this milieu. The prejudice in Detroit in those days, which I inherited from the mores and folkways of the people of the community, was directed against the Italians, who were the immigrants then coming to Detroit and who were competing for jobs with the local inhabitants. Back in Detroit in 1914, one could observe all the stereotypes about the Italian population which are applied to any unwanted group. This has happened also in other parts of the country, up in New England, for example, where in the last century, the same sort of stereotypes applied to the Irish.

At that time in Detroit, there was little or no prejudice against Negroes, because there were then not enough of us there. The Negro migration from the South came during the First World War. In fact, Detroit was so free of Negro prejudice in my childhood days that even the Y.M.C.A.'s were mixed. That in itself has an ironical significance. Later, they became segregated; but I learned to swim in a pool in a mixed Y.M.C.A. in Detroit.

My father was a barber, and one winter he got a job in Toledo, Ohio, so we moved to Toledo. There the feelings were very strong against the newly arriving Polish immigrants and there were community tensions. Later, we went for a winter to Knoxville, Tennessee. I think I was about six years old at the time. I've never been to Knoxville since. I imagine it is a very nice community, but I have only one impression of Knoxville, Tennessee, or rather, two. I relate it because it reveals how one experience of an unhealthy kind in a bad race-relations atmosphere can actually poison one's whole feeling. All I remember are these two things: First, that there were huge, delicious yams which grew in the red clay and which I liked very much. Secondly, that there was a park very close to where we lived into which I wandered one day and was promptly ordered out, because Negroes were not admitted. Whenever Knoxville has been mentioned in my presence in the intervening years, this early experience has been all that was registered in my mind about this community. This, obviously, is no healthy attitude for anyone to have. However, it is inescapable, because one's attitudes are based upon one's experiences and impressions.

Then we moved out West for my parents' health. We went to Albuquerque, New Mexico, and here again there was not much prejudice against Negroes, since they were so few in the community. There was very great feeling against Mexicans, however. As a matter of fact, one of my first direct experiences with racial prejudice was because my mother and I were probably mistaken for Mexicans. My mother took me to the Busy Bee Theater in Albuquerque in 1915. It was what we called in those days a "nickelodeon." My mother, crippled with rheumatism, took a seat in a middle row on the aisle. Very soon the usher came and tapped my mother on the shoulder and told her that he was very sorry but it was the rule of the house that Mexicans sit in the last row. My mother looked at him, and, in a most friendly way, thanked him for his kind consideration and said that the seats were quite comfortable and that she preferred to remain in them. We did remain in them, and that made quite an impression upon me as a youth.

Then we went out to Los Angeles. There we came in contact with prejudice against the Chinese and the Japanese, against the Mexican, and also against the Negro. In southern California in those days they drew no distinctions among minority groups in applying prejudice.

I recall one of my early experiences there. I had a newspaper route for one of the Los Angeles papers, and the newsboys were taken on an outing one day down to the beach, Venice or Santa Monica, as I recall. Two of us in the group were Negroes— Charles Matthews, now a prominent and highly successful attorney in Los Angeles, and myself. We had a very good time until we went to the bathhouses for the ocean bathing. There Matthews and I, because of our race, were met with refusal; we were not permitted to change. We had to sit outside the bathhouse until the other boys finished their swim. That made quite an impact upon me.

Later, I graduated from high school—Jefferson High School in Los Angeles. My high-school principal was a very fine man. I believe that although he had no prejudice he had never done much thinking about this problem. At my graduation, he came to me and said, quite sincerely, "We're sorry to see you go, Ralph. You know, we have never thought of you as a Negro."

I knew this was wrong, was incensed by it, but had not the words to express my feeling. But fortunately, my grandmother, who was a tiny woman of great spiritual strength and character, and who never lacked for words, was standing by and overheard this. Then in a very quiet way, for about five minutes, she lectured the principal of Jefferson High School, on what it means for a people to be proud of their origin and why we as Negroes were proud, were never apologetic, and that therefore, he was insulting not only her grandson, but the entire Negro race by saying that he had never thought of me as a Negro. After that, there followed what perhaps was one of the longest and most profuse apologies any grandmother ever received for any reason whatsoever.

I remember, also, at U.C.L.A., how an early stand which the Provost of the university took had so much to do with determining the policy of that school, which has ever since been one of the very best in the country on the question of race relations. This was about 1923, when a Negro student, Leon Whittaker, was the Pacific Coast intercollegiate lightweight boxing champion. In those days, Stanford had what might be called an unwritten rule about not meeting Negroes in sports which involved direct personal contact. Their boxing team came down to meet U.C.L.A.'s. The Stanford coach announced that their lightweight boxer could not meet Whittaker, since Whittaker was a Negro. The U.C.L.A. coach this time was a little weak and substituted a white boxer for Whittaker, the Pacific Coast champion.

Unfortunately for the individual, but fortunately for the cause of democracy and the cause of racial justice, the U.C.L.A. white boy got the stuffings beaten out of him by the Stanford entrant. This incited the students of U.C.L.A. no little, because that was the decisive match, and they lost it to Stanford. Consequently, bright and early the next morning they were petitioning and circulating protests against the actions of the coach in making this substitution and thereby causing U.C.L.A. to lose the match and, also, causing one of our good students to get quite beaten up.

The Provost by noon of that day had a notice on the bulletin board in which he stated the simple principle on which the university would be run, namely, that there would be complete equality for all in the university community, irrespective of race or creed, that this principle would be observed by every teacher in the university, and anyone who could not act on that basis did not belong there. Very soon the boxing coach was out. That one act set the tone for this university, and has no little to do with the fact that in subsequent years Jackie Robinson, Kenny Washington and so many other Negroes have won distinction in that institution.

I might mention that chance may often be an important factor in hurdling racial barriers—for example the chance fact that a man cannot see very well. When I graduated from U.C.L.A. and went to Cambridge to do graduate work, I was given a letter by a man who ran a bookstore near the campus addressed to a friend of his who ran a bookstore in Cambridge. The intent was that I would use this letter to get my books at a discount in Cambridge. That was all. But when I got to Cambridge, I visited the bookshop and presented the letter to the owner—an extremely nearsighted man with heavy-lensed glasses. He pored over the letter, identified his friend's signature and said to me, "Sure, I'll give you a job." I had not come for a job, but I took it. Several weeks later, after the owner's wife had come into the shop and seen me, the owner called me aside and said, "Ralph, are you a Negro?" I replied affirmatively and expressed surprise that he did not know it. Explaining that he could not see well enough to tell, he said that had he known this originally he would not have hired me, since he would have thought that it would hurt his business. He found that it did not, however, and kept me on. Thus, the fact that a man may be a little blind can sometimes carry one over a racial obstacle. It is a pity that more people are not color blind in this respect.

Then I came to Washington, D. C., the nation's capital. You can well imagine that I had many problems there. Of Washington, I could tell at great length about experiences, but I select only a few.

I have three children, my two daughters being the oldest. Washington, as you know, has separate schools. We had built a house out in Brookland in a section in which the races were mixed. There had been a number of Negro families living there for a good many years and the relations in the area were not at all tense. But there had not been enough Negroes in that section to warrant building a Negro school, so I had to send my daughters three miles to the nearest Negro school, although there was a white public school nearby. I was paying taxes just like my white neighbors.

During the war, as a government employee, I used my car in a car pool and en route to the office I was able to take my youngest daughter to her school. In my car pool I carried two of my white colleagues. Soon I noticed that though I went directly past the door of my daughter's school, which was in the middle of the block, she began to insist that I let her out on the corner which was a good hundred and fifty feet from the entrance to the school. No matter how inclement the weather might be, she asked to be let out on the corner. I knew that there was something wrong, and finally, I wormed it out of her. I found that the reason she was insisting that she be let out on the corner was because when I dropped her at the entrance to the school, other children would see the white passengers in my car, and thereupon would chide, deride and scorn her, because her father was carrying white people in his car. My wife and I knew that this was an unhealthy, unwholesome, diseased attitude for our child to have and that if she came up in this atmosphere, being quite sensitive, she might become warped as so many others have been.

I remember one occasion when my other daughter came to me with a copy of *Life*, which had in it—it was during one of the campaigns—some pictures of leading Negro politicians. She said to me quite innocently, "Daddy, I thought *Life* was a *white* magazine," assuming that a white magazine should not have pictures of Negroes in it. Because of these and similar experiences we finally sent our daughters away to school since we felt this was a very unwholesome atmosphere in which to rear them.

As I relate such experiences, I reflect on how significantly they would be regarded by Edwin Embree.*

A couple of years ago, in New York, I was invited to dinner— a very formal dinner, white tie and tails. At this dinner, I found myself seated between two ladies, one of whom was an American. At the beginning of the dinner, our host asked for a standing toast to the President of the United States, who at that time was Harry Truman. We rose, drank the toast, and as we were about to sit down the American lady whispered, or rather hissed, "I hope he chokes."

Well, that sort of startled me and I said, "Who, our host?"

"No, the President," she said.

That excited my interest and I asked, "Why, because of himself or his politics?" She said that politics had nothing to do with it. "I don't like him." She then went into an explanation, citing his humble origin, the fact that he came from nothing and had failed as a haberdasher. I pointed out that this was all in the American tradition, the log cabin, et cetera. This incensed her a bit and she look me straight in the eye and said, "You talk like some of those people who believe that Negroes ought to be equal."

This astounded me no little, as you may well imagine, because it had never occurred to me that my neighbor was unaware of my racial identification. Rather ungallantly, I led her on and encouraged a discussion of race. I cited scientific books, the biologists, the sociologists, the social anthropologists, the physical anthropologists. She listened impatiently and finally said, "Now, Mr. Bunche, I've heard all of that before and I don't believe it any more than you do. Now tell me this. You told me

* Edwin Embree, president of the Julius Rosenwald Fund, formerly secretary and then vice-president of the Rockefeller Foundation, was the author of *Brown Americans: The Story of a Tenth of the Nation*, *American Negroes* and *13 Against the Odds*.

you had two daughters. Would you wish your daughters to marry Negroes?"

I have been active in race relations most of my life and have been very seldom without words. But this question floored me. When I recovered my poise, I said, "My dear lady, I don't know what you took me for, what you thought I might be, but I couldn't possibly object to my daughters marrying Negroes, because you see, whatever you may have thought I was, I am a Negro, and therefore, my daughters are Negroes and you can understand that I could have no objection."

I thought this would startle her, but not at all. "But you're different," she said.

"Look," I said, "you've known me for about a half an hour. There are fifteen million Negroes in this country. I'm one of fifteen million and you tell me on the basis of a half-hour acquaintance, and obviously not knowing any other Negroes before, and in fact, not being able to identify them anyhow, that I'm different. Really, does this make sense?"

We bandied this about and she finally admitted that it did not make sense, and she said quite earnestly that she had never thought much about the question, did not really know much about it and would like to know more. She asked me for suggestions as to how she might learn. I told her to join the N.A.A.C.P. I told her further that it seemed to me that people who are bent on exercising prejudice ought to adhere to a minimum degree of logic, that is, that they at least ought to identify those against whom they are exercising the prejudice. She agreed.

One of the stock questions I often hear is: "How does it feel to be a Negro?" To tell the truth, I really do not know, but I have developed a pretty good stock answer to that stock question:

"I dislike and resent discrimination, segregation and humiliation in any form, and as a Negro I have experienced all of these. But on the whole I find that it feels very good indeed to be a Negro, because the Negro knows positively that he is right, and that his cause is right, and that logic and justice and decency are altogether on his side."

A far more significant question in my view is how does it feel to be an American who is *not* a Negro? How does it feel to have the Negro problem, and the Jewish, Indian, Mexican and Oriental problem, on one's mind and conscience? How must it feel to know that logic and justice and decency are against you? To be self-conscious about wrongs to one's fellow men and fellow citizens and to know that all the world is raising its eyebrows about you?

Thought of in this context, I am not at all sure that the Negro is entitled to all the pity he receives. The penalties of prejudice are assessed against those who harbor prejudice as well as those who are victimized by it.

The existence of racial prejudice, the practice of religious bigotry, whether anti-Semitism, anti-Catholicism or "anti" anything, in our midst today should be the active concern of every American who believes in our democratic way of life. Such attitudes and practices subvert the foundation principles of our society. And they are most costly and more dangerous today than ever before in our history.

Indeed, it is impossible to calculate the tremendous costs to the nation of such attitudes and their shameful manifestations. They are a seriously divisive influence among our people. They create resentments, tensions, unrest and disturbances in our communities. They deprive us of our maximum national unity at a time when our way of life and all that we stand for are gravely threatened from without. They play into the hands of our Communist enemies. They prevent us from using a substantial part of our manpower effectively, even though we are seriously short of manpower.

With regard to this problem which has bedeviled our society for too long already, we have reason, I think, for looking to the future with real hopefulness, and I do so because we Americans are a people with a conscience. We are frank with ourselves and we know that racial prejudice and religious bigotry are in violent contradiction to our cardinal beliefs. We pride ourselves on our sense of justice and fair play. Practices of prejudice and bigotry, therefore, must inevitably weigh heavily on the American conscience. They cause us to be self-conscious and defensive about the imperfections in our society and they sap our moral strength. They provide the raw material for damaging propaganda against us throughout the world by our enemies. They affect adversely our prestige and moral leadership abroad, even among our friends. At home, as well as abroad, these attitudes and practices raise doubts about the sincerity and the virility of our democracy.

These are the costs which every American pays, whatever his color, his race or his creed. They are as inescapable as taxes, and they are much more burdensome. They are the penalties of injustice. Americans of all colors in all sections of the country are beginning to realize this more acutely than ever before. And this, indeed, accounts for the fact that remarkable progress, dramatic progress, has been made in the last decade—more than in the previous seventy-five years of our history.

Our nation is a union of peoples more diversified in origin than any society in history. From our earliest beginnings, we have been diversified, racially and culturally. We have set out on a great experiment on these shores, the greatest, I believe, in the history of human society—an experiment to demonstrate that peoples of all races, colors, creeds and cultures can live and work and play together and be welded into a firm unity by the sheer force of a great and compelling ideal—the democratic way of life. We have made remarkable progress and have had remarkable success with that experiment. This is, in fact, the true source of our unparalleled national growth and strength.

I believe that differences in race, in religion and in culture enrich the society. Surely there is nothing so inspired or inspiring as men and women of all races and religions working together as free men in a common cause and with common interests, ideals and objectives.

In concluding, may I say that the ideal of men and women living together in peace and brotherhood is the noblest ideal of human history. It is the Christian ideal, indeed it is the ideal of all the great religions. It is the ideal also which the United Nations has embraced. In view of the instruments of destruction which man's inventive genius now makes available to war, the ability of mankind to approach this ideal in the realm of day to day human relationships has become the decisive challenge of all time.

This challenge can be met only if each of us is willing, in mind and heart, to accord to our fellow men, of whatever race or creed, that respect and good will to which every human being is entitled. We are in an age in which the price of survival is the earnest application of the spirit of human brotherhood.

THE CONSPIRACY TO DENY EQUALITY

By Roy Wilkins

On May 17, 1954, the Supreme Court, in the landmark decision Brown v. *Board of Education, declared: "We conclude that in the field of public education the doctrine of 'separate but equal' has no place. Separate educational facilities are inherently unequal." In overruling the* Plessy v. *Ferguson decision of 1896, which had established the "sep-*

arate but equal" doctrine as Constitutional, the Supreme Court opened a new era in the legal struggle for Negro equality. When the N.A.A.C.P., which had led the legal fight that produced the 1954 decision, met at its forty-sixth annual convention in 1955, Roy Wilkins, Executive Secretary, delivered a speech in which he both hailed the significance of the Supreme Court's action and reminded the delegates that there was no room for complacency. Already the foes of Negro equality were organizing to resist the 1954 decision and renewed efforts and struggles were necessary to prevent them from achieving their goals. Wilkins' warning against complacency was to be borne out by events, for ten years after the 1954 decision the Constitutional declaration against school segregation was still only a paper right in many parts of the country. Only 2.14 percent of the nearly three million Negroes in Southern schools were receiving anything approaching a desegregated education. Many communities of the North, by de facto school segregation resulting from residential patterns, the organized efforts by white citizens to block measures designed to promote desegregation, the flight to the suburbs of middle-class white families, and the transfer to parochial and other nonpublic schools of white children in cities, effectively avoided integration of their public schools.

Roy Wilkins was born August 30, 1901, in St. Louis, Missouri, and received his education in St. Paul and at the University of Minnesota, where he majored in journalism and sociology. From 1923 to 1931 he was managing editor of the Kansas City Call, a Negro weekly. In 1930, after a vigorous campaign against an anti-Negro United States Senator from Kansas, he was appointed to the N.A.A.C.P. staff. In 1931 he became assistant secretary of the Association and after 1934 served as editor of The Crisis, the official organ of the organization. In 1955 he replaced Walter White as executive secretary.

Wilkins' address to the 1955 convention is taken from his The Conspiracy to Deny Equality, National Association for the Advancement of Colored People, August, 1955. It is reprinted here with permission of the author.

LAST YEAR at Dallas we had a celebration. The convention theme was victory, for we had just had the pronouncement of the United States Supreme Court that segregation in the public schools was unconstitutional.

Most of us knew that the victory was sweet, not because it immediately desegregated the Jim Crow schools, but because it gave us the prize we had been seeking for fifty-eight years: the declaration by the nation's highest court that such segregation was now unlawful. Hitherto, we had had the moral conviction that these schools were wrong and contrary to the guarantees of American citizenship; we had had outrage and frustration as our companions while we went up and down the land seeking recruits to our army of moral and spiritual devotees.

But we had not had the law. We had no means of enforcing our moral convictions except through preachment and persuasion. We secured converts, but they—and we—were helpless without the law. On May 17, 1954, we got the law. On May 31, 1955, we got the decree as to how the law would have to be carried out.*

With the May 31 opinion, it has become apparent that we have entered a new era, an era where racial discrimination and segregation are to be not merely morally wrong, but contrary to the law and the Constitution. A description of this era has been given by an editorial writer for the Charlotte, N. C., *News*, in its issue of June 1, 1955. Under the heading, "End of An Era," its opening paragraph states:

The stark, elementary realities of the Supreme Court decision on segregation in the public schools can be avoided no longer. Racial barriers which have existed for generations must be dissolved. A massive change . . . is about to take place.

I should like to borrow this for my general theme. We have come to the end of an era and the beginning of a new one. Our great Association, which has carried the fight thus far, is faced with new challenges, new responsibilities, new and more pressing calls to duty, to devotion, intelligence and skill. Each and every officer and member, wherever he may be, shares the heavy burden of the transition. None may shirk his duty, for that would be to betray the ones who come after. Let no one in tomorrow's world be able to say that in the years of decision, when destiny was in our hands, we failed to measure up. The people of 1903 had no such challenge and opportunity; nor did those of 1923, or 1943. This great day is ours. Upon us depend the speed, the order and the completeness of the victory.

We have emerged from more than a half-century of the doctrine of "separate but equal" set forth in the now-famous *Plessy*

---

* On May 31, 1955, the Supreme Court ruled that states must end racial segregation in public schools in "reasonable" time.

v. *Ferguson* case of 1896.* We Negroes always knew the Plessy doctrine to be wrong and we fervently believed it to be unconstitutional. But it was not until our attorneys carried to the highest court the challenge to its legality that we finally shook off the shackles that had hobbled our progress since the turn of the century.

What did the Plessy era hold for us? To what kind of life were we committed by it? Discrimination and segregation were our lot. In his great dissenting opinion in the Plessy case, Mr. Justice Harlan said the result would be "mischievous." At another point he used the word "pernicious." He spoke also of state enactments regulating the enjoyment of civil rights as being "cunningly devised" to defeat the legitimate results of the Civil War.

It is pertinent to quote some of his words because they were so prophetically true, because they described so accurately, that day in 1896, what we as a group were destined to suffer for more than fifty years. Said Mr. Justice Harlan:

In my opinion, the judgment this day rendered will, indeed, prove to be quite as pernicious as the decision made by this tribunal in the Dred Scott case. . . .

I am of the opinion that the statute of Louisiana is inconsistent with the personal liberty of citizens, white and black, in that state and hostile to both the spirit and letter of the Constitution of the United States. If laws of like character should be enacted in the several states of the Union, the effect would be in the highest degree mischievous. Slavery as an institution tolerated by law would, it is true, have disappeared from our country, but there would remain a power in the states, by sinister legislation, to interfere with the full enjoyment of the blessings of freedom; to regulate civil rights

---

* The *Plessy v. Ferguson* case dealt with a Louisiana law which required the separation of the races in railroad cars. Plessy, who was one-eighth Negro, refused to sit in a car set aside for Negroes. He was convicted of violating the Lousiana law, and the case was appealed to the Supreme Court. The court, in an 8 to 1 decision, upheld the Louisiana law, ruling that "legislation is powerless to eradicate racial instincts," and that racial segregation was not a violation of the Fourteenth Amendment if the facilities were equal. In a dissenting opinion, Justice John Marshall Harlan predicted that the majority decision would open the door to all forms of discrimination against Negroes, a prediction all too soon to come true. But the facilities provided for Negroes were never "equal" though always "separate." In 1954, the year that the Supreme Court held that racial segregation was unconstitutional, the state of Mississippi was spending $98.15 yer year for each white pupil and $43.14 for each Negro pupil.

common to all citizens, upon the basis of race; and to place in a condition of legal inferiority a large body of American citizens . . .

Mark well that last phrase—"to place in a condition of legal inferiority a large body of American citizens."

For us it was all this and more. We have been subject to the whims and fancies of white persons, individually and collectively. We went to back doors and were forced to live in hollows and alleys and back streets. We stepped off sidewalks and removed our hats and said "Sir" to all and sundry, if they were white. If schools were provided, our children went to shanties and whites to schools. We rode in the rear seats of buses and trolleys and in the dirty, dangerous front-end coaches of the trains. We could not vote. Our health and our recreation were of little or no concern to the responsible officials of government. In time of war we were called to serve, but were insulted, degraded and mistreated even as we fought to defend the flag that flew over every American. We were beaten, shot, lynched and burned, and no man was punished for what he did to us.

Slowly in this fifty-eight years, we have lifted ourselves by our own bootstraps. Step by halting step, we have beaten our way back. It has been a long and tortuous road since the Dred Scott decision of 1857, which branded us as noncitizens and which, by the Plessy decision, gave the states and the nation as a whole the green light to treat us as they pleased.

But we are here, through the grace of God, through our refusal to quit, through the strength and skill of our own right arms, and through the burning spirit from father to son, from mother to daughter, that persisted in hope and prayer to the precious goal of freedom.

We need only recall, not recount the victories along the way. We wiped out lynching. We knocked out the strongest barriers to voting, as well as the widely used restrictive covenants on housing. We have clothed our fighting men with dignity. Travel is no longer an ordeal of both the body and the spirit. The courts, in the South as well as in the North, are becoming places where color-blind justice is dispensed. Our men and women are working at more and better jobs and at better and better wages.

Now our children, at long last, are to have equality in education. They are to have a chance in the race of life without being penalized before they are born.

Truly, we are at the beginning of a new era. But just as the old order did not pass without prayer and struggle and sacrifice even unto death—so the new order will not come into being unless we accomplish it by our own efforts. This is the beginning, not the end. This is a time for action, not for resting. Some have complained that they thought May 17 settled everything and that now they could retire and enjoy. Freedom never came to any people in that fashion.

We cannot be complacent as we see before our eyes the outlines of a conspiracy to deny, in 1955, the equality we have won for ourselves. For this school decision heralds the death of all inequality in citizenship based upon race. The Richmond, Virginia, editor, Virginius Dabney, correctly stated in 1953 that public-school segregation was the keystone in the arch of segregation. It has been knocked out and the arch will fall.

The conspirators know this, hence the desperation of their tactics. To us who have known the refined as well as the brutal methods of persecution, the emerging pattern is not new.

First they are organizing. Here and there, dotting the South, organizations have sprung up overnight, some with fancy names like Virginia's Defenders of State Sovereignty and Individual Liberty and others like the White Citizens' Councils in Mississippi,* which frankly declare their anti-Negro purpose.

Terror and intimidation are the weapons being used. The Mississippi Councils—now spreading to Alabama—seek to freeze Negroes economically and frighten them bodily.

"We intend," said one organizer, "to see that no Negro who believes in equality has a job, gets credit, or is able to exist in our communities."

"Is able to exist"—that means agree and knuckle under, or flee, or die.

It is not strange that in such an atmosphere, Rev. George W. Lee was murdered by a shotgun blast on May 7 in his home town of Belzoni, Mississippi. The Reverend Mr. Lee's "crime" was that he was the first Negro to register to vote in his county, and he had refused orders from whites to remove his name from the voting list. The state headquarters of the White Citizens' Councils is a scant sixty miles from Belzoni, in Winona.

But naked terror alone will not do the job. Even murder will not guarantee victory to the conspirators.

* In the fall of 1955, racists in Mississippi organized White Citizens' Councils. These Councils aimed to maintain a segregated school system and otherwise restrict the rights of Negroes. Soon the Councils spread across the South. Their chief weapon was economic pressure. Negroes (and whites) suspected of favoring integration lost their jobs and, if they were sharecroppers, were thrown off the land, were denied credit and were refused services in shops and stores.

They have a well-oiled system, rooted in politics, by which they hope to stave off defeat. All these years the system has worked. Today they are trying to use it still.

At the local and state levels they have enforced disfranchisement of Negroes, which in turn has permitted the election of local and state officers wholly indifferent to the plight, wishes and demands of our citizens. No better illustration of the effectiveness of this technique at this level can be found than the actions of the South Carolina, Georgia, Louisiana and Mississippi legislators during the past year in passing legislation frankly and brazenly labeled as efforts to deny the Negro equality and to prevent him from voting.

This same disfranchisement has permitted the election of Congressmen and Senators to Washington who are pledged to block any executive or legislative moves which recognize the needs of Negroes as citizens. These Southern Congressmen and Senators have used their committee posts to smother legislation and, in the Senate, the filibuster to kill legislation.

While hamstringing Presidents and choking off legislation they have not had as much success in hampering the courts, although they have done their best through their power to confirm judicial appointees. With but few exceptions they are now in full cry against the courts and especially the Supreme Court. If they had a ghost of a chance they would emulate South Africa in making Supreme Court decrees subject to ratification by the Congress.

Thus we have had a two-pronged political operation, one prong bottling up the Negro vote in the South at the ballot box level, and the other nullifying the Negro vote in the North by the use of blackjack tactics in both Houses of the Congress.

This system has worked through the decades whether a Democratic or Republican President has been in office. The only Chief Executive to buck it was Harry S Truman, who split his party rather than keep silent on his recommendations as to civil rights for Negro Americans.*

* In December, 1946, President Harry S Truman issued Executive Order 9808, in which he established the President's Committee on Civil Rights. Truman incorporated the basic recommendations of the Committee in his special message on February 2, 1948, but Congress refused to act. Again, in July, 1948, Truman established the President's Committee of Equality of Treatment and Opportunity in the Armed Services, which led eventually to the abolition of segregation in the armed forces. On July 17, 1948, the so-called Dixiecrats, Southern Democrats who opposed President Truman's renomination because of his stand against segregation, met in Birmingham, Alabama, formed the States' Rights Democratic

The system has been aided by Northern Democrats who seek "party unity" as they play poker politics with the civil rights of Negroes as the joker card.

The system is aided also by the Republicans, who seek support for their program and who also continue to hope that they will be able to build a permanent party structure in the South. It might be added here that if they continue to talk like Dixiecrats, act like Dixiecrats, and vote like Dixiecrats, they will not have to infiltrate the South; it will have taken them over.

One of our principal objectives as an Association is the smashing of this iniquitous network of political strangulation, which has its base in the choking off of Negro citizenship rights at the precinct or county level through denial of the ballot. During the past year we have stimulated increased registration by Negro citizens in many Southern states. Intensive campaigns have been underway in Virginia, Alabama, North Carolina and South Carolina. We expect to increase this activity in these and other states between now and the 1956 election.

Along with the effort to broaden the voting base in the South will go a campaign to use the Northern Negro's voting strength to break the hold of the Dixiecrat system. Northern Democratic officeholders may continue to receive Negro votes on the basis of their individual records, and many, like Senator Herbert Lehman of New York, have most excellent records. But increasingly, Negro voters—as far as the Democratic party is concerned—are demanding less unity with the system that disfranchises, insults, terrorizes, and generally creates an atmosphere in which violence can flourish. They want no unity with the White Councils of Mississippi; no unity with areas that murder men as the Reverend Mr. Lee was murdered, for wanting to vote; no unity with the forces of slander, as exemplified by a nationwide radio talk of Senator Allen J. Ellender of Louisiana branding Negroes as ignorant, diseased and crime-ridden; no unity with those who defy the law of the land as laid down by the Supreme Court, as exemplified by the recent television broadcast of Senator James O. Eastland of Mississippi.

On the other hand, the Republicans, who hope and hope, cannot expect substantial support as long as they "play footsie" with Southern Democrats on civil rights. They wonder why the Negro vote does not return to the G.O.P. fold. Well, thousands want to return because they are not comfortable in the party of Herman Talmadge, but they cannot see any percentage in

---

party and nominated Governor J. Strom Thurmond of South Carolina for President.

changing as long as the Republicans play ball with the Dixie-crats.

These conspirators about whom I have been talking—the conscious as well as the unconscious ones—went so far as to enlist the prestige of the White House in their demands to maintain segregation and circumvent the national policy of no discrimination in the armed services. On June 8 the President in his press conference lashed out at those who seek anti-segregation amendments to pending legislation including the military reserves bill.*

We who seek such amendments were accused of placing our special desires above the security of the nation. We want to say here plainly and unmistakably that it is not we who seek our own way at the expense of the country. It is the Southern Democratic bloc, which openly threatened to kill the military-reserves bill unless it contained their provision for segregation. The President has every right to demand the legislation he deems necessary for the welfare of the nation, but in all fairness the blame for the delay on that legislation should be placed at the doorstep of those who are guilty.

We love our country. We have fought for it in the past and we will fight for it in the future, but we do not relish our patriotism being called into question because we demand our rights as American citizens.

We feel the same way about the antisegregation amendment to the housing bill and to the bill which would provide aid to the states for the construction of public schools. We do not believe that housing which is provided out of the funds or the credit of all the people of the United States should be denied to any citizen because of his race or color. We do not believe that the tax funds of all the people of the United States should be given to any state or locality for the purpose of subsidizing these in defying the Supreme Court ruling on segregated schools.

Our legislative goals, of course, are not limited to amendments to pending bills. Although the President expressed the opinion in 1953 that the states should pass fair-employment-practice bills, only the states with Democratic administrations have so far complied, the latest being Minnesota and Michigan. Two state governments of the President's own party—Illinois

---

* At his press conference on June 8, 1955, President Eisenhower came out against attaching riders to legislation to achieve indirectly what might not be achieved directly. It was an attack upon the attempt of Congressman Adam Clayton Powell, Jr., to attach to the military reserves bill a rider outlawing segregation in schools and public housing.

and Pennsylvania—have defeated F.E.P.C. Neither the 83rd nor the 84th Congress has done anything on F.E.P.C., nor has the President made any recommendation on this or any other civil-rights bill.

Our Department of Justice will remain almost impotent in prosecuting civil-rights crimes, such as the murders of Mr. and Mrs. Harry T. Moore of Florida,* and the Reverend Mr. Lee of Mississippi, until Congress passes a bill to strengthen the civil-rights laws.

These and other bills to make secure the rights of all our citizens form the continuing objective of our members, who will make their likes and dislikes known in the polling booths.

Yes, in fashioning the new era we shall use all the weapons at our disposal. Thurgood Marshall, our general counsel, has outlined how we will use the courts. We shall continue to use education and persuasion and moral pressure. Heartened by the support of millions of our white fellow citizens in all sections of the country, we welcome their participation in the crusade, which is one not alone for us, but for our nation as a whole. And we shall use all the political power we can muster, for this is the most vital ingredient in a government of, by and for the people, not the white people, but all the people.

As the new era dawns there are those who say "it shall never be." The Richmond, Virginia, *News Leader*, a long-established and apparently responsible journal, declared in an angry editorial after the May 31 opinion:

When the court proposes that its social revolution be imposed upon the South "as soon as practicable" there are those of us who would respond that "as soon as practicable" means never at all.

But my friends, the Richmond paper and others like it say "never" like the Romans before the coming of Christ; like King John before Magna Charta; like the emperors of France before 1789; like George III of England before the Declaration of Independence; like the Southern plantation owners before the Civil War.

We know them. How we know them! They are wicked, and wickedness shall not prevail, though for a time it shall spread itself like the green bay tree.

The time of the wicked is fast approaching. We shall never return to bondage, with or without shackles. We shall heed the word of God as set forth in Leviticus 26:13:

* On Christmas night, 1951, Harry T. Moore and his wife were killed by a bomb placed beneath their Florida home. Both had been leaders in the

I am the Lord your God which brought you forth out of the land of Egypt, that you should not be their bondsmen; and I have broken the bands of your yoke, and made you go upright.

We shall go upright. We shall go in faith, without hatred of any man, but with determination in the righteousness of our cause, armed with the weapons provided for us. We shall not— we cannot—fail. We shall, we will, be free men.

THE NEGRO PEOPLE ON THE MARCH

By Benjamin J. Davis

Benjamin J. Davis, former New York City Councilman and chairman of the Negro Commission of the Communist party, delivered one of the leading speeches at a meeting of the party's National Committee in New York City on June 23–24, 1956. Below is a portion of the speech dealing with "Recent Gains of the Negro People."

Davis was born in Dawson, Georgia. He attended public schools in Atlanta, but had to quit because provision for public education for Negroes ended at the sixth grade. He attended Morehouse College (the equivalent of high school), then graduated from Amherst College and Harvard Law School. He joined the International Labor Defense as a lawyer for Angelo Herndon, and the celebrated case of the young Negro victim of Georgia's slave law was the turning point of his life, for he joined the Communist party. Davis went on to join the famous legal and mass defense of the nine Scottsboro boys, to defend the Atlanta Six, who faced a conspiracy charge similar to Herndon's, and to help edit the Southern Worker, *a Communist publication. Later, he came to New York to edit the* Negro Liberator *and joined the editorial board of the* Daily Worker. *In 1943 he was elected as the Communist candidate to the New York City Council and was reelected two years later. One of his achievements while councilman was the fight he led to end Jim Crow in baseball. It was Davis who made possible the official City Hall proclamation of Negro His-*

drive of the state N.A.A.C.P. to register more Negroes to vote. Those guilty of the crime have never been brought to justice.

*tory Week. Indicted under the Smith Act, he was impris-
oned for five years for his belief in Communism. After his
release from prison he returned to work in the Communist
party until his death in 1962.
Davis' 1956 National Committee speech, presented here
in part, is taken from the pamphlet by him,* The Negro
People on the March, *New York, 1956, pp. 23–28.*

. . . CHARACTERISTIC OF the Negro people's movement
today is that it is demanding more and more. While every small
gain encourages the Negro people, it only whets their appetites
and demands for more, for their full, unconditional equality and
human dignity now. This is not only correct, but our party
should welcome and encourage it, for it has contributed to these
growing aspirations of the Negro. The great virtue of this movement is that the Negroes are moving as a people from top to
bottom, despite the many currents within it. Communists and
other left forces should work in the Negro people's movement,
not through claiming any superiority of ideology, but modestly
by the performance of the most simple concrete tasks in a most
principled, efficient and loyal manner. Our party in many states
has begun in recent months to make important contributions
to the mass struggle for Negro rights, strengthening its ties with
broader labor and people's organizations. . . .

Over the last six years the Negro people and their white supporters have won a number of important and significant gains
in their battle against Jim Crow. These gains are an extension
of those begun during the Roosevelt New Deal and World War
II periods. A precise and detailed examination of these gains
is still to be made, but their pattern is somewhat apparent. They
touch virtually every field of American life; they are uneven
and too often merely token.

Among the most dramatic are the integration of the armed
forces; the federal court decisions against school segregation
and bus transportation; the elections and appointment of Negroes to previous lily-white offices, et cetera. They extend to
jobs, health and nursing facilities, to sports and culture, trade-
unions, increase of Negroes in state and federal government
agencies and branches, and to the South. A twenty-seven-year-
old young American Negro* is today one of the greatest tennis
players in the world, if not the greatest. Lynchings have decreased, and the lynch class has been compelled to change its

* Althea Gibson was the black woman tennis champion, who won several
international tournaments in the 1950's.

tactics. There are only five states in the Deep South with the poll tax—Alabama, Arkansas, Virginia, Mississippi and Texas. Important victories have been won against the white primaries in the South, increasing the Negroes' voting strength.

The least gains, in my opinion, have been made in the field of housing, where the ghettos of the Northern urban centers still exist, and have even become more stiflingly dense, reflecting the mass migration of the Negroes to the North. Nearly every effort on the part of the Negro people is met by bomb violence, inspired by the realty lords. Although restrictive covenants cannot be enforced in the courts, they have not been outlawed. Today they are enforced by force and violence.

Breaking into new industries and upgrading for Negro workers is very spotty. Negroes have made little or no progress in the skilled trades. They are still predominantly in the heaviest, dirtiest and most dangerous jobs with the lowest wages. There has been an absolute improvement in the Negro family's economic position, and this is extremely important, even though within the framework of job Jim Crow. But relative to the white workers there's been little narrowing the gap and in some areas it has gotten wider. This is especially true in the Deep South. There, the Negro sharecroppers, farmers and agricultural workers live on a subhuman wage which must be improved while they're on the farms. An estimated five million Negroes are still in the rural farm areas, and they are the most forgotten men of the boasted American high living standards. The advancement of Negro women from domestic service is three times less than white women.

The civil-rights gains have amounted largely to a relaxation of only the rawest forms of racist persecution of the Negro people. But they are of important significance. While the economic ones are important they have been made within the framework of the basic Jim Crow system still existing against the Negro people. The Negroes of the United States are still an oppressed people, and the area of their most brutal oppression is still the Southern Black Belt. The Till murder,* the Autherine Lucy case,† the legal whitewash of the lynchers show how unbearable that oppression is—and so does the bus boy-

---

* In the summer of 1955, fourteen-year-old Emmett Till was kidnaped and lynched at Money, Mississippi, for allegedly whistling at a white storekeeper's wife.
† Autherine Lucy, a Negro applicant to the University of Alabama, entered the university early in 1956 by court order. But she was met with violence and was expelled by the university officials.

cott, which was provoked by the unendurable brutality toward Negro passengers.

These gains were the result of the struggles of the Negro people themselves, supported by their white labor and progressive allies on a nationwide scale. They were powerfully influenced by world socialist and other democratic pressures, led by the Soviet Union, China and the colonial struggles in Asia and Africa. They were assisted by the influence of the neutralist countries led by India. They were helped by the early pioneering, the present existence and self-sacrificing contributions of our party.

Other American pressures had effect. In the first place the existence of a fifteen-billion-dollar market among the Negro people—a market larger than that of Canada and Latin America combined. The Wall Street monopolists are compelled to utilize and enhance this market, faced as they are by the shrinkage in their world markets and by competition from the Soviet Union and the world socialist system. Secondly, the monopolists need to exploit more fully the Negro potential, driving it into certain utilizable contradictions with the backward plantation economy in the South. A study financed by several Wall Street corporations advocates that Negroes and whites live and mingle together from childhood. Certain Northern-owned and new industries in the Deep South, like the Montgomery bus company, have offered to end segregation on the bus in order to guarantee its operational profits. In certain Northern-owned plants, where unions exist, there has been integration in the heart of the South. Such coincidences of interests between the Negro people and specific industrial interests can and should be utilized, no matter how temporary.

The reforms in the armed forces during the Korean war showed a combination of at least four factors. Under fire from the Asian colonial and socialist-led peoples, the government could not appear as a defender of democracy with a Jim Crow army as its ambassador in the Far East. Secondly, integration increased the efficiency and fighting potential of the Army, which we always advocated. Thirdly, the Negro people pointedly struggled against Jim Crow in the armed forces, conscious of the gap between actual democracy and United States imperialist pretensions in the war. Fourthly, the numerous brutalities and injustices against Negro soldiers in the Far East, resulting in brutal courts-martial, death sentences and filling the federal prisons. Our party was among the first to raise sharply the Jim Crow injustices against Negro troops in the Korean war. The positive effects of integrating Negroes and whites together in the armed forces will ultimately be far-reaching and especially in the South. This was a blow against the white-supremacist neurosis against social equality.

The handed-down character of these concessions, beginning with the Bourbon-led armed forces, revealed at once its design to allay international pressure—one of the most powerful allies of Negro liberation. But we should not underestimate the specific American pressures for these reforms, nor fail to use all internal contradictions of American society and policy to maintain and extend them.

The very fact that these gains were extended through the executive and judicial branches of the federal government and not through the legislative is of particular significance. The United States monopolists were speedily trying to mobilize allies for a projected atomic war on the socialist countries; this had to be done quickly and with the least basic uprooting of the national oppression of the Negro.

To have utilized the Congress would have required defeating the Dixiecrats, breaking up the Dixiecrat-Republican alliance and enfranchising ten million Negroes and whites in the South. But this makes the Congressional elections and the pending civil-rights legislation in Congress a thousand times more important. Nor should the contradictions between the various branches of the federal government escape exploitation.

The basic significance of these gains is that they relieve in some small way some of the most humiliating and spectacular practices of Jim Crow brutality against the Negro people. Moreover, they have unleashed a flood of democratic currents designed to undermine the whole Jim Crow system. Secondly, they radically improve the conditions and atmosphere for the Negro people and their white allies to pursue with all vigor the struggle for full Negro liberation. They help to multiply the allies of the Negro people among millions of even prejudiced whites. The Supreme Court decision in the school cases outlawed in principle the whole legal basis of segregation, undermined the whole myth of white supremacy even though it set the stage for another big betrayal by its dillydallying with enforcement and implementation of the decision. In enforcing the decree, it's the old story of leaving the cat to watch the milk. . . .

These gains must be maintained and extended. The whole rotten system of Jim Crow segregation and white-chauvinist persecution must be destroyed. Nothing less will satisfy the Negro's vital interests nor the needs of American democracy. . . .

AMERICA'S WINDOW TO THE WORLD: HER RACE PROBLEM

By John Hope Franklin

To most black Americans the role the United States assumed as leader of the free world in upholding the principles of liberty and equality smacked of hypocrisy, since racism still prevailed in this country and Negroes still faced discrimination in nearly all phases of American life. The fact that chronic racism made absurd the whole posture of the United States in world affairs and was the major drawback in its influence abroad was effectively presented in a speech by John Hope Franklin, the distinguished black historian, delivered at the presentation of the J. J. Hoey Awards by the Catholic Interracial Council of New York, October 26, 1956.

Born in Oklahoma in 1915, John Hope Franklin was graduated from Fisk University in 1935. He received his doctorate from Harvard University in 1951. Professor Franklin has been a member of the history faculties at Fisk and Howard universities, and Chairman of the Department of History at Brooklyn College. At present he is Chairman of the History Department at the University of Chicago. Among his published works are From Slavery to Freedom: A History of Negro Americans, The Emancipation Proclamation, *and* Reconstruction After the Civil War.

Here is the major portion of Professor Franklin's speech, excerpted from the text in Roy L. Hill, editor, Rhetoric of Racial Revolt, *Denver, 1964, pp. 202–10.*

. . . THERE WAS a time when we in the United States could make a sharp distinction between those problems and policies having to do with our foreign relations and those having to do with our domestic relations. That distinction was always more apparent than real. Now it can hardly be said to exist at all. The contraction of the world that has come with the transportation and communication revolution and the worldwide drive toward political, social and economic democracy have certainly reduced any apparent distinctions between foreign and domestic problems. I believe, too, that there has been an increasing recognition on the part of the countries of the world

of the ramifications and implications of the most intimate domestic problems and their inevitable involvement, under certain
conditions, with the most delicate and difficult problems in foreign affairs. Thus, an American delegate to the current General
Assembly to the United Nations can argue before an Assembly
Committee that when any nation violates the human-rights
pledges of the Charter its violation is "a matter of concern to
all of us."

This comment was in connection with the question of
whether or not apartheid in South Africa was the business of
the United Nations or any of its members other than the Union
of South Africa. Twelve years ago, when a group of American
Negroes called the attention of the United Nations to some of
the more sordid aspects of the American race problem in a
document called "An Appeal to the World,"* the effort was almost universally condemned here as a deliberate attempt to
embarrass the United States by holding up to ridicule a problem
that was peculiarly and exclusively domestic. It may be seriously doubted that the people of the United States would relish
such a discussion of the American race problem any more today than they did twelve years ago. The likelihood is, however,
that today they would argue that national governmental policy
here looks toward the elimination of race distinctions, whereas
it is the governmental policy of South Africa to maintain and,
perhaps, to increase the race distinctions written into the law
of the country. In other words, we want other countries to stay
out of our so-called domestic affairs, but today we do not say
that it is none of their business, but that we are doing all right
and do not need their intervention.

This is a clear acknowledgment, it would seem, of the indi-
visibility of domestic and foreign problems. If additional proof
is needed it can be seen in the interest of other countries in the
problem of race relations in the United States and their reaction to it. Whether we like it or not, many peoples of the world
study race relations in the United States not merely because of
their interest in the advancement of interracial justice but also
to discover, if they can, the good faith or lack of it on the part
of the United States in its relations with other countries. They
are convinced that they can get a *better* understanding of the
position of the United States on a vital matter by examining the
status of race relations than by reading a lengthy and learned
pronouncement. While they are not altogether correct in this

* In 1947 the N.A.A.C.P. presented this document to the United Nations.
It was edited by W. E. B. Du Bois.

conviction it is nevertheless a firm one with many peoples in other parts of the world. Thus they continue to peer through the window of race relations that gives a remarkable picture of American life to the world.

For four weeks during August and September I had the privilege of lecturing at the Seminar in American Studies in Salzburg, Austria. The general theme for that session of the Seminar was "Races and Minorities in American Life." The interest of the fifty-five Europeans from fifteen countries was high, and I am told that many more wanted to come but could not be accommodated. I would suppose that the interest was high for the reason that Europeans, as peoples elsewhere, seek in American race relations some index to the policy of this country in its relations with peoples everywhere. As one of them put it to me, "As your country grows in military and industrial strength its every move takes on increasing importance. As she strides across the world, the great colossus she is, we wonder how we, as ordinary individuals, will be affected. Thus, how the least of her own citizens gets along becomes terribly important to us."

It should be added that these Europeans did not come to Salzburg to criticize race relations in the United States. They had, of course, the kind of critical interest that intelligent people have in any problem, but there were no acrimonious or bitter condemnations of American practices. They had many questions that they asked frankly because they honestly wanted answers and because they flattered us by believing that we from the United States would give them honest answers. They were there primarily to learn, and they welcomed our descriptions and analyses of the problem. We talked about the history of the problem, with its numerous economic, sociological and psychological ramifications. We talked about its constitutional, legal and political aspects. We were not defending but explaining, not rationalizing or justifying but describing and analyzing. In this spirit of candor and of pursuing the truth we were able to examine the problem in an atmosphere of calm and good will. In these exchanges we learned as much about ourselves and our problems as Europeans learned about us and our problems. We learned, among many other things, how the problem of race in the United States serves as one of the most important windows through which the world looks in upon us and studies our national character and conscience.

The questions that Europeans asked revealed their deep concern about how the United States was using its enormous power to further the cause of human relations. A Norwegian asked, "Is the difference between the race problem of South Carolina and the race problem of South Africa one merely of degree, if indeed there is a difference?" It was not a complete and satisfactory answer to indicate to the Norwegian that he was comparing the policy of a sovereign power with the policy of a mere state within the United States. Nor was it satisfactory to suggest that the Union of South Africa had a policy of apartheid and white supremacy, whereas its counterpart here, the federal government, had no such policy. At that point a French participant intervened with this observation. "You have big government in Washington that is growing more powerful all the time. Your government builds houses, finances highway construction, produces and sells electricity. It is difficult for me to accept any argument based on federalism and states' rights. It appears to the outsider that federalism stands in the way of nothing that the national government actually wants to do; but it is always used as an excuse for the national government's not protecting the rights of Negroes."

I indicated that federal intervention to protect the rights of Negroes was not unheard of or unthinkable. I reminded my friends that federal troops were called out last year when law and order broke down in Little Rock.* Then, displaying a remarkable fund of information about developments here, they reminded me that the calling out of troops came *after* law and order broke down, *after* the Negro children had been barred from Central High School, and *after* federal authority had been flagrantly and brazenly flouted. These were the facts in the case and, even if one wanted to do so, it would have been folly not to have faced them. Close on the heels of this clear embarrassment was an even more difficult question raised by a member of the Seminar from Yugoslavia. "It is all very strange to me," he began. "The leader of the free world can dispatch at a moment's notice thousands of troops to Lebanon to prevent the overthrow of the government there.† Yet, it has great difficulty

---

* When Arkansas Governor Orval Faubus ordered National Guard units to Central High School to prevent desegregation, on September 3, 1957, Little Rock became a national and even international issue. Three weeks later President Dwight D. Eisenhower authorized the use of federal troops to enforce desegregation of the Little Rock School. Soldiers stood on the high-school steps to escort nine Negro children to their classes and protect them on their way to and from school.

† On July 15, 1958, a vast American armada of ships and planes appeared off the port of Beirut, Lebanon, and landed several thousand Marines. More were landed in the following days. The action was taken because of the sudden collapse of the Government of Iraq, headed by President Camille Chamoun; the United States intervened to prevent a

POST-WORLD WAR II: 1945-1963

in protecting the Constitutional rights of eight or nine Negro
children who seek an education. When troops were reluctantly
and finally dispatched to Little Rock, the howls of objection and
resentment could be heard around the world. Why this willingness, even anxiety, of Americans to send troops to protect the
rights of peoples in remote places and, at the same time, this
loathing to use force to protect the rights of its own citizens?"
It was a question worth thinking about and one to which there
was no ready answer.

There were numerous other questions and much discussion
of the problems related to race relations in America. The total
experience impressed one with the fact that the interest in
America is enormous and that the answers that peoples obtain
to the questions in their minds on this problem will greatly
determine the conclusions they draw about the policies of the
United States in many areas. At times one gets the impression
that most attitudes toward the United States are tentative, pending the manner in which this problem is solved. Until that time
they will watch and scrutinize with the greatest care every
development in this area.

Even the local newspaper in a city no larger than Salzburg
bore testimony to this point of view. Despite the fact that the
Middle East crisis had not subsided and there were several other
incidents in international relations in which the United States
had a role, the paper's main attention was focused on race relations in the United States. To be sure, the situation was unusually tense, with some schools closing and the future course
of action of several states quite uncertain. Even so, one had to
marvel at the attention and space devoted to race relations in
the United States by a paper of limited circulation in a moder-
ate-sized city in Central Europe. For more than a week there
were front-page articles touching on some aspect of the race
problem in the United States. Today it would be an article on
the special session of the Supreme Court to make a ruling in
the Little Rock school controversy. Tomorrow it would be an
article on the possibility of Alabama's Governor Folsom com-
muting the death sentence of the illiterate Negro Jimmy Wilson
to life imprisonment. The following day it would be a piece
on the anti-integration laws passed by the special session of the
Arkansas legislature, and so on, through the days and weeks.
My friends at the Seminar told me that it was the same at their

revolutionary upheaval which might have endangered American interests
in the country and threatened the anti-Soviet Baghdad Pact.

homes; and frequently they showed me the papers from Holland, France, England or Italy to illustrate their assertions.

The kind of interest manifested by these and numerous other groups in the problem of race in the United States should be instructive to us. It tells us a great deal about the significance of this problem and what it means to people looking in our window. It is not too much to say that the significance does not lie in their humanitarian concern for the welfare of seventeen million Negroes in the United States despite the fact that the concern is doubtless very great. Nor does the significance lie in an objective interest in a very complex social problem, despite the fact that the interest is very great indeed. Rather, its significance lies in the lively, critical interest in the way in which the United States approaches and solves its own problems. This, they are certain, tells them a great deal about the way in which the United States might approach the social problems of the hundreds of millions of peoples who are affected by the dominant position the United States occupies in the world today.

These peoples are constantly asking themselves if the United States can be trusted to lead the world toward greater freedom for all and toward a greater recognition of the dignity of the individual. They are convinced that the answer is not to be found in the amount of military, financial and material aid given so generously by this country to the less fortunate. Rather the answer is to be found in the manner in which this country seeks to protect the rights of human beings in the areas of equality, freedom and justice. And the real test is obviously this nation's treatment of its own less privileged groups.

When one calls our attention to the fact that the inability of the people of the United States to extend equality and justice to all its citizens is losing friends for the United States throughout the world, we frequently shout that this is a Communist line. People who have cautioned this country that its relations were hurting an effective and constructive foreign policy have frequently been criticized as having fallen under some foreign, un-American spell. But outrage or disgust with the criticism cannot wash it away. Nor can the sins of this country be expiated by the search, in which so many have indulged in recent years, for racial discrimination in the Soviet Union. It should be no consolation to any American to learn that there is racial discrimination in the Soviet Union, if such exists. It would seem quite irrelevant to any discussion of America's position, anyway.

In the first place, we, not the Russians, have been proclaiming to the world for more than a century and a half that we sub-

scribe to the doctrine of the equality of all men. We have, therefore, set for ourselves a goal that we have not attained and
which a considerable number of Americans actively oppose.
And this the entire world knows. In the second place, with all
the controls over speech, press and other forms of communication in the Soviet Union, it is inconceivable that the problem of
race there could become a factor in international relations, regardless of what was happening. If there are lynchings or riots,
segregation and discrimination there, the information does not
flow freely out of the country, and we would, therefore, not
have the opportunity to be outraged by such injustices. It seems,
moreover, that the Soviet Union manages not to insult foreign
visitors on the basis of race, as this country all too frequently
does. This, of course, could arise from the fact that foreign visitors in Russia are more carefully "looked after" than they are
in this country. On the other hand, every racial incident in this
country is front-page news throughout the world. This is the
price we pay for freedom of communication. It can be the
bombing of a Negro church in Birmingham or Montgomery or
the expulsion of the Indian ambassador to the United States
from a Houston, Texas, restaurant. It immediately becomes
front-page news throughout the world. It immediately becomes
an ingredient in the formulation of attitudes toward the United
States and hampers, to a considerable extent, the execution of
a constructive foreign policy.

It would seem, then, that this is one of the grim facts of life
with which we must live in our present stage of development.
We are extremely vulnerable not merely because we have our
deficiencies but also because we do have our strengths, one of
which is our willingness to let the world know what goes on
here. It is a clear sign of weakness, however, to ascribe to Soviet
influence every foreign eyebrow that is raised, every criticism
that is voiced about the race problem in the United States. There
is no need for us to fall into the trap of thinking that the status
of race relations in the United States is, somehow, a factor in
the relations between the so-called free world and the so-called
Communist world. It solves nothing for the people of the United
States to defend their position on the ground that the critics
are under Communist influence. Indeed, it merely suggests to
these critics that this country is not willing to face its problem
honestly and do something about it. This would be an unfortunate turn, and the efforts of the United States to solve its race
problem deserve more sympathetic consideration and more
favorable judgment than this.

I suppose that it is fair to assume that most Americans are

honestly interested in moving as rapidly as possible toward the achievement of interracial justice *and* in securing the support and good will of all freedom-loving peoples in the world. If this is a valid assumption we should be able to profit by questions, comments, observations and criticisms of racial policies and practices in the United States. Often, the vantage point of the critical outsider gives us a perspective on ourselves that we otherwise would not have. One cannot listen to the comments of a European or Asian on the American race problem without realizing that in the eyes of some we appear rather ridiculous, inconsistent and hypocritical. That should not disturb us too much, despite the fact that as a nation and as a people we naturally want to appear in the most favorable light. We should ask ourselves if there are grounds for their having this view of us. We should try to look at ourselves as they do and see if their view is as fantastic as it would appear at first glance. If it is, we should be happy to rectify the conditions that give rise to these unhappy impressions.

Some who look at us believe that our position is ridiculous as we dash about the world seeking to eradicate every manifestation of injustice that we find and, in doing so, overlook or disregard injustices at home. Some regard us as inconsistent when we argue for the enfranchisement of peoples behind the Iron Curtain and stand by and see a community like Tuskegee, Alabama, revise its boundaries for the specific purpose of excluding every Negro citizen from participating in the affairs of the community. Some accuse us of hypocrisy when we claim that we believe in the equality and dignity of all men and, at the same time, make either half-hearted attempts or no attempt at all to eradicate the inequalities and tolerate one indignity after another directed to people because of race or creed. We can plead that we are not guilty, but the plea in itself is not convincing to those on the outside who are looking at us.

In so many respects, then, race relations is our big window, our picture window, to the world. What would we like for those who gaze in upon us to see? We would, of course, like to have our observers see us as a people who not only subscribe to the principles of equality but who put these principles into practice in every conceivable way. We would want them to see us making no discrimination or segregation among peoples on the highly questionable grounds of race or creed. We would want them to see us extending to every person in the United States the rights and privileges to which we as a nation are committed: the right to equality of opportunity to make of oneself what one can, to security of one's person, to be free of the indignities that degrade human beings, to move freely among one's fellows, and to exercise all the responsibilities and privileges of citizenship. If they could look in on us and see these practices, they would then have more confidence in our preachments and would attach more importance and meaning to them. They would also have infinitely more confidence in our seriousness of purpose as we set up goals of equality and freedom for peoples in other parts of the world.

We can be certain that what people see in our window to the world will be a pleasing picture if we work diligently and conscientiously to correct the evils that produce a bad picture. Happily, we are realizing in increasing numbers the importance of this point. But there can be no doubt that much remains to be done. We must make it unmistakably clear that as a nation we will tolerate no amount of discrimination or segregation based on race. It is not enough that the Supreme Court should establish the principle and give legal sanction to it. Every arm of the government must be committed to the same principle and must use its resources to translate the principle into practice. The executive and legislative branches of the federal government that have done so little to promote equality and to further interracial justice must take a much more active role than they have done. States and local governments have responsibilities; and if they do not understand what they are they must be taught what the principles of racial justice involve in the context of the American creed.

The achievement of real interracial justice involves not merely the establishment and maintenance of rights under the law, although that is an indispensable step toward interracial justice. It also involves the most drastic modification of *individual* attitudes and actions in the area of human relations. After all, laws merely establish minimal requirements; and after all, even these can be evaded and nullified if there is no individual commitment to the principles underlying the law. This is one area in which laws alone are inadequate. The enforcement of the law, the respect for the law, the belief in those fundamentals in human relations that are even above and outside the law are the tests of popular commitment. These are the tests by which we as a people will be judged.

Perhaps there are those among us who do not care what others think of us. We have all seen the shrug of the shoulder of some of our fellows when it was suggested that the esteem in which we were held abroad was low because of our inhumanity to each other. If enough of us shrug our shoulders and assume an attitude of indifference in this matter we shall speed

the process of disrespect of other peoples for us and add to the
lack of confidence they have in us. In less time than we can
imagine we shall have lost our position as a moral leader in
the world and when that is gone our military and economic
leadership will have little value. If people begin to regard us as
fundamentally incapable of achieving interracial justice at
home, they will begin to turn their faces from us. It will then be
too late to make explanations based on legalisms and the split-
ting of hairs.

What other peoples see as they look through our window
should be of interest to us because, after all, the national self-
esteem dictates that we should want the picture to be a favorable one. We are hardly deserving of their respect and confidence if we do not have respect and esteem for ourselves and
for each other. One hopes that for the sake of ourselves as well
as for the sake of others who desire to place themselves under
our leadership, we shall be able to present a true, healthy picture of interracial justice before those who look in upon
us. . . .

NEGRO WRITERS HAVE BEEN ON THE
BLACKLIST ALL THEIR LIVES

By Langston Hughes

*In May, 1957, Langston Hughes delivered the following
speech at the National Assembly of the Authors' League of
America. It is reprinted from the* National Guardian, *June
3, 1957.*

BRUCE CATON spoke of the writer's chance to be heard.
My chance to be heard as a Negro writer is not so great as your
chance. I once approached the Play Service of the Dramatists
Guild as to the handling of some of my plays. No, was the
answer, they would not know where to place plays about Negro
life. I once sent one of my best-known short stories, before it
came out in book form, to one of our oldest and most famous
American magazines. The story was about racial violence in the
South. It came back to me with a very brief little note saying the
editor did not believe his readers wished to read about such

things. Another story of mine, which did not concern race problems at all, came back to me from one of our best-known editors
of anthologies of fiction with a letter praising the story but
saying that he, the editor, could not tell if the characters were
white or colored. Would I make them definitely Negro? Just a
plain story about human beings from me was not up his alley,
it seems. So before the word *man* I simply inserted "black," and
before the girl's name, the words "brown skin"—and the story
was accepted. Only a mild form of racial bias. But now let us
come to something more serious.

Censorship, the black list: Negro writers, just by being black,
have been on the blacklist all our lives. Do you know that there
are libraries in our country that will not stock a book by a
Negro writer, not even as a gift? There are towns where Negro
newspapers and magazines cannot be sold—except surreptiti-
ously. There are American magazines that have *never* published
anything by or about Negroes. There are film studios that have
never hired a Negro writer. Censorship for us begins at the
color line.

As to the tangential ways in which many white writers may
make a living: I've already mentioned Hollywood. Not once in
a blue moon does Hollywood send for a Negro writer, no matter
how famous he may be. . . . When you go into your publishers'
offices, how many colored editors, readers, or even secretaries
do you see? In the book-review pages of our Sunday supplements and our magazines, how often do you see a Negro reviewer's name? And if you do, ninety-nine times out of a hundred the Negro reviewer will be given a book by another Negro
to review—seldom, if ever, "The Sea Around Us" or "Auntie
Mame"—and yet a reviewer of the caliber of Arna Bontemps
or Anne Petry or J. Saunders Redding could review anybody's
books, white or colored, interestingly. Take lecturing: There are
thousands and thousands of women's clubs and other organizations booking lectures that have never had, and will not have,
a Negro speaker—though he has written a best seller.

We have in America today about a dozen top-flight, frequently published, and really good Negro writers. Do you not
think it strange that of that dozen, at least half of them live
abroad, far away from their people, their problems, and the
sources of their material: Richard Wright (*Native Son*) in
Paris; Chester Himes (*The Primitives*) in Paris; James Baldwin
(*Giovanni's Room*) in Paris; William Denby (*Beetle Creek*) in
Rome; Ralph Ellison (*Invisible Man*) in Rome; Frank Yerby (of
the dozen best sellers), South of France; Willard Motley (*Knock
on Any Door*), Mexico.

Why? *Why?* Because the stones thrown at Autherine Lucy at
the University of Alabama are thrown at them, too. Because the
shadow of Montgomery and the bombs under Reverend King's
house shadow them and shatter them, too. Because the body
of little Emmett Till drowned in a Mississippi river and no one
brought to justice, haunts them, too. Because the Jim Crow
schools from New York to New Orleans Jim-Crow them, too.
One of the writers I've mentioned, when last I saw him before
he went abroad, said to me, "I don't want my children to grow
up in the shadow of Jim Crow."

And so let us end with children. And let us end with poetry—
since somehow the planned poetry panel, of which I was to
have been a part, did not materialize. So, therefore, there has
been no poetry in our National Assembly. Forgive me, then, if
I read a poem. It's about a child—a little colored child. I imagine her as being maybe six or seven years old. She grew up in
the Deep South, where our color lines are still legal. Then her
family moved to a Northern or Western industrial city—one
of those continual migrations of Negroes looking for a better
town. There in this Northern city—maybe a place like Newark,
New Jersey, or Omaha, Nebraska, or Oakland, California—the
little girl goes one day to a carnival, and she sees the merry-go-
round going round, and she wants to ride. But being a little
colored girl, and remembering the South, she doesn't know if
she can ride or not. And if she can ride, where? So this is what
she says:

> Where is the Jim Crow section
> On this merry-go-round,
> Mister, cause I want to ride?
> Down South where I come from
> White and colored
> Can't sit side by side.
> Down South on the train
> There's a Jim Crow car,
> On the bus we're put in the back
> —But there ain't no back
> To a merry-go-round!
> Where's the horse
> For a kid that's black?

GIVE US THE BALLOT—WE WILL TRANSFORM THE SOUTH

By Martin Luther King, Jr.

On December 1, 1955, Rosa Parks refused to move to the back of the bus in Montgomery, Alabama, and accommodate white passengers getting on. Rather than accept this form of discrimination, she was ready to go to jail. Her action brought on the great Montgomery bus boycott and brought into prominence a new and dynamic black leader —the Reverend Dr. Martin Luther King, Jr. After Mrs. Parks was arrested, convicted and fined ten dollars, the Montgomery Improvement Association was formed and Dr. King was chosen as its president.

Martin Luther King, Jr., was born at Atlanta, Georgia, January 15, 1929, the son of a Baptist minister. He was educated at Morehouse College, Crozer Theological Seminary, studied at the University of Pennsylvania and Harvard University, and completed his theological training at Boston University. He then came to Montgomery as pastor of the Dexter Avenue Baptist Church. King believed in the nonviolent, direct-action approach and had been greatly influenced by the nonviolent philosophy of love fashioned by Ghandi. King made it the basis of the movement which sponsored the Montgomery bus boycott, and even after his home had been bombed by racists, he refused to abandon his advice that nonviolence was the way to victory. On November 13, 1956, almost a year after the boycott had started, the United States Supreme Court affirmed the decision of a lower federal court and declared Alabama's state and local laws requiring segregation on buses unconstitutional.

The success of the Montgomery bus boycott was followed by other victories against segregation in the South, many of them influenced by the nonviolent movement headed by Dr. King. As his reputation grew, Dr. King was hailed as the leader of the civil-rights revolution. An effective and moving speaker, he influenced large masses with his oratory.

Dr. King, together with Roy Wilkins, Executive Secre-

tary of the N.A.A.C.P., and A. Philip Randolph, a vice-
president of the A.F.L.-C.I.O., sponsored a Prayer Pilgrim-
age to Washington, D. C., on May 17, 1957, after President
Eisenhower rebuffed a plea by sixty Negro leaders that he
use the weight of his office to underscore the "moral na-
ture of the problems posed at home and abroad by the un-
resolved civil-rights issue." Below is the text of the address
made by Dr. King on that occasion; it is reprinted from
The Worker, *June 2, 1957.*

THREE YEARS AGO the Supreme Court of this nation
rendered in simple, eloquent and unequivocal language a decision which will long be stenciled on the mental sheets of succeeding generations. For all men of good will, this May 17
decision came as a joyous daybreak to end the long night of enforced segregation. It came as a great beacon light of hope to
millions of distinguished people throughout the world who had
dared only to dream of freedom. It came as a legal and sociological deathblow to the old Plessy doctrine of "separate-but-
equal." It came as a reaffirmation of the good old American
doctrine of freedom and equality for all people.

Unfortunately, this noble and sublime decision has not gone
without opposition. This opposition has often risen to ominous
proportions. Many states have risen up in open defiance. The
legislative halls of the South ring loud with such words as "interposition" and "nullification." Methods of defiance range from
crippling economic reprisals to the tragic reign of violence and
terror. All of these forces have conjoined to make for massive
resistance.

But, even more, all types of conniving methods are still being
used to prevent Negroes from becoming registered voters. The
denial of this sacred right is a tragic betrayal of the highest
mandates of our democratic traditions and it is democracy
turned upside down.

So long as I do not firmly and irrevocably possess the right to
vote I do not possess myself. I cannot make up my mind—it is
made up for me. I cannot live as a democratic citizen, observing
the laws I have helped to enact—I can only submit to the edict
of others.

So our most urgent request to the President of the United
States and every member of Congress is to give us the right to
vote.

Give us the ballot and we will no longer have to worry the
federal government about our basic rights.

Give us the ballot and we will no longer plead to the federal government for passage of an antilynching law; we will by the power of our vote write the law on the statute books of the Southern states and bring an end to the dastardly acts of the hooded perpetrators of violence.

Give us the ballot and we will transform the salient misdeeds of bloodthirsty mobs into the calculated good deeds of orderly citizens.

Give us the ballot and we will fill our legislative halls with men of good will, and send to the sacred halls of Congress men who will not sign a Southern Manifesto,* because of their devotion to the manifesto of justice.

Give us the ballot and we will place judges on the benches of the South who will "do justly and love mercy," and we will place at the head of the Southern states governors who have felt not only the tang of the human, but the glow of the divine.

Give us the ballot and we will quietly and nonviolently, without rancor or bitterness, implement the Supreme Court's decision of May 17, 1954.

In this junction of our nation's history there is an urgent need for dedicated and courageous leadership. If we are to solve the problems ahead and make racial justice a reality, this leadership must be fourfold.

First, there is need for a strong, aggressive leadership from the federal government. So far, only the judicial branch of the government has evinced this quality of leadership. If the executive and legislative branches of the government were as concerned about the protection of our citizenship rights as the federal courts have been, then the transition from a segregated to an integrated society would be infinitely smoother. But we so often look to Washington in vain for this concern.

In the midst of the tragic breakdown of law and order, the executive branch of the government is all too silent and apathetic. In the midst of the desperate need for civil-rights legislation, the legislative branch of the government is all too stagnant and hypocritical.

This dearth of positive leadership from the federal government is not confined to one particular political party. Both parties have betrayed the cause of justice. The Democrats have betrayed it by capitulating to the prejudices and undemocratic

---

* In March, 1956, more than ninety Southerners, led by Senator Walter George presented in Congress their "Declaration of Constitutional Principles," commonly known as the "Southern Manifesto." The document condemned the Supreme Court decision on segregation in education as a usurpation of the powers of the states and encouraged the use of "every lawful means" to resist its implementation.

practices of the Southern Dixiecrats. The Republicans have betrayed it by capitulating to the blatant hypocrisy of right-wing, reactionary Northerners. These men so often have a high blood pressure of words and an anemia of deeds.

In the midst of these prevailing conditions, we come to Washington today pleading with the President and the members of Congress to provide a strong, moral and courageous leadership for a situation that cannot permanently be evaded. We come humbly to say to the men in the forefront of our government that the civil-rights issue is not an ephemeral, evanescent domestic issue that can be kicked about by reactionary guardians of the status quo; it is rather an eternal moral issue which may well determine the destiny of our nation in the ideological struggle with Communism. The hour is late. The clock of destiny is ticking out. We must act now, before it is too late.

A second area in which there is need for strong leadership is from the white Northern liberals. There is a dire need today for a liberalism which is truly liberal. What we are witnessing today in so many Northern communities is a sort of quasi liberalism which is based on the principle of looking sympathetically at all sides. It is a liberalism so bent on seeing all sides that it fails to become committed to either side. It is a liberalism that is so objectively analytical that it is not subjectively committed. It is a liberalism which is neither hot nor cold, but lukewarm.

We call for a liberalism from the North which will be thoroughly committed to the ideal of racial justice and will not be deterred by the propaganda and subtle words of those who say, "Slow up for a while; you are pushing too fast."

A third area that we must look to for strong leadership is from the moderates of the white South. It is unfortunate, indeed, that at this time the leadership of the white South stems from the closed-minded reactionaries. These persons gain prominence and power by the dissemination of false ideas, and by deliberately appealing to the deepest hate responses within the human mind. It is my firm belief that this closed-minded, reactionary, recalcitrant group constitutes a numerical minority. There are in the white South more open-minded moderates than appears on the surface. These persons are silent today because of fear of social, political and economic reprisals. God grant that the white moderates of the South will rise up courageously, without fear, and take up the leadership in this tense period of transition.

I cannot close without stressing the urgent need for strong, courageous and intelligent leadership from the Negro community. We need leadership that is calm and yet positive. This is no day for the rabble-rouser, whether he be Negro or white. We must realize that we are grappling with the most weighty social problem of this nation, and in grappling with such a complex problem there is no place for misguided emotionalism. We must work passionately and unrelentingly for the goal of freedom, but we must be sure that our hands are clean in the struggle. We must never struggle with falsehood, hate or malice. Let us never become bitter.

There is another warning signal. We talk a great deal about our rights, and rightly so. We proudly proclaim that three fourths of the peoples of the world are colored. We have the privilege of noticing in our generation the great drama of freedom and independence as it unfolds in Asia and Africa. All of these things are in line with the unfolding work of providence.

But we must be sure that we accept them in the right spirit. We must not seek to use our emerging freedom and our growing power to do the same thing to the white minority that has been done to us for so many centuries. We must not become victimized with a philosophy of "black supremacy." Our aim must never be to defeat or to humiliate the white man, but to win his friendship and understanding, and thereby create a society in which all men will be able to live together as brothers.

We must also avoid the temptation of being victimized with a psychology of victors. In our nation, under the guidance of the superb legal staff of the N.A.A.C.P., we have been able, through the courts, to remove the legal basis of segregation. This is by far one of the most marvelous achievements of our generation. Every person of good will is profoundly indebted to the N.A.A.C.P. for its noble work. We must not, however, remain satisfied with a court "victory" over our white brothers.

We must respond to every decision with an understanding of those who have opposed us and with an appreciation of the difficult adjustments that the court orders pose for them.

We must act in such a way as to make possible a coming-together of white people and colored people on the basis of a real harmony of interest and understanding. We must seek an integration based on mutual respect.

I conclude by saying that each of us must keep faith in the future. Let us realize that as we struggle alone, but God struggles with us. He is leading us out of a bewildering Egypt, through a bleak and desolate wilderness, toward a bright and glittering promised land. Let us go forth into the glorious future with the words of James Weldon Johnson resounding in our souls:

God of our weary years,
God of our silent tears,
Thou who has brought us thus far on the way;
Thou who has by thy might,
Led us into the light,
Keep us forever in the path, we pray.
Lest our feet stray from the places, our God,
    where we met thee.
Lest our hearts, drunk with the wine of the world
    we forget thee;
Shadowed beneath thy hand, may we forever stand
True to our God, true to our native land.*

"FREE BY '63"

By William L. Patterson

In a speech delivered in 1960 at a dinner sponsored by the Civil Rights Congress, of which he was head, William L. Patterson analyzed the significance of the slogan raised in 1953 by the N.A.A.C.P.—"Free By '63"—and examined the various forces in the black liberation struggle at this time.

Patterson was born in California, lived three years in the Soviet Union during the 1920's and, after his return, served as attorney for the Metal Workers Industrial Union and the National Miners Union. He was attorney in 1932 for several black Army veterans arrested following the expulsion of the Bonus Expeditionary Force from Anacostia Flats. In the fall of that year, Patterson was the Communist party's candidate for Mayor of New York City. Patterson was National Secretary of the International Labor Defense from 1932 to 1936, years during which he played a leading role in the defense of the Scottsboro youths.

The Civil Rights Congress speech presented here is taken from a copy of the speech in the possession of Mr. Patterson and is published with permission of the author.

* The verses quoted are from Johnson's famous poem set to music, "Lift Every Voice and Sing," which was also known as the Negro national anthem.

. . . IF THE SLOGAN "Free by '63" is to have more than propaganda value, if it is to have a value which can be measured in terms of daily human relations, it must be implemented by a program of action calculated to defeat the social forces responsible for racist ideology and oppression. "Free by '63" can be, it must be, made the property of the people. It cannot be effective if only a slogan of propaganda.

"Free by '63" must become the property of all the people regardless of creed, color, sex, age, or political affiliation. The slogan, expressive of the aims and desires of the Negro people, is expressive also of the needs of all American citizens. The people who were part of the "Scottsboro Boys" defense, those who made history in Montgomery, Alabama, Little Rock, Arkansas, and a hundred smaller struggles that have not been widely publicized, these people have a duty and responsibility to make "Free by '63" a slogan of militant, democratic action.

The several hundred thousand members of the N.A.A.C.P. who have steadfastly stood behind their leadership through many legal battles, will learn through experience the wisdom in the words of Dean George S. Johnson when, in the report of the Eisenhower Civil Rights Commission, he said:

The achievement of equal justice under the law and equality of opportunity should not be left to the federal judiciary. The legislative and executive branches of the federal government also have basic responsibilities to secure and protect the Constitutional rights of all citizens. The public interest is not best served if private citizens and organizations are left to vindicate Constitutional rights of national significance through litigation in federal courts.

Dean Johnson is profoundly correct. Coordination of the three branches of government is essential to the enforcement of law and a democratic interpretation of the Constitution in the interests of the people. For that coordination the pressure of an aroused citizenry is more effective than a decision of the judiciary. The famous decision of the Supreme Court in the case of *Plessy v. Ferguson,* 1896, made an impossible doctrine of "separate but equal" consistent with bourgeois democracy. Violation of the Constitution was consistent with democracy when it served the interests of those in power.

Racism has become a menace to the democratic processes of Constitutional government. Under a fiction of states' rights, the racist has ignored the 1954 desegregation decision of the Supreme Court. Racism has brought about the prostitution of American culture. History, art and science have been distorted or flagrantly falsified. Paid ideologists in the highest seats of

learning deny the black man's contributions to human development. This, in order to create belief in the inherent inferiority
of Negroes and to create an image of the Negro in art and
literature that will give credence to the myths of white superiority. Racism has become a barrier to the nation's intellectual
growth. It has become a policy of government in the government's relations with the Negro people. But millions of white
Americans are tired of this policy. They lack leadership and a
knowledge of how effectively to wage the struggle against it.

James P. Warburg, in *The West in Crisis*, says, "The moral
challenge to democracy [bourgeois democracy] is to rid itself
of the cancer of racial and religious discrimination; to dissociate
itself from colonial exploitation and from expedient alliances
with antidemocratic forces and to associate itself firmly with
the aspirations of all men everywhere seeking human betterment under justice, dignity and freedom."

The challenge to democracy is, in more concrete terms, a
challenge to a policy of government.

A hundred years of unsuccessful struggles to complete the
unfinished tasks of a revolution which capitalism started and
then betrayed has left a mark on every institution in American
life. The fight against racist ideas is now a fight to save the
country from moral decay and to prevent political and social
corruption from becoming a way of life. Racism thus becomes
the concern of enlightened peoples everywhere.

Those changes are possible under capitalism. But profound
changes in the relation of forces in American society are needed.
Imperialist morality, economics and politics are not geared to
bring equality of opportunity to men of color. Hitler's myths of
Aryan superiority were in part patterned after American imperialism's myths of white supremacy. Many do not see that the
dangers inherent in one are not foreign to the other. Racism
carries both the germs of war and massive internal discord
and violence, especially to Constitutional government.

The unity of the black and white people in struggle is
essential if those changes are to be realized.

History has no respect for timetables that reflect only the
wishful thinking of leaders who fear militant, democratic movements of the people. History is people in motion, people, millions
of people demanding change and harnessing their demands to
democratic political action. The people of Africa and Asia are
making history, through movements involving millions.

Freedom from the horrors of racist savagery and barbarism is
the right of the Negro people and American democracy now.

Those who have set the calendar for 1963 obviously have not clearly seen the political possibilities of the moment. They do not appreciate the vitality and power of militant action. Their dependence is not upon the people, the Negro people, and the allies who find in the enemies of the Negro people their own enemies. Indeed, free by '63 without the accompaniment of an action program that permeates every phase of American life may well become a hoax of monstrous proportions. Here the danger lies.

Those who lead the liberation struggles of the Asian-African and Latin-American peoples recognize the menacing character of American democracy with its racist ingredient. They are deeply sympathetic to the struggles of the Negro people against white supremacy. The struggles of a world demanding an end to colonialism and racism have merged spiritually if not yet on an organic basis. A further step is possible.

The peoples of Asia, Africa and semicolonial America are working ever more closely in the United Nations in the interest of peace. Peace and racism are incompatible. In joint actions these people are breathing life into the Charter of the U. N. They are slowly making a reality of the Universal Declaration of Human Rights. A magnificent Declaration of the Rights of the Children has emerged from the U. N. Anti-Semitism has been condemned by one of its organs in a resolution that calls for a struggle against the incidents and forms of "racial and national hatred and religious and racial prejudices." These facts demand the most serious consideration.

These steps make for the centralization and unification of the drive toward human freedom. True, the United States of America has not ratified the Universal Declaration of Human Rights. Its observance of the U. N. conventions has never been of a positive character and for that reason every effort to eliminate Jim Crow and segregation from American life strengthens the fight for peace and freedom the world over. The Negro people should bring the matter of racism back to the U. N.

The decade of the sixties opens up on an amazing new world. Its tensions have relaxed under the incessant demands of the socialist lands for permanent peace. Science is beginning to flourish in countries whose people under colonialism and racism were restricted in development even more than is the Negro. Imperialism and racism are everywhere under attack.

Freed from exploitation, the peoples of the socialist world are opening limitless frontiers. In the light of the selfless aid the socialist world is rendering the countries capitalism has left undeveloped after years of exploitation, a monstrous shadow of doubt is cast on the values of capitalist democracy to peoples seriously seeking freedom. But in the United States of America, possibilities remain for putting an end to racism under capitalism.

The Report of the United States Commission on Civil Rights, 1959, quotes Abraham Lincoln to the effect that "the legitimate object of government is to do for the people what needs to be done, but which they cannot, by individual effort, do at all or do so well themselves."

The direction of this government regardless of the party in power has been to serve the interests of monopoly. It will serve the interests of the people only when the demands of the people are expressed through independent political action guided by a labor movement conscious of its power and determined to defend its interests and its rights.

"Free by '63" is possible. Three years is an extremely short time when compared with the seeming magnitude of the struggle against racism. But American monopoly reaction is weaker than it appears. The victory of the steel union is proof of that.

Crucial to victory by '63 is the unity of the Negro people. Unity irrespective of political outlook.

The freedom demanded is from every kind and form of racism in the realms of economics, the industrial life of America, politics and culture. In 1953 the N.A.A.C.P. said the target was "the complete elimination of all vestiges of second-class citizenship under which Negro Americans still suffer."

The Negro people cannot permit itself to be split along political lines. This is the aim and desire of the enemy. Its success in achieving such a split is a necessary condition for its continuance of racial exploitation. The Negro people's struggle is an all-class struggle. All differences of a political character can be settled when the burden of racism has been thrown from our shoulders.

Within the realm of political affairs the Negro people must be free from the policy that permits the substitution of fictional states' rights for the federal Constitution. The fourteenth and fifteenth amendments must be rigidly enforced. There are sufficient laws upon the statute books for such enforcement now.

The desire of the Negro to vote must be registered, his vote received and counted, and every agency of government, particularly in the Department of Justice, must be used at once to ensure this end. Proportional representation should determine the election of officers throughout the Southern states.

All organizations of racist terror, the K.K.K. and the White Citizens Councils, must at once be outlawed. It is the responsibility of the Executive branch of government to demand such legislation and of Congress to enact it.

Congressmen who use their immunity to teach racism or in Congress fail to defend impartially the rights of all citizens regardless of race or color shall be impeached. The President of the United States shall call upon members of his party to move the impeachment.

The Supreme Court shall have presented to it by the Department of Justice cases involving all laws infringing upon the Constitution and human dignity of citizens because of race or color. It shall declare the same to be unconstitutional.

No branch of the federal government shall make any contract with any firm or business enterprise that follows a policy of discrimination in employment.

It shall be unlawful for any public utility or any institution of public service to practice discrimination because of color in any of its relations with the public. The 1960 election campaign offers a magnificient opportunity to mount nationwide struggles to end racism.

Workers, employees of every category shall be hired on the basis of merit. Upgrading on the job shall determine the same principles.

Any trade-union organization or subdivision thereof which shall exclude from its membership because of race or color workers in the trade otherwise eligible to join is taking a position that can only defeat progressive American principles. All steps necessary to enforce this principle, including legal action, should be regarded as proper and in due course if resorted to by an aggrieved party.

Everywhere in the world experience has shown that reaction seeks with every weapon at hand to split the working class off from other strategic groups within the population. Unity of the working class and Negro people can only be viewed as the most essential step on the American front of democratic struggle. With that unity achieved through an alliance of equals, the historical tasks left undone by American capitalism and now blocked through its racist practices can be completed. The degree to which the realization of this historic step can further the people's interests is immeasurable.

The myths of white superiority must be relentlessly expelled from all institutions of learning.

All attempts at caricaturing the Negro people shall be prohibited by law. Any attempts through art, literature, science or any cultural form to demean another because of race or color shall be made an offense punishable by law.

These are positions that can be taken before the city council of every major American city, before every state assembly, before the Congress of the United States.

The unity of labor and the Negro people is crucial if these ends are to be achieved. Labor is the key factor in any relation of forces in American life. United in struggle with the Negro people, its economic problems as well as the political problems of the Negro people, can be resolved. Together these two social forces can put an end to racism in every sphere of life and in doing so effect a decisive change in Constitutional procedure and respect for human rights.

The realization of a vast network of American Negro Labor Councils* can have an amazing impact on labor and do much to link labor-community struggles together in a powerful bloc.

"Free by '63" must become a slogan of action. Inherent in it is a solution to the question of peace and domestic tranquillity.

"Free by '63" sets forth no impossible tasks. History has put this matter on the order of business.

IN PRAISE OF THE SIT-IN STRIKES

By *Thurgood Marshall*

Despite Supreme Court decisions, Presidential orders and federal legislation, the pace of change for black Americans was too slow to satisfy their demand for "Freedom Now!" a demand stimulated after World War II by the emergence of new nations in Africa. No longer content to wait for gradual elimination of discrimination through the courts and step-by-step victories, black Americans decided to act, and a new tactic, the direct-action mass demonstration emerged. Early in 1960 four students from North Carolina A. and T. College decided to sit in at a segregated lunch counter in Greensboro, North Carolina. Within a few weeks, sit-ins against segregated facilities spread throughout the South. White sympathizers often demonstrated

* For the Negro Labor Council see pp. 843–49.

*with Negroes, but the bulk of the demonstrators were
black. These nonviolent mass protests were met by violence, police brutality and arrests, but the demonstrators
persisted and went to jail singing "We Shall Overcome,"
the theme song of their movement. In a speech at a
N.A.A.C.P. mass meeting held in Charlotte, North Carolina, March 20, 1960, Thurgood Marshall hailed the sit-in
strikes and denounced those who violently interfered with
the right of the strikers to lawfully protest. Later the constitutionality of the sit-in tactic was upheld by the Supreme
Court in several cases.*

Here is an excerpt from the speech; it is taken from
Rhetoric of Racial Revolt, *Roy L. Hill, ed., pp. 318–20.*

WHILE THE CRY is against apartheid in South Africa, is
for one man, one vote in Kenya, is for the right to register and
vote in Mississippi and Alabama, the right to nondiscriminatory
service in stores throughout the South, the right to nonsegregated education in the South or the ending of subtle
segregation in the North, the cry for freedom is increasing in
tempo throughout the world. Thus, the sit-in strikes of young
people throughout the South is the latest evidence of this wave.
We believe that those of us in the N.A.A.C.P. and other organizations who have fought so long in this fight must continue the
type of leadership that brings about the lawful and orderly
step-by-step march toward freedom from racial discrimination
wherever it exists.

One writer, in commenting upon the situation in sit-in strikes
says, "It seems rather ridiculous when you can buy a nice hat
for eight or ten dollars in the store and yet you can't satisfy,
without discrimination, the very fundamental need of your
own hunger with a cup of coffee and a sandwich."

Thus young people, in the true tradition of our democratic
principles, are fighting the matter for all of us and they are
doing it in a most effective way. Protest—the right of protest—is basic to a democratic form of government. The right
of petition; the right of assembly; the right of freedom of
speech are so basic to our government that they are enshrined
in the very first amendment to the Constitution. And the Fourteenth Amendment says that no state shall throttle these freedoms.

These young people are just simply sick and tired of waiting patiently without protest for the rights they know to be
theirs. Consequently, they settled upon the right of peaceful
protests. And what is wrong with that?

As a result of these peaceful protests, the whole force of state government has been arrayed behind the private store owner to prevent peaceful protests. The students have been arrested on every possible type of criminal charge.*

In some areas they are charged with trespassing because they refuse to leave the establishment, because they came on the property when told not to do so, or are charged with having threatened someone. Secondly, many of them have been charged with violation of fire-department regulations such as blocking of aisles of a store despite the fact that no one has ever been charged with the same crime before;

Thirdly, some are charged with assault for refusing to move or allegedly brushing against someone;

Fourth, some are charged with failure to obtain licenses for public meetings or parades; and

Fifth, authorities have dragged out the old disorderly-conduct procedure.

There will be many others thought up by lawyers well paid and well trained in the law. And here we have once again the example of the full strength of a state government, paid for by white and black taxes, arrayed against young people solely because of their race and color.

In Orangeburg, South Carolina, 450 students were arrested walking down the street before they had even started to picket or to parade and everyone is to be tried in blocs of fifteen per day. This is obviously done in the hope of wearing our legal staff and our pocketbook down. We have news for them. We are prepared to stay in court after court, in city after city and in state after state as long as they can stay there.

On Thursday, March 17, in Little Rock, Arkansas, fifteen students peacefully protesting were seized and fined $250 and sentenced to thirty days in jail.

Each of these instances can be cited in state after state wherever the protests have been made. To all of this, we have but one reply, even one word and the word is *shame*.

Whenever you read about it—Whenever you hear about it—Whenever you hear it discussed, say "Shame"—Shame on those who under the guise of states' rights or state law seek to throttle young people lawfully protesting.

Say "Shame" on the white people of the South, the good white people, the so-called moderates who sit idly by and allow

---

* By this time seventy-five cities in twelve states had had sit-ins, and nearly 1,300 arrests had been made. Most of those arrested were Negroes.

young people to be persecuted solely because of their race or color. And when you hear a Negro who has been adequately brainwashed say that this is too much to do just to get a hamburger or a frankfurter, to him say "Shame." For this that the young people are doing is for the best interest of all of us and indeed for the country itself.

THE AMERICAN DREAM

By Martin Luther King, Jr.

One of Dr. King's greatest speeches was delivered on June 6, 1961, at Lincoln University, where he received an honorary degree of Doctor of Laws. Here is the text of the commencement address he gave there. It has been published as a pamphlet by Lincoln University, Pennsylvania.

. . . TODAY YOU BID FAREWELL to the friendly security of this academic environment, a setting that will remain dear to you as long as the cords of memory shall lengthen. As you go out today to enter the clamorous highways of life, I should like to discuss with you some aspects of the American dream. For in a real sense, America is essentially a dream, a dream as yet unfulfilled. It is a dream of a land where men of all races, of all nationalities and of all creeds can live together as brothers. The substance of the dream is expressed in these sublime words, words lifted to cosmic proportions: "We hold these truths to be self-evident, that all men are created equal, that they are endowed by their Creator with certain unalienable rights, that among these are life, liberty, and the pursuit of happiness." This is the dream.

One of the first things we notice in this dream is an amazing universalism. It does not say some men, but it says all men. It does not say all white men, but it says all men, which includes black men. It does not say all Gentiles, but it says all men, which includes Jews. It does not say all Protestants, but it says all men, which includes Catholics.

And there is another thing we see in this dream that ultimately distinguishes democracy and our form of government from all of the totalitarian regimes that emerge in history. It says that each individual has certain basic rights that are neither

conferred by nor derived from the state. To discover where they
came from it is necessary to move back behind the dim mist of
eternity, for they are God-given. Very seldom if ever in the
history of the world has a sociopolitical document expressed
in such profoundly eloquent and unequivocal language the
dignity and the worth of human personality. The American
dream reminds us that every man is heir to the legacy of
worthiness.

Ever since the founding fathers of our nation dreamed this
noble dream, America has been something of a schizophrenic
personality, tragically divided against herself. On the one hand
we have proudly professed the principles of democracy, and on
the other hand we have sadly practiced the very antithesis of
those principles. Indeed slavery and segregation have been
strange paradoxes in a nation founded on the principle that all
men are created equal. This is what the Swedish sociologist,
Gunnar Myrdal, referred to as the American dilemma.*

But the shape of the world today does not permit us the
luxury of an anemic democracy. The price America must pay
for the continued exploitation of the Negro and other minority
groups is the price of its own destruction. The hour is late; the
clock of destiny is ticking out. It is trite, but urgently true, that
if America is to remain a first-class nation she can no longer
have second-class citizens. Now, more than ever before, America is challenged to bring her noble dream into reality, and
those who are working to implement the American dream are
the true saviors of democracy.

Now may I suggest some of the things we must do if we are
to make the American dream a reality. First I think all of us
must develop a world perspective if we are to survive. The American dream will not become a reality devoid of the larger dream
of a world of brotherhood and peace and good will. The world
in which we live is a world of geographical oneness and we
are challenged now to make it spiritually one.

Man's scientific genius and technological ingenuity has
dwarfed distance and placed time in chains. Jet planes have
compressed into minutes distances that once took days and
months to cover. It is not common for a preacher to be quoting
Bob Hope, but I think he has aptly described this jet age in
which we live. If, on taking off on a nonstop flight from Los
Angeles to New York City, you develop hiccups, he said, you
will hic in Los Angeles and cup in New York City. That is really
moving. If you take a flight from Tokyo, Japan, on Sunday

* Gunnar Myrdal's *The American Dilemma* was published in 1944.

morning, you will arrive in Seattle, Washington, on the preceding Saturday night. When your friends meet you at the airport and ask you when you left Tokyo, you will have to say, "I left tomorrow." This is the kind of world in which we live. Now this is a bit humorous but I am trying to laugh a basic fact into all of us: the world in which we live has become a single neighborhood.

Through our scientific genius we have made of this world a neighborhood; now through our moral and spiritual development we must make of it a brotherhood. In a real sense, we must all learn to live together as brothers, or we will all perish together as fools. We must come to see that no individual can live alone; no nation can live alone. We must all live together; we must all be concerned about each other.

Some months ago, Mrs. King and I journeyed to that great country in the Far East known as India. I will never forget the experiences that came to us as we moved around that great country, or the opportunity of meeting and talking with the great leaders of India and with people all over in the cities and the villages throughout India. Certainly this was an experience that I will always remember, but there were depressing moments. How can one avoid being depressed when he sees with his own eyes millions of people going to bed hungry at night? How can one avoid being depressed when he sees with his own eyes millions of people sleeping on the sidewalk at night?

In Calcutta alone, more than a million people sleep on the sidewalks every night; in Bombay, more than six hundred thousand people sleep on the sidewalks every night. They have no beds to sleep in; they have no houses to go into. How can one avoid being depressed when he discovers that of India's 400 million people, more than 365 million make an annual income of less than sixty dollars a year? Most of these people have never seen a doctor or a dentist.

As I looked at these conditions, I found myself saying that we in America cannot stand idly by and not be concerned. Then something within me cried out, "Oh, no, because the destiny of the United States is tied up with the destiny of India—with the destiny of every other nation." And I remembered that we spend more than a million dollars a day to store surplus food in this country. I said to myself, "I know where we can store that food free of charge—in the wrinkled stomachs of the millions of people who go to bed hungry at night." Maybe we spend too much of our national budget building military bases around the world, rather than bases of genuine concern and understanding.

All this is simply to say that all life is interrelated. We are caught in an inescapable network of mutuality; tied in a single garment of destiny. Whatever affects one directly, affects all indirectly. As long as there is poverty in this world, no man can be totally rich even if he has a billion dollars. As long as diseases are rampant and millions of people cannot expect to live more than twenty or thirty years, no man can be totally healthy, even if he just got a clean bill of health from the finest clinic in America. Strangely enough, I can never be what I ought to be until you are what you ought to be. You can never be what you ought to be until I am what I ought to be. This is the way the world is made. I didn't make it that way, but this is the interrelated structure of reality. John Donne caught it a few centuries ago and could cry out, "No man is an island entire of itself; every man is a piece of the continent, a part of the main . . . any man's death diminishes me, because I am involved in mankind, and therefore never send to know for whom the bell tolls; it tolls for thee." If we were to realize the American dream we must cultivate this world perspective.

There is another thing quite closely related to this. We must keep our moral and spiritual progress abreast with our scientific and technological advances. This poses another dilemma of modern man. We have allowed our civilization to outdistance our culture. Professor MacIver follows the German sociologist, Alfred Weber, in pointing out the distinction between culture and civilization. Civilization refers to what we use; culture refers to what we are. Civilization is that complex of devices, instrumentalities, mechanisms and techniques by means of which we live. Culture is that realm of ends expressed in art, literature, religion and morals for which at best we live.

The great problem confronting us today is that we have allowed the means by which we live to outdistance the ends for which we live. We have allowed our civilization to outrun our culture, and so we are in danger now of ending up with guided missiles in the hands of misguided men. This is what the poet Thoreau meant when he said, "Improved means to an unimproved end." If we are to survive today and realize the dream of our mission and the dream of the world, we must bridge the gulf and somehow keep the means by which we live abreast with the ends for which we live.

Another thing we must do is to get rid of the notion once and for all that there are superior and inferior races. Now we know that this view still lags around in spite of the fact that many great anthropologists, Margaret Mead and Ruth Benedict and Melville Herskovits and others have pointed out and made it clear through scientific evidence that there are no superior races and there are no inferior races. There may be intellectually superior individuals within all races. In spite of all this evidence, however, the view still gets around somehow that there are superior and inferior races. The whole concept of white supremacy rests on this fallacy.

You know, there was a time when some people used to argue the inferiority of the Negro and the colored races generally on the basis of the Bible and religion. They would say the Negro was inferior by nature because of Noah's curse upon the children of Ham. And then another brother had probably read the logic of Aristotle. You know Aristotle brought into being the syllogism which had a major premise and a minor premise and a conclusion, and one brother had probably read Aristotle and he put his argument in the framework of an Aristotelian syllogism. He could say that all men are made in the image of God. This was a major premise. Then came his minor premise: God, as everybody knows, is not a Negro; therefore the Negro is not a man. And that was called logic!

But we don't often hear these arguments today. Segregation is now based on "sociological and cultural" grounds. "The Negro is not culturally ready for integration, and if integration comes into being it will pull the white race back a generation. It will take fifty or seventy-five years to raise these standards." And then we hear that the Negro is a criminal, and there are those who would almost say he is a criminal by nature. But they never point out that these things are environmental and not racial; these problems are problems of urban dislocation. They fail to see that poverty, and disease, and ignorance breed crime whatever the racial group may be. And it is a tortuous logic that views the tragic results of segregation and discrimination as an argument for the continuation of it.

If we are to implement the American dream we must get rid of the notion once and for all that there are superior and inferior races. This means that members of minority groups must make it clear that they can use their resources even under adverse circumstances. We must make full and constructive use of the freedom we already possess. We must not use our oppression as an excuse for mediocrity and laziness. For history has proven that inner determination can often break through the outer shackles of circumstance. Take the Jews, for example, and the years they have been forced to walk through the long and desolate night of oppression. This did not keep them from rising up to plunge against cloud-filled nights of oppression, new and blazing stars of inspiration. Being a Jew did not keep Einstein from using his genius-packed mind to prove his theory of relativity.

And so, being a Negro does not have to keep any individual from rising up to make a contribution as so many Negroes have done within our own lifetime. Human nature cannot be catalogued, and we need not wait until the day of full emancipation. So from an old clay cabin in Virginia's hills, Booker T. Washington rose up to be one of the nation's great leaders. He lit a torch in Alabama; then darkness fled.

From the red hills of Gordon County, Georgia, from an iron foundry at Chattanooga, Tennessee, from the arms of a mother who could neither read nor write, Roland Hayes rose up to be one of the nation's and the world's greatest singers. He carried his melodious voice to the mansion of the Queen Mother of Spain and the Palace of King George the Fifth. From the poverty-striken areas of Philadelphia, Pennsylvania, Marian Anderson rose up to be the world's greatest contralto, so that Toscanini could say that a voice like this comes only once in a century. Sibelius of Finland could say, "My roof is too low for such a voice."

From humble, crippling circumstances, George Washington Carver rose up and carved for himself an imperishable niche in the annals of science. There was a star in the sky of female leadership. Then came Mary McLeod Bethune to let it shine in her life. There was a star in the diplomatic sky. Then came Ralph Bunche, the grandson of a slave preacher, and allowed it to shine in his life with all of its radiant beauty. There were stars in the athletic sky. Then came Joe Louis with his educated fists, Jesse Owens with his fleet and dashing feet, Jackie Robinson with his powerful bat and calm spirit. All of these people have come to remind us that we need not wait until the day of full emancipation. They have justified the conviction of the poet that:

> Fleecy locks and dark complexion
> Cannot forfeit nature's claim.
> Skin may differ but affection
> Dwells in black and white the same.
> Were I so tall as to reach the pole
> Or to grasp the ocean at a span,
> I must be measured by my soul,
> The mind is standard of the man.

Finally, if we are to implement the American dream, we must continue to engage in creative protest in order to break down all of those barriers that make it impossible for the dream to be realized. Now I know there are those people who will argue that we must wait on something. They fail to see the necessity for creative protest, but I say to you that I can see no way to break loose from an old order and to move into a new order without standing up and resisting the unjust dogma of the old order.

To do this, we must get rid of two strange illusions that have been held by the so-called moderates in race relations. First is the myth of time advanced by those who say that you must wait on time; if you "just wait and be patient," time will work the situation out. They will say this even about Freedom Rides.* They will say this about sit-ins: that you're pushing things too fast—cool off—time will work these problems out. Well, evolution may hold in the biological realm, and in that area Darwin was right. But when a Herbert Spencer seeks to apply "evolution" to the whole fabric of society, there is no truth in it.† Even a superficial look at history shows that social progress never rolls in on the wheels of inevitability. It comes through the tireless effort and the persistent work of dedicated individuals. Without this hard work, time itself becomes an ally of the primitive forces of irrational emotionalism and social stagnation. And we must get rid of the myth of time.

There is another myth, that bases itself on a species of educational determinism. It leads one to think that you can't solve this problem through legislation; you can't solve this problem through judicial decree; you can't solve this problem through executive orders on the part of the President of the United States. It must be solved by education. Now I agree that education plays a great role, and it must continue to play a great role in changing attitudes, in getting people ready for the new order. And we must also see the importance of legislation.

It is not a question either of education or of legislation. Both legislation and education are required. Now, people will say, "You can't legislate morals." Well, that may be true. Even though

---

* In May, 1961, the Congress of Racial Equality, an interracial direct-action group founded in 1942, sent buses of "Freedom Riders" into the South to test segregation laws and practices in interstate transportation. In Alabama and Mississippi the Freedom Riders were attacked by white racist mobs and arrested, but on September 22, 1961, the Interstate Commerce Commission ruled that passengers on interstate carriers would be seated without regard to race and that such carriers could not use segregated terminals.

† Herbert Spencer (1820–1903) was the formulator of "social Darwinism," an effort to apply Darwinism to society; he stressed, among other points, that Anglo-Saxon civilization was a superior development out of previous civilizations and the result of competition.

morality may not be legislated, behavior can be regulated. And this is very important. We need religion and education to change attitudes and to change the hearts of men. We need legislation and federal action to control behavior. It may be true that the law can't make a man love me, but it can keep him from lynching me, and I think that's pretty important also.

And so we must get rid of these illusions and move on with determination and with zeal to break down the unjust systems we find in our society, so that it will be possible to realize the American dream. As I have said so often, if we seek to break down discrimination, we must use the proper methods. I am convinced more than ever before that, as the powerful, creative way opens, men and women who are eager to break the barriers of oppression and of segregation and discrimination need not fall down to the levels of violence. They need not sink into the quicksands of hatred. Standing on the high ground of non-injury, love and soul force, they can turn this nation upside down and right side up.

I believe, more than ever before, in the power of nonviolent resistance. It has a moral aspect tied to it. It makes it possible for the individual to secure moral ends through moral means. This has been one of the great debates of history. People have felt that it is impossible to achieve moral ends through moral means. And so a Machiavelli could come into being and so force a sort of duality within the moral structure of the universe. Even Communism could come into being and say that anything justifies the end of a classless society—lying, deceit, hate, violence—anything. And this is where nonviolent resistance breaks with Communism and with all of those systems which argue that the end justifies the means, because we realize that the end is preexistent in the means. In the long run of history, destructive means cannot bring about constructive ends.

The practical aspect of nonviolent resistance is that it exposes the moral defenses of the opponent. Not only that, it somehow arouses his conscience at the same time, and it breaks down his morale. He has no answer for it. If he puts you in jail, that's all right; if he lets you out, that's all right too. If he beats you, you accept that; if he doesn't beat you—fine. And so you go on, leaving him with no answer. But if you use violence, he does have an answer. He has the state militia; he has police brutality.

Nonviolent resistance is one of the most magnificent expressions going on today. We see it in the movement taking place among students in the South and their allies who have been willing to come in from the North and other sections. They have taken our deep groans and passionate yearnings, filtered them in their own souls, and fashioned them into the creative protest, which is an epic known all over our nation. They have moved in a uniquely meaningful orbit, imparting light and heat to a distant satellite. And people say, "Does this bring results?" Well, look at the record.

In less than a year, lunch counters have been integrated in more than 142 cities of the Deep South, and this was done without a single court suit; it was done without spending millions and millions of dollars. We think of the Freedom Rides, and remember that more than sixty people are now in jail in Jackson, Mississippi. What has this done? These people have been beaten; they have suffered to bring to the attention of this nation, the indignities and the injustices Negro people still confront in interstate travel. It has, therefore, had an educational value. But not only that—signs have come down from bus stations in Montgomery, Alabama. They've never been down before. Not only that—the Attorney General of this nation has called on I.C.C. to issue new regulations making it positively clear that segregation in interstate travel is illegal and unconstitutional.

And so this method can bring results. Sometimes it can bring quick results. But even when it doesn't bring immediate results, it is constantly working on the conscience; it is at all times using moral means to bring about moral ends. And so I say we must continue on the way of creative protest. I believe also that this method will help us to enter the new age with the proper attitude.

As I have said in so many instances, it is not enough to struggle for the new society. We must make sure that we make the psychological adjustment required to live in that new society. This is true of white people, and it is true of Negro people. Psychological adjustment will save white people from going into the new age with old vestiges of prejudice and attitudes of white supremacy. It will save the Negro from seeking to substitute one tyranny for another.

I know sometimes we get discouraged and sometimes disappointed with the slow pace of things. At times we begin to talk about racial separation instead of racial integration, feeling that there is no other way out. My only answer is that the problem never will be solved by substituting one tyranny for another. Black supremacy is as dangerous as white supremacy, and God is not interested merely in the freedom of black men and brown men and yellow men. God is interested in the freedom of the whole human race and in the creation of a society where all men can live together as brothers, where every man will respect the dignity and the worth of human personality.

By following this method, we may also be able to teach our world something that it so desperately needs at this hour. In a day when Sputniks and Explorers are dashing through outer space, and guided ballistic missiles are carving highways of death through the stratosphere, no nation can win a war. The choice is no longer between violence and nonviolence; it is either nonviolence or nonexistence. Unless we find some alternative to war, we will destroy ourselves by the misuse of our own instruments. And so, with all of these attitudes and principles working together, I believe we will be able to make a contribution as men of good will to the ongoing structure of our society and toward the realization of the American dream. And so, as you go out today, I call upon you not to be detached spectators, but involved participants, in this great drama that is taking place in our nation and around the world.

Every academic discipline has its technical nomenclature, and modern psychology has a word that is used, probably, more than any other. It is the word *maladjusted*. This word is the ringing cry of modern child psychology. Certainly all of us want to live a well-adjusted life in order to avoid the neurotic personality. But I say to you, there are certain things within our social order to which I am proud to be maladjusted and to which I call upon all men of good will to be maladjusted.

If you will allow the preacher in me to come out now, let me say to you that I never did intend to adjust to the evils of segregation and discrimination. I never did intend to adjust myself to religious bigotry. I never did intend to adjust myself to economic conditions that will take necessities from the many to give luxuries to the few. I never did intend to adjust myself to the madness of militarism, and the self-defeating effects of physical violence. And I call upon all men of good will to be maladjusted because it may well be that the salvation of our world lies in the hands of the maladjusted.

So let us be maladjusted, as maladjusted as the prophet Amos, who in the midst of the injustices of his day could cry out in words that echo across the centuries, "Let justice run down like waters and righteousness like a mighty stream." Let us be as maladjusted as Abraham Lincoln, who had the vision to see that this nation could not exist half slave and half free. Let us be maladjusted as Jesus of Nazareth, who could look into the eyes of the men and women of his generation and cry out, "Love your enemies. Bless them that curse you. Pray for them that despitefully use you."

I believe that it is through such maladjustment that we will be able to emerge from the bleak and desolate midnight of man's inhumanity to man into the bright and glittering daybreak of freedom and justice. That will be the day when all of God's children, black men and white men, Jews and Gentiles, Catholics and Protestants, will be able to join hands and sing in the words of the old Negro spiritual, "Free at last! Free at last! Thank God almighty, we are free at last!"

THE PHILOSOPHY OF THE STUDENT NONVIOLENT MOVEMENT

By Martin Luther King, Jr.

As black Americans became increasingly dissatisfied with the emphasis placed by the N.A.A.C.P. upon gradual change through the courts, new protest groups emerged. These included the Congress of Racial Equality (CORE), the Southern Christian Leadership Conference (S.C.L.C.) and the Student Nonviolent Coordinating Committee (S.N.C.C.). S.N.C.C. was organized by students who had carried through the sit-in movement, and in its early stages it was greatly influenced by the nonviolent philosophy of Martin Luther King, Jr. It later repudiated basic elements of the nonviolent philosophy and changed its name to Student National Coordinating Committee.

In an address to the annual meeting of the Fellowship of the Concerned, November 16, 1961, Dr. King explained the philosophy behind the student nonviolent movement. It is one of his major speeches. It is reprinted here with the permission of Mrs. Martin Luther King, Jr.

. . . I HAVE BEEN ASKED to talk about the philosophy behind the student movement. There can be no gainsaying the fact that we confront a crisis in race relations in the United States. The crisis in 1954 outlawing segregation in the public schools has been precipitated on the one hand by the determined resistance of reactionary forces in the South to the Supreme Court's decision. And we know that at times this resistance has risen to ominous proportions. At times we find the legislative halls of the

South ringing loud with such words as "interposition" and "nullification." And all these forces have developed into massive resistance. But we must also say that the crisis has been precipitated on the other hand by the determination of hundreds
and thousands and millions of Negro people to achieve freedom
and human dignity. If the Negro stayed in his place and accepted discrimination and segregation, there would be no crisis.
But the Negro has a new sense of dignity, a new self-respect
and new determination. He has reevaluated his own intrinsic
worth. Now, this new sense of dignity on the part of the Negro
grows out of the same longing for freedom and human dignity
on the part of the oppressed people all over the world. Now, we
must say that this struggle for freedom will not come to an
automatic halt, for history reveals to us that once oppressed
people rise up against that oppression, there is no stopping
point short of full freedom. On the other hand, history reveals
to us that those who oppose the movement for freedom are
those who are in privileged positions, who very seldom give up
their privileges without strong resistance. And they seldom do it
voluntarily. So the sense of struggle will continue. The question
is, How will the struggle be waged?

Now, there are three ways that oppressed people have generally dealt with their oppression. One way is the method of
acquiescence, the method of surrender; that is, the individuals
will somehow adjust themselves to oppression, they adjust
themselves to discrimination or to segregation or colonialism or
what have you. The other method that has been used in history
is that of rising up against the oppressor with corroding hatred
and physical violence. Now, of course, we know about this
method in Western civilization, because in a sense it has been
the hallmark of its grandeur, and the inseparable twin of
Western materialism. But there is a weakness in this method
because it ends up creating many more social problems than it
solves. And I am convinced that if the Negro succumbs to the
temptation of using violence in his struggle for freedom and
justice, unborn generations will be the recipients of a long and
desolate night of bitterness. And our chief legacy to the future
will be an endless reign of meaningless chaos.

But there is another way—namely, the way of nonviolent
resistance. This method was popularized in our generation by
a little man from India, whose name was Mohandas K. Gandhi.
He used this method in a magnificent way to free his people
from the economic exploitation and the political domination
inflicted upon them by a foreign power.

This has been the method used by the student movement in

the South and all over the United States. And naturally whenever I talk about the student movement I cannot be totally objective. I have to be somewhat subjective, because of my great admiration for what the students have done. For in a real sense they have taken our deep groans and passionate yearnings for freedom, and filtered them in their own tender souls, and fashioned them into a creative protest which is an epic known all over our nation. As a result of their disciplined, nonviolent, yet courageous struggle, they have been able to do wonders in the South, and in our nation. But this movement does have an underlying philosophy, it has certain ideals that are attached to it, it has certain philosophical precepts. These are the things that I would like to discuss for the few moments left.

I would say that the first point or the first principle in the movement is the idea that means must be as pure as the end. This movement is based on the philosophy that ends and means must cohere. Now this has been one of the long struggles in history, the whole idea of means and ends. Great philosophers have grappled with it, and sometimes they have emerged with the idea, from Machiavelli on down, that the end justifies the means. There is a great system of thought in our world today, known as Communism. And I think that with all of the weakness and tragedies of Communism, we find its greatest tragedy right there, that it goes under the philosophy that the end justifies the means that are used in the process. So we can read or we can hear the Leninists say that lying, deceit, or violence, that many of these things justify the ends of the classless society.

This is where the student movement and the nonviolent movement that is taking place in our nation would break with Communism and any other system that would argue that the end justifies the means. For in the long run, we must see that the end represents the means in process and the idea in the making. In other words, we cannot believe, or we cannot go with the idea that the end justifies the means, because the end is preexistent in the means. So the idea of nonviolent resistance, the philosophy of nonviolent resistance, is the philosophy which says that in history, immoral destructive means cannot bring about moral and constructive ends.

There is another thing about this philosophy, this method of nonviolence which is followed by the student movement. It says that those who adhere to or follow this philosophy must follow a consistent principle of noninjury. They must consistently refuse to inflict injury upon another. Sometimes you will read the literature of the student movement, and see that, as they are getting ready for the sit-in or stand-in, they will read something like this, "If you are hit do not hit back, if you are cursed do not curse back." This is the whole idea, that the individual who is engaged in a nonviolent struggle must never inflict injury upon another. Now this has an external aspect and it has an internal one. From the external point of view it means that the individuals involved must avoid external physical violence. So they don't have guns, they don't retaliate with physical violence. If they are hit in the process, they avoid external physical violence at every point. But it also means that they avoid internal violence of spirit. This is why the love ethic stands so high in the student movement. We have a great deal of talk about love and nonviolence in this whole thrust.

Now when the students talk about love, certainly they are not talking about emotional bosh, they are not talking about merely a sentimental outpouring; they're talking something much deeper, and I always have to stop and try to define the meaning of love in this context. The Greek language comes to our aid in trying to deal with this. There are three words in the Greek language for love, one is the word *eros*. This is a beautiful type of love, it is an aesthetic love. Plato talks about it a great deal in his Dialogue, the yearning of the soul for the realm of the divine. It has come to us to be a sort of romantic love, and so in a sense we have read about it and experienced it. We've read about it in all the beauties of literature. I guess in a sense Edgar Allan Poe was talking about *eros* when he talked about his beautiful Annabel Lee, with the love surrounded by the halo of eternity. In a sense Shakespeare was talking about *eros* when he said "Love is not love which alters when it alteration finds, or bends with the remover to remove: O, no! it is an ever-fixed mark that looks on tempests and is never shaken; it is the star to every wandering bark. . . ." (You know, I remember that because I used to quote it to this lady when we were courting; that's *eros*.) The Greek language talks about *Philia* which was another level of love. It is an intimate affection between personal friends, it is a reciprocal love. On this level you love because you are loved. It is friendship.

Then the Greek language comes out with another word which is called the *agape*. *Agape* is more than romantic love; *agape* is more than friendship. *Agape* is understanding, creative, redemptive, good will to all men. It is an overflowing love which seeks nothing in return. Theologians would say that it is the love of God operating in the human heart. So that when one rises to love on this level, he loves men not because he likes them, not because their ways appeal to him, but he loves every man because God loves him. And he rises to the point of loving the person who does an evil deed while hating the deed that the person does. I think this is what Jesus meant when he said "love your enemies." I'm very happy that he didn't say like your enemies, because it is very difficult to like someone bombing your home; it is pretty difficult to like somebody threatening your children; it is difficult to like Congressmen who spend all of their time trying to defeat civil rights. But Jesus says love them, and love is greater than like. Love is understanding, redemptive, creative, good will for all men. And it is this whole ethic of love which is the idea standing at the basis of the student movement.

There is something else; that one seeks to defeat the unjust system, rather than individuals who are caught in that system. And that one goes on believing that somehow this is the important thing, to get rid of the evil system and not the individual who happens to be misled, who was taught wrong. The thing to do is to get rid of the system and thereby create a moral balance within society.

Another thing that stands at the center of this movement is another idea: that suffering can be a most creative and powerful social force. Suffering has certain moral attributes involved, but it can be a powerful and creative social force. Now, it is very interesting at this point to notice that both violence and nonviolence agree that suffering can be a very powerful social force. But there is this difference: violence says that suffering can be a powerful social force by inflicting suffering on somebody else; so this is what we do in war, this is what we do in the whole violent thrust of the violent movement. It believes that you achieve some end by inflicting suffering on another. The nonviolent say that suffering becomes a powerful social force when you willingly accept that violence on yourself, so that self-suffering stands at the center of the nonviolent movement and the individuals involved are able to suffer in a creative manner, feeling that unearned suffering is redemptive, and that suffering may serve to transform the social situation.

Another thing in this movement is the idea that there is within human nature an amazing potential for goodness. There is within human nature something that can respond to goodness. I know somebody's liable to say that this is an unrealistic movement if it goes on believing that all people are good. Well, I didn't say that. I think the students are realistic enough to believe that there is a strange dichotomy of disturbing dualism within human nature. Many of the great philosophers and thinkers through the ages have seen this. It caused Ovid, the Latin poet, to say, "I see and approve the better things of life, but the evil things I do." It caused even Saint Augustine to say, "Lord, make me pure, but not yet." Plato centuries ago said that the human personality is like a charioteer with two headstrong horses, each wanting to go in different directions, so that within our own individual lives we see this conflict and certainly when we come to the collective life of man, we see a strange badness. But in spite of this there is something in human nature that can respond to goodness. So that man is neither innately good nor is he innately bad; he has potentialities for both. So, in this sense, Carlyle was right when he said that "there are depths in man which go down to the lowest hell, and heights which reach the highest heaven, for are not both heaven and hell made out of him, ever-lasting miracle and mystery that he is?" Man has the capacity to be good, man has the capacity to be evil.

And so the nonviolent resister never lets this idea go, that there is something within human nature that can respond to goodness. So that a Jesus of Nazareth or a Mohandas Gandhi can appeal to human beings and appeal to that element of evil within them, and a Hitler can appeal to the element of evil within them. But we must never forget that there is something within human nature that can respond to goodness, that man is not totally depraved; to put it in theological terms, the image of God is never totally done. And so the individuals who believe in this movement and who believe in nonviolence and our struggle in the South, somehow believe that even the worst segregationist can become an integrationist. Now sometimes it is hard to believe that this is what this movement says, and it believes it firmly, that there is something within human nature that can be changed, and this stands at the top of the whole philosophy of the student movement and the philosophy of nonviolence.

It says something else. It says that it is as much a moral obligation to refuse to cooperate with evil as it is to cooperate with good. Noncooperation with evil is as much a moral obligation as the cooperation with good. So that the student movement is willing to stand up courageously on the idea of civil disobedience. Now I think this is the part of the student movement that is probably misunderstood more than anything else. And it is a difficult aspect, because on the one hand the students would say, and I would say, and all the people who believe in civil rights would say: Obey the Supreme Court's decision of 1954 and at the same time, we would disobey certain laws that exist on the statutes of the South today.

This brings in the whole question of how can you be logically consistent when you advocate obeying some laws and disobeying other laws? Well, I think one would have to see the whole meaning of this movement at this point by seeing that the students recognize that there are two types of laws. There are just laws and there are unjust laws. And they would be the first to say obey the just laws, they would be the first to say that men and women have a moral obligation to obey just and right laws. And they would go on to say that we must see that there are unjust laws. Now the question comes into being, what is the difference, and who determines the difference, what is the difference between a just and an unjust law?

Well, a just law is a law that squares with a moral law. It is a law that squares with that which is right, so that any law that uplifts human personality is a just law. Whereas that law which is out of harmony with the moral is a law which does not square with the moral law of the universe. It does not square with the law of God, so for that reason it is unjust, and any law that degrades the human personality is an unjust law.

Well, somebody says that that does not mean anything to me; first, I don't believe in these abstract things called moral laws, and I'm not too religious, so I don't believe in the law of God; you have to get a little more concrete, and more practical. What do you mean when you say that a law is unjust, and a law is just? Well, I would go on to say in more concrete terms that an unjust law is a code that the majority inflicts on the minority that is not binding on itself. So that this becomes difference made legal. Another thing that we can say is that an unjust law is a code which the majority inflicts upon the minority, which that minority had no part in enacting or creating, because that minority had no right to vote in many instances, so that the legislative bodies that made these laws were not democratically elected. Who could ever say that the legislative body of Mississippi was democratically elected, or the legislative body of Alabama was democratically elected, or the legislative body even of Georgia has been democratically elected, when there are people in Terrell County and in other counties, because of the color of their skin, who cannot vote? They confront reprisals and threats and all of that; so that an unjust law is a law that individuals did not have a part in creating or enacting because they were denied the right to vote.

Now by the same token, a just law would be just the opposite. A just law becomes saneness made legal. It is a code that the majority, who happen to believe in that code, compel the minority, who don't believe in it, to follow, because they are willing to follow it themselves, so it is saneness made legal. Therefore the individuals who stand up on the basis of civil disobedience realize that they are following something that says that there are just laws and there are unjust laws. Now, they are not anarchists. They believe that there are laws which must be followed; they do not seek to defy the law, they do not seek to evade the law. For many individuals who would call themselves segregationists and who would hold on to segregation at any cost seek to defy the law, they seek to evade the law, and their process can lead on into anarchy. They seek in the final analysis to follow a way of uncivil disobedience, not civil disobedience. And I submit that the individual who disobeys the law, whose conscience tells him it is unjust and who is willing to accept the penalty by staying in jail until that law is altered, is expressing at the moment the very highest respect for law.

This is what the students have followed in their movement. Of course there is nothing new about this; they feel that they are in good company and rightly so. We go back and read the Apology and the Crito, and you see Socrates practicing civil disobedience. And to a degree academic freedom is a reality today because Socrates practiced civil disobedience. The early Christians practiced civil disobedience in a superb manner, to a point where they were willing to be thrown to the lions. They were willing to face all kinds of suffering in order to stand up for what they knew was right, even though they knew it was against the laws of the Roman Empire.

We could come up to our own day and we see it in many instances. We must never forget that everything that Hitler did in Germany was "legal." It was illegal to aid and comfort a Jew, in the days of Hitler's Germany. But I believe that if I had the same attitude then as I have now I would publicly aid and comfort my Jewish brothers in Germany if Hitler were alive today calling this an illegal process. If I lived in South Africa today in the midst of the white-supremacy law in South Africa, I would join Chief Luthuli* and others in saying, break these unjust laws. And even let us come up to America. Our nation in a sense came into being through a massive act of civil disobedience, for the Boston Tea Party was nothing but a massive act of civil disobedience. Those who stood up against the slave laws, the Abolitionists, by and large practiced civil disobedience. So I think these students are in good company, and they feel that by practicing civil disobedience they are in line with men and women through the ages who have stood up for something that is morally right.

* Chief Albert John Luthuli was a distinguished champion of the rights of the black people of South Africa, and for this work he was imprisoned by the racist South African government. He received the Nobel Peace Prize in 1960.

Now there are one or two other things that I want to say about this student movement, moving out of the philosophy of nonviolence, something about what it is a revolt against. On the one hand it is a revolt against the negative peace that has encompassed the South for many years. I remember when I was in Montgomery, Alabama, one of the white citizens came to me one day and said—and I think he was very sincere about this—that in Montgomery for all of these years we have been such a peaceful community, we have had so much harmony in race relations and then you people have started this movement and boycott, and it has done so much to disturb race relations, and we just don't love the Negro like we used to love him, because you have destroyed the harmony and the peace that we once had in race relations. And I said to him, in the best way I could say and I tried to say it in nonviolent terms: We have never had peace in Montgomery, Alabama, we have never had peace in the South. We have had a negative peace, which is merely the absence of tension; we've had a negative peace in which the Negro patiently accepted his situation and his plight, but we've never had true peace, we've never had positive peace, and what we're seeking now is to develop this positive peace. For we must come to see that peace is not merely the absence of some negative force, it is the presence of a positive force. True peace is not merely the absence of tension, but it is the presence of justice and brotherhood. I think this is what Jesus meant when he said, "I come not to bring peace but a sword." Now Jesus didn't mean he came to start war, to bring a physical sword, and he didn't mean, I come not to bring positive peace. But I think what Jesus was saying in substance was this, that I come not to bring an old negative peace, which makes for stagnant passivity and deadening complacency, I come to bring something different, and whenever I come, a conflict is precipitated between the old and the new, whenever I come, a struggle takes place between justice and injustice, between the forces of light and the forces of darkness. I come not to bring a negative peace, but a positive peace, which is brotherhood, which is justice, which is the Kingdom of God.

And I think this is what we are seeking to do today, and this movement is a revolt against a negative peace and struggle to bring into being a positive peace, which makes for true brotherhood, true integration, true person-to-person relationships. This movement is also revolt against what is often called tokenism. Here again, many people do not understand this; they feel that in this struggle the Negro will be satisfied with tokens of integration, just a few students and a few schools here and there and a few doors open here and there. But this isn't the meaning of the movement, and I think that honesty impels me to admit it everywhere I have an opportunity, that the Negro's aim is to bring about complete integration in American life. And he has come to see that token integration is little more than token democracy, which ends up with many new evasive schemes and it ends up with new discrimination, covered up with such niceties of complexity. It is very interesting to discover that the movement has thrived in many communities that had token integration. So this reveals that the movement is based on a principle that integration must become real and complete, not just token integration.

It is also a revolt against what I often call the myth of time. We hear this quite often, that only time can solve this problem; that if we will only be patient, and only pray—which we must do, we must be patient and we must pray—but there are those who say just do these things and wait for time, and time will solve this problem. Well, the people who argue this do not themselves realize that time is neutral, that it can be used constructively or destructively. At points the people of ill will, the segregationists, have used time more effectively than the people of good will. So individuals in the struggle must come to realize that it is necessary to aid time, that without this kind of aid, time itself will become an ally of the insurgent and primitive forces of social stagnation. Therefore, this movement is a revolt against the myth of time.

There is a final thing that I would like to say to you: This movement is a movement based on faith in the future. It is a movement based on a philosophy, the possibility of the future bringing into being something real and meaningful. It is a movement based on hope. I think this is very important. The students have developed a theme song for their movement, maybe you've heard it. It goes something like this: "We shall overcome, deep in my heart, I do believe, we shall overcome," and they go on to say another verse, "We are not afraid today, deep in my heart, I do believe, we shall overcome." So it is out of this deep faith in the future that they are able to move out and adjourn the councils of despair, and to bring new light in the dark chambers of pessimism. I can remember the times that we've been together, I remember that night in Montgomery, Alabama, when we had stayed up all night, discussing the Freedom Rides, and that morning came to see that it was necessary to go on with the Freedom Rides, that we would not in all good conscience call an end to the Freedom Rides at that point. And I remember the first group got ready to leave, to take a bus for Jackson, Mississippi, we all joined hands and started singing together. "We shall overcome, we shall overcome." And something within me said, now how is it that these students can sing this? They are going down to Mississippi, they are going to face hostile and jeering mobs, and yet they could sing, "We shall overcome." They may even face physical death, and yet they could sing, "We shall overcome." Most of them realized that they would be thrown into jail, and yet they could sing, "We shall overcome, we are not afraid." Then something caused me to see at that moment the real meaning of the movement. That students had faith in the future. That the movement was based on hope, that this movement had something within it that says somehow even though the arc of the moral universe is long, it bends toward justice. And I think this should be a challenge to all others who are struggling to transform the dangling discords of our Southland into a beautiful symphony of brotherhood. There is something in this student movement which says to us, that we shall overcome. Before the victory is won, some will lose jobs, some will be called Communists and Reds, merely because they believe in brotherhood, some will be dismissed as dangerous rabble rousers and agitators merely because they're standing up for what is right. But we shall overcome. That is the basis of this movement, and as I like to say, there is something in this universe that justifies Carlyle in saying no lie can live forever. We shall overcome because there is something in this universe which justifies William Cullen Bryant in saying truth crushed to earth shall rise again. We shall overcome because there is something in this universe that justifies James Russell Lowell in saying, truth forever on the scaffold, wrong forever on the throne. Yet that scaffold sways the future, and behind the dim unknown standeth God within the shadows, keeping watch above His own. With this faith in the future, with this determined struggle, we will be able to emerge from the bleak and the desolate midnight of man's inhumanity to man, into the bright and glittering daybreak of freedom and justice. Thank you.

A CHALLENGE TO ARTISTS

By Lorraine Hansberry

In 1938 a temporary investigation unit of Congress, the House Un-American Activities Committee, was created mainly to advance the political career of its chairman, Martin Dies, Democratic Congressman from Texas. In January, 1947, the Committee was revived by the Republican leadership and, with the eager support of California Republican Congressman Richard M. Nixon, proceeded to investigate the Communists, alleged Communists, and all Americans who believed in progressive causes. Opposition to the un-American activities of the House Un-American Activities Committee mounted in the nation, and on October 27, 1962, a rally to abolish the Committee was held in Manhattan Center, New York City. One of the speakers was Lorraine Hansberry.

Lorraine Hansberry was born to an upper-class Negro family in Chicago, where her father was a wealthy businessman and a former United States Marshal. Miss Hansberry graduated from the University of Wisconsin, where she gained practical knowledge of dramatics from university and community theaters. At the age of twenty-seven, she wrote A Raisin in the Sun, *which, directed by Negroes and performed by an all-Negro cast headed by Sidney Poitier, became a Broadway hit, won the New York Drama Critic's Award for 1958, and was produced as a motion picture by Columbia Pictures. Miss Hansberry died of cancer in 1966. Two years later, excerpts from her published and unpublished works were performed in an off-Broadway production called* To Be Young, Gifted, and Black.

Here is Miss Hansberry's speech, reprinted from Freedomways, *Winter, 1963, pp. 31–35, with the permission of the Estate of Lorraine Hansberry.*

I AM AFRAID that I haven't made a speech for a very long time, and there is a significance in that fact, which is part of what I should like to talk about this evening.

A week or so ago I was at my typewriter working on a scene in a play of mine in which one character, a German novelist, is trying to explain to another character, an American intellectual, something about what led the greater portion of the German intelligentsia to acquiesce to Nazism. He says this: "They [the Nazis] permitted us to feel, in return for our silence, that we were nonparticipants—merely irrelevant if inwardly agonized observers who had nothing whatsoever to do with that which was being committed in our names."

Just as I put the period after that sentence, my own telephone rang and I was confronted with the voice of Dr. Otto Nathan, asking this particular American writer if she would be of this decade and this nation and appear at this rally this evening and join a very necessary denunciation of a lingering *American* kind of travesty.

It is the sort of moment of truth that dramatists dearly love to put on the stage but find as uncomfortable as everyone else in life. To make it short, however, I am here.

I mean to say that one can become detached in this world of ours; we can get to a place where we read only the theater or photography or music pages of our newspapers. And then we wake up one day and find that the better people of our nation are still where they were when we last noted them: in the courts defending *our* Constitutional rights for us.

This makes me feel that it might be interesting to talk about where are our artists in the contemporary struggles. Some of them, of course, are being heard and felt. Some of the more serious actresses such as Shelley Winters and Julie Harris and a very thoughtful comedian such as Steve Allen have associated themselves with some aspect of the peace movement and Sidney Poitier and Harry Belafonte have made significant contributions to the Negro struggle. But the vast majority—where are they?

Well, I am afraid that they are primarily where the ruling powers have always wished the artist to be and to stay: in their studios. They are consumed, in the main, with what they consider to be larger issues—such as "the meaning of life," et cetera. . . . I personally consider that part of this detachment is the direct and indirect result of many years of things like the House Committee and concurrent years of McCarthyism in all its forms. I mean to suggest that the climate of fear, which we were once told, as I was coming along, by wise men, would bear a bitter harvest in the culture of our civilization, has in fact come to pass. In the contemporary arts, the rejection of this particular world is no longer a mere grotesque threat, but a fact.

Among my contemporaries and colleagues in the arts the search for the roots of war, the exploitation of man, of poverty and of despair itself, is sought in any arena other than the one which has shaped these artists. Having discovered that the world is incoherent, they have—some of them—also come to the conclusion that it is also unreal and, in any case, beyond the corrective powers of human energy. Having determined that life is in fact an absurdity, they have not yet decided that the task of the thoughtful is to try and help impose purposefulness on that absurdity. They don't yet agree, by and large, that simply being against life as it is is not enough; that simply *not* being a "rhinoceros" is not enough. That, moreover, replacing phony utopianisms of one kind with vulgar and cheap little philosophies of accommodation is also not enough. In a word, they do not yet agree that it is perhaps the task, I should think certainly the joy, of the artist to chisel out some expression of what life can conceivably be.

The fact is that this unwitting capitulation really does aim to be a revolt; really does aim to indict—*something*. Really does aim to be partisan in saying no to a world which it generally characterizes as a "brothel." I am thinking now, mainly, of course, of writers of my generation. It is they, upon whom we must depend so heavily for the refinement and articulation of the aspiration of man, who do not yet agree that if the world is a brothel, then someone has built the edifice; and that if it was the hand of man, then the hand of man can reconstruct it— that whatever man renders, creates, imagines, he can render afresh, re-create and even more gloriously re-imagine. But, I must repeat, that anyone who can even think so these days is held to be an example of unparalleled simple-mindedness.

Why? For this is what is cogent to our meeting tonight; the writers that I am presently thinking of come mainly from my generation. That is to say that they come from a generation which was betrayed in the late forties and fifties by the domination of McCarthyism. We were ceaselessly told, after all, to be everything which mutilates youth: to be silent, to be ignorant, to be without unsanctioned opinions, to be compliant and, above all else, obedient to all the ideas which are in fact the dregs of an age. We were taught that agitational activity in behalf of changing this world was nothing but an expression, among other things, of our "neurotic compulsions" about our own self-dissatisfactions because our mothers dominated our fathers or some such as that. We were told in an age of celebrated liberations of repressions that the repression of the *urge* to protest against war was surely the only *respectable* repression left in the universe.

As for those who went directly into science or industry it was all even less oblique than any of that. If you went to the wrong debates on campus, signed the wrong petitions, you simply didn't get the job you wanted and you were forewarned of this early in your college career.

And, of course, things are a little different than in my parents' times—I mean, with regard to the candor with which young people have been made to think in terms of money. It is the only single purpose which has been put before them. That which Shakespeare offered as a curse, "Put money in thy purse," is now a boast. What makes me think of that in connection with what we are speaking of tonight? Well, I hope that I am wise enough to determine the nature of a circle. If, after all, the ambition in life is merely to be rich, then all which might threaten that possibility is much to be avoided, is it not? This means, therefore, not incurring the disfavor of employers. It means that one will not protest war if one expects to draw one's livelihood from, say, the aircraft industry if one is an engineer. Or, in the arts, how can one write plays which have either implicit or explicit in them a quality of the detestation of commerciality, if in fact one is beholden to the commerciality of the professional theater? How can one protest the criminal persecution of political dissenters if one has already discovered at nineteen that to do so is to risk a profession? If all one's morality is wedded to the opportunist, the expedient in life, how can one have the deepest, most profound moral outrage about the fact of the condition of the Negro people in the United States? Particularly, thinking of expediency, when one has it dinned into one's ears day after day that the only reason why, perhaps, that troublesome and provocative group of people must some day be permitted to buy a cup of coffee or rent an apartment or get a job—is *not* because of the recognition of the universal humanity of the human race, but because it happens to be extremely expedient international politics to now *think* of granting these things!

As I stand here I know perfectly well that such institutions as the House Committee, and all the other little committees, have dragged on their particular obscene theatrics for all these years not to expose "Communists" or do anything really in connection with the "security" of the United States, but merely to create an atmosphere where, in the first place, I should be afraid to come here tonight at all and, secondly, to absolutely guarantee that I will not say what I am going to say, which is this:

I think that my government is wrong. I would like to see them

turn back our ships from the Caribbean.* The Cuban people, to
my mind, and I speak only for myself, have chosen their destiny
and I cannot believe that it is the place of the descendants of
those who did not ask the monarchists of the eighteenth century
for permission to make the United States a republic, to interfere with the twentieth-century choice of another sovereign
people.

I will go further, speaking as a Negro in America, and impose
a little of what Negroes say all the time to each other on what I
am saying to you. And that is that it would be a great thing if
they would not only turn back the ships from the Caribbean but
turn to the affairs of our country that need righting. For one
thing, empty the legislative and judicial chambers of the victims
of political persecution so we know why that lamp is burning
out there in the Brooklyn waters. And, while they are at it, go on
and help fulfill the American dream and empty the Southern
jails of the genuine heroes, practically the last vestige of dignity
that we have to boast about at this moment in our history; those
students whose imprisonment for trying to insure what is already on the book is our national disgrace at this moment.

And I would go so far—perhaps with an over sense of drama,
but I don't think so—to say that maybe without waiting for another two men to die, that we send those troops to finish the
Reconstruction in Alabama, Georgia, Mississippi, and every
place else where the fact of our federal flag flying creates the
false notion that what happened at the end of the Civil War was
the defeat of the slavocracy at the political as well as the military level. And I say this not merely in behalf of the black and
oppressed but, for a change—and more and more thoughtful
Negroes must begin to make this point—also for the white and
disinherited of the South, those poor whites who, by the millions, have been made the tragic and befuddled instruments of
their own oppression at the hand of the most sinister political
apparatus in our country. I think perhaps that if our government would do that it would not have to compete in any wishful
way for the respect of the new black and brown nations of the
world.

Finally, I think that all of us who are thinking such things,
who wish to exercise these rights that we are here defending
tonight, must really exercise them. Speaking to my fellow artists in particular, I think that we must paint them, sing them,

* The reference is to the blockade imposed upon Revolutionary Cuba
by the United States. American naval vessels were regularly stationed
outside the coastal limits of Cuba.

write about them. All these matters which are not currently fashionable. Otherwise, I think, as I have put into the mouth of my German novelist, we are indulging in a luxurious complicity —and no other thing.

I personally agree with those who say that from here on in, if we are to survive, we, the people—still an excellent phrase— we the people of the world must oblige the heads of all governments to become responsible to us. I personally do not feel that it matters if it be the government of China presently engaging in incomprehensible and insane antics at the border of India or my President, John F. Kennedy, dismissing what he knows to be in the hearts of the American people and engaging in overt provocation with our sister people to the South. I think that it is imperative to say "No" to all of it—"No" to war of any kind, anywhere. And I think, therefore, and it is my reason for being here tonight, that it is imperative to remove from the American fabric any and all such institutions or agencies as the House Committee on Un-American Activities which are designed expressly to keep us from saying "No!"

INTEGRATION MUST WORK—NOTHING ELSE CAN

By Rev. Milton A. Galamison

On its March 27, 1963, Court of Reason program, New York City's educational television station, WNDT, broadcast a debate on the subject, "The Negro in American Life: Can Integration Be Achieved?" Speaking for the affirmative was Rev. Milton A. Galamison and for the negative Malcolm X, New York leader of the Muslims. Dr. Galamison is the pastor, Siloam Presbyterian Church, Brooklyn, New York, and in addition to his religious duties, was the leader of the fight in New York City for desegregation in the public schools, heading the Parents' Workshop for Equality in New York City Schools. Later, he became a member of the New York City Board of Education.

Here is Dr. Galamison's five-minute opening statement in the debate, reprinted with permission from Freedomways, *Spring, 1963, pp. 215–17.*

THERE IS NOTHING in America which does not belong to me. There is no public office, however high; no employment opportunity, however lucrative; no community, however restricted; no marriage, however interracial, which is not a part of my heritage as a citizen of these United States. The fact that I have been historically deprived of my birthright by the majority of majority America and am unable to overcome the frustrations to my pursuit of happiness is an indictment of our national culture. But there is yet a deeper tragedy that could befall me. It is that I should *voluntarily* surrender my birthright. It is that I should elect life in a corner of America which my black forefathers rejected to the death. It is that I should retreat from the battlefield and abandon the prize to those who denied my father's father and who would deny my children's children.

Some five thousand Negroes, slave and free, fought in the War for Independence. Many thousands more fought in the War to preserve the Union. The story of our sacrifice and loyalty is written in blood tracks around the world. The soil has been fertilized by our sweat, the factories built on our backs, the machines oiled by our tears, the homes maintained by our servitude and the nation carved by our suffering. When, then, we speak of integration or separation as alternatives, we must consider the degree to which the Negro is already woven into the pattern of American life. We have been integrated at the level of sowing. It is in the area of reaping that we have been short-changed. We have paid the fare. The question is whether we shall fight for the ride. We have planted the tree. Shall we not demand the fruit?

The distress I feel for the segregationist mentality is unspeakable. We have, in this nation, seized on a monstrous evil like racism and exalted it as a great good. We have taught our children this immorality as a moral imperative. We have made hatred a holy thing. Our Senators and Congressmen win public office on the basis of a pledge to perpetuate deprivation against black children. Our churches have made race a religion above all other religions. Our immorality and crime against human life continues unabated and unmodified by even repentance. Our society is too sick to understand the depth of our sickness.

This sickness, like any sickness, knows no bounds. Its contagion recognizes no class or color lines. We have infected Europe and all the lands of our tourism with our disease. Why should it be thought a thing incredible that the victims of our own ghettos should also mistake this sickness for health, this insanity for sanity, this death for life? The new nationalists are saying to the racists, "I will show you what it is to be the object

of race arrogance. I will be just as you are." The integrationists
are saying, on the other hand, "Nothing could make me want
to be as you are." The worst harm white supremacy could inflict
on me is to mold me in the image of its buffoonery. Yet white
supremacy has achieved the supreme stroke of perverted genius
in convincing some Negroes that the desire for racial unity is
symptomatic of inferiority and pridelessness.

It follows, therefore, that I cannot see black arrogance as an
antidote for, or negation of, white arrogance. The proposed cure
so resembles the illness that it expands rather than reduces the
problem. Americans have been living for three hundred years
by the fraud of race supremacy. It has taken its toll on our individual and national character. It will represent more than a
footnote in the story of our decline and fall. Racism will ultimately fail no matter who practices it. Only when we stop
thinking about who is wrong and turn our attention to what is
wrong does the course for future action become clear.

Integration must work, because nothing else can. There is a
comradeship of suffering, a fellowship of pain across the world,
which knows no race. There can be no racial interpretation of
history or of the future. Whites will never solve the riddle of
their existence save through the Negro. As times past called for
a common front against slavery, the present calls for a common
front against bigotry and oppression. Segregation has been dead
for years. The task of its burial only awaits people of good will
who, in spite of evidence to the contrary, still believe that love
is the greatest force in the world.

THE SOCIAL REVOLUTION: CHALLENGE TO THE NATION

By Whitney M. Young, Jr.

*Organized in 1911 in New York City, the National Urban
League concentrated on the problems of urban Negroes.
The League sought, through an alliance with the white
business community, to open opportunities for Negroes in
industry, to train Negro social workers and to assist black
migrants from the South in adjusting to life in the Northern cities. Dominated by white businessmen and conserva-*

tive Negroes, the League did not attract a mass following. However, after World War II the League began slowly to move toward a more militant outlook. This change was reflected in an address delivered by Whitney M. Young, Jr., Executive Secretary of the League, at its 1963 National Conference, in which he interpreted the meaning of the Negro demand for "Freedom Now!"

Whitney M. Young was born in Kentucky. He did his undergraduate work at Kentucky State College and received his Master's degree in social work from the University of Minnesota in 1947. During the academic year 1960–61 he was a visiting scholar at Harvard under a special Rockefeller grant. He became Dean of the Atlanta University School of Social Work and Executive Director of the National Urban League on October 1, 1961. He died of a heart attack on March 14, 1971, while on a mission to Nigeria.

Here are extracts from his 1963 Conference address, reprinted with the permission of the National Urban League, from Whitney M. Young, Jr., The Social Revolution: Challenge to the Nation, Address at the 1963 National Conference of the Urban League, New York, National Urban League, 1963.

. . . EVERY MAJOR CITY in the United States has felt some manifestation of the unrest and burning desire of its Negro citizens for equality—now!* And hundreds of smaller communities have had reflected in their mirror the discontent that has spread like wildfire and that has illuminated the land with the flames of a modern revolution the counterpart of which neither this nation nor any nation has ever witnessed.

This revolution bears no similarity, however, to the American Revolution or to the French Revolution or to the Russian Revolution. There is no attempt here to overthrow a government. This is a revolution against historic injustice, against a way of life, against persons who maintain that the measure of achievement of man is determined by and related to the color of his skin. This is a revolution peculiarly characterized by a heroic drive and a courageous fight to gain the rights and respect that

---

* In 1963 there were riots in scores of cities, North and South, as police and vigilantes battled Negroes and whites determined to make the centennial celebration of the Emancipation Proclamation the occasion for the achievement of meaningful freedom. There were more than ten thousand racial demonstrations in 1963, and more than five thousand Negroes were arrested.

should be synonymous with the word "American." It is a revolution not by black people against white people, but by people who are right against those who are wrong.

This revolution is unlike any other also because, after three hundred years of deprivation, the deprived seek redress for their grievances in an expression of faith in a nation that has done very little to develop and nurture such faith. Their demands are simple and elemental, and those who would describe them as difficult and complicated do a disservice to America and to Americans.

This revolution is what I chose last year at our National Conference to call a "Revolution of Expectation." Today I would call it a "Revolution of Witnessing."

A review by me now of the events in this conflict as they have occurred since we met together last year is unnecessary. For there is not a person in this room tonight who cannot recall with his mind's eye, and with vividness and recurring horror, the photographs of brutality and barbarism. There is not a person in this room tonight who cannot remember with pride and humility the pictures of the bright-eyed children and courageous youth participants in the events of recent months.

For the Negro citizen, therefore, these are acts of bearing witness to his faith in democracy through peaceful nonviolent demonstration, and by channeling in constructive ways justified resentments and pent-up, frustrated emotions that have been born out of age-old abuses and contemptuous indignities.

For the white citizen these events mean bearing witness to the fact that democracy is more than a convenient institution through which privileges and material products flow to him.

For both, democracy is a way of life, an ideal in which all share its rewards, as well as its responsibilities. Indeed, without this concept, democracy has no meaning and certainly no permanence.

For the church and its membership, this is a time of witnessing that piety rests not in credal affirmation, but in the confirmation of deeds.

For the public official—whether city, state or federal—witnessing means greater concern for broad, democratic promises and human rights, rather than preoccupation with technical, Constitutional details and states' rights.

For the private sector of our society—whether business, labor, or health and welfare—this is a time for witnessing that the free-enterprise system works equally well for *all* American citizens.

For the Urban League this is a time to express willingness to witness that, while our past contributions need no defense or apology, our future challenges and opportunities are greater and more demanding than any we have ever faced. These are times that call for us to be frank, not only with the perpetuators of injustice as to their responsibilities, but equally frank and forthright with the victims of injustice as to their responsibilities in this new day that is full with promise of a brighter destiny for those whom we are committed to serve.

It is not enough to remind white Americans that for fifty-three years the Urban League has warned them of this inevitable consequence of indifference; neither is it necessary to boast of League contributions that now help to make it possible for Negro Americans to express their grievances so courageously.

The past is prologue. Today the nation and its Negro citizens ask of the Urban League: "What have you done for me recently? What will you be doing for me tomorrow?"

We in the Urban League are in the position of being able to answer these questions in language and with machinery possessed by no other agency. Our job is clear. Our job is to give meaning and reality to the revolution to which we all now serve as witnesses.

As we win the battle for civil rights, we can, and might well, lose the war for human rights.

In this age of automation and urbanization, the demands on Americans differ. The victories so courageously won in the streets can easily become an empty, hollow mockery if we do not simultaneously equip ourselves with the skills, the values, and the sense of community responsibility and participation which the future will demand.

At the risk of being misunderstood by the currently immature; by those who are merely seeking to remove the symbols that disturb their consciences; or even by the naïve who believe that equality is a condition automatically arrived at through the lowering of overt barriers, the League hereby announces its intent to pursue what we know to be a necessary program.

We have this year shared our identity with all others who struggle for the goal of equality, and we will continue to do so. But while we applaud and respect the victories which they have won, by the use of methods different from those of the Urban League, we will continue to seek their understanding and mutual respect for the long-range and vitally necessary programs and methods of the Urban League—programs and methods which can only be achieved by a professionally structured agency, devoting itself full time to this problem.

This we see not as competitive or in any way discrediting but rather as complementing and supplementing. To put it bluntly, we say that while there must be those who in the interest of justice and equality must walk the picket line in front of restaurants, hotels, theaters, business establishments—these same persons, and others, with equal zest and determination, must walk to the libraries, to the adult-education classes, and to the voting registrar's office. And they must take time to serve on policy-making bodies of agencies and institutions. For reality now dictates that we must recognize that those who would enter the new doors of opportunity must have the skills to qualify, the money to pay, and the confidence and security of knowing that they are, in fact, equal citizens.

I am not offering a substitute, or an "either-or" suggestion. Both are necessary; both must be done. The real test, therefore, of the sincerity and the maturity of all of us now participating in this struggle will be our willingness to labor in the vineyards where we are not televised and photographed, and in those places where our contributions may not be popular news copy.

I feel very deeply that the increasing numbers of Negro women, as well as our allies among men and women of other racial groups, who are willing to volunteer a few hours a week to tutor youngsters who bear the scars of generations of deprivation, are making a lasting contribution to the struggle—a contribution as lasting as that made by the gallant heroes who go to jail, or those who lie in the streets.

The Urban League is challenged, therefore, to see that the barriers of yesterday—the barriers built by prejudice, fear and indifference which are now crumbling—are not replaced by new barriers of apathy, of underdeveloped skills, of lack of training. If this happens, our gains will be but temporary, our victories hollow.

Protest we must. Demonstrate if necessary. These are the time-tested weapons for correcting injustices and righting historic wrongs. But these alone are not enough. We will only have cleared the site. The next task is to build upon that site the new house of true democracy. This requires different skills—but equal commitment and equal energy. This we will do. This we must do. The same faith and determination that have been responsible for the Negro's survival in a hostile and cruel society will respond to the new challenge. That faith and determination will respond if given reasonable understanding and assistance from a total society more sympathetic and honest than heretofore. . . .

As George Bernard Shaw has said, "America has relegated

the Negro citizen to be a bootblack, and now condemns him because his hands are dirty."

There is today great talk among our many new and self-
appointed advisers about self-help and personal responsibility
on the part of the Negro citizen himself. The curious, if not
tragic, aspect of this is that this talk comes from so many white
Americans who themselves have been passive participants in,
or passive observers of, the age-old denials responsible for the
lacks which they now deplore.

If this is not done, then Negro America will have less need to
be defensive, and its leadership will not run the risk of being
misunderstood when it addresses itself to this aspect. Today
nothing is more discouraging or inhibiting to responsible Negro
leadership, and to discussion of self-help and self-responsibility,
than the fact that this has become the chief theme song of
many self-appointed advisers who would claim now to be our
friends, but who for all these years have never raised their
voices against the obvious racial injustices—those who even today say little about the real responsibilities of white Americans.

As President Kennedy noted recently—demonstrations would
be minimized, if not eliminated, if there were as much concern
and indignation about the injustices and the discrimination
against Negro citizens to which these demonstrations are addressed, as there is to the demonstrations themselves.

The present and future test of the concern and sincerity of
the responsible white leadership of America will be the degree
to which they assume what seems to me clear-cut and obvious
tasks. Let me indicate them.

1. White leadership must be honest about the fact that
throughout the history of this country there has existed a special, privileged class of citizens who have received special pref-
erential treatment over other citizens purely on the basis of an
accident of birth. The problems of social disorganization and
racial unrest which we face today are the direct result of this
fact. Honesty and decency should compel our mass media and
responsible majority leadership to admit a long-established sociological fact: that the high ratio of dependency, crime and
social disorganization among Negro citizens which so many of
them deplore actually occurs in the same degree among white
citizens of the same socioeconomic class. Negro citizens representing the middle-income group have actually less social disorganization than white citizens in similar economic circumstances. These problems, therefore, are problems not of race, but
of socioeconomic condition.

2. Responsible white leadership and the mass media must,

with honesty and sincerity, promote and teach the idea that integration should and can be viewed as an opportunity for all Americans, rather than an irritating and uncomfortable problem—that integration can provide for all of us the creative experience that flows from inclusiveness, rather than the stagnating and damaging effects that accompany exclusiveness. . . . It is poignantly tragic that American citizens debate the rights of fellow Americans to live in the same neighborhoods, attend the same schools, eat in the same restaurants, or attend the same houses of worship.

This is a time when great minds and great nations will reflect their true greatness by concentrating on the multitude of things we have in common. For the truth is that today white Americans and black Americans are equally and mutually dependent upon each other.

3. Responsible white leadership in this nation can demonstrate the sincerity of its desire to accelerate constructive transition, by enthusiastic support of the Urban League's massive "domestic Marshall Plan," as the only fair and realistic way of closing the gap and correcting historic abuses. This is little indeed to ask of a great nation if it is to truly provide world leadership in the brief time allowed us by a fast-moving world society. . . .

In broad terms this plan calls for a transitional period of intensified special effort of corrective measures in education, in training and employment, in housing and in health and welfare. It calls for the same kind of expression of generosity and understanding which motivated this country to spend twelve billion dollars under the original Marshall Plan in a four-year period to rehabilitate war-torn Europe.* It calls for the same kind of concern that has motivated our nation more recently to spend millions of dollars in providing special help for Hungarian and Cuban refugees fleeing oppression. Should this nation—can this nation do less for its own citizens whose blood, sweat and tears have gone into building and preserving this great country which is ours?

4. Responsible white leadership must provide support—unprecedented support—both morally and financially, to existing responsible Negro agencies and their leadership. As Winston

---

* In April, 1948, Congress passed a bill providing $5.3 billion for the aid of European countries under the European Recovery Program, better known as the Marshall Plan, after Secretary of State George C. Marshall, who outlined it in his commencement address at Harvard University on June 5, 1947. The appropriation was for the first twelve months of the Plan.

Churchill said so forthrightly to America during the moment of England's gravest crisis in World War II: "Give us the tools and we will do the job."

For fifty-three years the Urban League has valiantly endeavored to provide America with responsible leadership. But the League was forced to do so with token financial support offered with the subtle inference that even such meager support might be jeopardized if there was too close identification with the legitimate aspirations of the masses of Negro citizens for equality, dignity and first-class citizenship.

Today, however, there is strong evidence that a different and more mature point of view is now being adopted by corporations, government, labor and enlightened community funds. It is becoming clear now, that if the impatience and the heightened aspirations of the masses of Negro citizens are to be protected and to be channeled along constructive lines, then the Urban League must of necessity be involved in this feat of social engineering. To divorce ourselves from this would be an expression of irresponsibility; to isolate our organization from this activity would be to deny corporations, foundations and community funds a unique opportunity for representation and participation in a new era of social planning. The Urban League will be valueless to responsible institutions in our society if it does not maintain communication with and the respect of other responsible Negro organizations and the respect of the masses of Negro citizens.

The final aspirations of Negro citizens can never be realized unless they too respect the distinctive and vital role which the Urban League can play—a role which the Urban League is peculiarly and uniquely qualified for, and can perform. Only the Urban League has the professional equipment and the knowhow for this role, and the contacts and machinery to implement. In this moment of grave racial crisis, the Urban League is gearing itself for accelerated activity in its traditional role and girding itself to maintain identity with all other responsible groups in the struggle for human rights. In this process we will be enabled to understand motives and test the sincerity of our friends and supporters.

5. And, finally, responsible white leadership must not permit itself to be drawn into anxiety around an increasingly popular phrase "reverse reactions." For to do so is to suggest that there are still degrees of citizenship to which society is committed to grant Negro Americans.

Our expression must be loud and clear. Once and for all we must state it: Human rights and civil rights in America are not negotiable. There does not exist in the hands of any one group of citizens either the divine right or the Constitutional authority to give or withhold from another, rights that are God-given and legally implemented.

WE MUST HAVE JUSTICE

By Elijah Muhammad

While most Negroes were involved in one form or another in the civil-rights revolution of the 1950's and early 1960's, one organization remained aloof. This was The Lost-Found Nation of Islam in the Wilderness of North America —known commonly as the Black Muslims. The Black Muslims condemn integration. Their solution to the Negro problem is separation. They reject white American society and wish to separate and form a black nation within the United States. Elijah Muhammad, leader of the militant black nationalist organization, expresses their philosophy in a brief address delivered on June 21, 1963.

Born Elijah Poole, in Georgia, the son and the grandson of Baptist ministers, he became leader of the movement in 1934. In less than three decades after taking control, he transformed the movement from a small black sect in the slums of Detroit into a nationwide organization which claimed in 1963 over a quarter million members. Believers are required to abide by a strict code of behavior and are offered the heritage of Islamic civilization and a religion which is a deliberate rejection of the white man's Christianity.

Elijah Muhammad's speech, which is presented here, is reprinted from Rhetoric and Racial Revolt, Roy L. Hill, ed., *pp. 292–93.*

THIS IS the question of today among the black people of America: Shall we have or get justice? The answer is yes; if you seek it from the right source and the right source is from Allah (God), truth and self.

Everything except the above three has failed us in the way of justice.

Let us then, all (leaders) meet together and see how best

we can get justice for our people without selling their birth-rights for a "mess of porridge," as Jacob did Esau.

We want justice for the so-called Negroes regardless of the price. We are fast learning that nonviolence is not respected. Church services, praying and singing glory hallelujah are not regarded any more than singing the blues.

It was pitiful to look at college students headed by a college leader, Mr. Martin Luther King, on TV singing and praying to the devils to allow him and his followers to share in with them (whites), respect the Negroes, and be able to dine and have everything in common together, while the devils were shaking their heads saying no, no.

One poor brother leading the others said to the devil, "Why not? Why not? Am I not a human being?"

The police and his dogs were sicked upon the whole group of beggars, and the poor people were driven off without the respect of dogs. Shall we have justice? Since everything fails but Allah, truth and self, unite on the side of Allah and truth and come follow me and you will get justice, money, good homes, and friendship in all walks of life, and some of the earth that we can call our own, separated from people that have brought us to disgrace and shame.

We are falling on our knees praying to a merciless enemy (the white American), begging and pleading with blood and tears streaming down our bodies, without the slightest sympathy from the universally known murderers (the white race of devils). The so-called Negroes have been fooled in the knowledge of the American white race. The average so-called Negro thinks he is dealing with a people that are of the God of righteousness, but they (white race) have just become rich and wicked.

The so-called Negroes must remember the poorer the whites are, the more wicked they are when it comes to the so-called Negroes. The entire black nation must know that God has revealed this race of people to be the true race of devils, and there is no righteousness in them. Nature did not give them any righteousness, says Allah to me.

They know to do good but cannot. Their religious teachings mean nothing in the way of being righteous people. A few here and there wish to go all right, but they are outnumbered a thousand to one.

Now, let us go from them and build a nation ourselves that God and the nations of the earth will respect. Your loving to live and become one of the race of devils, who have proven to you for four hundred years that they do not want you for anything but to enslave you in their behalf, is outright foolish and ignorant. Do not you want your own black nation to see you in a better light of understanding?

The government wants to enforce integration, and will be successful after some bloodshed, wherein, the so-called Negro will lose the most blood. The government is and will do anything to keep the blind, deaf and dumb Negroes from going over to Allah and the Islamic nation (the Black Muslims).

What future will we, the twenty million blacks in America, have in a forced integration? Seeking equal employment and equal recognition would only be temporary, but some of this earth that you can call your own where you can build your own employment would be permanent!

This is the desire of God for us. He did it for Israel, and made a triple job of it in Belshazzar. To give you some of this earth is the purpose of His (Allah's) coming.

I HAVE A DREAM

By Martin Luther King, Jr.

On August 28, 1963, more than two hundred and fifty thousand Americans—about sixty thousand of them white —participated in a March on Washington for Jobs and Freedom, to demand immediate passage of a civil-rights bill and immediate implementation of basic guarantees in the Declaration of Independence, and the thirteenth, fourteenth, and fifteenth amendments. It was the largest demonstration in the history of the nation's capital. The orderly procession moved from the Washington Monument to the Lincoln Memorial, where A. Philip Randolph, Martin Luther King, Roy Wilkins, Walter Reuther and others addressed the immense gathering. Dr. King's address had a tremendous effect on the audience and has been widely published; it is reprinted here by permission of Mrs. Martin Luther King, Jr.

FIVE SCORE YEARS AGO, a great American, in whose symbolic shadow we stand, signed the Emancipation Proclamation. This momentous decree came as a great beacon light of hope to millions of Negro slaves who had been seared in the flames of withering injustice. It came as a joyous daybreak to end the long night of captivity.

But one hundred years later, we must face the tragic fact that the Negro is still not free. One hundred years later, the life of the Negro is still sadly crippled by the manacles of segregation and the chains of discrimination. One hundred years later, the Negro lives on a lonely island of poverty in the midst of a vast ocean of material prosperity. One hundred years later the Negro still languishes in the corners of American society and finds himself an exile in his own land. So we have come here today to dramatize an appalling condition.

In a sense we have come to our nation's capital to cash a check. When the architects of our republic wrote the magnificent words of the Constitution and the Declaration of Independence, they were signing a promissory note to which every American was to fall heir. This note was a promise that all men would be guaranteed the unalienable rights of life, liberty, and the pursuit of happiness.

It is obvious today that America has defaulted on this promissory note insofar as her citizens of color are concerned. Instead of honoring this sacred obligation, America has given the Negro people a bad check; a check which has come back marked "insufficient funds." But we refuse to believe that the bank of justice is bankrupt. We refuse to believe that there are insufficient funds in the great vaults of opportunity of this nation. So we have come to cash this check—a check that will give us upon demand the riches of freedom and the security of justice. We have also come to this hallowed spot to remind America of the fierce urgency of *now*. This is no time to engage in the luxury of cooling off or to take the tranquilizing drug of gradualism. *Now* is the time to make real the promises of democracy. *Now* is the time to rise from the dark and desolate valley of segregation to the sunlit path of racial justice. *Now* is the time to open the doors of opportunity to all of God's children. *Now* is the time to lift our nation from the quicksands of racial injustice to the solid rock of brotherhood.

It would be fatal for the nation to overlook the urgency of the moment and to underestimate the determination of the Negro. This sweltering summer of the Negro's legitimate discontent will not pass until there is an invigorating autumn of freedom and equality. Nineteen sixty-three is not an end, but a beginning. Those who hope that the Negro needed to blow off steam and will now be content will have a rude awakening if the nation returns to business as usual. There will be neither rest nor tranquillity in America until the Negro is granted his citizenship rights. The whirlwinds of revolt will continue to shake the foundations of our nation until the bright day of justice emerges.

But there is something that I must say to my people who stand on the warm threshold which leads into the palace of justice. In the process of gaining our rightful place we must not be guilty of wrongful deeds. Let us not seek to satisfy our thirst for freedom by drinking from the cup of bitterness and hatred. We must forever conduct our struggle on the high plane of dignity and discipline. We must not allow our creative protest to degenerate into physical violence. Again and again we must rise to the majestic heights of meeting physical force with soul force. The marvelous new militancy which has engulfed the Negro community must not lead us to a distrust of all white people, for many of our white brothers, as evidenced by their presence here today, have come to realize that their destiny is tied up with our destiny and their freedom is inextricably bound to our freedom. We cannot walk alone.

And as we walk, we must make the pledge that we shall march ahead. We cannot turn back. There are those who are asking the devotees of civil rights, "When will you be satisfied?" We can never be satisfied as long as the Negro is the victim of the unspeakable horrors of police brutality. We can never be satisfied as long as our bodies, heavy with the fatigue of travel, cannot gain lodging in the motels of the highways and the hotels of the cities. We cannot be satisfied as long as the Negro's basic mobility is from a smaller ghetto to a larger one. We can never be satisfied as long as a Negro in Mississippi cannot vote and a Negro in New York believes he has nothing for which to vote. No, no, we are not satisfied, and we will not be satisfied until justice rolls down like waters and righteousness like a mighty stream.

I am not unmindful that some of you have come here out of great trials and tribulations. Some of you have come fresh from narrow jail cells. Some of you have come from areas where your quest for freedom left you battered by the storms of persecution and staggered by the winds of police brutality. You have been the veterans of creative suffering. Continue to work with the faith that unearned suffering is redemptive.

Go back to Mississippi, go back to Alabama, go back to South Carolina, go back to Georgia, go back to Louisiana, go back to the slums and ghettos of our modern cities, knowing that somehow this situation can and will be changed. Let us not wallow in the valley of despair.

I say to you today, my friends, that in spite of the difficulties and frustrations of the moment I still have a dream. It is a dream deeply rooted in the American dream.

I have a dream that one day this nation will rise up and live out the true meaning of its creed: "We hold these truths to be self-evident; that all men are created equal."

I have a dream that one day on the red hills of Georgia the sons of former slaves and the sons of former slaveowners will be able to sit down together at the table of brotherhood.

I have a dream that one day even the state of Mississippi, a desert state sweltering with the heat of injustice and oppression, will be transformed into an oasis of freedom and justice.

I have a dream that my four little children will one day live in a nation where they will not be judged by the color of their skin but by the content of their character.

I have a dream today.

I have a dream that one day the state of Alabama, whose governor's lips are presently dripping with the words of interposition and nullification, will be transformed into a situation where little black boys and black girls will be able to join hands with little white boys and white girls and walk together as sisters and brothers.

I have a dream today.

I have a dream that one day every valley shall be exalted, every hill and mountain shall be made low, the rough places will be made plains, and the crooked places will be made straight, and the glory of the Lord shall be revealed, and all flesh shall see it together.

This is our hope. This is the faith with which I return to the South. With this faith we will be able to hew out of the mountain of despair a stone of hope. With this faith we will be able to transform the jangling discords of our nation into a beautiful symphony of brotherhood. With this faith we will be able to work together, to pray together, to struggle together, to go to jail together, to stand up for freedom together, knowing that we will be free one day.

This will be the day when all of God's children will be able to sing with new meaning, "My country 'tis of thee, sweet land of liberty, of thee I sing. Land where my fathers died, land of the pilgrim's pride, from every mountainside, let freedom ring."

And if America is to be a great nation this must become true. So let freedom ring from the prodigious hilltops of New Hampshire. Let freedom ring from the mighty mountains of New York. Let freedom ring from the heightening Alleghenies of Pennsylvania!

Let freedom ring from the snowcapped Rockies of Colorado!
Let freedom ring from the curvaceous peaks of California!
But not only that; let freedom ring from Stone Mountain of
Georgia!
Let freedom ring from Lookout Mountain of Tennessee!
Let freedom ring from every hill and molehill of Mississippi.
From every mountainside, let freedom ring.

When we let freedom ring, when we let it ring from every
village and every hamlet, from every state and every city, we
will be able to speed up that day when all of God's children,
black men and white men, Jews and Gentiles, Protestants and
Catholics, will be able to join hands and sing in the words of
the old Negro spiritual, "Free at last! Free at last! Thank God
Almighty, we are free at last!"

WE ARE IN A SERIOUS REVOLUTION

By John Lewis

*Another less-widely publicized speech delivered at the
March on Washington was given by John Lewis, then
chairman of the Student Nonviolent Coordinating Committee (S.N.C.C.). Lewis' speech reflected the rising disillusionment among young black Americans with the tactic
of nonviolence and their suspicion of the Kennedy administration. In February, 1963, President John F. Kennedy
had recommended legislation to strengthen voting rights,
and in June he had submitted to Congress a new civil-
rights bill. But organizations like S.N.C.C. believed that
these measures did not go far enough, and Lewis was determined to express this dissatisfaction in his speech.
However, because of objections of some of the march's
cosponsors, the speech was altered just before delivery to
soften its criticism of the federal government.*

The speech is reprinted here from Joanne Grant, ed.,
Black Protest: History, Documents, and Analyses, *1619
to the Present, New York, 1968, pp. 375–77.*

WE MARCH TODAY for jobs and freedom, but we have
nothing to be proud of, for hundreds and thousands of our
brothers are not here—for they have no money for their trans-

portation, for they are receiving starvation wages . . . or no wages at all.

In good conscience, we cannot support the administration's civil-rights bill, for it is too little, and too late. There's not one thing in the bill that will protect our people from police brutality.*

The voting section of this bill will not help the thousands of citizens who want to vote; will not help the citizens of Mississippi, of Alabama and Georgia who are qualified to vote, who are without a sixth-grade education. "One Man, One Vote," is the African cry. It is ours, too.

People have been forced to move for they have exercised their right to register to vote. What is in the bill that will protect the homeless and starving people of this nation? What is there in this bill to insure the equality of a maid who earns five dollars a week in the home of a family whose income is a hundred thousand dollars a year?

This bill will not protect young children and old women from police dogs and fire hoses for engaging in peaceful demonstrations. This bill will not protect the citizens in Danville, Virginia, who must live in constant fear in a police state.† This bill will not protect the hundreds of people who have been arrested on trumped-up charges, like those in Americus, Georgia, where four young men are in jail, facing a death penalty, for engaging in peaceful protest.

For the first time in a hundred years this nation is being awakened to the fact that segregation is evil and it must be destroyed in all forms. Our presence today proves that we have been aroused to the point of action.

We are now involved in a serious revolution. This nation is still a place of cheap political leaders allying themselves with open forms of political, economic and social exploitation.

In some parts of the South we have worked in the fields from sun-up to sun-down for twelve dollars a week. In Albany, Georgia, we have seen our people indicted by the federal government for peaceful protest, while the Deputy Sheriff beat Attorney C. B. King and left him half-dead; while local police officials

---

* This was changed to read: "True, we support the administration's civil-rights bill, but this bill will not protect young children and old women from police dogs and fire hoses. . . ."
† In Danville, Virginia, policemen, armed with submachine guns and in armored cars, regularly broke up mass demonstrations by Negroes. After each demonstration, scores of Negroes were taken to hospitals with fractured skulls and lacerations.

kicked and assaulted the pregnant wife of Slater King, and she lost her baby.

It seems to me that the Albany indictment is part of a conspiracy on the part of the federal government and local politicians for political expediency.

I want to know, Which side is the federal government on?

The revolution is at hand, and we must free ourselves of the chains of political and economic slavery. The nonviolent revolution is saying, "We will not wait for the courts to act, for we have been waiting hundreds of years. We will not wait for the President, nor the Justice Department, nor Congress, but we will take matters into our own hands, and create a great source of power, outside of any national structure that could and would assure us victory." For those who have said, "Be patient and wait!" we must say, "Patience is a dirty and nasty word." We cannot be patient, we do not want to be free gradually, we want our freedom, and we want it now. We cannot depend on any political party, for both the Democrats and the Republicans have betrayed the basic principles of the Declaration of Independence.

We all recognize the fact that if any radical social, political and economic changes are to take place in our society, the people, the masses must bring them about. In the struggle we must seek more than mere civil rights; we must work for the community of love, peace and true brotherhood. Our minds, souls and hearts cannot rest until freedom and justice exist for *all the people*.

The revolution is a serious one. Mr. Kennedy is trying to take the revolution out of the streets and put it in the courts. Listen, Mr. Kennedy, listen, Mr. Congressman, listen, fellow citizens— the black masses are on the march for jobs and freedom, and we must say to the politicians that there won't be a "cooling-off period."

We won't stop now. All of the forces of Eastland, Barnett and Wallace won't stop this revolution. The next time we march, we won't march on Washington, but we will march through the South, through the Heart of Dixie, the way Sherman did. We will make the action of the past few months look petty. And I say to you, *Wake up America!!*

All of us must get in the revolution—get in and stay in the streets of every city, village and hamlet of this nation, until true freedom comes, until the revolution is complete. The black masses in the Delta of Mississippi, in Southwest Georgia, Alabama, Harlem, Chicago, Philadelphia and all over this nation are on the march.

SECTION VI

Civil Rights to Black Power

September 1963 to 1971

LET YOUR SON FIGHT FOR FREEDOM

By Dick Gregory

*In September, 1963, S.N.C.C. was conducting a voter regis-
tration drive in Selma, Alabama, and asked Dick Gregory,
the black humorist and civil-rights activist, to help. Gregory
found the adult black population frightened by police
brutality and worried over the participation of their sons
and daughters in the voter registration drive. In a speech
to the black citizens of Selma, in the Negro church, Gregory urged them to support the young freedom fighters.*

*Dick Gregory was born in 1932, in St. Louis, the second-
eldest in a family of six. His home environment was typical of the majority of the blacks in the country: his family
was on welfare. As a child of the streets, young Gregory,
as he wrote later, "shined shoes, swiped coal and learned
how to play the game with the Man." At the age of eighteen,
he was able to run the mile faster than anyone in Missouri.
On the strength of this, Southern Illinois University, in
Carbondale, gave him an athletic scholarship, and he spent
four years there with time out for military service. He
moved on to Chicago, worked for a time in the Post Office,
but by 1961 he had become a successful comedian. Soon
he became actively involved in the civil-rights struggle in
the South and has been active in most black protest
activities ever since. Gregory calls himself a "nonviolent
revolutionary."*

*Here is a major part of his Selma speech, taken from
Nigger: An Autobiography, by Dick Gregory with Robert
Lipsyte, New York, 1964, pp. 216–20.*

IT'S AMAZING how we come to this church every Sunday
and cry over the crucifixion of Christ, and we don't cry over
these things that are going on around and among us. If He was
here now and saw these things, He would cry. And He would
take those nails again. For us. For this problem.

It just so happened that in His day and time, religion was the
big problem. Today, it is color.

What do you think would happen to Christ tonight if He arrived in this town a black man and wanted to register to vote on Monday? What do you think would happen? Would you be there? You would? Then how come you're not out there with these kids, because He said that whatever happens to the least, happens to us all. . . .

Let's analyze the situation.

We're not saying, "Let's go downtown and take over City Hall."

We're not saying, "Let's stand on the rooftops and throw bricks at the white folks."

We're not saying, "Let's get some butcher knives and some guns and make them pay for what they've done."

We're talking to the white man, and this is what we're saying.

We're saying, "We want what *you* said belongs to us. You have a constitution. I'm a black man, and you make me sit down in a black school and take a test on the United States Constitution, a constitution that hasn't worked for anyone but you. And you expect me to learn it from front to back. So I learned it.

"You made me stand up as a little kid and sing 'God Bless America,' and 'America the Beautiful,' and all those songs the white kids were singing. I Pledge Allegiance to the Flag. That's all I'm asking you for today."

Something important happened in 1963, and the sooner we wake up and realize it, the better off this whole world is going to be. Because for some reason God has put in your hands the salvation of not just America—this thing is bigger than just this country—but the salvation of the whole world. . . .

The Negro in America has the highest standard of living, the highest educational standard, the highest medical standard of any black man the world over and of most white men outside America. And yet there are backward countries getting more respect from this American white man than you people could ever command. Do you know why?

It's because we grinned when he wanted us to grin. We cried when he wanted us to cry. We've spent money when he wanted us to spend money. And we've done without when he said do without.

He owns all the missiles in the world, and when he talks to you about owning a switchblade you become ashamed.

He started all the wars, and when he talks to you about cutting somebody on Saturday night you become ashamed.

He makes me feel small. He calls me everything on the job but my name, so I'm aggravated before I get home.

Then he tells me about my education. Well, if it takes education his-style to produce a clown that would throw dynamite in a church, I hope we never get that.

I have a newspaper and I wish I brought it tonight. It embarrasses me just to look at it. It's a newspaper from 1848, a New Orleans newspaper.

On the back page are ads offering rewards for the return of runaway slaves. Can you believe in 1848 we were running away, rebelling, and we didn't have any place to run to? Eighteen forty-eight. Slaves were running away.

Can you imagine what this old Negro had to go through? Can you imagine the day a Negro woman went to a black man and said, "Honey, I'm pregnant," and both of them fell on their knees and prayed that their baby would be born deformed? Can you imagine what this Negro went through, hoping his baby is born crippled?

Because if he was born crippled, he would have less chance of being a slave and more chance of having freedom.

Think about that. Think about the woman you love coming to you and saying she's pregnant with your baby and you both pray the baby is born crippled.

This is what the slaves went through. And a hundred years later, we have parallels.

A hundred years later and you people are worrying about your kids being in jail overnight, being in jail because they demonstrated for freedom. So many parents who don't even know where their kids are, for the first time they'll know where their kids are twenty-four hours a day. In jail. And know that they're there for a good cause and a good reason.

How many mothers let their sons play football, and all he can get from that is a chance to help his team win a victory. A victory that will be forgotten tomorrow. So can't you let your son fight for freedom, something that the whole world will profit from, forever?

Sometimes I wonder how much this system has corrupted us. Sometimes I wonder when we will wake up to see that the day is over when we can say, "I'm not involved."

Those four kids who were killed in that church in Birmingham, they weren't demonstrating.*

You don't have to participate. Just be black. Or be white, and for our cause. When the bomb is thrown, somebody has to die.

---

* In September, 1963, a Negro church in Birmingham, Alabama, was bombed and four Negro children were killed.

And do you know that 50 percent of the killings are our fault? That's right. We let this white man go crazy on us, instead of straightening him out when we should have.

Each one of us scratched our heads five years too long.

Sure, Tomming was good once upon a time. That's how we got here. The old folks knew that was the only way they could raise you. What we call Uncle-Tomism today was nothing but finesse and tact then. The old folks had to scratch their heads and grin their ways into a white man's heart. A white man who wouldn't accept them any other way.

But at what point do we stop Tomming?

A Negro is better off going to a foreign country fighting for America than he is coming to the South fighting for the Negro cause. When he's in a foreign country, fighting to give those people rights he doesn't even get, the whole of America is behind him. When he comes down here, there are only a few behind him.

So it's coming down to this. You have to commit. You're going through the same thing today that the folks went through when the Lord was crucified.

"Who else is with Christ?" the Romans asked.

And everybody just stood there. And prayed silently. And they went back and said, "I prayed."

No, sister, I didn't even see your lips move.

Were you there when they crucified the Lord? It's a nice song to sing. But this time, you have an opportunity to be there.

Sure would be a heck of a thing, twenty, thirty years from now when they're singing a song about these days, and your grandkids and great-grandkids can stand up and say, "Yeah, baby, he was there, my grandfather was there."

And when they ask you, you can nod your head and say, "Yeah, I was there."

I'd like to tell you a story before I leave. I talked to the father of one of the kids who died in that church in Birmingham. He said to me, "You know, Gregory, my daughter begged me to let her demonstrate, and I told her No. I told her she was too young. And she looked at me, and she said, 'Then you do it, Daddy.'" . . .

And that's what that man will have to live with for the rest of his life. Because if Birmingham had had enough Negroes behind them, there wouldn't have been a bombing. . . .

These kids here in Selma aren't doing anything just for themselves. There's nothing selfish about what they're doing here. Freedom will run all over this town. But you have to get behind

them. Because there are too many white folks in front of them.
Get behind your kids in this town.
Goodbye and God bless you and good night.

THE BALLOT OR THE BULLET

By Malcolm X

*While the post-World War II Negro protest movement did
bring important results it had little actual effect on the
lives of the vast majority of Negroes living in the North.
The Northern ghettos swelled, and discrimination in employment, housing and education continued.*

*The spokesman for the militant Northern urban Negro
ghetto dweller was Malcolm X, one of the most significant
black leaders of our century. He was born Malcolm Little
in Omaha, Nebraska, on May 19, 1925. He dropped out of
school at fifteen and went to prison for burglary at twenty-
one. While there he was converted to the Black Muslims.
When he left prison in 1952, he adopted the name Malcolm X and devoted himself to expanding the movement.
He soon became the chief spokesman for the black nationalist group. In addition to presiding over the organization's New York temple, Malcolm X made frequent appearances on the air and at leading colleges and universities.
He predicted explosions in every major American city. In
late 1963 Malcolm X was suspended as a Muslim minister.
He soon broke with Elijah Muhammad, the Black Muslim
leader, to form his own organizations, first the Muslim
Mosque, Inc., and later the nonreligious Organization of
Afro-American Unity. Malcolm X visited Mecca and Africa
during 1964, and on his return began to move away from
his earlier separatist and antiwhite approach. On February
21, 1965, he was assassinated by the Black Muslims in
New York.*

*"The Ballot or the Bullet" is considered one of his most
important speeches. It was delivered on April 3, 1964, at
the Cory Methodist Church in Cleveland, at a meeting
sponsored by the Congress of Racial Equality on "The Negro Revolt—What Comes Next?" Malcolm X claimed that
the elements of black nationalism were present and grow-*

ing in such organizations as the N.A.A.C.P. and CORE and advised all blacks to join any organization which practiced "the gospel of black nationalism." A major part of the speech is presented here, reprinted from Malcolm X, Malcolm X Speaks, New York, 1965, pp. 23–44.

MR. MODERATOR, brothers and sisters, friends and enemies: I just can't believe everyone in here is a friend and I don't want to leave anybody out. The question tonight, as I understand it, is "The Negro Revolt, and Where Do We Go from Here?" or "What Next?" In my little humble way of understanding it, it points toward either the ballot or the bullet.

Before we try and explain what is meant by the ballot or the bullet, I would like to clarify something concerning myself. I'm still a Muslim, my religion is still Islam. That's my personal belief. Just as Adam Clayton Powell is a Christian minister who heads the Abyssinian Baptist Church in New York, but at the same time takes part in the political struggles to try and bring about rights to the black people in this country; and Dr. Martin Luther King is a Christian minister down in Atlanta, Georgia, who heads another organization fighting for the civil rights of black people in this country; and Reverend Galamison —I guess you've heard of him—is another Christian minister in New York who has been deeply involved in the school boycotts to eliminate segregated education; well, I myself am a minister, not a Christian minister, but a Muslim minister; and I believe in action on all fronts by whatever means necessary.

Although I'm still a Muslim, I'm not here tonight to discuss my religion. I'm not here to try and change your religion. I'm not here to argue or discuss anything that we differ about, because it's time for us to submerge our differences and realize that it is best for us to first see that we have the same problem, a common problem—a problem that will make you catch hell whether you're a Baptist, or a Methodist, or a Muslim, or a nationalist. Whether you're educated or illiterate, whether you live on the boulevard or in the alley, you're going to catch hell just like I am. We're all in the same boat and we all are going to catch the same hell from the same man. He just happens to be a white man. All of us have suffered here, in this country, political oppression at the hands of the white man, economic exploitation at the hands of the white man, and social degradation at the hands of the white man.

Now in speaking like this, it doesn't mean that we're anti-white, but it does mean we're anti-exploitation, we're antidegradation, we're antioppression. And if the white man doesn't want us to be anti-*him*, let him stop oppressing and exploiting and degrading us. Whether we are Christians or Muslims or nationalists or agnostics or atheists, we must first learn to forget our differences. If we have differences, let us differ in the closet; when we come out in front, let us not have anything to argue about until we get finished arguing with the man. If the late President Kennedy could get together with Khrushchev and exchange some wheat, we certainly have more in common with each other than Kennedy and Khrushchev had with each other.

If we don't do something real soon, I think you'll have to agree that we're going to be forced either to use the ballot or the bullet. It's one or the other in 1964. It isn't that time is running out—time has run out! Nineteen sixty-four threatens to be the most explosive year America has ever witnessed. The most explosive year. Why? It's also a political year. It's the year when all of the white politicians will be back in the so-called Negro community jiving you and me for some votes. The year when all of the white political crooks will be right back in your and my community with their false promises, building up our hopes for a letdown, with their trickery and their treachery, with their false promises which they don't intend to keep. As they nourish these dissatisfactions, it can only lead to one thing, an explosion; and now we have the type of black man on the scene in America today—I'm sorry, Brother Lomax*—who just doesn't intend to turn the other cheek any longer.

Don't let anybody tell you anything about the odds are against you. If they draft you, they send you to Korea and make you face 800 million Chinese. If you can be brave over there, you can be brave right here. These odds aren't as great as those odds. And if you fight here, you will at least know what you're fighting for.

I'm not a politician, not even a student of politics; in fact, I'm not a student of much of anything. I'm not a Democrat, I'm not a Republican, and I don't even consider myself an American. If you and I were Americans, there'd be no problem. Those Hunkies that just got off the boat, they're already Americans; Polacks are already Americans; the Italian refugees are already Americans. Everything that came out of Europe, every blue-eyed thing, is already an American. And as long as you and I have been over here, we aren't Americans yet.

Well, I am one who doesn't believe in deluding myself. I'm not going to sit at your table and watch you eat, with nothing

---

* The reference is to Louis E. Lomax, author of *The Negro Revolt*, published in 1962.

on my plate, and call myself a diner. Sitting at the table doesn't make you a diner, unless you eat some of what's on that plate. Being here in America doesn't make you an American. Being born here in American doesn't make you an American. Why, if birth made you American, you wouldn't need any legislation, you wouldn't need any amendments to the Constitution, you wouldn't be faced with civil-rights filibustering in Washington, D. C., right now. They don't have to pass civil-rights legislation to make a Polack an American.

No, I'm not an American. I'm one of the twenty-two million black people who are the victims of democracy, nothing but disguised hypocrisy. So, I'm not standing here speaking to you as an American, or a patriot, or a flag-saluter, or a flag-waver— no, not I. I'm speaking as a victim of this American system. And I see America through the eyes of the victim. I don't see any American dream; I see an American nightmare.

These twenty-two million victims are waking up. Their eyes are coming open. They're beginning to see what they used to only look at. They're becoming politically mature. They are realizing that there are new political trends from coast to coast. As they see these new political trends, it's possible for them to see that every time there's an election the races are so close that they have to have a recount. They had to recount in Massachusetts to see who was going to be governor, it was so close. It was the same way in Rhode Island, in Minnesota, and in many other parts of the country. And the same with Kennedy and Nixon when they ran for President. It was so close they had to count all over again. Well, what does this mean? It means that when white people are evenly divided, and black people have a bloc of votes of their own, it is left up to them to determine who's going to sit in the White House and who's going to be in the dog house.

It was the black man's vote that put the present administration in Washington, D. C. Your vote, your dumb vote, your ignorant vote, your wasted vote put in an administration in Washington, D. C., that has seen fit to pass every kind of legislation imaginable, saving you until last, then filibustering on top of that. And your and my leaders have the audacity to run around clapping their hands and talk about how much progress we're making. And what a good President we have. If he wasn't good in Texas, he sure can't be good in Washington, D. C. Because Texas is a lynch state. It is in the same breath as Mississippi, no different; only they lynch you in Texas with a Texas accent and lynch you in Mississippi with a Mississippi accent. And these Negro leaders have the audacity to go and have some

coffee in the White House with a Texan, a Southern cracker—
that's all he is—and then come out and tell you and me that
he's going to be better for us because, since he's from the South,
he knows how to deal with the Southerners. What kind of logic
is that? Let Eastland be President, he's from the South too. He
should be better able to deal with them than Johnson.*

In this present administration they have in the House of
Representatives 257 Democrats to only 177 Republicans. They
control two thirds of the House vote. Why can't they pass something that will help you and me? In the Senate, there are 67
Senators who are of the Democratic party. Only 33 of them are
Republicans. Why, the Democrats have got the government
sewed up, and you're the one who sewed it up for them. And
what have they given you for it? Four years in office, and just
now getting around to some civil-rights legislation. Just now,
after everything else is gone, out of the way, they're going to
sit down now and play with you all summer long—the same old
giant con game that they call filibuster.† All those are in cahoots together. Don't you ever think they're not in cahoots together, for the man that is heading the civil-rights filibuster is
a man from Georgia named Richard Russell. When Johnson
became President, the first man he asked for when he got back
to Washington, D. C., was "Dicky"—that's how tight they are.
That's his boy, that's his pal, that's his buddy. But they're playing that old con game. One of them makes believe he's for you,
and he's got it fixed where the other one is so tight against you,
he never has to keep his promise.

So it's time in 1964 to wake up. And when you see them coming up with that kind of conspiracy, let them know your eyes
are open. And let them know you got something else that's wide
open too. It's got to be the ballot or the bullet. The ballot or the
bullet. If you're afraid to use an expression like that, you should
get on out of the country, you should get back in the cotton
patch, you should get back in the alley. They get all the Negro
vote, and after they get it, the Negro gets nothing in return. All
they did when they got to Washington was give a few big Negroes big jobs. Those big Negroes didn't need big jobs, they
already had jobs. That's camouflage, that's trickery, that's
treachery, window-dressing. I'm not trying to knock out the
Democrats for the Republicans, we'll get to them in a minute.

* President Johnson was from Texas and had represented the state in the
Senate.
† To prevent passage of a civil-rights bill in 1964, Southerners in
Congress began a long filibuster. The bill was finally passed in a
modified form.

But it is true—you put the Democrats first and the Democrats
put you last.

Look at it the way it is. What alibis do they use, since they
control Congress and the Senate? What alibi do they use when
you and I ask, "Well, when are you going to keep your promise?"
They blame the Dixiecrats. What is a Dixiecrat? A Democrat. A
Dixiecrat is nothing but a Democrat in disguise. The titular head
of the Democrats is also the head of the Dixiecrats, because
the Dixiecrats are a part of the Democratic Party. The Democrats have never kicked the Dixiecrats out of the party. The
Dixiecrats bolted themselves once, but the Democrats didn't put
them out. Imagine, these low-down Southern segregationists
put the Northern Democrats down. But the Northern Democrats
have never put the Dixiecrats down. No, look at that thing the
way it is. They have got a con game going on, a political con
game, and you and I are in the middle. It's time for you and me
to wake up and start looking at it like it is, and trying to understand it like it is; and then we can deal with it like it is.

The Dixiecrats in Washington, D. C., control the key committees that run the government. The only reason the Dixiecrats
control these committees is because they have seniority. The
only reason they have seniority is because they come from states
where Negroes can't vote. This is not even a government that's
based on democracy. It is not a government that is made up of
representatives of the people. Half of the people in the South
can't even vote. Eastland is not even supposed to be in Washington. Half of the Senators and Congressmen who occupy
these key positions in Washington, D. C., are there illegally, are
there unconstitutionally.

I was in Washington, D. C., a week ago Thursday, when they
were debating whether or not they should let the bill come onto
the floor. And in the back of the room where the Senate meets,
there's a huge map of the United States, and on that map it
shows the location of Negroes throughout the country. And it
shows that the Southern section of the country, the states that
are most heavily concentrated with Negroes, are the ones that
have Senators and Congressmen standing up filibustering and
doing all other kinds of trickery to keep the Negro from being
able to vote. This is pitiful. But it's not pitiful for us any longer;
it's actually pitiful for the white man, because soon now, as
the Negro awakens a little more and sees the vise that he's in,
sees the bag that he's in, sees the real game that he's in, then
the Negro's going to develop a new tactic.

These Senators and Congressmen actually violate the Constitutional amendments that guarantee the people of that particular state or county the right to vote. And the Constitution itself has within it the machinery to expel any representative from a state where the voting rights of the people are violated. You don't even need new legislation. Any person in Congress right now, who is there from a state or a district where the voting rights of the people are violated, that particular person should be expelled from Congress. And when you expel him, you've removed one of the obstacles in the path of any real meaningful legislation in this country. In fact, when you expel them, you don't need new legislation, because they will be replaced by black representatives from counties and districts where the black man is in the majority, not in the minority.

If the black man in these Southern states had his full voting rights, the key Dixiecrats in Washington, D. C., which means the key Democrats in Washington, D. C., would lose their seats. The Democratic party itself would lose its power. It would cease to be powerful as a party. When you see the amount of power that would be lost by the Democratic party if it were to lose the Dixiecrat wing, or branch, or element, you can see where it's against the interests of the Democrats to give voting rights to Negroes in states where the Democrats have been in complete power and authority ever since the Civil War. You just can't belong to that party without analyzing it.

I say again, I'm not anti-Democrat, I'm not anti-Republican, I'm not antianything. I'm just questioning their sincerity, and some of the strategy that they've been using on our people by promising them promises that they don't intend to keep. When you keep the Democrats in power, you're keeping the Dixiecrats in power. I doubt that my good Brother Lomax will deny that. A vote for a Democrat is a vote for a Dixiecrat. That's why, in 1964, it's time now for you and me to become more politically mature and realize what the ballot is for; what we're supposed to get when we cast a ballot; and that if we don't cast a ballot, it's going to end up in a situation where we're going to have to cast a bullet. It's either a ballot or a bullet.

In the North, they do it a different way. They have a system that's known as gerrymandering, whatever that means. It means when Negroes become too heavily concentrated in a certain area, and begin to gain too much political power, the white man comes along and changes the district lines. You may say, "Why do you keep saying white man?" Because it's the white man who does it. I haven't ever seen any Negro changing any lines. They don't let him get near the line. It's the white man who does this. And usually, it's the white man who grins at you the most, and pats you on the back, and is supposed to be your friend. He may be friendly, but he's not your friend.

So, what I'm trying to impress upon you, in essence, is this: You and I in America are faced not with a segregationist conspiracy, we're faced with a government conspiracy. Everyone who's filibustering is a Senator—that's the government. Everyone who's finagling in Washington, D. C., is a Congressman—that's the government. You don't have anybody putting blocks in your path but people who are a part of the government. The same government that you go abroad to fight for and die for is the government that is in a conspiracy to deprive you of your voting rights, deprive you of your economic opportunities, deprive you of decent housing, deprive you of decent education. You don't need to go to the employer alone, it is the government itself, the government of America, that is responsible for the oppression and exploitation and degradation of black people in this country. And you should drop it in their lap. This government has failed the Negro. This so-called democracy has failed the Negro. And all these white liberals have definitely failed the Negro.

So, where do we go from here? First, we need some friends. We need some new allies. The entire civil-rights struggle needs a new interpretation, a broader interpretation. We need to look at this civil-rights thing from another angle—from the inside as well as from the outside. To those of us whose philosophy is black nationalism, the only way you can get involved in the civil-rights struggle is to give it a new interpretation. That old interpretation excluded us. It kept us out. So, we're giving a new interpretation to the civil-rights struggle, an interpretation that will enable us to come into it, take part in it. And these handkerchief-heads who have been dillydallying and pussyfooting and compromising—we don't intend to let them pussyfoot and dillydally and compromise any longer.

How can you thank a man for giving you what's already yours? How then can you thank him for giving you only part of what's already yours? You haven't even made progress, if what's being given to you, you should have had already. That's not progress. And I love my Brother Lomax, the way he pointed out we're right back where we were in 1954. We're not even as far up as we were in 1954. We're behind where we were in 1954. There's more segregation now than there was in 1954. There's more racial animosity, more racial hatred, more racial violence today in 1964, than there was in 1954. Where is the progress?

And now you're facing a situation where the young Negro's

coming up. They don't want to hear that "turn-the-other-cheek" stuff, no. In Jacksonville, those were teen-agers, they were throwing Molotov cocktails. Negroes have never done that before. But it shows you there's a new deal coming in. There's new thinking coming in. There's new strategy coming in. It'll be Molotov cocktails this month, hand grenades next month, and something else next month. It'll be ballots, or it'll be bullets. It'll be liberty, or it will be death. The only difference about this kind of death—it'll be reciprocal. You know what is meant by "reciprocal"? That's one of Brother Lomax's words, I stole it from him. I don't usually deal with those big words because I don't usually deal with big people. I deal with small people. I find you can get a whole lot of small people and whip hell out of a whole lot of big people. They haven't got anything to lose, and they've got everything to gain. And they'll let you know in a minute: "It takes two to tango; when I go, you go."

The black nationalists, those whose philosophy is black nationalism, in bringing about this new interpretation of the entire meaning of civil rights, look upon it as meaning, as Brother Lomax has pointed out, equality of opportunity. Well, we're justified in seeking civil rights, if it means equality of opportunity, because all we're doing there is trying to collect for our investment. Our mothers and fathers invested sweat and blood. Three hundred and ten years we worked in this country without a dime in return—I mean without a *dime* in return. You let the white man walk around here talking about how rich this country is, but you never stop to think how it got rich so quick. It got rich because you made it rich.

You take the people who are in this audience right now. They're poor, we're all poor as individuals. Our weekly salary individually amounts to hardly anything. But if you take the salary of everyone in here collectively it'll fill up a whole lot of baskets. It's a lot of wealth. If you can collect the wages of just these people right here for a year, you'll be rich—richer than rich. When you look at it like that, think how rich Uncle Sam had to become, not with this handful, but millions of black people. Your and my mother and father, who didn't work an eight-hour shift, but worked from "can't see" in the morning until "can't see" at night, and worked for nothing, making the white man rich, making Uncle Sam rich. . . .

By ballot I only mean freedom. Don't you know—I disagree with Lomax on this issue—that the ballot is more important than the dollar? Can I prove it? Yes. Look in the U.N. There are poor nations in the U.N.; yet those poor nations can get together with their voting power and keep the rich nations from making a move. They have one nation, one vote—everyone has an equal vote. And when those brothers from Asia, and Africa and the darker parts of this earth get together, their voting power is sufficient to hold Sam in check. Or Russia in check. Or some other section of the earth in check. So, the ballot is most important.

Right now, in this country, if you and I, twenty-two million African-Americans—that's what we are—Africans who are in America. In fact, you'd get farther calling yourself African instead of Negro. Africans don't catch hell. You're the only one catching hell. They don't have to pass civil-rights bills for Africans. An African can go anywhere he wants right now. All you've got to do is tie your head up. That's right, go anywhere you want. Just stop being a Negro. Change your name to Hoogagagooba. That'll show you how silly the white man is. You're dealing with a silly man. A friend of mine who's very dark put a turban on his head and went into a restaurant in Atlanta before they called themselves desegregated. He went into a white restaurant, he sat down, they served him, and he said, "What would happen if a Negro came in here?" And there he's sitting, black as night, but because he had his head wrapped up the waitress looked back at him and says, "Why, there wouldn't no nigger dare come in here."

So, you're dealing with a man whose bias and prejudice are making him lose his mind, his intelligence, every day. He's frightened. He looks around and sees what's taking place on this earth, and he sees that the pendulum of time is swinging in your direction. The dark people are waking up. They're losing their fear of the white man. No place where he's fighting right now is he winning. Everywhere he's fighting, he's fighting someone your and my complexion. And they're beating him. He can't win any more. He's won his last battle. He failed to win the Korean War. He couldn't win it. He had to sign a truce. That's a loss. Any time Uncle Sam, with all his machinery for warfare, is held to a draw by some rice-eaters, he's lost the battle. He had to sign a truce. America's not supposed to sign a truce. She's supposed to be bad. But she's not bad any more. She's bad as long as she can use her hydrogen bomb, but she can't use hers for fear Russia might use hers. Russia can't use hers, for fear that Sam might use his. So, both of them are weaponless. They can't use the weapon, because each's weapon nullifies the other's. So the only place where action can take place is on the ground. And the white man can't win another war fighting on the ground. Those days are over. The black man knows it, the brown man knows it, the red man knows it, and the yellow man knows it. So they engage him in guerrilla warfare. That's not his style. You've got to have heart to be a guerrilla warrior, and he hasn't got any heart. I'm telling you now.

I just want to give you a little briefing on guerrilla warfare, because, before you know it, before you know it— It takes heart to be a guerrilla warrior because you're on your own. In conventional warfare you have tanks and a whole lot of other people with you to back you up, planes over your head and all that kind of stuff. But a guerrilla is on his own. All you have is a rifle, some sneakers and a bowl of rice, and that's all you need—and a lot of heart. The Japanese on some of those islands in the Pacific, when the American soldiers landed, one Japanese sometimes could hold the whole Army off. He'd just wait until the sun went down, and when the sun went down they were all equal. He would take his little blade and slip from bush to bush, and from American to American. The white soldiers couldn't cope with that. Whenever you see a white soldier that fought in the Pacific, he has the shakes, he has a nervous condition, because they scared him to death.

The same thing happened to the French up in French Indochina. People who just a few years previously were rice farmers got together and ran the heavily mechanized French army out of Indochina. You don't need it—modern warfare today won't work. This is the day of the guerrilla. They did the same thing in Algeria. Algerians, who were nothing but Bedouins, took a rifle and sneaked off to the hills, and de Gaulle and all of his highfalutin' war machinery couldn't defeat those guerrillas. Nowhere on this earth does the white man win in a guerrilla warfare. It's not his speed. Just as guerrilla warfare is prevailing in Asia and in parts of Africa and in parts of Latin America, you've got to be mightly naïve, or you've got to play the black man cheap, if you don't think some day he's going to wake up and find that it's got to be the ballot or the bullet.

I would like to say, in closing, a few things concerning the Muslim Mosque, Inc., which we established recently in New York City. It's true we're Muslims and our religion is Islam, but we don't mix our religion with our politics and our economics and our social and civil activities—not any more. We keep our religion in our mosque. After our religious services are over, then as Muslims we become involved in political action, economic action and social and civic action. We become involved with anybody, anywhere, any time and in any manner that's designed to eliminate the evils, the political, economic and social evils that are afflicting the people of our community.

The political philosophy of black nationalism means that

the black man should control the politics and the politicians in his own community; no more. The black man in the black community has to be reeducated into the science of politics so he will know what politics is supposed to bring him in return. Don't be throwing out any ballots. A ballot is like a bullet. You don't throw your ballots until you see a target, and if that target is not within your reach, keep your ballot in your pocket. The political philosophy of black nationalism is being taught in the Christian church. It's being taught in the N.A.A.C.P. It's being taught in CORE meetings. It's being taught in S.N.C.C. meetings. It's being taught in Muslim meetings. It's being taught where nothing but atheists and agnostics come together. It's being taught everywhere. Black people are fed up with the dillydallying, pussyfooting, compromising approach that we've been using toward getting our freedom. We want freedom *now*, but we're not going to get it saying "We Shall Overcome." We've got to fight until we overcome.

The economic philosophy of black nationalism is pure and simple. It only means that we should control the economy of our community. Why should white people be running all the stores in our community? Why should white people be running the banks of our community? Why should the economy of our community be in the hands of the white man? Why? If a black man can't move his store into a white community, you tell me why a white man should move his store into a black community. The philosophy of black nationalism involves a reeducation program in the black community in regard to economics. Our people have to be made to see that any time you take your dollar out of your community and spend it in a community where you don't live, the community where you live will get poorer and poorer, and the community where you spend your money will get richer and richer. Then you wonder why where you live is always a ghetto or a slum area. And where you and I are concerned, not only do we lose it when we spend it out of the community, but the white man has got all our stores in the community tied up; so that though we spend it in the community, at sundown the man who runs the store takes it over across town somewhere. He's got us in a vise.

So the economic philosophy of black nationalism means in every church, in every civic organization, in every fraternal order, it's time now for our people to become conscious of the importance of controlling the economy of our community. If we own the stores, if we operate the businesses, if we try and establish some industry in our own community, then we're developing to the position where we are creating employment for our own kind. Once you gain control of the economy of your own community, then you don't have to picket and boycott and beg some cracker downtown for a job in his business.

The social philosophy of black nationalism only means that we have to get together and remove the evils, the vices, alcoholism, drug addiction, and other evils that are destroying the moral fiber of our community. We ourselves have to lift the level of our community, the standard of our community to a higher level, make our own society beautiful so that we will be satisfied in our own social circles and won't be running around here trying to knock our way into a social circle where we're not wanted.

So I say, in spreading a gospel such as black nationalism, it is not designed to make the black man reevaluate the white man—you know him already—but to make the black man reevaluate himself. Don't change the white man's mind; you can't change his mind. And that whole thing about appealing to the moral conscience of America—America's conscience is bankrupt. She lost all conscience a long time ago. Uncle Sam has no conscience. They don't know what morals are. They don't try and eliminate an evil because it's evil, or because it's illegal, or because it's immoral; they eliminate it only when it threatens their existence. So you're wasting your time appealing to the moral conscience of a bankrupt man like Uncle Sam. If he had a conscience, he'd straighten this thing out with no more pressure being put upon him. So it is not necessary to change the white man's mind. We have to change our own mind. You can't change his mind about us. We've got to change our own minds about each other. We have to see each other with new eyes. We have to see each other as brothers and sisters. We have to come together with warmth so we can develop unity and harmony that's necessary to get this problem solved ourselves. How can we do this? How can we avoid jealousy? How can we avoid the suspicion and the divisions that exist in the community? I'll tell you how.

I have watched how Billy Graham comes into a city, spreading what he calls the gospel of Christ, which is only white nationalism. That's what he is. Billy Graham is a white nationalist; I'm a black nationalist. But since it's the natural tendency for leaders to be jealous and look upon a powerful figure like Graham with suspicion and envy, how is it possible for him to come into a city and get all the cooperation of the church leaders? Don't think because they're church leaders that they don't have weaknesses that make them envious and jealous—no, everybody's got it. It's not an accident that when they want to choose a cardinal [as Pope] over there in Rome, they get in a closet so you can't hear them cussing and fighting and carrying on.

Billy Graham comes in preaching the gospel of Christ, he evangelizes the gospel, he stirs everybody up, but he never tries to start a church. If he came in trying to start a church, all the churches would be against him, So, he just comes in talking about Christ and tells everybody who gets Christ to go to any church where Christ is; and in this way the church cooperates with him. So we're going to take a page from his book.

Our gospel is black nationalism. We're not trying to threaten the existence of any organization, but we're spreading the gospel of black nationalism. Anywhere there's a church that is also preaching and practicing the gospel of black nationalism, join that church. If the N.A.A.C.P. is preaching and practicing the gospel of black nationalism, join the N.A.A.C.P. If CORE is spreading and practicing the gospel of black nationalism, join CORE. Join any organization that has a gospel that's for the uplift of the black man. And when you get into it and see them pussyfooting or compromising, pull out of it because that's not black nationalism. We'll find another one.

And in this manner, the organizations will increase in number and in quantity and in quality, and by August, it is then our intention to have a black nationalist convention which will consist of delegates from all over the country who are interested in the political, economic and social philosophy of black nationalism.* After these delegates convene, we will hold a seminar, we will hold discussions, we will listen to everyone. We want to hear new ideas and new solutions and new answers. And at that time, if we see fit then to form a black nationalist party, we'll form a black nationalist party. If it's necessary to form a black nationalist army, we'll form a black nationalist army. It'll be the ballot or the bullet. It'll be liberty or it'll be death.

It's time for you and me to stop sitting in this country, letting some cracker Senators, Northern crackers and Southern crackers, sit there in Washington, D. C., and come to a conclusion in their mind that you and I are supposed to have civil rights. There's no white man going to tell me anything about *my* rights. Brothers and sisters, always remember, if it doesn't take Senators and Congressmen and Presidential proclamations to give freedom to the white man, it is not necessary for legislation or proclamation or Supreme Court decisions to give freedom to the black man. You let that white man know, if this is a coun-

* For various reasons, the black nationalist convention projected for August, 1964, was not held.

try of freedom, let it be a country of freedom; and if it's not a country of freedom, change it.

We will work with anybody, anywhere, at any time, who is genuinely interested in tackling the problem head-on, nonviolently as long as the enemy is nonviolent, but violent when the enemy gets violent. We'll work with you on the voter-registration drive, we'll work with you on rent strikes, we'll work with you on school boycotts—I don't believe in any kind of integration; I'm not even worried about it because I know you're not going to get it anyway; you're not going to get it because you're afraid to die; you've got to be ready to die if you try and force yourself on the white man, because he'll get just as violent as those crackers in Mississippi, right here in Cleveland. But we will work with you on the school boycotts, because we're against a segregated school system. A segregated school system produces children who, when they graduate, graduate with crippled minds. But this does not mean that a school is segregated because it's all black. A segregated school means a school that is controlled by people who have no real interest in it whatsoever.

Let me explain what I mean. A segregated district or community is a community in which people live, but outsiders control the politics and the economy of that community. They never refer to the white section as a segregated community. It's the all-Negro section that's a segregated community. Why? The white man controls his own school, his own bank, his own economy, his own politics, his own everything, his own community—but he also controls yours. When you're under someone else's control, you're segregated. They'll always give you the lowest or the worst that there is to offer, but it doesn't mean you're segregated just because you have your own. You've got to *control* your own. Just like the white man has control of his, you need to control yours.

You know the best way to get rid of segregation? The white man is more afraid of separation than he is of integration. Segregation means that he puts you away from him, but not far enough for you to be out of his jurisdiction; separation means you're gone. And the white man will integrate faster than he'll let you separate. So we will work with you against the segregated school system because it's criminal, because it is absolutely destructive, in every way imaginable, to the minds of the children who have to be exposed to that type of crippling education.

Last but not least, I must say this concerning the great controversy over rifles and shotguns. The only thing that I've ever said is that in areas where the government has proven itself either unwilling or unable to defend the lives and the property of Negroes, it's time for Negroes to defend themselves. Article number two of the Constitutional amendments provides you and me the right to own a rifle or a shotgun.* It is constitutionally legal to own a shotgun or a rifle. This doesn't mean you're going to get a rifle and form battalions and go out looking for white folks, although you'd be within your rights—I mean, you'd be justified; but that would be illegal and we don't do anything illegal. If the white man doesn't want the black man buying rifles and shotguns, then let the government do its job. That's all. And don't let the white man come to you and ask you what you think about what Malcolm says—why, you old Uncle Tom. He would never ask you if he thought you were going to say, "Oh, man!" No, he is making a Tom out of you.

So, this doesn't mean forming rifle clubs and going out looking for people, but it is time, in 1964, if you are a man, to let that man know. If he's not going to do his job in running the government and providing you and me with the protection that our taxes are supposed to be for, since he spends all those billions for his defense budget, he certainly can't begrudge you and me spending $12 or $15 for a single-shot, or double-action. I hope you understand. Don't go out shooting people, but any time, brothers and sisters, and especially the men in this audience—some of you wearing Congressional Medals of Honor, with shoulders this wide, chests this big, muscles that big—any time you and I sit around and read where they bomb a church and murder in cold blood, not some grownups, but four little girls while they were praying . . . if you never see me another time in your life, if I die in the morning, I'll die saying one thing: the ballot or the bullet, the ballot or the bullet.

If a Negro in 1964 has to sit around and wait for some cracker Senator to filibuster when it comes to the rights of black people, why, you and I should hang our heads in shame. You talk about a march on Washington in 1963, you haven't seen anything. There's some more going down in '64. And this time they're not going like they went last year. They're not going singing "We Shall Overcome." They're not going with white friends. They're not going with placards already painted for them. They're not going with round-trip tickets. They're going with one-way tickets.

* The reference is to the Second Amendment of the Constitution. The first ten amendments, known collectively as the Bill of Rights, were ratified December 15, 1791. The Second Amendment reads: "A well regulated militia being necessary to the security of a free State, the right of the people to keep and bear arms, shall not be infringed."

And if they don't want that non-nonviolent army going down there, tell them to bring the filibuster to a halt. The black nationalists aren't going to wait. Lyndon B. Johnson is the head of the Democratic party. If he's for civil rights, let him go into the Senate next week and declare himself. Let him go in there right now and declare himself. Let him go in there and denounce the Southern branch of his party. Let him go in there right now and take a moral stand—right now, not later. Tell him, don't wait until election time. If he waits too long, brothers and sisters, he will be responsible for letting a condition develop in this country which will create a climate that will bring seeds up out of the ground with vegetation on the end of them looking like something these people never dreamed of. In 1964, it's the ballot or the bullet. Thank you.

WHITE LIBERALS AND THE BLACK REVOLUTION

By John O. Killens

As the Negro Freedom Movement became more militant and radical, a number of white liberals who had been helping it with funds and other forms of support became increasingly upset by the emphasis of a growing number of black militants on the theme that blacks should rely on themselves more than they were doing and that the goal of integration into American society was not necessarily the correct path for blacks to follow. As the question kept being asked what role whites should play in the Negro Freedom Movement, a forum was sponsored by the Association of Artists for Freedom at Town Hall, New York, June 15, 1964, to debate this very issue. Panel members were Ossie Davis, Ruby Dee, Lorraine Hansberry, Leroi Jones, John O. Killens and Paule Marshall, representing blacks, and Charles E. Silberman and James Wechsler, representing white liberals. The moderator was David Susskind.

Below are excerpts from the presentation of the distinguished black novelist John O. Killens, author of Youngblood *and* And Then We Heard the Thunder. *The excerpts are reprinted from the* National Guardian, *July 4, 1964.*

I THINK the first thing I'd like to say is that there is a misnomer here. There is no black revolution yet. . . . There is a black revolt. White liberals have become disturbed. I understand there was a white newspaper writer who first dubbed the Negro revolt as a revolution. White liberals have called this revolt a revolution when they get upset because of an inconvenience when we stalled their motor car on the bridge. In revolutions, people blow up bridges.

One white patriot, a long time ago, almost two centuries ago, said that these are the times that try men's souls. It was Tom Paine who said this almost two hundred years ago. Well, certainly he could have been talking about today. These are the times that try men's souls, these are the times that divide, indeed, the men from the boys. These are the times when the Cold War liberal must somehow, somewhere down the line, make up his mind, make a choice between the Cold War and the freedom movement. Because the struggle is to free America and not to help the downtrod Negro, which is the way many of the white liberals and white Americans like to look at it. . . .

So many liberals in the freedom movement are long on advice and short on action. Too many are willing to lead us down the freedom road but not to follow black leadership. But in the final analysis, that is how it must be, that is how it will be. American black folk will—with white assistance great or small—change America if it can be changed, and that's what it's all about—to change the country fundamentally and lead her out of the muck and mire of obsolescence of nineteenth-century racialism into the new world of the freedom century, which is already magnificently here all over the world. You know, I really marvel at the patience and fortitude displayed by many liberal Americans in the face of other peoples' degradation. They remind me of that great liberal, William Faulkner, the great Nobel Prize winner, exponent of *noblesse oblige*, and plantation owner. His advice to the American Negro is still typical of the complacency of the Cold War liberal. You remember those three great revolutionary slogans he gave us: "Patience, courtesy and cleanliness"—or words to that effect. . . .

How many white liberals are prepared to go all the way? How many will fall on the side, fall on the wayside at the first turn of the road? How many will be like Gideon's army? You know, Gideon was testing his army out, I believe. He asked for all—he put them through quite a few tests and when he got ready to fight, he had only about three hundred.

How many are the winter soldiers of white America? How many are the sunshine patriots? How many cold-war liberals will desert our ranks when we assert the right of self-defense? Because we must assert this right. We must affirm this right. This is one of the most fundamental rights recognized by all men everywhere, because we must dispel this new myth. You know, Negroes have always been trapped in so many myths. Now there's a myth that the Negro is nonviolent. . . .

Will the liberals of white America desert our ranks when we say that we will not love our enemies? That's a pretty sick bit, anyhow. Unrequited love.

For example, what if Harlem organized a vigilante group? Would the newspapers and the police be so tolerant? To defend themselves.

And another big test is where will the Cold War liberals be when we place our case before the United Nations, which we must do in due time since it is a case of a denial of human rights? I believe there is a Human Rights Commission.* When we assert our rights to political power, when we assert our rights to speak for ourselves and for the nation in all the halls of the legislatures throughout the land, how many white liberals care about the nation enough to criticize us fundamentally? Because I got a feeling the white liberals that—you know, America is sick, America is sick and is in need of basic surgery,

---

* The idea of an appeal by black Americans to the United Nations began soon after the international organization was formed. The N.A.A.C.P. presented the document "An Appeal to the World" to the U. N. in 1947. Written under the editorial supervision of W. E. B. Du Bois, the document was subtitled "A Statement on the Denial of Human Rights to Minorities in the Case of Citizens of Negro Descent in the United States of America and an Appeal to the United Nations for Redress." In 1951 the petition "We Charge Genocide" was presented to the U. N. by William L. Patterson, national executive secretary of the Civil Rights Congress. The petition was a catalog of lynchings and other acts of violence against Negroes and asked for U. N. action under Article II, the Genocide Convention. In 1964 Malcolm X attended the conference of the Organization of African Unity to urge African nations to bring the question of Negro rights to the United Nations. On July 19, 1964, Jesse Gray, leader of the Harlem Rent Strike, told the press that he planned to lead a demonstration at United Nations Plaza "to ask the U. N. to intervene in the 'police terror in the United States.'" In 1970, the Committee to Petition the United Nations announced a plan to submit another petition to the U. N. to end United States genocide against black, yellow, red and brown Americans. A million signatures were sought for the petition. Members of the committee which drafted the petition included Ossie Davis; Huey P. Newton, Minister of Defense of the Black Panther party; Black Congresswoman Shirley Chisholm; Dr. Nathan Wright; Roger Littlehorn, of the Indians of All Tribes; Dick Gregory; and Carl Blakley, of the Saulteaux tribe.

while the Madison Avenue fellows with more sense than anybody sitting here try to cure the world with plastic surgery, with
a face-lifting job when she needs basic surgery.

There are a few myths we must be willing to relinquish. The
one that I mentioned before, that there is no revolution yet; another one, that we have let the establishment get by a long time
on, is telling us that we are second-class citizens. Who in the
hell ever heard of a second-class citizen until they were in-
vented in the United States? A person is either a citizen or he
is not a citizen. You are either free or you are a slave. Thank
you. It's like being a woman that is half pregnant.

The backlash is a counterrevolution before the revolution
has gotten underway.

Another myth—and we've kept ourselves in this trap too—
is to imagine that we are all one big happy family. We're not
even all one big unhappy family. You know, if we're all one big
happy family, this means, of course, that the Negro must not
think of embarrassing big daddy before the world, you see.

The United Nations—with this big-family approach, the
United Nations and a lot of other avenues of protest are ruled
out. It's like a woman whose husband beats her and she doesn't
cry out loud because she doesn't want the neighbors to know.
Well, if we play that role, we deserve to be beaten. . . .

Fortunately or unfortunately—depending on your point of
view—the black move, generally speaking, is one of great impatience to emancipate the country.

TO YOUNG PEOPLE

By Malcolm X

*The following is part of a speech by Malcolm X on Decem-
ber 31, 1964, at New York's Hotel Theresa. It was delivered to a delegation of thirty-seven teen-agers from
McComb, Mississippi, who had come to New York for their
Christmas vacation. The trip was sponsored by S.N.C.C.,
and those chosen were young people who had been leaders
of the civil-rights struggle in their home town.*

*The excerpts from Malcolm X's speech are reprinted
from* Malcolm X Speaks, *New York, 1965, pp. 145–54.*

ONE OF THE FIRST THINGS I think young people, especially nowadays, should learn is how to see for yourself and listen for yourself and think for yourself. If you form the habit of going by what you hear others say about someone, or going by what others think about someone, instead of searching that thing out for yourself and seeing for yourself, you will be walking west when you think you're going east, and you will be walking east when you think you're going west. This generation, especially of our people, has a burden, more so than any other time in history. The most important thing we can learn to do today is think for ourselves.

It's good to keep wide-open ears and listen to what everybody else has to say, but when you come to make decisions, you have to weigh all of what you've heard on its own, and place it where it belongs, and come to a decision for yourself; you'll never regret it. But if you form the habit of taking what someone else says about a thing without checking it out for yourself, you'll find that other people will have you hating your friends and loving your enemies. This is one of the things that our people are beginning to learn today—that it is very important to think out a situation for yourself. If you don't do it, you'll always be maneuvered into a situation where you are never fighting your actual enemies, where you will find yourself fighting your own self.

I think our people in this country are the best examples of that. Many of us want to be nonviolent and we talk very loudly, you know, about being nonviolent. Here in Harlem, where there are probably more black people concentrated than any place in the world, some talk that nonviolent talk too. But we find that they aren't nonviolent with each other. You can go out to Harlem Hospital, where there are more black patients than any hospital in the world, and see them going in there all cut up and shot up and busted up where they got violent with each other.

My experience has been that in many instances where you find Negroes talking about nonviolence, they are not nonviolent with each other, and they're not loving with each other, or forgiving with each other. Usually when they say they're nonviolent, they mean they're nonviolent with somebody else. I think you understand what I mean. They are nonviolent with the enemy. A person can come to your home, and if he's white and wants to heap some kind of brutality on you, you're nonviolent; or he can come to take your father and put a rope around his neck and you're nonviolent. But if another Negro just stomps his foot, you'll rumble with him in a minute. Which shows you that there's an inconsistency there.

If the leaders of the nonviolent movement can go into the white community and teach nonviolence, good. I'd go along with that. But as long as I see them teaching nonviolence only in the black community, we can't go along with that. We believe in equality, and equality means that you have to put the same thing over here that you put over there. And if black people alone are going to be the ones who are nonviolent, then it's not fair. We throw ourselves off guard. In fact, we disarm ourselves and make ourselves defenseless. . . .

Around that time—1939, or '40 or '41—they weren't drafting Negroes in the Army or Navy. A Negro couldn't join the Navy in 1940 or '41. They wouldn't take a black man in the Navy except to make him cook. He couldn't just go and join the Navy, and I don't think he could just go and join the Army. They weren't drafting him when the war first started. This is what they thought of you and me in those days. For one thing, they didn't trust us; they feared that if they put us in the Army and trained us how to use rifles and other things, we might shoot at some targets that they hadn't picked out. And we would have. Any thinking man knows what target to shoot at. If a man has to have someone else choose his target, then he isn't thinking for himself—they're doing the thinking for him.

The Negro leaders in those days were the same type we have today. When the Negro leaders saw all the white fellows being drafted and taken into the Army and dying on the battlefield, and no Negroes were dying because they weren't being drafted, the Negro leaders came up and said, "We've got to die too. We want to be drafted too, and we demand that you take us in there and let us die for our country too." That was what the Negro leaders did back in 1940, I remember. A. Philip Randolph was one of the leading Negroes in those days who said it, and he's one of the "Big Six" right now; and this is why he's one of the Big Six.

So they started drafting Negro soldiers then, and started letting Negroes get into the Navy. But not until Hitler and Tojo and foreign powers were strong enough to put pressure on this country, so that it had its back to the wall and needed us, [did] they let us work in the factories. Up until that time we couldn't work in the factories; I'm talking about the North as well as the South. And when they let us work in the factories, at first they let us in only as janitors. After a year or so passed by, they let us work on machines. We became machinists, got a little more skill. If we got a little more skill, we made a little more money, which enabled us to live in a little better neighborhood. When we lived in a little better neighborhood, we went to a little better school, got a little better education and could come out and get a little better job. So the cycle was broken somewhat.

But the cycle was not broken out of some kind of sense of moral responsibility on the part of the government. No, the only time that cycle was broken even to a degree was when world pressure was brought to bear on the United States government. They didn't look at us as human beings—they just put us into their system and let us advance a little bit farther because it served their interests. They never let us advance a little bit farther because they were interested in us as human beings. Any of you who have a knowledge of history, sociology or political science, or the economic development of this country and its race relations—go back and do some research on it and you'll have to admit that this is true.

It was during the time that Hitler and Tojo made war with this country and put pressure on it that Negroes in this country advanced a little bit. At the end of the war with Germany and Japan, then Joe Stalin and Communist Russia were a threat. During that period we made a little more headway. Now the point that I'm making is this: Never at any time in the history of our people in this country have we made advances or progress in any way based upon the internal good will of this country, only when this country was under pressure from forces above and beyond its control. The internal moral consciousness of this country is bankrupt. It hasn't existed since they first brought us over here and made slaves out of us. They make it appear they have our good interests at heart, but when you study it, every time, no matter how many steps they take us forward, it's like we're standing on—what do you call that thing?—a treadmill. The treadmill is moving backward faster than we're able to go forward in this direction. We're not even standing still; we're going backward.

In studying the process of this so-called progress during the past twenty years, we of the Organization of Afro-American Unity realized that the only time the black man in this country is given any kind of recognition, or even listened to, is when America is afraid of outside pressure, or when she's afraid of her image abroad. So we saw that it was necessary to expand the problem and the struggle of the black man in this country until it went above and beyond the jurisdiction of the United States . . .

I was fortunate enough to be able to take a tour of the African continent during the summer. I went to Egypt, then to

Arabia, Kuwait, Lebanon, Sudan, Ethiopia, Kenya, Tanganyika, Zanzibar, Nigeria, Ghana, Guinea, Liberia and Algeria. I found, while I was traveling on the African continent—I had already detected it in May—that someone had very shrewdly planted the seed of division on this continent to make the Africans not show genuine concern with our problem, just as they plant seeds in your and my minds so that we won't show concern with the African problem. . . .

I also found that in many of these African countries the head of state is genuinely concerned with the problem of the black man in this country; but many of them thought if they opened their mouths and voiced their concern that they would be insulted by the American Negro leaders. Because one head of state in Asia voiced his support of the civil-rights struggle (in 1963) and a couple of the Big Six had the audacity to slap his face and say they weren't interested in that kind of help— which in my opinion is asinine. So the African leaders only had to be convinced that if they took an open stand at the governmental level and showed interest in the problem of black people in this country, they wouldn't be rebuffed.

And today you'll find in the United Nations—and it's not an accident—that every time the Congo question or anything on the African continent is being debated, they couple it with what is going on, or what is happening to you and me, in Mississippi and Alabama and these other places. In my opinion, the greatest accomplishment that was made in the struggle of the black man in America in 1964 toward some kind of real progress was the successful linking together of our problem with the African problem, or making our problem a world problem. Because now, whenever anything happens to you in Mississippi, it's not just a case of somebody in Alabama getting indignant, or somebody in New York getting indignant. The same repercussions that you see all over the world when an imperialist or foreign power interferes in some section of Africa—you see repercussions, you see the embassies bombed and burned and overturned—nowadays, when something happens to black people in Mississippi, you'll see the same repercussions all over the world.

I wanted to point this out to you, because it is important for you to know that when you're in Mississippi, you're not alone. As long as you think you're alone, then you take a stand as if you're a minority or as if you're outnumbered, and that kind of stand will never enable you to win a battle. You've got to know that you've got as much power on your side as the Ku Klux Klan has on its side. And when you know that you've got as much power on your side as the Klan has on its side, you'll talk the same kind of language with that Klan as the Klan is talking with you. . . .

I think in 1965—whether you like it, or I like it, or they like it, or not—you will see that there is a generation of black people becoming mature to the point where they feel that they have no more business being asked to take a peaceful approach than anybody else has, unless everybody's going to take a peaceful approach.

So we here in the Organization of Afro-American Unity are with the struggle in Mississippi one thousand percent. We're with the efforts to register our people in Mississippi to vote one thousand percent. But we do not go along with anybody telling us to help nonviolently. We think that if the government says that Negroes have a right to vote, and then some Negroes come out to vote, and some kind of Ku Klux Klan is going to put them in the river, and the government doesn't do anything about it, it's time for us to organize and band together and equip ourselves and qualify ourselves to protect ourselves. And once you can protect yourself, you don't have to worry about being hurt. . . .

That doesn't mean we're against white people, but we sure are against the Ku Klux Klan and the White Citizens Councils; and anything that looks like it's against us, we're against it. Excuse me for raising my voice, but this thing, you know, gets me upset. Imagine that—a country that's supposed to be a democracy, supposed to be for freedom and all of that kind of stuff when they want to draft you and put you in the Army and send you to Saigon to fight for them—and then you've got to turn around and all night long discuss how you're going to just get a right to register and vote without being murdered. Why, that's the most hypocritical government since the world began! . . .

I hope you don't think I'm trying to incite you. Just look here: Look at yourselves. Some of you are teen-agers, students. How do you think I feel—and I belong to a generation ahead of you —how do you think I feel to have to tell you, "We, my generation, sat around like a knot on a wall while the whole world was fighting for its human rights—and you've got to be born into a society where you still have the same fight." What did we do, who preceded you? I'll tell you what we did: Nothing. And don't you make the same mistake we made.

You get freedom by letting your enemy know that you'll do anything to get your freedom; then you'll get it. It's the only way you'll get it. When you get that kind of attitude, they'll label you as a "crazy Negro," or they'll call you a "crazy nigger" —they don't say Negro. Or they'll call you an extremist or a subversive, or seditious, or a red or a radical. But when you stay radical long enough, and get enough people to be like you, you'll get your freedom. . . .

So don't you run around here trying to make friends with somebody who's depriving you of your rights. They're not your friends, no, they're your enemies. Treat them like that and fight them, and you'll get your freedom: and after you get your freedom, your enemy will respect you. And we'll respect you. And I say that with no hate. I don't have hate in me. I have no hate at all. I don't have any hate. I've got some sense. I'm not going to let somebody who hates me tell me to love him. I'm not that way-out. And you, young as you are, and because you start thinking, you're not going to do it either. The only time you're going to get in that bag is if somebody puts you there. Somebody else, who doesn't have your welfare at heart. . . .

MALCOLM WAS OUR MANHOOD, OUR LIVING BLACK MANHOOD

By Ossie Davis

At the funeral of Malcolm X, held at Faith Temple, Church of God, in Harlem, February 27, 1965, Ossie Davis delivered the eulogy below. The brief, eloquent tribute aroused widespread criticism among those who viewed Malcolm X as a black racist and a danger to American society. Davis answered the criticism in an article, "Why I Eulogized Malcolm X" (Negro Digest, February, 1966, pp. 64–66).

Ossie Davis, the noted actor, made his Broadway debut in Jeb, *presented by Herman Shumlin. Subsequently he appeared with Helen Hayes in* The Wisteria Trees; *with Lena Horne in the musical* Jamaica; *and he replaced Sidney Poitier in Lorraine Hansberry's* A Raisin in the Sun. *He is the author of* Purlie Victorious, *in which he costarred with his wife, Ruby Dee. Mr. Davis has also appeared in many Hollywood films and on television. He was Master of Ceremonies at the historic March on Washington in*

1963, and was host and narrator of a National Education TV series on the history of the Negro people.
Davis' eulogy is presented here with the permission of the author, who kindly provided a copy of the speech.

HERE, at this final hour, in this quiet place, Harlem has come to bid farewell to one of its brightest hopes—extinguished now and gone from us forever.

For Harlem is where he worked and where he struggled and fought—his home of homes; where his heart was, and where his people are—and it is, therefore, most fitting that we meet once again—in Harlem—to share these last moments with him.

For Harlem has been ever gracious to those who have loved her, have fought for her and have defended her honor even to the death. It is not in the memory of man that this beleaguered, unfortunate, but nonetheless proud, community has found a braver, more gallant young champion than this Afro-American who lies before us—unconquered still.

I say the word again, as he would want me to: *Afro-American; Afro-American* Malcolm, who was a master, was most meticulous in his use of words. Nobody knew better than he the power words have over the minds of men. Malcolm had stopped being "Negro" years ago.

It had become too small, too puny, too weak a word for him. Malcolm was bigger than that. Malcolm had become an *Afro-American*, and he wanted—so desperately—that we, that all his people would become Afro-Americans too.

There are those who still consider it their duty, as friends of the Negro people, to tell us to revile him, to flee, even from the presence of his memory, to save ourselves by writing him out of the history of our turbulent times.

Many will ask what Harlem finds to honor in this stormy, controversial and bold young captain. And we will smile.

Many will say turn away, away from this man, for he is not a man but a demon, a monster, a subverter and an enemy of the black man. And we will smile.

They will say that he is of hate—a fanatic, a racist who can only bring evil to the cause for which you struggle.

And we will answer and say unto them: Did you ever talk to Brother Malcolm? Did you ever touch him, or have him smile at you? Did you ever really listen to him? Did he ever do a mean thing? Was he ever himself associated with violence or any public disturbance? For if you did, you would know him. And if you knew him, you would know why we must honor him.

Malcolm was our manhood, our living black manhood! This was his meaning to his people. And, in honoring him, we honor the best in ourselves.

Last year, from Africa, he wrote these words to a friend:

My journey [he says] is almost ended, and I have a much broader scope than when I started out, which I believe will add new life and dimension to our struggle for freedom and honor, and dignity in the States. I'm writing these things so that you will know for a fact the tremendous sympathy and support we have among the African states for our Human-Rights Struggle. The main thing is that we keep a United Front wherein our most valuable time and energy will not be wasted fighting each other.

However much we may have differed with him—or with each other about him and his value as a man—let his going from us serve only to bring us together now. Consigning these mortal remains to earth, the common mother of all, secure in the knowledge that what we place in the ground is no more now a man, but a seed, which, after the winter of discontent, will come forth again to meet us. And we shall know him then for what he was and is—a Prince, our own black shining Prince, who didn't hesitate to die, because he loved us so.

THE AMERICAN DREAM IS AT THE EXPENSE OF THE AMERICAN NEGRO

By James Baldwin

On the anniversary of its founding one hundred fifty years before, the Cambridge Union Society of Cambridge University in England invited two United States visitors to join two undergraduates in debating the motion, "The American Dream is at the Expense of the American Negro." The debate took place in February, 1965. Speaking for the proposition was novelist and essayist James Baldwin; opposing it was William F. Buckley, Jr., editor of The National Review *and a spokesman for American Conservatives. More than seven hundred students crowded the debating chamber, and five hundred others packed other rooms to watch over closed-circuit TV. Here, slightly condensed, is Baldwin's argument.*

James Baldwin was born in New York City, where he grew up and attended school, graduating from De Witt Clinton High School. He has held, as he put it, "all kinds of jobs, mostly in New York, but one job in Paris, where I lived for nearly ten years." Baldwin is the winner of a number of literary fellowships—a Eugene F. Saxton Memorial Trust Award, a Rosenwald Fellowship, a Guggenheim Fellowship, a National Institute of Arts and Letters Fellowship, and a Ford Foundation Grant-in-Aid. His stories and essays have appeared in leading magazines here and in Europe. With his books of essays, Notes of a Native Son and The Fire Next Time, and his novels, James Baldwin has established himself as one of the leading writers of his time.

Baldwin's statement is reprinted from The New York Times Sunday Magazine, March 7, 1965.

I FIND MYSELF, not for the first time, in the position of a kind of Jeremiah. It would seem to me that the question before the house is a proposition horribly loaded, that one's response to that question depends on where you find yourself in the world, what your sense of reality is. That is, it depends on assumptions we hold so deeply as to be scarcely aware of them.

The white South African or Mississippi sharecropper or Alabama sheriff has at bottom a system of reality which compels him really to believe, when they face the Negro, that this woman, this man, this child must be insane to attack the system to which he owes his entire identity. For such a person, the proposition which we are trying to discuss here does not exist.

On the other hand, I have to speak as one of the people who have been most attacked by the Western system of reality. It comes from Europe. That is how it got to America. It raises the question of whether or not civilizations can be considered equal, or whether one civilization has a right to subjugate—in fact, to destroy—another.

Now, leaving aside all the physical factors one can quote— leaving aside the rape or murder, leaving aside the bloody catalogue of oppression which we are too familiar with anyway— what the system does to the subjugated is to destroy his sense of reality. It destroys his father's authority over him. His father can no longer tell him anything, because his past has disappeared.

In the case of the American Negro, from the moment you are

born every stick and stone, every face, is white. Since you have not yet seen a mirror, you suppose you are, too. It comes as a great shock around the age of five, six or seven to discover that the flag to which you have pledged allegiance, along with everybody else, has not pledged allegiance to you. It comes as a great shock to see Gary Cooper killing off the Indians and, although you are rooting for Gary Cooper, that the Indians are you.

It comes as a great shock to discover that the country which is your birthplace and to which you owe your life and identity has not, in its whole system of reality, evolved any place for you. The disaffection and the gap between people, only on the basis of their skins, begins there and accelerates throughout your whole lifetime. You realize that you are thirty and you are having a terrible time. You have been through a certain kind of mill and the most serious effect is again not the catalogue of disaster—the policeman, the taxi driver, the waiters, the landlady, the banks, the insurance companies, the millions of details twenty-four hours of every day which spell out to you that you are a worthless human being. It is not that. By that time you have begun to see it happening in your daughter, your son or your niece or your nephew. You are thirty by now, and nothing you have done has helped you to escape the trap. But what is worse is that nothing you have done, and as far as you can tell nothing you *can* do, will save your son or your daughter from having the same disaster and from coming to the same end.

We speak about expense. There are several ways of addressing oneself to some attempt to find out what that word means here. From a very literal point of view, the harbors and the ports and the railroads of the country—the economy, especially in the South—could not conceivably be what they are if it had not been (and this is still so) for cheap labor. I am speaking very seriously, and this is not an overstatement: I picked cotton; I carried it to the market; I built the railroads under someone else's whip for nothing. For nothing.

The Southern oligarchy which has still today so very much power in Washington, and therefore some power in the world, was created by my labor and my sweat and the violation of my women and the murder of my children. This in the land of the free, the home of the brave. None can challenge that statement. It is a matter of historical record.

In the Deep South you are dealing with a sheriff or a landlord or a landlady or the girl at the Western Union desk. She doesn't know quite whom she is dealing with—by which I mean, if you are not part of a town and if you are a Northern nigger, it shows in millions of ways. She simply knows that it is an unknown quantity and she wants to have nothing to do with it. You have to wait a while to get your telegram. We have all been through it. By the time you get to be a man it is fairly easy to deal with.

But what happens to the poor white man's, the poor white woman's, mind? It is this: they have been raised to believe, and by now they helplessly believe, that no matter how terrible some of their lives may be and no matter what disaster overtakes them, there is one consolation like a heavenly revelation —at least they are not black. I suggest that of all the terrible things that could happen to a human being that is one of the worst. I suggest that what has happened to the white Southerner is in some ways much worse than what has happened to the Negroes there.

Sheriff Clark in Selma, Alabama, cannot be dismissed as a total monster;* I am sure he loves his wife and children and likes to get drunk. One has to assume that he is a man like me. But he does know what drives him to use the club, to menace with the gun and to use the cattle prod. Something awful must have happened to a human being to be able to put a cattle prod against a woman's breasts. What happens to the woman is ghastly. What happens to the man who does it is in some ways much, much worse. Their moral lives have been destroyed by the plague called color.

This is not being done a hundred years ago, but in 1965, and in a country which is pleased with what we call prosperity, with a certain amount of social coherence, which calls itself a civilized nation and which espouses the notion of freedom in the world. If it were white people being murdered, the government would find some way of doing something about it. We have a civil-rights bill now. We had the Fifteenth Amendment nearly a hundred years ago. If it was not honored then, I have no reason to believe that the civil-rights bill will be honored now.

The American soil is full of the corpses of my ancestors, through four hundred years and at least three wars. Why is my freedom, my citizenship, in question now? What one begs the American people to do, for all our sakes, is simply to accept our history.

It seems to me when I watch Americans in Europe that what they don't know about Europeans is what they don't know about me. They were not trying to be nasty to the French girl, rude to

---

* Sheriff Clark of Selma, Dallas County, was especially brutal in opposing civil-rights demonstrators during the summer and fall of 1964.

the French waiter. They did not know that they hurt their feelings; they didn't have any sense that this particular man and woman were human beings. They walked over them with the same sort of bland ignorance and condescension, the charm and cheerfulness, with which they had patted me on the head and which made them upset when I was upset.

When I was brought up I was taught in American history books that Africa had no history and that neither had I. I was a savage about whom the least said the better, who had been saved by Europe and who had been brought to America. Of course, I believed it. I didn't have much choice. These were the only books there were. Everyone else seemed to agree. If you went out of Harlem the whole world agreed. What you saw was much bigger, whiter, cleaner, safer. The garbage was collected, the children were happy. You would go back home and it would seem, of course, that this was an act of God. You belonged where white people put you.

It is only since World War II that there has been a counter-image in the world. That image has not come about because of any legislation by any American government, but because Africa was suddenly on the stage of the world and Africans had to be dealt with in a way they had never been dealt with before. This gave the American Negro, for the first time, a sense of himself not as a savage. It has created and will create a great many conundrums.

One of the things the white world does not know, but I think I know, is that black people are just like everybody else. We are also mercenaries, dictators, murderers, liars. We are human, too. Unless we can establish some kind of dialogue between those people who enjoy the American dream and those other people who have not achieved it, we will be in terrible trouble. This is what concerns me most. We are sitting in this room and we are all civilized; we can talk to each other, at least on certain levels, so that we can walk out of here assuming that the measure of our politeness has some effect on the world.

I remember when the ex-Attorney General, Mr. Robert Kennedy, said it was conceivable that in forty years in America we might have a Negro President. That sounded like a very emancipated statement to white people. They were not in Harlem when this statement was first heard. They did not hear the laughter and bitterness and scorn with which this statement was greeted. From the point of view of the man in the Harlem barbershop, Bobby Kennedy only got here yesterday and now he is already on his way to the Presidency. We were here for four hundred years and now he tells us that maybe in forty years, if you are good, we may let you become President.

Perhaps I can be reasoned with, but I don't know—neither does Martin Luther King—none of us knows how to deal with people whom the white world has so long ignored, who don't believe anything the white world says and don't entirely believe anything I or Martin say. You can't blame them.

It seems to me that the City of New York has had, for example, Negroes in it for a very long time. The City of New York was able in the last fifteen years to reconstruct itself, to tear down buildings and raise great new ones and has done nothing whatever except build housing projects, mainly in the ghettos, for the Negroes. And, of course, the Negroes hate it. The children can't bear it. They want to move out of the ghettos. If American pretensions were based on more honest assessments of life, it would not mean for Negroes that when someone says "urban renewal" some Negroes are going to be thrown out into the streets, which is what it means now.

It is a terrible thing for an entire people to surrender to the notion that one ninth of its population is beneath them. Until the moment comes when we, the Americans, are able to accept the fact that my ancestors are both black and white, that on that continent we are trying to forge a new identity, that we need each other, that I am not a ward of America, I am not an object of missionary charity, I am one of the people who built the country—until this moment comes, there is scarcely any hope for the American dream. If the people are denied participation in it, by their very presence they will wreck it. And if that happens it is a very grave moment for the West.

BEN IS GOING TO TAKE HIS BIG BROTHER'S PLACE

By Fannie Lee Chaney

In the summer of 1964, three young civil-rights workers—James Chaney, Andrew Goodman and Michael Schwerner, the first a Negro from Meridian, Mississippi, and the others whites from New York City—were brutally mur-

dered in Philadelphia, Mississippi. The three had been suddenly released from detention in the county jail so that they might be shot by an alerted white mob, which included the town officials. The parents of the boys all vowed to continue the struggle for which their sons had sacrificed their lives. In a moving speech at a memorial meeting in New York City, Fannie Lee Chaney, the mother of James Chaney, announced that she and the rest of her family were going to continue in the Movement, and that her son Ben would take his big brother's place. Her speech is reprinted here from Freedomways, *Second Quarter, 1965, pp. 290–91.*

I AM HERE to tell you about Meridian, Mississippi. That's my home. I have been there all of my days. I know the white man; I know the black man. The white man is not for the black man—we are just there. Everything to be done, to be said, the white man is going to do it; *he* is going to say it, right or wrong. We hadn't, from the time that I know of, been able to vote or register in Meridian. Now, since the civil-rights workers have been down in Mississippi working, they have allowed a lot of them to go to register. A lot of our people are scared, afraid. They are still backward. "I can't do that; I never have," they claimed. "I have been here too long. I will lose my job; I won't have any job." So, that is just the way it is. My son, James, when he went out with the civil-rights workers around the first of '64 felt it was something he wanted to do, and he enjoyed working in the civil-rights movement. He stayed in Canton, Mississippi, working on voter registration from February through March. When he came home he told me how he worked and lived those few weeks he was there; he said, "Mother, one half of the time, I was out behind houses or churches, waiting to get the opportunity to talk to people about what they needed and what they ought to do." He said, "Sometime they shunned me off and some would say, 'I want you all to stay away from here and leave me alone.'" But he would pick his chance and go back again. That is what I say about Mississippi right now. There is one more test I want to do there. I am working with the civil-rights movement, my whole family is, and my son, Ben, here, he is going to take his big brother's place.

He has been working for civil rights. Everything he can do, he does it. For his activities, he had been jailed twice before he was twelve years old. He told me when he was in jail he wasn't excited. He is not afraid; he would go to jail again! I am too, because we need and we've got to go to jail and we've got to get where the white man is. The white man has got Mississippi and we are just there working for the white man. He is the one getting rich. And when he gets rich, we can be outdoors or in old houses and he is going to knock on the door and get his rent money.

This is not something that has just now started, it has been going on before my time and I imagine before my parents' time. It is not just *now* the white man is doing this; it was borne from generation to generation. So, as I say, Ben is going to take his big brother's place, and I am with him and the rest of the family also. You all read about Mississippi—all parts of Mississippi—but I just wish it was so you could just come down there and be able to see; just try to live there just for one day, and you will know just how it is there.

WE'VE DECIDED TO STOP BEGGING

By John Hulett

In his article, "What We Want," published in New York Review of Books *in 1966 and reprinted many times, Stokely Carmichael explained: "S.N.C.C. is working in both the North and the South on programs of voter registration and independent political organizing. In some places, such as Alabama, Los Angeles, New York, Philadelphia and New Jersey, independent organizing under the black panther symbol is in progress." The first of these movements for independent political action by blacks occurred in Lowndes County, Alabama, where blacks are a majority. The movement led to the formation of the Lowndes County Freedom Party, whose chairman was John Hulett and whose symbol was the black panther. In a speech delivered in Los Angeles, May 22, 1966, entitled "How the Black Panther Party Was Organized," Hulett described the conditions which brought about independent political action in Lowndes County. Hulett was addressing a meeting sponsored by nine different antiwar committees.*

Seven black candidates ran as independents under the Black Panther emblem in Lowndes County, Alabama, in the election of 1966. All were defeated by margins ranging from 273 votes to 677 votes. Frank Ryals, incumbent white

*sheriff, defeated Sidney Logan, the black candidate, 2,320
to 1,643. The county had 2,681 black and 2,100 white
voters.*

*The symbol of the black panther was later used by
Huey P. Newton and Bobby Seale when they organized
the Black Panther Party for Self-Defense, at Oakland,
California.*

Hulett's speech is reprinted here from The Black Panther Party, *New York, 1966, pp. 7–15.*

I'M HAPPY to have the opportunity to come and share
this evening with you. I'd like to give you a general idea of
what's happening in the state of Alabama and in Lowndes
County. This county, as far as I'm concerned, is one of the
worst counties in the state of Alabama, and not only that, it is
one of the poorest counties in the nation.

Lowndes County consists of a population of about 15,000
people. Out of these 15,000 people, 80 percent are Negroes, 20
percent white. The entire county is controlled entirely by
whites. It has always been this way. . . .

Last year in March, some thirty people assembled at the
courthouse in Haynesville to make an attempt to get registered.
They were talked about and many people were sitting by their
radios that day and their televisions, waiting to see what would
happen in Lowndes County. We made the attempt and two
weeks later, two people became registered voters. Today we
have at least 2,500 registered Negro voters.

According to the 1960 statistics, there are only 1,900 possible
white registered voters in the county. Today, all of these people
are registered. Two years ago, 118 percent of these white people voted. In the general elections this year for governor, I
learned that there will be even more white people voting.

Last year, we started a group in Lowndes County known as
the Lowndes County Christian Movement for Human Rights.
This was a civil-rights group. We fought for integration in this
county. We fought that Negroes might have a right to get registered to vote. We protested at the school so that all the people
could have education—and for this we got nothing. . . .

We sat down together and discussed our problems. We
thought about what we were going to do with these 2,500 registered voters in the county, whether or not we were going to
join Lyndon Baines Johnson's party. Then we thought about the
other people in the state of Alabama who were working in this
party. We thought of the city commissioner of Birmingham,
Eugene "Bull" Conner; George Wallace who is now the Governor

of the state of Alabama; Al Lingo, who gave orders to those who beat the people when they got ready to make the march from Selma to Montgomery; the sheriff of Dallas County, known as Jim Clark—these people control the Democratic party in the state of Alabama.

So the Negroes in Lowndes County decided that it's useless to stay in the Democratic party or the Republican party in the state of Alabama. Through the years, these are the people who kept Negroes from voting in the South and in the state of Alabama. Why join the Democratic party?

A POLITICAL GROUP OF OUR OWN

Some time ago, we organized a political group of our own known as the Lowndes County Freedom Organization, whose emblem is the Black Panther.

We were criticized, we were called Communists, we were called everything else, black nationalists and what not, because we did this. Any group which starts at a time like this to speak out for what is right—they are going to be ridiculed. The people of Lowndes County realized this. Today we are moving further . . .

Too long Negroes have been begging, especially in the South, for things they should be working for. So the people in Lowndes County decided to organize themselves—to go out and work for the things we wanted in life—not only for the people in Lowndes County, but for every county in the state of Alabama, in the Southern states, and even in California.

You cannot become free in California while there are slaves in Lowndes County. And no person can be free while other people are still slaves—nobody.

In Lowndes County, there is a committee in the Democratic party. This committee not only controls the courthouse, it controls the entire county. When they found out that the Negroes were going to run candidates in the primary of the Democratic party on May 3, they assembled themselves together and began to talk about what they were going to do. Knowing this is one of the poorest counties in the nation, what they decided to do was change the registration fees in the county.

Two years ago, if a person wanted to run for sheriff, tax collector or tax assessor, all he had to do was pay fifty dollars and then he qualified to be the candidate. This year, the entrance fee is about nine hundred dollars. If a person wants to run, he has to pay five hundred dollars to run for office. In the primary, when they get through cheating and stealing, then the candidate is eliminated. So we decided that we wouldn't get into such a primary, because we were tired of being tricked by the Southern whites. After forming our own political group today, we feel real strong. We feel that we are doing the right thing in Lowndes County.

We have listened to everybody who wanted to talk, we listened to them speak, but one thing we had to learn for ourselves. As a group of people, we must think for ourselves and act on our own accord. And this we have done.

Through the years, Negroes in the South have been going for the bones while whites have been going for the meat. The Negroes of Lowndes County today are tired of the bones. We are going to have some of the meat too.

FIGHTING THE "TRICKS" OF THE RACISTS

At the present time, we have our own candidates which have been nominated by the Lowndes County Freedom Organization. And we fear that this might not be enough to avoid the tricks that are going to be used in Lowndes County against us. . . .

In Lowndes County, the sheriff is the custodian of the courthouse. This is a liberal sheriff, too, who is "integrated," who walks around and pats you on the shoulder, who does not carry a gun. But at the same time, in the county where there are only eight hundred white men, there are five hundred and fifty of them who walk around with a gun on them. They are deputies. This is true; it might sound like a fairy tale to most people, but this is true.

After talking to the sheriff about having the use of the courthouse lawn for our mass nominating meeting, not the courthouse but just the lawn, he refused to give the Negroes permission. We reminded him that last year in August, that one of the biggest Klan rallies that has ever been held in the state of Alabama was held on this lawn of this courthouse. And he gave them permission. A few weeks ago an individual who was campaigning for governor, he got permission to use it. He used all types of loudspeakers and anything that he wanted.

But he would not permit Negroes to have the use of the courthouse. For one thing he realized that we would build a party, and if he could keep us from forming our own political group then we would always stand at the feet of the Southern whites and of the Democratic party. So we told him that we were going to have this meeting, we were going to have it here, on the courthouse lawn. And we wouldn't let anybody scare us off. We told him, we won't expect you to protect us, and if you don't, Negroes will protect themselves.

Then we asked him a second time to be sure he understood what we were saying. We repeated it to him the second time. And then we said to him, sheriff, if you come out against the people, then we are going to arrest you.

And he said, I will not give you permission to have this meeting here. I can't protect you from the community.

Then we reminded him that according to the law of the state of Alabama, that this mass meeting which was set up to nominate our candidates must be held in or around a voters' polling place. And if we decide to hold it a half a mile away from the courthouse, some individual would come up and protest our mass meeting. And our election would be thrown out.

So we wrote the Justice Department and told them what was going to happen in Lowndes County.

All of a sudden the Justice Department started coming in fast into the county. They said to me, John, what is going to happen next Tuesday at the courthouse?

I said, We are going to have our mass meeting. And he wanted to know where. And I said on the lawn of the courthouse.

He said, I thought the sheriff had told you you couldn't come there. And I said, Yes, but we are going to be there.

Then he wanted to know, if shooting takes place, what are we going to do? And I said, that we are going to stay out here and everybody die together.

And then he began to get worried, and I said, Don't worry. You're going to have to be here to see it out and there's no place to hide, so whatever happens, you can be a part of it.

And then he began to really panic. And he said, There's nothing I can do.

And I said, I'm not asking you to do anything. All I want you to know is we are going to have a mass meeting. If the sheriff cannot protect us, then we are going to protect ourselves. And I said to him, through the years in the South, Negroes have never had any protection, and today we aren't looking to anybody to protect us. We are going to protect ourselves.

That was on Saturday. On Sunday, at about two o'clock, we were having a meeting, and we decided among ourselves that we were going to start collecting petitions for our candidates to be sure that they got on the ballot. The state laws require at least twenty-five signatures of qualified electors and so we decided to get at least a hundred, for fear somebody might come up and find fault. And we decided to still have our mass meeting and nominate our candidates.

About 2:30, here comes the Justice Department again, and he was really worried. And he said he wasn't satisfied. He said to me, John, I've done all I can do, and I don't know what else I can do, and now it looks like you'll have to call this meeting off at the courthouse.

And I said, we're going to have it.

He stayed around for a while and then got in his car and drove off, saying, I'll see you tomorrow, maybe. And we stayed at this meeting from 2:30 until about 11:30 that night. About 11:15 the Justice Department came walking up the aisle of the church and said to me, Listen. I've talked to the Attorney General of the state of Alabama, and he said that you can go ahead and have a mass meeting at the church and it will be legal.

Then we asked him, Do you have any papers that say that's true, that are signed by the Governor or the Attorney General? And he said no. And we said to him, Go back and get it legalized, and bring it back here to us and we will accept it.

And sure enough, on Monday at three o'clock, I went to the courthouse and there in the sheriff's office were the papers all legalized and fixed up, saying that we could go to the church to have our mass meeting.

To me, this showed strength. When people are together, they can do a lot of things, but when you are alone you cannot do anything. . . .

There are six hundred Negroes in the county who did not trust in themselves and who joined the Democratic party. We warned the entire state of Alabama that running on the Democratic ticket could not do them any good, because this party is controlled by people like Wallace; and whoever won would have to do what these people said to do. . . .

Now, to me, the Democratic party primaries and the Democratic party is something like an integrated gambler who carries a card around in his pocket and every now and then he has to let somebody win to keep the game going. To me, this is what the Democratic party means to the people in Alabama. It's a gambling game. And somebody's got to win to keep the game going every now and then.

There is another guy who was running on the ticket calling himself a liberal, the Attorney General of the state of Alabama, Richmond Flowers. Most of you have heard about him. When he started campaigning to the people of Alabama, especially the Negro people, he assembled all their leaders and he made all kinds of promises to them—if you elect me for your governor, I'll do everything in the world for you.

And at the same time, he never made a decent campaign speech to the white people of this state. We kept warning our people in the state of Alabama that this was a trick and many Negroes listened to their so-called leaders, who profess to speak for the state of Alabama, and they got caught in the trap too.

I would like to say here, and this is one thing I am proud of, the people in Lowndes County stood together, and the six hundred people who voted in the Democratic primary have realized one thing, that they were tricked by the Democratic party. And now they too are ready to join us with the Lowndes County Freedom Organization whose emblem is the black panther.

We have seven people who are running for office this year in our county; namely, the coroner, three members of the board of education—and if we win those three, we will control the board of education—tax collector, tax assessor, and the individual who carries a gun at his side, the sheriff.

Let me say this—that a lot of persons tonight asked me, Do you really think if you win that you will be able to take it all over and live?

I say to the people here tonight, yes, we're going to do it. If we have to do like the present sheriff, if we have to deputize every man in Lowndes County twenty-one and over, to protect people, we're going to do it.

There was something in Alabama a few months ago they called fear. Negroes were afraid to move on their own, they waited until the man, the people whose place they lived on, told them they could get registered. They told many people, Don't you move until I tell you to move and when I give you an order, don't you go down and get registered. . . .

EVICTIONS AND THREATS

Then all the people were being evicted at the same time and even today in Lowndes County, there are at least seventy-five families that have been evicted, some now are living in tents while some are living in one-room houses, with eight or nine in a family. Others have split their families up and are living together with their relatives or their friends. But they are determined to stay in Lowndes County, until justice rolls down like water.

Evicting the families wasn't all. There were other people who live on their own places who owe large debts, so they decided to foreclose on these debts to run Negroes off the place. People made threats, but we're going to stay there, we aren't going anywhere.

I would like to let the people here tonight know why we chose this black panther as our emblem. Many people have been asking this question for a long time. Our political group is open to whoever wants to come in, who would like to work with us. But we aren't begging anyone to come in. It's open, you come at your own free will and accord.

But this black panther is a vicious animal as you know. He never bothers anything, but when you start pushing him, he moves backward, backward, and backward into his corner, and then he comes out to destroy everything that's before him.

Negroes in Lowndes County have been pushed back through the years. We have been deprived of our rights to speak, to move, and to do whatever we want to do at all times. And now we are going to start moving. On November 8 of this year, we plan to take over the courthouse in Haynesville. And whatever it takes to do it, we're going to do it.

We've decided to stop begging. We've decided to stop asking for integration. Once we control the courthouse, once we control the board of education, we can build our school system where our boys and girls can get an education in Lowndes County. There are eighty-nine prominent families in this county who own 90 percent of the land. These people will be taxed. And we will collect these taxes. And if they don't pay them, we'll take their property and sell it to whoever wants to buy it. And we know there will be people who will buy land where at the present time they cannot buy it. This is what it's going to take.

We aren't asking any longer for protection—we won't need it—or for anyone to come from the outside to speak for us, because we're going to speak for ourselves now and from now on. And I think not only in Lowndes County, not only in the state of Alabama, not only in the South, but in the North. I hope they too will start thinking for themselves. And that they will move and join us in this fight for freedom.

"CAN THERE ANY GOOD THING COME OUT OF NAZARETH?"

By Adam Clayton Powell, Jr.

*In May, 1966, during a demonstration in Jackson, Missis-
sippi, Stokely Carmichael, head of S.N.C.C., concluded a
fiercely militant speech with the slogan, "Black Power!"
The slogan hit the headlines of newspapers, and aroused
fear in the white community that an era of "black racism"
was emerging. Actually, the slogan indicated that an era
was passing, the era of nonviolence and white paternalism
which had characterized the integrated civil-rights revolution. It signaled the emergence of a separatist trend
among militant Negroes—the concept that blacks must
develop a base of political and economic power from
which to identify and define their own needs in their own
terms. Most black leaders identified with the civil-rights
movement were at first cool if not hostile to the idea of
"Black Power," but Adam Clayton Powell, Jr., Harlem
Congressman, did not hesitate to identify himself with the
slogan. He made this clear in the baccalaureate he delivered before the graduating class of Howard University,
Washington, D. C., May 29, 1966.*

*Powell's father had been the minister of the Abyssinian
Baptist Church in Harlem, a director of the N.A.A.C.P.
and a political leader in New York City. Once out of college, Powell took over his father's post in the Harlem
church, and led the fight for jobs for Negroes during the
early 1930's through the Greater New York Coordinating
Committee. In 1941 he was elected as the first Negro member of the City Council, and three years later he won an
easy election to the House of Representatives. His militant
stand for civil rights and other legislation for Negroes won
him regular reelection, and not even repudiation by the
regular Democratic organization in 1958 could stop his
election for an eighth term. As chairman of the Education
and Labor Committee of the House of Representatives,
Powell focused national attention on the problem of job
discrimination against Negroes. Although Powell has been
criticized for absenteeism in Congress and was refused his
seat in the House in 1967 for supposed irregularities in*

finances, he has until recently consistently received the overwhelming support of his constituents. On June 16, 1969, the Supreme Court, in a 7-to-1 decision, ruled the removal of Congressman Powell from his seat in Congress unconstitutional. He was again seated as a member of Congress, though no longer as chairman of the Education and Labor Committee. Defeated in the Democratic primary in 1970, Powell sought nomination as an independent, but his petitions were held to be insufficient to win him a place on the ballot.

Here is the speech Powell delivered to the Graduating Class of Howard University. It is reprinted here from a copy of the speech provided by the office of Congressman Adam Clayton Powell, Jr., and with his permission. Powell's sermons have been published in his Keep the Faith, Baby! *New York, 1967.*

ALMOST TWO THOUSAND years ago, that question was a contemptuous inquiry in the book of John.

"And Nathanael said unto Philip, 'Can there any good thing come out of Nazareth?' Philip saith, 'Come and see.'" Nazareth was the Mississippi of Galilee. There were no great artists or philosopher-kings or musicians. There was no center of learning such as Howard University. In this commencement of your life, the world will ask: Can there any good thing come out of Howard?

As black students educated at America's finest black institution of higher learning, you are still second-class citizens. A mere one hundred years in the spectrum of time separates us from the history of slavery and a lifetime of indignities. Next year, on March 2, 1967, Howard will celebrate the centennial of its founding.* Next year, on March 21, 1967, the Committee on Education and Labor of which I am the chairman will also celebrate its hundredth anniversary.

How ironic that the Committee on Education and Labor, which was formed immediately after the Civil War to help black slaves make the transition into freedom, should have a black man one hundred years later as its chairman. One of the purposes of the committee's founding was to take care of Howard University. It is too late for you who are graduating to know

* Howard University was founded on March 2, 1867, with aid from the Freedmen's Bureau. It was named after Oliver Otis Howard (1830–1900), who was head of the Bureau of Refugees, Freedmen, and Abandoned Lands, commonly known as the Freedmen's Bureau. Howard was president of the university from 1869–1874.

this, unless you plan to pursue graduate work here, but it is not too late for the faculty to know it: the Education and Labor Committee is in charge of Howard University. Howard, along with other federal institutions such as St. Elizabeth's and Gallaudet College, is under the jurisdiction of my committee. While both Howard and I as chairman of this committee will celebrate our one hundred years together, joy of our success is tempered by the sobering fact that our status as black people has been denied first-class acceptance.

Keith E. Baird, writing in the spring edition of *Freedomways*, gives eloquent voice to these thoughts in his poem "Nemesis":

> You snatched me from my land,
> Branded my body with your irons
> And my soul with the slave-name, "Negro."
> (How devilish clever to spell it upper case
> And keep me always lower!)*

To possess a black skin today in America means that if you are in Los Angeles driving your pregnant wife to a hospital, you'll be shot to death by a white policeman.

A black skin means that if your family lives in Webster County, Mississippi, your average family income will be $846 a year—$16.30 a week for an entire family.

A black skin today is an unemployment rate twice that of whites, despite a skyrocketing gross national product of 714 billion dollars and an unprecedented level of employment.

A black skin means you are still a child, that all the white liberals who have helped you to take your first steps toward freedom and manhood now believe they own your soul, can manage your lives and control your civil-rights organizations. Only S.N.C.C. has been able to resist the seductive blandishments of white liberals.

So beware not only of Greeks bearing gifts, but colored men seeking loans and Northern white liberals!

At this graduation today, this is the reality of self you must face. Your graduation comes at a particularly critical period of the black man's searching reassessment of who he is, what he should become and how he should become it. The history of the last twenty-five years of the freedom struggle has been capsuled in only two concepts: integration and civil rights.

During those years, our leaders—and black people are the only people who have "leaders"; other groups have politicians,

---

* Quoted from "Nemesis," *Freedomways*, Second Quarter, Spring, 1966, p. 136.

statesmen, educators, financiers and businessmen—but during those years, our leaders drugged us with the LSD of integration. Instead of telling us to seek audacious power—more black power—instead of leading us in the pursuit of excellence, our leaders led us in the sterile chase of integration as an end in itself, in the debasing notion that a few white skins sprinkled amongst us would somehow elevate the genetics of our development.

As a result, ours was an integration of intellectual mediocrity, economic inferiority and political subservience. Like frightened children, we were afraid to eat the strong meat of human rights and instead sucked the milk of civil rights from the breasts of white liberals, black Uncle Toms and Aunt Jemimas. From the book of Hebrews, a diet of courage is offered to black people:

> For every one that useth milk is unskilled in the work of righteousness: for he is a babe. But strong meat belongeth to them that are of full age, even those who by reason of use have their senses exercised to discern both good and evil.

Historically, strong meat was too risky for most black people, for it would have enabled them to discern both good and evil, the difference between civil rights and human rights.

Human rights are God-given. Civil rights are man-made. Civil rights has been that grand deception practiced by those who have not placed God first, who have not believed that God-given rights can empower the black man with superiority as well as equality.

Our life must be purposed to implement human rights:

> The right to be secure in one's person from the excessive abuses of the state and its law-enforcing officials.
> The right to freedom of choice of a job to feed one's family.
> The right to freedom of mobility of residence.
> The right to the finest education man's social order can provide.
> And most importantly, the right to share fully in the governing councils of the state as equal members of the body politic.

To demand these God-given human rights is to seek black power—what I call audacious power; the power to build black institutions of splendid achievement.

Howard University was once well on its way toward becoming a lasting black institution of splendid achievement when it struggled to contain the intellectual excitement and dynamic creativity of such black scholars as Alain Locke, Sterling

Brown, E. Franklin Frazier, Sam Dorsey, Eugene Holmes, James Nabrit and Rayford Logan—all on the campus at the same time. What glorious symbols they were of black creativity!

But where are the black symbols of creativity of 1966? Where is the greatness of our yesteryears? Where are the sonnets black poets once sang of the black man's agony of life? Can any good thing come out of Howard today?

There can and there must. I call today for a black renaissance at Howard University. Resurrect black creativity, not only in literature, history, law, poetry and English, but more so in mathematics, engineering, aerodynamics and nuclear physics. Like Nicodemus, Howard must be born again—born again in the image of black greatness gone before.

Will one black woman here today dare to come forth as a pilgrim of God, a Sojourner Truth—as a black Moses, Harriet Tubman, or a Nannie Burroughs?* Will one black man here today dare be a Denmark Vesey, a Nat Turner, a Frederick Douglass, a Marcus Garvey, a W. E. B. Du Bois or a Malcolm X?

One with God is a majority.

This divine oneness can restore Howard to the Glory of Charlie Houston, whose classrooms were the womb of the civil-rights movement, a womb that birthed a Thurgood Marshall. But the womb has aborted and the good thing which must come out of Howard must also come out of black people. Ask yourselves that higher question: Can any good thing come of black people?

We are the last revolutionaries in America—the last transfusion of freedom into the bloodstream of democracy. Because we are, we must mobilize our wintry discontent to transform the cold heart and white face of this nation.

Indeed, we must "drop our buckets" where we are.† We must stop blaming "Whitey" for all our sins and oppressions and deal from situations with strength. Why sit down at the bargaining table with the white man when you have nothing with which to bargain? Why permit social workers and various leagues and associations to represent us when they are representing the decadent white power structure which pays their salaries, their rent, and tells them what to say? Such men cannot possess the noble arrogance of power that inspires men, moves nations and decides the fate of mankind.

I call for more arrogance of power among black people, but

* Nannie H. Burroughs, a member of the President's Conference on Home Building, was the author of *Negro Housing*.
† The sentence refers to an expression used by Booker T. Washington in his Atlanta Exposition speech of 1895.

an arrogance of power that is God-inspired, God-led and God-daring. As Cassius said, "The fault, dear Brutus, is not in our stars, but in ourselves, that we are underlings."

"So, every bondman in his own hand bears the power to cancel his captivity." We can cancel the captivity of our souls and destroy the enslavement of our minds by refusing to compromise any of our human rights. The era of compromise for the black man is gone! Birmingham, Harlem and Watts* have proved this. You cannot compromise man's right to be free, nor can you sit down and "reason together" whether man should have some rights today and full rights tomorrow.

Let somebody reason with Mrs. Barbara Deadwyler, in Los Angeles, that a white policeman really did not intend to kill her black husband. Let somebody tell her that the passion of her love for her husband should bow to the reason of diaphanous official alibis. Only God can reason with her and soothe her grief. And there is a "God who rules above with a hand of power and a heart of love, and if I'm right He'll fight my battle and I shall be free this day."

This same God calls us first to the conference table, and His Son, when the word of reason was no longer heeded, went into the temple and "began to cast out those that sold." Those that sell black people down the river must be cast out. Those conference tables which defile the human spirit must be overturned.

Conferences are for people who have time to contemplate the number of angels dancing on a civil-rights pin. Conferences are for people who seek a postponement until tomorrow of a decision which screams for a solution today. Conferences are an extravagant orgy of therapy for the guilt-ridden and a purposeless exercise in dialectics for the lazy. America has been holding too many conferences, conducting too many seminars, writing too many books and articles about the black man and his right to freedom for over a century.

This week, three thousand black and white people will gather once again in our nation's capital to whisper words of futility into the hurricane of massive indifference. Certainly the federal government should cease to be a partner in this cruel, historic charade with the black man's rights.

To fulfill these rights? Let us begin with first things first. The largest single employer in the United States is the federal government—2,574,000 employees. Yet, racial discrimination

* Watts, the black ghetto in Los Angeles, exploded in a riot in August, 1965. By the time the police, assisted by the California National Guard, restored order, 34 were dead, 1,032 injured, and 3,953 arrested. Property damage was estimated at forty million dollars.

within the government—more subtle, more sophisticated, more elegantly structured—continues almost as rampant as yesterday. The times have changed, but the system hasn't.

Though racial persecution presses its crown of thorns on our brows, our faith in God must never falter. We must sustain that faith which helps us to cast off the leprosy of self-shame in our black skins and lift us up to the glorious healing power of belief in the excellence of black power. We must have the faith to build mighty black universities, black businesses and elect black men as governors, mayors and senators. Our faith must be sustained by our passion for dignity and our trust in God, not man's faithless reason in himself.

What is easier—"to say to the sick of the palsy, Thy sins be forgiven thee, or to say, Arise and take up thy bed and walk?"

Black children of Howard, take up thy beds and walk into the new era of excellence.

Arise, and walk into a new spirit of black pride.

"Can there any good thing come out of Nazareth?" "Come and see," said Philip.

Nathanael came and saw Jesus and the world felt, as he did, the power of his love and the beauty of his words.

Can there any good thing come out of Howard University here today?

"Come and see," you Howard graduates must say.

"Come and see" us erect skyscrapers of economic accomplishment, scale mountains of educational excellence and live among the stars of audacious political power.

"Come and see" us labor for the black masses—not the black leaders, but the black masses, who have yearned for audacious leadership.

BLACK POWER

By Stokely Carmichael

On November 16, 1966, Stokely Carmichael spoke on "Black Power" at the University of California, Berkeley, and discussed the charge that Black Power meant violence, racial hatred and racial separatism.

Stokely Carmichael was born in the West Indies and attended Howard University. He is the coauthor (with

Charles Hamilton) of Black Power. *Today he lives in Guinea.*
Carmichael's speech at Berkeley is reprinted here from the abridged text in Joanne Grant, Black Protest, *pp. 459–466.*

. . . IT SEEMS to me that the institutions that function in this country are clearly racist, and that they're built upon racism. And the question, then, is how can black people inside this country move? And then, how can white people, who say they're not a part of those institutions, begin to move, and how then do we begin to clear away the obstacles that we have in this society that keep us from living like human beings. How can we begin to build institutions that will allow people to relate with each other as human beings? This country has never done that. Especially around the concept of white or black.

Now several people have been upset because we've said that integration was irrelevant when initiated by blacks and that in fact it was a subterfuge, an insidious subterfuge for the maintenance of white supremacy. We maintain that in the past six years or so this country has been feeding us a thalidomide drug of integration, and that some Negroes have been walking down a dream street talking about sitting next to white people, and that that does not begin to solve the problem. When we went to Mississippi, we did not go to sit next to Ross Barnett; we did not go to sit next to Jim Clark; we went to get them out of our way, and people ought to understand that. We were never fighting for the right to integrate, we were fighting against white supremacy. . . .

Now we are engaged in a psychological struggle in this country and that struggle is whether or not black people have the right to use the words they want to use without white people giving their sanction to it. We maintain, whether they like it or not, we gon' use the words "black power" and let them address themselves to that. We are not gonna wait for white people to sanction black power. We're tired of waiting. Every time black people move in this country, they're forced to defend their position before they move. It's time that the people who're supposed to be defending their position do that. That's white people. They ought to start defending themselves, as to why they have oppressed and exploited us.

It is clear that when this country started to move in terms of slavery, the reason for a man being picked as a slave was one reason: because of the color of his skin. If one was black, one was automatically inferior, inhuman, and therefore fit for slavery. So that the question of whether or not we are individually suppressed is nonsensical and is a downright lie. We are oppressed as a group because we are black, not because we are lazy, not because we're apathetic, not because we're stupid, not because we smell, not because we eat watermelon and have good rhythm. We are oppressed because we are black, and in order to get out of that oppression, one must feel the group power that one has. Not the individual power which this country then sets the criteria under which a man may come into it. That is what is called in this country as integration. You do what I tell you to do, and then we'll let you sit at the table with us. And then we are saying that we have to be opposed to that. We must now set a criterion, and that if there's going to be any integration it's going to be a two-way thing. If you believe in integration, you can come live in Watts. You can send your children to the ghetto schools. Let's talk about that. If you believe in integration, then we're going to start adopting us some white people to live in our neighborhood. So it is clear that the question is not one of integration or segregation. Integration is a man's ability to want to move in there by himself. If someone wants to live in a white neighborhood and he is black, that is his choice. It should be his right. It is not because white people will allow him. So, vice versa, if a black man wants to live in the slums, that should be his right. Black people will let him, that is the difference.

It is this difference which points up the logical mistakes this country makes when it begins to criticize the program articulated by S.N.C.C. We maintain that we cannot afford to be concerned about 6 percent of the children in this country. I mean the black children who you allow to come into white schools. We have 94 percent who still live in shacks. We are going to be concerned about those 94 percent. You ought to be concerned about them, too. The question is, Are we willing to be concerned about those 94 percent. Are we willing to be concerned about the black people who will never get to Berkeley, who will never get to Harvard and cannot get an education, so you'll never get a chance to rub shoulders with them and say, "Well, he's almost as good as we are; he's not like the others." The question is How can white society begin to move to see black people as human beings? I am black, therefore I am. Not that I am black and I must go to college to prove myself. I am black, therefore I am. And don't surprise me with anything and say to me that you must go to college before you gain access to X, Y and Z. It is only a rationalization for one's oppression.

The political parties in this country do not meet the needs

of the people on a day-to-day basis. The question is How can we build new political institutions that will become the political expressions of people on a day-to-day basis? The question is How can you build political institutions that will begin to meet the needs of Oakland, California? And the needs of Oakland, California, are not one thousand policemen with submachine guns. They don't need that. They need that least of all. The question is How can we build institutions where those people can begin to function on a day-to-day basis, where they can get decent jobs, where they can get decent housing, and where they can begin to participate in the policy and major decisions that affect their lives? That's what they need. Not Gestapo troops. Because this is not 1942. And if you play like Nazis, we're playing back with you this time around. Get hip to that.

The question, then, is How can white people move to start making the major institutions that they have in this country function the way they are supposed to function? That is the real question. And can white people move inside their own community and start tearing down racism where, in fact, it does exist? It is you who live in Cicero and stop us from living there.* It is white people who stop us from moving into Grenada. It is white people who make sure that we live in the ghettos of this country. It is white institutions that do that. They must change. In order for America to really live on a basic principle of human relationships, a new society must be born. Racism must die, and the economic exploitation of this country, of nonwhite people around the world, must also die.

There are several programs that we have in the South among some poor white communities. We're trying to organize poor whites on a base where they can begin to move around the question of economic exploitation and political disenfranchisement. We know we've heard the theory several times, but few people are willing to go into this. The question is Can the white activist not try to be a Pepsi generation who comes alive in the black community, but that he be a man who's willing to move into the white community and start organizing where the organization is needed? . . .

We've been saying that we cannot have white people working in the black community and we've based it on psychological grounds. The fact is that all black people often question

* The reference is to the attack upon nonviolent black demonstrators who sought to integrate housing in Cicero, Illinois. Instead of condemning the white racists who used violence against the peaceful blacks, Mayor Daley of Chicago attacked Martin Luther King, Jr., and others who led the demonstrations.

whether or not they are equal to whites, because every time they start to do something white people are around showing them how to do it. If we are going to eliminate that for the generations that come after us, then black people must be seen in positions of power doing and articulating for themselves. . . .

Now, then, the question is How can we move to begin to change what's going on in this country? I maintain, as we have in S.N.C.C., that the war in Vietnam is an illegal and immoral war. And the question is What can we do to stop that war? What can we do to stop the people who, in the name of our country, are killing babies, women and children? What can we do to stop that? And I maintain that we do not have the power in our hands to change that institution, to begin to recreate it so that they learn to leave the Vietnamese people alone, and that the only power we have is the power to say "Hell, no!" to the draft. . . . There isn't one organization that has begun to meet our stand on the war in Vietnam. Because we not only say we are against the war in Vietnam; *we are against the draft.** We are against the draft. No man has the right to take a man for two years and train him to be a killer. . . .

It is impossible for white and black people to talk about building a relationship based on humanity when the country is the way it is, when the institutions are clearly against us. We have taken all the myths of this country and we've found them to be nothing but downright lies. This country told us that if we worked hard we would succeed, and if that were true we would own this country lock, stock and barrel. It is we who picked the cotton for nothing; it is we who are the maids in the kitchens of liberal white people; it is we who are the janitors, the porters, the elevator men; it is we who sweep up your college floors; yes, it is we who are the hardest working and the lowerst paid. And that it is nonsensical for people to start talking about human relationships until they're willing to build new institutions. Black people are economically insecure. White liberals are economically secure. Can you begin an economic coalition? Are the liberals willing to share their salaries with the economically insecure black people who they so much love? Then if you're not, are you willing to start building new institutions that will provide economic security for black people? That's the question we want to deal with. . . .

* On January 6, 1966, the Student Nonviolent Coordinating Committee issued a statement opposing United States involvement in the war in Vietnam and supporting all Americans who were unwilling to respond to the military draft. It was the first anti-Vietnam statement by a major civil-rights organization.

We have to raise questions about whether or not we need new types of political institutions in this country and we in S.N.C.C. maintain that we need them now. We need new political institutions in this country. And any time Lyndon Baines Johnson can head a party which has in it Bobby Kennedy, Wayne Morse, Eastland, Wallace and all those other supposedly liberal cats, there's something wrong with that party. They're moving politically, not morally. And if that party refuses to seat black people from Mississippi and goes ahead and seats racists like Eastland and his clique,* then it is clear to me that they're moving politically and that one cannot begin to talk morality to people like that. We must begin to think politically and see if we can have the power to impose and keep the moral values that we hold high. We must question the values of this society. And I maintain that black people are the best people to do that, because we have been excluded from that society and the question is, we ought to think whether or not we want to become a part of that society. That's what we want. And that is precisely what, it seems to me, the Student Nonviolent Coordinating Committee is doing. We are raising questions about this country. I do not want to be a part of the American pride. The American pride means raping South Africa, beating Vietnam, beating South America, raping the Philippines, raping every country you've been in. I don't want any of your blood money. I don't want it . . . don't want to be part of that system. And the question is How do we raise those questions? . . . How do we raise them as activists?

We have grown up and we are the generation that has found this country to be a world power, that has found this country to be the wealthiest country in the world. We must question how she got her wealth. That's what we're questioning. And whether or not we want this country to continue being the wealthiest country in the world at the price of raping everybody across the world. That's what we must begin to question. And because black people are saying we do not now want to become a part of you, we are called reverse racists. Ain't that a gas?

How do we raise the questions of poverty? The assumptions of this country is that if someone is poor, they're poor because of their own individual blight, or they weren't born on the right side of town. They had too many children; they went in the

* In 1964 the Mississippi Freedom Party challenged the legitimacy of the regular Democratic members of Congress from Mississippi on the ground that Negroes could not participate in elections. The challenge was rejected.

Army too early; their father was a drunk; they didn't care about school; they made a mistake. That's a lot of nonsense. *Poverty is well calculated in this country*. It is well calculated. And the reason why the poverty program won't work is because the calculators of poverty are administering it. That's why it won't work.

So how can we, as the youth in this country, move to start tearing those things down? We must move ino the white community. We are in the black community. We have developed a movement in the black community that challenges the white activist who has failed miserably to develop the movement inside of his community. The question is Can we find white people who are going to have the courage to go into white communities and start organizing them? Can we find them? Are they here? And are they willing to do that? Those are the questions that we must raise for white activists.

We are never going to get caught up with questions about power. This country knows what power is and knows it very well. And knows what black power is, because it's deprived black people of it for four hundred years. So it knows what black power is. But the question is, why do white people in this country associate black power with violence? Because of their own inability to deal with blackness. If we had said Negro power, nobody would get scared. Everybody would support it. And if we said power for colored people, everybody would be for that. But it is the word *black*, it is the word *black* that bothers people in this country, and that's their problem, not mine. . . .

So that in conclusion, we want to say that first, it is clear to me that we have to wage a psychological battle on the right for black people to define their own terms, define themselves as they see fit and organize themselves as they see fit. Now, the question is How is the white community going to begin to allow for that organizing? Because once they start to do that, they will also allow for the organizing that they want to do inside their communities. It doesn't make any difference. Because we're going to organize our way anyway. We're going to do it. The question is how we're going to facilitate those matters. Whether it's going to be done with a thousand policemen with submachine guns or whether or not it's going to be done in the context where it's allowed to be done by white people warding off those policemen. That is the question.

And the question is How will white people who call themselves activists get ready to start moving into the white communities on two counts? On building new political institutions, to destroy the old ones that we have, and to move around the concept of white youth refusing to go into the Army. So that we can start then to build a new world.

It is ironic to talk about civilization in this country. This country is uncivilized. It needs to be civilized. We must begin to raise those questions of civilization—what it is. And we'll do it. And so we must urge you to fight now to be the leaders of today, not tomorrow. We've got to be the leaders of today. This country is a nation of thieves. It stands on the brink of becoming a nation of murderers. We must stop it. *We* must stop it.

And then, in a larger sense, there is the question of black people. We are on the move for our liberation. We have been tired of trying to prove things to white people. We are tired of trying to explain to white people that we're not going to hurt them. We are concerned with getting the things we want, the things that we have to have to be able to function. The question is Can white people allow for that in this country? The question is Will white people overcome their racism and allow for that to happen in this country? If that does not happen, brothers and sisters, we have no choice, but to say very clearly, move on over, or we're going to move on over you.

THE "MOVEMENT" NOW

By James Farmer

In 1942 James Farmer was the Race-Relations Secretary of the Quaker-Pacifist Fellowship of Reconciliation, and at his suggestion, the Fellowship's national council organized the Congress of Racial Equality (CORE). As national director of CORE, Farmer launched the original Freedom Bus Ride to Alabama and Mississippi in 1961. Gradually Farmer moved away from his early pacifism and his belief in nonviolence as the only method to be used by the black liberation movement. However, he always opposed separatism, and he spoke out in favor of integration in a debate with Malcolm X at Cornell University on March 7, 1962.

Farmer served as national director of CORE until January, 1966. In February, 1969, President Nixon appointed him Assistant Secretary of the Department of Health, Education and Welfare. Farmer resigned that post late in 1970.

On February 25, 1967, Dr. Farmer addressed the American Studies Conference at Lincoln University, Pennsylvania, and analyzed the reasons for the growing disillusionment in black communities with the results of the civil-rights revolution of the late 1950's and early 1960's. Here is a major portion of this address, reprinted from Lincoln University Bulletin, *Winter, 1967, pp. 6-9.*

IF OUR MOVEMENT these past years has been a revolution, as it has been called, then we are forced to say that the revolution has failed. We are forced to say that the victories have not yet been meaningful to the masses of people, and this is precisely the present dilemma of the movement now, and the present crisis.

I spend a lot of time—too much time—traveling around the country. I sort of feel the pulse of the segment of the Negro community that I come in contact with, and the white community. The impression I get is that we are now indeed in an area of pessimism in the whole movement. And the pessimism, indeed, has some basis and reality. We have won victories. One cannot travel through the South without seeing those victories —in voting rights, in public places.

I was in Little Rock, Arkansas, not too long ago. I stopped a Negro on the street and asked him if things had changed there greatly, over the last few years. The last time I was in the city, about ten years ago, there were screaming mobs in the streets as those children were trying to get into Central High. He looked me in the face and said: "Brother Farmer, everything has changed, but everything remains the same. Yes, I can now buy a hot dog at that lunch counter. Big deal." Somehow that hot dog doesn't seem nearly so important as it did a few years ago.

A footnote here: I think that this is one of the problems with which we must deal. The fact that a little progress like a hot dog does not satisfy the appetite. It merely whets the appetite. Although, I think that this is of such stuff that further progress is made.

But my friend went on talking. He said: "Yes, I can go downtown and check into a hotel, if I had the money, which I don't. I have been out of work for six months. And furthermore, if I go three miles outside the city, I won't know that there ever was a Civil Rights Act of 1964. And yes, we can sit on the front seat of a bus. We can go to the theater and sit in the audience; we can buy a hot dog and a hamburger. Everything has changed but everything remains the same."

And I think it has, essentially. There has been no substantial change in the plight or the position of the black man in our country. And that is why the age of pessimism has come upon the movement. And that is why the "little people" in the ghetto community feel so completely frustrated and left out. As Richard Wright put it in one of his novels: "Sometimes I feel like I am on the outside of the world looking in through a knothole in the fence." And I think that this is the feeling among the people in the ghetto who, literally, have not been substantially relieved by our battle.

In 1942, when there was no real movement of CORE, we had a small band of young idealists, mostly college students, who had been studying Gandhi, his programs and methods, and had come to the conclusion that his techniques of nonviolence really worked. And they used them in those days, for sitting-in, waiting-in, et cetera, and nonviolence became, for a long time, the watchword for a large segment of the movement. Now nonviolence is under considerable fire. And to a great extent, I would say that it is repudiated by the masses of people in the ghetto, essentially because the movement has not yet won victories which have changed their life situations. They live in the same tenement slums, in the Northern cities; in the rural areas of the South, in the same sharecropper–tenant-farmer shacks, and they are equally unemployed. This is as they were a few years ago before the movement got started.

Then what have we accomplished? Nothing? By no means. We have succeeded in elevating life for those of us who are in the middle classes. We have given greater mobility to the Negro middle-class man in our society . . .

Economically, the Negro has improved—but in absolute terms, not in relative terms. Relatively, we are becoming increasingly aware that the plot has worsened. I wouldn't go around the country as George Wallace does—he's one of the governors of Alabama—saying that our colored people have a high and rapidly rising standard of living. He says that black people have a standard of living higher than any place in Africa, as though that is any basis for comparison. The only basis for comparison is that of a Negro in the United States and one will find that the gap between the average Negro and the average white has widened since World War II.

During the war, there was a narrowing of the gap, but since the war, there has been a widening of the gap. The average income of Negroes in 1950 was 53% of the average income of whites; 1961, 52%. In spite of the fact that hundreds of thousands of Negroes have migrated from rural areas in the South to urban centers in the North and normally one would expect an improvement in the standard of living. In spite of the fact also that the educational gap had slightly closed in that period of time. One would expect that to correct itself in the closing of the income gap. That did not happen.

Segregation in our land is not decreasing, it is increasing. I said that if our struggle had been a revolution, then it is a revolution that has failed. The integration fight has not been successful. It has failed too. Residential segregation is increasing all over the country. Recently I was in various cities in the Northwest which I visited twenty years ago. I observed much more segregation there than when they had few Negroes who had been there for generations. They lived just about any place they wanted. As the Negro population increased following the war, the ghettos were established. The rigid lines were set up and Negroes were excluded from other areas. In other places in the North one finds that the old pattern of the black core and the white noose is still perpetuated and the Negro population increases and the flight to the suburbs of whites presents that pattern. This results in an increase of segregation and an increase of de facto school segregation as a result. One finds in the South that many of the Southern cities are now trying to imitate the North, and now Southern cities are seeking through urban renewal and other devices to create a de facto segregation —relocation to relocate black here and white here. In a few years they will be able to say, as our Northern cities now say, "We have no segregation here; anybody who lives in this school zone is perfectly free to go to this school; it just so happens that they are all white or all black."

We have to face the stark fact that segregation is increasing, not decreasing. The anger and frustration in the ghetto community is growing. As I travel around the country, I find a greater sense of alienation than was true a few years ago. There have been so many promises and broken promises, they say. And they are right. There was a wave of optimism at the outset of the poverty program. A wave of optimism which I shared. That optimism has dissipated itself as far as the masses are concerned, it seems to me, because of the controversy, in part, of the maximum feasible participation and the fear of many of the politicians in city halls that maximum feasible participation might mean making visible those who hitherto have been invisible, making vocal those who have been silent, and that they might indeed come to identify their plight with city hall, in a cause-and-effect relationship, and that controversy has continued. Today with the cutback in antipoverty funds the situation has not been improved, and on my last trip into Minnesota, the few Negroes who were there expressed to me some concern about the Civil Rights Bill which is to be introduced in Congress. They say what we need now is some money to get rid of the slums. I had not been aware that they had any sizable slums in Minnesota, but they said we need to get rid of the slums and so forth, and instead we get another bill. One would not have heard such comments a few years ago. . . .

There is also the talk about power. The interpretation is that the power means military power and thus means violence. I think all kinds of threatening images have been conjured up in everybody's mind, and much of this is due to the press, which has strongly misinterpreted what the spokesmen have been trying to say as they speak of power. Now, I didn't choose the slogan and am not sure that I would have chosen it, but it is most important to understand the concepts that are underneath it: He is American and he is black. A few years ago I looked at the preschool books of my little girl. She had gotten quite a group of them as gifts. I wanted to see how she would see herself and what kind of image she would get. I found that in most cases she couldn't see herself at all, unless she was carrying somebody else's bag or was in some absurd position with a string tied around her toe with other kids poking fun at her and laughing. Not an acceptable image.

This occurred to me that, as we walked through the streets and looked at the billboards, she would not see herself. She would see another image. Why couldn't she identify with it? Very simply, because society has pounded into her from the very beginning of consciousness that that is not she and she is not that and thus it becomes a virtual impossibility for her to identify herself.

I think today the most aggravating struggle in the black community is this quest for identity. As Jimmy Baldwin puts it "Who am I? Who am I? In America."

With this must go the realization in our nation that we have had such a deep split for 350 years, there is a racist aspect in our culture. One that we cannot get away from by denying, but only by facing. It is extremely difficult for any of us in our land to grow to adulthood without having at least some residual racial prejudice back of us, black or white. It takes great feats of empathy and great qualities of sensitivity for one to approach the point of overcoming it. Pick any white person at random, and probably he knows no Negroes; or perhaps only the Negro who works for him as a domestic and that is not a basis for understanding in spite of the stereotype of their being closer together and therefore understanding each other better. They actually understand each other less because of the racism that exists. Pick any Negro in the street and in all probability he knows no white people, except his boss, who pushes him around if he doesn't pull the mop fast enough; or the landlord or the merchant who exploit. And so, he develops the negative image too.

I say that because of this the polarization in our national community has grown so deep that now it becomes extremely difficult if not impossible for any of us to overcome it or to be free from it. And this speeds up the necessity of the black people to find identity. How do we find it? Well, by developing pride. Certainly, we need pride. We need to know more about the Negro and the contribution of the Negro to American history. We need to know more about African history and about the roots—our heritage and our tradition. That, of course, is not enough in itself. If that is all that we do, then it will be a form of intellectual masturbation. We need also to have a program to deal with the very real issue that is confronting us in the ghetto community. Pride, yes. There is nothing wrong with group pride. It only becomes bad or destructive if it becomes chauvinistic. And I oppose this.

Other groups in American history have developed pride. They have strengthened those things as they faced discrimination. I recall reading of the great wave of Irish immigration more than a century ago—at the time of the potato-crop failure in Ireland, when the Irish faced all kinds of things, signs in windows saying "Man Wanted: No Irishmen Need Apply." That sign became so widespread that they didn't have to spell it out. "Man Wanted NINA." The Irish, of course, of necessity, drew tighter together. It was inevitable. They sang songs; some bitter. One song they sang was about its being an honor to be born an Irishman. And it is. It is good. It is essential for those who are pushed around. It is an honor to be born an Irishman so long as it is not a dishonor not to be born one. In other words, so long as it doesn't become chauvinism.

I see the same thing in black identity and black pride. Let us find that pride and let us develop it and let us think of ourselves and we can answer the question what it means to be black, and from there we can find the answer to the question what it means to be an American. I don't think that we can do it the other way around. I think it has to be done in that way. A few years ago after the Supreme Court decision on desegregation of schools, there was a far too simple view of the goals that we seek in the movement. That view is now changing.

After 1954 it was somehow assumed that Negroes were going

to disappear; that they would be thoroughly dispersed in our society. You wouldn't be able to find a Negro. This was a kind of self-abdication. It was assumed then that there would be no more Negro colleges. I understand the United Negro College Fund had difficulty raising funds. People asked why money was needed when there would be no more Negro colleges. Negroes would be scattered around. There would no longer be any Negro colleges. If any civil-rights leader had in those days spoken of elevating the housing accommodations within the ghetto community, he would have been charged with being an advocate of segregation. What we wanted to do (this was the feeling) was to get rid of the ghetto community. There would be no more Harlem. Phil Randolph, Brotherhood of Sleeping Car Porters, proposed a Negro Labor Council; he was immediately shot down by the A.F. of L. and everybody else. This was nonsense. Segregation. This was ignoring the fact that other ethnic groups had labor councils and there was no reason why there should not be a Negro-American Labor Council. This was in the day of color blindness. Of the color-blind theater. And I would say that this was a kind of self-abdication, for black people.

Some would say now that we don't want any more integration. And since integration has failed, and furthermore, since we want identity, then there must be separatism. I don't think now that there is a possibility of separation. Our lives are so intertwined economically and every other way that separation is an impossibility. But I think that now the place has to be found for the pendulum to come to rest between those two. Between the two extremes. I would guess it would come to rest by finding the great truth that lies in both camps. Truth in that we are black people—and must be proud of it—but we are also Americans and that if a black man should want to live in the suburbs or any place in the city that must be his right and his color must not be a bar. But if he wants to live in what is considered the ghetto, then that too must be his choice but I would deny that he has a right to keep others from living there too. There must be this element of freedom within the American society. That is what I mean by the swinging of the pendulum coming to rest somewhere between the two. That would be my dream of America.

Black power advocates the saying of something else that is of great truth now, and that is that the appeal to conscience of the past has not been enough. The appeal to conscience has not moved the masses off dead center. The poor have gained no

more mobility; the middle class has. The appeal to conscience
has not improved their plight significantly. In addition to the
appeal to conscience, there must be added the element of
strength. Economic strength and political strength. We must
be in a position to sit at a table and bargain in a position of
strength instead of weakness. The civil-rights organizations
are moving more and more in that direction now. . . .

I do not think that there can be political strength unless there
is economic strength along with it, because of the cost of campaigns, et cetera. In addition, until Negroes have developed
some economic strength they will not be in a power position in
the United States along with other power groups. This economic
strength means starting businesses, small, middle-size, pooling
resources, mergers, purchasing stocks to try to have some influence on the policies of those organizations. I think, most of
all, owning property that is income-producing is most important
if Negroes are going to seek to develop some economic strength
within the American concept. That can be done. That is where
the civil-rights movement is today. Those are the issues which
are being discussed.

I would be less than candid and frank if I expressed to you
an optimism. At least for the next few years. I see a deepening
of the split and probably a growing polarization. Even this
polarization can be a creative polarization if the time is used by
black and white to examine American culture as we are doing
here today, and examining the depths of division and the split
and seeking to understand what American means with reference
to the black man here. He must be a part of American culture,
but not an assimilated or merged part. The movement now
feels that he will be a part by coming in through a pluralistic
culture; a black culture, subculture part of a broader culture of
the nation. In other words, he is black and he is American.

The white man too is American. The white man with the
black man will have to explore the meaning of that fact, and the
period of polarization can be used for that purpose toward that
end. I would hope that after the black man has answered his
burning question, he and the white man can answer the question which must burn both of them—what it means to be American—and then go on to an even broader, more profound question—what it means to be human in our world today. Then the
new ethnocentricism, Negritude culturally and politically, will
have made a real contribution to the nation; and to the world.
As Langston Hughes put it, "Let America be America again;
it has never been America for me. Home of the Brave? Land of

the Free. Free? Who said Free? Not me. Surely not me. Yes, I say it plain. America never was America for me. But by this oath I swear. America will be."

A TIME TO BREAK SILENCE

By Martin Luther King, Jr.

Martin Luther King, Jr., spoke frequently in favor of world peace. For many months, however, he was reluctant to voice opposition to United States involvement in the war in Vietnam, believing that this would alienate supporters of the movement he was leading for greater freedom for the Negro. But as he saw the funds which were to be used in the war against poverty directed toward fighting the war in Vietnam, and as he observed the increasing brutality of the war, he became convinced that he had to speak out. In February, 1967, Dr. King publicly joined the anti-Vietnam-war coalition. On March 25, he led thousands in Chicago in a parade and rally for peace, and told some four thousand persons at the Chicago Coliseum that he opposed the war in Vietnam "because I love America." "The war," he declared, "is a blasphemy against all that America stands for. . . . This is a great nation, but in this war she seems bent on her own destruction." On April 4, 1967, Dr. King delivered an address against the war at a meeting sponsored by Clergymen and Laymen Concerned about Vietnam and held at Riverside Church, New York City. Here are excerpts from King's passionate plea for ending the war in Vietnam, reprinted from Freedomways *(Second Quarter, 1967, pp. 104–11) with the permission of Mrs. Martin Luther King, Jr., and the Southern Christian Leadership Conference.*

I COME to this magnificent house of worship tonight, because my conscience leaves me no other choice. I join with you in this meeting because I am in deepest agreement with the aims and work of the organization which has brought us together: Clergy and Laymen Concerned About Vietnam. The recent statement of your executive committee is the sentiment of my own heart, and I found myself in full accord when I read its opening lines: "A time comes when silence is betrayal." That time has come for us in relation to Vietnam.

The truth of these words is beyond doubt, but the mission to which they call us is a most difficult one. Even when pressed by the demands of inner truth, men do not easily assume the task of opposing their government's policy, especially in time of war. Nor does the human spirit move without great difficulty against all the apathy of conformist thought within one's own bosom and in the surrounding world. Moreover, when the issues at hand seem as perplexed as they often do in the case of this dreadful conflict, we are always on the verge of being mesmerized by uncertainty; but we must move on.

Some of us who have already begun to break the silence of the night have found that the calling to speak is often a vocation of agony, but we must speak. We must speak with all the humility that is appropriate to our limited vision, but we must speak. And we must rejoice as well, for surely this is the first time in our nation's history that a significant number of its religious leaders have chosen to move beyond the prophesying of smooth patriotism to the high grounds of a firm dissent based upon the mandates of conscience and the reading of history. Perhaps a new spirit is rising among us. If it is, let us trace its movements well and pray that our own inner being may be sensitive to its guidance, for we are deeply in need of a new way beyond the darkness that seems so close around us.

Over the past two years, as I have moved to break the betrayal of my own silences and to speak the burnings of my own heart, as I have called for radical departures from the destruction of Vietnam, many persons have questioned me about the wisdom of my path. At the heart of their concerns this query has often loomed large and loud: Why are *you* speaking about the war, Dr. King? Why are *you* joining the voices of dissent? Peace and civil rights don't mix, they say. Aren't you hurting the cause of your people? they ask. And when I hear them, though I often understand the source of their concern, I am nevertheless greatly saddened, for such questions mean that the inquirers have not really known me, my commitment or my calling. Indeed, their questions suggest that they do not know the world in which they live.

In the light of such tragic misunderstanding, I deem it of signal importance to try to state clearly, and I trust concisely, why I believe that the path from Dexter Avenue Baptist Church —the church in Montgomery, Alabama, where I began my pastorate—leads clearly to this sanctuary tonight.

I come to this platform tonight to make a passionate plea to my beloved nation. This speech is not addressed to Hanoi or to the National Liberation Front. It is not addressed to China or to Russia.

Nor is it an attempt to overlook the ambiguity of the total situation and the need for a collective solution to the tragedy of Vietnam. Neither is it an attempt to make North Vietnam or the National Liberation Front paragons of virtue, nor to overlook the role they can play in a successful resolution of the problem. While they both may have justifiable reason to be suspicious of the good faith of the United States, life and history give eloquent testimony to the fact that conflicts are never resolved without trustful give and take on both sides.

Tonight, however, I wish not to speak with Hanoi and the N.L.F., but rather to my fellow Americans who, with me, bear the greatest responsibility in ending a conflict that has exacted a heavy price on both continents.

Since I am a preacher by trade, I suppose it is not surprising that I have seven major reasons for bringing Vietnam into the field of my moral vision. There is at the outset a very obvious and almost facile connection between the war in Vietnam and the struggle I and others have been waging in America. A few years ago there was a shining moment in that struggle. It seemed as if there was a real promise of hope for the poor— both black and white—through the Poverty Program. There were experiments, hopes, new beginnings. Then came the buildup in Vietnam and I watched the program broken and eviscerated as if it were some idle political plaything of a society gone mad on war, and I knew that America would never invest the necessary funds or energies in rehabilitation of its poor so long as adventures like Vietnam continued to draw men and skills and money like some demonic destructive suction tube. So I was increasingly compelled to see the war as an enemy of the poor and to attack it as such.

Perhaps the more tragic recognition of reality took place when it became clear to me that the war was doing far more than devastating the hopes of the poor at home. It was sending their sons and their brothers and their husbands to fight and to die in extraordinarily high proportions relative to the rest of the population. We were taking the black young men who had been crippled by our society and sending them eight thousand miles away to guarantee liberties in Southeast Asia which they had not found in Southwest Georgia and East Harlem. So we have been repeatedly faced with the cruel irony of watching Negro and white boys on TV screens as they kill and die together for a nation that has been unable to seat them together in the same schools. So we watch them in brutal solidarity burning the huts of a poor village, but we realize that they would never live on the same block in Detroit. I could not be silent in the face of such cruel manipulation of the poor.

My third reason moves to an even deeper level of awareness, for it grows out of my experience in the ghettos of the North over the last three years—especially the last three summers. As I have walked among the desperate, rejected and angry young men I have told them that Molotov cocktails and rifles would not solve their problems. I have tried to offer them my deepest compassion while maintaining my conviction that social change comes most meaningfully through nonviolent action. But they asked—and rightly so—what about Vietnam? They asked if our own nation wasn't using massive doses of violence to solve its problems, to bring about the changes it wanted. Their questions hit home, and I knew that I could never again raise my voice against the violence of the oppressed in the ghettos without having first spoken clearly to the greatest purveyor of violence in the world today—my own government. For the sake of those boys, for the sake of this government, for the sake of the hundreds of thousands trembling under our violence, I cannot be silent.

For those who ask the question, "Aren't you a civil-rights leader?" and thereby mean to exclude me from the movement for peace, I have this further answer. In 1957 when a group of us formed the Southern Christian Leadership Conference, we chose as our motto: "To save the soul of America." We were convinced that we could not limit our vision to certain rights for black people, but instead affirmed the conviction that America would never be free or saved from itself unless the descendants of its slaves were loosed completely from the shackles they still wear. . . .

Now, it should be incandescently clear that no one who has any concern for the integrity and life of America today can ignore the present war. If America's soul becomes totally poisoned, part of the autopsy must read Vietnam. It can never be saved so long as it destroys the deepest hopes of men the world over. So it is that those of us who are yet determined that America *will* be are led down the path of protest and dissent, working for the health of our land.

As if the weight of such a commitment to the life and health of America were not enough, another burden of responsibility was placed upon me in 1964; and I cannot forget that the Nobel Prize for Peace was also a commission—a commission to work harder than I had ever worked before for "the brotherhood of man." This is a calling that takes me beyond national allegiances, but even if it were not present I would yet have to live with the meaning of my commitment to the ministry of Jesus Christ. To me the relationship of this ministry to the making of peace is so obvious that I sometimes marvel at those who ask me why I am speaking against the war. Could it be that they do not know that the good news was meant for all men— for communist and capitalist, for their children and ours, for black and for white, for revolutionary and conservative? Have they forgotten that my ministry is in obedience to the one who loved his enemies so fully that he died for them? What, then, can I say to the Viet Cong or to Castro or to Mao as a faithful minister of this one? Can I threaten them with death, or must I not share with them my life?

Finally, as I try to delineate for you and for myself the road that leads from Montgomery to this place I would have offered all that was most valid if I simply said that I must be true to my conviction that I share with all men the calling to be a son of the Living God. Beyond the calling of race or nation or creed is this vocation of sonship and brotherhood, and because I believe that the Father is deeply concerned especially for his suffering and helpless and outcast children, I come tonight to speak for them.

This I believe to be the privilege and the burden of all of us who deem ourselves bound by allegiances and loyalties which are broader and deeper than nationalism and which go beyond our nation's self-defined goals and positions. We are called to speak for the weak, for the voiceless, for victims of our nation and for those it calls enemy, for no document from human hands can make these humans any less our brothers.

And as I ponder the madness of Vietnam and search within myself for ways to understand and respond to compassion my mind goes constantly to the people of that peninsula. I speak now not of the soldiers of each side, not of the junta in Saigon, but simply of the people who have been living under the curse of war for almost three continuous decades now. I think of them too because it is clear to me that there will be no meaningful solution there until some attempt is made to know them and hear their broken cries.

They must see Americans as strange liberators. The Vietnamese people proclaimed their own independence in 1945 after a combined French and Japanese occupation, and before the Communist revolution in China. They were led by Ho Chi Minh. Even though they quoted the American Declaration of Independence in their own document of freedom, we refused to recognize them.* Instead, we decided to support France in its reconquest of her former colony.

Our government felt then that the Vietnamese people were not "ready" for independence, and we again fell victim to the deadly Western arrogance that has poisoned the international atmosphere for so long. With that tragic decision we rejected a revolutionary government seeking self-determination, and a government that had been established not by China (for whom the Vietnamese have no great love) but by clearly indigenous forces that included some Communists. For the peasants this new government meant real land reform, one of the most important needs in their lives.

For nine years following 1945 we denied the people of Vietnam the right of independence. For nine years we vigorously supported the French in their abortive effort to recolonize Vietnam.

Before the end of the war we were meeting 80 percent of the French war costs. Even before the French were defeated at Dien Bien Phu, they began to despair of the reckless action, but we did not. We encouraged them with our huge financial and military supplies to continue the war even after they had lost the will. Soon we would be paying almost the full costs of this tragic attempt at recolonization.

After the French were defeated it looked as if independence and land reform would come again through the Geneva agreements.† But instead there came the United States, determined that Ho should not unify the temporarily divided nation, and the peasants watched again as we supported one of the most vicious modern dictators—our chosen man, Premier Diem. The peasants watched and cringed as Diem ruthlessly routed out all opposition, supported their extortionist landlords and refused even to discuss reunification with the North. The peasants watched as all this was presided over by United States influence

* In September, 1945, the Republic of Vietnam was established. The Constitution proclaimed its independence from all colonial rule and incorporated the famous principle of the American Declaration of Independence—the "self-evident" truths that "all men are created equal," and are endowed with "certain inalienable rights; that among these are life, liberty, and the pursuit of happiness."

† The Geneva Conference ended the war between France and the Republic of Vietnam. At Geneva, Vietnam was clearly established as a single sovereign nation, temporarily divided into regrouping zones for truce purposes. While the United States refused to sign the Agreement, it did pledge that it would "refrain from use of force to upset the agreement," and it acknowledged its U. N. obligation to respect Vietnam's territorial integrity and independence.

and then by increasing numbers of United States troops who
came to help quell the insurgency that Diem's methods had
aroused. When Diem was overthrown they may have been
happy, but the long line of military dictatorships seemed to
offer no real change—especially in terms of their need for land
and peace.

The only change came from America as we increased our
troop commitments in support of governments which were
singularly corrupt, inept and without popular support. All the
while the people read our leaflets and received regular promises
of peace and democracy—and land reform. Now they languish
under our bombs and consider us—not their fellow Vietnamese
—the real enemy. They move sadly and apathetically as we herd
them off the land of their fathers into concentration camps
where minimal social needs are rarely met. They know they
must move or be destroyed by our bombs. So they go—primarily
women and children and the aged.

They watch as we poison their water, as we kill a million
acres of their crops. They must weep as the bulldozers roar
through their areas preparing to destroy the precious trees.
They wander into the hospitals, with at least twenty casualties
from American firepower for one Vietcong-inflicted injury. So
far we may have killed a million of them—mostly children.
They wander into the towns and see thousands of the children,
homeless, without clothes, running in packs on the streets like
animals. They see the children degraded by our soldiers as they
beg for food. They see the children selling their sisters to our
soldiers, soliciting for their mothers.

What do the peasants think as we ally ourselves with the
landlords and as we refuse to put any action into our many
words concerning land reform? What do they think as we test
out our latest weapons on them, just as the Germans tested out
new medicine and new tortures in the concentration camps of
Europe? Where are the roots of the independent Vietnam we
claim to be building? Is it among these voiceless ones?

We have destroyed their two most cherished institutions: the
family and the village. We have destroyed their land and their
crops. We have cooperated in the crushing of the nation's only
non-Communist revolutionary political force—the unified Bud-
dhist Church. We have supported the enemies of the peasants
of Saigon. We have corrupted their women and children and
killed their men. What liberators!

Now there is little left to build on—save bitterness. Soon the
only solid physical foundations remaining will be found at our

military bases and in the concrete of the concentration camps we call fortified hamlets. The peasants may well wonder if we plan to build our new Vietnam on such grounds as these? Could we blame them for such thoughts? We must speak for them and raise the questions they cannot raise. These too are our brothers.

Perhaps the more difficult, but no less necessary, task is to speak for those who have been designated as our enemies. What of the National Liberation Front—that strangely anonymous group we call V.C. or Communists? What must they think of us in America when they realize that we permitted the repression and cruelty of Diem which helped to bring them into being as a resistance group in the South? What do they think of our condoning the violence which led to their own taking-up of arms? How can they believe in our integrity when now we speak of "aggression from the North" as if there were nothing more essential to the war? How can they trust us when now we charge them with violence after the murderous reign of Diem and charge them with violence while we pour every new weapon of death into their land? Surely we must understand their feelings even if we do not condone their actions. Surely we must see that the men we supported pressed them to their violence. Surely we must see that our own computerized plans of destruction simply dwarf their greatest acts.

How do they judge us when our officials know that their membership is less than 25 percent Communist and yet insist on giving them the blanket name? What must they be thinking when they know that we are aware of their control of major sections of Vietnam and yet we appear to allow national elections in which this highly organized political parallel government will have no part? They ask how we can speak of free elections when the Saigon press is censored and controlled by the military junta. And they are surely right to wonder what kind of new government we plan to help form without them— the only party in real touch with the peasants. They question our political goals and they deny the reality of a peace settlement from which they will be excluded. Their questions are frighteningly relevant. Is our nation planning to build on political myth again and then shore it up with the power of new violence?

Here is the true meaning and value of compassion and non-violence when it helps us to see the enemy's point of view, to hear his questions, to know his assessment of ourselves. For from his view we may indeed see the basic weaknesses of our own condition, and if we are mature, we may learn and grow and profit from the wisdom of the brothers who are called the opposition.

So, too, with Hanoi. In the North, where our bombs now pummel the land and our mines endanger the waterways, we are met by a deep but understandable mistrust. To speak for them is to explain this lack of confidence in Western words, and especially their distrust of American intentions now. In Hanoi are the men who led the nation to independence against the Japanese and the French, the men who sought membership in the French commonwealth and were betrayed by the weakness of Paris and the willfulness of the colonial armies. It was they who led a second struggle against French domination at tremendous costs, and then were persuaded to give up the land they controlled between the 13th and 17th parallels as a temporary measure at Geneva. After 1954 they watched us conspire with Diem to prevent elections which would have surely brought Ho Chi Minh to power over a United Vietnam,* and they realized they had been betrayed again. . . .

At this point I should make it clear that while I have tried in these last few minutes to give a voice to the voiceless on Vietnam and to understand the arguments of those who are called enemy, I am as deeply concerned about our own troops there as anything else. For it occurs to me that what we are submitting them to in Vietnam is not simply the brutalizing process that goes on in any war where armies face each other and seek to destroy. We are adding cynicism to the process of death, for they must know after a short period there that none of the things we claim to be fighting for are really involved. Before long they must know that their government has sent them into a struggle among Vietnamese, and the more sophisticated surely realize that we are on the side of the wealthy and the secure, while we create a hell for the poor.

Somehow this madness must cease. We must stop now. I speak as a child of God and brother to the suffering poor of Vietnam. I speak for those whose land is being laid waste, whose homes are being destroyed, whose culture is being subverted. I speak for the poor of America who are paying the double price of smashed hopes at home and death and corruption in Viet-

* With the backing of the United States, President Ngo Dihn Diem of South Vietnam refused to allow the people of South Vietnam to vote in the elections scheduled under the Geneva Agreement to be held in 1956. The reason was clear to all. As President Eisenhower later conceded, "possibly 80 percent of the population would have voted for the Communist Ho Chi Minh."

nam. I speak as a citizen of the world, for the world as it stands aghast at the path we have taken. I speak as an American to the leaders of my own nation. The great initiative in this war is ours. The initiative to stop it must be ours. . . .

If we continue there will be no doubt in my mind and in the mind of the world that we have no honorable intentions in Vietnam. It will become clear that our minimal expectation is to occupy it as an American colony and men will not refrain from thinking that our maximum hope is to goad China into a war so that we may bomb her nuclear installations. If we do not stop our war against the people of Vietnam immediately the world will be left with no other alternative than to see this as some horribly clumsy and deadly game we have decided to play.

The world now demands a maturity of America that we may not be able to achieve. It demands that we admit that we have been wrong from the beginning of our adventure in Vietnam, that we have been detrimental to the life of the Vietnamese people. The situation is one in which we must be ready to turn sharply from our present ways.

In order to atone for our sins and errors in Vietnam, we should take the initiative in bringing a halt to this tragic war. I would like to suggest five concrete things that our government should do immediately to begin the long and difficult process of extricating ourselves from this nightmarish conflict:

1. *End all bombing in North and South Vietnam.*
2. *Declare a unilateral cease-fire in the hope that such action will create the atmosphere for negotiation.*
3. *Take immediate steps to prevent other battlegrounds in Southeast Asia by curtailing our military buildup in Thailand and our interference in Laos.*
4. *Realistically accept the fact that the National Liberation Front has substantial support in South Vietnam and must thereby play a role in any meaningful negotiations and in any future Vietnam government.*
5. *Set a date that we will remove all foreign troops from Vietnam in accordance with the 1954 Geneva Agreement.*

Part of our ongoing commitment might well express itself in an offer to grant asylum to any Vietnamese who fears for his life under a new regime which included the Liberation Front. Then we must make what reparations we can for the damage we have done. We must provide the medical aid that is badly needed, making it available in this country if necessary.

Meanwhile we in the churches and synagogues have a continuing task while we urge our government to disengage itself from a disgraceful commitment. We must continue to raise our voices if our nation persists in its perverse ways in Vietnam. We must be prepared to match actions with words by seeking out every creative means of protest possible.

As we counsel young men concerning military service we must clarify for them our nation's role in Vietnam and challenge them with the alternative of conscientious objection. I am pleased to say that this is the path now being chosen by more than seventy students at my own Alma Mater, Morehouse College, and I recommend it to all who find the American course in Vietnam a dishonorable and unjust one. Moreover I would encourage all ministers of draft age to give up their ministerial exemptions and seek status as conscientious objectors. These are the times for real choices and not false ones. We are at the moment when our lives must be placed on the line if our nation is to survive its own folly. Every man of humane convictions must decide on the protest that best suits his convictions, but we must all protest. . . .

THE CAUSE of CIVIL RIGHTS

By Edward W. Brooke

The 1967 convention of the N.A.A.C.P. was held in Boston in July, and one of the events was the awarding of the Spingarn Medal to Edward W. Brooke, Negro Senator from Massachusetts. (The Spingarn Medal, instituted in 1914 by J. E. Spingarn, Chairman of the Board of Directors of the N.A.A.C.P., was given annually by the organization for the "highest or noblest achievement by an American Negro.") In response, Senator Brooke delivered an address on the Cause of Civil Rights, the major portion of which is published here with the permission of the N.A.A.C.P.

Edward William Brooke was born in Washington, D. C., on October 26, 1919, and was educated in the public schools of Washington and at Howard University, where he received a B.S. degree in 1940. He fought in World War II with the 366th Combat Infantry Regiment as a second lieutenant, and was awarded the Bronze Star and the Combat Infantryman's Badge. After graduating from Boston

University Law School, where he edited the Law Review, Brooke was admitted to the Massachusetts bar in 1948. He was elected Attorney General of Massachusetts in 1962 and was reelected two years later. He was elected Senator from Massachusetts on the Republican ticket in November, 1966, the first Negro to serve in that body since Blanche K. Bruce in 1881 and the first to be elected by popular vote, the previous two black Senators (Revels and Bruce) having been elected by the state legislatures of Mississippi as was the custom until the adoption of the Seventeenth Amendment on May 31, 1913.

. . . MANY VICTORIES for the cause of civil rights have been won, many of them attributable directly to the work of the N.A.A.C.P. Your decades of ceaseless labor have written themselves into the fabric of contemporary American history. You and the men and women who were your predecessors in this freedom movement have helped to change American society. The responsible narration and responsible promotion of plans for the improvement of the relations between the Negro and the white American within our society for over fifty years has largely been guided by your organization and the wisdom of such outstanding men as W. E. B. Du Bois, James Weldon Johnson, Walter White, and your present, inspired leader, Roy Wilkins. Unprecedented and unexcelled is the N.A.A.C.P. contribution to equal justice under law through the legal talent of distinguished constitutional lawyers, such as Thurgood Marshall, Robert Carter, Jack Greenberg, and other N.A.A.C.P. attorneys throughout the nation. You have helped to achieve for colored people what never could have been accomplished by courts or legislatures alone.

But the civil-rights movement in the United States is not simply a movement for the advancement of colored people. It springs from the very essence of the concept of democracy in America. It is an attempt to fulfill the promises this nation made at the time of its birth to generations of Americans yet to be born. The civil-rights movement is a bringing-together of people with those promises and a testing of our belief in the principle on which the promises are founded: the belief in the worth and dignity of every individual and the promise that every individual would have the opportunity to develop his capacities to the fullest in a free society.

The civil-rights movement awakened the nation to the fact that we were far from keeping the promises of America.

Into that gap between promise and performance walked the Negro schoolchildren, the women, the clergy, the old, the students, the committed, the makers of the second American Revolution.

The names Little Rock, Montgomery, Selma, Birmingham burned deep into the American conscience. When the history of this nation is reviewed, these times will stand among the most significant moments of courage and sacrifice in behalf of the rights and dignity of man. Whatever the events and problems which accompany us today, what has only so recently passed should not be so soon forgotten.

But our focus *is* different in July of 1967 from that in July of 1963. The names Watts, Hough, Roxbury, Buffalo have burned more literally and set more than the American conscience aflame.

We witness at this time the opposite of the national consensus of the early 1960's which resulted in the passage of the Civil Rights Act of 1964. At that time, the country was moved and stirred by the peaceful demonstrations of a people long deprived of the most elementary rights of free men. The national conscience was reached, and it reacted to the attacks perpetrated upon peaceful civil-rights workers and demonstrators. Today, alarmed by riots and cries of Black Power, which have often meant violence, the mood of the nation is resistant to progress in civil rights, and is bent toward protecting what is being threatened.

Many cannot realize that the federal legislation which has been adopted is simply a beginning. How much, the question is asked, is necessary to satisfy the demands of civil-rights activists? A larger and larger bloc of Americans resent the fomenting of trouble and unrest in the name of civil rights when it appears, at least to them, that real progress has already been made. As a result, there is quickly developing in this country a reaction to the civil-rights movement which appears to be a "punitive reaction."

I see this reaction reflected in the Congress of the United States. In 1966, Congress defeated proposed civil-rights legislation. Last year's proposals, including the extremely important open-housing provisions, have been resubmitted in this session as the Civil Rights Act of 1967. The first session of the 90th Congress has now been in existence for more than six months, and no action of any kind has been taken on these proposals.* In fact, the only so-called civil-rights legislation

* This act, much revised, was passed in 1968.

which has made serious progress in the Congress is a bill to make promoting a riot a federal crime. . . .

I am not an advocate of Black Power. Nor do I believe that violence, bloodshed, and the destruction of property will lead the Negro or any other minority to equality. The traditional objective of the civil-rights movement has been the effective and impartial enforcement of the law. Riots and violence are the mortal enemies, not the servants, of the civil-rights movement.

Summer or winter violence must not be used as an excuse for stopping the progress of the nation toward equality and justice for Negro Americans. The "punitive reaction" punishes not only the Negro community but also the white community. A halt in progress in the field of civil rights means an end to the domestic tranquillity to which all Americans are entitled. The social and economic factors which cause riots multiply in direct proportion to the preservation of the social, economic and psychological status quo in the Negro community. To stand still is to regress. The word *wait* engenders hate. If Congress, out of fear or anger, continues to choose the path of inaction, racial violence in the United States will not only continue, it will recur with ever-increasing intensity. The lightning of violence will strike again and again. . . .

Those of us who serve in the Congress have a duty to lead, not simply to follow public reaction. We must do more than mirror the present fears and antagonisms of the electorate. We must do what we believe to be legally and morally right. The Negro community has been petitioning the United States government for a redress of grievances for more than one hundred years. It is time—*it is past time*—that the petition "was"—not "is"—granted.

The federal legislation which is necessary to implement Constitutional guarantees of equality should not be passed simply because there has been a demonstration. Nor should such legislation be rejected because there has been a riot. These laws should be passed because they are just. They should be passed because they are necessary to the well-being of this nation's people. There are few demonstrators. There are fewer rioters. But there are many in the United States who do not have the basic rights which rightfully belong to every American citizen.

Many who are denied those basic rights are serving this nation in Vietnam. Before a member of the Congress casts a "nay" vote for the Civil Rights Act of 1967, he should write to his Negro constituents in Vietnam explaining why the federal government cannot assure them the right to live where they choose or why racial unrest in their community makes it politically inopportune to vote for civil-rights legislation at this time.

I have said that the focus of the civil-rights movement in July of 1967 is different from that in July of 1963. The energy and direction in the early years was concentrated on guaranteeing basic civil rights.

But the issues in Selma and Birmingham are not the issues in Watts or Hough. The problems are different. The problems of Watts and Hough are the problems of the urban Negro poor.

Seventy-five percent of the Negro population live in cities. One half of the Negro population is poor. That means that one out of every two Negro citizens is denied the minimal levels of health, housing, food and education that our present state of scientific knowledge specifies for life as it is now lived in the United States.

Guaranteeing the right of a Negro to be served at an integrated lunch counter is of little significance to a man who is unemployed and unable to adequately feed his family.

Assuring education in an integrated school will accomplish little if the school still follows a pattern of internal segregation. We must achieve more than merely technical compliance with the laws requiring integration in public schools. We should seek integration which is *de facto* not simply *de jure*. We should make certain that Negro children in the public schools at all times receive the same quality of education that is available to white children.

The power of the Negro vote in Northern cities is dissipated and fragmented if, because of gerrymandering, Negroes are unable to achieve representation consistent with their numbers. This further denies the Negro minority the ability to obtain responsiveness to its needs through the political process.

In many cities, little is done to deal with the legitimate grievances of the Negro population. As a result, activists turn increasingly to violence in reaction to community indifference. In turn, the community, angered by and fearful of the demands which have been made, becomes even more insensitive to the problems confronted by the Negro and even more reluctant to provide meaningful solutions for them. Much of the responsibility for this frustrating stand-off must be borne by state and local governments. . . .

State and local governments have been extremely shortsighted. They have failed to provide the most elementary services for the Negro communities within their cities. Legitimate grievances are legion. Action to eliminate them lags. A disgruntled and potentially revolutionary class grows at a record pace. The very public officials who most deplore the rise of militant civil-rights leadership are often its unwitting partners. Each time that extremism compels a state or municipal government to take long-overdue but desirable and necessary action upon grievances, moderation suffers another defeat in the eyes of the Negro community.

The answer to extremism is clear. Government at all levels must respond to the legitimate requests of responsible civil-rights leadership. Black power is a response to white irresponsibility. The Lemberg Center for the Study of Violence at Brandeis University has, in a report released only two weeks ago, concluded that the key factor in determining a community's susceptibility to racial violence is the attitude, as the Negro community understands it, of the municipal government toward the subject of integration and toward increased opportunities for Negro citizens.

State and local governments have a clearly defined choice. They can continue to ignore moderate requests for reasonable governmental action submitted by responsible members of the Negro community, or they can recognize that their responsibility extends to all parts of the state or the municipality, thus enlarging the scope of governmental action to include many who have traditionally been deprived of the most elementary forms of public service. The failure to respond to responsible requests means the promotion of militancy. It is an invitation to violence. But constructive action can be the beginning of a society which has seen the end of racial violence because every man receives an equal share of the attention of his government.

The civil-rights movement must continue to be the vehicle for the assertion of the legitimate claims of Negro citizens, not only at all levels of government but also within the private segments of the community which are not yet partners in progress toward human rights. If the civil-rights movement is to be a functioning and effective vehicle for moving this country forward, it must draw its strength, as it has in the past, from every part of the American society which recognizes the justness and importance of its cause. This is not simply a Negro movement. It is an American movement for the attainment of an American ideal. And it encompasses the commitment, the efforts and the energy of Negro Americans and white Americans alike. Any effort to exclude white Americans from the prosecution of this cause is, first, a betrayal of the most profound beliefs and principles of the movement itself, and second, a barrier to its ultimate success.

Who would be so foolish to think that an end to discrimination, the creation of jobs, and housing, the provision of better education, the survival and over-all success of the civil-rights movement can be achieved by Negroes without the cooperation, the active support, and the good will of the white community? Even if Negroes could isolate themselves and achieve their goals separated from whites, who, as an American, would relish such a sterile victory? The symbol of the Congress of Racial Equality has always been a black hand and a white hand extended and embracing one another. I support that symbol and its significance. It, and all it implies and promises, is the only meaningful goal of the civil-rights movement in this nation. It is the commitment to that goal which brought forth such men as the namesake of the award which you bestow upon me tonight. And it is the commitment to that goal which engages men such as your dedicated president, Kivie Kaplan, in the continuation of this effort. Their commitment, and that of thousands of other white Americans, is not merely one of sympathy. It is a commitment not to a race, but to the principles upon which this nation was founded. They are working to keep promises that were made, not only to others but also to themselves. We must not accept a division between Negro and white within the civil-rights movement. We must give our full attention to the unfinished business which is still on the civil-rights agenda.

It is somewhat ironic, but I think true, that the existence of the civil-rights movement is both an affirmation and an indictment of what we believe about America and about ourselves as Americans.

The movement exists because of the lag between what was promised nearly two centuries ago and what is actually accorded to Negro Americans in terms of their rights and dignity and the opportunity to lead significant lives.

The way in which peaceful progress has been made toward that ideal is possible because of an American system which allows for change. But no thinking American can take comfort from that fact and counsel patience because some progress has been made. What the civil-rights movement seeks is the promise of today, not the hope of tomorrow.

For the one Negro who is elevated to the highest court in the land, there are thousands of Negroes who are denied the protection of laws which have been interpreted by that court.

For every celebrated Negro educator, there are thousands of Negroes who are denied the basic education to equip them for life in a technological society.

For the one Negro who serves as Secretary of Housing, there

are thousands who must tolerate dilapidated, inadequate, and overcrowded housing conditions.

For every Negro writer or artist, there are thousands who will never have the opportunity to develop their talents and their potential for creativity.

For the Negro United States Senator, there are thousands who are locked out of the political process and whose right to vote is exercised at the peril of their lives or livelihood.

This is the indictment of America, and its sad loss. The potential for greatness of this country has, for more than a century, been diminished by a system which denies citizens the opportunity to enrich their nation as well as fulfill their own capabilities.

The cause of civil rights moves forward in the deepest interests of America and its people. It is a profound affirmation of all that we are and all that we hope to become.

WHY THE NEGRO MUST REBEL

By Floyd B. McKissick

On July 20–23, 1967, the National Conference of Black Power convened in Newark, New Jersey, scene of the "riot" in which twenty-five black Americans were killed in what the 1,100 delegates to the Conference called a "public massacre." Among the delegates were bishops, ministers, ghetto organizers, scholars, professionals, students, trade-unionists, teachers, unemployed, and "revolutionaries." The Conference grew from the 1966 Labor Day weekend planning session in Washington, called together by Congressman Adam Clayton Powell, Jr. The committee appointed at that time agreed to organize a national conference limited to four hundred delegates, but in the wake of the Newark "massacre," the number grew quickly and all fifteen Conference workshops and plenary sessions were jammed with angry blacks.

A leading speech to the Conference was delivered by Floyd B. McKissick, executive director of the Congress of Racial Equality (CORE). In addition to defending the right of the black ghettos to revolt, McKissick criticized black civil-rights leaders who had condemned the "riots." Al-

though he did not mention names, he was obviously refer-
ring to Roy Wilkins, Whitney M. Young, Dr. Martin Luther
King, Jr., and A. Philip Randolph, who had publicly criti-
cized the ghetto rebellions.

In a news conference in Harlem, July 31, 1967, McKis-
sick continued the points he made in his speech to the
Black Power Conference, issuing a "Black Manifesto re-
garding recent rebellions across the country." He urged
"release of all political prisoners," making it clear that he
meant "those seized during the recent rebellions. Halt all
prosecutions." McKissick also urged defeat of the federal
antiriot bill, resubmission of urban rat-control legislation
in Congress, and ten-billion-dollar increase in funds for
the Office of Economic Opportunity. In analyzing the
"riots" of the summer of 1967, McKissick said:

"History will likely record the explosions of this summer
as the beginning of the black revolution. The criminal con-
notation of the term 'riots' will be erased. They will be
recognized for what they are—rebellions against oppres-
sion and exploitation." (The New York Times, Aug. 1,
1967)

Here are excerpts from Floyd B. McKissick's speech to
the National Conference of Black Power, as published in
The New York Times, July 30, 1967.

WE ARE GIVEN rhetoric about power sharing: "The Land
of the Free. Home of the Brave. With liberty and justice for
all." I could name dozens of others that sound beautiful, but
mean absolutely nothing for black people, here or on any other
continent. They were never intended to mean anything for
black people. They were written when we were still slaves.

There are black people starving in Mississippi, millions of
colored people starving in India while white Americans bask in
luxury, spending millions to go to the moon, billions on a war
in Vietnam which pits yellow people against yellow people.

There are rebellions throughout the United States—black
people demanding that they no longer be exploited, that they
be free—free to live in dignity. . . .

In America, as we have seen, the belief in white superiority
runs deep. It was a dominant factor in the slave trade. The
black African wasn't recognized as a human being. A belief
ferocious enough to allow human slavery cannot be dissipated
by a mere century, and, in America, it has been quietly reinforced.

Although slavery as a recognized legal institution has been abolished, economic slavery, economic exploitation, has not. Black people in this country have never been allowed to share in the economic riches of America. A few get in—here and there—a few get rich, but their success has no effect on the masses of black people.

White landlords, white storekeepers, white corporate managers and a white, Anglo-Saxon Wall Street, conspire to keep the black man in his place. As whites quietly exit to the comfortable suburbs, they do not relinquish the economic control of the ghetto; they maintain control of the city agencies and the political scene. They determine what opportunities will be available and what will be reserved for whites only—and, occasionally, one or two good "Negroes."

With the climate existing in the United States, we would be foolish, as leaders, to think that black people are not being politically oppressed. If black people got political power, they might be able to merge their values with the values of the dominant culture. And the white man wants to protect his values—particularly his economic values. The materialism which has distorted his dealings with the entire world . . .

And who is to blame for the rebellions? This point we need not argue. The white man is the judge, jury and the executioner in his system, and he made the law so as to control us. We are called the violators of his "law and order"—"criminals."

Yet he knows that the white racist society is to blame for all of the conditions which force a man to rebel. His concept of "law and order" means the legal methods of exploiting blacks. We object and we resist.

Some so-called Negro leaders even have the audacity to join the man—by calling a liberation struggle a riot, his brothers hoodlums and criminals, and damning his brothers who seek to overthrow the yoke of oppression. . . . In this country, the ghetto is not defined by barbed wire; the ghetto follows the black man wherever he goes. . . .

Yes, black people know fear and live with it each and every day of their lives—in deadly fear of the white man's potential. We know he can kill, we know he will—because of his hurt pride—we know that his personality demands that he control whatever he sees, we know that normal dissent is treason in his blue eyes.

In fact, we know the man better than he knows himself. We know him for what he is. We know he will kill us if he can—one by one or all at once. . . .

Even our friends in the peace movement find it too easy to look thousands of miles away from home and, with much indignation, see the extermination of the Vietnamese.

On the other hand, they cannot see ten blocks away, where many black people are the walking dead—dead in mind and spirit, because of lack of hope and lack of chance.

We cannot look elsewhere for help. We cannot lean on the crutch of religion. We cannot depend on phony "coalitions." We must work out our own methods. We must draw our own conclusions.

To those queasy individuals who are afraid of the resolutions presented here, let me state my unequivocal opinion: The right of revolution is a Constitutional right, condoned by the creation of the American Constitution itself. When we assert the right of revolution, we are asserting a Constitutional right.

Revolution in America is justified by all standards of morality —religious and ethical. It is required to fulfill the basic, natural rights of man.

Even white men recognized the need for revolution when, in 1776, they revolted because they were oppressed. And today— 1967—black people are more oppressed than any white man has ever been, in the history of the world.

This is the time when we must unite, brothers and sisters. We must join in making plans. . . .

WHERE DO WE GO FROM HERE?

By Martin Luther King, Jr.

By the summer of 1967 the civil-rights revolution was practically over, and Dr. King was preparing to move in new directions. While still a firm believer in nonviolence, he was beginning to understand that the Movement (as the civil-rights revolution had been called) "must address itself to the question of restructuring the whole of American society." In the presidential address to the Tenth Anniversary Convention of the Southern Christian Leadership Conference, Atlanta, Georgia, August 16, 1967, Dr. King projected the issues which led eventually to his proposal of a Poor People's March on Washington. This speech is important for understanding the evolution of Dr. King's think-

ing on crucial problems facing his people and all other
oppressed peoples in the United States. The following ex-
cerpt from the speech is reprinted by special arrangement
with Mrs. Martin Luther King, Jr., and the S.C.L.C., At-
lanta, Georgia.

Now, in order to answer the question, "Where do we go
from here?" which is our theme, we must first honestly recognize where we are now. When the Constitution was written, a
strange formula to determine taxes and representation declared
that the Negro was 60 percent of a person. Today another
curious formula seems to declare he is 50 percent of a person.
Of the good things in life, the Negro has approximately one half
those of whites. Of the bad things of life, he has twice those of
whites. Thus half of all Negroes live in substandard housing.
And Negroes have half the income of whites. When we view the
negative experiences of life, the Negro has a double share. There
are twice as many unemployed. The rate of infant mortality
among Negroes is double that of whites and there are twice as
many Negroes dying in Vietnam as whites in proportion to their
size in the population.

In other spheres, the figures are equally alarming. In elementary schools, Negroes lag one to three years behind whites,
and their segregated schools receive substantially less money per
student than the white schools. One twentieth as many Negroes
as whites attend college. Of employed Negroes, 75 percent hold
menial jobs.

This is where we are. Where do we go from here? First, we
must massively assert our dignity and worth. We must stand up
amidst a system that still oppresses us and develop an unassail-
able and majestic sense of values. We must no longer be
ashamed of being black. The job of arousing manhood within a
people that have been taught for so many centuries that they
are nobody is not easy.

Even semantics have conspired to make that which is black
seem ugly and degrading. In Roget's *Thesaurus* there are 120
synonyms for blackness and at least 60 of them are offensive,
as for example, blot, soot, grim, devil and foul. And there are
some 134 synonyms for whiteness and all are favorable, expressed in such words as purity, cleanliness, chastity and innocence. A white lie is better than a black lie. The most degenerate
member of a family is a "black sheep." Ossie Davis has suggested that maybe the English language should be reconstructed
so that teachers will not be forced to teach the Negro child 60
ways to despise himself, and thereby perpetuate his false sense

of inferiority, and the white child 134 ways to adore himself, and thereby perpetuate his false sense of superiority.

The tendency to ignore the Negro's contribution to American life and to strip him of his personhood, is as old as the earliest history books and as contemporary as the morning's newspaper. To upset this cultural homicide, the Negro must rise up with an affirmation of his own Olympian manhood. Any movement for the Negro's freedom that overlooks this necessity is only waiting to be buried. As long as the mind is enslaved, the body can never be free. Psychological freedom, a firm sense of self-esteem, is the most powerful weapon against the long night of physical slavery. No Lincolnian Emancipation Proclamation or Johnsonian Civil Rights Bill can totally bring this kind of freedom. The Negro will only be free when he reaches down to the inner depths of his own being and signs with the pen and ink of assertive manhood his own Emancipation Proclamation. And, with a spirit straining toward true self-esteem, the Negro must boldly throw off the manacles of self-abnegation and say to himself and to the world, "I am somebody. I am a person. I am a man with dignity and honor. I have a rich and noble history. How painful and exploited that history has been. Yes, I was a slave through my foreparents and I am not ashamed of that. I'm ashamed of the people who were so sinful to make me a slave." Yes, we must stand up and say, "I'm black and I'm beautiful," and this self-affirmation is the black man's need, made compelling by the white man's crimes against him.

Another basic challenge is to discover how to organize our strength in terms of economic and political power. No one can deny that the Negro is in dire need of this kind of legitimate power. Indeed, one of the great problems that the Negro confronts is his lack of power. From old plantations of the South to newer ghettos of the North, the Negro has been confined to a life of voicelessness and powerlessness. Stripped of the right to make decisions concerning his life and destiny he has been subject to the authoritarian and sometimes whimsical decisions of this white power structure. The plantation and ghetto were created by those who had power, both to confine those who had no power and to perpetuate their powerlessness. The problem of transforming the ghetto, therefore, is a problem of power—confrontation of the forces of power demanding change and the forces of power dedicated to the preserving of the status quo. Now power properly understood is nothing but the ability to achieve purpose. It is the strength required to bring about social, political and economic change. Walter Reuther defined power one day. He said, "Power is the ability of a labor union like the

U.A.W. to make the most powerful corporation in the world, General Motors, say 'Yes' when it wants to say 'No.' That's power."

Now a lot of us are preachers, and all of us have our moral convictions and concerns, and so often have problems with power. There is nothing wrong with power if power is used correctly. You see, what happened is that some of our philosophers got off base. And one of the great problems of history is that the concepts of love and power have usually been contrasted as opposites—polar opposites—so that love is identified with a resignation of power, and power with a denial of love.

It was this misinterpretation that caused Nietzsche, who was a philosopher of the will to power, to reject the Christian concept of love. It was this same misinterpretation which induced Christian theologians to reject the Nietzschean philosophy of the will to power in the name of the Christian idea of love. Now, we've got to get this thing right. What is needed is a realization that power without love is reckless and abusive, and love without power is sentimental and anemic. Power at its best is love implementing the demands of justice, and justice at its best is power correcting everything that stands against love. And this is what we must see as we move on. What has happened is that we have had it wrong and confused in our own country, and this has led Negro Americans in the past to seek their goals through power devoid of love and conscience.

This is leading a few extremists today to advocate for Negroes the same destructive and conscienceless power that they have justly abhorred in whites. It is precisely this collision of immoral power with powerless morality which constitutes the major crisis of our times.

We must develop a program that will drive the nation to a guaranteed annual income. Now, early in this century this proposal would have been greeted with ridicule and denunciation, as destructive of initiative and responsibility. At that time economic status was considered the measure of the individual's ability and talents. And, in the thinking of that day, the absence of worldly goods indicated a want of industrious habits and moral fiber. We've come a long way in our understanding of human motivation and of the blind operation of our economic system. Now we realize that dislocations in the market operations of our economy and the prevalence of discrimination thrust people into idleness and bind them in constant or frequent unemployment against their will. Today the poor are less often dismissed, I hope, from our consciences by being branded as inferior or incompetent. We also know that no matter how dynamically the economy develops and expands, it does not eliminate all poverty.

The problem indicates that our emphasis must be twofold. We must create full employment or we must create incomes. People must be made consumers by one method or the other. Once they are placed in this position we need to be concerned that the potential of the individual is not wasted. New forms of work that enhance the social good will have to be devised for those for whom traditional jobs are not available. In 1879 Henry George anticipated this state of affairs when he wrote in *Progress and Poverty:**

> The fact is that the work which improves the condition of mankind, the work which extends knowledge and increases power and enriches literature and elevates thought, is not done to secure a living. It is not the work of slaves driven to their tasks either by the task, by the taskmaster, or by animal necessity. It is the work of men who somehow find a form of work that brings a security for its own sake and a state of society where want is abolished.

Work of this sort could be enormously increased, and we are likely to find that the problems of housing and education, instead of preceding the elimination of poverty, will themselves be affected if poverty is first abolished. The poor transformed into purchasers will do a great deal on their own to alter housing decay. Negroes who have a double disability will have a greater effect on discrimination when they have the additional weapon of cash to use in their struggle.

Beyond these advantages, a host of positive psychological changes inevitably will result from widespread economic security. The dignity of the individual will flourish when the decisions concerning his life are in his own hands, when he has the means to seek self-improvement. Personal conflicts among husbands, wives and children will diminish when the unjust measurement of human worth on the scale of dollars is eliminated.

Now our country can do this. John Kenneth Galbraith said that a guaranteed annual income could be done for about twenty billion dollars a year. And I say to you today, that if our nation can spend thirty-five billion dollars a year to fight an unjust, evil war in Vietnam, and twenty billion dollars to put a man on the moon, it can spend billions of dollars to put God's

---

* Henry George (1839–1897) was the father of the single-tax system, which he set forth in his *Progress and Poverty*, published in 1879. The book argued that the land belonged to society, which created its value and properly taxed that value, not improvements on the land.

children on their own two feet right here on earth.

Now, let me say briefly that we must reaffirm our commitment to nonviolence. I want to stress this. The futility of violence in the struggle for racial justice has been tragically etched in all the recent Negro riots. Yesterday, I tried to analyze the riots and deal with their causes. Today I want to give the other side. There is certainly something painfully sad about a riot. One sees screaming youngsters and angry adults fighting hopelessly and aimlessly against impossible odds. And deep down within them, you can even see a desire for self-destruction, a kind of suicidal longing.

Occasionally Negroes contend that the 1965 Watts riot and the other riots in various cities represented effective civil-rights action. But those who express this view always end up with stumbling words when asked what concrete gains have been won as a result. At best, the riots have produced a little additional antipoverty money allotted by frightened government officials, and a few water-sprinklers to cool the children of the ghettos. It is something like improving the food in the prison while the people remain securely incarcerated behind bars. Nowhere have the riots won any concrete improvement such as have the organized protest demonstrations. When one tries to pin down advocates of violence as to what acts would be effective, the answers are blatantly illogical. Sometimes they talk of overthrowing racist state and local governments and they talk about guerrilla warfare. They fail to see that no internal revolution has ever succeeded in overthrowing a government by violence unless the government had already lost the allegiance and effective control of its armed forces. Anyone in his right mind knows that this will not happen in the United States. In a violent racial situation, the power structure has the local police, the state troopers, the National Guard and, finally, the Army to call on—all of which are predominantly white. Furthermore, few if any violent revolutions have been successful unless the violent minority had the sympathy and support of the nonresistant majority. Castro may have had only a few Cubans actually fighting with him up in the hills, but he could never have overthrown the Batista regime unless he had the sympathy of the vast majority of Cuban people.*

* In 1956 Fidel Castro landed on the coast of Cuba in the vessel, *Gramma*, to overthrow the despot Fulgencio Batista. Twelve men survived the counterattack and went on to lead the Cuban people to victory over Batista, who fled the island on New Year's Day, 1959, which ushered in the Cuban revolutionary victory.

It is perfectly clear that a violent revolution on the part of American blacks would find no sympathy and support from the white population and very little from the majority of the Negroes themselves. This is no time for romantic illusions and empty philosophical debates about freedom. This is a time for action. What is needed is a strategy for change, a tactical program that will bring the Negro into the mainstream of American life as quickly as possible. So far, this has only been offered by the nonviolent movement. Without recognizing this we will end up with solutions that don't solve, answers that don't answer and explanations that don't explain.

And so I say to you today that I still stand by nonviolence. And I am still convinced that it is the most potent weapon available to the Negro in his struggle for justice in this country. And the other thing is that I am concerned about a better world. I'm concerned about justice. I'm concerned about brotherhood. I'm concerned about truth. And when one is concerned about these, he can never advocate violence. For through violence you may murder a murderer but you can't murder murder. Through violence you may murder a liar but you can't establish truth. Through violence you may murder a hater, but you can't murder hate. Darkness cannot put out darkness. Only light can do that.

And I say to you, I have also decided to stick to love. For I know that love is ultimately the only answer to mankind's problems. And I'm going to talk about it everywhere I go. I know it isn't popular to talk about it in some circles today. I'm not talking about emotional bosh when I talk about love, I'm talking about a strong, demanding love. And I have seen too much hate. I've seen too much hate on the faces of sheriffs in the South. I've seen hate on the faces of too many Klansmen and too many White Citizens Councilors in the South to want to hate myself, because every time I see it, I know that it does something to their faces and their personalities and I say to myself that hate is too great a burden to bear. I have decided to love. If you are seeking the highest good, I think you can find it through love. And the beautiful thing is that we are moving against wrong when we do it, because John was right, God is love. He who hates does not know God, but he who has love has the key that unlocks the door to the meaning of ultimate reality.

I want to say to you as I move to my conclusion, as we talk about "Where do we go from here," that we honestly face the fact that the Movement must address itself to the question of restructuring the whole of American society. There are forty million poor people here. And one day we must ask the question, "Why are there forty million poor people in America?" And when you begin to ask that question, you are raising questions about the economic system, about a broader distribution of wealth. When you ask that question, you begin to question the capitalistic economy. And I'm simply saying that more and more, we've got to begin to ask questions about the whole society. We are called upon to help the discouraged beggars in life's market place. But one day we must come to see that an edifice which produces beggars needs restructuring. It means that questions must be raised. You see, my friends, when you deal with this, you begin to ask the question, "Who owns the oil?" You begin to ask the question, "Who owns the iron ore?" You begin to ask the question, "Why is it that people have to pay water bills in a world that is two thirds water?" These are questions that must be asked.

Now, don't think that you have me in a "bind" today. I'm not talking about Communism.

What I'm saying to you this morning is that Communism forgets that life is individual. Capitalism forgets that life is social, and the Kingdom of Brotherhood is found neither in the thesis of Communism nor the antithesis of capitalism but in a higher synthesis. It is found in a higher synthesis that combines the truths of both. Now, when I say question the whole society, it means ultimately coming to see that the problem of racism, the problem of economic exploitation, and the problem of war are all tied together. These are the triple evils that are interrelated.

If you will let me be a preacher just a little bit— One night, a juror came to Jesus and he wanted to know what he could do to be saved. Jesus didn't get bogged down in the kind of isolated approach of what he shouldn't do. Jesus didn't say, "Now Nicodemus, you must stop lying." He didn't say, "Nicodemus, you must stop cheating if you are doing that." He didn't say, "Nicodemus, you must not commit adultery." He didn't say, "Nicodemus, now you must stop drinking liquor if you are doing that excessively." He said something altogether different, because Jesus realized something basic—that if a man will lie, he will steal. And if a man will steal, he will kill. So instead of just getting bogged down in one thing, Jesus looked at him and said, "Nicodemus, you must be born again."

He said, in other words, "Your whole structure must be changed." A nation that will keep people in slavery for 244 years will "thingify" them—make them things. Therefore they will exploit them, and poor people generally, economically. And a nation that will exploit economically will have to have foreign investments and everything else, and will have to use its military might to protect them. All of these problems are tied together. What I am saying today is that we must go from this convention and say, "America, you must be born again!"

So, I conclude by saying again today that we have a task and let us go out with a "divine dissatisfaction." Let us be dissatisfied until America will no longer have a high blood pressure of creeds and an anemia of deeds. Let us be dissatisfied until the tragic walls that separate the outer city of wealth and comfort and the inner city of poverty and despair shall be crushed by the battering rams of the forces of justice. Let us be dissatisfied until those that live on the outskirts of hope are brought into the metropolis of daily security. Let us be dissatisfied until slums are cast into the junk heaps of history, and every family is living in a decent sanitary home. Let us be dissatified until the dark yesterdays of segregated schools will be transformed into bright tomorrows of quality, integrated education. Let us be dissatisfied until integration is not seen as a problem but as an opportunity to participate in the beauty of diversity. Let us be dissatisfied until men and women, however black they may be, will be judged on the basis of the content of their character and not on the basis of the color of their skin. Let us be dissatisfied. Let us be dissatisfied until every state capitol houses a governor who will do justly, who will love mercy and who will walk humbly with his God. Let us be dissatisfied until from every city hall, justice will roll down like waters and righteousness like a mighty stream. Let us be dissatisfied until that day when the lion and the lamb shall lie down together, and every man will sit under his own vine and fig tree and none shall be afraid. Let us be dissatisfied. And men will recognize that out of one blood God made all men to dwell upon the face of the earth. Let us be dissatisfied until that day when nobody will shout "White Power!"—when nobody will shout "Black Power!"—but everybody will talk about God's power and human power.

I must confess, my friends, the road ahead will not always be smooth. There will still be rocky places of frustration and meandering points of bewilderment. There will be inevitable setbacks here and there. There will be those moments when the buoyancy of hope will be transformed into the fatigue of despair. Our dreams will sometimes be shattered and our ethereal hopes blasted. We may again with tear-drenched eyes have to stand before the bier of some courageous civil-rights worker whose life will be snuffed out by the dastardly acts of bloodthirsty mobs. Difficult and painful as it is, we must walk on in the days ahead with an audacious faith in the future. And as we continue our charted course, we may gain consolation in the words so nobly left by that great black bard who was also a great freedom fighter of yesterday, James Weldon Johnson:

> Stony the road we trod,
> Bitter the chastening rod
> Felt in the days
> When hope unborn had died.
>
> Yet with a steady beat,
> Have not our weary feet
> Come to the place
> For which our fathers sighed?
>
> We have come over the way
> That with tears hath been watered.
> We have come treading our paths
> Through the blood of the slaughtered,
>
> Out from the gloomy past,
> Till now we stand at last
> Where the bright gleam
> Of our bright star is cast.

Let this affirmation be our ringing cry. It will give us the courage to face the uncertainties of the future. It will give our tired feet new strength as we continue our forward stride toward the city of freedom. When our days become dreary with low hovering clouds of despair, and when our nights become darker than a thousand midnights, let us remember that there is a creative force in this universe, working to pull down the gigantic mountains of evil, a power that is able to make a way out of no way and transform dark yesterdays into bright tomorrows. Let us realize the arc of the moral universe is long but it bends toward justice.

Let us realize that William Cullen Bryant is right: "Truth crushed to earth will rise again." Let us go out realizing that the Bible is right: "Be not deceived, God is not mocked. Whatsoever a man soweth, that shall he also reap." This is our hope for the future, and with this faith we will be able to sing in some not too distant tomorrow with a cosmic past tense, "We have overcome, we have overcome, deep in my heart, I did believe we would overcome."

A WAY OUT OF THE EXPLODING GHETTO

By Bayard Rustin

Bayard Rustin, a pacifist, Socialist, formerly executive secretary of the War Resisters League, and active in the League for Industrial Democracy, has been a leading civil-rights activist for more than two decades. He became nationally prominent as chief organizer of the 1963 March on Washington. A firm believer in a Negro-labor alliance and in political action as a major protest weapon, Rustin lost favor with more militant blacks when he spoke out against violence and attacked refusal to work with white liberals in the Freedom Movement. As Executive Director of the A. Philip Randolph Institute, Rustin addressed many audiences throughout the country. Here is one of his speeches, delivered in Detroit shortly after the riots of the summer of 1967. Rustin discussed the question of whether the uprising in the ghettos represented revolutionary struggles and offered A. Philip Randolph's $185-billion "Freedom Budget for all Americans" as the solution for the ghetto uprisings. A. Philip Randolph had presented the "Freedom Budget" in a speech on October 26, 1966, calling upon Congress to pass legislation making $185 billion available over the next ten years in federal funds to substantially eliminate poverty in America, raise living standards and increase cultural opportunities, especially for low-income families.

The speech on the ghetto uprisings is reprinted, with permission of Bayard Rustin, from a pamphlet published by the A. Philip Randolph Institute, 1967.

THERE is no longer any denying that this country is in the throes of a historic national crisis. Its ramifications are so vast and frightening that even now, shocked into numbness and disbelief, the American people have not yet fully grasped what is happening to them.

The grim data are clear enough and still coming in. Since this summer began, thirty of our cities, big and small, have been racked by racial disorder; scores of citizens, almost all of them black, have been killed, thousands injured and even more arrested. Property damage has exceeded a billion dollars; total income loss is incalculable.

As a people, we are not unaccustomed to violence. Frontier lawlessness, Southern vigilanteism, Chicago gangsterism: these are images and themes embedded in the American tradition. We have only just lost a President to an assassin's bullet.* But, having escaped the bombs of two world wars, we are not familiar with the horror of burned-out buildings, smoking rubble, tanks in our streets, the blasts of Molotov cocktails, the ring of snipers' bullets from rooftops. Today we look at sections of Detroit and think of war-torn Berlin. We see rampaging, looting mobs and think of the unstable politics of underdeveloped countries. A nation's identity has been overturned.

In our own history we can find no precedent in this century for the massive destruction the past three years have brought to our cities—no precedent since the Civil War. But the greatest toll is not in property damage or even in lives lost. Nor is the greatest danger that the violence will go on indefinitely, any more than the Civil War did. It is that the aftermath of that war will be repeated, that as in the Compromise of 1877 the country will turn its back on the Negro, on the root causes of his discontent, on its own democratic future.

Not since the Great Depression have social policy, our national institutions, our political order been more severely tested than at present. The coming months will shape the character of America in the remainder of the twentieth century —and I am trying to speak with the utmost sobriety, precision and restraint.

Why does the Republic find itself at a crossroads? What has actually happened?

The term "race riot" is unilluminating and anachronistic. It describes the Detroit disorders of 1943, when the Negro and white communities were locked in combat. White mobs invaded the ghetto. Negroes forayed downtown. Men were beaten and murdered for the color of their skins. In the upheavals of the last four summers, destruction has been confined to the ghetto; nor, discounting the police, were black and white citizens fighting. In fact, in Detroit whites joined in the looting and sniping. And I am told that whites were free to walk through the embattled ghetto without fear of violence from Negroes.

This is not to deny the importance of antiwhite hostility. One has only to hear the sick racial epithets "honkey" and "whitey" to recognize the deep and bitter hatred that is loose on the streets of the ghettos. But if white blood was what the rioters

* President John F. Kennedy was assassinated in Dallas, Texas, on November 22, 1963.

thirsted for, they didn't go very far to get it. What they assaulted were the symbols of white power—police and property, the latter embracing the entire ghetto. These are traditional targets of rebellions and in that sense the riots can be called rebellions.

That sense, however, must be sharply qualified. Is it correct to speak of "race rebellion," or "Negro rebellion"? Are America's Negroes on the verge of revolution? More than one newspaper and television commentator has already begun to draw comparisons between the ghetto uprisings and the French, Russian, Algerian, Irish and Black African independence revolutions. Some Black Power advocates have proclaimed the beginnings of guerrilla warfare and see the urban Negro as a counterpart to the Viet Cong. And in Paris it has become fashionable to speak of the *"révolution des noires"* in the United States.

The reality is that the revolutionary rhetoric now employed by some young Negro militants cannot create the preconditions for successful, or even authentic, revolution. The independence movements in colonial territories provide no model, for the simple reason that American Negroes can have no geographical focus for nationalist sentiment.

Moreover, American Negroes do not constitute a popular majority struggling against a relatively small white colonial ruling group—the ideal condition for guerrilla warfare. Whatever separatist impulses exist among American Negroes cannot find appropriate models in the colonial world.

If independence revolutions are no model, what of social revolutions? This is a more interesting subject because the phrase "social revolution" has been widely used by the civil-rights and liberal movements generally. But in this sense in which I have been using it for thirty years—the phrase designates fundamental changes in social and economic class relations resulting from mass political action. Such action would be democratic. That is, it would aim to create a new majority coalition capable of exercising political power in the interest of new social policies. By definition the coalition has to be interracial.

As a minority, Negroes by themselves cannot bring about such a social revolution. They can participate in it as a powerful and stimulating force; or they can provoke a counter-revolution. In either case the decisive factor will be the political direction in which the majority will move.

Numbers are not the only issue. Also important is the class content of revolt. At least in the French and Russian revolutions, revolutionary leaders and parties sought to mobilize fairly definable and cohesive socioeconomic classes—workers, peasants, the middle class—which, though oppressed or aggrieved, were part of the society they sought to transform. Upon what classes do the advocates of rioting, the voices of the apocalypse, base their revolutionary perspective? This is another way of posing the question I left hanging earlier: Who is rioting?

Daniel Patrick Moynihan is correct in locating the riots in the "lower class" or in the words of another controversial man, Karl Marx, in the *lumpenproletariat,* or "slum proletariat." Lower class does not mean working class; the distinction is often overlooked in a middle-class culture that tends to lump the two together.

The distinction is important. The working class is employed. It has a relation to the production of goods and services; much of it is organized in unions. It enjoys a measure of cohesion, discipline and stability lacking in the lower class. The latter is unemployed or marginally employed. It is relatively unorganized, incohesive, unstable. It contains the petty criminal and antisocial elements. Above all, unlike the working class, it lacks the sense of a stake in society. When the slum proletariat is black, its alienation is even greater.

From the revolutionist point of view, the question is not whether steps could be taken to strengthen organization among the *lumpenproletariat* but whether that group could be a central agent of social transformation. Generally, the answer has been no.

The black slum proletariat has been growing in numbers and density. As agricultural mechanization and other factors continue pushing Negroes out of the South, the urban ghettos expand each year by half a million; only forty thousand Negroes annually find their way into the suburbs. This trend has not been affected at all by any antipoverty or Great Society programs.

When the migration of Negroes to Northern and Western cities was at its height during World War II, factory jobs were available at decent wages. With the advent of advanced technology eliminating many semiskilled and unskilled jobs, and with the movement of plants from the central cities to the suburbs (New York lost 200,000 factory jobs in a decade), urban Negroes suffered rising joblessness or employment in low-paying service jobs.

The depth of the unemployment problem in the slum ghettos is indicated in a recent United States Department of Labor report on "subemployment" in cities and slums. While the traditional unemployment rate counts only those "actively looking" but unable to find work, the subemployment index reflects in addition: (1) those who have dropped out of the labor market in despair; (2) those who are working part time but want full-time jobs; (3) heads of households under 65 working full time but earning poverty wages (less than $60 a week); (4) individuals under 65 who are not heads of households and earn less than $56 a week in full-time jobs; and (5) a conservatively estimated portion of males known to be living in the slums but who somehow do not show up in employment or unemployment counts.

The report states: "If the traditional statistical concept of 'unemployment' (which produced the nationwide average of 3.7 percent unemployment rate for January, 1967) is applied to the urban slum situation, the *unemployment rate* in these areas is about 10 percent . . . three times the average for the rest of the country." [Original italics.] The figure for Detroit's Central Woodward area, incidentally, is 10.1 percent.

The subemployment rate in the ten cities surveyed yields an average figure of almost 35 percent. Though possibly in need of further refining, the subemployment rate is the more meaningful figure. Not only does it include the categories listed above, but it also tends to reflect the number of people who experience unemployment over a period of time. By contrast, the official rate counts those unemployed at a point in time (i.e., the time the survey is taken).

High unemployment and low income are not the only problems afflicting the black slum proletariat, but they are the crucial ones. Without adequate income, there is no access to the decent housing market, educational opportunity, even proper health care. (In 1964, East and Central Harlem, comprising 24 percent of Manhattan's population, accounted for 40 percent of its TB deaths, 33 percent of its infant deaths; in Bedford-Stuyvesant, which contains 9 percent of Brooklyn's population, the respective figures were 24 and 22 percent.)

The tendency of much current antipoverty rhetoric to create a multitude of disparate problems out of a central multifaceted one is a mistake. It is precisely in the expansion of public facilities and social services that new employment opportunities can be generated, at varying skill levels. High subemployment rates and the lack of decent housing in the slums are two sides of the same coin.

Meanwhile, within the slum proletariat, youth constitutes a subdivision of increasing economic and political importance. While according to the official unemployment rates the joblessness gap between Negro and white men over twenty has been narrowing since 1961, even this official rate records a widening of the gap between Negro and white teen-agers since 1957. Right now the national Negro unemployment rate is 25 percent nationally but for 16-to-19-year-olds in the ten slum areas surveyed, it is over 38 percent! Moreover, this rate was unaffected by the downward trend of the nation's over-all unemployment rate late last year. For white teen-agers, on the other hand, unemployment since 1957 never went beyond 15 percent and is now at 10 percent.

Nor is there any evidence that Negro teen-agers do not want to work. Whenever job programs have been announced, they have turned out in large numbers, only to find that the jobs weren't there. In Oakland, a "Job Fair" attracted 15,000 people; only 250 were placed. In Philadelphia, 6,000 were on a waiting list for a training program.

What Negro teen-agers are not inclined to accept are dead-end jobs that pay little and promise no advancement or training. Many would prefer to live by their wits as hustlers or petty racketeers, their version of the self-employed businessman or salesman. That their pursuit of this distorted entrepreneurial ideal only mires them deeper in the slum proletariat is not the point. They want to be part of the white-collar organization man's world that is America's future, not trapped behind brooms and pushcarts.

Nor can they fairly be blamed by a society which has itself produced these yearnings, reveled in its affluence, encouraged the consumption of trivia and proclaimed the coming of computerized utopias. The middle classes may nostalgically extol their immigrant parents' fortitude and perseverance in manual labor, but they do not steer their own children toward the construction gang or the garment district. They show them the push buttons, not the pushcart. Might they not then show some compassionate understanding of black youngsters who dream of better things even when crippled by poor education, broken families and the disabilities bred by slum life. If it is true that a Negro boy is nobody unless he owns alligator shoes and an alpaca sweater, who created these symbols? Who whetted this appetite? Who profited from the sale of these commodities, and who advertised them? And who is victimized?

The ghetto youth who is out of school, unemployed and rejected even by the draft (as 52 percent are in Harlem) is the extreme embodiment of the bitter frustration in the slum proletariat. He is utterly propertyless, devoid of experience in the productive process and without a stake in existing social arrangements. At the same time, because he is young and not beaten down, he is irreverent, filled with bravado, hostile to the alien authority of the police and determined to "make it" in any way that he can. He is at the core of the rioting.

In Detroit, the riot begins when pimps and prostitutes taunt police who are raiding a "blind pig" at 5 A.M. In Minneapolis, two women fight over a wig, the police try to break it up and a riot erupts in an atmosphere already charged by delays in the mailing of Federal Youth Opportunity Program paychecks to youths in the ghetto area. In Cairo, Illinois, a Negro soldier dies in the city jail; police say it was suicide but order the body embalmed without an autopsy, and fire bombing and shooting follow.

In these cases, the police figure prominently in the incidents that triggered the rioting. Sometimes they are not directly involved, but rumors of police brutality flood through the ghetto. Although it may be of some interest to search for a pattern, no very profound purpose is served by concentrating on who struck the match. There are always matches lying around. We must ask why there was also a fuse and why the fuse was connected to a powder keg.

To pursue this analogy: Whether the match is struck by police misconduct or by an "extremist" exhorting his listeners to violence, the fuse is the condition of life among the black slum proletariat—hostile, frustrated and with nothing to lose. The powder keg is the social background against which the riots break out and which extends their scope. They become more than riots pure and simple, yet less than politically coherent rebellions. They are *riotous manifestations of rebellion.*

The social background is defined by the fact that the black slum proletariat is part of a larger community of oppressed and segregated citizens—the overwhelming majority of the Negro population. Were it not for this the riots could be dismissed merely as wild, inchoate sprees of looting and violence, the expressions of criminal greed, a carnival of destruction to be suppressed by police force. Such actions, detached from political policies, programs and goals—and, make no mistake about it, the riots were not on behalf of the Black Power ideology; the latter is an after-the-fact justification employed by people in search of a constituency—do not properly constitute a rebellion. But because of the social background, the riots, while not *the rebellion* of the Negro people, are charged with manifestations of rebellion.

It is because of this background that the riots can set off a chain reaction, fan out from the slum proletariat and, as Detroit showed, involve people who ordinarily would not be found looting stores. It is because of this background that snipers and the most violent elements can feel that their actions are in some sense heroic. And it is because of this background that the riots have enormous implications for the future of all Negroes.

As Martin Luther King, A. Philip Randolph, Roy Wilkins and Whitney Young pointed out in their recent statement,* the most severe and immediate damage has been to the Negro community itself. In addition to those who lost their lives, thousands lost their homes, food supplies, access to schools. There is danger of a counterreaction enlisting the most bigoted, vigilante-minded elements in the white community. Ammunition has been given to the reactionaries in an already backlash-dominated Congress. Many whites sincerely in favor of integration will be silenced out of fear and confusion. Riots do not strengthen the power of black people; they weaken it and encourage racist power.

But why, asks white America, do the Negroes riot now—not when conditions are at their worst but when they seem to be improving? Why now, after all of the civil-rights and anti-poverty legislation? There are two answers.

First, "progress" has been considerably less than is generally supposed. While the Negro has won certain important legal and Constitutional rights (voting, desegregation of public accommodations, etc.), his relative socioeconomic position has scarcely improved. There simply has not been significant, visible change in his life.

Second, if a society is interested in stability, it should either not make promises or it should keep them. Economic and social deprivation, if accepted by its victims as their lot in life, breeds passivity, even docility. The miserable yield to their fate as divinely ordained or as their own fault. And, indeed, many Negroes in earlier generations felt that way.

Today, young Negroes aren't having any. They don't share the feeling that something must be wrong with them, that they are responsible for their own exclusion from this affluent society. The civil-rights movement—in fact, the whole liberal trend beginning with John Kennedy's election—has told them otherwise.

Conservatives will undoubtedly seize the occasion for an attack on the Great Society, liberalism, the welfare state and Lyndon Johnson. But the young Negroes are right: the

---

* In a joint statement on July 26, 1967, Martin Luther King, Jr., A. Philip Randolph, Roy Wilkins and Whitney Young urged Negroes to end mob violence and denounced riots.

promises made to them were good and necessary and long, long overdue. The youth were right to believe in them. The only trouble is that they were not fulfilled. Prominent Republicans and Dixiecrats are demanding not that the promises be fulfilled, but that they be revoked.

What they and the American people absolutely must understand now is that the promises cannot be revoked. They were not made to a handful of leaders in a White House drawing room; they were made to an entire generation, one not likely to forget or to forgive. If Republican leaders Everett Dirksen and Gerald Ford, hand in glove with the die-hards of the Confederacy, continue their contemptible effort to exploit partisan political advantage, they will sow the dangerous seeds of race hate and they will discredit themselves morally in the eyes of the coming generations and of history. This is not a wise policy for a party that only yesterday reduced itself to a shambles by catering to the most backward and reactionary elements in the country.

It is ironic that in a nation which has not undertaken a massive social and economic reform since the New Deal one now hears even liberal voices asking: "Don't the causes of the riots go deeper than economics, than jobs, housing, schools? Aren't there profound moral, cultural, psychological and other factors involved—powerlessness, an identity crisis?"

Of course, but in the present context such questions smack of a trend toward mystification which, if it gains ascendancy, will paralyze public policy. Then, too, I cannot help but suspect that they are rationalizations for the yearning of some white liberals to withdraw. "Obviously," they are saying, "there seems to be nothing we can do. We're not even wanted. Why not give the ghettos over to the Black Power people?"

I have no hesitation in saying that this recommendation simply aids and abets the Congressional reactionaries, who would have no objection to letting Negroes run their own slum tenements, dilapidated schools and tax-starved communities. Isn't this in the best tradition of rugged self-help, Horatio Alger and all that? Haven't Barry Goldwater and William F. Buckley endorsed this notion of Black Power? Just so long as white people are left alone. Just so long as the total society is not forced to examine its own inner contradictions. Just so long as the federal government isn't challenged to launch radical and massive programs to rebuild our cities, end poverty, guarantee full employment at decent wages, clear out polluted air and water and provide mass transportation.

This is just the challenge posed by A. Philip Randolph's $185-

billion "Freedom Budget for all Americans"—a carefully designed, economically feasible program for the obliteration of poverty in ten years. Unless the nation is prepared to move along these lines—to rearrange its priorities, to set a timetable for achieving them and to allocate its resources accordingly—it will not be taking its own commitments seriously. Surely it cannot then turn amazedly to responsible Negro leaders, whose pleas for large-scale programs it has failed to heed, for an explanation of the consequences.

The present administration has a grave responsibility. It is very well for it to proclaim that we can have guns *and* butter, that we can pursue our course in Vietnam and still make progress at home. We do have the economic capacity for both, as the Freedom Budget itself shows. But we are not doing both. Let us stop proclaiming that we *can* do what we *don't* do and start *doing* it.

If administration actions are not to mock its own rhetoric, the President must now take the lead in mobilizing public opinion behind a new resolve to meet the crisis in our cities. He should now put before Congress a National Emergency Public Works and Reconstruction bill aimed at building housing for homeless victims of the riot-torn ghettos, repairing damaged public facilities and in the process generating maximum employment opportunities for unskilled and semiskilled workers. Such a bill should be the first step in the reconstruction of all our decaying center cities.

Admittedly, the prospects for passage of such a bill in the present Congress are dismal. Congressmen will cry out that the rioters must not be rewarded, thereby further penalizing the very victims of the riots. This, after all, is a Congress capable of defeating a meager forty-million-dollar rat-extermination program the same week it votes ten million dollars for an aquarium in the District of Columbia!

But the vindictive racial meanness that has descended upon this Congress, already dominated by the revived coalition of Republicans and Dixiecrats, must be challenged, not accommodated. The President must go directly to the people, as Harry Truman did in 1948. He must go to them, not with slogans, but with a timetable for tearing down every slum in the country.

There can be no further delay. The daydreamers and utopians are not those of us who have prepared massive Freedom Budgets and similar programs. They are the smugly "practical" and myopic Philistines in the Congress, the state legislatures and the city halls who thought they could sit it out. The very practical choice now before them and the American people is whether we shall have a conscious and authentic democratic social revolution or more tragic and futile riots that tear our nation to shreds.

THE THIRD WORLD AND THE GHETTO

By H. Rap Brown

The most revolutionary of the leaders of S.N.C.C. was H. Rap Brown, who replaced Stokely Carmichael as chairman in May, 1967. In a speech in Detroit shortly after the riots in that city during the summer of 1967, Brown set forth his views on the black liberation struggle. The speech soon became famous because of one sentence: "Violence is as American as cherry pie."

H. Rap Brown was born on October 4, 1943, in Louisiana. He was educated in an Orphanage House operated by white missionaries and at Southern High which was associated with Southern University, a Negro college in Baton Rouge, Louisiana. Brown entered Southern University in 1960 at the age of fifteen. He became active in the civil-rights movement, joined S.N.C.C. and participated in the Mississippi Summer Project. In 1965 he was chosen chairman of NAG, Nonviolent Action Group, in Washington, D. C. By the time he was elected chairman of S.N.C.C., Brown had abandoned his belief in nonviolence and often carried a gun for self-protection. He was repeatedly arrested and in July, 1967, was wounded by police bullets in Cambridge, Maryland. Accused of creating a riot in Cambridge, Brown was indicted and ordered to trial in Maryland in April, 1970. After a bomb explosion killed two of his co-workers, Brown disappeared. Although he had not yet been convicted of a crime, he was placed on the F.B.I.'s list of the most-wanted criminals.

Brown is the author of a widely praised autobiography, Die Nigger Die!

The following are excerpts from a speech Brown delivered at a dinner held by the National Guardian, *a radical weekly, in October, 1967, and are reprinted from the* National Guardian *of November 4, 1967.*

I CANNOT TALK about "The Third World and the Ghetto," for black people who comprise the ghetto *are* the Third World. You see, we make up the Third World. And we have to understand the revolution, and it is a revolution that America is about to undergo, before we can relate to the Third World internationally. . . . Black people are saying we're not talking about equality, we're talking about freedom, and we're going to be free by any means necessary. A lot of white people who can be participants of the revolution—participants of the Third World, if they would—became offended because they saw the doors being closed on liberals. Well, we don't need liberals, we need revolutionaries. We cannot afford to sit and talk about politics in the form of legality, politics in the form of the '68 elections, that does not address itself to the problems of black people. How can you choose between Johnson and Reagan? Camus raises a very good point. He says, What better way to enslave a man than to give him the vote and call him free? Black people have never been free. We're still experiencing slave revolt; and you have to understand that, if you choose to be a revolutionary. You see, the movement is not merely a black movement, it is a movement of the dispossessed of America. That includes the Puerto Ricans; that includes the Mexican-Americans; that includes the poor whites; that includes any dispossessed man. But we happen to be the vanguard of that movement because we are the most dispossessed. . . . We are not against all wars. We are against some wars. We are in favor of wars of liberation. There is no justice in this country for black people. Justice is a joke. . . . You see, the power structure in America, the man, the police force, the governors serve the ruling class in America as does General Westmoreland in Vietnam. The very same thing. So we are members of the Third World. Now you have to understand the key role of black people. The liberation of oppressed people across the world depends upon the liberation of black people in this country. . . . It is not only Lyndon Johnson—he is the most visible—but it's the ruling class of America that the fight must be fought against. You have to understand that Standard Oil or Chase Manhattan Bank is as much an enemy to oppressed people as is Lyndon Johnson. I have a bit of advice to the left. That advice is: Don't get left. Because the revolution is going to go on with or without you. The *National Guardian* is an invaluable paper to the movement, but we don't need sympathetic journalism, we need revolutionary journalism. You have to see yourself as being a part of that revolution. If you can't see yourself in the context of being John Brown then bring me the guns. . . . So your role is not in the black movement, it is not in the American Indian movement. If you're white your role is in Appalachia, your role is with the poor white people. We cannot talk about coalitions. We talk about alliances and we talk about alliances from the position of power. We will not make the same mistake that was made with the Populist movement.* Now, if you choose to align with black people it has to be from a position of power. . . . Another reason that the *National Guardian* is invaluable is that *The New York Times* is a weapon against freedom, a weapon against people, and every other journal in America that is published by the top people in America is controlled by the government and is a weapon against people.

So when you look at the black revolution, the black rebellion, when you see a brother in the streets throwing a Molotov cocktail, he's not out there for his health; he's out there for his freedom. Understand that when America raises the question of law and order, it's very easy for Johnson to raise the question of law and order, because he never talks about justice. So the question really becomes whether you choose to be an oppressor or a revolutionary. And if you choose to be an oppressor, then you are my enemy—not because you are white, but because you choose to oppress me. We are not an antiwhite movement. We are anti*anybody* who is antiblack. Johnson says every day, If Vietnam don't come 'round, Vietnam will be burnt down. I say that if America don't come 'round, America should be burned down. It's the same thing. But you have to begin to associate, you have to begin to find your identity in your own movement. I cannot go to Appalachia and talk about developing an alliance with poor whites, because racism is rampant in America. I cannot go to American Indians and talk about organizing American Indians. My role is in the black community. Once these communities are organized then we can talk about alliances and maybe coalitions. But not until then. . . . You see, the hippies are a lesson. These were people who were supposed to inherit. They are rejecting America. They say we reject your barbarism, we reject your decadence. So black people are saying the same thing. But we don't choose to use drugs. We choose to fight. Though the hippies are rejecting society, they are apolitical in the way they are going about it, and so we cannot feel a strong alliance with the hippie movement. . . . So we must choose

* The reference is to the fact that blacks who supported the Populist Party in the 1890's discovered to their dismay that white Populists were fundamentally racists and that white Populist leaders were in the forefront of the movement in the South to disfranchise Negroes.

who we are going to align with. That's what we were talking about in Chicago. That's what black people talked about at the black conference in Newark. Another thing about the movement at this point, the black movement, is that the black movement is a leaderless movement. I am not the leader of the black movement. I only speak about the temperament of the black community, and only because I have a forum, because there are people who speak about it much better than I do—people in Detroit for example. . . . No one person, no black person in America could have stopped Detroit from burning. So, while the movement is now a leaderless movement, it says it needs an ideology. That's the role of black so-called intellectuals. You must develop an ideology for that movement. If not, then we will become oppressors in the end, because we will fight the other dispossessed. So, therefore, the role of revolutionaries is to make revolution. . . . So when you talk about a third world, you have to understand the role that you play in the third world. You have to understand that you are not to be a missionary. We don't need missionaries, we don't need "images" in the revolution, we need revolutionaries. If you can't give a gun, then give a dollar to somebody who can buy a gun. See, you sit out there and you pretend violence scares you, but you watch TV every night and you can't turn it on for five minutes without seeing somebody shot to death or karate-ed to death. Violence is part of your culture. . . . There's no doubt about it. You gave us violence and this is the only value that black people can use to their advantage to end oppression. . . .

THE PRESENT DILEMMA OF THE NEGRO

By Kenneth B. Clark

With the rising influence of the Black Muslim movement and the growing demand for "Black Power," interest in integration declined among black militants, and separatism became increasingly popular. Dr. Kenneth B. Clark, professor of psychology at the City College of New York and author of the seminal study, Dark Ghetto, *critically analyzed the separatist tendencies among black militants in an address to the Second Carter G. Woodson Memorial Luncheon, 52nd Annual Meeting of the Association for the Study of Negro Life and History, October 14, 1967, at Greensboro, North Carolina. Below is the major portion of the address.*

Dr. Clark was born July 14, 1914, in the Canal Zone, Panama, where his father was an employee of the United Fruit Company. His mother moved back to New York with Kenneth when he was five years old. After graduation from George Washington High School, he attended Howard University, earning a bachelor's degree and a master's and then went to Columbia University for a Ph.D. in psychology in 1940. Dr. Clark joined the faculty of City College in 1940, spent a year during World War II with the Office of War Information, and then returned to the college, becoming in 1960 the first black to receive a permanent appointment as professor at the college—the post he still holds. In 1946, Dr. Clark and his wife founded the Northside Center for Child Development, at first for black children alone, but since 1949 for both black and white. In 1954, when the Supreme Court ruled against school segregation, part of that decision was based on Dr. Clark's studies showing that racial segregation in the schools caused psychological damage to children.

Dr. Clark's Woodson Memorial speech is reprinted from The Journal of Negro History, Vol. LIII, No. 1 (January, 1968), pp. 1–11.

THE "nuclear" irony of American history and the American social, political and economic system is that the destiny of the enslaved and disadvantaged Negro determines the destiny of the nation. The fundamental fact around which all questions of national survival pivot is the fact of inherent racial interrelatedness—or integration, if you please—in spite of the persistent demands and attempts to impose racial separatism. The problems of the American Negro are problems of America. The conflicts, aspirations, confusions and doubts of Negro Americans are not merely similar but are identical to those of white Americans. The Negro need not yearn to be assimilated into American culture—he is and determines American culture. In the face of rapid and at times frightening historical, economic, political, technological, social and intellectual changes, the Negro remains the constant, and at times irritating reality that is America. He remains the essential psychological reality with which America must continuously seek to come to terms—and in so doing is formed by.

The moral and ethical aspirations of America have been accepted totally by Negroes. The moral schizophrenia of America is reflected most clearly in the status of Negroes, starting with slavery and continuing to the contemporary ghettos which blight the powerful and affluent cities of our nation. The dilemmas of America are the dilemmas of Negro Americans. One cannot, therefore, discuss the dilemmas of the contemporary American Negro without at the same time becoming involved in an analysis of the historical and psychological fabric of American life. This is the thesis reflecting the bias of a social psychologist—a bias which might be rejected by more sophisticated historians, political and economic theorists, or tougher-minded social critics. I nonetheless base my thesis on the psychological premise that the values, attitudes and behavior of individual human beings and groups of human beings are determined by the complex socialization process—that normal human beings are modifiable and are determined by their environment and culture—and not by any inherent genetic or racial determinants.

Let us now be specific:

A basic dilemma of America is whether the Negro should be accepted and taken seriously as a human being and permitted the rights and privileges accorded other human beings in our political system. America has endured slave rebellions, developed an underground railroad, fought one of the most bloody wars in human history and is now undergoing a series of urban ghetto implosions in the attempt to resolve this persistent bedeviling question.

The Negro's form of this basic dilemma is whether to persist in his insistence upon his unqualified rights as a human being without regard to the risks or consequences—or whether to accommodate to the resistances by subtle or flagrant forms of withdrawal from the fray. The general acceptance of slavery, the many psychological adjustments and deflection of aggressive reactions to subjugation, the varieties of back-to-Africa movements, the cults, fads, and the recent series of riots in our ghettos are among the many ways in which American Negroes have sought to deal with this basic American dilemma.

The gnawing doubts of white Americans as to their status and worth as human beings—the deep feelings of inferiority coming out of the actual inferior status in the land of their origin in Europe—impelled American whites to develop and enforce social and institutional arrangements designed to inflict upon Negroes an inferior status in American life. This was necessary to bolster the demanding status needs of whites. These needs were powerful enough to counteract the logic, the morality and the powerful political ethics of the egalitarian and democratic rhetoric which is also an important American reality. I differ with early Myrdal only in my belief that the American democratic creed and ideals are not psychologically contradictory to American racism. In terms of dynamics and motivation of the insecure, they are compatible.

This critical American dilemma is reflected in Negroes not only in terms of acceptance of the creeds and its promises literally, but also in terms of deep doubts concerning the worth of self. The former aspect of the dilemma stems from the fact of general indoctrination which transcends even the barriers of racially segregated schools and is reinforced by the development of the mass media in the twentieth century. The latter component of the Negro's dilemma arises out of the reality of the inferior status to which he has been subjugated. The walls of segregation are not only humiliating, but, given this type of chronic humiliation, there develops self-doubt, subtle and flagrant forms of self-hatred, personal and group frustrations, internalized hostility, aggressions, self-denial or bombast. Under these conditions the walls of segregation become pathetically protective. Within them the subjugated individuals need not meet the tests of free and open competition—need not expose vulnerable egos to single standards of competence.

The anguish and resistance of anxious, self-doubting white segregationists and the cautious timidity of striving middle-class whites with the psyche of affluent peasants are matched only by the anxieties, doubts and vacillation of vast numbers of Negroes—working and middle class—as they stand at the threshold of nonsegregated society and are confronted by the tremendous psychological challenges for which American history not only did not prepare them but erected seemingly insurmountable barriers. The demand for racial justice on the part of American Negroes is balanced by an almost equal psychological reality of the fear of the removal of racial barriers.

Within this context—disturbing and painful but, I believe, psychologically valid—one can now attempt an analysis of the contemporary manifestations of the dilemma of America and the dilemma of Negro Americans. The value of such an analysis will be determined by whether it provides a basis for constructive, realistic, democratic and humane resolutions of some of the racial and social problems which afflict America and threaten its survival.

In many disturbing ways the problems of race relations in America today are similar to those of the post-Reconstruction period of the late nineteenth century which continued and intensified through World War I. This period, which Rayford Logan and John Hope Franklin have described as the "nadir" of the Negro in American life,* came as a seemingly abrupt and certainly cruel repudiation of the promises of Reconstruction for inclusion of the Negro into the political and economic life of the nation. This was a period:

—when the white crusaders for racial justice and democracy became weary as the newly freed Negroes could no longer be considered a purely Southern problem;

—when the aspirations for and movement of Negroes toward justice and equality were curtailed and reversed by organized violence and barbarity perpetrated against them;

—when, as a result of their abandonment and powerlessness, the frustrations, bitterness and despair of Negroes increased and displaced optimism and hope.

This period culminated in the institutionalization of rigid forms of racism—the enactment and enforcement of laws requiring or permitting racial discrimination and segregation in all aspects of American life. This retrogression in racial democracy in America was imposed by white segregationists with the apathy, indifference, or quiet acceptance of white liberals and moderates as necessary accessories.

The parallel with the state of race relations in America today is stark and frightening. The promises and optimism of the Second Reconstruction, initiated by the pattern of litigation which resulted in the Brown decision of 1954—which precipitated the high morale mark of the successful boycotts and sit-ins, and which reached its climax in the emotional catharsis of the 1963 March on Washington—were also cruelly aborted by stepped-up violence against Negro and white civil-rights workers in the resistant Southern states and the related weariness, racial anxieties and latent racism of Northern whites which emerged under the guise of "white backlash."

The hopes and beliefs of the Negro that racial equality and democracy could be obtained through litigation, legislation, executive action and negotiation, and through strong alliances with various white liberal groups, were supplanted by disillusionment, bitterness and anger which erupted under the anguished cry of "Black Power" which pathetically sought to disguise the understandable desperation and impotence with bombast and rhetoric.

* Dr. Rayford W. Logan, Professor of History, Howard University, was the first to apply the term *nadir* to this period, in his book *The Negro in American Life and Thought, The Nadir 1877–1901*, New York, 1954.

A critical danger—and probably a difference without a pragmatic distinction—between the determinants of retrogression in the first post-Reconstruction period and the present is that whereas the promises of racial progress were reversed in the nineteenth century by the fanaticism, irrationality and cruel strength of white segregationists, the impending racial retrogression of today might come about largely through self-hatred leading to the fanaticism, dogmatism, rigidity and self-destructive cruelty of black separatists. If this comes about, it will not be enough to excuse this monstrous perpetuation of the lie of racism and postponement of the goals of democracy and humanity by asserting that the frustrations and bitterness of the victimized Negro account for his present irrationality and rigidity. A similar and equally valid psychological explanation could be offered to explain the racial cruelties of desperate and miserable poor whites of the past and present. Understanding is not acceptance.

White segregationists were able to inflict and perpetuate racial injustices upon Negroes, because rational, sophisticated and moderate whites were silent in the face of barbarities. They permitted themselves to be intimidated and bullied by white extremists until they were morally and almost functionally indistinguishable from their worst and most ignorant elements. A similar threat and dilemma face the rational, thoughtful Negro today. If he permits himself to be cowed into silence by unrealistic Negro racists, he will be an active partner in fastening the yoke of impossible racial separatism more tightly around the neck of America. He—you, through your silence, will permit the difficult goals of a racially nonsegregated society to be lost by default. You would have given to black racists what you, your fathers and grandfathers fought and died to prevent giving to white racists. The victories which white segregationists, in spite of all their material and political power, could not have won for themselves, black separatists would have won for them; and we through our silence would make this possible.

To prevent the repetition of the tragedy of racial retrogression and a return to the "nadir" of race relations in America, we must be realistic in our appraisal of the present state of race relations in America. . . . We must analyze as tough-mindedly as possible the dynamics and symptoms of our times if we are to develop effective and realistic remedies.

During the past few years it became excruciatingly clear for the Negro that the more things changed the more they remained the same—or worsened. The promises and hope for progress became a relentless quagmire of words.

The drama of direct action, nonviolent confrontation of the more obvious signs of Southern racial injustice became trite, and was not particularly relevant or effective in dealing with the persistent, pervasive and subtle problems of racism which afflicted the Northern Negro. More appropriate and effective methods have not yet been found to deal with Northern racism.

The guilt and indignation of some Northern whites against Southern forms of racism turned into white backlash or mutism when the Northern Negro began to take seriously the claims of civil-rights progress and sought some observable signs of them in Northern cities.

The anguish and desperation of the Northern Negro have been expressed in the latest series of ghetto eruptions which started in the Harlem riot of the summer of 1964,* reached a crescendo in the Watts riot of 1965 and continued through the current series of riots in Newark and Detroit of this past summer.† Another significant expression of the Northern Negro's "no-win" fatalism is found in the rise of the "Black Power" slogan and momentum which skyrocketed at the time of the Meredith shooting in Mississippi in June of 1966,‡ and continues as an obbligato to the sounds of ghetto violence and futility.

It is important to keep in mind the date (June, 1966) when the "Black Power" slogan became nationally advertised—in order not to be confused about the cause-and-effect relationship between "Black Power" and "white backlash."

Whatever may be its tactical, strategic and rational shortcomings and its ambiguity, "Black Power" did not cause "white backlash.". . . The existence of "white backlash," the unwilling-

* The Harlem Riot began on July 18, 1964, and lasted over the weekend. The riot followed the slaying of a fifteen-year-old Negro schoolboy by a white policeman.
† The Newark Riot began on July 12, 1967, after a Negro cab driver was reported to have been beaten by police. By the time the riot ended on July 17, twenty-three persons were killed, twenty-one of them Negroes.
The Detroit Riot began on July 22, 1967, after police had raided a Negro private social club. It lasted until July 27. Thirty-three Negroes and ten whites were killed.
‡ James Meredith was the first Negro to be admitted to the University of Mississippi. He entered in 1962 under the protection of federal marshals and the Mississippi National Guard. In June, 1966, he began a lone march through Mississippi to dramatize the lack of freedom for his people. He was shot during the march, but recovered and continued, this time joined by many black and white sympathizers. It was during this march that Stokely Carmichael first introduced the slogan "Black Power."

ness of whites to be serious in meeting the demands of Negroes for the same rights and responsibilities granted as a matter of course to all other Americans—including the newest refugee from European, Latin American, or Asiatic oppression—caused the outbursts of hysterical bitterness and random hostility inherent in the cry of "Black Power."

"Black Power" emerged as a response to the following facts:

—a recognition of the fact that the center of gravity of the civil-rights movement had moved to the Northern urban racial ghettos, where it was now immobilized by ambiguous intensified white resistance to any meaningful change in the predicament of Negroes;

—the recognition of the fact that successful litigation, strong legislation, free access to public accommodations, open housing laws, strong pronouncements on the part of the President, governors or mayors, and even the right to vote or to hold office were not relevant to the overriding fact that the masses of Negroes were still confined to poverty and to the dehumanizing conditions of the ghetto;

—and that in spite of the promises of a Great Society and the activity of the war on poverty, the Negro's children were still doomed to criminally inferior schools and his youth and males the victims of unemployment, underemployment and stagnation.

"Black Power" is the cry of defiance of what its advocates have come to see as the hoax of racial progress—of the cynicism of the appeals to the Negro to be patient and to be lawful as his needs are continually subordinated to more important national and international issues and to the needs, desires and conveniences of more privileged groups.

Whites, by virtue of their numerical, military and economic superiority, reinforced by historical American racism which grants higher status to whites by virtue of skin color alone, do have the power to decide whether the future of Negroes—the Negro masses, the Negro middle class, or the Negro elected official—will be positive, negative or stagnant.

This core reality of the dynamics of power is not likely to be influenced by sentimental and idealistic appeals for justice, by smiles or promises or by emotional sloganeering.

"Black Power," in spite of its ambiguity, its "no-win" premise, its programmatic emptiness and its pragmatic futility, does have tremendous psychological appeal for the masses of Negroes who have "nothing to lose" and some middle-class Negroes who are revolted by the empty promises and the moral dry-rot of affluent America.

"Black Power" is a bitter retreat from the possibility of the attainment of the goals of any serious racial integration in America. . . .

It is an attempt to make a verbal virtue of involuntary racial segregation. . . .

It is the sour-grapes phenomenon on the American racial scene. . . .

"Black Power" is the contemporary form of the Booker T. Washington accommodation to white America's resistance to making democracy real for Negro Americans. While Booker T. made his adjustment to and acceptance of white racism under the guise of conservatism, many if not all of the "Black Power" advocates are seeking to sell the same shoddy moral product disguised in the gaudy package of racial militance.

Nonetheless, today "Black Power" is a reality in the Negro ghettos of America, increasing in emotional intensity, if not in rational clarity. And we, if we are to be realistic, cannot afford to pretend that it does not exist. Even in its most irrational and illusory formulations—and particularly when it is presented as a vague and incoherent basis upon which the deprived Negro can project his own pathetic wishes for a pride and an assertiveness which white America continues mockingly or piously to deny him—"Black Power" is a powerful political reality, which cannot be ignored by realistic Negro or white political officials.

It is all too clear that among the casualties of the present phase of American race relations are reason, clarity, consistency and realism. Some "Black Power" spokesmen, like their white segregationist counterparts, demand the subjugation of rational and realistic thought and planning to dogmatism and fanaticism. By their threats and name calling, they seek to intimidate others into silence or a mindless mouthing of their slogans.

To be effective and to increase his chances of survival in the face of name-calling verbal racial militants, the trained Negro must demonstrate that he is concerned and can bring about some positive changes in the following intolerable areas of ghetto life:

1. criminally inefficient and racially segregated public schools;
2. dehumanizingly poor housing;
3. pervasive job discrimination and joblessness;
4. shoddy quality of goods and high prices in local stores;
5. the dirt, filth and stultifying drabness of ghetto streets and neighborhoods;
6. the adversary relationship between police and the residents of the ghettos.

This requires the mobilization and use of human intelligence to define the problems, to study and analyze them and to develop practical and implementable solutions to them. This cannot be done on the basis of race; whites and Negroes must join together in an experiment to determine whether systematic and empathic use of human intelligence and training can be a form of power which can be used constructively in the quest for solutions of long-standing urban and racial problems. This is the rationale of The Metropolitan Applied Research Center.* We are under no illusions that this will be easy. . . . We know that power confrontation brings risks not found in the cloistered halls of academia. We know that we cannot expect the protections and safety of the detached isolated scholars. But we believe that human intelligence is a social thrust and that the stakes are worth the risks.

Another dilemma, not related to the dilemmas and inconsistencies of "Black Power," is the fact that in the present doldrums of the civil-rights movement the cleavage between the masses of Negroes and the middle class has become more clear and exacerbating. The masses of Negroes are now starkly aware of the fact that recent civil-rights victories benefited primarily a very small percentage of middle-class Negroes, while their predicament remained the same or worsened. Added to Ralph Bunche and our traditional civil-rights leaders who are invited to Washington, we now have Thurgood Marshall, Robert Weaver, Walter Washington as the appointed mayor of Washington, D. C., a few vice-presidents in private industry, a few more Negroes in New England prep schools and Ivy League colleges, and more white colleges and universities are looking for one or two "qualified Negroes" for their faculties. These and other tokens of "racial progress" are not only rejected by the masses of Negroes but seem to have resulted in their increased and more openly expressed hostility toward middle-class Negroes. They see the advances of the middle-class Negroes as being at their expense, at worst, or obscuring their plight or, at best, not being in any way relevant to their being condemned indefinitely to their dehumanizing predicament. There are some clues which suggest that the recent ghetto implosions were not only antiwhite, but also involved vague stirrings of anti-Negro middle-class sentiment among the rioters.

The present dilemma of the Negro is focused for the trained

* The Metropolitan Applied Research Center was organized in New York City on March 8, 1967, "to influence social and political decisions by government officials and agencies in behalf of the urban poor." Dr. Clark was chosen president of the Center.

Negro intellectual. He must now choose sides. He must now clarify the nature of the enemy. He must dare to say that the enemy was never to be understood in terms of color . . . but in the more difficult and abstract terms of human irrationality, ignorance, superstition, rigidity and arbitrary cruelty.

These are the common enemies which underlie all forms of tyranny—racism, authoritarianism, McCarthyism. . . .

They are no less enemies when being sold or offered as truth or salvation by blacks, yellows or whites. . . .

If Negroes and whites who understand this can make it clear, we can help to save America. We will use the power of disciplined intelligence combined with respect for moral values and humanity to save Negroes from the destructive possibilities of white and black dilemmas and thereby contribute to the survival of America. . . . For America cannot survive if Negroes do not. . . . And no Negroes and no other group of human beings are likely to survive if America does not.

REVOLUTION IN THE WHITE MOTHER COUNTRY AND NATIONAL LIBERATION IN THE BLACK COLONY

By Eldridge Cleaver

Elridge Cleaver was born in Wabaseka, Arkansas, in 1935, to Leroy and Thelma Cleaver, his father a pianist, his mother a grade-school teacher. When Leroy Cleaver became a waiter on the Super Chief, the family moved to Phoenix and then on to Los Angeles. By the time Eldridge was enrolled in Abraham Lincoln Junior High School, his parents had separated, and he was arrested for stealing a bicycle and shipped off to the Fred C. Nelles School for Boys, where he learned about hustling pot. It was for this crime that he was sent to the Preston School of Industry in 1953 and then to Soledad. His secondary education, begun at Belmont High School, was completed in prison. During eleven months of freedom, he set about raping white women, was apprehended, and sentenced to 2-to-14 years in prison for assault with intent to kill.

At first a member of the Black Muslims, Cleaver broke
with the movement after the assassination of Malcolm X.
In 1967 he joined the Black Panther Party for Self-Defense.
The party was organized in October, 1966, in Oakland,
California, by two black militants, Bobby Seale and Huey
Newton, with Seale as chairman and Newton as minister
of defense. The Black Panther party emphasized self-
defense for the black community against indiscriminate
police violence. In the summer of 1968, the California
Peace and Freedom party designated Eldridge Cleaver,
now the Black Panther minister of information, as its
Presidential candidate. Cleaver's best-selling Soul on Ice,
written in prison, made him the Black Panther's most
widely known member.

Nationwide harassment of Black Panthers by the police
and F.B.I. caused the death of a number of leading Panthers and the imprisonment of scores of others. It also
forced Eldridge Cleaver into exile. About to be returned to
jail on a charge of probation violation, Cleaver vowed he
would never go back behind bars, and disappeared from
sight. After living for several months in Cuba, he went to
Algeria, and there in 1971 he broke with the leadership of
the Black Panther Party in the United States and formed
a separate unit of the Black Panthers.

The following is an address Cleaver delivered at the
Peace and Freedom Founding Convention, Richmond, California, March 16, 1968. It is reprinted from a pamphlet
by the Black Panther Party for Self-Defense, N.D., Oakland, California.

THE BLACK PANTHER PARTY believes that the era in
which we now struggle can be characterized as the Age of the
Showdown—between oppressed people everywhere and the racist imperialist power structure. This era can be further defined
as that in which significant sectors of the exploiting population
have turned away from the system, have declared war upon the
system that has warped their lives and tainted their existence at
the same time that it was doing the same thing and worse to
those whom it oppresses. We recognize these alienated people
as allies or potential allies in a struggle against a common enemy.

We start with the basic definition—that black people in America are a colonized people in every sense of the term and that
white America is an organized imperialist force holding black
people in colonial bondage. From this definition our task becomes clearer: what we need is a revolution in the white mother

country and national liberation for the black colony. To achieve these ends we believe that political and military machinery that does not exist now and has never existed must be created. We need functional machinery that is able to deal with these two interrelated sets of political dynamics which, strictly speaking, make up the total political situation on the North American continent. Ideally, we need a revolutionary organization that is able, guided by a revolutionary ideology and comprehending the necessity involved, to move in two directions at the same time. We are here tonight because we believe that the Peace and Freedom Party is the beginning of the answer to one half of this equation and that the Black Panther party is the beginning of the answer to the other half. We do not delude ourselves with the notion that we have found or that we represent or that anybody else has found or represents any final solutions to age-old problems, but we do feel that the Peace and Freedom Party and the Black Panther Party have made a significant breakthrough and have indisputably upped the ante.

THE COALITION

The Black Panther Party and the Peace and Freedom Party in the Bay Area have been experimenting over the past few months with a very narrow coalition around a very broad subject. The focal point of the coalition is now, and has always been, the case of Huey P. Newton, Minister of Defense, Creator and Leader of the Black Panther Party.* Although the coalition has been narrow and limited, tentative and viewed with mutual suspicion, it has in fact unleashed political forces with explosive local impact and national implications. It is a fact that in a very short time these infant political facts have become forces with which the old, established forces must contend. We must recall that the Peace and Freedom Party has been on the ballot only a couple of months, it is less than a year old, and is still wearing the diaper of its liberal democratic parentage. The Black Panther Party is less than two years old and the coalition of which we speak is less than five months old. For newborn children, we are already doing a man-size job. This is a source of great optimism and enthusiasm for us, because if in our infancy we are able to do a man-size job, we can dream that when we grow to

---

* Huey P. Newton was involved in a shoot-out with police on October 28, 1967, during which he was wounded. He was charged with murder and kidnaping, and one of the demands of the Peace and Freedom Party was "Free Huey." Newton was sentenced to two to fifteen years in jail, but on May 29, 1970, the California Court of Appeals reversed the conviction.

maturity we can do the giant-size work that history has cut out for us.

The coalition between our two fraternal parties is based upon Carmichael's dictum of specific coalitions for specific purposes.* We think that this dictum is functional and proper and that it provides a basis for unlimited action with no strings attached. On the basis of this dictum, we think that ultimately we can develop a specific coalition for the specific purpose of destroying capitalistic exploitation and racism. We have freedom to move as far and with such speed as our understanding and imagination and commitment will allow us. We believe that cooperation between revolutionary forces in the mother country and their counterpart in the black colony is absolutely and unequivocally desirable and necessary. We believe that it is suicidal and nonsensical for such potential allies to remain aloof and isolated from each other any longer. All that is needed is for those who fulfill the vanguard function to supply the form of this cooperation. We believe that henceforth the form of cooperation between revolutionary forces in the mother country and those in the colony must be on a coalition basis. We believe that all black colonial subjects should be members of the Black Panther Party, and that all American citizens should be members of the Peace and Freedom Party. We invite other oppressed and colonized people in America to organize themselves and to join our coalition as equal partners. We feel that it is a political mistake of the first order to try and develop a multinational, all-inclusive political party at this time; to do so would only compound existing confusion and erect new obstacles to the real work that can and must be done.

THE DUAL STATUS OF BLACK PEOPLE IN BABYLON

Black people in North America have always been plagued by a dual status. We were both slave and Christian, we were both free and segregated, we are both integrated and colonized. In the past this duality has worked to our disadvantage. It kept us running around in circles. Today we propose to turn it to our advantage, in the manner that we have turned our blackness from a disadvantage into a rallying point of advantage. Yesterday we were black and oppressed; today our blackness is a tool

* However, during the summer of 1969, Stokeley Carmichael announced from Africa that he had resigned from the Black Panthers because of their work with white radicals. Carmichael asserted that the only path to liberation lay in effecting a united front of black people in Africa and in the United States.

for our liberation. Our dual status gives us a mythical right of citizenship and the concrete reality of our situation has given us the national consciousness of an oppressed and colonized people. We intend to use them both wisely. The citizenship that we have on paper we will use through the mechanism of our coalition with the Peace and Freedom Party. We will use our papier-mâché right to vote to help strengthen the Peace and Freedom Party and to help it attain its objectives within the framework of political realities in the mother country. Our major emphasis, or direction, and our perspective, however, are inward—into the black heart of the colony. Our goal is to organize black people for national liberation. In this, our primary task, political reality in the white mother country can only have peripheral and supportive importance. The duality of our status dictates the duality of our strategy.

THE BLACK PLEBISCITE

As our major political objective, the Black Panther Party is calling for a black plebiscite, a United Nations-supervised plebiscite to be held throughout the black colony, in which only colonial subjects will be allowed to participate. The plebiscite is for the purpose of determining the will of black people as to their national destiny. In the past many people and organizations have stated what they believed the will of black people to be. The Black Panther Party believes that it is the right of black people to state for themselves the destiny that they desire. We feel that the burning question to which only such a plebiscite can supply the answer is: Whether the black people want to be integrated into Babylon, or whether they want to be separated into a sovereign nation of their own, with full status and rights with the other nations of the world, including U.N. membership and diplomatic recognition by the other nations of the world. Through our Minister of Foreign Affairs, James Forman, we have conducted a preliminary poll of certain key members of the U.N. and have learned to our utter satisfaction but not to our surprise, that they are receptive to the idea of the black plebiscite. In our perspective on our struggle for liberation, the black plebiscite would play a key function. In the colonial analogy, it would correspond to the role of the first or the key political campaign that happened in all countries emerging from colonial bondage. In Guinea the political focus was provided by the campaign against De Gaulle's Constitution. In Ghana it was the national election that placed Kwame Nkrumah at the head of the government. The campaign leading to the plebiscite would be the means of solidly organizing Afro-America along national lines. Committees organized by people on both sides of the national question will spring up throughout the black colony. The issue will be hotly debated, and people will be organized around the issues involved. The entire political fabric of the mother country would be thrown into a crisis. The argument of those who oppose black national independence would be that blacks do not need it because they are citizens of white America. Our argument would be simply to point out the facts, the reality of the black man's status in white America. Here our coalition with the Peace and Freedom Party will become functional, because the members of the Peace and Freedom Party whom we will have strategically helped to elect could argue for our position within the Senate and House of Representatives, the state legislatures, and the city councils.

For those who view the land question, that is, the absence of geographical boundaries of our dispersed colony, as an insuperable obstacle to nationhood, we say that we will hold the land question in abeyance. We follow the dictum of Osagyefo Kwame Nkrumah, "Seek ye first the political kingdom, and all other things shall be added unto you." What the black man in Babylon needs is organized black power, and with that political power he can carve out his place in the sun—and it won't be on a reservation or in the gas chambers, as certain madmen propose and certain other panic-stricken people fear.

ELECTORAL POLITICS

We have offered our leader, Minister of Defense Huey P. Newton, as a candidate for the Seventh Congressional District of Alameda County and we have offered our Chairman, Bobby Seale, as a candidate for the 17th Assembly District. In San Francisco, we have offered our Communications Secretary, Kathleen Cleaver, for a candidate in the 18th Assembly District. The advantages in doing this are manifold. First and foremost, we are interested in setting Huey P. Newton free. By running Huey P. Newton for Congress we are uniting the revolutionary political arena with the conventional political arena, and thereby obliterating the distinction between the two. We are able to focus attention in all our campaigns on a revolutionary leader with a revolutionary program within the conventional political context. In oversophisticated and decadent "revolutionary" circles, this is called "heightening the consciousness of the masses." In practical terms, this kind of campaign becomes another tool for political organization for black power. Our purpose in entering the political arena is to send the jackass back to the farm and the elephant back to the zoo. We want to put the Establishment up tight. We want to put the black lackeys and bootlickers of the Demo/Republican party out of business; some of them will be sent back to the farm, and others can also go to the zoo with the elephants. We want to pull people out of the Democratic party, out of the Republican party, and swell the ranks of the Black Panther Party and the Peace and Freedom Party on the basis outlined above.

PROGRAM OF THE PANTHERS

1. We believe that every human being on the face of the planet Earth has a right to live. Therefore, when it is necessary to work to live, every human being has a right to work in order that he may eat and provide himself with basic necessities. If he is physically incapable of work, then society has an obligation to support him for life, or for as long as his disability remains. We demand for every human being the highest standard of living that the present-day level of technological development is capable of providing. This encompasses the traditional demand for decent housing, decent clothing, decent food and decent schooling.

2. Withdraw the troops—replace the occupying army of the police with a public force of black men who live in the community to maintain order and harmony; also, station U.N. observers in the black colony to observe and halt the police-gestapo actions against black people—prevent genocide and racist extermination violating not only the U.N. Charter of Human Rights but the lives and right to life and peace of black people.

3. Ten Point Program—Ten Point Platform—Ten Point Organizational Structure (10–10–10).*

* The 10-point program adopted by the Black Panther Party on October, 1966, presented the following objectives: (1) We want freedom; we want the power to determine the destiny of our Black Community; (2) We want full employment for our people; (3) We want an end to the robbery of our Black Community by the white man; (4) We want decent housing, fit for shelter of human beings; (5) We want for our people education that exposes the true nature of this decadent American society . . . that teaches us our true history and our role in the present-day society; (6) We want all black men to be exempt from military service; (7) We want an immediate end to *police brutality* and *murder* of black people; (8) We want freedom for all black men held in federal, state, county and city prisons and jails; (9) We want all black people when brought to trial to be tried in court by a jury of their peer group or people from their black communities, as defined by the Constitution of the

OUR SPECIFIC PROPOSALS

We propose that:

1. The Peace and Freedom Party run our proposed candidates;
2. The Peace and Freedom Party support our call for the black plebiscite;
3. The Peace and Freedom Party support our call for U.N. observers to be stationed in the major cities or in areas of concentrated black population to halt the *aggression* and the provocative tactics of the racist pig gestapo police who occupy our colony as foreign troops occupying conquered territory;
4. The Peace and Freedom Party join with the Black Panther Party and the Stop the Draft Week organizers and participate in the Stop the Draft Week demonstrations in April to focus attention and to supply pressure on the demands that the troops of the power structure be withdrawn from Vietnam and from the black colony, *and from the black colony,* AND FROM THE BLACK COLONY;
5. The Peace and Freedom Party support the Black Community's demand that those who police the black communities must live in the black communities.

I SEE THE PROMISED LAND

By *Martin Luther King, Jr.*

In the early spring of 1968, Dr. King was organizing a march of the poor—black and white—on Washington to "dramatize the whole economic problem of the poor. . . . We need an Economic Bill of Rights so as to guarantee a job to all people who want to work and are able to work and guarantee an income for all who are not able to work." He came to Memphis, Tennessee, interrupting his work for the March of the Poor, to support the strike of 1,300 black sanitation men.

On April 4, 1968, Martin Luther King, Jr., was assassi-

United States; (10) We want land, bread, housing, education, clothing, justice and peace. And as our major political objective, a United Nations–supervised plebiscite to be held throughout the black colony in which only black colonial subjects will be allowed to participate, for the purpose of determining the will of black people as to their national destiny.

*nated as he stood on the balcony of a motel in Memphis.
After Dr. King's assassination, his co-worker, the Reverend
Ralph Abernathy, continued the movement for a poor people's march, and in June, 1968, poor black and white
marchers established "Resurrection City" in the nation's
capital. On June 24, Resurrection City was torn down by
the National Guard and hundreds were arrested, among
them the Reverend Ralph Abernathy.*

*The night before his assassination, Dr. King told an au-
dience that he had "seen the promised land" of victory in
his fight for equality and justice, but "I may not go with
you." Here are excerpts from his last speech, taken from
the* Sacramento Observer, *April 11, 1968, memorial issue
in honor of Martin Luther King, Jr.*

. . . I DON'T KNOW what will happen now. We have got
difficult days ahead, but it doesn't matter with me, because I've
been to the mountain top. Like anyone else, I would like to live a
long life. But I'm not concerned with that. I just want to do
God's will, and He has allowed me to go up the mountain.

I see the Promised Land. I may not get there with you, but I
want you to know tonight that we as a people will get to the
Promised Land. I am happy tonight that I am not worried about
anything. I'm not fearing any man. Mine eyes have seen the
glory of the coming of the Lord.

You all know the story of Rip Van Winkle. . . . Everyone
remembers that Winkle slept for twenty years. But what is important is that when he went up on that mountain to sleep
there was a picture of King George hanging in the town. When
he came down, there was a picture of George Washington in its
place.

Rip Van Winkle slept through a revolution, but we cannot
afford to remain asleep. . . .

Our world is as a neighborhood. We must all learn to live together as brothers or we will all perish as fools. . . .

There are two challenges to America. The challenges are
racism and poverty. In a few weeks a few of us are coming to
Washington to see if the will to meet these challenges still lives
among us. We are going to bring those who have known long
years of hurt and neglect. We're not coming to engage in any
historic action. We are not coming to tear up Washington. We
are coming to engage in dramatic, nonviolent action.

We are coming, and we will stay as long as we have to. . . .

We will suffer and die if we have to. For I submit, nothing
will be done until people put their bodies and souls into this.

WHICH IS THE PATH OF CHANGE?

By Richard Gordon Hatcher

*In an address before a gathering for the N.A.A.C.P. Legal
Defense Fund, in May, 1968, Mayor Richard Gordon
Hatcher of Gary, Indiana, assessed what he termed the
"forces for change" in United States society: the black and
white liberals; the Black Power advocates; and the white
radicals. Hatcher was elected mayor of Gary in the spring
of 1968, the first Negro to occupy that office and one of the
first two Negro mayors of any major United States city. In
his speech he offered a keen and valuable evaluation of the
significance of his election. Here is a major portion of the
address, reprinted from* The Worker, *June 9, 1968, by permission of Richard Gordon Hatcher.*

MORE THAN three decades ago, several thousand hungry,
poorly clad veterans of World War I, walked, rode freight cars
and battered jalopies, and converged on our nation's capital.
They came to bring into visual focus the suffering and agony of
the millions of America's poor.* That march set in motion the
forces out of which industrial unions grew, the "New Deal"
swept into power and social security became law. The power of
the people had pushed the Establishment to save itself by meeting the immediate, surface needs of the people.

"The Establishment" has never initiated change. It only responds to the explosive forces gathering underneath it, and if
it moves at all, like the lid on a kettle of boiling water, it jiggles
to avoid an explosion.

I would like to analyze . . . three broad groupings which
profess an interest in change. For ease of reference, they are
the black and white liberals; the Black Power advocates; and
the white radicals. By black and white liberals, I mean all those
who believe that it is possible, by some modification of the
existing social system, to achieve an end to racism and poverty.
The advocates of Black Power are those who believe that only by
a drastic change in present black–white relationships can blacks
be liberated. White radicals, the third group, believe that not

---

* In the spring of 1932, fifteen to twenty thousand unemployed veterans
of World War I marched on Washington, D. C., to demand a bonus.
They were dispersed without their bonus by the U. S. Army under
President Hoover's order.

only must black–white power relationships be changed, but the entire society must be reorganized.

Each of these groups has exhibited some strength and some weakness in their efforts to achieve a better community. I propose to review these strengths and weakness now, so that we may, on the basis of such analysis, understand how we can effectuate change.

First, then, the liberals. Who are they? Let us name them. They are the N.A.A.C.P. and the A.D.A. [Americans for Democratic Action], they are the *New Republic* and *The Crisis*, the A.C.L.U. [American Civil Liberties Union], and the Urban League. They are that segment of trade-union leadership which has retained some degree of decency and a memory of its own origins. They are the New Dealers who have not been absorbed by the Great Society. They are men and women to whom we all owe some debt, for they have been trying.

During the dark and dismal late forties and early fifties this coalition of liberals was most notable for the humanistic thrust of their endeavors. They worked hard and long because they were aware of the injustices toward black people that pervaded our society, because they honestly opposed the misuse of excessive power by the rich and the privileged. With great organizational skill they put together a coalition which often acted as the national conscience, the voice of reason when all else seemed chaos and the land was inhabited by lotus-eaters, drugged with the powerful intoxicant of buck-making. Theirs was a holding action, the only thing that was happening in Eisenhowerland.

The tools honed by these liberals have proven invaluable. The use of the courts for the advancement of freedom was developed into a fine art, which boasts among its masterpieces the Brown decision. They used the Congress when they could. All the classical channels for advocating change in our society were their tools, and they used these tools with skill, although with limited effectiveness.

The liberals wanted the good life for all, as they saw it, and had the best of intentions. But built into the liberal world-view were tragic flaws which made for failure. The first of these flaws was—perhaps still is—their basic middle-class view of the world. They conceived of leadership as coming only from those who have made it in society. Consequently, they emphasized the problems of those who have made it; hence the drive for integration in housing conditions of the poor; hence the emphasis on hiring pretty black girls for front-office jobs, and not on a guaranteed annual wage for those who were casualties in a cruel antihuman job market; hence the emphasis on Brotherhood Month, and not on "Black is beautiful, Baby." Coupled with the middle-class orientation of the liberals was their assumption that the highest good was the integration of black culture into a sick, white society.

The liberals' desire to make it in the white middle-class world, was a source of another weakness. They became the chief persecutors of those who went too far or too fast in threatening the comfort of the Establishment. The liberals believe that if we reason with the Establishment, if we employ the weapons the system gives us with gentlemanly bearing, we will soon convince the Establishment that it ought to give us our rights. Based on such reasoning, the liberals shuddered when radical black voices were raised, calling for more militant, dramatic action, involving not negotiations but *people's power*. Thus, Dr. W. E. B. Du Bois,* whose voice from the grave still speaks in tones more cogent and more powerful than those of most of our leadership today, found his picture removed from the walls of the office of the very organization he had helped to bring into existence, and was fired as the editor of *The Crisis*.

He was a "Red," a "pro-Soviet agent," all the names the Establishment could think of calling him—and all these names were echoed by liberal voices. That history shames the name "liberal."

And Du Bois is not the only one. When Paul Robeson, who had thrilled the black middle class as actor and singer, turned his magnificent bass-baritone to more profound issues, he too was scorned. In the words of one of his own songs, "They scandalized his name." In 1949, when Robeson said in Paris, "Hell no, we won't go," he was saying what black young men are chanting today in Harlem and Watts and on college campuses up and down the land. And when he wrote the following in 1958, he was a decade ahead of his time. He said, in his book *Here I Stand:*

I am not suggesting, of course, that the Negro people should take law enforcement into their own hands, but we have the right, and above all, we have the duty, to bring the strength and support of our entire community to defend the lives and property of each indi-

---

* In 1961, Dr. Du Bois, at the invitation of President Nkrumah, took up residence in Ghana, and in 1963, after renouncing his American citizenship, he became a citizen of Ghana. He died on August 23, 1963, in his ninety-sixth year, on the eve of the huge "March on Washington for Jobs and Freedom." Dr. Du Bois lies buried in Accra.

vidual family. Indeed, the law itself will move a hundred times quicker whenever it is apparent that the power of our numbers has been called forth. The time has come for the great Negro communities throughout the land—Chicago, Detroit, New York, Birmingham and all the rest—to demonstrate that they will no longer tolerate mob violence against one of their own.

The liberals helped to silence Robeson's voice, helped hound him out of the country, under the guise of helping to protect the country against the Communist menace.

What, in fact, liberalism, black and white, did was to help silence voice after voice of protest out of a mistaken notion that the way to progress was to agree with the white power structure on everything—its foreign policy, its ethics, its witch hunting, and its paranoid anti-Communism, How they damaged white militancy! How they dampened the spirit of black men! How the attitudes they fostered carry over today! For what the liberals did to Robeson and Du Bois they have done to the three voices in our own day which have most clearly articulated the demands of black people.

Malcolm X's voice was the voice of pride for the black poor. That ex-addict, that ex-numbers runner, that superlative hater and superlative lover, had to be listened to, not derided by the liberals. He gave pride, he gave hope, he gave manhood back to poor black men who have been castrated by their own world. He spoke for them, and they loved him; and the liberals, the middle-class thinkers, tried to do to him what they had done to Robeson and Du Bois. They failed, for, despite the assassin's bullet, his voice is louder today than ever—ask the black kids at Columbia and Northwestern and Southern Illinois University.

And what was true of Malcolm is true of Stokely. Whether or not you agree with the tactics of Carmichael and H. Rap Brown, they have made us aware that we have to talk less about love and more about power. They have taught us that the rulers do not respect reason as the ultimate weapon, but that they respect power more. When Stokely says "get guns" one might argue against this thesis. But the liberals have not argued. They have simply followed the line of the power structure and called him crazy or rabid. They have carried, once again, the message of the rulers of the people. The liberals fear that the wave Carmichael seeks to unleash may sweep aside not only the power structure, but the liberals as well.

Finally I want to talk of our martyred Dr. King, for he too felt the lash of liberal censure. Oh yes, he was a hero when he spoke for nonviolence in Montgomery, and when he fought Bull Conner with freedom songs in Birmingham.* But how quickly the liberals abandoned him when he said that the struggle for justice at home and for an end to the war in Vietnam were one and the same. The liberals could hardly wait to accuse him of jeopardizing the movement by linking the two issues. But he didn't heed them, that preacher who went to the top of the mountain, that dreamer of the dream, who saw clearly that the dream at home could not be fulfilled as long as we were engaged in a costly, cruel and unjust war abroad. And now these liberals rally to the Bobbies and the Genes, who are saying just what Dr. King said—three years ago, when it took guts to stand on a public platform and say it.

Where were the liberals when Lumumba† died, and the black world cried out in anguish? Where were they when America played its shameful colonial game in the Dominican Republic and Guatemala? Is it not a disservice to Black America to encourage it to believe that American power is right and righteous everywhere except in Harlem and Watts? But the liberals didn't see it that way then, and probably don't now.

The second group I wish to discuss—the Black Power advocates—has come on the scene quite recently. It too has its share of strengths and weaknesses.

To begin with, it must be said that the logic of its case is irrefutable. Black Power advocates have pointed out that the response to love—in Selma, in Montgomery, in Georgia bus stations, and in New York and Gary ghettos, was usually a policeman's club or a county political chairman's vilification and perfidy. Martyrdom is hardly a nourishing diet. Black Power advocates have taught us a fundamental lesson, that black people must learn to exercise their power for their own advantage, to demonstrate their unity, use their vote, their numbers to achieve their objectives. This lesson can no longer be denied. It has been proved in Gary, it has just been proved again at Columbia Uni-

* Eugene "Bull" Conner, police chief of Birmingham, led the police violence against civil-rights demonstrators with mass arrests, police dogs, nightsticks, and high-pressure fire hoses.
† Patrice Lumumba, head of the Congolese National Movement, which had led the fight for independence of the Belgian Congo, became head of the Congo after it was granted independence by Belgium in June, 1960. But Lumumba enraged European and American imperialists by insisting that independence meant total control of their nation, including their economy, by the Congolese people. Lumumba was assassinated on February 14, 1961.

versity,* and is in the process of being proved today by the poor encamped in Washington.

Black Power has had other salutary results. Black men, especially young men, find themselves filled with a new pride and self-respect, a new sense that their struggle need not end in futility, but might end in victory. The Black Power advocates have fostered a sense of oneness and completeness. They have made "Black is beautiful, Baby" a meaningful slogan of pride. They have tapped the same resources which Africans, under the leadership of Senghor and Kenyatta, call *Negritude*. They have helped our young find themselves.

Black Power has taught us that the power structure is not some inscrutable emotionless sphynx. Rulers are just ordinary people; they tremble when they are afraid. And when frightened they are much more prone to yield. Black Power has reminded us that fear can be an important ingredient for change; that fear reaches its zenith when black people choose not to play by the rules of the game—rules they never made and the powerful never obeyed.

Threats from the Stokelys and Raps, the Deacons† and Black Panthers, have made the power structure more attentive to the demands of the less militant. "We'd better give in to the moderates," whites say, "because if we don't, the Mau Mau's will get us." Let us be grateful for the whirlwind they have sown; for, like it or not, we have all been the beneficiaries of its harvest.

But the Black Power advocates too have not completely fulfilled the needs of the black liberation movement. The slogan "Get guns," while provocative, hardly spells out a program of action. Get guns for what, we want to know? One can see guns for self-defense. That slogan was clearly announced by Robert E. Williams in a book he wrote as long ago as 1962.‡ But beyond that? Are we to engage in guerrilla warfare in the cities? If we do, what are our hopes of success? Regis Debray on guerrilla

---

* The reference is to the role of the Harlem community in forcing Columbia University to abandon construction of a gymnasium on the site of Morningside Park.

† Deacons for Defense and Justice was an organization established by black militants to protect the Negro people and civil-rights workers from vigilante terrorism. Several chapters were established in the South in 1965.

‡ The reference is to *Negroes with Guns*, published in 1962. It was written while Williams was in Cuba, where he was forced to flee after he organized the defense of his Monroe, North Carolina, community against Ku Klux Klan gangs in 1961.

warfare in the Cuban mountains,* Frantz Fanon on the Algerian
revolution and the purifying quality of violence, raise vital questions.† But the applicability of these theories to the American
ghetto has not yet been seriously probed.

Ghetto uprisings are really not always manifestations of
Black Power in planned organized fashion, they are not insurrections in the sense of violent revolts aimed at the seizure of
power. They are the angry lashing-out of frustration and fury,
not studied tactics leading to a clear goal. It is very hard to see
a full-blown insurrectionary movement in the looting of that
bromide dispenser known as color TV by nine-year-old kids.

There is much talk about black control of the ghetto. What
does that mean? I am mayor of a city of roughly 90,000 black
people, but we do not control the possibilities of jobs for them,
of money for their schools, or state-funded social services. These
things are in the hands of the United States Steel Corporation
and the County Department of Welfare, the State of Indiana.
Will the poor in Gary's worst slums be helped because the
pawnshop owner is black, not white? It may be less demeaning
to be robbed by a Soul Brother, but it leaves the belly just as
empty. In some instances, black control has meaning: in neighborhood school board or community-action councils; in Gary,
efforts to take the economic opportunity program out of county-
wide hands so that the ghetto may shape programs to fit its
own needs. But in a larger sense, black control is at this point
a mystique and not a program of action.

The last manifestation of Black Power I wish to discuss briefly
is the one in which I have the most experience: black politics.
At the risk of sounding immodest, I believe the black people
of Gary have gotten a terrific lift out of electing one of their
own as mayor of the city, after years of living under the leadership of white men. We have attempted to institute meaningful
changes in the life of the city. Model-cities programs, job training, ghetto renewal—all these I am attempting within the
scope of my abilities and resources. But not for a moment do I
fool myself that black political control of Gary or of Cleveland,
or of any other city in and of itself can solve the problems of

* The reference is to Regis Debray's *Revolution in the Revolution?* published early in 1967 in Cuba and France and later that year in the United
States.
† In *The Wretched of the Earth,* the Martinique-born, French-speaking
Negro psychiatrist and revolutionary Frantz Fanon suggested that
violence may be the only recourse left to the exploited and humiliated
masses.

the wretched of this nation. The resources are not available to the cities to do the job that needs doing.

But the election of fifty black mayors in fifty major cities could lead to a new national-movement system. Only by such change can the needed resources be made available.

Obviously, the next step for the Black Power movement is to develop ideology and program.

In the third category of progressives are the white radicals. Who are they, and what, if anything, distinguishes them from the liberals?

Although in practice the distinctions between liberals and radical are often blurred, the philosophical differences are striking and can be stated with some precision.

The liberal has been described as one who exhibits a decent concern for those he deems to be oppressed. However—and this is crucial—he does not see himself as one of the oppressed. Life and the times have been good to him, he thinks; and all he really asks is that others, less fortunate than he, have the same opportunity to share in the good life with him.

Since the philosophical source of liberalism is humanist, the liberal view is not meant to be condescending—not at all.

But by definition, and in theory and practice, that is just what it is, a form of condescension. For the underlying assumptions of the liberal doctrine—that all is well with me, but unfortunately not with you—lead almost inevitably, in both strategy and tactics, to the extension of the helping hand.

But the white radical views himself not as one of the liberated, but as one of the oppressed. The thesis is that most of us, irrespective of our station in life, are oppressed.

A man may be free, white and twenty-one, comfortably ensconced in his split-level home on an acre of ground somewhere in suburbia; possessed of a $25,000-a-year income, and loaded with stock options. Yet he too may be oppressed. For he lives in an alienated society. And in such a society it is not unlikely that, in some respects at least, he too is alienated. Alienated from his work, which may have little social life, if often geared to business relationships; alienated, finally, even from himself, painfully groping for answers thrice a week in prone position on a couch somewhere on Park Avenue. Yes, he too may be oppressed. For "The world is too much with him, late and soon. Getting and spending he lays waste his powers."

What of the student in the university, where curriculum, pedagogy and policies seem to have little relevance to a meaningful education? He too is oppressed.

A man may have creative musical talents which he devotes

exclusively to clever advertising jingles, or literary skills wholly diverted to public relations. Such men are also oppressed. What of the housewife preoccupied with sterile middle-class trivia? She too is oppressed.

Consider the emerging black middle class, with newly acquired merchandise and comforts galore, yet burdened with the pervasive effects of white racism.

For all these people, in all these walks of life, there is a world of difference between what they are and what they could be. That is the nature of their oppression.

The radical, on the other hand, is aware of his own oppression. Consequently, he relates it to the oppression of others, personally identifies with their struggle, and finally commits himself to joining in those struggles.

What I have just presented is a kind of existential distinction between liberal and radical. It is a view about which thoughtful people may differ.

There is, of course, a less personal, more classical radical thesis related to what I have just outlined; it asserts that the evils of the society emerge from the economic system; that nothing short of a radical transformation of that system can metamorphose our society.

One respected proponent of this theory has written that in the final analysis, capitalism has no solution to the ghetto:

No one ever decides to build ghettos and to crowd them with angry black people; no one decided to deprive these people of education and jobs; no one decided to treat them as subhuman, to oppress them with racist cops, to condemn them to a life of frustration and hopelessness. And by the same token no one can decide to undo these situations or reverse these trends. They are the cumulative consequences of millions of decisions directed to the seemingly unrelated aim of making as much money as possible by responding to the opportunities and penalties of the market—in other words, obeying the most fundamental law of the established social order.

Another crucial component of the radical thesis is that foreign and domestic policy are facets of each other, forming one integrated whole. Each feeds on and is formed by the other.

The liberal espouses the policies of the welfare state at home, while often supporting an imperial policy abroad. The radical rejects this dichotomy and opposes such ventures as the overthrow of Mossadegh in Iran, Arbenz in Guatemala, Lumumba in the Congo, and Jagan in British Guiana, not to mention the ill-fated invasion at the Bay of Pigs.*

In summation, then, the distinction between liberal and radical is that the liberal wishes to preserve the present system, while attempting to humanize it at home. The radical thinks the present system cannot be humanized and must therefore be transformed.

The white radical movement in America today finds its strength primarily among youth on and off campus. In some respects, this is healthy. For the movement now has the attributes of youth: it is not yet burdened with vested interests; it has *élan;* it is vigorous, fresh, experimental, inconoclastic and undoctrinaire.

Except for the growing participation of youth, the size of the white radical movement is extremely limited. There are, to be sure, older members, whose tenets were, in main, forged out of the experiences of the 1930's. Due to the passage of time, the McCarthyite badgering of the fifties and the Establishment's co-opting of labor unions, the ranks of adult white radicals have not swelled, but thinned to the point where their impact on the contemporary scene is limited. To that extent, then, they too have failed.

I have tried to delineate the contours of current political forces in American life from center to left. I have carved out the categories of black and white liberals, Black Power advocates, and white radicals, because they lend themselves to useful discourse, not because they are easily defined and neatly packaged groups. Quite obviously they are not. There are in fact blurred lines, gradations and nuances.

I have deliberately dealt with that segment of America which, unlike the purveyors of reaction and racism, has consciously adopted a political and philosophical approach related to the improvement of man's condition. I have rarely mentioned, but certainly do not minimize, the immense significance of that

---

* Lumumba, Mossadegh, Arbenz and Chedi Jagan were all the targets of C.I.A.—inspired revolts and conspiracies which resulted in the overthrow of their governments, assassination in the case of Lumumba, and exile in the case of Arbenz.

The Bay of Pigs refers to the attack launched against Revolutionary Cuba by 1,500 anti-Castro Cuban exiles who had been secretly trained under C.I.A. men for an invasion of the island. The invaders, assisted by American air support, attempted a landing at the Bay of Pigs in April, 1961, but met defeat. Over 1,200 of the invaders were taken prisoner and held for almost two years.

vast portion of the American populace, which for one reason or another has not yet hacked out its ideological niche. It is for the allegiance of that uncommitted group that the battle will be waged.

What then is the outlook? What the prognosis?

Black people in America, by themselves, may be able to muster the means to defend themselves against absolute repression —a kind of survival action. But alone they cannot liberate the total society. For such a function they may act as a catalyst or a leading force; but the completion of the revolution will require an alliance with broad and diverse sectors of American life. To bring about that consummation, the logic of numbers necessarily comes into play.

From the black and white liberals we need the organizational skills and the knowledge of how to use existing institutions. From the Black Power advocates we need the new sense of black pride, the awareness of the crucial importance of power relationships, the concern for the poor and the disinherited, the plain, courageous militancy. From the white radicals we need their willingness to commit themselves to total change, their conviction that only a true, fraternal alliance with black militants can restructure this society. If we can combine these forces, then we have the opportunity to win over the uncommitted millions in our nation, to build a community recently described by Professor Mason Drukman:

A community in which none would suffer the degradation of want, where all would enjoy equally the advantages of education, progress and public service, where all could link arms as brothers and strike together to achieve a nation whose greatness was not only material but aesthetic and spiritual, where equality and justice would not be regarded as the shibboleths of institutionalized hypocrisy.

To that I say, Amen.

A CASE FOR SEPARATION

By Robert S. Browne

By the spring of 1968, a debate was raging in the Negro community around the integration-versus-separation issue. A calm, reasoned exposition of the arguments in favor of separatism or black nationalism was presented by Robert S. Browne in a speech before the Plenary Session of the National Jewish Community Relations Advisory Councils, June 30, 1968. (The case for integration was presented at the same session by Bayard Rustin.) Robert S. Browne is an assistant professor of economics at Fairleigh Dickinson University. His speech is taken from a pamphlet published by the A. Philip Randolph Institute, N.D., and is reprinted with permission of the Institute.

THERE IS a growing ambivalence in the Negro community which is creating a great deal of confusion both within the black community itself and within those segments of the white community that are attempting to relate to the blacks. It arises from the question of whether the American Negro is a cultural group, significantly distinct from the majority culture in ways that are ethnically rather than socioeconomically based.

If one believes the answer to this is yes, then one is likely to favor emphasizing the cultural distinctiveness and to be vigorously opposed to any efforts to minimize or to submerge the differences. If, on the other hand, one believes that there are no cultural differences between the blacks and whites or that the differences are minimal and transitory, then one is likely to resist the placing of great emphasis on the differences and to favor accentuating the similarities.

These two currents in the black community are symbolized, and perhaps oversimplified, by the factional labels of "separatists" and "integrationists."

The separatist would argue that the Negro's foremost grievance is not solvable by giving him access to more gadgets, although this is certainly a part of the solution, but that his greatest thirst is in the realm of the spirit—that he must be provided an opportunity to reclaim his own group individuality and to have that individuality recognized as having equal validity with the other major cultural groups of the world.

The integrationist would argue that what the Negro wants,

principally, is exactly what the whites want—that is, that the Negro wants "in" to American society and that operationally this means providing the Negro with employment, income, housing and education comparable to that of the whites. This having been achieved, the other aspects of the Negro's problem of inferiority will disappear.

The origins of this ideological dichotomy are easily identified. The physical characteristics that distinguish blacks from whites are obvious enough; and the long history of slavery, supplemented by the postemancipation pattern of exclusion of the blacks from so many facets of American society, are equally undeniable. Whether observable behavioral differences between the mass of the blacks and the white majority are more properly attributable to this special history of the black man in America or are better viewed as expressions of racial differences in life style is an arguable proposition.

What is not arguable, however, is the fact that at the time of the slave trade the blacks arrived in America with a cultural background and a life style that was quite distinct from that of the whites. Although there was perhaps as much diversity amongst those Africans from widely scattered portions of the continent as there was amongst the European settlers, the differences between the two racial groups was unquestionably far greater, as attested by the different roles which they were to play in the society.

INTEGRATIONIST AND SEPARATIST VIEWPOINTS

Over this history there seems to be little disagreement. The dispute arises from how one views what happened during the subsequent 350 years.

The integrationist would focus on the transformation of the blacks into imitators of the European civilization. European clothing was imposed on the slaves; eventually their languages were forgotten; the African homeland receded ever further into the background. Certainly after 1808, when the slave trade was officially terminated, thus cutting off the supply of fresh injections of African culture, the Europeanization of the blacks proceeded apace. With emancipation, the national Constitution recognized the legal manhood of the blacks, United States citizenship was unilaterally conferred upon the ex-slave, and the Negro began his arduous struggle for social, economic and political acceptance into the American mainstream.

The separatist, however, takes the position that the cultural transformation of the black man was not complete. Whereas the integrationist is more or less content to accept the destruction of the original culture of the African slaves as a *fait accompli,* irrespective of whether he feels it to have been morally reprehensible or not, the separatist is likely to harbor a vague sense of resentment toward the whites for having perpetrated this cultural genocide and he is concerned to nurture whatever vestiges may have survived the North American experience and to encourage a renaissance of these lost characteristics. In effect, he is sensitive to an identity crisis which presumably does not exist in the mind of the integrationist.

To many observers, the separatist appears to be romantic and even reactionary. On the other hand, his viewpoint strikes a harmonious chord with mankind's most fundamental instinct— the instinct for survival. With so powerful a stimulus, and with the oppressive tendencies congenitally present in the larger white society, one almost could have predicted the emergence of the burgeoning movement toward black separatism. Millions of black parents have been confronted with the poignant agony of raising black, kinky-haired children in a society where the standard of beauty is a milk-white skin and long, straight hair. To convince a black child that she is beautiful when every channel of value formation in the society is telling her the opposite is a heart-rending and well-nigh impossible task. It is a challenge that confronts all Negroes, irrespective of their social and economic class, but the difficulty of dealing with it is likely to vary directly with the degree to which the family leads an integrated existence. A black child in a predominantly black school may realize that she doesn't look like the pictures in the books, magazines, and TV advertisements, but at least she looks like her schoolmates and neighbors. The black child in a predominantly white school and neighborhood lacks even this basis for identification.

THE PROBLEM OF IDENTITY

This identity problem is not peculiar to the Negro, of course, nor is it limited to questions of physical appearance. Minorities of all sorts encounter it in one form or another—the immigrant who speaks with an accent; the Jewish child who doesn't celebrate Christmas; the vegetarian who shuns meat. But for the Negro the problem has a special dimension, for in the American ethos a black man is not only "different," he is classed as ugly and inferior.

This is not an easy situation to deal with, and the manner in which a Negro chooses to handle it will be both determined by

and a determinant of his larger political outlook. He can deal
with it as an integrationist, accepting his child as being ugly
by prevailing standards and urging him to excel in other ways
to prove his worth; or he can deal with it as a black nationalist,
telling the child that he is not a freak but rather part of a larger
international community of black-skinned, kinky-haired people
who have a beauty of their own, a glorious history, and a great
future. In short, he can replace shame with pride, inferiority
with dignity, by imbuing the child with what is coming to be
known as black nationalism. The growing popularity of this
latter viewpoint is evidenced by the appearance of "natural"
hair styles among Negro youth and the surge of interest in
African and Negro culture and history.

BLACK POWER, BLACK CONSCIOUSNESS, AND AMERICAN SOCIETY

Black Power may not be the ideal slogan to describe this
new self-image that the black American is developing, for to
guilt-ridden whites the slogan conjures up violence, anarchy
and revenge. To frustrated blacks, however, it symbolizes unity
and a newly found pride in the blackness with which the Creator endowed us and which we realize must always be our mark
of identification. Heretofore this blackness has been a stigma,
a curse with which we were born. Black Power means that
henceforth this curse will be a badge of pride rather than of
scorn. It marks the end of an era in which black men devoted
themselves to pathetic attempts to be white men and inaugu-
rates an era in which black people will set their own standards
of beauty, conduct and accomplishment.

Is this new black consciousness in irreconcilable conflict with
the larger American society?

In a sense, the heart of the American cultural problem always
has been the need to harmonize the inherent contradiction between racial (or national) identity and integration into the
melting pot which was America. In the century since the Civil
War, the society has made little effort to find a means to afford
the black minority a sense of racial pride and independence
while at the same time accepting it as a full participant in the
larger society.

Now that the implications of that failure are becoming apparent, the black community seems to be saying "Forget it!
We'll solve our own problems." Integration, which never had a
high priority among the black masses, now is being written off

by them as not only unattainable but as actually harmful—
driving a wedge between those black masses and the so-called
Negro elite.

To these developmets has been added the momentous realization by many of the "integrated" Negroes that in the United
States full integration can only mean full assimilation—a loss
of racial identity. This sobering prospect has caused many a
black integrationist to pause and reflect, even as have his similarly challenged Jewish counterparts.

INTEGRATION—A PAINLESS GENOCIDE?

Thus, within the black community there are two separate
challenges to the traditional integration policy which long has
constituted the major objective of established Negro leadership.
There is the general skepticism that the Negro, even after having transformed himself into a white blackman, will enjoy full
acceptance into American society; and there is the longer-
range doubt that, even should complete integration somehow be
achieved, it would prove to be really desirable, for its price may
be the total absorption and disappearance of the race—a sort
of painless genocide.

Understandably, it is the black masses who have most vocif-
erously articulated these dangers of assimilation, for they have
watched with alarm as the more fortunate among their ranks
have gradually risen to the top only to be promptly "integrated"
off into the white community—absorbed into another culture,
often with undisguised contempt for all that had previously constituted their racial and cultural heritage. Also, it was the black
masses who first perceived that integration actually increases
the white community's control over the black one by destroying
black institutions and by absorbing black leadership and coin-
ciding its interests with those of the white community.

The international "brain drain" has its counterpart in the
black community, which is constantly being denuded of its best-
trained people and many of its natural leaders. Black institutions of all sorts—colleges, newspapers, banks, even community
organizations—are experiencing the loss of their better people
to the newly available openings in white establishments, thereby lowering the quality of the Negro organizations and in some
cases causing their demise or increasing their dependence on
whites for survival. Such injurious, if unintended, side effects of
integration have been felt in almost every layer of the black
community.

NEGRO DISTRUST OF WHITE AMERICA

If the foregoing analysis of the integrationist-versus-separatist conflict exhausted the case, we might conclude that all the problems have been dealt with before by other immigrant groups in America. (It would be an erroneous conclusion, for while other groups may have encountered similar problems, their solutions do not work for us, alas.) But there remains yet another factor which is cooling the Negro's enthusiasm for the integrationist path: he is becoming distrustful of his fellow Americans.

The American culture is one of the youngest in the world. Furthermore, as has been pointed out repeatedly in recent years, it is essentially a culture that approves of violence, indeed enjoys it. Military expenditures absorb roughly half the national budget. Violence predominates on the TV screen and the toys of violence are best-selling items during the annual rites for the much-praised but little-imitated Prince of Peace. In Vietnam, the zeal with which America has pursued its effort to destroy a poor and illiterate peasantry has astonished civilized people around the globe.

In such an atmosphere the Negro is understandably restive about the fate his white compatriots might have in store for him. The veiled threat by President Johnson at the time of the 1966 riots, suggesting that riots might beget pogroms and pointing out that Negroes are only 10 percent of the population was not lost on most blacks.* It enraged them, but it was a sobering thought. The manner in which Germany herded the Jews into concentration camps and ultimately into ovens was a solemn warning to minority peoples everywhere. The casualness with which America exterminated the Indians and later interned the Japanese suggests that there is no cause for the Negro to feel complacent about his security in the United States. He finds little consolation in the assurance that if it does become necessary to place him in concentration camps it will only be as a means of protecting him from uncontrollable whites. "Protective incarceration" to use governmental jargonese.

The very fact that such alternatives are becoming serious topics of discussion has exposed the Negro's already raw and

---

* At a press conference on November 10, 1966, President Johnson also warned that ghetto riots had produced a backlash of Republican gains in Congress, and he urged Negro leaders to show a "sense of responsibility."

sensitive psyche to yet another heretofore unfelt vulnerability—
the insecurity he suffers as a result of having no homeland
which he can honestly feel is his own. Among the major ethno-
cultural groups in the world he is unique in this respect.

NEED FOR NATIONHOOD

As the Jewish drama during and following World War II
painfully demonstrated, a national homeland is a primordial
and urgent need for a people, even though its benefits do not
always lend themselves to ready measurement. For some, the
homeland constitutes a vital place of refuge from the strains
of a life led too long within a foreign environment. For others,
the need to reside in the homeland is considerably less intense
than the need merely for knowing that such a homeland exists.
The benefit to the expatriate is psychological, a sense of security
in knowing that he belongs to a culturally and politically identifiable community. No doubt this phenomenon largely accounts
for the fact that both the West Indian Negro and the Puerto
Rican exhibit considerably more self-assurance than does the
American Negro, for both of the former groups have ties to an
identifiable homeland which honors and preserves their cultural
heritage.

It has been marveled that we American Negroes, almost alone
among the cultural groups of the world, exhibit no sense of
nationhood. Perhaps it is true that we do lack this sense, but
there seems to be little doubt that the absence of a homeland
exacts a severe if unconscious price from our psyche. Theoreti-
cally, our homeland is the U.S.A. We pledge allegiance to the
Stars and Stripes and sing the national anthem. But from the
age when we first begin to sense that we are somehow "different," that we are victimized, these rituals begin to mean less
to us than to our white compatriots. For many of us they become form without substance; for others they become a cruel
and bitter mockery of our dignity and good sense; for relatively
few of us do they retain a significance in any way comparable
to their hold on our white brethren.

The recent coming into independence of many African states
stimulated some interest among Negroes that independent Africa might become the homeland which they so desperately
needed. A few made the journey and experienced a newly found
sense of community and racial dignity. For many who went,
however, the gratifying racial fraternity which they experienced
was insufficient to compensate for the cultural estrangement
that accompanied it. They had been away from Africa for too

long, and the differences in language, food and custom barred
them from experiencing that "at home" sensation they were
eagerly seeking. Symbolically, independent Africa could serve
them as a homeland: practically, it could not. Their search
continues—a search for a place where they can experience the
security that comes from being a part of the majority culture,
free at last from the inhibiting effects of cultural repression and
induced cultural timidity and shame.

"THIS LAND IS OUR RIGHTFUL HOME"

If we have been separated from Africa for so long that we
are no longer quite at ease there, then we are left with only one
place to make our home, and that is in this land to which we
were brought in chains. Justice would indicate such a solution
in any case, for it is North America, not Africa, into which our
toil and effort have been poured. This land is our rightful home
and we are well within our rights in demanding an opportunity
to enjoy it on the same terms as the other immigrants who have
helped to develop it.

Since few whites will deny the justice of this claim, it is paradoxical that we are offered the option of exercising this birthright only on the condition that we abandon our culture, deny
our race, and integrate ourselves into the white community.
The "accepted" Negro, the "integrated" Negro, are mere euphe-
misms, hiding a cruel and relentless cultural destruction which
is sometimes agonizing to the middle-class Negro but which is
becoming intolerable to the black masses. A Negro who refuses
to yield his identity and to ape the white model finds he can
survive in dignity only by rejecting the entire white society,
which ultimately must mean challenging the law and the law-
enforcement mechanisms. On the other hand, if he abandons
his cultural heritage and succumbs to the lure of integration,
he risks certain rejection and humiliation along the way, with
absolutely no guarantee of ever achieving complete acceptance.

That such unsatisfactory options are leading to almost continuous disruption and dislocation of our society should hardly
be cause for surprise.

PARTITION AS A SOLUTION

A formal partitioning of the United States into two totally
separate and independent nations, one white and one black,
offers one way out of this tragic situation. Many will condemn
it as a defeatist solution, but what they see as defeatism may

better be described as a frank facing up to the realities of American society. A society is stable only to the extent that there exists a basic core of value judgments that are unthinkingly accepted by the great bulk of its members. Increasingly, Negroes are demonstrating that they do not accept the common core of values that underlies America—whether because they had little to do with drafting it or because they feel it is weighted against their interests.

The alleged disproportionately large number of Negro law violators, of unwed mothers, of illegitimate children, of non-working adults *may* be indicators that there is no community of values such as has been supposed, although I am not unaware of racial socioeconomic reasons for these statistics also. But whatever the reasons for observed behavioral differences, there clearly is no reason *why* the Negro should not have his own ideas about what the societal organization should be. The Anglo-Saxon system of organizing human relationships certainly has not proved itself to be superior to all other systems, and the Negro is likely to be more acutely aware of this fact than are most Americans.

This unprecedented challenging of the "conventional wisdom" on the racial question is causing considerable consternation within the white community, especially the white liberal community, which has long felt itself to be the sponsor and guardian of the blacks. The situation is further confused because the challenges to the orthodox integrationist views are being projected by persons whose roots are authentically within the black community—whereas the integrationist spokesmen of the past often have been persons whose credentials were partly white-bestowed. This situation is further aggravated by the classical intergenerational problem, with black youth seizing the lead and speaking out for nationalism and separatism, whereas their elders look on askance, a development which has at least a partial parallel within the contemporary white community, where youth is increasingly strident in its demands for thoroughgoing revision of our social institutions.

THE BLACK NATIONALISTS

If one were to inquire as to who the principal spokesmen for the new black nationalism or for separatism are, one would discover that the movement is essentially locally based rather than nationally organized. In the San Francisco Bay area, the Black Panther Party is well known as a leader in the tactics of winning recognition for the black community. Their tactic is *via* a separate political party for black people, a format which I suspect we will hear a great deal more of in the future. The work of the Black Muslims is well known, and perhaps more national in scope than that of any other black nationalist group. Out of Detroit there is the Malcolm X Society, led by attorney Milton Henry, whose members reject their United States citizenship and are claiming five Southern states for the creation of a new Black Republic. Another major leader in Detroit is the Reverend Albert Cleage, who is developing a considerable following for his preachings of black dignity and who has also experimented with a black political party, thus far without success.

The black students at white colleges are one highly articulate group seeking for some national organizational form. A growing number of black educators are also groping toward some sort of nationally coordinated body to lend strength to their local efforts for developing educational systems better tailored to the needs of the black child. Under the name of Association of Afro-American Educators, they recently held a national conference in Chicago which was attended by several hundred public-school teachers and college and community workers.

This is not to say that every black teacher or parent-teacher group that favors community control of schools is necessarily sympathetic to black separatism. Nevertheless, the general thrust of the move toward decentralized control over public schools, at least in the larger urban areas, derives from an abandoning of the idea of integration in the schools and a decision to bring to the ghetto the best and most suitable education that can be obtained.

GHETTO IMPROVEMENT EFFORTS

Similarly, a growing number of community-based organizations are being formed for the purpose of facilitating the economic development of the ghetto, for replacement of absentee business proprietors and landlords by black entrepreneurs and resident owners. Again, these efforts are not totally separatist in that they operate within the framework of the present national society, but they build on the separatism that already exists in the society rather than attempting to eliminate it. To a black who sees salvation for the black man only in a complete divorce of the two races, these efforts at ghetto improvement appear futile—perhaps even harmful. To others, convinced that coexistence with white America is possible within the national framework if only the white will permit the Negro to develop as he wishes and by his own hand rather than in accordance with a white-conceived and white-administered pattern, such physically and economically upgraded black enclaves will be viewed as desirable steps forward.

Finally, those blacks who still feel that integration is in some sense both acceptable and possible will continue to strive for the color-blind society. When, if ever, these three strands of thought will converge toward a common outlook I cannot predict. In the meanwhile, however, concerned whites wishing to work with the black community should be prepared to encounter many rebuffs. They should keep ever in mind that the black community does not have a homogeneous vision of its own predicament at this crucial juncture.

RACISM IN THE LAW

By Judge George W. Crockett, Jr.

"There is no equal justice for black people today; there has never been," wrote Judge Crockett of Detroit Recorder's Court in the Journal of the American Judicature Society *(April–May, 1970). "To our everlasting shame, the quality of justice in America has always been and is now directly related to the color of one's skin as well as to the size of one's pocketbook. Our Constitution and the entire body of our written law say it shall not be that way, but our judges have made it that way."*

In a speech delivered on October 15, 1968, to a seminar on "A Black Looks at White America," held at Wayne State University, Detroit, Judge Crockett discussed the racist features of law in the United States. Judge Crockett was a nationally known civil-rights attorney before he was appointed to the bench, a member of the bars of Florida, West Virginia, Michigan and the United States Supreme Court, and Vice-President of the National Lawyers Guild. Judge Crockett spent the summer of 1964 in Mississippi directing the activities of sixty-five volunteer civil-rights lawyers. On March, 1969, Judge Crockett gained nationwide attention (and nationwide condemnation by racists) for his courageous action in upholding the Constitutional rights of 142 blacks, including some forty women and children, arrested by the Detroit police in a raid on a meeting of the Republic of New Africa, an organization of black militants whose program calls for separatism—geographical, social and economic—from white America.

Here are excerpts from Judge Crockett's speech at Wayne State University, reprinted from Science & Society, *Spring, 1969, pp. 223–30.*

RACISM HAS BEEN an integral part of American law since the first slaves arrived in Virginia in 1619. A century and a half later, a new nation, composed in large part of slaveholders, made a Declaration of Independence in which they bore witness to the world that "all men are created equal."

Eleven years later the citizens of the new nation experienced neither logical nor moral difficulty when they adopted a Constitution that sanctioned human slavery based upon race and color, and decreed that persons of color who were held in bondage should be counted as three-fifths of a man. Thus, the false principle of the inferiority of black people because of their race or color, which over the years had become imbedded in our national consciousness, now became part of our country's fundamental law.

The significance of this and its effect upon whites was well stated in a recent address by Rudolf B. Schmerl to a University of Michigan seminar on "The Urban Crisis":

Absolutely *everything* in the development of the social system of this country, in law, religion, education, politics, commerce, and most certainly in human intercourse, for two hundred years, was a further refinement of this doctrine, that the slave was not a man. This was possible, in part, because the people who were enslaved were reduced to such utter wretchedness, so numbed with shock and despair in a series of experiences which took two lives out of every three persons originally captured for sale, that they did indeed appear less than human. So did the concentration camp inmates appear less than human to their Nazi captors and tormentors. Define a man in line with certain assumptions about dignity, bearing, pride, and courage; create conditions in which such attributes are utterly impossible, for example, a slave ship in which slaves are shackled between decks as little as eighteen inches apart; and you cannot help but conclude that slaves are not men. If slaves are not men, they are inferior to men, and therefore slavery is justified; and since slavery is justified, it needs to be defended, and the best way to do that is to make sure that slaves do not become men.

Racism prospered and persisted in this country not because of racial prejudice, as some would have us believe, but, rather, because racism and the stimulation of color prejudice in whites and blacks was economically profitable to the propertied class, while also satisfying the "status" craving of the poor whites.

Traditionally law has functioned as the handmaiden of the propertied class in our society. So it was to be expected that lawyers in the legislative halls, lawyers on the bench, and lawyers in the executive branch of government would combine their talents to perpetuate by law this peculiarly American doctrine of racism predicated upon a claimed color inferiority.

Initially, control of racial contacts and race relations was a matter of and was maintained by the force of social sanctions and without benefit of law. This was true for more than two centuries after 1619, but with North and South becoming more and more divided upon the question of slavery, it became more and more necessary to amplify the Constitution's concept of racial inferiority. This was accomplished through such landmarks of legal racism as the Fugitive Slave Act, the Missouri Compromise, and, of course, Chief Justice Taney's opinion in the Dred Scott case.

Habits of thought nurtured over centuries and handed down from one generation to another are not easily uprooted. Racism in our law has created a national psychosis. Historically and by sacred pledges contained in our Declaration of Independence and our Constitution we are the world's greatest exponents of the democratic ideal—the equality and the brotherhood of all men. And yet, by law and in practice, we have segregated and declared inferior, and therefore unequal, a tenth of the population because of their black skin. As a nation and as an individual, by the middle of the nineteenth century the white American had developed a split personality that nothing short of human fratricide could hope to remedy. So entrenched had racism become in American law that a Civil War had to be fought. Following the war, three Constitutional amendments were added to the nation's charter abolishing the principle of Negro inferiority before the law and proclaiming for white and black alike a new national right to freedom and to the equal protection of the laws.

Even these drastic measures did not cure our national malady. And they failed precisely because their failure was in the interest of the rich, the powerful, and the well-to-do in our society—those who dreaded, economically, the cost of employing free men to do what slaves formerly did for nothing; who dreaded, politically, the combined power of the poor white's ballot and the free black's ballot; and who dreaded, socially, the downfall of the inferiority concept and the inevitable intermingling, integration and intermarriage that would result from the black man's new sense of dignity, self-respect, and self-reliance and the poor white's liberation from the shackles imposed upon him by the lie of black inferiority.

And, again, the law functioned as the handmaiden of the propertied class. The Supreme Court in a series of cases—including *Plessy v. Ferguson*—literally gutted each of these Civil War amendments by reading into them such delimiting concepts as "state citizenship rights versus federal citizenship rights," "separate-but-equal treatment under law," and "state or public action versus individual or private action."

An abolitionist-minded Congress attempted in a series of civil-rights enactments to restate the Congressional intent in waging the Civil War and in subsequently proposing the amendments which the people had adopted. Thus in the Civil Rights Act of 1875 the meaning of these amendments was spelled out by a preamble which stated that Congress deemed it essential to just government that "we recognize the equality of all men before the law, and hold that it is the duty of government in all its dealings with the people to mete out equal and exact justice to all, of whatever nativity, race, color or persuasion, religious or political. . . ."

But notwithstanding this clear Congressional restatement of the American creed of equality, the specter of "racial inferiority" buttressed by law persisted, aided especially by these propertied-class—oriented decisions of the United States Supreme Court.

It has taken the Supreme Court more than a hundred years to come around to a repudiation of these cases and to an acceptance of those principles of equality proclaimed in the 1875 Civil Rights Act. And while the Supreme Court waited and obstructed, thousands of black folk were lynched; tens of thousands were kept in a state of peonage; hundreds of thousands never learned to read or write; and untold millions eked out a precarious survival amid the crime, and poverty, the filth, and the disease of a hundred urban ghettos.

In the process of this hundred years of waiting, black people, too, have developed a split personality. The supreme law of the land establishes their freedom and guarantees them equality of treatment; but they accept and act upon this guarantee at their peril. And this is so because each day the men who are charged with interpreting and applying the law equally give the lie to this guarantee. So the black man even now is in doubt from day to day and from community to community what the law of the day, as applied to him, really is.

The Warren Supreme Court and the Kennedy-Johnson administration have returned our written law to the original intention of the Civil War amendments. It is hoped this return is permanent. Today with such opinions as the St. Louis case outlawing private discrimination in housing (*Jones v. Mayer Co.*, 392 U. S. 409 [1968]), the school desegregation cases and others abolishing the "separate but equal" doctrine in all aspects of public life (*Brown v. Bd. of Ed.*, 347 U. S. 483 [1954]), the Virginia interracial-marriage case outlawing antimiscegenation statutes (*Loving v. Virginia,* 388 U. S. 1 [1968]), and the several Federal Civil Rights Acts enacted during the last seven years, we think we see a clear intention by the national government to eradicate all racial distinctions from American law. Much will depend upon the actions of the new administration.

Our task as lawyers and judges is no longer one of erasing racial connotations from our statutory and decisional law; our task now is to change first our own subconscious racial biases and the practices which flow from this, and then to change the habits, the thinking and the practices of those who are charged with implementing the law. This is no mean task. Our "split personality" manifests itself whenever we are confronted with issues involving or related to race or color. Three and a half centuries still call out to us that black is black and white is white "and never the twain shall meet." We must turn our backs, resolutely, against this call.

How else do you get people to discard 350 years of believing in separatism? that black people are property? that they have no rights? that they are inferior? and that they can and should be treated differently and separately with impunity?

How else can we hope to change the thinking of officials who still believe that any discrimination based on race or color is legal so long as it is not "State action"? and that "equal protection of the laws" does not mean the *same* protection for everyone?

How else can you expect to change the mores of the policeman on the street, or the sergeant at the precinct station, who clings to a belief in black "inferiority" because that belief feeds his ego and is essential to the maintenance of his own "superior" image of himself?

How else do you get the message over to white employers, school administrators, housing developers, hospital boards, and the like, that "tokenism" will not satisfy the demands of equality under law; that too frequently it tends to exacerbate the situation by showing that racial barriers *can* be broken down if there is a *will* to do so?

And how, except through more and more personal communication, do you change the thinking of that black nationalist whose despair has turned to bitter hatred of all white people? who asserts his claim for a "Black Republic" in the South? and who suspects and sees sinister motives in everything that a white person says or does?

That white policeman who bristles at the sight of a black male and a white female walking hand in hand down an urban thoroughfare never heard of the Supreme Court's decision in *Loving v. Virginia.* When he insults the white girl and physically abuses her Negro escort, he is reflecting 350 years of indoctrination at the hands of lawyers and judges, as well as laymen.

That Negro who feels uncomfortable and "out of place" in the presence of whites; that black man or woman who is prone to interpret every act and expression of a white person as a sign of his personal racial bias; that Negro and all others like him or her are reflecting what fifteen generations of white Americans have never permitted them to forget, namely, that in their eyes he is different; he is "inferior" to all whites regardless of his accomplishments or their deficiencies.

So that while the "Supreme Law of the Land" no longer countenances racial distinctions, the day-to-day "law" as understood, accepted and acted upon by the people and the forces who really control our social order remains still very much racist.

Relatively few decision-making officials in government today will openly concede this. Instead, racism in the law today is camouflaged under such terms as "administrative" or "judicial discretion."

Thus, when our civil-service laws provide for the appointment of any one of the "top three" on the list of eligibles and the black one of the three is repeatedly passed over, this is not racism; rather, it is officially referred to as an example of "administrative discretion" exercised for the "good of the service"! When, during an urban racial upheaval, as in Detroit in 1967, the overwhelming bulk of those arrested are black people and the prosecutor and the judges insist that, as a matter of policy, bail in every case should be not less than $10,000, this is not "racism" in the law; it is publicly justified as an acceptable legal device to keep "those people off the streets"! And when politicians of the Strom Thurmond and George Wallace stripe seek to undermine the Negroes' recent judicial gains by castigating the Warren Supreme Court and calling for the election of candidates who support "law and order" and "separate but equal," they are not trying to turn back the judicial clock a hundred years and restore racism in our law; instead, to hear them explain it, they are genuinely concerned about "crime in the streets" and the maintenance of safety of the individual.

One might inquire parenthetically why such genuine concern does not lead these politicians to support more adequate appropriations to eradicate the conditions of poverty, ignorance, alienation, and hopelessness which feed crime and which bring about a disrespect and a disregard for "law and order"; and why, instead, they persist in the wanton squandering of our national resources upon a racist war in Vietnam?

Finally, there is another aspect of our subject which must not be overlooked. This aspect is seen in a combination of developments which, taken together, demonstrate the revolutionary changes in black-white relations in recent years; developments which, if allowed to continue, signify an end to racism in our law in theory and in practice.

First and foremost among these revolutionary developments is the black man's growing consciousness of himself as a person and as a group to be reckoned with in the affairs of this nation. This is the true meaning of Black Power. It is just as simple as that. And its most potent manifestation thus far has been at the ballot box in the election of black public officials. If this trend continues—and it will, unless we are to have a violent revolution—racism in the administration of our laws will soon be a thing of the past.

The second revolutionary development to be noted is that black people and poor white people are beginning to identify more and more. They are beginning to understand that the interests of the two groups are not and need not be in conflict (as they necessarily were during slavery and for the one hundred years of post–Civil War black second-class citizenship) and that racism, which began in this country as a *caste* distinction, is today a matter of *class* distinction. There is, therefore, no longer any justifiable basis for a race struggle or racial conflicts in which black is pitted against white. Instead, the struggle today is a class struggle in which black and white are to be found on both sides of our national issues; and the most pressing of these issues is the expeditious elevation of 35,000,000 poor people—black and white—from a level of poverty so as to bring them into the mainstream of life in the most affluent society the world has ever known. Integration, intermingling, and intermarriage (which is frowned on by black nationalists and white "backlash" alike) is a key to our continued progress in this area—for it is only through such social contact and communication that we shall each overcome our "split personality" on the question of race.

The third and last of these revolutionary developments is apparent in the reaction of the Establishment itself. It is a reaction characterized by fear; a fear of moving too fast and at the same time a fear of not moving fast enough. It is a fear that was more or less dormant for a century under the shelter of the delimiting Supreme Court decisions mentioned above, but which is now revitalized by the freedom-expanding rulings of the High Courts and also by the racial upheavals in our cities.

The real significance of this fear is that, at long last, the Establishment feels compelled to face up to what one writer has called

a lie . . . we have lived for a hundred years . . . the unspoken fact that a nation with such high pretensions to world leadership in science, culture, and democratic government could have tolerated for so long, in every section of the country, and in every aspect of its national existence, a way of life inherited from a system of human chattel slavery . . . It is an unpleasant fact, an upsetting fact, one which is easier submerged than recognized, easier ignored than acknowledged. [Prof. Arthur Kinoy of Rutgers University Law School.]

Today, at least, the Establishment acknowledges the lie. It remains to be seen if they are still frightened enough to go ahead with corrective measures.

THE MEANING OF BLACK HISTORY

By John Henrik Clarke

As the civil-rights struggle grew, black Americans, especially black students, began to demand education relevant to their background, that would correct many of the misconceptions of the Negro's role in American history and would teach about the African background of black Americans and their contributions to the development of this country. In an address at the Jewish Currents Conference in New York, February 15, 1969, John Henrik Clarke de-

*scribed the struggle of black people to reenter the main-
stream of history.*

Mr. Clarke is Associate Editor of Freedomways, *a
quarterly review of the Freedom Movement, a teacher of
African history, and the compiler and editor of* Harlem:
A Community in Transition, American Negro Short
Stories, *and* William Styron's Nat Turner: 10 Black
Writers Respond. *He is director of the Heritage Teaching
Program of Haryou-Act, the antipoverty program in Har-
lem, and special consultant to the CBS television series,*
Black Heritage: A History of Afro-Americans.

*Here is the major portion of Mr. Clarke's address, re-
printed from* Jewish Currents, *May, 1969, pp. 4–9.*

. . . IN THESE BRIEF REMARKS, I am going to see if I can
address myself to how a whole people got lost from the commentary of human history and how, at this present juncture of
history, they are finding themselves and demanding things you
never dreamed they would demand. These demands and this
self-assertion are the basis of a whole lot of problems that need
not be problems.

Now, let us look at how and why the slave trade came, because it was during this period that the African was lost, consciously, from the commentary of human history. To answer
the question, you have to study something other than the slave
trade as such. As a teacher, I never teach this area of history
and call it the slave trade, because this is not what it's about.
My subject, in teaching this, is: The Consequences of the Second Rise of Europe. Until we study the consequences of the
second rise of Europe, we are not going to understand current
events, because, during the first rise of Europe, after the first
decline of Africa, the European, the Graeco-Roman, was not a
racist. There were many African emperors of Rome. This might
come as a complete surprise to you. There were many African
fathers of the early Church. There were many African leaders
of Islam, and the original conqueror of Spain was a black African, not an Arab, Berber or Moor, but a black African who came
from inner Africa.

My point is that we played a major role in human history, in
the shaping of the destiny of man, before the coming of the
slave trade. To understand what did happen to us, you have to
understand, once more, certain things that happened in Europe
between the decline of Rome in the seventh and the eighth centuries and the resurgence of Europe in the fifteenth and six-
tenth centuries. When Europe resurged, reentered the world and

began to expand in the broader world, Europe had endured a number of family quarrels. Europeans not only had no sentimental attachment to the nonwhite world; Europeans did not have too much of a sentimental attachment to each other. The Crusades, the famines, the internal disputes within the Church, all of this had drained Europe of sentiment. Hence the decline in the agricultural output and the need to push out into the broader world in search of something to eat.

There was Henry the Navigator, who never went to sea, incidentally. He began to send his captains down the East Coast and the West Coast of Africa in search of gold and new things. When Columbus stumbled quite by accident upon what is called the New World and introduced the idea of using African labor to develop the New World, this came at a time when the Africans had had a number of family disputes which had weakened the structure of the African countries.

Then the Berbers, the Moors, settlements of Arabs, came back into Africa. As Africans with no sentimental attachment to Africa, they began to prey upon the independent states in East Africa and West Africa. Finally, they broke the structure of these states and made Africa open for the slave trade.

Europe needed a rationale to oppress that many people, to destroy civilizations that were old before Europe was born, to destroy a people that had contributed to the early development of Europe, so they turned to the Church, and the Church obliged them. In 1455, Portugal and Spain went to Pope Callistus III to settle a dispute. He told them: "As for the lines of demarcation, you take the East and you take the West." They didn't quite know which one was supposed to take what, because the Pope's gestures were somewhat ambiguous. Finally, Spain began to gravitate toward the West and Portugal toward the East, and Europe began to expand into the broader world.

Another fight ensued in 1492, and they went back to the Pope. This time, Alexander VI said, "You are both authorized to reduce to servitude all infidel peoples." It just so happened that most of the so-called infidels were nonwhite people. Europe had its rationale now, to go out and subjugate most of the people of the world.

You cannot subjugate a man and recognize his humanity, his history and his personality; so, systematically, you must take this away from him. You begin by telling lies about this man's role in history. You deny that from time immemorial you married into royal families of the very people that you are now enslaving; you deny that you accepted their scholars and gave them homage in the universities of your country. You now set out to prove that they never had any universities, they never had any scholars, they never had any kings, they never had any structured country or any country that's worthy of respect.

It is necessary to take this man out of consideration as a fellow and as a brother under humanity, because, if you acknowledge a man as being totally a man, served by the same humanity that you are served by, no matter what his color may be, you are saying, "That man is an extension of me"; and if the man is an extension of you, there is nothing you can do to him lest you do it to yourself. So, the idea of oppressing people is first to reduce them to nonmen, to insignificant cipher statistics; and this is how African history was lost. Many African history books were gone through and stripped of everything complimentary to Africa; many Africans were turned white. All of a sudden, we see many Africans who were black in history portrayed in the movies as white. The mass media began, when they came into being, to contribute greatly to reading the African out of human history as a hero.

Let me mention a recent example. In a silly movie called *Khartoum*, the leader of the rebellion in the Sudan is a babbling Arab and an idiot. In real life, he was a black African, a Dongula from the Sudan, not an Arab at all. At issue was a people that were members of the Moslem faith fighting a war against England. The people of the Sudan have never been Arabs and are not Arabs now. I say this not to degrade or denigrate the Arab in the slightest. My point is that when an African rises to great magnificence he is depicted as anything but black African. He has to be something else; he has to be Hamitic or Semitic, and these are linguistic terms, not ethnic terms. It took evil genius to set this trend in motion and to set the world up the way it is now. You will not understand it or our present conflict until you understand the rise of a monster called racism.

Nature created no races. Nature created people and people did not refer to themselves as belonging to a race until the rise of the colonial system and of the slave trade concurrent with that system. People belonged to groups and religions, they belonged to clans, they belonged to regional groupings, they belonged to blacksmith guilds and carvers' guilds, but they did not belong to a race in the general sense that we are now talking about. This concept was created to justify European colonialism. I am not saying that prejudice is a European invention, but I am saying that Europeans began prejudice based solely on color of the skin. The European could not acknowledge the role that the African played in the making of the New World.

But for the exploitation of African labor, the capitalist system could never have emerged the way it did. The first large-scale investment in anything, this intercontinental investment, was investment in the slave trade. This was an investment touching three continents, South America, Europe and Africa. The development of embryo technology, principally the gun, gave the Europeans an advantage over most of the peoples in the world.

What we are witnessing now is a people who have been systematically read out of history demanding reentry into history and demanding compensation. This demand is at the basis of so much of the dissension between black people and white people. And white people, who have lived so long thinking and seeing black people in an oppressed servant role, are not ready to see them in a decision-making position effecting paramount change and making the whole new Age of Man.

The reaction of white people is somewhat tragic, because they are throwing away the best possible ally they could ever have— this newly emerged man reentering the mainstream of history and demanding at the very base the respect for his dignity and his humanity as a human being. This reaction is part of the conflict in the school system and is part of what is going into the cry for black history and black power—which is somewhat "old hat" with us. A negative reaction to this cry proves how little you know about the fight that we had in the latter part of the eighteenth and the whole nineteenth century to regain our total self as a human being and to restore the history that has been taken away from us.

This is not a new fight at all and black power is not a new fight at all. We all know that power has no color, power is neutral; but we put a word *black* together with *power* and start frightening people. Then we say, well, now, that's a new weapon so we might as well use this new weapon. But David Walker, in his dramatic appeal to the colored people of the world in 1829, laid the theoretical basis for what you are calling black power.* And the Black Petitioners of the latter eighteenth and throughout the nineteenth century up to the Civil War were demanding the same thing many of our youth are demanding today—that we must be treated and regarded as total human beings.

We seem to have come to some kind of crossroads in our re-

---

* David Walker was the black author of a powerful tract, published in Boston at his own expense in 1829, called *Walker's Appeal, in Four Articles,* addressed to the "coloured citizens" of the world, but particularly to those of the United States. Walker called upon the Negro slaves to revolt and overthrow their oppressors.

lationship because of this demand and yet the demand is not monumental at all. The demand is that when a black child goes to school and reads about heroes, he reads something about the heroes of his own who look like him.

It might break a lot of people's hearts to know that America has been set up as a white Anglo-Saxon Protestant country. A careful scrutiny of the founding fathers, nearly all slaveholders, and of the direction of America shows this is what this country was intended to be. It was intended to be a haven for the white Anglo-Saxon Protestant, and the people not falling into this category seem to have upset the basic pattern of the country.

I tend to believe that the American promise was made only to that branch of America and that this is what makes America such a contradiction at this juncture in history—because this is a multiethnic nation. It is a multiethnic nation that has never made the best use of the fact that is multiethnic. It is throwing away its golden opportunity in the world. Because this country ethnically relates to most of the people in the world, we have some kind of calling card on most of the people of the world and you will be in serious trouble so long as you keep thinking of America as not only a white nation, but as a white Anglo-Saxon Protestant nation. This description is not true; and if it ever was, it is no more.

America must bring all of these components into some kind of concerted effort that can be used for America's projection on the world; and that projection cannot be solely under our present economic system, which is not good for most of the people in the world. Africans have no money to buy out gold mines and oil fields. They have no choice but to nationalize; and no matter what I personally believe, there is absolutely no road for them other than socialism—and I am *not* speaking of Communism. I am speaking of a socialism that would be based on the best socialist values of an African communal society. If this leads them to cooperation with Communism, it is a decision for them to make, but that is not really what I am talking about.

Let me see if I can conclude this by explaining what, then, is the meaning of African history and Afro-American history for today?

The young black kids demanding black-studies programs, even black dormitories, are saying to America and the world, "I am a total human being and I want the respect that is due a total human being." This being the case, you would wonder, why are they demanding black dormitories when their families fought for generations to get integrated dormitories. They are not demanding black dormitories in the general sense. They need to go through a period when something is being done on their terms. They live in a world and a country where everything is being done on somebody else's terms. They want to make the decision. Now, once you give them the black dormitory, chances are most of them won't even live in it; but they would have participated in the decision about whether they should or should not live in it. And this is what so much of the fight is about: our participation in the decision-making apparatus.

I remember a case of two girl students in one of the smaller colleges in New England, an Afro-American student and a white student who were roommates. In jest, the Afro-American girl put on the door, "In this room lives one piece of white trash and black me." She was kidding. The white girl, a nice, naïve, middle-class girl said, "Why would you do this? I accept you, I like you." The black girl answered, "Who gave you permission to like me? You are under consideration as a friend and I haven't finished deliberating on it. I'll let you know whether you'll be accepted or not."

What are they doing? Reversing the procedure. They want to make the decision about whether you should or should not be their friend—because decision making is adulthood and this is the basis of what they are claiming. It is not really monumental at all.

A people in search of themselves and their history are not looking for concessions—concessions can always be taken away. They are seeking acknowledgment of their inalienable right to certain things, the right to make mistakes and correct them and suffer from them—even this.

We are going to enter the mainstream of history. We are going to enter it as some of the decision makers. I am not saying all of these decisions are going to be good. I am saying that, in the light of some of the decisions made by others, they probably could not be worse.

The role of history in the life of a people is to give them a kind of measurement as to where they have been and where they are; and, if they understand history correctly, they will have some definition of what they still must be. At this juncture in history, this is the major search of the black people—finding out where they have been, where they are and what they still must be. This search is going to cause even more trouble before it is finally settled, but it can be settled comparatively easily. If you accept our total human-beingness, then you must accept the fact that our good is equal to your good and, at least sometimes, our bad is equal to your bad.

And what does this prove? Nothing more or less than that we are human beings. And, as human beings, we are now demanding the right to reenter world history and this is what most of the fight is all about. The tragedy of the fight is that *it need not be a fight at all.*

THE KERNER REPORT, PROMISES AND REALITIES

By Ralph David Abernathy

The Reverend Ralph David Abernathy was Martin Luther King's chief lieutenant, and second-in-command in the Southern Christian Leadership Conference. After Dr. King's assassination on April 4, 1968, Dr. Abernathy took over leadership of S.C.L.C. On March 5, 1969, he participated in a symposium at Georgetown University on the Report of the National Advisory Commission on Civil Disorders, or the Kerner Report. His speech was a blunt and frank reminder that other reports had preceded the Kerner Report and had ended up gathering dust on library shelves, and a conviction that this would probably be the same fate of the latest report. Dr. Abernathy keenly examined a number of basic contradictions in American society, and concluded with a call for less talk and more action.

Dr. Abernathy's speech is presented here in part and is excerpted from a copy of the text furnished by, and reprinted with the permission of, the Southern Christian Leadership Conference.

STUDENTS OF Georgetown University, members of the faculty, distinguished guests, ladies and gentlemen:

As your chairman of the Committee organizing this Symposium, Mr. T. Stephen Cheston, said when he invited me, "The Kerner Report will be remembered as one of the major documents in twentieth-century American history. It was comprehensive in its study, incisive in its analysis, and courageous in expressing its findings."

But today, one year after the release of the Kerner Report, I am deeply troubled by a question: Will that report be remembered by all Americans as a call to national action that will save America?

Unhappily, but in candor, I must say to you today that the answer thus far is that the Kerner Report is just another piece of paper gathering dust on a shelf littered with similarly hopeful and promising reports—reports that have been consistently, cynically, cruelly ignored by America.

Let me begin by reminding you of some of these reports. One report, if I may give it that term, was issued 193 years ago. It said in ringing words that were to shake the world for the next two centuries: "We hold these truths to be self-evident, that all men are created equal, that they are endowed by their Creator with certain unalienable rights, that among these are life, liberty, and the pursuit of happiness."

That document, the Declaration of Independence, held great promise, but the reality even today is that no one can pretend that all men are considered equal in America, and that millions of poor people are in fact denied their right to life, liberty and the pursuit of happiness.

The Constitution of the United States took effect 180 years ago, on March 4, 1787, and specifically stated an intention to establish justice, welfare and liberty for all. Yet that same Constitution upheld slavery and condemned my people to a life of injustice, insecurity and bondage.

One hundred and six years ago, in 1863, Lincoln issued the Emancipation Proclamation. The promise was an end to slavery, but what was the reality? The reality was that only the slaves in parts of the South unoccupied by Northern troops were set free, as a military strategy to disrupt the Confederacy. But in Missouri, General Fremont was fired because he set the slaves free.* And the reality also is that my people have been kept in virtual slavery—the slavery of segregation, discrimination and economic exploitation—ever since, in spite of the Emancipation and the Thirteenth Amendment, which was ratified abolishing slavery in 1865.

Next, in 1868, 101 years ago, the Fourteenth Amendment guaranteeing the right of *all people* to life, liberty and property, was ratified. What was the reality? The reality was, for ex-

---

* On August 30, 1861, General John C. Fremont, Commander of the Western Department, issued a proclamation instituting martial law in Missouri and freeing the slaves of every rebel in the state. President Lincoln modified Fremont's proclamation to make it conform with the Confiscation Act of August 6, which confiscated only those slaves who had directly aided the Confederate military forces. When Fremont refused to comply, Lincoln issued an order that he do so.

ample, in that same year, forty thousand black people in South Carolina were promised four hundred thousand acres of farm land. But do you think they ever got it? No! And the reality to this day is that we never did get our rights to life, liberty and property—not even our little forty acres and a mule.

In 1870—ninety-nine years ago—the Fifteenth Amendment, guaranteeing the right to vote, was ratified. In 1890—seventy-nine years ago—Congress passed a bill providing for federal registrars in the South. In 1944—twenty-five years ago—the Supreme Court outlawed the white primary election in Texas. But what happened to all these promises? The reality is that black people were denied the right to vote, and lily-white elections continued in fact, until we in the Southern Christian Leadership Conference put so much pressure on Congress with the Selma-to-Montgomery March that the Voting Rights Act was passed in 1965. Black people now vote in the South, but not without risking harassment, abuse and retaliation, because the Voting Rights Act is not adequately enforced. And another glaring gap between promise and reality is that the Voting Rights Act of 1965 expires in 1970.* And another gap can be seen in the fact that last summer, in the national conventions of both major parties, black people and other poor people were systematically denied proportional representation in their state delegations.

When the Kerner Commission began its hearings, Dr. Kenneth Clark, a very distinguished scholar, pointed out some other promises and realities. He recalled similar reports that had been issued with great fanfare and promise, but ignored in reality: reports on the Chicago riot of 1919, the Harlem riot of 1935, another Harlem riot in 1943, the McCone Commission on Watts three years ago.

We have had the promise of the Supreme Court's school-desegregation order of 1954, fifteen years ago, and the reality of de facto segregation in the South *and* North. We have the promise of a new President saying he wants to "bring us together," but failing to make himself clear on whether he is going to keep our children apart.

* The Voting Rights Act of 1965 made voters of thousands of Southern blacks previously prevented by discrimination from registering or voting. It also put on the voting rolls a number of black illiterates who had not previously been eligible. In 1970 the voting-rights legislation was renewed, and for the next five years literacy tests of qualification for voting in any state were suspended. The legislation also eased residency and other requirements that had limited the right to vote in Presidential elections.

We had the promises of many recent analyses of our racial and economic problems—including recommendations from established business leaders, the report of the White House Conference on Civil Rights, President Johnson's vision of a "Great Society," the repeated eloquent calls to action from my predecessor, Dr. Martin Luther King, Jr., and, finally, the Kerner Report.

And again, what are the realities? All of these studies and reports and calls have been turned aside. Instead of a Great Society, we have a nation gone mad in an evil, unwinnable war in Vietnam. Instead of reforms recommended by moderate business and political leaders, we have the same old subsidies and protections for the rich and oppression of the poor—what I call socialism for the rich and rugged free enterprise for the poor. Instead of investment in life-giving measures for peace and justice, we have investment in death-dealing war, assassination, and daily violence to poor people. Instead of meaningful action on the Kerner Report, one year later we only have another study of the Kerner Report.

Ladies and gentlemen, I am here today to tell you that *I am sick and tired of promises, and I am sick and tired of the realities of war, poverty and racism.* I am also here to tell you that the time has come for more action and fewer words.

I am also here to tell you that Ralph David Abernathy has his own promise to make and a new reality to create. I promise today that I am going to take action to make the recommendations of the Kerner Report, the Poor People's Campaign, and the dozens of other reports I have mentioned a living reality. I am going to confront this nation and the world with the reality of massive, ceaseless confrontation until America deals with the reality of her evils. I am going into the streets of our cities and the plantations of the Southland, and I will take every student, every housewife, every businessman, every working man, the old and young, the robust and the weak, black and white—everyone who believes in justice and who is willing to stand and march with me. I am tired of the promises of Kerner reports. I want the reality of action.

To find out what this nation must do, we need only turn to the Kerner Report. That report recommended, first of all, that full opportunities, rights and benefits be extended to *all* Americans in the areas of jobs, education, welfare and housing. The Kerner Commission disposed of the myths that America cannot afford these reforms and the myth that problems in jobs, education, welfare and housing do not exist. But let me just remind you of a few facts.

In the case of jobs, it was recently disclosed that the Johnson

Administration suppressed a study which found that black workers are held down not so much by inadequate education as by racial discrimination, even among Negroes with superior education. And we all know that black men, particularly young black men, suffer from Depression-level unemployment rates. I say that we must follow the Kerner recommendation to create at least one million new jobs in the public sector and one million in the private sector during the next three years, and to enact massive recruiting and training programs for the poor. We must also have full enforcement of antidiscrimination laws, not the lip-service promises of the past. Did you know that the President signed an order three years ago which would remove defense contracts from companies which practice racial discrimination—and that not one single contract has been withheld, not even in the South?

To anyone who asks, can we afford to create these jobs? My answer is this: If Congress can raise its own pay by 40 percent in 1969, spend two and a half billion dollars a month on the war in Vietnam, give jobs to an army of political patronage workers, and build 1,710 I.C.B.M.'s with nuclear bombs, then America can create the jobs that are so desperately needed.

In education, the Kerner Report stated that we must eliminate segregation and provide the best modern education for all, from preschool to college and vocational training. If you doubt the need for this, go into any black school in Washington, D. C., and see the terribly inadequate facilities, teachers and curriculum for black children. Or go into any white school and see the failure to teach the evils of racism, economic oppression and war. Or go to a public hospital and see poor people dying because we have not educated enough doctors, black or white.

If you ask, can we afford to educate our children? Check into the massive spending on schools in the affluent suburbs—for example, Montgomery County, Maryland, a few miles from this campus. I say, if Mr. Nixon can spend fifteen times as much on guns and war as he does on education, the time has come to reduce the killing and escalate the teaching.

The Kerner Report recommended in the field of welfare and incomes that federal standards be adopted to insure full rights and benefits to all recipients, and that the United States of America, the richest country in history, should follow the example of all other industrialized and civilized nations by providing a guaranteed income.

When I talk about welfare, I think the very word "welfare" is a joke. As it exists today, the welfare system degrades and punishes people, it has no policy for helping people get out of the welfare cycle (which they desperately want to do), it denies most recipients as much as half of the benefits to which they are entitled by law, and it prevents hundreds of thousands of people eligible for welfare from getting any benefits at all. When I talk about income, I do not mean the family allowances proposed by Mr. Daniel Patrick Moynihan.* The vast majority of people who would be helped by his scheme are not poor at all, and even the rich would get the allowances. I think the rich already receive too many tax advantages and government handouts. The poor should be guaranteed a decent annual income.

Once again, people ask: Can we afford a decent welfare system and a guaranteed income? My answer is that if we can pay Senator Eastland $13,000 a month *not* to grow food or fiber on his plantation, we can pay more than the nine dollars a month that a hungry child receives in welfare in the state of Mississippi. And if we can guarantee the incomes of retired Congressmen and Presidents, we can guarantee incomes to people who cannot get jobs and mothers of infants and old folks and sick people. If we can guarantee a few thousand cotton, tobacco and sugar farmers more subsidy payments than forty million poor people get in the entire antipoverty program, we can have a guaranteed income for all. Finally, if we really believe in equality in America, we can ask ourselves why there is nothing close to equality of income for black people. Americans now receive 550 billion dollars in personal income each year. If black people make up 11 percent of the population—actually, the census does not count millions of us—but if we had even 11 percent of the income, we would be earning 60.5 billion dollars. But in reality, we receive only 27 billion.

In the field of housing, the Kerner Commission found that open-housing laws and building codes must be enforced, and we need massive housing programs for the poor—including Model Cities, rent supplements, and modern, decent low-cost housing. None of these things have been done. Earlier, I mentioned the many gaps between promises and realities in America. You may not know that one of these gaps has been in enforcing housing laws. Congress passed an open-housing law covering all housing in the nation in 1866—one hundred three years ago.†

* Daniel Patrick Moynihan, author of a controversial report on the Negro family during the administration of Lyndon Johnson, and an adviser on urban problems to President Nixon, proposed a family allowance to replace the welfare system. The amount the government would provide under his plan was limited to $1,200 for a family.
† The Federal Civil Rights Act of 1866 contained the following provision: "All citizens of the United States shall have the same right, in

It has never been enforced, even in spite of the open-housing act of 1968 and the Supreme Court's decision for open housing last summer. Similarly, existing housing programs have never really served poor and black people. More people have been made homeless by urban renewal than have been provided with new homes. Public-housing projects are prisons, where the occupants have no rights and are terrorized by rats. Privately owned slum housing is ruled by the human form of rats, the absentee slum landlord. Model Cities and rent supplements have never been fully funded, and the existing ceilings for these programs should be greatly increased.

Once again, it is asked: Can we afford decent housing? If we can subsidize the whole middle class of America with tax concessions for buying homes, then we can certainly provide housing for poor people. If we give free housing to military people, why not the poor? If we can talk piously about "law and order," how about starting by enforcing open-housing laws and cracking down on the crimes of slum landlords?

Those are my conclusions in reference to the Kerner Report's recommendations on jobs, education, welfare, income and housing.

I now turn briefly to its two other major recommendations.

The first is that black people and other poor and oppressed people should control their own lives and communities, so that the great frustrations of powerlessness will be removed. What is supposedly more traditional in America than local control? The majority of Americans enjoy a significant measure of control over their lives. Let us extend this to all. Let us give the poor —not mayors, governors and bureaucrats—control of the poverty program. Let us extend this to all. Let poor tenants control the management and upkeep of their homes. Let black businesses and services develop—not as in a phony "black capitalism" to make a few men rich, but as a kind of "black socialism" of cooperative efforts to serve the entire community. Let poor workers organize collectively into a powerful bargaining force. Let poor people unite for political control of their communities. Let the poor develop police protection in their own neighborhoods and eliminate the police state now imposed on the ghettos of America by the white power structure. And let the students of America demand, demonstrate, win, and exercise

---

every state and territory, as is enjoyed by white citizens thereof to inherit, purchase, lease, sell, hold and convey real and personal property." In 1968 the Supreme Court ruled that this forbade discrimination in all real-estate sales.

their rights to, an education that is not dehumanizing and oppressive, but humane and free and truthful. We need to close the generation gap in America, and the way to do it is not to beat students' heads, but to teach older people how to be young again.

The last objective stated by the Kerner Report was simply that we must have increased communication across racial lines "to destroy stereotypes, to halt polarization, to end distrust and hostility, and to create common ground for efforts toward goals of public order and social justice."

The need for this is so obvious that I need not elaborate on it except to say this: In the case of all of the Kerner Commission's recommendations, the important thing now is to *go ahead and do it.* I am confident that students and young people especially are ready, willing and able to seek the interracial communications we are talking about. Indeed, this process began among young people long ago, and it is continuing. I only urge you to accelerate this.

My other challenge to you today is to take action with me for the kinds of reforms suggested by the Kerner report. We must admit the white racism in America, just as the Kerner Commission did,* and we must take action to end it.

No amount of talk, and certainly no report, will produce the changes we need in America.

I urge you to join me, the Southern Christian Leadership Conference, and many national, regional and local organizations of the rich and poor, young and old, in a new movement to save America. . . .

IT IS TIME FOR A CHANGE

By Shirley Chisholm

Shirley St. Hill Chisholm *was born in 1925 in Brooklyn, New York. She has been a teacher, director of nursery schools and child-care centers and a lecturer in education at Brooklyn College. She was elected to the New York State*

* In its report, the Kerner Commission noted, in discussing the black ghettos: "White institutions created it, white institutions maintain it, and white society condones it." (*U. S. Riot Commission Report. Report of the National Advisory Commission on Civil Disorders*, New York, 1968, p. 145.)

Assembly in 1964 and served there until her election to Congress. Mrs. Chisholm was elected from the 12th Congressional District, centered in the heavily black Bedford-Stuyvesant neighborhood. Assigned to a House Agricultural subcommittee on Forestry and Rural Villages, she fought to change her assignment to something more relevant to her Bedford-Stuyvesant community, and she was assigned to the Veterans Affairs Committee.

In her first speech before the House of Representatives, March 26, 1969, the first black woman member of Congress, known as Fighting Shirley Chisholm, called for a change in American values and priorities. She vowed to vote "No" on every money bill that came before the House until the nation "starts to use its strength, its tremendous resources, for people and peace, not for profits and war." Here is Mrs. Chisholm's first speech in the House; it is reprinted from the Congressional Record, 91st Congress, 1st Session, pp. H2242–43.

MR. SPEAKER, on the same day President Nixon announced he had decided the United States will not be safe unless we start to build a defense system against missiles, the Headstart program in the District of Columbia was cut back for the lack of money.

As a teacher, and as a woman, I do not think I will ever understand what kind of values can be involved in spending nine billion dollars—and more, I am sure—on elaborate, unnecessary and impractical weapons when several thousand disadvantaged children in the nation's capital get nothing.

When the new administration took office, I was one of the many Americans who hoped it would mean that our country would benefit from the fresh perspectives, the new ideas, the different priorities of a leader who had no part in the mistakes of the past. Mr. Nixon had said things like this:

"If our cities are to be livable for the next generation, we can delay no longer in launching new approaches to the problems that beset them and to the tensions that tear them apart."

And he said, "When you cut expenditures for education, what you are doing is shortchanging the American future."

But frankly, I have never cared too much what people say. What I am interested in is what they do.* We have waited to

---

* Congresswoman Chisholm was paraphrasing President Nixon's frequent remark when dealing with the problems of black Americans: "Don't watch what I say; watch what I do."

see what the new administration is going to do. The pattern now is becoming clear.

Apparently launching those new programs can be delayed for a while, after all. It seems we have to get some missiles launched first.

Recently the new Secretary of Commerce spelled it out. The Secretary, Mr. Stans, told a reporter that the new administration is "pretty well agreed it must take time out from major social objectives" until it can stop inflation.

The new Secretary of Health, Education and Welfare, Robert Finch, came to the Hill to tell the House Education and Labor Committee that he thinks we should spend more on education, particularly in city schools. But, he said, unfortunately we cannot "afford" to, until we have reached some kind of honorable solution to the Vietnam war. I was glad to read that the distinguished Member from Oregon [Mrs. Green] asked Mr. Finch this:

"With the crisis we have in education, and the crisis in our cities, can we wait to settle the war? Shouldn't it be the other way around? Unless we can meet the crisis in education, we really can't afford the war."

Secretary of Defense Melvin Laird came to Capitol Hill, too. His mission was to sell the antiballistic-missile insanity to the Senate. He was asked what the new administration is doing about the war. To hear him, one would have thought it was 1968, that the former Secretary of State was defending the former policies, that nothing had ever happened—a President had never decided not to run because he knew the nation would reject him, in despair over this tragic war we have blundered into. Mr. Laird talked of being prepared to spend at least two more years in Vietnam.

Two more years, two more years of hunger for Americans, of death for our best young men, of children here at home suffering the lifelong handicap of not having a good education when they are young. Two more years of high taxes, collected to feed the cancerous growth of a Defense Department budget that now consumes two thirds of our federal income.

Two more years of too little being done to fight our greatest enemies, poverty, prejudice and neglect, here in our own country. Two more years of fantastic waste in the Defense Department and of penny pinching on social programs. Our country cannot survive two more years, or four, of these kinds of policies. It must stop—this year—now.

Now, I am not a pacifist. I am deeply, unalterably opposed to this war in Vietnam. Apart from all the other considerations—

and they are many—the main fact is that we cannot squander there the lives, the money, the energy that we need desperately here, in our cities, in our schools.

I wonder whether we cannot reverse our whole approach to spending. For years, we have given the military, the defense industry, a blank check. New weapons systems are dreamed up, billions are spent, and many times they are found to be impractical, inefficient, unsatisfactory, even worthless. What do we do then? We spend more money on them. But with social programs, what do we do? Take the Job Corps. Its failure has been mercilessly exposed and criticized. If it had been a military research and development project, they would have been covered up or explained away, and Congress would have been ready to pour more billions after those that had been wasted on it.

The case of Pride, Inc., is interesting. This vigorous, successful black organization, here in Washington, conceived and built by young inner-city men, has been ruthlessly attacked by its enemies in the government, in this Congress. At least six auditors from the General Accounting Office were put to work investigating Pride. They worked seven months and spent more than $100,000. They uncovered a fraud. It was something less than $2,100. Meanwhile, millions of dollars—billions of dollars, in fact—were being spent by the Department of Defense, and how many auditors and investigators were checking into their negotiated contracts? Five.

We Americans have come to feel that it is our mission to make the world free. We believe that we are the good guys, everywhere—in Vietnam, in Latin America, wherever we go. We believe we are the good guys at home, too. When the Kerner Commission told white America what black America had always known, that prejudice and hatred built the nation's slums, maintain them and profit by them, white America would not believe it.* But it is true. Unless we start to fight and defeat the enemies of poverty and racism in our own country and make our talk of equality and opportunity ring true, we are exposed as hypocrites in the eyes of the world when we talk about making other people free.

I am deeply disappointed at the clear evidence that the

* The National Advisory Commission on Civil Disorders was appointed by President Johnson following the racial disorders in American cities during the summer of 1967. President Johnson directed the Commission to answer three basic questions: What happened? Why did it happen? What can be done to prevent it from happening again? The Commission was headed by Otto Kerner, Governor of Illinois, and its report, submitted in March, 1968, was widely published and discussed.

number-one priority of the new administration is to buy more and more weapons of war, to return to the era of the cold war, to ignore the war we must fight here—the war that is not optional. There is only one way, I believe, to turn these policies around. The Congress can respond to the mandate that the American people have clearly expressed. They have said, "End this war. Stop the waste. Stop the killing. Do something for your own people first." We must find the money to "launch the new approaches," as Mr. Nixon said. We must force the administration to rethink its distorted, unreal scale of priorities. Our children, our jobless men, our deprived, rejected and starving fellow citizens must come first.

For this reason, I intend to vote "No" on every money bill that comes to the floor of this House that provides any funds for the Department of Defense. Any bill whatsoever, until the time comes when our values and priorities have been turned right side up again, until the monstrous waste and the shocking profits in the defense budget have been eliminated and our country starts to use its strength, its tremendous resources, for people and peace, not for profits and war.

It was Calvin Coolidge, I believe, who made the comment that "the Business of America is Business." We are now spending eighty billion dollars a year on defense—that is two thirds of every tax dollar. At this time, gentlemen, the business of America is war, and it is time for a change.

THE "BLACK MANIFESTO": TOTAL CONTROL AS THE ONLY SOLUTION TO THE ECONOMIC PROBLEMS OF BLACK PEOPLE

By James Forman

In 1967 the Interreligious Foundation for Community Organization was founded in New York City with Protestant, Catholic, Mexican-American, black and one Jewish group (the American Jewish Committee) participating. In two years the I.F.C.O. gave $885,831 to thirty-seven organizations to promote worthy efforts to improve the lot of the black people. One allotment was for a National Black Eco-

nomic Development Conference, held in Detroit, April
25–27, 1969. It was here that black militant leader James
Forman brought forth his controversial "Black Manifesto"
calling for American churches and synagogues to pay
blacks five hundred million dollars—a sum later raised to
three billion—in reparations for the evils of slavery. The
"Black Manifesto" stated that "even if these demands were
met in full these inequities and injustices (suffered by the
Negro people) would not be rectified." The "Black Mani-
festo" was adopted by the Conference by a vote of 183–63
after heated discussion, with many of the six hundred dele-
gates abstaining.

On May 4, 1969, Forman startled the religious com-
munity, as well as the entire nation, when he and his sup-
porters disrupted services at Manhattan's Riverside Church
to read the "Black Manifesto." Below is the text of James
Forman's speech introducing the "Black Manifesto" to the
Conference; it is taken from Action Training Clearing-
House Notes, Metropolitan Urban Service Training
(MUST), New York City.

BROTHERS AND SISTERS: We have come from all over
the country, burning with anger and despair not only with the
miserable economic plight of our people, but fully aware that
the racism on which the Western world was built dominates our
lives. There can be no separation of the problems of racism
from the problems of our economic, political and cultural
degradation. To any black man, this is clear.

But there are still some of our people who are clinging to the
rhetoric of the Negro and we must separate ourselves from
those Negroes who go around the country promoting all types
of schemes for black capitalism.

Ironically, some of the most militant black nationalists, as
they call themselves, have been the first to jump on the band-
wagon of black capitalism. They are pimps—black power
pimps and fraudulent leaders, and the people must be educated
to understand that any black man or Negro who is advocating a
perpetuation of capitalism inside the United States is in fact
seeking not only his ultimate destruction and death, but is
contributing to the continuous exploitation of black people all
around the world. For it is the power of the United States
government, this racist, imperialist government, that is choking
the life of all people around the world.

We are an African people. We sit back and watch the Jews
in this country make Israel a powerful conservative state in

the Middle East, but we are not concerned actively about the plight of our brothers in Africa. We are the most advanced technological group of black people in the world, and there are many skills that could be offered to Africa. At the same time, it must be publicly stated that many African leaders are in disarray themselves, having been duped into following the lines as laid out by the Western imperialist governments.

Africans themselves succumbed to and are victims of the power of the United States. For instance, during the summer of 1967, as the representatives of S.N.C.C., Howard Moore and I traveled extensively in Tanzania and Zambia. We talked to high, very high, governmental officials. We told them there were many black people in the United States who were willing to come and work in Africa. All these governmental officials, who were part of the leadership in their respective governments, said they wanted us to send as many skilled people as we could contact. But this program never came into fruition and we do not know the exact reason, for I assure you that we talked and were committed to making this a successful program. It is our guess that the United States put the squeeze on these countries, for such a program directed by S.N.C.C. would have been too dangerous to the international prestige of the United States. It is also possible that some of the wild statements by some black leader frightened the Africans.

In Africa today, there is a great suspicion of black people in this country. This is a correct suspicion, since most of the Negroes who have left the States for work in Africa usually work for the Central Intelligence Agency (C.I.A.) or the State Department. But the respect for us as a people continues to mount, and the day will come when we can return to our homelands as brothers and sisters. But we should not think of going back to Africa today, for we are located in a strategic position. We live inside the United States which is the most barbaric country in the world and we have a chance to help bring this government down.

Time is short and we do not have much time, and it is time we stop mincing words. Caution is fine, but no oppressed people ever gained their liberation until they were ready to fight, to use whatever means necessary, including the use of force and power of the gun to bring down the colonizer.

We have heard the rhetoric, but we have not heard the rhetoric which says that black people in this country must understand that we are the vanguard force. We shall liberate all the people in the United States and we will be instrumental in the liberation of colored people the world around. We must understand this point very clearly, so that we are not trapped into diversionary and reactionary movements. Any class analysis of the United States shows very clearly that black people are the most oppressed group of people inside the United States. We have suffered the most from racism and exploitation, cultural degradation and lack of political power. It follows from the laws of revolution that the most oppressed will make the revolution, but we are not talking about just making the revolution. All the parties on the left who consider themselves revolutionary will say that blacks are the vanguard, but we are saying that not only are we the vanguard, but we must assume leadership, total control and we must exercise the humanity which is inherent in us. We are the most humane people within the United States. We have suffered and we understand suffering. Our hearts go out to the Vietnamese, for we know what it is to suffer under the domination of racist America. Our hearts, our soul and all the compassion we can mount goes out to our brothers in Africa, Santo Domingo, Latin America and Asia who are being tricked by the power structure of the United States, which is dominating the world today. These ruthless, barbaric men have systematically tried to kill all people and organizations opposed to its imperialism. We no longer can just get by with the use of the word *capitalism* to describe the United States, for it is an imperial power, sending money missionaries and the Army throughout the world to protect this government and the few rich whites who control it. General Motors and all the major auto makers see no relationship to the exploitation of black people in South Africa and the exploitation of black people in the United States. If they understand it, they certainly do not put it into practice, which is the actual test. We as black people must be concerned with the total conditions of all black people in the world.

But while we talk of revolution, which will be an armed confrontation and long years of sustained guerrilla warfare inside this country, we must also talk of the type of world we want to live in. We must commit ourselves to a society where the total means of production are taken from the rich and placed into the hands of the state for the welfare of all the people. This is what we mean when we say total control. And we mean that black people who have suffered the most from exploitation and racism must move to protect their black interest by assuming leadership inside the United States of everything that exists. The time has passed when we are second in command and the white boy stands on top. This is especially true of the welfare agencies in this country, but it is not enough to say that a

black man is on top. He must be committed to building the new
society, to taking the wealth away from the rich people such as
General Motors, Ford, Chrysler, the Duponts, the Rockefellers,
the Mellons, and all the other rich white exploiters and racists
who run this world.

Where do we begin? We have already started. We started the
moment we were brought to this country. In fact, we started on
the shores of Africa, for we have always resisted attempts to
make us slaves and now we must resist the attempts to make
us capitalists. It is the financial interest of the United States
to make us capitalists, for this will be the same line as that of
integration into the mainstream of American life. Therefore,
brothers and sisters, there is no need to fall into the trap that we
have to get an ideology. We have an ideology. Our fight is
against racism, capitalism and imperialism, and we are dedicated to building a socialist society inside the United States
where the total means of production and distribution are in the
hands of the state, and that must be led by black people, by
revolutionary blacks who are concerned about the total humanity of this world. And therefore, we obviously are different from
some of those who seek a black nation in the United States, for
there is no way for that nation to be viable if in fact the United
States remains in the hands of white racists. Then, too, let us
deal with some arguments that we should share power with
whites. We say that there must be a revolutionary black vanguard and that white people in this country must be willing to
accept black leadership, for that is the only protection that
black people have to protect ourselves from racism rising again
in this country.

Racism in the United States is so pervasive in the mentality
of whites that only an armed, well-disciplined, black-controlled
government can insure the stamping out of racism in this
country. And that is why we plead with black people not to
be talking about a few crumbs, a few thousand dollars for this
cooperative, or a thousand dollars which splits black people
into fighting over the dollar. That is the intention of the government. We say . . . think in terms of total control of the United
States. Prepare ourselves to seize state power. Do not hedge,
for time is short and all around the world, the forces of liberation are directing their attacks against the United States. It is
a powerful country, but that power is not greater than that of
black people. We work the chief industries in this country and
we could cripple the economy while the brothers fought guerrilla warfare in the streets. This will take some long-range planning, but whether it happens in a thousand years is of no con-

sequence. It cannot happen unless we start. How, then, is all of this related to this conference?

First of all, this conference is called by a set of religious people, Christians, who have been involved in the exploitation and rape of black people since the country was founded. The missionary goes hand in hand with the power of the states. We must begin seizing power wherever we are, and we must say to the planners of this conference that you are no longer in charge. We the people who have assembled here thank you for getting us here, but we are going to assume power over the conference and determine, from this moment on, the direction in which we want it to go. We are not saying that the conference was planned badly. The staff of the conference have worked hard and have done a magnificent job in bringing all of us together, and we must include them in the new membership which must surface from this point on. The conference is now the property of the people who are assembled here. This we proclaim as a fact and not rhetoric, and there are demands that we are going to make and we insist that the planners of this conference help us implement them.

We maintain we have the revolutionary right to do this. We have the same rights, if you will, as the Christians had in going into Africa and raping our Motherland and bringing us away from our continent of peace into this hostile and alien environment where we have been living in perpetual warfare since 1619.

A NEW MOVEMENT AND A NEW METHOD

By Julian Bond

In a speech he gave before the Lexington Democratic Club Annual Dinner in New York City, May, 1969, Julian Bond, twenty-nine, member of Georgia's House of Representatives, analyzed the situation facing black Americans in 1969.

Julian Bond helped found the Student Nonviolent Coordinating Committee, and he worked as publicity chairman from 1961 to 1965, throughout the voter-registration drives in Mississippi and Alabama. He dropped out of college to devote his time to civil-rights work, and then ran for the Georgia House of Representatives. He came into the national spotlight in January, 1966, when he was denied his seat in the legislature because he refused to withdraw endorsement of a statement denouncing United States involvement in the Vietnam war issued by S.N.C.C. He was seated a year later as a result of a Supreme Court decision. In 1968, running unopposed, he was reelected. At the 1968 Democratic National Convention in Chicago he was spokesman of the Southern Challenge Coordinating Committee and leader of Georgia's loyalist delegation, challenging Governor Lester Maddox's hand-picked delegation, and winning half the state's seats.

Here are excerpts from Julian Bond's speech, taken from Daily World, *May 31, 1969.*

BEFORE I BEGIN, I must admit to a prejudice, a bias. That is race. Most of my life has been colored by race, so you will pardon me if most of my address is colored by race.

Let me begin by trying to describe exactly where black Americans find themselves in 1969, and go from there to list some of the ways we have tried to improve that condition.

To begin with, we are becoming, with most of America, an urban population. In Washington, D. C., where we can't elect a dogcatcher, much less a mayor, we are over 60 percent of the population.* In Richmond, Nashville, New Orleans, Jacksonville and Birmingham, we are over 40 percent of the population. Atlanta; Compton, California; Gary, Indiana; Baltimore; St. Louis; Newark; Detroit and Trenton will have majority black populations by 1970.

We know, too, that some things in America over the past several years have gotten better for some few of us.

We can eat where we never ate before, go to school where we never went to school before, and can sit in the front of buses that never used to stop. There are more Negroes holding

---

* During the late 1870's residents of the District of Columbia were disfranchised when Congress abolished the District government. It was abolished, *The Christian Recorder* editorialized on February 26, 1880, "for the reason that the strength of the colored vote was such as would result in filling one-half of the offices with colored officers. This was too much for the whites, and rather than have it so, they readily assented to their own disfranchisement. What is it that prejudice to the colored man will not do?"

In 1971 the vote was partially restored to residents of the District of Columbia when they obtained the right to vote for a nonvoting delegate to Congress.

elective office today in all parts of this country, and more Negroes making more money now than ever before. More of us are registered to vote and more of us are voting.

But for most of us, things have not gotten better. Let me quote America's authority on race relations, President Lyndon B. Johnson:

In 1948 [the President said] the 8 percent unemployment rate for Negro teen-age boys was actually less than that of whites. By 1964, the rate for Negroes had grown to 23 percent as against 13 percent for whites. Between 1949 and 1959, the income of Negro men relative to white men declined in every section of the country. From 1952 to 1963, the median income of Negro families compared to white actually dropped from 57 to 53 percent. Since 1947, the number of white families living in poverty has decreased 27 percent, while the number of nonwhite families living in poverty has decreased only 3 percent. The infant mortality of nonwhites in 1940 was 70 percent greater than whites. In 1962, it was 90 percent greater.

To use President Johnson's figures, the rate of unemployment for Negroes and whites in 1930 was about the same. In 1965, the Negro rate was twice as high.

We must in all candor admit that poverty is not the exclusive province of America's blacks. There are poor white people as well. They, however, enjoy the dubious distinction of knowing they are not poor because they are white, but rather they are poor in spite of their whiteness.

Since 1954, there have been various sorts of methods and techniques directed at solving America's white problem. These have included the sit-in demonstration and nonviolent march, the pursuit of education as a barrier breaker, the use of violence as an inducement to change, the challenging in the courts of segregation by law, and the thrust for power through political action.

In the immediate past few years, the country at large has begun to change.

In 1964, the poor American community was promised that poverty would end. By 1967, a foreign war had rendered that promise—if it was ever meant—nearly useless. Between 1961 and 1964, the country officially denounced violence and war as a means of settling disputes between persons or nations. From 1965 to the present, violence has been the official policy of the government of the United States in settling her own disputes with other nations, and that belief has seeped into the police stations and slums across the land.

In 1964, a young black man thought he might get a job, but in 1968, the only job open to him was being a soldier. War brewed anger in the black community, and it gave birth to the belief that nonviolence was only a joke to be played on, or played by, the black community.

Is not the status quo as violent as any Watts or Newark or Detroit? Is it not violent to condemn to death twice the proportion of black babies as white babies in their first year? Is it not violent to send twice the proportion of black men as white men to Vietnam every year?

There are those in America who believe that a nonviolent confrontation will force a reluctant government to turn its attention homeward and toward a real solution of the white problem in America.

There are those who are convinced that nothing good will come tomorrow unless the structure of today is changed, and who will willingly kill and die on these streets either in frustration and rage or in the faint hope that from destruction will come a newer, better day.

There are those who believe that giving some small power— the appearance of control of neighborhood schools, decision making in some forms of government—will hold off the day of Armageddon that many think is coming.

And there are those for whom the major problem has become the right to smoke pot, to throw flowers, while for others the fight is for the right to breathe air or to throw bombs.

When one looks for an answer to what is called the domestic crisis, or the urban crisis, one ought to look at the places where these problems are the most concentrated. That place is what Dr. Kenneth Clark has called the "dark ghetto."

"The dark ghettos," Clark writes, "are social, political, educational and, above all, economic colonies. Their inhabitants are subject people, victims of the greed, cruelty, insensitivity, guilt and fear of their masters."

Using that description, the terms "colony" and "colonized people" will correctly describe the condition of those dark millions who even today are deserting the mechanized feudal system of the South for the more highly mechanized—and more highly segregated, in a sophisticated way—ghettos of the North and West.

From the colonies must come a new movement and a new method.

We ought to remind ourselves of the method an earlier colony on these shores took to free itself from oppression; that method was armed rebellion, insurrection, seizure of property, death and destruction—the American war of 1776.

If a new sort of movement springs from the active protests and organizing drives of the early sixties, it must be first of all (small d) democratic. It must extend to every member of the black community the opportunity to have a say in who gets how much of what from whom. It must cast its votes in a unit, it must deal with problems on a local, regional, national and international basis, and it must decide that freedoms not enjoyed in Watts or Sunflower County cannot be enjoyed in Westchester County.

It must declare itself in the interest of laboring people, but not become the mistress of organized labor.

It has to seek out its natural allies in the Spanish-speaking community, but must not close its eyes to potential allies in middle-class suburbia.

It must pay as much attention to a street light in a 50-foot alley as it does to national legislation involving millions of people, and international complication involving the future of the world.

It must maintain a militance and an aggressiveness that will earn it the respect of those it hopes to lead.

If there are any rules peculiar to this new movement in politics, they would be these:

1. That social, economic, educational, political and physical segregation and discrimination fill a very real need for the white majority;

2. That appeals to justice and fair play are outmoded and useless when power, financial gain and prestige are at stake;

3. That positions of segregation and discrimination will be adhered to until change is forced through coercion, threats, power or violence;

4. That initiative for black political education and organization must come from within the Negro community and must be sustained on a day-by-day basis;

5. That the geographical distribution of Negroes makes Negrowhite coalitions desirable, but only when based on racial self-interest and genuine equality between the coalescing groups; but

6. That racial self-interest, race consciousness and racial solidarity must always be paramount in the deeds and words of the black political animal; when self-interest is forgotten, organized racism will continue to dominate and frustrate the best-organized political actions of any black political unit, and will leave it powerless and defenseless.

This new movement must address itself to solving America's white problem, to developing a new sophistication and consciousness in the black and white communities, and in making democracy safe for the world.

Peaceful protests—and the bloodied heads of anonymous thousands—have won the lunch-counter seat, the bus-station bench, the integrated toilet and the vote.

This new movement can be a tool for further, more meaningful gains, the gains that fill bellies and build homes and schools, but only if we reject the dangerous sort of equality that we are winning today.

That equality gives us an equal chance to be poor, and equal chance to be unemployed, an equal chance to drop out of school, and a more-than-equal chance to fight for someone else's freedoms thousands of miles from home.

That equality must be suppressed and replaced with an equality that provides full employment of guaranteed incomes, and makes the American nightmare the American dream.

Only when we have gotten ourselves together, only when we shall have decided who our enemies are and where the battleground ought to be, only when we know in our hearts we are right and only when we demand that our worse-off are treated as well as white America's best-off will we begin to see whether this system and this method can make a difference in our lives.

Having done all that, having built a new movement; having forged a new majority coalition, having put people in motion, one further thing will be needed, from black and white, rich and poor alike.

That one further thing is something simple. It is what high school and college graduation speakers urge upon their charges. It is called *commitment*.

In our terms, it means the kind of commitment from young people that would have kept the South in ferment from the heady days of 1964 till the present; it is the kind of commitment that takes over the dean's office one day, but the welfare office the next, the kind of commitment that will mean year-round participation in a new politics, a people politics, a politics that will insure a choice, and not an echo, at the top of the ballot in November, 1972.

WE ARE GOING TO MAKE IT BETTER FOR BLACKS AND WHITES

By Charles Evers

On June 12, 1963, Medgar Evers, field secretary of the Mississippi N.A.A.C.P., was assassinated by a white racist in the driveway of his home in Jackson. Charles Evers, his brother, picked up the struggle for the rights of the blacks in Mississippi where Medgar Evers had been forced to abandon it. In the spring of 1969, Charles Evers was elected mayor of the town of Fayette—the first Negro mayor to be elected in Mississippi since Reconstruction. Eleven black aldermen were also elected.

In May, 1969, Charles Evers was the guest of honor at a party in New York City. He delivered a speech; and, although he had not prepared his remarks, the speech was recorded by a reporter for The New Yorker, *where it was published. "We think what he said," declared* The New Yorker, *"is the best speech we have ever heard by anyone running for or elected to the office of mayor." Here is the speech, reprinted from* The New Yorker, *June 14, 1969, with the permission of Mr. Evers and* The New Yorker.

ALL OF US have won a victory in Mississippi. All the poor blacks, and all the concerned, scared whites. I'm not going to belittle the whites, because they need help, just as we need help. Whatever we have done was made possible by men like Medgar, John, Dr. King, and Bobby.* Their lives made it possible not for Charles Evers to get elected, but for all Americans in the state of Mississippi to have the right to go to the polls. They wanted to end hate and destruction in our country. This past Tuesday, part of their hope became a reality. Others came and helped us, too. John Lewis came, and he'd just got married. Paul O'Dwyer came all the way from New York, just to be there. And many others helped us with their work and their prayers. This is not a celebration for Charles Evers but for all of us—the lesser-known and the better-known. I did nothing special. I don't deserve a pat on the back. It's my duty to do it. Everyone did it—

---

* Medgar Evers, John F. Kennedy, Dr. Martin Luther King, Jr., and Robert F. Kennedy—all victims of assassination.

doctors, mothers, fathers, pool sharks and cabdrivers. I pray
every day that I never become anything special. We've also got
to mention Governor Rockefeller. He's one of the few whites
who over the years has done something for the poor folks. We
know that whatever happens in Mississippi affects the people in
New York, and that whatever happens in New York affects the
people in Mississippi. We're all God's children. He brought us
all here. And those of us who are more affluent have something
special to do. I don't mean being braggadacios. But He equipped
us to go out and help our brothers. We're going to show the
whites down there—the whites who have done so much to hurt
us—that it's so easy to do good. We're going to say to all the
blacks: Don't get mad, get smart. Don't shoot our brother, and
don't bomb him. Just vote him out of office. Because the right
will prevail. All the mean folks in this country will someday be
gone. And then the country will belong to the good folks.

You can't blame the kids for what is happening in this country, and you can't blame the blacks. It is the system which has
kept us in the corner. But the black mayor and the black aldermen of Fayette are going to behave the same to everyone:
young, in-between, old; black, white; rich, poor. We're going to
prove this to white America. When you whites come to Fayette,
you'll be able to drive there. And if you speed, we'll charge you
the same amount we charge anyone. White and black, in our
town, will pay the same cost of speeding—a dollar a mile per
hour. Now, the mayor gets his salary from traffic fines. And
when you win, I lose. I hope they put me out of business. When
you get arrested in Fayette, you're not going to be abused. No
policeman is going to strike anyone. If I ever hear of any policeman hitting any man, he will be fired in a moment. We are not
going to tolerate any brutality.

We need industry in Fayette. We got no jobs down there.
We're seventy-five percent of the population of that town, and
sixty-five percent of us blacks are on welfare. Twenty percent
of us are unemployed. The average level of education is less
than the fifth grade. The average income is under a thousand
dollars. There is not a single playground or swimming pool in
town. It's not just the black folks who don't have these things.
Nobody does. There are shack houses and no sewers. This is
what white America has done to us. But we twelve blacks are
going to make it better for blacks and whites. My dad always
said, "Don't ever destroy anything or anybody." So we're all going to live and struggle together to make it a decent town. There
are thirty-nine million poor folks in this country, and we blacks
are only twenty-two million. That means there are a lot of poor

Mexicans, poor Indians, poor Puerto Ricans, and poor whites—millions of all of us. That's why we're going to be mayor and aldermen for all our citizens. On July the seventh, we take office. On July the eighth, we are going to enforce a law that will read something like this: "Anyone found carrying a gun in this town will be sent to jail for six months." There ain't nobody going to practice violence in our town. Then we'll issue an order saying that there will be no more discrimination in this town. And any contractor or shopkeeper—anyone—who doesn't comply is going to be prosecuted. Our schools will be open to everybody. There will be one school system, and that's all. Maybe what we do in Mississippi will help our black brothers and our white brothers all over the country. I'm only here to say: Let's help ourselves. Let's not cast anybody off, and let's not hate anybody. I'm not even going to hate that old chief of police, whom I'm going to fire on July the eighth.

It can be done. It's got to be done. We got no choice. Please, any of you here who are sitting on the fence, get down off it on the right side. Thank you so much. Come visit us in Fayette. Have no fear.

WE NEED TO BE UNITED

By Mrs. Martin Luther King, Jr.

On April 22, 1970, at the twenty-second Automobile Workers' Constitutional Convention in Atlantic City, Mrs. Martin Luther King, Jr., accepted the United Automobile Workers' Social Justice Award to her late husband. Here are excerpts from the speech she delivered in response, reprinted with permission of Mrs. King and the international union, United Automobile, Aerospace and Agricultural Implement Workers of America.

IT IS a heart-warming privilege to accept this posthumous award to my husband from an organization that always made itself part of our struggle whether the scene of action was in Birmingham, Selma, Detroit or Washington. . . .

Before moving on to my principal topic, because the men at this convention outnumber the women, I would like to call to their attention that this year, 1970, marks the fiftieth anniversary of woman's suffrage. This landmark amendment to the Constitution was a vastly important step in the liberation of women, but unfortunately even now, half a century after its enactment, it is only partially effective. Not until the fifties and sixties did black women become voters in large numbers despite the mandates of the law. It is also noteworthy that the five states which rejected the Nineteenth Amendment were all Southern states, once again demonstrating where the roots of reaction are in the nation. . . .

My husband in his lifetime, as many of you know, had a special affinity for the labor movement. His understanding of society was too profound to permit him to be caught up in superficial prejudices. Though part of the labor movement has joined in the oppression of black people, another part of it pioneered in welding a coalition of rights and opportunities. He knew both truths. My husband knew that in much of basic industry black people through unions have relatively more freedom than in other sectors of the economy.

His memorial thus could not be merely a shrine, though it had to be that. It developed from planning, necessarily complex as he was complex.

It is not an accident that my husband was assassinated while leading a strike, nor is it coincidental that the time of his assassination came when he was calling for a coalition of all the poor black and white, and urging that they create a union organization. He was arousing a sleeping giant when he was cut down.

The trade-union movement was never a movement merely to protect and advance living standards. It had noble objectives beyond these limitations. From its birth it sought to attain social justice in its broadest sense. A wage increase was important, but important too was its elevating effect on human dignity. It was under that banner that the U.A.W. made workers more than mere appendages to machines and attained for them the status of dignified, proud men. When the U.A.W. in the thirties made trade-unionism an instrument of social reform, it won the respect of a majority of the nation. In holding today to this larger vision of the trade-union movement, it is providing the base of leadership desperately needed in a divided and confused land.

It was your union and others of the C.I.O. that pioneered to admit black people to your ranks. By standing for equal justice you not only opened doors to blacks, but you defeated the employer's strategy to make black people a distinct group of strikebreakers. Thus you strengthen yourselves while you enlarge the democratic rights of others.

We would be less than candid, however, if we refused to recognize that the coalition of blacks and the trade-union movement faces tensions.

Some trade-unionists are hostile to the freedom movement, and some blacks are spreading the illusion that a separatist road exists in the journey to emancipation. Even worse, some blacks out of frustration and despair play with notions of terrorism, and some whites are no less drawn to solutions of violence.

It is not black workers or white workers who will profit if they fight each other. Only those will profit who wish to dominate all workers. Blacks are not looking for advancement at the expense of other working people. Industry and government have enough control of wealth to provide decent employment for every man, black and white. If we don't identify the right problems and isolate the right adversary, we will all play the role of fools. Our trade-unions torn by division can lose their independence, fighting strength and leadership.

More than ever in the past we need to be united, because in all the dimensions of our lives, not just in race relations, we are in serious jeopardy. It is an illusion to think routine or formal trade-unionism can solve the vast problems of society today. Indeed, today a union need not be broken to become ineffectual; your living standards are not solely in your wage envelope. . . .

Taxes, swollen by an insane war in Vietnam, can shrink the envelope as you hold it in your hand. Inflation empties it further. Beyond these, the quality of life is diminished by the dying of our cities. Though our nation is the richest on the earth, and more opulent than any in world history, our slums are among the worst of any industrial nation. Our health services are primitive compared with European standards. We are choked by transportation, sickened by poisoned air and polluted rivers, lakes and seaways. The leisure time you fought for is nullified by narrowed opportunities for recreation and relaxation. Before long, the shortage of water and the diminished volume of breathable air will begin to threaten the lives of all.

We are now surrounded by dirt, congestion and impure air in all walks of our daily life which you fought to eliminate in the factories because they were barbarous and inhuman.

Today, April 22, is an appropriate day to mention these things, because it is Earth Day, designed to remind all people that our planet can die.

Trade-unions will have to come out of the plants and move on the state houses and centers of power if our nation is to survive. We are at a new crossroad of responsibility. You who make the wheels of society turn will have to apply your strength and dynamism to broader social problems, if a suicidal course is to be avoided.

The whole population cannot flee to the suburbs, or they too will become the inner city. In many suburbs unmanageable problems are catching up.

Thus, black communities and white communities will have to unite and write new laws of urban development. If they fail, America has to go into a decline no matter what wage scales it can afford, and many of the features of the nineteenth-century mill towns in all their bleakness and ugliness will overtake our cities. We will see again the dark, dismal municipalities where families cannot breathe, children cannot play or learn, order cannot be maintained because it is cheaper to let some live in squalor while others seek individual havens of retreat.

To fight the decomposition of the cities, to fight poisoned air, accumulating garbage, filthy rivers and dying schools constitute the battle of the seventies. You fought out of the depression thirties for yourselves and everyone. You will have to repeat that victory, if an expanding industrial nation almost out of control is not to stagger into social catastrophe.

This social leadership is your special responsibility, first of all because it involves your own direct interests. More than this, you have the power, experience and a tradition of moral sense. This nation was in a more severe moral crisis in the thirties, when it was rescued by the vision and boldness of the young labor movement. The nation needs that quality of leadership today as it faces new perils. Black people in the large majority are ready for a new crusade for radical reform; they will be a powerful force in a militant struggle for decent conditions of life, and they are ready for an honorable partnership in a progressive coalition. Divided, neither one of us can win; deluded by myths and prejudices, we will fail; but united we can put this nation together and restore social sanity, inspire hope and achieve the interracial harmony my husband always believed was possible.

I think such a crusade of decency and progress is also part of a memorial to Martin Luther King. He believed people would always fight for their rights against all prophets of doom and despair. As long as we lift ourselves to new heights of human dignity and equality the sacrifice will deepen in meaning and his life will be renewed in our own growth and development.

THE NIXON ADMINISTRATION'S ANTI-NEGRO POLICY

By Bishop Stephen G. Spottswood

At the annual convention of the N.A.A.C.P., June 19, 1970, the keynote address by Bishop Stephen G. Spottswood, chairman of the Association's Board of Directors, was a carefully documented history of the Nixon Administration's policies toward black Americans, which added up to a definite anti-Negro policy. Bishop Spottswood is associated with the African Methodist Episcopal Zion Church. The following are portions of his keynote address, excerpted from The New York Times, *June 20, 1970.*

TWO YEARS AGO, former Attorney General Ramsey Clark, speaking for the Kerner Commission, called for "the reaffirmation of our faith in one society," and the commission itself sounded a warning that the nation is moving in the direction of two societies—one black, one white—separate and unequal.

Today, the signs are even more ominous. On every hand, the commentators and the politicians, the faint-hearted liberals and the tragically misguided black separatists are announcing the end of integration, especially in the schools.

For the first time since Woodrow Wilson, we have a national administration that can be rightly characterized as anti-Negro.*

This is the first time since 1920 that the national administration has made it a matter of calculated policy to work against the needs and aspirations of the largest minority of its citizens.

Here are a few instances supporting our contention of the administration's anti-Negro policy:

1. Signing of defense contracts with textile companies long in violation of contract requirements versus our recommendations that these contracts be canceled.

---

* For a discussion of segregation practices during the Wilson Administration, *see* pp. 703–706. *See also* Morton Sosna, "The South in the Saddle: Racial Politics during the Wilson Years," *Wisconsin Magazine of History,* Vol. LIV, Autumn, 1970, pp. 30–49, and Nancy J. Weiss, "The Negro and the New Freedom: Fighting Wilsonian Segregation," *Political Science Quarterly,* Vol. LXXXIV, March, 1969, pp. 61–79.

2. The pull-back on school desegregation. The Administration went into court to secure delays in already ordered desegregation. Thank God, the Supreme Court struck down these attempts.

3. The nominations of Clement Haynsworth and G. Harrold Carswell to the United States Supreme Court (which nominations were defeated by the leadership of the N.A.A.C.P., along with other organizations, including the Leadership Conference on Civil Rights, of which Roy Wilkins is chairman and in which fight our Clarence Mitchell demonstrated his superb skills on Capitol Hill as truly the 101st Senator).

4. The administration at Washington attempted to weaken our hard-won Voting Rights Act in the House, but in a demonstration of our power we met the racist and beat him in his own house.

5. The administration opposed the cease-and-desist-order power of the Equal Employment Opportunity Commission.

6. The administration supported the Stennis amendment on the school appropriation bill.

7. The administration produced the Moynihan memorandum calling for "benign neglect."

8. The administration supports tax exemption for white, separate private schools, designed to avert desegregation of the public schools.

9. On April 9, after the rejection of his nominee, Judge Carswell, for the Supreme Court, the President described the ideal judge as "someone who believes in the strict construction of the Constitution, as I do—a judge who will not use the power of the Court to seek social change by freely interpreting the law or constitutional clauses." This is the administration's expressed opposition to the equal protection clauses of the Fourteenth Amendment.

The effect of this has been exactly what was predicted. It has given encouragement to the Southern racists, whose full-page advertisements have exposed their radical retreat to the calendar level of the 1870's, such as produced by Senator [John C.] Stennis of Mississippi and Governor [John J.] McKeithen of Louisiana, to say nothing of the melodramatic pose of Florida's Governor [Claude R.] Kirk in defying the federal court's orders to desegregate the public schools of the Everglades State.

Before us today, in the solution of the problem of a single society, are the issues arising from what seems to many the futility of our effort toward integration. There is a tremendous white backlash as we have forged a difficult path through the metallic barriers in housing, employment and politics.

A small but vociferous number of Negroes has effected the black retreat, as indicated in the black college students' demands for separate dormitories, separate cafeterias, separate curricula and separate facilities. Incidentally, we should sympathize—even as we disagree—with young black youth whose bitter and bloody experiences on white college campuses have driven them to the black retreat.

The white backlash on the one hand and the black retreat on the other hand have combined to accentuate the racial polarity of which the Kerner Commission warned.

At this juncture in our national life, we of the N.A.A.C.P., recalling Abraham Lincoln's declaration that "this nation cannot endure half free and half slave," emphatically paraphrase Mr. Lincoln and declare "this country cannot endure half white and half black." If American democracy is to survive, we shall be one society, as the Declaration of Independence visioned and the Constitution declares.

Ours is a national problem affecting all Americans, and no matter where we live, the problem of one society is before us. For instance, it is easy for Northern Negroes to forget the South, because local needs are urgent and desperate, but they do so at their own peril.

Fifty-two percent of black Americans still live in the South, mostly in cities, where the problems of overcrowding, housing, crime, discrimination, poor education are the same as the North's. In addition, they have the Southern segregation traditions, white supremacy ideology and wanton murderousness.

Even as lynching was the Roman holiday sport of the nineteenth-century America, killing black Americans promiscuously has been the twentieth-century pastime of our police, whose primary duty is law enforcement and keeping the peace.

I'm thinking of the six Negroes killed in Augusta, Georgia, all shot in the back; of the Panthers slain in their beds in Chicago; of the students slain at Jackson State College;* of the almost daily news stories of the indiscriminate, ruthless slaying of black Americans by police and civilians, under the guise of "law

* In the spring of 1970, seven blacks were killed by police in Augusta, Georgia, and two black students at Jackson State College. Those at Augusta were shot in the back while fleeing armed police.

On December 4, 1969, Fred Hampton, chairman of the Illinois Black Panther Party, was murdered in a police raid on an apartment in Chicago. Mark Clark, Panther member, was also killed; four other Panthers were critically wounded, and three were arrested, unharmed. One policeman was slightly wounded. State's Attorney Edward V. Hanrahan held a press conference later that day, displaying what he said was the arms cache recovered from the apartment and saying that the police had fired because they had been attacked by the Black Panthers. But it soon became clear that the police had massed a heavy concentration of machine-gun and shotgun fire at one living-room wall and into two bedrooms, and that there was little if any sign of return fire. A federal grand jury investigating the murders reached the conclusion that and order," but actually fulfilling the guidelines of a bitter, white majority, whose vain effort to keep us "in our place" leads them to resort to the policeman's pistol and kangaroo court trials.

The white liberals and the churches have not been conspicuous in the fight for freedom lately. No one questions the demand for an immediate end of the Vietnam war. We ask again, why is it that white people always manage to find some issue other than race to which they give their priority attention, the latest of which is pollution and the ecology?

If racial justice and civil rights had commanded just 10 percent of the attention that white liberals have given to the Vietnam war, we would not be in the position we are today—and it is unlikely that we would have Nixon in the White House either.

We must counteract some black authors who have tried to show that bad English grammar and slurred consonants and special terminology found among poorly educated Negroes (and poorly educated white people) are really a different language which should be learned and used in ghetto school teaching. Recently a black architect has been working on the theory that Negroes should have distinctive-type housing—one which adequately accommodates their tribal instincts inherited from our African past—*reductio ad absurdum*.

Then, after the long series of suggestions of self-imposed apartheid, we must beware of those who once stood on the solid ground of full freedom for all Americans and have now retreated to the wabbling field of compromise and sinking sands of surrender.

For example, Roy Innis, national director of CORE, recently made a Deep South visit where he was warmly received by John Bell Williams of Mississippi, John J. McKeithen of Louisiana, Albert Brewer of Alabama and Lester (Ax-Handle) Maddox of Georgia.*

He was there to solicit their interest and support of the Innis plan to reestablish a dual school system. His scheme is not to have separate black and white systems by race—oh, no—but to split the city in half along residential lines, with the white half under its school system and the black half under its system.

---

the police charge that they had fired in self-defense was false, but no police officials were indicted.

* Before he became governor of Georgia, Lester Maddox won notoriety as restaurant owner who wielded an ax handle to repel blacks who wished to enter his restaurant. Thereafter, he handed out ax handles to his white customers as souvenirs, a practice he continued while governor.

You can just imagine how the governors were delighted with the Innis proposal.

There are others who advocate a separate nation, to be set up somewhere, or for autonomous neighborhoods or districts in the cities—to run our own police, fire department, hospitals, schools and everything else. But they always make it clear that they expect to get the money from the rest of the community. There is no such thing as autonomy on someone else's money.

No major problem afflicting black Americans can be solved except by solving them for all Americans.

We have worked too long and too hard, made too many sacrifices, spent too much money, shed too much blood, lost too many lives fighting to vindicate our manhood as full participants in the American system, to allow our victories to be nullified by phony liberals, die-hard racists, discouraged and demoralized Negroes and power-seeking politicians.

I AM A BLACK REVOLUTIONARY WOMAN

By Angela Davis

In the spring of 1969, Angela Davis, a graduate student at the University of California, San Diego, accepted a two-year contract as Assistant Professor of Philosophy at the University of California, Los Angeles. When it was discovered she was a member of the Communist Party, the Regents voted to dismiss her under a twenty-nine-year-old university rule barring employment of Communists. Miss Davis gained the support of faculty and students, and on October 20, 1969, a Superior Court judge ruled that the dismissal was unconstitutional and ordered Miss Davis reinstated. On June 8, 1970, the Regents voted not to renew her contract for the coming year, this time citing her "extramural activities" on behalf of the Soledad Brothers and the Black Panther party. The U.C.L.A. faculty voted to support Miss Davis and even to pay her salary out of their own pockets.

In August, 1970, Jonathan Jackson, the brother of one of the three black "Soledad Brothers"—so named for Cali-

fornia's notorious Soledad prison, where they had been accused of murdering a white guard—invaded a court-room in Marin County. He took several hostages, including a judge, and demanded the release of the prisoners. The guards opened fire, and Jackson and the judge were killed. Angela Davis was later charged with buying the guns used by young Jackson. Placed on the F.B.I.'s "ten most-wanted" list, Miss Davis, who had gone into hiding, was arrested in New York City on October 13, 1970. Indicted by a Marin County grand jury, which charged her with conspiracy, kidnaping and murder, Miss Davis was sneaked out of prison in New York City and extradited to California to await trial. On January 13, 1971, the N.A.A.C.P.'s National Board officially announced: "We are appalled at the obvious effort to deny the presumption of innocence and thereby convict Miss Angela Davis of murder long before the first witness had been called. We are deeply concerned that the American judicial system provide a fair trial for a young, black American woman who admits to being a member of the Communist party." The Board warned the State of California "that we shall watch closely the trial of Miss Davis and we invite the whole nation to do like-wise. . . . We call on all other Americans, black and white, to join us in assuring a fair and impartial trial for Miss Davis." Protests demanding either a fair trial or the release of Miss Davis poured into this country from all parts of the world.

Below are two statements by Angela Davis. The first was made while Miss Davis was in prison and is reprinted from Muhammad Speaks, *December, 1970, and the* Guardian, *December 26, 1970. The second, the brief speech Miss Davis delivered to the court in Marin County Courthouse, January 5, 1971, is issued by the National United Committee to Free Angela Davis.*

BEFORE ANYTHING else I am a black woman. I dedicated my life to the struggle for the liberation of black people—my enslaved, imprisoned people.

I am a Communist because I am convinced that the reason we have been forcefully compelled to eke out an existence at the very lowest level of American society has to do with the nature of capitalism. If we are going to rise out of our oppression, our poverty, if we are going to cease being the targets of the racist-minded mentality of racist policemen, we will have to destroy the American capitalist system. We will have to obliterate a system in which a few wealthy capitalists are guaranteed the privilege of becoming richer and richer, whereas the people who are forced to work for the rich, and especially Black people, never take any significant step forward.

I am a Communist because I believe that black people, with whose labor and blood this country was built, have a right to a great deal of wealth that has been hoarded in the hands of the Hugheses, the Rockefellers, the Kennedys, the DuPonts, all the superpowerful white capitalists of America.

Further, I am a Communist because I believe Black men should not be coerced into fighting a racist, imperialist war in Southeast Asia, where the United States government is violently denying a nonwhite people the right to control their own lives, just as they violently suppressed us for hundreds of years.

My decision to join the Communist party emanated from my belief that the only true path of liberation for black people is the one that leads toward a complete and total overthrow of the capitalist class in this country and all its manifold institutional appendages which insure its ability to exploit the masses and enslave black people. Convinced of the need to employ Marxist-Leninist principles in the struggle for liberation, I joined the Che-Lumumba Club, which is a militant, all-black collective of the Communist party in Los Angeles committed to the task of rendering Marxism-Leninism relevant to black people. But mindful of the fact that once we as black people set out to destroy the capitalist system we would be heading in a suicidal direction if we attempted to go at it alone. The whole question of allies was crucial. And furthermore aside from students, we need important allies at the point of production. I do not feel that all white workers are going to be inveterate conservatives. Black leadership in working class struggles is needed to radicalize necessary sectors of the working class.

The practical perspective of the Che-Lumumba Club is based on an awareness of the need to emphasize the national character of our people's struggle and to struggle around the specific forms of oppression which have kept us at the very lowest levels of American society for hundreds of years, but at the same time to place ourselves as black people in the forefront of a revolution involving masses of people to destroy capitalism, to eventually build a socialist society and thus to liberate not only our own people but all the downtrodden in this country. And further, recognizing the international character of the revolution especially in this period when the battle against our home-grown capitalists is being carried out all over the world, in Indochina, Africa and Latin America. My decision to join the Communist party was predicated in part on the ties the party has established with revolutionary movements throughout the world. . . .

The American judicial system is bankrupt. In so far as black people are concerned, it has proven itself to be one more arm of a system carrying out the systematic oppression of our people. We are the victims, not the recipients of justice.

It is obvious that democracy in America is hopelessly deteriorated, when the courts, allegedly guardians of the rights of the people, have been enlisted to play an active role in the genocidal war against black people.

We must reject the right of the courts to further oppress us. The only way we can get justice is demand it and to create a mass movement which will give notice to our enemy that we will use all means at out disposal to secure justice for our people. This is the only way we can expect to free all our brothers and sisters held captive in America's dungeons. This is the only way we can expect to ultimately gain total liberation.

. . . no revolutionary should fail to understand the underlying significance of the dictum that the success or failure of a revolution can almost always be gauged by the degree to which the status of women is altered in a radical, progressive direction. After all, Marx and Engels contended that there are two basic facts around which the history of mankind revolves: production and reproduction. The way in which people obtain their means of subsistence on one hand, and the way in which the family is organized on the other hand.

Further, if it is true the outcome of a revolution will reflect the manner in which it is waged, we must unremittingly challenge anachronistic bourgeois family structures and also the oppressive character of women's role in American society in general. Of course, this struggle is part and parcel of a total revolution. Led by women, the fight for the liberation of women must be embraced by men as well. The battle for women's liberation is especially critical with respect to the effort to build an effective black liberation movement. For there is no question about the fact that as a group, black women constitute the most oppressed sector of society.

Historically we were constrained not only to survive on an economic level as slaves, but our sexual status was that of a breeder of property for the white slave master as well as being the object of his perverse sexual desires. Our enemies have attempted to mesmerize us, to mesmerize black people, by propounding a whole assortment of myths with respect to the black woman. We are inveterate matriarchs, implying we have worked in collusion with the white oppressor to insure the emasculation of our men. Unfortunately, some black women have accepted these myths without questioning their origin and without being aware of the counter-revolutionary content and effect. They're consequently falling into behind-the-scenes positions in the movement and refuse to be aggressive and take leadership in our struggle for fear of contributing to the oppression of the black male.

As black women, we must liberate ourselves and provide the impetus for the liberation of black men from this whole network of lies around the oppression of black women, which serve only to divide us, thus impeding the advance of our total liberation struggle. . . .

I think it is important to link up the struggle for my freedom with the fight to free other black political prisoners . . . I maintain that the fight should call for the freedom of all black men and women. For few of us have received fair trials. We certainly have not been judged by juries from among our peers.

Even if I am eventually allowed to leave the dungeon, I will not consider myself free. My freedom will become a reality when we as a people have destroyed our enemies, when we black people have broken the yokes of our oppression and can freely erect a society which reflects our needs and our dreams. I will not be free until all black people are free.

As a preface to my brief remarks I now declare publicly before the court, before the people of this country that I am innocent of all charges which have been leveled against me by the State of California. I am innocent and therefore maintain that my presence in this courtroom today is unrelated to any criminal act.

I stand before this court as a target of a political frame-up which, far from pointing to my culpability, implicates the State of California as an agent of political repression. Indeed the state reveals its own role by introducing as evidence against me my participation in the struggles of my people—black people—against the many injustices of society. Specifically my involvement with the "Soledad Brothers Defense Committee." The American people have been led to believe that such involvement is Constitutionally protected.

In order to insure that these political questions are not obscured, I feel compelled to play an active role in my own defense as the defendant, as a black woman and as a Communist. It is my duty to assist all those directly involved in the proceedings, as well as the people of this state and the American people in general, to thoroughly comprehend the substantive issues at stake in my case. These have to do with my political beliefs, affiliations and my day-to-day efforts to fight all the conditions which have economically and politically paralyzed black America.

No one can better represent my political beliefs and activities than I. A system of justice which virtually condemns to silence the one person who stands to lose most would seem to be self-defeating.

It is particularly crucial to black people to combat this contradiction inherent in the judicial system, for we have accumulated a wealth of historical experience which confirms our belief that the scales of American justice are out of balance.

In order to enhance the possibility of being granted a fair trial, of which at present I am extremely doubtful, it is imperative that I be allowed to represent myself. I might add that my request is not without legal precedent.

If this court denies our motion to include me as co-counsel in this case, it will be aligning itself with the forces of racism and reaction which threaten to push this country into the throes of fascism, and the many people who have become increasingly disillusioned with the court system in this country will have a further reason to solidify their contention that it is no longer possible to get a fair trial in America.

THE TRANSFORMATION OF THE BLACK PANTHER PARTY

By Huey P. Newton

Huey P. Newton was born in Louisiana in 1942. When he was a year old, his family moved to California. Although he was graduated from high school, he became literate by "self determination," attended Merritt Junior College and went to law school for six months. Newton met Bobby G. Seale at Merritt College, and in the fall of 1966, these two black militants formed the Black Panther Party for Self-Defense in Oakland, California. Seale became Chairman and Newton Minister of Defense. Newton wrote the Party's famous ten-point program after asking the residents of Oakland's ghetto what they needed and wanted. For the history and ideologies of the Black Panther Party from its inception to the fall of 1970, see Philip S. Foner, editor, The Black Panthers Speak (*New York, 1970*).

In 1971 the Black Panther Party, its influence eroded by factional fights, seemed to many observers spent and dead, and discussion now dealt with who would succeed the Panthers. However, Huey P. Newton, following his release on bail from prison to await a new trial on the charge of having slain a police officer (one trial had ended in a hung jury), insisted that the Party was still alive and functioning but had only been transformed. In a speech at the Center for Urban-Black Studies, Graduate Theological Union, University of California, Berkeley, May 19, 1971, Newton spelled out what this transformation meant, and spoke in detail of the Party's changed attitude toward the black church. Here are excerpts from Newton's speech; they are taken from the text printed in The Black Panther, *May 29, 1971.*

. . . The Black Panther Party was formed because we wanted to oppose the evils in our community. Some of the members in the Party were not so refined—we were grasping for organization. It wasn't a college campus organization; it was basically an organization of the grass roots, and anytime we organize the most victimized of the victims, we run into a problem. To have a Party or a church or any kind of institution, whether we like it or not, we have to have administrators. The institution, the organization, or the Party in this case—how it functions, how effective it is—will depend upon how knowledgeable, how advanced in thinking the administrators will be. We attempt to apply the administrative skills—if you are a grass-roots organization—to the problems that are most heard in the community. When we do this, it is somewhat abstract in a way.

History shows that it's there, and because most of the parties that have led people out of their difficulties to change the situation have administrators that have what we sometimes call the traits of the bourgeoisie or else declassed intellectuals. In other words they are the people who have gone through the established institutions, rejected them, and then applied their skills to the community. They gave it to the community, therefore making their skill not a bourgeoisie skill, but a people's skill.

It was transformed through the contradiction of applying what's usually bourgeoisie to the person who is oppressed; and that itself is a kind of transformation.

With our Party we're not so blessed with this. History does not repeat itself; it goes on also transforming itself through its dialectical process. We see that our Party, while we have administrators (we need them in the Party), the victims have not received that bourgeoisie training. So I will not apologize for our mistakes, our lack of a scientific approach that we tried to use and put into practice. It was a matter of not knowing, of learning, but also starting out with a loss, a loss that history has never seen. That is, that a group attempting to influence and change the society so much and at the same time have its administrators as much in the dark much of the time as the people that they are trying to change. In our Party we have now what we call the Ideological Institute, where we are teaching these skills. And we also invite those people who have received a bourgeois education to come and help us, letting them know that they will, by their contribution, make their need to exist—as they exist—null and void. In other words, after we learn the skills they will not be bourgeois anymore, because that will evaporate with its application.

I explain this to show some of the mistakes. I won't go into particulars but I will show you generally what happens, because it's also happened to the Church. I say that everything seems to negate itself through contradiction. Remember, it is transformed by the contradiction, so therefore its old quality, its old composition is transformed so much until it has a new composition. We call it a thing negating itself; sometimes we call it the negation of the negation, because just as it is formed, it is also being negated by something else, and we see that this goes on in the process of development.

As far as the Church is concerned, the Black Panther Party, and other community groups who call themselves concerned with the political and not the spiritual, criticize the spiritual. We say that it's only a ritual; it's irrelevant, and therefore we have nothing to do with it. We say this in the context of the whole community having something to do with the Church, usually on one level or another. That is one way of defecting from the community, and that is exactly what we did. Once we stepped outside of the Church with that criticism we stepped outside of the thing that the community was involved in and said to them, "You follow our example; your reality is not true and you don't need it." I think that people do the thing that they think they need and they probably do it on that level, one way or another.

Now without judging whether the Church is operating in a total reality, I'll venture to say that if we judge whether the Church operates in a situation of relevance to the total community, we would all agree that it does not. That is why you develop new programs and become more relevant so your pews will be filled on Sunday.

So we will say that the Church is in its developmental process, then; first it needs to exist. We feel that with our new direction, which is an old direction as far as I am concerned, but we'll call it new, because there has been a reversal in the dominance in the Central Committee of our Party, because of reasons that you probably know about. So we go to church and we are involved in the Church, and we're not doing it in any hypocritical way. I think that it is a thing that man needs at this time, and he needs it because of what? Because we scientists cannot answer all of the questions. As far as I am concerned when all of the questions are answered, when the odd is not answered, when the unknown is not answered, then there is room for God because that unknown is God. God is a thing that we know nothing about really, and that is why as soon as the scientist develops or points out a new way of controlling the universe or part of it, suddenly that thing is not God. In other words, at one point when thunder clashed it was God's clap, putting his hands together. As soon as we found out that it was not God, then we say that God has other attributes but not that one. So in that way we took on what was His before, you see? But you still haven't answered all of the questions, so He exists. And those scientists that say they can answer them are dishonest.

So we go into the Church realizing that we cannot answer the questions at this time, that the answers will be delivered at some time, and we feel that when they are delivered they will be explained in a way that we can understand and that we can control. We noticed—I went to church for years; my father is a minister, and I spent fifteen years in the church; this was my life as a child—we saw one thing. That is, as we approach the unknown, we see that sometimes a group of people will find something out or feel that they have discovered something they can control and say this is not God, while the other group will say that we have to approach my God differently for the simple reason that they attribute other characteristics to God. So we get many denominations, you see, all struggling to understand.

When I was going to church I used to hear much of the time, they would say that God is within us and so therefore God is some part of us. And God is that part of us that's very mystical, in the sense that we don't understand it. But as man develops and understands more and more then he will approach God, and finally he will reach heaven and therefore he will merge with the universe. I've never heard one preacher say that there is a need for the Church in heaven; the Church would negate itself. As man approaches his development and becomes larger and larger, the Church therefore becomes smaller and smaller because it is not needed any longer. Then if we really get ministers who will deal with the social realities that cause the misery, so that we can solve them, so that man will become larger and larger, then their God within will come out, we can see it and merge with it. Then we will be one with the universe.

So I think it was rather arrogant of my Party to criticize the community for indulging in a practice to deliver this answer. The only thing we will criticize in the future is when the Church does not act upon these evils that we feel cause man to go on his knees. The man goes on his knees and humbles himself under the awe, that large force that he cannot control. But as man becomes stronger and stronger, his understanding greater and greater, he will have a closer walk with thee. *You note they say "walk" and not "crawl."*

So with the Church we will all start again to control our lives and control our communities. Even with the black Church we have to really create a community spirit. We say that the Church is an institution, but in itself it is not a community according to sociology. The sociological definition of a community is that a community is a comprehensive collection of institutions that will deliver our whole life, provided that we can reach most of our goals within it. It serves us, and we create it in order to carry out our desires. In the black community we have the Church as an institution that we created, they let us create. They warred against us, but finally we got that compromise and we worship as a unit, as a people concerned with satisfying their needs. At the time the white Church was not satisfying our needs, because the actual questions could not be answered in human terms, because they felt we were not human beings. So therefore the white Church does not answer our cause or our problem at all, so we formed our own. They let us form it because they felt if we're not human beings then why should we go to church? So through that negative thing a positive thing came out again. We started to administer fraternities, antilynching groups and so forth, but they still would not let our community exist. We came here in chains, and I guess they thought we were meant to stay in chains. But this wasn't the case, and the way we started to move out and have that forward thrust was to organize a political machine or trying to develop a community so that we could have the apparatus in order to fight back. You cannot fight an organized machine back individually, so we would work with the Church in order to establish a community to satisfy most of our needs so that we can live and operate as a community group.

The Black Panther Party, with its survival programs, plans to develop the institutions in the community. We have a clothing factory we are just erecting on Third Street, where we will soon give away about three hundred to four hundred new clothes a month. And we can do this by robbing Peter to pay Paul. What we will do is start to make golfing bags under contract to a company, and with the surplus we will buy material to make free clothes. Our members will do this. We will have no overhead, because our collective—we'll exploit our collective by making them work free. We'll do this not just to satisfy ourselves—like the philanthropist—or to serve, to save someone from going without shoes, even though this is a part of the cause of our problem. People make the revolution; we will give the process a forward thrust. If we suffer genocide we won't be around to change things. So in this way our survival program is very practical.

What we are concerned with is the larger problem, so we will be honest and say that we will do like the churches, we will negate our necessity for existing. In other words, after we accomplish our goals then the Black Panther Party will not need to exist because we have already created our heaven right here on earth. What we're going to do is administer to the community the things they need in order to get their attention, in order to organize them into a political machine. In other words the community will then look to the Party and look to those people who are serving their needs in order to give them guidance and direction, whether it is political, whether it is judicial, or whether it is economic.

So our real thing is to organize across this country. We have thirty-eight chapters and branches, and I would like to inform you that the so-called split is only a myth, that it does not exist. We lost two chapters in that so-called split, and I will tell you that the burden is off my shoulders, I was glad to lose them because it was like a yoke, I was frozen. Even though I couldn't make a move I already told you that I wouldn't get out of the whole thing then, because certain people had such an influence over the Party. For me to have taken that stand, it would have been an individual stand. So now we're about three years behind in our five-year plan, but we will now move to start to organize the community around the survival programs, like administering shoes.

We have a shoe factory that we're opening up on Fourteenth and Jefferson. We have the machines and everything else donated. We'll use it to get inmates out of prison, because most of us know how to make shoes through making shoes in the prison. So it will serve two purposes. We can give them a position in the shoe factory and therefore get somebody out on parole; secondly they'll come out with the idea of giving a certain amount of shoes away each week, and we'll have a right-to-wear-shoes program. We'll point out that everyone in the society should have shoes, and we should not have a situation like in Beaufort County, South Carolina, where the children—many of them—70 percent of the children suffer brain damage because of malnutrition. They have malnutrition because of the combination of not enough food and parasites in the stomach. The worm eats up half the food that they take in. Why? Because the ground is infested with the eggs of the worms and they don't have shoes to wear. So as soon as we send a doctor there to cure them they get the parasites again. So we think that a shoe program is a very relevant thing, first to make them live, to create those conditions so that they will grow up and be able to work out a plan to change things. If they have brain damage, they will never be revolutionists, because they cannot plan, because they have already been killed. That is genocide in itself.

So we will do this and we will point out to this government, to this social order, that they must administer to its people because they say that they're supposed to be a representative government, representing the needs of the people. Then serve them. If they don't do this, then they have a right to be criticized. What we will not do in the future is jump too far ahead. We can jump too far ahead and say that the system absolutely cannot give us anything, which is not true, the system can correct itself to a certain extent. What we are interested in is for it to correct itself as much as it can do and after that if it doesn't do everything that the people think is necessary then we'll think about reorganizing things.

To be very honest again, I think there's great doubt whether the particular arrangements can do this. But until the people feel the same way I feel, then I'll be rather arrogant to say dump the whole thing, just as we were arrogant to say dump the Church. Let's give it a chance, let's work with it in order to twist as many contributions and compromises out of all the institutions as possible and then criticize after the fact. We'll know when that time comes, when the people tell us so.

We have a program attempting to get the people to do all they will do. It's too much to ask the people to do all they can do, because we know we can do everything. But that is not the point, the point is how do we get them to do all they will do, until they eventually get to the point they will have to be doing all they can do because they will be satisfied with everything else? This is the kind of program we have.

When the Party started we started, because we recognized that what was growing out of the movement was what we called a cultural cult group. We defined a cultural cult group as an organization that disguised itself as a political organization, but really it was more interested in the cultural rituals of Africa in the 1100's before the contact with the European. Instead of administering to the community and organizing it, they would rather wear bubas and get African names and use this and demand that the community do the same and do nothing about the survival of the community. Sometimes they say that "well if we get our culture back then all things will be solved." This is like saying to be regenerated and born again is to solve everything. We know that it is not solved.

. . . We went into a thing just as closed in as the cultural cultist group. You might know many churches that are very reactionary and you might call them a religious cult. They go through many rituals but they're divorced from reality. Even though we have many things in common with them we say they isolate themselves from reality because they're so miserable and reality is so hard to take. We know that by us operating within the reality does not mean that we accept it; we're operating within it, so that we can change it, because what we do as revolutionists we're somewhat abstract in our approach. The people are always real. They think they are real, but we know that reality is changing all the time, but what we want to do is harness those forces that are causing the change in order to direct them in a desirable direction. In other words the development will go on, but we have no guarantee that it will develop so man can live. We have no guarantee that the bomb won't be dropped, but we know that there are certain ways that we can plan for the new reality, and in order to do this, we have to take some control over the now. So the people

who withdraw, like I mentioned the religious cultist group, do
the same thing as the cultural cultist group.

These are new words that we have coined. The Panthers are
always defining words, because we have to keep defining the
new reality, the new phenomena. The old words confuse us
sometimes, because things have changed so much. So we try
to stay abreast, by developing or stipulating definitions, the old
lexical definitions become so outdated after the qualitative leap
(the transformation) that it doesn't match at all what we're
talking about now.

The new word that we are talking about now is what I was
guilty of. I was guilty of this when I offered the black troops to
Vietnam—I won't talk about whether it was morally right or
wrong—I will say that anything that you say or do as a revolutionist that does not spur or give the forward thrust to the
process (of revolution) is wrong. Remember that the people
are the makers of history, the people make everything in their
society. They are the architects of the society and if you don't
spur them on then I don't care what phrases you use, whether
they are political or religious, you cannot be classified as being
relevant to that process. You might be reactionary, because if
you know you're wrong and do these things then you're reactionary, because you are very very guilty. You serve many
stripes. Some of us didn't know. I'm probably more guilty than
anyone. I keep searching myself to see whether I knew we were
going wrong. I couldn't influence them (the Central Committee) and maybe I should have been charged with an individual
violation and gotten out that they didn't know. I think most of
them didn't know, so they're not as guilty as I am. But anyway,
the new word that we call what we went into for a short length
of time—a couple of years—is "revolutionary cultist."

The revolutionary cultist uses the words *social change;* they
use words for being interested in the development of society,
he uses that terminology, you see. But his actions are so far
divorced from the process, and organizing the community until
he is living in a fantasy world. So we talk to each other on the
campuses, or we talk to each other in the conspiracy of the
night, with concentration upon the weapons thinking that
these things will produce change, without the people themselves changing it. Of course people will do courageous things
and call themselves the *vanguard.* But the people who do things
like that are either heroes or criminals. They are not the vanguard, because the vanguard means spearhead, and the spearhead has to spearhead something; if nothing is behind it, then

you are divorced from all the masses, and not the vanguard.

I am going to be very criticized now by the revolutionary cultists and probably even more in the future, because I view the process as going in stages. I feel that we can't jump from A to Z, we have to go through all that development. So even though I could see a thing is not the answer, I don't think it's dishonest to involve myself in it for the simple reason that the people tend to take not even one step higher, they take a half a step higher. Then hang on to the reality or what they view as the reality, because they can't see that it is constantly changing and when it finally changes (qualitatively) they don't know why. Remember that part of the reason it changes around them is because they are there, so they participate whether they like it or not.

So what we will do now is involve ourselves in anything or any stage of development in the community, support that and try to introduce some insight into it. Then we will work very hard with the people in the community and with this institution so that it can negate itself. We will be honest about this and we hope they are honest. They will be honest if they accept this thing, that is the reality that everything is negated and this is how we go on to higher levels. . . .

THE LEGACY OF GEORGE JACKSON

By Angela Davis

On August 21, 1971, twenty-nine-year-old black militant George Jackson, who was serving a life term at San Quentin Prison for having eleven years before pleaded guilty to armed robbery of seventy dollars, was shot and killed. The prison authorities said that Jackson had been shot while racing toward the wall in an escape attempt, but many black Americans were soon convinced that he had been deliberately murdered by prison guards because of his militancy. At his death Jackson was world-famous as one of the three Soledad Brothers who were facing trial on charges of having murdered a white guard while they were inmates at Soledad Prison, and because of the eloquent presentation of his development into a revolutionary black militant in his book, Soledad Brother. *From her own prison cell, Angela Davis issued the following tribute to George Jackson to be read at the memorial service for Jackson held at St. Augustine's Episcopal Church in the heart of West Oakland's black ghetto. It was at the same church just a year before that funeral services were held for seventeen-year-old Jonathan Jackson, George's younger brother. Angela Davis' tribute to George Jackson is reprinted from the* Daily World, *August 25, 1971.*

An enemy bullet has once more brought grief and sadness to black people and to all who oppose racism and injustice and who love and fight for freedom. On Saturday, August 21, a San Quentin guard's sniper bullet executed George Jackson and wiped out that last modicum of freedom with which he had persevered and resisted so fiercely for eleven years.

Though deprived so long of the freedom of movement enjoyed by his oppressors, even as he died, George was far more free than they. Like he lived, he died resisting. A field marshal of the Black Panther Party, George belongs to a very special breed of fallen black leaders, for his struggle was the most perilous.

He was recognized as a leader of the movement which sought to deepen the political consciousness of black and brown prisoners who constitute 30 to 40 percent of California's prison population. His impact on the community outside was and continues to be boundless. George's example of courage in the face of the specter of summary execution, his insights honed in the torment of seven years of solitary confinement, his perseverance in the face of overwhelming odds will continue to be a source of inspiration to all our sisters and brothers inside prison walls and outside.

His book, *Soledad Brother*, a stirring chronicle of the development of the highest form of revolutionary fortitude and resistance, serves as a primer to captured brothers and sisters across the world. Equally important, his volume, perhaps more than any other, has given impetus to, and shaped the direction of, the growing support movement outside the prisons.

George, from behind seemingly impenetrable walls, has placed the issue of the prison struggle squarely on the agenda of the people's movement for revolutionary change. His book reveals the indivisible nature of the struggle on the outside of the prison system with the one inside.

Whether in prison or not, black and third-world people are the victims and targets of a common system of oppression and exploitation. Only the methods used are different.

The prevailing conditions of race and class exploitation invariably result in the captivity of a disproportionate number of black and third-world people. Our brothers and sisters are usually locked up for crimes they did not commit, or for crimes against property—crimes for which white youths receive prosecutorial, judicial, and penal leniency.

George himself was an eighteen-year-old man-child when he was sentenced to serve from one to life for a robbery involving seventy dollars—one to life—or eleven years' enslavement and sudden death. Through George's life and the lives of thousands of other brothers and sisters, the absolute necessity for extending the struggle of black and third-world people into the prison system itself becomes unmistakably clear.

The legacy left us by George and his dead brother, Jon, means that we must strengthen the mass movement which alone is capable of freeing all of our brothers and sisters in prisons. We know that the road to freedom has always been stalked by death. George knew that the price of his intense revolutionary commitment was having to live each day fighting off potential death blows. He had repeatedly seen death used as a standard reprisal for blacks who "stepped out of line." In January of 1970, he had seen his brother prisoners, Nolan, Miller and Edwards, warrantlessly and viciously murdered in the Soledad Prison yard. In *Soledad Brother,* George graphically told of the manner in which he had learned to thwart the many past attempts to murder him.

The dimensions of the task which lies ahead of us are clearer now, but the price of our new vision has been the death of two brilliant and brave revolutionaries, brothers in blood.

Associate Warden James Park promises us that the new wave of repression which has been unleashed within San Quentin will not halt with George's death. Rather, he has ushered in new terrorism by openly inviting guards to make a show of force and fully exhaust their vengeance on the prisoners themselves. Efforts to squelch revolutionary prison activity will not stop with one murder, Park tells us, but will continue until San Quentin is purged of all revolutionaries and every revolutionary thought.

The newspaper of George's party, the Black Panther Party, is hereafter forbidden within San Quentin's walls. "Old-fashioned prison methods," namely raw brutality, without its cosmetic dressings, is officially the new regime. Brothers Ruchell Magee, Fleeta Drumgo, and John Clutchette are identified targets; others in the so-called Adjustment Center who have taken sides are equally in danger.

Our responsibility extends to all these brothers upon whom war has been declared. The people must secure their safety and ultimately their freedom. Prison authorities seek only to cover up their own murderous crimes by attempting to initiate new frame-ups. These efforts must be swiftly and forcefully countered.

The Jackson family must be saluted. Their grief is deep. In little more than a year, two of their sons, George and Jonathan, were felled by fascist bullets. I express my love to Georgia and Robert Jackson, Penny, Frances and Delora.

For me, George's death has meant the loss of a comrade and revolutionary leader, but also the loss of an irretrievable love. This love is so agonizingly personal as to be indescribable. I can only say that in continuing to love him, I will try my best to express that love in the way he would have wanted—by reaffirming my determination to fight for the cause George died defending. With his example before me, my tears and grief are rage at the system responsible for his murder. He wrote his epitaph when he said:

"Hurl me into the next existence, the descent into hell won't turn me. I'll crawl back to dog his trail forever. They won't defeat my revenge, never, never. I'm part of a righteous people who anger slowly, but rage undammed. We'll gather at his door in such a number that the rumbling of our feet will make the earth tremble."

Index